Modernization and Postmodernization

Modernization and Postmodernization

CULTURAL, ECONOMIC, AND

POLITICAL CHANGE IN 43 SOCIETIES

RONALD INGLEHART

PRINCETON UNIVERSITY PRESS

PRINCETON, NEW JERSEY

Library of Congress Cataloging-in-Publication Data

Inglehart, Ronald.
Modernization and postmodernization : cultural, economic, and
political change in 43 societies / Ronald Inglehart.
p.   cm.
Includes bibliographical references (p.   ) and index.
ISBN 0-691-01181-8 (cloth : alk. paper). — ISBN 0-691-01180-X (pbk. : alk. paper)
1. Progress—Cross-cultural studies.   2. Political development—
Cross-cultural studies.   3. Economic development—Cross-cultural
studies.   4. Social change—Cross-cultural studies.   I. Title.
HM101.I554   1997
303.44—dc21   96-53839   CIP

This book has been composed in Times Roman expanded 5%

Princeton University Press books are printed on acid-free paper and meet the guidelines for
permanence and durability of the Committee on Production Guidelines for Book
Longevity of the Council on Library Resources

http:// pup.princeton.edu

Printed in the United States of America

1   2   3   4   5   6   7   8   9   10

2   3   4   5   6   7   8   9   10
(pbk)

THIS BOOK IS DEDICATED WITH LOVE TO

MY WIFE, MARITA, AND MY CHILDREN,

ELIZABETH, RACHEL, RONALD, AND MARITA

CONTENTS

A C K N O W L E D G M E N T S

THIS BOOK WAS MADE POSSIBLE by the combined efforts of more than 80 principal investigators who carried out the World Values surveys in 43 societies. The author expresses his deep gratitude to Rasa Alishauskiene, Vladimir Andreyenkov, Soo Young Auh, David Barker, Miguel Basanez, Elena Bashkirova, Marek Boguszak, Pi-chao Chen, Marita Carballo de Cilley, Eric da Costa, Juan Diez Nicolas, Karel Dobbelaere, Mattei Dogan, Javier Elzo, Ustun Erguder, Yilmaz Esmer, Blanka Filipcova, Michael Fogarty, Luis de Franca, Christian Friesl, Yuji Fukuda, Ivan Gabal, Alec Gallup, George Gallup, Renzo Gubert, Peter Gundelach, Loek Halman, Elemer Hankiss, Stephen Harding, Gordon Heald, Felix Heunks, Carlos Huneeus, Kenji Iijima, J. C. Jesumo, Fridrik Jonsson, Ersin Kalaycioglu, Jan Kerkhofs, Hans-Dieter Klingemann, Renate Koecher, Marta Lagos, Max Larsen, Ola Listhaug, Jin-yun Liu, Nicolae Lotreanu, Leila Lotti, V. P. Madhok, Robert Manchin, Carlos Eduardo Meirelles Matheus, Anna Melich, Ruud de Moor, Neil Nevitte, Elisabeth Noelle-Neumann, Stefan Olafsson, Francisco Andres Orizo, R. C. Pandit, Juhani Pehkonen, Thorleif Petterson, Jacques-Rene Rabier, Andrei Raichev, Vladimir Rak, Helene Riffault, Ole Riis, Andrus Saar, Renata Siemienska, Kancho Stoichev, Kareem Tejumola, Noel Timms, Mikk Titma, Niko Tos, Jorge Vala, Andrei Vardomatski, Christine Woessner, Jiang Xingrong, Vladimir Yadov, Seiko Yamazaki, Catalin Zamfir, Brigita Zepa, Xiang Zongde, and Paul Zulehner. The World Values surveys build on the 1981 European Values Systems Survey directed by Jan Kerkhofs, Ruud de Moor, Juan Linz, Elisabeth Noelle-Neumann, Jacques-Rene Rabier, and Helene Riffault. Thanks are also due to Karlheinz Reif and Anna Melich of the Commission of the European Union, who directed the Euro-Barometer surveys which constitute another major data source. Finally, I would like to acknowledge the contributions made by my colleagues in the two-wave Political Action study, Samuel Barnes, Dieter Fuchs, Jacques Hagenaars, Felix Heunks, M. Kent Jennings, Max Kaase, Hans-Dieter Klingemann, Jacques Thomasson, and Jan Van Deth.

Chapter 5 builds on a long-term collaboration with Paul Abramson; a much more detailed analysis of the shift toward Postmaterialist values appears in our jointly authored book, *Value Change in Global Perspective* (1995). Chapters 6 and 7 draw on collaborative work with James Granato, David Leblang, and Sue Ellis. I wish to express my deep appreciation to Abramson, Ellis, Granato, and Leblang, who are co-authors of these chapters. This book benefited from criticism and suggestions from David Appel, Sylvia Evers, Judy Federbush and Marita Inglehart, and from extensive discussions with Kazufumi Manabe, with whom I am exploring Japanese political culture.

I am also indebted to a number of people who have written criticism of my work: their efforts stimulated me to rethink various aspects of social change, to carry out new analyses, and sometimes even to change my mind. I appreciate the contributions of Thomas Baldino, Ferdinand Boeltken, Wilhelm Buerklin, Harold Clarke, Russell Dalton, Raymond Duch, Nitish Dutt, Scott Flanagan, James Gibson, Nan Dirk de Graaf, Thomas Herz, Nobutaka Ike, Wolfgang Jagodzinski, Max Kaase, Helmut Klages, Markus Klein, Oddbjorn Knutsen, William Lafferty, Alan Marsh, Sidney Milkis, Edward Muller, Rafaella Nardi, Achim Russ, James Savage, Elinor Scarbrough, Mitchell Seligson, Michaell Taylor, Jacques Thomassen, Thomas Trump, Jan Van Deth, and others who provided stimulation and ideas through scholarly debate.

Data from both the World Values surveys and the Euro-Barometer surveys are available from the ICPSR survey data archive at the University of Michigan. The processing and documentation of these surveys was made possible by a National Science Foundation grant to the author, SES 91–22433. Thanks are due to Julio Borquez, Georgia Aktan, Alejandro Moreno, and Bettina Schroeder for skillful and effective research assistance, and to Judith Ottmar for outstanding secretarial and administrative assistance.

Modernization and Postmodernization

INTRODUCTION

CHANGING VALUES AND CHANGING SOCIETIES

DEEP-ROOTED CHANGES in mass worldviews are reshaping economic, political, and social life. This book examines changes in political and economic goals, religious norms, and family values, and it explores how these changes affect economic growth rates, political party strategies, and the prospects for democratic institutions.

Throughout advanced industrial society, freedom of expression and political participation are becoming increasingly important to a growing share of the public. The literature on democratic theory suggests that mass participation, interpersonal trust, tolerance of minority groups, and free speech are important to the consolidation and stability of democracy. But until recently it has not been possible to analyze the linkages between individual-level attitudes such as these and the persistence of democratic institutions at the societal level: most of the research on political culture has been limited to democratic societies, with a small number of cases and little or no time series data. Reliable cross-level analysis requires data from a large number of societies that vary across the full economic and political spectrum. This book draws on a unique database, the World Values surveys, which opens up new possibilities for analyzing how peoples' worldviews influence the world.

These surveys cover a broader range of variation than has ever before been available for analyzing the impact of mass publics on political and social life. They provide data from 43 societies representing 70 percent of the world's population and covering the full range of variation, from societies with per capita incomes as low as $300 per year to societies with per capita incomes 100 times that high, and from long-established democracies with market economies to authoritarian states and ex-socialist states. The 1990 wave of this survey was carried out in Argentina, Austria, Belarus, Belgium, Brazil, Bulgaria, Canada, Chile, China, Czechoslovakia, Denmark, Estonia, Finland, France, Germany (with separate samples in the East and West regions), Great Britain, Hungary, Iceland, India, Ireland, Northern Ireland, Italy, Japan, South Korea, Latvia, Lithuania, Mexico, greater Moscow, the Netherlands, Nigeria, Norway, Poland, Portugal, Russia, Romania, Slovenia, South Africa, Spain, Sweden, Switzerland, Turkey, and the United States. The 1981 surveys provide time series data for 22 of these societies, enabling us to analyze the changes in values and attitudes that took place from 1981 to 1990. Figure 0.1 shows the countries covered in these surveys. We also analyze data from the Euro-Barometer surveys, carried out annually in all member countries of the European Union from 1970 to the 1990s; this provides a longer and more detailed time series with which to analyze change.

The World Values survey measures mass attitudes in a sufficiently large number of countries so that it is possible to carry out statistically significant analyses of cross-level linkages, such as those between political culture and democratic institutions. We find remarkably strong linkages between macro-level characteristics such as stable democracy, and micro-level characteristics, such as trust, tolerance, Postmaterialist values, and subjective well-being among individuals. Many other important societal-level variables—ranging from divorce rates to the emergence of environmentalist movements—also show strong cross-level linkages with underlying values and attitudes. One could argue that cultural changes are caused by societal changes, or that cultural changes are contributing to societal changes, or that the influences are reciprocal; but these data make it clear that mass belief systems and global change are intimately related.

The World Values surveys explore the hypothesis that mass belief systems are changing in ways that have important economic, political, and social consequences. We do not assume either economic or cultural determinism: our findings suggest that the relationships between values, economics, and politics are reciprocal, and the exact nature of the linkages in given cases is an empirical question, rather than something to be decided a priori.

The design of these surveys was influenced by various theories, including a theory of intergenerational value change (Inglehart, 1971, 1977, 1990). They explore the hypothesis that, as a result of the rapid economic development and the expansion of the welfare state that followed World War II, the formative experiences of the younger birth cohorts in most industrial societies differed from those of older cohorts in fundamental ways that were leading them to develop different value priorities. Throughout most of history, the threat of severe economic deprivation or even starvation has been a crucial concern for most people. But the historically unprecedented degree of economic security experienced by the postwar generation in most industrial societies was leading to a gradual shift from "Materialist" values (emphasizing economic and physical security above all) toward "Postmaterialist" priorities (emphasizing self-expression and the quality of life). Evidence of intergenerational value change began to be gathered cross-nationally in 1970; a long time series has now been built up with which to test these hypotheses.

This theory has been controversial: during the past 20 years, scores of critiques of various aspects of the theory have been published in this country and abroad. Much of the research on value change has been designed to disprove the thesis of a Postmaterialist shift or to propose alternative explanations of why this shift is occurring.

Some of the conceptualization underlying this debate is outdated: evidence from the World Values surveys indicates that the shift toward Materialist/ Postmaterialist values is only one component of a much broader cultural shift. About 40 of the variables included in these surveys seem to be involved in this shift. These variables tap a variety of orientations from religious outlook to sexual norms; but they all display large generational differences, are strongly correlated with Postmaterialist values, and in most societies moved in a predictable direction from 1981 to 1990. We use the label "Postmodernization" to describe this pervasive change in worldviews. The shift from Materialist to Postmaterialist values is by far the best documented component of this broader cultural change, but it is not necessarily the most important one: changing gender roles and changes in attitudes toward gays and lesbians have been even more dramatic.

The evidence accumulated so far indicates that pervasive changes are taking place in basic values of the publics of industrialized and industrializing societies throughout the world. Moreover, these changes seem to be linked with intergenerational population replacement processes, which means that they are gradual but have a good deal of long-term momentum.

This book argues that economic development, cultural change, and political change go together in coherent and even, to some extent, predictable patterns. This is a controversial claim. It implies that some trajectories of socioeconomic change are more likely than others—and consequently, that certain changes are foreseeable. Once a society has embarked on industrialization, for example, a whole syndrome of related changes, from mass mobilization to diminishing differences in gender roles, are likely to occur.

This, of course, is the central claim of Modernization theory; it was proposed by Marx and has been debated for well over a century. Although any simplistic version of this claim has long since been exploded, we *do* endorse the idea that some scenarios of social change are far more probable than others—and we will present a good deal of empirical evidence supporting this proposition. The World Values surveys reveal coherent cultural patterns that are closely linked with economic development.

At the same time, it seems clear to us that Modernization is not linear. In advanced industrial societies, the prevailing direction of development has changed in the last quarter century, and the change in what is happening is so fundamental that it seems appropriate to describe it as "Postmodernization" rather than "Modernization."

Modernization is, above all, a process that increases the economic and political capabilities of a society: it increases economic capabilities through industrialization, and political capabilities through bureaucratization. Modernization is widely attractive because it enables a society to move from being poor, to being rich. Accordingly, the core process of Modernization is industrialization; economic growth becomes the dominant societal goal, and achievement motivation becomes the dominant individual-level goal. The transition from preindustrial society to industrial society is characterized by "the pervasive rationalization of all spheres of society" (as Weber put it), bringing a shift from Traditional, usually religious values, to Rational-Legal values in economic, political, and social life.

But Modernization is not the final stage of history. The rise of advanced industrial society leads to another fundamentally different shift in basic values—one that de-emphasizes the instrumental rationality that characterized industrial society. Postmodern values become prevalent, bringing a variety of societal changes, from equal rights for women to democratic political institutions and the decline of state socialist regimes. The emergence of this Postmodern value syndrome is described in the following chapters.

This book demonstrates that there are powerful linkages between belief systems and political and socioeconomic variables such as democracy or economic growth rates. It also demonstrates coherent and to some extent predictable patterns of change in values and belief systems. These changes in worldviews reflect changes in the economic and political environment, but they take place with a generational time lag and have considerable autonomy and momentum of their own. Major cultural changes are occurring. They have global implications that are too important to ignore.

CHAPTER 1

Value Systems: The Subjective Aspect of Politics and Economics

MODERNIZATION AND POSTMODERNIZATION

Economic, cultural, and political change go together in coherent patterns that are changing the world in predictable ways.

This has been the central claim of Modernization theory, from Karl Marx to Max Weber to Daniel Bell. The claim has given rise to heated debate during the last two centuries. This book presents evidence that this claim is largely correct: though we cannot predict exactly what will happen in a given society at a given time, some major trends are predictable in broad outline. When given processes of change are set in motion, certain characteristics are likely to emerge in the long run.

The idea that social and economic change go together on coherent trajectories has been attractive but controversial ever since it was proposed by Marx. It is intellectually exciting because it not only helps *explain* economic, social, and political change, but may even provide a certain degree of predictability. So far, most efforts at prediction in human affairs have been exercises in hubris; it is common knowledge that many of Marx's predictions were wrong. Human behavior is so complex and influenced by such a wide range of factors, operating on so many levels, that any claim to provide precise, unqualified predictions is likely to go unfulfilled.

We do not make such promises: one cannot foretell the precise course of social change. Nevertheless, certain syndromes of economic, political, and cultural changes go together in coherent trajectories, with some trajectories being more probable than others. In the long term, across many societies, once given processes are set in motion, certain important changes are likely to happen. Industrialization, for example, tends to bring increasing urbanization, growing occupational specialization, and higher levels of formal education in any society that undertakes it (Lerner, 1958; Deutsch, 1964). These are core elements of a trajectory that is generally called "Modernization."

This trajectory also tends to bring less obvious but equally important long-term consequences, such as rising levels of mass political participation. Thus, although we cannot predict the actions of specific leaders in given countries, we *can* say that (at this point in history) mass input to politics is likelier to play a decisive role in Sweden or Japan than in Albania or Burma. And we can even specify, with far better than random success, what issues are likely to be most salient in the politics of the respective types of societies.

The Modernization trajectory is linked with a wide range of other cultural changes. As we will see, certain cultural values are conducive to the economic accumulation and investment that make industrialization possible, and the sharply contrasting gender roles that characterize all preindustrial societies almost inevitably give way to increasingly similar gender roles in advanced industrial society.

But social change is not linear. Although a specific Modernization syndrome of changes becomes probable when societies move from an agrarian mode to an industrial mode, no trend goes on in the same direction forever. It eventually reaches a point of diminishing returns. Modernization is no exception. In the past few decades, advanced industrial societies have reached an inflection point and begun moving on a new trajectory that might be called "Postmodernization."

With Postmodernization, a new worldview is gradually replacing the outlook that has dominated industrializing societies since the Industrial Revolution. It reflects a shift in what people want out of life. It is transforming basic norms governing politics, work, religion, family, and sexual behavior. Thus, the process of economic development leads to two successive trajectories, Modernization and Postmodernization. Both of them are strongly linked with economic development, but Postmodernization represents a later stage of development that is linked with very different beliefs from those that characterize Modernization. These belief systems are not mere consequences of economic or social changes, but shape socioeconomic conditions and are shaped by them, in reciprocal fashion.

Modernization Theory: The Linkages between
Culture, Economics, and Politics

The study of Modernization played a major role in social science in the late 1950s and early 1960s. Severely criticized subsequently, since the 1970s the Modernization concept has been widely considered discredited. As Pye (1990) has argued, it may be time to reexamine it. This chapter does so, presenting new empirical evidence and proposing a modified view of how Modernization works.

The central claim of Modernization theory is that industrialization is linked with specific processes of sociopolitical change that apply widely: though preindustrial societies vary immensely, one can meaningfully speak of a model of "modern" or "industrial" society toward which all societies tend to move if they commit themselves to industrialization. Economic development is linked with a syndrome of changes that includes not only industrialization, but also urbanization, mass education, occupational specialization, bureaucratization, and communications development, which in turn are linked with still broader cultural, social, and political changes.

One reason why Modernization theory aroused such great interest was its promise of predictive power: it implied that once a society entered the trajectory of industrialization, certain types of cultural and political change were likely to take place, ranging from lower birth rates to greater penetration by government, higher life expectancies, increased mass political participation, and perhaps even democracy. Some critics caricatured Modernization theory as implying that economic development would easily and automatically produce liberal democracies, and they dismissed this outlook as naive ethnocentrism. In fact, most Modernization theorists made more qualified prognoses than this, but if we drop the gratuitous assumption that Modernization is easy and automatic, even this claim does not seem totally implausible today.

Modernization theory has been developing for over a century. A wide variety of social theorists have argued that technological and economic changes are linked with coherent and predictable patterns of cultural and political change. But there has been continuing debate over the causal linkages: does economic change cause cultural and political change, or does it work in the opposite direction?

Marx emphasized economic determinism, arguing that a society's technological level shapes its economic system, which in turn determines its cultural and political characteristics: given the technological level of the windmill, a society will be based on subsistence agriculture, with a mass of impoverished peasants dominated by a landed aristocracy; the steam engine brings an industrial society in which the bourgeoisie becomes the dominant elite, exploiting and repressing an urban proletariat.

Weber, on the other hand, emphasized the impact of culture: it was not just an epiphenomenon of the economic system, but an important causal factor in itself; culture can shape economic behavior, as well as being shaped by it. Thus, the emergence of the Protestant Ethic facilitated the rise of capitalism, which contributed to both the Industrial Revolution and the Democratic Revolution: this view held that belief systems influence economic and political life, as well as being influenced by them.

Some of Marx's successors shifted the emphasis from economic determinism (which suggests that the revolutionary Utopia will come spontaneously) toward greater emphasis on the impact of ideology and culture. Thus Lenin argued that by itself, the working class would never develop sufficient class consciousness for a successful revolution; they needed to be led by an ideologically aware vanguard of professional revolutionaries.

Mao emphasized the power of revolutionary thinking even more strongly. Breaking with Marxist orthodoxy, he held that China need not wait for the processes of urbanization and industrialization to transform it; if an ideologically committed cadre could instill sufficient enthusiasm among the Chinese masses, a communist revolution could succeed even in an agrarian society. Mao's faith in the power of ideological fervor to triumph over material obstacles seemed justified by the Chinese communist victory in 1949 over forces with vastly superior financial resources and manpower. On the other hand, the fact that ideological determinism has limits was demonstrated by the disastrous failure of the Great Leap Forward in 1959: to develop a complex society, it seems, one needs experts with specialized knowledge, as well as right-thinking masses. When building a drainage system or constructing a steel mill, there are ways that work and ways that do not work, regardless of one's ideological perspective.

While conceding an important role to cultural factors, recent Modernization theorists such as Bell (1973) viewed changes in the structure of the workforce as the leading cause of cultural change. For Bell, the crucial milestone in the coming of "Postindustrial society" is reached when a majority of the workforce is in the tertiary sector of the economy, producing neither raw materials, nor manufactured goods, but services. This leads to a massive expansion of formal education, driven by the need for an increasingly skilled and specialized workforce. Other writers such as Lerner (1958) and Inkeles and Smith (1974) emphasized the importance of formal education as the main factor shaping a "modern" worldview.

Does Modernization lead to democracy? In the late 1950s, Khrushchev's reforms gave rise to hopes that the communist bloc might be on the brink of democratizing. The emergence of scores of newly independent postcolonial nations in the 1960s intensified these hopes. But optimism collapsed after the communist elite drove Khrushchev from power in 1964, the Soviet world settled down into a seemingly permanent authoritarian regime under Brezhnev, and authoritarian regimes took over in most postcolonial nations. Rostow (1961) had argued that economic development was inherently conducive to democratization, but by the 1970s most social scientists were skeptical of the idea. Authoritarian regimes seemed to be a permanent feature of the world—even (or perhaps especially) in those communist states that had achieved impressive economic growth. Industrialization could give rise to either democracy or dictatorship.

We propose a revised view of Modernization theory. We agree with the Modernization theorists on their most central point: that economic development, cultural change, and political change are linked in coherent and even, to some extent, predictable patterns. Some trajectories of change are more probable than others because certain configurations of values and beliefs, and political and economic institutions, are mutually supportive—while others are not. Thus, if one knows one component of a society, one can predict what other components will be present with far better than random success.

But while we follow Marx, Weber, and their successors in believing that change tends to take predictable rather than random trajectories, we differ from most Modernization theorists on four essential points:

1. Change is not linear. It does not move in one continuous direction until the end of history. Instead, it eventually reaches points of diminishing returns and has begun to move in a fundamentally new direction during the past few decades.

2. Previous versions of Modernization theory were deterministic, with the Marxist version tending toward economic determinism and the Weberian version sometimes tending toward cultural determinism. We believe that the relationships between economics and culture and politics are mutually support-

ive, as are the various systems of a biological organism. It would be senseless to ask whether the behavior of the human body is "really" determined by the muscular system, the circulatory system, the nervous system, or the respiratory system: each plays an essential role, and all activity ceases if any of them breaks down. Similarly, political systems and economic systems require a supportive cultural system—otherwise they would need to rely on naked coercion, which almost never endures for long. Conversely, a cultural system that was incompatible with its economic system would be unlikely to endure. Economic determinism, cultural determinism, and political determinism are *all* oversimplified: the causal linkages tend to be reciprocal. Unless these systems are mutually supportive, they are unlikely to survive.

3. We reject the ethnocentric perspective of those who equated Modernization with "Westernization": At one point in history, Modernization *was* concentrated in the West; today it is evident that the process is global, and that in some ways East Asia is now leading the process of Modernization. In keeping with this outlook, we propose a modified interpretation of Weber's (1904–5) thesis concerning the role of the Protestant Ethic in economic development. Weber was correct in viewing the rise of Protestantism as a crucial event in the Modernization of Europe. However, its impact was not unique to Protestantism but was mainly due to the fact that its acquisitive rationality supplanted a set of religious norms that are common to most preindustrial societies and that inhibit economic achievement. Protestantism was uniquely Western, but acquisitive rationality is not. Although industrialization occurred first in the West, the rise of the West was only one version of Modernization.

4. Democracy is not inherent in the Modernization phase, as some Modernization theorists suggested. There are alternative outcomes, with fascism and communism being the most prominent alternatives as Moore (1966) has pointed out. But democracy *does* become increasingly likely as societies move beyond the Modernization phase into Postmodernization. In the Postmodern phase, a distinctive syndrome of changes occur that make democracy increasingly likely—to the point where it eventually becomes costly to avoid.

We have stated four ways in which our view—which might be termed Postmodernization theory—differs from Modernization theory. Let us provide more detail on these points. Chapter 3 will present empirical evidence that supports the central claim underlying both Modernization theory and Postmodernization theory: that technological and economic changes tend to be linked with specific types of cultural, political, and social change. In other words, history tends to move in coherent and to some extent predictable patterns.

Socioeconomic Change Is Not Linear

The prevailing direction of development has changed in the last quarter century, and this shift is so distinctive that, rather than continuing to use the term "Modernization," we prefer to speak of "Postmodernization." The term "Postmodern" has been used with scores of different meanings, some of which are associated with a cultural relativism so extreme that it approaches cultural determinism: it asserts that culture shapes human experience almost entirely, unlimited by any external reality. Nevertheless, the term conveys an important insight, suggesting that the process known as Modernization is no longer at the cutting edge, and that social change is now moving in a fundamentally different direction. Moreover, the literature on Postmodernism suggests some of the specific attributes of this new direction: it is a move away from the emphasis on economic efficiency, bureaucratic authority, and scientific rationality that characterized Modernization, toward a more human society with more room for individual autonomy, diversity, and self-expression.

Unfortunately, the word "Postmodern" has become loaded with so many meanings that it is in danger of conveying everything and nothing. In architecture, the term has a clear meaning, designating a style of architecture that departs strikingly from the bare functionalism of "modern" architecture, which had become sterile and aesthetically repelling. The first glass box was a stunning tour de force, but by the one-hundredth box, the novelty had worn thin. Postmodern architecture reintroduced a human scale, with touches of adornment and references to the past, but incorporating new technology. In a similar vein, we suggest that Postmodern society is moving away from the standardized functionalism and the enthusiasm for science and economic growth that dominated industrial society during an era of scarcity—giving more weight to aesthetic and human considerations and incorporating elements of the past into a new context.

Neither Cultural Determinism Nor Economic Determinism

We disagree with the cultural determinism that is sometimes linked with the concept of Postmodernism. Postmodern writers are certainly correct in thinking that everyone perceives reality through some kind of cultural filter. Moreover, these cultural factors are steadily becoming a more *important* component of experience as we move from societies of scarcity, in which economic necessity limits one's behavior rather narrowly, to a world in which human will increasingly prevails over the external environment, allowing broader room for individual choice: this is a major reason why the Postmodern perspective has become increasingly credible.

But we reject the notion that cultural construction is the *only* factor shaping human experience. There is an objective reality out there too, and it applies to social relations as well as to natural science. External reality is crucial when it comes to the ultimate political resource, violence: when you shoot someone, that person dies regardless of whether he or she believes in ballistics or bullets. Similarly, though an architect has considerable scope for choice and imagination, if one forgets objective engineering principles, the building may collapse. Partly for this reason, architecture has preserved a healthy respect for reality. Similarly again, among physicists and astronomers, cultural biases play a minimal role. Despite some nonscientists' garbled references to the Heisenberg uncertainty principle, there is a worldwide consensus among natural scientists that they are studying a reality that exists independently of their preconceptions;[1] a theory eventually triumphs or is rejected depending on how well it models and predicts that reality—even if it violates people's long-standing beliefs.

The fact that some Postmodern writers' grasp of the physical sciences is a bit shaky was demonstrated rather strikingly in 1996, when Alan Sokal, a physicist irked with Postmodernist claims that objective reality had dissolved in the physical sciences, submitted an article to *Social Text*, one of this school's leading reviews. His article, entitled "Transgressing the Boundaries: Toward a Transformative Hermeneutics of Quantam Gravity," began: "There are many natural scientists, and especially physicists, who . . . cling to the dogma . . . that there exists an external world, whose properties are independent of any individual human being. . . . It has thus become increasingly apparent that physical 'reality,' no less than social 'reality,' is at bottom a social and linguistic construct; that scientific 'knowledge,' far from being objective, reflects and encodes the dominant ideologies and power relations of the culture that produced it" (Sokal, 1996: 217–18).

Though the text that followed was full of nonsense, this viewpoint was all too congenial to many Poststructuralists. Sokol went on to solemnly proclaim a long series of palpable absurdities about physical reality, including claims that the force of gravity and pi were socially constructed.

According to the *New York Times* account, this article was reviewed by a half dozen members of the review's editorial board, none of whom seemed to realize that the piece was a broad self-parody; they caught on shortly after the article was published, when the author himself revealed that it was a hoax.

This is not the first time that an august body has taken pi to be a social construct. In the nineteenth century, the Indiana state legislature passed a resolution officially declaring that pi would henceforth be a round 4.0, instead of the

---

[1] The Heisenberg principle is often misread as indicating that the laws of physics do not really govern the universe, which is fundamentally disorderly and unpredictable. At the ultimate level of smallness, the universe *is* probabilistic, not deterministic. Thus, the behavior of individual photons is unpredictable. But large numbers of photons behave in ways that are indistinguishable from being deterministic; and since human beings normally only deal with enormous numbers of photons, the behavior of light can be predicted very accurately by deterministic physical laws.

Other laws of physics are also slight oversimplifications of reality. For example, though the laws of gases say otherwise, it is conceivable that all of the air molecules in the reader's vicinity could suddenly rush to the far end of the room and remain there until you died a horrible death. The reader need not worry. This is technically possible, but the probability is so overwhelmingly low that it would not be expected to occur even once during the entire lifetime of the universe (or even in many lifetimes of the universe). At the microlevel, the universe is probabilistic; this is a very significant fact. But it is extremely misleading to leap from this fact to the conclusion that Newton and Avogadro had it all wrong, and that the universe is disorderly and your brain could spontaneously explode at any moment. Technically, it could. But it's not likely to happen until long after the sun and the stars have all disappeared from the sky.

inconvenient 3.1416; but this may be the first time that the proposition has been accepted by a panel of Ph.D.'s.

Despite this bit of entrapment, Postmodern thinkers are making a valid and profoundly important point in emphasizing that everyone's perception of reality is shaped by his or her subjective values and preconceptions. Moreover, these factors help shape even natural scientists' perceptions of reality—though not quite to the extent that some Postmodernists seem to think it does.

As Kuhn (1962) pointed out, objective tests alone do not immediately cause an entire scientific paradigm to be rejected; as inconsistent observations accumulate, the dominant paradigm may increasingly be called into question and new explanations proposed, but the new paradigm generally comes to be accepted through intergenerational replacement of scientists, more than through conversion of the older scientists. This reflects the fact that the cognitive structures of the older generation are organized around the old paradigm; it is far easier for the new generation to integrate their thinking according to the new paradigm than it is for the older generation, which would have to dismantle elaborate cognitive structures of inconsistent previous learning. At any given time, natural science reflects a cross-cultural consensus depending, ultimately, on how well given interpretations model and predict an external reality. The fine arts are at the opposite extreme. Aesthetic preferences largely *are* a matter of cultural predispositions.

Social phenomena fall between these extremes. Human behavior is heavily influenced by the culture in which one has been socialized. But objective factors set limits too, a recent example being the collapse and abandonment of state-run economies from Czechoslovakia to China: in running an economy, there are ways that work and ways that do not work.

Nevertheless, the term "Postmodern" is potentially useful: it implies that social change has moved beyond the instrumental rationality that was central to Modernization and is now taking a fundamentally different direction. This book does not discuss in any detail the various writers who have been labeled Postmodern: it is not about them. It deals with a set of empirical changes that are taking place among mass publics and will examine some specific ways in which the direction of social change has shifted. They include the fact that, while Modernization was not necessarily linked with democratization, Postmodernization *does* seem to be inherently conducive to the emergence of democratic political institutions.

Functional Analysis and Predictable Syndromes of Change

Economic, cultural, and political change go together in coherent patterns. The two most influential proponents of Modernization theory, Marx and Weber, agreed on this point. They disagreed profoundly on *why* economic, cultural, and political changes go together. For Marx and his disciples, they are linked because economic and technological change determines political and cultural changes. For Weber and his disciples, they are linked because culture shapes economic and political life.

Both Marx and Weber had major insights. We believe that economics shapes culture and politics—*and* vice versa. The causal linkages tend to be reciprocal. Political, economic, and cultural changes go together because societies without mutually supportive political, economic, and cultural systems are unlikely to survive for long: in the long run, the respective components either adapt to each other or the system flounders. And systems do indeed flounder: most of the societies that have ever existed are now extinct.

A culture is a system of attitudes, values, and knowledge that is widely shared within a society and is transmitted from generation to generation. While human nature is biologically innate and universal, culture is learned and varies from one society to another. The more central and early learned aspects of culture are resistant to change, both because it requires a massive effort to change central elements of an adult's cognitive organization, and because abandoning one's most central beliefs produces uncertainty and anxiety. In the face of enduring shifts in socioeconomic conditions, even central parts of culture may be transformed, but they are more likely to change through intergenerational population replacement than by the conversion of already socialized adults.

By culture, we refer to the *subjective* aspect of a society's institutions: the beliefs, values, knowledge, and skills that have been *internalized* by the people of a given society, complementing their external systems of coercion and exchange. This is a narrower definition of culture than is generally used in anthropology, because our purpose here is empirical analysis. We will examine the degree to which internal cultural orientations and external social institutions are linked empirically, rather than simply assume that they are. Building everything into one's definition of culture would make the concept useless for this type of analysis.

Any stable economic or political system has a compatible and supportive cultural system which legitimates that system. The people of that society have internalized a set of rules and norms. If they had not, the rulers could only get their subjects to comply with their rules by external coercion, which is costly and insecure. Moreover, to be effective in legitimating the system, cultures set limits to elite as well as mass behavior—shaping the political and economic systems, as well as being shaped by them. The process is not teleological, but it operates as if it were: societies with legitimate authority systems are more likely to survive than those without them.

Like Axelrod (1984), we find the evolutionary perspective a useful way to analyze how cultures and institutions develop: certain characteristics survive and spread because they have functional advantages in a given environment. Elster (1982) argues that functionalist interpretations of institutions are fundamentally flawed because they anthropomorphize institutions, postulating a purpose without a purposive actor—a view that has become widely accepted. But this criticism actually only applies to a crude and naive type of functionalist interpretation. Biologists today regularly use functionalist interpretations, especially when dealing with evolution. For example, plants are said to have developed bright flowers and nectar in order to attract bees so that the bees will fertilize them. Other plants are said to have developed poisonous leaves to discourage animals and insects from eating them. The newly hatched cuckoo chick pushes the other eggs out of the nest so that the parent birds will devote all their efforts to nourishing the cuckoo. And mammals living in the far North have developed white fur in order to be less visible against the snow.

Although they use this interpretation, neither biologists nor social scientists accept the crude teleological assumptions that Elster attributes to functional analysis. This mode of explanation is not used because biologists think that flowers or newly hatched cuckoos are consciously planning ahead or because they believe that evolution is guided by an anthropomorphic force. They use it because it is the most direct and parsimonious way to discuss the interaction between random mutations and natural selection that causes most mutations to die out—except for those with some functional advantage that enhances the organism's chances for survival. The mutations do not occur in order to serve some function; but they survive and spread because they do. A similar principle applies to functional interpretations of society. Dawkins (1989) argues convincingly that cultural traits or "memes" that function relatively well in a given environment replicate and spread for the same basic reason as do genes: they confer a survival advantage. Axelrod (1984) has demonstrated that certain strategies of conflict or cooperation function better than others and eventually drive out competing strategies.

Among the numerous types of societies that ever existed, the great majority have disappeared and the process is still going on. At the start of the twentieth century, absolute monarchy was the most widespread form of government. Today it has dwindled to a handful of surviving cases. Fascism spread rapidly in the 1920s and 1930s, and then all but disappeared in the 1940s, with a few loosely fascistic regimes surviving until the 1970s. The most recent case of mass extinction among societies has been the sudden collapse of communist regimes, which until recently controlled one-third of the world's population. Authoritarian state-run economies proved to be unworkable and uncompetitive in a high-technology environment. Although many of the ex-communist societies are still run by ex-communist elites, even the hard-liners among them are unlikely to return to the Stalinist model: it is a type of society that eventually proved to be dysfunctional.

Political institutions are also shaped by processes of natural selection. Some institutions survive for long periods, but most do not: three-quarters of the national constitutions now in effect were written since 1965. And even the surviving institutions undergo mutations. Thus, legislatures no longer initiate much legislation in most societies, but they do fill a legitimating function. Legislatures themselves do not possess a conscious will to serve a legitimating function—but the fact that they fill this function is a major reason why they survive and spread. A great many new constitutions have been written in the past decade, and virtually all of them give prominent roles to legislatures. This reflects a widespread awareness that in the contemporary world those political systems that have legislatures are more likely to enjoy legitimacy and to survive and flourish than are those without them.

Is the Modernization Concept Ethnocentric?

A standard criticism of Modernization theories is that they are either ethnocentric or teleological or both. Some of the early Modernization literature *did* simplistically equate Modernization with becoming (1) morally superior and (2) like the West. The flaws in this perspective are pretty obvious. Few people would attribute moral superiority to Western society today, and it is evident that East Asia is now at the cutting edge of Modernization in many respects.

But there is nothing ethnocentric in the concept that social change tends to take coherent, broadly predictable trajectories. In a given economic and technological environment, certain trajectories *are* more probable than others: it is clear that in the course of history, numerous patterns of social organization have been tried and discarded, while other patterns eventually became dominant. At the dawn of recorded history, a wide variety of hunting and gathering societies existed, but the invention of agriculture led to their almost total disappearance. They were displaced because agriculture has functional advantages over hunting and gathering. An account of the displacement of hunting-gathering societies by farming societies in precolonial Africa attributes this shift to an interaction between economic, biological, and cultural factors:

> Farming and herding yield far more calories per acre than does hunting wild animals or gathering wild plants. As a result, population densities of farmers and herders are typically at least 10 times those of hunter-gatherers. That's not to say that farmers are happier, healthier or in any way superior to hunter-gatherers. They are, however, more numerous. And that alone is enough to allow them to kill or displace hunter-gatherers.
>
> In addition, human diseases such as smallpox and measles developed from diseases plaguing domestic animals. The farmers eventually became resistant to those diseases, but hunter-gatherers do not have the opportunity. So when hunter-gatherers first come into contact with farmers, they tend to die in droves from the farmers' diseases.
>
> Finally, only in a farming society—with its stored food surpluses and concentrated villages—do people have the chance to specialize, to become full-time metalworkers, soldiers, kings and bureaucrats. Hence the farmers, and not the hunter-gatherers, are the ones who develop swords and guns, standing armies and political organization. Add that to their sheer numbers and their germs and it is easy to see how the farmers in Africa were able to push the hunter-gatherers aside. (Diamond, 1993)

Although a few hunting and gathering societies still survive today, they comprise less than one one-thousandth of the human population. After supplanting them, agricultural societies were dominant for many centuries, until the industrial revolution finally gave rise to a fundamentally new pattern of society. The transition to industrial society is far from complete, but today almost every society on earth has at least begun to industrialize, and it seems likely that within the next century, most of humanity will live in predominantly urban industrialized societies.

This does not mean that all societies will be identical. Industrial societies have a wide variety of cultures and institutions. But their common characteristics are also striking: virtually without exception, they are characterized by high degrees of urbanization, industrialization, occupational specialization, the use of science and technology, bureaucratization, reliance on legal-rational authority, relatively high levels of social mobility and emphasis on achieved rather than ascribed social status, high levels of formal education, diminishing sex role specialization, high standards of material well-being, and much higher life expectancies than were ever achieved in agrarian or hunting and gathering societies. Hunting and agriculture will not disappear from the earth—but they will no longer be the predominant way of life. They will shape the worldview of a small minority of the population (and even the remaining hunters and farmers will have their lives transformed by the fact that they live in a predominantly urban industrial world).

It is neither ethnocentric nor teleological to assert that hunting and gathering societies gave way to agricultural societies. It is a simple historical fact. It *would* be ethnocentric to assert that the people living in one type of society are inherently wiser, nobler, or morally superior to those living in another—but that gratuitous claim has nothing to do with the logic of the effort to discern which type of society is most likely to survive and spread in a given economic and technological environment. The people of industrial society are not more admirable than those of agrarian society, nor does history have an anthropomorphic preference for the former; but it *is* clear that a majority of the world's population once shifted from hunting and gathering into the agrarian mode—and are now moving into the industrial mode. They have done so because in a given technological and economic environment, certain forms of society have functional advantages over others. Moreover, modern industrial society is not the end of history. The process of cultural evolution is still going on. This book will explore the cultural changes that go with both Modernization and Postmodernization.

For many years, it has been alleged that cultural interpretations of society are inherently conservative. This is a half-truth. The Marxist Left did indeed view emphasis on cultural factors as reactionary, but more recently the Postmodern Left has strongly emphasized the crucial role played by subjective perceptions and cultural values. From this perspective, recognizing the decisive influence of cultural factors is considered a prerequisite to social progress.

Nevertheless, there is some truth in the idea that culture *itself* tends to be a conservative influence. The cultural approach argues that (1) people's responses to their situation are shaped by subjective orientations that vary cross-culturally and within subcultures, and (2) these variations in subjective orientations reflect differences in one's socialization experiences, with early learning conditioning later learning, making the former more difficult to undo. Consequently, action does not simply reflect external situations. Enduring differences in cultural learning also play an essential part in shaping what people do and think.

These postulates of the cultural approach have important implications for social change. Cultural theory implies that a culture *cannot* be changed overnight. One may change the rulers and the laws, but to change basic aspects of the underlying culture generally takes many years. Even then, the long-run effects of revolutionary transformation are likely to diverge widely from revolutionary visions and to retain important elements of the old pattern of society. Furthermore, when basic cultural change does occur, it will take place more readily among younger groups (where it does not need to overcome the resistance of inconsistent early learning) than among older ones, resulting in intergenerational differences. An awareness of the inertia linked with cultural factors may be dismaying to those who would like to believe they have a quick fix for deep-rooted social problems. But this awareness is essential to any realistic strategy of social change, and therefore is likely to produce policies that are more effective in the long run, than a perspective which simply denies that cultural factors are important. An awareness of the fact that deep-rooted values are not easily changed is essential to any realistic and effective program for social change.

The Marxist Left saw cultural factors as opiates of the people—forms of false consciousness that could only distract the attention of the masses from the real problems, which were economic. They found it attractive to believe that the proper indoctrination could speedily wash away all previous orientations: if the right elite, guided by the one true ideology, could take power and enforce the right programs, all social problems could be quickly solved.

Unfortunately, Marxist programs designed to bring swift and massive change to entire societies overlooked the reality of cultural persistence. When these programs did not correspond to the deep-rooted values and habits of the peoples on whom they were targeted, they could be implemented only through massive coercion. The most ambitious programs of rapid social change required enormous coercion and failed nevertheless: Stalin's Forced Collectivization and Great Purges and Mao's Great Leap Forward and Great Cultural Revolution not only failed to create a New Soviet Man, or a new Chinese culture, but led to enormous human suffering and ultimately were immensely counterproductive.

The Postmodern Left tends toward the other extreme, sometimes presenting culture as virtually supreme. There are no objective limits or standards: everything is determined by one's cultural perspective—to such an extent that any reference to objective reality is viewed as almost reactionary.

Both of these extremes distort the role of culture. This book presents empirical evidence that culture *is* a crucial part of reality. But it is only part of it.

CHANGE IS NOT LINEAR: POSTMODERNIZATION

Another way in which early versions of Modernization theory were deficient lay in the fact that they presented a linear view of social change: the future, everywhere, would simply be more of the same. Marx's tendency to do this is particularly well known, but he had plenty of company. With the advantages of a longer time perspective, it has become evident that such linear projections are far too simple. Although industrial society has become widespread (as Marx correctly predicted), it is not the end of the road. This book presents evidence that, beyond a certain threshold, social change takes a fundamental change in direction. In the past few decades, advanced industrial societies have moved through an inflection point, from the Modernization phase into a Postmodernization phase.

This book does not examine the intellectual history of Postmodern thought and will refer to Postmodern writers only in passing. It is, instead, an empirical analysis of how a Postmodern worldview is spreading among mass publics: as it will demonstrate, a Postmodern cultural shift is taking place that manifests many of the key characteristics discussed by Postmodern thinkers. This book will not discuss how Postmodern thought developed among these writers; but we *will* examine the reasons why they have become widely influential. No one has fully explained *why* Postmodern culture has emerged: a vast amount has been written about it, but the explanation has been almost entirely at the level of the intellectual history and permeation of Postmodernism. This is an important aspect of Postmodernism, but it is not an adequate explanation of why popular culture today is strikingly different from what it was a generation or two ago. Should we assume that the masses have been profoundly influenced by the writings of Foucault and Derrida? They may have had some (largely indirect) impact. But the change is mainly due to the fact that the firsthand life experience of mass publics in recent decades has been profoundly different from that of earlier generations. Deep-rooted changes in mass worldviews have taken place that enabled Postmodern ideas to find a receptive audience. This is why a Postmodern worldview that would almost certainly have been generally rejected a generation earlier has gained widespread acceptance in the last few decades.

It is not easy to give a brief account of Postmodern thought: there are several different versions of Postmodernism, and multiple readings of given authors. The literature is complex, contradictory, full of hyperbole, and sometimes reads like gibberish. *Question*: What is the difference between the Mafia and a deconstructionist? *Answer*: A deconstructionist makes you an offer you can't understand.

Ambiguity is a central component of Postmodern worldviews, and some writers seem to consider it a virtue. This is unfortunate because, underlying the ambiguous rhetoric, a real and important phenomenon is emerging. Another key tenet of Postmodernism is incredulity toward all metanarratives: all ideologies, religions, and other overarching explanations including natural science (and Postmodernism itself) cannot be believed. There is no external standard against which theories can be tested.

This perspective is carried to an extreme by Lyotard (1979) who depicts natural science as having dissolved into a relativism characterized by abrupt ruptures and sudden unforeseen changes of direction. His interpretation, which has had wide influence, implies that science, like normative thought, is no longer oriented by any external reality. Baudrillard (1983) also tends toward this extreme, implying that there is no objective reality out there.[2] This picture of science is one that few natural scientists would recognize. It is true, as Kuhn (1962) pointed out, that the development of knowledge is partly a social enterprise in which, when paradigm shifts occur, there is a temporary breakdown of the prevailing theoretical consensus. Kuhn's finding concerning the structure of scientific revolutions is frequently misinterpreted to mean that science itself is culture-bound. This is not the case: as we have noted, when a paradigm shift occurs, the split in acceptance is mainly along generational lines, based on different degrees of commitment to prior learning. The fact that science has a hermeneutic aspect does not mean that Indian or Chinese scientists are rejecting an interpretation that is accepted by French or German scientists. Instead, what occurs is an intergenerational culture lag.

But even these historic paradigm shifts involve much less discontinuity than Lyotard seems to imagine. Thus, Einstein's astonishing and paradigm-shifting breakthrough did *not* cause the previous body of scientific knowledge to be discarded. Newtonian physics continued (and continues) to function quite adequately: it simply became a special case within a broader Einsteinian framework. Many decades later, Newtonian calculations were used to take people safely to and from the moon: Einstein's limits become significant only under far more extreme conditions than are normally experienced on earth, or even in lunar voyages.

The way for Einstein's revolution was prepared by a series of findings that were inconsistent with the implications of Newtonian physics. Einstein developed a new theory that resolved these inconsistencies and generated a number of precise predictions that were then confirmed by a series of empirical tests that left little room for doubt that Einstein was right. These findings (with some delay) gave rise to a new theoretical consensus that gained acceptance from Buenos Aires to Tokyo.

Today, we seem to be on the brink of a new paradigm shift in physics—but it is unlikely to consign previous research to oblivion. Instead, the work of both Newton and Einstein will continue to apply, though within a still broader the-

[2] Thus, in 1991 Baudrillard asserted with characteristic hyperbole that the Gulf War did not take place: it was all a media event (Baudrillard, cited in Lyon, 1994: 52). But whether or not the war took place was not simply a question of one's cultural perspective: thousands of corpses testified to the fact that it was a reality. From the opposite end of the ideological spectrum, German revisionist historians have argued that the Holocaust did not really take place—it is just a case of the victors writing history. In this case, millions of corpses constitute a fact that goes beyond questions of interpretation.

oretical framework. The emerging Grand Unified Theory is designed to integrate all of the laws of physics into one coherent theory that will account for everything that has happened in the physical world from the birth of the universe to the present moment. Far from disintegrating into discontinuous and mutually incomprehensible islands of short-lived insights, natural science seems to be moving toward a mega-metanarrative. This is precisely the opposite of what Lyotard's followers seem to believe.

Nevertheless, stripped of its hyperbolic extremes, the literature on Postmodernity is dealing with a very real and important phenomenon: the world (or, at least, large parts of it) has moved onto a different trajectory from the one it had been following since the industrial revolution. And this new trajectory corresponds, in many respects, to what Postmodern observers claim is happening. Although there still is an external reality out there, culture does indeed have a tremendous influence on how reality is perceived. Moreover, the relative importance of culture seems to be increasing. On this new Postmodern trajectory, economic rationality determines human behavior less narrowly than before: the realm of the possible has expanded, and cultural factors are becoming more important. An empirically demonstrable cultural shift is taking place. The great religious and ideological metanarratives are losing their authority among the masses. The uniformity and hierarchy that shaped modernity are giving way to an increasing acceptance of diversity. And the increasing dominance of instrumental rationality that characterized Modernization is giving way to a greater emphasis on value rationality and quality of life concerns.

As this book will demonstrate with empirical evidence, a Postmodern shift in mass values and attitudes actually *is* taking place. This is why the ideas of Postmodern writers have found a receptive audience in recent decades. Although our analysis of empirical evidence cannot solve Postmodernity's normative questions, it does enable us to identify where the Postmodern shift is occurring and how fast it is moving, and it helps explain why it is taking place.

Has the entire world suddenly turned Postmodern, as some writers seem to assume? The empirical answer is No. Instead, some societies (such as Nigeria) are starting to modernize; others (such as China) are now modernizing very rapidly; still others (such as South Korea), seem to be reaching a turning point where they may be about to begin Postmodernization; and still others, such as Britain, Germany, and the United States, are well into the Postmodernization process—but even they do not lead the world in this respect. As we will see, the evidence indicates that the Nordic countries and the Netherlands are now the most Postmodern societies on earth.

This book will not merely chart the progress of Postmodernization; we will propose a theoretical explanation of *why* it is taking place. Before doing so, let us try to categorize Postmodernist thought: to a large extent, the changes that are occurring among mass publics correspond to these ideas. But how true this is depends on what version of Postmodernism one has in mind.

One could start by dividing Postmodern thought into three broad schools:

1. Postmodernism is the rejection of modernity: that is, of rationality, authority, technology, and science. Within this school, there is a widespread tendency to equate rationality, authority, technology, and science with Westernization. From this perspective, Postmodernism is considered to be the rejection of Westernization.

2. Postmodernism is the revalorization of tradition. Since Modernization drastically devalued tradition, its demise opens the way for this revalorization.

3. Postmodernism is the rise of *new* values and lifestyles, with greater tolerance for ethnic, cultural, and sexual diversity and individual choice concerning the kind of life one wants to lead.

These three versions of Postmodernism all capture important elements of what is taking place; though they are not incompatible, they emphasize different things.

Let us start with the rejection of modernity. Modernization offers great rewards, but imposes huge costs. It dismantles a traditional world in which the meaning of life is clear; warm, personal communal ties give way to an impersonal competitive society geared to individual achievement. Industrialization vastly increases human productivity; but (especially before labor unions and working-class political parties bring countervailing pressures to bear against capitalism) it gives rise to inhuman working conditions. Marx criticized not only the ruthless economic exploitation of early capitalism, but also the tremendous psychological costs of industrialization.

Decades later, Weber saw the rationalization of society as an inexorable aspect of Modernization; though it facilitated economic growth and public order, ever-increasing rationalization was disenchanting the world, forcing humanity into a painfully narrow iron cage of bureaucracy and mass production. What Weber deplored was the ubiquitous penetration of *instrumental* rationality: the rationality of immediate means was driving out the rationality of ultimate ends. Subsequently, Heidegger (1946, 1949) and Horkheimer and Adorno (1947) carried the critique of modernity farther, arguing that the instrumental rationality of industrialization had, ironically, undermined any absolute moral standards and given rise to new forms of irrationality and repression, culminating in the horrors of Hitler and Stalin. Instrumental rationality had virtually banished value rationality.

Today, this trend is beginning to reverse itself: instrumental rationality gained an exaggerated predominance during the rise of industrialization, but today, for reasons we will discuss in this book, a growing segment of society is concluding that the price is too high. Rationality, science, technology, and authority are here to stay; but their relative priority and their authority among mass publics are declining.

Within this first version of Postmodernism, there is a widespread tendency to confound rationality, authority, technology, and science with Westernization. Some of the (now outmoded) Modernization literature also equated Modernization with Westernization. If Postmodernism is the rejection of modernity, it would logically follow that Postmodernism is the rejection of

Westernization. This perspective is found in the work of Lyotard and Derrida, who tend to equate modernization with Western imperialism.

Western imperialism was an important phenomenon: it was brutally imposed on the rest of the world, it deserved to be rejected, and it deserves the scorn with which Postmodern writers treat it. But equating Modernization with Westernization is not a useful way to proceed. It emphasizes superficial and accidental aspects of Modernization and ignores the core process. Wearing Western clothing was not crucial; industrialization was. Moreover, it is inaccurate to equate modern imperialism with Westernization. In the number of people it subjugated, the Japanese empire was the second largest colonial empire in history and was fully as oppressive as any Western empire.

The essential core of Modernization is a syndrome of changes closely linked with industrialization: this syndrome includes urbanization, the application of science and technology, rapidly increasing occupational specialization, rising bureaucratization, and rising educational levels. It also includes one more thing, which was the motivating force behind the whole process: industrialization was a way to get rich.

By getting rich, one could dispel hunger, acquire military strength, and obtain a number of other desirable things, including a much longer life expectancy than was possible in preindustrial society. Adopting a life strategy aimed at getting rich becomes compellingly attractive from the perspective of low-income societies, once it has been demonstrated that it can be done. Furthermore, as we will show in this chapter, economic development actually seems to be conducive to subjective well-being (though only up to a certain point in history). In short, industrialization and the Modernization syndrome that goes with it were an attractive package. It carries a high cost, and from the viewpoint of advanced industrial society these costs may seem excessive. But from the perspective of most preindustrial societies, it seemed worth the price.

This constitutes another crucial difference between Modernization and Westernization: Western imperialism was imposed on non-Western societies, which almost universally rejected it when they were free to do so. By contrast, the goal of Modernization (that is, the industrialization syndrome) has now been adopted by almost every society on earth—and non-Western societies show no sign of wishing to abandon it. Quite the contrary, it is being pursued today with far more enthusiasm in the non-Western world than in the West. The Postmodern critique of Modernization comes overwhelmingly from within *Western* societies.

By the 1960s, the tendency to equate Modernization with Westernization had been abandoned by most Modernization theorists. And even if one goes by obvious external indicators, this concept has been outdated since at least 1980, when Japan became the world's leading automobile producer—outdoing the United States at Fordism itself. During the ensuing decade, Japan also attained the highest GNP per capita of any major nation, leading the world in attaining the fruits, as well as the tools, of Modernization. Historically, the Industrial Revolution occurred first in the West. But there is nothing uniquely

Western about technology and industrialization, or even bureaucratic rationality. Mathematics came to Europe from India and Egypt. China was the technologically most advanced society in the world for most of the past 2,000 years, losing its technological lead only in the seventeenth century (and it is not inconceivable that the nation will regain it). Similarly, another key aspect of modernity—bureaucracy—originated in China. The idea that rationality and technology are Western inventions is simply a myth. In the modern era, Westerners raised them to unprecedented levels and applied them to production to an unprecedented degree, but they are part of the human heritage, not something uniquely European. Today, East Asian and Southeast Asian societies are achieving the world's highest rates of economic growth and are at the cutting edge of Modernization in numerous other respects. Japan has become the world leader in various aspects of modernity, from consumer electronics to human life expectancy. And in recent years a growing flow of Western experts have made the pilgrimage to Japan to study the secrets of Japanese management, just as the Japanese earlier made the reverse voyage to learn industrialization from the West.

Another perspective views Postmodernism as the revalorization of tradition. This reverses one of the most prominent trends associated with Modernization. In the early modern era, the astonishing achievements of science and industry gave rise to a myth of Progress and radically discredited tradition. "New" became virtually synonymous with "good." But more recently, the instrumental rationality of modernity has lost its prestige. This has not only opened the way for tradition to regain status, but created a need for a new legitimating myth. In the Postmodern worldview, tradition once again has positive value—especially non-Western traditions. But the revalorization of tradition is sharply selective. Despite their ubiquitous presence in the traditional societies of both the Western and non-Western world, the norm that "Women's place is in the home" and the stern prohibition of extramarital sex are not among the aspects of premodern tradition that Postmodern writers admire.

The rise of new values and lifestyles is a profoundly important aspect of what is taking place today, throughout advanced industrial society. Derrida (1979, 1981) emphasizes this aspect of Postmodernity. Although Postmodernization *does* involve a downgrading of modernity and a revalorization of tradition, the emergence of a new culture is even more crucial, in our view. The best documented example of the rise of new values is the intergenerational shift from Materialist to Postmaterialist value priorities that seems to be taking place throughout advanced industrial society (Inglehart, 1971, 1977, 1990); but the rise of new values and lifestyles is taking place across many other aspects of life, from sexual orientation to religion.

Critical Theory

Apart from the Postmodern thinkers, Habermas (1984, 1987) has developed the most influential recent philosophical critique of modernity. Habermas differs from the Postmodern school on a number of points. One major disagreement is that, while Postmodernism tends to depict Modernization as a basically bad choice and rejects it, Habermas argues that while it imposed high costs, it also brought major benefits. Modernization is an unfinished project; we should build on it rather than reject it. Although we think that the process of change has taken a fundamentally new Postmodern turn, we agree with Habermas on this point. Industrialization provided more than just noisy, polluting automobiles and mindless television sitcoms. It provided two things that would be considered valuable from almost any cultural perspective: (1) greatly enhanced chances for survival, as measured by human life expectancy, and (2) higher levels of subjective well-being. Empirical evidence will be presented below in support of these assertions.

Another major disagreement centers on the fact that Postmodern thinkers conclude that there is no longer any basis by which universal moral standards could be validated: both God and Marx are dead. Habermas has not given up: he argues that moral norms may be merely social conventions, but if they are, it is imperative to develop rules for arriving at universally acceptable conventions. In a new version of the social contract, Habermas argues that a rational basis for collective life can be achieved only when social relations are organized so that the validity of every norm depends on a consensus arrived at in communication free from domination. Against the Postmodern position that moral rules are simply myths created by the ruling elite to justify the social order they control, Habermas argues that it *is* possible to reach a moral consensus that is not simply dominated by the ruling elites. Here again, we think he is right, and this debate raises a crucial question: Are cultural norms simply tools of the ruling elite? In order to answer this question, let us examine the relationship between authority and culture.

Authority and Culture

Marx defined ideology as false consciousness—that is, a consciousness shaped by power-holders to justify their right to rule (and to exploit), and to make it seem inevitable. The insight that culture is closely linked with power is important. It would be naive to believe that culture is neutral: in virtually every society, it legitimates the established social order—partly because the dominant elite try to shape it to help perpetuate their rule.

One of the leading themes in the literature on Postmodernism is the claim that culture is used to legitimate political authority; Foucault is a prominent advocate of this view. An extreme version of this position would hold that every reality is a politically constructed system of myths, and the key task of the social critic is to deconstruct these myths, which are simply a means to justify privilege and exploitation.

Without a doubt, culture serves to legitimate the social order. From an elite perspective, this may even be the most important thing it does. But it certainly is not the *only* thing it does. Culture integrates society in terms of common goals, satisfies intellectual and aesthetic needs, and finally—no insignificant point—also places some restraints on elites.

The extreme position, that mass belief systems are completely dominated by elite interests, assumes a degree of mass manipulability that is simply unrealistic. Recent historical developments illustrate this point. Thus, after 70 years of controlling the Soviet Union's educational systems, public discussion, the mass media, churches, and all other channels of communication to an historically unprecedented extent, the Soviet elite ultimately was not able to shape the worldviews of their people to conform to their goals: toward the end, not even the Soviet elite really believed the official ideology.

Western advanced industrial societies are also changing—whether their elites like it or not. A modern worldview that was once firmly established has gradually given way to Postmodern values that emphasize human autonomy and diversity instead of the hierarchy and conformity that are central to modernity. In both cases, a major factor leading to basic cultural change was the fact that the life experience of a new generation gave rise to new perceptions of reality. For the reality of one's firsthand experience ultimately intrudes. The official truth, propagated by the dominant elite, usually has a great deal of influence. But the firsthand life experience of ordinary people *also* counts—and ultimately may have even greater credibility than the official truth. How do established worldviews begin to crumble?

WHY IS THE POSTMODERN SHIFT OCCURRING?

The shift toward Postmodern values is not the first time that a major cultural shift has occurred. The transition from agrarian society to industrial society was facilitated by a shift from a worldview shaped by a steady-state economy. This worldview discouraged social mobility and emphasized tradition, inherited status, and communal obligations, backed up by absolute religious norms; it gave way to a worldview that encouraged economic achievement, individualism, and innovation, with increasingly secular social norms. Today, some of these trends linked with the transition from "Traditional" to "Modern" society have reached their limits in advanced industrial society, where change is taking a new direction.

This change of direction reflects the principle of diminishing marginal utility. Industrialization and Modernization required breaking the cultural constraints on accumulation that are found in any steady-state economy. In Western European history, this was achieved by the rise of the Protestant Ethic, which (though it had a long intellectual history) was like a random mutation from a functional perspective. If it had occurred two centuries earlier it might have died out. In the environment of its time, it found a niche: technological developments were making rapid economic growth possible, and the Calvinist worldview complemented these developments beautifully, forming a cultural-economic syndrome that led to the rise of capitalism and eventually to the industrial revolution. Once this had occurred, economic accumulation (for individuals) and economic growth (for societies) became the top priorities for an increasing part of the world's population; they are still the central goals for much of humanity. But eventually, diminishing returns from economic growth lead to a Postmodern shift that in some ways constitutes the decline of the Protestant Ethic.

Advanced industrial societies are now changing their sociopolitical trajectories in two fundamental respects:

1. Value systems. Increasing emphasis on individual economic achievement was one of the crucial changes that made Modernization possible. This shift toward Materialistic priorities entailed a de-emphasis on communal obligations and an acceptance of social mobility: increasingly, social status became something that an individual could achieve, rather than something into which one was born. Economic growth came to be equated with progress and was seen as the hallmark of a successful society.

In Postmodern society this emphasis on economic achievement as the top priority is now giving way to an increasing emphasis on the quality of life. In a major part of the world, the disciplined, self-denying, and achievement-oriented norms of industrial society are giving way to an increasingly broad latitude for individual choice of lifestyles and individual self-expression. The shift from "Materialist" values, emphasizing economic and physical security, to "Postmaterialist" values, emphasizing individual self-expression and quality of life concerns, is the most amply documented aspect of this change; but it is only one component of a much broader syndrome of cultural change.

2. Institutional structure. We are also reaching limits to the development of the hierarchical bureaucratic organizations that helped create modern society. The bureaucratic state, the disciplined, oligarchical political party, the mass-production assembly line, the old-line labor union, and the hierarchical corporation all played enormously important roles in mobilizing and organizing the energies of masses of people; they made the industrial revolution and the modern state possible. But they have come to a turning point for two reasons: first, they are reaching limits in their functional effectiveness; and second, they are reaching limits in their mass acceptability. Let us consider both factors.

Functional Limits to the Expansion of the Bureaucratic State

The rise and fall of the Soviet Union illustrates the limits of the centralized, hierarchical state. In its early decades, the USSR was remarkably efficient in mobilizing masses of relatively unskilled workers and vast quantities of raw materials to build the world's largest steel mill and the world's largest hydroelectric dam, and to attain one of the fastest rates of economic growth in the world. Although Stalin starved and murdered millions of Soviet citizens, the economic and military achievements of the Soviet state were so impressive that they convinced many people throughout the world that this type of society was the irresistible wave of the future. Soviet economic growth was remarkable in the 1950s, was still impressive in the 1960s, tapered off in the 1970s, and stagnated in the 1980s. Partly, this happened because a hypertrophied bureaucracy paralyzed adaptation and innovation. Bureaucracy is inherently deadening to innovation, and this problem became acute once the Soviet Union had moved past the stage of simply importing already proven technology from the West and was attempting to innovate in competition with the West and Japan. But the problem was not only the failure of central economic planning to cope with an increasingly complex and rapidly changing society. It also reflected a collapse of motivation and morale. Absenteeism rose to massive proportions, alcoholism became a tremendous problem, and confidence in government eroded until finally the entire economic and political system collapsed. Although the Soviet example is the most striking case, similar manifestations of the diminishing effectiveness of hierarchical, centralized bureaucratic institutions can be seen throughout industrial society. State-run economies are giving way to market forces; old-line political parties and labor unions are in decline; and bureaucratic corporations are losing ground to more loosely organized and participatory types of organization.

These organizational and motivational changes are intimately related. One reason for the decline of the classic bureaucratic institutions of industrial society is the fact that they are inherently less effective in high-technology societies with highly specialized workforces than they were in the earlier stages of industrial society. But another reason for their decline is the fact that they also became less *acceptable* to the publics of Postmodern society than they were earlier, because of changes in these people's values.

The mass production assembly line broke down manufacturing into simple standardized routines that were repeated endlessly. This was marvelously effective in turning out masses of relatively simple, standardized products. But a price was paid for the increased productivity that resulted: the workers became cogs in huge centrally coordinated machines. Marx, Weber, and others were concerned with the alienation and depersonalization of industrial society that made one's work uninteresting, dehumanizing, devoid of meaning. In societies of scarcity, people were willing to accept these costs, for the sake of economic gains. In affluent societies, they are less willing to do so.

Modern bureaucracy makes a similar tradeoff involving loss of individual identity and autonomy for the sake of increased productivity; this enables it to process thousands or millions of people, using standardized routines. It, too, is inherently depersonalizing: in a rational bureaucracy, individuals are reduced to interchangeable roles. Bureaucracy strips away spontaneity, personal likes and dislikes, individual self-expression and creativity. Nevertheless it was an effective tool for coordinating the efforts of hundreds or even millions of individuals, in the large organizations of modern society.

But its effectiveness and its acceptability are eroding. Postmodern values give a higher priority to self-expression than to economic effectiveness: people are becoming less willing to accept the human costs of bureaucracy and of rigid social norms. As this book will demonstrate, Postmodern society is characterized by the decline of hierarchical institutions and rigid social norms, and by the expansion of the realm of individual choice and mass participation.

Up to the middle of the twentieth century, "Modernization" was an unambiguous term. It referred to urbanization, industrialization, secularization, bureaucratization, and a culture based on bureaucratization—a culture that requires a shift from ascriptive status to achieved status, from diffuse to specific forms of authority, from personalistic obligations to impersonal roles, and from particularistic to universalistic rules. In some areas this Modernization process is still going on. But elsewhere, trends that were central to the Modernization process have undergone a fundamental change of direction.

For example, one of the most striking phenomena of the past two hundred years was the rapidly expanding scope of government. Industrial societies became increasingly centralized, hierarchical, and bureaucratized. Until recently, highly centralized state-run economies and societies like the Soviet Union seemed to be the logical end point of Modernization. One might view this trend as profoundly progressive, with the Marxists, or deplore it as threatening to human liberty, with Schumpeter (1947) and Orwell (1949)—but the growth of government seemed inexorable. At the start of the twentieth century, government spending in most societies consumed from 4 to 10 percent of gross domestic product. By 1980, it ranged from 33 to 60 percent of a much bigger output in Western societies, and 70 to 80 percent in some socialist societies. Increasing government ownership and control of the economy seemed to be the wave of the future.

It was not. During the 1980s, further expansion of the state reached a point of diminishing returns, both functionally and in terms of mass acceptance. It first ran into growing political opposition in the West and then collapsed in the Eastern bloc.

The mass production assembly line and the mass production bureaucracy were the two key organizational instruments of industrial society, and in the early phase of Modernization they had a high payoff—enabling factories to produce millions of units and governments to process millions of individuals through standardized routines. But the trend toward bureaucratization, centralization, and government ownership and control has reversed itself. Modern economies lose their effectiveness when the public sphere becomes overwhelmingly large. And public confidence in hierarchical institutions is eroding throughout advanced industrial society.

Cultural Changes Leading to Postmodernization

An equally basic change in the direction of change has been a shift in the predominant norms and motivations underlying human behavior. Virtually all agrarian societies were characterized by value systems that stigmatized social mobility. This was inevitable, given their steady-state economies. The main source of wealth was land, which is in fixed supply: the only way to become rich was by seizing someone else's land—which probably required killing the owner. Such internal violence was threatening to the survival of any society and was repressed by norms that emphasized acceptance of the status into which one was born and stigmatized the ambitious and the arriviste. At the same time, traditional societies emphasized duties of sharing and charity—which helped compensate the poor for the absence of social mobility, but further undermined the legitimacy of economic accumulation.

The rise of a Materialistic value system that not only tolerated economic accumulation but encouraged it as something laudable and heroic was a key cultural change that opened the way for capitalism and industrialization. Weber (1904–5) examined this process in *The Protestant Ethic and the Spirit of Capitalism*, but his work can be seen as a case study of a more general phenomenon. Today the functional equivalent of the Protestant Ethic is operating most vigorously in East Asia and is fading away in Protestant Europe, as technological development and cultural change have become global phenomena.

Precisely because they attained high levels of economic security, the populations of the first nations to industrialize have gradually come to emphasize Postmaterialist values, giving higher priority to the quality of life than to economic growth. This shift has been taking place throughout advanced industrial society during the past few decades, as we will see in chapter 4. With this has come a shift from the politics of class conflict, to political conflict based on such issues as environmental protection and the status of women and sexual minorities. Marxist ideology, based on economic determinism, was an immensely influential guide for interpreting the transition from agrarian to "modern" or industrial society. It is outmoded for the analysis of "Postmodern" society.

To clarify what we mean by this term, let us examine the specific changes that are linked with Postmodern values. Some of these trends differ radically from those of Modernization.

The Origins of Postmodern Values: Existential Security

A new worldview is gradually replacing one that has dominated Western society since the Industrial Revolution. The consequences of this transformation are still taking shape, and elements of the older culture are still widespread, but the major features of the new pattern can be discerned.

This shift in worldview and motivations springs from the fact that there is a fundamental difference between growing up with an awareness that survival is precarious, and growing up with the feeling that one's survival can be taken for granted.

The urge to survive is common to all creatures, and normally survival is precarious. This reflects a basic ecological principle: the population of any organism tends to rise to meet the available food supply; it is then held constant by starvation, disease, or predators. Throughout most of history, this principle has governed the lives of all organisms, including humanity. Until very recently, the survival of most human beings was precarious.

Eventually, culture began to soften the competition for survival among humans. Although the ways in which this was done varied enormously from one society to another, virtually all traditional societies established cultural norms that limited the use of violence and repressed aspirations for social mobility. On one hand, they emphasized sharing and charity among those who were relatively well-off, stigmatizing accumulation as greed; and on the other hand, they justified acceptance of the existing social order by the poor. And cultural norms limiting reproduction softened the ruthless competition for survival that overpopulation brought.

A few centuries ago, cultural changes in Protestant Europe led to the reversal of the traditional stigma against economic accumulation, and a Materialistic worldview began to spread. Using new technology and organizational techniques, production began to outpace population growth. Nevertheless, well into the twentieth century, severe economic scarcity still prevailed widely: the Marxist view that people and history were motivated primarily by the struggle for economic goods was a fairly accurate first approximation of the driving force underlying the modernizing phase of industrial society.

The economic miracles and the welfare states that emerged after World War II gave rise to a new stage of history, and ultimately laid the way for the rise of Postmodern values. Fundamental changes in formative experiences have given rise to a distinct value system among a growing segment of those raised in advanced industrial societies during the years since World War II. The postwar birth cohorts in these societies grew up under conditions profoundly unlike those that shaped previous generations. They differed in two respects: first, the postwar economic miracles produced levels of prosperity that were literally unprecedented in human history. Real per capita income in most industrial societies rose to levels several times as high as had ever been experienced before the war, and in some cases (such as Japan) to levels 20 or 30 times higher than ever before. The economic pie became much bigger; this alone would tend to encourage a greater sense of economic security.

But the impact of unprecedented prosperity interacted with a second factor: the emergence of the modern welfare state. A sense of existential security, not absolute wealth, is the crucial variable, and the welfare state reinforced economic growth in producing a sense of security. The pie was much bigger than ever before, and it was distributed more evenly and more reliably than before. For the first time in history, a large share of the masses grew up with the feeling that survival could be taken for granted.

This led to a process of intergenerational value change that is gradually transforming the politics and cultural norms of advanced industrial societies. The best documented aspect of this process is the shift from giving top priority to economic and physical security, to giving top priority to self-expression and the quality of life. This shift from Materialist to Postmaterialist priorities has been measured annually since 1970 in surveys carried out in a number of Western societies. A massive body of evidence is now available, and it demonstrates that an intergenerational shift has been taking place in the predicted direction. This shift from Materialist to Postmaterialist value priorities has brought new political issues to the center of the stage and provided much of the impetus for new political movements.

More recent research indicates that the rise of Postmaterialism itself is only one aspect of a still broader process of cultural change that is reshaping the political outlook, religious orientations, gender roles, and sexual mores of advanced industrial society (Inglehart, 1990). These changes are related to a common concern: the need for a sense of security that religion and absolute cultural norms have traditionally provided. In advanced industrial societies during the decades since World War II, the emergence of unprecedentedly high levels of prosperity, together with the relatively high levels of social security provided by the welfare state, have contributed to a decline in the prevailing sense of vulnerability. For the general public, one's fate is no longer so heavily influenced by unpredictable forces as it was in agrarian and early industrial society. This has been conducive to the spread of Postmodern orientations that place less emphasis on traditional cultural norms—especially those norms that limit individual self-expression.

THE THEORY OF INTERGENERATIONAL VALUE CHANGE

Let us reexamine the theory of intergenerational value change in light of recent findings. Our theory is based on two key hypotheses (Inglehart, 1977):

1. *A Scarcity Hypothesis*. An individual's priorities reflect the socioeconomic environment: one places the greatest subjective value on those things that are in relatively short supply.

2. *A Socialization Hypothesis*. The relationship between socioeconomic environment and value priorities is not one of immediate adjustment: a substantial time lag is involved because, to a large extent, one's basic values reflect the conditions that prevailed during one's preadult years.

The scarcity hypothesis is similar to the principle of diminishing marginal utility in economic theory. The complementary concept of a need hierarchy (Maslow, 1954) helped shape the survey items used to measure value priorities. In its simplest form, the idea of a need hierarchy would probably command almost universal assent. The fact that unmet physiological needs take priority over social, intellectual, or aesthetic needs has been demonstrated all too often in human history: starving people will go to almost any length to obtain food. The rank ordering of human needs varies as we move beyond those needs directly related to survival; Maslow's need hierarchy does not hold up in detail. But there does seem to be a basic distinction between the "material" needs for physiological sustenance and safety, and nonphysiological needs such as those for esteem, self-expression, and aesthetic satisfaction.

The recent economic history of advanced industrial societies has significant implications in light of the scarcity hypothesis. For these societies are a striking exception to the prevailing historical pattern: they still contain poor people, but most of their population does *not* live under conditions of hunger and economic insecurity. This has led to a gradual shift in which needs for belonging, esteem, and intellectual and aesthetic satisfaction became more prominent. Other things being equal, we would expect prolonged periods of high prosperity to encourage the spread of Postmaterialist values; economic decline would have the opposite effect.

But it is not quite that simple: there is no one-to-one relationship between economic level and the prevalence of Postmaterialist values, for these values reflect one's *subjective* sense of security, not one's economic level per se. While rich individuals and nationalities tend to feel more secure than poor ones, these feelings are also influenced by the cultural setting and social welfare institutions in which one is raised. Thus, the scarcity hypothesis must be interpreted in connection with the socialization hypothesis.

One of the most pervasive concepts in social science is the notion of a basic human personality structure that tends to crystallize by the time an individual reaches adulthood, with relatively little change thereafter. This concept permeates the literature from Plato through Freud and extends to the findings of contemporary survey research. Early socialization seems to carry greater weight than later socialization.

This, of course, does not imply that no change occurs during adult years. In individual cases, dramatic behavioral shifts are known to occur, and the process of human development never comes to a complete stop (Erikson, 1982; Levinson et al., 1979; Brim and Kagan, 1980). Nevertheless, human development seems to be far more rapid during the preadult years than afterward, and the great bulk of the evidence points to the conclusion that the statistical likelihood of basic personality change declines sharply after one reaches adulthood (Block, 1981; Costa and McCrae, 1980; Jennings and Niemi, 1981; Jennings and Markus, 1984).

Taken together, these two hypotheses generate a clear set of predictions concerning value change. First, while the scarcity hypothesis implies that prosperity is conducive to the spread of Postmaterialist and Postmodern values, the socialization hypothesis implies that neither an individual's values nor those of a society as a whole are likely to change overnight. Instead, fundamental value change takes place gradually; largely it occurs as a younger generation replaces an older one in the adult population of a society.

Consequently, after a period of sharply rising economic and physical security, one would expect to find substantial differences between the value priorities of older and younger groups: they would have been shaped by different experiences in their formative years. But there would be a sizable time lag between economic changes and their political effects. Ten or 15 years after an era of prosperity began, the age cohorts that had spent their formative years in prosperity would begin to enter the electorate. A decade or so might pass before these groups began to occupy positions of power and influence in their society; another decade or so would pass before they reached the level of top decision makers. But their influence would become important long before this final stage. Postmaterialists are more highly educated, more articulate, and politically more active than Materialists. Consequently, their political impact tends to outweigh that of the Materialists.

The socialization hypothesis complements the scarcity hypothesis. It helps account for apparently deviant behavior: on one hand, the miser who experienced poverty in early years and relentlessly continues piling up wealth long after attaining material security; and on the other hand, the saint who remains true to the higher-order goals instilled by his or her culture, even in the face of severe deprivation. In both instances, an explanation for the seemingly deviant behavior of such individuals lies in their early socialization.

The unprecedented economic and physical security of the postwar era has led to an intergenerational shift from Materialist to Postmaterialist values. The young emphasize Postmaterialist goals to a far greater extent than do the old, and cohort analysis indicates that this reflects generational change rather than aging effects. At the time of our first surveys, in 1970–71, Materialists held an overwhelming numerical preponderance over Postmaterialists, outnumbering them by nearly four to one. By 1990, the balance had shifted dramatically, to a point where Materialists outnumbered Postmaterialists by only four to three. Projections based on population replacement suggest that by the year 2000 Materialists and Postmaterialists will be about equally numerous in many Western countries (Abramson and Inglehart, 1992).

Postmaterialists are not non-Materialists, still less are they anti-Materialists. The term "*Post*-materialist" denotes a set of goals that are emphasized *after* people have attained material security, and *because* they have attained material security. Thus, the collapse of security would lead to a gradual shift back toward Materialist priorities. The emergence of Postmaterialism does not reflect a reversal of polarities, but a change of *priorities*: Postmaterialists do not place a negative value on economic and physical security—they value it positively, like everyone else; but unlike Materialists, they give even higher priority to self-expression and the quality of life.

Thus, Inglehart (1977: 179–261) found that an emerging emphasis on quality of life issues was being superimposed on the older, class-based cleavages of industrial society. Although social class voting was declining, it had by no means disappeared (and was unlikely to do so). But while the old class-based polarization over ownership and control of the means of production had once dominated politics, it was increasingly sharing the stage with new Postmaterialist issues. Both industrial and preindustrial cleavages persisted, beside cross-cutting new issues.

The shift from Materialist to Postmaterialist priorities is a core element of the Postmodernization process. In early industrial society, emphasis on economic achievement rose to unprecedented levels. While traditional societies stigmatized social mobility and individual economic accumulation, modern industrial societies provided a positive evaluation of economic achievement. The Captain of Industry became a cultural hero, and the nineteenth-century U.S. Supreme Court interpreted "the pursuit of happiness" to mean "freedom to accumulate property." The core societal goal of the Modernization process was economic growth. This made a good deal of sense. Early industrializing nations had only recently acquired the technological means to cope with chronic scarcity. In such societies, where malnutrition is the main cause of death, economic achievement is an overwhelmingly important part of the pursuit of happiness. The transition from preindustrial society to advanced industrial society brings a change from a life expectancy of 35 or 40 years, to one of 75 or 80 years. This is a huge improvement.

As the possibility of starvation receded from being a major concern to an almost insignificant prospect for most people, prevailing values gradually changed. Economic security is still something that everyone wants, but it is no longer a synonym for happiness. Increasingly, the publics of advanced industrial societies have come to emphasize quality of life concerns, sometimes giving environmental protection priority over economic growth. Thus, emphasis on economic achievement rises sharply with the Modernization process, but then levels off as Postmodernization occurs. Societies in which Postmaterialists are most numerous have lower growth rates than those in which Materialists are overwhelmingly predominant—but the former tend to have higher levels of subjective well-being. Postmodernization brings declining emphasis not only on economic growth itself, but also on the scientific and technological developments that make it possible; emphasis shifts from coping with survival, to maximizing subjective well-being.

The Risk Society

Ironically, as survival has become unprecedentedly secure, the peoples of advanced industrial societies have become increasingly sensitive to risk. Indeed, one of the most influential critics of postmodern society characterizes it as Risk Society (Beck, 1992). According to this diagnosis, the distributional conflicts over "goods" (such as property, income, and jobs) that characterized industrial society have given way to distributional conflicts over "bads," such as the risks of nuclear technology, genetic research, and the threat to the environment. With industrialization, the religious certainties of feudal society were eroded, but they gave rise to an increasing degree of existential security; with the rise of Postmodern society, the risks of life have become incalculable and increasingly escape the control mechanisms of society. In this updated version of the doctrine of late capitalism, the ecological crisis takes over the role previously played by the legitimation crisis of late capitalism.

It is ironic that in societies where human life expectancy has risen by 20 years during the last century, concerns about risk have become central political issues. It is ironic, but logical: for it is precisely *because* the risk of starvation has receded almost to the vanishing point that people have been able to redirect their concerns from pervasive daily uncertainty concerning survival to more remote concerns such as the ecological crisis. The very success of the welfare states of advanced industrial society in providing an unprecedented degree of existential insecurity has given rise to the expectation that the state can and should ensure everyone against all uncertainties. As Samuelson has put it,

> The reason for this paradox is entitlement: a postwar word and concept. By entitlement, I mean more than the catalogue of well-known government benefits (Social Security being the most prominent) or various modern "rights" (such as the "right" of those in wheelchairs to public ramps). Entitlement expresses a modern conviction, a broader sensibility, that defines Americans' attitudes toward social conditions, national institutions and even the world. Increasingly, we have come to believe that certain things are (or ought to be) guaranteed to us. We feel entitled. Among other things, we expect secure jobs, rising living standards, enlightened corporations, generous government, high-quality health care, racial harmony, a clean environment, safe cities, satisfying work, and personal fulfillment. (Samuelson, 1995: 4)

What Samuelson attributes to American society holds true of other Postmodern societies. As long as people were overwhelmingly engaged in coping with survival, more remote concerns had little salience. But the attainment of existential security does not bring Nirvana. Postmodern society has brought increasing attention to quality of life problems, and far more demanding standards for societal performance. As a net result, people probably worry as much as ever, but they worry about different things: there are profound differences in the behavior and worldviews of people who feel insecure about their personal survival and people who worry about global warming.

Stress, Coping Stategies, and Belief Systems

Far-reaching though it is, the rise of Postmaterialist values is only one aspect of a still broader process of cultural change that is reshaping orientations toward authority, religion, politics, gender roles, and sexual norms among the publics of advanced industrial society. What is driving this broad shift from survival values toward well-being values? This question is illuminated by recent research in social psychology on the relationships between stress, coping strategies, and belief systems.

People who feel that their survival is threatened react with stress; this stimulates efforts to cope with the threat. But high levels of stress can become dysfunctional and even life-threatening. One's belief system mediates the response to new or threatening situations, helping the individual deal with stress and shaping the strategy used to cope with the threat. If one *has* a belief system that provides a sense of predictability and control, it reduces stress to a level conducive to coping behavior (Rotter, 1966). In the absence of such a belief system, people experience a sense of helplessness, leading to withdrawal instead of coping behavior; these withdrawal responses may take the form of depression, fatalism, resignation, or alcohol or drug abuse (M. Inglehart, 1991).

Virtually all of the world's major cultures have belief systems which provide reassurance that, even though the individual alone cannot understand or predict what lies ahead, it is in the hands of a benevolent higher power. One's future may be unpredictable, but this higher power will ensure that things work out. Both religion and secular ideologies provide assurance that the universe is not random, but follows a plan which guarantees that (in this world or the next) everything will turn out well. This belief reduces stress, enabling one to shut out anxiety and focus on some immediate coping strategy. Without such a belief system, extreme stress is likely to produce withdrawal reactions.

Religion is the dominant influence on the belief systems of most preindustrial societies. In religious worldviews, the higher power is an omniscient and benevolent God. Stress is reduced by a system of absolute rules that govern many aspects of life and maximize predictability. In secular societies, the state or a strong political leader fills the role of the higher power. Under conditions of great unpredictability, people have a powerful need to see authority as not only strong, but also benevolent—even in the face of evidence to the contrary.

Communist ideology provided a functional equivalent to religion, furnishing an explanation of how the universe functioned and where history was going. Although many of Marx's predictions eventually turned out to be wrong, the ideology provided a sense of predictability and reassured people that infallible leaders were in charge.

The Authoritarian Reflex

In societies undergoing an historical crisis, a phenomenon has been observed that might be called the Authoritarian Reflex. Rapid change leads to severe insecurity, giving rise to a powerful need for predictability. Under these circumstances, the Authoritarian Reflex takes two forms:

1. Fundamentalist or nativist reactions. This phenomenon frequently occurs in preindustrial societies when they are confronted with rapid political and economic change through contact with industrialized societies; and it is often found among the more traditional and less secure strata in industrial societies, especially during times of stress. In both cases, the reaction to change takes the form of a rejection of the new, and a compulsive insistence on the infallibility of old, familiar cultural patterns.

2. Adulation of strong secular leaders. In secularized societies, severe insecurity brings a readiness to defer to strong secular leaders, in hopes that superior men of iron will can lead their people to safety. This phenomenon frequently occurs in response to military defeat or economic or political collapse.

Thus, disintegrating societies often give rise to authoritarian and xenophobic reactions. Pogroms broke out in the declining years of Czarist Russia, and after its collapse power was seized by rulers who were even more ruthlessly authoritarian than the czars. Similarly, the Great Depression of the 1930s helped bring Hitler to power in Germany and contributed to the rise of fascistic dictators in a number of other countries, from Spain to Hungary to Japan.

Massive insecurity is conducive not only to a need for strong authority figures to protect one from threatening forces, but also to xenophobia (Tajfel,

1978; Tajfel and Turner, 1979; Hamilton, 1981; Jackson and Inglehart, 1996). Frighteningly rapid change breeds an intolerance of cultural change, and of different ethnic groups. Thus, in the United States during the late nineteenth and early twentieth centuries, when the price of cotton went down, lynchings of Blacks went up in the South. This was a reaction to insecurity, not a cognitive response to the belief that Blacks were manipulating the price of cotton: the lynchers were aware that Blacks had little influence on the cotton market (Beck, Massey, and Tolnay, 1989). Similarly, the Great Depression of the 1930s gave rise to the twin phenomena of Hitler and anti-Semitism—and ultimately, to the Holocaust. There was nothing inevitable in this horror story. It occurred in a society that previously had been more tolerant toward Jews than had Russia or France and had one of the most socially integrated Jewish communities in Europe. It reflected traumatic insecurity caused by military defeat and political and economic collapse, rather than anything uniquely German. In a hauntingly parallel phenomenon, the collapse of the economic and political systems of what used to be the Soviet Union and Yugoslavia has given rise to ultranationalism and "ethnic cleansing."

Postmodernism: Declining Emphasis on Political, Economic, and Scientific Authority

All societies depend on some legitimating formula for authority: unless their leaders' decisions are seen as legitimate, they rest solely on coercion. A central component of Modernization was the shift from religious authority to rational-bureaucratic authority, justified by claims that the governing institutions were conducive to the general good.

A major component of the Postmodern shift is a shift away from *both* religious and bureaucratic authority, bringing declining emphasis on all kinds of authority. For deference to authority has high costs: the individual's personal goals must be subordinated to those of a broader entity. But under conditions of insecurity, people are more than willing to do so. Under threat of invasion, internal disorder, or economic collapse, people eagerly seek strong authority figures who can protect them.

Conversely, conditions of prosperity and security are conducive to pluralism in general and democracy in particular. This helps explain a long-established finding: rich societies are much likelier to be democratic than poor ones. This finding was pointed out by Lipset (1960) and has been confirmed most recently by Burkhart and Lewis-Beck (1994). The reasons why this is true are complex (we will examine them in chapter 5); but one factor is that the authoritarian reflex is strongest under conditions of insecurity.

Until recently, insecurity was a central part of the human condition. Only recently have societies emerged in which most of the population did *not* feel insecure concerning survival. Thus, both premodern agrarian society and modern industrial society were shaped by survival values. But the Postmodern shift has brought a broad de-emphasis on all forms of authority.

Changing Religious Orientations, Gender Roles, and Sexual Norms

The rise of Postmodernism is the reverse of the Authoritarian Reflex: Postmaterialist values characterize the most *secure* segment of advanced industrial society. Postmaterialist values developed in the environment of the historically unprecedented economic growth and the welfare states that emerged after World War II. And they are a core element of a Postmodern shift that is reshaping the political outlook, religious orientations, gender roles, and sexual norms of advanced industrial society. Two factors contribute to the decline of traditional political, religious, social, and sexual norms in advanced industrial societies.

The first is that an increasing sense of security brings a diminishing need for absolute rules. Individuals under high stress have a need for rigid, predictable rules. They need to be sure of what is going to happen because they are in danger—their margin for error is slender and they need maximum predictability. Postmaterialists embody the opposite outlook: raised under conditions of relative security, they can tolerate more ambiguity; they are less likely to need the security of absolute rigid rules that religious sanctions provide. The psychological costs of deviating from whatever norms one grew up with are harder to bear if a person is under stress than if a person feels secure. Taking one's world apart and putting it together again is extremely stressful. But Postmaterialists—people with relatively high levels of security—can more readily accept deviation from familiar patterns than can people who feel anxiety concerning their basic existential needs. Consequently, Postmaterialists accept cultural change more readily than others.

The second reason is that societal and religious norms usually have a function. Such basic norms as "Thou shalt not kill" (the Judeo-Christian version of a virtually universal social norm) serve an important societal function. Restricting violence to narrow, predictable channels is crucial to a society's viability. Without such norms, a society would tear itself apart.

Many religious norms such as "Thou shalt not commit adultery" or "Honor thy father and mother" are linked with maintaining the family unit. Various versions of these norms are also found in virtually every society on earth because they serve crucial functions. But in advanced industrial society, some of these functions have dwindled.

The role of the family has become less crucial than it once was. Although the family was once the key economic unit, in advanced industrial society one's working life overwhelmingly takes place outside the home. Similarly, education now takes place mainly outside the family. Furthermore, the welfare state has taken over responsibility for survival. Formerly, whether children lived or died depended on whether their parents provided for them, and the parents' survival depended on their children when they reached old age. Today, though the family is still important, it is no longer a life or death relationship; its role has largely been taken over by the welfare state. The new generation can survive if the family breaks up—or even if neither parent is around. One-parent families and childless old people have vastly better chances for survival under contemporary conditions than ever before. As long as it threatens the survival of children, society is apt to view divorce as absolutely wrong: it undermines the long-term viability of society itself. Today, the functional basis of this norm and other norms reinforcing the two-parent family has eroded: does that mean that society changes its values? No—at least, not immediately.

Cultural norms are usually internalized very firmly at an early age, and backed up by prerational sanctions. People's opposition to divorce does not simply reflect an individual's rational calculation that "the family is an important social unit, so I should stay married." Instead, divorce tends to be made a question of good and evil, through absolute norms. Norms that constrain people's behavior even when they strongly want to do something else are norms that have been taught as absolute rules, and inculcated so that their consciences torture them if these norms are violated. Such societal norms have a great deal of momentum. The mere fact that the function of a given cultural pattern has weakened or disappeared does not mean that the norm immediately disappears. But it opens the way for that norm to weaken gradually, especially if those norms conflict with strong impulses to the contrary.

Norms supporting the two-parent heterosexual family are weakening for a variety of reasons, ranging from the rise of the welfare state to the drastic decline of infant mortality rates, which means that a couple no longer needs to produce four or five children in order for the population to reproduce itself. Experimentation and testing of the old rules takes place; gradually, new forms of behavior emerge that deviate from traditional norms, and the groups most likely to accept these new forms of behavior are the young more than the old, and the relatively secure, more than the insecure.

The Postmodern shift involves an intergenerational change in a wide variety of basic social norms, from cultural norms linked with ensuring survival of the species, to norms linked with the pursuit of individual well-being. For example, Postmaterialists and the young are markedly more tolerant of homosexuality than are Materialists and the old. This is part of a pervasive pattern. Postmaterialists have been shaped by security during their formative years and are far more permissive than Materialists in their attitudes toward abortion, divorce, extramarital affairs, prostitution, and euthanasia. Materialists, conversely, are likely to adhere to the traditional societal norms that favored childbearing, but only within the traditional two-parent family—and that heavily stigmatized any sexual activity outside that setting.

Traditional gender role norms from East Asia to the Islamic world to Western society discouraged women from taking jobs outside the home. Virtually all preindustrial societies emphasized childbearing and childrearing as the central goal of any woman, her most important function in life, and her greatest source of satisfaction. In recent years, this perspective has been increasingly called into question, as growing numbers of women postpone having children or forego them completely in order to devote themselves to careers outside the home.

EXISTENTIAL SECURITY AND THE RISE OF POSTMODERN VALUES

Throughout advanced industrial society, there is evidence of a long-term shift away from traditional religious and cultural norms. This decline of traditional norms is closely linked with the shift from Materialist toward Postmaterialist values. In terms of face content, this is not obvious: none of the survey items used to measure Materialist/Postmaterialist values makes any reference whatever to religion or to sexual or gender norms. Nevertheless, all of these values are components of a broad cultural change linked with the transition from industrial to postindustrial society. The shift to Postmaterialism and the decline of traditional religious and sexual norms go together because they share a common cause: the unprecedented levels of existential security attained in contemporary advanced industrial society that grows out of the economic miracles (both Western and Asian) of the past several decades, and the rise of the welfare state.

In the highly uncertain world of subsistence societies, the need for absolute standards and a sense that an infallible higher power will ensure that things ultimately turn out well filled a major psychological need. One of the key functions of religion has been to provide a sense of certainty in an insecure environment. Not only economic insecurity gives rise to this need: the old saying that "there are no atheists in foxholes" reflects the fact that physical danger also leads to a need for belief in a higher power. But in the absence of war, prosperity and the welfare state have produced an unprecedented sense of security concerning one's survival. This has diminished the need for the reassurance that religion traditionally provided.

These same factors have weakened the functional basis of a pervasive set of norms linked with the fact that, throughout most of history, the traditional two-parent family was crucial to the survival of children, and thus, of society. These norms ranged from disapproval of divorce, abortion, and homosexuality, to negative attitudes toward careers outside the home for married women. As we will see, it is precisely in the most advanced welfare states that mass adherence to traditional religious and family norms has declined most rapidly. This is no coincidence. These factors are also changing another major aspect of people's worldviews: respect for authority is declining throughout advanced industrial society.

The difference between feeling secure or insecure about survival is so basic that it has led to a wide-ranging but coherent syndrome of changes, from the "survival" values that characterized agrarian and early industrial society, to the "well-being" values that characterize advanced industrial society.

The difference between whether one views survival as uncertain, or assumes that it can be taken for granted, is central in shaping people's life strategies, giving rise to very distinct worldviews. Throughout most of history, in both agrarian and early industrial society, survival has been uncertain for the great majority of the population; consequently, they have emphasized survival values. Postmodern values grow out of the unprecedented mass prosperity of advanced industrial societies in which, for the first time in history, large segments of the public take survival for granted. These contrasting value systems have ramifications that extend across politics, economics, sexual and family norms, and religion, as table 1.1 illustrates.

The shift from modern to Postmodern values is eroding many of the key institutions of industrial society, through the following changes:

1. In the political realm, the rise of Postmodern values brings declining respect for authority, and growing emphasis on participation and self-expression. These two trends are conducive to democratization (in authoritarian societies) and to more participatory, issue-oriented democracy (in already democratic societies). But they are making the position of governing elites more difficult.

Respect for authority is eroding. And the long-term trend toward increased mass participation is not only continuing, but has taken on a new character. In large-scale agrarian societies, political participation was limited to a narrow minority. In industrial society, the masses were mobilized by disciplined elite-led political parties. This was a major advance for democratization, and it resulted in unprecedented numbers of people taking part in politics by voting—but mass participation rarely went much beyond this level. In Postmodern society the emphasis is shifting from voting, to more active and issue-specific forms of mass participation. Mass loyalties to long-established hierarchical political parties are eroding; no longer content to be disciplined troops, the pub-

TABLE 1.1
Security and Insecurity: Two Contrasting Value Systems

	Survival Is Seen as	
	Insecure	*Secure*
1. Politics		
Need for strong leaders	De-emphasis on political authority	
Order	Self-expression, participation	
Xenophobia/fundamentalism	Exotic/new are stimulating	
2. Economics		
Priority to economic growth	Quality of life = top priority	
Achievement motivation	Subjective well-being	
Individual vs. state ownership	Diminishing authority of both private and state ownership	
3. Sexual/Family Norms		
Maximize reproduction—but only in two-parent heterosexual family	Individual sexual gratification Individual self-expression	
4. Religion		
Emphasis on higher power	Diminishing religious authority	
Absolute rules	Flexible rules, situational ethics	
Emphasis on predictability	Emphasis on meaning and purpose of life	

lic has become increasingly autonomous and elite-challenging. Consequently, though voter turnout is stagnant or declining, people are participating in politics in increasingly active and more issue-specific ways. Moreover, a growing segment of the population is coming to value freedom of expression and political participation as things that are good in themselves, rather than simply as a possible means to attain economic security.

But these changes have had a traumatic impact on the old-line political machines of industrial society, which are in disarray almost everywhere. Throughout the history of industrial society, the scope of state activities had been growing rapidly; it seemed to be a law of nature that government control of economy and society would continue to expand. That trend has now reached a set of natural limits—both for functional reasons and because of eroding public trust in government and a growing resistance to government intrusion. The people of each society tend to assume that this erosion of confidence is due to factors unique to their own country; in reality, it is taking place throughout advanced industrial society.

Xenophobia thrives under conditions of rapid change and insecurity. Today, this is especially evident in what used to be Yugoslavia and the Soviet Union, and ethnic hatred has not disappeared even in more secure industrial societies. But xenophobia is less widespread in secure societies than in insecure ones; and in long-term perspective, the more secure societies seem to be moving toward increasing acceptance of diversity. Finally, Postmodern politics are distinguished by a shift from the class-based political conflict that characterized industrial society, to increasing emphasis on cultural and quality of life issues.

2. In the economic realm, existential security leads to increasing emphasis on subjective well-being and quality of life concerns; for many people, these become higher priorities than economic growth. The core goals of Modernization, economic growth, and economic achievement are still positively valued, but their relative importance is declining.

There is also a gradual shift in what motivates people to work: emphasis shifts from maximizing one's income and job security toward a growing insistence on interesting and meaningful work. Along with this comes a twofold shift in the relationship between owners and managers. On one hand, we find a growing emphasis on more collegial and participatory styles of management. But at the same time, there is a reversal of the tendency to look to government for solutions to such problems and a growing acceptance of capitalism and market principles. Both trends are linked with a growing rejection of hierarchical authority patterns and rising emphasis on individual autonomy. Ever since the era of laissez-faire capitalism, people have almost automatically turned to government to offset the power of private business. Today, there is a widespread feeling that the growth of government is becoming functionally ineffective and a threat to individual autonomy.

3. In the realm of sexual behavior, reproduction, and the family, there is a continued trend away from the rigid norms that were a functional necessity in

agrarian society. In these societies, traditional methods of contraception were unreliable, and children born outside a family with a male breadwinner were likely to starve; sexual abstinence except in marriage was a key means of population control. The development of effective birth control technology, together with prosperity and the welfare state, have eroded the functional basis of traditional norms in this area; there is a general shift toward greater flexibility for individual choice in sexual behavior, and a dramatic increase in the acceptance of homosexuality. This not only continues some of the trends associated with modernity, but breaks through to new levels. Gays and lesbians have come out of the closet, and unmarried parenthood is a normal part of prime time television.

4. In the realm of ultimate values, we also find both continuity and striking change. One of the key trends associated with Modernization was secularization. This trend has continued, where established religious institutions are concerned: the publics of most advanced industrial societies show both declining confidence in churches and falling rates of church attendance and are placing less emphasis on organized religion. This does not mean that spiritual concerns are vanishing, however: for we also find a consistent cross-national tendency for people to spend *more* time thinking about the meaning and purpose of life. The dominance of instrumental rationality is giving way to growing concern for ultimate ends.

These trends reflect the unprecedented security that has developed in Postmodern society. Economic accumulation for the sake of economic security was the central goal of industrial society. Ironically, their attainment set in motion a process of gradual cultural change that has made these goals less central—and is now bringing a rejection of the hierarchical institutions that helped attain them.

PREDICTING CULTURAL CHANGE

The theory of value change generates a number of clear predictions. Table 1.1 outlines a set of qualitative shifts linked with growing existential security. This table shows what *kinds* of values we would expect to become more widespread as Postmodernization takes place. But the theory is not limited to qualitative predictions concerning the general direction of cultural change. It also generates a set of quantitative predictions concerning where and how fast these changes should occur. The scarcity hypothesis postulates that a sense of existential security is conducive to Postmodern values. This gives rise to the following predictions:

1. In cross-national perspective, Postmodern values will be most widespread in the richest and most secure societies; the publics of impoverished societies will place more emphasis on survival values.

2. Within any given society, Postmodern values will be most widespread

among the more secure strata: the wealthier and better educated will be most likely to hold a whole range of security values, including Postmaterialism; the less secure strata will emphasize survival priorities.

3. Short-term fluctuations will follow the implications of the scarcity hypothesis: prosperity will enhance the tendency to emphasize well-being values; economic downturn, civil disorder, or war will lead people to emphasize survival values.

4. Long-term changes will also reflect the scarcity hypothesis. In societies that have experienced high levels of security for several decades, we should find a long-term shift from survival values toward well-being values. This is not a universal trend that sweeps the entire world, like the popularization of pop culture fostered by the global mass media. Instead, the shift toward well-being values is occurring mainly in those societies that have attained such a high level of prosperity and safety that a substantial share of the population takes survival for granted; it is not found in societies that have not experienced rising prosperity. On the other hand, it is *not* a uniquely Western phenomenon: it should appear in any society that *has* experienced the transition to high mass security.

The socialization hypothesis postulates that neither an individual's values nor those of a society as a whole will change overnight. In connection with the scarcity hypothesis, this generates three additional predictions:

5. In societies that have experienced a long period of rising economic and physical security, we will find substantial differences between the value priorities of older and younger groups: the young will be much likelier to emphasize well-being values than the old. This reflects the fact that the young experienced greater security during their formative years than did the old. Fundamental value change takes place mainly as younger birth cohorts replace older ones in a given society.

6. These intergenerational value differences should be reasonably stable over time: though immediate conditions of security or insecurity will produce short-term fluctuations, the underlying differences between younger and older birth cohorts should persist over long periods of time. The young will not take on the values of the old as they age, as would happen if the intergenerational differences reflected life-cycle effects; instead, after two or three decades have passed, the younger cohorts should still show the distinctive values that characterized them at the start of the period.

7. In cross-national perspective, large amounts of intergenerational *change* will be found in those countries that have experienced relatively high rates of economic *growth*: if differences between the values of young and old were a normal feature of the human life cycle, they would be found everywhere. But if, as our theory implies, this process of value change is driven by historical changes in the degree of security experienced during one's preadult years, then the age differences found in a given society will reflect that society's economic history: the difference between the values of young and old will be largest in countries like Western Germany or South Korea that experienced the greatest

increases in prosperity during the past 40 years; and conversely, the difference between the values of young and old will be small or nonexistent in such countries as Nigeria and India, which experienced relatively little increase in per capita income from 1950 to 1990.

Thus, high *levels* of prosperity should be conducive to high *levels* of Postmaterialism and other Postmodern values; high rates of economic *growth* should produce relatively rapid rates of value *change* and relatively large intergenerational *differences*.

8. Finally, the theory of intergenerational value change not only yields predictions about what kinds of values should be emerging and where, but even predicts how much value change should be observed in a given period of time. Since the change is based on intergenerational population replacement, if one knows the distribution of values across birth cohorts in a given nation and the sizes of the cohorts, one can estimate how much change will be produced in a given time span, as a result of intergenerational population replacement. With the four-item Materialist/Postmaterialist values battery, for example, population replacement should produce a shift toward Postmaterialism of approximately one point per year on the Materialist-Postmaterialist percentage difference index (Abramson and Inglehart, 1992).

Authoritarianism and the Postmodern Shift

We have just described a syndrome of cultural changes through which people are shifting from one belief system to another. Under conditions of insecurity people seek strong authority; this is part of a worldview that also embraces ethnocentrism, traditional gender roles, and traditional religious norms.

This is not the first time that such a configuration of orientations has been observed. Several decades ago, Adorno et al. (1950) demonstrated that orientations toward authority, aggression toward outgroups, and a high degree of adherence to social conventions go together in a syndrome that they called *The Authoritarian Personality*. This work was controversial, evoking numerous critiques on both theoretical and methodological grounds. Despite massive criticism, this thesis generated an immense body of research that has survived and evolved over the years, with particularly significant recent contributions being made by Altemeyer (1981, 1988).

From the outset of our research, the Authoritarian Personality thesis seemed potentially relevant to the rise of Materialist/Postmaterialist values that are at the core of Postmodern values. A standardized set of authoritarianism items was used in a cross-national exploration of nationalism and internationalism. The results were disappointing: dimensional analysis showed that the authoritarianism items did not cluster together as they theoretically should (Inglehart, 1970).

Subsequent pilot tests gave similar results. Authoritarianism items showed relatively weak relationships with each other; some were closely related to the Materialist/Postmaterialist dimension, but others tapped quite different dimensions. Authoritarianism, as originally operationalized, has a poor empirical fit with Materialism/Postmaterialism.

The theoretical basis of authoritarianism is not necessarily incompatible with that of Materialism/Postmaterialism, but there are important differences in focus. The initial concept of authoritarianism emphasizes the psychodynamics of harsh discipline in early childrearing, rather than influences from the broader economic and political environment. On the other hand, Hyman and Sheatsley (1954), in their critique of the original study, argue a cognitive explanation: certain respondents, especially those from a lower socioeconomic level, may show an authoritarian-type response because this is a more or less accurate reflection of the conditions governing their adult lives; Altemeyer also endorses this interpretation. Our own interpretation of the genesis of Materialist/Postmaterialist values contains elements of both positions. It emphasizes the importance of early experiences, but links them with one's formative experiences as a whole, and not just parental discipline.

The original authoritarianism hypothesis does not predict either the age-group differences or the social class differences that are strikingly evident in our data. Quite the contrary, studies of authoritarianism have found that children tend to be *more* authoritarian than adults. It would not be impossible to reinterpret the *Authoritarian Personality* hypothesis in such a way as to explain the age and class differences. One might argue that childrearing practices vary according to social class and have changed over time. But if one did so, one would then need to seek an explanation of *why* they vary and *why* they have changed. Quite probably, one would eventually trace this explanation to the economic and political changes on which we rest our own interpretation.

Another important distinction between authoritarianism and Materialist/Postmaterialist values lies in the way they are measured: authoritarianism reflects *levels* of support for given positions; Materialist/Postmaterialist values deal with *priorities*—that is, the relative *rank* of various goals. This distinction is crucial, and will be discussed at some length in chapter 3. Our theory implies that an intergenerational change in *priorities* is taking place—and *not* that people no longer value economic security. Nevertheless, the two streams of research agree on one major point: orientations toward authority are related to a broad range of other orientations, forming the core of a coherent worldview.

Changing Mass Values: Testing Our Predictions

We now have a large body of empirical evidence on cultural change, from surveys carried out in more than 40 societies over the past 25 years. Using these data, this book will test these predictions. Chapter 4 focuses on the relatively detailed and abundant body of data concerning the Materialist/Postmaterialist value shift; chapters 8 and 9 examine the evidence of a much broader process of cultural change involving religious, civic, sexual, and economic norms as well as Materialist/Postmaterialist values.

The following chapters examine survey data from societies containing 70

percent of the world's population. For 21 of these societies, we have time series data from the World Values surveys carried out in 1981 and 1990. For several societies, we also have detailed time series data on value changes from
1970 to 1994. The evidence from these surveys indicates that advanced industrial societies are moving on a common trajectory. To a striking degree, societies in Western Europe, North America, Latin America, Eastern Europe, and
East Asia are undergoing similar cultural changes in politics, economics, sex
and gender norms, and religion. Although they have widely varying cultural
traditions and start from very different levels, they are generally moving in the
same direction.

Do the values linked with secure survival actually move in the predicted direction from 1981 to 1990? As we will see below, on the whole our predictions
hold up very well when tested against data from the 21 nations surveyed in
both 1981 and 1990. About 40 variables were strongly correlated with existential security. These variables move in the predicted direction in most countries for which data are available. Moreover our predictions hold up best in
those countries that experienced relatively prosperous circumstances; they fail
to apply in those countries that experienced economic decline and political upheaval—precisely as the theory implies.

These findings suggest that social science can sometimes have predictive
power: when we are dealing with relatively enduring aspects of the outlook of
given birth cohorts, we can anticipate that change will tend to move in a specific direction, as intergenerational population replacement occurs. Other factors such as the rise and fall of the economic cycle or war and peace will also
shape the outlook of a given society at a given time. But in the long run, across
many societies, such situational factors tend to cancel each other out: the influence of intergenerational population replacement, on the other hand, tends
to work in a specific direction for many decades, and its cumulative impact can
be great.

This study was motivated by the belief that mass belief systems have important economic, political, and social consequences. Although it has long
been believed that given cultural patterns tend to go with given economic and
political systems, this belief has rested mainly on impressionistic evidence: it
has been difficult to demonstrate empirically because, until recently, cross-culturally comparable measures of beliefs and values have not been available on
a global scale. Empirical evidence from 43 societies demonstrates that cultural
patterns are, indeed, linked with important economic and political variables—
and that the cross-level linkages are astonishingly strong.

Chapter 5 examines the causal linkages between culture and democracy in
greater detail; chapter 6 focuses on the linkages between culture and economic
growth. In both cases, the evidence suggests that culture is not just a dependent variable, but has an important impact on both democracy and economic
growth.

The evidence we will examine makes it clear that—as both Marx and Weber
argued—belief systems, economics, and politics *are* intimately related. Their

linkages seem to reflect neither a simple Marxian causality (with economics driving culture and politics) nor a simple Weberian causality (with culture driving economics and politics), but reciprocal causal relationships. Cultural, economic, and political systems tend to be mutually supportive in any society that survives for long. They help shape each other, and they are changing the world in ways that are to some extent predictable.

Individual-Level Change and Societal-Level Change

THE NEXT SEVERAL CHAPTERS examine the linkages between individual-level value change and changes at the societal level. This chapter investigates how economic development brings changes in human life strategies—and then examines the ways in which cultural changes can give rise to legal and institutional changes. Chapter 5 will analyze how belief systems influence the emergence of democratic institutions, chapter 6 examines the impact of values on economic growth, and chapter 7 examines their impact on political cleavages.

In analyzing the linkages between belief systems and societal variables, the first question one is likely to ask is, Do the values and attitudes of individuals affect their behavior? If they *do not*, then changes in these values and attitudes could scarcely have any impact on the society as a whole. And it has often been claimed that people's attitudes have no impact on their behavior.

DO ATTITUDES SHAPE BEHAVIOR?

In the 1930s, an American social scientist reported that, in response to a written inquiry, most of the restaurant owners whom he contacted said they would not serve Chinese customers; but when he appeared at these same restaurants with a young Chinese couple, almost all of them actually did so (LaPiere, 1934). He concluded that attitudes were irrelevant to actual behavior. This finding was so counterintuitive and so interesting that it was widely cited for several decades. And as recently as the 1960s, a review of empirical studies concluded that attitudes were generally "unrelated or only slightly related to overt behaviors" (Wicker, 1969: 65).

A more recent review of 88 attitude-behavior studies comes to a very different conclusion: Kraus (1995) finds that attitudes significantly and substantially predict future behavior. Furthermore, the most important factor associated with high attitude-behavior correlations was whether the research design used the same level of specificity in the attitudinal and behavioral measures— as Fishbein and Ajzen (1975) had suggested 20 years earlier. Not surprisingly, broad global attitudes do not necessarily predict specific behaviors. For example, one's answer to the question "Are you a liberal or a conservative?" is not nearly as good a predictor of voting behavior, as is one's voting intention. And the question "Do you believe in God?" does not predict church attendance as well as the question "Do you think it's important to go to church?" Belief in God is a more global attitude than is emphasis on church attendance. On the other hand, global attitudes *are* relatively good at predicting global patterns of behavior. In short, low levels of attitude-behavior consistency are largely a measurement problem.

The situation in which behavior occurs *does* influence one's behavior. It is even possible to contrive situations in which the underlying attitude is completely irrelevant to the behavior being measured: for example, regardless of their attitudes, no one votes for environmentalist parties in countries where no such parties exist. It is equally true, however, that if people give low priority to environmental protection (as was generally the case until a few decades ago), there is little support for environmentalist movements or parties, even if they *do* exist. As criminologists discovered long ago, both the motive and the opportunity must be present for behavior to take place. In appropriately designed studies, one generally *does* find significant and substantial linkages between attitudes and behavior.

Furthermore, it is important to distinguish between central and strongly held attitudes, and peripheral and fleeting ones. In the early 1930s, when the classic LaPiere study was carried out, there were very few Chinese in most parts of the United States. Some respondents may have responded to LaPiere's hypothetical question on the basis of vague and rarely examined stereotypes of coolie laborers. When confronted with a well-dressed young couple accompanied by a college professor, they served them without hesitation.

But at precisely the same time, attitudes toward African Americans were highly salient and strongly held in most parts of the United States If exactly the same experiment had been held in 1934 using Blacks instead of Chinese as the test case, it seems likely that a large proportion of the restaurant owners would have said that they would not serve Blacks—and then proceeded to *do* exactly what they had said. To anyone who recalls the lunch counter sit-ins and the protracted desegregation struggles of the 1960s, it is evident that attitudes and behavior were all too consistent (and all too racist) where African Americans were concerned. During the first half of this century even more than today, a large proportion of the American people had negative attitudes toward Blacks *and* went to great lengths to exclude them from all aspects of their lives.

In short, attitudes do not determine behavior in any one-to-one fashion. One must also take situational factors into account. But the same is true of situations: by themselves, they do not determine what happens. Behavior requires both motive and opportunity.

CULTURE AND COERCION: TWO ASPECTS OF POLITICAL AUTHORITY

Value systems play an important role in any society. They provide the cultural basis for loyalty to given economic and political systems. And value systems interact with external economic and political factors in shaping social change. One cannot understand social change without taking it into account.

Culture has a crucial relationship to political authority. Culture is not just a random collection of the values, beliefs, and skills of the people in a given society. It constitutes a survival strategy. In any society that has survived for long, the cultural system is likely to have a mutually supportive relationship with the economic and political systems (see Bell, 1976). As Eckstein (1961, 1988) argues in his theory of stable democracy, a society's authority patterns and its political system must be congruent, for democracy to survive over the long term. Almond and Verba (1963) make a similar argument in *The Civic Culture*. Though they approach the question from a very different perspective, Marx and various Postmodernist thinkers also make essentially the same claim: a society's belief system tends to justify its social order, legitimating a given elite's right to rule. This is a crucial function.

A government is a decision-making system for a society. And the people in that society comply with their government's decisions either (1) because of external coercion, or (2) because they have internalized a set of norms that justifies compliance. All societies depend on some mixture of the two, though there are crucial differences in the *degree* to which given societies depend on coercion or on enculturated legitimacy. This is the crucial difference between unstable dictatorships and stable democracies. This balance between culture and coercion is so central to politics that Weber (1925) defined the political realm in terms of the *legitimate* use of *violence*, emphasizing the complementary roles of the two factors. As figure 2.1 indicates, legitimacy and violence (or culture and coercion) are at opposite poles of the political spectrum.

Any sociopolitical system that endures for long is supported by an underlying moral order. A warlord or military dictator can stay in power for a limited time through naked repression, but doing so is risky. It is costly to keep a soldier on every corner, enforcing government edicts at bayonet point; it is costly to maintain a massive repressive apparatus; and it is costly to buy loyalty that is not culturally internalized, but maintained only by external payoffs. Ultimately, the society's entire economic surplus may be diverted into maintaining the loyalty of the military elite. Moreover, the absence of culturally based loyalties means that the dictator is dependent on some kind of Praetorian Guard to stay in power, and therefore chronically vulnerable to a coup. Number one in the power structure lives in perpetual fear of number two.

Any elite that aspires to hold power for long will seek to legitimate itself—usually by conforming to established cultural norms, but sometimes by trying to reshape these norms so as to justify its right to rule. Conformity is much easier and less coercive than reshaping the culture; but when a truly revolutionary elite seizes power, it may attempt to reshape the cultural system to conform with its new ideology. This is a huge undertaking that generally requires the coercive capabilities of a totalitarian state. In the real world, all regimes rely on coercion to some extent, but it is far cheaper and safer to rely on inter-

CULTURE ◄─────────────────────► **COERCION**

Figure 2.1. Legitimacy and violence in politics.
The continuum from internalized controls to external coercion.

nalized values and norms than to depend on naked force in order to get people to comply with one's policies. While newly established totalitarian regimes tend to be located near the pole labeled "coercion" on figure 2.1, democracies enjoying widespread legitimacy are located near the pole labeled "culture."

One of the most important functions of culture is its role in legitimating the society's political and economic systems. Indeed, Wilson (1992) goes so far as to define political culture as "a dominant ideology justifying compliance with a society's institutional system." This *is* one of political culture's most important functions, but not the only thing it does: in a democracy, for example, it may also legitimate dissent, through such norms as "the loyal opposition." In most systems, culture also has norms that place limits and obligations on elite behavior—and by doing so in the long run help legitimate the elites' right to rule.

Any political system that endures for long is virtually certain to be supported by an appropriate moral order, which shapes the political and the economic systems as well as being shaped by them. In preindustrial societies the moral order usually takes the form of a religion.

This moral order shapes all aspects of life, not just politics. It integrates the society through injunctions against internal violence (some variation of "Thou shalt not kill" is a basic principle in any society), and by instilling norms protecting private property (such as "Thou shalt not steal")—but balancing them with norms of charity and sharing that soften the struggle for survival.

These norms perform crucial functions in traditional societies. In order to be compelling enough to bring compliance even in the face of strong temptations to disobey, these norms are inculcated as absolute values, usually as rules that reflect the divine will. This is workable in relatively unchanging agrarian societies, but absolute values are inherently rigid and difficult to adjust to a rapidly changing environment. Breaking down at least some components of traditional value systems was necessary in order for Modernization to occur. This is one reason why the Protestant Reformation was so important in modernizing Western Europe, and why similar challenges to traditional values have been crucial elsewhere. In China, for example, key norms of the Confucian system (those stigmatizing manual work and mercantile and technological work as incompatible with the role of the refined scholar-bureaucrat) had to be broken down through successive waves of reform (first liberal and then Maoist) before modern economic development could take place. Similarly, the traditional virtue of unreservedly helping one's relatives and fellow villagers must be reined in: it becomes a major vice—nepotism—in a modern bureaucratic society.

THE BALANCE BETWEEN CULTURE AND COERCION

Throughout history most regimes have been initiated by conquest, and as recently as 1970, most of the world's societies were governed by military dictatorships. Even after the recent global wave of democratization, the military still threaten to play a crucial role in politics, from Latin America to the former Soviet Union to Africa, if the new democratic regimes flounder. It is often asked, "Why do the military so often take over?" One might better ask, "Why doesn't the military *always* take power?" Control of the means of coercion is central to politics; it is only when cultural norms are strongly enough entrenched to prevent domination by force of arms that any *other* type of regime emerges. Without a strongly internalized cultural system, rule by the military is the simplest solution: in politics, clubs are trumps.

The question, then, is "How do you *prevent* the military from taking over?" The answer is, by instilling cultural norms that support other types of authority. It is especially important to instill these norms among the military elite. In a monarchy, these norms emphasize unquestioning obedience and loyalty to the king or queen. In the United States, they emphasize fidelity to the constitutional chain of command, with the president as commander-in-chief. And in Marxist regimes, the ideological taboo on "Bonapartism" played a crucial role: the founder of the Red Army, Leon Trotsky, accepted it even though it cost him political power and ultimately his life. These norms amount to a quasi-religious commandment, "Thou Shalt Not Carry Out a Military Coup."

Since coercion and culture are simply different aspects of political power, the elite most likely to dominate any society (after the military) is the priesthood or the other ideologues who provide the authoritative interpretation of the society's cultural norms. In ancient Egypt and Sumeria, Medieval Europe and the Aztec empire, the priesthood was dominant or ruled on equal terms with military elites; in Soviet Russia and Maoist China, Marxist ideologues played a dominant role. And in legalistic societies, lawyers rule: as the authoritative interpreters of American society's legitimating myth, lawyers are the functional equivalent of the priesthood.

Culture is the subjective component of a society's equipment for coping with its environment: the values, attitudes, beliefs, skills, knowledge of its people. Economic, political, and other external factors are equally important, but they are not decisive by themselves. When dealing with human beings, there is a continual interaction between subjective and objective factors—between culture and environment. What goes on inside people's heads is as important as what goes on outside them. Although it usually changes slowly, culture does change through interaction with the environment (as processed through subjective cultural filters).

Culture does not simply consist of the myths propagated to justify those in power (though this is always an important component). It reflects the entire historical heritage and life experiences of a given people. Some Postmodern theorists collapse the continuum from culture to coercion, making culture simply a disguised form of coercion. We reject this position. With Habermas, we believe that uncoerced communication is also possible—and that this possibility expands in advanced industrial society.

Changing Values and Changing Family Patterns

Postmodern values reflect the assumption that survival can be taken for granted, which leads to a growing emphasis on self-expression. In preindustrial society, the two-parent family was crucial to the survival of children; in advanced industrial societies, growing numbers of people have come to see the family as an optional aspect of one's lifestyle. Postmodern values place top priority on self-fulfillment through careers, rather than childbearing. Nevertheless, they are relatively permissive toward single parenthood, because they tend to take the economic viability of the single mother for granted.

This changing cultural outlook among individuals is reflected in changes at the societal level. Starting in the mid-1960s, birth rates declined throughout advanced industrial societies. Meanwhile, divorce rates, abortion rates, and illegitimate births rose sharply. By 1990, fertility rates were below the population replacement level in almost all advanced industrial societies. Such demographic phenomena are complex, involving economic, political, and other factors, but it seems clear that cultural change has played a significant role in this shift (see Lesthaeghe and Meekers, 1986).

Although birth rates fell, the proportion of births that took place outside of marriage *rose* tremendously, tripling in the United States and increasing by 250 percent from 1960 to 1990 in the European Union as a whole. Here, too, it appears that cultural factors play a major role.

Finally, divorce rates rose in almost all advanced industrial societies but one—the Republic of Ireland, where divorce remained illegal until 1995. In Italy and Spain, it became legal only recently. For Western Europe as a whole, however, the divorce rate more than quadrupled from 1960 to 1990. Aggregate statistical data support the interpretation that norms linked with religion and the inviolability of the family have been growing weaker.

Here, as with any major social change, the causes can be interpreted on more than one level. One could argue, for example, that the dramatic decline in birth rates is due to advances in contraceptive technology. There is no question that developments in contraceptive technology played an important instrumental role—but effective birth control techniques have existed for many decades. Nevertheless, in the 1950s birth rates rose to levels far above those of previous years; and the decline that is now so dramatically apparent set in after 1965. The emergence of below-replacement-level birth rates reflects a combination of two things: 1. The availability of effective birth control technology, and 2. The fact that people choose to use it. The fact that people increasingly choose to have children later in life or not at all seems to reflect a gradual change in underlying norms. Both the technology and the fact that people choose to use it are essential, and to ask which one was the real cause is to pose false alternatives.

Similarly, one might argue that the recent surge in divorces in Italy and Spain is the result of legal changes: divorce used to be illegal, but is no longer. This interpretation is perfectly true, but superficial. If one probes deeper, the first question that arises is *"Why* did divorce become legal in these countries?" Divorce had been illegal for centuries because it violated deeply held religious norms in those cultures. This still was true in the Republic of Ireland until 1995: a majority of the public had voted against legalizing divorce as recently as 1987. But, as our data suggest, these norms have gradually been weakening over time. Public support for legalizing divorce became increasingly widespread and articulate in Italy and Spain, until the laws themselves were changed in the 1970s. And by 1995, even the Irish finally accepted divorce in a national referendum. One consequence was a sudden surge of divorces in these countries immediately after the laws were changed. Although this *behavioral* change was sudden and lumpy, it reflected a long process of incremental value change.

Some writers have interpreted the lumpiness of the behavioral symptoms of cultural change as meaning that no long-term decline in traditional norms is taking place. For example, Hout and Greeley (1987) point out that in the United States church attendance among Protestants has not declined in recent decades; and, while it fell sharply among Catholics from 1968 to 1975, it has not declined subsequently. They conclude that the lack of a steady downward trend contradicts the secularization thesis.

This argument is not compelling: church attendance rates provide only a very rough indicator of underlying cultural changes. More important, this argument assumes that there must be a one-to-one relationship between the pace of attitudinal changes and their behavioral consequences. Since they operate on different levels, with behavioral patterns often more subject to institutional and situational constraints, this is not necessarily the case. The sudden decline in Catholic church attendance, for example, may have been precipitated by the strong opposition to artificial birth control that Pope Paul VI voiced in 1968. But the public's negative reaction to papal authority also reflected the fact that a majority of American Catholics had come to *disagree* with the church's longstanding position on birth control by that point in time—a change that had taken place gradually, over a long period of time.

The rise of the Greens in West Germany provides another illustration of the disparity between the incremental pace of cultural change and the sudden emergence of its behavioral symptoms. In 1983 the Greens suddenly achieved worldwide prominence when they won enough votes to enter the West German parliament for the first time, bringing a fundamental change in the equilibrium of West German politics. But this abrupt breakthrough reflected a gradual intergenerational rise of mass support for environmentalist policies. Institutional barriers, such as the fact that a party must win at least 5 percent of the vote to gain seats in the Bundestag, made the party's breakthrough to prominence sudden and dramatic. But its rise reflected long-term processes of incremental change. If one focuses only on the immediate causes, a society's electoral rules appear to be the decisive factor: the Greens had little visibility until they surmounted the 5 percent threshold; and in societies without proportional representation, such as the United States and Great Britain, ecology parties may never play an important role. But even in these countries, a rising concern for environmental protection has transformed the agendas of existing parties. In most societies, the activists of Green parties are mainly Postmaterialists, and it seems unlikely that Green parties or environmentalist movements would have emerged without the cultural changes that gave rise to a Postmaterialist worldview.

In the United States, there has recently been a renewed emphasis on religious issues, including a heated antiabortion movement and a campaign to allow prayer in public schools. This has been interpreted as a manifestation of a swing to the Right on cultural issues.

This interpretation seems to be mistaken. Our evidence points to a pervasive tendency toward secularization. Clearly, the pro-prayer and Right to Life movements *do* have devoted partisans. But their revival of religious issues reflects a reaction among a gradually dwindling traditionalist sector, rather than a surge toward cultural conservatism among the population at large. Glenn (1987) has examined long-term trends in American survey data on this subject. He finds only a moderate overall decline in church membership, but a substantial decline in endorsement of traditional Christian beliefs. For example, the share of the American public who considered religion very important in their lives declined from 75 percent in the 1950s to 56 percent in the 1980s. This book will present additional evidence from many countries, indicating that for the past several decades adherence to traditional cultural norms has been in retreat. The societal-level consequences of this retreat have become manifest in rising rates of divorce and abortion—and in institutional changes that have made them easier to obtain. The intensity with which religious issues have been raised in recent years reflects their adherents' alarmed and passionate conviction that some of their most basic values are rapidly eroding—and not the growth of mass support for traditional religion.

Institutional determinists (e.g., Skocpol, 1982, Jackman and Miller, 1996) argue that institutions are exogenous while culture is endogenous—in other words, that institutions always shape attitudes and beliefs, never the other way around. This attempt to solve an empirical question by definitional fiat is begging the question. And historical evidence indicates that the assumption that institutions are always exogenous is simplistic. It works both ways: sometimes institutions shape cultural values, and sometimes culture shapes institutions.

Switzerland, for example, has a federal structure with extreme decentralization of authority and a seven-person council instead of one individual as prime minister. If one knows Swiss history, it is obvious that its ethnic diversity gave rise to these institutions, and not the other way around (they are a means of avoiding the appearance that one ethnic group dominates the others). Belgium, India, and Canada have somewhat similar institutions for similar reasons. To anyone familiar with these societies, the claim that the institutions gave rise to the culture would seem preposterous. Historically, the ethnic diversity preceded the federal structure and other institutions that help these societies cope with diversity. In a variety of ways, from Spain to Canada to India, it is clear that culture often shapes institutions, as well as the other way around.

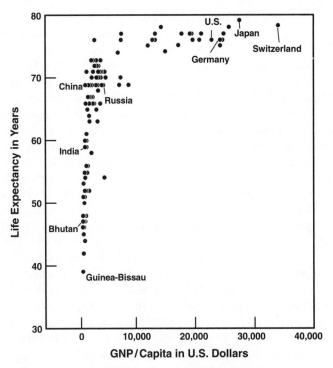

Figure 2.2. Life expectancy by economic development level.
Mean life expectancy at birth, by GNP per capita in 124 countries.
Source: Data from World Bank, *World Development Report, 1993*.

The Societal Roots of the Postmodern Shift: Diminishing Marginal Returns from Economic Development

Although culture can shape economic and political life, it is equally true that major socioeconomic changes reshape culture. The shift from Modernization to Postmodernization reflects the diminishing marginal utility of economic determinism: economic factors tend to play a decisive role under conditions of economic scarcity, but as scarcity diminishes, other factors shape society to an increasing degree. Thus, through processes of random mutation and natural selection, culture adapts to a given environment. Chapter 4 examines how this process works at the individual level, through intergenerational population replacement. Here, let us briefly examine it at the societal level.

Figure 2.2 illustrates the diminishing impact of economic development on human life expectancy. As it demonstrates, life expectancy is closely linked to a nation's level of economic development, especially at the low end of the economic continuum. The people of poor nations have relatively short average life spans. Guinea-Bissau falls at the low end of the spectrum on both income and life expectancy, with a per capita gross national product of $180 and a life expectancy of 39 years. Just above this level is a cluster of nations having per capita GNPs of less than $300 and life expectancies of about 45 years. Next comes a group of societies with GNPs of $1,000 to $3,000 and life expectancies of 60 to 75 years. At the high end of the spectrum are Japan and Switzerland, with per capita GNPs of $28,000 and $33,000, respectively, and life expectancies of 79 and 78 years, respectively—twice that of Guinea-Bissau. A cross-national relationship like this does not always reflect developmental change, but in this case it does: historical evidence demonstrates that life expectancies have indeed risen as economic development took place.

The curve rises steeply with relatively modest increases in wealth, until it reaches about $3,000 per capita. Thereafter, the curve levels off. Economic factors become less decisive, and lifestyle factors more so. Among the poorer nations in figure 2.2, GNP per capita explains 51 percent of the variance in life expectancy; among the richer half it accounts for only 15 percent. There is still a good deal of cross-national variation, but longevity becomes less and less a question of adequate nutrition and sanitary facilities, and more and more a question of cholesterol intake, tobacco and alcohol consumption, exercise, levels of stress, and environmental pollution. Increasingly, life expectancy is determined by lifestyle and behavioral patterns, rather than by economics.

Some striking recent cultural phenomena could be interpreted as a rational response to this shift from economic factors to lifestyle factors as the main determinants of survival. For example, a generation ago, Americans were notorious for their unwillingness to walk even short distances. Some people jokingly claimed that the next generation would be born with wheels instead of legs. It did not work out that way. Quite the contrary, two decades later jogging and emphasis on physical fitness became widespread. There has also been a growing concern for avoiding cholesterol and food additives, an increasingly successful movement to reduce environmental pollution and to ban smoking in public places, and a growing interest in less stressful lifestyles—all of which reflect a spreading awareness that, today, longevity has more to do with lifestyle than with sheer income.

The leveling off of the curve does not simply reflect ceiling effects. In 1975 only a few nations had male life expectancies above 70 years, but in the ensuing years life expectancies in most nations went up by several years. By 1990, female life expectancy in Switzerland and Japan had risen above 80 years, and this almost certainly does not represent the ultimate biological ceiling. In advanced industrial society, the most rapidly growing demographic segment is the group 100 years of age and over. Most developed nations still have considerable room for improvement—but changes in life expectancy are no longer as closely tied to economic development as they were when starvation was the leading cause of death. Thus male life expectancy in the former Soviet Union declined sharply during the 1970s and 1980s and continued to fall after the collapse of the USSR. In large part, this seems to reflect cultural-historical factors, such as rising alcoholism rates and psychological stress. By contrast, East

Asian countries have long been overachievers in life expectancies. China, North Korea, South Korea, Taiwan, Hong Kong, and Japan (now the world leader in life expectancy) all have historically shown higher life expectancies than their economic level would predict. The nations of the former Soviet Union have shown the opposite tendency: for decades, nearly all of them have shown lower life expectancies than their economic level would predict. Recent changes have accentuated these tendencies to the point where—although Russia's GNP/capita is still much higher than China's—China now shows a higher life expectancy than Russia. The reasons are complex, but they seem to have a significant cultural component, with a tradition of alcohol abuse having a negative impact on the life expectancy of Russian males, while the low-cholesterol diet traditionally prevalent in East Asia may have a positive effect on life expectancies in that region.

As our diminishing returns hypothesis implies, a logarithmic transformation of GNP per capita shows a much better fit with life expectancy than does a linear model. Figure 2.2 shows untransformed GNP per capita in order to demonstrate the diminishing impact of economic gains. Similar patterns of diminishing returns from economic development are found with numerous other social indicators. Caloric intake, literacy rates, the number of physicians per capita, and other objective indicators all rise steeply at the low end of the scale, but level off among advanced industrial societies (Hirsch [1976], in *Social Limits to Growth*, makes a loosely related point, arguing that development brings no gain in *positional* goods). In short, a narrow focus on economic achievement has a tremendous payoff in the early stages of industrialization: the instrumental rationality associated with Modernization had high rewards. But when a society reaches a fairly high level of industrialization (at a per capita GNP of $6,000 to $7,000 in 1990 dollars) it reaches a point of diminishing returns.

This pattern of diminishing marginal returns from economic development is not limited to objective aspects of life, such as caloric intake and life expectancy. New evidence from the 1990 World Values Survey indicates that this applies to subjective well-being too. Figure 2.3 demonstrates this point. It is based on the responses of 43 publics to questions concerning their happiness and satisfaction with their lives as a whole—questions that have been shown to be excellent indicators of overall subjective well-being, and relatively stable cultural characteristics (Andrews and Withey, 1976; Inglehart, 1990, ch. 7).

As one might expect, subjective well-being rises with rising levels of economic development: the people of rich and secure societies such as Sweden are happier and more satisfied with their lives as a whole than are those living in societies where disease and starvation are widespread, such as India. The overall relationship has impressive strength (r = .74). But here again, we find a marked leveling off above a certain threshold. This effect is so pronounced that earlier studies, carried out mainly in rich societies, concluded that there was no cross-national relationship between economic development and subjective well-being. Above a threshold of about $6,000 (in 1991 dollars), there

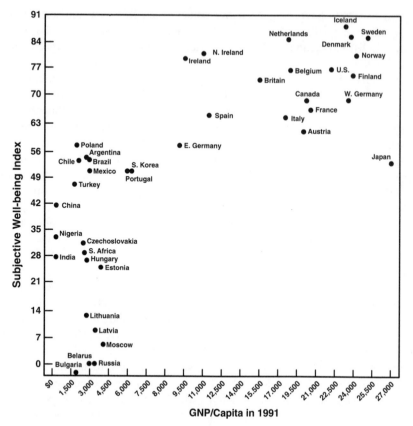

Figure 2.3. Economic development and subjective well-being.

N = 40, r = .74, p < .00001. *Source*: subjective well-being data from 1990–91 World Values Survey; GNP/capita data from World Bank, *World Development Report, 1993*. *Note*: The subjective well-being index reflects the average between the percentage of the public in each country who (1) describe themselves as "Very happy" or "happy," minus the percentage who describe themselves as "not very happy" or "unhappy," and (2) the percentage placing themselves in the 7–10 range, minus the percentage placing themselves in the 1–4 range, on a 10-point scale on which "1" indicates that the person is strongly dissatisfied with his or her life as a whole, and "10" indicates that the person is highly satisfied with his or her life as a whole.

is virtually no relationship between wealth and subjective well-being. Thus, the Irish show a higher level of subjective well-being than do the Western Germans, though the latter are more than twice as rich; and the South Koreans show subjective well-being levels as high as the Japanese, although the Japanese are more than four times as rich.

Our interpretation here is more speculative than it was with the relationship between economic development and life expectancy. We know for certain that numerous objective indicators (from calories consumed per person to telephones per capita and automobiles per capita to human life expectancy) follow a curve of diminishing returns: ample historical data demonstrate that as given societies underwent economic development, all of these things increased sharply at first, but then reached a point of diminishing returns, with further economic growth producing only modest increases. But we simply do not have this kind of historical information concerning the relationship between economic development and subjective well-being: subjective well-being only began to be measured a few decades ago, and until recently it was measured only in a handful of rich Western societies. The 1990 World Values Survey was the first study to measure it in representative national samples of a majority of the world's population.

One possible interpretation of figure 2.3 would be that the pattern has nothing to do with economic development: one might argue that for some reason (perhaps cultural or climatic or geographic), Nigeria, India, and Russia may have *always* ranked low on subjective well-being, while Sweden, Denmark, and the Netherlands have always had high levels of well-being, for reasons having nothing to do with economic development.

We cannot disprove this interpretation, but it seems extremely unlikely. The relationship between economic development level and subjective well-being is remarkably strong and is significant at the .00001 level: it could scarcely have resulted from sheer chance. Furthermore, the linkage between economic level and subjective well-being manifests itself not only at the cross-national level but also within given societies: as common sense might lead one to expect, people with high incomes tend to have higher levels of subjective well-being than do those with low incomes. Moreover, Eastern and Western Germany provide a sort of controlled experiment, in which nationality and culture are held constant, but in Eastern Germany, per capita income is much lower than in Western Germany: as our interpretation implies, the Western Germans show substantially higher levels of subjective well-being than do the Eastern Germans. Moreover, this same comparison helps explain why the impact of economic development eventually levels off: in terms of what they consider important, economic factors (such as income) rank much higher among Eastern Germans than among Western Germans; and conversely, noneconomic aspects of life (such as leisure time) are considered much more important by the Western Germans than by the Eastern Germans (Staatistisches Bundesamt, 1994: 441).

The interpretation that prosperity and security are conducive to subjective well-being is further supported by the extremely low levels of well-being shown by the former Soviet societies. Here again, one might attribute this finding to something inherent in Slavic (and Baltic) culture, or to something inherent in the Soviet type of socialism. But a much more obvious interpretation would see it as linked with the disintegration of the economic, political, and social fabric of these societies that was taking place when these surveys were carried out in 1990. In the 1981 World Values Survey, a sample from the Tambov region of Russia showed relatively low levels of subjective well-being; but the levels found here are lower than any ever registered before, either in the Tambov region of Russia or in any other country. We should note that these phenomenally low levels of subjective well-being manifested themselves *before* the political disintegration of the Soviet Union in December 1991: they were a leading indicator of deep-rooted demoralization and dissatisfaction among the masses, and not simply a response to political collapse. Our interpretation is that the Soviet successor states are experiencing a profound malaise that could have dramatic consequences.

Until we have a longer time series, it will not be possible to conclusively prove or disprove our interpretation that economic growth is conducive to increased subjective well-being, but eventually reaches a point of diminishing returns. But this interpretation is supported by the fact that, among prosperous European Union societies, subjective well-being has been roughly constant since 1973: as figure 6.4 indicates, subjective well-being has risen slightly in some of these societies (e.g., Western Germany) and fallen slightly in others (especially, Belgium), but there is no clear overall trend. Within wealthy societies, the correlation between income and subjective well-being is relatively weak. In societies where a higher income may make the difference between survival and starvation, a good income is a pretty good first approximation of what well-being really means. But in rich societies, income differences have a surprisingly small impact on subjective well-being: the rich are slightly happier and more satisfied than the poor, but only to a modest extent (Andrews and Withey, 1976; Campbell, Converse, and Rodgers, 1976; Inglehart, 1990).

The overall evidence supports the thesis of diminishing marginal utility from economic gains. As figure 2.3 suggests, the transition from a society of scarcity to a society of security brings a dramatic increase in subjective well-being. But (at roughly the economic level of Ireland in 1990) we find a threshold at which economic growth no longer seems to increase subjective well-being significantly. This may be linked with the fact that at this level starvation is no longer a real concern for most people. Survival begins to be taken for granted. Significant numbers of Postmaterialists begin to emerge, and for them further economic gains no longer produce an increase in subjective well-being. Indeed, if further economic growth brings deterioration in the nonmaterial quality of life, it may actually lead to *lower* levels of subjective well-being. Beyond this level, economic development no longer seems to bring rising subjective well-being. The stage is set for the Postmodern shift to begin.

From a rational actor's perspective, one would expect economic development to eventually bring a shift in survival strategies. Figure 2.4 suggests how this works. At low levels of economic development, even modest economic gains bring a high return in terms of caloric intake, clothing, shelter, medical care, and ultimately in life expectancy itself. For individuals to give top priority to maximizing economic gains, and for a society to give top priority to economic growth, is a highly effective survival strategy. But once a society has reached a certain threshold of development—at about the level where the Soviet Union was before its collapse, or where Portugal or South Korea are today—one reaches a point at which further economic growth brings only min-

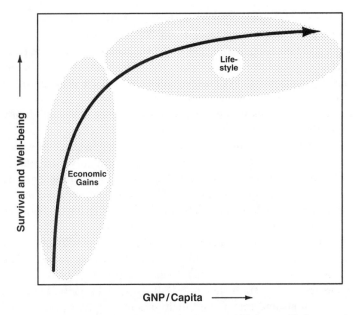

Figure 2.4. Economic development leads to a shift in survival strategies.

imal gains in both life expectancy and in subjective well-being. There is still a good deal of cross-national variation, but from this point on, noneconomic aspects of life become increasingly important influences on how long, and how well, people live. Beyond this point, a rational strategy would be to place increasing emphasis on quality of life concerns, rather than to continue the inflexible pursuit of economic growth as if it were a good in itself. Instrumental rationality begins to give way to value rationality.

Normally, culture changes slowly; but it does eventually respond to a changing environment. Changes in the socioeconomic environment help reshape individual-level beliefs, attitudes, and values through their impact on the life experience of individuals. Cultures do not change overnight. Once they have matured, people tend to retain whatever worldview they have learned. Consequently, the impact of major changes in the environment tends to be most significant on those generations that spent their formative years under the new conditions.

The best documented case of this phenomenon is the shift from Materialist to Postmaterialist values in Western societies during the last few decades. This intergenerational cultural shift is one of the few cases in which we can follow a gradual cultural shift based on intergenerational population replacement, through times of prosperity and times of recession, and under widely varying conditions in different societies. Comparable data are available for few if any other cultural variables, but there is no reason to assume that this pattern does not apply to changes in other basic values.

Culture is resistant to change, partly because people tend to believe whatever their society's institutions teach them. But one's worldview is also influenced by one's firsthand experience—and if the two are in conflict, one's firsthand experience may have even greater credibility than what one is told. This is one reason why political systems, even totalitarian ones, have limited ability to reshape their culture. People are sensitive to those aspects of reality that directly affect them. This was crucial in the shift toward Postmodern values. The younger birth cohorts in advanced industrial societies perceived, during their formative years, that survival was *not* precarious and that they could take it more or less for granted. This experience was profoundly different from the conditions that have shaped most people's lives throughout most of history. It led to pervasive changes in worldviews. For these birth cohorts, maximizing their economic gains no longer maximized their subjective well-being as it had for earlier generations.

People did not consciously set out to change their worldviews. New outlooks and new modes of behavior, like random mutations, arose for a variety of reasons—and some of them spread. Even within a given birth cohort, many continued to accept the established norms of industrial society; but others took on new orientations and transmitted them to some of their peers through social learning processes. Change has been uneven. But the new lifestyles have spread gradually—and in the last analysis, they have done so because they represent more effective ways to maximize survival and subjective well-being under new conditions. At a much earlier stage of history, new norms linked with the rise of modern society (such as the Protestant Ethic) gradually spread in somewhat similar fashion. We lack detailed information on how this took place, but it seems to have occurred more slowly than the rise of Postmodern values, which in some ways represents its reversal. In both cases, culture was gradually reshaped by changes in the socioeconomic environment; and these cultural changes eventually produced feedback that helped reshape political and economic life.

Postmodernization is a shift in survival strategies. It moves from maximizing economic growth to maximizing survival and well-being through lifestyle changes. Once industrialization had become possible, Modernization focused on rapid economic growth as the best way of maximizing survival and well-being. But no strategy is optimal for all times. Modernization was dramatically successful in raising life expectancies, but it has begun to produce diminishing returns in advanced industrial societies. Emphasizing competition, it reduces the risk of starvation, but increases psychological stress. With the transition from Modernization to Postmodernization, the trajectory of change has shifted from maximizing economic growth to maximizing the quality of life.

Modernization and Postmodernization in 43 Societies

INTRODUCTION

As we have seen, Modernization theory falls into two main schools: (1) a Marxist version, which claims that economics, politics, and culture are closely linked because economic development determines the political and cultural characteristics of a society, and (2) a Weberian version, which claims that culture shapes economic and political life. Despite an enduring debate between the two schools, they agree on one crucial point: that socioeconomic change follows coherent and relatively predictable patterns. This means that key social, political, and economic characteristics are not randomly related; they tend to be closely linked so that by knowing one such trait, one can predict the presence of other key traits with much better than random success.

Cultural relativists, on the other hand, claimed that it would be ethnocentric not to believe that all cultures are equally conducive to economic development and democracy. And dependency theorists viewed a given society's culture as irrelevant to economic development and democracy, which were determined by the forces of global capitalism. Both of these views imply that the relationships between culture and economics and politics are more or less random.

This chapter presents a broad overview of a huge body of data from more than 40 societies. It demonstrates that, far from being randomly related, specific cultural, economic, and political variables are closely correlated. Although this chapter does not attempt to demonstrate whether causality flows in the Marxist or the Weberian direction, the linkages we find indicate that at least one version of Modernization theory was right. Subsequent chapters will probe more deeply into the causal linkages.

Although we find strong support for the central claim of Modernization theory, we disagree with it on several narrower points—above all, the notion that socioeconomic change is linear. Instead, we find evidence that a major change of direction occurs when societies reach an advanced level of industrial development. The Modernization phase involves the familiar syndrome of industrialization, occupational specialization, bureaucratization, centralization, rising educational levels, and beliefs and values that support high rates of economic growth; but among advanced industrial societies, a second syndrome of cultural and institutional changes emerges in which economic growth becomes less central, and there is rising emphasis on the quality of life and democratic political institutions.

CROSS-SECTIONAL EVIDENCE OF CHANGE OVER TIME

This chapter will undertake something that verges on heresy: we will examine hypotheses about changes over time in the light of cross-sectional evidence. This procedure has been criticized (quite appropriately) in the past: taken by itself, cross-sectional evidence is an uncertain indicator of change. There is no substitute for time series data if one hopes to draw firm conclusions about social change. In keeping with this idea, much of this book is devoted to analyzing time series data concerning sociocultural change.

Nevertheless, we are convinced that the World Values surveys can usefully supplement the available time series evidence, providing additional insight on patterns of cultural change. Global cross-national data are needed because the available survey data on this topic are largely drawn from advanced industrial societies and limited to the past few decades. The World Values survey provides a much broader range of variation than has ever before been available, bringing together data from 43 nations throughout the world, covering the full range of economic and political variation.

If we had survey data covering the entire period from the early nineteenth century to the present we could analyze the interplay between changing cultural values and economic and political Modernization over many decades. We could then determine which came first, cultural change or economic or political change. But such data are not available. The analysis of cross-sectional data offers the nearest substitute. Examining the orientations of people in poor societies gives some sense of what prevailing mass orientations in today's rich democracies may have been like when these countries were poor and predemocratic.

Conversely, comparing the worldviews of rich and poor countries provides some idea of how the outlook of the publics of poorer countries may change if their societies become industrialized and economically secure. We do not view these changes as deterministic: economic and technological changes interact with political, cultural, and other variables. The cultural heritage of a given society may facilitate or retard Modernization; and determined leaders can repress or accelerate social change. Nevertheless, as we will demonstrate, it is possible to identify a specific syndrome of cultural values and beliefs that is likely to be present, if urbanization, industrialization, higher education, and other components of Modernization become widespread.

Inkeles and Smith (1974) suggested that this should be true, but their conclusion was based on a comparison of the belief systems of those working within the "modern" and premodern sectors of six developing societies, and it did not compare societies at various levels of development. This analysis, for the first time, demonstrates the existence of fundamentally different worldviews between the publics of preindustrial and industrial societies, confirming Inkeles and Smith's insight. But our analysis goes a step farther: it also analyzes the cultural differences between societies of scarcity (both preindustrial and early industrial) and economically affluent "Postmodern" societies.

MODERNIZATION AND POSTMODERNIZATION
IN CROSS-SECTIONAL PERSPECTIVE

The concepts of both Modernization and Postmodernization are based on two key assumptions:

1. Various cultural elements tend to go together in coherent patterns. For example, do societies that place relatively strong emphasis on religion also tend to favor large families (or respect for authority or other distinctive attitudes)? If each culture goes its own way, elements such as these would be uncorrelated, and one would find no consistent patterns of constraint.

2. Coherent cultural patterns exist, *and* they are linked with economic and technological development. For example, industrialization was accompanied by secularization in Western history. But some observers argue that, since some Islamic countries such as Iran and Libya have grown rich without secularization, there is no linkage between economic development and secularization. This argument ignores the fact that Modernization is not just the possession of large oil deposits: it is a syndrome of cultural, economic, and technological changes closely linked with industrialization—a syndrome that Iran and Libya have not experienced, and which *does* tend to be linked with secularization.

Together, these two postulates imply that some patterns are more probable than others—and hence, that development is to some extent predictable. *Is* economic development linked with coherent cultural patterns, distinct from those found in less developed societies? If so, then cross-national surveys should reveal clear patterns, with one syndrome of orientations being found in economically developed societies, and another syndrome being found in less developed societies. If such patterns are found, the evidence would support Modernization theory. Furthermore, it would imply that sociopolitical change has an element of predictability.

Do coherent cultural patterns exist, and are they linked with levels of economic development? To answer this question, we will analyze the World Values survey data on key values and beliefs among representative national samples of publics around the world. This survey was designed to test the hypothesis that economic development leads to specific changes in mass values and belief systems—which in turn produce feedback, leading to changes in the economic and political systems of these societies. We do not assume that *all* elements of culture will change, leading to a uniform global culture: we see no reason to expect that the Chinese will stop using chopsticks in the foreseeable future, or that Brazilians will learn to polka. But certain cultural and political changes *do* seem to be logically linked with the dynamics of a core syndrome of Modernization, involving urbanization, industrialization, economic development, occupational specialization, and the spread of mass literacy.

Change is not linear in any system subject to feedback. This complicates our analysis. If the process of economic-cultural-political change moved smoothly in one continuous direction, a cross section of the world's societies would show a simple developmental progression of cultural changes as one moved from the least developed to the economically most developed societies. Analogously, a cross section of the earth's surface sometimes reveals neatly ordered geological layers, with the oldest stratum of rock lowest and the newer strata located above the older ones. But reality is not this simple: social change produces feedback, which eventually changes the direction of change. Thus, we are likely to find patterns similar to those produced by tectonic upheavals, in which identifiable geological layers are shifted and juxtaposed with other strata. The result is not chaos, but neither is it a simple layering from oldest to newest strata.

We suggest that we will find the residue of two major waves of change (along with many lesser ones) mirrored in the World Values survey's cross section of the world's cultures: the distribution of these cultural traits reflects the processes of Modernization and Postmodernization, respectively.

The literature on Modernization focuses on the first of these two processes. It argues (correctly, we believe) that a broad syndrome of changes has been linked with modern economic development. These changes include urbanization, industrialization, occupational specialization, mass formal education, development of mass media, secularization, individuation, the rise of entrepreneurs and entrepreneurial motivations, bureaucratization, the mass production assembly line, and the emergence of the modern state. The material core of this process is industrialization; and though the industrial revolution originated in the West, this process is not inherently Western and should not be confused with Westernization. Although there are arguments about what the "real" driving force is behind this syndrome, there is widespread agreement that these changes include technological, economic, cultural, and political components.

RELIGION AND ECONOMIC GROWTH

We propose a modified interpretation of Weber's thesis concerning the role of the Protestant Ethic in economic development. Weber was correct in arguing that the rise of Protestantism was a crucial event in modernizing Europe. But this was not due to factors unique to Protestantism—it has been argued that everything Weber ascribed to Puritanism might equally well be ascribed to Judaism (Sombart, 1913). European Judaism had an outlook that was in some ways modern, but it could not transform Europe because it held a marginal position there. The crucial impact of Protestantism was due to the fact that it supplanted a set of religious norms that are common to most preindustrial societies, and which inhibit economic achievement; and it replaced them with norms favorable to economic achievement.

Because they experience little or no economic growth, preindustrial economies are zero-sum systems: upward social mobility can only come at someone else's expense. In any preindustrial society that has endured for some time, the cultural system is likely to have adapted accordingly: social status is hereditary rather than achieved, and the culture encourages people to accept their social position in this life, emphasizing that meek acceptance and denial of worldly aspirations will be rewarded in the next life. Aspirations toward social mobility are sternly repressed. Such value systems help to maintain social solidarity and discourage economic accumulation in a variety of ways, ranging from norms of sharing and charity, to the norms of noblesse oblige, to the potlatch and similar institutions in which one attains prestige by recklessly giving away one's worldly goods.

For Weber, the central element in the rise of modernity was the movement away from traditional religious authority to secular rational-legal authority: a shift from ascriptive status to impersonal, achievement-based roles, and a shift of power from society to state. Traditional value systems must be shattered in order for modern economic development to take place. In a society undergoing rapid economic expansion, social mobility is acceptable, even a virtue. But in hunting and gathering or agrarian societies, the main basis of production—land—is a fixed quantity, and social mobility can only occur if an individual or group seizes the lands of another. To preserve social peace, virtually all traditional cultures discourage upward social mobility and the accumulation of wealth. They help to integrate society by providing a rationale that legitimates the established social order, in which social status is hereditary; but these cultures also inculcate norms of sharing, charity, and other obligations that help mitigate the harshness of a subsistence economy.

The Confucian system was an exception in one important respect. Although (like virtually all traditional cultures) it inculcated the duty to be satisfied with one's station in life and to respect authority, it did permit social mobility based on individual achievement, through the Confucian examination system. Moreover, it did not justify meek acceptance of one's lot in this world, by stressing the infinitely greater rewards that this would bring in the next world. It was based on a secular worldview: if one were to rise, one would do so in this world or not at all.

On the whole, however, the traditional value systems of agrarian society (China included) are adapted to maintaining a stable balance in unchanging societies. Accordingly, they tend to discourage social change in general and accumulative entrepreneurial motivation in particular, which is stigmatized and relegated to pariah groups if tolerated at all. Economic accumulation is characterized as ignoble greed. To facilitate the economic accumulation needed to launch industrialization, these cultural inhibitions must be relaxed.

In Western society, the Protestant Reformation helped break the grip of the medieval Christian worldview on a significant part of Europe. It did not do this by itself. The emergence of scientific inquiry had already begun to undermine this worldview. But Weber's emphasis on the role of Protestantism captures an important part of reality. Prior to the Reformation, Southern Europe was economically more advanced than Northern Europe. During the three centuries after the Reformation, capitalism emerged—mainly in Protestant countries, and among the Protestant minorities in Catholic countries. Within this cultural context, economic accumulation was no longer despised. Quite the contrary, it was highly respected because it was taken as evidence of divine favor: those whom God had chosen, he made rich.

Protestant Europe manifested a subsequent economic dynamism that was extraordinary, moving it far ahead of Catholic Europe. Shifting trade patterns, declining food production in Southern Europe, and other factors also contributed to this shift, but the evidence suggests that cultural factors played a major role. Throughout the first 150 years of the Industrial Revolution, industrial development took place almost entirely within the Protestant regions of Europe, and the Protestant portions of the New World. This began to change only during the second half of the twentieth century, when those regions that had been most strongly influenced by the Protestant Ethic—and had become economically secure—began to deemphasize economic growth. As we will argue, they did so precisely *because* they had become economically secure. At the same time, an entrepreneurial outlook had emerged in Catholic Europe and (even more strikingly) in East Asia, both of which are now showing higher rates of economic growth than Protestant Europe. The concept of the Protestant Ethic is outdated if we take it to mean something that can only exist in Protestant countries. But Weber's more general concept that culture influences economic growth is a crucial insight.

MODERNIZATION: THE SHIFT FROM RELIGIOUS AUTHORITY TO STATE AUTHORITY

Secularization is inherently linked with Modernization. This holds true despite frequent assertions that a rapid growth of fundamentalist religion is taking place throughout the world. This interpretation reflects a misconception of what is happening, generalizing from two very different phenomena. The apparent rise of religious fundamentalism reflects two disparate elements:

1. Advanced industrial societies in North America, Western Europe, and East Asia, traditional forms of religion have been, *and still are*, declining, as we will demonstrate. During the past 40 years, church attendance rates have been falling and adherence to traditional norms concerning divorce, abortion, suicide, single parenthood, and homosexuality have been eroding—and continue to erode. Resurgent fundamentalist activism has indeed been dramatic: gay bashing and the bombing of abortion centers have received widespread coverage in the mass media, encouraging the perception that these actions have a rapidly growing constituency. They do not. Instead, precisely because fundamentalists correctly perceive that many of their central norms are rapidly eroding, they have been galvanized into unprecedented activism. But this reflects the rearguard action of a dwindling segment of the population, not the wave of the future.

2. Islamic fundamentalism, on the other hand, does have a growing mass constituency. But it is growing in societies that have *not* modernized: though

some of these societies are rich, they have not become rich by moving along the Modernization trajectory of industrialization, occupational specialization, rising educational levels, and so on, but simply by virtue of the fact that they have large oil revenues. Even without modernizing, it is possible to become rich if one possesses large petroleum reserves that can be sold to industrialized countries, enabling traditional elites to buy the external trappings of Modernization.

The possession of this wealth is important: it has enabled oil-rich fundamentalist regimes to obtain such things as automobiles, air conditioning, modern medical treatment for elites, and, above all, modern weapons: without them, the fundamentalist regimes would be perceived as militarily weak and technologically backward—and their mass appeal and prospects for survival would be far weaker.

Modernization involves more than the shift away from cultural traditions (usually based on religious norms) that emphasize ascribed status and sharing, toward placing a positive value on achievement and accumulation. For Weber, the key to Modernization was the shift from a religion-oriented worldview to a rational-legal worldview. There were two key components of Modernization.

1. *Secularization*. Weber emphasized the *cognitive* roots of secularization. For him, the rise of the scientific worldview was the crucial factor that led to the decline of the sacred/prerational elements of religious faith. We suggest that, more recently, the rise of a sense of *security* among mass publics of advanced welfare states has been an equally important factor in the decline of traditional religious orientations. This difference in emphasis has important implications. The cognitive interpretation implies that secularization is inevitable: scientific knowledge can diffuse across national boundaries rapidly, and its spread is more or less irreversible. By contrast, the rise of a sense of security among mass publics takes place only after a society has successfully industrialized; and it can be reversed to some extent by rapid change or economic decline. Thus although scientific knowledge has been permeating throughout the world for many decades, religious fanaticism continues to flourish in societies that are still in the early stages of industrialization; and fundamentalist movements continue to emerge among the less secure strata of even the most advanced industrial societies, especially during times of stress.

2. *Bureaucratization*. The process of secularization paved the way for another key component of Modernization, Bureaucratization, the rise of "rational" organizations, based on rules designed to move efficiently toward explicit goals, and with recruitment based on impersonal goal-oriented achievement standards. A prerequisiite for bureaucratization was the erosion of the belief systems supporting ascriptive traditional authority and zero-sum economies; and their replacement by achievement-oriented, rational, and scientifically oriented belief systems that supported the authority of large, centralized bureaucratic states geared to facilitating economic growth. The core of cultural Modernization was the shift from traditional (usually religious) authority to rational-legal authority.

   Along with this went a shift of prestige and socioeconomic functions away from the key institutions of traditional society—the family and the church—to the state, and a shift in economic activity from the small family enterprise to mass production that was state-regulated or even state-owned. Globally, it was a shift of prestige and power from society to state.

   During the modernizing phase of history, it seemed (to Marxists and non-Marxists alike) that the direction of social evolution was toward the increasing subordination of the individual to a Leviathan state having superhuman powers. The state would become an omnipotent and benevolent entity, replacing God in a secular world. And for most of the nineteenth and twentieth centuries, the dominant trend (the wave of the future, as it was sometimes called) was a shift from societal authority toward state authority, manifested in the apparently inexorable growth of the economic, political, and social role of government. Even non-Marxist thinkers such as Schumpeter (1947) reluctantly considered the triumph of socialism to be inevitable. And until recently, even such mainstream figures as Lindblom (1977) thought that the only question was whether socialism would triumph over capitalism, or whether capitalism and socialism would continue to coexist. The possibility that socialism might give way to capitalism was not even entertained.

THE POSTMODERN SHIFT

The socialist leviathan-state *was* the logical culmination of the Modernization process, but it did not turn out to be the wave of the future. Instead, the expansion of the bureaucratic state eventually approached a set of natural limits, and change began to move in a new direction. Figure 3.1 illustrates what happened. From the Industrial Revolution until well into the second half of the twentieth century, industrial society underwent Modernization. This process transformed political and cultural systems from traditional regimes legitimated by religious belief systems to rational-legal states legitimated by their claim to maximize the welfare of their people through scientific expertise. It was a transfer of authority from family and religious institutions to political institutions.

   Within the last 25 years, a major change in the direction of change has occurred that might be called the Postmodern shift. Its origins are rooted in the economic miracles that occurred first in Western Europe and North America, and later in East Asia and now in Southeast Asia. Coupled with the safety net of the modern welfare state, this has produced unprecedentedly high levels of economic security, giving rise to a cultural feedback that is having a major impact on both the economic and political systems of advanced industrial societies. This new trajectory shifts authority away from *both* religion and the state to the individual, with an increasing focus on individual concerns such as friends and leisure. Postmodernization deemphasizes all kinds of authority,

Figure 3.1. The shift from Modernization to Postmodernization: changing emphasis on key aspects of life.

whether religious or secular, allowing much wider range for individual autonomy in the pursuit of individual subjective well-being.

The core function of culture in traditional society was to maintain social cohesion and stability in a steady-state economy. Norms of sharing were crucial to survival in an environment where there was no social security bureau and no unemployment benefits: in bad times, one's survival depended on how strongly the norms of sharing were inculcated.

The importance of these norms is almost certain to be underestimated by anyone brought up in an individualistic society. In relatively traditional societies such as Nigeria, even today people feel a strong obligation to help take care of not only their immediate family, but their brothers, sisters, cousins, nieces, nephews, and old friends and neighbors. These norms are highly functional in traditional societies: they enable people to survive who would otherwise starve. In industrial societies, this sense of obligation has eroded almost to the point of extinction.

The core project of Modernization is economic growth, and the means to attain it is through industrialization—the systematic application of technology

TABLE 3.1

Traditional, Modern, and Postmodern Society: Societal Goals and Individual Values

	Traditional	*Modern*	*Postmodern*
Core Societal Project	Survival in a steady-state economy	Maximize economic growth	Maximize subjective well-being
Individual Value	Traditional religious and communal norms	Achievement motivation	Postmaterialist and Postmodern values
Authority System	Traditional authority	Rational-legal authority	De-emphasis of *both* legal and religious authority

to maximize the output of tangible things, such as wheat, textiles, coal, steel, and tractors.

In Postmodernization, the core project is to maximize individual well-being, which is increasingly dependent on subjective factors. Human behavior shifts from being dominated by the economic imperatives of providing food, clothing, and shelter toward the pursuit of quality of life concerns.

Even economic behavior becomes less a matter of meeting the survival needs and becomes increasingly oriented toward attaining subjective well-being. Economic growth continues, but output consists less and less of tangible things that contribute directly to survival, and more and more of intangibles whose value is subjective. The Postmodernization writers are on target in emphasizing the increasingly subjective nature of life experience in advanced industrial society.

For example, government has become an enormous sector, now employing a larger proportion of the U.S. workforce than does industrial manufacturing. Government services are intangible, and their value is highly subjective—people even disagree about whether their value is positive or negative. Computer software, education, research, entertainment, and tourism have all become major industries. Unlike food, clothing, and shelter, their products are intangible and their value is largely subjective. Computer software, microchips, and entertainment have become three of the United States' largest exports, but the value of the film or silicon or disk on which they are stored is negligible. A successful motion picture or computer program may be worth hundreds of millions of dollars; another film or program that costs just as much to produce may be virtually valueless. Ideas and innovation are the crucial component—and their value is whatever people feel it is worth. With psychotherapy and tourism, this is equally true: they have become major economic activities, and their value lies almost entirely in their contribution to subjective well-being.

Table 3.1 compares the societal goals and individual value systems underlying traditional, modern, and postmodern society. As it indicates, the core societal goal of traditional society is survival under the conditions of a steady-state economy, in which social mobility is a zero-sum game. During the

Modernization phase, by contrast, the core societal project is maximizing economic growth—and, in both capitalist and socialist societies, it tends to be carried out by ruthlessly extracting the necessary capital from an impoverished populace, regardless of the costs to the environment and quality of life. In Postmodern society, by contrast, the top priority shifts from maximizing economic growth to maximizing subjective well-being.

From Survival Values to Well-being Values

Individual-level value systems reflect the core societal project of the three respective types of societies. Traditional societies vary enormously, but virtually all of them emphasize individual conformity to societal norms limiting violence, sexual behavior, and economic accumulation; and encouraging acceptance of the existing economic and social order. These norms are usually codified and legitimated within a religious framework. Perhaps the most central individual-level change linked with Modernization is the rise of achievement motivation; but the broad shift toward instrumental rationality weakens all traditional norms.

During the Modernization era, there was a consensus throughout industrial society that economic growth was not only a good thing, but virtually the ultimate good: though Marxists and capitalists disagreed sharply about how the fruits of production should be distributed, both sides shared an implicit consensus that economic growth was desirable. This consensus was unquestioned because it seemed self-evident. Economic growth and scientific discoveries constituted Progress: they were good almost by definition.

During the Cold War there was a similar shared sentiment that the question of whether East or West was the better society would be decided by which one achieved the most economic growth. And during the first half of the Cold War, the Eastern bloc seemed to be winning by the test that really counted: high growth rates. In 1972 Meadows et al.'s *The Limits to Growth* called this consensus into question, arguing that economic growth was *not* desirable and should be brought to a stop before it was too late. Shortly afterward, Schumacher's (1973) *Small Is Beautiful* questioned another key principle of the Modernization era: the tendency to equate Biggest with Best—a tendency that was widespread, but especially strong in the socialist bloc, where bigness and centralization were elevated almost to the rank of moral virtues. Both of these critiques reflected the emergence of well-being values, a core element of Postmodernism.

From Achievement Motivation to Postmaterialist Motivation

In the Postmodern shift, values that played a key role in the emergence of industrial society—economic achievement motivation, economic growth, economic rationality—have faded in salience. At the societal level, there is a radical shift from the priorities of early industrialization, and a growing tendency for emphasis on economic growth to become subordinate to concern for its impact on the environment. At the individual level, maximizing economic gains is gradually fading from top priority: self-expression and the desire for meaningful work are becoming even more crucial for a growing segment of the population. And the motivations for work are changing, from an emphasis on maximizing income as the top priority, toward increasing emphasis on the quality of the work experience. There is even some willingness to accept ascriptive criteria rather than achievement criteria for recruitment, if it is justified by social goals.

Scarcity has prevailed throughout most of history: it follows from the ecological principle that population normally rises to meet the available food supply and is then held in check by starvation, disease, and war. The result has been chronic scarcity, with the possibility of starvation shaping the daily awareness and life strategies of most people. Both traditional and modern societies were shaped by scarcity, but industrial society developed the belief that scarcity could be alleviated by individual achievement and economic growth, a radical change in outlook.

The root *cause* of the Postmodern value shift has been the gradual withering away of value systems that emerged under conditions of scarcity, and the spread of security values among a growing segment of the publics of these societies. This, in turn, grows out of the unprecedentedly high levels of subjective well-being that characterize the publics of advanced industrial society, as compared with those of earlier societies. In advanced industrial societies, most people take survival for granted. Precisely *because* they take it for granted, they are not aware of how profoundly this supposition shapes their worldviews.

Starvation is no longer a real concern for most of the people in high-technology societies, where production has been increasing much faster than the rate of population growth. These societies have attained unprecedentedly high life expectancies and unprecedentedly high levels of subjective well-being. One consequence of this fact is the rise of Postmaterialist values, but this is only one component of a broader cultural shift. The emergence and spread of Postmaterialist values is only the tip of the iceberg—one component of a much broader syndrome of cultural changes that we term Postmodernization. There are several additional important components.

GROWING EMPHASIS ON INDIVIDUAL FREEDOM AND REJECTION OF BUREAUCRATIC AUTHORITY

The shift from traditional society to industrial society brought a shift from traditional authority to rational bureaucratic authority. In most societies, this simply substituted political authority for religious authority. But in Postmodern society, authority, centralization, and bigness are all under growing suspicion. They have reached a point of diminishing effectiveness; and they have reached a point of diminishing acceptability.

Every stable culture is linked with a congruent authority system. But the Postmodern shift is a move away from *both* traditional authority and state authority. It reflects a declining emphasis on authority in general—regardless of whether it is legitimated by societal or state formulae. This leads to declining confidence in hierarchical institutions. Today, political leaders throughout the industrialized world are experiencing some of the lowest levels of support ever recorded. This is not simply because they are less competent than previous leaders. It reflects a systematic decline in mass support for established political institutions, and a shift of focus toward individual concerns.

Because Postmaterialists view self-expression and political participation as things that are valuable in themselves, the Postmodern phase of development is inherently conducive to democratization. There is nothing easy or automatic about this tendency. Determined authoritarian elites can repress it almost indefinitely, though at growing cost to the morale and cooperativeness of their subjects. Similarly, the institutional structure and cultural heritage of a given society can facilitate or retard this tendency, as can external pressures and other macropolitical factors. But as economic development takes place, mass input to the political process becomes increasingly widespread and effective. Economic development leads mass publics to place growing emphasis on participatory values.

In addition to the changes in core societal goals, individual values, and authority systems outlined in table 3.1, the Postmodern shift has two other aspects.

First, as Postmodern philosophers argue, an essential attribute of postmodernity is a diminishing faith in science, technology, and rationality. One of the core components of Modernization was a growing faith in the power of science and rational analysis to solve virtually all problems. At the elite level (especially among Postmodern writers) Postmodernization is linked with a diminishing faith in rationality and a diminishing confidence that science and technology will help solve humanity's problems. This change in worldview has advanced farthest in the economically and technologically most advanced societies. And insofar as industrial society's culture of instrumental rationality is identified with the West, Postmodernity is linked with a rejection of the West. But for mass publics, Postmodernity has *also* brought a rejection of the Soviet model, which was even more hierarchical and instrumentally oriented than the Western version of industrial society.

Initially, Postmodernism focused on discontent with the dehumanizing aspects of modernity as manifested in the *West*. Many of the most prominent Postmodernist thinkers even considered themselves Marxists (and some still do). But it was inevitable that Postmodernization would eventually lead to the rejection of hierarchical, bureaucratic, centralized big government in the socialist world as well, where it was most extreme. This contributed to an unexpected development: the collapse of socialism. State socialism failed because (1) it no longer functioned well, in advanced industrial society—though it *had* functioned relatively well during the Modernization era, and (2) because it was no longer acceptable. The declining effectiveness and acceptability of massive, centralized bureaucratic authority contributed to the collapse of state socialism, as did the fact that Postmodernization brings an inherent tendency toward democratization, linked with its growing emphasis on individual autonomy.

ELEMENTS OF CONTINUITY BETWEEN MODERNIZATION
AND POSTMODERNIZATION

Postmodernization continues some of the trends that were launched by Modernization, particularly the processes of specialization, secularization, and individuation. The growing complexity of advanced industrial society results in increasing specialization in all areas of life. But the processes of secularization and individuation have taken on a new character.

Secularization

Weber attributed the decline of religious belief largely to the rise of the scientific worldview, which gradually replaced the sacred/mystical prerational elements of religious faith. Although the scientific worldview has lost its glamor, secularization continues—but for a new reason: the emergence of a sense of security among the economically more advanced societies diminishes the need for the reassurance that has traditionally been provided by absolute belief systems, which purport to provide certainty and the assurance of salvation, if not in this world at least in the next.

It would be a major mistake to equate either Modernization or Postmodernization with the decline of religion. Modernization does require the dismantling of some core aspects of traditional religion—in particular, it abolishes traditional tendencies to equate the old with the good, and the rigid rejection of social mobility and individual economic achievement. But—significantly—in the Protestant Ethic thesis, Weber argued that this was accomplished by having one type of religion replace another. The Marxist route to modernity achieved this by replacing traditional religion with a secular ideology that initially inspired widespread Utopian hopes and expectations of a new sort of Judgment Day that would come with the revolution. As it lost its ability to inspire such hopes, Marxism began to crumble.

In some form or other, spiritual concerns will always be a part of the human condition. This remains true after the shift from Modernization to Postmodernization. A core element in Postmodernization is the decline of instrumental rationality (equating economic growth with the good) to value rationality, seeking human happiness itself, rather than the economic means to that end. Although Postmodernism goes with a continuing decline in traditional religious beliefs, it is linked with a *growing* concern for the meaning and purpose of life.

Individuation

With industrialization, the erosion of religious social controls opened up a broader space for individual autonomy, but this space was largely taken up by growing obligations to the state. The Postmodern shift away from *both* religious and state authority continues this long-standing shift toward individuation, but in a much stronger form. Increasingly, individual rights and entitlements take priority over any other obligation.

Globally, there is a great deal of cross-national variation in degrees of Modernization: even today, only a minority of the world's population live in industrialized societies. An even smaller proportion of humanity live in the rich and secure advanced industrial societies in which Postmodern value systems have taken root.

Consequently, we would expect to find two main dimensions of cross-cultural variation across the 43 societies we are about to analyze. During the past two centuries, the two most pervasive and important processes that have shaped them have been (1) Modernization and (2) Postmodernization. Accordingly, we would expect the world's societies to vary according to the degree to which they have been transformed by these two processes. Furthermore, a given society's position on these two dimensions should be closely linked with its level of economic and technological development: societies that are only beginning to industrialize should manifest relatively traditional belief systems; those that are now in the stage of rapid industrialization should manifest value systems keyed to maximizing economic growth; and societies that had already attained high levels of existential security some time ago should have undergone an intergenerational value shift toward Postmodern values that give priority to subjective well-being over economic growth.

MODERNIZATION AND POSTMODERNIZATION DIMENSIONS:
EMPIRICAL FINDINGS

We have outlined the patterns of cross-cultural variation we expect to find, and why. Now let us examine cross-cultural variation empirically, as reflected in survey data from 43 societies. Our first question is whether the various religious, social, economic, and political components of given cultures are randomly related, or whether they go together, with certain coherent combinations being more probable than others. Figure 3.2 shows the results of a principal components factor analysis of the data from representative national surveys in the 43 societies included in the 1990–91 World Values Survey. The responses to each of the variables used here are boiled down to a mean score for each country; using the society as the unit of analysis, we can examine cross-cultural variation in a wide range of norms and values.

Figure 3.2 sums up an immense amount of information. It presents an overview of findings from the World Values surveys, showing the relationships

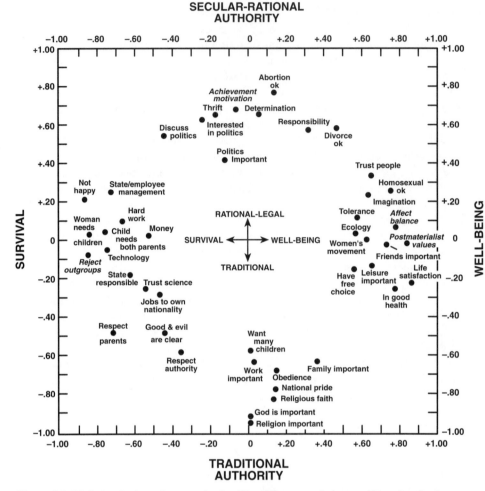

Figure 3.2. Variation in the values emphasized by different societies: traditional authority vs. rational-legal authority and scarcity values vs. Postmodern values. *Source*: 1990–93 World Values Survey. This figure shows the first and second principal components emerging from a factor analysis of data from representative national surveys of 43 societies, aggregated to the national level. The scales on the margins show each item's loadings on the two respective dimensions. The items in italics (e.g., "reject outgroups") are multi-item indicators.

between scores of items. Subsequent chapters will probe more deeply into the causal relationships between key variables and examine changes over time. This figure is based on the responses given by nearly 60,000 respondents in 43 societies. We do not provide the full text of each question used here. A short phrase (such as "Abortion OK") is used to convey the gist of each item on figure 3.2; for the full text, see Appendix 2. The 43 variables used here reflect a much larger number of questions: some of them are based on responses to whole batteries of questions. "Affect balance," for example, sums up each respondent's answers to the 10 questions in the Bradburn Affect Balance Scale; "Postmaterialist Values" sums up the responses to a series of questions through which each respondent ranks a set of 12 basic goals; and "Achievement Motivation" sums up responses to four items concerning important values for a child to learn; "Reject outgroups" also sums up the responses to several questions.

Furthermore, these variables were chosen to reflect a considerably larger number of related items that show similar patterns. "God is important," for example, taps a cluster of more than 30 items that measure the extent to which religion is, or is not, an important part of the respondent's life. Similarly, "Life satisfaction," "Affect balance," and "Not happy" reflect a larger cluster of items that tap subjective well-being. To avoid redundancy, and to limit figure 3.2 to a readable size, we have only included the most sensitive indicators of each cluster. Figure 3.2 depicts the structure underlying responses to more than 100 questions dealing with many aspects of life in 43 societies, providing a global overview of basic cultural patterns.

Figure 3.2 shows the relationships between scores of variables covering a wide variety of topics ranging from religion to politics to sexual norms to attitudes toward science. These diverse orientations tend to go together in coherent patterns. For example, certain societies place relatively heavy emphasis on religion: the people of these societies also show high levels of national pride, prefer to have relatively large families, would like to see more respect for authority, tend to rank relatively low on achievement motivation and political interest, oppose divorce, and have a number of other distinctive cultural orientations. The people of other societies consistently fall toward the opposite end of the spectrum on all of these orientations, giving rise to a vertical dimension that reflects Traditional versus Secular-Rational orientations.

Figure 3.2 greatly simplifies a complex reality—in a sense, it is a one-page summary of the entire 1990 World Values Survey. It is, of course, an oversimplification. The present author has written two books on Postmaterialist values alone, and in this analysis, these values serve as only one indicator of a much broader Survival–well-being dimension. Nevertheless—to a surprising degree—reality fits this simplified model: over half of the cross-national variance among these variables can be explained by two dimensions that reflect the Modernization and Postmodernization processes, respectively.

Our first major finding is that there is a great deal of constraint among cultural systems. The pattern found here is anything but random. The first two dimensions that emerge from the principal components factor analysis depicted in figure 3.2 account for fully 51 percent of the cross-national variation among these variables. Additional dimensions explain relatively small amounts of variance. Moreover, these two main dimensions are robust, showing little change when we drop given items, even high-loading ones. The vertical axis reflects the polarization between Traditional authority and Secular-Rational authority; the horizontal axis depicts the polarization between a cluster of items labeled Survival Values and another cluster labeled Well-being Values.

The scales on the borders of figure 3.2 indicate each item's loadings on these two dimensions.

Just two dimensions account for over half of the cross-national variance among these items: this also means that about half of the variance in these values and orientations is *not* explained by the Modernization and Postmodernization dimensions. It is important to keep this in mind. Historical change cannot be entirely reduced to universal processes: to a great extent, each society works out its history in its own unique fashion, influenced by the culture, leaders, institutions, climate, geography, situation-specific events, and other unique elements that make up its own distinctive heritage. General explanatory factors can never account for everything in cross-cultural research. Just as each individual is unique, each society is unique (and each historical moment is unique). Thus, while we find the metaphor of evolution useful in describing how social change works, we do not equate evolution with determinism. Certain strategies for coping with a given environment are far more probable than others: such a strategy represents a mutually supportive combination of economic, technological, political, and cultural factors, and one that is likely to survive—while other, almost limitless, dysfunctional combinations prove abortive. But social change also involves less systematic factors that make each society unique.

Brilliant and instructive books have been written about the ways in which given societies differ from others. This book focuses on the general themes underlying the cross-national pattern, not because we are uninterested in the unique aspects of given societies—few things are more fascinating—but because the common themes are *also* interesting, and because any book that undertakes to deal with more than 40 societies almost inevitably *must* focus on what is common, rather than on what is unique. The evidence examined here indicates that common underlying themes *do* exist: it suggests that roughly half of the cross-national variance in these values and attitudes can be accounted for by the processes of Modernization and Postmodernization, while the remaining half of the variation reflects factors that are more or less nation-specific.

Religion plays a much more important role in some societies than in others. In Nigeria, fully 85 percent of the population said that religion is "very important" in their lives; in South Africa, the figure was 66 percent; in Turkey, 61 percent; in both Poland and the United States, 53 percent; in Italy, the figure was only 34 percent; in Great Britain, France, and Germany, the figures were 16, 14, and 13 percent, respectively; in Russia, it was 12 percent; in Denmark, 9 percent; in Japan, it was 6 percent; and in China, 1 percent.

"Do societies that place relatively strong emphasis on religion also tend to favor large families?" The answer is an unequivocal "Yes," as the proximity of "Religion important" and "Want many children" near the bottom of figure 3.2 suggests: the correlation between these two items is $r = .51$ (significant at the .001 level). Moreover, societies characterized by an emphasis on religion also tend to place relatively strong emphasis on work, as the proximity between "Work important" and "Religion important" suggests ($r = .62$, significant at the .0000 level). The emphasis here is on *having* work, for the sake of survival; in economically more developed societies, people place much greater emphasis on work as a source of personal *satisfaction*. Relatively traditional societies also tend to stress "Obedience" as an important quality to teach a child (r = .58), and to view the family as relatively important ("Family important," r = .56). And, as one would expect, those societies in which the public considers "Religion important" also tend to be those in which the public believe that "God is important," and to say that religious faith is an important quality to teach a child ("Religious faith"): these are almost 1:1 relationships (r = .95 and .87, respectively). These last two linkages are obvious; the others, though intuitively plausible, are not. All of these items have high loadings on the vertical dimension, labeled "Traditional Authority" vs. "Secular-Rational Authority."

Societies that place relatively strong emphasis on religion are characterized by very distinctive norms concerning sexual behavior, childrearing, the role of women, and fertility rates; they have distinctive attitudes toward divorce, abortion, and homosexuality; they also place relatively strong emphasis on deference to authority; and they have distinctive norms concerning economic achievement and distinctive motivations for work.

It is not particularly surprising that societies in which religion is relatively important have distinctive norms concerning abortion, childbearing, and the role of women. But these differences also extend to areas in which the connection is far from obvious. For example, societies in which religion is important are characterized by much higher levels of national pride than those in which it is not, as figure 3.3 demonstrates. Here, the horizontal axis shows the percentage in each society who say that God plays an important role in their lives. The people of societies that rank high on this variable show much higher levels of national pride than do those that rank low. China is a deviant case, with a high level of national pride despite being overwhelmingly secular, and West Germany deviates in the opposite direction, showing a lower level of national pride than its level of religiosity would predict. But the overall linkage is remarkably strong and significant at the .0000 level (see figure 3.3).

As these findings suggest, high levels of constraint exist between various cultural attributes. For example, if we know that a society ranks high on national pride, we can pretty accurately predict its position on childrearing practices, religiosity, and a number of other important attributes. But the pattern extends even farther. Societies that emphasize the importance of religion tend to attach low importance to politics, as the locations of "Religion important" and "Politics important" (far apart from each other on the vertical dimension) suggests: the correlation between the two is −0.39. And these same societies tend to place *low* emphasis on "Thrift" and "Determination" as important qualities to teach a child (r = −.57 and −.59, respectively). As we will see in a more detailed analysis in chapter 5, emphasis on these values is part of an Achievement Motivation syndrome that is strongly linked with the economic growth rates of given societies.

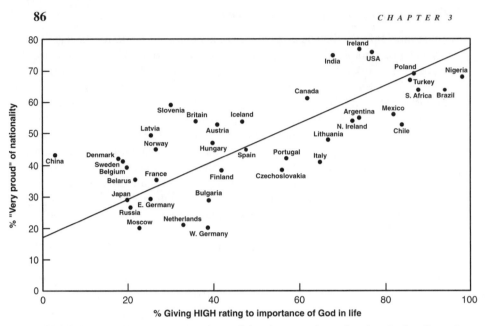

Figure 3.3. Coherent values patterns on the traditional vs. secular-rational authority dimension: the linkage between religiosity and national pride.
Horizontal dimension shows percentage ranking importance of God in their lives as relatively high (i.e., scores of 7–10 on a 10-point scale ranging from "not at all important" [1] to "very important" [10]). r = .71, significant at .0000 level.

COHERENT VALUE PATTERNS: THE POSTMODERNIZATION DIMENSION

In the Postmodernization phase of development, emphasis shifts from maximizing economic gains to maximizing subjective well-being. This gives rise to another major dimension of cross-cultural variation, on which a wide range of orientations are structured. So far, we have been discussing items with high loadings on the second principal component, labeled "Traditional Authority" vs. "Rational-Legal Authority." This dimension reflects the Modernization process, in which authority moves away from a traditional (usually religious) basis, toward increasing emphasis on impersonal bureaucratic authority. This is an important dimension, accounting for 21 percent of the variance among these 47 variables. But it is overshadowed by the first principal component, which accounts for 30 percent of the total variance. This dimension taps "Survival Values" versus "Well-being Values." A very sensitive indicator of this dimension is "Postmaterialist Values" (located near the right-hand pole of the horizontal axis on figure 3.2). This is a central element in a much broader cultural configuration.

Societies with large numbers of Postmaterialists tend to be characterized by a relatively strong sense of subjective well-being. Their publics tend to express high levels of satisfaction with their lives as a whole ("Postmaterialist Values" has a .68 correlation with "Life satisfaction"). Moreover, they report relatively high levels of positive affect (saying that within the past few days they felt interested in something, or proud, or pleased about having accomplished something) rather than negative affect (reporting that they were restless, or felt lonely, or upset because someone criticized them), which produces high scores on the Bradburn "Affect balance" scale. Furthermore, the publics of societies with high levels of Postmaterialism are likely to rate themselves as "In good health," (r = .58) and are *not* likely to describe themselves as "Not happy" (the correlation with "Postmaterialist Values" is −.71).

Subjective well-being is a condition, not a value, and is not correlated with Postmaterialism at the individual level. But high levels of subjective well-being are a key element in the cultural syndrome called Postmodernism. When a society attains high levels of economic security and subjective well-being, it is conducive to Postmaterialist values; but further economic development does not necessarily bring increased subjective well-being.

The linkage between Postmaterialism and subjective well-being is a cultural syndrome, not an individual-level ideology. It reflects the fact that societies with high levels of economic development not only have relatively high levels of *objective* need satisfaction (being relatively well-nourished, in good health, and having relatively high life expectancies); but their publics also experience relatively high levels of *subjective* security and well-being, which leads to an intergenerational shift toward Postmaterialist values. This cultural syndrome has gone largely unnoticed in previous Modernization literature, but manifests itself clearly when one has survey data covering a sufficiently broad range of countries.

At the individual level, however, Postmaterialists do *not* report relatively high levels of subjective well-being. Far from being a paradox, this is central to their nature: Postmaterialists have experienced relatively high levels of economic security throughout their formative years. They develop Postmaterialist priorities precisely because further economic gains do *not* produce additional subjective well-being: they take economic security for granted and go on to emphasize other (nonmaterial) goals. Moreover, they have relatively demanding standards for these other aspects of life—to such an extent that they often manifest *lower* levels of overall life satisfaction than do Materialists in the same society.

This leads to another finding that at first seems paradoxical. Generally, within any given society, the rich show higher levels of subjective well-being than the poor, as common sense might suggest. But Postmaterialists are an exception: they are richer (and have better education, more prestigious occupations, etc.) than most people—but they do *not* rank higher on subjective well-being than other people. This is significant. It reflects the fact that, as given nations become advanced industrial societies, they reach a point of diminishing marginal utility at which maximizing economic gains (for the individual) or economic growth (for the society) no longer results in higher levels of subjective well-being (we noted this phenomenon in chapter 2). From this perspective, it is perfectly rational to cease making economic efficiency and economic growth top priorities, and give increasing emphasis to quality of life concerns.

This cultural syndrome is pervasive and lies at the heart of Postmodernization. The publics of societies with high proportions of Postmaterialists do *not* emphasize "Hard work" as one of the most important qualities to teach a child (reflected in a loading of -0.67 on the Scarcity-Security dimension); instead, they emphasize "Tolerance" and "Imagination." Similarly, their publics do not view more emphasis on "Money" as a desirable change.

The polarization between survival values and well-being values extends to family values as well. The publics of societies with high proportions of Postmaterialists tend to reject the proposition that "A woman needs children" to be fulfilled, and disagree that "A child needs both parents," in a home with both a father and a mother, to grow up happily. There is a growing emphasis on self-realization for women, linked with a shift of emphasis from the role of mother to emphasis on careers.

"Respect parents" and "Respect authority" show strong loadings on both dimensions in figure 3.2. Their loadings indicate that *both* the Modernization process and the Postmodernization process are linked with declining respect for authority. And "Good and Evil are clear" has a negative relationship with both the shift from traditional authority to rational-legal authority and the shift from survival values to well-being values. A growing moral relativism is linked with both Modernization and Postmodernization. In traditional societies, moral rules are absolute truths, revealed by God. At the opposite extreme, in Postmodern society, absolute standards dissolve, giving way to an increasing sense of ambiguity.

We have argued that these two dimensions reflect the Modernization process and the Postmodernization process, respectively. And the fit is generally good. For example, the rise of Achievement Motivation is strongly linked with the vertical (Modernization) dimension. Moreover, the rankings of the global domains of life fit the expected configuration: as we move up the vertical dimension we see a shift in emphasis from family and religion (as indicated by "Family important" and "Religion important") toward increasing emphasis on the state ("Politics important"). Then, as we move from left to right on the horizontal dimension, we move away from emphasis on *both* traditional authority and state authority, toward increasing emphasis on individual concerns: "Leisure important" and "Friends important" show loadings of .66 and .72, respectively, on the Postmodernization dimension.

An emphasis on science and technology was a core element of modernity. But the publics of societies with high proportions of Postmaterialists (at the Postmodern end of the continuum) tend to have little confidence that scientific advances will help, rather than harm, humanity ("Trust science" has a negative correlation with "Postmaterialist values" that is significant at the .001 level); similarly, they tend to doubt that more emphasis on "Technology" would be a good thing. Conversely, these same societies have relatively high levels of support for the "Ecology" movement. The fact that societies shaped by security tend to reject science and technology is a major departure from the basic thrust of Modernization—another reason why this dimension reflects change in a *Post*-modern direction.

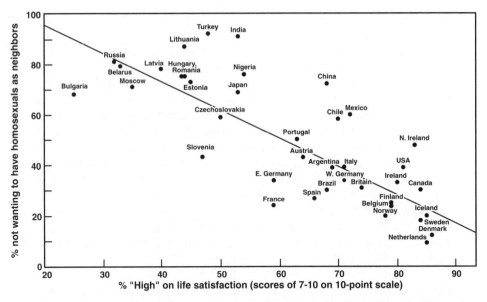

Figure 3.4. Coherent values patterns on the survival vs. well-being dimension: the linkage between life satisfaction and rejection of homosexuals as neighbors (part of the "Reject outgroups" cluster).
r = −.75, significant at .0000 level.

Societies influenced by Postmodern or well-being values tend to be markedly more tolerant than are those characterized by survival values. These societies emphasize "Tolerance" as an important quality to teach a child. Similarly, their publics are less likely to "Reject outgroups," saying that they would not like to have foreigners, people with AIDS, or homosexuals as neighbors; and they are relatively likely to feel that homosexuality is acceptable ("Homosexual OK"). Both of these correlations with "Postmaterialist values" are significant at the .001 level. Moreover, societies with relatively high levels of subjective well-being rank relatively low on intolerance of outgroups, as figure 3.4 illustrates.

The outgroup dealt with here is homosexuals, but the same pattern applies to rejection of other outgroups. In Russia and Belarus, where subjective well-being was extremely low in 1990, fully 80 percent of the public said they would not like to have homosexuals as neighbors. In such societies as Denmark or the Netherlands, where overall life satisfaction was much higher, only about 10 percent of the public were unwilling to have homosexuals as neighbors. Numerous other orientations are closely related to whether a society has high or low levels of subjective well-being.

Security is conducive to tolerance and conversely, insecurity is conducive to xenophobia. The narrower one's margin for survival is, the more likely one is to fear that strangers are threatening. This is especially true if the strangers speak a foreign language or hold different values and therefore seem incomprehensible and unpredictable.

In an agrarian or hunting and gathering society in which the land supply is just sufficient to feed the existing population, the arrival of a foreign group poses a direct threat to survival: in such a situation, xenophobia is realistic and almost certain to arise. In a technologically advanced society with a growing economy, foreigners may be tolerated or even welcomed. They do not pose a threat to survival and may even enhance the standard of living. But in times of economic or political crisis, even advanced industrial societies are prone to xenophobia, as the rise of fascism during the Great Depression demonstrated, and as recent events in Western Europe and the United States continue to demonstrate. But the severity of xenophobia tends to be proportionate to the degree of insecurity; hence, ethnic conflict is far more severe in Eastern Europe, where the economic systems and political systems have collapsed, than in Western Europe: far more people have been killed in ethnic conflicts in Eastern Europe, by several orders of magnitude.

No culture is immune to xenophobia, but it tends to be most intense where insecurity is most severe. Conversely, at the individual level, Postmaterialists—those who have grown up under conditions of relative economic and physical security—tend to be relatively tolerant of people with different ethnicity or sexual orientations. Similarly, they are relatively supportive of the "Women's movement." The rise of security values seems conducive to increasing tolerance of diversity, an essential component of democracy.

An environment of security and subjective well-being seems to foster not only tolerance, but a whole cluster of traits that are conducive to democracy. For example, well-being values are linked with high levels of interpersonal trust (as reflected in the .66 loading of "Trust people" on this dimension). Moreover, a participant public is an essential component of democracy—and one of the defining characteristics of Postmaterialist values is the fact that they give a high priority to self-expression and participation in decision making at all levels, including the political. Postmaterialism constitutes a central component of Postmodern values. Are these values linked with stable democracy? As we will see shortly, the answer is Yes.

In addition to its emphasis on science and technology, another key characteristic of Modernization was its tendency to bureaucratize all aspects of life, with the biggest bureaucracy of all resulting from the seemingly inexorable growth of government. But Postmodern values are linked with *declining* support for big government: believing that the state (rather than the individual) should take more responsibility to ensure that everyone is provided for ("State responsible") is linked with survival values, and not with well-being values; the same is true of support for "State/employee management" rather than owner management. Support for big government was a central component of Modernization. It does *not* go with Postmodern values, which is another indication that Postmodernization reflects a fundamental change of direction.

The analysis presented here is not the only possible way to slice the data. If one applies varimax rotation to the factors, one gets a somewhat different solution. Similarly, one can generate a three-dimensional or six-dimensional or even a 30-dimensional solution. Doing so produces a far more complicated result that might superficially seem more scholarly. But if one is looking for the *simplest* possible configuration, a reasonable approach is to use principal components analysis and focus on the first dimensions. Figure 3.2 is what emerges then—a structure that sums up a surprisingly wide range of phenomena in just two dimensions that capture over half of the total cross-national variance in this array of orientations. Additional dimensions exist, but they explain relatively small amounts of additional variance. The reality is that cross-cultural variation is surprisingly orderly and can be interpreted with a relatively parsimonious model.

Another critique of this approach would be to point that it is based on the assumption that our questions have comparable meaning to people from 43 widely varying societies, who were interviewed in 31 different languages. Our questionnaire was, of course, designed with this in mind: building on extensive previous cross-national survey research and extensive pilot testing, with input from social scientists on five continents, it was designed to ask questions that *do* have a shared meaning across many cultures. If we had asked questions about nation-specific issues, the cross-cultural comparability would have broken down. In France, for example, a recent hot political issue (linked with Islamic immigration) was the question whether or not girls should be allowed to wear scarves over their heads in school. This question would have had totally different meanings (or would have seemed meaningless) in other societies. On the other hand, a question about whether religion is important in one's life *is* meaningful in virtually every society on earth, including those in which most people say it is not. The same is true of questions about respect for authority, or about how many children one would like to have, or whether or not one is satisfied with one's life as a whole.

Moreover, the cross-national placement of societies underlying this configuration of worldviews is astonishingly coherent. As we will see below, societies that show similar cultural orientations in our surveys fall into compact and theoretically meaningful clusters. Working independently and without knowledge of each other's findings, the World Values survey investigators in the five Nordic countries came up with relatively similar results. So did our colleagues in Nigeria and South Africa, and so did those in the four Latin American countries and in Eastern Europe. The evidence suggests that the World Values survey group was generally successful in framing cross-nationally meaningful questions. If these items had idiosyncratic meanings in each society, we would not have attained such a parsimonious and coherent structure. Instead, the orientations that went together in one society would be unrelated in other societies, and it would take 15 or 20 dimensions to explain half of the variance.

WHERE ARE GIVEN SOCIETIES LOCATED ON THESE DIMENSIONS?
A CULTURAL GEOGRAPHY OF THE WORLD

In most respects, the two dimensions in figure 3.2 show a good fit with the attributes we would expect to find if they reflected the shift from Traditional to
Modern values, and from Modern to Postmodern values, respectively. But in
one important way the pattern seems wrong: the growth of big government was
a central aspect of Modernization. For many decades, the all-encompassing socialist state was thought to be the wave of the future: it was the logical culmination of the trend toward bureaucratization and state authority. If so, we
would expect to find emphasis on "State/employee management" and "State
responsibility" located near the top of the vertical dimension. Instead, we find
them occupying roughly neutral positions on this dimension. Why? In order to
understand the answer, let us examine the specific national cultures underlying this pattern.

Figure 3.5 shows the location of each society on the two dimensions we have
been examining. To locate them in this space, dummy variables were created
for each of our 43 societies; these variables were mapped onto the two dimensions shaped by the worldviews of the respective publics. Because these
dummy variables are extremely skewed (each having one country coded "1"
and 42 countries coded "0"), the correlations with the cultural dimensions are
modest; but if we combine countries into larger groups (such as the Nordic
group or the Latin American group) the correlations with the ideological space
become quite strong. The societies that show similar cultural orientations in
our surveys (and therefore are near each other on this figure) fall into intuitively plausible clusters.

Our broadest generalization is that the value systems of richer countries differ systematically from those of poorer countries. The poorer countries tend to
be located toward the lower left on figure 3.5, with the richer ones falling into
the upper right-hand quadrant. Although there are some deviant cases (the
United States having much more traditional values than its GNP per capita
would predict), the overall correlation between values and economic development is very strong.

But the pattern is coherent in many additional respects. For example, all four
of the Latin American societies included in the 1990 World Values Survey fall
into one cluster, reflecting the fact that, in global perspective they have relatively similar value systems. The two African societies fall into another cluster; and the three Confucian-influenced societies of East Asia fall into another
cluster—which partly overlaps with another cluster containing the former
communist societies. The historically Catholic societies of Western Europe fall
into another compact cluster. Although church attendance in Western Europe
has collapsed, the historically Protestant societies of Northern Europe fall into
another cluster (with Eastern Germany located at the intersection of the Northern European cluster and the ex-communist cluster, as its historical experience
might suggest). The United States and Canada constitute a North American

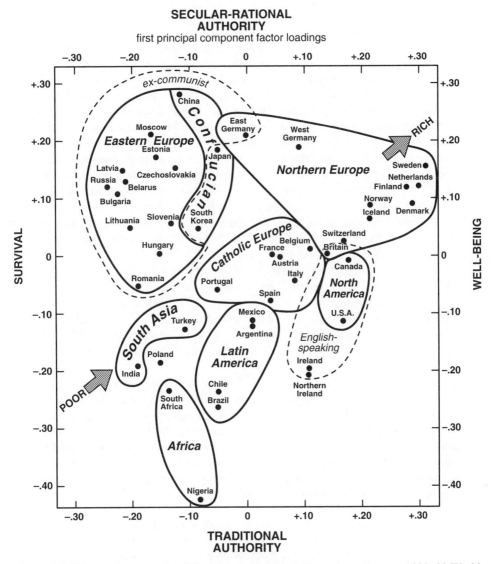

Figure 3.5. Where given societies fall on two key cultural dimensions. *Source*: 1990–93 World Values Survey. Positions are based on the mean scores of the publics of the given nation on each of the two dimensions.

cluster—that could be expanded to include the other English-speaking societies. Poland is an outlier, having more traditional values than the other ex-communist societies of Eastern Europe: it does not fit into any coherent cluster. But on the whole, the value systems of a majority of the world's people are anything but random: though shaped by a variety of factors, they manifest a remarkably coherent pattern that can be interpreted parsimoniously.

Societies that are close to each other on figure 3.5 show relatively similar responses to most of the questions that were asked in the World Values survey. For example, though the peoples of the United States and Canada differ in many ways, they have relatively similar basic values in comparison with most other societies: accordingly, they are located close to each other on figure 3.5.

Just how close are they? To answer this question, let us examine the responses to the first six questions asked in the survey. The publics of each society were asked "Please say, for each of the following, how important it is in your life." They rated the relative importance of "Work," "Family," "Friends," "Leisure," "Politics," and "Religion." This list covers a broad range of human concerns, and the various publics differed a great deal in how much importance they attached to the respective aspects of life. The cross-national rankings for nearly 350 variables are shown in Basanez, Inglehart, and Moreno (1997), and they support the claim that societies that are close to each other on figure 3.5 tend to show similar values and beliefs in many other ways; here, we will limit ourselves to these six variables.

Since 43 societies are ranked here, the greatest possible distance between any two societies would occur if one of them were ranked first and the other were ranked forty-third: all 41 of the other societies would fall between them. Conversely, the smallest possible distance would occur if the two societies had consecutive ranks, with *none* of the other societies falling between them. Finally, if the two societies were randomly distributed, about 20 societies would fall between them.

The publics of the United States and Canada give relatively similar ratings to these six aspects of life: on the average, only 3.3 other societies fall between them. The values of Canadians and Americans are much more similar to each other than they are to those of most other peoples. The British are also relatively close to the Americans, but by no means as close as the Canadians. On the other hand, the publics of the United States and China generally give these six domains quite different ratings: on the average, they are separated by nearly 24 societies, as the following ratings show:

CULTURAL DISTANCE FROM THE UNITED STATES
(mean number of societies between the
United States and given society)

United States–Canada	3.3
United States–Britain	9.0
United States–France	16.7
United States–Japan	21.8
United States–Russia	22.2
United States–China	23.8

This principle applies generally. One finds a similar pattern if one views the world from a Swedish perspective, for example. Sweden, Norway, and Denmark are located relatively near each other on figure 3.5, and they make rather similar ratings of the six aspects of life. On the average, only 3.8 societies fall between Sweden and Norway in these rankings, and only 5.8 societies fall between Sweden and Denmark. On the other hand, Sweden and France are separated by a mean of 13.6 societies, while Sweden and Russia are separated by an average of 17.8 societies, Sweden and Japan by 18.2 societies, and Sweden and China are separated by an average of more than 19 societies.

Given groups of nations take coherent positions on the two dimensions. For example, Norway, Iceland, Denmark, Finland, and Sweden—the five Nordic countries—form a compact cluster located in the upper right-hand quadrant of figure 3.5: all five have related histories and similar cultures, ranking fairly high on the cultural outlook associated with rational-legal authority, and ranking very high on Postmodern values. To some extent, these countries are geographically proximate, but the fact that they are prosperous and traditionally Protestant welfare states seems more important than their geographic proximity. Thus the Netherlands, which is not a Nordic country but was historically Protestant and is today a prosperous welfare state, falls squarely into the middle of the Nordic group. Although geographically located next door to Belgium and sharing a common language with half of Belgium, the Netherlands is culturally much closer to the Nordic countries than to Belgium. Historically, the Netherlands has been shaped by Protestantism; even the Dutch Catholics today are remarkably Calvinist. And although the churches themselves are now a fading influence in Western European society, religious traditions helped shape enduring *national* cultures that persist today. Thus, culturally, the Netherlands is located somewhere between Norway and Sweden.

Belgium, France, Italy, Spain, Portugal, and Austria constitute another cluster in the cultural space of figure 3.5. Although church attendance has declined drastically, all of these countries were historically Roman Catholic. Furthermore, this cluster is adjacent to a Latin American (and overwhelmingly Catholic) cluster containing Mexico, Argentina, Chile, and Brazil. These predominantly Catholic countries form a fairly coherent group. One could even expand it to include the four other historically Roman Catholic countries, Poland, Hungary, Slovenia, and Lithuania. The last four countries are outliers, probably because of their divergent histories since 1945: the rising prosperity experienced by Western European Catholic countries in recent decades had much less impact on them, and they are more permeated by survival values than are the rest of the Catholic group. On the Modernization dimension, however, their values are almost as traditional as those of other Catholic countries (and they have more traditional values than the other exsocialist countries). As Basanez (1993) demonstrates, the Protestant-Catholic differences do not simply reflect the fact that the historically Protestant countries tend to be richer than the Catholic ones: controlling for GDP/capita, the value differences between them remain significant at the .001 level.

Nevertheless, there is no question that traditional orientations *are* closely related to a society's level of economic development. Almost all of the economically less-developed countries fall into the lower left-hand quadrant of figure

3.5, with cultures that emphasize traditional authority and survival values. But interestingly enough, all five of the English-speaking societies (Britain, Canada, the United States, Ireland, and Northern Ireland) fall into a cluster located in the lower right-hand quadrant: these countries have relatively strong security values, but much more religious-traditional values than most other countries at their economic level. This is particularly true of Ireland and Northern Ireland, which have a traditional/religious outlook that is fully as strong as that found in India, South Africa, or Brazil—with only Nigeria being markedly more traditional.

The former West German and East German regions of Germany were still independent states when these surveys were carried out and were sampled separately. Although West Germany falls into the upper right-hand quadrant with the other Western European societies, and East Germany into the upper left-hand quadrant containing most of the historically communist societies, the two societies are relatively close to each other on the two main cultural dimensions. This is significant. From 1945 to 1990, the communist regime made a massive effort to reshape East German culture to support a Marxist and atheistic authoritarian regime. Simultaneously, the Western powers launched massive efforts in West Germany to remake political culture to support a market-oriented Western liberal democracy. The evidence indicates that 45 years under radically different regimes did have an impact: by 1990 the two societies were some distance apart, especially along the Postmodernization dimension. But even more impressive is the fact that, in global perspective, the basic cultural values of the two societies were still relatively similar. This natural experiment indicates that, even when it makes a conscious and concerted effort to do so, the ability of a regime to reshape its underlying culture is limited. After 45 years under diametrically opposed political and economic institutions, in their basic values East Germany and West Germany remained as similar to each other as are the United States and Canada.

Almost all of the socialist or ex-socialist societies fall into the upper left-hand quadrant: these societies are characterized by survival values and a strong emphasis on state authority, rather than traditional authority. Poland is a striking exception, distinguished from the other socialist societies by its strong traditional-religious values. China is an outlier in the opposite direction—the least religious and most state-oriented society for which we have data. These societies' positions reflect their distinctive cultural heritages. On one hand, adherence to the Catholic church has been a mainstay of the Polish struggle for independence since 1792. The church continued to play a vital role in this struggle throughout the 1980s, revitalizing the role of religion in the national culture.

China, on the other hand, has had a relatively secular cultural system for 2,000 years; and bureaucratic authority developed within the Confucian system long before it reached the West. Thus China and the other Confucian-influenced societies of East Asia have had one major component of modern culture for a very long time. Until recently, they lacked the emphasis on science and technology and the esteem for economic achievement that are its other main components; but their secular, bureaucratic heritage probably helped to facilitate their rapid economic development once these were attained. China's traditional emphasis on the state may have been reinforced by four decades of socialism. Japan, another Confucian-influenced society, and both Eastern and Western Germany are also characterized by relatively strong emphasis on rational-legal authority.

Most of the socialist and ex-socialist societies are oriented toward rational-legal, rather than traditional-religious, authority. Their people have experienced four to eight decades of socialist regimes in which religion has been systematically repressed and in which it is perfectly realistic to consider politics important because economic life, cultural life, and even one's chances of survival depend on the state. The socialist states were probably the most heavily bureaucratized, centralized, and secularized societies in history, and they held science and technology in such esteem that their elites legitimated their power by the claim that they ruled, not through the unscientific and fallible process of majority rule, but according to the principles of scientific socialism. By these standards, the socialist states represented the culmination of Modernization—and the fact that, on figure 3.5, they are located near the Modernization pole of the Traditional Authority–Rational-Legal Authority dimension seems appropriate. But figure 3.2 revealed one surprising anomaly: one would expect that such key ideological components of the socialist state as its tendency to hold the "State responsible" for providing for everyone's needs should *also* cluster near the Modernization pole and gain maximum support in the socialist societies. It does not. Why?

We suspect that if these surveys had been carried out a decade or two earlier, support for state management and state responsibility *would* have been relatively strong in the ex-socialist societies. Most of them had experienced relatively high economic growth rates from 1945 to 1975 or 1980. Up to this point, they seemed to be functioning well: they had done a good job of providing the basic necessities for nearly everyone and were able to conceal or repress criticism of their shortcomings in other aspects of life. Support for a state-run economy and society was probably a good deal higher then, in socialist countries, than it was in 1990. In this simpler, more orderly world, we would have found "State responsible" located near the Modernization pole. And the empirical picture may now again be closer to this model than it was in 1990: as the transition to market economies proved unexpectedly traumatic, reform communist elites returned to power in a number of ex-communist societies during the early 1990s.

But reality is complex. In 1990–91, when these surveys were carried out, the socialist economic and political systems were collapsing; and mass support for state-run economies had withered away in these societies. The classic model of state socialism was surviving only in North Korea and Cuba, and paradoxically mass support for socialism was no longer the wave of the future for industrial society, but had become a Third World phenomenon.

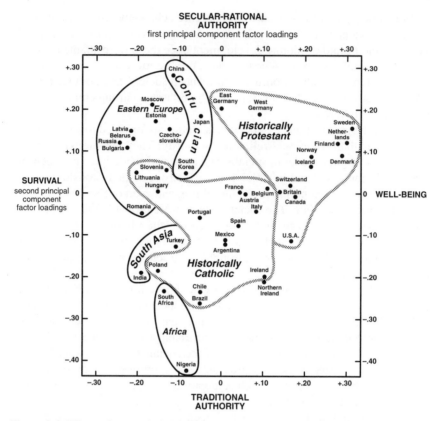

Figure 3.6. Where given societies fall on two key cultural dimensions: religious influences. *Source*: 1990–93 World Values Survey. Positions are based on the mean scores of the publics of the given nation on each of the two dimensions.

INSTITUTIONAL DETERMINISM OF CULTURE?

As we have seen, the historically Protestant countries of both Northern Europe and North America tend to cluster together to form one large group; similarly, the historically Roman Catholic countries of Western Europe, Latin America, and Eastern Europe tend to cluster together, forming another broad but reasonably cohesive cluster. Despite the enormous recent changes linked with economic and social Modernization, and despite the tremendous sociopolitical changes linked with communist domination of four traditionally Catholic societies throughout the Cold War, in global perspective the historically Catholic societies still have relatively similar cultural values—as do the historically Protestant societies. As figure 3.6 illustrates, the Catholic societies form a group characterized by more traditional values, and by greater emphasis on survival values, than holds true of most Protestant societies. At first glance, this might seem to constitute strong evidence for an institutional determinist interpretation: the religious institutions of these societies led them to develop different cultures.

If institutional determinism is simply taken to mean that a society's institutions are among the factors that help shape its culture, it is undoubtedly correct. But institutional determinism is often pushed to a much more extreme claim than this. It is taken to mean that institutions alone determine a society's cultural values, so one need not really take cultural factors into account: if one changes the institutions, the culture automatically changes to fit it. If one examines the evidence more closely, it is clear that this position is untenable.

There are tremendous cultural differences between Protestant and Catholic societies, but for the most part they do not reflect the direct influence of the Catholic and Protestant churches today. For the direct influence of the church today is very slight in many of these countries. Although church attendance remains relatively high in Poland and Ireland (and the United States), it has fallen drastically in most of the historically Catholic countries of both Western and Eastern Europe; and it has fallen even more drastically in most historically Protestant European societies, to the point where some observers now speak of the Nordic countries as post-Christian societies: church attendance has plummeted toward zero. The societies that were traditionally Catholic still show very distinct values from those that were traditionally Protestant—even among segments of the population who have no contact with the church. But these values persist as part of the cultural heritage of given nations, and not through the direct influence of the religious institutions. This cultural heritage has been shaped by the economic, political, and social experience of the people, including the fact that the Protestant societies industrialized earlier than most of the Catholic societies—which at an even earlier stage of history may, in turn, have been linked with religious differences (as Weber suggests), but is certainly not a case of mere institutional determinism.

There is a remarkable degree of coherence to this pattern. Forty of the 43 societies fall into compact and historically meaningful clusters, such as Latin America or Eastern Europe or East Asia. There are only three outliers from this perspective: Poland plus Ireland and Northern Ireland (with the two parts of Ireland being closely linked). Both Poland and Ireland might be described as hyper-Catholic societies: they are Roman Catholic societies that for centuries were occupied and dominated by more powerful non-Catholic neighbors and that responded to pressures toward cultural assimilation by an intense reemphasis on their Roman Catholic heritage as a means of preserving their national identity. Ironically, this may have led to a similar reaction on the part of the Irish Protestants, who constitute a small minority within Ireland as a whole and might be described as hyper-Protestants. Poland and both parts of Ireland strongly emphasize traditional cultural values concerning not only religion, but also politics, gender roles, sexual norms, and family values. They illustrate the fundamentalist reaction to threat.

In most countries, these cultural differences reflect the entire historical experience of given societies, and *not* the influence of the respective churches today. This point becomes vividly evident when we examine the value systems of such societies as the Netherlands and Germany—both of which were historically predominantly Protestant societies, but (as a consequence of different birth rates and different rates of religious attrition) have about as many practicing Catholics as Protestants today. Despite these changes in their religious makeup today, both the Netherlands and Germany manifest typically Protestant values. Moreover, the Catholics and Protestants *within* these societies do not show markedly different value systems: the Dutch Catholics today are as Calvinist as the members of the Dutch Reformed Church.

The historically Protestant and Catholic societies are not randomly distributed on our cultural map—far from it, they constitute coherent clusters. The communist ideology has been described as a secular religion, and the historically communist societies also make up a coherent cluster, which partly overlaps with the Catholic cluster: 13 of the 14 formerly communist societies fall into a compact cluster in the upper left-hand quadrant, and this Eastern European cluster could easily be expanded to include China and Eastern Germany. And as we have noted, though they are located on two different continents and span the Catholic-Protestant divide, the five English-speaking societies are also relatively near to each other on this cultural map: a common language is the unifying factor in this case. But the most pervasive influence of all seems to be economic development. If one draws a diagonal from the lower-left corner to the upper-right corner of figures 3.5 or 3.6, it traces the transition from poorer to richer societies. Both the Modernization dimension and the Postmodernization dimension are strongly correlated with a society's level of economic development: the values of richer societies differ systematically from those of poorer societies on both dimensions. Clearly, institutional determinism would be a far too simple interpretation of the evidence. Although the impact of religious institutions is evident, economic, political, geographic, linguistic, and other factors also play important roles. The worldview of a given people reflects its entire historical heritage.

To What Extent Was Modernization Theory Correct?

Coherent Cultural Patterns Exist

We have found that constraint *does* exist among cultural patterns. To get a sense of just how true this is, let us imagine two extreme models, ranging from a world wholly without cultural constraint, to one with total constraint. In the former model, each society goes its own way: the fact that it possesses one specific cultural attribute has no influence on whether other attributes are present. Cultural components are randomly related. The other extreme model is one of total determinism: only a few cultural patterns are possible, and if one major component of a pattern is present, all the other elements are also present in every case.

As one would expect, the empirical findings do not fit either extreme model, but they come much closer to the constrained model than to the random one. Fully half of the cross-cultural variation among this broad array of variables can be captured in just two dimensions. This picture is certainly not one of complete determinism: these two dimensions do not explain *all* of the variation among these 43 cultural indicators. But they do account for 51 percent of the variance—vastly more than the less than 5 percent that they would explain in a random model.

These Coherent Cultural Patterns Are Linked with a Society's Level of Economic Development

The fact that constrained cultural patterns exist does not, by itself, demonstrate that Modernization theory is correct: coherent cultural patterns might be found exclusively in given regions (such as Western Europe) as a result of given historical or religious traditions (such as Protestantism or Buddhism) without having any relationship to economic and technological change. Modernization theory, by contrast, implies that economic development *is* strongly linked with given cultural patterns—either because economic development produces specific types of culture, or because certain cultural patterns produce economic development. In short, Modernization theory implies that coherent cultural patterns exist, *and* that these patterns are linked with a given society's level of economic development. As figure 3.7 demonstrates, this clearly *is* the case.

We argued that the vertical dimension on figures 3.2 and 3.3 reflects the Modernization process, while the horizontal dimension reflects Postmodernization. The evidence presented in figure 3.7 indicates that economic development is conducive to *both* Modernization and Postmodernization, which are two successive stages of development: a society's per capita GNP is correlated with Modernization values at the .60 level, and at the .78 level with Postmodernization values. But other economic indicators show quite different relationships to these two respective dimensions. For example, the percentage of the labor force in the manufacturing sector is strongly correlated with the vertical (Modernization) dimension ($r = .63$) but much less strongly linked with the horizontal (Postmodernization) dimension ($r = .22$); but Postmodern values are strongly linked with the percentage of the labor force in the *service* sector ($r = .79$).

Bell argues that Postindustrial society has arrived when a majority of a society's workforce is employed in the service sector. There is a good deal of overlap between Postmodern society and Postindustrial society. But Bell's concept of Postindustrial society emphasizes changes in the structure of the workforce, while the term "Postmodern society" emphasizes cultural changes linked with economic security; we have argued that existential security is a key factor underlying Postmodernization. In keeping with this contention, we find that prosperity has as strong a relationship with Postmodern culture as does the composition of the workforce.

Similarly, the percentage of a given society's population having a secondary

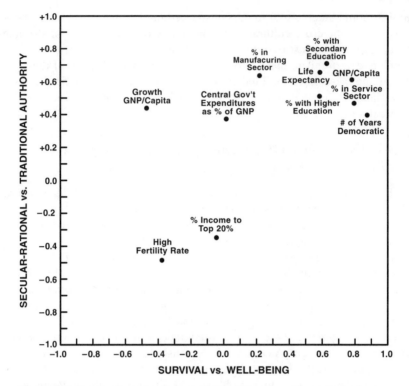

Figure 3.7. Economic and social correlates of two key dimensions of cross-cultural variation. *Source*: 1990–93 World Values Survey.

or higher education shows a .71 correlation with the Rational-Legal pole of the Modernization dimension—and a .63 correlation with the Well-being pole of the Postmodernization dimension. These findings support the claim by Lerner (1958), Inkeles and Smith (1974), and others that rising educational levels have contributed to major cultural changes.

The consequences of growing up in a setting in which one can take satisfaction of one's survival needs for granted, rather than in a society of scarcity, seems to have been underestimated by Bell, Inkeles and Smith, and others. The strong linkage between Postmodern values and a society's GDP/capita supports the interpretation that these are, indeed, *security* values: they have an extremely strong tendency to be found in relatively prosperous societies.

An even more striking contrast between the economic correlates of Modernization and Postmodernization is the fact that Modernization values have a substantial positive linkage with economic growth rates, while Postmodern values have a *negative* linkage with economic growth: Postmodern societies are even richer than modernizing societies, but they show lower economic growth rates.

Overall, the evidence in figure 3.7 suggests that if educational levels con-

tinue to rise and the workforce continues to move out of farming and manufacturing into the service and knowledge sectors, and if per capita income continues to rise, then we can expect to see a gradual modernization of preindustrial societies and a shift toward Postmodern values, in advanced industrial
societies.

Is Cultural Change Taking Place?

The fact that Postmodern values are strongly linked with economic development does not necessarily prove that as economic development takes place,
these values will become more widespread. The linkage might be spurious.
Long-term time series data are needed to demonstrate whether or not the predicted changes are taking place and help sort out the causal relationships. We
don't have extensive time series data for most of the variables examined here,
but we do have some—and virtually all of the available evidence points to the
conclusion that a shift toward Postmodern culture *is* taking place in advanced
industrial societies.

The most abundant time series data (by far) relate to Materialist/Postmate-
rialist values. Though this is only one component of the much larger syndrome
of Postmodern values, it is a key indicator of this broader syndrome. Evidence
of a shift from Materialist to Postmaterialist values will be presented in chapter 4; it shows that Postmaterialist values have increased in the past quarter
century, and that they have increased at almost exactly the rate predicted by
the intergenerational population replacement model (about one point on the
values percentage difference index per year).

If Postmaterialist values are moving in the predicted direction, this suggests
that the entire set of closely correlated Postmodern values may be moving in
the same direction, since theoretically they share a common set of causes: the
transition from conditions of scarcity to the relative security of Postmodern
society.

This broader shift toward Postmodern values in general *does* seem to be taking place. In chapters 7 and 8 we test the hypothesis that all values having reasonably strong correlations with Postmaterialism are part of an intergenerational shift linked with population replacement. To do so, we first identified 40
variables that were strongly correlated with Postmaterialist values and were
included in both the 1981 and 1990 World Values surveys. Our expectation was
that whatever values were positively correlated with Postmaterialism would
become more widespread over time, other things being equal. When we compare the 1981 responses, with responses to the same questions in the same
countries in 1990, we find that in the great majority of cases these values
shifted in the predicted direction. The available evidence suggests that cultural
change is taking place in the predicted direction.

As hypothesized, the apparent decline of traditional values is strongly linked
with economic growth: as figure 3.7 indicates, a country's growth rate from

104

1965 to 1990 shows a .44 correlation with emphasis on Rational-Legal Authority (and a corresponding negative correlation with Traditional Authority). In chapter 6 we probe into the relevant causal linkages: the findings suggest that culture shapes economic life, as well as being shaped by it. In the early stages of industrialization, achievement motivation seems to contribute to economic growth. But insofar as this growth produces prosperity, in the long run it leads to cultural changes that tend to de-emphasize achievement motivation, leading to *lower* rates of economic growth. This points to still another contrast between Modernization and Postmodernization: while the Modernization process is linked with high *rates* of economic growth, Postmodernization is not. Quite the contrary, relatively high growth rates show a *negative* linkage (r = −.47) with well-being values. In part, this reflects the fact that Postmaterialists do not emphasize economic growth, and they tend to give priority to protecting the environment, if forced to choose.

Traditional values are negatively linked with economic growth, but positively linked with high fertility rates, as figure 3.7 demonstrates (r = .48). As we saw earlier, societies with Traditional values tend to emphasize the family and have relatively large numbers of children. It seems that this is not just a matter of lip service. A society's values and its actual fertility rate are closely linked, probably in a causal relationship. This tends to set up a self-reinforcing process: traditional values not only seem to inhibit a set of norms that are conducive to economic growth, they also encourage population growth rates that tend to offset the effects of whatever economic growth *does* occur, making it still more difficult to raise per capita income. Conversely, both Modernization and Postmodernization are linked with declining birth rates, so the pie gets divided up among fewer people—another example of how cultural and economic factors constitute mutually reinforcing syndromes.

MODERNIZATION, POSTMODERNIZATION, AND DEMOCRATIZATION

Finally, the Postmodernization process has important political implications. Inkeles and Diamond (1980), Inglehart (1990), and others have argued that economic development is linked with cultural changes that are conducive to democracy, an argument that has been disputed by dependency theorists, neo-Marxists, and some rational choice theorists. As figure 3.7 indicates, there is no correlation whatever between the Modernization axis and the number of years for which a given society has been democratic. As Moore (1966) pointed out, modernization can give rise to either democratic or authoritarian regimes.

But there is an amazingly strong correlation between the Postmodernization dimension and democracy: r = .88. We suggested earlier that high levels of subjective well-being, coupled with Postmodern values, including interpersonal trust, tolerance, and Postmaterialist values, should be conducive to democracy. The empirical evidence is remarkably strong: this cluster of cultural traits clearly *is* linked with stable democracy. One could argue that this cultural syndrome is conducive to democracy, or that democracy somehow gives rise to a culture of trust, tolerance, subjective well-being, and Postmaterialist values, or that the cultural syndrome and the political institutions are mutually supportive. We will analyze the causal linkages more closely in chapter 5; for the moment, we will simply observe that Postmodern values and stable democracy go together very closely.

It has been known for some time that democracy is more likely to be found among relatively prosperous countries than among poorer ones (Lipset, 1960). The present body of evidence supports that conclusion. But the linkage between culture and democracy found here is even stronger than the linkage between economic development and democracy. This finding suggests that economic development by itself does not automatically produce democracy; it does so only insofar as it gives rise to a specific syndrome of cultural changes.

Putnam (1993) supports this interpretation, using aggregate time series data from 20 regions of Italy, extending from 1860 to the mid-1980s. He finds that given regions have varying degrees of a cultural syndrome termed "Civic Community" (characterized by trust, tolerance, solidarity, civic engagement, political equality, and civic associations), which is strongly correlated with the effectiveness of democratic institutions in the given regions. Economic development is also related to democratic effectiveness; but controlling for civic traditions, economic development has no impact whatever. On the other hand, a region's level of civic involvement in 1900 not only predicts subsequent civic involvement and institutional performance, but also helps explain subsequent economic development.

WHY DOES CHANGE FOLLOW PREDICTABLE PATTERNS?

Coherent trajectories of cultural change exist, with some cultural patterns being far more probable than others. Why?

The evidence suggests that in the long run, cultural change behaves as if it were a process of rational choice—subject to substantial cultural lags, and subject to the fact that the goals being maximized vary from one culture to another and can only be understood through empirical knowledge of the specific culture. In this loosely rational process, peoples are maximizing a variety of goods, the most basic of which is survival—and their cultures are survival strategies for a given people. Cultural variation tends to follow predictable patterns because some ways of running a society work better than others. If one is willing to concede that most people prefer survival to nonsurvival, then both Modernization and Postmodernization are linked with outcomes that almost anyone would consider "better." As figure 3.7 indicates, there is a .59 correlation between a society's female life expectancy and its level of Modernization, and a .65 correlation between life expectancy and Postmodernization. Neither process bestows moral superiority, but both Modernization and Postmodernization are linked with a markedly lower likelihood of dying prematurely from disease or malnutrition. Life expectancy today ranges from as low as 39 years in the poorest countries to almost 80 years in developed ones. This is a difference that few people would fail to appreciate, regardless of cultural orientation. It is one reason why the modernization syndrome had such pervasive appeal. Successful industrialization requires a relatively competitive, impersonal, bureaucratic, achievement-oriented form of social relations that tends to be dehumanizing and stressful; but in societies of scarcity around the globe, it came to be viewed as a worthwhile trade-off. Islamic fundamentalism remains an alternative model insofar as oil revenues make it possible to obtain many of the advantages of modernization *without* industrializing; but we would not expect this model's credibility and mass appeal to outlast the oil reserves.

The Modernization process brought substantial gains in life expectancy by maximizing economic growth, making it possible to sharply reduce the two leading causes of death in preindustrial societies—malnutrition and disease. But the linkage between economic development and rising life expectancy eventually reached a point of diminishing returns.

Postmodernization represents a shift in survival strategies, from maximizing economic growth to maximizing survival and well-being. Modernization focused on rapid economic growth, which provided a means to maximize survival and well-being under the conditions that emerged when rationalization and industrialization first became possible. But no strategy is optimal for all time. Modernization was dramatically successful in raising life expectancies, but it has begun to produce diminishing returns in advanced industrial societies. By emphasizing competition it reduced the risk of starvation—but it probably also increased psychological stress. As we have seen, subjective well-being levels are lower in the communist and ex-communist societies—which are, by some criteria, the most "modern" of all societies—than in the most traditional societies. These low levels of subjective well-being in the ex-socialist world are almost certainly linked with the current crisis in the former communist societies, but the 1981 World Values Survey found low levels there even before the collapse of communism. During the decade before 1990, symptoms of severe demoralization and psychological stress were evident in the former Soviet Union and were manifest in high rates of alcoholism and declining life expectancies.

Postmodernization, on the other hand, has a mildly negative linkage with economic growth, but a strong positive linkage with subjective well-being. With the transition from Modernization to Postmodernization, the trajectory of change seems to have shifted from maximizing economic growth to maximizing the quality of life.

CROSS-SECTIONAL EVIDENCE OF SOCIAL CHANGE

Cross-sectional data can be a useful supplement to time series data in understanding processes of socioeconomic change. Although time series data provide the only reliable measurements of changes over time, appropriate cross-sectional data can extend the scope of one's perspective in time and space: its configuration may reflect processes that occurred over many decades or even centuries.

Interpreted in connection with the available time series data, the cultural configurations found in the 43-nation World Values survey suggest that coherent, and even to some extent predictable, trajectories of political and cultural change are linked with given socioeconomic developments. These trajectories are not deterministic: the leaders and institutions, and the cultural and geographic heritage, of a given society also help shape its course. And development does not move in a simple, linear fashion: all trends eventually change direction.

But neither is socioeconomic change random and unpredictable, with each society following its own idiosyncratic course. On the contrary, change tends to follow clear configurations, in which specific clusters of cultural characteristics go together with specific types of political and economic change. The familiar Modernization syndrome of urbanization, industrialization, and mass literacy tends to have foreseeable consequences such as increasing mass mobilization. Modernization is linked with given cultural changes, such as a growing emphasis on Achievement Motivation, and a shift from Traditional to Rational-Legal Authority, which encompasses dozens of more specific changes.

Similarly, the emergence of advanced industrial society, with an increasing share of the public having higher education, being employed in the service sector, and feeling assured that their survival needs will be met, gives rise to a process in which high levels of subjective well-being and Postmodern values emerge—and in which a variety of attributes, from equal rights for women to democratic political institutions, become increasingly likely.

Measuring Materialist and Postmaterialist Values

MATERIALIST/POSTMATERIALIST VALUE PRIORITIES are only one component of the much broader configuration that constitutes the Postmodernization dimension. But Materialist/Postmaterialist values are by far the best documented aspect of this broader configuration, having been measured in cross-national surveys carried out regularly since 1970. The initial research on intergenerational value change was based on this dimension, and it continues to play an important role in research on cultural change. This chapter examines the nature of Postmaterialist values and the controversy over how these values can be measured most effectively; the next chapter analyzes the intergenerational shift from Materialist to Postmaterialist priorities during the past quarter century.

Over the years since these values were first investigated, there has been considerable controversy about what they were tapping, how values should be measured, and how many dimensions one should use to analyze Materialist/Postmaterialist value priorities. This controversy continues; several important critiques of measurement techniques have appeared recently. The 1990 World Values Survey measured Materialist/Postmaterialist value priorities by asking the respondents in more than 40 societies a series of questions that began as follows: "There is a lot of talk these days about what the aims of this country should be for the next ten years. On this card are listed some of the goals which different people would give top priority. Would you please say which one of these you, yourself, consider the most important? And which one would be the next most important?"

Twelve goals were rated, but in order to reduce the task to manageable proportions, they were presented in three groups of four items; each set of four goals contained two items designed to tap Materialist priorities, and two designed to tap Postmaterialist priorities. These 12 goals are shown in abbreviated form in figure 4.1; the full text of this battery appears in Appendix 2.

The choices deal with broad societal goals rather than the immediate needs of the respondent: we wanted to tap long-term concerns, not one's response to the immediate situation. Among these 12 goals, six items were intended to emphasize survival needs: "Rising prices," "Economic growth," and "Stable economy" designed to tap emphasis on economic security, and "Maintain order," "Fight crime," and "Strong defense forces" designed to tap emphasis on physical security. These items tap two distinct types of needs, but both are "Materialist," in that they are directly related to physiological survival. We hypothesized that they would tend to go together, with only those who feel secure about the satisfaction of both needs being likely to give top priority to belonging, self-expression, and intellectual and aesthetic satisfaction—Post-

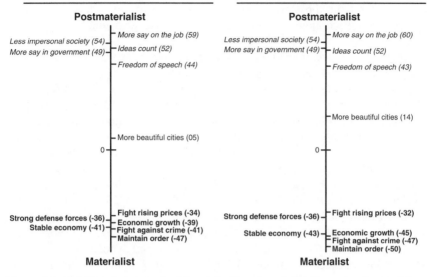

Figure 4.1. Stability over time: the Materialist/Postmaterialist dimension in nine Western nations in 1973 and 1978.
Mean factor loadings from each of the nine European Union countries surveyed in September 1973 and October–November 1978. Items with Materialist polarity are in boldface type; items with Postmaterialist polarity are in italics. Based on principal components analyses of ranking of the 12 goals. *Source*: Inglehart, 1990: 140.

materialist needs that the remaining six items are designed to tap. We view all of these needs as universal: every human being needs sustenance and safety—but also desires self-expression, esteem, and aesthetic satisfaction and has a sense of intellectual curiosity. Thus one finds art and music and other products of the search for beauty in all societies, and one finds magic, religion, myths, or philosophy, reflecting the desire to understand and interpret the meaning of life in even the poorest societies. Hungry people may not give top priority to self-expression and intellectual concerns, but given some respite from the struggle for survival, people will act on these needs unless circumstances stifle them. Our expectation, therefore, is that emphasis on the six Materialist items will tend to form one cluster, with the Postmaterialist items in another distinct cluster.

All cultures are multidimensional. Change can occur in sexual norms, tastes in food or music, political party preferences, trust in government, religious outlook, and numerous other aspects of life. The question is not whether the Materialist/Postmaterialist dimension is the only dimension along which change can occur, but whether such a dimension exists—and if so, whether significant change has been taking place in the predicted direction.

Our theoretical framework implies that emphasis on economic security and on physical security will tend to go together—and that those who feel insecure about these survival needs have a fundamentally different outlook and political behavior from those who feel secure about them. The latter are likely to give top priority to nonmaterial goals such as self-expression, belonging, and intellectual or aesthetic satisfaction.

Emphasis on economic and physical security were expected to go together for two reasons: (1) From a macrosocietal perspective, war tends to produce both economic and physical insecurity—both hunger and loss of life. Consequently, those generations that have experienced war are likely to feel less secure about both. (2) From a microsocietal perspective, poor individuals tend to be exposed to both economic and physical insecurity—both poverty and relatively high crime rates. The more affluent strata have resources that shield them, to some extent, from *both*.

Satisfaction of the survival needs, we hypothesized, leads to growing emphasis on nonphysiological or "Postmaterialist" goals. A large share of the public in Western societies have been socialized in an environment that provides an unprecedentedly secure prospect that one's physiological needs will be met. Consequently, Western publics' responses should tend to polarize along a Materialist/Postmaterialist dimension, with some individuals consistently emphasizing Materialist goals, while others tend to give priority to Postmaterialist goals.

To test this hypothesis, we performed principal components analyses of the rankings of these goals in each of the countries surveyed in 1990–93. For this analysis, each item was recoded as a separate variable with codes ranging from "1" to "3," indicating whether the given item was ranked as most important in its group of four items, as second most important, or as one of the two least important items.

Our variables are based on relative rankings, not absolute scores. This is crucial to operationalizing our hypothesis, but it means that the items are not independent, which raises problems for factor analysis. If one were rating only two items, for example, the rank of the first item would determine the rank of the second, automatically generating a -1.0 correlation between them. With three items, one would expect negative correlations of about .5. With a pool of four items, random answering would generate negative correlations of about .3 between all four items. Thus, there is a tendency for the ratings of all these items to be negatively correlated, which tends to spread any four items over more than one dimension. Nevertheless, as our empirical results show, this effect is dominated by an even stronger tendency for Materialist items to be chosen together, on one hand, and for Postmaterialist items to be chosen together, on the other.

The Materialist/Postmaterialist dimension has proven to be remarkably robust over time. As figure 4.1 demonstrates, factor analyses of survey data from the nine countries that were members of the European Community in 1973 reveal two clear clusters: at the top of the continuum, five Postmaterialist items cluster together, showing positive polarity; and at the opposite pole, all six Materialist items cluster together, showing negative polarity. This pattern is remarkably uniform across all nine nations (detailed country-by-country results appear in Inglehart, 1977: 44–47). Moreover, this battery was used again in a subsequent survey in these same countries in 1978, and as figure 4.1 shows, the results were very similar to those from 1973. The results show a cross-national consistency that is truly remarkable. In survey after survey, five items—the same five items in every country—cluster near the positive end of the continuum. Six items—again, the same six in every country—are grouped near the negative pole. The remaining item falls near the midpoint.

The items that cluster toward the negative pole are the six Materialist items, and five of the six Postmaterialist items fall into the opposite group. A single item—the one concerning "More beautiful cities"—does not fall into either cluster. This item does not behave according to our expectations, a fact that we must explore in more detail. But the other 11 items live up to expectations to an almost uncanny degree. The consistency of responses to these items cannot be attributed to such common sources of spurious correlation as response set, which often occurs when respondents simply rate a series of items as either "good" or "bad" (or "very important" or "less important"): some respondents give similar ratings to a whole series of items. In the present case, this is impossible: one must rank each goal as being *more* important or *less* important than the others, in a format that gives no cues to the "right" answer.

Given respondents tend to be preoccupied with a consistent set of needs located toward either the Materialist or Postmaterialist side of the continuum. Eleven of the 12 items fall into two separate clusters, reflecting Materialist and Postmaterialist priorities, respectively. The item designed to tap aesthetic needs ("more beautiful cities") fits into neither cluster; with the same consistency by which the eleven other items did fit into their expected places, this one fails to show a strong positive loading in any of these countries. Why?

The answer is that this item does not simply evoke aesthetic needs, as it was intended to do. Instead, it also taps an Urban/anti-Urban dimension on which collective economic development is seen as conflicting with one's personal security. Here, this item shows a surprisingly strong relationship with the safety needs (see Inglehart, 1977:45–50). For many people, the term "cities" evokes fears of crime.

The relationship between aesthetic concerns and Postmaterialist values is clarified by another analysis utilizing the Rokeach Terminal Values Survey (see Rokeach, 1973) together with the Materialist/Postmaterialist battery, both of which were included in the American component of the Political Action study (Barnes et al., 1979). Factor analysis of the 12-item Materialist/Postmaterialist battery plus the 18-item Rokeach battery reveals an interesting structure. As we would expect, a number of dimensions are needed to capture the configuration of responses. But the Materialist/Postmaterialist dimension remains clearly recognizable, and several of Rokeach's items show substantial loadings on it. In the Postmaterialist cluster of this dimension, we find "Equality" and "Inner Harmony," plus a pair of items relating to the intellectual and aesthetic needs—"Wisdom" and "A World of Beauty." Ironically, the item we

TABLE 4.1

The Materialist/Postmaterialist Dimension in 15
Western Nations, 1990 (Loadings on First Principal
Component in Factor Analysis)

Less Impersonal Society	.60
More Say on Job	.62
More Say in Government	.50
Ideas Count More than Money	.51
Freedom of Speech	.34
More Beautiful Cities	.18
Strong Defense Forces	−.26
Fight Rising Prices	−.28
Fight against Crime	−.39
Maintain Order	−.55
Economic Growth	−.59
Maintain Stable Economy	−.63

Note: Items with Materialist polarity are in boldface type;
items with Postmaterialist polarity are in italics.

Source: 1990–91 World Values Survey data from France,
Britain, West Germany, Italy, the Netherlands, Denmark, Bel-
gium, Ireland, Norway, Sweden, Denmark, Finland, Iceland,
Canada, and the United States.

designed to tap the aesthetic needs fails to show the expected empirical relationships—but the item developed by Rokeach *does*. Analysis of the responses
to our own item concerning "more beautiful cities" revealed an unexpected
tendency for this item to be linked with emphasis on "the fight against crime."
Including the word "cities" in this context seems to evoke a concern with safety
among some respondents; for them, the cities are unbeautiful not only because
they are dirty but because they are dangerous. Rokeach's item makes no reference to cities and evokes aesthetic concerns in unmixed form—and consequently falls into the Postmaterialist cluster as the need hierarchy hypothesis
would suggest. In short, the anomalous results obtained with this item seem to
reflect imperfect formulation of our "aesthetic" alternative, rather than an indication that aesthetic concerns are not part of the Postmaterialist syndrome.
When unambiguously formulated, they *are*.

   The pattern found in 1973 and 1978 continues to manifest itself in the 1990s.
The loadings on the first factor in 15 Western countries are shown in table 4.1
(the detailed results for each country are shown in Abramson and Inglehart,
1995). In this table, the goals designed to tap Materialist priorities appear in
boldface; the goals intended to tap Postmaterialist priorities appear in italics.
With almost incredible consistency, in nation after nation, emphasis on the six
items designed to tap economic and physical security goes together, forming
a coherent Materialist cluster; in every case, emphasis on the five items de-

signed to tap belonging, self-expression, and intellectual satisfaction also goes together, forming a clearly defined Postmaterialist cluster.

A "UNIDIMENSIONAL" THEORY OF VALUE CHANGE?

The Materialist/Postmaterialist thesis postulates that an intergenerational value shift is taking place along a dimension defined by two poles, termed "Materialist" and "Postmaterialist" values, respectively. This space is, by definition, one-dimensional and, though human values are almost infinitely multidimensional, the theory focuses on this one dimension. In this sense only, the theory might be called "unidimensional," though this is a potentially misleading label.

Just how misleading this label can be becomes evident in a recent analysis by Buerklin, Klein, and Russ (1994). Claiming that the Materialist/Postmaterialist value change theory is "unidimensional," they interpret this term to mean that we believe *all* human values constitute one dimension. If this claim were true, then the analysis carried out by Buerklin et al. would be a valid test of the theory: if the Materialist/Postmaterialist value change thesis actually *did* hold that all human values constitute a single dimension and that everything on it is undergoing intergenerational change, then if one can find any value that *is not* undergoing an intergenerational shift, the thesis would be disproven. Buerklin et al. analyze a battery of questions that measures a number of different things and have no difficulty in finding various values that are *not* undergoing intergenerational change, so, they conclude, they have refuted the thesis.

But do we really believe that human values are unidimensional, in the sense that Buerklin et al. claim? Demonstrably, no: though our analyses focus mainly on the Materialist/Postmaterialist dimension, we have, from the start, also analyzed various other value dimensions.

Our analysis of the Materialist/Postmaterialist shift focuses on one dimension. It does so because the theory generates clear predictions about the type and direction of change one should find along this specific dimension: unprecedentedly high levels of security are producing an intergenerational shift from giving top priority to security, to giving top priority to self-expression. The investigation focuses on this one dimension because the theory does not predict what might be happening in other value domains. The Materialist/Postmaterialist dimension is a central and important part of mass value systems, but (obviously) it does not cover everything. There are almost limitless numbers of other values, and changes might conceivably be occurring in almost any of them, ranging from communism versus capitalism, to whether people prefer Madonna to Mozart, or chocolate to vanilla, but the theory does not deal with them. Nevertheless, it is clear that we recognized from the start that other value dimensions also exist and discussed them at some length (Inglehart,

1977: 45–51). In subsequent publications, (Inglehart, 1978, 1979) we analyzed the relationships between Materialist/Postmaterialist values and the 18 Rokeach Terminal Values which are designed to tap the full range of human concerns. And in Inglehart (1990) we explored the relationships between Materialist/Postmaterialist values and a wide variety of other values, extending from religion to politics to sexual norms. Clearly, the claim that the theory is "unidimensional" in the sense of considering the Materialist/Postmaterialist dimension to be the only value dimension that exists, or the only dimension worth analyzing, is groundless.

THE STUDY OF VALUE PRIORITIES: RANKINGS VERSUS RATINGS

The Materialist/Postmaterialist thesis deals with priorities, not levels: this a crucial distinction. We did not think that people had never before valued freedom of expression: history makes it clear that it has been valued for centuries. Nor did we think that the new generation no longer valued economic security and order, but now preferred crime and deprivation: it is pretty obvious that most Postmaterialists want peace and prosperity, like everyone else. In other words, we did not think it likely that there had been a reversal of polarity in core societal goals. But it did seem possible that a more subtle change had occurred: though both old and young still valued both prosperity *and* freedom, there had been a change in the relative priority attached to such goals. While the older generation were likely to give top priority to economic and physical security over self-expression if they had to choose, we hypothesized that a growing segment of the postwar generation would give self-expression priority over economic and physical security, if it came to a crunch.

In short, the shift is *not* a reversal of polarities, in which most people formerly were opposed to freedom of speech or having more say on the job, but now favor them; nor is it one in which the Postmaterialists no longer like the items with Materialist priority, but have come to prefer crime and high inflation. It is, instead, a shift in priorities—something that would not necessarily be revealed in favorable/unfavorable ratings of given goals but would, nevertheless, have a crucial impact on the choices they made.

The intergenerational change is based on a shift in *priorities*. Consequently, we set out to determine which, among a set of almost universally desired goods, have top priority among different generations. Priorities reflect the way in which one *ranks* various goals (all of which may be considered desirable and important). Consequently, they are best measured by a ranking method. One can, under some circumstances, infer priorities from ratings, but ratings are generally not well suited to that task.

Building on criticisms made earlier by Herz (1979), Flanagan (1982, 1987), and Klages (1988, 1992), Buerklin et al. imply that the ranking technique is a means of forcing respondents to say things they do not really mean: "We wish to make it clear that the so-called 'Ranking' procedure violates the principle of Independence of Measurement. One obtains from this 'extreme forced-choice situation' (Klages, 1992: 26) only a distorted and imperfect picture of the value space. . . . The ranking procedure forces the respondent to differentiate value items along a single dimension" (Buerklin et al., 1994: 585; my translation).

Contrary to this claim, the use of ranking techniques is a commonly used and widely accepted method in survey research. It is virtually unavoidable in any well-designed study of basic values. Thus, it was used by Milton Rokeach in his classic studies of human values. Rokeach is quite explicit about why he used ranking instead of ratings. Even though rankings are a far more time-consuming method than simple ratings, he required his respondents to rank each of his 18 terminal values and 18 instrumental values because he realized that practically everyone attached positive polarity to all 36 items and would score almost all of them as "important" or "very important" if they were simply asked to rate them. He did so because he understood that one's value *priorities* are a genuine and crucial aspect of one's motivation—and something quite distinct from what is measured by ratings.

As we have noted, the ranking method tends to cause each item in a given pool to be negatively correlated with all of the other items in that pool. With random answering, each item in a pool of four items would have a negative correlation of about $-.33$ with each of the other items. This means that the first two items will tend to fall at the opposite poles of the first dimension; but the third item will be negatively correlated with *both* of them, which tends to force it off the first factor and onto another. The same is true of all additional items: ipsivity tends to force them *off* the first factor. We get a Materialist/Postmaterialist dimension not because of, but *in spite of*, the ranking format. The fact that we nevertheless obtain a clear Materialist-Postmaterialist dimension as the first principal component in survey after survey reflects the fact that people are not answering these items randomly: certain people tend to choose Materialist goals consistently, while others tend to emphasize Postmaterialist goals consistently. The format gives no cue concerning which are which: they cluster together because of their content, not their format.

By contrast, the rating method tends to produce a one-dimensional solution: insofar as it encourages response set, it produces a first principal component on which everything is positively correlated with everything else, regardless of content, so that all items have high positive loadings on the first principal component. As we will see below, this is exactly the pattern that appears in the data collected by both Buerklin et al. and Bean and Papadakis (1994) when they employ the rating technique (see table 4.4, first unrotated factor). These authors interpret this as simply meaning that people want all of these goals, overlooking the fact that this tendency is inflated by response set.

It is perfectly true that most people would like to eat their cake and have it too—and this poses no problem when no choice is necessary. But the crucial situations in politics (and life in general) arise when choices are necessary—when one must choose between civil liberties and maintaining order, or between building highways and protecting the environment, or choosing which of two attractive people one will marry. In such situations, ratings may provide little or no guidance: one may like both alternatives. The choice is determined by one's priorities.

We certainly do not claim that the rating method is never useful; we often use it. But any battery designed to measure changes in *basic value priorities* will, almost inevitably, be extremely vulnerable to response set. This is true because any such battery will (and should) consist of items that have the following characteristics: (1) almost everyone considers them desirable, and (2) almost everyone considers them important. They would not *be* basic human values unless they had these characteristics.

It is conceivable that one might, for some reason, want to measure people's priorities among superficial and unimportant values, but it would make no sense to do so in connection with the study of intergenerational change. Such values would not be central and deep-rooted enough to show enduring intergenerational differences: they would change readily, in response to the immediate environment.

Ratings are a perfectly valid means of collecting some types of information, but they are not well suited to measuring priorities: people can and do give equally high ratings to many goals, without revealing their underlying priorities. This does not mean that one does not *have* any underlying priorities— they can be readily and reliably measured with properly framed questions. The question is not whether one should always use ratings or always use rankings: both techniques are useful, but it is important to be aware that they measure two different aspects of reality.

THE PROBLEM OF RESPONSE SET

One of the classic methodological problems associated with having respondents rate a long series of items in identical format is the danger that the ratings will be shaped, not by the items' content (as the investigator assumes), but by the fact that they are asked in an identical format: the similarity of format cues the respondent into giving similar responses to a whole series of items, especially if they appear near each other in the questionnaire. Respondents with relatively little education are especially prone to do this, since this way of responding requires no cognitive effort or information—but, of course, it yields misleading data. This problem has been well known for decades, having been revealed as a major problem in the research underlying the classic *Authoritarian Personality* study; partly because the problem was already recognized so long ago, it is sometimes lost sight of in contemporary research. It remains as real as ever.

The ratings obtained from the battery used by Buerklin et al. seem to reflect the questionnaire format as much as the content of the items used. The ranking method is much less vulnerable to response set: by its very nature, one cannot simply run down the list, giving similar scores to a series of consecutive items: one is forced to select one item for top priority, another for second priority, and so on. This method has the disadvantages of ipsivity, but it is capable of measuring values or attitudes with much less noise than tends to be present in responses to rating scales.

It also is more useful for testing a specific theory. It targets the inquiry much more sharply than do ratings. It enables one to focus on measuring the respondents' priorities along a specific dimension. This, of course, implies that one has a specific theory in mind that one wishes to test: it is too tightly focused to be useful at the exploratory stage, or if one is not guided by some clear theory.

RANKINGS VERSUS RATINGS: AN EMPIRICAL COMPARISON

As we have pointed out, this theory is about priorities, not levels of support. Consequently, the items in the Materialist/Postmaterialist battery need to be ranked, not simply rated. The ranking method has two real disadvantages: (1) it is much more time consuming than ratings, and (2) it produces ipsitive data, which violate one of the assumptions of some statistical models; this is a difficulty, though not an insuperable one (Jackson and Alwin, 1980). Ranking, however, has two major advantages that, for present purposes, far outweigh the disadvantages: first, rankings are not determined by response set: when the respondent ranks the items, it is impossible to simply race down the list, giving relatively high (or relatively low) ratings to all of them. One is forced to consider each item separately, in relation to the others. Response set seems to be such a serious problem in the ratings obtained by Buerklin et al. that it is unclear if any but the first item in their battery is rated primarily in terms of its content: after the first item in the series, all of the succeeding items get uniformly high ratings (Inglehart and Klingemann, 1996). Second—and even more important—rankings are a fundamentally different approach, which is more suitable for the measurement of priorities than are ratings: rankings enable one to measure an aspect of reality that ratings may completely fail to uncover.

Buerklin et al. (1994) have raised an important and basic methodological question, but their database does not enable them to answer it since they employed neither the format nor the items used to measure Materialist/Postmatearialist values. What would they have found if they had used items that actually *did* tap the Materialist/Postmaterialist dimension—and then had also taken the precaution to ask them as both ratings and rankings, to test the effects of response set? Fortunately, this question is not merely hypothetical: exactly this was done in an article published almost simultaneously with the one by Buerklin et al. The results are extremely interesting.

Bean and Papadakis (1994) also argue that the Materialist/Postmaterialist dimension can better be measured by ratings than by rankings, and they pro-

TABLE 4.2
Factor Analysis of Materialism-Postmaterialism
Items Based on Rankings: First Principal Component

Less Impersonal Society	.61
Ideas Count More than Money	.58
More Say in Government	.48
Freedom of Speech	.45
More Say on Job	.44
More Beautiful Cities	.21
Maintain Stable Economy	−.19
Fight Rising Prices	−.22
Strong Defense Forces	−.29
Fight against Crime	−.35
Economic Growth	−.48
Maintain Order	−.55

Note: Items with Materialist polarity are in boldface type;
items with Postmaterialist polarity are in italics.
Source: National survey of Australians' Attitudes toward
Welfare, 1988 (N = 1,814), in Bean and Papadakis, 1994: 275.

ceed to carry out an appropriate and well-designed test of this claim. To do so, they first administered a national survey in Australia that measured Materialist/Postmaterialist values both by rankings (as advocated by Inglehart) and by ratings. They find that when the respondent uses the ranking method, one obtains a first principal component on which all six of the items designed to tap Materialist priorities form a cluster having negative polarity, and all six items designed to tap Postmaterialist priorities show positive polarity. In short, the authors find a clear Materialist-Postmaterialist dimension, with the Materialist items near one pole and the Postmaterialist items near the other pole. Table 4.2 shows their results. As this table indicates, the fit with theoretical expectations is virtually perfect. Although two of the items have relatively weak loadings on their respective factors, all 12 items show the polarity predicted by the theory. And although these results come from Australia, they show a pattern that is almost identical to results obtained by other investigators using the same methodology, in dozens of other countries.

Using a rating format, however, the authors get a completely different set of results: the first principal component is one on which all 12 items are given relatively high (or relatively low) ratings. When subjected to varimax rotation, this factor breaks down into a Materialist factor and a Postmaterialist factor (which are uncorrelated since varimax rotation was used). Using this approach, there seems to be no such thing as a Materialist/Postmaterialist dimension. Table 4.3 shows the results obtained from ratings.

The results seem contradictory. The authors argue that the rating approach reflects reality better than the ranking approach because most respondents are really in favor of all 12 goals: they want freedom of speech *and* law and

TABLE 4.3
Factor Analysis of Materialism-Postmaterialism Items Based on Ratings:
First Principal Component Analysis with Varimax Rotation

	First Unrotated Factor	Rotated Factors	
		Postmaterialism	Materialism
Materialist Items			
Maintain Order	.47	.06	.67
Fight Rising Prices	.56	.39	.41
Economic Growth	.46	.04	.69
Strong Defense	.42	.04	.63
Stable Economy	.56	.24	.59
Fight Crime	.51	.09	.70
Postmaterialist Items			
More Say in Government	.53	.52	.19
Protect Free Speech	.49	.51	.14
More Say in Jobs	.61	.70	.11
Beautify Cities and Countryside	.54	.65	.05
More Humane Society	.64	.75	.08
Society Where Ideas Count	.56	.74	−.04

Source: National survey of Australians' Attitudes toward Welfare, 1988 (N = 1,814), in Bean and Papadakis, 1994: 278.

order—*and* economic growth *and* environmental protection *and* low inflation *and* more say in government *and* strong defense forces. The rating approach is more "flexible" than the ranking approach because it enables respondents to give high ratings to all 12 goals. Most respondents give priority to the Materialist goals over the Postmaterialist goals (or vice versa) only when they are constrained to do so by a ranking format.

Which approach captures reality? It depends on which aspect of reality you want to capture. Ultimately, it comes down to the question, Do you want to measure priorities or response levels?

It is perfectly true, as Bean and Papadakis point out (together with Klages and Buerklin et al.), that nearly everyone would like to attain all of these goals. All 12 goals were designed to tap things that nearly everyone considers desirable: this is inherent in any battery designed to measure changing priorities among basic values. Thus, in an unconstrained format, people can give positive ratings to virtually everything. This tendency is strengthened by the fact that a rating approach puts a dozen positive goals in an identical format, creating a series where the easiest thing to do is run down the list, giving similar ratings to item after item. This is a perfect setting for response set to occur. The rating list is a convenient way to quickly elicit a long stream of responses. It seems extremely quick and efficient. The problem is that it can yield virtually meaningless responses. This format systematically tends to create or inflate positive correlations between the items in a series. Furthermore, it provides a systematic bias: less-educated people are particularly likely to be influenced by response set. It is cognitively undemanding: one need not differentiate between the items—one can simply give a series of high (or low) ratings.

The less educated are particularly prone to response set, and in keeping with this fact it is very significant that Bean and Papadakis find (when, and *only* when they use ratings) that the less educated constitute the high scorers on both their Materialist dimension and their Postmaterialist dimension (Bean and Papadakis, 1994: 280). In striking contrast to this finding, in virtually every survey ever carried out, the Postmaterialists identified by the *ranking* method consist of those with relatively high educational levels—to such an extent that some analysts have even suggested that Postmaterialist values simply reflect high educational levels (Duch and Taylor, 1993). This is a remarkably clear illustration of the fact that the rating method fails to identify those with Postmaterialist priorities: the "Postmaterialists" identified by ratings have a mean educational level *below* that of the sample as a whole. Needless to say, the "Postmaterialists" identified in this manner do not show the other demographic characteristics of true Postmaterialists: most strikingly, they are not concentrated among the young.

Ratings elicit information quickly—but they are not well suited to measuring priorities. Rankings, on the other hand, are much more time-consuming and difficult than ratings. With this format, the respondent cannot simply race down the list giving similar (usually high) ratings to every item. He or she must painstakingly decide which, among a series of desirable goals, is most important, which ranks second, and which are least important. This is a more demanding method. But for analyzing politics, this provides much more useful information than simply knowing that given individuals rate almost everything as "extremely important."

This is true because politics is, above all, a question of choices. True, environmental protection does *not* always conflict with economic growth; nor does maximizing individual freedom necessarily conflict with maintaining order. But these are the easy situations, when the solution is obvious and everyone can be satisfied. The crunch comes when two or more highly important and desirable goals *do* conflict with each other: it is precisely then that important political issues arise. Sometimes you cannot eat your cake and have it too. Under these circumstances, one is forced to make choices. And it is then that priorities become crucial.

The ratings approach is quite appropriate for many purposes. But it is not an appropriate way to measure value priorities—which is the topic on which the Materialist/Postmaterialist value change thesis focuses. The theory does not hypothesize that some people are opposed to economic and physical security, while others like it. It assumes that these are goals sought by almost everyone. The shift from Materialist to Postmaterialists priorities occurs when a given segment of the population has been raised with a sufficiently high level of economic and physical security that further emphasis on them has diminishing marginal utility. It is precisely because Postmaterialists have security (and *not* because they reject it) that they give top priority to other goals.

Thus, Bean and Papadakis (1994) and Buerklin et al. (1994) are perfectly correct in saying that most people (Materialists and Postmaterialists alike) would like to have all of these goals—and that, if they were unconstrained, they would give positive ratings to nearly all of them. The ratings results that they obtain from Australia and Germany, respectively, demonstrate this point. This is, indeed, one aspect of reality. Hence, the ratings approach produces a first principal component on which all 12 goals have positive polarity.

But this does not mean that there is no such thing as Materialist-Postmaterialist priorities. Quite the contrary, the data collected by Bean and Papadakis (1994) demonstrate clearly that these very same respondents are perfectly capable of differentiating between Materialist and Postmaterialist priorities, and they do so when the question is posed in a way that measures priorities. Priorities tap a different aspect of reality from that measured by ratings; and priorities are important because reality often constrains individuals to make choices.

Priorities are not an artifact of survey research. They exist inside people's minds and can be measured reliably—and they emerge even when (as with Bean and Papadakis) the investigators have a skeptical attitude toward them. Indeed, their data replicate the pattern that was predicted by the theory of Materialist/Postmaterialist value change with a remarkable fidelity. This theory was developed 25 years ago, by an American working in Western Europe. Over the past two decades, literally scores of surveys in dozens of countries have discovered an almost identical configuration, in which one segment of the population (which tends to be the older and the economically less secure strata) gives top priority to the items that were designed to tap Materialist priorities; while another segment (the younger, more prosperous and better educated) give priority to a set of items that were designed to tap Postmaterialist priorities. These findings, from 43 societies not including Australia, are presented below. This latest set of findings, from a survey in Australia, indicates that a virtually identical configuration of societal priorities emerges in yet another country on another continent.

The study by Bean and Papadakis (1994) adds a well-executed methodological study to the picture, and it provides convincing evidence that the format in which the questions are posed is crucial. The authors conclude that the rating method is a more appropriate way to measure Materialist/Postmaterialist values than the ranking method, since it "allows for a more flexible and realistic account of the choices made by most social actors." The authors have demonstrated that, free from any constraint, people will give high ratings to both Materialist and Postmaterialist goals. They interpret this to mean that the rating format taps reality more faithfully than the ranking format.

But it depends on which aspect of reality one wishes to understand. If one is asking the question, Do people want to attain all of these goals, or only some of them? then the rating format is appropriate, and the answer is clear: most people want all of them. But if one is interested in the question, What priorities do people act on, when forced to choose between two desirable goals? then the ranking method is appropriate.

Comments on Bean and Papadakis's study by both Inglehart (1994) and Hellevik (1994) appeared with the original article. Both comments noted, independently, that the results from the ratings approach gave strong indications of response set. Hellevik commented,

> Bean and Papadakis see the correlated indexes of Materialism and Postmaterialism as a substantively interesting result of allowing a choice of "both-and" instead of forcing the respondent to make priorities. In my view they overlook methodological problems of the rating method, problems which actually may explain their results. Through my work with national and comparative analyses of cultural indicators, using mainly scales, we have reached exactly the opposite conclusion: ranking is preferable to rating. The reasons for this are both substantive and methodological. The two measurement methods give information on separate aspects of value preferences which are both of interest. Rating indicates absolute levels of support, while ranking indicates the *priorities* among values—even if they have similar levels of support. (Hellevik, 1994: 293)

In their reply to these critiques, Bean and Papadakis (1994) reported that they had tried to correct for response set by using a standard method—anchoring the responses around each respondent's mean score across the set of items and analyzing the extent to which a given response was higher or lower than this mean. When they did so, they found, to their surprise, that their result mirrors the result based on rankings, with the Materialist items at one pole, and the Postmaterialist items at the opposite pole (Bean and Papadakis, 1994: 297). They took this to mean that their correction for response set had failed. There is no reason to believe that it had: a more straightforward interpretation is that response set is, indeed, responsible for the pattern they get using ratings—and that when it is corrected, one obtains the Materialist/Postmaterialist dimension that these items were designed to tap.

WHAT IS THE RIGHT LEVEL OF ANALYSIS: ONE DIMENSION? OR TWO, FOUR, OR N DIMENSIONS?

The Materialist/Postmaterialist concept is unidimensional by definition and operates at a relatively high level of generality. This level of analysis has proven productive. It is perfectly possible, however, either to ascend to higher levels of generality—examining the degree to which Materialist/Postmaterialist values are themselves part of a still broader configuration of values (as we did in chapter 3)—or to descend to lower levels of generality, examining its component subclusters, as Herz (1979), Flanagan (1982, 1987), and Van Deth (1984) have done.

Herz (1979) used multidimensional scaling to obtain a two-dimensional structure from the Materialist-Postmaterialist rankings. But this two-dimensional array revealed a clear watershed, with all of the Materialist items on one side and all of the Postmaterialist items on the other side (see Inglehart, 1990:143).

Van Deth (1986) went even farther: he used factor analysis, smallest space analysis, multidimensional scaling, and unfolding techniques to explore the structure of the standard 12-item battery Materialist/Postmaterialist values battery based on rankings. He found that, although the detailed placement of individual items varied, these methods all produced basically the same result: here, too, the most prominent feature was a clear watershed, with all of the Materialist items at one side of the graph and all of the Postmaterialist items at the other side. The results indicated that the use of an additive index, based on the distinction between Materialist and Postmaterialist items, was justified.

As all of these analyses demonstrate, the Postmaterialist dimension can, indeed, be broken down into its constituent subclusters. But, at the same time, they confirm the robustness of the broader Materialist-Postmaterialist dimension: if one measures people's priorities, then no matter how you slice the data, one comes up with an overall pattern on which the Materialist items are at one side, and the Postmaterialist items are on the opposite side.

Klages (1988, 1992) prefers to deal with two dimensions that he describes as "Duty/Acceptance" and "Self Realization." His analysis does not deal with a change in priorities, but with high or low levels of support for two more or less unrelated dimensions. He is free to do so, and he may well come up with interesting findings concerning changes in levels of support for these goals: it is not an either/or choice.

Varimax rotation will usually do what it was designed to do—break a dimension down into its components; but it is absurd to interpret this fact as meaning that the dimension in question "really" has two or more subcomponents, and that, consequently, one is obliged to operate at the lower level of generality. The reality is not only that the battery used to measure Materialist/Postmaterialist values has subclusters that were designed to tap economic and physical security, respectively, but that each of these subclusters can also be broken down further, until one reaches the individual items that make them up. It is perfectly legitimate to operate at the lowest possible level of generality, examining attitudes toward "The fight against crime," for example, or any other individual item that interests one. Similarly, it is perfectly possible to operate at Flanagan's slightly higher level of generalization, or at the level of the Materialist/Postmaterialist dimension, or (since Materialist/Postmaterialist priorities prove to be correlated with a broad range of other values) to examine whether these values themselves fit into a still broader configuration such as "Survival Values" versus "Well-being Values." It depends on the theoretical purpose one has in mind.

To date, dimensional analysis of data from more than 40 countries around the world has demonstrated that, underlying the value systems of many different peoples, a Materialist/Postmaterialist dimension *does* exist. Furthermore, as the Materialist/Postmaterialist value change theory implies, and as we will see in the next chapter, the values measured by this dimension are linked with economic security, both at the microlevel—with individuals from relatively prosperous families being more likely to be Postmaterialists—and at the macrolevel—with Postmaterialist values being far more widespread in rich countries than in poor ones. In addition, as the theory implies, these values show evidence of intergenerational change, with Postmaterialist values being far more widespread among the young than among the old.

A number of critics implicitly assume that one must *either* focus on levels of support for given values, as measured by ratings; *or* value priorities, which are best measured by rankings. They overlook the fact that value priorities and levels of support reflect two distinct aspects of reality. One is free to measure either. A good deal of empirical evidence indicates that the most important intergenerational value change now taking place involves a change in priorities: this does not rule out the possibility that important changes may *also* be occurring in levels of support for given goals. For value *priorities* and relative levels of support for given goals are two distinct aspects of reality. Both are worth studying. It is not an either/or choice.

The Postmaterialist Dimension in Global Perspective

The 1990 World Values Survey measured Materialist/Postmaterialist priorities in 43 societies, using the ranking method. As we saw above in figure 4.1, the results from 16 Western democracies show remarkable cross-national similarity. In every case, the same five items clustered near one pole of the first principal component. These items deal with such goals as freedom of expression and having more say on the job or in political life. All five of these items had been designed to tap Postmaterialist priorities. Six items—again the same six in every country—clustered near the opposite pole. These items emphasize economic and physical security. All six were designed to tap Materialist priorities. The remaining item fell near the midpoint.

Exactly the same pattern holds true in 16 Western European and North American societies—including several that had not previously been surveyed. People respond to the five Postmaterialist items (shown in italics) as if they tapped a similar underlying value, placing them in one cluster. People also respond to the six Materialist items (shown in boldface type) as if they tapped something very different. The one remaining item is ambivalent. The detailed results for each of the 43 societies included in the 1990 World Values Survey are reported in Abramson and Inglehart (1995).

There is strong evidence that the Materialist/Postmaterialist battery taps a cross-nationally comparable phenomenon throughout the Western world. Is it *merely* a Western phenomenon, however, or does it, as the theory implies, emerge in any society that is undergoing an intergenerational shift toward higher levels of prosperity and security?

TABLE 4.4
The Materialist/Postmaterialist Dimension in Four
Latin American Countries (Loadings on First
Principal Component in Factor Analysis)

More Say in Government	.67
More Say on Job	.60
Less Impersonal Society	.52
Freedom of Speech	.36
Ideas Count More than Money	.34
Economic Growth	−.15
More Beautiful Cities	−.27
Strong Defense Forces	−.27
Maintain Stable Economy	−.31
Fight Rising Prices	−.37
Fight against Crime	−.49
Maintain Order	−.56

Note: Items with Materialist polarity are in boldface type; items with Postmaterialist polarity are in italics.
Source: 1990–91 World Values Survey data from Mexico, Argentina, Brazil, and Chile.

Do non-Western publics see things from a completely different perspective? Apparently not. Four Latin American societies were included in the 1990–91 World Values Survey, and the same basic structure applies (see table 4.4). There are some variations from the pattern found in advanced industrial societies: already known to be a deviant item, "More beautiful cities" shows negative polarity here, and "Economic growth" is only very weakly linked with the Materialist cluster. But all five of the Postmaterialist items show positive polarity and fall into the predicted cluster.

More strikingly still, the pattern that emerges in Japan and South Korea is practically identical to the pattern we find in Western Europe and Latin America. Although these two East Asian societies started with profoundly different cultural traditions from those of the West, they have both become advanced industrial societies—and their publics respond in a fashion that is almost indistinguishable from that of Western respondents. As table 4.5 demonstrates, the five Postmaterialist items cluster at one pole, and the six Materialist items cluster at the opposite pole. Moreover, the item concerning "More beautiful cities and countryside," which gave ambiguous results in the West, shows a clear Postmaterialist polarity in both Japan and South Korea. The two East Asian countries not only conform to theoretical expectations, they actually show a slightly better fit than do most Western countries. This is a very interesting finding. It indicates that the emergence of a polarization between Materialist goals and Postmaterialist goals is *not* a uniquely Western phenomenon. It is a phenomenon of advanced industrial society that emerges with high levels of

TABLE 4.5
The Materialist/Postmaterialist Dimension in East
Asia (Loadings on First Principal Component in
Factor Analysis)

Less Impersonal Society	.70
More Say on Job	.60
More Say in Government	.50
More Beautiful Cities	.38
Freedom of Speech	.45
Ideas Count More than Money	.24
Fight against Crime	−.30
Fight Rising Prices	−.31
Strong Defense Forces	−.45
Maintain Order	−.50
Maintain Stable Economy	−.61
Economic Growth	−.62

Note: Items with Materialist polarity are in boldface type;
items with Postmaterialist polarity are in italics.
Source: Pooled 1990–91 World Values Survey data from
Japan and South Korea.

economic development—even among societies that started with very different
cultural heritages.

There are societies in which the polarization between Materialist and Postmaterialist values is less distinct, but the division is *not* between Western and
non-Western cultures. The countries that deviate most from the Materialist/
Postmaterialist configuration are the ex-socialist countries, even those that
have historically had close ties with the West.

The 1990–91 World Values Survey includes samples from 11 societies of
the former Soviet bloc, as well as China (see table 4.6). In 11 of these 12
countries the five Postmaterialist items cluster together in one group. Poland
is the sole exception, and even there, four of the five Postmaterialist items
cluster together. Thus, even in the communist and ex-communist societies,
we find a clear and consistent Postmaterialist cluster. But there is a tendency
for emphasis on "economic growth" to fall into the Postmaterialist cluster.
This is a striking deviation from what we find everywhere else, and it would
be surprising if we found it in societies with market economies. But within
the societies that have had state-run economies, it is understandable. "Economic growth" (like everything connected with the economy) has quite different connotations in a state-socialist society from what it has in a market
economy.

In 1990 the socialist societies had authoritarian political systems and state-
run economies that had become stagnant to the point of paralysis. The existing system of state controls had widely come to be seen as incompatible with
economic growth. Even in China, which continued to experience rapid growth,

TABLE 4.6
The Materialist/Postmaterialist Dimension in 11
Ex-socialist or Socialist Countries (Loadings on
First Principal Component in Factor Analysis)

More Say in Government	.73
Less Impersonal Society	.46
More Say on Job	.44
Freedom of Speech	.27
Economic Growth	.18
Ideas Count More than Money	.17
Maintain Stable Economy	−.02
Strong Defense Forces	−.37
More Beautiful Cities	−.38
Fight Rising Prices	−.43
Maintain Order	−.50
Fight against Crime	−.57

Note: Items with Materialist polarity in Western countries
and East Asia are in boldface type; items with Postmaterialist
polarity in Western countries and East Asia are in italics.
Source: Pooled 1990–91 World Values Survey data from
Belarus, Bulgaria, China, Czechoslovakia, East Germany, Estonia, Hungary, Latvia, Lithuania, Poland, Russia, and greater
Moscow.

this growth was taking place entirely in the private sector. State-run industries
were stagnant. In this context, as of 1990, economic growth had come to be
seen as something that could only be attained by breaking free from a massive
and sclerotic state bureaucracy and turning the economy over to individual initiative. In contrast with the West, where an emphasis on economic growth was
linked with loyalty to the established order, in the state-socialist world many
viewed economic growth as a goal that could only come through radical socioeconomic change. Moreover, these changes were closely linked with the
Postmaterialist emphasis on individual autonomy: they required the liberation
of the individual from state authority. Hence we find the apparent paradox that,
in many of the former state-socialist societies and in China, respondents who
gave high priority to economic growth were the same people who emphasized
"giving the people more say in government," "more say on the job," "freedom
of speech," and "a less impersonal, more humane society."

   Further analyses support the conclusion that in these societies Postmaterialist values are linked with support for reduced government involvement in the
economy. In the 1990–91 World Values Survey, respondents were asked to
place themselves on a 10-point scale measuring their attitudes toward governmental versus private ownership of business and industry. In the non-socialist
countries, people with Postmaterialist values tend to be slightly more favorable to the idea of a state-run economy than are those with Materialist values.

This is not a strong relationship, but it reflects the traditional ideological heritage of the Left.

The situation is dramatically different in Eastern Europe, the societies of the former Soviet Union, and the People's Republic of China. In all 12 of these societies, people with Postmaterialist values are *less* favorable to a state-run economy than are the Materialists. The polarity of "progressive" values has reversed. Throughout the ex-socialist societies, people who place themselves on the Left *and* those with Postmaterialist values reject the idea of a state-run economy.

There are also cross-national differences in the polarity of the goal of "trying to make our cities and countryside more beautiful." This item was designed to tap aesthetic values. But analyses of Western societies showed that it had a surprisingly strong linkage with safety needs.

The "beautiful cities" goal has differing associations in different societies in the World Values survey. The variations follow a consistent pattern. When the 12-item measure was first developed in 1973, the "beautiful cities" item was more or less neutral, with a slight Postmaterialist polarity (Inglehart, 1977). In the 1990 surveys, this item has a slightly stronger Postmaterialist polarity than it had previously, in most Western societies. And, as we noted, the goal has an even clearer Postmaterialist polarity in Japan and South Korea. In the four Latin American countries, on the other hand, the goal of "more beautiful cities" clearly emerges as a Materialist value; and it is even more clearly a Materialist goal in the societies of the former Soviet bloc.

In the West this goal, originally designed to tap aesthetic values, now appears to be performing its original mission, though still only weakly. The fact that this item falls into the Materialist cluster in Eastern Europe seems to reflect severe environmental deterioration in these societies (see Inglehart and Abramson, 1992b). In these societies, environmental pollution has become a massive and life-threatening problem, one that is far more severe than in the West. In the former state socialist countries, pollution is not perceived primarily as an aesthetic problem, but as one that is directly life-threatening. This perception is far from groundless. The death rates in some regions of Russia, the former East Germany, Poland, and the former Czechoslovakia are shockingly high, for reasons attributable to massive industrial pollution. In the West the goal of "more beautiful cities" has an ambivalent meaning, tapping aesthetic needs to some extent, but also having secondary connotations of urban disorder and crime. In Japan and Korea, where urban crime rates are much lower than in most Western countries, this item unequivocally taps Postmaterialist concerns. In the former Soviet bloc countries, with life-threatening levels of pollution, it tends to tap basic Materialist concerns for the effects of industrial pollution on human survival.

In the former communist world, economic and physical security cannot be taken for granted nearly as much as in the rich industrial societies of the West and East Asia. Hence, as one might expect, the Materialist-Postmaterialist dimension is less consistent, and less clearly crystallized in the ex-socialist so-

TABLE 4.7

The Materialist/Postmaterialist Dimension in India
(Loadings on Second* Principal Component in
Factor Analysis)

More Say in Government	.61
Less Impersonal Society	.58
More Say on Job	.43
Ideas Count More than Money	.38
Freedom of Speech	.06
Strong Defense Forces	−.01
Economic Growth	−.08
Maintain Order	−.19
Maintain Stable Economy	−.34
More Beautiful Cities	−.35
Fight Rising Prices	−.46
Fight against Crime	−.49

Note: Items with Materialist polarity are in boldface type; items with Postmaterialist polarity are in italics.

Source: Pooled 1990–91 World Values Survey data from India.

*In India, the first principal component reflects a polarization between emphasis on economic priorities and emphasis on maintaining military and domestic order; all of the Postmaterialist items are neutral on this dimension.

cieties than it is in the West and East Asia. Although a recognizable Materialist/Postmaterialist dimension does emerge in the former Soviet bloc, it accounts for less variance than it does in richer advanced industrial societies. In three of these societies (Lithuania, Czechoslovakia, and Hungary) this dimension emerges only as the second principal component in the factor analysis.

The Postmaterialist phenomenon is only marginally present in such low-income societies as India and Nigeria, both of which had per capita incomes of approximately $300 in 1990. As the theory implies, there are very few Postmaterialists in these countries, and mass values do not crystallize along this dimension as strongly as they do in richer societies (see Abramson and Inglehart, 1995, for country-by-country results). A recognizable Materialist/Postmaterialist dimension emerges in India, but it accounts for less variance than in almost any other country and is the second principal component instead of the first (see table 4.7).

Although interesting cross-national differences in the structure of these values exist, the evidence suggests that the core meaning of Materialism/Postmaterialism is similar across this wide range of societies. The quest for economic security is much more politicized in societies with state-run economies than in societies with market economies, which gives a distinctive meaning to items that refer to the economy. Apart from this, however, the Materialist goals show consistent results, and the five Postmaterialist items behave in a similar way in all types of societies, East and West, as well as North and South. The results indicate that an additive index, based on summing up the five Postmaterialist items (producing an index having scores ranging from 0 to 5) can be used in virtually any of the 43 societies included in the World Values survey. Consequently, we can construct a cross-nationally comparable index of Materialist/Postmaterialist values, based on the nine items that do have globally consistent polarity (assigning neutral polarity to the two items referring to the economy, and the item referring to "more beautiful cities"). This index is used throughout this book, except when only the original four-item index is available.

On the whole, the cross-national similarities underlying mass responses to the Materialist/Postmaterialist values items are far more striking than the cross-national differences.

The Shift toward Postmaterialist Values, 1970–1994

INTRODUCTION

The basic values of publics throughout advanced industrial society have been undergoing a gradual intergenerational shift during the past several decades. Although different countries have shifted at different rates, economic and technological changes have had a broadly similar impact across these societies. As Postmodernization theory implies, the process applies to advanced industrial society in general.

In 1970 we hypothesized that the value priorities of Western publics were shifting from Materialist values toward Postmaterialist values—from giving top priority to physical sustenance and safety, toward heavier emphasis on belonging, self-expression, and the quality of life (Inglehart, 1971). The predicted intergenerational value shift could not be demonstrated until many years had passed; and whether or not it was occurring has been hotly disputed (Böltken and Jagodzinski, 1985; Thomassen and Van Deth, 1989; Trump, 1991; Clarke and Dutt, 1991). Only in recent years has a sufficiently long time series become available to test the prediction reliably. This chapter examines cross-national survey data over a 24-year period. The results show a clear and statistically significant trend toward Postmaterialist values in almost all of the societies for which we now have detailed time series measurements over this period. These values also show short-term fluctuations linked with changing rates of inflation and unemployment, as the value change thesis implies; but the long-term trend seems to result mainly from intergenerational replacement.

Evidence from the 43 societies surveyed in the World Values surveys enables us to test the value change hypothesis on a broader basis than has ever before been possible. The thesis implies that we should observe two quite different findings, both of which are important: societies with high *levels* of economic development should have relatively high *levels* of Postmaterialist values, and societies that have experienced relatively high rates of economic *growth* should show relatively large *differences* between the values of younger and older generations. As we will see, the evidence supports both hypotheses. It appears that this value shift occurs in any society that has experienced sufficient economic development in recent decades so that the preadult experiences of younger birth cohorts have been significantly more secure than those of older cohorts. Large intergenerational differences are found in societies that have experienced rapid growth in GNP per capita and are negligible in societies that have had little or no growth. And these value differences are enduring characteristics of given birth cohorts. Accordingly, as intergenerational population replacement has occurred, Materialist priorities have become less prevalent and Postmaterialism has increased in 18 of the 20 societies for which we have comparable data over the past decade.

The shift toward Postmaterialist values has far-reaching implications. It is only one part of a broader shift toward Postmodern values, involving changing orientations toward politics, work, family life, religion, and sexual behavior. Far more data are available on the evolution of Postmaterialist values than on any other component of this cultural shift, but a broad range of orientations are linked with Materialist/Postmaterialist values, and most of them seem to be moving on the same trajectory. Thus, charting the transition to Postmaterialist values can help us understand the entire Postmodern shift.

THE RISE OF POSTMATERIALIST VALUES

As noted earlier, research on the Materialist/Postmaterialist value change has been guided by two key hypotheses (Inglehart, 1977):

1. *A Scarcity Hypothesis*. An individual's priorities reflect the socioeconomic environment: one places the greatest subjective value on those things that are in relatively short supply.

2. *A Socialization Hypothesis*. The relationship between socioeconomic environment and value priorities is not one of immediate adjustment: a substantial time lag is involved, because, to a large extent, one's basic values reflect the conditions that prevailed during one's preadult years.

The scarcity hypothesis is similar to the principle of diminishing marginal utility. And it implies that recent economic developments have significant consequences. During the period since World War II, advanced industrial societies have attained much higher real income levels than ever before in history. Coupled with the emergence of the welfare state, this has brought about a historically unprecedented situation: most of their population does *not* live under conditions of hunger and economic insecurity. This has led to a gradual shift in which needs for belonging, self-expression, and a participant role in society became more prominent. Prolonged periods of prosperity tend to encourage the spread of Postmaterialist values; economic decline tends to have the opposite effect.

But there is no simple one-to-one relationship between economic level and the prevalence of Postmaterialist values. These values reflect one's *subjective* sense of security, not one's economic level per se. While rich people tend to feel more secure than poor people, one's sense of security is also influenced by the cultural setting and social welfare institutions in which one is raised. Thus, the scarcity hypothesis must be supplemented with the socialization hypothesis: a basic personality structure tends to take shape by the time an individual reaches adulthood, and changes relatively little thereafter.

Taken together, these two hypotheses generate a set of predictions concerning value change. First, while the scarcity hypothesis implies that prosperity is conducive to the spread of Postmaterialist values, the socialization hypothesis implies that neither an individual's values nor those of a society as a whole will change overnight. For the most part, fundamental value change takes place as younger birth cohorts replace older ones in the adult population of a society. Consequently, after a long period of rising economic and physical security, one should find substantial differences between the value priorities of older and younger groups: they have been shaped by different experiences in their formative years.

This thesis was first tested in surveys carried out in 1970 with representative national cross sections of the publics of Great Britain, France, West Germany, Italy, the Netherlands, and Belgium. The people interviewed chose the goals they considered most important among a set of items designed to tap economic and physical security, on the one hand, or self-expression and the nonmaterial quality of life, on the other hand.

In the original four-item Materialist/Postmaterialist values battery, each respondent was asked to select what their country's two top goals should be among the following choices: (1) maintaining order in the nation, (2) giving the people more say in important government decisions, (3) fighting rising prices, (4) protecting freedom of speech. Respondents who select "maintaining order" and "fighting inflation" are classified as Materialists; those who choose "giving the people more say" and "freedom of speech" are classified as Postmaterialists. The four remaining combinations are classified as "Mixed."

As the preceding chapter indicates, the Materialist/Postmaterialist dimension travels well cross-culturally. It taps an almost universal concern: feeling secure or insecure about survival is meaningful in virtually any culture. Consequently, the Materialist/Postmaterialist dimension emerges in such societies as South Korea or Turkey with a basic structure roughly similar to that found in Western industrial societies. There are very few Postmaterialists in low-income societies, so the dimension is less important and less strongly structured there, accounting for a smaller percentage of the variance than it does in advanced industrial societies. But these items seem to tap comparable concerns in poor countries and in rich countries.

Not only do the Postmaterialist items have similar connotations within this 12-item battery, but they also have similar demographic correlates: in all societies that have experienced substantial increases in economic security during the past several decades, these values tend to be emphasized more heavily by the younger birth cohorts.

Our theory of value change generates a number of predictions. The most basic prediction specifies what kind of cultural change should take place under given conditions: existential security leads to the rise of Postmodern values. This chapter focuses on the shift from Materialist to Postmaterialist values, while chapters 9 and 10 test this prediction concerning various other aspects of the Postmodern shift. In addition to predicting what kinds of values should become more widespread, chapter 1 spelled out a series of detailed predictions concerning when, where, and how fast value change should occur. This chapter tests the following predictions, connected with the shift from Materialist to Postmaterialist values:

1. Postmaterialist and other Postmodern values will be most widespread in the richest and otherwise most secure societies. The publics of impoverished and insecure societies will emphasize survival values to a much greater extent.

2. Within any given society, Postmodern values will be most widespread among the more secure strata: the wealthier and better educated will be most likely to hold a whole range of security values, including Postmaterialism; the less secure strata will emphasize survival priorities.

3. Short-term fluctuations will follow the scarcity hypothesis: prosperity will enhance the tendency to emphasize well-being values; economic downturn, civil disorder, or war will lead people to emphasize survival values.

4. Long-term changes will also reflect the scarcity hypothesis: in societies that have experienced high levels of security for several decades, we should find a long-term shift from survival values toward well-being values. This shift is not universal: it should occur only in those societies that have attained sufficient existential security so that a substantial share of the population takes survival for granted; but it is not uniquely Western: it appears in any society that *has* experienced the transition to high mass security.

5. In those societies that have experienced a long period of rising economic and physical security, we will find substantial differences between the value priorities of older and younger groups, with the young being much likelier to emphasize well-being values than the old.

6. These intergenerational value differences should be reasonably stable over time: though immediate conditions of security or insecurity will produce short-term fluctuations, the underlying differences between younger and older birth cohorts should persist over long periods of time.

7. In cross-national perspective, large amounts of intergenerational *change* will be found in countries that have experienced relatively high rates of economic *growth*; conversely, the difference between the values of young and old will be small or nonexistent in countries that experienced relatively little increase in per capita income. Thus, high *levels* of prosperity should be conducive to high *levels* of Postmaterialism and other Postmodern values; high rates of economic *growth* should produce relatively rapid rates of value *change*, and relatively large intergenerational *differences*.

8. If one knows the distribution of values across birth cohorts in a given nation at a given time, one can estimate how much change will be produced in a given time span as a result of intergenerational population replacement. Thus for Western Europe, using the four-item Materialist/Postmaterialist values battery, population replacement should produce a shift toward Postmaterialism of approximately one point per year on the Materialist-Postmaterialist percentage difference index.

The 1970 European Community surveys were the first to test the value change thesis. The results showed the age group differences that the social-

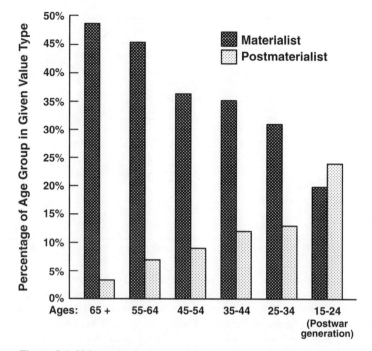

Figure 5.1. Value type by age group, among the publics of Britain, France, West Germany, Italy, Belgium, and the Netherlands in 1970. *Source*: European Community survey of February 1970; based on original four-item Materialist/Postmaterialist values battery. Reprinted from Inglehart, 1990: 76.

ization hypothesis predicts. Figure 5.1 depicts this pattern in a pooled sample of six Western European publics. The basic pattern is similar in all six countries: among the older groups, Materialists outnumber Postmaterialists enormously; as we move to younger groups, the proportion of Materialists declines and that of Postmaterialists increases. Thus, among the oldest cohort, Materialists outnumber Postmaterialists by more than 12 to 1; but among the youngest cohort, Postmaterialists are more numerous than Materialists.

The age differences shown here are striking. But does this pattern reflect life-cycle effects, birth cohort effects, or some combination of the two? Our theory predicts that we will find birth cohort differences; but these differences between the priorities of young and old *could* reflect some inherent tendency for people to become more materialistic as they age. If so, then as time goes by, the values of the younger groups will eventually become just like those of the older groups, producing no change in the society as a whole. Does aging make one place ever-increasing emphasis on economic and physical security? The only way to answer this question is by following given birth cohorts over time, to see if they become more Materialist as they age. We can do so: the four-item Materialist/Postmaterialist values battery has been asked in cross-national sur-

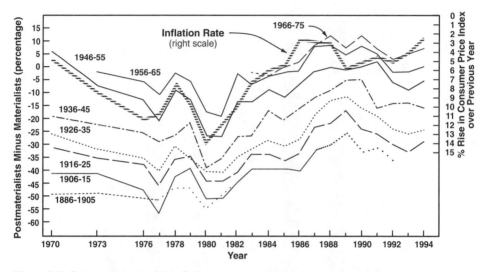

Figure 5.2. Cohort analysis with inflation rate superimposed (using inverted scale on right): percent Postmaterialists minus percent Materialists in eight birth cohorts in six Western European societies, 1970–94. *Source*: Based on combined weighted sample of European Community surveys carried out in West Germany, France, Britain, Italy, the Netherlands, and Belgium, in given years (N = 243,356), and based on the four-item values index, which was included in each of these surveys. Inflation data from statistical office of the European Communities.

veys carried out by the European Community at least once a year in almost every year from 1970 to the present.

Figure 5.2 traces the balance between Materialists and Postmaterialists within given birth cohorts from February 1970 to fall 1994, using the pooled data from the surveys carried out in Britain, France, West Germany, Italy, Belgium, and the Netherlands (an analysis based on more than 240,000 interviews). Each cohort's position at a given time is calculated by subtracting the percentage of Materialists in that cohort from the percentage of Postmaterialists. Thus, at the zero point on the vertical axis, the two groups are equally numerous (the cohort born in 1946–55 was located near this point in 1970). On this graph, the proportion of Postmaterialists increases as we move up the vertical axis; the proportion of Materialists increases as we move down. If the age differences reflected a life-cycle effect, then each of the cohort lines should move downward, toward the Materialist pole, as we move from left to right across this 24-year period.

We find no such downward movement. Instead, the younger birth cohorts remain relatively Postmaterialist throughout the period from 1970 to 1994: given cohorts did not become more Materialist as they aged by almost a quarter of a century—instead, many of these cohorts were slightly *less* Materialist at the end of this period than they were at the start.

WHAT CAUSES THE PERIOD EFFECTS?

In addition to presenting the results of a cohort analysis from 1970 to 1994, figure 5.2 shows the current rate of inflation, superimposed as a heavy shaded line. Since the theory predicts that Postmaterialist values will rise when inflation falls, the inflation index runs from low rates at the top of the graph to high rates toward the bottom. This makes it easy to see that (as predicted) inflation and Postmaterialist values move up and down together, bearing in mind that a *downward* movement of the inflation line indicates *rising* rates of inflation on this graph.

Striking period effects are evident: there was a clear tendency for each cohort to dip toward the Materialist pole during the recession of the mid-1970s and again during the recessions of the early 1980s and the early 1990s. These effects are implicit in the theory, which links Postmaterialist values with economic security. High inflation rates tend to make people feel economically insecure, and as the graph demonstrates, there is a remarkably close fit between current economic conditions and the short-term fluctuations in Materialist/ Postmaterialist values. High levels of inflation depress the proportion of Postmaterialists. But these period effects are transient; they disappear when economic conditions return to normal. In the long run, the values of a given birth cohort are remarkably stable. Despite the fluctuations linked with current economic conditions, the intergenerational differences persist: at virtually every point in time, each younger cohort is significantly less Materialist than all of the older ones. These enduring generational differences reflect differences in the formative conditions that shaped the respective birth cohorts: the older ones were influenced by the hunger and insecurity that prevailed during World War I, the Great Depression, and World War II; the younger ones have grown up in an era of historically unprecedented prosperity.

Strictly speaking, these data do not prove that generational change is taking place: one can never distinguish between cohort effects, period effects, and aging effects on statistical grounds alone, since any one of them is a perfect linear function of the other two. Theoretically, the pattern in figure 5.2 might reflect a combination of life-cycle (or aging) effects plus some mysterious period effect that somehow prevented each cohort from becoming more Materialist as it aged from 1970 to 1994. So far, no one has identified a period effect that might have done this (for a debate on this point, see Clarke and Dutt, 1991; and Inglehart and Abramson, 1994); and if someone did, it would be an ad hoc explanation, designed to fit an existing set of observations.

The generational change hypothesis, on the other hand, was published long before these data were collected—and it predicted both the robust cohort differences subsequently observed, and the period effects. If one agrees that the downward swings toward Materialist values found in the mid-1970s, the early 1980s, and the early 1990s were probably due to the economic fluctuations that occurred in those years (and the empirical fit is very good), then the pattern looks like a clear case of intergenerational value change. If this is true, it has

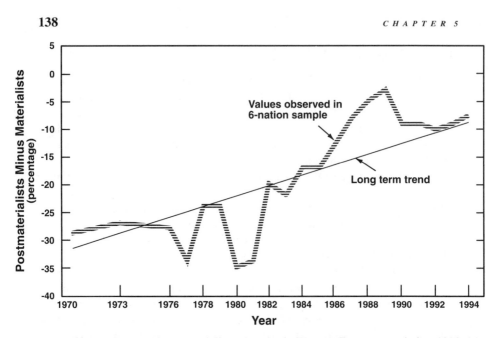

Figure 5.3. The trend toward Postmaterialist values in six Western European societies, 1970–94. The trend toward Postmaterialism is significant at the .001 level. Beta = .61, p < .001. *Source*: Based on combined weighted sample of European Community surveys carried out in West Germany, France, Britain, Italy, the Netherlands, and Belgium, in given years (N = 243,356).

far-reaching implications: in the long run the values of these societies should shift in the predicted direction.

VALUE CHANGES OBSERVED IN WESTERN COUNTRIES, 1970–1994

A good deal of intergenerational population replacement has taken place since 1970. The intergenerational value change thesis predicts that in the long run this should produce a shift from Materialist toward Postmaterialist values among the populations of these societies. More than a quarter century has passed since these values were first measured in 1970. Do we find the predicted value shift? As the following evidence demonstrates, we do indeed. In a companion volume to this book, Abramson and Inglehart (1995) present a far more detailed analysis of the shift from Materialist to Postmaterialist values than is given here. This chapter summarizes and updates the key findings.

Figure 5.3 shows the overall trend among the populations of the six nations first surveyed in 1970. Like the cohort trajectories in the preceding figure, the trend line shown here dips steeply downward in each of the three recent recessions; but the long-term trajectory shows a clear upward trend, and regression analysis reveals that this trend is statistically significant at the .001 level (see Abramson and Inglehart, 1995: ch. 4). Although each given birth cohort in the preceding figure shows relatively little net movement upward or downward from 1970 to 1994, the line for the *total* sample shows a strong upward movement, reflecting intergenerational population replacement: by 1994, the two oldest cohorts had almost completely disappeared from the sample and had been replaced by two younger (and much more Postmaterialist) cohorts. In 1970, the mean position for the sample as a whole was located about halfway between the cohort born in 1916–25 and the cohort born in 1926–35; by 1994 this point had moved up more than two cohorts and was located slightly below the position of the 1946–55 birth cohort. A substantial value shift had occurred in the population as a whole.

In 1970, Materialists outnumbered Postmaterialists overwhelmingly in all of these countries, but by 1994, the balance had shifted markedly toward Postmaterialist values. In 1970, within these six Western European nations as a whole, Materialists outnumbered Postmaterialists by a ratio of about 4 to 1. By 1994, this ratio had fallen to less than 1.5 to 1: Postmaterialists had become almost as numerous as Materialists.

Figure 5.3 shows the trend in six European countries for which detailed time series data are available from more than 40 European Community surveys that were carried out in *each* of these countries from 1970 to 1994. An almost equally detailed time series is available for Denmark and Ireland, from the surveys that were carried out in each country from 1973 to 1994. Figure 5.4 shows the net shift in these eight countries, plus the United States. Eight of the nine countries show a shift from Materialist toward Postmaterialist values, with only Belgium remaining unchanged. In the early 1970s, Materialists heavily outnumbered Postmaterialists in all nine of these countries. By the early 1990s, Postmaterialists had increased almost everywhere and had become more numerous than Materialists in the United States, Denmark, and the Netherlands.

If one knows the relative proportions of Materialists and Postmaterialists in each birth cohort of a given nation, plus the size of each cohort (obtainable from census figures), one can calculate the amount of value shift that would take place each year as a result of intergenerational population replacement. Abramson and Inglehart (1987) have done so, finding that in Western Europe, the population replacement process would bring a shift toward Postmaterialism of slightly more than one point per year in the percentage difference index or PDI (this constitutes the vertical axis in figures 5.2, 5.3, and 5.4). This is a relatively modest gain; in any given year, it could easily be swamped by fluctuations in current conditions linked with security or insecurity. But these short-term fluctuations move in both directions: in the long run, they tend to cancel each other out. The impact of intergenerational population replacement, on the other hand, moves in one continuous direction for decades. In the long run, its cumulative effects can be substantial. This seems to be the case with the data at hand. For these nine countries as a whole, over the 24-year period from 1970 to 1994 the PDI shows a mean shift toward the Postmaterialist pole

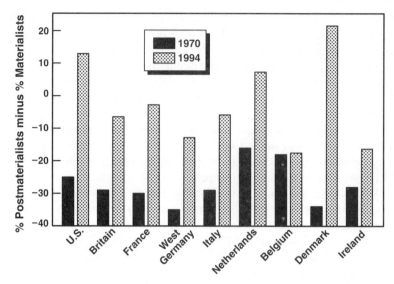

Figure 5.4. The shift toward Postmaterialist values among the publics of nine Western Societies, 1970–94. *Source*: European Community surveys, February 1970 and fall 1994; and U.S. national election surveys from 1972 and 1992.

of 23 points: this is almost exactly the amount of change that would be expected to occur solely as a result of intergenerational population replacement.

Economic conditions were *not* more favorable in 1994 than they were at the start of the series, in 1970; they were worse. The early 1990s were a period of recession, and as figure 5.2 indicates, the levels of Postmaterialism in most cohorts reached a peak about 1989 and declined during the next few years. Nevertheless, as younger, more Postmaterialist cohorts replaced older ones, the population as a whole showed a long-term shift toward Postmaterialist values in almost every country. Despite substantial short-term fluctuations, and despite the fact that the surveys in our most recent year, 1994, occurred when Western Europe was still recovering from a major recession, the predicted shift toward Postmaterialist values took place—and its magnitude was just about the size that would be predicted by an intergenerational population replacement model.

Figure 5.4 shows only the starting point and the end point of each country's time series from 1970 to 1994. In a more detailed analysis of this time series, consisting of at least 33 surveys for each nation, Inglehart and Abramson (1994) examine the trends in each of the eight countries; then, using regression analysis, they demonstrate that Britain, France, West Germany, Italy, the Netherlands, Ireland, and Denmark all show large and statistically significant long-term trends from Materialist to Postmaterialist values over this period. In the eighth case (Belgium), they find no trend. But a time series analysis controlling for the joint effects of inflation and unemployment demonstrates that there is a statistically significant trend toward Postmaterialism in *all eight* of the Western European countries for which a detailed time series is available over the past two decades: Belgium showed no shift toward Postmaterialism because it has suffered much higher levels of unemployment in recent years than in the 1970s, which has largely offset the effects of intergenerational population replacement. When they control for inflation and unemployment, Belgium is no longer a deviant case: it too shows a significant shift toward Postmaterialism. Controlling for inflation and unemployment largely explains the period effects: as the theory implies, high levels of inflation and unemployment encourage an emphasis on economic security, rather than on Postmaterialist values (Inglehart and Abramson, 1994). As we have seen, a substantial shift toward Postmaterialist values also took place in the United States. These data come from the six NES presidential election surveys carried out from 1972 to 1992. Six surveys do not provide a sufficient number of time points to test the trend's statistical significance, but the net effect in the United States seems to be about as large as in most Western European countries.

THE POSTMATERIALIST PHENOMENON: EVOLVING OVER TIME

Much of the literature on Postmaterialism deals with whether it is a deep-rooted phenomenon having a long-term impact on political behavior or simply a transient epiphenomenon. We will reexamine this issue in the light of recent evidence. If a society's basic values change mainly through intergenerational population replacement, we would expect them to change at a gradual pace. But though short-term changes may be small, close examination of their societal location can provide valuable insight into their long-term implications. Contrary to what some observers assumed (Kesselman, 1979), Postmaterialism did not dwindle away in the face of diminished economic and physical security. In most countries its numbers grew, and in many ways its political influence is greater now than it was a decade or two ago; but its character and tactics have changed significantly.

By 1970, Postmaterialists had attained numerical parity with Materialists only among the postwar generation. Furthermore, they were concentrated among the more affluent strata of this age group: among university students, they heavily outnumbered the Materialists. This helps explain the widespread popular perceptions of a generation gap that emerged in the late 1960s and early 1970s. Even among the postwar generation, Materialists were about as numerous as Postmaterialists. But in this age group's most articulate and most visible segment—the university students—there was an overwhelming preponderance of Postmaterialists. The students lived in a distinct milieu: they had highly developed communications networks with other students but were largely isolated from their nonstudent peers. The priorities prevailing in this milieu were fundamentally different from those shaping the society as a whole.

The existence of such a milieu can play an important part in the evolution and propagation of a given set of values. Indeed, Habermas (1979) argues that the rise of Postmaterialism is not due to the different formative experiences of different generation units, but to exposure to the specific worldviews inculcated by distinct communications networks (see also Jaeggi, 1979). But this explanation seems to complement, not substitute for, the one proposed here. It helps account for the spread of values in a given milieu, but provides no explanation of *why* given generation units were disposed to accept given values in the first place, while others rejected them. It seems clear that in virtually all Western nations, the student milieu of the late 1960s *did* constitute a distinct communications network, propagating a distinctive viewpoint. Given these circumstances, it is not surprising that the student elite saw themselves as part of a counterculture that was engaged in an irreconcilable clash with the culture of an older generation: From their viewpoint, the dictum "Don't trust anyone over 30" seemed plausible. Our hypotheses imply that as time went by, the Postmaterialists would become older and more evenly distributed across the population. Hence, the plausibility of a monolithic generation gap would fade away. But in 1970, conditions were optimal to sustain belief in a generation gap, with all youth on one side and all older people on the other.

One of the most important changes derives from the simple fact that, today, Postmaterialists are older than they were when they first emerged as a major political factor in the 1960s. Initially manifested mainly through student protest movements, their most important impact now comes through the activities of elites. For the students have grown older, and Postmaterialism has penetrated deeply into the ranks of professionals, civil servants, managers, and politicians (Inglehart, 1990: ch. 9). It seems to be a major factor in the rise of a "new class" in Western society—a stratum of highly educated and well-paid young technocrats who take an adversarial stance toward their society (Ladd, 1978; Gouldner, 1979; Lipset, 1979). The debate between those giving top priority to economic growth, versus those who emphasize environmentalism and the quality of life, reflects persisting value cleavages.

The Postmaterialists among the protest generation of the 1960s were much more likely to enter academic life, the mass media, and nonprofit foundations than were Materialists: these occupations provided relatively great opportunities for self-expression. By contrast, the Materialists were more likely to go into career paths that maximized one's earning power and financial security, such as business, engineering, and technical fields.

One consequence has been that, as they aged and moved into adult careers, Postmaterialists have become the dominant force in most universities. In the 1960s, they were student protesters; by the 1990s, they were the department chairs and deans. The emergence of the phenomenon of Political Correctness reflects this transition in the dominant culture within universities: values that were controversial in the 1960s had became the values of the establishment in the 1990s. Although some of these values were still controversial in the society as a whole, there was pressure to conform to them within the universities.

VALUE CHANGE BEYOND WESTERN DEMOCRACIES

Although the highly industrialized democracies of Western Europe and North America historically led the shift toward Postmaterialist values, our theory implies that this process should also occur in other nations that develop high levels of prosperity and advanced social welfare networks. Consequently, it should be at work in East Asia (parts of which have now attained Western levels of prosperity) and even in Eastern Europe. The value change theory implies that we should find a higher proportion of Postmaterialists among the younger cohorts than among the old, in *any* society that has had sufficient economic growth during the past four or five decades so that the younger cohorts experienced substantially greater economic security during their preadult years than did those who are now in their fifties, sixties, or seventies.

At first glance, it might seem unlikely that intergenerational value change would be at work in Eastern European countries, since they are far less prosperous than Western Europe and the United States, and their economies are currently in decline. But a country's absolute level of wealth is not the crucial variable: the value change thesis implies (1) that countries with high *levels* of prosperity should have relatively high *levels* of Postmaterialist values, and (2) that countries that have experienced relatively high rates of economic *growth* should show relatively large *differences* between the values of young and old, reflecting the fact that the formative conditions of the respective generations have undergone relatively large amounts of *change*.

Thus, we would indeed expect Russia and other Eastern European countries to show relatively low absolute *levels* of Postmaterialism. But they should also show substantial intergenerational *change* in these values, reflecting the massive differences between the conditions that shaped the formative years of those who grew up during World War I, the Great Depression, and World War II and those who grew up subsequently. The crucial factor governing the emergence of Postmaterialist values is whether one experienced a sense of economic and physical security during one's formative years. Accordingly, we would expect Postmaterialist values to have developed during the past 50 years in Eastern Europe and the former Soviet Union. Though their GNP per capita lags behind that of Western countries, it is far above the subsistence level (and several times as high as that of such countries as China, Nigeria, or India). Throughout the ex-socialist world, the younger birth cohorts have generally experienced greater security during their formative years than did older ones.

In the Russian case, for example, those born in 1920 experienced the civil war and the mass starvation linked with forced collectivization during the 1920s, followed by the terror and Stalinist purges of the 1930s, and mass starvation and the loss of 27 million lives in the Soviet Union during World War II. The 1950s and 1960s, by contrast, were an era of recovery and rapid economic growth at rates that exceeded those of most Western countries. This was the era that led Khrushchev to boast "We will bury you" economically—and at the time, many Western observers thought it a plausible claim. Recent years have been calamitous, creating a period effect that tends to drive all of the Russian cohorts downward toward the Materialist pole. But the formative years of the younger cohorts were far more secure than those of the older cohorts, and if the intergenerational *differences* reflect differences in preadult experience rather than current conditions, we would indeed expect to find evidence of intergenerational change in Eastern Europe.

From 1945 to about 1980, most Eastern European countries had impressive rates of economic growth; in the early decades, it seemed likely that they would catch up with and surpass the West. Since 1980, their economies have decayed, but there is no question that the average Pole or Russian experienced far greater economic and physical *security* during the era from 1950 to 1980 than during the period from 1915 to 1945.

The emergence of Postmaterialist values in Eastern Europe might be reinforced by the fact that the welfare systems of socialist states partially compensated for their relatively low levels of prosperity. The key factor in value change is not one's absolute income, but the degree of *security* experienced during one's formative years. The communist regimes of Eastern Europe provided a relatively secure existence during most of the postwar era: job security was very high, rents were low, basic foods were provided at subsidized prices, and medical care and education were free. The quality of what one got was poor, but one was sure of getting it.

East Asia contrasts with Eastern Europe. Fifty years ago, it was far less developed than Eastern Europe; as recently as 1950, Japan's annual per capita income was only a fraction of that in such Eastern European countries as Czechoslovakia, Poland, or Hungary—and the Chinese and South Korean per capita incomes were a fraction of Japan's. But in recent decades, East Asia (including China, since the pragmatists took power in 1976) has shown the most rapid economic growth rates in the world. By 1990, per capita income in South Korea and Taiwan had reached Eastern European levels and Japan was one of the richest countries in the world. Even China was experiencing annual growth rates of around 10 percent, enough to double GNP every seven years.

Thus, the older East Asian birth cohorts grew up under conditions of extreme scarcity, while the youngest ones have experienced relatively secure circumstances throughout their formative years. Consequently, we would expect these countries to show low proportions of Postmaterialists overall, but relatively steep rates of intergenerational change. The Eastern European countries, by comparison, started out at much higher levels but have grown less rapidly: we would expect to find higher proportions of Postmaterialists than in East Asia, but less intergenerational change. Figure 5.5 shows the value differences across the respective birth cohorts, using 1990 World Values Survey data from countries in Eastern Europe and East Asia, together with the European Union and the United States, using the 12-item values indicator.

As figure 5.5 illustrates, the younger birth cohorts do, indeed, show considerably higher proportions of Postmaterialists than the older cohorts in most of these societies. The intergenerational shift from Materialist to Postmaterialist

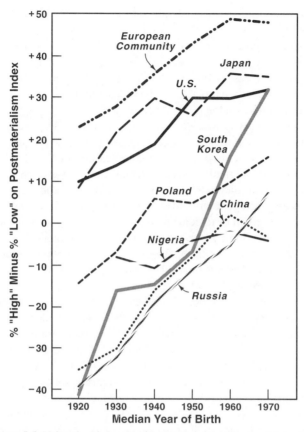

Figure 5.5. Values by birth cohort in Western democracies, Eastern Europe, East Asia, and Africa. *Source*: 1990–93 World Values Survey. *Note*: Respondents are classified as "high" on the 12-item Materialist/Postmaterialist values index used here if they gave high priority to at least three of the five Postmaterialist goals (ranking them among the two most important in each group of four goals). They are classified as "low" if they gave high priority to none of the five Postmaterialist goals.

values is not limited to Western democracies: it is found across advanced industrial societies with a wide variety of political and economic institutions, and a wide variety of cultural traditions. Although the richer countries have much higher absolute proportions of Postmaterialists than the poorer ones, we also find a steep slope reflecting intergenerational value differences in poor countries that have experienced a rapid increase in prevailing standards of living during the past several decades.

Results from several European Union countries have already been examined in detail and are combined into a single line on figure 5.5 to simplify the picture. Overall, the European Union shows the highest proportion of Postmaterialists on this graph, with the United States and Japan also ranking high. Even the oldest birth cohorts in these advanced industrial societies rank higher than even the youngest cohorts in most other countries. But an upward slope, reflecting a rising proportion of Postmaterialists to Materialists as we move from old to young, is also found in Eastern Europe and East Asia.

In virtually every case, from North America to Western Europe to Eastern Europe to East Asia, as we move from the oldest cohorts at the left of the graph to the youngest cohorts at the right, the ratio of Postmaterialists to Materialists rises. This is exactly what we would expect to find if intergenerational value change were occurring. To prove that it is, we would need data from a long time series, and thus far such data are available only for Western Europe and, to a lesser extent, the United States and Japan. But in every country for which substantial time series data *are* available, the evidence indicates that these age differences reflect intergenerational change, rather than life-cycle effects: there is no tendency for given birth cohorts to become more Materialist as they age. Furthermore, as this finding implies, the ratio of Postmaterialists to Materialists has gradually risen over time. We believe that the other countries shown in figure 5.5 are on a trajectory similar to that on which Western nations and Japan have been moving in recent decades.

Figure 5.5 presents a great deal of information, reflecting the twentieth-century history of each nation; it could be discussed at considerable length. The data reveal huge cross-national differences. Thus, there are far more Postmaterialists in the United States and the European Union than in South Korea, but the slope rises steeply in South Korea, suggesting that a very rapid process of intergenerational change is taking place there. During the past quarter century, only one country in the world (Singapore) has had a higher rate of economic growth than South Korea, which shows the steepest slope in the graph. Among its oldest birth cohort there are literally *no* Postmaterialists; 70 percent fall into the pure Materialist category and 30 percent are mixed types (producing an index of -40 on the vertical axis). Among its youngest cohort, Materialists outnumber Postmaterialists by only 10 points.

If Postmaterialist values simply reflected current conditions, one would not expect to find a shift from Materialist to Postmaterialist values in such countries as Russia and Poland, which experienced economic stagnation during the decade preceding these surveys and by 1990 were in a state of economic collapse. But the theory postulates a long-term process of intergenerational change based on the differences experienced during a given cohort's preadult years. From this perspective, we *would* expect to find intergenerational value differences in Eastern Europe, for it is clear that the formative experiences of the cohorts born in the 1950s, the 1960s, and the 1970s were characterized by far more secure circumstances than is true of those who experienced the traumatic upheavals of the 1920s, 1930s, or 1940s. And we do find evidence of intergenerational change. As figure 5.5 demonstrates, the Russian results show an upward slope. Although the Russian cohort line starts and ends at a level far below that of the richer countries, intergenerational differences in Russia are even steeper than those found in Western Europe, the United States, or Japan.

China shows an equally steep slope, reflecting sharp intergenerational differences that may have contributed to the spring 1989 clash between young intellectuals and the aging leadership still in control of the army. These intergenerational differences reflect the massive differences between the formative experiences of the older generation in China, who lived through an era of mass starvation and civil war that went on almost continuously from the 1920s to 1949, and those of the younger cohorts, brought up in conditions of relative stability and prosperity—broken by the severe but relatively brief upheavals of the Great Leap Forward and the Cultural Revolution in the late 1960s. China has had a series of wild swings since 1949, including periods of extremely rapid economic growth and periods of severe economic decline. As recently as 1959–60, millions of people starved to death; but this was a relatively brief period, compared with the decades of slaughter and starvation that dominated the warlord period, the civil war, and World War II. By these standards, the communist victory in 1949 brought a distinct improvement. And for the past two decades, China has experienced exceptional economic growth, with an average rate higher than Japan's. Our data reflect these facts: China starts out with an extremely low proportion of Postmaterialists among its oldest cohorts, but then shows a steep upward slope (though not as steep as that found in South Korea) as we move to its younger cohorts. Although its absolute level of Postmaterialism remains far below that of most Western countries, China seems to be on a similar trajectory, and (as we will argue in the following chapter) further economic development should bring expanding mass support for democratization.

The European Union countries show a steeper rate of change than does the United States, reflecting their higher growth rates since World War II. While among the older Western European cohorts, Materialists substantially outnumber Postmaterialists (and thus fall well below the zero level on this graph), all three of the cohorts born after 1945 rise above this threshold—indeed, the two youngest European Union cohorts rank well above their American counterparts.

The value differences across age groups are greater in Western Europe than in the United States—which implies that Western Europe is manifesting a more rapid rate of value change over time. This has indeed been the case. In 1972, when the American public was first surveyed, it showed a considerably higher proportion of Postmaterialists than did the combined six European Union countries for which data were then available; but subsequently, Western Europe has caught up. Nevertheless, the United States has shown a significant movement in the predicted direction.

For the most part, the findings from Japan fit theoretical expectations. Its overall proportion of Postmaterialists ranks just after the United States and Western Europe and well above most of the other countries in figure 5.5, as one would expect of a country that has now attained a high per capita income. Moreover, in Japan as in virtually all advanced industrial societies, Postmaterialist values are more widespread among the younger cohorts than among the

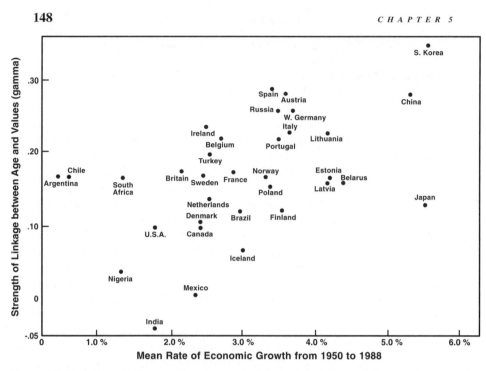

Figure 5.6. Societies with fast-growing economies have relatively large differences between the values of young and old.

r = .52, p < .001. *Source*: 1990–93 World Values Survey. Based on 12-item Materialist/Postmaterialist values index. *Note*: Data on economic growth were not available for several Eastern European countries.

older ones. Furthermore, the ratio of Postmaterialists to Materialists has gradually risen over time, in Japan as in the United States and Western Europe. In 1972, the first Japanese survey to measure these values found 43 percent Materialists and only 5 percent Postmaterialists—a preponderance of more than 8 to 1 (Watanuki, 1977). In the 1981 World Values Survey, the figures had shifted to 37 and 6 percent, respectively, a ratio of 6 to 1. And the 1990 World Values Survey found 29 percent Materialists and 10 percent Postmaterialists: the ratio had fallen to less than 3 to 1. In these respects, the Japanese findings confirm the theory's predictions. One finding is surprising, however: as one of the world's most rapidly growing economies, we would expect to find a steeper slope for Japan than for most other countries, but we do not.

Figure 5.5 would be unreadable if it included the results from all 43 societies for which data are available, but we should note that two important countries do *not* show any indication of intergenerational change: India and Nigeria. The data for Nigeria are plotted on figure 5.5. The line is almost horizontal, reflecting virtually no intergenerational change. The Indian data are not shown here, but as figure 5.6 demonstrates, the relationship between values and age is even weaker there, with younger groups being slightly *less* Postmaterialist than the old. A combination of relatively slow industrialization and rapid population growth during most of the period from 1945 to 1990 kept India from developing at anything approaching the East Asian rate. Nigeria has had virtually no increase in GNP per capita since 1965, and its public also shows a flat relationship between age and values. These findings indicate that intergenerational value change is not inherent in the human condition: as our theory implies, we find it in those countries where the formative years of the younger cohorts were shaped by significantly higher levels of economic security than those of the older cohorts. In countries that have *not* experienced economic development, intergenerational value differences are absent.

ECONOMIC GROWTH AND VALUE CHANGE

The value change thesis implies that large amounts of intergenerational *change* will be found in countries that have experienced relatively high rates of economic *growth*. Figure 5.6 tests this hypothesis against the data from all of the societies for which we have data, and not just the selected examples just discussed. To present the findings from more than 40 societies on one graph, figure 5.6 condenses the relationship between age and values for each country into a single coefficient. As this figure demonstrates, the selected examples shown in figure 5.5 reflect the overall pattern: intergenerational value differences tend to be largest in countries that have experienced the greatest amounts of economic growth during the past 40 years. Accordingly, the correlation between age and values is strongest in such countries as South Korea and China, and weak or even negative in such countries as Nigeria and India—which have not only experienced much lower rates of economic growth than China or South Korea, but which also have much more unequal income distributions, so that substantial proportions of the population live at the edge of starvation.

Note that the intergenerational value differences are also relatively weak in the United States: though it has a relatively high absolute *level* of Postmaterialism, its rate of intergenerational *change* is relatively small. Although the United States has been one of the world's richest countries since the nineteenth century, it has not experienced dramatic changes between the formative experiences of younger and older cohorts like those found in Europe and East Asia. The United States has been a relatively rich country throughout the lifetime of everyone in the sample and was not devastated by World War II—but the United States has had relatively slow growth in recent decades.

As usual, we find deviant cases. Argentina and Chile are "overachievers," showing larger intergenerational differences than their economic growth rates would predict; and, as we have seen, Japan is an "underachiever," showing smaller intergenerational value differences than its historic economic growth rate would predict. But overall, the pattern fits our theoretical expectations. High rates of economic growth tend to go with large intergenerational value differences (r = .41, statistically significant at the .01 level).

ECONOMIC SECURITY AND VALUE CHANGE:
NEW EVIDENCE FROM 40 SOCIETIES

The value change thesis also implies that high *levels* of prosperity should be conducive to high *levels* of Postmaterialism, so rich countries should tend to have more Postmaterialists than poor ones.

Disputing this thesis, Trump (1991) and Duch and Taylor (1993), drawing on data from only three societies, have claimed that Postmaterialist values are *not* more likely to be found in prosperous countries or regions than in poor ones. The World Values surveys provide strong evidence that they *are*. These surveys cover an unprecedentedly broad range of the economic spectrum, with data from low-income nations, middle-income countries, and advanced industrial democracies having per capita incomes 60 or 70 times as high as those of the poorest countries.

Our theory implies that the shift from Materialist to Postmaterialist priorities is potentially universal: it should occur in any country that moves from conditions of economic insecurity to relative security (though during a transitional period, older generations will continue to reflect the conditions that characterized their preadult experiences). This has clear implications: people living in rich countries generally experience more economic security than those in poor nations, where the pie is not only smaller but also tends to be less evenly distributed, and many people live on the edge of starvation. Accordingly, we would expect high levels of GNP/capita to be linked with relatively high levels of Postmaterialist values.

Although this implication is straightforward, until recently it was not possible to test it adequately because most of the surveys exploring values (like most surveys in general) have been carried out in relatively developed societies. Using the 1990–91 World Values Surveys we can now test this hypothesis across the full range of economic development. The results confirm that hypothesis, as figure 5.7 demonstrates (using the 12-item values index). Rich countries tend to have much higher proportions of Postmaterialists than poorer countries. Although some rich countries such as Norway and the United States are "underachievers" and some poorer countries such as Mexico and Turkey are "overachievers," the overall correlation is remarkably strong: r = .68, significant at the .0001 level.

Diez Nicolas (1994) demonstrates that this relationship also holds true at the regional level, within a given nation. He has included the Materialist/Postmaterialist values battery in *monthly* national surveys of the Spanish public since 1988, obtaining nearly 55,000 interviews in the period 1989–92. Cumulating large numbers of interviews from each region enables him to perform statistically reliable analyses of the relationship between values and economic security at the regional level, in a country that has large amounts of regional variation. This provides a much more reliable base on which to test this hypothesis than the 741 secondary school students on which Trump (1991) relied for ev-

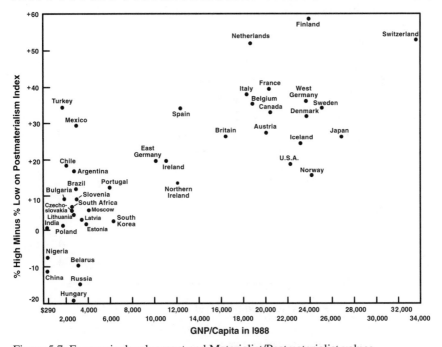

Figure 5.7. Economic development and Materialist/Postmaterialist values.
r = .68, p < .0001. *Source*: 1990–93 World Values Survey. GNP/capita from World
Bank, *World Development Report, 1993. Note*: Respondents are classified as "high" on
the 12-item Materialist/Postmaterialist values index used here if they gave high priority to at least three of the five Postmaterialist goals (ranking them among the two most
important in each group of four goals). They are classified as "low" if they gave high
priority to none of the five Postmaterialist goals.

idence that regional economic variations in the United States are unrelated to
Postmaterialist values.

Diez Nicolas finds that the relative level of Postmaterialism varies a good
deal from region to region and is quite stable from one year to the next. The
wealthiest regions (the Basque country and greater Madrid) consistently have
the highest proportions of Postmaterialists; and the poorest regions (Andalu-
sia, Extremadura, and Castille-La Mancha) show the lowest proportions of
Postmaterialists in virtually every year. As figure 5.8 shows, this relationship
is very strong, and it shows a particularly good fit with a given region's level
of economic development 25 years prior to the survey, during the median respondent's preadult years (r = .83). Here again, the evidence indicates that
economic security has a powerful linkage with the emergence of Postmaterialist values.

Duch and Taylor (1993) and Davis (1996) suggest that the value shift we observe is due simply to rising levels of education. Do richer countries and richer

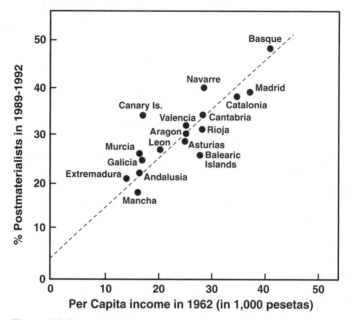

Figure 5.8. Postmaterialist values by economic level of Spanish regions one generation before surveys.
N = 54,557, r = .83. *Source*: Juan Diez Nicolas, "Postmaterialismo y Desarrollo Economico en Espana," paper presented at World Conference on Social Values, Madrid, September 27–October 1, 1993.

regions have larger numbers of Postmaterialists simply because their publics are better educated?

As our theory implies, we do indeed find that the better educated in every country are likelier to have Postmaterialist values than the less educated. In large part, this reflects the fact that one's educational level is an excellent indicator of how economically secure one was during one's *formative* years. For the great majority of people, one's education is completed in their preadult years; and how much education they get is closely related to how well-off their parents were during that period: economically secure families give their children more years of education than economically insecure ones. We would also expect the upper-income and occupational groups to be more Postmaterialist than the lower ones, but one's educational level is a considerably better indicator of security during one's formative years than is one's *current* income or occupation. Education gets closer to the key causal factor, which is *formative* security. One's income or occupation reflects one's *current* economic level. But one's education not only taps current prosperity but is also an excellent indicator of how prosperous one's *parents* were.

An alternative explanation would focus on some form of indoctrination: the better educated are more likely to have Postmaterialist values because their teachers teach them these values. Some version of this seems to be what Duch and Taylor, and Davis have in mind—though this interpretation fails to explain why (as our data demonstrate) those who received a higher education in the era before World War II are *not* predominantly Postmaterialists.

Still another possible explanation for why we would expect the better educated to be more Postmaterialistic lies in the fact that the better educated generally have better jobs and higher incomes than the less educated: they have relatively high levels of *current* economic security, which, the theory implies, should also be conducive to Postmaterialist values. We don't rule out either indoctrination or current prosperity as possible contributing factors: our theory holds that security during one's formative years is conducive to the emergence of Postmaterialist values, and not that it is the *only* influence on these values. The question is "What is the relative importance of these factors?"

Our theory emphasizes the role of formative security. But one's educational level is linked with current prosperity, exposure to indoctrination, and how well-off one's family was during a person's formative years. In order to separate these mingled influences, we will perform a multiple regression analysis. But we have a problem in doing so: this approach will almost inevitably underestimate the impact of formative experiences. The reason why it will do so is simple: recall data virtually always contain a good deal more measurement error than do reports of one's own current characteristics. Most respondents can give pretty accurate information concerning their own income, occupation, or educational level at the time of the survey. But their report of their parents' characteristics when they were growing up almost inevitably is contaminated with a good deal of measurement error. First, there is the simple fact that they are not reporting their own characteristics now—they are reporting someone else's characteristics when they were growing up—which may have been 30 or 40 years ago. These problems are especially acute with recall data concerning one's parents' *income*: this is something that may have varied a good deal from one year to the next and, quite often, was something that the parents did not discuss with their children. We ask the reader, "What was your parents' income level when you were growing up?" Hardly anyone can give a precise figure—but most people can provide a pretty accurate account of their *own* income at the time of the survey. Consequently, recall data on parental income will almost certainly explain less of the variance in one's attitudes than data on one's own current income: its explanatory power is weakened by a great deal of measurement error. Recall data on one's parents' occupation has some of these same problems—it deals with something that may be quite distant in time, may have varied, and may not have been clearly conveyed to the child; but most people can give at least a fairly accurate idea of what their parents' occupation was when they were growing up. The same is true of one's parents' educational level: it suffers from the measurement problems inherent in recall data about someone else's characteristics, possibly a long time ago; but one's parents' educational level was a fixed characteristic in most cases, and one can get a more accurate measurement of it than of parental income during one's formative years.

In short, it is considerably more difficult to get an accurate measure of "formative security" than it is to get one of one's current economic characteristics—which tends to weaken the relative explanatory power of formative security in any regression analysis that runs one against the other. Nevertheless, let us carry out the test, using the best measure of formative security that we can get. For this purpose, the best data we know of are those from the *Political Action* surveys (Barnes et al., 1979) carried out in the 1970s. In order to obtain a relatively good indicator of formative security, we construct a multi-item index based on the reported educational level of the respondent's mother and father, plus the reported occupation of the respondent's father (most respondents' mothers didn't have one, when they were growing up). Table 5.1 shows the results of multiple regression through the origin, in each of the six countries for which these data are available.

As table 5.1 demonstrates, our theory is clearly upheld in every one of the six societies. For our indicator of formative security not only reduces the correlation between the respondent's educational level and his or her values: in all six societies, our indicator of formative security, based on recall data concerning the respondent's parents' educational and occupational level when the respondent was growing up, actually explains *more* of the variance in his or her values than does the respondent's own educational level.

This is a truly remarkable set of findings. Normally, one would expect an individual's own current characteristics to provide a far stronger explanation of his or her own values or attitudes than the status of some other person—particularly since our measure of parental SES is based on recall data reporting the status of another person at a time that may be several decades in the past. But despite all the problems inherent in recall data, we find that the respondent's *parents'* SES consistently provides an even stronger explanation of the respondent's values, than does his or her *own* educational level.

These two variables, by themselves, explain most of the variance in Materialist/Postmaterialist values in every country; across the six societies, they account for 79 percent of the variance. And the most important factor is Formative Security, not the respondent's education. This holds true only rather narrowly in Italy, where (as the respective beta coefficients demonstrate) Formative Security accounts for slightly more of the variance in values than does the respondent's educational level. In Germany, the Netherlands, Austria, the United States, and Finland, the predominance of Formative Security is one-sided; and for the six nations as a whole, the beta coefficient for Formative Security is .635—more than twice the size of the coefficient for respondent's educational level, which is .266.

One could scarcely hope for a clearer demonstration of the fact that these values are *not* simply the result of indoctrination in the schools, or a reflection of the fact that the better educated tend to have higher incomes. The impact of one's *formative* experiences seems to have a considerably greater impact on Materialist/Postmaterialist values than the individual's educational level. For-

TABLE 5.1
Dependent Variable: VAR0340 INDEX1 — Materialist/Postmaterialist Values: 4 pt
Independent Variables: Formative Security, Computed According to the Following Formula:
INDEX1 = [2 × (VAR0162/25) + VAR0168 + VAR0172]/4,
where   VAR0162—Father's Occupation: Standard Prestige Scores
        VAR0168—Father's Education Type
        VAR0172—Mother's Education Type
VAR0214 Respondent's Educational Level

| | | | | Simple Regression Beta Coefficients (for Respondent's Educational Level) | Multivariate Analysis | | | | | |
| | | | | | Regression Coefficients | | Beta Coefficients | | |
Number	Country	Number of Cases	Number of Valid Cases		Formative Security	Educational Level	Formative Security	Educational Level	R Square
1	Germany	2,307	1,841	.868	.724 (.040)	.427 (.040)	.566	.338	.794
2	Netherlands	1,201	993	.871	1.171 (.059)	.485 (.062)	.665	.260	.828
3	Austria	1,585	1,205	.872	.956 (.054)	.411 (.051)	.628	.286	.812
4	United States	1,719	1,246	.857	.788 (.056)	.328 (.045)	.590	.305	.783
5	Italy	1,779	1,385	.876	.742 (.046)	.601 (.040)	.475	.442	.808
6	Finland	1,224	1,005	.870	1.113 (.065)	.443 (.062)	.649	.268	.816
	All Countries	12,558	7,675	.858	.952 (.021)	.365 (.020)	.635	.266	.789

Notes: Standard errors in parentheses. All regressions are significant at 1% level (based upon regression through the origin). No data available for VAR0172 (Mother's Education Type) in the British and Swiss surveys.
Source: "Political Action—An Eight Nation Study," 1979.

mative Security seems to play a key role in the emergence of Postmaterialist values.

CHANGES IN THE WORLD VALUES SURVEY, 1981–1990

Data from a long time series would be needed to demonstrate directly that economic development tends to produce an intergenerational shift toward Postmaterialist values globally, and such data are not available for most of these countries. Although the time series evidence that *is* available has a remarkably good fit with the predictions of the Postmaterialist value shift thesis, most of it comes from nine Western nations. We can supplement it with a modest amount of additional time series data from the World Values surveys: for 21 of these countries, data from the four-item values battery is available from both the 1981 and the 1990–91 surveys.

Table 5.2 shows the distribution of Materialist and Postmaterialist values in 1981 and 1990 for 21 countries. We also have World Values survey data from these time points for one additional country, Denmark, but we do not present them here. The 1981 Danish sample seems to have been unrepresentative: its results are far out of line with the results from other countries, and also with the results from other Danish surveys carried out at the same time. Consequently we do not use this survey as a basis of cross-time comparisons in this book (details concerning the 1981 Danish sample are presented in Appendix 2).

As table 5.2 shows, 18 out of these 21 countries show a shift in the predicted direction, from 1981 to 1990–91. South Korea shows no net shift, which is surprising. Only two countries (Iceland and South Africa) show shifts in the opposite direction from the one predicted. We have no explanation for why Iceland is a deviant case, but it is not surprising that South Africa shows a shift toward Materialist goals. A society's values at any given time point reflect a combination of long-term trends and current period effects—and South Africa experienced a period of severe insecurity during the 1980s. Its economy, suffering from international boycott and low commodity prices, experienced economic stagnation throughout the 1980s. Moreover, widespread violence and political instability gave rise to growing concern for physical security among both blacks and whites. Powerful period effects were working to produce a sense of insecurity, rather than the security that contributes to Postmaterialist values.

A generalized shift toward Postmodern values seems to be taking place. With only two time points available, the World Values surveys database does not enable one to distinguish period effects from long-term trends, but it does provide data from a wide range of nations. Here again, the findings show a shift from Materialist to Postmaterialist values, complementing the findings from the much more detailed time series available from eight Western European countries.

TABLE 5.2

The Shift Toward Postmaterialist Values: Results from the 1981 vs. 1990 World Values Surveys (Percentage Postmaterialist Minus Percentage Materialist)

	1981	*1990*	*Net Shift*
Finland	21	23	+2
Netherlands	−2	26	+28
Canada	−6	14	+20
Iceland	−10	−14	−4
Sweden	−10	9	+19
W. Germany	−11	14	+25
Britain	−13	0	+13
France	−14	4	+18
Belgium	−16	2	+18
S. Africa	−16	−33	−17
Mexico	−19	−14	+5
Ireland	−20	−4	+16
Argentina	−20	−6	+14
Norway	−21	−19	+2
U.S.*	−24	6	+30
Japan	−32	−19	+13
S. Korea	−34	−34	0
Italy	−39	7	+46
Spain	−41	−6	+35
N. Ireland	−45	−7	+38
Hungary	−50	−41	+9

*The values question was not asked in the U.S. in the 1981 survey; results are from the 1980 NES survey.

Source: 1981 and 1990 World Values surveys.

CONCLUSIONS

The value change thesis predicts a gradual intergenerational shift from Materialist values toward Postmaterialist values. During the years from 1970 to 1994, a statistically significant shift toward Postmaterialist values took place in all eight Western European countries for which a detailed time series is available; similar shifts seem to have occurred in the United States, Japan, and many other countries around the world.

The trend toward Postmaterialism is not automatic. It does not seem to be taking place in Nigeria or India. Although generational replacement tends to push Postmaterialism upward throughout advanced industrial society, such economic factors as inflation and unemployment also affect value change. The consequences of the breakup of the Soviet Union have been massive, and current conditions there are harrowing. In settings of extreme uncertainty such as the former Soviet Union, with falling living standards and declining life expectancy, we would *not* expect to find a movement toward Postmaterialism. On the contrary, our theory implies that current conditions in Russia or Belarus would bring increasing emphasis on Materialist values.

The data we have examined make two points clear: first, the shift from Materialist to Postmaterialist values is not a uniquely Western phenomenon. It is found in societies with widely different institutions and cultural traditions. The rise of Postmaterialist values is closely linked with prosperity and seems to occur wherever a society has experienced enough economic growth in recent decades so that the younger birth cohorts have experienced significantly greater economic security during their formative years than did the older cohorts. In societies that are not yet well launched on industrialization, on the other hand, there are few Postmaterialists and little difference between the values of young and old: intergenerational value differences reflect a society's rate of economic growth. Economic growth, of course, is only one factor that contributes to security or insecurity. Other events such as war, domestic upheaval, and ethnic conflict can also have a major impact, but they tend to be situation-specific (and are less readily quantified), making them more difficult to analyze empirically.

Second, where value change has occurred, intergenerational differences are remarkably robust. In Western Europe, clear and sizable differences between the values of younger and older birth cohorts persisted through the recessions of the mid-1970s and the early 1980s. More remarkably still, in Russia and Eastern Europe sizable intergenerational value differences have persisted through the collapse of the economic and political systems in recent years. These values show predictable period effects in response to current economic conditions. But the Postmaterialist value shift does not simply reflect current conditions. It also has a long-term component that seems to reflect the distinctive formative circumstances that given birth cohorts experienced as much as 40 or 50 years ago.

As we have seen, cultural change has a rational component: it tends to follow the principle of diminishing marginal utility. But the enduring intergenerational differences found here undermine any simplistic version of rational choice theory that would seek to explain behavior as a response to one's immediate situation, unshaped by internal cultural differences. For we find persisting generational differences that seem to reflect the enduring legacy of the distinctive formative experiences of given generations. At any point in time, the respective birth cohorts in a given society are in the same situation as their elders but respond to it in fundamentally different ways because they evaluate it by different values. These different responses to the same situation do not simply reflect that fact that the respective cohorts are of different ages, for their distinctive values continue to characterize given cohorts even after they have aged over many years.

Inglehart (1990) found that orientations concerning a wide variety of domains, from politics to religion, to sexual norms to childrearing values, were correlated with Materialist/Postmaterialist values. Evidence presented in chapters 9 and 10 indicates that this broader cluster of Postmodern values is undergoing an intergenerational value shift, similar to the shift from Materialist toward Postmaterialist values. Thus, the detailed evidence now available about the Postmaterialist shift may help us understand the far broader cultural shift from survival values to Postmodern values.

Economic Development, Political Culture, and Democracy: Bringing the People Back In

A GENERATION AGO, Lipset (1959), Rostow (1961), Dahl (1971), and others argued that economic development leads to democracy. This claim was disputed by dependency school writers, who argued that development was more likely to lead to bureaucratic authoritarianism than to democracy; and more recently, Arat (1988) and Gonick and Rosh (1988) claimed to have disproven Lipset's thesis on the basis of empirical analyses. Nevertheless, the evidence indicates that development is indeed conducive to democracy (Bollen, 1979, 1980, 1993; Bollen and Jackman, 1985; Brunk, Caldeira, and Lewis-Beck, 1987).

Figure 6.1 shows one piece of the evidence. It reveals that as of 1987, out of the 42 countries with per capita incomes under $500 only one (India) was democratic. Among countries with incomes from $500 to $1,000, only four out of 15 were democracies. But among countries with incomes over $6,000, 20 of the 26 were democratic (the exceptions being then East Germany, Czechoslovakia, Kuwait, Saudi Arabia, United Arab Emirates, and Singapore). Although there is no one-to-one relationship between economic development and democratization, rich countries are much likelier to have democratic institutions than are poor countries.

This relationship between democracy and economic development is not merely cross-sectional—it helps predict which countries are most likely to *become* democratic. Thus, during the avalanche of democratization that took place during the four years after 1987, most of the countries that began the transition to democracy were drawn from the upper middle income group, with per capita incomes from $1,000 to $6,000. This includes such countries as Chile, Nicaragua, Turkey, South Korea, and most of Eastern Europe (including both Czechoslovakia and East Germany). By 1992, democracy remained very rare in low-income countries, but a majority of the countries in the upper middle income group had governments that came to power through free elections.

Burkhart and Lewis-Beck (1994) have provided the latest and most conclusive demonstration of the fact that economic development is conducive to democracy, using more reliable time series data and more rigorous methodology than that of Arat (1988) or Gonick and Rosh (1988), and finding (1) that economic development is conducive to democracy, and (2) but democracy is *not* conducive to economic development. On the latter point they confirm Helliwell's (1994) finding that, despite the spectacular success of the authoritarian model of development in East Asia, economic development is about as likely to take place in democratic as in authoritarian regimes.

These are important findings, but they leave a major question unanswered:

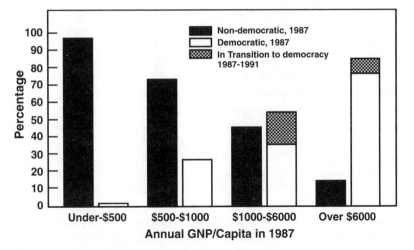

Figure 6.1. Economic development and the transition to democracy. *Source*: GNP per capita from World Bank, *World Development Report, 1989*, pp. 164–65. "Democracies" consist of countries coded as "free" in Raymond D. Gastil (ed.), *Freedom in the World*, 1986–87 (New York: Freedom House, 1987): 30–34. This figure includes only those countries for which data are available for both variables.

Why does economic development lead to democracy? Is the linkage between development and democracy due to wealth per se? Apparently not: if democracy automatically resulted from simply becoming wealthy, then Kuwait and Libya would be model democracies. It is important to bear this point in mind: wealth *alone* does not automatically produce democracy. It seems clear that additional steps are involved. This chapter argues that economic development is conducive to democracy *provided* that it brings certain changes in culture and social structure.

Lerner (1958), Deutsch (1964), and others had argued that modern economic development brings social mobilization, facilitating mass participation in politics, which helps prepare the way for democracy. We believe that they were right, but this is only part of the story. Building on the work of Almond and Verba (1963), Inglehart (1988, 1990), Diamond, Linz, and Lipset (1990), and Putnam (1993), we will demonstrate that economic development is conducive to democracy not only because it mobilizes mass publics, but also because it tends to give rise to supportive cultural orientations. Our analysis utilizes empirical measures of culture from the 1990–93 World Values surveys carried out in 41 societies around the world representing 70 percent of the world's population, to demonstrate that both social structure and political culture play important roles in the emergence and survival of democracy.

The idea that political culture was linked with democracy had great impact following the publication of *The Civic Culture* (Almond and Verba, 1963), but went out of fashion during the 1970s for a variety of reasons. The political culture approach raised an important empirical question: whether given societies had political cultures that were relatively conducive to democracy. Some critics alleged that this approach was "elitist" in finding that some cultures were more conducive to democracy than others: any right-minded theory should hold that all societies are equally likely to be democratic. The problem is that by tailoring one's theory to fit a given ideology, one may come up with a theory that does not fit reality, in which case, one's predictions will eventually go wrong, and the theory will provide misleading guidance to those who are trying to cope with democratization in the real world.

By the 1980s, though the concept of political culture was still unfashionable in American academic circles, observers in other countries, from Latin America to Eastern Europe to East Asia, were coming to the conclusion that cultural factors played an important role in the problems they were encountering with democratization. Thus Mikhail Gorbachev observed, "We are now, as it were, going through the school of democracy afresh. We are learning. Our political culture is still inadequate. Our standard of debate is inadequate; our ability to respect the point of view of even our friends and comrades—even that is inadequate" (Gorbachev, cited in Brzezinski, 1989: 44). Even in Latin America, where the dependency perspective had been extremely influential, cultural factors are now being accorded a key role in democratization. Thus in 1990, a conference of leading politicians and intellectuals from throughout Latin America concluded

> Democracy and sustainable development will depend in large measure on the ability of individual societies to modernize from within. . . . Changes in the practical exercise of power and the reorganization of systems of production give rise to changes not only in political, social and economic institutions, but also in culture and in the behavior of individuals molded by that culture. The other vital dimension of the challenge facing societies in the early stages of democratization is the forging of a democratic political culture. (Declaration of Montevideo, 1990, cited in Albala-Bertrand, 1992: 156–57)

Cultural factors have been omitted from most empirical analyses of democracy—partly because, until now, we have not had reliable measures of them from more than a handful of countries. When cultural factors *are* taken into account, as in Inglehart's (1990) and Putnam's (1993) work, they seem to play an important role.

We will briefly describe which factors are important to democracy and why, and discuss the nature of our dependent variable, democracy, in presenting the theory underlying this analysis. We claim that economic development leads to two types of changes that are conducive to democracy: it gives rise to social structural changes that *mobilize* mass participation; and cultural changes that help *stabilize* democracy.

Structural changes. Industrialization tends to transform a society's social structure, bringing urbanization, mass education, occupational specialization, growing organizational networks, greater income equality, and a variety of associated developments that mobilize mass participation in politics. Two aspects of this "Modernization" syndrome are particularly relevant to democracy:

1. Rising educational levels, which produce a more articulate public that is better equipped to organize and communicate, and

2. Rising occupational specialization, which first shifts the workforce into the secondary sector and then into the tertiary sector. These changes produce a more autonomous workforce, accustomed to thinking for themselves on the job and having specialized skills that enhance their bargaining power against elites.

Cultural changes. Economic development is also conducive to *cultural* changes that help stabilize democracy. We find two particularly central factors:

1. *A culture of trust.* In authoritarian regimes, the usual way to handle opposition is to imprison or execute its leaders. A crucial element in the rise of democracy is the emergence of the norm of the "loyal opposition": instead of being viewed as traitors who are conspiring to overthrow the government, the opposition is trusted to play by the rules of the democratic game. This means that if the opposition wins an election, the governing elite will turn power over to them, trusting that they will not be imprisoned or dispossessed, and that (after a given time) the new elite will hold elections in which they can freely compete for power.

2. *Mass legitimacy.* Legitimacy, or diffuse mass support, can help sustain democratic institutions through difficult times. It is an asset to any regime, but it is crucial to democracies. Democratic institutions can be imposed by elites or even by foreign conquest—but whether they survive depends on whether they take root among the public. With democratization, the public becomes a crucial political factor.

Positive outputs from a political system can generate mass support for the political incumbents. In the short term, this support is based on calculations concerning "What have you done for me lately?" But if a given regime's outputs are seen as positive over a long time, the regime may develop "diffuse support" (Easton, 1963)—the generalized perception that the political system is inherently good, quite apart from its current outputs. This type of support can endure even through difficult times. As we will demonstrate, a sense of subjective well-being among the public of a given society is an excellent indicator of whether or not that regime possesses legitimacy—indeed, it is a *better* indicator than responses to direct questions about how strongly one supports democratic political institutions.

THREE ASPECTS OF DEMOCRACY: STABILITY, LEVEL AT A GIVEN TIME, AND SHORT-TERM SHIFTS

Democracy is a multidimensional phenomenon. But to date, most empirical analyses have focused on a single aspect of democracy as the dependent variable. Thus, Inglehart (1990) analyzed the *stability* of democracy—operationally, the number of years that democratic institutions had functioned continuously in a given society. But this is just one aspect of democracy; many other analyses have focused on *levels* of democracy at a given time. This chapter examines the linkages between economic development, sociocultural change, and three different aspects of democracy:

1. The long-term *stability* of democracy,
2. The *level* of democracy at given points in time, and
3. Short-term *changes* in levels of democracy: for example, the causes of the sudden surge of democracy that followed the collapse of socialist regimes in Eastern Europe and the former Soviet Union in 1989–91.

Careful specification of the aspect of democracy to be examined is crucial, since different causal factors are important with each aspect of democratization. These factors may even reverse their polarity in connection with different aspects of democratization. Thus, though there is strong evidence that prosperity is conducive to democracy, the fall of authoritarian regimes may be precipitated by economic *collapse*. Political culture tends to be most important in consolidating democracy and enabling it to endure through difficult times. Situation-specific factors (such as the death of Franco) are often the immediate cause of the transition to democracy. But once democratic institutions are in place, their long-term survival depends on the presence or absence of supportive orientations among the citizens. The growing importance of mass preferences is inherent in the very nature of democracy. If democratic institutions do not attain enough deep-rooted mass support to weather difficult times, the citizens can simply vote democracy out of existence: they did so in Weimar; they would have done so in Algeria if democracy had not been suspended there; and they may do so in some of the Soviet successor states.

Long-Term Stability of Democracy

Mass political culture's most crucial role concerns the long-term *stability* of democracy: political culture stabilizes democracy by providing an enduring base of mass support.

Democratic institutions can be implanted by a handful of elites or even imposed by foreign conquest, as they were in Germany and Austria at the end of World War I, and in Germany, Japan, and elsewhere at the end of World War II. Democracy can be imposed from above or from outside, but whether or not it survives through good times and bad depends on whether its institutions have built up deep-rooted cultural attachments among the citizens. Various writers have stressed the importance of this factor. Weber emphasized the importance of legitimacy; Easton spoke of "diffuse support"; Almond and Verba discussed the "Civic Culture"; Putnam (1993) showed how "Civic Orientations" contributed to the effectiveness of democracy in Italy; and in an analysis based on data from 24 societies surveyed in the 1981 World Values Survey, Inglehart (1990) demonstrated that interpersonal trust and subjective well-being were closely linked with the long-term survival of democratic institutions.

The appropriateness of analyzing the stability of democracy has been debated. Lipset (1959), Muller (1988), and others measured democracy in ways that included stability along with measures of political rights and civil liberties. This practice was criticized by Jackman (1973), Bollen (1980), and Bollen and Jackman (1985). "The fusion of stability and democracy measures," Bollen and Jackman argue, "makes it impossible to interpret observed associations of 'democratic stability' with other variables, because it is never clear whether degree of stability or degree of democracy is the operative factor at work" (Bollen and Jackman, 1985: 612). For example, in answering the question "Does democracy lead to greater income equality?" this procedure can be confusing—possibly leading one to conclude that *democracy* leads to income equality, when it is actually due to *stability*. Bollen and Jackman's writings make a strong case for not confusing the *stability* of democracy with the *extent* of democracy—which, we emphatically agree, are two distinct things. But they do not constitute a blanket injunction against studying the stability of democratic institutions—which is an important variable in itself.

Our analysis does not confuse these two aspects of democracy: we will carry out analyses in which the dependent variable is the *extent* or level of democracy. But we will also analyze the *stability* of democracy. This analysis does not use democratic stability as a proxy for *degree* of democracy; instead, it is explicitly designed to focus on the factors that enable democratic institutions to survive over time, addressing the question "What factors enable given societies to remain above the threshold at which the top political leaders are chosen by free and competitive elections?"[1]

Levels of democracy at a given point in time and the stability of democracy in given societies are both significant. Whether or not democratic institutions survive through good times and bad depends on whether they have built up deep-rooted cultural attachments among the citizens. Weimar Germany had a constitution that was, on paper, as democratic as that of any society on earth; the *level* was high. But democratic norms did not take root, and these institutions proved unstable. In 1933 the German people turned power over to Adolf Hitler. Similarly, although Bulgaria and Slovenia today are coded by Freedom House as having virtually the same levels of democracy as Britain and Swe-

---

[1] Our measure of the stability of democratic institutions is the number of continuous years from 1920 to 1990 during which top leadership was chosen by free and competitive elections and ranges from 0 to 70. Accordingly, it reflects a wide range of degrees of *stability* (without attempting to simultaneously capture the relative *extent* of democracy across the various societies). Coding it requires that one determine whether top leadership was selected by free and competitive elections. This is a judgment call, which may be uncertain in marginal cases, but in most instances there is almost universal agreement on whether or not given elections were free and competitive. But any system for measuring either the extent *or* the stability of democracy requires human judgments about whether or not given societies fall above given thresholds. Competent coders usually *can* decide whether a given society did, or did not, hold genuinely competitive elections—and probably can do so with even greater reliability than they would attain in judging whether a given society falls at level "3" or level "4" on the Freedom House ratings of political rights or political liberties—which many analysts (ourselves included) use.

den, democratic institutions have functioned much longer in Britain and Sweden than in Bulgaria or Slovenia—a fact that no prudent analyst would ignore in assessing the prospects for survival of democratic institutions in the respective societies. Stability and levels of democracy are two different things, and both are important.

Levels of democracy have risen repeatedly during the nineteenth and twentieth centuries. When modern democracy first emerged in Great Britain and the United States, suffrage was limited to the middle class. In subsequent waves, it was extended to the lower middle class, the working class and to exslaves; in the 1920s, it was extended to women; and in the 1970s, to 18–20-year-olds. In subsequent years, mass political participation has continued to become more active and more issue-specific, as increasingly educated electorates have extended their repertory of techniques designed to influence elite decision making.

Jackman and Miller (1996) claim that this expansion of mass participation makes it impossible to measure democratic stability: one cannot start counting the number of years during which a given society has been "democratic" until it has become completely democratic by today's standards. In fact, this constitutes a problem only if one adheres to a unidimensional concept of democracy. Dahl (1971) distinguishes between two key aspects of democracy, contestation and inclusion; and he argues that democracy is more likely to survive over time if contestation *precedes* broad mass inclusion. Thus, in British history, elite contestation began with the Magna Charta, which forced the king to share power with the nobility, and which constitutional authorities accord an important role in introducing pluralist norms into the British political culture. Mass democracy began to emerge in the nineteenth century, and democratic norms had become widespread and generally accepted long before the latest major extension of the franchise, to 18-year-olds in the 1970s. It would be absurd to claim that British democracy began only in the 1970s (or even in the 1920s, when women obtained suffrage). These were indeed important stages in the extension of mass inclusion, but genuine contestation (in the form of freely contested elections) existed well before that time. To insist that democracy does not exist until the process of mass inclusion has been completed would be to define democracy as an empty cell: the process is probably not yet complete even now, because levels of democratic participation will almost certainly continue to rise.

Shifts to (and from) Democracy

In contrast with its role in sustaining democracy over the long run, political culture has a very different relationship to short-term changes to and from democracy. Indeed, the same cultural factors that stabilize and sustain democracy can also help stabilize authoritarian regimes. Thus, though high levels of legitimacy and trust are crucial to the survival of democracy, they would not explain short-term shifts toward democracy. Instead, one would expect *low* levels of legitimacy and trust to be linked with the collapse of authoritarian regimes, possibly opening the way for a transition to democracy. Thus, the short-term consequences of cultural factors are very different from their long-term functions. Gradual cultural changes can give rise to conditions that become increasingly favorable to the rise of democratic institutions, but the immediate precipitating factor is likely to be some macroevent such as defeat in war or an intergenerational transfer of power from hard-line leaders to reformist leaders. Accordingly, the literature on transitions to democracy tends to focus on elite-level events rather than on underlying changes in culture or social structure (e.g., O'Donnell, Schmitter, and Whitehead, 1986).

Levels of Democracy at a Given Time Point

Most empirical analyses of the factors conducive to democracy have used the level of democracy at a given point in time as the dependent variable. Although the most crucial function of cultural factors is their role in sustaining democratic institutions over time, they are also linked with the level of democracy found at given points in time. But clearly, the strength of this relationship will vary from one time point to another.

In 1790, there were three democracies in the world. In 1900, there were about a dozen. In 1919, there were about two dozen, and by 1991 there were more than 60. After each wave of democratization, many of the new democracies failed to survive. Thus, the number of democracies declined sharply during the period between the two World Wars, and again in the 1960s and 1970s; and some of today's new democracies will probably not survive.

Each major wave of democratization weakens the correlation between cultural factors and democracy, because a massive surge of democratization tends to bring into the "democratic" category a large new group of societies that rank lower on prodemocratic culture than the long-established democracies: the latter are societies in which democracy has survived for a long time partly *because* they have high levels of these cultural characteristics. If, by some happy stroke, every nation in the world were suddenly to adopt democratic constitutions, the correlation between culture and democracy would automatically drop to zero—but this would probably be a temporary situation. Unless the new democracies developed such cultural attributes as interpersonal trust and legitimacy, their democratic institutions would be unlikely to survive major economic or political crises; and the processes of cultural change and attrition would eventually bring back a correlation between civic culture and democracy. Thus (as we will demonstrate) the strength of the relationship between polit-ical culture and democracy differs sharply before and immediately after a major wave of democratization. This means that when one uses *levels* of democracy as a dependent variable, the time point one chooses is crucial.

The number of democracies in the world has been increasing and, in the long run, we think the trend will continue. It will do so because economic development tends to bring changes in social structure and culture that are favorable to democracy. Let us examine these processes in more detail.

CHANGES IN SOCIAL STRUCTURE: COGNITIVE MOBILIZATION
AND THE RISE OF CITIZEN INTERVENTION

The literature on social mobilization has chronicled how industrialization and urbanization led to mass literacy, the rise of organized labor, mass political parties, and the emergence of universal suffrage (Lerner, 1958; Deutsch, 1964; Inkeles and Smith, 1974). These were profoundly important developments that brought previously parochial masses into political relevance. These processes increased mass political participation, but they did not necessarily bring about democracy. Instead, depending on the social and economic context of the given society, they could either give rise to mass democracy, or to fascism or communism. All three forms of government emphasized mass participation; indeed, both fascism and communism regularly attained higher levels of mass attendance at political rallies and higher voting turnout than liberal democracies ever did. But with fascism and communism, it was almost entirely elite-led participation, designed to mobilize mass support for policies already chosen by the elites—and not participation through which the masses chose between competing elites and alternative elite policies.

Democratic theory emphasizes two central elements: elite competition and mass participation. In the first half of the twentieth century, democracy (unlike fascism and communism) was based on genuine elite competition; but mass participation was still largely orchestrated by elites even in the democracies. Democracy continues to evolve. In advanced industrial society, the process of cognitive mobilization gives rise to more active and more demanding types of mass participation. This makes it increasingly difficult for democracies to limit mass publics to an elite-directed role, and increasingly difficult for authoritarian systems to *survive*: they face rising mass pressures for liberalization.

The coming of advanced industrial society leads to a syndrome of intergenerational changes that bring significant further increases in citizen intervention in politics. A long-term rise in educational levels and in mass political skills has characterized all industrial societies. An extension of social mobilization beyond the transformations brought by urbanization and early industrialization, this process has been termed "cognitive mobilization" (Inglehart, 1977). While social mobilization manifested itself in visible changes of location and occupation, cognitive mobilization is based on invisible changes that upgrade individual skills. These changes have momentous political consequences.

Cognitive Mobilization reflects rising levels of education and changes in the nature of work, from simple routine operations to tasks requiring specialized knowledge and autonomous judgment. The publics of advanced industrial societies become accustomed to thinking for themselves in their everyday jobs; at the same time, they become more articulate and skilled at organizing people. The skills they learn through higher education and in their work life make them increasingly skillful political participants.

Democracies existed before the industrial era. But in polities that are too large for face-to-face interaction, political participation was limited to a minority of the population. Ancient Athens was a democracy by the standards of its time, but one that excluded a large slave population, a large foreign population, and all women. Even as recently as the eighteenth century, democracy in the United States was limited to a minority of the population which excluded Blacks, women, and, in some states, those who fell below certain property-ownership thresholds. By contemporary standards, neither classical Athens nor the early United States would qualify as democracies. Mass mobilization is a prerequisite for the contemporary version of democracy.

Mass political participation develops in two major stages, one based on an older mode of elite-led political participation, and the other on a newer mode linked with cognitive mobilization. The institutions that mobilized mass political participation in the late nineteenth and early twentieth century—labor union, church, and mass political party—were hierarchical organizations in which a small number of leaders or bosses led masses of disciplined troops. These institutions were effective in bringing large numbers of newly enfranchised citizens to the polls in an era when universal compulsory education had just taken root and the average citizen had a low level of political skills. But while these elite-directed organizations could mobilize large numbers, they produced only a relatively low *level* of participation, rarely going beyond mere voting.

By itself, voting is not necessarily an effective way for citizens to exert their control over national decisions. It can be, and sometimes is, manipulated by elites. The extreme example is the communist people's democracies which regularly attained far higher levels of electoral participation than any liberal democracy—but did so in an institutional framework that kept real decision making entirely in the hands of the elites. Voting can be an effective step toward empowering the citizens, but it is not a very discriminating one. In one-party states, it is nothing more than a way for the ruling elite to elicit mass endorsement. And even when competing parties are present, it may only mean that the citizens get to choose one set of elites or another, and then let them make the actual decisions for the next several years.

A newer elite-challenging mode of participation is emerging that expresses the individual's preferences with far greater precision than the old. It is issue-oriented and based on ad hoc groups rather than on established bureaucratic organizations. It seeks specific policy changes, rather than simply giving a blank check to the elites of a given party. This mode of participation requires relatively high skill levels.

The most readily available indicator of political skills is one's level of formal education. In part, participation levels reflect skill levels, and sheer literacy seems sufficient to produce voting. The citizens of most Western democracies reached this threshold generations ago. But while mere literacy may be sufficient to produce high rates of voting, taking the initiative to seek specific policy changes at the national level seems to require higher education. This is particularly true of the more elite-challenging types of political behavior: as Barnes et al. (1979) demonstrate, high educational levels are closely associated with participation in elite-challenging forms of political action. But the

Barnes et al. study goes a step farther and develops measures of political skills; they prove to be an even stronger predictor of unconventional political behavior than is education—and far stronger than social class.

Educational statistics give a good indication of the progress of cognitive mobilization over time, since governments have kept records of the numbers of students enrolled at various levels for many decades. These statistics tell a dramatic story. Early industrial society introduced universal primary education, bringing widespread literacy, and as industrial societies have developed knowledge-based economies, enrollment in higher education has increased enormously.

As a result of the explosive expansion of higher education during the past 50 years, younger cohorts have much higher educational levels than older ones, throughout advanced industrial society. In the United States, for example, only about a third of the cohort born during the decade before 1925 received any secondary or higher education. Among the cohort born from 1966 to 1972, over 90 percent have done so. In Russia, the rise is even steeper, moving from about 10 percent among the oldest cohort, to almost 90 percent among the youngest.

Because its educational attainment is a relatively stable attribute of a given birth cohort, intergenerational population replacement has foreseeable consequences. One can project the educational level of a given population 10 or 20 years into the future with considerable accuracy. And the consequences are significant.

The rise of postindustrial society or information society (Bell, 1973, 1976) leads to a growing potential for citizen participation in politics. Increasingly, not only one's formal education but also one's job experience helps develop politically relevant skills. The assembly-line worker produced material objects, working in a hierarchical system that required (and allowed) very little autonomous judgment. Workers in the service and information sectors deal with people and concepts; operating in an environment where innovation is crucial, they need autonomy for the use of individual judgment. It becomes inherently ineffective to attempt to prescribe innovation from above, in hierarchical fashion. Accustomed to working in less hierarchical decision-structures in their job life, people in the tertiary, or information and service, sectors are relatively likely to have both the skills and the inclination to take part in decision-making in the political realm as well.

Inglehart (1990) presents evidence of a long-term rise in mass skills in coping with politics that is transforming the mass basis of politics in Western industrial societies. Throughout advanced industrial society, publics are becoming more apt to *want* democratic institutions, and more adept at applying pressures to *get* them. These changes in mass skills and values are not the only factors that matter. A determined elite can repress public demands for democratization for a long time. But as an industrial society matures, the costs of repression rise: it stultifies initiative, bringing a demoralized, inefficient economy, and a technology that falls behind world standards.

The new mode of political participation is far more issue-specific than voting is, and more likely to function at the higher thresholds of participation. It is new in the sense that only recently has a large percentage of the population possessed the skills required for this form of participation. And it is new in that it makes the public less dependent on permanent, oligarchic organizations.

Thus, as cognitive mobilization proceeds, the established organizations become progressively less effective. Possessing a wide range of alternative channels of information and input, people rely less and less on permanent organizational networks such as labor unions, churches, and urban political machines. Both union membership rates and church attendance have been falling in most Western countries, and traditional political party ties have also been weakening. This tends to depress voter turnout, which is heavily dependent on elite-directed mobilization, and may require little or no cognitive response to current issues. High rates of voter turnout are a good thing, to be sure. But we should bear in mind that the one-party communist regimes regularly reported voting rates of 98 or 99 percent. Electoral turnout is desirable, but it is *not* a reliable indicator of citizen input. Although electoral turnout has stagnated, elite-directing types of participation, aimed at influencing specific policy decisions, are becoming more widespread.

The Iron Law of Oligarchy is being weakened. Advanced industrial society brings an increasingly educated and occupationally specialized public. As the workforce shifts from doing routine tasks, toward becoming specialists, doing tasks that require individual judgment and autonomy, they become less amenable to centralized hierarchical control.

Cultural Changes Conducive to Democracy

The spread of democracy reflects not only changes in social structure, but also cultural changes. The study of political culture grew out of the tragic events that led up to World War II. In the aftermath of World War I, democratic regimes were set up in Germany, Italy, Poland, Spain, and many other formerly authoritarian societies. On paper, some of them looked like ideal democracies. But when they encountered the severe economic difficulties of the 1920s and 1930s, democracy failed to survive in many cases. Why did this happen? Great Britain, the United States, and the Nordic countries also experienced severe economic distress during the Great Depression, but democracy survived there; in contrast, democracy gave way to fascist regimes in Germany, Italy, Japan, Spain, Hungary, and elsewhere, preparing the way for the greatest bloodbath the world had ever known.

The classic Civic Culture study (Almond and Verba, 1963) addressed the question "Why did democratic institutions survive in some countries but not in others?" Manifestly, it was not just a question of constitutional engineering. The laws and constitution of the Weimar Republic were as democratic as those of any nation in the world—but they did not take root. An authoritarian outlook remained widespread throughout German society, and when distress and insecurity became severe, the Germans voted Hitler into power in free elections. Facing comparable problems, the British, Americans, and various other peoples were relatively steadfast in their support for democracy. Democracy, apparently, is not just a matter of elite-level arrangements; the basic cultural orientations of the citizens also play a crucial role in its survival. Almond and Verba set out to measure the relevant orientations empirically, to determine whether there really were underlying differences in the political cultures of stable democracies, as compared with those of unstable democracies.

Ideally, to explain the role of cultural factors in the survival of democracy, Almond and Verba would have used data on cultural conditions from the period *before* the rise of fascism: a cause must precede its effect. But survey research techniques had not yet been developed in that period, and they would have needed a time machine in order to go back and collect such data. However, culture is by definition a relatively stable aspect of a society. If so, one would expect to find significant elements of the cultural differences that contributed to the survival of democracy in Britain and the United States, and to its failure in Germany and Italy, that were still visible in the orientations of the respective mass publics in 1959, when their fieldwork was carried out. Almond and Verba set out to determine whether such differences existed.

Democratic institutions had recently been transplanted to Germany, Italy, and Japan. Would they take root this time, or would they fail again?

This basic question is of far more than academic interest again today, when democratic institutions have recently been installed in scores of formerly authoritarian societies, from Argentina to Russia—and where their fate remains uncertain. Authoritarian forces seem to be making a comeback in a number of the Soviet successor states; and a protofascist party won more votes than any other party in the 1993 Russian parliamentary elections, which gives rise to the chilling question: Will Russia's fate be like that of the Weimar Republic?

THE IMPORTANCE OF SOCIETAL TRUST

Partly, the answer depends on the development of a culture of trust. Interpersonal trust plays a crucial role in democracy. Democratic institutions depend on trust that the opposition will accept the rules of the democratic process. One must view one's political opponents as a *loyal* opposition who will not imprison or execute you if you surrender political power to them, but can be relied on to govern within the laws, and to surrender power if your side wins the next election.

Banfield (1958) found that Southern Italian society had much lower levels of trust than Northern Italy; this severely hindered the large-scale cooperation between strangers that is essential to both economic development and successful democratic institutions. Almond and Verba (1963) also argued that a sense of interpersonal trust is a prerequisite for effective democracy. They found that the

publics of Italy and West Germany were characterized by lower levels of interpersonal trust, readiness to participate, and other attitudes conducive to democracy than were the British and American publics. The relative weakness of the
"Civic Culture" in Germany and Italy presumably contributed to the failure of
democracy in those societies in the period before World War II.

Testing these ideas in a broader cross-national context, Inglehart (1990)
found that interpersonal trust and related cultural orientations were strongly
linked with both economic development and with stable democracy. He emphasized, however, that culture is a variable, not a constant: though cultural
characteristics tend to change slowly, they can and do change. Thus, while
Southern Italians were still markedly less trusting than Northern Italians in
1990, and the Italian public still had lower levels of interpersonal trust than the
British or Americans, levels of trust had gradually risen in Italy. Starting from
an almost incredibly low level in the 1959 Almond and Verba survey, only 8
percent of the Italian public had agreed that "most people can be trusted"; but
this figure rose to 27 percent in 1981 and to 30 percent in 1986. Even in 1990
Italy ranked lower than the United States or Britain, but it showed a gradual
upward trend.

As the classic literature on political culture implied (but could not demonstrate directly), trust is linked with the survival of democratic institutions. The
1990 World Values data reveal a strong positive correlation between interpersonal trust and the functioning of democratic institutions throughout the world,
as figure 6.2 demonstrates. The vertical axis reflects the number of years during which democratic institutions have functioned continuously in a given
country. This measure ranges from long-established stable democracies to authoritarian states and societies in which democratic institutions have just been
established—and may or may not survive.

The overall pattern in figure 6.2 confirms theoretical expectations that have
never before been tested against a global database. Levels of interpersonal trust
among mass publics are closely linked with the number of years for which democratic institutions have functioned continuously in those societies, showing a
highly significant .72 correlation globally. In most stable democracies, at least
35 percent of the public express the opinion that "most people can be trusted";
in almost all of the nondemocratic societies, or those that have only recently
started to democratize, interpersonal trust is below this level.[2]

It seems likely that democratic institutions are conducive to interpersonal

---

[2] Because the 1990 World Values Survey finds a surprisingly high level of interpersonal trust
among the Chinese public (higher than in any other nondemocratic society), we checked these results against another national survey carried out in China, using the same question. An October
1993 survey of urban China carried out for Ichiro Miyake and Kazufumi Manabe by the Institute
for Public Opinion Research of the People's University of China, with an N of 1,920, also shows
higher levels of interpersonal trust in China than in any other nondemocratic or newly democratic society (for further details, see Manabe, 1995). The level of interpersonal trust shown for China
in figure 6.2 reflects the combined results from the 1990 World Values Survey and the 1993 survey by Manabe and Miyake.

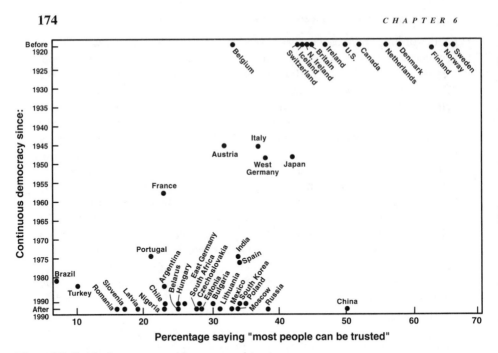

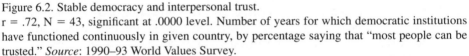

Figure 6.2. Stable democracy and interpersonal trust.
r = .72, N = 43, significant at .0000 level. Number of years for which democratic institutions have functioned continuously in given country, by percentage saying that "most people can be trusted." *Source*: 1990–93 World Values Survey.

trust, as well as trust being conducive to democracy. We do not have the long time series database that would be needed to sort out the causal linkages between culture and institutions. But there is no reason to simply assume that institutions determine culture, rather than the other way around. As Putnam (1993) has demonstrated in the Italian case, cultural patterns already present in the nineteenth century seem to have helped shape the economic and political developments of given regions in the twentieth century. We suspect that culture and social structure tend to have a mutually supportive relationship in any stable social system. The available evidence cannot determine the causal direction, but it does indicate that culture and political institutions have a strong tendency to go together—with trust and stable democracy being closely linked, as the political culture literature has long claimed.

STABLE DEMOCRACY AND LEGITIMACY

In recent years, formerly authoritarian regimes from East Asia to Central Europe and the former Soviet Union have held their first free elections. But it is one thing to adopt formal democracy and another to attain stable democracy.

Immediately after World War I, a number of new democracies were established, many of which did not survive the stresses of the interwar era. The most tragic and fateful case was that of Germany. Democratic institutions were seen by many Germans as a foreign element that had been forced on them by defeat in World War I. Authoritarian elites still held influential positions, and the underlying mass political culture was not congruent with democratic institutions (Eckstein, 1961, 1988). Democracy failed to develop the deep-rooted allegiance among the mass public that might have enabled it to weather difficult times. Formal democracy can be established by elites—but once politics is decided by free elections, the orientations of the masses become crucial. In Weimar Germany, Hitler became chancellor through free elections.

The Weimar Republic collapsed in the face of economic difficulties because it lacked legitimacy and because an authoritarian political culture persisted. But culture is a variable, not a constant. It can change gradually, as the history of Germany after World War II demonstrates. Democracy slowly established roots among the West German people after 1945 (Boynton and Lowenberg, 1973; Baker, Dalton and Hildebrandt, 1981). By the 1980s, West Germany had become a stable democracy.

Weimar Germany never had a chance to develop this kind of legitimacy. Associated with defeat from its start, it soon faced the hyperinflation of the 1920s; it was unable to maintain internal order; and it finally collapsed under the impact of the Great Depression in the 1930s. Several decades later, the Bonn regime did develop legitimacy, but it did so gradually. Throughout the first decade of its existence, a large proportion of the German public continued to agree with the statement that "the Nazi regime was a good idea, badly carried out." As recently as 1956, a plurality of the West German public still rated Hitler as one of Germany's greatest statesmen; 1967 was the first year in which an absolute majority of respondents rejected that claim (Conradt, 1993: 51–52).

Democratic institutions gradually won acceptance. At first this acceptance was based on the postwar economic miracle; by the late 1950s, the Bonn republic had achieved remarkable economic success. The 1959 *Civic Culture* survey showed that while many British and American citizens expressed pride in their political institutions, few Germans did. But the West Germans *did* take pride in their economic success (Almond and Verba, 1963). Mass support for the democratic regime in Bonn continued to grow with continued economic achievement, though economic success was not the only reason for its growing legitimacy. The institutions of the Federal Republic (unlike those of Weimar) maintained domestic order and provided for a peaceful transfer of political power from a hegemonic party to the opposition in the 1960s. By the late 1970s, the West German public was *more* apt to express satisfaction with the way their political system was functioning than were most other Western European peoples, including the British. Democracy had finally developed roots in West German society.

SUBJECTIVE WELL-BEING AND LEGITIMACY

Political economy research deals with similar processes leading to the development of mass support, but it normally has a short-term focus. If the economic cycle has been going well, support for the incumbents increases; if the economy has done poorly, support for the incumbents declines. In the short run, the response is to "throw the rascals out" (Kramer, 1971; Lewis-Beck, 1986; Markus, 1988). Support for a democratic regime has similar dynamics but is based on deeper long-term processes. Recent economic success may enhance support for the individuals in office. But if, in the long run, people feel that *life* has been good under a given regime, it enhances feelings of diffuse support for that regime. Thus, feelings of overall subjective well-being play a key role in the growth of legitimacy. Legitimacy is, of course, helpful to any regime, but authoritarian systems can survive through coercion; democratic regimes *must* be legitimate in the eyes of their citizens, or, like the Weimar Republic, they are likely to collapse.

In preindustrial society, chronic poverty was taken for granted as a normal part of life. But in industrial society, mass publics have come to expect their governments to provide for their well-being. Thus, in industrial society, reasonably high levels of subjective well-being have become a necessary though not sufficient condition for stable democracy: societies with high levels of subjective well-being *can* function as democracies, though they do not necessarily become democratic unless they also have high levels of trust and other preconditions; societies with low levels of subjective well-being are likely to have coercive governments or to collapse in the face of mass demands for radical change.

Satisfaction with one's life as a whole is one of the best available indicators of subjective well-being, and it has been surveyed regularly in the Euro-Barometer studies. A society's prevailing level of subjective well-being is a reasonably stable cultural attribute—and one that has important political consequences. If a society has a high level of subjective well-being, its citizens feel that their entire way of life is fundamentally good. Their political institutions gain legitimacy by association.

Surprising as it may seem at first glance, satisfaction with one's *life as a whole* is far more conducive to political legitimacy than is a favorable opinion of the political system itself. Mass satisfaction with the way the *political system* is currently functioning has only a modest linkage with stable democracy; but satisfaction with one's life as a *whole* is a strong predictor of stable democracy (Inglehart, 1990). On reflection, it makes sense that satisfaction with one's life as a whole is a stronger predictor of stable democracy than is satisfaction with the political system. For politics is a peripheral aspect of most people's lives; and satisfaction with this specific domain can rise or fall over night. But if one feels that one's life as a *whole* has been going well under democratic institutions, it gives rise to a relatively deep, diffuse, and enduring basis of support for those institutions. Such a regime has built up a capital of mass support that can help the regime weather bad times. Precisely because overall life satisfaction is deeply rooted and diffuse, it provides a more stable basis of sup-

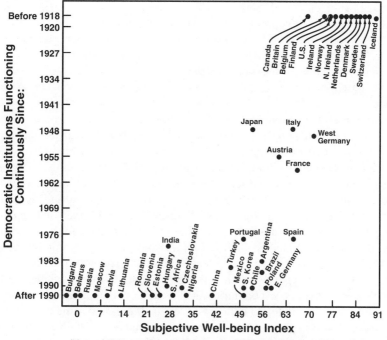

Figure 6.3. Stable democracy and subjective well-being.
r = .82, N = 42, significant at .0000 level. Number of years for which democratic institutions have functioned continuously in given country, by percentage ranking "high" on subjective well-being index. *Source*: 1990–93 World Values Survey.

port for a given regime than does political satisfaction. The latter is a narrower orientation that taps support for specific incumbents at least as much as support for the regime. Accordingly, political satisfaction may fluctuate rapidly over time, with adherents of the Left expressing higher levels when their party is in office, and supporters of the Right showing higher levels when their party is in power—but overall life satisfaction is relatively stable. Political satisfaction mainly taps support for the current incumbents; life satisfaction taps support for the type of political system, or regime.

Figure 6.3 shows levels of subjective well-being in more than 40 societies, based on combined responses to questions about life satisfaction and personal happiness. It examines a broader range of societies than ever before, including a number of authoritarian societies and new democracies. As this figure shows, societies characterized by a relatively strong sense of subjective well-being are far likelier to be stable democracies than societies characterized by a low sense of well-being, confirming earlier findings (Inglehart, 1990). The correlation (r = .82) is remarkably strong. Our interpretation is that, because a sense of subjective well-being is diffuse and deep-rooted, it provides a relatively stable basis of support for a given type of regime.

When people are dissatisfied with politics, they may change the parties in office. When the people of a given society become dissatisfied with their *lives*, they may reject the regime—or even the political community, as in the case of the Soviet Union and Yugoslavia. Only rarely does mass dissatisfaction reach this level.

Research on subjective well-being in many countries has virtually always found that far more people describe themselves as "happy" than as "unhappy" and far more people describe themselves as satisfied with their lives as a whole than as dissatisfied (see, for example, Andrews, 1986). The data from the 1990 World Values Survey reveal the lowest levels of subjective well-being ever recorded in research on this subject. In the surveys carried out in Russia, Belarus, and Bulgaria, as many people described themselves as "unhappy" as "happy"; and as many said they were "dissatisfied with their lives as a whole" as said they were "satisfied." This is an alarming finding. Normally, people tend to describe themselves as at least fairly satisfied with their lives as a whole, even in very poor societies. But in 1990, these three societies ranked far below even the poorest countries such as India, Nigeria, or China. Subjective well-being had fallen to unheard-of levels. It seems significant that in all three societies, the system of government collapsed during the year following these surveys—and in the Soviet case, the political community itself also collapsed, breaking up into successor states.

POSTMATERIALIST VALUES, PEOPLE POWER, AND DEMOCRACY:
THE INTERACTION BETWEEN MASS PUBLICS AND ELITES

Democratization is not something that automatically occurs when a society's people attain given skill levels and a given threshold of value change. The process can be blocked or triggered by societal events. For Eastern Europe, Gorbachev's accession to power was important: he made it clear that the Red Army would no longer intervene to stop liberalization in these countries. This, together with economic failure, was a triggering event that explains why liberalization suddenly took place throughout the region in 1989–91, rather than a decade earlier or later. But this catalyst would not have worked if underlying societal preconditions had not developed. These preconditions were not present earlier: with the possible exception of Czechoslovakia (the most developed society), none of the Eastern European countries were stable democracies before World War II.

Ironically, an unintended consequence of the relative security and rising educational levels provided by four decades of communist rule was to make Eastern European publics less willing to accept authoritarian rule and increasingly adept at resisting it. Such cultural changes can be repressed by domestic elites or by external military force. But by the late 1980s, such countries as Poland, Czechoslovakia, Hungary, and East Germany were ripe for democratization.

Once it became clear that the threat of Soviet military intervention was no longer present, mass pressures for democracy surfaced almost overnight.

These forces interact with the elites in control of a given society. The generational transition that brought Gorbachev to power could, conceivably, have brought some other less flexible leader to the top. This might have delayed the process of reform for some years, but it would not have held back the clock forever.

The impact of changing values on mass potential for unconventional political action is not limited to Western societies. East Asian societies show the same phenomenon; indeed, rising mass participation began to manifest itself in South Korea *before* the recent surge of democratization in Eastern Europe. In 1987 an unprecedented wave of demonstrations swept South Korea, demanding direct election of the president. The government yielded, and the ensuing elections in December 1987 were the fairest in South Korean history, with the opposition actually winning a clear majority of the vote. Only the fact that the two main opposition candidates split their vote almost evenly enabled the governing party's candidate to win. In the early 1990s, Taiwan, facing similar pressures from an increasingly educated and articulate populace, also adopted freely contested elections.

China went through a somewhat similar crisis in 1989, but it ended with bloody repression of the dissidents. This illustrates an important point: democratization is never automatic. It reflects the interaction of underlying social changes and specific historical events and leaders. A resolute authoritarian elite can respond to demands for reform by slaughtering the citizens involved. But in choosing this course, one pays a price: the loss of legitimacy and citizen cooperation. In part, the Chinese leadership's choice of this option was feasible because China was still at a considerably less advanced level of development than the other nations we have discussed. Its per capita income was only a fraction of that in South Korea, Taiwan, or most of Eastern Europe. China's prodemocracy movement, in 1989, was mainly based on the younger and better educated strata in the urban centers. Its repression brought little repercussion among China's vast rural masses, which still comprise the great majority of the population.

Subjective well-being levels seem to have been falling throughout the socialist world during the 1980s. The most reliable evidence comes from Hungary, the only ex-socialist nation in which the World Values survey was carried out in 1981 as well as 1990. Both happiness and life satisfaction fell by about 20 points from 1981 to 1990: in the former year, Hungary ranked at about where Turkey and Mexico are on figure 6.3; but by 1990, it had fallen to the level of India. A local survey was also carried out in one region (Tambov oblast) of the Russian republic in 1981, using the World Values survey questionnaire. Comparing these results with those from the 1990 survey of Russia indicates that subjective well-being fell even more markedly in Russia than in Hungary.

A large decline in the subjective well-being of a given public is unusual and may portend major changes in the society. The decline in subjective well-being in Hungary and Russia probably was linked with the deepening economic and political crises of the socialist world in the 1980s. In the Soviet case, it is clear that the decline of subjective well-being was not simply a mass reaction to elite-level events, for our findings of unprecedentedly low subjective well-being among the Russian people were registered *before* the economic and political system broke down in August 1991. The decline of subjective well-being among mass publics *preceded* the collapse of communism and the breakup of the Soviet Union.

We suspect that under the Weimar Republic, the German public also manifested low levels of subjective well-being. It is too soon to say whether the former Soviet Union will follow the path of Weimar or that of Bonn. The Russian economy is beginning to recover. But it is clear that in 1990–91 diffuse support was at alarmingly low levels; it would be rash to assume that democracy is safely installed in the former Soviet Union.

Although dependency theory itself has largely been abandoned, the heritage of its efforts to discredit political culture still lingers. Recent interpretations of democratization tend to focus on elite bargaining or on economic factors outside the individual, de-emphasizing the role of mass publics. This is one-sided. It is also ironic, because democracy is, by definition, a system in which mass preferences determine what happens. Mass political culture is certainly not the only factor; but, we argue, it plays a crucial role—particularly in consolidating democracy and enabling it to survive over the long term. It is time to reevaluate the role of political culture. We are in a better position to do so than ever before, because we now have a database that makes it possible to examine the linkages between mass belief systems and political institutions in global perspective.

EMPIRICAL ANALYSES: THREE ASPECTS OF DEMOCRACY

Let us summarize our key theoretical points. Our central claim is that economic development is linked with democracy because it tends to bring social and cultural changes that help democracy emerge and flourish. The assertion that *cultural* factors play an important role in sustaining democracy is the most controversial part of this claim, but we believe that social change is also important. These two types of change play quite different roles in relation to different aspects of democracy. Economic development may encourage democracy, but democracy does not emerge automatically. It emerges and flourishes insofar as economic growth produces the social and cultural changes we have just discussed. These factors impact differently on three different aspects of democracy: (1) the amount of *change* toward democracy in a given period, (2) the *level* (or extent) of democracy, and (3) the *persistence* of democracy over time.

Table 6.1 examines the impact of cultural factors on each of these three aspects of democracy, using multiple regression analysis. We have already seen (in figures 6.1 and 6.2) that well-being and trust are closely linked with the stability of democratic institutions. Table 6.1 demonstrates that (controlling for each other's effects) they both have powerful linkages with stable democracy,

TABLE 6.1

Cultural Values and Democracy: Multiple Regression Model

Independent Variable	Stability of Democracy 1920–95	Level of Democracy 1990	Level of Democracy 1995	Change in Level 1990–95
Culture				
Well-being	0.74**	0.14**	0.05**	−0.09**
	(6.34)	(7.77)	(2.95)	(−4.08)
Trust	82.91**	−1.17	−0.07	1.10
	(4.00)	(−0.35)	(−0.02)	(0.28)
Intercept	−37.13	3.09	8.82	5.73
Adjusted R^2	.76	.66	.20	.33
Number of Cases	41	43	43	43

Notes: Entry is unstandardized OLS coefficient. Coefficient divided by standard error is in parentheses.

*Variables significant at .05 level

**Variables significant at .01 level

giving preliminary support to Inglehart's (1990) findings from the narrower range of countries in the 1981 World Values Survey, that trust and well-being are conducive to stable democracy. But well-being and trust have quite different relationships with each of our three dependent variables. They explain a very large proportion (76 percent) of the variance in stability of democracy, and a large proportion (66 percent) of the variance in levels of democracy in 1990; but their linkage with levels of democracy in 1995 is much weaker (explaining only 20 percent of the variance). The relatively weak linkage between culture and levels of democracy in 1995 reflects the fact that a major historical change took place from 1989 to 1995: an avalanche of new democracies emerged, partly through the collapse of communism in the former Soviet Union and Eastern Europe, but also through a major wave of democratization in other societies from South Korea to South Africa. Among the 41 independent polities in the 1990–93 World Values Survey, more than *one-third* began a transition to democracy during this period.

Virtually all of these new democracies had much lower levels of well-being and trust than the already established democracies, which greatly weakened the relationship between political culture and democratic institutions in 1995. But whether or not democratic institutions survive in these new democracies will depend, in large part, on the extent to which their publics develop a sense of well-being and interpersonal trust.

The change in the relationship between these cultural variables and *changes* in level of democracy from 1990 to 1995 is even more dramatic. Subjective well-being shows a strong *negative* linkage with this variable: the societies that were most likely to shift toward democracy were those in which the public

TABLE 6.2
Social Structure and Democracy: Multiple Regression Model

Independent Variable	Stability of Democracy 1920–95	Level of Democracy 1990	Level of Democracy 1995	Change in Level 1990–95
Social Structure				
Percent Service	1.50**	0.33**	0.12**	−0.21**
Sector	(3.54)	(6.51)	(2.96)	(−3.24)
Percent Higher	0.82**	0.03	0.08**	0.04
Education	(2.95)	(1.02)	(2.85)	(0.97)
Intercept	−62.50	−6.84	3.86	10.70
Adjusted R^2	.55	.65	.48	.19
Number of Cases	41	42	42	42

Notes: Entry is unstandardized OLS coefficient. Coefficient divided by standard error is in parentheses.
*Variables significant at .05 level
**Variables significant at .01 level

showed the *lowest* levels of subjective well-being. Thus subjective well-being shows strong relationships with all four dependent variables, but reverses its role in connection with short-term changes. While *high* levels of well-being are linked with stable democracy and high levels of democracy, *low* levels of well-being are linked with short-term shifts away from authoritarian institutions. This finding supports our interpretation that subjective well-being is crucial to the legitimacy of political institutions: when it is absent, neither democratic nor authoritarian institutions are likely to endure.

Table 6.2 shows the linkages between democracy and our two indicators of cognitive mobilization, occupational structure, and educational level. As hypothesized, both variables have strong positive linkages with the stability of democratic institutions: societies with a large service sector and societies in which a relatively large proportion of the given age cohort receives "tertiary" education (as defined by the World Bank) are much likelier to be stable democracies than are other societies. Both variables are also linked with levels of democracy in both 1990 and 1995 (though the linkage with education falls below significance in the former year). But these two variables explain relatively little of the variance in the *changes* that took place from 1990 to 1995—and here again, we find a reversal of polarity: the proportion of the economy in the service sector shows a rather strong but negative relationship with change.

Let us now undertake a more comprehensive analysis of how culture and social structure relate to economic development, and to each of the three aspects of democracy. Table 6.3 shows the results of OLS regression analyses measuring the impact of culture, social structure, and economic development on democratic stability. Model 3.1 includes all three types of independent variables,

TABLE 6.3
Stability of Democracy: Multiple Regression Model

Independent Variable	Model 3.1	Model 3.2	Model 3.3	Model 3.4
Culture				
Well-being	0.25	—	0.36**	0.44**
	(1.90)		(3.09)	(3.03)
Trust	57.07**	—	47.51**	82.43**
	(3.08)		(2.74)	(4.02)
Social Structure				
Percent Service	0.51	0.53	—	0.78*
Sector	(1.59)	(1.67)		(2.00)
Percent Higher	0.05	0.12	—	0.30
Education	(0.30)	(0.56)		(1.47)
Economic				
GNP/capita, 1990	0.15**	0.25**	0.18**	—
($100s)	(3.91)	(6.87)	(5.23)	
Intercept	−44.40	−24.96	−24.02	−66.19
Adjusted R^2	.86	.80	.86	.81
Number of Cases	41	41	41	41

Notes: Dependent variable is the number of years for which democratic institutions functioned continuously in the given society from 1920 to 1995. Entry is unstandardized OLS coefficient. Coefficient divided by standard error is in parentheses.
  *Variables significant at .05 level
  **Variables significant at .01 level

and it explains fully 86 percent of the variance in the number of years for which democratic institutions have functioned consecutively in these 41 societies. Taking the other variables into account, interpersonal trust and GDP/capita emerge as the key factors, both being significant at well above the .01 level. Subjective well-being also seems important, being significant at very near the .05 level. Neither occupational structure nor educational level shows significant effects.

When we drop the two cultural variables (in model 3.2), the proportion of explained variance drops to .80 and the impact of economic development rises markedly, taking up most of the slack. But when we drop the two social structural variables (in model 3.3), the proportion of explained variance remains unchanged, at .86; the cultural and economic variables take up all of the slack, with subjective well-being and interpersonal trust both being significant at above the .01 level. Finally, when we drop GNP/capita from the regression, the proportion of explained variance falls to .81; the two cultural variables take up most of the slack, though the percentage in the service sector also rises to the .05 level of significance.

Our model is robust and indicates that the impact of economic development on stable democracy seems to work mainly through its tendency to bring cultural and (to a lesser degree) social changes. Dropping GNP/capita from the model reduces the explained variance by only five percentage points; though the linkage between development and democratic stability is very strong, most of its impact seems to pass through the cultural variables (and excluding them reduces the explained variance even more than does excluding GNP/capita).

Burkhart and Lewis-Beck (1994) have argued convincingly that economic development leads to democracy, and not the other way around. Building on their analysis, we would conclude that the most plausible interpretation of these results is that economic development leads to stable democracy mainly (though not entirely) insofar as it brings changes in political culture and social structure. This model could be depicted as follows:

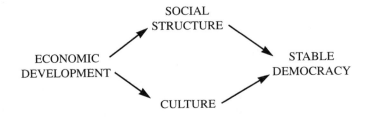

Can We Use 1990 Measures of Trust and Well-being as Indicators of Their Levels at an Earlier Time? The Stability of Cultural Variables

Before we go any farther, let us take up a basic problem involved in any endeavor to measure the impact of political culture on long-term democratic stability. Empirical measures of political culture from most of the world's societies have not been available until quite recently; consequently, any analysis of culture's impact on long-term stability must necessarily use recent measures to help explain events that took place in earlier years. Thus, the analysis in table 6.3 uses cultural measures carried out in 1990 to explain democratic stability from 1920 to 1995: obviously, we would prefer to have cultural measures from 1920 or earlier for this analysis, but such data are not available.

Using a 1990 measure of culture to explain the stability of democracy from 1920 to 1995 depends on the assumption that the cultural variables are relatively stable. But this assumption (though fortified by countless anecdotes about the stability of the cultural characteristics of given nationalities through the ages) has never been proven empirically. As we will show, there is strong empirical evidence that the cultural characteristics dealt with here actually *are* relatively stable. We have already seen one piece of this evidence: the fact that, from the Almond and Verba study in 1959 to the present survey in 1990, South-

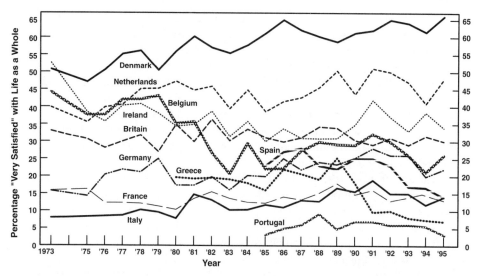

Figure 6.4. Cultural differences are relatively enduring but not immutable: cross-national differences in satisfaction with one's life as a whole, 1973–95. *Source*: Euro-Barometer surveys carried out in each respective year.

ern Italy has been characterized by much lower levels of interpersonal trust than Northern Italy—a finding that is entirely consistent with Putnam's (1993) evidence that the contemporary differences in political performance that he found between Northern and Southern Italy can be traced back to cultural differences that already existed more than a century earlier.

Although we have only fragmentary evidence concerning the long-term persistence of interpersonal trust, we have much more detailed evidence concerning another of our key variables. Overall life satisfaction has been measured in the Euro-Barometer surveys carried out in the member countries of the European Union every spring and fall from 1973 to the present. As figure 6.4 demonstrates, overall life satisfaction shows an impressive degree of cross-national stability in the European Union countries, from 1973 to 1995. Although a society's level of subjective well-being can and does change gradually over time, high or low levels are a relatively stable attribute of given societies. The correlation between a given country's level of life satisfaction at the first time point for which data are available, and its level in 1995 (the latest time point for which we have data), is .81: for most societies, this covers a 22-year time span, and it represents a truly impressive level of stability. Furthermore, as inspection of figure 6.4 demonstrates, this stability maintains itself throughout the period from 1973 to 1995, and not just at the two endpoints: in every year for which we have data, the Dutch and the Danes always rank near the top, while the Italians, French, and Portuguese always rank near the bottom.

To provide a yardstick by which to evaluate the stability of this basic cultural orientation, let us ask: How does it compare with the stability of the most frequently used of all economic indicators, per capita GNP? Relative levels of wealth are generally considered to be very stable. This assumption is well founded: with few exceptions, the relatively rich nations of 1900 were also the relatively rich nations of 1995; and most of the societies that were relatively poor in 1900 were still relatively poor in 1995. Accordingly, during the 20-year period from 1970 to 1990, GNP/capita was relatively stable, showing a correlation of .73 among the societies in the 1990 World Values Survey. But—surprising as it may seem to those who view economic data as "hard" and cultural data as "soft"—our cultural indicator shows even *greater* stability over time than does the economic indicator!

The data from the 1981 and 1990 World Values surveys enable us to test the stability of key cultural characteristics on a broader scale, using the data from the 24 societies on five continents included in both of these surveys. The results are impressive. Our index of subjective well-being (based on overall life satisfaction and reported happiness) shows a correlation of .86 between the levels measured in 1981 and the levels measured in 1990: this is even higher than the .81 correlation shown in figure 6.4. Moreover, interpersonal trust (as measured in the 1981 surveys) shows an amazingly high correlation of .91 with interpersonal trust in 1990. By comparison, the per capita GNP of these same countries in 1980 shows a correlation of .88 with their per capita GNP in 1990: a stability level about as high as that of our two cultural indicators. All of these figures are high. When one speaks of "rich countries" versus "poor countries," one is indeed dealing with a relatively stable attribute of most societies. But this is equally true of our two political culture variables. Relative levels of interpersonal trust and subjective well-being seem to be as stable attributes of given societies as are their economic levels.

Cultural variables are often thought of as vague and ethereal simply because we usually have only vague, impressionistic *measures* of them. When measured quantitatively, basic orientations such as these display impressive stability. This is an important finding, which supports the claim that cultural variables have an autonomy and momentum of their own.[3] Moreover, it suggests that our measures of political culture carried out in the 1980s and 1990s may be reasonably good indicators of how these societies ranked in earlier decades: though we cannot go back in time and measure the orientations of these publics in the 1920s, we need not abandon the effort to understand how political culture contributes to the long-term survival of democratic institutions.

Let us examine this problem from another perspective. The question is "How well can data from 1990 be used in multivariate analysis, to stand in for data measuring the same variable at an earlier point in time?" In table 6.3 we

---

[3] Culture has a significant degree of autonomy from economic factors. Though affected by economic events, culture is not simply a consequence of economic change: (1) it is shaped by many other factors besides economic ones, including wars, great leaders, major diseases, and other historical events; and (2) even insofar as they *are* shaped by economic factors, cultural changes have significant time lags. Thus culture has a momentum of its own and can influence economic factors as well as being influenced by them.

TABLE 6.4

Stability of Democracy, Using GNP/Capita in 1990, 1980, 1970, and 1957
as Independent Variables: Multiple Regression Model

Independent Variable	*Model 4.1*	*Model 4.2*	*Model 4.3*	*Model 4.4*
Culture				
Well-being	0.25	0.34**	0.45**	0.46**
	(1.90)	(2.59)	(3.42)	(3.35)
Trust	57.07**	63.75**	66.86**	73.33**
	(3.08)	(3.43)	(3.51)	(3.77)
Social Structure				
Service Sector	0.51	0.57	0.68*	0.67
	(1.59)	(1.79)	(2.06)	(1.95)
Higher Education	0.05	0.07	−0.06	−0.09
	(0.30)	(0.35)	(−0.26)	(−0.37)
Economic				
GNP/capita, 1990 ($100s)	0.15** (3.91)	—	—	—
GNP/capita, 1980 ($100s)	—	0.25** (3.56)	—	—
GNP/capita, 1970 ($100s)	—	—	1.20** (3.11)	—
GNP/capita, 1957 ($100s)	—	—	—	0.02* (2.53)
Intercept	−44.40	−54.96	−62.05	−60.31
Adjusted R^2	.86	.85	.84	.83
Number of Cases	41	41	41	41

Notes: Dependent variable is the number of years for which democratic institutions functioned continuously in the given society from 1920 to 1995. Entry is unstandardized OLS coefficient. Coefficient divided by standard error is in parentheses.

*Variables significant at .05 level

**Variables significant at .01 level

used 1990 GNP/capita to measure the impact of economic development on cultural and social change, and on democracy. We used the 1990 data to be on the same footing with the cultural variables, which were also measured in 1990. But this means that the economic data have the same problem of chronology as the cultural data: causes precede effects, and we are using economic data from 1990 to explain democratic stability from 1920 to 1995.

In fact, we get essentially the same results when we employ economic indicators from much earlier time points: GNP/capita is a relatively stable attribute of given societies and, although absolute levels of income vary from one year to the next, the relative positions of given societies are reasonably stable. Thus, our regression model yields virtually identical results when we use GNP/capita in 1990, as when we use GNP/capita from earlier times.

Table 6.4 shows the results of multiple regression analyses of democratic stability, using GNP/capita in 1990, 1980, 1970, and 1957, respectively, as our indicators of economic development levels. Although the coefficients vary slightly, the same basic model emerges: GNP/capita, subjective well-being, and interpersonal trust are the key variables in every case. Moreover, our various models all explain approximately the same amounts of variance, ranging from a low of 83 percent (using GNP/capita in 1957) to a high of 86 percent (using GNP/capita in 1990).

As we have seen, our two cultural variables are fully as stable over time as is GNP/capita. Although we do not have measures of well-being and trust from earlier decades, we suspect that if we could obtain them our analysis would produce similar results, with the same basic model emerging. This, at any rate, is what happens when we use economic indicators from earlier points in time. Our model proves to be robust, suggesting that relatively stable cultural indicators from 1990 can serve as surrogates for cultural indicators from earlier points in time.

TESTING ADDITIONAL VARIABLES

Let us now examine the impact of a variety of additional variables that the literature suggests may play important roles in democracy. After preliminary discussion, each of these variables will be tested in multivariate analyses.

The Importance of Organizational Networks

Alexis de Tocqueville stressed the importance of networks of voluntary associations, arguing that democracy had emerged and flourished in America because its people participated in numerous and extensive networks of voluntary associations. This fostered cooperation and trust, which were essential to the successful functioning of democratic institutions. Putnam (1993) also emphasized this factor, arguing that Social Capital plays a crucial role in both political and economic cooperation. Social Capital consists of a culture of trust and tolerance, in which extensive networks of voluntary associations emerge. These networks provide contacts and information flows that are, in turn, supportive of a culture of trust and cooperation: economics does not unilaterally determine culture *nor* does culture determine economics. The two are intimately intertwined and mutually supportive in any society that flourishes for any length of time.

Putnam's work makes an important contribution to sorting out the causal linkages between economic and cultural factors, facilitated by his development of an exceptionally long time series of economic and cultural indicators. Analyzing Italian regional-level data from the nineteenth century to the 1980s, Putnam found that certain regions had relatively high levels of social capital, while others had much lower levels. These levels were fairly stable attributes of given regions; and they were strongly linked with the economic development level of those regions. But Putnam's analysis dispels any assumption that these regional cultural differences are simply a consequence of their respective levels of economic development. Putnam found that levels of civic involvement around 1900 predicted civic involvement levels 60 or 70 years later far better than did economic factors. More strikingly still, he also found that levels of civic involvement around 1900 predicted subsequent levels of *economic* development even better than did economic variables. Putnam's analysis indicates that cultural factors help shape economic life, as well as being shaped by it.

The World Values surveys provide information about organizational memberships. The respective publics were shown or read a list of 16 types of voluntary associations and asked, "To which, if any, of these organizations do you belong?" The surveys cover the following types of organizations: labor unions, religious organizations, sports/recreation organizations, educational/cultural organizations, political parties, professional associations, social welfare organizations, youth groups, environmental organizations, health volunteer groups, community action groups, women's organizations, Third World development groups, animal rights groups, and peace movements.

Rates of organizational memberships vary greatly across societies. The lowest level of membership was recorded in Argentina, where only a cumulative 23 percent belonged to *any* of the 16 types of organizations: the average rate of membership was slightly over 2 percent. The society with the highest rate of organizational membership was the Netherlands, where membership in these organizations averages 16 percent.

These data underrepresent the low-income societies. This battery was not asked in India or Turkey because many of these organizations scarcely existed there; it was asked in Nigeria, but was framed to imply "Do you *sympathize* with these organizations?" Consequently, we do not have comparable data from these cases. These questions *were* asked in a number of relatively low-income countries, however, with particularly interesting results from China. Although China shows a lower rate of organizational memberships than most advanced industrial societies, it has a high rate for a largely rural society.

These data enable us to examine the relationship between organizational membership and stable democracy in an unprecedentedly broad perspective. Figure 6.5 shows the overall relationship between rates of membership in these 16 types of organizations and the number of years for which democratic institutions have functioned in the given society.

Our findings support the Tocqueville-Putnam hypothesis: membership in voluntary associations is strongly linked with stable democracy. The overall regression coefficient is .65, significant at the .0001 level. Societies with high

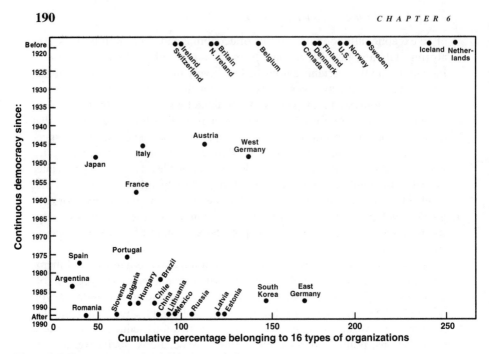

Figure 6.5. Democracy and voluntary associations.
r = .65, N = 35, significant at .0001 level. Number of years for which democratic institutions have functioned continuously in given nation since 1920, by cumulative percentage belonging to 16 types of voluntary associations (e.g., the Dutch public report a cumulative 259 percent belonging to the 16 types of organizations, for a mean 16 percent belonging to each type). *Source*: 1990–93 World Values Survey.

rates of membership are far more likely to be stable democracies than those with low rates of membership. Subsequent analyses will examine whether this holds up in multivariate analysis.

Support for Revolutionary Change and Support for Gradual Reform

Inglehart (1990) used a political culture index composed of interpersonal trust, subjective well-being, and the percentage supporting revolutionary change to explain democratic stability, finding that societies characterized by relatively high levels of support for revolutionary change are less likely to be stable democracies than other societies. Muller and Seligson (1994), in a reanalysis of Inglehart's data (plus six Central American countries), used support for gradual reform in their analysis instead of support for revolutionary change, arguing that the former provides a stronger explanation of shifts toward democracy than does the latter. Both of these variables show reasonably high levels of stability over time—though not as high as that found with subjective well-being and interpersonal trust. Among the 24 societies included in both the

1981 and 1990 World Values surveys, the correlations between levels in 1981 and levels in 1990 for each of these four variables were:

Interpersonal trust	.91
Subjective well-being	.86
Support for gradual reform	.80
Support for revolutionary change	.74

Thus, although there is an enduring tendency for certain societies to be characterized by relatively high levels of support for revolutionary change, this is a less stable variable than interpersonal trust or subjective well-being. These variables will also be examined in multivariate analyses.

Income Inequality

Much of the literature on democracy has emphasized income equality as an important factor in connection with stable democracy. This literature points out that very high levels of income inequality lead to extremist politics in which the dispossessed have nothing to lose and a great deal to gain by radical change—and the privileged elite has an enormous stake in maintaining the status quo at almost any cost. This is a recipe for extremist politics. Conversely, a reasonable degree of income equality is conducive to the spirit of compromise and moderation that is crucial to democratic politics. Furthermore, a diverse economy with many attractive jobs in the tertiary sector makes the elite more willing to accept rotation out of office: in such a setting, government is not the only route to prosperity and power; one may even have greater opportunities to earn a high income out of office than in office. Cross-sectional evidence suggests that economic development tends to produce greater income equality—which could be one reason why economic development is linked with democracy. We would expect income equality to be positively correlated with democracy.

Ethnolinguistic Fractionalization

Muller and Seligson (1994) used an Index of Ethnolinguistic Fractionalization from Taylor and Jodice (1983) in their analysis, finding that ethnic diversity makes democratization less likely. We will examine whether this finding holds up when tested in the context of the much broader database provided by the 1990 World Values Survey.

EMPIRICAL RESULTS

As table 6.5 demonstrates, none of these additional factors has a significant impact on stable democracy; and in no case does adding them to the regression analysis increase the percentage of variance explained. The basic model shown in table 6.3 explains 86 percent of the variance in democratic stability; none

TABLE 6.5
Stability of Democracy: Multiple Regression Models Testing Impact of Support
for Revolutionary Change, Support for Gradual Reform, Income Equality,
and Organizational Memberships

Independent Variable	*Model 5.1 (Revolution)*	*Model 5.2 (Reform)*	*Model 5.3 (Income Equality)*	*Model 5.4 (Organizational Membership)*
Culture				
Well-being	0.27	0.32	0.32*	0.25
	(1.90)	(2.05)	(1.96)	(1.46)
Trust	59.90**	56.49**	54.79*	49.44*
	(3.01)	(2.88)	(2.27)	(2.24)
For Revolutionary Change	0.16 (0.51)	—	—	—
For Gradual Reform	—	−0.22 (−0.90)	—	—
Social Structure				
Percent Service Sector	0.59 (1.71)	0.56 (1.71)	0.51 (1.25)	0.62 (1.62)
Percent Higher Education	0.02 (0.09)	0.04 (0.21)	0.05 (0.23)	0.02 (0.01)
Percent Income to Top 20%	—	—	−0.36 (−0.95)	—
Membership, 16 Types of Organizations	—	—	—	0.05 (1.05)
Economic				
GNP/capita, 1990 ($100s)	0.16** (3.47)	0.16** (3.42)	0.14** (3.18)	0.14** (3.31)
Intercept	−52.44	−35.01	−30.87	−51.21
Adjusted R^2	.85	.85	.86	.85
Number of Cases	39	39	32	34

Notes: Dependent variable is the number of years for which democratic institutions functioned continuously in the given society from 1920 to 1995. Entry is unstandardized OLS coefficient. Coefficient divided by standard error is in parentheses.
  *Variables significant at .05 level
  **Variables significant at .01 level

of the models shown in table 6.5 explain more than this proportion of the variance. Thus, neither support for revolutionary change nor support for gradual reform has a significant independent impact on stable democracy.

It seems likely that income equality is conducive to democracy. To test this hypothesis, the percentage of a country's income going to the top 20 percent of the population was included as an explanatory factor in this analysis.[4] The findings were interesting. There is a clear tendency for advanced industrial democracies to have higher levels of income equality than preindustrial or newly industrializing societies, most of which are not stable democracies. But the *highest* levels of income equality were found among the ex-socialist countries—and when they are included in the analysis, the zero-order correlation between income inequality and stable democracy dwindles almost to zero ($r = -.06$). Democracies tend to have reasonably high levels of income equality, and we believe that this is conducive to democracy (though it may also be a consequence of democracy to some extent, since democracy shifts political power to the public, enabling them to press for more egalitarian social policies). But income equality does not seem to be the main cause of democracy.

Moreover, the relationship between income equality and democracy is not linear. Very low levels of income inequality lead to economic inefficiency and political instability. But, apparently, extremely high levels of income equality can only be attained by coercive governments.

We also tested the impact of membership in voluntary associations, our indicator of Putnam's concept of Social Capital. Although it is strongly correlated with stable democracy, this variable did not show a statistically significant impact when we control for the effects of other variables. This does not prove that it plays no role; it simply indicates that it is not among the two or three variables most strongly linked with stable democracy. Putnam (1993) views organizational membership as contributing to democracy largely because it is conducive to interpersonal trust and cooperation: consequently, we would expect organizational membership to be highly correlated with interpersonal trust, and it is. With only 41 observations and a good deal of overlapping variance (as is the case here), only a few variables are likely to have a statistically significant impact, and in this analysis organizational membership shows a positive but not statistically significant linkage with stable democracy. It also shows positive but not statistically significant linkages with levels of democracy in 1990 and 1995; but, as we will see below, organizational membership *does* show a statistically significant linkage with changes in levels of democracy from 1990 to 1995.

Although the results are not shown in table 6.5, we also examined the impact of ethnolinguistic fractionalization, finding that it does not show a signif-

[4] Data on income equality are from World Bank (1993). These data were not available for the Soviet successor states, which were assigned the mean score observed across the Eastern European ex-communist societies. This is only roughly accurate but should be in the right ballpark: income equality was certainly higher in these societies than in non-communist societies.

icant effect on stable democracy, and that adding it to the model does not increase the percentage of variance explained. Although one can point to horror stories about the difficulties that ethnic diversity may pose for democratic governance, from Nigeria in the 1960s to Bosnia in the 1990s, diversity does not seem to rank among the most crucial factors. In global perspective, multiethnic societies are only slightly less likely to be stable democracies than are more homogeneous societies.

Interpersonal trust, subjective well-being, reasonable levels of income equality, low levels of extremism, relatively high levels of political participation and organizational membership, and Postmaterialist values are all part of a highly intercorrelated syndrome that might be called a "prodemocratic culture." And all of these variables are closely correlated with stable democracy. But interpersonal trust and subjective well-being have the highest correlations with stable democracy. In this regression analysis, with a huge amount of shared variance and only 40 cases, only these two variables show statistically significant relationships with stable democracy. We think it highly unlikely that trust and well-being are the only relevant parts of this syndrome. Social reality is usually more complex than that. Quite possibly, all or many of the other elements of this closely related cluster of variables help sustain democratic institutions. The present analysis indicates that cultural variables play an important role in the survival of democracy over time, with trust and well-being constituting the two most prominent cultural variables. It seems unlikely that these two variables alone shape the outcome: more probably, they serve as indicators of a broader cultural configuration that is conducive to democracy.

LEVELS OF DEMOCRACY: 1990 AND 1995

Table 6.6 analyzes the factors linked with level of democracy in 1990, using the five variables in our basic model. There are some interesting changes from the results in table 6.3. Subjective well-being has a highly significant linkage with levels of democracy in 1990, as it does with democratic stability. But social structure plays a more important role, and economic development a less important one, than it did with stable democracy. The percentage of the economy in the service sector is the most important single factor shaping levels of democracy in 1990.

Interpersonal trust does not have a significant impact on levels in 1990—indeed, it shows a weakly negative linkage with it. The same occurs with the percentage receiving higher education: though it has a strong positive zero-order relationship with democracy in 1990, it shows a weakly negative relationship in this regression analysis. The education finding seems to reflect a familiar phenomenon: education and the size of the service sector are highly correlated, and under certain conditions, including both of them in the regression causes a reversal of the sign on the variable with the larger measurement error—in this case, education (Achen, 1985).

TABLE 6.6
Level of Democracy in 1990: Multiple Regression Model

Independent Variable	Model 6.1	Model 6.2	Model 6.3	Model 6.4
Culture				
Well-being	0.07**	—	0.11**	0.08**
	(2.93)		(3.98)	(3.49)
Trust	−1.30	—	−4.75	0.29
	(−0.39)		(−1.40)	(0.09)
Social Structure				
Percent Service	0.18**	0.27**	—	0.20**
Sector	(3.18)	(5.31)		(3.44)
Percent Higher	−0.01	−0.02	—	0.01
Education	(−0.18)	(−0.51)		(0.42)
Economic				
GNP/capita, 1990	0.01	0.02**	0.02**	—
($100s)	(1.60)	(3.08)	(2.64)	
Intercept	−2.79	−4.40	4.10	−4.12
Adjusted R^2	.76	.71	.70	.75
Number of Cases	42	42	42	42

Notes: Dependent variable is the level of democracy in 1990 as measured by the Freedom House ratings for Political Rights and Civil Liberties, combined into an additive index. Entry is unstandardized OLS coefficient. Coefficient divided by standard error is in parentheses.

  *Variables significant at .05 level
  **Variables significant at .01 level

The importance of economic level diminishes markedly here, by comparison with its linkage to democratic stability. When both culture and social structure are included in the model, GNP per capita does not show a significant impact on the 1990 level of democracy (though it does show a powerful linkage when either of these factors is dropped). Moreover, eliminating GNP/capita from the model reduces the percentage of explained variance by only one percentage point, from 76 to 75: here again, we find indications that, although economic development is strongly linked with democracy, its effects work mainly through the changes it brings in culture and social structure.

We also examined the impact of several additional variables, including support for revolutionary change, support for gradual reform, levels of income inequality, organizational memberships, and ethnolinguistic fractionalization. None of these variables shows a statistically significant linkage with level of democracy in 1990, and none of them greatly increases the proportion of variance explained.

TABLE 6.7

Level of Democracy in 1995: Multiple Regression Model

Independent Variable	Model 7.1	Model 7.2	Model 7.3	Model 7.4
Culture				
Well-being	−0.01	—	0.01	−0.01
	(−0.64)		(0.55)	(−0.02)
Trust	−3.20	—	−4.34	−1.23
	(−1.03)		(−1.36)	(−0.40)
Social Structure				
Percent Service	0.10	0.10*	—	0.12*
Sector	(1.90)	(2.16)		(2.20)
Percent Higher	0.06	0.05	—	0.08**
Education	(1.89)	(1.79)		(2.72)
Economic				
GNP/capita, 1990	0.01*	0.08	0.02**	—
($100s)	(2.11)	(1.52)	(3.74)	
Intercept	5.76	4.90	10.94	4.11
Adjusted R^2	.50	.50	.39	.46
Number of Cases	42	42	42	42

Notes: Dependent variable is the level of democracy in 1995 as measured by the Freedom House ratings for Political Rights and Civil Liberties, combined into an additive index. Entry is unstandardized OLS coefficient. Coefficient divided by standard error is in parentheses.

　*Variables significant at .05 level

　**Variables significant at .01 level

Table 6.7 analyzes the factors linked with level of democracy in 1995. When we compare the percentage of variance explained by these variables with the percentage explained by the democracy level in 1990, the proportion drops from .76 to .50. Although this analysis is based on levels of democracy only five years later than the previous analysis, it reflects the state of the world after an avalanche of changes that brought democratization to fully one-third of the nations in our sample. Consequently, structural factors explain much less than they did in the analysis of levels of democracy in 1990: in the new democracies that had emerged by 1995, democratic institutions were less firmly anchored in social structure and culture, and much more contingent on situation-specific factors (such as historical events, elite maneuvering, and the role of specific leaders) than they were in the longer-established democracies. The only statistically significant influence on levels of democracy in 1995 is level of economic development: richer societies were likelier to be democracies than were poorer ones. But when GNP per capita is dropped from the regression, social structural variables take up most of the slack: societies with a relatively large service sector and (even more important) societies with a relatively well-educated population were likelier to show high levels of democracy than were those with lower levels of these variables.

Our indicators of political culture are virtually unrelated to levels of democracy in 1995. The massive number of new democracies washes out the linkage between culture and democracy: as we have argued, democratic institutions can be *adopted* in virtually any setting. But our interpretation implies that democracy is most likely to survive and flourish in societies that rank high on subjective well-being and interpersonal trust. A culture of trust and well-being will probably develop in some of the new democracies; and democracy may fail to survive in others that rank low on trust and well-being. In the long run, both processes tend to reinstate the linkage between political culture and democracy.

As additional analyses indicate, none of the additional variables examined in table 6.5 (support for revolution, support for gradual reform, income inequality, organizational membership, and ethnolinguistic fractionalization) has a statistically significant impact on levels of democracy in 1995, although income inequality comes close to the .05 level of significance: societies with relatively low levels of income inequality were likelier to have higher levels of democracy in 1995 than those with greater inequality.

ANALYZING RECENT CHANGES IN LEVELS OF DEMOCRACY

Inglehart (1988, 1990) argued that political culture plays a crucial role in sustaining democratic political institutions: economic development is linked with democracy, in large part, because it leads to changes in social structure and political culture that are conducive to democracy.

Muller and Seligson (1994) argue that Inglehart's political culture data were collected in 1981 and therefore cannot be used to explain the persistence of stable democracy before that time (unless, of course, they tap stable cultural differences that were present even earlier). Consequently, they drop Inglehart's dependent variable and analyze changes in levels of democracy that occurred after 1981. They claim to be testing Inglehart's thesis, but their analysis is based on a model in which the dependent variable is democracy at time 2 (the 1980s), controlling for democracy at time 1 (the 1970s). This means that they are not analyzing either the *extent* of democracy or the *stability* of democracy among the societies in their sample: they are analyzing recent *changes* (from the 1970s to the 1980s). The authors do not attempt to conceal this fact: they refer to their dependent variable as "change in level of democracy." But their choice of recent *change* as a test of whether political culture is conducive to democracy has important implications that they seem to have overlooked. They use this dependent variable to address the question "Is political culture conducive to democracy?" But their analysis actually addresses the question "Is political culture conducive to the *shifts* in levels of democracy observed

TABLE 6.8

Shifts in Levels of Democracy, Muller-Seligson Model: Impact of Income Inequality, Support for Gradual Reform, and Ethnolinguistic Fractionalization

Independent Variable	Model 8.1 (1970s–1980s shifts) (Muller-Seligson, 1994: 642)	Model 8.2 (1990–95 shifts)
Culture		
For Gradual	.62**	−.05
Reform	(2.82)	(−.75)
Social Structure		
Ethnolinguistic	−.17*	−.01
Fractionalization	(2.13)	(−.59)
Income to Top 20%	−1.60**	−.09
	(4.10)	(−1.23)
Level of Democracy,	.32*	.61**
1980s (1990)	(2.46)	(3.11)
Intercept	93.1	13.1
Adjusted R^2	.87	.37

Notes: Dependent variable is the level of democracy in 1980s (1995), controlling for level in 1970s (1990). Entry is unstandardized OLS coefficient. Coefficient divided by standard error is in parentheses.

*Variables significant at .05 level

**Variables significant at .01 level

from one decade to another?" It does not and cannot determine whether a given political culture is conducive to stable democracy or to high levels of democracy during a given period.

Table 6.7 replicates the Muller-Seligson analysis, using their model to analyze shifts in levels of democracy from 1990 to 1995. Model 8.1 in table 6.8 shows the results they obtained, using the data from the 1981 World Values Survey (plus six Central American societies) to analyze shifts from the 1970s to the 1980s. In their analysis, they found that income inequality was the most important influence on democratization from the 1970s to the 1980s. Support for gradual reform, ethnolinguistic fractionalization, and level of democracy at the earlier time point also had statistically significant effects. Their model explained fully 87 percent of the variance in democratization during this time period.

But their model is completely time bound. The factors governing *shifts* in levels of democracy from one decade to the next are largely situation-specific (in the period they analyzed, such events as the death of Franco and Argentina's defeat in the Falklands War triggered democratization). Accordingly, their model does not hold up when used to analyze the shifts toward democracy in other time periods. As model 8.2 demonstrates, using the same variables with the 1990 World Values Survey data, we get completely different results when we apply their model to analyze shifts toward democracy during the period from 1990 to 1995. Neither income inequality nor support for gradual reform nor ethnolinguistic fractionalization has a statistically significant impact on the shifts that took place in this broader sample of countries from 1990 to 1995. Not surprisingly, level of democracy at time 1 *does* have a significant linkage with level of democracy at time 2, but this is the only element of their model that survives. And the proportion of variance explained by their model drops precipitously—falling from 87 to 37 percent. A completely different group of countries shifted toward democracy in the 1980s, from those that shifted toward democracy during the 1990s—and the two groups of countries were very different in social structure and culture.

Is the breakdown of the Muller-Seligson model due to the fact that we use a broader set of nations in the analysis in model 8.2? No, it is not. Table 6.9 replicates their analysis, using the *same* set of nations that they examined. The results demonstrate that their findings are indeed time bound. When we focus on the same time span that they examined, we get similar results (see model 9.1). But when we analyze shifts toward democracy among these same societies during other time periods, we get quite different results. Income equality, support for gradual reform, and level of democracy at time 1 were the main influences on the shifts toward democracy that took place from the 1970s to the 1980s, in Muller and Seligson's analysis (with ethnolinguistic fractionalization approaching the 0.05 level of significance). None of these variables consistently shows a significant impact on democratization during the other time periods. Level of democracy at time 1 has a significant effect in two of the four other time periods; income equality has a significant effect in one of the four other time periods; and neither support for gradual reform nor ethnolinguistic fractionalization has a significant effect in any of the four other time periods. The factors that explain shifts toward democracy from the 1970s to the 1980s are *not* the same as those that explain shifts toward democracy in those same countries from the 1980s to the 1990s, or from the 1970s to the 1980s, or from the 1970s to 1995, or from 1990 to 1995. Situation-specific factors dominate structural factors, in explaining short-term change.

To understand why we get such volatile results, let us look more closely at the changes on which the Muller and Seligson analysis focuses. Figure 6.6 shows which societies changed the most during the period Muller and Seligson analyzed, based on their own data. As figure 6.6 makes clear, their approach does not analyze which nations are most democratic, or which nations have the most stable democratic institutions. Instead, their analysis focuses on the difference between two distinct sets of countries: one group consisting of Spain, Argentina, Honduras, Portugal, Greece, and Panama, which had experienced large recent changes; and another group of 21 societies that showed little or no change in level of democracy from the 1970s to the 1980s—and which lumps together the stable democracies *and* the stable authoritarian states and any marginally democratic societies that did not undergo major changes

TABLE 6.9
Effects of Civic Culture Attitudes and Macrosocietal Variables

Independent Variable	Equations Explaining Level of Democracy	
	Model 9.1 1970s–1980s (Muller-Seligson Analysis)	Model 9.2 1980s to 1990
Level, 1970s	0.32 (2.23)*	—
Level, 1980s	—	0.96 (6.36)**
Level, 1990	—	—
Gradual Reform	0.62 (2.49)*	0.16 (0.78)
Interpersonal Trust	0.04 (0.20)	−0.19 (−1.44)
GDP/capita	−0.01 (−0.05)	−0.07 (−0.72)
Income Inequality	−1.61 (−3.21)**	−0.20 (−0.44)
Ethnolinguistic Fractionalization	−1.62 (−1.78)	0.65 (0.91)
Intercept	93.13	14.10
Adjusted R^2	.85	.92
Number of Cases	25	25

Independent Variable	Equations Explaining Level of Democracy		
	Model 9.3 1970–95	Model 9.4 1980s–95	Model 9.5 1990–95
Level, 1970s	0.01 (0.07)	—	—
Level, 1980s	—	0.53 (2.83)**	—
Level, 1990	—	—	0.15 (0.76)
Gradual Reform	−0.13 (−0.47)	0.50 (−1.93)	−0.25 (−0.80)
Interpersonal Trust	0.12 (0.57)	0.06 (0.35)	0.13 (+0.66)
GDP/capita	0.07 (0.46)	0.03 (0.23)	0.07 (+0.50)
Income Inequality	−1.20 (−2.20)*	−0.08 (−0.14)	−0.89 (−1.38)
Ethnolinguistic Fractionalization	−0.39 (−0.39)	0.08 (0.88)	−0.19 (−0.19)
Intercept	144.47	76.57	125.45
Adjusted R^2	.61	.73	.62
Number of Cases	25	25	25

Notes: Entry is unstandardized OLS coefficient. Coefficient divided by standard error is in parentheses. Estimates are based on 25 cases. Greece and Luxembourg are excluded because data on income inequality is unavailable.

*Significant at .05 level

**Significant at .01 level

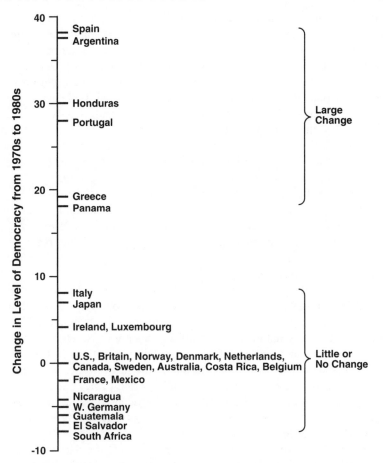

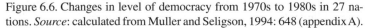

Figure 6.6. Changes in level of democracy from 1970s to 1980s in 27 nations. *Source*: calculated from Muller and Seligson, 1994: 648 (appendix A).

in this period. Most of the variance on which Muller and Seligson's analysis is based reflects the contrast between six societies that, for various reasons, showed major changes in the 1980s—and a heterogeneous group of societies that did not. Their analysis ranks Spain and Argentina at the top of the scale, far above the Nordic countries or the English-speaking democracies, even though the latter countries rank much higher on both *level* of democracy and *stability* of democracy: for Spain and Argentina happen to be the societies that showed the most dramatic *changes* during this period. Their analysis focuses on recent fluctuations that cultural differences would be unlikely to explain since culture is, by definition, relatively stable.

Muller and Seligson's dependent variable is so volatile that any cultural variables that *did* explain the pattern they find in the 1980s could not very well explain the pattern found in the 1970s or 1990s: the societies that make a breakthrough to democracy in one decade are not likely to be the same ones that make it a decade earlier or a decade later. For example, Spain falls at the high end of the scale in Muller and Seligson's analysis, since it adopted democratic institutions during this period. South Africa falls at the *opposite* end of the scale. Nevertheless, shortly after 1990 South Africa began a transition to democracy: today it would rank near the high end of their scale, having shown large recent changes. Conversely, Spain and Argentina would now drop toward the low end of the scale, since they did not show large *shifts* toward democracy in the last few years but declined slightly in the Freedom House ratings. When applied to a different time period, their dependent variable becomes radically different from the one they examined in the 1980s.

Muller and Seligson present a thoughtful analysis that addresses a very real problem: causes precede effects, which means that any attempt to analyze the contributions of political culture to democratic stability before 1960 (when political culture began to be measured empirically) faces difficult measurement problems. But their analysis has two flaws, either of which would be fatal to a test of political culture theory.

First, it is based on a dependent variable that does not address the question of whether cultural factors are responsible for the long-term survival or failure of democracy—instead, it focuses on the fluctuations from the 1970s to the 1980s. By their very nature, cultural differences are relatively stable aspects of given societies and hence unlikely to explain fluctuations in a given society's level of democracy from one decade to the next. Muller and Seligson's analysis controls for the long-term component of democracy and analyzes *only* the recent fluctuations. This gives them a dependent variable that was measured after the 1981 surveys were carried out, but it is clearly the wrong dependent variable to test the role of culture.

Their analysis is further distorted by an artifact of the data they use. The Freedom House codings of levels of democracy use the stable democracies to define the top level of their scales: from the start, they have been assigned the maximum possible score. This means that they literally *cannot* rise any farther—and since Muller and Seligson's analysis is based on change, this means that they cannot attain high scores on their dependent variable. This explains the bizarre pattern that is visible in figure 6.5: in virtually every case, the stable democracies get scores near (or exactly at) zero, reflecting no change. Muller and Seligson nevertheless argue that the cultural characteristics associated with stable democracy should be linked with large amounts of *change* on this measure. Their model specification virtually guarantees that they will not find it, and they don't.

It is perfectly legitimate and useful to analyze short-term changes in levels of democracy, as Muller and Seligson have done; but when one does so, it is important to be aware that this is a very different dependent variable from either *levels* of democracy or *stability* of democracy—and one that is mainly shaped by situation-specific factors.

With this in mind, let us examine the shifts in levels of democracy that took

TABLE 6.10

Shifts in Levels of Democracy from 1990 to 1995: Multiple Regression Model

Independent Variable	Model 10.1	Model 10.2	Model 10.3	Model 10.4
Culture				
Well-being	−0.09*	—	−0.10**	−0.08*
	(−2.49)		(−3.68)	(−2.56)
Trust	−1.90	—	0.41	−1.53
	(−0.41)		(0.09)	(−0.35)
Social Structure				
Service Sector	−0.08	−0.18*	—	−0.08
	(−0.99)	(−2.50)		(−0.97)
Higher Education	0.06	0.07	—	0.07
	(1.38)	(1.46)		(1.60)
Economic				
GNP/capita, 1990	0.01	−0.01	0.01	—
($100s)	(0.26)	(−1.26)	(0.67)	
Intercept	8.55	9.30	6.19	8.23
Adjusted R^2	.32	.20	.32	.34
Number of Cases	42	42	42	42

Notes: Dependent variable is the shift from 1990 to 1995 on the Freedom House combined index of Political Rights and Civil Liberties. Entry is unstandardized OLS coefficient. Coefficient divided by standard error is in parentheses.

*Variables significant at .05 level

**Variables significant at .01 level

place from 1990 to 1995, using change scores instead of level at time 2, controlling for level at time 1, as Muller and Seligson do: change scores provide a more straightforward measure of change, and one that is comparable to the other dependent variables used in this analysis.

Table 6.10 shows the results of a regression analysis of changes in level of democracy from 1990 to 1995, using the same cultural and social structural explanatory variables as in our previous analyses. One striking contrast with these previous analyses is the relatively small proportion of variance that these variables explain: while our analyses of levels of democracy and stability of democracy explained from 50 to 85 percent of the variance, the same variables explain only 32 percent of the variance in the shifts from 1990 to 1995. This reflects the fact that these recent shifts are not firmly rooted in the social or economic structure of the societies. Controlling for other factors, rich societies were as likely to shift as were poor ones, and highly educated publics were as likely to shift as were poorly educated ones. The most important influence on change is subjective well-being, but it has a reversed polarity in comparison with the previous analyses: the societies that underwent regime changes were

TABLE 6.11
Shifts from 1990 to 1995 (Change Scores): Multiple Regression Models Testing
Impact of Support for Revolutionary Change, Support for Gradual Reform, Income
Inequality, and Organizational Memberships

Independent Variable	Model 11.1 (Revolution)	Model 11.2 (Reform)	Model 11.3 (Income Inequality)	Model 11.4 (Organizational Membership)
Culture				
Well-being	−.07	−.08*	−.09*	−.08*
	(−1.91)	(−1.99)	(−2.33)	(−2.60)
Trust	−.69	−1.48	.54	−11.6*
	(−.01)	(−.29)	(.10)	(−2.68)
For Revolutionary Change	.13 (−1.75)	—	—	—
For Gradual Reform	—	−.02 (−.29)	—	—
Social Structure				
Service Sector	−.03	−.07	.04	−.11
	(−.35)	(−.83)	(.45)	(−1.60)
Higher Education	.06	.08	.02	.02
	(1.23)	(1.44)	(.41)	(.46)
Income to Top 20%	—	—	−.13 (−1.45)	—
Membership, 16 Types of Organizations	—	—	—	.03* (2.74)
Economic				
GNP/capita, 1990 ($100s)	.004 (.32)	.001 (.09)	.001 (−.09)	.005 (.65)
Intercept	3.02	8.99	8.32	11.93
Adjusted R^2	.34	.28	.36	.62

Notes: Dependent variable is the shift in level of democracy from 1990 to 1995. Entry is un-
standardized OLS coefficient. Coefficient divided by standard error is in parentheses.
  *Significant at .05 level
  **Significant at .01 level

societies in which the mass publics had *low* levels of subjective well-being.
When well-being and trust are dropped from the analysis, the percentage of
variance drops to only 20 percent (see model 10.2). When this is done, the role
of the occupational structure becomes significant: societies with a relatively
low proportion of the economy in the tertiary sector are most likely to have
shifted. But when the social structure variables are dropped and well-being and

trust are restored, the percentage of variance explained recovers fully, return-ing to 32 percent. Dropping GNP/capita from the analysis does not reduce the explanatory power of the model (it actually rises slightly). Far from confirm-ing Muller and Seligson's finding that subjective well-being is irrelevant to democracy, this analysis suggests that the authoritarian regimes fell, in part, because they had lost mass legitimacy.

We also tested the impact of a number of other variables, with the results shown in table 6.11. When we add "support for revolutionary change" to the regression (in model 11.1), this new variable almost reaches the .05 level of significance, while subjective well-being drops just below that threshold: both of these variables tap regime legitimacy and they share a good deal of vari-ance, reducing each others' explanatory power.

When we drop "support for revolutionary change" and add "support for gradual reform," however, the latter variable has very little explanatory power (and subjective well-being rises above the .05 significance level). Contrary to the findings of Muller and Seligson (1994), support for revolutionary change seems to have a stronger impact on short-term changes than does support for gradual reform, though neither of them increases the proportion of explained variance significantly.

Model 11.3 shows what happens when we add income inequality to the re-gression model. Countries with less inequality are somewhat more likely to change than those with greater inequality, but the effect is not significant and this variable does not add much to the percentage of variance explained.

Model 11.4 adds our indicator of Social Capital, organizational member-ships, to the regression. Doing so increases the percentage of variance ex-plained markedly, almost doubling the adjusted R^2. In this model, interper-sonal trust, subjective well-being, and organizational memberships all have significant effects: societies that are low on trust and well-being, but high on social capital, are the ones that are most likely to have shifted toward democ-racy from 1990 to 1995. Social Capital had shown the predicted polarity but had not attained a significant level in our previous analyses. Its inclusion here brings a dramatic change, producing what seems to be a model that is much stronger than those that lack it. This analysis is based on a significantly smaller number of cases than the other models, because we have data on organizational memberships for eight fewer societies than those included in the other analy-ses in table 6.11. Nevertheless, these findings tend to support the hypothesis that social capital plays a significant role in democratization.

WHICH COMES FIRST: DEMOCRATIC POLITICAL CULTURE OR DEMOCRACY?

We have found strong evidence that political culture and the level and stabil-ity of democracy are closely linked. But determining the causal direction of relationships in social science is always difficult. One way to explain away the linkages between culture and democracy would be to argue that they reflect a spurious effect of economic determinism, in which economic development gives rise to a specific type of culture, *and* to democratic institutions, without culture being an intervening variable. This interpretation does not hold up in the light of the analyses we have just carried out: economic development is indeed important, but its effect seems to work mainly through changes that it brings in culture and social structure.

Another interpretation that might explain away the relationships we have observed between culture and democracy could be termed Institutional Determinism. This interpretation would argue that the linkages between culture and democracy exist because democratic institutions determine the underlying culture.

This model contains a grain of truth: institutions *do* help shape their society's culture—along with many other factors. But the plausibility of the interpretation that institutional determinism is the major explanation is severely undermined by the findings of Burkhart and Lewis-Beck (1994) that economic development leads to democracy, but democracy does not bring economic development. The causal process seems to run from economic factors to institutions, rather than the other way around—and, as we have seen, the economic factors work mainly through changes in culture and social structure.

Institutions do influence politics and economics. But they do not explain them by themselves, and the importance of their role varies greatly according to the kind of behavior in question. For example, institutions have a major impact on relatively narrow and highly formalized behavior such as voting turnout. Voting is an activity that engages the average citizen briefly once every four or five years and is highly amenable to institutional control. By simply changing the laws, for example, one can expand the electorate overnight to include women or 18–20-year-olds. Or by applying severe sanctions against nonvoting, one can produce extremely high rates of turnout. Thus, the ex-communist societies regularly reported voter turnout rates of 98 or 99 percent, and Albania may hold the world's record for electoral participation, with a reported turnout of 99.99 percent in one of Enver Hoxha's last elections. Although they were voting for a one-party slate, the regime got almost every living citizen to the polls. The point is that voting turnout is relatively easily manipulated by elites: it does not necessarily reflect any real choice or deep-rooted preferences on the part of the masses.

Stable democracy, by contrast, depends on a deeply rooted sense of legitimacy among the public. Simply making it illegal not to trust people or legally requiring everyone to be satisfied with their lives would not produce governmental legitimacy or a society of trust.

Trust and legitimacy are much more diffuse characteristics than voter turnout, and much less amenable to institutional manipulation. They reflect the entire historical heritage of the given society, with the political institutions being only one of many relevant factors. Similarly, economic growth does not seem to result from simply getting the right institutions: societies with a wide variety of institutions have failed to attain it. And conversely, high rates of economic growth have been achieved by societies with institutions ranging from democratic to authoritarian ones, with market economies or state-run economies, and with small-scale enterprises or huge industrial conglomerates.

The same is true of stable democracy: if it were simply a question of getting the right institutions, the world would be much nicer. One could simply xerox the U.S. Constitution and mail it out to all the governments of the world. Unfortunately, reality is not that simple: the fact that each society has a distinctive economic and social structure and cultural heritage can have a decisive impact on whether or not democracy survives in that society.

Thus, the former Soviet Union had one of the most democratic constitutions in the world (on paper), guaranteeing high levels of civil rights and political freedom, together with referenda, recall of judges, and other enlightened features. Great Britain, on the other hand, has no written constitution: the basic rules of democracy exist only as unwritten norms. But in the Soviet Union, the constitutional guarantees had no real effect, while in Britain, they were generally observed—with results that were as different as day and night. The current debate between advocates of an institutional approach and the advocates of a behavioral approach wrongly assumes that the two are separable. They are not. Formal institutions and political culture have a symbiotic relationship, with institutions becoming a behavioral reality only insofar as they become a part of the political culture.

An Institutional Determinist interpretation of these findings would argue that a society's level of interpersonal trust is determined by how long it has lived under democratic institutions. Our position, by contrast, is that interpersonal trust reflects a society's entire historical heritage, with its political institutions being merely one contributing factor. Although we lack sufficient time series data for a conclusive test, the institutional determinist model fails to hold up in those cases where we do have a substantial time series. For example, the peoples of Northern and Southern Italy have lived together under the same political institutions since unification 125 years ago. Nevertheless (as we have seen), Northern Italian society continues to show much higher levels of interpersonal trust than Southern Italy: clearly, these differences in trust levels reflect something other than the presence or absence of democratic institutions. The United States furnishes an even stronger refutation of the institutional determinist thesis. It is one of the oldest democracies in the world and shows relatively high levels of interpersonal trust (though by no means the highest in the world). But are these high levels of trust due to its democratic institutions? Apparently not—for trust in government has shown a sharp decline among the American public during the past few decades: in 1958, only 24 percent of the American public expressed distrust in the national government; in 1992, fully 80 percent expressed distrust. But this collapse of trust in government was *not* mirrored in a similar collapse of interpersonal trust which was relatively stable, declining only slightly. Interpersonal trust apparently moved on a different trajectory, which suggests that interpersonal trust was *not* determined by the American people's experience in the political sphere. Moreover, it is perfectly clear that stable democracy does not necessarily produce high levels of trust. In the United States, it has actually been declining.

In addition to these empirical findings, there are theoretical grounds to doubt the institutional determinism model. To illustrate this point, let us turn to our other main variable, subjective well-being. There are clear reasons why democratic regimes cannot survive unless they are supported by the masses: if they are not, the public can simply vote them out of existence. The classic example was that of Weimar Germany, when Hitler came to power in 1933; this happened again most recently in Algeria, where the military took over to prevent a democratically elected Islamic Fundamentalist party from taking power; and it came close to happening in Russia in 1996 and could still conceivably happen there. But when we try to reverse the causal arrow, there is no obvious reason why democratic regimes would necessarily be more successful than authoritarian regimes in *producing* high levels of subjective well-being for their citizens. History indicates that they sometimes do and sometimes do not. In Germany, the Weimar regime apparently did not produce high levels of subjective well-being, but the Bonn regime did. Subjective well-being was higher under the authoritarian Soviet regime than it is under the current, more democratic, Russian regime. The World Values survey data show that in 1990 (the year before the collapse of the Soviet dictatorship), 33 percent of the Russian public were dissatisfied with their lives as a whole (scores of 1–4 on a 10-point scale). A 1995 survey of the Russian public replicated this question; it found that 51 percent of the Russian public—an absolute majority—were dissatisfied with their lives as a whole.[5] Far from automatically producing subjective well-being, the experience of the Russian people with democracy so far has been linked with a *decline* in overall life satisfaction.

The Euro-Barometer surveys provide a less dramatic but more broadly based demonstration of the fact that living under democratic institutions does not automatically produce rising life satisfaction. As we saw in figure 6.4, subjective well-being levels were remarkably stable among established Western European democracies throughout the period from 1973 to 1995. More than 20 years of being democracies *did not* significantly raise their levels of subjective well-being. The evidence suggests that high levels of subjective well-being are a prerequisite for stable democratic institutions, rather than an automatic consequence of them.

Even apart from this strong empirical evidence, it seems highly unlikely that the extremely strong correlation ($r = .82$) that we find between subjective well-being and democracy is *simply* a consequence of having democratic institutions: to accept this interpretation, one would need to believe (1) that whether the masses are experiencing desperate misery or high levels of well-being has no impact on the survival of democratic institutions, but (2) that democratic institutions have almost magical powers to make people happy.

---

[5] Results from a representative national survey of the adult population of the Russian Republic ($N = 2,040$), carried out by the Russian Institute of Public Opinion (ROMIR) in November 1995.

The latter proposition simply is not plausible. To assume that a society's subjective well-being is determined by its political institutions is to assume that the tail is wagging the dog. Andrews and Withey (1976) have demonstrated that among the American public, subjective well-being is determined mainly by one's level of satisfaction with one's family life, one's marriage, job, home, friends, and leisure time—with politics making only a relatively minor contribution to overall subjective well-being. This accords with a large body of evidence that politics plays only a peripheral role in most people's lives.

Findings from the 1990 World Values Survey demonstrate that this holds true not only in America but in the world as a whole: politics is only of relatively minor subjective importance to most people. When asked how important various things were in their lives, the following percentages of the publics of our 43 societies rated the six following domains "very important":

1. Family   83%
2. Work   59%
3. Friends   38%
4. Leisure   33%
5. Religion   28%
6. Politics   13%

Politics ranked dead last, with only one person in eight considering it very important. Six times as many people emphasized the family, as emphasized politics. This may be dismaying to political scientists, but it seems to be a global reality. Politics was rated least important in almost every country.

Unlike totalitarian systems, democracies make only modest efforts to reshape their underlying cultures: the very essence of democracies is that they *reflect* the preferences of their citizens, rather than attempting to dictate them. It seems highly unlikely that the powerful correlation that we have found between culture and democracy exists because democratic institutions somehow create a new culture. Democratic institutions probably encourage feelings of interpersonal trust to some extent and may have some tendency to enhance subjective well-being, but the process seems to work mainly in the opposite direction: mass well-being and trust are crucial to the viability of democratic institutions.

POSTMATERIALIST VALUES AND THE FUTURE
OF ADVANCED INDUSTRIAL SOCIETY

In advanced industrial society, prolonged prosperity and the welfare state contribute to an increasingly widespread sense that survival can be taken for granted, giving rise to another cultural factor conducive to democracy: the spread of Postmaterialist values. This is a relatively recent development, and it may be a major reason why, although early industrial societies were almost equally likely to mobilize their publics into democratic, fascist, or communist forms of political participation, advanced industrial society gives rise to democracy almost exclusively, rather than to either of the two other forms of modern political regimes.

Both theory and empirical evidence indicate that Postmaterialist values did not become a significant factor in politics until about two decades after World War II; clearly, Postmaterialist values cannot explain the stability of democracy throughout the period since 1920. Moreover, even today these values are widespread only in advanced industrial societies; they could not very well be the main factor explaining the *levels* of democracy found throughout the world. Nevertheless, there is reason to believe that they are conducive to democracy in advanced industrial societies, contributing to a growing demand for higher levels of mass participation in politics.

Our theory implies that a shift toward Postmaterialist values should occur in any nation that develops high levels of economic security. As we have seen, this process seems to be at work not only in the West but also in East Asia (parts of which have now attained Western levels of prosperity) and even to some extent in Eastern Europe.

Postmaterialist values are conducive to democracy for three reasons: (1) They entail an emphasis on self-expression and participation that is inherently conducive to political participation, and, as we will see, Postmaterialists are relatively likely to act to attain democracy. (2) Postmaterialists view democracy as something that is intrinsically desirable—and not just as a possible means to become wealthy and successful. Thus, their support for democracy is more secure than that of Materialists, many of whom were initially attracted to democracy simply because it was associated with being rich. (3) In addition to their emphasis on participation and free speech, Postmaterialists tend to hold a wide range of basic democratic norms, as recent research demonstrates. Thus, Rohrschneider (1993) finds that Postmaterialist values are an important factor accounting for the presence or absence of democratic attitudes among the elites of both the former German Democratic Republic and the Federal Republic of Germany.

Research by Gibson and Duch in the former Soviet Union also demonstrates this point. Gibson and Duch (1994) developed a broad based scale of support for democratic values. This scale integrates seven subscales measuring (1) valuation of liberty, (2) support for democratic norms, (3) rights consciousness, (4) support for dissent and opposition, (5) support for independent mass media, (6) support for competitive elections, and (7) political tolerance. In their 1990 survey of the European Soviet Union, Gibson and Duch find that

> Those who hold Postmaterialist values are markedly more likely to support these democratic values. In the European USSR data the percentage high in support for democratic values ranges from 14 percent for the Materialists to 80 percent for the Postmaterialists, a truly remarkable difference. This is quite strong support for Inglehart's theory: Postmaterialists are much more likely to support core democratic values such as tolerance, competitive elections, etc. To what degree, though, are these findings

spurious—that is, are they a function of other factors that contribute to the development of *both* democratic and Postmaterialist values? We can consider the effect of Postmaterialism on democratic values controlling for a number of attributes of the respondents that might well account for both sets of values. . . . We find that Postmaterialism has a substantial impact on democratic values beyond the effect of these demographic attributes. Those who are more highly educated, and who are younger are more likely to support democratic processes and institutions, and these variables alone can account for a respectable amount of variance in the dependent variable. Yet when the Postmaterialism indicator is added to the equation, *an additional 10 percent of the variance can be explained*. Even while controlling for age, education, social class, etc., Postmaterialists are considerably more supportive of democratic values than are Materialists. (Gibson and Duch, 1994: 20–21)

Since Postmaterialists emphasize individual freedom and self-expression, it is not surprising that Postmaterialist values correlate with democratic values, but Gibson and Duch's finding is far from tautologous. By demonstrating the linkages between democratic values and Postmaterialist values, Gibson and Duch help integrate democratic theory and the theory of value change. Their findings imply that we should find an intergenerational trend toward increasing support for basic democratic values in societies that experience economic growth and attain higher levels of mass security.

THE GROWING ROLE OF MASS POLITICAL ACTION

Value change has important behavioral implications. In any setting, Postmaterialists are relatively ready to act to attain their political goals—but in authoritarian systems, they are the ones most likely to act in order to attain democracy.

Representative samples of the publics interviewed in the World Values survey were asked about their readiness to take part in four forms of political action: (1) joining in boycotts, (2) attending lawful demonstrations, (3) joining unofficial strikes, (4) occupying buildings or factories. Using similar questions in eight Western democracies, Barnes et al. (1979) demonstrated that Materialist/Postmaterialist values are strongly related to one's willingness to participate in unconventional political activities such as these, in order to press for some political goal.

The spread of citizen activism is not merely a Western phenomenon. Postmaterialist values show the same linkages with unconventional political protest potential in Eastern Europe and East Asia as they do in Western countries. The data from the World Values surveys reveal that in country after country, Postmaterialists are two to four times as likely to engage in unconventional political action, as are Materialists. Figure 6.7 shows the percentage of the Russian public who said (in 1990–91) that they "have done" or "might do" all four of these activities.

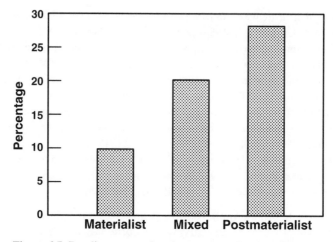

Figure 6.7. Readiness to undertake unconventional political action, by value type: Russia, 1990–91.
Percentage saying they "have done" or "might do" all four of the following: (1) join in boycotts, (2) attend lawful demonstrations, (3) join unofficial strikes, and (4) occupy buildings or factories. *Source*: World Values Survey carried out in Russia, December 1990–January 1991.

The spread of Postmaterialist values seems to be increasing the degree to which mass publics engage in elite-challenging political action. From 1981 to 1990, public readiness to engage in these activities became more widespread in the great majority of societies for which we have data, as we will see in chapter 10. In nondemocratic regimes, unconventional political action may play an even *more* important role than it does in the West: it may serve as the proximate cause by which the public obtains democratization. From Seoul to Warsaw to Budapest to East Berlin, mass participation in strikes, demonstrations, and boycotts—precisely the activities examined here—played a crucial part in the transitions to democracy launched throughout Eastern Europe in 1989, and in recent moves toward democratization in East Asia and Latin America.

People power has become an unprecedentedly important factor in politics. It proved its effectiveness again six months after these surveys, in August 1991, when hard-liners in the Soviet Union attempted to seize power, arresting Gorbachev and rolling tanks into Moscow. But to widespread surprise, this time the Russian people did not resign themselves to authoritarian rule. Instead, citizens poured into the streets, defying the reactionary coup's leaders and building barricades around the Russian Parliament building where Yeltsin had organized resistance. Crowds of citizens brought armored columns to a halt. Miners went on strike. And entire units of tanks and paratroops went over to the resistance.

Both economic and noneconomic motives played a part in motivating mass resistance to communism. Its economic failures contributed to its downfall.

But it is equally important that the desire for freedom of speech and self-determination have become high-priority goals, for more people, than ever before in history. Postmaterialists are far likelier than Materialists to have taken part in the strikes, demonstrations, and other unconventional protest actions which brought down the communist regimes (or helped maintain the reform regime, in the Soviet case).

As the younger, better-educated, and more Postmaterialistic birth cohorts replace the older, less-educated ones in the adult population, we would expect elite-challenging political action to increase. Does it? In virtually all societies for which we have time series data, the answer is yes. In almost every country included in both waves of the World Values surveys, we find the predicted shift. The proportion of people who have actually done elite-challenging political actions during the past five years rose substantially from 1981 to 1990, as we will see below. One frequently reads journalistic accounts that mass publics have become politically apathetic, citing evidence that voter turnout has stagnated or declined. These accounts are accurate about voting, but miss the point that people display a rising potential for elite-challenging action. Voting turnout statistics convey a misleading impression of political apathy. Mass publics *are* becoming less likely to vote, which is a relatively elite-controlled form of participation; but throughout industrial society they are becoming *more* likely to engage in elite-challenging behavior.

THE IMPACT OF MASS VALUES ON DEMOCRATIZATION, POLITICAL CULTURE, AND STABLE DEMOCRACY

Do individual-level values have an impact on the societies in which people live? The evidence we have just examined suggests that democracy should be more likely to emerge (and survive) in societies with relatively large numbers of Postmaterialists than elsewhere. Is this the case?

The horizontal axis on figure 6.8 reflects the balance between Materialists and Postmaterialists in each country. The pattern is clear. Nations with relatively high proportions of Postmaterialists are much more likely to have had continuously functioning democratic institutions than other societies. Those with heavily Materialist publics tend to be not democratic, or to be recent (and possibly unstable) democracies. All but one of the countries that were not yet democratic in 1990 show scores *below* +10 on the Materialist/Postmaterialist values index on figure 6.8 (the sole exception being Mexico). All but one of the democracies had scores *above* that level (the sole exception being India).

One consequence of this cultural transformation is rising mass pressure for more democratic and participatory institutions. Although mass preferences *alone* do not determine when democratization takes place, there is a remarkably strong correlation between the ratio of Postmaterialists to Materialists and the existence of stable democracy (r = .71). Correlation is not causation. But the evidence of a causal link between Postmaterialist values and stable democ-

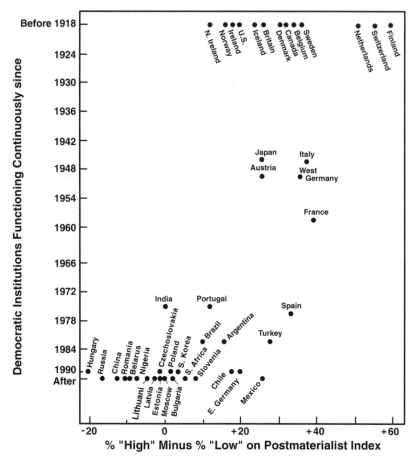

Figure 6.8. Stable democracy and Materialist/Postmaterialist values.
N = 43, r = .71, significant at .0000 level. *Source*: 1990–91 World Values Survey. *Note*:
Respondents are classified as "high" on the 12-item Materialist/Postmaterialist values
index used here if they gave high priority to at least three of the five Postmaterialist
goals (ranking them among the two most important in each group of four goals). They
are classified as "low" if they gave high priority to none of the five Postmaterialist goals.

racy goes well beyond cross-sectional evidence. It is reinforced by individual-
level findings that suggest *why* countries with relatively Postmaterialist publics
should be likelier to become stable democracies: (1) their publics give relatively high priority to individual freedom and to democratic values, and (2)
their publics are relatively likely to engage in direct political action that can
help bring a shift from authoritarian to democratic regimes.

When we entered Postmaterialist values into the regression analyses above,
they showed positive but not significant linkages with stable democracy and
high levels of democracy. These values are part of a highly intercorrelated syn-

drome consisting of interpersonal trust, subjective well-being, a large tertiary sector, a highly educated population, and well-developed organizational networks. This syndrome is strongly linked with democracy; but Postmaterialism is not among the two or three independent variables that show significant effects. Thus far, it seems to have played only a secondary role in the emergence and spread of democracy. But if advanced industrial societies continue to produce an increasingly widespread feeling that survival can be taken for granted among a growing proportion of their populations, the political implications of Postmaterialist values may be far-reaching.

CONCLUSION

The evolution of industrial society makes democracy more likely. It brings gradual cultural changes that make mass publics increasingly likely to want democratic institutions and more supportive of them once they are in place. This transformation does not come easily or automatically. Determined elites, in control of the army and police, can resist pressures for democratization. But the emergence of prosperous welfare states leads to gradual long-term changes in which mass publics give an increasingly high priority to autonomy and self-expression in all spheres of life including politics. And as they mature, industrial societies develop increasingly specialized and educated labor forces, which become increasingly adept at exerting political pressure. It becomes more difficult and costly to repress demands for political liberalization. Moreover, economic development is also linked with relatively high levels of subjective well-being and interpersonal trust, which also seem to play a crucial role in democracy. With rising levels of economic development, cultural patterns emerge that are increasingly supportive of democracy, making mass publics more likely to *want* democracy, and more skillful at *getting* it.

Although rich societies are much likelier to be democratic than poor ones, wealth alone does not automatically bring democracy. But the process of industrialization does have an inherent tendency to produce changes that are conducive to democracy. In the long run, the only way to avoid the growth of increasingly articulate and effective mass demands for democratization would be to reject industrialization. Very few ruling elites in the contemporary world are willing to do so. Those societies that do move onto the trajectory of industrial society will eventually face increasingly powerful pressures for democratization.

Our findings suggest that political culture plays a much more crucial role in democracy than the literature of the past two decades would indicate. Although it does not seem to be the immediate cause of the *transition* to democracy, political culture does seem to be a central factor in the survival of democracy. In the long run, democracy is not attained simply by making institutional changes or through clever elite-level maneuvering. Its survival also depends on what ordinary people think and feel.

The Impact of Culture on Economic Growth[1]

Introduction

Do cultural factors influence economic development? If so, can they be measured and their effect compared with that of standard economic factors such as savings and investment? This chapter examines the explanatory power of the standard growth model based on economic variables and compares it with that of cultural variables such as achievement motivation, Postmaterialist values, and social capital factors such as membership in associations. We argue that it is not an either/or proposition: cultural and economic variables play complementary roles and both are needed to produce growth. This hypothesis is tested empirically, using recently developed econometric techniques to assess alternative interpretations of economic growth.

In chapter 2 we found that a major dimension of cross-cultural variation—the Modernization dimension—was closely linked with the long-term economic growth rates of the 43 societies examined there. Although this suggests that basic values may be an important factor in economic development, we did not analyze causal relationships in that chapter, which simply presented a broad overview of the cross-national patterns. We return to that finding here, probing more deeply into the linkages between values and economic growth.

It is clear that cultural factors alone do not explain all of the cross-national variation in economic growth rates. Every economy experiences yearly fluctuations in growth rates as a result of short-term factors; these are not attributable to cultural factors, which fluctuate relatively little. It is evident that a given society's economic and political institutions are also important: for example, North Korea and South Korea had a common culture until 1945, but South Korea's economic performance has been vastly superior since then. Similarly, though China experienced some periods of high growth rates during the Maoist era, its economic performance has been much stronger since the pragmatists took control after the death of Mao. And Chile experienced low growth rates throughout the period from World War II to the 1970s, but has shown high growth rates since adopting structural reforms. Obviously, cultural factors *alone* do not explain why economic growth rates vary.

But there is equally strong evidence that cultural differences are an important part of the story. For example, during the 45 years of the Cold War, West Germany had the strongest economy in Western Europe, while East Germany had the most advanced economy in the Soviet bloc. Even more strikingly, over

---

[1] Ronald Inglehart, James Granato, and David Leblang are coauthors of this chapter.

the past five decades the Confucian-influenced societies of East Asia have out-performed the rest of the world by a wide margin. This holds true despite the fact that they have had an enormous variety of economic and political institutions—ranging from the extreme laissez-faire capitalism of Hong Kong to the state-run economy of Maoist China, and from the highly concentrated capitalist conglomerates of South Korea to the fragmented small enterprises of Taiwan, and under political institutions that ranged from liberal democracy to some of the world's most authoritarian regimes. The linkage between Confucian culture and economic achievement also manifests itself at the individual level, under a variety of institutional settings. East Asian minorities throughout the world—operating under a wide range of political and economic institutions—have achieved remarkable rates of social mobility and economic achievement. The performance of East Asian minorities has been a striking success story from Southeast Asia to Western Europe, North America, and Latin America. Institutions alone do not determine economic growth, any more than do cultural factors alone. Both societal-level and individual-level evidence suggests that a society's economic and political institutions are shaped by cultural factors as well as by economics.

We hypothesize that cultural and economic factors play complementary roles in economic growth. Surprisingly enough, this position has rarely been taken previously: the literature has tended to present culture and economic determinants of growth as mutually exclusive. One reason for this is because until now we have had inadequate measures of the cultural factors. Most previous attempts to establish the role of culture have either inferred culture from economic performance, which is circular and proves nothing, or have attempted to estimate cultural factors from impressionistic historical evidence. Since this evidence was not quantitative, it was usually used to support sweeping all-or-nothing claims: its relative impact could not be measured against that of economic factors, so its advocates felt obliged to assert that it was decisive all by itself. Debate centered on the question whether cultural factors determined economic growth, or whether economic factors were decisive. It is perfectly conceivable that *both* types of factors are important, but until cultural factors could be used in quantitative analysis, this possibility could not be tested.

By culture, we refer to a system of common basic values that help shape the behavior of the people in a given society. In most preindustrial societies, this value system takes the form of a religion and changes very slowly; but with industrialization and accompanying processes of Modernization, these worldviews tend to become more secular, rational, and open to change.

For reasons discussed earlier, the cultures of virtually all preindustrial societies are hostile to social mobility and individual economic accumulation. Thus, both medieval Christianity and traditional Confucian culture stigmatized profit-making and entrepreneurship. But (as Weber argued) a revised Protestant version of Christianity played a key role in the rise of capitalism; and at a later stage of history, a modernized version of Confucian society encouraged economic growth through its support of education and achievement.

We will first discuss theories that deal with the impact of culture on economic growth; next we will present some data demonstrating the surprisingly strong empirical linkages between cultural variables measured in the World Values survey and economic growth rates. We will then discuss the baseline endogenous growth model, which attempts to explain economic growth on the basis of economic factors alone. This approach has demonstrated that a given country's investment rate plays a key role in economic growth rates. But it has been unable to explain why some countries have high investment rates while others have low ones: standard economic variables, such as GNP per capita, are only weakly related to growth rates and explain very little. Why do some societies save and invest to a much greater extent than others? And why have the investment rates of some societies (such as the United States) gradually declined over time? We suggest that cultural factors help provide answers to both questions. Finally, we will integrate cultural and economic variables into a multivariate analysis that analyzes the contributions of both sets of factors.

Theories dealing with the impact of culture on economic development go back to Max Weber and Alexis de Tocqueville, respectively. The first set of ideas stresses the importance of motivational factors while the second emphasizes the importance of networks of voluntary associations. We will refer to these two bodies of theory as dealing with motivation and social capital, respectively.

MOTIVATIONAL FACTORS AND ECONOMIC GROWTH

The motivational literature stresses the degree to which given cultures emphasize or stigmatize economic accumulation and achievement. It grows out of Weber's (1904–5) Protestant Ethic thesis, which has been controversial for 90 years and continues to be influential. This school of thought gave rise to historical research from Tawney (1922) to Harrison (1992), and to empirical work by McClelland (1953, 1961) on Achievement Motivation, and continued with Inglehart's (1971, 1977, 1990) work on the shift from Materialist to Postmaterialist value priorities—a process that could be viewed as the erosion of the Protestant Ethic among populations that have experienced high levels of economic security.

Chapter 1 proposed a modified interpretation of Weber's thesis concerning the role of the Protestant Ethic in economic development. Briefly, we argued that Weber was correct in viewing the rise of Protestantism as a crucial event in modernizing Europe. He emphasized the fact that the Calvinist version of Protestantism encouraged norms favorable to economic achievement. But the rise of Protestantism was only one case of a more general phenomenon. It was important not simply because of the specific content of early Protestant beliefs, but because it undermined a set of religious norms that inhibit economic achievement and that are common to most preindustrial societies. Let us consider how this works.

Preindustrial economies are zero-sum systems: because they experience little or no economic growth, upward social mobility can only come at someone else's expense. Traditional cultural norms generally reflect this fact: social status is hereditary rather than achieved, and social norms encourage one to accept one's social position in this life, emphasizing that the denial of one's worldly aspirations will be rewarded in the next life. Aspirations toward social mobility are sternly repressed. Such value systems help to maintain social solidarity and discourage economic accumulation in a variety of ways, ranging from norms of sharing and charity, to the norms of noblesse oblige, to the potlatch and similar institutions found from pre-Columbian North America to Africa, in which one attains prestige by recklessly giving away one's worldly goods.

The traditional value systems of agrarian societies are adapted to maintaining a stable balance in an unchanging technological environment. They discourage social change in general and accumulative entrepreneurial behavior in particular, which tends to be relegated to pariah groups if tolerated at all. Economic accumulation is viewed as greed. To facilitate the economic accumulation needed to launch industrialization, these cultural inhibitions must be relaxed.

In Western society, the Protestant Reformation helped break the grip of the medieval Christian worldview on a significant part of Europe. Throughout the first 150 years of the Industrial Revolution, industrial development took place almost entirely within the Protestant regions of Europe and the Protestant portions of the New World. This began to change only during the second half of the twentieth century, when precisely those regions that had been most strongly influenced by the Protestant Ethic—and had become economically secure— began to de-emphasize economic growth, gradually turning toward Postmaterialist values. Meanwhile, an entrepreneurial outlook had emerged in Catholic Europe and (even more strikingly) in the Far East, both of which now show higher rates of economic growth than Protestant Europe. Today, the concept of the Protestant Ethic would be outdated if we took it to mean something that can only exist in historically Protestant countries. But Weber's more general insight that cultural factors can influence economic growth is valid.

McClelland's (1953, 1961) work on Achievement Motivation built on the Weberian thesis but focused on the values that were encouraged in children by their parents, schools, and other agencies of socialization. He hypothesized that some societies (whether Protestant, Catholic, Islamic, or other) tend to emphasize economic achievement as a positive goal, while others give it little emphasis. Since he could not directly measure the values emphasized in given societies through representative national surveys, McClelland attempted to measure them indirectly, through content analysis of the stories and school books used to educate children in various societies. He found that some cultures *did* emphasize achievement in their school books more heavily than others— and that the former showed considerably higher rates of economic growth (as measured by rates of electric power consumption) than did the latter.

McClelland's work has been criticized on various grounds. It was questioned whether his approach really measured the values actually taught to children, or simply those of textbook writers. And subsequently, writers of the dependency school argued that any attempt to trace differences in economic growth rates to factors within a given culture, rather than to global capitalist exploitation, was simply a means of justifying capitalist exploitation of the peripheral economies. Such criticism served to denigrate this type of research but was hardly an empirical refutation.

Survey research by Lenski (1963) and by Alwin (1986) found that Catholics and Protestants in the United States showed significant differences in the values they emphasized as the most important things to teach children, and that these differences followed the lines of the Protestant Ethic thesis, with Protestants being more likely to emphasize determination and individual autonomy, while Catholics tended to emphasize obedience. But Alwin also demonstrated that these differences have been eroding over time, with Protestants and Catholics in the United States gradually converging toward a common belief system (somewhat as Catholic Europe and Protestant Europe gradually became less dissimilar).

Building on this line of research, the World Values survey asked representative national samples of the publics in 43 societies, "Here is a list of qualities that children can be encouraged to learn at home. Which, if any, do you consider to be especially important?" This list included qualities that reflected emphasis on autonomy and economic achievement, such as "thrift, saving money and things" and "determination," and others that reflected emphasis on conformity to traditional social norms, such as "obedience" and "religious faith."

We constructed an index of Achievement Motivation that sums up the percentage in each country emphasizing the first two goals, minus the percentage emphasizing the latter two goals. This method of index construction offsets the tendency of respondents in some societies to place relatively heavy emphasis on *all* of these goals, while respondents in other countries mention relatively few of them. We thus obtain an index that ranges from −200 (which would result if 100 percent of the people in a given society emphasized "obedience," and 100 percent emphasized "religious faith," while no one emphasized either "thrift" or "determination") to +200 (which would result if everyone emphasized "thrift" and "determination" while no one emphasized "obedience" or "religious faith"). A score of zero results if there is exactly as much emphasis on the two traditional goals, as on the two achievement motivation goals.

Do different societies emphasize different qualities in raising their children? And are these values related to their economic growth rates? The answer to both questions is Yes. The societies examined here show tremendous variation, ranging from scores of −100 on the achievement motivation scale, to scores of +100. And the relationship that we find between childrearing values and economic growth is surprisingly strong. Our four-item Achievement Motivation index shows a .66 correlation (significant at the .001 level) with the economic growth rates observed from 1960 to 1990 in these societies.

Our dependent variable in this analysis is the given society's mean annual rate of real growth in GDP per capita, using data from Levine and Renelt (1992) covering the period from 1960 to 1990. Using a long time period such as this is appropriate when testing the linkages between economic growth and long-term attributes such as culture and social structure: this minimizes the impact of short-term fluctuations. We end the series in 1990, the year in which the World Values surveys were carried out.

The ex-socialist societies other than China are excluded from the analysis shown here because data on their economic growth rates are of uncertain reliability; including them, using the best available data, produces similar results (which are reported in Appendix 3).[2]

Although frequently stereotyped as having authoritarian cultures, China, Japan, and South Korea all emerge near the pole that emphasizes thrift rather than obedience. The three East Asian societies in this survey rank highest on Achievement Motivation, while the two African societies included in this survey rank near the opposite end of the continuum, emphasizing obedience and religious faith. The publics of India and the United States also fall toward the low end of the achievement motivation scale. This scale reflects the balance between two types of values: one type of values—emphasizing thrift and determination—supports economic achievement, while the other—emphasizing

---

[2] In Appendix 3, we include 11 ex-socialist societies in a similar analysis, using growth rates from the *World Handbook of Political and Social Indicators* (1st, 2d, and 3d editions). Figure A.3 shows the overall relationship between values and economic growth rates in this larger pool of societies. For the period 1965–88, our data for most countries come from the *World Development Report, 1990* (World Bank, 1990), but the data for all ex-communist societies (not including China) come from the *World Bank Atlas, 1992* and cover only 1980–91. The data for China in the earlier period cover only the period from 1952 through 1961. Our analysis is based on a weighted average of the growth rates for the earlier and later time periods.

The data from the ex-communist countries are less reliable than those from market economies. They are based on different accounting systems and tend to exaggerate growth rates. Furthermore, since separate growth figures are not available for the Soviet (or Yugoslav) successor states prior to 1980, we use the Soviet (or Yugoslav) growth rates for these societies in the earlier period. Clearly, these data are imperfect. But they reflect the best available estimates, from widely recognized sources; and we believe that they are in the right ballpark for purposes of global comparisons. Soviet sources claimed a 13 percent annual growth rate for the Soviet Union during the 1950s. The *World Handbook* credits the USSR with a much more plausible 4.9 percent growth rate in 1950–65; this is a higher rate than that of most Western democracies, but considerably lower than the 7.8 percent rate which the World Handbook estimates for Japan, or the 5.5 percent rate given for West Germany. In recent years, the Soviet economy slowed down, stagnated, and then, during the transition from a command economy to a market economy, collapsed: the World Bank estimates that Russia had a growth rate of only 1.3 percent during 1981–90 and negative growth more recently (China continued to grow at an estimated 7.8 percent). The recent collapse of most communist economies has been dramatic, but it should not obscure the fact that these societies once had some of the world's highest growth rates. Though the growth rates for the ex-socialist societies and China from 1950 through 1988 have relatively high error margins, few informed observers doubt that these countries experienced much higher growth during most of this period than did such countries as Argentina, Chile, Nigeria, and India; or the United States, Canada, and Great Britain.

obedience and religious faith—tends to discourage it, stressing conformity to traditional authority and norms. These two types of values are not necessarily incompatible: some societies rank high on both, while others rank relatively low on both. But the relatively *priority* accorded to these two types of values is strongly related to a society's growth rate.

Correlation is not causation, of course. In the remainder of this chapter, we will examine other possible causal factors that might account for the striking linkage we have found between Achievement Motivation and economic growth. Unless we can prove these linkages to be spurious, the no-relationship thesis seems untenable. But what third factor could be causing a spurious relationship here?

One possible candidate is suggested by the dependency school, which holds that the dominant factor is international economic exchanges: foreign investment and trade undermine economic growth in peripheral countries. This is the opposite of what economic theory would predict. Economists, citing the benefits of comparative advantage, argue that foreign investment and trade work to *enhance* the wealth of any country. While certain jobs and occupations will lose out, they tend to be replaced by new jobs and occupations that have even higher productivity levels than their predecessors. This increase in productivity leads to greater prosperity. This theoretical expectation is borne out empirically: Hein (1992) and Dollar (1992) analyze economic data from 150 countries and demonstrate that foreign trade and investment variables actually have a rather modest relationship to growth—but that their polarity is the opposite of that proposed by dependency theory: those nations that traded more and had more investment from capitalist countries showed higher, not lower, subsequent rates of economic growth.

Another possible way to explain away the strong linkage between culture and economic growth shown in figure 7.1 would be by arguing that economic growth determines values, rather than the other way around. Do cultural factors lead to economic growth, or does economic growth lead to cultural change? We believe that the causal flow can work in both directions, with the predominant influence varying from case to case. For example, there is strong evidence that Postmaterialist values emerge when a society has attained relatively high levels of economic security: in this case, economic change reshapes culture. On the other hand, once these values become widespread, they are linked with relatively low subsequent rates of economic growth. Here, culture seems to be shaping economics.

In the present case, the most plausible interpretation is that determination and thrift are conducive to economic growth. For some time, economists have been aware that a nation's rate of gross domestic investment is a major influence—generally, the *most* important influence—on its long-term growth rate. Investment, in turn, depends on savings. Thus, a perfectly straightforward reading of the evidence would be that a society that encourages thrift, produces savings; this leads to investment, which brings economic growth.

Emphasis on obedience is negatively linked with economic growth for the

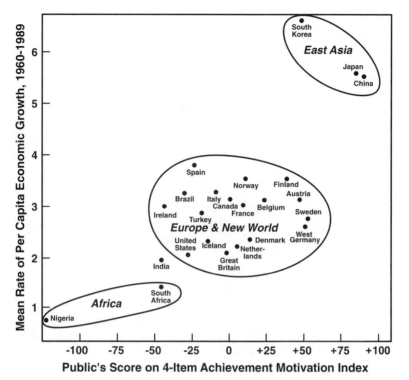

Figure 7.1. Economic growth rate by achievement motivation scores of publics.
Note: Achievement Motivation index is based on percentage in each society who emphasized "Thrift" and "Determination" as important things for a child to learn, *minus* the percentage emphasizing "Obedience" and "Religious faith."

converse reason. In preindustrial societies, obedience means conformity to traditional norms that stigmatize economic accumulation and instead emphasize obligations to share with one's relatives, friends, and neighbors. Such communal obligations are strongly felt in preindustrial societies; within the given culture, they are important virtues. But from the perspective of a bureaucratized rational-legal society, these norms are antithetical to capital accumulation and conducive to nepotism. Furthermore, this conformity to authority inhibits innovation and entrepreneurship.

The motivational component is also tapped by Materialist/Postmaterialist values, with Postmaterialism having a negative linkage with growth. Achievement motivation has a moderate negative linkage with the Materialist/Postmaterialist dimension (r = −.39). Although both Achievement Motivation and Postmaterialist values have significant linkages with economic growth, they affect it in different ways: Achievement Motivation seems to reflect the transition from preindustrial to industrial value systems, linked with the Modernization process. Materialist/Postmaterialist values, on the other hand, reflect the transition from industrial to postindustrial society, bringing a shift *away* from emphasis on economic growth, toward increasing emphasis on protection of the environment and on the quality of life in general. Previous research demonstrates that (1) a gradual shift from Materialist toward Postmaterialist goals has been taking place throughout advanced industrial society, (2) this shift is strongly related to the emergence of democracy, but (3) Postmaterialist values tend to be *negatively* linked with economic growth.

Do these cultural variables add anything to an explanation of economic growth, beyond what is explained by the standard economic variables? To answer this question, we will perform multivariate analyses below. But, first, let us examine the impact of "social capital," that is, propensities toward membership in voluntary associations—something distinct from the "human capital" factor in the endogenous growth model, which refers to skills and is usually operationally measured by the educational level of the given population.

SOCIAL CAPITAL AND ECONOMIC GROWTH

The importance of social capital was first stressed by Tocqueville, who argued that democracy had emerged and flourished in America because the American people participated in numerous and extensive voluntary associations. This fostered cooperation and trust, which were essential to the successful functioning of democratic institutions. Almond and Verba (1963) made similar findings.

In contemporary social science, this idea was reprised by Banfield (1958), who found that Italian society was characterized by low levels of interpersonal trust, especially in Southern Italy, where the prevailing outlook was "amoral familism": the absence of feelings of trust or moral obligation toward anyone outside the nuclear family. The Southern Italian subculture seemed to lack such norms, which severely hindered the large-scale cooperation among strangers that is essential to both economic development and successful democratic institutions.

Testing these ideas in a broader cross-national context, Inglehart (1990) found that interpersonal trust and related cultural orientations were strongly linked with both economic development and stable democracy. He emphasized, however, that culture is a variable, not a constant: though cultural characteristics tend to change slowly, they can and do change. Thus, while the Italian public in the 1980s continued to be characterized by relatively low levels of interpersonal trust (and Southern Italians remained much less trusting than Northern Italians), overall levels of trust had gradually risen.

Putnam (1993) argued that Social Capital plays a crucial role in both political and economic cooperation. Social Capital consists of a culture of trust and tolerance, in which extensive networks of voluntary associations emerge. These networks, in turn, provide contacts and information flows that are supportive of a culture of trust and cooperation: it would be mistaken to assume that economics unilaterally determines culture *or* that culture determines economics. The two are intimately intertwined, and mutually supportive in any society that flourishes for any length of time.

Putnam's work helped clarify the causal linkages between economic and cultural factors, utilizing his exceptionally long time series of both economic and cultural indicators. Analyzing Italian regional-level data from the nineteenth century to the 1980s, Putnam found that certain regions had relatively high levels of social capital, while others had much lower levels. These levels were fairly stable attributes of given regions; and they were strongly linked with the economic development level of those regions. Moreover Putnam's analysis dispels any assumption that these regional cultural differences are simply a consequence of their respective levels of economic development. He found that levels of civic involvement around 1900 predicted civic involvement levels 60 or 70 years later far better than did economic factors. More strikingly still, he also found that levels of civic involvement around 1900 predicted subsequent levels of *economic* development even better than did economic variables. While Putnam rejects cultural determinism as an interpretation of Italian development, his analysis provides strong evidence that cultural factors help shape economic life, as well as being shaped by it.

Another analysis of longitudinal data indicates that individuals' attitudes and expectancies influence their economic outcomes. Szekelyi and Tardos (1993) analyzed the 25-year database of the Panel Study of Income Dynamics carried out by the Institute for Social Research at the University of Michigan. They first identified a syndrome consisting of a long-term time perspective, confidence that one's long-term plans will work out, an emphasis on saving rather than spending now, and interpersonal trust. Analyzing the panel data, they found that those individuals who scored high on this syndrome subsequently earned significantly higher incomes than those who scored low, after controlling for initial levels of income, education, age, sex, race, residence, and region.

Tocqueville had argued that membership in voluntary associations was conducive to democracy. Putnam extends this to argue that a culture characterized by trust, cooperativeness, and extensive networks of secondary associations was conducive to *both* democracy and economic development.

Mancur Olson (1982), by contrast, argues that as a society's networks of secondary association become highly developed, they strangle economic growth. The behavior of individuals and firms in stable societies leads to the formation of dense networks of collusive, cartelistic and lobbying organizations that make economies less efficient and dynamic and polities less governable. The longer a society goes without an upheaval, the more powerful such organizations become—and the more they slow down economic expansion. Societies in which these narrow interest groups have been destroyed by war or revolution enjoy the highest rates of growth. The implications of Putnam's and Olson's theories seem diametrically opposed: does the growth of voluntary associations favor or strangle economic growth?

In fact, the two sets of ideas may not be as incompatible as they at first seem. For Olson emphasizes the negative consequences of organizational networks among *highly developed* societies; at earlier stages of development, they may play an innocuous or even useful role. Putnam, on the other hand, examines the roots of economic development in nineteenth-century Italy and even much earlier. Although he does not discuss the effects of associational networks at various stages of development, his analysis focuses on consequences that result from the presence or absence of these networks in the *early* stages. This, of course, is the phase which seems most relevant to development in contemporary developing nations.

VOLUNTARY ASSOCIATIONS AND ECONOMIC GROWTH IN 43 SOCIETIES

Although Tocqueville developed his thesis in the context of the nineteenth-century United States, and Putnam in the context of nineteenth- and twentieth-century Italy, their implications extend far beyond those settings. Thus, Esman and Uphoff (1984), Cernea (1993), and Landell-Mills (1992) have argued that local associations play a crucial role in the development of agrarian societies throughout the world.

Data from the 1990–91 World Values Survey enable us to examine the impact of membership in voluntary associations in a global perspective. Although this database does not have the long time series that makes Putnam's analysis so powerful, it enables us to test his hypotheses across a much broader spectrum of societies than was available to him or any previous analyst. The World Values survey provides cultural measures from societies throughout the world, covering the full range of economic and political variation.

These surveys provide information about organizational memberships: the respective publics were read a list of 16 types of voluntary associations and asked, "To which, if any, of these organizations do you belong?" They were also asked if they did voluntary work for any of these organizations. The types of organizations that were covered (listed from those with the most members to those with the fewest) are labor unions, religious organizations, sports and recreational organizations, educational/cultural organizations, political parties, professional associations, social welfare organizations, youth work (Scouts, etc.), environmental/conservation organizations, health volunteer work, community action groups, women's organizations, Third World development organizations, animal rights organizations, and peace organizations.

These data were not designed to test the Tocqueville-Putnam hypothesis. Also, they underrepresent the less developed societies, a problem that is exacerbated by the fact that comparable data are not available for three of the four lowest-income countries in our sample. This battery was not asked in India or Turkey because many of these organizations scarcely existed there. It was asked in Nigeria, but was framed to imply "Do you *sympathize* with these organizations?" Consequently, we do not have comparable data from some key cases.

These questions *were* asked in some low-income countries, however, and the results from China are particularly interesting. Although China shows a lower rate of organizational memberships than most advanced industrial societies, it has a high rate for a predominantly rural society. This may reflect the heavy emphasis that the Chinese government has placed on organizing rural populations since the start of the Maoist era.

Does associational membership have the same linkage with economic growth as it does with democracy? The answer is no. The correlates of high economic growth rates prove to be quite different from the syndrome of high levels of associational membership, plus high levels of trust, prosperity, and stable democracy.

High rates of membership in the 16 types of organizations for which we have data are *not* linked with high rates of economic growth during the period from 1950 to 1988; indeed, we find a modest *negative* correlation between associational membership and economic growth ($r = -.22$). What is good for democracy is not necessarily good for economic growth. As Przeworski and Limongi (1993) and Helliwell (1994) have demonstrated, there is no clear relationship between the two: democracies are no likelier (and no less likely) to have high rates of growth than are authoritarian regimes.

Thus far, the evidence seems to support Olson rather than Putnam et al.: membership in organizations is *negatively* related to economic growth (though only weakly so).

But the Olson thesis does not imply that voluntary associations are inherently detrimental to economic growth—only that they are detrimental when they become hypertrophied. Olson is mainly interested in the impact of organized interest groups in advanced industrial societies, where they tend to have stultifying effects. In the early stages of economic development, however, organizations may have a positive impact on growth, as Putnam argues.

We suspect that an interaction effect is involved in the impact of voluntary associations on economic growth. When we test this hypothesis, we find that it is confirmed. Let us compare the relationship between membership rates and economic growth, in relatively rich and relatively poor countries, respectively, dichotomizing our sample between those with a GNP/capita above $8,300 (the median income level for the 43 societies in our sample) and those with a lower GNP/capita. When we do so, we find that the correlation between cumulative membership in the 16 types of organizations included in the survey is *negative* among the more developed societies ($r = -.35$) but *positive* among the less developed ones ($r = .24$). Although neither of these correlations is very strong, they work in opposite directions, as Olson and Putnam together could be taken to imply: their net difference amounts to a substantial .59.

Our data were not designed to test Putnam's hypothesis, and, as we have noted, data are lacking for some particularly interesting cases. Moreover, different types of associations and different intensities of participation show different linkages with economic growth. In the lower-income societies in our sample, active participation in political parties, labor unions, and professional associations shows a particularly strong relationship with economic growth (r = .69) (among richer societies, this relationship disappears). Nevertheless, our findings suggest that Olson's and Putnam's theses are not actually incompatible, provided that they are specified according to a country's level of economic development. Relatively dense networks of associational membership seem to be conducive to economic growth in the earlier stages of development, as Putnam has argued; but (as Olson has argued) these associations can become hypertrophied and excessively powerful in advanced industrial societies, distorting policy to defend well-organized interests at the expense of overall economic growth.

Future research should attempt to improve our measurement of associational membership, and to obtain these measures for a larger number of less-developed societies. For now, the available evidence supports an interpretation that integrates the hypotheses of Olson and Putnam, specifying that they operate at different levels of economic development.

Let us briefly consider another factor that may be related to economic growth. Various writers have argued that reasonably equal income distributions are more conducive to economic growth than highly unequal ones. We measured income inequality using the percentage of income going to the top 20 percent of the population and examined its linkage with economic growth rates from 1950 to 1988. This thesis is supported by the data: the two variables show a significant relationship in the predicted direction (r = −.41). As anticipated, income inequality is linked with relatively low rates of economic growth; but this relationship is not nearly as strong as the relationship between Achievement Motivation and growth. Here again, we find that cultural factors can have even stronger linkages with economic growth than do purely economic variables.

Let us now test the relative impact of economic and cultural factors on economic growth.

THE BASELINE ENDOGENOUS GROWTH MODEL

Neoclassical growth models today build on the work of Solow (1956) and Swan (1956). These models focus on savings, population growth, and shifts in technology as the key influence on growth. Accordingly, one can trace the economic growth consequences resulting from a shift in the rate of saving, the population growth rate, or the level of technology. But these models all have a logical weakness: they show a paradoxical steady-state result. In these models aggregate savings produce a level of capital formation such that gross investment exceeds depreciation, and thereby increases capital per worker. Consequently, at the limit the marginal product of capital declines to the point where the savings (revenue) generated by the capital falls to a level just large enough to replace old equipment and provide new machines for new workers. The result is an unchanging standard of living.

This result is clearly not supported by evidence from the real world. Consequently, economists began searching for ways to augment the neoclassical model that would allow sustainable growth and increases in the standard of living. These models have been termed endogenous growth models. At the heart of the endogenous growth literature is an emphasis on the productivity of the population (Barro, 1990, 1991; Lucas, 1988; Romer, 1986, 1990). Unlike earlier neoclassical models, endogenous growth models show that reproducible capital need not have decreasing returns to scale; they assume constant returns to scale to a broad range of reproducible inputs, including human capital. Consequently, growth can be sustained.

The two leading schools of thought, however, differ in their emphasis. Romer (1990) argues that increased research and development spending is the key to new technological developments, which result in increasing social returns to social knowledge. Lucas (1988) argues that expansion of human capital in terms of both education and "learning by doing" also plays a pivotal role in economic growth.

Empirical endogenous growth models virtually always include initial levels of wealth and investment in human capital (as well as investment rates and growth rates), since studies by Barro (1991), Helliwell (1994), Levine and Renelt (1992), and Mankiw, Romer, and Weil (1992) all find that they have robust and positive partial correlations with economic growth.

Including initial levels of wealth (each society's Gross Domestic Product per capita) enables us to test the proposition that a society's absolute level of wealth is a significant determinant of its growth rates. There are two contrasting hypotheses concerning why this might be true. First, dependency theory implies that it is inherently easier for already developed ("core") countries to achieve growth than it is for the poorer ("peripheral") ones: the already established core economies dominate the world economy and can prevent the newcomers from developing. The second model takes exactly the opposite view: it is inherently easier for *less* developed countries to attain high growth rates than it for developed ones. The former can import already proven technology from richer countries; whereas the more developed societies can only grow by developing new technology—which is costly and often does not pay off. The empirical findings clearly support the latter interpretation: poorer countries show higher growth rates.

Levine and Renelt (1992) find that the initial level of per capita income, the initial level of human capital investment, and the period share of investment to GDP have robust correlations with economic growth. Their investigation uses a variant of Leamer's (1983) Extreme Bounds Analysis (EBA) which emphasizes the stability of various focus parameters when variables are removed or added. They find that most other exogenous variables are fragile to alterations in the conditioning set of information. Thus, the conclusions of most empirical work rest on parameter estimates that fluctuate enough to make scholars wary. Levine and Renelt's work is also useful because they provide a straightforward way to evaluate the sensitivity of the cultural variables; we implement this procedure below.

Multivariate Analysis

Our empirical approach is straightforward: we begin by using ordinary least squares regression to estimate a baseline endogenous growth model that includes the variables identified by Levine and Renelt (1992) as having robust partial correlations with economic growth. Using data for 25 countries, we first test the endogenous growth specification (model 1 in table 7.1).[3] Each nation's rate of per capita economic growth is regressed on its initial level of per capita income and human capital investment (education spending) as well as on its rate of physical capital investment. As expected, the results fit the predictions of endogenous growth theory. The results can be summarized as follows: (1) the significant negative coefficient on the initial level of per capita income indicates that controlling for human and physical capital investment, poorer nations grow faster than richer nations; (2) investment in human capital (education spending) has a positive and statistically significant effect on subsequent economic growth; and (3) increasing the rate of physical capital investment increases a nation's rate of economic growth. Overall, this baseline model performs well: it accounts for 55 percent of the variation in cross-national growth rates and is consistent with prior cross-national tests of the conditional convergence hypothesis (e.g., Barro, 1991; Mankiw et al., 1992). Model 1 also passes all diagnostic tests, indicating that the residuals are not serially correlated (LM test), are normally distributed (Jarque-Bera test), and are not heteroskedastic (White test).

Model 2 in table 7.1 regresses the rate of per capita economic growth on a constant and the two cultural variables. As expected, both achievement motivation and Postmaterialism are significant predictors of economic growth and have the expected sign: achievement motivation has a positive linkage with growth, while Postmaterialist values have a negative linkage with growth. Thus, the evidence tends to support the arguments of both the Protestant Ethic and Postmaterialist theses. Moreover, these variables, taken by themselves, account for 59 percent of the variance in growth rates—even more than is explained by the economic variables alone. A glance at the diagnostics again indicates that the residuals are well behaved.

COMPARING COMPETING EMPIRICAL MODELS: ENCOMPASSING RESULTS

Both the economic and cultural models give similar goodness-of-fit performance; and each model's regressors are statistically significant. But which model is superior? Or does each model possess explanatory factors that are missing in the other? Mizon and Richard (1986) have devised the encompassing approach, a set of statistical procedures that can guide us in building a theoretically parsimonious and statistically efficient model of economic growth

---

[3] The data used in the regression analyses in table 7.1 are provided in Appendix 3.

TABLE 7.1

OLS Estimation of Economic Growth Models Dependent Variable: Mean Rate of per Capita Economic Growth (1960–89)

Model Variable	Model 1	Model 2	Model 3	Model 4
Constant	−0.70 (1.08)	7.29* (1.49)	3.16 (1.94)	2.4* (0.77)
Per Capita GDP in 1960	−.63* (0.14)	—	−0.42* (0.14)	−0.43* (0.10)
Primary Education in 1960	2.69* (1.22)	—	2.19* (1.06)	2.09* (0.96)
Secondary Education in 1960	3.27* (1.01)	—	1.21 (1.08)	—
Investment	8.69* (4.90)	—	3.09 (4.40)	—
Achievement Motivation	—	2.07* (0.37)	1.44* (0.48)	1.88* (0.35)
Postmaterialism	—	−2.24* (0.77)	−1.07 (1.03)	—
R^2 Adjusted	.55	.59	.69	.70
SEE	.86	.83	.72	.71
LM [$\chi^2(1)$]	.42	.65	.68	.87
Jarque-Bera [$\chi^2(2)$]	.05	.30	.18	.57
White [$\chi^2(1)$]	.28	.24	.37	.18
SC	.119	−.117	−.095	−.352

Notes: Mean of dependent variable: 3.04. N is 25 for all models. Standard errors in parentheses.
*t test: $p < .05$

that answers these questions. The encompassing principle investigates the validity of a model relative to an alternative by determining whether a model statistically accounts for the main features of a rival, enabling analysts to choose one explanation over another and to assess the relative credibility of theoretical and empirical models. Granato, Inglehart, and Leblang (1996; see also Granato and Suzuki, 1995) use encompassing analysis to test various theories of economic growth, presenting a detailed explanation of this technique and illustrates its usefulness. We summarize their findings here. They find that neither model 1 nor model 2 is an efficient substitute for the other, and both models explain aspects of growth that the other cannot. In short, growth rates are best understood as a consequence of *both* economic and cultural factors. Accordingly, they combine the two models, with the results shown in table 7.1, model 3.

Some dramatic changes take place when we analyze the joint effects of cultural factors and economic factors. The most striking finding is the fact that the coefficient for investment decreases dramatically, falling from 8.69 in model 1 to 3.09 in model 3: while it still has the expected sign, it is now well below significance. Why is physical capital investment, which was robustly correlated with economic growth in other studies, now insignificant? We have suggested that achievement motivation is conducive to economic growth partly because it encourages relatively high rates of investment (one of its components is an emphasis on thrift—and, as this suggests, achievement motivation and investment are highly correlated). Consequently, when we take achievement motivation into account, we are controlling for investment to a considerable extent. Presumably, the direct path from culture to economic growth reflects the effect of motivational factors on entrepreneurship and effort.

Model 3 in table 7.1 indicates that achievement motivation is positively and significantly related to economic growth. But the coefficient for Postmaterialist values is now insignificant. This is probably due to the fact that Postmaterialism is most widespread in relatively rich countries, as we saw in chapter 4. The bivariate correlation between Postmaterialism and initial level of wealth is .75, which means that by controlling for wealth (and education) we have largely controlled for Postmaterialism as well. Secondary school enrollment also drops below significance in model 3: it is highly correlated with primary school enrollment, which continues to show significant effects.

Model 4 eliminates the three insignificant variables from model 3 to check the stability of the remaining parameters. Model 4 is quite clearly the most parsimonious and efficient model, explaining 70 percent of the variance in economic growth rates with only three variables (considerably more than either the economic or the cultural factors did alone) and generating a Schwartz criterion (SC) value of $-.352$, which indicates that this is the most robust of our four models. In addition, the residuals are well behaved, and the model passes tests for serial (spatial) correlation, normality, and heteroskedasticity.

Granato et al. (1996) test the robustness of this model in a number of additional ways, examining what happens when influential observations are removed (see Jackman, 1987), and when alterations are made in the set of variables included (see Levine and Renelt, 1992). The robustness of these results were further validated using a variant of Leamer's Extreme Bounds Analysis and nonparametric methods including robust regression and bootstrap resampling. By all of these tests, this model proves to be robust—and, in particular, Achievement Motivation continues to have a significant impact on economic growth.

A number of theoretically interesting variables showed significant zero-order relationships with economic growth, but were dropped from these models because they did not show statistically significant relationships in competition with other key independent variables. These variables include both income inequality and organizational memberships. And, as we have seen, though Postmaterialist values showed a significant impact on economic growth, in the predicted direction, its impact drops below statistical significance in our final model. This does not prove that these variables do not have an impact on economic growth—but simply that they are not among the two or three strongest predictors. When analyzing 2,000 cases, many independent variables can have statistically significant effects. But with an N of only 25 countries and a good deal of shared variance, as we have here, only the few variables that have the strongest relationships are likely to reach statistical significance. We think it likely that these other factors also play a role; but the encompassing analysis indicates that the most *important* influences on economic growth are (1) Achievement Motivation values, (2) human capital investment, and (3) the initial level of per capita GDP.

STRUCTURAL EQUATION MODELS

We have found that both Achievement Motivation and Gross Domestic Investment are closely linked to economic growth rates—and that the two are closely related. It seems likely that Achievement Motivation is conducive to economic growth at least partly because it encourages relatively high rates of investment. In order to examine the extent to which a multistage process such as this is at work, we tested a number of structural equation models based on this principle. The best-fitting model is shown in figure 7.2.

This model shows a chi-square of 3.56 and p = .313 with 3 degrees of freedom and an RMSR of .034, indicating a good fit with the data, and it explains 57 percent of the cross-national variance in economic growth. This model not only explains a higher percentage of the variance in economic growth than does a similar model based on economic variables alone (which accounts for only 45 percent of the variance), it also helps explain why gross domestic investment occurs: cultural differences lead to different investment rates. The model containing economic variables alone does not do so: investment rates are not significantly related to GNP/capita or to other purely economic variables.

This model has a number of interesting features. The most important finding, however, is that the data are consistent with a model positing that high levels of Achievement Motivation are conducive to high levels of investment, and to high levels of economic growth. Human capital (operationally, a high percentage of the population having secondary or higher education) is also conducive to investment (both represent forms of deferred gratification, building up two different types of capital for the future). But Achievement Motivation plays an even more important role, apparently having a major impact on Gross Domestic Investment. Achievement Motivation also has an important direct effect on economic growth rates, quite apart from its tendency to increase domestic investment: the direct path from Achievement Motivation to Growth

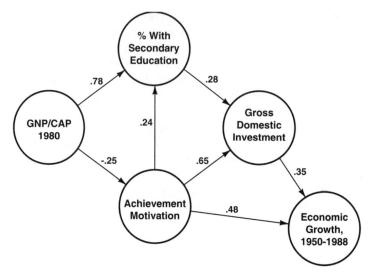

Figure 7.2. Economic and cultural influences on economic growth:
structural equation model.
N = 43, Chi squared = 3.56, p = .313, df = 3, RMSR = .034. *Source*:
World Bank data and 1990–91 World Values Survey data, aggregated to
national level.

probably reflects the effect of motivational factors on entrepreneurship and effort.

CONCLUSIONS: CULTURAL FACTORS IN ECONOMIC GROWTH

The idea that economic growth is partly shaped by cultural factors has been
highly controversial. One reason why this idea has been resisted is because culture is often thought of as a diffuse and permanent feature of given societies:
if culture determines economic growth, then the outlook for economic development seems hopeless, because culture cannot be changed.

When we approach culture as something to be measured by quantitative empirical means, this illusion of diffuseness and permanence disappears. We no
longer need deal with gross stereotypes, such as the idea that "Germans have
always been militaristic," or "Hispanic culture is unfavorable to development." We can move, instead, to the analysis of specific components of given
cultures at given times. Research carried out in this manner finds that, from
1945 to 1975, West German political culture underwent a striking transformation, from being relatively authoritarian to becoming increasingly democratic
and participant (Baker et al., 1981). We find that, from 1970 to 1995, the United
States and a number of Western European societies experienced a gradual intergenerational shift from having predominantly Materialist priorities toward
having increasingly Postmaterialist priorities. Although these changes have

been gradual, they demonstrate that central elements of culture can and do change.

Furthermore, empirical research can help identify the specific components of culture that are most relevant to economic development. One need not seek to change a society's entire way of life. The present findings suggest that one specific component—Achievement Motivation—plays a key role in economic growth. In the short run, it is not easy to change even a relatively narrow and well-defined cultural component such as this, but it seems far easier than attempting to change a society's entire culture. Simply making parents, schools, and other organizations aware of the relevant attitudes may be a step in the right direction.

As Weber suggested more than 90 years ago, cultural factors seem to play an important role in economic development: societies differ in the extent to which they emphasize thrift, savings, and individual economic achievement, as opposed to traditional communal obligations—and those that emphasize the former tend to show higher rates of growth.

Does this mean that societies that emphasize traditional values are doomed to remain permanently less developed? By no means. Only the old, carved-in-marble view of culture would point to this conclusion. As we have argued throughout this book, culture is a variable, not a constant. Although the Industrial Revolution was launched in predominantly Protestant countries, the "Protestant Ethic" spread to Catholic Europe, which today has a higher growth rate than Northern Europe. Moreover, precisely because they are less developed, low-income countries eventually develop one advantage over rich ones: they possess a pool of relatively low-cost labor, which eventually begins to attract investment from their richer neighbors. Thus, during the postwar era, the richer countries of Northern Europe began to build plants in Southern Europe, and remittances from "guest workers" in the North helped fuel the economic takeoff of the southern countries. More recently, this happened in East Asia, when the Japanese labor force became high-cost in comparison with that of its neighbors. Japanese investment (and outsourcing of components for Japanese products) flowed into the rest of East Asia—and more recently into Southeast Asia and South Asia.

This tendency for economic development to spread to countries having a cheap and efficient labor force is complemented by another process: cultural changes in the developed societies eventually bring a shift in emphasis away from economic growth at any cost, toward greater emphasis on environmental protection.

The present analysis suggests that a given society's culture plays an important role in economic growth—with a specific and clearly defined Achievement Motivation dimension being particularly significant. Although this is the only cultural variable that shows a statistically significant impact on economic growth in this analysis, much the same situation holds true here as in connection with stable democracy. Achievement Motivation is part of a cultural syndrome linked with growth. With a large amount of shared variance and only

25 cases, only this variable shows a statistically significant relationship, but it seems unlikely that it is the only relevant cultural variable. Postmaterialist values may also play an important role in shifting emphasis away from thrift and saving, though their effect tends to be confounded with the fact that they are found in relatively wealthy countries, which tend to have low growth rates for a variety of reasons. Also potentially important, though they do not show statistically significant results in this analysis, are a society's associational networks—which seem to play contrasting roles in developed and developing societies.

Since we do not yet have time series data on these values, we cannot reach definitive conclusions about the causal relations between culture and economic growth. An alternative interpretation to our own would be that high rates of economic growth somehow give rise to a culture that emphasizes thrift and determination. This is conceivable. But there is an obvious logic to the hypothesis that cultures that emphasize thrift and determination should tend to show high growth rates: thrift makes high investment rates possible. If we try to turn the causal arrow around, however, there is no obvious reason why rapid growth would bring increasing emphasis on thrift: quite the contrary, one would expect it to give rise to higher rates of *spending*. Until we have cultural time series data, we cannot regard the matter as settled, but the evidence strongly suggests that certain cultural values play an important role in economic growth.

The question "Is economic growth due to cultural factors or to economic factors?" misses the point. Cultural factors are intimately linked with economic factors; and they provide a strong explanation of why, over the long term, some societies have shown much higher rates of economic growth than others. Both the encompassing tests and the structural equation models demonstrate that a model that includes both cultural factors and economic factors has a significantly better fit and explains more of the variance than does a model that relies on economic variables alone.

Economic theory has already begun to incorporate social norms and cultural factors into its models (Cole, Malaith, and Postlewaite, 1992; Fershtman and Weiss, 1993). The logical next step is to determine how cultural and motivational factors can be used to augment existing economic models in order to gain a better understanding of economic growth.

The collapse of the Soviet economy illustrates how costly it can be in the long run to refuse to consider the importance of individual incentives and motivations. Our results indicate that both cultural and economic factors are crucial to economic growth. Neither supplants the other. Future research will be best served by treating the two types of explanation as complementary.

The Rise of New Issues and New Parties

THE GOALS OF BOTH INDIVIDUALS and of societies are changing as a result of the diminishing marginal utility of economic growth. This is changing the political agenda of advanced industrial societies, giving rise to new issues, new political movements, and new political parties. This chapter examines how this is happening at both the individual and societal levels.

CHANGING VALUES AND A CHANGING POLITICAL AGENDA

The shift toward Postmodern values has brought a shift in the political agenda throughout advanced industrial society, moving it away from an emphasis on economic growth at any price, toward increasing concern for its environmental costs. It has also brought a shift from political cleavages based on social class conflict toward cleavages based on cultural issues and quality of life concerns. Huntington (1994) has gone so far as to argue that the main basis of global political conflict from now on will no longer be economic or ideological issues, but cultural issues: world politics will revolve around a "Clash of Civilizations." While this projection may be overdrawn, there is no question that ethnic and cultural issues are becoming more prominent. Economic conflicts are likely to remain important. But, while in the past they dominated the scene to such a degree that many influential thinkers accepted the Marxist view that economics was virtually the whole story, today this seems less plausible. Economic conflicts are increasingly sharing the stage with new issues that were almost invisible a generation ago: environmental protection, abortion, ethnic conflicts, women's issues, and gay and lesbian emancipation are heated issues today—while the central element of the Marxist prescription, nationalization of industry, is almost a forgotten cause.

As a result, a new dimension of political conflict has become increasingly salient. It reflects a polarization between modern and postmodern issue preferences. This new dimension is distinct from the traditional Left-Right conflict over ownership of the means of production and distribution of income. Its growing salience is transforming the meaning of Left and Right and changing the social bases of Left and Right. Historically, the Left was based on the working class and the Right on the middle and upper classes. Today, increasingly, support for the Left comes from middle-class Postmaterialists, while a new Right draws support from less secure segments of the working class. A new Postmodern political cleavage pits culturally conservative, often xenophobic, parties, disproportionately supported by Materialists, against change-oriented parties, often emphasizing environmental protection, and disproportionately supported by Postmaterialists.

Throughout most of the twentieth century, it was generally agreed that support for more state intervention in the economy was the crucial distinction between Left and Right. From a Marxist perspective, private ownership was the root problem, and nationalization of industry and state control of the economy constituted the core solution to all social problems. Abolishing private ownership of the means of production, it was thought, would eradicate exploitation, oppression, alienation, crime, and war.

Although they called themselves "liberals," the American Left also tended to view more state regulation and control of the economy as inherently good: liberals were those who supported a growing role for the state; conservatives were those who opposed it. Well into the 1970s, Western political elites continued to define the meanings of "Left" and "Right" in terms of state intervention in the economy and society (see Aberbach et al., 1981, 115–69).

This consensus has dissolved. It no longer seems self-evident that more state authority constitutes progress, even to those on the Left. One of the key developments of recent years has been a growing skepticism about the desirability and effectiveness of state planning and control, a growing concern for individual autonomy, and a growing respect for market forces. In recent years this outlook has been endorsed not only by conservatives but also by growing segments of the Left. As early as the 1960s, New Left groups emerged in the West that were highly critical of big government, viewed bureaucracy as dehumanizing, and called for devolution of decision-making power to local communities and to those directly affected by the decisions.

In an even more dramatic change, post-socialist Eastern European governments have been drastically reducing the role of the state. And in China, the pragmatists who came to power after the death of Mao, though still nominally communists, have been allowing more and more scope for individual enterprise and an increased role for market forces, though continuing to repress political pluralism. The last attempt to apply the classic policies of the Left in a major Western nation occurred in 1981, when a socialist-communist coalition won office in France. After two years of unrewarding experience with nationalization of industry and other traditional policies of the Left, the socialists abandoned the classic Marxist approach and shifted to market-oriented policies. Similar shifts toward market economies have been occurring in Asia, Africa, and Latin America, even in states led by elites who were shaped by Marxism. Today, almost no one views nationalization of industry as a panacea. While the economic Left-Right dimension still exists, its meaning has changed radically.

The transition from a state-run economy to a market economy often entails traumatic costs. In a number of ex-communist societies, this has brought former communist elites back into power under new labels. But even in these cases, there has not been a return to a Soviet-style state-run economy; instead, the policies of former communist elites have generally been limited to slow-ing down the pace of change and attempting to soften its shock. Where change is occurring in this area today, it is predominantly a movement toward *privatization* of former state functions. The Right consists of those who are pushing for faster or more widespread privatization; the Left consists of those who resist privatization or urge that it be done more slowly.

Russia is an exception: here, in a reversal of meanings, the "Left" label now designates the reformers who are seeking a market economy with private ownership. Russia is torn between reformers on the Left, seeking a greater role for individual initiative and individual self-expression, and the still-entrenched Nomenklatura on the Right, clinging to power and privilege based on their control of the economy. Well into the 1990s, Russia was trapped between two eras, with its state-run economy collapsing but with its market economy not yet fully established. Halfway measures to move toward a more open but more competitive and less predictable society brought suffering and insecurity to a large part of the Russian people. In the 1993 elections to the Russian parliament, a majority of seats were won by a coalition of former communist hardliners and xenophobic protofascists. The future of the reform movement, and of democracy itself, is uncertain there, but the old lines of confrontation have changed irrevocably.

This change in orientations toward state authority can be analyzed on two levels. At the individual level these changes reflect the Postmodern shift in basic values; and at the societal level, they reflect the fact that the expansion of the state has reached a point of diminishing returns. The two developments are mutually supportive.

In the ex-socialist countries, overexpansion of the state eventually paralyzed innovation and economic growth, bringing their economies to the point of collapse. In the West, the problem is more limited; economic growth continues, but the welfare state is in crisis. Paradoxically, this crisis does not reflect the failure of the welfare state so much as the fact that it has succeeded in alleviating those problems it can most readily solve—and thereby helped pave the way for new types of problems to become central. The expansion of the welfare state tempered the ruthless exploitation of laissez-faire capitalism, helping it evolve into a stabler and more viable form of society. Today, in contrast with previous history, the masses do not starve even in times of severe economic decline; their standard of living has been stabilized at a modest level of economic security, reducing social class tensions. This helps explain why—in contrast to the widespread political extremism that arose during the Great Depression of the 1930s—Western nations' politics remained on a relatively even keel during the recent recessions, even though unemployment in some countries exceeded the levels experienced during the Great Depression.

But the growth of the welfare state has begun to reach its limits. When government expenditures exceed 55 percent of gross national product, as is now the case in many Western societies, there is little room for further expansion; taxation becomes massive, and the majority of the public feels the burden.

INDIVIDUAL-LEVEL CHANGES: THE POSTMODERN SHIFT AND THE RISE
OF THE POSTMODERN POLITICS CLEAVAGE

The goals of both individuals and of societies are changing as a result of the
diminishing marginal utility of economic growth. In this respect, cultural
change behaves as if it were a rational response to the changing physical and
socioeconomic environment. But culture exists in the minds and feelings of
given peoples. Accordingly, it changes only insofar as what people learn and
experience reshapes prevailing beliefs and values. It can be analyzed at both
the individual and societal levels, which are simply two sides of the same coin.

The rise of a new axis of political cleavage started with changes in the values of individuals—which then brought new issues such as abortion, environmental protection, and women's issues to a central place in the political arena.
Only gradually and a good deal later did these changes reshape political cleavages and lead to the emergence of new political parties. Long-established institutions have considerable inertia and are slow to change.

For most of the twentieth century, the dominant axis of political cleavage
was the Left-Right polarization based on economic issues, with the working
class supporting the Left and the middle class supporting the Right. In his 1960
classic *Political Man*, Lipset correctly described this polarization as the most
important single fact about political cleavages throughout the industrial world.
In a predominantly materialistic world, conflict over income and ownership of
the means of production was the central issue.

But significant numbers of Postmaterialists moved into political relevance,
as the postwar generation began to reach adulthood. Postmaterialists first became visible as student protesters, during the 1960s, bringing a variety of new
issues into the political arena. At that point in time their values differed sharply
from those of the dominant establishment; they were outsiders and invented a
whole repertory of (then) unconventional protest tactics to bring their goals to
national notice. But as they reached maturity and began to occupy positions of
power, Postmaterialists adopted new strategies. By the 1980s, they were becoming powerful within established political parties, or were founding successful political institutions of their own. As Postmaterialist elites took over
established institutions, political extremism became less and less associated
with the Left, and increasingly a tactic used by the Right.

For most of the past three decades, Postmaterialists have dominated the political agenda in most Western democracies: overwhelmingly, the new issues
that were introduced during the 1960s and 1970s reflected Postmodern priorities. It was only recently that the Right staged a counterattack, often utilizing
the same political techniques that the Postmaterialists had introduced during
the 1960s, when they were a relatively powerless minority.

The Modern/Postmodern dimension described in chapter 3 reflects the wide
array of new issues that have become prominent with the rise of Postmodern
politics: these issues range from abortion to cultural change and ethnic diversity as figure 3.2 demonstrated. Although a variety of issues became salient

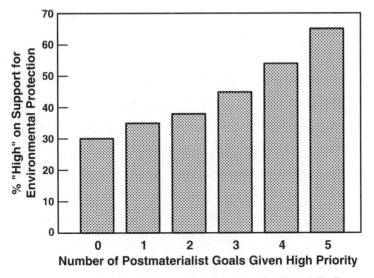

Figure 8.1. Support for environmental protection, by Materialist/Post-materialist values in five advanced industrial societies. *Source*: 1990–93 World Values Survey data from United States, Britain, France, West Germany, and Sweden (N = 7,473). *Note*: Respondents are classified as "high" on the environmental protection index if they (1) agreed with *both* of the following: (a) "I would give part of my income if I were certain that the money would be used to prevent environmental pollution," and (b) "I would agree to an increase in taxes if the extra money were used to prevent environmental pollution," *and* (2) they also disagreed with *both* of the following: (a) "The government should reduce environmental pollution but it should not cost me any money," and (b) "Protecting the environment and fighting pollution is less urgent than often suggested."

with the emergence of Postmodern culture, the central issue initially was the Peace Movement. But as the war in Vietnam receded into the past, environmental causes became the flagship issue. Throughout advanced industrial society (though not necessarily in developing societies), Postmaterialists are far more favorable to environmental protection than are Materialists, as figure 8.1 demonstrates.

Postmaterialist Values and Environmental Attitudes

The rise of Postmaterialist values helps account for the spectacular rise in the salience of environmental issues which has taken place during the past two decades. Postmaterialism became a significant political force during the past 25 years, as the postwar generation emerged into political relevance. Shortly afterward, environmental concerns took on an unprecedented salience throughout advanced industrial society.

Postmaterialist goals are not the only factor motivating concern for the quality of the environment. In advanced industrial society, environmental protection is primarily a Postmaterialist concern; but in many developing countries, from China to Mexico, air pollution and water pollution levels are far worse than in advanced industrial societies, posing immediate problems to health. In such settings, environmental protection is not a quality of life issue, but a matter of survival; it is as likely to be supported by Materialists as by Postmaterialists. The highest levels of support for environmental protection, however, are found in the Nordic countries and the Netherlands—which have the most Postmaterialist publics in the world (Inglehart, 1995).

Figure 8.1 shows the relationship between Materialist/Postmaterialist values and support for environmental protection in advanced industrial societies. This figure uses a 12-item battery in which the following five items tap Postmaterialist priorities across virtually all 43 societies included in the World Values surveys (see Abramson and Inglehart, 1995):

Protecting freedom of speech
Giving people more say in important government decisions
A less impersonal, more humane society
Giving people more say on the job and in their communities
A society in which ideas count more than money

A given individual may choose anywhere from zero to all five of these items among his or her high-priority goals.

In advanced industrial societies, these values are strongly related to support for environmental protection: as figure 8.1 demonstrates, among those who give high priority to none of the Postmaterialist goals, only 29 percent rank high on support for environmental protection; among those who give high priority to all five Postmaterialist goals, fully 68 percent rank high on support for environmental protection. This relationship has impressive strength across advanced industrial societies, especially considering the fact that none of the five Postmaterialist items makes any direct reference to environmental concerns.

It is relatively easy to give lip service to environmental protection, and many people do so. Do these attitudes have behavioral consequences? The relatively favorable attitude of Postmaterialists toward environmental causes is not just a matter of lip service: their behavior reflects their distinctive values to an even *greater* extent than do their attitudes. Although Postmaterialists are only about twice as likely as Materialists to favor environmental protection, they are four to 10 times as likely to be active members of environmental protection groups. And Postmaterialists are four to six times as likely to vote for environmentalist parties (in countries that have them) as are Materialists. Figure 8.2 shows the evidence from four Western societies.

The Materialist/Postmaterialist dimension has become the basis of a major new axis of political polarization in Western Europe, leading to the rise of the Green Party in West Germany, and to a realignment of party systems in a number of other countries (Inglehart, 1977, 1990; Dalton, Flanagan, and Beck,

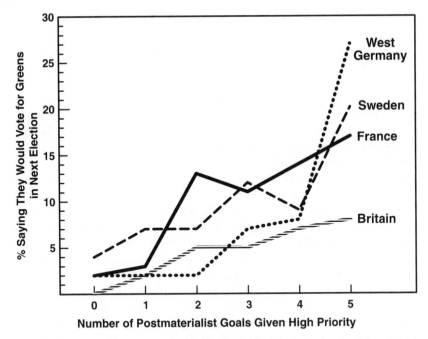

Figure 8.2. Intent to vote for environmentalist political parties, by Materialist/ Postmaterialist values in four countries having such parties. *Source*: 1990–93 World Values Survey.

1984). During the 1980s, environmentalist parties emerged in West Germany, the Netherlands, Belgium, Austria, and Switzerland. In the 1990s they made breakthroughs in Sweden and France and are beginning to show significant levels of support in Great Britain. In every case, support for these parties comes from a disproportionately Postmaterialist constituency. As figure 8.2 demonstrates, as we move from the Materialist to the Postmaterialist end of the continuum, the percentage intending to vote for the environmentalist party in their country rises steeply: from 0 to 8 percent in Britain, from 2 to 17 percent in France, from 4 to 20 percent in Sweden, and from 2 to 27 percent in Western Germany. Pure Postmaterialists are five to 12 times as likely to vote for environmentalist parties as are pure Materialists. Environmentalist parties are not yet strong enough to govern independently and may never be so; but they have successfully advocated environmental protection policies in each of these countries and have forced the established parties to adopt stronger environmental protection policies in order to compete for their voters.

A New Axis of Political Cleavage: Postmodern versus Fundamentalist Values

Although it is more difficult to change long-established institutions than individuals' attitudes, environmentalist parties have begun to emerge in many societies in which the electoral system does not tend to strangle new parties. Why? The environmentalist cause is only one of many Postmodern issues favored by Postmaterialists. This electorate is distinctive in its entire worldview: they are relatively favorable to women's rights, disabled groups, gay and lesbian emancipation, ethnic minorities, and a number of other causes. But the environmental cause has emerged as the symbolic center of this broad cultural emancipation movement: while many of the other Postmodern causes tend to be divisive, practically everyone likes clean air and green trees. Although these parties reflect an entire worldview, environmental symbols captures the issue on which they have the widest potential appeal.

Nevertheless, the rise of Postmaterialist causes has given rise to negative reactions from the very start. The French student protest movement was able to paralyze the entire country in May 1968; but it led to a massive shift of working-class voters, who rallied behind De Gaulle as the guarantor of law and order, giving the Gaullists a landslide victory in the June 1968 elections. In the same year, student protesters in the United States were able to bring down Lyndon Johnson, but they alienated much of the traditional Democratic Party electorate—many of whom threw their support to a reactionary candidate, George Wallace, enabling Richard Nixon to win the presidency. The 1972 elections were something of a replay, except that this time normally Democratic voters who were repelled by the seeming radicalism of the McGovern campaign supported Nixon: for the first time in history, white working-class voters were about as likely to vote for the Republican as for the Democratic candidate. The aftermath of these events transformed the two parties, but the United States still has a two-party system, with the same party labels as before: superficially, the system seems unchanged.

Although Postmaterialist-led parties emerged in both the Netherlands and Belgium during the 1970s, West Germany was the scene of the first breakthrough by an environmentalist party in a major industrial nation. Postmaterialist protest had manifested itself as dramatically in Germany as in the United States or France, but it was only in 1983 that the Greens were sufficiently strong and well organized to surmount West Germany's 5 percent hurdle and enter the West German parliament—bringing a significant structural change to West German politics. But more recently, the Greens have been countered by a Republikaner party characterized by cultural conservatism and xenophobia. In the 1994 national elections, the Greens won 7 percent of the vote. The Republikaner, on the other hand, were stigmatized as the heirs of the Nazis and won only 2 percent of the vote, too little to win parliamentary representation. Nevertheless, xenophobic forces have already had a substantial impact on German politics, motivating the established parties to shift their policy positions in order to co-opt the Republikaner electorate. These efforts even included an amendment to the German constitution: to cut down the influx of foreigners, the clause guaranteeing free right of political asylum was revised in 1993, in a decision supported by a two-thirds majority of the German parliament.

The rise of the Green Party in Germany has also had a major impact even

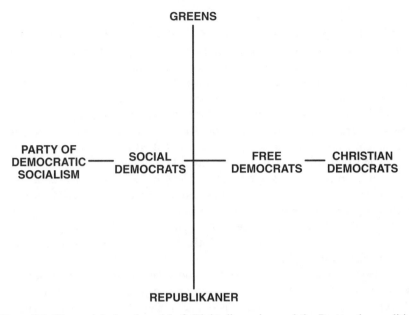

Figure 8.3. The social class-based Left-Right dimension and the Postmodern politics dimension in Germany.

though only a small portion of the electorate votes for it. For the Greens, like other New Left parties and movements, reflect an entire worldview which differs fundamentally from that of the traditional Left. Despite their name, the Greens are much more than an ecological party. They seek to build a basically different kind of society from the prevailing industrial model. During the Cold War, their most massive demonstrations were directed against nuclear weapons and NATO. They have actively supported a wide range of Postmodern causes, from unilateral disarmament to women's' emancipation, gay and lesbian rights, rights for the physically disabled, Palestinian liberation, and citizenship rights for non-German immigrants. But their greatest impact on German politics has been in forcing the established parties, from the Christian Democrats to the Social Democrats, to adopt pro-environmentalist positions in order to compete for the Greens' voters.

The Greens and the Republikaner are located at opposite poles of a new political dimension, as figure 8.3 suggests. If we simply judged by their labels, this might not seem to be the case: the Republikaner do not call themselves the Anti-Environment Party; nor do the Greens call themselves the Pro-Immigrant Party. But, in fact, their constituencies are disproportionately Materialist and Postmaterialist, respectively; and these parties adopt opposite policies on the relevant issues. The older parties are arrayed on the traditional Left-Right axis, established in an era when political cleavages were dominated by social class conflict. On this axis (the horizontal dimension of figure 8.3) both elites and mass electorates place the Party of Democratic Socialism (the Eastern German ex-communists) on the extreme Left, followed by the Social Democrats and the Free Democrats, with the Christian Democrats at the Right of the spectrum. This figure is schematic. As Kitschelt (1995) has demonstrated, the new politics dimension is not perpendicular to the long-established Left-Right dimension. Instead, the Greens are closer to the old Left on key issues, while the Republikaner are closer to the Right. But, although both elites and masses tend to think of the Greens as located on the Left, they represent a fundamentally new Left. Traditionally, the Left parties have been based on a working-class constituency and advocated a program that called for nationalization of industry and redistribution of income. In striking contrast, the Postmaterialist Left appeals primarily to a middle-class constituency and is only faintly interested in the classic program of the Left. For example, Postmaterialists are not necessarily more favorable to state ownership than are Materialists, as figure 8.12 indicates. But Postmaterialists *are* intensely favorable to the Left position on Postmodern issues—which frequently repel the traditional working-class constituency of the Left.

The vertical axis on figure 8.3 reflects the polarization between Postmodern and Fundamentalist values, reflecting differences in people's subjective sense of security. At one end, we find a Postmodern openness to ethnic diversity and changing gender roles; at the opposite pole we find an emphasis on familiar values (often rooted in traditional religion) in the face of insecurity. This cleavage tends to pit the Postmaterialists against those with traditional religious values. Although the classic interpretation of secularization attributed it to the cognitive spread of a scientific worldview, we have argued that the rise of a sense of *security* among mass publics of advanced welfare states is an equally important factor in the decline of traditional religious orientations. The cognitive interpretation implies that secularization is inevitable and more or less irreversible. By contrast, the rise of a sense of security among mass publics is far from inevitable and can be undermined by economic decline or rapid change. Fundamentalist movements continue to emerge among the less secure strata of even the most advanced industrial societies, with people reemphasizing traditional values in times of stress.

As figure 8.4 demonstrates, across five advanced industrial societies, 70 percent of the pure Materialists support a policy of reverse affirmative action— that is, the position that "When jobs are scarce, employers should give priority to [one's own nationality] over immigrants." Among the pure Postmaterialist type, only 25 percent are in favor of giving preference to native-born citizens.

Figure 8.5 presents a similar comparison, based on the proportion saying that they would not like to have immigrants or foreign workers as neighbors: 19 percent of the pure Materialists take the xenophobic position, as compared with only 3 percent of the pure Postmaterialists.

On this issue, value priorities have even more impact than they do on the environmental protection issue: Materialists are almost three times as likely as the Postmaterialists to favor employment discrimination favoring the native-

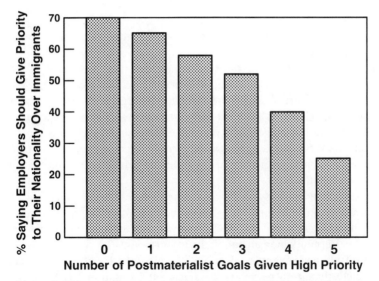

Figure 8.4. Support for giving preference to one's own nationality over immigrants when jobs are scarce, in the United States, Britain, France, West Germany, and Sweden. *Source*: 1990–93 World Values Survey. *Note*: The question was "Do you agree or disagree with the following statement: When jobs are scarce, employers should give priority to [one's nationality] over immigrants."

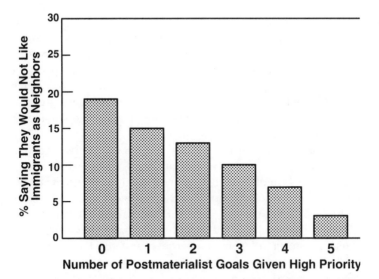

Figure 8.5. Rejection of immigrants as neighbors, in United States, Britain, France, West Germany, and Sweden. *Source*: 1990–93 World Values Survey. *Note*: The question was: "On this list are various groups of people. Could you please sort out any that you would not like to have as neighbors? Just call off the letters, please." The list included 15 groups, such as "heavy drinkers" or "homosexuals," with "immigrants/foreign workers" as one item.

born over foreigners, and six times as likely to say they would not want to have foreigners as neighbors.[1]

Like Materialist/Postmaterialist values (with which it is linked), our measure of xenophobia shows strong differences across age groups, with the younger birth cohorts being more tolerant of foreigners, homosexuals, and other outgroups. But this holds true only in societies that have experienced rising security: in societies that have not experienced economic growth, the young are *not* more tolerant than the old. In low-income societies that have not experienced economic growth, the young are actually *less* tolerant of outgroups than are the old.

A Postmodern Politics axis has also taken shape in other countries, such as France, where an Ecologist Party has recently emerged at the Postmaterialist pole, and the xenophobic National Front at the other. In contrast to Germany, where the Republikaner are unlikely to surmount the 5 percent hurdle, in France's 1993 parliamentary elections, the National Front won 12 percent of the vote. Reflecting a pervasive decline of the traditional Left in the early 1990s, the French Socialist Party won only 18 percent of the vote, and the communists won only 9 percent. Meanwhile, the Ecologists got 8 percent of the vote, the strongest performance they had ever made in elections to the National Assembly. Throughout the postwar era, the communists had been the strongest party in France. In 1993 they were outpolled by the National Front and came in only slightly ahead of the Ecologists. Figure 8.6 depicts the alignment of French parties on the two respective dimensions of political cleavage.

The once-dominant Left-Right dimension based on social class and religion is increasingly sharing the stage with a Postmodern politics dimension. Although support for environmentalist parties has grown in many Western societies, there has also been a right-authoritarian reaction at the opposite pole of the Postmodern Politics dimension. Right-wing extremist parties, such as Le Pen's National Front, have been gaining votes by appealing to antiforeign sentiments. This appeal has been particularly effective among blue-collar workers who formerly voted for parties of the Left.

The social base of such parties consists disproportionately of economically and psychologically marginal segments of society, manifesting a reaction of the insecure in the face of change. Parties of cultural autonomy, on the other hand, are not necessarily xenophobic and sometimes have a very cosmopolitan outlook: thus, though they emphasize a specific cultural identity, the Flemish and Catalan "nationalists" are actually more favorable to European integration than are most of their compatriots; and the Quebecois are more

[1] The "reject neighbors battery" referred to here was included in both waves of the World Values Survey, but the data are not reliable for cross-time comparisons. This battery used a scaleless format, which is very sensitive to context and interviewer effects. Moreover in 1981 it had an interviewer instruction to "code all mentions," while in 1990 each item had codes for "mentioned" or "not mentioned," with the interviewer instruction "Check a response for each item"; this attracted more choices for all items. In addition, "People with AIDS" was added to the battery in 1990.

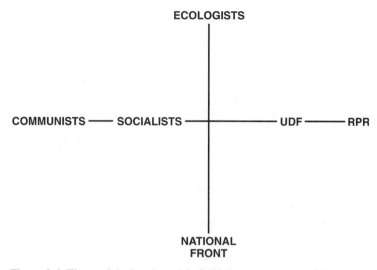

Figure 8.6. The social class-based Left-Right dimension and the Post-modern politics dimension in France.

supportive of North American free trade than are Canadians in general. These parties are motivated not by xenophobia so much as by a concern for cultural identity and for autonomy in decision making, and their social base consists disproportionately of the young, the well-educated, and Postmaterialists.

In the Netherlands—one of the most Postmaterialist societies in the world— Postmodern parties have been making growing inroads for more than two decades. In the 1994 Dutch parliamentary elections, two heavily Postmateri-alist parties—Democrats '66 and the Green Left—won nearly 20 percent of the vote; while at the opposite pole of the Postmodern politics spectrum, sev-eral small fundamentalist religious parties won over 5 percent of the vote.

The ex-communist resurgence in former socialist countries reflects the fact that these parties are associated with the Good Old Days of relative stability and security in the minds of their voters. But parties tied to the classic program of the Left have been faring poorly in Western countries. This is partly due to the Postmaterialist shift, and partly due to the loss of legitimacy of the eco-nomic philosophy of socialism that accompanied the collapse of Marxism in Eastern Europe and the former Soviet Union. It also reflects the fact that the electoral appeal of the long-established Western parties was based on class-based economic issues, which have a diminishing ability to mobilize voters today.

For most of the postwar era, the Italian Communist Party won 30 to 35 per-cent of the vote in Italian elections, but starting in the late 1970s, it went into a steady decline. As Italy's 1994 elections approached, the situation seemed to offer a golden opportunity for the communists to stage a comeback. The Chris-tian Democratic coalition, which had dominated Italian politics throughout the period since World War II, had finally self-destructed. Most of the top leaders of both the Christian Democrats and their socialist allies were either in jail or under indictment for flagrant corruption—a classic opportunity for the opposition to come to power. In the 1994 elections, the Christian Democratic vote plummeted to 11 percent and that of their socialist allies fell to 2 percent. But the communists were unable to capitalize on this opportunity. The Democratic Party of the Left won only 20 percent of the vote, and the hard-line communists won only 6 percent. The vacuum created by the collapse of the governing coalition was filled by new parties, some of which appeared almost overnight. The traditional Left-Right axis sunk to an unprecedented low point. The leading party was the newly established Forza Italia, with 21 percent of the vote; a regional party, the Northern League, won 8 percent; and the neofascist vote rose to an appalling 14 percent, while at the other pole of the Postmodern politics dimension, the Greens won 3 percent. In Italy's 1996 elections, a reform Communist Party (renamed as the Democratic Party of the Left) emerged as the largest party in parliament, but it was a profoundly transformed party, dedicated to a market economy and to Italian membership in NATO.

In Britain's 1992 general elections, the Left was in an ideal position to win. The Conservatives had been in power for three consecutive terms, and the British economy was in the throes of a deep recession; moreover, the Conservative Party had an unappealing leader who ran a dull campaign. Nevertheless, Labour lost for a fourth consecutive time. The party was widely seen as still committed to old-line policies of the Left, such as state ownership of business and industry—which it was still officially endorsing even after it had been abandoned within the ex-socialist bloc. A succession of Labour Party leaders tried to drag the party back to the mainstream, but it was only in 1995, under the leadership of Tony Blair, that the party finally officially abandoned the goal of state ownership of business and industry. With its return to the mainstream, the prospect of a Labour electoral victory was finally within reach.

The rise of Postmodern values has not led to the emergence of new parties in societies like the United States, where the absence of proportional representation makes it difficult for new parties to survive. Nevertheless, it has forced the existing parties to reposition themselves. Both major parties now claim to be pro-environmentalist, and both parties are trying to find just the right balance between cultural permissiveness and traditional family values. The success of Clinton in 1992 owed much to a skillful balancing act within the future First Family. Clinton himself, a Southern WASP male, took positions on social and economic issues that were almost indistinguishable from those of the Republicans, promising a middle-class tax cut and a balanced budget, while his wife made a subtly differentiated appeal to the Postmodern constituency. Although Postmodern political parties have not emerged in the United States, it is clear that the issues that launch such parties are as powerful here as anywhere. Concern for environmental protection has a large and active constituency; but opposition to illegal immigration also has broad and increasingly articulate support. In the United States, Postmodern politics plays itself out within the two long-established dominant parties.

In France, as we have seen, the National Front became prominent by appealing to nativist sentiment among working-class voters who formerly supported the parties of the Left. Its nearest parallels on the American scene are the Christian Coalition and the anti-immigration movements. These movements represent reactions against rapid cultural change which has been occurring throughout advanced industrial society. During the past 25 years, divorce rates rose by as much as 300 percent in Western societies, while during the same period, fertility rates fell to well below the population replacement rate. Similarly, a generation ago homosexuality was something that was only whispered about. Today, gay and lesbian groups are officially organized under government and university sponsorship and are beginning to obtain legal protection of the right to follow their own sexual orientations. This change is part of a broad intergenerational cultural shift. As we have seen, younger groups are far more permissive toward divorce, homosexuality, and abortion than older groups and place much less emphasis on having children.

In addition to these cultural changes, massive immigration flows, especially those from Third World countries, have changed the ethnic makeup of most advanced industrial societies. The newcomers speak different languages and have different religions and lifestyles from those of the native population— further compounding the impression that the culture one grew up in is being swept away. The rise of militant religious fundamentalism in the United States, and of xenophobic movements in Western Europe, represents a reaction against rapid cultural changes that seem to be eroding some of the most basic values and customs of the more traditional and less secure groups in these countries. The emergence of highly visible New Right groups has led some observers to conclude that they reflect the mainstream trend. They are important phenomena—but they do not represent the wave of the future. On the contrary, New Right groups are a reaction against broader trends that are moving faster than these societies can assimilate them. This reaction against cultural change has reinforced the Postmodern politics cleavage, pitting predominantly Materialist-oriented parties against Postmaterialist parties and giving rise to a Postmodern versus Fundamentalist cleavage dimension.

The foregoing interpretation is supported by empirical analyses by some leading scholars of comparative politics. Thus, Knutsen (1989, 1995) has demonstrated that in most Western European countries, a new dimension of political cleavage has emerged, which he describes as a Materialist/Postmaterialist values cleavage; tapping a number of issues such as environmentalism and nuclear power, the core variable in this cluster is Materialist/Postmaterialist values. This new dimension cuts across the traditional Left-Right dimension and has become an increasingly important influence on party choice in many societies—and has become the most important variable shaping political cleavages in some countries.

Similarly, in an insightful analysis of the rise of Postmodern parties in Western democracies, Kitschelt refers to parties based on Postmaterialist constituencies as "Left Libertarian parties," and those at the opposite pole, with disproportionately Materialist constituencies, as "Right Authoritarian parties" (Kitschelt, 1994, 1995). Although we use different labels, our interpretations converge with those of Knutsen and Kitschelt on the key points.

The Rise of Postmaterialist Issues and the Decline of Social Class Voting

Most of the major political parties in Western countries were established in an era dominated by social class conflict, and to a considerable extent the main established political parties are still aligned along a social class-based axis. But support for new political movements and new political parties largely reflects the tension between Materialist and Postmaterialist goals. Accordingly, social class-based voting has been declining, and there has been a growing tendency for Western electorates to polarize according to Materialist versus Postmaterialist values. This development imposes a difficult balancing act on party leaders, especially those of Left parties. If they adapt to this new polarization too slowly, they lose their young Postmaterialist activists; but if they move too fast in this direction, they risk losing their traditional working-class constituency.

The rise of a new axis of politics, based on polarization between Postmodern values and traditional cultural values and the decline of class-based polarization, has left Western political systems in a schizophrenic situation. Most of the major political parties have been aligned along the class-based axis of polarization for decades, and established party loyalties and group ties still hold much of the electorate to this alignment. But the most heated political issues today are mainly Postmodern issues, on which support for change comes mainly from a Postmaterialist, middle-class base. This creates a stress that can be resolved in two ways: by repositioning the established parties or by creating new parties. Both have been taking place.

Klingemann, Hofferbert, and Budge (1994) find that there has been a gradual repositioning of party positions along the Postmodern politics axis: in an analysis of party programs in Western democracies during the last several decades, the percentage of references to social class conflict steadily declined, and the percentage of references to Postmaterialist issues increased sharply.

In the 1940s and 1950s, socialist policies were a major theme in the political party programs of Western democracies. As figure 8.7 demonstrates, socialist economic policies were mentioned in party manifestos about 15 times as often as were environmentalist policies: during 1944–59, the average party program referred to socialist economic policy about five times (socialist parties, of course, mentioned them more often than conservative parties), while the average party platform mentioned environmental matters .3 times: two-thirds of the party platforms did not mention environmental policy at all. Since then, a radical shift in emphasis has taken place. By the 1980s, environmental policy had overtaken socialist economic policy as a campaign issue (receiving

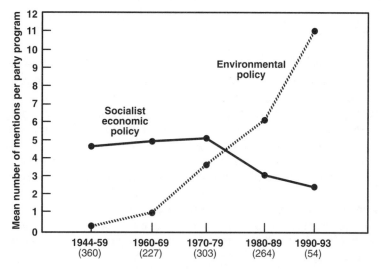

Figure 8.7. Emphasis on socialist economic policy vs. environmental policy in political party programs: 1944–93. *Source*: Comparative Manifestos
Project. Based on content analysis of 1,208 party programs issued during
this period by political parties in the following countries: France, Italy,
(West) Germany, Austria, Switzerland, Great Britain, Ireland, the United
States, Canada, Sweden, Norway, Denmark, Finland, Iceland, Belgium,
the Netherlands, Luxembourg, Australia, and New Zealand. For details,
see Klingemann et al., *Parties, Policies and Democracy* (Boulder: Westview Press, 1994).

almost twice as much emphasis). By the 1990s, environmental policy dominated socialist economic policy as an electoral theme: the average party program mentioned environmental policy eleven times; socialist economic policy
was mentioned only 2.5 times (with much of the mention being negative).

This seems to reflect political influences moving from the microlevel to the
macrolevel: though we cannot directly demonstrate that the changes at the
mass level preceded the shifts at the party program level, it seems implausible
that this was a case of mass values following elite cues. For, as we saw in chapter 5, the changes at the mass level reflect a deep-rooted intergenerational
change that can be traced back to the postwar economic miracles and was set
in motion long before the party programs began to shift. At the elite level, the
changes manifest themselves only in the 1960s and 1970s, when the postwar
generation became an increasingly important segment of the electorate—and
of the political activists. According to Carkoglu and Blinn (1994), by 1989 the
Materialist-Postmaterialist issue dimension had become the first factor in the
party programs of Western democracies, explaining more of the variance in
party programs than the traditional Left-Right dimension based on the classic
Marxist social class polarization over ownership of the means of production
and redistribution of income. Although the *parties* were still perceived as po-

sitioned along a Left-Right dimension, the dominant *issue* polarization had shifted from social class issues to Postmodern issues (Huber and Inglehart, 1995).

The rise of the Postmodern politics dimension tends to bring a reversal of social class positions: on the old Left-Right dimension, the upper income strata supported the Right or conservative position: they were the Haves and acted to preserve their economically privileged position against the Have-nots. But the Postmodern politics dimension is based not on ownership of property, but on one's subjective sense of security. It pits a Modern/Materialist worldview against a Postmodern/Postmaterialist worldview. On this dimension, those with *higher* levels of income, education, and occupational status are relatively secure, and increasingly, they tend to support the Left position.

Postmaterialists come from middle-class backgrounds, but they support change (Inglehart, 1977). This is conducive to a decline of social class voting, as middle-class Postmaterialists move left—and working-class Materialists move to the right.

For decades, one of the basic axioms of political sociology was the fact that working-class voters tend to support parties of the Left, and middle-class voters those of the Right (Alford, 1963; Lipset, 1960). This was an accurate description of reality a generation ago, but the tendency has been getting steadily weaker. As figure 8.8 illustrates, social class-based voting has declined markedly during the past 40 years. If 75 percent of the working class voted for the Left and only 25 percent of the middle-class voters did so, one would obtain an Alford class voting index of 50 (the difference between the two figures). As figure 8.8 shows, this is about where the Swedish electorate fell in 1948—but by 1990 the index had fallen to 26. The Scandinavian countries have traditionally shown the world's highest levels of social class voting, but it has declined sharply in all of them. In the United States, Britain, France, and West Germany, during the late 1940s and early 1950s, working-class voters were more apt to support the Left than were middle-class voters by margins that ranged from 30 to 45 points. By the 1990s, this spread had shrunken to the range from 1 to 25 points. In the 1992 U.S. presidential elections, social class voting had virtually disappeared. There were short-term fluctuations in given countries: the 1980s produced a partial resurgence of social class voting in Great Britain, for example. But all five of the countries for which we have data over this long time period show pronounced long-term declines in class voting. Overall, class voting indices in the 1990s were about half as large as they were in the postwar era. By the 1990s, the country with the *highest* class-voting index (Sweden) showed weaker class polarization than did the country with the *lowest* level in the 1940s (France).

The class-conflict model of politics is not just a straw man: a few decades ago it provided a fairly accurate description of reality. But that reality has changed, gradually but pervasively, and partly through intergenerational population replacement processes. Throughout Western Europe, social class vot-

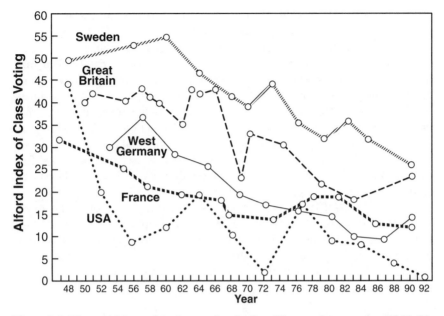

Figure 8.8. The trend in social class voting in five Western democracies, 1947–92. *Source*: Adapted from Lipset (1981): 505. Updated by author with results from France and from recent elections. American data based on whites only, for comparability over time, cited in Abramson et al., (1985, 1994). The 1990 figures for European countries are from the 1990 World Values Survey.

ing indices are about half as large among the postwar birth cohorts as they are among older groups.

There has been extensive recent debate over whether social class voting has really been declining. If one focuses on selected periods for selected countries, it is easy enough to demonstrate that there has been no decline. For example, if one focuses on Great Britain and uses the 1969 low point (shown in figure 8.8) as one's starting point, one can conclude that there has been no downward trend in that country. But if one examines the entire time series since World War II, one finds a statistically significant decline that brought class voting down to half its former size.

Another approach has been to argue that Alford's manual/nonmanual dichotomy is too simple: using various more complicated ways of measuring social class, or more complex statistical procedures than comparing the Alford index over time, various analysts have argued that they find no downward trend. The great advantage of Alford's index is precisely the fact that it *is* so simple and straightforward: the distinction between manual and nonmanual workers is theoretically clear and easy to operationalize. It indicates a clear and obvious cutting point in any industrial society. Hout, Brooks, and Manza

(1993) increase the number of measures of occupation and use logistic regression to test whether class voting has declined in the United States. Increasing the number of occupational categories does indeed increase the possibility that some combination of them may affect party choice. But their interpretation of their logistic regression results is questionable. They find, for example, that professionals voted predominantly for the Republicans in the 1950s, but for the Democrats in the 1990s. Ignoring this reversal of sign, they describe this as part of a pattern of "trendless fluctuation" because their various occupational groupings still explain about as much of the variance as ever (see Clark, 1995). Analyzing a massive database from 16 societies across four decades, and using more appropriate methodology, Nieuwbeerta and De Graaf (forthcoming) find a clear overall decline in class voting.

As social class-based voting has declined, the importance of the Postmodern political cleavage has increased. In the 1970s, Lijphart (1979) found "New Politics" parties (parties with a Postmaterialist constituency) in only three countries. In the 1989 elections to the European Parliament, New Politics parties won at least 10 percent of the vote in eight of the 12 European Community countries (Dalton, 1991b).

THE SOCIETAL LEVEL: DIMINISHING MARGINAL RETURNS FROM ECONOMIC DEVELOPMENT

Let us turn now from analyzing cultural change at the individual level, to view it at the societal level.

Although Karl Marx died in 1883, his analysis of political conflict continued to fascinate social scientists for most of the following century. His emphasis on politics as the struggle to own the means of production captured an important part of reality in the early phases of industrial society. But with the evolution of advanced industrial society, new conflicts and new worldviews have emerged, making the economic conflicts Marx emphasized less central to political life.

This development reflects the diminishing marginal utility of economic determinism: economic factors play a decisive role under conditions of economic scarcity; but as scarcity diminishes, other factors shape society to an increasing degree. We have examined this phenomenon from an individual-level perspective; now let us examine it at the aggregate cross-national level. Forces operating at both levels converge, bringing a diminishing degree of economic determinism and class-based political conflict, as advanced industrial society emerges.

As we saw in chapter 2, human life expectancy is closely linked to a nation's level of economic development. In poor societies, life expectancies are less than 40 years, but they rise steeply with relatively modest increases in wealth, until one reaches a threshold of about $3,000 per capita income; then the life expectancy curve levels off. Economic factors become less decisive, and

lifestyle factors more so. Similar patterns of diminishing returns from economic development are found with numerous other social indicators. Caloric
intake, literacy rates, and other indicators rise steeply at the low end of the scale
but level off among advanced industrial societies.

The pattern of diminishing marginal returns from economic development is
not limited to objective aspects of life: it extends to subjective well-being as
well. As we saw earlier, subjective well-being rises markedly with rising levels of economic development, and then levels off. Above a threshold of about
$6,000 per capita, there is virtually no cross-national relationship between
wealth and subjective well-being.

A rational strategy would dictate that at low levels of development, the individual should give top priority to maximizing one's income, and the society
should give top priority to economic growth. But more of the same indefinitely
is not a rational strategy. Beyond a certain threshold, there is a change in survival strategies, as Postmodern politics begins. Gradual cultural changes are
feeding back into the political process of advanced industrial societies, leading to a change in their political agenda.

The Diminishing Political Base of the Traditional Left

Political life is also responding to a curve of diminishing marginal returns—
in this case, the diminishing marginal utility of the classic program of the Left.

Equality of income distribution shows a curve of diminishing returns similar to those we saw for life expectancies and subjective well-being in chapter
2. Income equality increases sharply with economic development, up to a level
of about $3,500 per capita in 1978 dollars (see Inglehart, 1990: 251); above
that threshold, the curve levels off. In the overwhelming majority of countries
with a GNP per capita below $3,500 (as of 1978), the top tenth of the popula-
tion got more than one-third of the total income (in some cases as much as 57
percent). In *none* of the nations with a GNP per capita above $3,500 did the
top tenth of the population get more than one-third of the total income; their
share ranged from as low as 17 percent, in communist countries, to a high of
33 percent, in Finland.

Does this cross-sectional pattern reflect a longitudinal trend? The point has
been debated. The most reliable longitudinal data come from economically advanced countries, most of which have shown only modest increases in income
equality during the past 30 years. But if the shift is based on a curve of diminishing returns rather than a linear trend, this is exactly what we would expect.
It is only in the earlier stages of economic development that we would observe
large amounts of change. The United States, for example, moved toward substantially greater income equality from 1890 to 1950, but has shown some
reconcentration since then. Absolute levels of income continued to rise, but
relative shares changed only slightly. Most OECD countries moved toward
greater income equality during the 1960s and 1970s, but the trend seems to
have leveled off in the 1980s (Cusack, 1991). Conversely, Taiwan, South

Korea, Singapore, and Hong Kong all have made dramatic leaps from poverty to prosperity only recently—and all have shown substantial increases in income equality (Chen 1979).

Why do we find a curvilinear relationship between economic development and income equality? In the early phase, we believe, it reflects a process of social mobilization, engendered by economic development. Industrialization leads to urbanization and mass literacy, which facilitate the organization of labor unions and mass political parties and the enfranchisement of the working class. Economic development does not automatically bring equality, but it does tend to transform the masses from isolated and illiterate peasants into organized citizens with the power to bargain for a more equal share of the pie.

But why does the curve level off among mature industrial societies? There are two main reasons. First, as a society approaches perfect equality, it necessarily reaches a point of diminishing returns. At the point where the top tenth had only 10 percent of the income, any further transfer of income would be a move *away* from equality. None of these societies has actually reached this point, but some were getting close. In East Germany, for example, the top tenth got only 17 percent of the total income. Norway, Sweden, and Denmark have greater income equality than the United States, West Germany, or France, which suggests that the latter countries could move further toward equality without necessarily having ineffective economies or coercive societies. But the Scandinavian countries seem to be approaching the limit of what is possible in a democratic political system. By the 1980s they were already experiencing a sharp public reaction against any further expansion of the welfare state, and began to cut it back.

Why this is so reflects a second basic principle: political support for increased income equality reaches a point of diminishing returns at a level well short of perfect equality.

As a society moves closer to an equal income distribution, the political base of support for further redistribution becomes narrower. In a poor society where the top 10 percent get 80 percent of the total income, the vast majority would benefit from redistribution. In a society in which the top 50 percent get 80 percent of the total income, far fewer people will benefit from further redistribution, and they will benefit proportionately less; one eventually reaches the point at which a majority of the voters stand to lose more than they would gain by additional redistribution. This does not constitute a moral justification for not moving further toward equality, but it does constitute a major political barrier in democratic societies. Under these conditions, the political base for further development of the welfare state is simply not there—at least not insofar as the citizens are motivated solely by economic self-interest. Ironically, further progress toward equality would come *not* from an emphasis on materialistic class conflict, but through an appeal to the public's sense of justice, social solidarity, and other nonmaterial motivations. Thus in the long run, economic development makes a sense of economic deprivation both less widespread among mass publics, and a less powerful cause of political conflict.

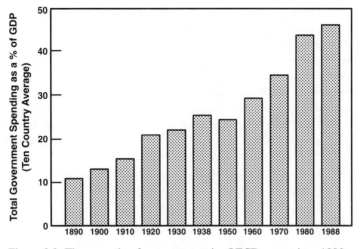

Figure 8.9. The growth of government in OECD countries, 1890–1988.
Average government spending rates over time from 10 OECD countries: Austria, Canada, Denmark, France, West Germany, Italy, Japan, Norway, United Kingdom, and the United States. *Source*: Cusack, 1991.

Stated in this way, this conclusion may seem self-evident. But it is not; it has been hotly debated and is not generally accepted even now. A quarter century ago, the "end of ideology" school concluded that growing prosperity was giving rise to the "politics of consensus in an age of affluence" (Lane 1965); the subsequent explosion of protest in the late 1960s led many to conclude that this school had been completely wrong. In fact, the "end of ideology" school's analysis of what had been happening was partly correct; like Marx, they simply failed to anticipate new developments. While economic cleavages did become less intense with rising levels of economic development, they gradually gave way to *other* types of conflict.

By 1988 government spending had risen to nearly 50 percent of GDP in OECD countries, as figure 8.9 illustrates. This is another point of diminishing returns. Obviously, this trend cannot continue much longer: it is impossible to go above 100 percent except by running large deficits, and the costs of debt service eventually eliminate even that option. But another limit begins to take effect long before a society reaches the 100 percent level: psychologically, the 50 percent level seems to be a significant threshold. As taxation moves above this level, people begin to realize that an hour spent on tax avoidance can be more remunerative than an hour spent on one's job. And the ratio shifts very rapidly as the curve rises. When government spending (and taxation) rises above 66 percent of GNP, it may become economically rational to devote two-thirds of one's time to lobbying or tax avoidance, and a third of one's time to working. One's job eventually becomes a sideline; dealing with the governmental bureaucracy becomes the major focus. For some time, people may continue to work diligently, from force of habit, but a mentality of "They pretend to pay us, and we pretend to work" increasingly permeates the society.

Consequently no economy even approaches the theoretical 100 percent limit; functional requirements call a halt well short of this point. Thus, even the USSR, though ideologically committed to the position that private enterprise was morally wrong, probably never went above the 75 percent level. The rulers were forced to tolerate a sizable private sector because private agriculture and the unofficial economy were essential in staving off economic collapse. Thus, for functional as well as political reasons, by the 1980s the growth of the state was reaching natural limits. An awareness that the Marxist model was no longer working began to permeate mass consciousness.

Diminishing Returns from the Traditional Program of the Left

We have seen indications that economic development leads to a diminishing impact of economic influences on such objective characteristics as life expectancy and economic equality. But do such changes actually reshape the subjective political preferences of mass publics? The evidence suggests that they do; at high levels of economic development, public support for the classic economic policies of the Left tends to diminish.

Everyone knows that Denmark is a leading welfare state, with advanced social legislation, progressive taxation, a high level of income equality, and well over half its GNP going to the public sector. Obviously, the Danish public must be relatively favorable to these traditional policies of the Left. Conversely, everyone knows that Ireland is a relatively rural nation, with a modest public sector and no significant communist or socialist movements. Clearly, Ireland must be a bastion of conservatism on the classic Left-Right issues.

In fact, the conventional stereotypes are wrong on both counts. These stereotypes reflect patterns that were true in the past, but precisely *because* Denmark has attained high levels of social security—and very high levels of taxation— the Danish public has little desire for further extension of these policies. Support for the classic economic policies of the Left tends to diminish as economic development rises.

As figure 8.10 demonstrates, Greece is by far the poorest country among 11 European Community societies surveyed in 1979–83, and the Greek public has by far the highest level of support for nationalization of industry, more government management of the economy, and reducing income inequality. Ireland is the second-poorest country, and overall Ireland ranks second in support for these policies. At the opposite end of the spectrum, Denmark is the richest country—and has the lowest level of support for these policies. Western Germany ranks next to Denmark in economic level—and also in support for the classic Left policies.

The principle of diminishing marginal utility applies at the societal level, as well as the individual level. Greece is an economically underdeveloped coun-

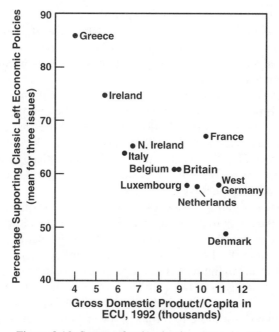

Figure 8.10. Support for the classic economic policies of the Left in 11 countries, by level of economic
development.
Based on responses to three questions asked in each
of three Euro-Barometer surveys in 1979, 1981, and
1983. *Source*: Inglehart, 1990: 256.

try, with many living in poverty and a small affluent elite. In such a context,
the balance between rich and poor can be redressed only by strong government
intervention. Denmark is a rich country that has long had some of the world's
most advanced social welfare policies—and one of the world's highest rates
of taxation. About 60 percent of Denmark's GNP is spent by the government;
it is reaching the point at which it becomes impossible to move much further
in this direction. In Denmark, further redistribution by the government seems
much less urgent than in Greece—and the costs of government intervention
impinge on a much larger share of the population. The incentives to press farther with the traditional economic policies of the Left become relatively weak,
and public resistance becomes relatively strong.

There may be still another factor behind the decline of the traditional program of the Left. Tanzi and Schuknecht (1995) argue that the human returns
on public spending are also subject to diminishing marginal returns. They analyze the increase in public spending in industrial economies over the past 125
years, assessing its social and economic benefits. They find that up to 1960,
higher government spending was linked with considerable improvements in
infant mortality rates, life expectancy, income equality, and educational lev-

els. But since 1960, further increases in public spending have gone with only modest social gains—and those countries in which spending has risen most have not performed any better than those in which spending rose least. Indeed, on some indicators such as unemployment rates, the low-spending countries have done significantly better.

These findings are sure to be controversial, and they do not demonstrate a causal link: it is possible, for example, that most of the improvement in social standards up to 1960 was mainly due to rising incomes rather than public spending, and that such gains diminish once a certain income threshold is reached. But regardless of whether increased public spending brings diminishing social returns beyond a certain level, it seems clear that it does eventually bring diminishing public support.

The evidence in figure 8.10 suggests that higher levels of economic development are linked with diminishing mass support for state intervention. This figure is based on data from Western Europe. Does this pattern hold up more broadly? Data from the 1990–93 World Values Survey suggest that the phenomenon is global. As figure 8.10 indicates, throughout the industrial world public sentiment today is in favor of less, not more, government ownership. But the degree of support is closely linked to a society's level of economic development. Support for more government ownership is highest in China and Nigeria and lowest in the United States, Canada, and Western Germany. The midpoint of this scale is 5.5, about where India is located on figure 8.11. The only countries in which a majority favor more (rather than less) government ownership are China, Nigeria, Turkey, Chile, and Belarus; and the publics of Russia and India are about evenly divided. The publics of the other 35 societies favor moving away from government ownership. Marxism has become a phenomenon for which the mass appeal is found mainly in developing nations.

As figure 8.12 shows, even in Western countries, Postmaterialists are not particularly interested in government ownership of industry: though relatively enthusiastic supporters of the Left position on practically all of the Postmodern issues, the Postmaterialist constituency is not significantly more favorable to government ownership of industry than are Materialists. And in the ex-socialist societies, the situation is dramatically different: Postmaterialists are far more favorable than other groups to moving *away* from state ownership of business and industry. They see privatization as a step away from the rigid authoritarianism of the past, toward a society in which individual autonomy is enhanced.

In many ex-socialist societies such as Lithuania, Poland, and Hungary, the trauma of the transition to a market economy has brought reform communists back to power in free elections—but even the former communists are now disillusioned with government ownership. As one leader of the newly elected reform communist regime in Poland commented, "If one of our leaders proposed going back to a state-run economy, we would have to drop him from the party—not because he was a communist, but because he was an idiot."

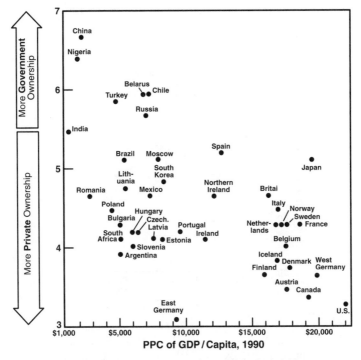

Figure 8.11. Economic development goes with diminishing support for state ownership.

Mean level of support for private vs. government ownership of business and industry, on a scale where 1 = "*Private* ownership of business and industry should be increased" and 10 = "*Government* ownership of business and industry should be increased." N = 43, r = −.54, p < .0001. *Source*: 1990–93 World Values Survey. Purchasing power estimates of GNP/capita from World Bank, *World Development Report, 1993*.

The policies that dominated the agenda of the Left throughout most of this century are running out of steam. Increased state intervention was desperately needed to alleviate starvation and social upheaval in the 1930s, was essential to the emergence of the welfare state in the postwar era, and still makes sense in some areas. But in others, it has passed a point of diminishing returns. The renewed respect for market forces that has emerged throughout most of the industrial world reflects this reality.

The neoconservative claim that the classic welfare state policies have failed is false, however. On the contrary, in such countries as Denmark these policies have largely solved the problems they are capable of solving—and have thereby reduced the demand for more of the same. Insofar as the *succeed*, they reach a point of diminishing returns, and begin to cede top priority to problems that have *not* been solved.

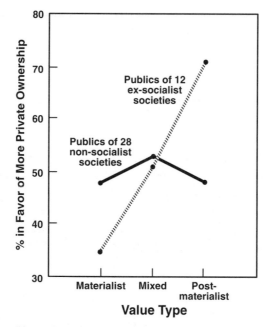

Figure 8.12. Percentage in favor of privatization of business and industry by value type, among publics of 12 ex-socialist societies vs. publics of 28 non-socialist societies.

Percentages are those placing themselves at points 1–4 on a 10-point scale on which 1 = "private ownership of business and industry should be increased" and 10 = "government ownership of business and industry should be increased."
Source: 1990–93 World Values Survey.

An attempt to turn back the clock to the savage laissez-faire policies of the early twentieth century would be self-defeating, ultimately leading to a resurgence of class conflict in all its former harshness. But the fundamentalists of the Left are equally self-defeating in their rigid adherence to a traditional program based on class conflict and state ownership and control of the means of production.

This does not mean that economic factors are no longer politically important. On the contrary, some very significant research has demonstrated strong linkages between fluctuations in the economies of Western nations and support for the incumbent political party (Kramer 1971; Tufte 1978; Hibbs, Rivers, and Vasilatos 1982). But this research has also produced a surprising finding: while support for the incumbents does reflect the performance of the national economy, it does *not* seem motivated by individual economic self-interest. The electorates of advanced industrial societies do not seem to be voting their pocketbooks, but instead seem primarily motivated by "sociotropic" concerns; rather than asking "What have you done for me lately?" they ask "What have you done for the *nation* lately?" (Kinder and Kiewiet 1979).

In short, economic factors remain an important influence on electoral behavior—but increasingly, they reflect sociotropic motivations rather than class conflict. The politics of advanced industrial societies no longer polarize primarily on the basis of working class versus middle class; and the old issues, centering on ownership of the means of production and government control of the economy, no longer lie at the heart of political polarization.

CONCLUSION

Marx set the agenda underlying modern political cleavages, which were based on ownership of the means of production and the distribution of income, and where support for the Left had a working-class base. With the emergence of advanced industrial society, the impact of economic factors reaches a point of diminishing returns. Postmodern issues take an increasingly important place on the national agenda, giving rise to a new axis based on the polarization between Postmodern and Fundamentalist worldviews; and support for sociopolitical change increasingly comes from a Postmaterialist, largely middle-class base.

The major established political parties in Western countries emerged in an era dominated by social class conflict, and to a considerable extent they are still aligned along a class-based axis. But support for new political movements and new political parties largely reflects the tension between traditional and Postmodern goals. Accordingly, social class-based voting has been declining, and there has been a growing tendency for Western electorates to polarize on a new axis, based on Postmodern issues. The established parties of the Left are trying to co-opt the Postmodern constituency, but if they move too far in this direction, they risk losing their traditional constituency, which reacts negatively to rapid change in sexual norms, gender roles, and massive immigration.

The Marxist model has lost its appeal in the industrialized world. Its emphasis on economic factors as the driving force of history provides a good first approximation of reality in the early stages of industrialization, but is of diminishing value as scarcity diminishes and new problems emerge. Similarly, the *policies* that are needed to counter the ruthless exploitation of capitalism in its laissez-faire stage reach a point of diminishing returns in advanced welfare states. Where government spending is already 40 to 60 percent of GNP, there is little potential to move further in this direction, and the massive power of big government itself becomes an increasingly serious problem. The old assumption of the Left that more government was automatically better has lost its credibility. But to elevate government nonintervention into a quasi-theological principle is equally untenable.

The meaning of "Left" and "Right" has been transformed. The key Marxist goal—nationalization of industry—has been abandoned by the publics of advanced industrial societies, though it remains attractive in less developed societies. Nationalization is not the panacea it once appeared to be. And insofar as it diverts attention from increasingly pressing problems concerning the quality of the physical and social environment, it can be downright counterproductive—for it provides no solution to these problems. Indeed, insofar as nationalization merges the political regulators with the military-industrial complex into one cozy elite, it may even make things worse. The nationalized factories of the Soviet bloc polluted even more than the private ones in the West. East Germany was the most severely polluted nation in Europe, with air and water pollutant levels two to three times as high as those in West Germany. And it is no coincidence that the only nuclear power plant accidents that have cost human lives occurred in the former Soviet Union, where environmentalist pressures for safety measures could not be freely organized. Although their environmental problems were even more severe, and their arms expenditures proportionately even higher than in Western societies, the political systems of the Eastern European countries made the emergence of independent environmentalist movements or peace movements far more difficult than in the West. It was relatively easy for the ruling elite to simply ignore such issues: officially, the problems underlying them existed only in capitalist countries.

The goals of individuals and the challenges facing society are different from those of a generation ago. For the past generation, Postmaterialists have controlled the agenda in advanced industrial societies, inserting a series of new causes into the political arena, and giving birth to new political movements and parties. After a generation of rapid social change, the opposition to Postmodern politics has become increasingly well organized and articulate, giving rise to movements and parties that systematically oppose the Postmodern agenda. The long-established political party institutions still reflect their origins in social class conflict, but the issues actually being debated today mainly concern support and opposition to Postmodernization.

CHAPTER 9

The Shift toward Postmodern Values: Predicted and Observed Changes, 1981–1990

A BROADER SHIFT TOWARD POSTMODERN VALUES

Not just postmaterialist values, but a whole range of Postmodern values are shifting in a predictable direction. This chapter and the next one examine this shift. Although we do not have year-by-year evidence of these changes (as we do for the shift from Materialist to Postmaterialist values), the 1981 and 1990 World Values surveys provide at least some evidence concerning how this broader shift toward a Postmodern worldview is moving.

The 1981 World Values Surveys showed that a wide variety of values and attitudes concerning politics, work, religion, sexual norms, and childrearing values were linked with Materialist/Postmaterialist values. They also showed significant differences between the preferences of young and old, with the old having attitudes similar to those of the Materialists, and the young having attitudes similar to those of the Postmaterialists.

These findings were based on the 1981 surveys alone: time series evidence was not yet available to show whether these age differences reflected an intergenerational shift. But we argued, on theoretical grounds, that these related attitudes were influenced by the same factors as those that motivated the Postmaterialist shift and were moving on a similar trajectory:

> Far-reaching though it is, the rise of Postmaterialist values is only one aspect of a still broader process of cultural change that is reshaping the political outlook, religious orientations, gender roles, and sexual mores of advanced industrial society. These changes are related to a common concern: the need for a sense of security, which religion and absolute cultural norms have traditionally provided. In the decades since World War II, the emergence of unprecedentedly high levels of prosperity, together with the relatively high levels of social security provided by the welfare state, have contributed to a decline in the prevailing sense of vulnerability. (Inglehart, 1990: 177)

Diminishing insecurity, it was claimed, is giving rise to a broad cultural shift, embracing not only Materialist/Postmaterialist values, but an entire syndrome of related attitudes. Emphasizing this prediction, the book that presented this thesis was entitled *Culture Shift in Advanced Industrial Society*.

We now have the cross-time data needed us to test this thesis. *Is* a broad cultural shift occurring?

We would not expect to find that *all* values are changing, of course: only those that are influenced by an underlying sense of security or insecurity. This means that we are dealing with the Postmodern shift discussed in chapter 3: we would expect to find systematic change among the values linked with the Scarcity-Postmodern values dimension described there (details of question wording are provided in Appendix 2).

Furthermore, we would not expect to find this shift taking place in every country. The rate of the shift toward Postmaterialist values is influenced by two sets of factors: (1) a long-term component, based on intergenerational value change, and (2) a short-term component that reflects current conditions.

The strength of intergenerational value change varies cross-nationally. Some countries are still undergoing the process of Modernization and have scarcely begun to move onto the Postmodernization trajectory. Among the countries for which data are available for at least two time points, South Africa is least likely to be moving rapidly toward Postmodern values. There are few Postmaterialists in South Africa, and relatively little difference between the values of young and old. Consequently, intergenerational population replacement would not bring much change there. The Nordic nations and the Nether-

TABLE 9.1
Variables Correlated with Materialist/Postmaterialist Values
in 1981 World Values Surveys (Correlations above .125 Level)

I. *Norms concerning (a) Respect for authority, (b) Sexual and marital behavior, and (c) Civil behavior*

1. "More respect for authority would be a good thing"
2. "Abortion is never justified"
3. "Divorce is never justified"
4. "Homosexuality is never justified"
5. "Prostitution is never justified"
6. "Sex under the legal age is never justified"
7. "Married men/women having an affair is never justified"
8. "Euthanasia is never justified"
9. "Suicide is never justified"
10. "Fighting with the police is never justified"
11. "Using marijuana is never justified"

II. *Religious norms*

12. Percentage attending church at least once a month
13. Percentage saying God is important in their lives
14. Percentage saying they believe in God
15. Percentage saying they believe in hell
16. Percentage saying they believe in heaven
17. Percentage saying they believe in sin
18. Percentage saying they get comfort and strength from religion
19. Percentage saying that the church in their country is giving adequate answers to moral problems

(continued)

TABLE 9.1   *Continued*

20. Percentage saying that the church in their country is giving adequate answers to problems of family life

21. Percentage saying that the church in their country is giving adequate answers to people's spiritual needs

22. Percentage saying that they "often" think about the meaning and purpose of life*

III. *Norms concerning parent-child ties*

23. Percentage saying "a child needs a home with both a father and a mother, to grow up happily"

24. Percentage saying "a woman has to have children in order to be fulfilled"

25. Percentage approving of a woman having a child as a single parent

26. Percentage believing one has a duty to love and respect one's parents, regardless of their faults

IV. *Norms concerning (a) Conventional political participation and (b) Unconventional political participation*

27. Percentage saying that they "often" or "sometimes" discuss politics with friends

28. Percentage saying that they are interested in politics

29. Percentage saying that they have signed a petition

30. Percentage saying that they have taken part in a boycott or might do so

31. Percentage saying that they have taken part in a demonstration or might do so

32. Percentage saying that they have taken part in an unofficial strike or might do so

33. Percentage saying that they have occupied a building or might do so

V. *Norms concerning (a) Control of business and industry, (b) Left-Right self-placement, and (c) Confidence in authoritarian institutions*

34a. Percentage favoring joint employee-owner participation in choosing managers in business and industry

34b. Percentage favoring state ownership of business and industry

34c. Percentage favoring owner's right to chose managers in business and industry

35. Percentage placing themselves on the Left half of a 10-point Left-Right ideological scale

36. Percentage expressing "a great deal" of confidence in the church in their country

37. Percentage expressing "a great deal" of confidence in their country's armed forces

38. Percentage expressing "a great deal" of confidence in their country's police forces

39. Percentage saying they are "very proud" of their nationality

40. Percentage saying "generally speaking, most people can be trusted"

Source: 1981 World Values survey, pooled data from 21 nations included in both 1981 and 1990 surveys.

*This item has a zero-order correlation with Materialist/Postmaterialist values of only .092 because of a tendency for older respondents to take the Postmaterialist position; controlling for age, the relationship rises above the .125 threshold.

lands are at the other extreme: Postmaterialists are numerous there, and values are strongly correlated with age, reflecting the presence of a steep gradient of intergenerational change. Most of the other nations of Western Europe and North America are well launched on the process of Postmodernization and seem likely to show relatively large amounts of change. East Asia might also show significant change on this dimension: though there are not yet many Post-materialists there, intergenerational differences are relatively large.

Do we actually observe systematic shifts among these values? Let us begin by testing a greatly oversimplified hypothesis: that all of the values that are linked with Postmaterialism will become more widespread over time. Reality is not this simple, of course. Current conditions will cause fluctuations, both in Materialist/Postmaterialist values and in other Postmodern orientations as well: secure and prosperous conditions should be conducive to Postmodern values, and economic decline, war, or domestic strife should be conducive to survival values. Nevertheless, to begin, let us ignore the impact of short-term factors and start with the deliberately oversimplified hypothesis that "Every-thing that goes with Postmaterialist values will increase."

We are testing the proposition that all values having reasonably strong cor-relations with Postmaterialism are part of an intergenerational shift linked with population replacement. To do so, we identified 40 variables that (1) had mean correlations of at least .125 with Postmaterialism in the 1981 World Values Survey and (2) were included in both the 1981 and 1990 World Values surveys (enabling us to see whether they had changed in the predicted direction). Table 9.1 lists these 40 items. They cover a wide range of topics, but all of them are correlated with Materialist/Postmaterialist values. Figure 9.1 gives some ex-amples, showing the relationships between four of these items and the Post-materialism dimension. Materialists are almost twice as likely to be intolerant of both homosexuality and abortion as are Postmaterialists and much likelier to believe that a woman needs children in order to be fulfilled; but they are only half as likely as Postmaterialists to say that God is not important in their lives.

The 40 norms and values in this diverse array of items go together because they are all influenced by one's sense of security. Chapter 3 gave an overview of the values involved in this cultural shift: we would expect most of the high-loading items on the Scarcity-Postmodern values dimension depicted in figure 3.2 to be moving in the Postmodern direction, in any society that has experi-enced a substantial intergenerational rise in its living standard during the past few decades.

To test our prediction, we will simply compare the responses to these 40 variables in 21 countries in 1981 with the responses to the same questions in the same 21 countries in 1990 to see if the predicted shift occurred.[1] Examin-ing the results from 40 variables in 21 different countries would produce a total

---

[1] Both World Values Surveys were also carried out in Denmark, which would provide a total of 22 countries except for the fact that the 1981 Danish survey does not seem to provide a reliable baseline for comparisons across time. See Appendix 1 for a discussion of this point.

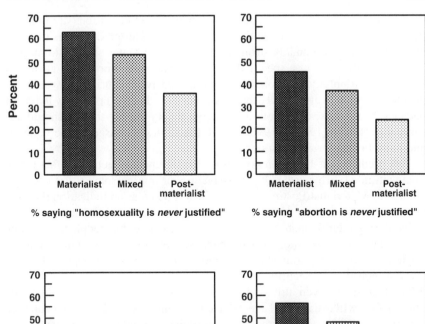

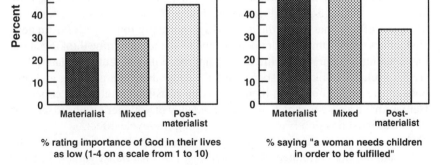

Figure 9.1. Some attitudes correlated with Materialist/Postmaterialist values. *Source*: Pooled cross-national data from 1990–93 World Values surveys.

of 40 × 21 = 840 separate tests. But since not all 40 items were asked in both years in every country, and one variable is broken down in two ways, we actually have 802 separate tests of the predicted change. This is a massive basis on which to test the hypothesized culture shift. As we are about to see, in most cases the publics did shift in the predicted direction.

CULTURAL CHANGE HAS A COMPONENT OF PREDICTABILITY

Successful prediction in the social sciences is rare, but our theory of intergenerational value change generates a set of systematic predictions that now can be tested. These predictions apply only when certain conditions are present; but (as we will see) these conditions apply widely. Our prediction is that any attitude having a reasonably strong correlation with Materialist/Postmaterialist values will move in a specified direction. And since our theory attributes these trends to intergenerational changes in perceived security, we would expect to find them in any society that has experienced rising prosperity in recent decades. When these conditions are met, our theory implies that we should observe a shift, from 1981 to 1990, toward the values espoused by the younger and more Postmaterialist respondents.

This prediction is based on population replacement effects. The fact that a given attitude (such as sexual permissiveness or interpersonal trust) is correlated with Materialist/Postmaterialist values is taken as an indication that this attitude is influenced by the degree of security that given birth cohorts experienced during their formative years. We do not assume that people are becoming more permissive or more trusting because they are Postmaterialists, but because the two orientations share common *causes*: they are shaped by one's level of security or insecurity.

The fact that a given attitude is correlated with Postmaterialist values implies that we will usually find age-related differences as well, with the younger cohorts more likely to have the Postmaterialists' attitudes. In most cases, we *do* observe such age-group differences, though a few attitudes are shaped by life-cycle effects that offset the age-linkage normally found with Postmaterialist values. For example, older people tend to spend more time thinking about the meaning and purpose of life as they approach its end; but Postmaterialists are *also* relatively likely to spend time thinking about the meaning and purpose of life, in keeping with their greater emphasis on intellectual concerns. Here we have a case in which the usual tendency of younger groups to take the Postmaterialist position is reversed by a strong life-cycle effect.

Conversely, some attitudes show age differences that reflect the human life cycle and are not correlated with Materialist/Postmaterialist values. In these cases, we would *not* expect to find any predictable trend over time. Consequently (paradoxical as it may seem), Materialist/Postmaterialist values are a better predictor of change than is age itself, even though these changes are based on population replacement effects. If a given attitude varies across age groups but is unrelated to Materialist/Postmaterialist values, we would *not* predict that it will change over time, since the age differences may simply reflect life-cycle effects. But if a given attitude is correlated with Materialist/Postmaterialist values, we *do* predict an intergenerational shift, even if we do not find age-group differences.

Short-term economic or political or social events can also have an impact on these attitudes, but they provide no basis for predicting long-term shifts. As we saw in chapter 5, short-term fluctuations influence the values of mass publics even when a long-term intergenerational shift *is* occurring: the impact of current events is superimposed on the long-term trend. This means that our predictions will not always be confirmed, especially over short time periods:

if period effects are sufficiently strong, they can neutralize the effects of inter-generational change. In the long run, however, our predictions should usually be valid. Negative period effects tend to conceal underlying intergenerational shifts, and positive period effects tend to exaggerate them. But in the long run, negative and positive period effects are likely to cancel each other out, leaving the underlying trend manifest.

The period from 1981 to 1990 is not very long from the perspective of in-tergenerational population replacement, but it is long enough so that at least moderate amounts of systematic change should become visible.

PREDICTED AND OBSERVED CHANGES

Norms concerning Authority

Let us examine some actual changes that were predicted and observed in the two waves of the World Values surveys. In the 1981 surveys, we found a sub-stantial correlation between attitudes toward authority and Materialist/Post-materialist values across nearly all of the 21 countries for which we have data. Materialists tend to support the proposition that "more respect for authority would be a good thing," while Postmaterialists tend to reject it. Consequently, we predicted a gradual shift toward the values of the Postmaterialists—that is, toward less emphasis on respect for authority.

Figure 9.2 presents the evidence that tests this prediction. It shows that from 1981 to 1990, emphasis on more respect for authority became less widespread in 17 of the 21 countries for which we have data. The absolute levels of sup-port for authority, and the size of the changes from 1981 to 1990, vary a good deal from country to country.

The prediction that this shift would occur is based on a simple population replacement model: as the younger, more Postmaterialist birth cohorts replace the older, more Materialist cohorts in the adult population, we should see a shift toward the Postmodern orientation. Moreover, since the size of the re-spective cohorts is known from census data, and since we have survey data on the attitudes of the various birth cohorts, we can also estimate the *size* of the attitudinal shift that population replacement should produce over a 10-year pe-riod. We do this by simply removing the oldest 10-year cohort from our sam-ple and replacing it with a new 10-year cohort at the youngest end. In creating this new cohort, we assume that it will have values similar to those of the youngest cohort in the sample—a conservative assumption, since younger co-horts usually show *more* Postmodern values than do older ones (for a more de-tailed discussion of how to estimate the effects of population replacement on mass attitudes, see Abramson and Inglehart, 1995).

When we perform this calculation it indicates that, for most of these coun-tries, we would expect to find a decline of only four or five points in the per-centage favoring more respect for authority. This is a small shift. If we found it in only one case, it would be an unimpressive finding: a difference between

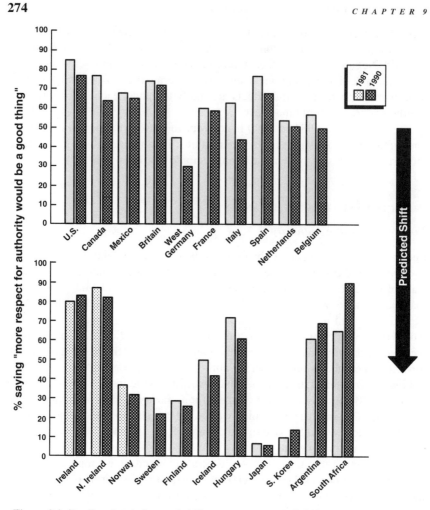

Figure 9.2. Predicted and observed shifts: percentages saying that "more respect for authority would be a good thing" in 1981 vs. 1990, in 21 countries. *Source*: 1981 and 1990 World Values surveys.

samples of this size is statistically significant at only about the .05 level. But if we observed several such consecutive shifts over 30 or 40 years, the finding would be highly significant, both statistically and substantively: over that time it could convert a 60:40 division of attitudes into a 40:60 split.

The same principle applies to a pattern of cross-cultural findings. Such a finding from only one country would hardly be worth mentioning. But if we had data from three or four countries and they all showed shifts of this size in the predicted direction, it would be highly significant. And if we found that the predicted shifts in values or attitudes generally held true across a score of societies, the probability of its being a random event would dwindle to the vanishing point. This chapter examines the shifts found with 40 variables, across

21 societies. Although the amount of change observed is usually small in any one case, the overall pattern is compelling and statistically significant at an enormously high level.

With attitudes toward authority, our theory predicts a shift of only four or five percentage points per country during this nine-year period. This is modest. In the short run, the impact of current economic or political events (or even sampling error) could easily swamp it in a given society. Thus, it would be astonishing if our predictions *did* hold up in every case. They do not: instead we find that in some countries, attitudes concerning authority moved in the predicted direction, while in others they did not. Moreover, some countries show shifts in the predicted direction that are too *large* to be due to population replacement alone: in these cases, situation-specific factors are probably adding to the results of population replacement, exaggerating the shift.

We can predict only one component of what is shaping mass attitudes, but we know that a number of factors are relevant. Consequently, we cannot predict precisely what will happen in every country. Nevertheless, because we *do* have information about one component of the process, our predictive power across many societies should be considerably better than random. And since there is a good chance that, in the long run, situation-specific factors or period effects will cancel each other out, in the long run, over many countries, our predictions should point in the right direction.

In the present case, the predicted shift toward less emphasis on respect for authority is actually observed in 17 out of 21 countries. With 81 percent success, this is far better than random prediction. We will not attempt to identify the nation-specific effects that were also at work here. Our point is that the values of most publics *did* move in the predicted direction.

Longitudinal research carried out in the United States over a much longer time confirms this finding, demonstrating that from the 1950s to the 1980s, there was a gradual decline in the American public's emphasis on conformity to authority as important things to teach a child; and there was a corresponding rise in emphasis on autonomy during this period (Alwin, 1986).[2]

Norms concerning respect for authority may be moving in the direction predicted by our theory, but does the prediction hold up in other realms as well?

The answer is yes—again and again. A wide variety of basic social norms are at least fairly strongly linked with Materialist/Postmaterialist values. And with impressive regularity, we observe shifts in prevailing values from 1981 to 1990 in which the outlook of the younger, more Postmaterialistic cohorts becomes increasingly widespread over time.

---

[2] The data from the World Values surveys show a similar shift in the relative balance between emphasis on obedience and autonomy as important values to teach a child (see figure A.3 in Appendix 3). However, these data are based on a set of unscaled questions, in which the interviewer is asked to "code all mentions." Such questions are very sensitive to interviewer effects and context. Moreover, there were changes in the other items on the list. Consequently, they cannot be considered reliable for comparisons across time and are not included in calculating the success rates of our predictions.

We find one major exception to this rule. In one domain (attitudes toward the importance of the traditional two-parent family), the values espoused by the more Postmaterialistic types did *not* become more widespread from 1981 to 1990. This is a significant phenomenon and is examined in more detail below. It reflects the fact that intergenerational population replacement is not the *only* factor that influences change. But this is a striking exception to the overall pattern. On the whole, the differences between the values of Postmaterialists and Materialists that we find in 1981 *do* generate accurate predictions of the direction in which values actually changed from 1981 to 1990.

Norms concerning Abortion, Divorce, Homosexuality, and Extramarital Sex

In face content, none of the items used to measure Materialist/Postmaterialist values makes any reference whatever to sexual or marital behavior; nevertheless, Postmaterialist values show strong correlations with a whole range of norms concerning sex and marriage. The underlying reason for this surprisingly strong linkage is the fact that both sets of values are heavily influenced by whether or not the individual feels secure concerning survival. Insecurity enhances the need for predictability and absolute norms; a sense of security, conversely, is conducive to relatively permissive and flexible norms.

Figure 9.3 shows the changes observed from 1981 to 1990 with one of these norms: attitudes toward abortion. This question (like the next several items) uses a 10-point scale, on which "1" indicates that the respondent feels that this behavior is "never justified" and "10" indicates that this behavior is "always justified." In most countries, a large share of the public felt that abortion was "never" justified and chose point "1" on this scale; figure 9.3 shows the percentages making that choice. Comparable data are not available from South Korea for this series of questions, because the 1990 survey in that country used four-point scales for these items. But across the societies for which we do have data, public attitudes moved mainly in the predicted direction, becoming more permissive toward abortion in 19 out of the 20 societies.

The South African public was the sole exception, moving against the prevailing trend both here and in the preceding case. This is part of a frequently recurring pattern that applies to both South Africa and Argentina: even when most countries were shifting in the direction predicted by the linkage with Postmaterialist values, the publics of these two societies shifted in the opposite direction. It is not surprising that South Africa and Argentina are exceptional. Theoretically, the Postmodern shift is driven by feelings of security, and during the 1980s these two societies were experiencing economic decline and a collapsing political order. They were moving from authoritarian regimes toward democracy, and the transition was filled with uncertainty.

Figure 9.4 shows the changes observed from 1981 to 1990 with attitudes toward divorce. The proportion saying that divorce is never justified was much smaller than the proportion saying that abortion is never justified, but the trend was similar: in 18 out of the 20 societies for which data are available, mass at-

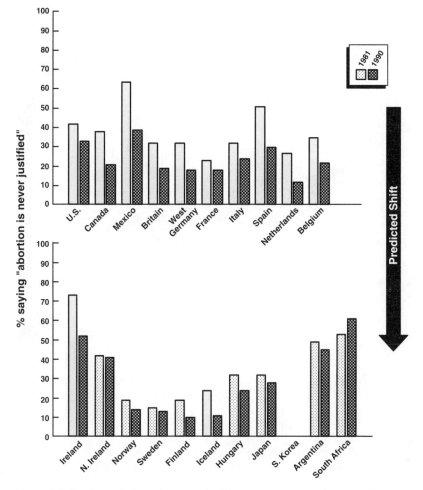

Figure 9.3. Predicted shifts and observed shifts: percentages holding that "abortion is *never* justified" in 1981 vs. 1990, in 20 countries. *Source*: 1981 and 1990 World Values surveys. Comparable data not available for South Korea (the 1990 South Korean survey used a four-point scale rather than a 10-point scale with this question).

titudes shifted in the predicted direction, becoming more permissive toward divorce (South Africa was again one of the exceptions).

Figure 9.5 shows a basically similar pattern of changes from 1981 to 1990, this time in attitudes concerning homosexuality. This attitude also is strongly correlated with Materialist/Postmaterialist values, with Postmaterialists being much less likely than Materialists to say that it is never justified. Here again, the publics of most societies shifted in the predicted direction, with 17 publics becoming more tolerant of homosexuality from 1981 to 1990: South Africa and Ireland were exceptions, moving in the opposite direction, and Northern Ireland showed no change.

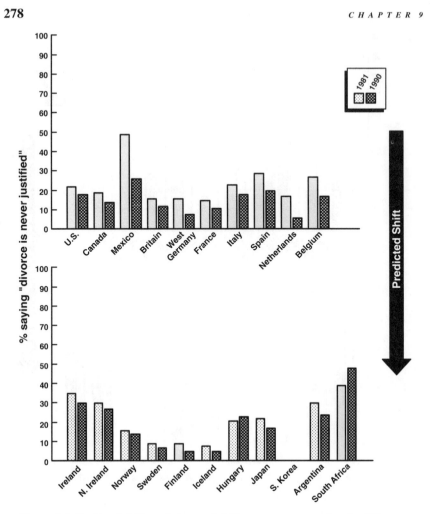

Figure 9.4. Predicted shifts and observed shifts: percentages saying that "divorce is *never* justified" in 1981 vs. 1990, in 20 countries. *Source*: 1981 and 1990 World Values surveys. Comparable data not available for South Korea.

Three more survey items in this category were strongly correlated with Post-materialist values: attitudes toward prostitution, sex under legal age, and extramarital affairs. To avoid burying the reader in an avalanche of data, and because these variables show patterns similar to those we have just seen, the relevant evidence is placed in Appendix 3, where the interested reader can examine the details (see figures A.4 through A.6). With all three attitudes, most publics shifted in the predicted direction: among those publics that showed any change, about two-thirds moved in the predicted direction. But with all three attitudes, the publics of Argentina and South Africa shifted in the opposite direction, becoming *less* permissive.

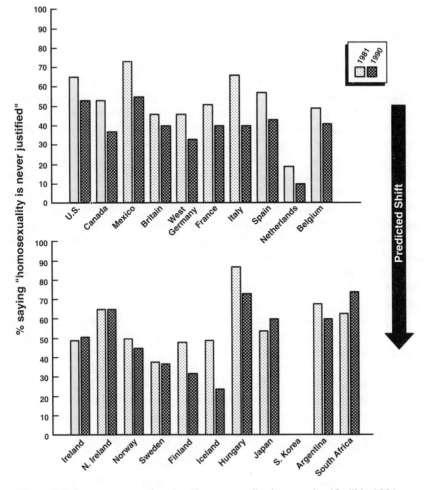

Figure 9.5. Percentages saying that "homosexuality is *never* justified" in 1981 vs. 1990, in 20 countries. *Source*: 1981 and 1990 World Values surveys. Comparable data not available for South Korea.

The publics of Norway and Sweden, who are generally rather permissive, overwhelmingly rejected "sex under the legal age." This probably reflects the fact that the translation used in these countries refers to "having sex with minors" (which could suggest child abuse), instead of the more neutral "sex under legal age." Attitudes toward sex under legal age had the lowest percentage of changes in the predicted direction among these norms, but even here 61 percent of the changes moved in the Postmodern direction. Argentina and South Africa, clearly, were *not* moving toward Postmodern values during the 1980s; nevertheless, with the seven attitudes that we have examined so far, 79 percent of the observed shifts were in the predicted direction.

Norms concerning Euthanasia, Suicide, Violence against Police, and Use of Marijuana

Four more variables that were strongly correlated with Materialist/Postmaterialist values could be described as civil norms: they concern attitudes toward euthanasia, suicide, fighting with police, and using marijuana. These questions used a 10-point scale like that just described; to avoid burdening the reader with excessive detail, the data on observed changes from 1981 to 1990 appear in Appendix 3.

Three of these four attitudes reveal a pattern of changes similar to that found above, with the overwhelming majority of publics shifting in the predicted direction from 1981 to 1990. Thus, 18 out of 20 publics became more tolerant toward euthanasia during this period (South Africa being one of the two exceptions); 16 out of 20 publics became more tolerant of suicide (with Argentina and South Africa being among the exceptions); and 17 out of 19 publics became more tolerant of fighting with the police (with Argentina and South Africa again being exceptions, and Hungary not asking this question in 1981). With these norms, observed changes are overwhelmingly in the predicted direction.

But attitudes concerning use of marijuana showed no consistent trend. The publics of nine countries became more tolerant, but the publics of nine other countries became less tolerant, and two publics showed no change. The World Values surveys do not show an undifferentiated shift toward greater permissiveness; orientations toward most norms did become more permissive, but these publics gave quite distinctive responses concerning some topics, and the use of marijuana was one of them. This finding runs counter to our predictions. Any explanation we might give for it would be ex post facto. We suspect that it may reflect a growing public awareness of the disastrous social consequences of drug abuse, but we did not predict this shift.

Despite the absence of the predicted trend with attitudes concerning use of marijuana, public responses to the four variables in this category overwhelmingly moved in the predicted direction: 78 percent of the observed shifts moved toward the position favored by those with Postmaterialist values. And more broadly, though we have encountered anomalies with some of the variables examined in this section, the responses to most items, in most countries, shifted in the predicted direction; across the norms concerning authority, sexual norms, and civil norms, fully 79 percent of the observed changes were toward the Postmodern pole.

Religious Norms

Most of the religious questions asked in 1981 showed strong correlations with Materialist/Postmaterialist values. Well before the 1990–91 data became available, we interpreted this as evidence that an intergenerational shift was taking place, making traditional religious values progressively less widely accepted in advanced industrial societies:

> Across the various societies included in this survey, Postmaterialists are about twice as likely as Materialists to indicate that God has little importance in their lives. From evidence presented in earlier chapters, it seems clear that an intergenerational shift is taking place from Materialist toward Postmaterialist values. Is a similar shift occurring, away from traditional Judeo-Christian religious and social values? This question cannot be answered conclusively because we do not yet have time series on these religious and cultural values that are comparable to those available on Materialist/Postmaterialist values. But the data that are available suggest that a major intergenerational shift in religious orientations is occurring. (Inglehart, 1990: 186–87)

The existence of such a trend is far from self-evident. In fact, the mass media tend to convey exactly the opposite impression—that we are witnessing a global trend toward fundamentalist religious values. Islamic fundamentalism and religious conflicts in India are cited as evidence of this trend, together with the revival of religion in Eastern Europe, and the Religious Right in the United States. Pulling together anecdotal evidence from a variety of sources, some observers have concluded that it all adds up to a worldwide fundamentalist trend. Which is taking place: a global trend toward fundamentalism—or a global trend toward secularization?

What is happening is more differentiated than either model. Our theory attributes the decline of religious values to a rising sense of security, which makes the need for the reassurance provided by traditional absolute belief systems less pressing. Thus, we *would* expect to find a trend toward secularization in advanced industrial societies. Indeed, we believe that it is precisely *because* traditional social and religious norms have been eroding rapidly in these societies during recent decades that people with traditional values (who are still numerous) have been galvanized into unusually active and disruptive forms of behavior, in order to defend their threatened values. But in advanced industrial societies, the numbers of those with traditional religious beliefs are diminishing, not growing. In these societies, fundamentalism does not represent the predominant trend, but a rearguard action by an aroused but slowly dwindling minority.

In much of the developing world, on the other hand, insecurity is pervasive. In much of Africa and some parts of Latin America, regimes are unstable and real per capita income has been declining in recent decades. The same has been true of the former Soviet states, though only recently. In such settings we *would* expect to see a heightened need for religious certainty.

So which do we find? A global trend toward traditional religious beliefs? Or two contrasting trends, with affluent and secure societies moving away from religion, but societies characterized by mass insecurity turning back to fundamentalist values?

The data from the 1990 World Values Survey helps us determine what has been happening in the realm of religion. Figure 9.6 shows one relevant indicator: reported attendance rates at religious services in 19 countries. The re-

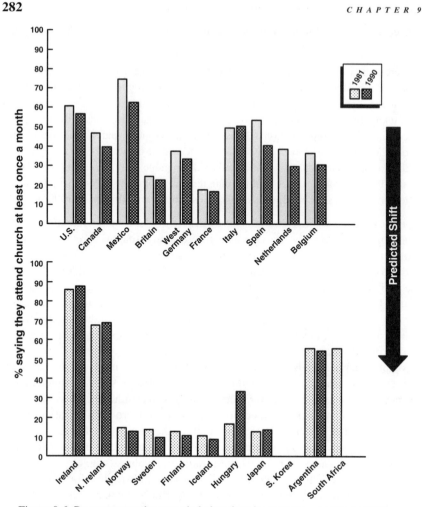

Figure 9.6. Percentages who attended church at least once a month, in 1981 vs. 1990, in 20 countries. *Source*: 1981 and 1990 World Values surveys. This question not included in 1990 South Korean survey.

sults show that from 1981 to 1990, church attendance rates *fell* in 14 of the 19 countries for which we have data. The South Korean surveys omitted most of the questions concerning religion; and data are not available for South Africa in 1981. Church attendance rose considerably in Hungary, and rose by a point or two in Ireland, Northern Ireland, Italy, and Japan. In 1981 participation in religious services already was extremely low in the Nordic countries, which are affluent welfare states—precisely the type of setting in which we would expect emphasis on religion to be minimal. In 1990 church attendance fell to even lower levels in all four countries.

Church attendance is one indicator of the priority which people accord to religion, but it measures external behavior that might be motivated by sociabil-

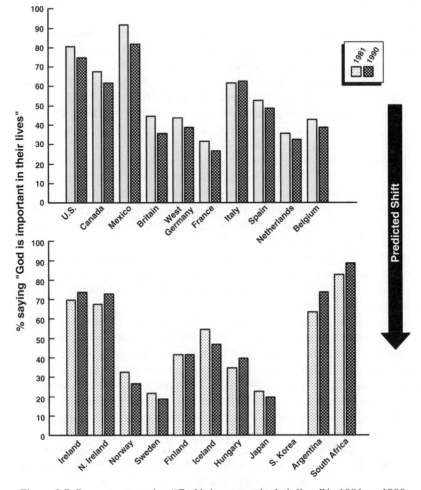

Figure 9.7. Percentages saying "God is important in their lives" in 1981 vs. 1990, in 20 countries. Based on percentage choosing cells 7–10 on a 10-point scale in which "1" means that God is not at all important in one's life and "10" means that God is very important in that person's life. *Source*: 1981 and 1990 World Values surveys. This question not included in 1990 South Korean survey.

ity, habit, or conformism, rather than genuine religious feeling. But we also have a number of indicators of how people feel about religion *internally*. Among them, the most sensitive indicator is a question that asks people to indicate how important God is in their lives, using a 10-point scale on which "1" means that God is not at all important, and "10" indicates that he is very important. Figure 9.7 shows the percentage in each country who give high ratings (scores of 7–10) to the importance of God in their lives.

This indicator of the subjective importance of religion tells the same story as the data on church attendance: emphasis on religion declined in 14 out of the 20 countries for which we have data. In keeping with the thesis that conditions of insecurity are conducive to a heightened need for the psychological reassurance that religion provides, the publics of both Argentina and South Africa showed significant *increases* in the importance attached to God in their lives. We suspect that similar changes would be found in many developing countries. Hungary, Ireland, Northern Ireland, and Italy show modest increases in the percentage placing great importance on religion, and Finland shows no change. But 70 percent of the observed changes are in the predicted direction, toward *less* emphasis on religion.

Thus we do find indications of a religious resurgence in Latin America, Africa, and Eastern Europe—but a marked *decline* in most advanced industrial societies. Within secure societies, some dramatic manifestations of militant fundamentalism have been seen recently; but this phenomenon reflects action by diminishing minorities who perceive that their way of life is threatened, and not the prevailing trend.

A substantial number of additional questions concerning religion show reasonably strong correlations with Materialist/Postmaterialist values. They include questions that measure belief in God, belief in hell, belief in heaven, belief in sin, the percentage saying that they get comfort and strength from religion, the percentage saying that the church in their country is giving adequate answers to moral problems and to problems of family life, and the percentage saying that the church is giving adequate answers to people's spiritual needs. The graphs showing the changes connected with each of these variables, in each country, are shown in Appendix 3. All but one of these variables show shifts in the predicted direction—toward less emphasis on religion—in most countries. One variable shows a countertrend: in a majority of countries, there was a rising perception that the church is giving adequate answers to people's spiritual needs. Nevertheless, the overall results are in keeping with theoretical expectations: 72 percent of the observed changes went in the predicted direction, toward *less* emphasis on religion.

Most of the countries that were surveyed in both 1981 and 1990 are relatively prosperous industrial societies that experienced modestly rising prosperity during the 1980s. This helps explain why the great majority of observed changes were in the direction of *diminishing* faith in the established religious institutions and traditional religious beliefs. Three societies were undergoing economic decay and political upheaval during this period—South Africa, Argentina, and Hungary; and in most instances, the publics of these countries shifted toward *greater* emphasis on religion.

The alleged global trend toward fundamentalist religion is based on a misconception. Fundamentalism is found mainly in less developed societies and in societies that are experiencing upheaval. In advanced industrial societies, fundamentalism has high visibility, but it seems to be a reaction by a declining minority that feels threatened by the pervasive and rapid cultural changes that are occurring in these societies.

Nevertheless, it would be inaccurate to speak of an undifferentiated trend away from religion, even in advanced industrial societies. As we commented in our analysis of the 1981 data,

> There is genuine irony in the fact that Postmaterialists seem relatively unattracted to organized religion in Western societies. Since they are less likely than Materialists to be preoccupied by the struggle for survival, theoretically they should have more intellectual and emotional energy to devote to the fulfillment of higher-order needs. And we find evidence that this is the case. Our respondents were asked, "How often, if at all, do you think about the meaning and purpose of life?" . . . Despite their relative alienation from traditional religion, in each of these societies Postmaterialists are *more* apt than the Materialists to spend time thinking about the meaning and purpose of life. This holds true despite the fact that older people are more likely to say they do so than younger ones. In this respect, Postmaterialists have more potential interest in religion than Materialists. (Inglehart, 1990: 192–93)

This implies that we should find an increase, not a decrease, in the percentage of the population who often think about the meaning and purpose of life. For religion serves a variety of functions. One of them is to provide a sense of orientation and certainty in an insecure world: no matter how threatening the situation may seem, one can have faith that things will ultimately turn out well if one adheres to a set of absolute traditional rules. For many people, that is the main function of religion. But religion has also traditionally helped satisfy intellectual and aesthetic needs, telling people where they come from and where they are going, and what is the meaning of life. Since the rise of modern science, traditional religious accounts of the origin and meaning of life have lost much of their credibility. But spiritual needs have not disappeared—indeed, interest in the meaning of life is more salient to Postmaterialists than to Materialists, and accordingly we would expect it to become *more* widespread even in advanced industrial societies. Our prediction is that interest in the meaning and purpose of life will be a rising concern, despite the general decline of traditional religious beliefs and behavior.

Figure 9.8 shows the changes observed from 1981 to 1990 in the percentage saying that they "often" think about the meaning and purpose of life. In 18 of the 21 societies, we find that a growing proportion of the population often thinks about the meaning of life; two societies show small decreases and one shows no change. Traditional beliefs and the established religious organizations may be losing their adherents, but spiritual concerns are becoming more widespread.

PARENT-CHILD TIES: A REVERSAL OF TRENDS

Now let us turn to an area in which our predictions do not hold up. This is not just a marginal failure. It is a striking reversal of the shift toward Postmodern values, not in just a few deviant cases, but across the great majority of soci-

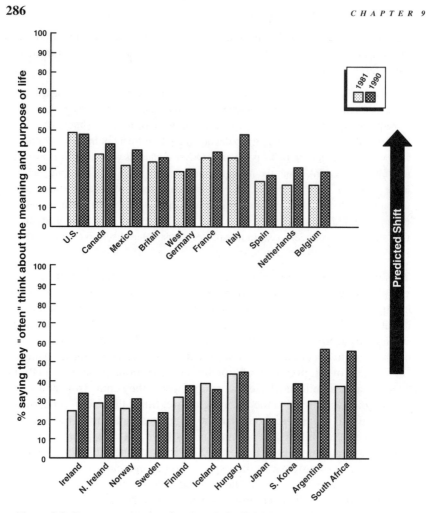

Figure 9.8. Percentages saying that they "often" think about the meaning and purpose of life, in 1981 vs. 1990, in 21 countries. *Source*: 1981 and 1990 World Values surveys.

eties for which we have data. It flatly contradicts our theoretical expectations,
but the finding is clear. And sometimes, one can learn just as much from the
failure of one's predictions as from their fulfillment.

The finding occurs with a set of four items concerning parent-child ties. The
first of these questions asks "If someone says a child needs a two-parent home
with both a father and a mother to grow up happily, would you tend to agree
or disagree?" Materialists are about twice as likely to agree with this proposition as are Postmaterialists, so our prediction is clear: we would expect to find
a shift in which the proportion agreeing that a child needs a two-parent family
diminishes over time. Figure 9.9 shows the actual findings.

In 16 of the 19 countries for which we have data, agreement with this propo-

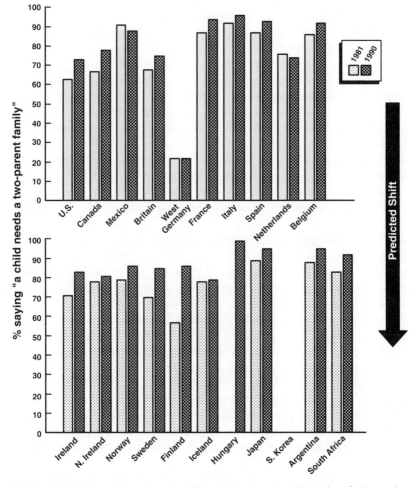

Figure 9.9. Percentages saying "a child needs a home with both a father and a mother, to grow up happily" in 1981 vs. 1990, in 19 countries. *Source*: 1981 and 1990 World Values surveys. Question not asked in South Korea, and 1981 data not available for Hungary.

sition rose, instead of falling, from 1981 to 1990. Two countries showed a slight decline and one showed no change. Overwhelmingly, the publics of these societies became more likely to believe that a child needs a home with both a father and a mother.

This is not an isolated fluke. The World Values surveys included three other questions about the importance of parent-child ties, and all three of them show roughly similar results. Figure A.19 (in Appendix 3) shows the changes over time in response to the question "Do you think that a woman needs to have children in order to be fulfilled, or is this not necessary?" Postmaterialists are much less likely than Materialists to think that a woman needs children in order to be fulfilled, so we would predict that this response would lose support; but in 14 of the 21 countries, agreement went up (with declines in six countries and no change in one). Figure A.20 (in Appendix 3) shows the changes registered in response to the question "If a woman wants to have a child as a single parent but doesn't want to have a stable relationship with a man, do you approve or disapprove?" Postmaterialists are much more likely to approve of single parenthood, so we would expect approval to rise—but it rose in 10 countries, and fell in 10 others. Finally, our respondents were asked whether they agreed that "Regardless of what qualities and faults one's parents have, one must always love and respect them" or "One does not have the duty to love and respect parents who have not earned it by their behavior and attitudes." Postmaterialists are substantially less likely to feel that one has a duty to love and respect one's parents, so we would expect this orientation to become more widespread. But, as figure A.21 demonstrates, this happened in only seven out of 21 countries.

Across the four items in this category, only 33 percent of the observed shifts were in the predicted direction. This is in startling contrast to the findings on other topics, where 75 to 80 percent of the shifts moved in the predicted direction. What accounts for the exceptional pattern of responses to questions concerning parent-child ties?

We must acknowledge that our response is ex post facto. We expected attitudes to shift toward less emphasis on family ties, but the bulk of the evidence contradicts our expectations. It may be that an intergenerational population replacement process is at work in the predicted direction, for not only is it true that Postmaterialists place less emphasis on parent-child ties, but both in 1981 and in 1990 we find clear and consistent age-group differences, with the younger cohorts placing relatively little emphasis on parent-child ties. Intergenerational differences may be present, but if so, something in the current socioeconomic environment is overwhelming their effects. What could this factor be?

Throughout advanced industrial societies, the traditional two-parent family has been breaking down. Only three decades ago, the vast majority of children were born into two-parent households. That is no longer true today, and in some countries, single-parent families have become extremely widespread. Figure 9.10 shows the rise in the percentage of children living with a never-married parent in the United States from 1960 to 1990. Figure 9.11 shows the percentage of children born to unmarried mothers in four Western European countries. The changes are dramatic. In many countries (including the United States), the proportion of children being raised by never-married parents is eight times as high as it was only 30 years ago.

A growing body of evidence from both sides of the Atlantic indicates that this phenomenon is linked with a wide range of social pathology. Recent studies show that virtually any kind of deviant behavior one can think of—from poor performance in school and early dropout rates, to drug use and criminal behavior, to obesity and psychological problems—are disproportionately high

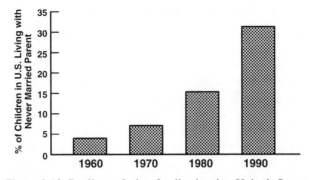

Figure 9.10. Decline of the family in the United States, 1960–90.
Percentage of children living with never-married parent. *Source*: U.S. Bureau of the Census.

among the children of never-married mothers. These linkages persist when one controls for such factors as race, income, and educational differences. Thus one recent study finds that "Children who grow up in a household with only one biological parent are worse off, on average, than children who grow up in a household with both of their biological parents, regardless of the parents' race or educational background. . . . Compared with teen-agers of similar background who grow up with both parents at home, adolescents who have lived apart from one of their parents during some period of childhood are more than twice as likely to drop out of high school, twice as likely to have a child before age twenty, and one and a half times as likely to be 'idle'—out of school and out of work—in their late teens and early twenties"(McLanahan and Sandefur, 1994: 1–2).

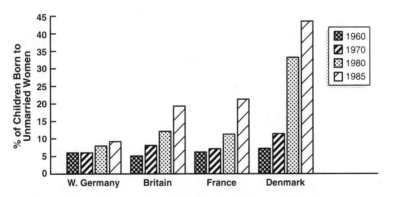

Figure 9.11. Decline of the family in Western Europe, 1960–85.
Percentage of children born to unmarried mothers. *Source*: European Community Statistical Office.

Another writer sums up recent findings as follows:

> Children in single-parent families are six times as likely to be poor. They are also likely to stay poor longer. Twenty-two percent of children in one-parent families will experience poverty during childhood for seven years or more, as compared with only 2 percent of children in two-parent families. A 1988 survey by the National Center for Health Statistics found that children in single-parent families are two to three times as likely as children in two-parent families to have emotional and behavioral problems. They are also more likely to drop out of high school, to get pregnant as teenagers, to abuse drugs and to be in trouble with the law. . . . Research shows that many children from disrupted families have a harder time achieving intimacy in a relationship, forming a stable marriage, or even holding a steady job. (Whitehead, 1993: 47)

Other recent studies present converging findings (Barton, 1992; McLanahan and Garfinkel, 1986; Wallerstein and Blakeslee, 1989): by almost any standard one might apply, children raised in single-parent families do not do as well as children raised in families where both parents are present.

It seems that social scientists are not the only people who have noticed these problems. One of the most interesting things about the resurgence of emphasis on family values is the fact that it started at the mass level and was picked up by political elites *later*. During the 1980s, mass publics throughout industrial society, reversing a long-established trend, were becoming less permissive toward parenthood outside of marriage and placing more emphasis on the importance of raising children in a setting where both a father and a mother were present.

In the late 1980s and early 1990s, growing numbers of social scientists were also coming to the conclusion that the breakdown of the traditional two-parent family was not progressive, after all, but was associated with a massive array of social pathologies.

In 1992, when Vice President Quayle criticized the mass media for irresponsibly glamorizing single parenthood, the immediate response was overwhelming ridicule. But within two years, cover stories were appearing in national magazines suggesting that the breakdown of the family really was a serious problem. And by 1994, President Clinton expressed great concern that "we are raising a whole generation of kids who aren't sure they're the most important person in the world to anybody"; while his Health and Human Services Secretary, Donna Shalala, stated in public that Dan Quayle was right when he condemned TV heroine Murphy Brown's attitude toward out-of-wedlock childbearing.

People learn from firsthand experience. Although few of them undoubtedly had read the scientific studies, it seems that on the basis of their own observations, the general publics in many countries were coming to the same conclusion as a growing number of social scientists: the traditional two-parent family was a relatively good way to raise children.

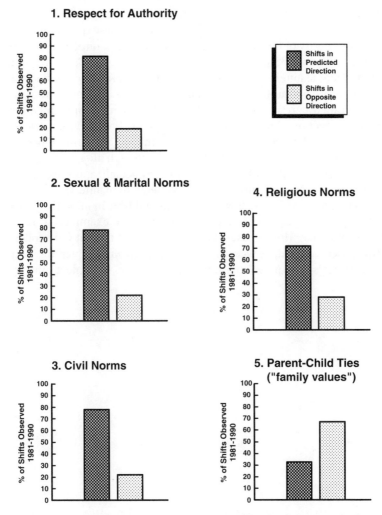

Figure 9.12. Predicted shifts and observed shifts: Overall results in five domains. *Source*: 1981 and 1990 World Values surveys.

PREDICTIONS AND OBSERVATIONS: OVERALL SUCCESS RATES

Figure 9.12 sums up the success rate of our predictions with five types of variables examined in this chapter. Across the first four categories, the great majority of the observed shifts moved in the predicted direction. This holds true for 81 percent of the shifts in respect for authority; of 79 percent of the shifts in sexual and marital norms, and also of 79 percent of the shifts in civil norms; and of 72 percent of the shifts in religious norms.

But, as we have just seen, our predictions did not hold up for the four questions dealing with parent-child ties. In response to these questions, the overwhelming majority of the publics shifted in the opposite direction from the one predicted, with only 33 percent of the observed shifts going in the predicted direction. Here again, it is clear that we are not dealing with an undifferentiated shift toward permissiveness in all things. Publics respond to what they experience in their current environment, as well as being shaped by a sense of security or insecurity during their formative years. Formative experiences remain important: the younger birth cohorts remained markedly more tolerant of single parenthood than the older ones, even though all age groups became less tolerant of it. But the influences of *both* early socialization effects and peoples' response to the contemporary environment are manifest.

To put this in perspective, however, we should bear in mind that this countershift applies to only four of the 26 items we have examined so far. In the overwhelming majority of cases, the predicted shift toward Postmodern values was observed. And, as we will see in the following chapter, the Postmodern shift was also the prevailing trend in connection with most other values.

The Erosion of Institutional Authority and the Rise of Citizen Intervention in Politics

INTRODUCTION

During the past four decades, the American public has become increasingly convinced that their government is not to be trusted. In 1958 the vast majority of Americans felt that their national government was basically honest. When asked, "Do you think that quite a few of the people running the government are crooked, not very many are, or do you think that hardly any of them are crooked?" only 24 percent of the American public said that "quite a few" of the people running the government were crooked. As figure 10.1 illustrates, this figure rose steeply during the 1960s and 1970s, leveled off during the 1980s, and reached an all time high in 1994, at which point an absolute majority—51 percent—of the American public said that quite a few of the people running the government were crooked.

A similar trend appears in response to the question "Would you say that the government is pretty much run by a few big interests looking out for themselves, or that it is run for the benefit of all the people?" In 1964 only 29 percent said that the government was run by a few big interests. This figure rose sharply until 1980, declined during the 1980s, and then reached an all-time high of 76 percent in 1994.

Figure 10.2 shows a similar pattern in response to a question concerning to what extent one can trust the government in Washington to do what is right. From 1958 to 1964, about 75 percent said that you can trust the government to do what is right "just about always" or "most of the time." A steep decline began in 1964 and continued throughout the 1970s, with a partial recovery in 1984–88, followed by further decline. By 1994 trust in the national government had fallen to an all-time low of 21 percent. In one generation, the prevailing outlook had changed from overwhelming trust to overwhelming cynicism.

This massive erosion of trust in government has given rise to a good deal of scholarly discussion since it was first noted by Miller (1974). But there is sharp disagreement about *why* it has occurred. Conservatives tend to attribute it to poor performance: the public has become fed up with the waste, corruption, and ineffectiveness of Big Government. Liberals tend to stress psychological or sociological explanations. Samuelson (1995), for example, argues that the postwar boom gave rise to expectations of economic progress that could not possibly be sustained. Both perspectives contain some truth. There is no question that good or bad performance is part of the story. For example, confidence

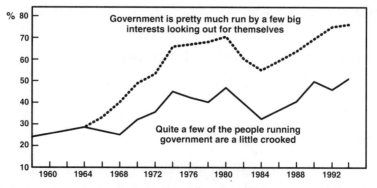

Figure 10.1. Rising distrust of government among the U.S. public, 1958–94. *Source*: University of Michigan National Election Studies, 1958–94.

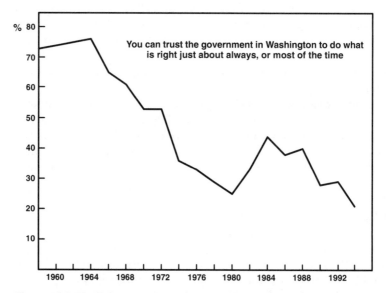

Figure 10.2. Declining trust in the federal government, 1958–94. *Source*: University of Michigan National Election Studies, 1958–94.

in the U.S. military dropped to extremely low levels during the disastrous intervention in Viet Nam—but subsequently recovered and rose to fairly high levels after the relatively quick and effective operations in Grenada and the Gulf War. But it is clearly not just a matter of government performance, for the United States was experiencing peace, steady economic growth, rising real income, low inflation, and relatively low unemployment in 1994—at which time confidence in the national government had fallen to an all-time low. It seems inconceivable that governmental performance would *not* influence public evaluations, but objective performance is always evaluated according to internalized standards—which have changed in recent decades.

If one believed in a simple one-to-one relationship between objective performance and mass evaluations, one would conclude that President Clinton must be the most inept and dishonest leader to have held office since these measurements were first taken. That interpretation doesn't hold water. The historical record suggests that governmental corruption hasn't increased over the past generation—it has probably diminished. But regardless of whether that is true, evidence presented in this chapter indicates that the phenomenon goes beyond the United States: we are witnessing a downward trend in trust in government and confidence in leaders across most industrialized societies. To explain these findings, one would need to assume that practically all of the leaders in power in the early 1990s—from Clinton to Major and Mitterrand and Gonzales and Mulroney and Andreotti and Hosokawa—all happened to be among the most incompetent and dishonest leaders their countries had ever seen. This is implausible. Instead, it seems that the rules have changed, and that the publics of these countries are now evaluating their leaders and institutions by more demanding standards than were applied in the past.

Nevertheless, there is reason to believe that governmental performance is also part of the story. Most Western governments are doing the old familiar tasks about as well as they ever did—but they are doing them in a profoundly changed setting. In the early twentieth century, industrial societies suffered from insufficient government regulation. As we argued in chapter 8, when government spending was rising from 10 percent to 20 or 30 percent of the economy, additional government regulation and redistribution had a relatively high payoff and benefited a large share of the population. But as government spending grew from 30 to 40 or 50 percent of the economy, it began to bring diminishing returns, and its costs became increasingly heavy for a growing share of the population. Entitlements tend to expand indefinitely; in the long run, the growth of government was on an unsustainable trajectory. More of the same did not have the same impact on public evaluations.

This trend has interacted with another factor: the rise of Postmodern political issues. In the 1950s, government policy was mainly aimed at securing economic growth and national security—public goods that practically everyone desired. Since the 1960s, politics has increasingly involved Postmodern issues, giving rise to a phenomenon that is sometimes described as the Culture Wars. Affirmative action, the right to abortion, and guaranteeing the rights of gays and lesbians are not viewed as public goods but involve goals that a substantial part of the public does not want to attain at all. Economic redistribution was also divisive, but was relatively amenable to compromise; issues like abortion tend to be seen as questions of good versus evil on which one cannot compromise.

Some observers have interpreted the decline of trust in government as a sign of general alienation. Pointing to declining rates of voter turnout, they argue that the American public has become disenchanted with the entire system and withdrawn from politics completely. The empirical evidence contradicts this interpretation. As we will see, though voter turnout has stagnated (largely because of weakening political party loyalties), Western publics have *not* become apathetic: quite the contrary, in the last two decades, they have become markedly more likely to engage in elite-challenging forms of political participation. Furthermore, the erosion of trust does not apply to all institutions: it is specifically a withdrawal of confidence from authoritarian institutions. During the same period that trust in political authority was fading, environmental protection movements rose from obscurity to attain remarkably high levels of public confidence: in the 1990–91 World Values survey, fully 93 percent of these publics approved of the environmentalist movement—with 59 percent approving "strongly." But support for certain types of institutions is sharply differentiated according to whether one has Materialist or Postmaterialist values, with Materialist being much more likely to support authoritarian institutions, and these institutions suffered from declining mass confidence throughout advanced industrial society.

THE AUTHORITARIAN REFLEX AND THE POSTMODERN SHIFT

Declining trust in government seems to be part of a broader erosion of respect for authority that is linked with the processes of Modernization and Postmodernization. Rapid change leads to severe insecurity, giving rise to an Authoritarian Reflex that may bring Fundamentalist or xenophobic reactions or adulation of strong leaders. As we have argued, insecurity leads to a need for strong authority figures to protect one from threatening forces and breeds an intolerance of cultural change and different ethnic groups.

Conversely, conditions of prosperity and security are conducive to greater emphasis on individual autonomy and diminishing deference to authority. Until recently, existential insecurity was a usual part of the human condition. Only recently have societies emerged in which most of the population does *not* have any fear of starvation (which is still a very real concern for much of humanity). Both premodern agrarian society and modern industrial society were shaped by survival values. The Postmodern shift has brought a broad de-emphasis on all forms of authority.

A major aspect of the Postmodern shift is a shift away from *both* religious and bureaucratic authority, bringing declining emphasis on all kinds of authority. Deference to authority has high costs: the individual's personal goals must be subordinated to those of a broader entity. Under conditions of insecurity, people are more than willing to do so. Under threat of invasion, internal disorder, or existential insecurity, people eagerly seek strong authority figures who can protect them. Conversely, the shift toward well-being values is linked with declining emphasis on political, religious and economic authority.

As we saw in figure 3.2, the idea that "more respect for authority would be a good thing" is closely linked with the Traditional pole of the Traditional-Secular-Rational values dimension. The peoples of low-income societies place much more emphasis on authority than do the peoples of advanced industrial societies: the correlation between the percentage who feel that "more respect for authority would be a good thing" and the society's per capita GNP is $-.66$. This suggests that as modernization and economic development take place, we will find declining respect for authority.

Similarly, as we saw in the preceding chapter, Materialists tend to support the proposition that "more respect for authority would be a good thing," while Postmaterialists tend to reject it. Consequently, we predicted a gradual shift toward the values linked with Postmaterialism—that is, toward less emphasis on respect for authority. And the data confirm this prediction: as figure 9.2 demonstrated, from 1981 to 1990, emphasis on more respect for authority became less widespread in 17 of the 21 countries for which we have data. Argentina, South Africa, Ireland, and South Korea were the only exceptions to this trend. The evidence indicates that respect for authority actually *is* declining in most advanced industrial societies. We suspect that this has contributed to the erosion of institutional authority. Performance still counts. But the tendency to idealize national leaders has been growing weaker, and their performance is being evaluated with a more critical eye.

Earlier in this book, we examined the curve depicting the relationship between subjective well-being and economic development. In the early phases of development, the curve rises steeply: additional income brings large increases not only in such things as life expectancy, but also in *subjective* well-being. After a certain point, however, the curve levels off, and additional economic growth is not associated with further increases in subjective well-being.

At this point, significant numbers of Postmaterialists begin to emerge. They take economic security for granted to such a degree that it has a relatively minor impact on their subjective well-being. Thus, despite the fact that Postmaterialists have higher levels of income, education, and occupational status than Materialists, they do *not* manifest higher levels of subjective well-being. They take their prosperity for granted and transfer their focus to other aspects of life, such as politics and the quality of the physical and social environment. These domains are subjectively more important to Postmaterialists than they are to Materialists, and they apply higher, more demanding standards to them. Thus, though Postmaterialists generally live in less noisy, less polluted neighborhoods than Materialists, they register lower levels of satisfaction with their environment.

They also evaluate politics by more demanding standards. Though they live in the same political systems as Materialists, and are more able to make these systems respond to their preferences (being more articulate and politically more active), they do not register higher levels of satisfaction with politics. The rise of Postmaterialist values is one symptom of a broader Postmodern shift that is transforming the standards by which the publics of advanced industrial societies evaluate governmental performance. It brings new, more demanding standards to the evaluation of political life and confronts political

298

leaders with more active, articulate citizens. The position of elites has become more difficult in advanced industrial society. Mass publics are becoming increasingly critical of their political leaders and increasingly likely to engage in elite-challenging activities.

This leads to a paradoxical finding: the publics of prosperous, stable, and democratic advanced industrial societies do *not* show higher levels of satisfaction with their political systems than do the publics of poor, authoritarian countries; quite the contrary, astonishing as it may seem, they show significantly *less* confidence in their leaders and political institutions than do their counterparts in developing countries. In the short run, economic development tends to bring rising levels of political satisfaction; in the long run, however, it leads to the emergence of new and more demanding standards by which governmental performance is evaluated.

THE EROSION OF INSTITUTIONAL AUTHORITY

Let us now examine the shifts that took place in political values from 1981 to 1990, testing the same type of prediction as in the previous chapter: all orientations linked with Postmaterialist values should become more widespread. We find that pervasive changes are taking place in political, as well as social, values. There is evidence of a long-term shift in which the publics of advanced industrial societies are becoming more likely to act in autonomous, elite-challenging fashion. These changes make mass publics less respectful of elites and more likely to challenge them. Confidence in established political and societal institutions is declining; but the participant potential of most publics is rising. Thus, we find two related trends: the erosion of institutional authority, and the rise of citizen intervention in politics.

When governmental authority declined in given countries in the past, it was usually attributed to the fact that the specific government then in office was less effective, and instilled less confidence, than the previous government. This undoubtedly *is* part of the explanation: incompetent and corrupt governments tend to evoke less confidence than do competent, honest ones. But we believe that a long-term component is also involved here, in addition to fluctuations linked with specific officeholders.

This erosion of political authority can be traced to some of the same factors that were examined in the previous chapter. It has often been observed that in time of national danger the public tends to seek the security of strong leaders and strong institutions. Thus, during the traumatic insecurity of the Great Depression, a wave of upheavals took place in newly established democracies, from Italy to Germany to Hungary to Spain, which led to the rise of authoritarian leaders such as Mussolini, Hitler, Horthy, and Franco. Even in the United States, with its deep-rooted democratic tradition, the American people rallied behind Franklin Roosevelt, who exercised exceptionally sweeping powers and was elected for an unprecedented four terms.

Long-enduring security paves the way for the reverse phenomenon: the public gradually sees less need for the discipline and self-denial demanded by strong governments. A Postmaterialist emphasis on self-expression and self-realization becomes increasingly central.

DECLINING CONFIDENCE IN HIERARCHICAL INSTITUTIONS

Evidence from the 1981 and 1990 surveys demonstrates the claims we have just laid out. Across nearly all of our societies, Materialists place more confidence in their country's hierarchical institutions—especially the armed forces, police, and church—than do Postmaterialists.

These findings are consistent with our argument that a sense of insecurity tends to motivate support for strong institutions and for strong political authority in particular. Having experienced a relatively high sense of economic and physical security throughout their formative years, Postmaterialists feel less need for strong authority than do Materialists. Moreover, Postmaterialists place relatively strong emphasis on self-expression—a value that inherently conflicts with the structure of hierarchical bureaucratic organizations.

The value-related differences point to the possibility of a shift over time, toward the outlook of the younger and more Postmaterialist respondents. Do we find it? The answer is yes. In most countries, we find lower levels of confidence in government institutions in 1990 than those that existed in 1981.

Our respondents were asked how much confidence they had in a dozen national institutions. Postmaterialists show lower levels of confidence in most established institutions than do Materialists, and in three cases the correlations were high enough to meet our criterion of "reasonably strong": Postmaterialist values are especially strongly linked with *low* levels of confidence in their country's police, armed forces, and church. Consequently, we predict that confidence in these institutions will decline.

As figure 10.3 demonstrates, from 1981 to 1990, confidence in the given society's police declined in 16 of the 20 countries for which we have data. Confidence rose only in Ireland and Iceland, and in Argentina and South Africa, two of the three societies in our sample that were undergoing regime changes (1981 data are not available for Hungary, the third such society).

Confidence in the country's armed forces shows a similar pattern (see figure 10.4). It declined in 17 of the 20 countries for which we have data—rising only in Northern Ireland and (again) in Argentina and South Africa. Confidence in one's country's church also moved on the predicted trajectory; as figure A.22 (in Appendix 3) demonstrates, it fell in 14 of the 20 cases where changes occurred; confidence in the churches rose only in the United States, Ireland, and Northern Ireland, and in Hungary, Argentina, and South Africa, the three countries undergoing regime changes.

Confidence in many other national institutions also showed a similar pattern of (1) being correlated with Materialist values and (2) declining over time. We

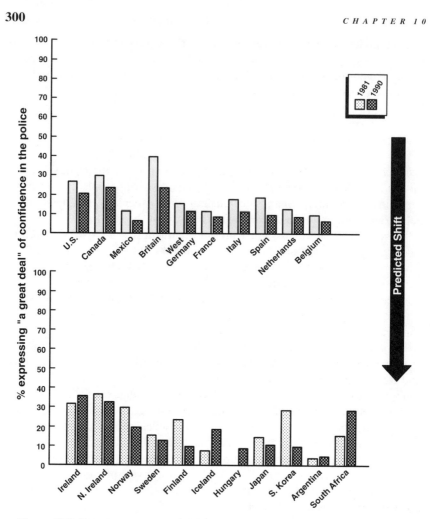

Figure 10.3. Percentages expressing "a great deal" of confidence in their country's police forces, in 1981 vs. 1990, in 20 countries. *Source*: 1981 and 1990
World Values surveys. 1981 data not available for Hungary.

do not analyze these attitudes here, however, since their correlation with Postmaterialist values falls below our .125 cutoff level.

Data from a number of other sources support the thesis that confidence in
hierarchical institutions is declining. The National Opinion Center at the University of Chicago has been measuring confidence in U.S. national institutions
every year since 1973. These institutions include Congress, the Executive
Branch, the Press, the Military, Organized Labor, the Supreme Court, Television, Education, and Organized Religion. Nearly all of these institutions have
suffered some decline since 1973. And in a number of cases, the 1993 levels
of confidence were the lowest ever recorded during this 20-year period. This
was true of the U.S. public's rating of Congress, the Press, Television, Educa-

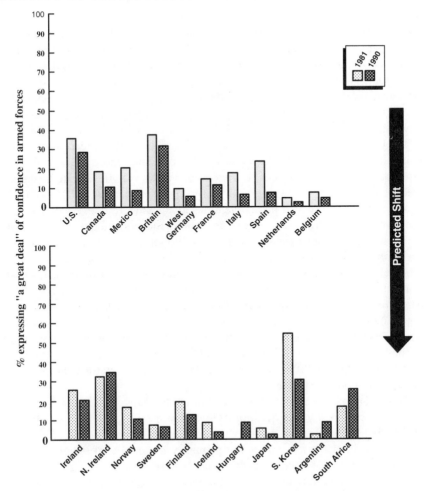

Figure 10.4. Percentages expressing "a great deal" of confidence in their country's armed forces, in 1981 vs. 1990, in 20 countries. *Source*: 1981 and 1990
World Values surveys.

tion, and Organized Religion. The decline in confidence was substantial. For
example, in 1973 only 15 percent of the public said that they had "hardly any"
confidence in Congress; in 1993, 41 percent said they had "hardly any" confidence. Similarly, though 1993 was not the low point of confidence in the Executive Branch (that was registered in 1974, when President Nixon resigned),
there was an overall downward trend here too: in 1973, only 18 percent said
they had "hardly any" confidence in the Executive Branch; in 1993, 32 percent
said they had "hardly any" confidence (NORC surveys reported in *The American Enterprise*, November/December, 1993: 94–95).

Another manifestation of the collapse of public faith in politicians is the recent emergence of massive support for term limitations on elected representa-

tives in Congress and, in some cases, in state legislatures as well. Although they probably are not constitutional, such proposals have been passed in every state where they have been on the ballot. Voters already have the right to limit the terms of their representatives by simply not reelecting them. But the mass mood seems to reflect a perception that, given the advantages incumbents have conferred on themselves, and given the fact that the voters have come to see them as a self-perpetuating privileged class, the only safe way to curtail their power is by placing formal limits on their tenure of power.

The old standards for evaluating elites no longer apply. A record that once would have ensured reelection is now insufficient. Thus, more than seven years after he had led allied forces to victory in World War II, a grateful nation elected Dwight Eisenhower president by a landslide margin. By contrast, shortly after the Cold War had come to a sudden and (from an American perspective) astonishingly successful conclusion, and immediately after a swift and (from an American perspective) almost bloodless victory in the Gulf War, and with an economy that was in relatively good shape, George Bush failed to win reelection in 1992. This was not just a failure of charisma on Bush's part. For within two years, his successor had become widely distrusted, and his party lost control of both houses of Congress. This happened though the economic indicators were doing even better than they were under Bush. It has become clear that the standard economic indicators no longer explain as much as they once did, in the realm of political behavior. Postmodern publics evaluate their leaders by different, and more demanding, standards than those applied throughout most of the modern era.

This phenomenon is not limited to the United States. Figure 10.5 shows changing responses to the question "Generally speaking, are you satisfied or dissatisfied with the way democracy is working in your country?" As we pointed out in chapter 4, this is not primarily a measure of whether the respondent supports democracy itself; it mainly taps his or her rating of how well the politicians currently in office are functioning. Although, as one would expect, these ratings tend to rise and fall with the economic cycle, they also show a long-term downward tendency. Thus, in the recessions of the early 1970s and the early 1980s, "dissatisfied" ratings became nearly as numerous as "satisfied" ratings among the combined European Community publics. But during the recession of the early 1990s, for the first time, negative ratings became more widespread than positive ratings. In 1993 dissatisfaction reached the highest level ever recorded. The economic downturn of the early 1990s seems to have contributed to this phenomenon, but it can't be the entire explanation: the recessions of the 1970s and 1980s were equally severe, but political dissatisfaction never rose to the heights it reached in 1993.

How deep does this dissatisfaction run? The respondents in the World Values surveys were asked how proud they were to be French, Mexican, Japanese, etc., answering on a scale that ran from "very proud" to "not at all proud" (see figure 10.6). In light of the evidence of a widespread decline of confidence in national institutions, one might reasonably expect pride in the nation itself

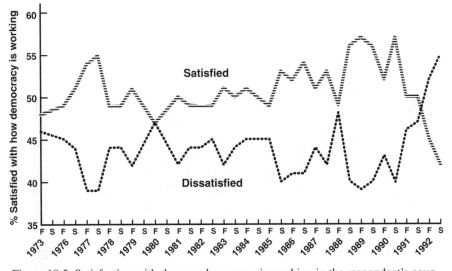

Figure 10.5. Satisfaction with the way democracy is working in the respondent's country, among the publics of the combined European Community countries, 1973–93.
"S" indicates surveys carried out in the spring of the given year, "F" indicates surveys carried out in the fall. *Source*: European Community survey and Euro-Barometer surveys from 1976 through 1993.

to decline too—especially since national pride *is* strongly correlated with confidence in national institutions and with the strength of one's religious convictions. Furthermore, we find that Postmaterialists express lower levels of national pride than do Materialists (and the correlation is "reasonably strong"). Hence, we would predict a decline in feelings of national pride.

On the other hand, running counter to this expectation, there is widespread belief that this is "an era of rising nationalism." But is it? The reality is more complex. We believe that the traditional form of nationalism is rising in many countries, but not in most advanced industrial societies. There *has* been a rising tide of one form of "nationalism"—that is, of xenophobia linked with insecurity—in poorer and less secure societies: it has had dramatic and tragic consequences in India, Sri Lanka, Azerbaijia, Armenia, Sudan, Nigeria, Rwanda and the former Soviet Union and Yugoslavia.

But in advanced industrial societies, we are witnessing a quite different phenomenon: we find demands to transfer authority *away* from the existing nation-states to smaller, more immediate units having greater cultural coherence: from Spain to Catalonia, for example, or from Canada to Quebec. The partisans of such movements tend to be Postmaterialists, motivated by concerns for cultural autonomy and a sense of community. Very confusingly, this completely different phenomenon is *also* called "nationalism." The fact that the term "nationalism" is used to denote both hyperloyalty to the nation-state *and* withdrawing one's loyalty away from it to smaller units has given rise to a good

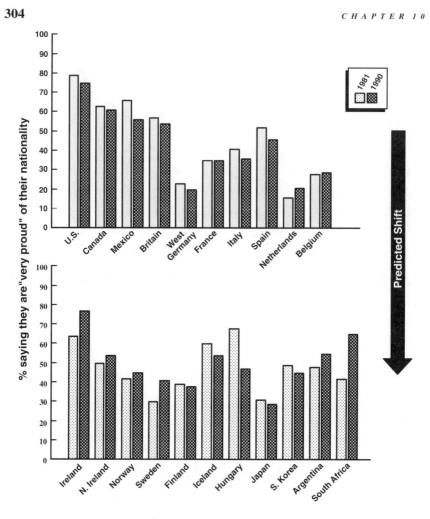

Figure 10.6. Percentages saying they are "very proud" of their nationality, in 1981 vs. 1990, in 21 countries. *Source*: 1981 and 1990 World Values surveys.

deal of confusion and misunderstanding; two quite different (indeed, almost opposite) things are lumped together as "rising nationalism." This usage equates contemporary Quebecois autonomists with the xenophobic nationalists of the nineteenth century. They are not at all the same thing. In advanced industrial societies, ethnic separatist movements generally do not involve an inward-looking parochialism. Instead, they represent a shift of focus away from the hierarchical nation-state in two directions: on one hand, a greater emphasis on community and local autonomy, and at the same time a growing openness to broader ties. Thus, the Quebecois separatists tend to be more favorable to North American free trade than are Canadians in general, and the Catalan "nationalists" tend to be partisans of European unification.

From 1981 to 1990, feelings of national pride tended to move on the same trajectory as did the other elements of this syndrome, but the results are mixed: in 12 out of 19 countries, we find a decline in the percentage expressing strong feelings of national pride, as figure 10.6 demonstrates. The results move in the predicted direction in 63 percent of the cases where change occurred. But there are a number of exceptions. In addition to the usual countertrends in Argentina and South Africa, national pride rose in Ireland, Northern Ireland, Norway, Sweden, the Netherlands, and Belgium. We do not find a simple split between secure and insecure societies.

Our predictions show a success rate of 63 percent; this is better than random, but it is not doing as well as with most political variables. It raises an interesting question: why is national pride not declining as much as we would expect in advanced industrial societies? We suspect that two major contemporary events are involved.

The first is a Western European reaction against massive non-European immigration. The immense disparity between living standards in Western Europe and developing countries, coupled with wide-bodied jet aircraft, has brought a large influx of visibly different immigrants into societies that never before had large numbers of them. Suddenly, most of these countries find themselves with large minorities of ethnically very distinct peoples, often coming from very far away. Interacting with the insecurity due to the recent recession, this has given rise to a wave of xenophobia—and the tendency to reemphasize one's own traditional ethnic identity. The other factor is the push toward European Union, which (like most major changes) has given rise to a traditionalist reaction in many countries.

An increase in feelings of national pride did not take place in North America during this period, despite the fact that the United States and Canada have had larger immigrant inflows than any Western European society. But more recently, the United States also has experienced strong pressures to limit further immigration.

The decline of confidence in established institutions and of trust in government does not represent a broad withdrawal of trust from the world in general: it is specifically a withdrawal of confidence from authoritarian institutions. National Election Study and General Social Survey data from the United States demonstrate that there was a significant downward movement in interpersonal trust from 1964 to 1994, but the United States seems to be exceptional in this respect. Interpersonal trust (as we have seen, a key element in pro-democratic political culture) is strongly linked with Postmaterialist values; consequently, we would predict rising, not falling, levels of interpersonal trust. As figure 10.7 demonstrates, this prediction is generally confirmed: interpersonal trust *rose* in 13 of the 19 countries in which change was observed. The exceptions include France, Northern Ireland, and South Korea, and the three societies undergoing regime change, Hungary, Argentina, and South Africa. Outside the United States, most publics are coming to trust people *more* but hierarchical institutions *less*.

Moreover, we find one striking exception to the decline of mass confidence

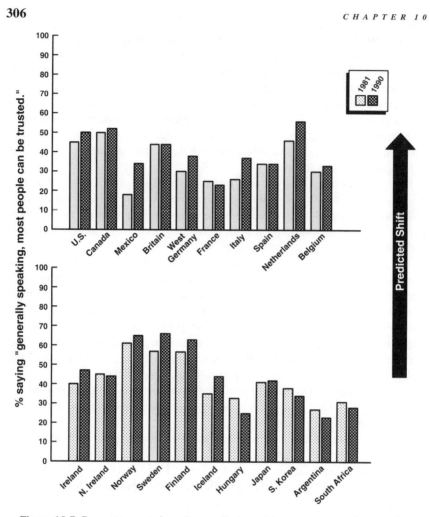

Figure 10.7. Percentage saying "generally speaking, most people can be trusted" in 1981 vs. 1990, in 21 societies. *Source*: 1981 and 1990 World Values surveys.

in established institutions: during the period 1981–90, confidence in "major corporations" did not decline. Though it started from relatively low levels in 1981, confidence in corporations showed a rising trend in most societies. This may have been linked with the collapse of state socialist economies, which made private enterprise look good by contrast. And in a sense, it is a logical reaction to the pronounced decline of trust in government: if the state is coming to be seen as the problem, rather than the solution, it becomes all the more important to have a strong countervailing force to offset the power of the state. In any case, it seems clear that one of the most pervasive defining tendencies of the modernization era—the tendency to look to the state as the solution to all problems—has reached its limits.

THE RISE OF CITIZEN INTERVENTION

Throughout advanced industrial democracies, voter turnout is stagnant or declining. In most countries, established political party machines are losing their grip on voters, and party membership has fallen to about half the level it had a few decades ago. And one frequently hears references to growing apathy on the part of the public. As we will demonstrate, these allegations of apathy are misleading: mass publics *are* deserting the old-line oligarchical political organizations that mobilized them in the modernization era—but, far from being apathetic, they are becoming more active than ever in a wide range of elite-challenging forms of political participation.

In contrast to widespread allegations of mass apathy, a more participant political role for mass publics has been predicted for some time. In 1977 it was suggested that Cognitive Mobilization (reflecting rising levels of formal education, political information, and cognitive skills) was making the publics of advanced industrial societies increasingly likely to engage in interventionist, elite-challenging politics (Inglehart, 1979: 291–321).

Throughout the world, the more educated tend to be more active in politics than the less educated (Milbrath and Goel, 1977; Verba, Nie, and Kim, 1978). And, throughout the world, younger birth cohorts are more educated than older ones. This implies that, as younger, more highly educated cohorts gradually replace the older, less educated ones in the adult population, we should witness a gradual rise in conventional political participation rates.

Moreover the *Political Action* study found a strong relationship between Postmaterialist values and "unconventional political behavior" (that is, elite-challenging action such as boycotts, unofficial strikes, and occupying buildings in order to press political demands), concluding "As relatively Postmaterialist younger age cohorts replace relatively Materialist ones in the adult electorate, we would anticipate a gradual rise in the public's propensity to employ 'unconventional' techniques of political protest (and, of course, a change in what is considered unconventional)" (Inglehart, 1979: 378–79).

Kaase and Barnes endorsed this prediction, in their conclusion to the same volume: "The dependence of unconventional political behavior on education, cognitive skills and Postmaterialism—well-documented in our analysis—displays too much of a structural component, and therefore permanence, to be considered just a fad of the young" (Barnes and Kaase, 1979: 524).

Because of changing values and skills levels, mass political participation was predicted to rise as intergenerational population replacement takes place. These predictions were published more than a decade before the data for the 1990 World Values Surveys were collected. They contradict the conventional wisdom that focuses on declining voting rates, concluding that citizens are losing interest in politics and the prevailing trend is toward mass apathy. But voting turnout largely reflects the parties' ability to mobilize their supporters and consequently is a misleading indicator of real mass interest and involvement. The World Values survey data show strong correlations between Material-

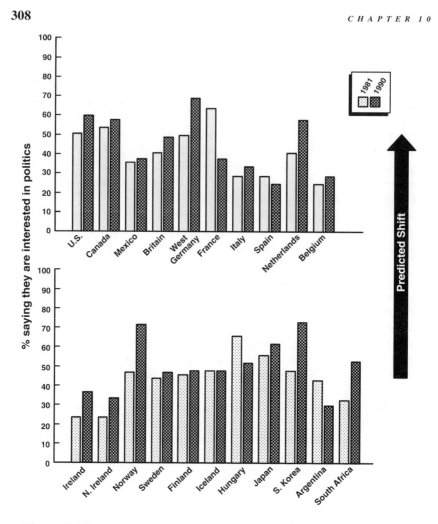

Figure 10.8. Percentages saying that they are interested in politics, in 1981 vs. 1990, in 21 countries. *Source*: 1981 and 1990 World Values surveys.

ist/Postmaterialist values and the more active forms of political participation (though not with voting). Accordingly, we predict that we will find rising, not falling, levels of mass political participation. Let us examine the evidence.

CONVENTIONAL POLITICAL PARTICIPATION

Evidence from the 21 countries surveyed in both 1981 and 1990 indicates that, though they may vote less regularly, most publics are *not* becoming apathetic; quite the contrary, they are becoming increasingly interested in politics. As figure 10.8 shows, political interest rates rose in 16 countries and fell in only four. The findings are unequivocal, and they contradict the conventional wisdom

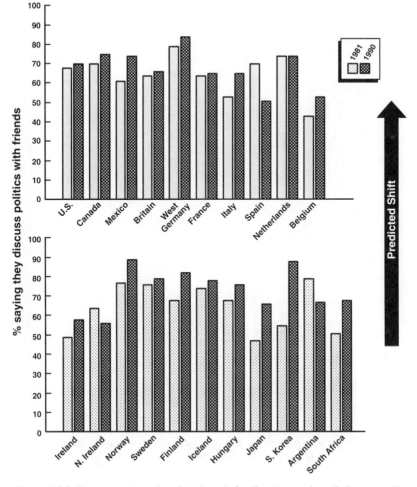

Figure 10.9. Percentages saying that they "often" or "sometimes" discuss politics with friends, in 1981 vs. 1990, in 21 countries. *Source*: 1981 and 1990 World Values surveys.

about mass apathy. Another good indicator of political interest is whether or not people discuss politics with others. Here, too, the predicted rise in conventional participation is taking place, as figure 10.9 indicates. The proportion of the population that discusses politics rose in 17 societies and fell in only three (with one country showing no change).

Another, more active form of conventional political participation also shows the predicted increase: as figure 10.10 demonstrates, from 1981 to 1990 the percentage reporting that they had signed a petition rose in 16 countries and fell in only four. When we examine trends over a still longer time period, the results are even more dramatic. Four of the countries that were included in both waves of the World Values survey were also surveyed for the 1974 Political

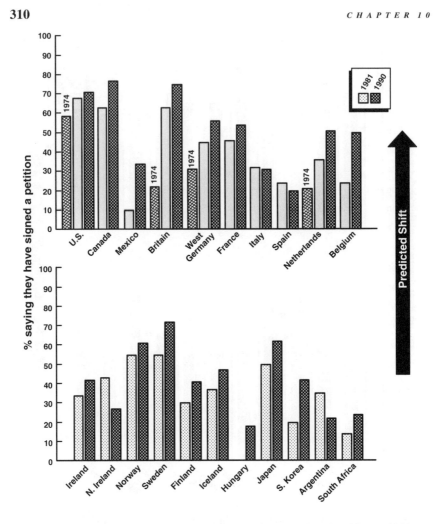

Figure 10.10. Percentages saying they have signed a petition, in 1981 vs. 1990, in 20 countries. *Source*: 1981 and 1990 World Values surveys. 1981 data not available for Hungary.

Action study (see Barnes et al., 1979: 548–49). The data for these countries (the United States, Britain, West Germany, and the Netherlands) are included in figure 10.10. In all four cases, we find even larger increases from 1974 to 1990 than we do from 1981 to 1990. In the United States, the percentage reporting that they had signed a petition rose from 58 percent in 1974, to 68 percent in 1981, to 71 percent in 1990; for Britain, they rose from 22 to 62 to 75 percent; for West Germany, the figures are 31, 43, and 56 percent; and in the Netherlands the percentage saying they had signed a petition rose from 21 percent in 1974 to 37 percent in 1981 to 50 percent in 1990.

This is dramatic evidence of rising mass political activism. How do we explain declining rates of voter turnout and falling political party membership, in light of these findings? The confusion over whether participation is rising or falling arises from the fact that we are dealing with two distinct processes: elite-directed participation is eroding, but more autonomous and active forms of participation are rising.

The decline in voter turnout reflects a long-term intergenerational decline in party loyalty. Although the younger, better-educated birth cohorts show higher rates of political interest, political discussion, and so forth than their elders, they have *lower* levels of party loyalty. Surveys from a number of Western European countries reveal that the postwar birth cohorts have considerably lower rates of political party loyalty than the older cohorts (Inglehart, 1990: 357–58). This finding parallels a pattern of intergenerational decline in party identification that has been found among the American electorate during the past two decades (Nie, Verba, and Petrocik, 1979; Abramson, 1979).

Although their higher levels of education and politicization predispose them to identify with *some* political party, the younger relatively Postmaterialist cohorts have less incentive to identify with any specific political party among the available choices. The established political parties were established in an era dominated by social class conflict and economic issues and tend to remain polarized along these lines. For the older cohorts, religion and social class still provide powerful cues in establishing one's political party loyalties. But the younger cohorts' loyalties are less strongly influenced by social class and religion. Moreover, in recent years, a new axis of polarization has arisen based on cultural and quality of life issues. Established parties have had difficulty in reorienting themselves in relation to this axis. Today, the established political party configurations in most countries do not yet adequately reflect the hottest contemporary issues; and those born in the postwar era have relatively little motivation to identify with the established political parties.

Even more important, however, is the fact that the younger birth cohorts are relatively Postmaterialist. This makes them less amenable to accepting the authority of hierarchical, oligarchical organizations like the old-line political parties. Accordingly, the last few decades have brought a decline of political party loyalties and membership in most advanced industrial societies.

But partisan loyalties and party organizations were the main reason for the high electoral turnout of earlier years. Hence, we find two divergent trends: on one hand, the bureaucratized and elite-directed forms of participation such as voting and party membership have declined, while on the other hand the individually motivated and elite-challenging forms of participation have risen.

The decline of partisanship need not continue indefinitely. A realignment of political party systems that made party polarization correspond more closely to issue polarization and less oligarchical forms of organization could stem the decline. Such a realignment seems to be under way with some Western parties, but it has not yet reversed the overall trend.

THE RISE OF UNCONVENTIONAL POLITICAL PARTICIPATION

Postmaterialists are much more likely to engage in unconventional political activities than are Materialists. Postmaterialists are those who have been raised under conditions of relative economic and physical security. Hence, they take survival for granted and devote more time and energy to relatively remote and abstract activities such as politics.

This has contributed to an international trend toward rising rates of unconventional, elite-challenging behavior. The World Values surveys included a battery of questions concerning one's readiness to take part in four forms of unconventional political action. The exact text of these questions asked, "I am going to read out some different form of political action that people can take and I'd like you to tell me, for each one, whether you have actually *done* any of these things, whether you might do it, or would never, under any circumstances, do it." The list includes (1) joining in boycotts, (2) attending lawful demonstrations, (3) joining unofficial strikes, and (4) occupying buildings or factories.

These questions are replicated from the *Political Action* study (Barnes et al., 1979). They were designed to test the hypothesis that intergenerational changes in values and skill levels are giving rise to a more activist public— one that is readier to intervene directly in political decision making, rather than limiting themselves to participation by voting, in which the public gives a blank check to a given set of elites, authorizing them to make all important political decisions for the next several years. In contrast with voting, unconventional participation is relatively disruptive and is designed to influence specific decisions.

Figure 10.11 shows the changes in the percentage saying that they actually have taken part in a boycott, or that they might do so. The former reports actual behavior, while the latter simply indicates a relative predisposition to do so. Both actual behavior and behavioral predispositions show clear upward trends from 1981 to 1990, but the numbers are larger and more reliable when we combine the two, as in this figure. Here again, we have 1974 data from four countries (the United States, Britain, West Germany, and the Netherlands) from the Political Action study, extending the time series over 16 years in these four cases. We predicted that we will observe an increase in this form of participation. And we find it: the percentage saying they have taken part in a boycott, or might do so, rose in 15 countries from 1981 (or from 1974) to 1990; it fell in five (we have no 1981 data from Hungary); the success rate for this prediction is 75 percent. Incidentally, the U.S. data in this figure constitute the sole anomaly in which the 1974 level was higher than the 1981 level (and even here, the overall trend is upward when continued to 1990). Generally, we find a steady upward trend, as this and the next two figures demonstrate. At the earliest time point, in 1974, such activities were still rare—which is why we used the label "unconventional political participation." Today, they have become so

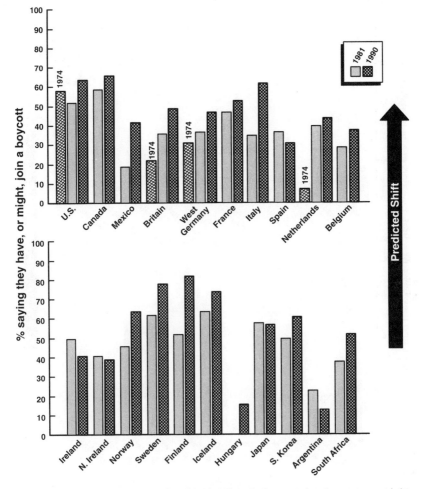

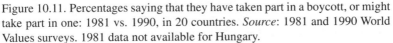

Figure 10.11. Percentages saying that they have taken part in a boycott, or might take part in one: 1981 vs. 1990, in 20 countries. *Source*: 1981 and 1990 World Values surveys. 1981 data not available for Hungary.

widespread that they are no longer unconventional. Another label such as "elite-challenging" participation seems appropriate.

Figure 10.12 shows the percentages that have taken part in demonstrations or are willing to do so. The percentage rises in 16 societies and declines in only one (three societies show no change, and 1981 data are lacking for Hungary). Here, and with both of the remaining "unconventional participation" variables, there is a perfectly monotonic rise from 1974 to 1990 in all four countries for which 1974 data are available.

Figures A.23 and A.24 (in Appendix 3) show the trends observed in the percentages saying they actually have taken part, or might take part, in an unoffi-

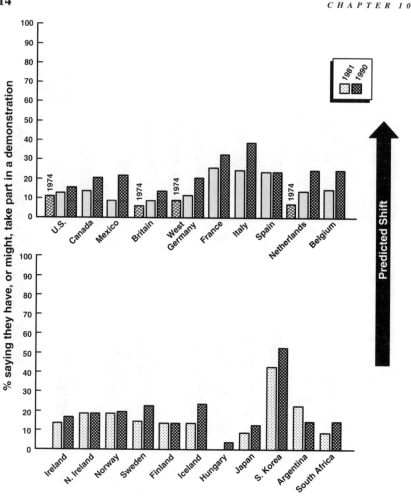

Figure 10.12. Percentages saying that they have taken part in a demonstration, or might do so, in 1981 vs. 1990, in 20 countries. *Source*: 1981 and 1990 World Values surveys. 1981 data not available for Hungary.

cial strike, and the percentage saying they actually have, or might, occupy a building. With unofficial strikes, the percentage rose in 14 societies and fell in four (with missing data for two countries and no change in one). And in regard to occupying buildings, the trend from 1981 (or from 1974) went up in 17 societies and declined in two (with 1981 missing data for one case and no change in another). The availability of a longer time series clearly improves our success rate with this variable, for both Britain and the Netherlands show slightly lower rates in 1990 than in 1981; but when we use 1974 as the base, the overall trend is markedly upward. This is in keeping with the principle that our predictions are uncertain for any given country over short time periods, but should hold up relatively well across many countries and over long periods. Across the four variables that measure changes in "unconventional" or elite-challenging political participation, the overall success rate for our predictions is 84 percent.

STATE CONTROL OF BUSINESS AND INDUSTRY,
LEFT-RIGHT SELF-PLACEMENT AND CONFIDENCE
IN AUTHORITARIAN INSTITUTIONS

We suggested earlier that since the industrial revolution, sociopolitical change has moved in two distinct phases. During the first (the Modernization phase), the dominant trend is a shift in salience and power from decentralized social institutions basing their legitimacy on the society's traditional culture heritage toward large centralized state institutions based on rational-legal authority. The leviathan state, of which the former USSR was the outstanding example, seemed to be the endpoint of this historical trend.

But this trend reverses itself in advanced industrial society. A Postmodern institutional and cultural shift takes place, in which there is increasing emphasis on individual autonomy, culturally, and a trend toward decentralization, marketization, and less hierarchical institutions.

We are witnessing a decline in the degree to which the individual is subordinated to society. We have seen evidence of the declining strength of traditional cultural norms that helped maintain the family and ensure the reproduction of society, and declining acceptance of the authority of hierarchical institutions, both political and nonpolitical. Related changes are taking place in the public's motivations to work and in their orientations toward the control of business and industry, as we will see. We find a pervasive trend toward weakening hierarchical controls over the individual.

But at the same time, we find indications of *rising* emphasis on society's responsibilities *to* the individual, and a tendency to blame society, rather than the individual, for social problems such as poverty. There has been rising emphasis on individual *rights* and entitlements, coupled with a declining emphasis on individual *responsibility*. The latter trend may be approaching its limits, however, in face of a growing awareness that giving the state responsibility for individual well-being may be beneficial in limited areas but tends to become oppressive and unworkable on a comprehensive scale. An awareness of these limits has emerged most acutely and most dramatically in the ex-communist societies of Central and Eastern Europe, but it has spread throughout industrial society.

Wildavsky (1987) and his associates (Thompson, Ellis, and Wildavsky, 1990) argue that the degree to which the individual is subordinated to the society is one of the two crucial dimensions on which cultures vary, and that there is a limited range of variation on this dimension because both extremes tend to be fatal: a viable society must maintain an equilibrium between the conflicting demands of individual freedom and conformity to societal norms.

But, we believe, in advanced industrial societies, the equilibrium point is significantly closer to the pole of individual freedom than it is in societies of scarcity. This is true because the emphasis can be skewed farther toward individual rights and entitlements when there are abundant resources; conversely, the need for tight social discipline is highest when the survival margin is narrow. Thus, one of the major concomitants of the rise of industrial society has been a long-term shift from social control toward individual freedom, and this shift is continuing. But there are limits to how far this or any other cultural change can move. Industrial society may currently be at an historical turning point where it is testing the limits to how much farther this trend can move.

The most important political event of the late twentieth century has been the withering away of communism. Although it was unexpected by most observers, it reflects underlying long-term forces that are common to all industrial societies.

One of these common factors has been a gradual decline in public support for state ownership and control of the economy. Already in 1981, this core element of the Marxist prescription for the good society had lost much of its mass appeal; by 1990, with the increasingly evident failure of Marxist societies, public support for state intervention fell still farther.

It would be a mistake to see the global movement away from communism as a move back to traditional capitalism, however. In most advanced industrial societies, though the trend in public preferences is away from Marxism, it is *not* back toward the laissez-faire capitalism that prevailed 60 to 90 years ago. Indeed, a key reason why capitalism is thriving today is the fact that it had already made a series of incremental but cumulatively massive reforms that brought about some much needed governmental regulation of the economy and society and developed extensive welfare state institutions through successive waves of change in the 1930s, the postwar era, the 1960s, and early 1970s. Today "Capitalism" is a misleading name for the welfare states of Western advanced industrial society, in which state expenditures range from a third to well over half of the given country's Gross National Product.

Clearly, the trend in these societies is not toward increasing the state hold on the economy; more often, it is toward privatization of functions carried out by a state that is now widely perceived as having grown too big. The idea that Small Is Beautiful was novel when it first emerged in the 1970s. It has gradually come to seem almost self-evident—and the beauty of smallness is being applied to government as well as to private organizations. Increasingly, big government is coming to be viewed with suspicion. Nevertheless, in some important ways, Western publics are still moving *away* from the traditional capitalist model, toward reducing the authority of owners. In other words, the wave of the future is *neither* communism nor traditional capitalism; instead, both types of societies are groping toward an optimal balance between state and society. Over time, it has become evident that neither laissez-faire capitalism nor a state-run society works well. At any given time, the optimal balance is uncertain, but a common model for industrial society is gradually emerging. This model cannot be defined a priori by some ideology; finding it is an empirical process, but it does seem to be emerging, and the tendency is toward convergence from both extremes. This global process can be seen throughout advanced industrial society.

The World Values surveys asked a question about who should own and manage business and industry. Four options were offered, ranging from the traditional capitalist position ("the owners should run their business or appoint the managers") to the classic Marxist position ("the state should be the owner and appoint the managers"), plus two other options, one giving employees a voice in selecting the managers, and the other giving employees full ownership and control.

First, let us examine changes in support for the Marxist alternative from 1981 to 1990. As figure 10.13 demonstrates, in 1981 public support for the Marxist option already was at extremely low levels in most countries. During the 1980s, its support eroded even further, approaching the vanishing point by 1990. Unfortunately, we do not have 1981 data from ex-socialist countries. At that time, one could not carry out this type of research in most state socialist countries, and even in Hungary, one of the most open societies, this question was not asked. But among publics of societies with market economies, support for state ownership was virtually a dead option in 1981. Iceland was an interesting exception, where 38 percent of the public favored state ownership in 1981, and the figure dropped only slightly in 1990. Mexico, Spain, Italy, and Argentina were the only other societies still having appreciable amounts of support for state ownership. In Mexico, for example, 9 percent of the public favored state ownership in 1981; but this fell to 3 percent in 1990. This was typical of the prevailing trend. In fact, Argentina was the *only* country of the 20 in which support for state ownership rose during this period.

For many years, the conventional wisdom was that youth naturally gravitated toward Marxism: "If my son were not a socialist at the age of 20, I would disown him; if he is still a socialist when he is 40, I will then disown him," as Clemenceau put it. This may have been true in the past, but our data indicate that it is not true today. The differences associated with age are extremely small in most countries.

We find a similar reversal of relationships when we cross-tabulate this attitude by Materialist/Postmaterialist values. Postmaterialists tend to support the conventional Left position on most social issues. They do *not* do so here. As we saw in chapter 8, in societies with market economies, there is practically no relationship between Materialist/Postmaterialist values and support for state ownership of business and industry. And in the formerly socialist countries the young, the better educated, and the Postmaterialists are *less* favorable to state ownership than are the old, the less educated, and the Materialists.

There is no reason why Postmaterialism should automatically be linked with support for state ownership. Traditionally, this was viewed as the Progressive or Leftist position; and probably for this reason, when Postmaterialists first appeared in significant numbers in Western Europe during the 1960s, they tended to think of themselves as Marxists. But this tendency weakened during the

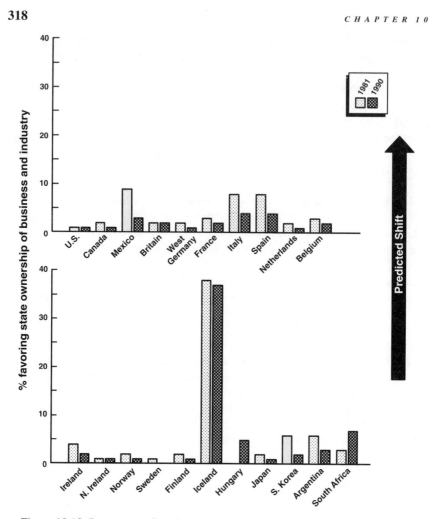

Figure 10.13. Percentages favoring state ownership of business and industry, in
1981 vs. 1990, in 20 countries. *Source*: 1981 and 1990 World Values surveys.
1981 data not available for Hungary.

1970s, and by the late 1980s it had all but vanished (Inglehart, 1990). In the
Eastern European context, this relationship has actually reversed itself: their
experience with the deadening repression of the socialist regimes under which
they have grown up has led Postmaterialists to see state ownership and control
as incompatible with the individual autonomy and self-expression that they
value so highly (Inglehart and Siemienska, 1988). For them, expansion of state
authority does not appear to be a progressive policy, but a repressive one.

This illustrates an important point: Postmaterialists do *not* automatically
adopt whatever happens to be the conventional Left position. On many issues,
they do gravitate toward the Left. But the rise of Postmaterialism has brought

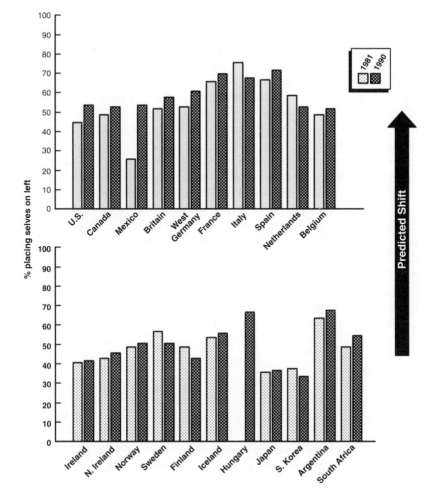

Figure 10.14. Percentages placing themselves on the Left half of a 10-point Left-Right ideological scale, in 1981 vs. 1990, in 20 countries. *Source*: 1981 and 1990 World Values surveys. 1981 data not available for Hungary.

a new perspective into play, one that sometimes runs against established political orthodoxy; it is reshaping the meaning of Left and Right.

Although Postmaterialists do not necessarily support state ownership of business and industry, they *do* tend to favor giving employees a say in the choice of managers. Materialists, conversely, are much more likely to support the owners' untrammeled right to run their enterprises. Hence, we would expect the former position to gain support and the latter to lose support over time. As figure A.25 shows (see Appendix 3), support for joint employee-owner choice of management did rise in 13 of the 18 countries in which changes were observed; conversely, as figure A.26 demonstrates (also in Appendix 3), support for the owners' right to determine management fell in 11 of the 19 countries in which changes were observed.

As we have seen, mass support for the classic Marxist prescription—state ownership of business and industry—had virtually disappeared by 1990. Especially to Marxist hard-liners, this seemed like the collapse of the Left itself. But is it? Not if we go by the self-perceptions of mass publics, rather than by outdated ideological formulations. Although Postmaterialists are no longer distinguished by their support for state ownership, they do—quite clearly—consider themselves to be located on the Left of the Left-Right political spectrum. Hence, despite the collapse of the Marxist alternative, we would predict rising levels of self-placement on the Left side of the scale. Figure 10.14 shows the changes observed in Left-Right self-placement from 1981 to 1990. As it demonstrates, Left self-placement actually rose from 1981 to 1990 in 14 out of the 20 countries for which we have data at both time points (the question was not asked in Hungary in 1981). As the foregoing findings make clear, this does *not* reflect an increase in support for the classic Marxist program. But it does reflect growing mass support for a variety of other issues, from environmental protection, to women's emancipation, to immigrants' rights, which today, to an increasing degree, constitute what people have in mind when they are asked whether they think of themselves as being on the Right or the Left.

CONCLUSIONS

Let us sum up the full array of changes observed across 21 nations. In the preceding chapter we found that with four types of items, the overwhelming majority of responses moved in the predicted direction from 1981 to 1990—that is, toward the pole that was correlated with Postmaterialist values. With one type of item, the overwhelming majority of responses moved in the opposite direction, defying our predictions and shifting in the direction preferred by the Materialists in 1981. This fifth category was by far the smallest category, however, based on only four questions.

In this chapter we have examined the changes found with several more types of variables. What is the overall success rate for all of our predictions? Table 10.1 shows the results for each category, including the Postmaterialist shift itself.

The results of this analysis reveal that in 72 percent of the 802 cases for which we have data, the values of the respective publics shifted in the direction specified by our deliberately oversimplified prediction.

But, as we have seen, the success rate of our predictions was highly differentiated cross-nationally. In most countries, the great majority of items moved in the predicted direction; but in both Argentina and South Africa, fully 78 percent of the items shifted in the *opposite* direction from that predicted by the intergenerational change model, bringing down the overall average considerably. But these deviant cases support our hypothesis that the shift is linked with

TABLE 10.1

Percentage of Shifts Moving in Predicted Direction, by Type of Variable

Category of Item	Number Moving in Predicted Direction	Total Number in Category	Percent Correctly Predicted
I. Authority, sexual, and civil norms	168	213	79
II. Religious Norms	143	199	72
III. Parent-Child Ties	25	76	33
IV. Political Behavior	114	137	83
V. State in Economy, Confidence in Institutions, Trust, Postmaterialism	129	177	73
Total	579	802	72

conditions of security. For both Argentina and South Africa experienced severe economic decline and political upheaval during the period 1981–90: powerful short-term influences offset the effects of intergenerational value change. One other country surveyed in both 1981 and 1990 (Hungary) experienced a nonviolent but wrenching transition from communism to democracy during the months before the 1990 survey, and here only half of the values items moved in the predicted direction. In the 18 remaining countries, almost 80 percent of the observed shifts were in the predicted direction.

As figure 10.15 shows, the cross-national differences in success rates for these predictions is systematic: in those that experienced rising prosperity during these years, the predicted Postmodern shift took place in the overwhelming majority of cases. In those countries that experienced economic stagnation or decline, this shift generally did not take place. In other words, predictable period effects were present. The linkage between economic growth rates and the percentage of values and norms shifting in the Postmodern direction is significant at the .01 level.

Our theory does *not* hold that, for some mysterious reason, there will always be a shift toward Postmodern values. It specifies that economic and physical security are conducive to these values and predicts that period effects will be present, in addition to the long-term effects of having experienced relatively secure conditions during one's formative years. Thus, we knew from the start that the prediction "everything correlated with Postmaterialism will move in that direction" was too simple. Even this oversimplified model correctly predicts 72 percent of the observed shifts. But this prediction is based on intergenerational population replacement effects alone; and we know that current conditions also matter. It is relatively easy to control for the effects of such economic factors as inflation and unemployment rates, for which quantitative indicators are readily available. It is more difficult to control for the effects of wars, civil unrest, the collapse of a regime,

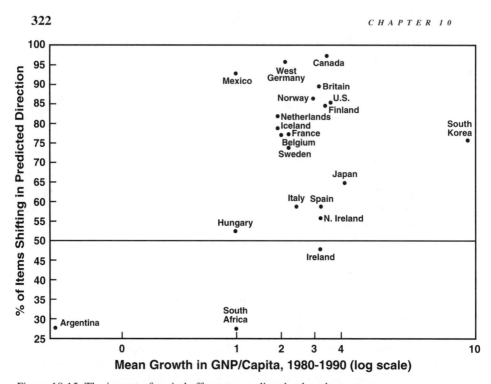

Figure 10.15. The impact of period effects on predicted value changes.
Proportion of items shifting in the predicted direction from 1981 to 1990, by rate of economic growth during that period. r = .47, significant at .01 level. *Source*: 1990 World Values Survey; economic growth data from World Bank, *World Development Report, 1993.*

and other types of political insecurity. Common sense suggests that political upheaval must have had a negative impact on the publics of Argentina, South Africa, and Hungary (all of which were experiencing regime transitions in 1990). We will not attempt to make a quantitative estimate of the impact of political upheaval here. We will simply note that when we exclude these three countries from our calculations (crudely controlling for societies undergoing massive political and economic upheaval), among the 18 societies that were *not* undergoing a change of regime, almost 80 percent of the observed shifts are in the predicted direction.

Political upheaval and regime change are part of reality. We do not, by any means, wish to exclude Argentina, South Africa, and Hungary from our broader analysis. Quite the contrary, they provide valuable clues concerning the kinds of changes that are probably taking place in Russia and much of Eastern Europe today. Our exercise in excluding them is not designed to pretend that they do not exist, but to provide a more differentiated view of cultural change. In the three societies that were undergoing major political and economic upheaval, the great majority of the observed changes moved *away* from Postmodern values; in the 18 societies that were experiencing relatively stable and prosperous conditions, about 80 percent of the changes moved *toward* Postmodernism.

The shift toward Postmodern values is based on a rising sense of mass security; accordingly, it takes place only in settings where countervailing period effects are not strong enough to reverse the effects of intergenerational population replacement. In societies that were enjoying reasonably secure circumstances (18 out of the 21 cases examined here), the predicted shift toward Postmodern orientations clearly *is* the prevailing trend.

These processes have both alarming and encouraging implications. On one hand, established institutions that have shaped industrial society for generations seem to be losing their authority over the average citizen. Public confidence is declining, not only in key governmental institutions such as parliament, police, civil service, and armed forces, but also in political parties, churches, educational systems, and the press. We even find a weakening sense of attachment to that most basic of all Western institutions, the nation-state itself.

There are potential dangers in this evolution. Societal institutions could become too atrophied to cope with a national emergency if one arose. But there are positive aspects as well. In societies characterized by too much respect for authority, it is conducive to democratization. For the erosion of state authority has been accompanied by a rising potential for citizen intervention in politics. Partly this is due to a shift in values, with a weakening emphasis on the goals of economic and physical security that favor strong authority; but another factor that favors rising citizen intervention is the long-term rise in educational levels and in mass political skills that have characterized all industrial societies. In the long run, industrialized societies of both East and West must cope with long-term changes that are making their publics less amenable to doing as they are told, and more adept at telling their governments what to do.

CHAPTER 11

Trajectories of Social Change

MODERNIZATION WAS ONCE an immensely influential concept, but it went out of fashion in the 1970s. A revised concept of Modernization still has an important role to play. But it is becoming increasingly clear that the phenomenon that Marx and Weber and Lerner and Deutsch wrote about is not the final stage of history. Socioeconomic change has begun to move in a new direction.

This book has examined changes in political and economic goals, religious norms, and family values—and how these changes affect economic growth rates, political party strategies, and the prospects for democratic institutions. A survey of the belief systems of most of the world's population reveals coherent cultural patterns that are closely linked with the economic levels of given societies. Economic development, cultural change, and political change go together in coherent and roughly predictable patterns: some trajectories of socioeconomic change are far more likely than others.

But change is not linear. In advanced industrial societies the prevailing direction of development is shifting from Modernization to Postmodernization. This new trajectory brings declining emphasis on the functional rationality that characterized industrial society, and increasing emphasis on self-expression and the quality of life. As Postmodern values become more widespread, various societal changes from equal rights for women to democratic political institutions and the decline of state socialist regimes become increasingly likely. With Postmodernization, a new worldview is gradually replacing the paradigm that has dominated industrializing societies since the Industrial Revolution. It reflects a shift in what people want out of life. It is transforming basic norms governing politics, work, religion, family, and sexual behavior.

Distinctive belief systems are linked with both the Modernization and Postmodernization trajectories. These belief systems are not mere consequences of economic or social changes, but integral parts of a broad syndrome in which culture shapes socioeconomic conditions and is also shaped by them, in reciprocal fashion. Let us sum up our findings.

The shift from the Modernization phase into the Postmodernization phase reflects the principle of diminishing marginal utility. Industrialization and Modernization required breaking the cultural constraints on accumulation that are found in any steady-state economy. In Western history, this break with traditional constraints was what Weber described as the rise of the Protestant Ethic. Eventually, when Western societies had become rich, diminishing returns from economic growth lead to a Postmodern shift, which in some ways is the decline of the Protestant Ethic.

The spread of materialistic motivations was one of the central characteristics of Modernization. In Postmodern society, emphasis on economic security and economic growth is giving way to an increasing emphasis on the quality of life. The disciplined, self-denying, and achievement-oriented norms of industrial society are yielding to an increasingly broad latitude for individual choice of lifestyles.

We are also reaching limits to the development of the hierarchical bureaucratic organizations that helped create modern society. The bureaucratic state, the disciplined, oligarchic political party, the mass-production assembly line, the old-line labor union, and the hierarchical corporation made the industrial revolution and the modern state possible. But the trend toward bureaucratization, centralization, and government ownership and control is now reversing itself, both because it is reaching limits to its effectiveness and because of changing priorities among the publics of advanced industrial societies. Public confidence in hierarchical institutions is eroding throughout these societies.

The Cultural Changes of Postmodernization

Having attained high levels of economic security, the populations of the first nations to industrialize have gradually come to emphasize Postmaterialist values; these groups give higher priority to the quality of life than to economic growth. This transformation has been taking place throughout advanced industrial society during the past few decades and is only one component of a broader cultural shift toward Postmodern values. This cultural change is bringing changes at the societal level, such as the shift away from the politics of class conflict, to political conflict based on such issues as environmental protection and the status of women and sexual minorities.

In the analysis of intergenerational cultural change, there is no substitute for long-term time series data. Although replication is not as exciting as asking new questions, it is crucial for the analysis of change. We have been extremely fortunate in having colleagues from many countries who were sufficiently interested in long-term social change to replicate and analyze key survey questions in exactly the same form over a period of many years. These colleagues are thanked at the beginning of this book, and this acknowledgment is far more than an empty formality. This many-sided effort has produced an unprecedentedly rich body of evidence concerning how mass values and motivations change and has led to cumulative progress in which some findings about social change are now rather clear.

In our first article on value change in 1971, we argued that a shift from Materialist to Postmaterialist values was taking place in advanced industrial societies, as a result of a process of intergenerational value change. This claim was highly controversial at the time; literally scores of articles and books attacked the thesis. The most widespread counterinterpretation argued that the observed age differences were not a permanent part of the outlook of given birth cohorts, but simply a life-cycle difference that would fade away as the younger cohorts aged. The intergenerational change thesis implied that a long-term shift in prevailing values would occur as the young replaced the older cohorts in industrial societies; the life-cycle interpretation implied that no societal change was taking place. In subsequent years, a large body of empirical evidence has emerged that demonstrates rather conclusively that the predicted shift has, indeed, taken place.

In 1995 a monumental five-volume analysis of the role of mass attitudes in politics was published. Sponsored by the European Science Foundation, it brings together the results of analyses by more than 50 social scientists from a dozen European countries. The evidence is now so strong that, although the volume on the political impact of values (Van Deth and Scarbrough, 1995) contains contributions by some of my most prominent earlier critics, one of its main conclusions is that the shift toward Postmaterialists values is, indeed, taking place. Thus, though highly critical of my theory, Scarbrough's evaluation of the empirical evidence concludes, "Indisputably, across much of Western Europe, value orientations are shifting. . . . The potency of Postmaterialist theory lies in providing us with one of the few explicated accounts of value change in contemporary West European societies" (Scarbrough, 1995: 157). A leading American critic comes to the same conclusion (Duch, 1996: 666). The debate has changed; the question no longer is, "Is an intergenerational shift to Postmaterialist values taking place?" but rather "*Why* is this intergenerational value shift taking place?"

Subsequent analyses in this massive work explore the impact of Postmaterialist values on political behavior. Summing up the findings from the entire five volumes, the project's coordinators, Kaase and Newton, conclude, "We find substantial support for the model which traces social changes to value changes, and value changes into changes in political attitudes and behavior, especially through the process of intergenerational replacement. . . . It is clear that the decline of religious values and the rise of Postmaterialist values have transformed the cultural composition of Western democracies in recent decades" (Kaase and Newton, 1995:63).

This book has examined the relevant time series evidence concerning this broad cultural transformation of advanced industrial society. We find that (in more than 800 tests) most variables moved in the predicted direction in most countries. Although this test is based on surveys from only two time points, 1981 and 1990, we also have a much more broader database indicating that the theoretically related Materialist/Postmaterialist shift is an enduring intergenerational change; this supports the interpretation that this may also hold true for the 40 variables examined in this book.

New societal goals are gradually replacing those that dominated Western society since the Industrial Revolution. This shift in motivations springs from the fact that there is a fundamental difference between growing up with the feeling that survival is precarious and growing up with the assumption that one's physical survival can be taken for granted. The difference between feeling secure or insecure about survival is so basic that it has led to a shift from the modern values that characterized industrial society, to the postmodern values that characterize advanced industrial society. This change is eroding many of the key institutions of industrial society.

Postmodern values bring declining confidence in religious, political, and even scientific authority; they also bring a growing mass desire for participation and self-expression. The two trends combine to make the task of political elites more difficult. What might have been a satisfactory performance by the old criteria is not considered satisfactory today. Especially in the political realm, respect for authority is weakening. Mass support for a bigger government role in society and confidence in government are both diminishing. In political participation, the emphasis is shifting from voting to more active and issue-specific forms of mass participation. Mass loyalties to long-established hierarchical political parties are eroding. No longer content to be disciplined troops, the public has become increasingly autonomous and elite-challenging. Consequently, though voting turnout is stagnant or declining, people are participating in politics in increasingly active and more issue-specific ways. Moreover, a growing segment of the population is coming to value freedom of expression and political participation as things that are good in themselves, rather than simply as a possible means to attain economic security. Overall, these changes are conducive to the expansion of democracy.

But these changes have had a traumatic impact on the old-line political machines of industrial society, which are in disarray almost everywhere. Until recently, it seemed to be almost a law of nature that government control of economy and society would continue to expand. That development has now reached its natural limits—both for functional reasons and because of declining mass confidence in government and a growing resistance to government intrusion.

In economic behavior, we find a gradual shift in what motivates people to work: emphasis is shifting from maximizing one's income and job security, toward a growing insistence on interesting and meaningful work. On one hand, we find a growing emphasis on more collegial and participatory styles of management. But simultaneously, there is a reversal of the tendency to look to government for solutions, and a growing acceptance of capitalism and market principles. Both trends are linked with a growing rejection of hierarchical authority patterns and increasing emphasis on individual autonomy. Ever since the rise of capitalism, people have almost automatically turned to government to offset the power of private business. Today there is a widespread feeling that the growth of government is reaching a point where it becomes ineffective and an even greater threat to individual autonomy than that presented by private corporations.

In sexual norms and gender roles, we find a continued movement away from the rigid norms that were a functional necessity in agrarian society, where children born outside a traditional two-parent family were likely to starve, and where sexual abstinence was a key means of population control. The development of effective birth control technology, together with unprecedented prosperity and the welfare state, have eroded the functional basis of traditional norms in this area; this has led to greater flexibility for individual choice in sexual behavior, with a particularly dramatic increase in the acceptance of sexual behavior outside marriage and of homosexuality. These changes reflect enduring long-term trends. But we also find one striking reversal: a trend toward reemphasizing the importance of the traditional two-parent family in child-rearing. Throughout advanced industrial society, there was a *growing* emphasis on the importance of parent-child ties during the period from 1981 to 1990. Many of the economic and social functions of the family have eroded, but society has not yet come up with a satisfactory substitute for the psychological role of the family in providing love, self-esteem, and socialization. Teachers and social workers play important roles, but they cannot provide the intense love and individual attention over a lifetime that parents usually give a child.

In the realm of ultimate values, we find both continuity and change. Secularization was one of the key trends associated with Modernization, and the publics of most advanced industrial societies show declining confidence in churches and falling rates of church attendance and are placing less emphasis on organized religion. But spiritual concerns are not vanishing: on the contrary, we find a consistent cross-national tendency for people to spend *more* time thinking about the meaning and purpose of life.

All of these trends are linked with the emergence of greater economic security. In the highly uncertain world of subsistence societies, the need for absolute standards and a sense that an infallible higher power will ensure that things ultimately turn out well filled a major psychological need. Today, the spiritual emphasis among mass publics is turning from security to significance: from a search for reassurance in the face of existential insecurity to a search for the significance of life.

CULTURAL CHANGE IS COHERENT, NOT RANDOM

This book has demonstrated that there are powerful linkages between belief systems and political and socioeconomic variables such as democracy or economic growth rates. It also demonstrated coherent and to some extent predictable patterns of change in values and belief systems.

Throughout the past century, a wide variety of social analysts have argued that a society's culture—that is, the basic values, beliefs, and skills of its people—are closely linked with its economic and political system. Although there has been continuing debate over the direction of causality, the concept that values are linked with economic and political behavior has gained widespread acceptance.

Although it has long been believed that given cultural patterns tend to go with given economic and political systems, in the past this belief has rested mainly on impressionistic evidence: it was difficult to demonstrate empirically because cross-culturally comparable measures of belief systems on a global scale were not available. This study has shown that cross-culturally similar syndromes of beliefs and values exist—and that they show astonishingly strong linkages with key economic and political variables. A given society's cultural system and its economic and political systems are opposite sides of the same coin.

Cultural Change Has Important Consequences

Cultural Factors in Economic Growth

We find strong evidence that cultural factors help shape the economic growth rates of given societies. This idea has been resisted in the past, partly because culture has generally been perceived as a diffuse and permanent feature of given societies: if culture determines economic growth, then the outlook for economic development would seem hopeless.

With the realization that culture is something that can be measured on a quantitative empirical basis, this illusion of diffuseness and permanence disappears. We no longer need deal with gross stereotypes. For the empirical evidence demonstrates that, though they change gradually, central elements of culture can and do change over time.

Our analysis suggests that two aspects of a given society's culture are particularly relevant to economic growth: the values emphasized in socializing children—with an Achievement Motivation cluster being especially significant—and the degree to which a society's people emphasize Materialist or Postmaterialist values.

The question "Is economic growth due to cultural factors or to economic factors?" misses the point. Cultural factors are intimately linked with economic factors; and the two sets of variables interact to provide a strong explanation of why, over the long term, some societies have shown much higher rates of economic growth than others. A model that includes both cultural factors and economic factors has a significantly better fit and explains more of the variance than does a model that relies on economic variables alone. Motivational factors seem to have a strong impact on economic growth, as Weber argued long ago.

Culture and Democracy

An analysis of empirical linkages between culture and democracy demonstrates that democracies have strikingly different political cultures from authoritarian societies. Almost without exception, stable democracies rank high on subjective well-being and interpersonal trust, and authoritarian societies rank low on them. These linkages persist when we control for economic level and social structure. Moreover, these cross-national differences are relatively stable over time. Economic development is conducive to democracy because it brings cultural changes and changes in social structure, and cultural factors seem to be even more important than occupational structure, educational levels, or income equality.

The evidence suggests that the remarkably strong linkage found between political culture and democracy is more a matter of culture contributing to democracy, than of democracy determining culture. With rising levels of economic development, cultural patterns tend to emerge that are increasingly supportive of democracy.

This transformation does not come easily or automatically. Determined elites, in control of the army and police, can resist pressures for democratization. But with economic development, mass publics tend to give an increasingly high priority to autonomy and self-expression. And as they mature, industrial societies develop increasingly specialized and educated labor forces, a culture of trust and well-being emerges, and Postmaterialist values begin to spread among the public. It becomes increasingly difficult and costly to repress demands for political liberalization.

In short, economic development leads to cultural changes that make mass publics more likely to *want* democracy and more skillful at *getting* it.

Changing Values and a Changing Political Agenda

The goals of both individuals and societies are changing as a result of the diminishing marginal utility of economic growth. In this respect, cultural change behaves as if it were a rational response to the changing socioeconomic environment. These shifts at both individual and societal levels are transforming the political agenda of advanced industrial societies, giving rise to new issues, new political movements, and new political parties.

The rise of Postmodern values changed the political agenda throughout advanced industrial society, moving it away from an emphasis on economic growth at any price, toward increasing concern for its environmental costs. It has also brought a shift from political cleavages based on social class conflict, toward cleavages based on cultural issues and quality of life concerns. Economic conflicts remain important. But in the past they dominated the scene to such a degree that many observers thought that economics was virtually the whole story. Today, this view seems less plausible. Economic conflicts are increasingly sharing the stage with new issues that were almost invisible a generation ago: environmental protection, abortion, ethnic conflicts, women's rights, and gay and lesbian rights are heated issues today. Conversely, the core of the Marxist program, state ownership and management of industry, has become virtually a forgotten cause.

A new dimension of political conflict has become increasingly salient: it reflects a polarization between Modern and Postmodern worldviews. This new dimension cuts across the traditional Left-Right conflict over ownership of the means of production and distribution of income. Its growing salience is transforming the meaning of Left and Right and changing the social bases of Left and Right. Historically, support for the Left was based on the working class, while the Right drew primarily on the middle and upper classes. Today, increasingly, support for the Left comes from middle-class Postmaterialists, while a new Right draws support from less secure segments of the working class. The new cleavage pits culturally conservative and xenophobic forces, disproportionately supported by Materialists, against change-oriented movements and parties, emphasizing gender and cultural issues and environmental protection, and disproportionately supported by Postmaterialists.

The role of cultural changes in the rise of new political cleavages is complex. The forces that gave rise to the Ecologists (on one hand) and the National Front (on the other) in France, or the Greens and the Republikaner in Germany, cannot give rise to similar parties in a society like the United States, because of institutional constraints that make it difficult for new parties to emerge here— even though the same forces clearly are present. And even in societies with proportional representation, the success of such parties partly depends on the strategies adopted by their leaders. But a less obvious change *has* taken place: the issues underlying U.S. politics have changed profoundly, with the old parties adopting the same new agenda as in other advanced industrial societies.

PREDICTABLE PATTERNS OF CHANGE

Changing cultural emphases on economic growth, global democratization, and the rise of new issues all reflect the fact that both Modernization and Postmodernization bring broad clusters of changes that are, to some extent, *predictable*. This predictability has three aspects:

1. We find predictable syndromes of economic, cultural, and political change: they are predictable in the sense that a broad range of characteristics are *linked*: if you know one component, you can predict the other components with far better than random success.

2. If the foregoing is true it follows that, when specific economic changes are known to be taking place, one can make predictions about future cultural and political changes. For example, if educational levels or income levels are rising, they may have predictable cultural consequences. And, as we have seen, rising levels of existential security also have predictable cultural consequences. These are probabilistic predictions. They will not come true in every case, because the predictions are based on only one component of reality, and reality is influenced by many factors. Nevertheless, over many societies, in the long run, certain outcomes tend to emerge with far greater likelihood than others.

3. When intergenerational population replacement processes are involved, they provide another element of predictability. Because important elements of culture, such as basic values and educational levels, tend to change through intergenerational population replacement, when intergenerational differences are observed one can predict the changes that will result from intergenerational population replacement. Furthermore, using a technique developed by Abram-

son, one can calculate not only the direction but the *amount* of change that intergenerational population replacement should produce—and the amount observed since 1970 is very near this predicted value.

Population replacement is not the only factor involved, but in the long run, a knowledge of intergenerational differences in basic values enables one to predict, with far better than random success, the direction of change, and even the amount of change, that will take place per year as a result of this process.

A broad cultural shift is occurring, involving orientations toward politics, work, religion, leisure, and norms governing childbearing, childrearing, and sexual behavior. The shift is not universal: it reflects the degree to which given birth cohorts have experienced security or insecurity during their preadult years. Intergenerational value differences are small or nonexistent in societies that have not experienced economic growth during the past three or four decades. But most societies around the world *have* experienced rising standards of living, and in them one finds significant intergenerational differences in many basic values. Thus, in 18 of the 21 societies for which we have data from both the 1981 and 1990 World Values surveys, most of these values shifted in the predicted direction during this period.

We are dealing with a coherent syndrome of changes which share a common cause: relative security during one's formative years. In the 1981 data, a number of variables showed a pattern that suggested intergenerational change: (1) young and old showed contrasting values, and (2) these variables were strongly correlated with Materialist/Postmaterialist values, with the young differing from the old in the same way as Postmaterialists differed from Materialists. When this pattern was present, we interpreted it as indicating a cultural shift, in which the values of the young and the Postmaterialists would become more widespread as time went by (Inglehart, 1988, 1990).

Intergenerational population replacement is not the only factor involved: period effects, reflecting current conditions, also have an impact—but the direction of their impact is predictable. Since our theory holds that these changes are driven by rising levels of security, we would expect the period effects to move accordingly: a major decline in the economic and physical security experienced by a given society would tend to retard or reverse the effects of intergenerational population replacement, and periods of exceptional prosperity would tend to magnify the effects of generational change.

A total of 40 variables in our 1981 survey showed strong correlations with Materialist/Postmaterialist values. These 40 variables ranged from values concerning work, to attitudes concerning gender roles, homosexuality, and political participation; though diverse, they all are influenced by the degree to which a sense of basic security or insecurity has shaped one's outlook. Our expectation was that intergenerational population replacement would tend to bring a shift toward whatever values were held by the younger, more Postmaterialist cohorts. On the whole these expectations were confirmed. We put our predictions to several hundred tests, examining the changes that took place from 1981 to 1990 in 21 countries. Our predictions were borne out most of the

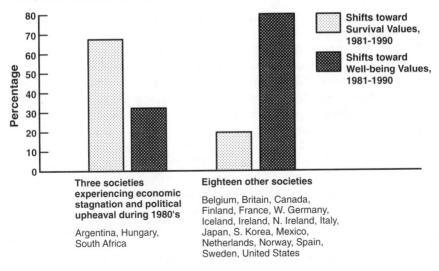

Figure 11.1. Security/Insecurity and cultural change. *Source*: 1981 and 1990 World Values surveys.

time. Economic, political, and cultural change seem to go together in coherent and broadly predictable patterns.

Nevertheless, the results of the World Values surveys show one major finding that runs counter to our predictions: four items dealing with the importance of parent-child ties were strongly correlated Postmaterialist values but did *not* move in the predicted direction from 1981 to 1990. This finding was not an isolated fluke: it appeared in society after society. It seems to reflect a reversal of trends, in which mass publics are now coming to attach more, not less, importance to parent-child ties. This may reflect a growing public awareness that the decline of the two-parent family has been linked with a wide range of social pathologies, from academic failure to drug abuse, poor health, and high crime rates.

Despite this anomaly, in most countries most items moved in the predicted direction. But in two countries, an overwhelming majority of variables moved in the other direction: in both Argentina and South Africa, fully 78 percent of the items shifted in the *opposite* direction from that predicted by the intergenerational change model. And in Hungary, only half of the values items moved in the predicted direction. These deviant cases support the hypothesis that the shift is connected with conditions of security. For all three of these countries experienced severe economic decline and political upheaval during 1981–90: powerful short-term influences offset the effects of intergenerational value change. In the 18 remaining countries, almost 80 percent of the observed shifts moved in the predicted direction.

Figure 11.1 illustrates our overall findings concerning cultural change. As it indicates, in the three societies that experienced economic stagnation and political upheaval during the 1980s, most of these variables shifted *away* from the Postmodern pole, toward greater emphasis on survival values. But these three societies were exceptional. In the 18 societies that experienced more or less normal conditions during the 1980s, these same variables overwhelmingly shifted toward the Postmodern pole. In other words, under conditions of insecurity we find a consistent and predictable cultural shift in one direction; under conditions of rising security, we find an equally coherent and overwhelming shift in the opposite direction.

This is an exciting finding: it suggests that social science can sometimes have predictive power. When dealing with relatively enduring aspects of the outlook of given birth cohorts, we can anticipate that change will tend to move in a specific direction, as intergenerational population replacement occurs. Other factors such as the rise and fall of the economic cycle and war or peace also shape the outlook of a given society at a given time. But in the long run, across many societies, such situational factors tend to cancel each other out: the influence of intergenerational population replacement, on the other hand, tends to work in a specific direction for many decades, and its cumulative impact can be decisive.

To sum up our findings about cultural change in cross-national perspective, let us turn to figure 11.2. This figure maps each of our more than 40 societies on the Modernization and Postmodernization dimensions, respectively. This map is similar to figure 3.5. But we go beyond this earlier figure here, presenting a dynamic perspective: with every society for which we have valid data from both 1981 and 1990, we show its position at both time points. Thus, figure 11.2 shows two dots for Sweden, labeled Sweden 81 and Sweden 90, showing the position of the Swedish public as measured in the 1981 and 1990 surveys, respectively.

This graph is based on a factor analysis that utilizes only about half as many variables as the one underlying figure 3.5, since we used only those indicators of the Modernization and Postmodernization dimensions that were included in both surveys. Figure A.27 (in Appendix 3) shows the variables we used in this analysis and their loadings on the two main axes. Although it uses 22 more surveys and 20 fewer variables than the corresponding analysis based on the 1990 data only, the resulting factor structure is a close approximation of the one shown in chapter 3 (see figure 3.2). And on the whole, the positions of the given societies are similar to those they had in 1990.

The massive database underlying figure 11.2 (based on 65 surveys, carried out in 44 societies) indicates that we are dealing with coherent and stable cross-cultural differences. Although we are particularly interested in the *changes* that occur from 1981 to 1990, let us emphasize the fact that the position of each society in 1981 is relatively close to its position in 1990: the societies' locations are anything but random. Thus, Sweden 81 is located relatively near to Sweden 90; and USA 81 is relatively close to USA 90; as are South Korea 81 and South Korea 90, Spain 81 and Spain 90, and so on. This reflects the fact that the basic cultural values of given societies are relatively stable.

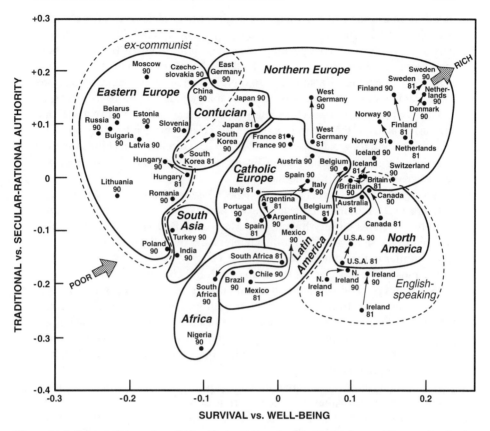

Figure 11.2. Where the peoples of 44 societies fall on the Modernization and Postmodernization dimensions in 1981 and 1990.
Positions are based on the mean scores of the respective publics on each of the two dimensions.
Source: 1981–93 World Values surveys.

Moreover, these societies fall into coherent clusters. Although we are dealing with 22 additional surveys, the same basic pattern emerges as the one we saw earlier, in figure 3.5. This pattern reflects a variety of influences: the broadest generalization is that the locations of these societies tends to reflect their levels of economic development, with the poorer societies located toward the lower left-hand corner and the richer ones near the upper right-hand corner of figure 11.2. But a society's religious heritage, language, geographic location, and whether or not it experienced communist domination all seem to influence the cultural locations of these societies. Thus the Nordic societies constitute a coherent cluster near the upper right; and they form part of a broader (historically Protestant) Northern European cluster. The countries of Catholic Europe form another coherent cluster, as do the Confucian-influenced societies of East Asia. Eastern Europe forms another cluster; and it falls into a broader ex-communist zone that incorporates Eastern Europe, plus culturally adjacent portions of Northern Europe and East Asia. The United States and Canada form a compact North American cluster into which all four surveys fall; but this in turn is part of a broader English-speaking zone that includes Great Britain (at both time points) and the Republic of Ireland and Northern Ireland (in both 1981 and 1990). Australia 81 also falls into this English-speaking zone, adding one more element of coherence: Australia was not included in the 1990 survey, so it did not appear in our previous analyses—but it was surveyed in 1981, and the basic values of the Australian public fall neatly into the English-speaking cluster. Despite its great geographical distance, culturally speaking Australia is a close neighbor of Britain and Canada. We find a stable and coherent pattern of cross-cultural differences.

But significant cultural changes have been taking place, and they are visible in figure 11.2. And though this analysis is based on a different set of variables from the 40 items closely linked with Materialist/Postmaterialist values that were analyzed in the two preceding chapters, the overall pattern of changes is fairly similar to that summarized in figure 11.1.

The most striking aspect of this map of cultural change is the fact that most of the arrows point upward or to the right: this means that most of the changes are moving away from the Traditional authority pole toward the Secular-rational authority pole; or from Survival values toward the Well-being values. In other words, the main shift is from the cultural values linked with *low* levels of economic development, toward the values linked with *higher* levels of economic development.

But some of these shifts move in the opposite direction, toward traditional values and survival values, and the pattern is far from random. All three of the societies that were undergoing economic stagnation and political collapse show shifts that are mainly downward or to the left. In the case of Argentina, the movement is minimal. In the case of Hungary, it is more substantial, with the main component of change being toward stronger emphasis on survival values, and a secondary component of secularization. The South African public shows the largest changes of all, with a sizable shift toward survival values and a lesser movement toward traditional religious authority.

The 18 remaining societies for which we have data on cultural change experienced relatively normal conditions. In 16 of these 18 cases the main shift is upward or to the right (or both)—that is, in the direction linked with economic development. Social change is influenced by many factors, and this generalization has some exceptions: Great Britain showed a net shift toward emphasis on survival values from 1981 to 1990; and the French public showed a slight movement toward emphasis on traditional religious authority (though the shift is so small that it may simply reflect sampling error). But in South Korea, Japan, Western Germany, Norway, Iceland, Finland, Sweden, the Netherlands, Ireland, Northern Ireland, Belgium, Italy, Spain, Canada, the United States, and Mexico, the main shift is either upward or to the right or both. Some of these shifts are minimal, but some are rather large. And to a considerably greater than random degree, cultural change has been moving in the direction of Modernization and Postmodernization: though it is far from perfect, there is some degree of predictability to cultural change.

Let us emphasize that this pattern of predominant shifts does not apply to the entire world. The subset of societies for which we have data from both 1981 and 1990 overrepresents the more prosperous and stable societies (it is generally difficult to carry out survey research in impoverished and unstable societies). Hungary and South Africa exemplify a trend that is underrepresented here: we would *not* expect to find a movement toward the secular and well-being values in societies undergoing traumatic changes. This is an important point. Much of the world, including most of the former Soviet Union, is currently in turmoil. We would *not* expect to find a shift toward Postmodern values in these societies; instead, we would expect to find a shift toward greater emphasis on traditional authority and survival values under these conditions.

On the other hand, after a difficult transition, Poland currently is enjoying the highest rate of economic growth in Europe; Eastern Germany (with massive aid from the West) is also rapidly rebuilding its economy; and the Czech Republic, Slovenia, and Estonia are in relatively good economic shape. Eastern Germany in 1990 was already relatively near to being a part of Northern Europe; we would expect it to move closer to Western Germany, and these other societies to gradually become part of Europe during the next decade. Future waves of the World Values survey will reveal whether these expectations are fulfilled.

WHY DID THE POSTMODERN SHIFT OCCUR? DIMINISHING MARGINAL RETURNS FROM ECONOMIC DEVELOPMENT

The shift from Modernization to Postmodernization reflects the diminishing marginal utility of economic determinism: economic factors tend to play a decisive role under conditions of economic scarcity, but as scarcity diminishes, other factors shape society to an increasing degree.

From a rational actor's perspective, economic development should eventually bring a shift in survival strategies. At low levels of economic development, even modest economic gains bring a high return in terms of caloric intake, clothing, shelter, medical care, and life expectancy itself. Under these conditions, giving top priority to economic growth is a highly effective survival strategy. Societies are not rational actors, but they behave as if they were—in the long run. Once a society has reached a certain threshold of development, further economic growth brings only minimal gains in both life expectancy and in subjective well-being. Noneconomic aspects of life become increasingly important influences on how long and how well a people live. Beyond this point, a rational strategy would be to place increasing emphasis on quality of life concerns, rather than to continue the inflexible pursuit of economic growth as if it were a good in itself.

Once industrialization became possible, modernizing societies focused on rapid economic growth as the best way of maximizing survival and well-being. But no strategy is optimal for all circumstances. Modernization was dramatically successful in raising life expectancies, but it has begun to produce diminishing returns in advanced industrial societies. Postmodernization is a shift in survival strategies, moving from maximizing economic growth to maximizing survival and well-being, through lifestyle changes.

BEYOND POSTMODERNISM?

Every stable culture is linked with a congruent authority system. But the Postmodern shift is a move away from both traditional authority and state authority. We find declining confidence in hierarchical institutions throughout advanced industrial society. By the early 1990s, political leaders around the world were experiencing some of the lowest levels of support ever recorded. This was not just because they were less competent than their predecessors: it reflects a systematic decline in the basis of mass support for established political institutions.

Such trends cannot continue forever. Political systems either adapt in ways that generate internalized support, or they collapse and are replaced by new political systems. Ultimately, the systems that emerge and survive will be systems that have found some effective legitimating formula. This formula, whatever it is, may mark the emergence of Post-Postmodern politics.

Similarly, the role of the family has been diminishing for many decades. The logical endpoint once seemed to be its complete disappearance, with reproduction and childrearing being taken over by the state as envisioned in *Brave New World* (Huxley, 1932). In the decade from 1981 to 1990, this trend seems to have reached its natural limits.

All societies that survive for long have social norms limiting reproduction and violence, based on a moral order that makes it possible to govern societies without depending solely on external coercion. Growing permissiveness and increasing room for individual autonomy from societal constraints have been the dominant trend in the evolution of social norms throughout the past century. The apparent reversal of this trend in the area of family values raises the question "Is the Postmodern trend approaching natural limits in other areas as well?" We do not yet find evidence that advanced industrial societies have reached a Post-Postmodern threshold in other domains. During the period from 1981 to 1990, the great majority of changes moved in the Postmodern direction. But no trend goes on in the same direction forever. Just as Modernization eventually gave way to Postmodernization, we can safely assume that Postmodernization is not the final stage of history. The past few decades have seen massive cultural change, and most of the innovation has come from the Postmodern side, which has largely controlled the agenda for change. But all trends eventually reach limits. The question is simply *when* this will happen with Postmodernism.

Postmodernism is many sided, and some components might continue while others taper off. One aspect of Postmodernism that seems likely to have a limited life span is the rejection of rationality itself. Since the species emerged, reason has been the key instrument for human coping with the environment. It will not be discarded. What is likely to happen, instead, is a shift away from the overemphasis on instrumental rationality that characterized industrial society, toward a more balanced synthesis of functional rationality and a renewed concern for ultimate ends, in which the pursuit of human well-being and self-expression is a major component.

Postmodern societies emerged as a consequence of Modernization, which eventually gave rise to such a high level of existential security that survival came to be taken for granted by growing segments of those societies. The application of reason through science and technology solved the problems of subsistence to such an extent that instrumental rationality eventually became less crucial. But the Postmodern worldview would ultimately collapse without the economic and technological base that it increasingly takes for granted. Some Postmodern thinkers may see themselves as antimodern, but they are, in fact, profoundly *post*modern: they reflect a worldview that could only come after the successful attainment of modernity.

Postmodern discourse sometimes claims that there is a radical discontinuity between modernity and postmodernity. Postmodernity does reflect a major change, but it grows out of modernity. Postmodern values would be difficult to sustain without a thriving industrial and technological infrastructure. Even in terms of Postmodern values, the rejection of modernity would be unattractive if it meant going back to a life expectancy of 35 years, coupled with the need for sexual abstinence before marriage and for women to spend their entire adult lives in childbearing and childrearing. Postmodernity must necessarily coexist with modernity.

Postmodernity reflects a rejection of instrumental rationality and an increased concern for ultimate ends, but, ironically, many Postmodern thinkers have given up on the quest for any universal moral consensus: moral rules are held to be merely conventions that simply reflect the interests of the dominant elite. All that is left for philosophers to do is to debunk whatever moral systems do appear.

Habermas has not given up: he believes that a valid moral consensus can be reached, provided that it is arrived at through communication free from domination—a goal that is difficult but not impossible. Evidence presented above indicates that, although belief systems generally do support a given political and economic order, value systems are not simply elite-dominated myths: the worldviews that eventually prevail also reflect the life experience of ordinary people, and official doctrine is not credible in the long run unless it also corresponds to this life experience. Thus, the ability of elites to manipulate the masses is limited. Elites are, by definition, people who have more influence than most people; but ordinary people are not always gullible. As Abraham Lincoln put it, "You may fool all the people some of the time; and you can even fool some of the people all the time; but you can't fool all of the people all the time." Moreover, evidence presented here suggests that, as ordinary people obtain greater resources, going from being illiterate peasants to become relatively secure, well-educated people, the balance between elites and masses shifts in favor of the masses. It is not as easy to manipulate highly educated publics, who have access to a wide variety of ideas, as it is an illiterate public who may be unaware of any alternative to the official truth. The goal of a consensus on ultimate goals, freely arrived at, is not totally unrealistic.

Habermas's quest for a new moral consensus, reached through free rational debate, is not an impossible goal. But it may be too intellectual an approach. There are two competing alternatives, both of which have the advantage of appealing to standards that are already present.

The ideologues of the ecology movement present nature as an objective standard that is a given, as natural law was claimed to be. Nature has a major asset: like tradition, it is not merely conventional but given to us from outside. Traditional belief systems held that "Whatever is, is Right" (either because it was ordained by God, or because it reflected the collective wisdom of the ages). High ecology holds that "Whatever is natural is Right," because it reflects the result of evolutionary and ecological equilibria. Ecology also has the advantage of universality—it transcends the cultural heritages of different societies: there is one Mother Earth for all of us.

The chief remaining alternative is the revival of tradition—including traditional religions. Tradition has the asset of hallowed age; for many people, its norms have been familiar since youth and were familiar to their parents and grandparents. But it also has a major disadvantage: the mythology of traditional religion is clothed in archaic symbols that emerged in pastoral or agrarian societies. The image of God as "the Good Shepherd" is less compelling in an era when most people have far more daily contact with computers than with sheep. Moreover, traditional religions can be dangerously divisive in an increasingly global society: they present the traditional normative system of a specific culture as absolute and universal values. The rigidity of any absolute belief system can give rise to fanatic intolerance, as the historical struggles between Christianity and Islam or between Protestant and Catholic demonstrate.

To function in Postmodern societies, religion would need to take on a universal perspective and become integrated with the intellectual heritage of natural science, which is an important part of most people's consciousness in these societies. Some thinkers have been moving in this direction. Teilhard de Chardin (1959), for example, views the universe as incomplete, with both human society and God still being constructed. Humanity is not a helpless puppet but plays a decisive role as the story unfolds. From this perspective, the account of creation in the book of Genesis could be seen as a first approximation, in pastoral imagery, of the more recent account provided by the Big Bang theory—which is also no more than a rough approximation of the ultimate account. Both traditional religion and modern science provide successive approximations of a truth that is vast beyond human comprehension: a thousand years from now humanity will probably know a great deal more than now, but still have an ant's view of the universe. Humans are rational beings that need both material sustenance and a moral orientation in order to function well. The search for meaning and purpose in life will continue.

At this point in time, the publics of advanced industrial societies are moving toward Postmodern values and placing increasing emphasis on the quality of life. Empirical evidence from around the world shows that cultural patterns are closely linked with the economic and political characteristics of given societies. The Modernization syndrome is linked with a shift from traditional to rational-legal values; but the emergence of advanced industrial society gives rise to a shift from survival values to postmodern values, in which a variety of changes, from equal rights for women to the emergence of democratic political institutions, become increasingly likely.

Economic, cultural, and political change go together in coherent patterns, and they are changing the world in broadly predictable ways.

APPENDIX 1

A NOTE ON SAMPLING; FIGURES A.1 AND A.2

THE WORLD VALUES SURVEYS provide a broader range of variation than has ever before been available for analyzing the values and attitudes of mass publics. The 1990–93 surveys were carried out in 43 societies representing almost 70 percent of the world's population and covering the full range of variation, from societies with per capita incomes as low as $300 per year to societies with per capita incomes as high as $30,000 per year, and from long-established democracies with market economies to ex-socialist states and authoritarian states. The 1981–84 surveys provide time series data for 22 of these societies, enabling us to analyze the changes in values and attitudes that took place during the years between the two sets of surveys.

The World Values surveys grew out of a study launched by the European Values Systems Study Group (EVSSG) under the leadership of Jan Kerkhofs and Ruud de Moor, with an advisory committee consisting of Gordon Heald, Juan Linz, Elisabeth Noelle-Neumann, Jacques Rabier, and Helene Riffault. In 1981 the EVSSG carried out surveys in 10 West European societies; it evoked such widespread interest that it was replicated in 14 additional countries.

Findings from these surveys suggested that predictable cultural changes were taking place: many variables showing large intergenerational differences were strongly correlated with Postmaterialist values. To monitor possible changes, a new wave of surveys was designed and pretested and went into the field in 1990. This second wave of surveys built on findings from the 1981 European Values Survey but was designed to be carried out globally. It was designed and coordinated by Karel Dobbelaere, Loek Halman, Stephen Harding, Felix Heunks, Ronald Inglehart, Jan Kerkhofs, Renate Koecher, Jacques Rabier, and Noel Timms, with Ruud de Moor serving as chair. Inglehart organized the surveys in the non-European countries and in several East European countries.

Most of the first-wave World Values surveys were carried out in spring 1981, but fieldwork for the South Korean survey took place in 1982, and fieldwork for the Argentine survey was in 1984. Similarly, most of the second-wave surveys were carried out in 1990, but two (the Swiss and Polish surveys) completed their fieldwork in 1989, and two surveys (those in Russia and Turkey) were completed in early 1991, while another (in Slovenia) was carried out in early 1992, and still another (in Romania) was carried out in spring 1993.

SAMPLING, FIELDWORK, AND PRINCIPAL INVESTIGATORS FOR THE 1990 SURVEYS

Survey organizations, sample sizes, fieldwork period, and the principal investigators for each country are shown below. If not otherwise noted, the investigator is affiliated with the institution that carried out fieldwork:

ARGENTINA—Instituto Gallup de la Argentina (Buenos Aires) N = 1,001; February–April 1991. Principal investigator, Marita Carballo de Cilley, Catholic University of Argentina.

AUSTRIA—Fessel + GFK Institut (Vienna) N = 1,460; June–July 1990. Principal investigators, Paul Zulehner and Christian Friesl, University of Vienna.

BELARUS—Institute of Sociology, Belarus Academy of Sciences (Minsk) N = 1,015; October–November 1990. Principal investigator, Andrei Vardomatski.

BELGIUM—Dimaraso-Gallup, Belgium (Brussels) N = 2,792; June 1990. Principal investigators, Jan Kerkhofs and Karel Dobbelaere, University of Leuven, and Jacques-Rene Rabier, formerly of the Commission of the European Communities.

BRAZIL—Instituto Gallup de Opiniao Publica (São Paolo) N = 1,782; October 1991–January 1992. Principal investigator, Carlos Eduardo Meirelles Matheus.

BRITAIN—Gallup (London) N = 1,484; June–September 1990. Principal investigators, David Barker, Stephen Harding, Gordon Heald, and Noel Timms, University of Leicester.

BULGARIA—National Public Opinion Center (Sofia) N = 1,034; August 1990. Principal investigators, Andrei Raichev and Kancho Stoichev.

CANADA—Gallup-Canada (Toronto) N = 1,730; May–June 1990. Principal investigators, Neil Nevitte, University of Calgary, and Ronald Inglehart, University of Michigan.

CHILE—Centro de Estudios de la Realidad Contemporanea (Santiago) N = 1,500; May 1990. Principal investigators, Carlos Huneeus and Marta Lagos, Academia de Humanismo Cristiano.

CHINA—China Statistical Information Center (Beijing), N = 1,000; July–December 1990. Principal investigators, Jiang Xingrong, Xiang Zongde, and Ronald Inglehart.

CZECHOSLOVAKIA—Association for Independent Social Analysis (Prague) N = 1,396; September 1990. Principal investigators, Vladimir Rak, Marek Boguszak, and Ivan Gabal, Association for Independent Social Analysis, Blanka Filipcova, Institute of Sociology, Czechoslovak Academy of Sciences, and Hans Dieter Klingemann, Berlin Science Center for Social Research.

DENMARK—Socialforskningsinstituttet [Danish National Institute of Social Research] (Copenhagen) N = 1,030; April–May 1990. Principal investigators, Ole Riis and Peter Gundelach, University of Aarhus.

ESTONIA—Mass Communication Research and Information Center (Tallinn) N = 1,008; June–August 1990. Principal investigators, Mikk Titma, Andrus Saar, and Hans-Dieter Klingemann.

FINLAND—Suomen Gallup [Gallup-Finland] (Helsinki) N = 588; April 1990. Principal investigators, Leila Lotti and Juhani Pehkonen.

FRANCE—Faits et Opinions (Paris) N = 1,002; June–July 1990. Principal investigator, Helene Riffault.

(EAST) GERMANY—Institut für Demoskopie (Allensbach) N = 1,336; fall 1990. Principal investigators, Renate Köcher and Elisabeth Noelle-Neumann.

(WEST) GERMANY—Institut für Demoskopie (Allensbach) N = 2,201; June–July 1990. Principal investigators, Renate Koecher and Elisabeth Noelle-Neumann.

HUNGARY—Gallup, Hungary (Budapest) N = 999; May–June 1990. Principal investigators, Elemer Hankiss and Robert Manchin, Center for Value Sociology, Hungarian Academy of Sciences.

ICELAND—University of Iceland, Social Science Research Institute, N = 702; April 1990. Principal investigators, Stefan Olafsson and Fridrik Jonsson.

INDIA—Indian Institute of Public Opinion (New Delhi) N = 2,500; July–December 1990. Principal investigators, Eric de Costa, V. P. Madhok, and Ronald Inglehart.

IRELAND—Economic and Social Research Institute (Dublin) N = 1,000; July–October 1990. Principal investigator, Michael Fogarty.

NORTHERN IRELAND—N = 304; July–September 1990. Principal investigators, David Barker, Stephen Harding, Gordon Heald, and Noel Timms.

ITALY—Centro internazionale di ricerche sociali sulle aree montane (Trento) N = 2,010; October–November 1990. Principal investigator, Renzo Gubert, University of Trento.

JAPAN—Nippon Research Center Ltd. [Gallup-Japan] (Tokyo) N = 1,011; September 1990. Principal investigator, Kenji Iijima, Nippon Research Center, and Yuji Fukuda and Seiko Yamazaki, Dentsu Institute for Human Studies.

SOUTH KOREA—Ewha University (Seoul) N = 1,251; June–July 1990. Principal investigator, Soo Young Auh, Ewha University.

LATVIA—Public Opinion Research Group, Latvian Sociological Association (Riga) N = 903; June–August 1990. Principal investigators, Brigita Zepa and Hans-Dieter Klingemann.

LITHUANIA—Vilnius State University Sociological Laboratory (Vilnius) N = 1,000; June–August 1990. Principal investigators, Rasa Alishauskiene and Hans-Dieter Klingemann.

MEXICO—Market and Opinion Research International [MORI de Mexico] (Mexico City) N = 1,531; May 1990. Principal investigators, Miguel Basanez, Instituto Tecnologico Autonomo de Mexico, and Ronald Inglehart.

MOSCOW—Institute of Sociology, Soviet Academy of Sciences (Moscow) N = 1,012; October–November 1990. Principal investigators, Elena Bashkirova and Vladimir Yadov.

NETHERLANDS—Institut voor Sociaal-Wetenschappelijk Onderzoek (Tilburg) N = 1,017; June–August 1990. Principal investigators, Ruud de Moor, Felix Heunks, and Loek Halman, University of Tilburg.

NIGERIA—Research and Marketing Services, Ltd. [Gallup-Nigeria] (Lagos) N = 939; May–June 1990. Principal investigators, Kareem Tejumola and Ronald Inglehart.

NORWAY—Survey division of Norwegian Central Bureau of Statistics (Oslo) N = 1,239; April–June 1990. Principal investigator, Ola Listhaug, University of Trondheim

POLAND—Osrodek Badania Opinii Publicznej [survey unit of Polish Radio-Television] (Warsaw) N = 938; November–December 1989. Principal investigator, Renata Siemienska, University of Warsaw.

PORTUGAL—EuroExpansao, S.A. (Lisbon) N = 1,185; May–July 1990. Principal investigators, Luis de Franca, Jorge Vala, and J. C. Jesumo, Instituto de Estudios para o Desenvolvimento.

RUSSIA—Institute for Social and Political Research, Soviet Academy of Sciences (Moscow) N = 1,961; January 1991. Principal investigator, Vladimir Andreyenkov.

ROMANIA—Institute for Research on Quality of Life, Romanian Academy of Sciences (Bucharest) N = 1,103; spring 1993. Principal Investigators, Catalin Zamfir, Nicolae Lotreanu, and Mattei Dogan.

SLOVENIA—Center for Public Opinion Research, University of Ljubljana N = 1,035; February 1992. Principal investigator, Niko Tos.

SOUTH AFRICA—Markinor (Johannesburg) N = 2,736; October–November 1990. Principal investigator, Christine Woessner.

SPAIN—DATA, Madrid N = 2,637; April–May 1990. Principal investigators, Francisco Andres Orizo and Javier Elzo, Deusto University.

SPAIN—Analisis Sociologicas, Economicos y Politicos (ASEP) (Madrid) N = 1,510; May 1990. Principal investigator, Juan Diez Nicolas, Complutense University, Madrid.

SWEDEN—Svenska Institutet for Opinionsundersokingar (SIFO)[Gallup-Sweden] (Stockholm) N = 1,047; April–May 1990. Principal investigator, Thorleif Petterson, University of Uppsala

SWITZERLAND—ISOPUBLIC, Institut Suisse d'Opinion Publique (Zurich) N = 1,400; November 1988–February 1989. Principal investigator, Anna Melich, University of Geneva and Commission, European Community.

TURKEY—Bogazici University, Department of Political Science (Istanbul) N = 1,030; November 1990–January 1991. Principal investigators, Ustun Erguder, Yilmaz Esmer, and Ersin Kalaycioglu.

U.S.A.—The Gallup Organization (Princeton) N = 1,839; May–June 1990. Principal investigators, George Gallup, Alec Gallup, and Max Larsen, the Gallup Organization, and Ronald Inglehart, University of Michigan.

Representative national samples were interviewed in all cases except for subnational surveys in Northern Ireland and the greater Moscow region (which was surveyed in addition to the entire Russian Republic); and in 1981 a survey was carried out in the Tambov region of the Russian Republic. The quality of the samples varies from country to country. Surveys in Western countries were carried out by professional survey organizations with a great deal of experience, most of them members of the Gallup chain. In other countries they were carried out by the respective national academies of sciences or university-based institutes, some of which had carried out few previous surveys.

All of these surveys were carried out through face-to-face interviews, with a sampling universe consisting of all adult citizens aged 18 and older. Apart from the regional samples mentioned above, national samples were targeted except in the following cases: In Chile, the sample covers the central portion of the country, which contains 63 percent of the total population; the income level of this region is about 40 percent higher than the national average. In Argentina, sampling was limited to the urbanized central portion of the country, where about 70 percent of the population is concentrated, and which also has above-average incomes. In India, the sample was stratified to allocate 90 percent of the interviews to urban areas and 10 percent to rural areas, and to have 90 percent of the respondents with literate respondents (who are slightly less than 50 percent of the population). In Nigeria, the fieldwork was limited to urban areas plus a sample of rural areas within 100 kilometers of an urban center. In China the sample is 90 percent urban. The samples have been weighted accordingly to make the samples replicate the national population parameters more closely. Similarly, the 1981 surveys in Western Europe, the United States, Canada, and Mexico oversampled the youngest group aged 16–24 (by approximately 50 percent). These respondents receive proportionately less weight in the weight variable. The samples from China, India, and Nigeria undersample the illiterate and rural portions of the public and oversample the more educated and urban portions; the weight variable is designed to correct for this problem by giving greater weight to the less educated. Both the 1981 and 1990 samples from both the United States and South Africa were stratified by race; the weight variable corrects for this. The Swiss survey is stratified by language group, producing a sample that overrepresents the French- and Italian-speaking groups; it is weighted to obtain a nationally representative sample. The weight variable also corrects for obvious deviations from national population parameters in age and education in other countries. In most cases, the more highly educated are oversampled and are accordingly weighted less heavily than the less educated. In the 1990 Italian sample, however, the more educated are substantially undersampled and are weighted more heavily to compensate for it.

The surveys from low-income countries tend to have larger error margins than those from other countries. The samples from India, Nigeria, and China by design undersampled the illiterate portion of the public and oversampled the urban areas and the more educated strata. Since the oversampled groups tend to have orientations relatively similar to those found in industrial societies, our data probably underestimate the size of cross-national differences involving these countries; nevertheless, these three countries frequently show very distinctive orientations. The present dataset is weighted to correct for these (and other) features of sampling; but it would be unrealistic to view the samples from these three countries as fully comparable to those from advanced industrial societies. We considered these societies extremely important, from both substantive and theoretic perspectives; though obtaining random probability samples from them would require far more funding than was available for this project, we accorded a high priority to including them and were willing to accept a higher error margin than is present elsewhere in order to do so.

Fieldwork was carried out by professional survey research organizations in all countries except South Korea and Turkey, where sampling was designed by faculty and interviewing was executed by students from Ewha University and Bogazici University, respectively. In most cases, stratified multistage random sampling was used, with the samples being selected in two stages. First, a random selection of sampling locations was made; this ensured that all types of locations were represented in proportion to their population. Next, a random selection of individuals was drawn up. In Great Britain, Northern Ireland, Italy, and the Republic of Ireland, individuals were selected from electoral rolls; in Slovenia they were selected from a central registry of citizens. In Norway, Sweden, and Denmark, stratified random samples were interviewed, with response rates averaging 71 percent. The United States and Canada used stratified random samples, with three callbacks. The Japanese used a stratified multistage random sample, drawing names from records maintained by local government agencies; completed interviews were obtained with 62 percent of the individuals drawn. In some other countries, the final selection was made by quota sampling with quotas assigned on the basis of sex, age, occupation, and region, using census data as a guide to the distribution of each group in the population. The Chinese survey used stratified multistage random sampling, first stratifying the provinces according to three levels of economic development, with several provinces being randomly selected within each of these strata. Within each province, approximately 20 sampling points were selected randomly, with five individuals being interviewed at each point. The population was stratified according to rural-urban residence, sex, age, occupation, and education, and within these sampling points, each stratum was sampled by quota, with a 10 percent subsample of illiterate persons. The Indian survey was stratified to cover 14 states representing different geographic and socioeconomic regions of the country, with 2,500 interviews distributed among these states in proportion to their population. Within these 14 states, about 10 percent of the Parliamentary Constituencies were selected and 50 interviews allocated to each one. The interviews were then stratified according to town size, allocating 90 percent to urban areas, but stratifying according to population within the urban sample. A quota sample was then designed that is representative in terms of age and sex, but not education, since the sample design called for 90 percent of the interviews to be carried out with the literate part of the public. Within this segment, interviews were stratified according to education. Interviews were carried out in the eight most widely spoken languages of India, but the rural 10 percent of the sample was confined to the five Hindi-speaking states in the sample. The Nigerian sample was stratified in a similar fashion, with 90 percent of the interviews being carried out with the urban and

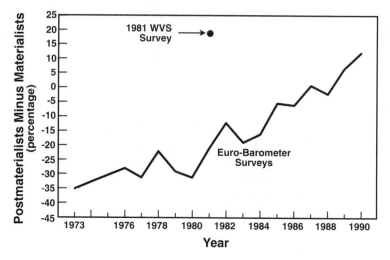

Figure A.1. Discrepancy between results from the 1981 Danish World Values Survey and the 30 Euro-Barometer surveys carried out in Denmark from 1973 to 1990.

literate segments of the population. It was then stratified by age, sex, and education within 17 provinces representing the major ethnic groups in the country. Most surveys in these countries undersample rural and illiterate respondents, who tend to give large numbers of "don't know" responses. Our samples from all three low-income countries underrepresent the rural and illiterate segments of the population; though the samples have been weighted accordingly, this compensates imperfectly. These samples do provide representative coverage of the various regions, cultural groups, and age and gender groups.

This project was a confederation of equal partners. It was carried out with very little central funding and hence with minimal central control. In most countries, funding for fieldwork and analysis was obtained from local sources. Inevitably, the quality of fieldwork varies cross-nationally; the problems are not restricted to low-income societies. The 1981 Danish survey heavily overrepresented the more educated strata; in this case, it was possible to compare certain key variables with results from other surveys, since Denmark is included in the Euro-Barometer surveys carried out each spring and fall. As figure A.1 illustrates, the results concerning Postmaterialist values from the 1981 Danish sample show major deviations from all of the other surveys carried out in that period. Hence, although the 1990 Danish sample (carried out by another institute) seems to be of excellent quality, we do not use the 1981 sample for cross-time comparisons.

Although, as we have just indicated, these data have numerous imperfections, our experience in analyzing them suggests that the results from most societies are in the right ballpark in global perspective. A variety of indications point to this conclusion. Figure A.2 provides one piece of evidence. It shows how the responses of the publics from these 43 societies compare with each other on the two major dimensions of cross-cultural variation (based on responses to scores of items) discussed in chapter 2. If there were a great deal of error in measurement, one might expect to find the various soci-

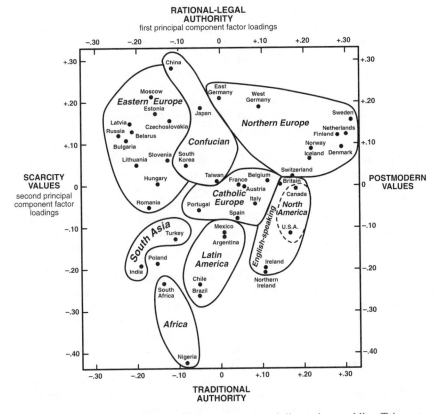

Figure A.2. Where given societies fall on two cultural dimensions: adding Taiwan to the picture. *Source*: 1990–93 World Values Survey. Positions are based on the mean scores of the publics of the given nation on each of the two dimensions.

eties scattered more or less randomly across these two key dimensions of cross-cultural variation. But the actual results show a remarkably clear and coherent pattern, as is immediately evident from inspection of figure A.2.

The four Latin American societies all fall into one coherent cluster. Though surveyed independently, they produce relatively similar results. The same is true of the United States and Canada, and of the two African societies. Their peoples' values were measured separately, by different organizations and by people who had no idea what the others were finding; nevertheless, the results from the four Latin American societies, the two African societies, or the United States and Canada are much more similar to each other than they are to other societies. They are not identical: excellent books have been written about the cultural differences between the United States and Canada, for example. But virtually all informed observers (including the authors of those books) would consider Canada to be culturally more similar to the United States than to almost any other country except, perhaps, Britain or Australia. If the Canadian public had instead shown values similar to those of China or Chile, or if Switzerland's nearest neighbor had been India, it would have given rise to understandable skepticism among informed observers. But the empirical findings are remarkably coherent.

Similarly, the Northern European societies form another cluster, with the five Nordic societies concentrated at one end and East and West Germany at the other; Catholic Europe constitutes another cluster, adjacent to Northern Europe but distinct from it. The four English-speaking societies form another cluster, with Britain next to the Northern European cluster but also proximate to Canada (which is adjacent to the United States). The three East Asian societies are also relatively close to each other. After this book had been completed, we received data from a survey carried out in Taiwan in 1994 in preparation for the 1995 World Values Survey. The results from Taiwan have been added to this figure. We find that Taiwan falls into the East Asian cluster: like the other three East Asian societies, it occupies a position on the cultural map between the Western European societies and most of the Eastern European societies. As we have seen, 10 of the 12 Eastern European societies fall into a common cluster. East Germany might seem to be an anomaly, since it falls just outside the Eastern European cluster, but its anomalous location fits historical reality perfectly: though a member of the Eastern bloc for several decades, it maintained exceptionally close ties with West Germany and is now again a part of Germany. East Germany's location on our cultural map of the world reflects this heritage, falling on the fringe of the East European cluster, and adjacent to West Germany.

Poland clearly is an outlier: though geographically and historically located in Eastern Europe, it is an intensely Catholic society, and the worldview of the Polish people emphasizes traditional cultural norms to a far greater extent than is true of other Eastern European societies, or other industrial societies more broadly. The other predominantly Roman Catholic societies of the Eastern European group (Lithuania, Hungary, and Slovenia) deviate in the same direction, but not to the same degree. We believe that Poland's deviant position reflects a genuine distinctiveness of that society; but even if we are wrong on this point, Poland is the only striking anomaly in a remarkably coherent overall pattern. The face validity of the cross-national pattern is high. With very few exceptions, 43 independently executed surveys produce results in which societies that informed observers would consider relatively similar show similar orientations.

There are a number of additional indications that the findings from these surveys are in the right ballpark. For the most part, when we can check our results against findings from other sources, they are reasonably consistent. Moreover, the pattern of internal correlations shows an excellent fit with theoretical expectations. For example, Postmaterialist values are more prevalent among the young than among the old in nearly all societies; but the strength of this relationship varies a good deal cross-culturally, being strong in those societies that have experienced rapid economic growth during the past several decades, and weak or nonexistent in those that have experienced little or no growth. This is true more broadly: the findings show remarkably coherent patterns in cross-level analyses. With a wide variety of variables, the values and attitudes of the respective publics show strong relationships with logically related macrosocietal characteristics, from economic development level to political institutions. The overall pattern of cross-national differences is remarkably coherent.

A P P E N D I X   2

(The short labels shown on Figure 3.2 appear in bold italics)

Please say, for each of the following, how important it is in your life:

		Very Important	Quite Important	Not Very Important	Not at All Important
Work Important	A) Work	1	2	3	4
Family Important	B) Family	1	2	3	4
Friends Important	C) Friends, acquaintances	1	2	3	4
Leisure Important	D) Leisure time	1	2	3	4
Politics Important	E) Politics	1	2	3	4
Religion Important	F) Religion	1	2	3	4

Discuss Politics
When you get together with your friends, would you say you discuss political matters frequently, occasionally or never?

    1 Frequently
    2 Occasionally
    3 Never

Not Happy
Taking all things together, would you say you are

    1 Very happy
    2 Quite happy
    3 Not very happy
    4 Not at all happy

Reject Outgroups *[Scores on this index range from 0 to 3, depending on how many of the following groups are mentioned]*
On this list are various groups of people. Could you please sort out any that you would not like to have as neighbors?

	Mentioned	Not Mentioned
I) Immigrants/foreign workers	1	2
J) People who have AIDS	1	2
L) Homosexuals	1	2

In Good Health
All in all, how would you describe your state of health these days? Would you say it is

1 Very good
2 Good
3 Fair
4 Poor
5 Very poor

Affect Balance [*Scores on the Bradburn Affect Balance Scale are the number of mentions of items A, C, E, G, and I minus the sum of items B, D, F, H, and J: in short, the number of positive feelings reported minus the number of negative feelings reported*]
We are interested in the way people are feeling these days. During the past few weeks, did you ever feel

	YES	NO
A) Particularly excited or interested in something	1	2
B) So restless you couldn't sit long in a chair	1	2
C) Proud because someone had complimented you on something you had done	1	2
D) Very lonely or remote from other people	1	2
E) Pleased about having accomplished something	1	2
F) Bored	1	2
G) On top of the world/feeling that life is wonderful	1	2
H) Depressed or very unhappy	1	2
I) That things were going your way	1	2
J) Upset because somebody criticized you	1	2

Trust People
Generally speaking, would you say that most people can be trusted or that you can't be too careful in dealing with people?

1 Most people can be trusted
2 Can't be too careful

Have Free Choice
Some people feel they have completely free choice and control over their lives, and other people feel that what they do has no real effect on what happens to them. Please use the scale to indicate how much freedom of choice and control you feel you have over the way your life turns out.

1   2   3   4   5   6   7   8   9   10
None at all   A great deal

Life Satisfaction
All things considered, how satisfied are you with your life as a whole these days? Please use this card to help with your answer.

1   2   3   4   5   6   7   8   9   10
Dissatisfied   Satisfied

State/Employee Management
There is a lot of discussion about how business and industry should be managed. Which of these four statements comes closest to your opinion?

1 The owners should run their business or appoint the managers
2 The owners and the employees should participate in the selection of managers
3 The government should be the owner and appoint the managers
4 The employees should own the business and should elect the managers

Jobs to Own Nationality
Do you agree or disagree with the following?

	Agree	Disagree	Neither
When jobs are scarce, employers should give priority to [American] people over immigrants [*countries other than U.S.: substitute own nationality*]	1	2	3

Good and Evil Are Clear
Here are two statements which people sometimes make when discussing good and evil. Which one comes closest to your own point of view?

A. There are absolutely clear guidelines about what is good and evil. These always apply to everyone, whatever the circumstances.
B. There can never be absolutely clear guidelines about what is good and evil. What is good and evil depends entirely upon the circumstances at the time.

1 Agree with statement A
2 Disagree with both
3 Agree with statement B

God Is Important
And how important is God in your life? Please use this card to indicate—10 means very important and 1 means not at all important.

1	2	3	4	5	6	7	8	9	10
Not at all									Very

Want Many Children
What do you think is the ideal size of the family—how many children, if any?

0 None
1 1 child
2 2 children
3 3 children
4 4 children
5 5 children
6 6 children
7 7 children
8 8 children
9 9 children
10 10 or more

Child Needs Both Parents
If someone says a child needs a home with both a father and a mother to grow up happily, would you tend to agree or disagree?

1 Tend to agree
2 Tend to disagree

Woman Needs Children
Do you think that a woman has to have children in order to be fulfilled or is this not necessary?

1 Needs children
2 Not necessary

Respect Parents
With which of these two statements do you tend to agree?

A. Regardless of what the qualities and faults of one's parents are, one must always love and respect them
B. One does not have the duty to respect and love parents who have not earned it by their behavior and attitudes

1 Tend to agree with statement A
2 Tend to agree with statement B

Here is a list of qualities which children can be encouraged to learn at home. Which, if any, do you consider to be especially important?

		IMPORTANT
Hard Work	C) Hard work	1
Responsibility	D) Feeling of responsibility	1
Imagination	E) Imagination	1
Tolerance	F) Tolerance and respect for other people	1
Thrift	G) Thrift, saving money and things	1
Determination	H) Determination, perseverance	1
Religious Faith	I) Religious faith	1
Obedience	K) Obedience	1

Interested in Politics
How interested would you say you are in politics?

1 Very interested
2 Somewhat interested
3 Not very interested
4 Not at all interested

Now I'd like you to tell me your views on various issues. How would you place your views on this scale? 1 means you agree completely with the statement on the left, 10 means you agree completely with the statement on the right, or you can choose any number in between.

State Responsible

Individuals should take more responsibility for providing for themselves							The state should take more responsibility to ensure that everyone is provided for		
1	2	3	4	5	6	7	8	9	10

Postmaterialist Values *[scores on this index range from 0 to 5, depending on how many of items C, F, H, J, and K are chosen as either first or second priority in their group]*

There is a lot of talk these days about what the aims of this country should be for the next 10 years. On this card are listed some of the goals which different people would give top priority. Would you please say which one of these you, yourself, consider the most important?

And which would be the next most important?

	First Choice	Second Choice
A Maintaining a high level of economic growth	1	1
B Making sure this country has strong defense forces	2	2
C Seeing that people have more to say about how things are done at their jobs and in their communities	3	3
D Trying to make our cities and countryside more beautiful	4	4

If you had to choose, which one of the things on this card would you say is most important?

And which would be the next most important?

	First Choice	Second Choice
E Maintaining order in the nation	1	1
F Giving people more say in important government decisions	2	2
G Fighting rising prices	3	3
H Protecting freedom of speech	4	4

Here is another list. In your opinion, which one of these is most important?

And what would be the next most important?

	First Choice	Second Choice
I A stable economy	1	1
J Progress toward a less impersonal and more humane society	2	2
K Progress toward a society in which ideas count more than money	3	3
L The fight against crime	4	4

Here is a list of various changes in our way of life that might take place in the near future. Please tell me for each one, if it were to happen, whether you think it would be a good thing, a bad thing, or don't you mind?

		Good	Don't Care	Bad
Money	A Less emphasis on money and material possessions	1	2	3
Technology	C More emphasis on the development of technology	1	2	3
Respect Authority	E Greater respect for authority	1	2	3

Trust Science

In the long run, do you think the scientific advances we are making will help or harm mankind?

1 Will help
2 Some of each
3 Will harm

There are a number of groups and movements looking for public support. For each of the following movements, which I read out, can you tell me whether you approve or disapprove of this movement?

		Approve		Disapprove	
		Strongly	Somewhat	Somewhat	Strongly
Ecology	A Ecology movement or nature protection	1	2	3	4
Women's Movement	E Women's movement	1	2	3	4

Please tell me for each of the following statements whether you think it can always be justified, never be justified, or something in between, using this card.

		Never Justified		In Between						Always Justified	
Homosexual OK	L Homosexuality	1	2	3	4	5	6	7	8	9	10
Abortion OK	N Abortion	1	2	3	4	5	6	7	8	9	10
Divorce OK	O Divorce	1	2	3	4	5	6	7	8	9	10

National Pride

How proud are you to be [French]? [*Countries other than France: substitute own nationality*]

1 Very proud
2 Quite proud
3 Not very proud
4 Not at all proud

SUPPLEMENTARY FIGURES FOR CHAPTERS 3, 9, AND 10;

FIGURES A.3 (CHAPTER 6), A.4–A.21 (CHAPTER 9),

A.22–A.26 (CHAPTER 10), AND A.27 (CHAPTER 11)

DATA ON DEMOCRATIZATION

Scores on democracy, cultural, macroeconomic, and social structure variables are reported in tables A.1, A.2, A.3, and A.4 for the 43 countries of this study. The countries are listed in alphabetical order. The scores on democracy are given in table A.1. The measures include (1) the number of years of continuous democracy since 1920 (as of 1995), with a maximum score of 75 years, (2) the level of democracy in 1990 and 1995, based on the Freedom House scores, which range from 2 (low) to 14 (high), and (3) the change in the level of democracy from 1990 to 1995, computed as the 1990 level subtracted from the 1995 level. For 1990, the scores are from Freedom House, *Freedom in the World 1990.* The 1995 political rights and civil liberties rankings are from *Freedom Review* 26, no. 1 (1995): 15–16. The scores for cultural variables in table A.2 include several measures based on the 1990–91 World Values Survey. The Postmaterialist values score is the mean percentage of respondents giving first choice (out of a group of four goals) to each of the five Postmaterialist goals. It ranges from 7 percent in China to 33 percent in Finland, with a mean of 19.6 percent. While each of the four goals would be given top priority by 25 percent of the sample on a random basis, the Postmaterialist goals get top priority only 20 percent of the time. The subjective well-being index is the mean of two differences—the percent of respondents answering happy minus the percent unhappy, and the percent satisfied minus the percent dissatisfied. The interpersonal trust score is the percentage of respondents saying "most people can be trusted." Another measure from the 1990–91 World Values Survey is the percentage of respondents favoring revolutionary change, as determined by the answer to the question "The entire way our society is organized must be changed by revolutionary action." The percentage of respondents favoring gradual reform is determined by the answer to the question "Our society must be gradually improved by reforms."

The macroeconomic variables in table A.3 include GNP per capita in 1957, 1970, 1980, and 1990. GNP per capita for 1957 is from *World Handbook of Political and Social Indicators* (Russett et al., 1964, 155–57). The values for 1970, 1980, and 1990 are from *World Bank World Development Report 1993* and earlier editions. Income inequality is measured by the size of the income share received by the upper quintile of households, from studies in the 1970s and 1980s. Income inequality measures are missing for 10 countries, and all former Soviet cases are scored as the mean of the other ex-socialist countries of Eastern Europe (34 percent). The first social structure variable in table A.4 is the percentage of the nation's GDP produced by the service sector in 1988. In the second column, the percentage of the college-age population enrolled in higher education in 1988 is from the World Bank, *World Development Report 1993*, 294–95. The cumulative percentage of citizens belonging to 16 types of voluntary associations is from the 1990–91 World Values Survey. The index of ethnolinguistic fractionalization, an indicator of subcultural pluralism, is from the *World Handbook of Political and Social Indicators* (Taylor and Jodice, 1983). Expressed as a fraction between 0 and 1, it is the probability that two randomly selected persons from one country will not speak the same language.

358

Table A.1
Scores on Democracy

Country	Years of Continuous Democracy	Level of Democracy, 1990	Level of Democracy, 1995	Change, 1990–95
Argentina	10	13	11	−2
Austria	49	14	14	0
Belarus	0	5	8	3
Belgium	75	14	14	0
Brazil	9	12	10	−2
Britain	75	14	13	−1
Bulgaria	3	2	12	10
Canada	75	14	14	0
Chile	4	9	12	3
China	0	2	2	0
Czechoslovakia	4	4	13	9
Denmark	75	14	14	0
E. Germany	4	4	13	9
Estonia	3	5	11	6
Finland	75	14	14	0
France	37	13	13	0
Hungary	4	9	13	4
Iceland	75	14	14	0
India	17	11	8	−3
Ireland	75	14	13	−1
Italy	49	14	13	−1
Japan	49	14	12	−2
Latvia	3	5	11	6
Lithuania	3	5	12	7
Mexico	0	9	8	−1
Moscow	MD	5	9	4
Netherlands	75	14	14	0
Nigeria	0	5	3	−2
N. Ireland	MD	9	9	0
Norway	75	14	14	0
Poland	4	9	12	3
Portugal	18	13	14	1
Romania	0	2	9	7
Russia	0	5	9	4
Slovenia	3	2	13	11
South Africa	1	5	11	6
South Korea	3	11	12	1
Spain	17	14	13	−1
Sweden	75	14	14	0
Switzerland	75	14	14	0
Turkey	0	10	6	−4
United States	75	14	14	0
W. Germany	46	14	13	−1

TABLE A.2
Scores on Cultural Variables

Country	Post-materialist Values	Subjective Well-being	Interpersonal Trust	Percent Support Revolution	Percent Support Reform
Argentina	19	59	23	8	81
Austria	22	59	32	2	78
Belarus	14	−2	26	26	46
Belgium	27	77	33	3	76
Brazil	19	55	7	16	74
Britain	24	75	44	5	81
Bulgaria	13	4	30	22	59
Canada	25	69	52	5	82
Chile	19	53	23	5	72
China	7	42	60	7	68
Czechoslovakia	16	32	28	42	42
Denmark	23	85	58	2	76
E. Germany	19	57	26	13	84
Estonia	13	25	28	22	61
Finland	33	76	63	3	88
France	27	67	23	4	74
Hungary	12	28	25	6	77
Iceland	21	89	44	3	82
India	13	28	34	11	72
Ireland	22	80	47	4	76
Italy	27	66	37	8	84
Japan	25	54	42	2	77
Latvia	12	10	19	31	59
Lithuania	16	13	31	32	59
Mexico	21	51	33	17	71
Moscow	15	6	34	33	41
Netherlands	32	85	56	2	75
Nigeria	13	33	23	26	62
N. Ireland	20	82	44	5	75
Norway	20	81	65	2	66
Poland	13	58	35	23	65
Portugal	17	51	21	4	85
Romania	12	20	16	MD	MD
Russia	11	−1	38	15	50
Slovenia	16	23	17	14	73
South Africa	18	30	28	19	60
South Korea	18	51	34	7	83
Spain	25	65	34	4	90
Sweden	25	86	66	6	86
Switzerland	30	86	43	MD	MD
Turkey	22	47	10	14	61
United States	22	77	50	7	76
W. Germany	25	70	38	2	66

Table A.3
Scores on Macroeconomic Variables

Country	GNP/ Capita 1957	GNP/ Capita 1970	GNP/ Capita 1980	GNP/ Capita 1990	Income Inequality
Argentina	490	770	2,390	2,380	MD
Austria	670	1,287	10,230	19,000	MD
Belarus	600	1,234	4,140	3,110	34
Belgium	1,198	1,804	12,180	17,580	MD
Brazil	293	267	2,050	2,920	MD
Britain	1,189	1,818	7,920	16,080	39
Bulgaria	380	829	4,150	1,840	32
Canada	1,947	2,473	10,130	20,380	40
Chile	379	565	2,150	1,950	MD
China	73	109	290	370	34
Czechoslovakia	680	1,561	5,820	3,190	33
Denmark	1,057	2,120	12,950	22,440	40
E. Germany	600	1,260	7,180	12,000	MD
Estonia	600	1,628	5,531	4,170	34
Finland	794	1,749	9,720	24,540	44
France	943	1,924	11,730	19,590	46
Hungary	490	1,094	4,180	2,780	34
Iceland	572	2,469	11,330	22,090	MD
India	73	101	240	360	45
Ireland	550	980	4,880	10,370	39
Italy	516	1,104	6,480	16,882	41
Japan	306	861	9,890	25,840	41
Latvia	650	1,425	4,778	3,590	34
Lithuania	650	1,234	4,140	3,110	34
Mexico	262	455	2,090	2,490	57
Moscow	650	MD	MD	MD	34
Netherlands	836	1,554	11,470	17,570	40
Nigeria	78	84	505	290	42
N. Ireland	600	1,273	5,544	1,125	MD
Norway	1,130	1,890	12,650	22,830	39
Poland	475	978	3,900	1,690	36
Portugal	224	406	2,370	4,950	56
Romania	360	778	2,340	1,620	MD
Russia	600	1,357	4,550	3,430	34
Slovenia	400	451	2,600	3,000	MD
South Africa	395	611	2,300	2,530	62
South Korea	144	105	1,520	5,450	40
Spain	293	561	5,400	11,010	41
Sweden	1,380	2,549	13,520	23,780	37
Switzerland	1,428	2,333	16,440	32,250	45
Turkey	220	292	1,470	1,640	57
United States	2,577	3,575	11,360	21,810	41
W. Germany	927	1,901	13,590	22,360	47

TABLE A.4
Scores on Social Structure Variables

Country	Percent in Service Sector	Percent in Higher Education	Organizational Membership (Cumulative Percent)	Ethnolinguistic Fractionization
Argentina	44	22	3	.307
Austria	51	33	112	.126
Belarus	41	20	MD	MD
Belgium	64	37	145	.551
Brazil	49	12	85	.071
Britain	56	25	116	.325
Bulgaria	37	31	70	.220
Canada	56	70	170	.755
Chile	56	19	81	.140
China	21	2	83	.118
Czechoslovakia	38	18	MD	.490
Denmark	58	32	175	.049
E. Germany	39	30	168	.017
Estonia	35	20	120	MD
Finland	50	47	175	.159
France	59	40	75	.261
Hungary	49	15	72	.098
Iceland	55	32	235	.054
India	38	6	MD	.886
Ireland	52	26	93	.045
Italy	56	20	77	.038
Japan	57	31	20	.015
Latvia	35	20	118	MD
Lithuania	35	20	87	MD
Mexico	56	14	93	.305
Moscow	50	MD	MD	MD
Netherlands	58	34	242	.102
Nigeria	29	3	MD	.733
N. Ireland	56	25	115	MD
Norway	51	43	188	.039
Poland	43	22	MD	.028
Portugal	54	18	68	.006
Romania	33	9	45	.252
Russia	41	20	105	MD
Slovenia	40	18	62	MD
South Africa	49	3	MD	.877
South Korea	46	39	145	MD
Spain	57	34	15	.436
Sweden	54	33	205	.083
Switzerland	56	26	95	.504
Turkey	46	14	MD	.255
United States	65	75	185	.505
W. Germany	47	32	135	.026

TABLE A.5
Data Used in Economic Growth Regressions

Country	Growth[a]	GDP[b]	Primary[c]	Secondary[d]	Investment[e]	Four-Item[f]	Postmaterialism[g]
Austria	3.141	3.908	1.05	0.5	0.24373	0.46	2.11
Belgium	3.0639	4.379	1.09	0.69	0.19595	0.22	2.02
Brazil	3.2383	1.313	0.95	0.11	0.20599	−0.32	1.67
Canada	3.0608	6.069	1.04	0.52	0.201	0	2.14
China	5.5	0.567	0.75	0.41	0.20163	0.9	1.36
Denmark	2.4935	5.49	1.03	0.65	0.21627	0.2	1.99
Finland	3.5184	4.073	0.97	0.74	0.25217	0.38	2.23
France	2.9729	4.473	1.44	0.46	0.2224	0.09	2.04
Germany	2.7082	5.217	1.33	0.53	0.20923	0.52	2.14
India	1.9398	0.533	0.61	0.2	0.19982	−0.46	1.58
Ireland	2.9652	2.545	1.1	0.35	0.22252	−0.44	1.96
Italy	3.5253	3.233	1.11	0.34	0.22909	−0.1	2.07
Japan	5.5539	2.239	1.03	0.74	0.31723	0.82	1.81
Korea	6.6378	0.69	0.94	0.27	0.2493	0.47	1.66
Mexico	2.26	2.157	0.8	0.11	0.20675	−0.15	1.86
Netherlands	2.3531	4.69	1.05	0.58	0.19853	0.13	2.26
Nigeria	0.7517	0.552	0.36	0.03	0.147	−1.24	1.67
Norway	3.551	5.001	1.18	0.53	0.29782	0.1	1.81
South Africa	1.428	2.627	0.89	0.15	0.2555	−0.46	1.73
Spain	3.6954	2.425	1.1	0.23	0.22484	−0.24	1.94

	Growth[a]	GDP[b]	Primary[c]	Secondary[d]	Investment[e]	Four-Item[f]	Postmaterialism[g]
Sweden	2.542	5.149	0.98	0.55	0.21237	0.5	2.09
Switzerland	1.9991	6.834	1.18	0.26	0.25747	−0.03	2.1
Turkey	2.8506	1.255	0.75	0.14	0.19792	−0.19	1.95
United Kingdom	2.1637	4.97	0.95	0.67	0.15317	−0.01	2
United States	2.0976	7.38	1.18	0.86	0.13906	−0.28	2.06

[a]Growth: Growth rate of real per capita GDP from 1960 to 1989. *Source:* Levine and Renelt (1992).

[b]GDP: The 1960 value of real per capita GDP (1980 base year). *Source:* Levine and Renelt (1992).

[c]Primary: The number of students enrolled in primary school grade level relative to the total population of that age group in 1960. *Source:* Levine and Renelt (1992).

[d]Secondary: The number of students enrolled in secondary school grade level relative to the total population of that age group in 1960. *Source:* Levine and Renelt (1992).

[e]Investment: Average from 1960 to 1989 of the ratio of real domestic investment (private plus public) to real GDP. *Source:* Levine and Renelt (1992).

[f]Four-Item: Four-Item Achievement Motivation Index comprised of (Thrift + Determination) − (Obedience + Religious Faith). *Source:* 1990 World Values Survey.

[g]Postmaterialism: Mean score of Postmaterialism. Source: 1990 World Values Survey.

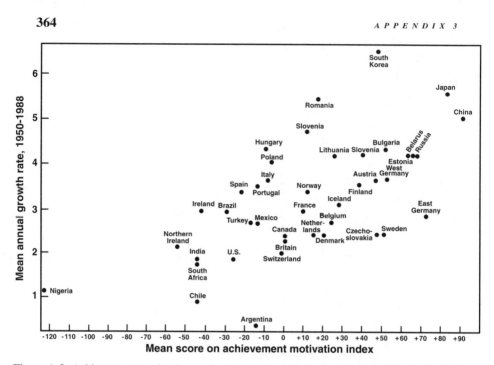

Figure A.3. Achievement motivation and economic growth (ex-socialist societies included). Mean annual economic growth rate, 1950–88, by achievement motivation index. r = .64, N = 42, significant at .0000 level. *Source*: 1981 and 1990 World Values surveys.

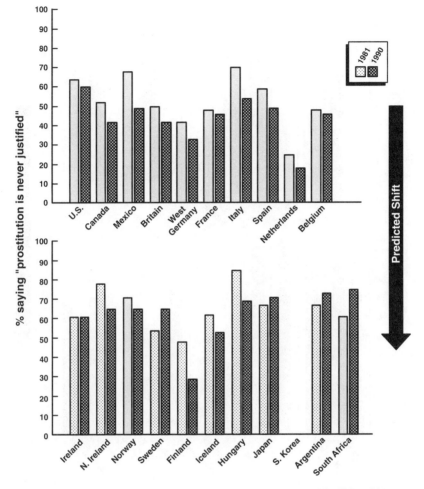

Figure A.4. Percentages saying that "Prostitution is *never* justified" in 1981 vs. 1990, in 20 countries. *Source*: 1981 and 1990 World Values surveys. Comparable data not available for South Korea.

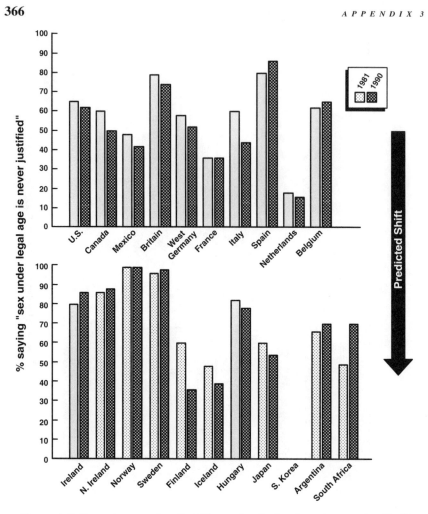

Figure A.5. Percentages saying that "Sex under the legal age is *never* justified" in 1981 vs. 1990, in 20 countries. *Source*: 1981 and 1990 World Values surveys.

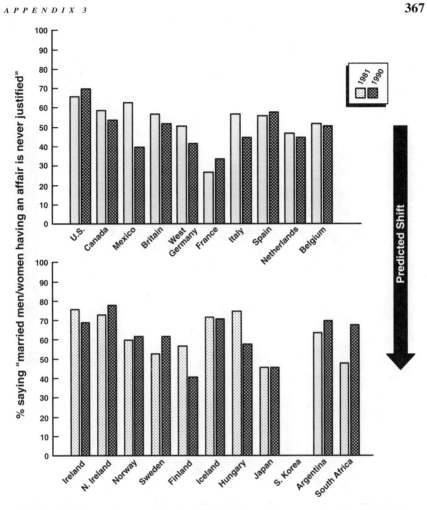

Figure A.6. Percentages saying that "Married men/women having an affair is *never* justified" in 1981 vs. 1990, in 20 countries. *Source*: 1981 and 1990 World Values surveys.

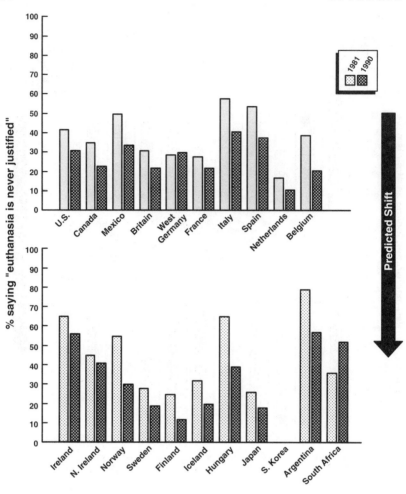

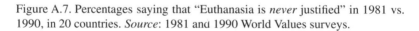

Figure A.7. Percentages saying that "Euthanasia is *never* justified" in 1981 vs. 1990, in 20 countries. *Source*: 1981 and 1990 World Values surveys.

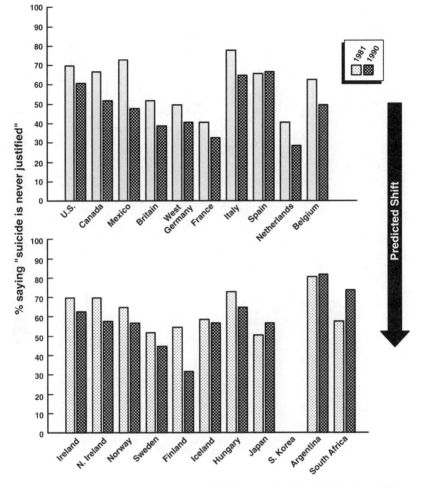

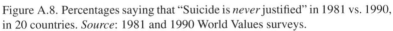

Figure A.8. Percentages saying that "Suicide is *never* justified" in 1981 vs. 1990, in 20 countries. *Source*: 1981 and 1990 World Values surveys.

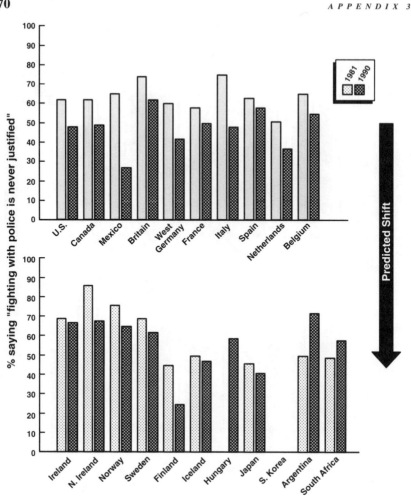

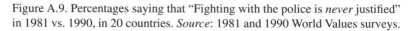

Figure A.9. Percentages saying that "Fighting with the police is *never* justified" in 1981 vs. 1990, in 20 countries. *Source*: 1981 and 1990 World Values surveys.

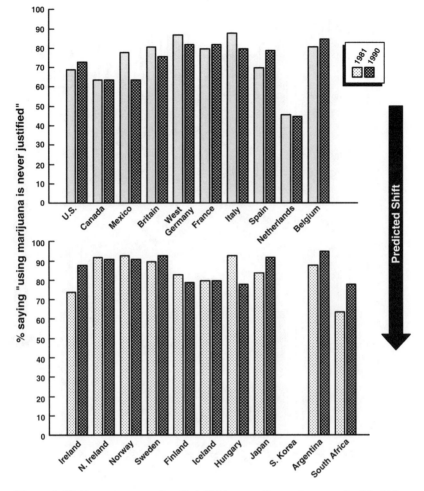

Figure A.10. Percentages saying that "Using marijuana is *never* justified" in 1981 vs. 1990, in 20 countries. *Source*: 1981 and 1990 World Values surveys.

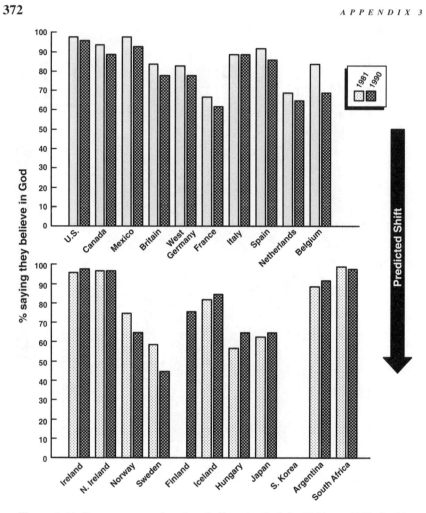

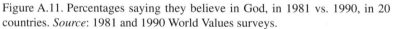

Figure A.11. Percentages saying they believe in God, in 1981 vs. 1990, in 20 countries. *Source*: 1981 and 1990 World Values surveys.

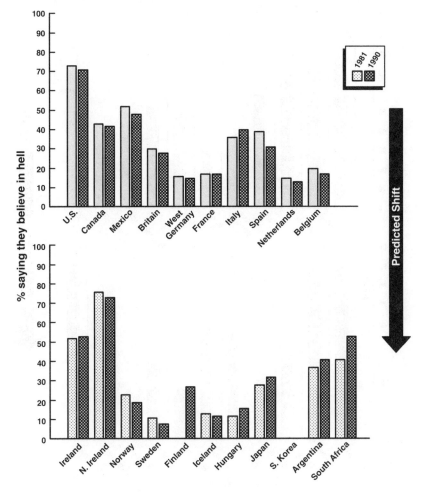

Figure A.12. Percentages saying they believe in hell, in 1981 vs. 1990, in 20 countries. *Source*: 1981 and 1990 World Values surveys.

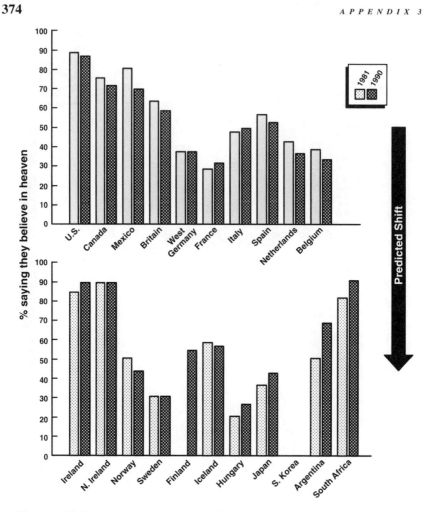

Figure A.13. Percentages saying they believe in heaven, in 1981 vs. 1990, in 20 countries. *Source*: 1981 and 1990 World Values surveys.

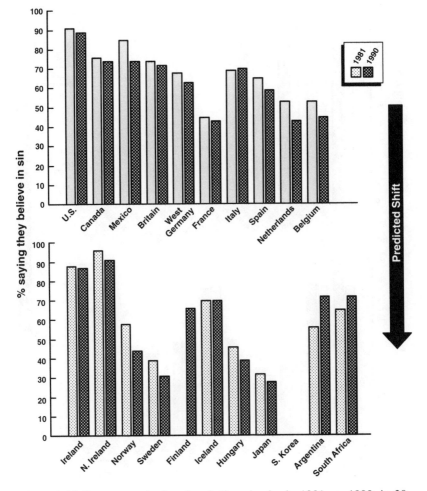

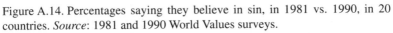

Figure A.14. Percentages saying they believe in sin, in 1981 vs. 1990, in 20 countries. *Source*: 1981 and 1990 World Values surveys.

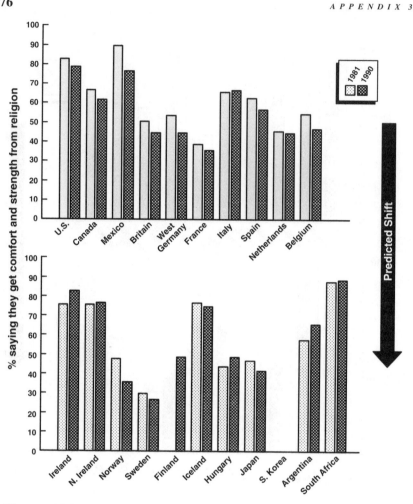

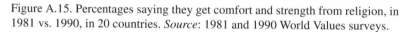

Figure A.15. Percentages saying they get comfort and strength from religion, in 1981 vs. 1990, in 20 countries. *Source*: 1981 and 1990 World Values surveys.

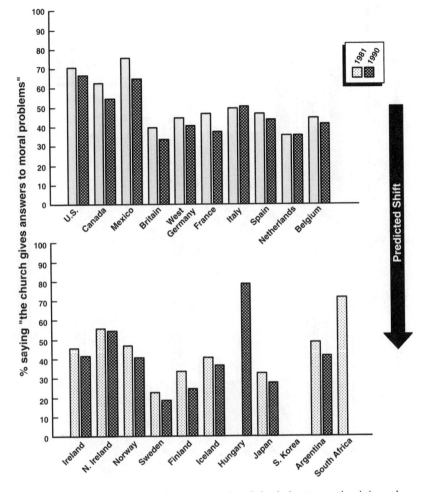

Figure A.16. Percentages saying that the church in their country is giving adequate answers to moral problems, in 1981 vs. 1990, in 20 countries. *Source*: 1981 and 1990 World Values surveys.

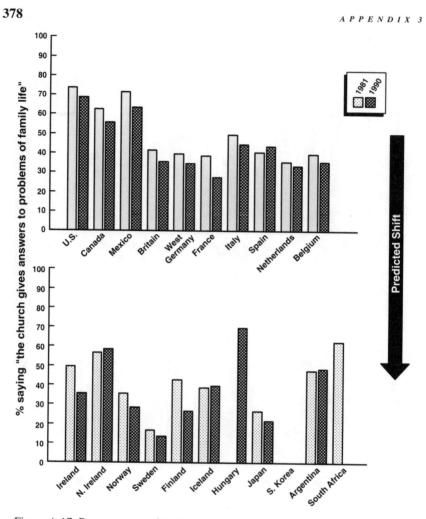

Figure A.17. Percentages saying that the church in their country is giving adequate answers to problems of family life, in 1981 vs. 1990, in 20 countries. *Source*: 1981 and 1990 World Values surveys.

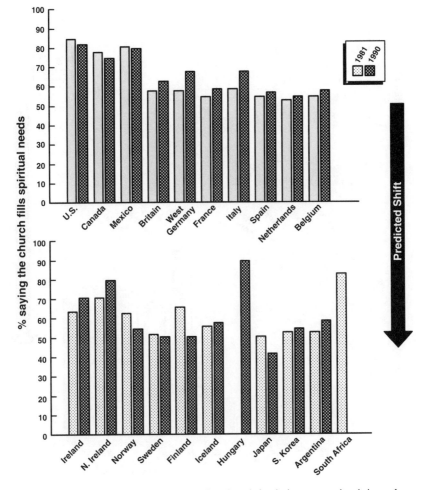

Figure A.18. Percentages saying that the church in their country is giving adequate answers to people's spiritual needs, in 1981 vs. 1990, in 20 countries. *Source*: 1981 and 1990 World Values surveys.

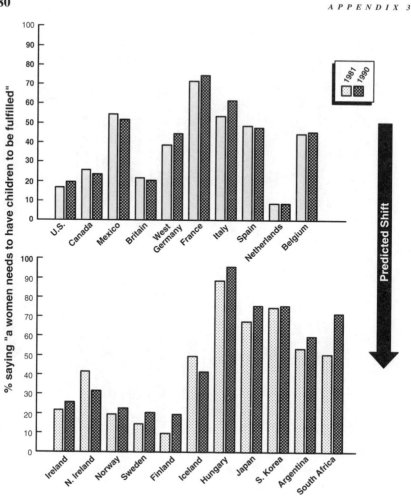

Figure A.19. Percentages saying "A woman has to have children in order to be fulfilled," in 1981 vs. 1990, in 21 countries. *Source*: 1981 and 1990 World Values surveys.

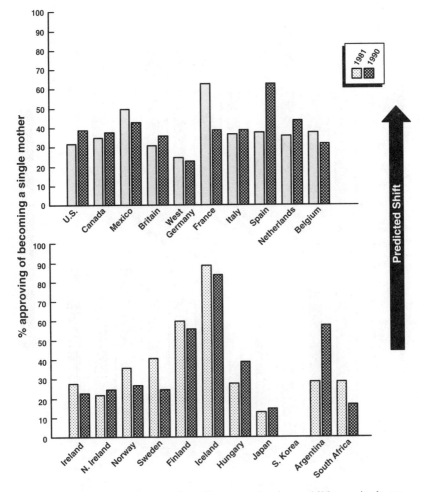

Figure A.20. Percentages approving of a woman having a child as a single parent, in 1981 vs. 1990, in 20 countries. *Source*: 1981 and 1990 World Values surveys. Not asked in South Korea.

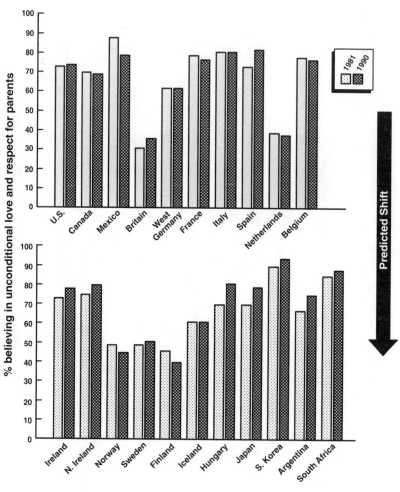

Figure A.21. Percentages believing one has a duty to love and respect one's parents, regardless of their faults, in 1981 vs. 1990, in 21 countries. *Source*: 1981 and 1990 World Values surveys.

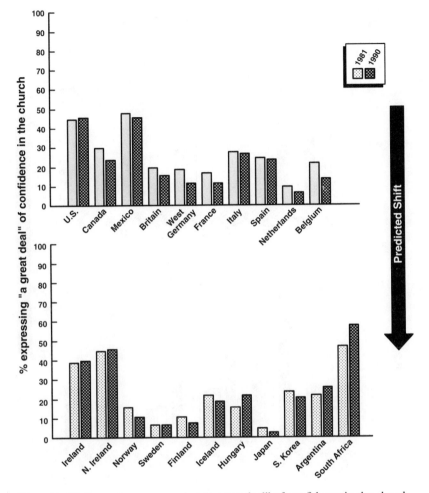

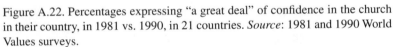

Figure A.22. Percentages expressing "a great deal" of confidence in the church in their country, in 1981 vs. 1990, in 21 countries. *Source*: 1981 and 1990 World Values surveys.

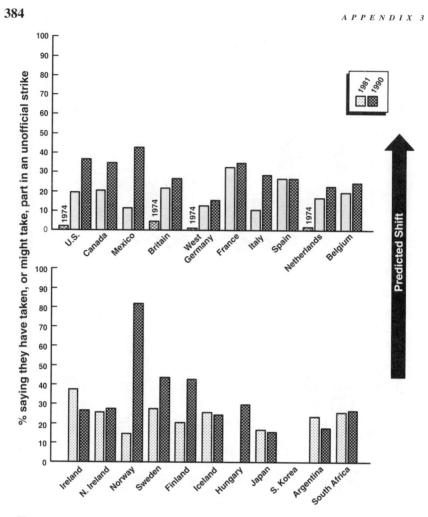

Figure A.23. Percentages saying that they have taken part in an unofficial strike, or might do so, in 1981 vs. 1990, in 20 countries. *Source*: 1981 and 1990 World Values surveys. 1981 data not available for Hungary.

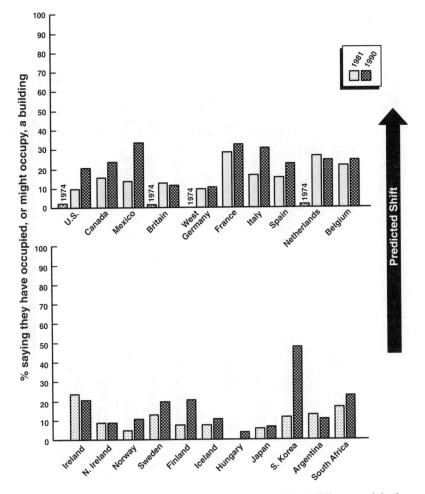

Figure A.24. Percentages saying that they have occupied a building, or might do so, in 1981 vs. 1990, in 20 countries. *Source*: 1981 and 1990 World Values surveys. 1981 data not available for Hungary.

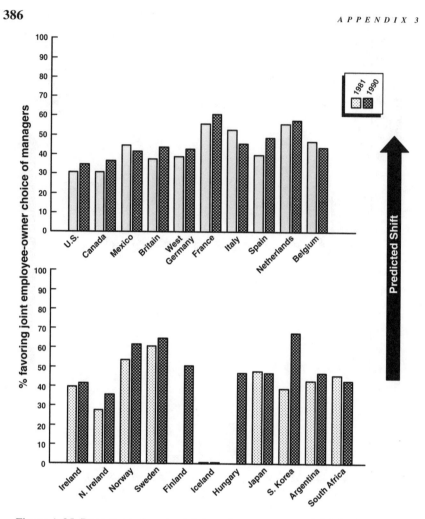

Figure A.25. Percentages favoring joint employee-owner participation in choosing managers in business and industry, in 1981 vs. 1990, in 20 countries. *Source*: 1981 and 1990 World Values surveys. 1981 data not available for Hungary.

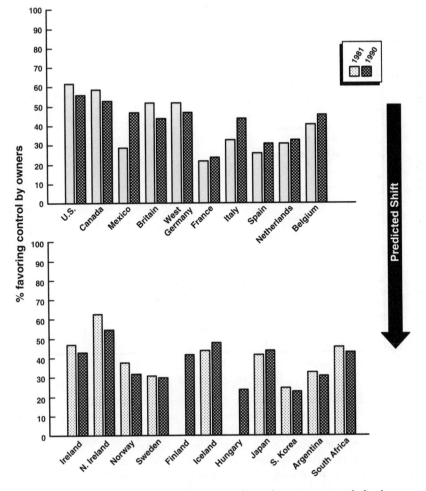

Figure A.26. Percentages favoring owner's right to choose managers in business and industry, in 1981 vs. 1990, in 20 countries. *Source*: 1981 and 1990 World Values surveys. 1981 data not available for Hungary.

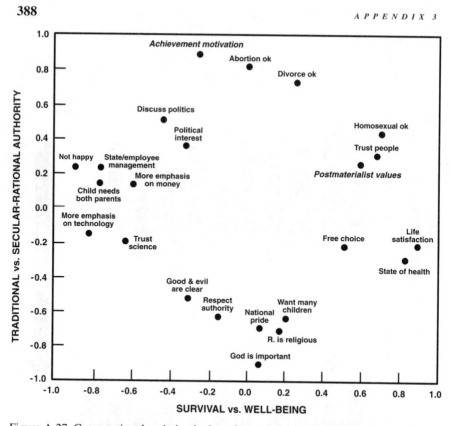

Figure A.27. Cross-national variation in the values emphasized in different societies: the Modernization and Postmodernization dimensions, based on the combined data from the 1981 and 1990 World Values surveys. *Source*: 1981–93 World Values surveys. This figure shows the first and second principal components emerging from a factor analysis of data from 65 representative national surveys of 44 societies, aggregated to the national level. The scales on the margins show each item's loadings on the two respective dimensions. The items in italics ("achievement motivation" and "Postmaterialist values") are multi-item indices.

APPENDIX 4

CONSTRUCTION OF KEY INDICES USED IN THIS BOOK

THE FOLLOWING SPSS INSTRUCTIONS show how key indices used in this book were created.

1. MATERIALIST/POSTMATERIALIST VALUES (FOUR-ITEM INDEX): [V1000]

COMPUTE V1000 = 2
IF ((V259 = 1 AND V260 = 3) OR (V259 = 3 AND V260 = 1)) V1000 = 1
IF ((V259 = 2) AND (V260 = 4)) OR ((V259 = 4) AND (V260 = 2)) V1000 = 3
(range = 1–3; missing data = 9)

This index is based on the respondent's first and second choices in the original four-item Materialist/Postmaterialist values battery. If both Materialist items are given high priority, the score is "1"; if both Postmaterialist items are given high priority, the score is "3"; if one Materialist item and one Postmaterialist item are given high priority, the score is "2." If the respondent makes only one or no choices, the result is missing data.

2. MATERIALIST/POSTMATERIALIST VALUES (12-ITEM INDEX): [V1010]

IF (V257 = 3 OR V258 = 3) V1001 = 1
IF (V259 = 2 OR V259 = 4) V1002 = 1
IF (V260 = 2 OR V260 = 4) V1003 = 1
IF (V261 = 2 OR V261 = 3) V1004 = 1
IF (V262 = 2 OR V262 = 3) V1005 = 1
COMPUTE V1010 = V1001 + V1002 + V1003 + V1004 + V1005

This index is based on all 12 items in the Materialist/Postmaterialist values battery; it simply sums up the total number of Postmaterialist items that were given high priority (i.e., ranked as either first or second most important in its group of four items). Accordingly, scores range from zero (none of the five Postmaterialist items was given high priority) to five (all five of the Postmaterialist items were given high priority).
(range = 0–5; missing data = 9)

3. BRADBURN AFFECT BALANCE SCALE: [V1032]

IF (V84 = 1) V1020 = 1
IF (V86 = 1) V1021 = 1
IF (V88 = 1) V1022 = 1
IF (V90 = 1) V1023 = 1
IF (V92 = 1) V1024 = 1

COMPUTE V1025 = V1020 + V1021 + V1022 + V1023 + V1024

IF (V85 = 1) V1026 = 1

IF (V87 = 1) V1027 = 1

IF (V89 = 1) V1028 = 1

IF (V91 = 1) V1029 = 1

IF (V93 = 1) V1030 = 1

COMPUTE V1031 = V1026 + V1027 + V1028 + V1029 + V1030

COMPUTE V1032 = V1025 − V1031

This index sums up the number of positive affect items that are chosen, and the number of negative affect items that are chosen, and then subtracts the negative affect score from the positive affect score.
(range = −5 to +5)

4. ACHIEVEMENT MOTIVATION SCALE (FOUR-ITEM INDEX): [V1046]

IF (V228 = 1) V1040 = 1

IF (V233 = 1) V1041 = 1

COMPUTE V1042 = V1040 + V1041

IF (V234 = 1) V1043 = 1

IF (V236 = 1) V1044 = 1

COMPUTE V1045 = V1043 + V1044

COMPUTE V1046 = V1042 − V1045

Respondents were asked, "Here is a list of qualities which children can be encouraged to learn at home. Which, if any, do you consider to be especially important?" Among the options were "Thrift" and "Determination," on one hand, and "Obedience" and "Religious faith," on the other hand. Each individual's score on this index represents the number of choices emphasizing the former two items, minus the number of choices emphasizing the latter two items.
(range = −2 to +2; missing data = 9)

5. ETHNOCENTRISM ("REJECT OUTGROUPS") [V1053]

IF (V77 = 1) V1050 = 1

IF (V78 = 1) V1051 = 1

IF (V80 = 1) V1052 = 1

COMPUTE V1053 = V1050 + V1051 + V1052

Respondents were asked, "On this list are various groups of people. Could you please sort out any that you would not like to have as neighbors?" The list included (among others) "Immigrants/foreign workers," "People who have AIDS," and "Homosexuals." Scores on this index range from 0 to 3, depending on how many of these three groups are mentioned.
(range = 0–3; missing data = 9)

6. SUBJECTIVE WELL-BEING INDEX

(This index is created at the national level, based on overall percentages scoring above given levels in the given nation. No SPSS instructions are provided, since this index is not created at the individual level.)

1. For each nation, calculate the percentage scoring HIGH on V18 (*"How happy are you these days?"*) minus the percentage scoring LOW on V18:

codes 1–2 = "high" ("very happy" + "quite happy");

codes 3–4 = "low" ("not very happy" + "not at all happy").

2. For each nation, calculate the percentage scoring HIGH on V95 minus the percentage scoring LOW on V95 ("How satisfied are you with your life as a whole these days? Please use this scale to answer: 1 = very dissatisfied . . . 10 = very satisfied"):

codes 1–4 = "low";

codes 7–10 = "high."

3. Sum the two figures obtained in (1) and (2) above.

4. Divide this result by 2.

On this index, a score of "0" indicates that as many people consider themselves unhappy or dissatisfied with their lives as a whole, as consider themselves happy or satisfied. A score of −100 would result if everyone in the given society considered themselves happy and satisfied with their lives as a whole; a score of +100 would mean that everyone considered themselves unhappy and dissatisfied with their lives as a whole. Range = −100 to +100.

All of these indices either measure priorities (rather than levels); or subtract the percentage high from the percentage low to control for the fact that respondents in some cultures have a tendency to give extreme scores, while those in others have a tendency to give moderate scores. This minimizes the impact of response set which, as chapter 4 demonstrates, is likely to be a particularly serious source of measurement error in cross-cultural research.

COMPLETE 1990 WVS QUESTIONNAIRE, WITH VARIABLE NUMBERS

IN ICPSR DATASET

Country Codes and Number of Interviews in 1981 and 1990

	1990-91 Surveys			**1981 Surveys**	
Code	*Country*	*N*	*Code*	*Country*	*N*
1	France	1,002	42	Austria	1,460
2	Britain	1,484	44	Turkey	1,030
3	W. Germany	2,101	45	Moscow	1,012
4	Italy	2,018	46	Lithuania	1,000
5	Netherlands	1,017	47	Latvia	903
6	Denmark	1,030	48	Estonia	1,008
7	Belgium	2,792	50	Russia	1,961
8	Spain	4,147	51	France81	1,200
9	Ireland	1,000	52	Britain81	1,231
10	N. Ireland	304	53	W. Germany81	1,305
11	U.S.	1,839	54	Italy81	1,348
12	Canada	1,730	55	Netherlands81	1,221
13	Japan	1,011	56	Denmark81	1,182
14	Mexico	1,531	57	Belgium81	1,145
15	S. Africa	2,736	58	Spain81	2,303
16	Hungary	999	59	Ireland81	1,217
18	Norway	1,239	60	N. Ireland81	312
19	Sweden	1,047	61	U.S. 81	2,325
21	Iceland	702	62	Canada81	1,254
22	Argentina	1,002	63	Japan81	1,204
23	Finland	588	64	Mexico81	1,837
24	S. Korea	1,251	65	S. Africa81	1,596
25	Poland	938	66	Hungary81	1,464
26	Switzerland	1,400	67	Australia81	1,228
28	Brazil	1,782	68	Norway81	1,246
29	Nigeria	1,001	69	Sweden81	954
30	Chile	1,500	70	Tambov81	1,262
31	Belarus	1,015	71	Iceland81	927
32	India	2,500	72	Argentina81	1,005
33	Czechoslovakia	1,396	73	Finland81	1,003
34	E. Germany	1,336	74	South Korea81	970
35	Slovenia	1,035			
36	Bulgaria	1,034			
37	Romania	1,103		V1= Study number	
39	China	1,000		V25 = Country code	
41	Portugal	1,185		V35 = Interview number	

WORLD VALUES SURVEY
1990 QUESTIONNAIRE

SHOW CARD A
Please say, for each of the following, how important it is in your life.

	Very Important	*Quite Important*	*Not Very Important*	*Not at All Important*	*DK*
V 4 A) Work	1	2	3	4	9
V 5 B) Family	1	2	3	4	9
V 6 C) Friends, acquaintances	1	2	3	4	9
V 7 D) Leisure time	1	2	3	4	9
V 8 E) Politics	1	2	3	4	9
V 9 F) Religion	1	2	3	4	9

Note: Throughout these surveys, "0" is used as a Not Ascertained (N.A.) code. With single-digit variables, "9" is also occasionally used as a N.A. code. An asterisk indicates items asked in both the 1981 and 1990 surveys.

V 10* When you get together with your friends, would you say you discuss political matters frequently, occasionally, or never?

1 Frequently
2 Occasionally
3 Never
9 Don't know

V 11 When you yourself hold a strong opinion, do you ever find yourself persuading your friends, relatives, or fellow workers to share your views? IF SO, does it happen often, from time to time, or rarely?

1 Often
2 From time to time
3 Rarely
4 Never
9 Don't know

SHOW CARD B

I am now going to read out some statements about the environment. For each one I read out, can you tell me whether you agree strongly, agree, disagree, or strongly disagree? (READ OUT EACH STATEMENT AND CODE AN ANSWER FOR EACH)

	Strongly Agree	Agree	Disagree	Strongly Disagree	DK
V 12 I would give part of my income if I were certain that the money would be used to prevent environmental pollution	1	2	3	4	9
V 13 I would agree to an increase in taxes if the extra money is used to prevent environmental pollution	1	2	3	4	9
V 14 The government has to reduce environmental pollution but it should not cost me any money	1	2	3	4	9
V 15 All the talk about pollution makes people too anxious	1	2	3	4	9
V 16 If we want to combat unemployment in this country, we shall just have to accept environmental problems	1	2	3	4	9
V 17 Protecting the environment and fighting pollution is less urgent than often suggested	1	2	3	4	9

V 18* Taking all things together, would you say you are (READ OUT, RE-VERSING ORDER FOR ALTERNATE CONTACTS)

   1 Very happy
   2 Quite happy
   3 Not very happy
   4 Not at all happy
   9 Don't know

SHOW CARD C*

Please look carefully at the following list of voluntary organizations and activities and say

(a) which, if any, do you belong to?
(CODE ALL 'YES' ANSWERS UNDER [a])
(b) which, if any, are you currently doing
unpaid voluntary work for?
(CODE ALL 'YES' ANSWERS UNDER [b])

		(a) *Belong to*	(b) *Do Unpaid Work for*
V 19 A)	Social welfare services for elderly, handicapped, or deprived people	1	V 37 1
V 20 B)	Religious or church organizations	1	V 38 1
V 21 C)	Education, arts, music, or cultural activities	1	V 39 1
V 22 D)	Trade unions	1	V 40 1
V 23 E)	Political parties or groups	1	V 41 1
V 24 F)	Local community action on issues like poverty, employment, housing, racial equality	1	V 42 1
V 25 G)	Third world development or human rights	1	V 43 1
V 26 H)	Conservation, the environment, ecology	1	V 44 1
V 27 I)	Professional associations	1	V 45 1
V 28 J)	Youth work (e.g., scouts, guides, youth clubs, etc.)	1	V 46 1
V 29 K)	Sports or recreation	1	V 47 1
V 30 L)	Women's groups	1	V 48 1
V 31 M)	Peace movement	1	V 49 1
V 32 N)	Animal rights	1	V 50 1
V 33 O)	Voluntary organizations concerned with health	1	V 51 1
V 34 P)	Other groups	1	V 52 1
V 35	None	1	V 53 -
V 36	Don't know	9	V 54 -

For V 19 to V 54, "1" indicates "mentioned," "2" indicates "not mentioned." The Chinese questionnaire translated "Trade unions" (V 22 and V 40) as "Trading associations," which was chosen by very few people. "Professional associations" was translated as "Occupational organizations," which evokes the (government-sponsored) labor unions; thus, for China, V 27 is functionally equivalent to V 22. The Swiss survey used the phrase "charitable organization" for "social welfare services" in V 19 and V 37.

SHOW CARD D

Thinking about your reasons for doing voluntary work, please use the following five-point scale to indicate how important each of the reasons below have been *in your own case*. (WHERE 1 IS UNIMPORTANT AND 5 IS VERY IMPORTANT)

		Unimportant				*Very Important*	DK
V 55 A)	A sense of solidarity with the poor and disadvantaged	1	2	3	4	5	9
V 56 B)	Compassion for those in need	1	2	3	4	5	9
V 57 C)	An opportunity to repay something, give something back	1	2	3	4	5	9
V 58 D)	A sense of duty, moral obligation	1	2	3	4	5	9
V 59 E)	Identifying with people who were suffering	1	2	3	4	5	9
V 60 F)	Time on my hands, wanted something worthwhile to do	1	2	3	4	5	9
V 61 G)	Purely for personal satisfaction	1	2	3	4	5	9
V 62 H)	Religious beliefs	1	2	3	4	5	9
V 63 I)	To help give disadvantaged people hope and dignity	1	2	3	4	5	9
V 64 J)	To make a contribution to my local community	1	2	3	4	5	9
V 65 K)	To bring about social or political change	1	2	3	4	5	9
V 66 L)	For social reasons, to meet people	1	2	3	4	5	9
V 67 M)	To gain new skills and useful experience	1	2	3	4	5	9
V 68 N)	I did not want to, but could not refuse	1	2	3	4	5	9

SHOW CARD E*
On this list are various groups of people. Could you please sort out any that you
would not like to have as neighbors? (CODE AN ANSWER FOR EACH)

		Mentioned	*Not Mentioned*
V 69 A)	People with a criminal record	1	2
V 70 B)	People of a different race	1	2
V 71 C)	Left-wing extremists	1	2
V 72 D)	Heavy drinkers	1	2
V 73 E)	Right-wing extremists	1	2
V 74 F)	People with large families	1	2
V 75 G)	Emotionally unstable people	1	2
V 76 H)	Muslims	1	2
V 77 I)	Immigrants/foreign workers	1	2
V 78 J)	People who have AIDS	1	2
V 79 K)	Drug addicts	1	2
V 80 L)	Homosexuals	1	2
V 81 M)	Jews	1	2
V 82 N)	Hindus	1	2

*The Slovenian survey and the Lithuanian, Latvian, and Estonian surveys asked about
"Gypsies," rather than "Hindus," in V 82.*
*The surveys in the Baltic countries asked about "extremists" (not "left-wing extrem-
ists") in V 71, and about "people of other nationalities" in V 73.*

V 83* All in all, how would you describe your state of health these days? Would you
say it is (READ OUT, REVERSING ORDER FOR ALTERNATE CONTACTS)

   1 Very good
   2 Good
   3 Fair
   4 Poor
   5 Very poor
   9 Don't know

We are interested in the way people are feeling these days. During the past few
weeks, did you ever feel (READ OUT AND MARK ONE CODE FOR EACH
STATEMENT)*

		YES	NO
V 84 A)	Particularly excited or interested in something	1	2
V 85 B)	So restless you couldn't sit long in a chair	1	2
V 86 C)	Proud because someone had complimented you on something you had done	1	2
V 87 D)	Very lonely or remote from other people	1	2
V 88 E)	Pleased about having accomplished something	1	2
V 89 F)	Bored	1	2

V 90 G) On top of the world/feeling that life is wonderful	1	2
V 91 H) Depressed or very unhappy	1	2
V 92 I) That things were going your way	1	2
V 93 J) Upset because somebody criticized you	1	2

V 94* Generally speaking, would you say that most people can be trusted or that you can't be too careful in dealing with people?

1 Most people can be trusted
2 Can't be too careful
9 Don't know

SHOW CARD F
V 95* Some people feel they have completely free choice and control over their lives, and other people feel that what they do has no real effect on what happens to them. Please use the scale to indicate how much freedom of choice and control you feel you have over the way your life turns out.

1   2   3   4   5   6   7   8   9   10
None at all   A great deal
                                         DK = 99

SHOW CARD G
V 96* All things considered, how satisfied are you with your life as a whole these days? Please use this card to help with your answer.

1   2   3   4   5   6   7   8   9   10
Dissatisfied   Satisfied
                                         DK = 99

SHOW CARD H
V 97 Why are there people in this country who live in need? Here are four possible reasons. Which one reason do you consider to be most important? (CODE ONE UNDER [a] BEL0W) And which reason do you consider to be the second most important? (CODE ONE UNDER [b] BELOW)

	V 97 (a) Most Important	V 98 (b) Second Most Important
Because they are unlucky	1	1
Because of laziness and lack of willpower	2	2
Because there is injustice in our society	3	3
It's an inevitable part of modern progress	4	4
None of these	5	5
Don't know	9	9

India only: additional codes 6 and 8 refer to ascetic and religious motivations.

SHOW CARD I*

Here are some aspects of a job that people say are important. Please look at them and tell me which ones you personally think are important in a job? (CODE ALL MENTIONED)

		Mentioned	Not Mentioned
V 99 A)	Good pay	1	2
V 100 B)	Pleasant people to work with	1	2
V 101 C)	Not too much pressure	1	2
V 102 D)	Good job security	1	2
V 103 E)	Good chances for promotion	1	2
V 104 F)	A job respected by people in general	1	2
V 105 G)	Good hours	1	2
V 106 H)	An opportunity to use initiative	1	2
V 107 I)	A useful job for society	1	2
V 108 J)	Generous holidays	1	2
V 109 K)	Meeting people	1	2
V 110 L)	A job in which you feel you can achieve something	1	2
V 111 M)	A responsible job	1	2
V 112 N)	A job that is interesting	1	2
V 113 O)	A job that meets one's abilities	1	2
V 114	None of these	1	2

ASK ALL WORKING; OTHERS SKIP TO V 118

How much pride, if any, do you take in the work that you do? (READ OUT)

V 115* 1 A great deal
2 Some
3 Little
4 None
9 Don't know

SHOW CARD J

Overall, how satisfied or dissatisfied are you with your job?

V 116* 1   2   3   4   5   6   7   8   9   10
      Dissatisfied   Satisfied
                                    DK = 99

SHOW CARD K

How free are you to make decisions in your job? Please use this card to indicate how much decision-making freedom you feel you have.

V 117*   1   2   3   4   5   6   7   8   9   10
        None at all   A great deal
                                       DK = 99

ASK ALL

SHOW CARD L

Here are some statements about why people work. Irrespective of whether you have a job, or not, which of them comes closest to what you think?

	Mentioned	Not Mentioned	
V 118	1	2	Work is like a business transaction. The more I get paid, the more I do; the less I get paid, the less I do
V 119	1	2	I will always do the best I can, regardless of pay
V 120	1	2	Working for a living is a necessity; I wouldn't work if I didn't have to
V 121	1	2	I enjoy working, but I don't let it interfere with the rest of my life
V 122	1	2	I enjoy my work; it's the most important thing in my life
V 123	1	2	I never had a paid job
V 124	1	2	Don't know

Imagine two secretaries, of the same age, doing practically the same job. One finds out that the other earns $50 a week more than she does. The better-paid secretary, however, is quicker, more efficient, and more reliable at her job. In your opinion, is it fair or not fair that one secretary is paid more than the other? (**Countries other than U.S.: Please use own currency**)

V 125* 1 Fair
        2 Unfair
        9 Don't know

SHOW CARD M

There is a lot of discussion about how business and industry should be managed. Which of these four statements comes closest to your opinion? (CODE ONE ONLY)

V 126* 1 The owners should run their business or appoint the managers
   2 The owners and the employees should participate in the selection of managers
   3 The government should be the owner and appoint the managers
   4 The employees should own the business and should elect the managers
   9 Don't know

SHOW CARD N

People have different ideas about following instructions at work. Some say that one should follow instructions of one's superiors even when one does not fully agree with them. Others say that one should follow one's superior's instructions only when one is convinced that they are right. With which of these two opinions do you agree?

V 127* 1 Should follow instructions
   2 Depends
   3 Must be convinced first
   9 Don't know

Do you agree or disagree with the following statements?

	Agree	Neither	Disagree	DK
V 128 A) When jobs are scarce, men have more right to a job than women	1	2	3	9
V 129 B) When jobs are scarce, people should be forced to retire early	1	2	3	9
V 130 C) When jobs are scarce, employers should give priority to British people over immigrants **(countries other than U.K.: please substitute your nationality)**	1	2	3	9
V 131 D) It is unfair to give work to handicapped people when able-bodied people can't find jobs	1	2	3	9

SHOW CARD O

How satisfied are you with the financial situation of your household?

V 132* 1   2   3   4   5   6   7   8   9   10
     Dissatisfied   Satisfied
                                     DK = 99

How often, if at all, do you think about the meaning and purpose of life? (READ OUT IN REVERSE ORDER FOR ALTERNATE CONTACTS)

V 133* 1 Often
       2 Sometimes
       3 Rarely
       4 Never
       9 Don't know

Do you ever think about death? Would you say

V 134 1 Often
      2 Sometimes
      3 Rarely
      4 Never
      9 Don't know

I am going to read out a list of statements about the meaning of life. Please indicate whether you agree or disagree with each of them. (READ OUT IN REVERSE ORDER FOR ALTERNATE CONTACTS)

	Agree	*Disagree*	*Neither*	*DK*
V 135 A) Life is meaningful only because God exists	1	2	3	9
V 136 B) The meaning of life is that you try to get the best out of it	1	2	3	9
V 137 C) Death is inevitable; it is pointless to worry about it	1	2	3	9
V 138 D) Death has a meaning only if you believe in God	1	2	3	9
V 139 E) If you have lived your life, death is a natural resting point	1	2	3	9
V 140 F) In my opinion, sorrow and suffering only have meaning if you believe in God	1	2	3	9
V 141 G) Life has no meaning	1	2	3	9

SHOW CARD P

Here are two statements which people sometimes make when discussing good and evil. Which one comes closest to your own point of view?

V 142*   A.   There are absolutely clear guidelines about what is good and evil. These always apply to everyone, whatever the circumstances.

        B.   There can never be absolutely clear guidelines about what is good and evil. What is good and evil depends entirely upon the circumstances at the time.

   1   Agree with statement A
   2   Disagree with both
   3   Agree with statement B
   9   Don't know

V 143*   (a)   Do you belong to a religious denomination?

        1   Yes—GO TO (b)
        2   No—GO TO (c)

      (b)   (IF YES) Which one? (CODE UNDER [b] BELOW)
      (c)   (IF NO) Were you ever a member of a religious denomination? Which one? (CODE UNDER [c] BELOW)

	V 144 (b) *Religious Denomination*	V 145 (c) *Before*
Roman Catholic	1	1
Mainline Protestant	2	2
Fundamentalist Protestant	3	3
Jew	4	4
Muslim	5	5
Hindu	6	6
Buddhist	7	7
Other	8	8
Never	—	0
No answer	9	9

NOTE: Japan, South Korea, and many Eastern European countries used different codes from these. For these and other deviations from the above, see V 144 and V 145 in the section on Nation-Specific Codes.

ASK ALL

V 146   Were you brought up religiously at home?

  1   Yes
  2   No

SHOW CARD Q

V 147* Apart from weddings, funerals, and christenings, about how often do you attend religious services these days?

1 More than once a week
2 Once a week
3 Once a month
4 Christmas/Easter day
5 Other specific holy days
6 Once a year
7 Less often
8 Never, practically never

Do you personally think it is important to hold a religious service for any of the following events?

		Yes	No	DK
V 148 A)	Birth	1	2	9
V 149 B)	Marriage	1	2	9
V 150 C)	Death	1	2	9

Independently of whether you go to church or not, would you say you are (READ OUT REVERSING ORDER)

V 151* 1 A religious person
2 Not a religious person
3 A convinced atheist
9 Don't know

Generally speaking, do you think that your church is giving, in your country, adequate answers to (READ OUT AND CODE ONE ANSWER FOR EACH)*

	YES	NO	DK
V 152 A) The moral problems and needs of the individual	1	2	9
V 153 B) The problems of family life	1	2	9
V 154 C) People's spiritual needs	1	2	9
V 155 D) The social problems facing our country today	1	2	9

Do you think it is proper for churches to speak out on

		YES	NO	DK
V 156 A)	Disarmament	1	2	9
V 157 B)	Abortion	1	2	9
V 158 C)	Third world problems	1	2	9
V 159 D)	Extramarital affairs	1	2	9
V 160 E)	Unemployment	1	2	9
V 161 F)	Racial discrimination	1	2	9
V 162 G)	Euthanasia	1	2	9
V 163 H)	Homosexuality	1	2	9
V 164 I)	Ecology and environmental issues	1	2	9
V 165 J)	Government policy	1	2	9

Which, if any, of the following do you believe in? (READ OUT AND CODE ONE ANSWER FOR EACH)*

		YES	NO	DK
V 166 A)	God	1	2	9
V 167 B)	Life after death	1	2	9
V 168 C)	A soul	1	2	9
V 169 D)	The Devil	1	2	9
V 170 E)	Hell	1	2	9
V 171 F)	Heaven	1	2	9
V 172 G)	Sin	1	2	9
V 173 H)	Resurrection of the dead	1	2	9
V 174 I)	Reincarnation	1	2	9

SHOW CARD R

Which of these statements comes closest to your beliefs? (CODE ONE ANSWER ONLY)

V 175*
1 There is a personal God
2 There is some sort of spirit or life force
3 I don't really know what to think
4 I don't really think there is any sort of spirit, God, or life force
9 Not answered

SHOW CARD S

And how important is God in your life? Please use this card to indicate—10 means very important and 1 means not at all important.

V 176*   1   2   3   4   5   6   7   8   9   10
       Not at all   Very
                              DK = 99

Do you find that you get comfort and strength from religion?

V 177*   1 Yes
       2 No
       9 Don't know

Do you take some moments of prayer, meditation or contemplation or something like that?

V 178*   1 Yes
       2 No
       9 Don't know

How often do you pray to God outside of religious services? Would you say

V 179 1 Often
      2 Sometimes
      3 Hardly ever
      4 Only in times of crisis
      5 Never
      9 Don't know

SHOW CARD T

Overall, how satisfied or dissatisfied are you with your home life?

V 180*   1   2   3   4   5   6   7   8   9   10
       Dissatisfied   Satisfied
                                       DK = 99

Are you currently (READ OUT AND CODE ONE ONLY)

V 181* 1   Married
      2   Living as married
      3   Divorced
      4   Separated
      5   Widowed
      6   Single

Have you been married before?

V 182 1   Yes—more than once
     2   Yes—only once
     3   No—never

NOTE: In the 1990 Dutch survey, V 182 was worded as "How often have you been married?" 1 = once, 2 = more than once, 3 = more than twice. This question gave rise to confusion in many countries; it was not clear whether being married before meant "have you ever been married?" or "have you ever been married before your present marriage?"

ASK ALL EXCEPT SINGLES

Do (did) you and your partner share any of the following? (READ OUT AND CODE ALL MENTIONED)*

V 183   1   Attitudes toward religion
V 184   1   Moral attitudes
V 185   1   Social attitudes
V 186   1   Political attitudes
V 187   1   Sexual attitudes
V 188   1   None of these
V 189   1   Don't know

For V 183–V 196, code "2" indicates "not mentioned."

ASK ALL

And how about your parents? Do (did) you and your parents share any of the following? (READ OUT AND CODE ALL MENTIONED)*

V 190   1   Attitudes toward religion
V 191   1   Moral attitudes
V 192   1   Social attitudes
V 193   1   Political attitudes
V 194   1   Sexual attitudes
V 195   1   None of these
V 196   1   Don't know

If someone said that individuals should have the chance to enjoy complete sexual freedom without being restricted, would you tend to agree or disagree?

V 197* 1 Tend to agree
      2 Neither/it depends
      3 Tend to disagree
      9 Don't know

SHOW CARD U
Here is a list of things which some people think make for a successful marriage. Please tell me, for each one, whether you think it is very important, rather important or not very important for a successful marriage:*

	Very Important	*Rather Important*	*Not Very Important*
V 198 A) Faithfulness	1	2	3
V 199 B) An adequate income	1	2	3
V 200 C) Being of the same social background	1	2	3
V 201 D) Mutual respect and appreciation	1	2	3
V 202 E) Shared religious beliefs	1	2	3
V 203 F) Good housing	1	2	3
V 204 G) Agreement on politics	1	2	3
V 205 H) Understanding and tolerance	1	2	3
V 206 I) Living apart from your in-laws	1	2	3
V 207 J) Happy sexual relationship	1	2	3
V 208 K) Sharing household chores	1	2	3
V 209 L) Children	1	2	3
V 210 M) Tastes and interests in common	1	2	3

Have you had any children? IF YES, how many?

V 211* 0 No child—skip to V 213
      1 1 child
      2 2 children
      3 3 children
      4 4 children
      5 5 children
      6 6 children or more
      9 No answer

How many of them are still living at home?

V 212 0 No child
      1 1 child
      2 2 children
      3 3 children
      4 4 children
      5 5 children
      6 6 children or more
      9 No answer

ASK ALL

What do you think is the ideal size of the family—how many children, if any?

V 213* 0 None
        1 1 child
        2 2 children
        3 3 children
        4 4 children
        5 5 children
        6 6 children
        7 7 children
        8 8 children
        9 9 children
       10 10 or more
       99 Don't know

If someone says a child needs a home with both a father and a mother to grow up happily, would you tend to agree or disagree?

V 214* 1 Tend to agree
        2 Tend to disagree
        9 Don't know

(*South Korean 1981 survey contains one undocumented code "4"*)

Do you think that a woman has to have children in order to be fulfilled, or is this not necessary?

V 215 1 Needs children
       2 Not necessary
       3 Don't know (in some countries)
       9 Don't know (in other countries)

Do you agree or disagree with the following statement? (READ OUT)

	YES	NO	DK
V 216* Marriage is an outdated institution	1	2	9

If a woman wants to have a child as a single parent but she doesn't want to have a stable relationship with a man, do you approve or disapprove?

V 217* 1 Approve
        2 Depends
        3 Disapprove
        9 Don't know

SHOW CARD V
People talk about the changing roles of men and women today. For each of the following statements I read out, can you tell me how much you agree with each. Please use the responses on this card.

		Strongly Agree	*Agree*	*Dis- agree*	*Strongly Disagree*	*DK*
V 218 A)	A working mother can establish just as warm and secure a relationship with her children as a mother who does not work	1	2	3	4	9
V 219 B)	A preschool child is likely to suffer if his or her mother works	1	2	3	4	9
V 220 C)	A job is all right, but what most women really want is a home and children	1	2	3	4	9
V 221 D)	Being a housewife is just as fulfilling as working for pay	1	2	3	4	9
V 222 E)	Having a job is the best way for a woman to be an independent person	1	2	3	4	9
V 223 F)	Both the husband and wife should contribute to household income	1	2	3	4	9

SHOW CARD W
With which of these two statements do you tend to agree? (CODE ONE ANSWER ONLY)

V 224*
A. Regardless of what the qualities and faults of one's parents are, one must always love and respect them
B. One does not have the duty to respect and love parents who have not earned it by their behavior and attitudes
1   Tend to agree with statement A
2   Tend to agree with statement B
9   Don't know

SHOW CARD X
Which of the following statements best describes your views about parents' responsibilities to their children? (CODE ONE ONLY)

V 225*

1 Parents' duty is to do their best for their children even at the expense of their own well-being
2 Neither
3 Parents have a life of their own and should not be asked to sacrifice their own well-being for the sake of their children
9 Don't know

SHOW CARD Y

Here is a list of qualities which children can be encouraged to learn at home. Which, if any, do you consider to be especially important? Please choose up to five. (CODE FIVE ONLY)*

		IMPORTANT
V 226 A)	Good manners	1
V 227 B)	Independence	1
V 228 C)	Hard work	1
V 229 D)	Feeling of responsibility	1
V 230 E)	Imagination	1
V 231 F)	Tolerance and respect for other people	1
V 232 G)	Thrift, saving money, and things	1
V 233 H)	Determination, perseverance	1
V 234 I)	Religious faith	1
V 235 J)	Unselfishness	1
V 236 K)	Obedience	1

(*V 226–V 236: code "2" indicates items that were not chosen*)

SHOW CARD Z

Do you approve or disapprove of abortion under the following circumstances?*

		Approve	*Disapprove*
V 237 A)	Where the mother's health is at risk by the pregnancy	1	2
V 238 B)	Where it is likely that the child would be born physically handicapped	1	2
V 239 C)	Where the woman is not married	1	2
V 240 D)	Where a married couple do not want to have any more children	1	2

How interested would you say you are in politics?

V 241 1 Very interested
     2 Somewhat interested
     3 Not very interested
     4 Not at all interested
     9 Don't know

The Swiss survey asked about interest in international politics, national politics, regional politics, and community politics. Responses to the question about community politics (which showed the highest levels of interest) were used here.

SHOW CARD AA

Now I'd like you to look at this card. I'm going to read out some different forms of political action that people can take, and I'd like you to tell me, for each one, whether you have actually done any of these things, whether you might do it or would never, under any circumstances, do it.*

	Have Done	*Might Do*	*Would Never Do*	*DK*
V 242 A) Signing a petition	1	2	3	9
V 243 B) Joining in boycotts	1	2	3	9
V 244 C) Attending lawful demonstrations	1	2	3	9
V 245 D) Joining unofficial strikes	1	2	3	9
V 246 E) Occupying buildings or factories	1	2	3	9

(For V 242, the normal N.A. code is "0," but "8" was used in some countries)

SHOW CARD BB

V 247* Which of these two statements comes closest to your own opinion?

    A. I find that both freedom and equality are important. But if I were to choose one or the other, I would consider personal freedom more important, that is, everyone can live in freedom and develop without hindrance.

    B. Certainly both freedom and equality are important. But if I were to choose one or the other, I would consider equality more important, that is, that nobody is underprivileged and that social class differences are not so strong.

    1 Agree with statement A
    2 Agree with neither/depends
    3 Agree with statement B
    9 Don't know

SHOW CARD CC

V 248 In political matters, people talk of "the Left" and "the Right." How would you place your views on this scale, generally speaking?*

    1 2   3   4   5   6   7   8   9   10
    Left   Right
                                DK 5 99
                    Not answered 5 98

SHOW CARD DD

V 249* On this card are three basic kinds of attitudes concerning the society we live in. Please choose the one which best describes your own opinion. (CODE ONE ONLY)

    1 The entire way our society is organized must be radically changed by revolutionary action
    2 Our society must be gradually improved by reforms
    3 Our present society must be valiantly defended against all subversive forces
    9 Don't know

SHOW CARD EE

Now I'd like you to tell me your views on various issues. How would you place your views on this scale? 1 means you agree completely with the statement on the left, 10 means you agree completely with the statement on the right, or you can choose any number in between.

V 250

1	2	3	4	5	6	7	8	9	10

DK = 99

A) Incomes should be
made more equal

There should be greater
incentives for individual effort

V 251

1	2	3	4	5	6	7	8	9	10

DK = 99

B) Private ownership of
business and industry
should be increased

Government ownership of
business and industry
should be increased

V 252

1	2	3	4	5	6	7	8	9	10

DK = 99

C) Individuals should take
more responsibility for
providing for themselves

The state should take more
responsibility to ensure that
everyone is provided for

V 253

1	2	3	4	5	6	7	8	9	10

DK = 99

D) People who are unemployed
should have to take any job
available or lose their
unemployment benefits

People who are unemployed
should have the right to
refuse a job they do not want

V 254

1	2	3	4	5	6	7	8	9	10

DK = 99

E) Competition is good. It
stimulates people to work hard
and develop new ideas

Competition is harmful. It
brings out the worst in people

V 255

1	2	3	4	5	6	7	8	9	10

DK = 99

F) In the long run, hard
work usually brings a better
life

Hard work doesn't generally
bring success—it's more a
matter of luck and connections

V 256

1	2	3	4	5	6	7	8	9	10

DK = 99

G) People can only accumulate
wealth at the expense of others

Wealth can grow so there's
enough for everyone

SHOW CARD FF

There is a lot of talk these days about what the aims of this country should be for the next 10 years. On this card are listed some of the goals which different people would give top priority. Would you please say which one of these you, yourself, consider the most important? (CODE ONE ANSWER ONLY UNDER [a] BELOW)

And which would be the next most important? (CODE ONE ANSWER ONLY UNDER [b] BELOW)

	V 257 (a) First Choice	V 258 (b) Second Choice
Maintaining a high level of economic growth	1	1
Making sure this country has strong defense forces	2	2
Seeing that people have more to say about how things are done at their jobs and in their communities	3	3
Trying to make our cities and countryside more beautiful	4	4
Don't know	9	9

SHOW CARD GG*

a) If you had to choose, which one of the things on this card would you say is most important? (CODE ONE ANSWER ONLY)

b) And which would be the next most important? (CODE ONE ANSWER ONLY)

	V 259 (a) First Choice	V 260 (b) Second Choice
Maintaining order in the nation	1	1
Giving people more to say in important government decisions	2	2
Fighting rising prices	3	3
Protecting freedom of speech	4	4
Don't know	9	9

SHOW CARD HH*

a) Here is another list. In your opinion, which one of these is most important?
(CODE ONE ANSWER ONLY)

b) And what would be the next most important? (CODE ONE ANSWER ONLY)

	V 261 (a) First Choice	V 262 (b) Second Choice
A stable economy	1	1
Progress toward a less impersonal and more humane society	2	2
Progress toward a society in which ideas count more than money	3	3
The fight against crime	4	4
Don't know	9	9

V 263 * Of course, we all hope that there will not be another war, but if it were to
come to that, would you be willing to fight for your country?

    1 Yes
    2 No
    9 Don't know

SHOW CARD II*

Here is a list of various changes in our way of life that might take place in the near future. Please tell me for each one, if it were to happen whether you think it would be a good thing, a bad thing, or don't you mind?

	Good	Don't Mind	Bad
V 264 A) Less emphasis on money and material possessions	1	2	3
V 265 B) Decrease in the importance of work in our lives	1	2	3
V 266 C) More emphasis on the development of technology	1	2	3
V 267 D) Greater emphasis on the development of the individual	1	2	3
V 268 E) Greater respect for authority	1	2	3
V 269 F) More emphasis on family life	1	2	3
V 270 G) A simple and more natural lifestyle	1	2	3

V 271 * In the long run, do you think the scientific advances we are making will help or harm mankind?

1 Will help
2 Some of each
3 Will harm
9 Don't know

SHOW CARD JJ*

Please look at this card and tell me, for each item listed, how much confidence you have in them: is it a great deal, quite a lot, not very much, or none at all? (CODE ONE ANSWER FOR EACH ITEM—READ OUT REVERSING ORDER FOR ALTERNATE CONTACTS)

	A Great Deal	Quite a Lot	Not Very Much	None at All
V 272 A) The church	1	2	3	4
V 273 B) The armed forces	1	2	3	4
V 274 C) The education system	1	2	3	4
V 275 D) The legal system	1	2	3	4
V 276 E) The press	1	2	3	4
V 277 F) Trade unions	1	2	3	4
V 278 G) The police	1	2	3	4
V 279 H) Parliament	1	2	3	4
V 280 I) Civil service	1	2	3	4
V 281 J) Major companies	1	2	3	4
V 282 K) The social security system	1	2	3	4
V 283 L) TV/European Community	1	2	3	4

V 284 M) NATO	1	2	3	4
V 285 N) The [American]* political system	1	2	3	4

*In Western European countries and China, V 283 refers to the European Community;
elsewhere, it refers to TV newscasters.*
The item concerning NATO (V 284) was not asked in some countries.
*In Slovenia, V 280 ("Civil service") was worded as "Local administration" to distin-
guish it from Yugoslav authority.*
*In Lithuania, Latvia, and Estonia, the following changes were made: V 276 = this re-
public's (Lithuanian, etc.) mass media, V 279 = this republic's parliament, V 281 =
cooperatives, V 283 the People's Front (Baltic independence movement), V 284 =
this republic's government, V 285 = government of the USSR.*
*In Russia, substitutions were made for V 279–V 285: V 279 Parliament (USSR),
V 281 = Government (USSR), V 282 = Parliament (Russia), V 283 = TV, V 284 =
Government (Russia), V 285 = Soviet political system.*

On this card are listed some things people have said make them proud of the [U.S.]*
Do any of these things make you proud of this country?
Is there anything else?
And is there anything else? (CODE UP TO TWO MENTIONS)

	V 286 First Choice	V 287 Second Choice
[American]* scientific achievements	1	1
The American political system	2	2
American sporting achievements	3	3
American culture and arts	4	4
American economic achievements	5	5
American health and welfare system	6	6
None of these things make me proud	7	7
DK	9	9

*In Spain (ASEP survey) only, the codes for V 286–V 287 were: 0 = scientific achieve-
ments, 1 = the political system, 2 = sporting achievements, 3 = culture and arts,
4 = economic achievements, 5 = health and welfare system, 6 = Spain's history,
7 = the language, 8 = none, 9 = don't know.*
*In China, the above codes were used, with the addition of code 8 = "the long, long
Chinese history."*

V 288 Generally speaking, would you say that this country is run by a few big interests looking out for themselves, or that it is run for the benefit of all the people?

  1 Run by a few big interests
  2 Run for all the people
  9 Don't know

V 289 How much do you trust the government in [Washington]* to do what is right?
Do you trust it almost always, most of the time, only some of the time, or almost
never?

1 Almost always
2 Most of the time
3 Only some of the time
4 Almost never

Substitute your nation for "U.S." or "American" or "Washington"

SHOW CARD KK

There are a number of groups and movements looking for public support. For each of
the following movements, which I read out, can you tell me whether you approve or
disapprove of this movement? (READ OUT AND CODE ONE ANSWER FOR
EACH) Please use the responses on this card!

	Approve		*Disapprove*		
	Strongly	*Somewhat*	*Somewhat*	*Strongly*	*DK*
V 290 A) Ecology movement or nature protection	1	2	3	4	9
V 291 B) Anti-nuclear energy movement	1	2	3	4	9
V 292 C) Disarmament movement	1	2	3	4	9
V 293 D) Human rights movement at home or abroad	1	2	3	4	9
V 294 E) Women's movement	1	2	3	4	9
V 295 F) Anti-apartheid movement	1	2	3	4	9

SHOW CARD LL*

Please tell me for each of the following statements whether you think it can always be justified, never be justified, or something in between, using this card. (READ OUT STATEMENTS REVERSING ORDER FOR ALTERNATE CONTACTS. CODE ONE ANSWER FOR EACH STATEMENT)

V 296 A) Claiming government benefits
which you are not entitled to   1 2 3 4 5 6 7 8 9 10
                                    Never   Always
                                                           DK = 99

V 297 B) Avoiding a fare on public
transport   1 2 3 4 5 6 7 8 9 10
                                                           DK = 99

V 298 C) Cheating on tax if you have
the chance   1 2 3 4 5 6 7 8 9 10
                                                           DK = 99

V 299 D) Buying something you knew
was stolen   1 2 3 4 5 6 7 8 9 10
                                                           DK = 99

V 300 E) Taking and driving away a car belonging
to someone else (joyriding)   1 2 3 4 5 6 7 8 9 10
                                                           DK = 99

V 301 F) Taking the drug marijuana or
hashish   1 2 3 4 5 6 7 8 9 10
                                                           DK = 99

V 302 G) Keeping money that you
have found   1 2 3 4 5 6 7 8 9 10
                                                           DK = 99

V 303 H) Lying in your own interest 1 2 3 4 5 6 7 8 9 10
                                                           DK = 99

V 304 I) Married men/women having
an affair   1 2 3 4 5 6 7 8 9 10
                                                           DK = 99

V 305 J) Sex under the legal age of
consent   1 2 3 4 5 6 7 8 9 10
                                                           DK = 99

V 306 K) Someone accepting a bribe in
the course of their duties   1 2 3 4 5 6 7 8 9 10
                                                           DK = 99

V 307 L) Homosexuality   1 2 3 4 5 6 7 8 9 10
                                                           DK = 99

V 308 M) Prostitution   1 2 3 4 5 6 7 8 9 10
                                                           DK = 99

V 309 N) Abortion   1 2 3 4 5 6 7 8 9 10
                                                           DK = 99

V 310 O) Divorce

1   2   3   4   5   6   7   8   9   10
DK = 99

V 311 P) Fighting with the police

1   2   3   4   5   6   7   8   9   10
DK = 99

V 312 Q) Euthanasia, terminating the
life of the incurably sick

1   2   3   4   5   6   7   8   9   10
DK = 99

V 313 R) Suicide

1   2   3   4   5   6   7   8   9   10
DK = 99

V 314 S) Failing to report damage you've done
accidentally to a parked vehicle

1   2   3   4   5   6   7   8   9   10
DK = 99

V 315 T) Threatening workers who refuse to
join a strike

1   2   3   4   5   6   7   8   9   10
DK = 99

V 316 U) Killing in self-defense

1   2   3   4   5   6   7   8   9   10
DK = 99

V 317 V) Political assassinations

1   2   3   4   5   6   7   8   9   10
DK = 99

V 318 W) Throwing litter in a public
place

1   2   3   4   5   6   7   8   9   10
DK = 99

V 319 X) Driving under the influence
of alcohol

1   2   3   4   5   6   7   8   9   10
Never   Always
DK = 99

SHOW CARD MM

(a) Which of these geographical groups would you say you belong to first of all?

(b) And the next?

	V 320 (a) First	V 321 (b) Next
Locality or town where you live	1	1
State or region of country where you live	2	2
The U.S. as a whole	3	3
North America	4	4
The world as a whole	5	5
(see nation-specific codes)	6	6
Don't know	9	9

V 322 How proud are you to be British?*
[*substitute your own nationality for British*]

1 Very proud
2 Quite proud
3 Not very proud
4 Not at all proud
9 Don't know

SHOW CARD NN

Now I want to ask you some questions about your outlook on life. Each card I show you has two contrasting statements on it. Using the scale listed, could you tell me where you would place your own view? 1 means you agree completely with the statement on the left, 10 means you agree completely with the statement on the right, or you can choose any number in between.

V 323   1 2 3 4 5 6 7 8 9 10   DK = 99
A) One should be cautious about   You will never achieve much
   making major changes in life   unless you act boldly

V 324   1 2 3 4 5 6 7 8 9 10   DK = 99
B) Ideas that have stood the test   New ideas are generally
   of time are generally best   better than old ones

V 325   1 2 3 4 5 6 7 8 9 10   DK = 99
C) When changes occur in my life,   When changes occur in my life,
   I worry about the difficulties   I welcome the possibility that
   they may cause   something new is beginning

SHOW CARD OO

A variety of characteristics are listed here. Could you take a look at them and select those which apply to you?

V 326 A) I usually count on being successful in everything I do   1
V 327 B) I enjoy convincing others of my opinion   1
V 328 C) I often notice that I serve as a model for others   1
V 329 D) I am good at getting what I want   1
V 330 E) I own many things others envy me for   1
V 331 F) I like to assume responsibility   1
V 332 G) I am rarely unsure about how I should behave   1
V 333 H) I often give others advice   1
V 334   None of the above   1

(For V 327-V 334, code "2" indicates "not mentioned")

SHOW CARD PP

I am going to read out some statements about the government and the economy. For each one, could you tell me how much you agree or disagree? Please use the responses on this card.

		Agree Completely	*Agree Somewhat*	*Neither Agree nor Disagree*	*Disagree Somewhat*	*Disagree Completely*	*Don't Know*
V 335 A)	This country's economic system needs fundamental changes	1	2	3	4	5	6
V 336 B)	Our government should be made much more open to the public	1	2	3	4	5	6
V 337 C)	We are more likely to have a healthy economy if the government allows more freedom for individuals to do as they wish	1	2	3	4	5	6
V 338 D)	If an unjust law were passed by the government I could do nothing at all about it	1	2	3	4	5	6
V 339 E)	Political reform in this country is moving too rapidly	1	2	3	4	5	6

SHOW CARD QQ

I now want to ask you how much you trust various groups of people: Using the responses on this card, could you tell me how much you trust: (READ OUT EACH AND CODE AN ANSWER FOR EACH)

	Trust Them Completely	*Trust Them a Little*	*Neither Trust nor Distrust Them*	*Do Not Trust Them Very Much*	*Do Not Trust Them at All*	*Don't Know*
V 340 A) Your family	1	2	3	4	5	9
V 341 B) The British in general *(substitute your nationality for British)*	1	2	3	4	5	9
V 342 C) Black Americans	1	2	3	4	5	9
V 343 D) Hispanic Americans	1	2	3	4	5	9
V 344 E) Canadians	1	2	3	4	5	9
V 345 F) Mexicans	1	2	3	4	5	9
V 346 G) Russians	1	2	3	4	5	9
V 347 H) Chinese	1	2	3	4	5	9

Here, as elsewhere, "0" indicates N.A.

Items C through H were asked in 15 of the 43 countries surveyed in 1990. The nationalities referred to in these items vary from country to country: items C and D indicate some important ethnic group within the given country; E and F indicate some neighboring nationality; G and H refer to the Americans, the Chinese, or the Russians. See Nation-Specific Variables section in ICPSR codebook for details.

V 348 Were you born in the United States [this country]?

 1   Yes
 No (If no): Where were you born?
 2   Latin America
 3   North America
 4   Asia
 5   Europe
 6   Africa
 7   Other

V 349 (If no) In what year did you come to the United States [to this country]?

 1 Within past 2 years
 2 Within past 3–5 years
 3 6–10 years ago
 4 11–15 years ago
 5 More than 15 years ago

V 350 To which of the following groups do you belong above all? Just call out one of the letters on this card. SHOW CARD

1 [A] Above all, I am an Hispanic American
2 [B] Above all, I am a black American
3 [C] Above all, I am a white American
4 [D] Above all, I am an Asian American
5 [E] I am an American first and a member of some ethnic group second

(the groups coded in V350 vary from country to country; see the section on Nation-Specific Codes in ICPSR codebook for codes used in countries other than the U.S.)

V 351 If there were a general election tomorrow, which party would you vote for? If DON'T KNOW: Which party appeals to you most?
(see Nation-Specific Codes in ICPSR codebook for codes used in given countries)

V 352 And which party would be your second choice?
(see Nation-Specific Codes in ICPSR codebook for codes used in given countries)

DEMOGRAPHICS

V 353* Sex of respondent

1 Male
2 Female

V 354* (a) Can you tell me your date of birth, please? _____
V 355* (b) This means you are ____ years old.

NOTE: The surveys carried out in Sweden, South Africa, and the Baltic countries did not ascertain the respondent's exact age, but did provide a collapsed six-category age variable; see V 404 in ICPSR codebook.

V 356* At what age did you or will you complete your full-time education, either at school, or at an institution of higher education? Please exclude apprenticeships. (WRITE IN AGE)

Except as noted, the following categories were used in all surveys (*see Nation-Specific Codes in ICPSR codebook for exceptions*)

0 N.A.
1 Completed formal education at 12 years of age or earlier
2 Completed education at 13 years of age
3 Completed education at 14
4 Completed education at 15
5 Completed education at 16
6 Completed education at 17
7 Completed education at 18
8 Completed education at 19
9 Completed education at 20
10 Completed education at 21 years of age or older
99 N.A., don't know

V 357* Do you live with your parents?

1 Yes

2 No

Are you yourself employed now or not?*
IF YES:
About how many hours a week? If more than one job: only for the main job
V358*

Has paid employment
30 hours a week or more	1
Less than 30 hours a week	2
Self-employed	3

If no paid employment
Retired/pensioned	4
Housewife not otherwise employed	5
Student	6
Unemployed	7
Other (PLEASE SPECIFY)	8

In which profession/industry do you or did you work? If more than one job, the main job (WRITE IN)*

_____

_____

What is/was your job there? (WRITE IN AND CODE BELOW)*

The following codes were used in most countries (see Nation-Specific Codes in ICPSR codebook for exceptions):

V 359
    1 Employer/manager of establishment with 10 or more employees
    2 Employer/manager of establishment with less than 10 employees
    3 Professional worker lawyer, accountant, teacher, etc.
    4 Middle level non-manual—office worker, etc.
    5 Junior level non-manual—office worker, etc.
    6 Foreman and supervisor
    7 Skilled manual worker
    8 Semiskilled manual worker
    9 Unskilled manual worker
    10 Farmer: employer, manager on own account
    11 Agricultural worker
    12 Member of armed forces
    13 Never had a job

V 360*   Are you the chief wage earner?

1 Yes—GO TO V 363

2 No—GO TO V 361

3 Equal wage earner (treated as "Yes")—(GO TO V 363)

V 361

(a) Is the chief wage earner employed now or not?

  1 Yes
  2 No

(b) In which profession/industry does/did he or she work? (WRITE IN)

_____

V 362 (c) What is/was his/her job? (WRITE IN AND CODE BELOW)

Most countries used the following codes (see Nation-Specific Codes in ICPSR code-book for exceptions):

  1 Employer/manager of establishment with 10 or more employees
  2 Employer/manager of establishment with less than 10 employees
  3 Professional worker lawyer, accountant, teacher, etc.
  4 Middle level non-manual—office worker, etc.
  5 Junior level non-manual—office worker, etc.
  6 Foreman and supervisor
  7 Skilled manual worker
  8 Semiskilled manual worker
  9 Unskilled manual worker
  10 Farmer: employer, manager on own account
  11 Agricultural worker
  12 Member of armed forces
  13 Never had a job

ASK ALL
SHOW INCOME CARD
V 363 Here is a scale of incomes and we would like to know in what group your household is, counting all wages, salaries, pensions, and other incomes that come in. Just give the letter of the group your household falls into, before taxes and other deductions.
(see Nation-Specific Codes in ICPSR codebook for categories):

1	2	3	4	5	6	7	8	9	10
C	D	E	F	G	H	I	J	K	L

No answer = 98

V 364* *INTERVIEWER CODE BY YOURSELF*
     Socioeconomic status of respondent
Most countries used the following codes (see Nation-Specific Codes in ICPSR code-book for exceptions):

  1 AB Upper, upper-middle class
  2 C1 Middle, non-manual workers
  3 C2 Manual workers—skilled, semiskilled
  4 DE Manual workers—unskilled, unemployed

V 365 (a) Time at the end of the interview: _____

V 366 (b) Total length of interview: Hours Minutes

V 367 During the interview the respondent was

1 Very interested
2 Somewhat interested
3 Not very interested

(a) Town where interview was conducted: _____

V 368 (b) Size of town:
Most countries used the following codes (see Nation-Specific Codes in ICPSR code-
book for exceptions):

1 Under 2,000
2 2,000–5,000
3 5–10,000
4 10–20,000
5 20–50,000
6 50–100,000
7 100–500,000
8 500,000 and more

V 369 Ethnic group (CODE BY OBSERVATION):
Unless otherwise noted, all countries used the following coding scheme:

1 Caucasian/white
2 Negro/Black
3 South Asian Indian, Pakistani, etc.
4 East Asian Chinese, Japanese, etc.
5 Arabic
6 Other
9 N.A.

V 370 Region where the interview was conducted:
(see Nation-Specific Codes section in the ICPSR codebook) The following is the U.S.
example:

1 New England
2 Middle Atlantic states
3 South Atlantic
4 East South Central
5 West South Central
6 East North Central
7 West North Central
8 Rocky Mountain states
9 Northwest
10 California

V 371 Citizenship
(see Nation-Specific Codes in ICPSR codebook)

V 372 Urban/Rural
(see Nation-Specific Codes in ICPSR codebook)

V 373 Language spoken by respondent
(see Nation-Specific Codes in ICPSR codebook)
(Canada, India, Switzerland, and Baltic nations only)

V 374 European Integration Scale
(This question was asked in Western Europe only)

There is much talk about what the individual member states of the European Community have in common and what makes each one distinct. [INTERVIEWER SHOWS CARD WITH SEVEN-POINT SCALE. STATEMENT A IS AT ONE END; STATEMENT B IS AT OPPOSITE END]

Statement A:
Some people say: If the European member states were truly to be united, this would mean the end of their national, historical, and cultural identities. Their national economic interests would also be sacrificed.

Statement B:
Others say: Only a truly united Europe can protect its states' national, historical, and cultural identities and their national economic interests from the challenges of the superpowers.

Which statement is closest to your own opinion, the first or the second? Please use the scale listed. "1" would mean that you agree completely with A, and "7" would mean that you agree completely with B. The numbers in between allow you to show where your own opinion falls, if you would place yourself somewhere in between.

1 Agree completely with statement A
2
3
4
5
6
7 Agree completely with statement B
9 Don't know, N.A.

V 375 Educational Level
(see Nation-Specific Codes in ICPSR codebook)

CONSTRUCTED VARIABLES

V 376   Weight Variable

This weight factor compensates for various features of sampling in given countries to make the samples replicate the national population parameters more closely. For example, the 1981 surveys in Western Europe, the United States, Canada, and Mexico oversampled (by approximately 50 percent) the youngest group aged 16–24. These respondents receive proportionately less weight in this variable. The samples from China, India, and Nigeria undersample the illiterate and rural portions of the public and oversample the more educated and urban portions; the weight variable is designed to correct for this problem by giving greater weight to the less educated. Both the 1981 and 1990 South African samples were stratified by race, interviewing approximately as many whites as Blacks; the weight variable corrects for this. This variable also corrects for obvious deviations from national population parameters in age and education in other countries. In most cases, the more highly educated are oversampled and are accordingly weighted less heavily than the less educated. In the 1990 Italian sample, however, the more educated are substantially undersampled and are weighted more heavily to compensate for it.

Finally, the 1990 Spanish sample has a much larger N than most other samples, which would give it disproportionate importance in any analysis involving pooled samples; it is down-weighted. Similarly, this study includes many small countries, and their combined Ns would far outweigh the results from the larger countries: unweighted, the Nordic countries plus the Baltic countries would outweigh India, China, the United States, and Russia. This weight factor gives greater weight to the more populous countries than to the less populous ones, so that pooled analyses (which are often convenient) more closely approximate global reality. The weighted N of the combined 67 surveys assembled here is 89,672, as compared with the unweighted N of 89,909.

REFERENCES

Aberbach, Joel D., Robert D. Putnam, and Bert A. Rockman. 1981. *Bureaucrats and Politicians in Western Democracies.* Cambridge, Mass.: Harvard University Press.

Abrams, Mark, et al. 1985. *Values and Social Change in Britain.* London: Macmillan.

Abramson, Paul R. 1979. "Developing Party Identification: A Further Examination of Life-cycle, Generational and Period Effects." *American Journal of Political Science* 23:78–96.

Abramson, Paul R., John H. Aldrich, and David W. Rohde. 1986. *Change and Continuity in the 1984 Elections.* Washington, D.C.: C. Q. Press.

———. 1994. *Change and Continuity in the 1992 Elections.* Washington: C. Q. Press.

Abramson, Paul R., and Ronald Inglehart. 1986. "Generational Replacement and Value Change in Six West European Societies." *American Journal of Political Science* 30:1–25.

———. 1987. "Generational Replacement and the Future of Post-Materialist Values." *Journal of Politics* 49:231–41.

———. 1992. "Generational Replacement and Value Change in Eight West European Societies." *British Journal of Political Science* 22:183–228.

———. 1994. "Education, Security, and Postmaterialism." *American Journal of Political Science* 38 (3): 797–814.

———. 1995. *Value Change in Global Perspective.* Ann Arbor: University of Michigan Press.

Achen, Christopher. 1985. "Proxy Variables and Incorrect Signs on Regression Coefficients." *Political Methodology* 11:299–316.

Adorno, Theodor W., et al. 1950. *The Authoritarian Personality.* New York: Harper.

Ajzen, Icek, and Martin Fishbein. 1974. "Factors Influencing Intentions and the Intention-behavior Relation." *Human Relations* 27:1–15.

Albala-Bertrand, Luis. 1992. *Democratic Culture and Governance: Latin America on the Threshold of the Third Millennium.* Paris: UNESCO/Hispanamerica.

Alford, Robert R. 1963. *Party and Society: The Anglo-American Democracies.* Chicago: Rand McNally.

Almond, Gabriel. 1983. "Communism and Political Culture Theory." *Comparative Politics* 13 (1): 127–38.

Almond, Gabriel, and Sidney Verba. 1963. *The Civic Culture: Political Attitudes and Democracy in Five Nations.* Princeton: Princeton University Press.

Almond, Gabriel, and Sidney Verba (eds.). 1990. *The Civic Culture Revisited.* Boston: Little, Brown.

Altemeyer, Bob. 1981. *Right-Wing Authoritarianism.* Winnepeg: University of Manitoba Press.

———. 1988. *Enemies of Freedom.* San Francisco: Jossey-Bass.

Alwin, Duane F. 1986. "Religion and Parental Child-Rearing Orientations: Evidence of A Catholic-Protestant Convergence." *American Journal of Sociology* 92:412–40.

Andrews, Frank (ed.). 1986. *Research on the Quality of Life.* Ann Arbor: ISR.

Andrews, Frank, and Stephen Withey. 1976. *Social Indicators of Well-Being in America.* New York: Plenum.

Arat, Zehra F. 1988. "Democracy and Economic Development: Modernization Theory Revisited." *Comparative Politics* 21:21–36.

Ashford, Sheena, and Noel Timms. 1992. *What Europe Thinks: A Study of Western European Values.* Aldershot: Dartmouth.

Auletta, Ken. 1982. *The Underclass.* New York: Random House.

Axelrod, Robert. 1984. *The Evolution of Cooperation.* New York: Basic Books.

Bahry, Donna. 1987. "Politics, Generations and Change in the USSR." In James R. Millar (ed.), *Politics, Work and Daily Life in the USSR.* Cambridge: Cambridge University Press.

Baker, Kendall L., Russell Dalton, and Kai Hildebrandt. 1981. *Germany Transformed.* Cambridge: Harvard University Press.

Banfield, Edward. 1958. *The Moral Basis of a Backward Society.* Chicago: Free Press.

Barnes, Samuel, et al. 1979. *Political Action.* Beverly Hills: Sage.

Barro, Robert. 1990. "Government Spending in a Simple Model of Endogenous Growth." *Journal of Political Economy.* 98:103–25.

———. 1991. "Economic Growth in a Cross Section of Countries." *Quarterly Journal of Economic Growth* 106:407–44.

Barton, Paul E. 1992. *America's Smallest School: The Family.* Princeton: Educational Testing Service.

Basanez, Miguel. 1993. "Protestant and Catholic Ethics: An Empirical Comparison." Paper presented at conference on "Changing Social and Political Values: A Global Perspective," Complutense University, Madrid, September 27–October 1.

Basanez, Miguel, Ronald Inglehart, and Alejandro Moreno. 1997. *Human Beliefs and Values: A Cross-Cultural Sourcebook.* Ann Arbor: University of Michigan Press.

Baudrillard, Jean. 1973. *Le miroir de la production.* Tournai: Castermans.

———. 1974. *La société de consommation: ses mythes, ses structures.* Paris: Gallimard.

———. 1983. *Simulations.* New York: Semiotext.

Bean, Clive, and Elim Papadakis. 1994. "Polarized Priorities or Flexible Alternatives? Dimensionality in Inglehart's Materialism-Postmaterialism Scale." *International Journal of Public Opinion Research* 6 (9): 264–88.

Beardsley, Richard K., John W. Hall, and Robert E. Ward. 1959. *Village Japan.* Chicago: University of Chicago Press.

Beck, Ulrich. 1992. *Risk Society: Towards a New Modernity.* London: Sage.

Beck, E. M., James L. Massey, and Stewart E. Tolnay. 1989. "Black Lynchings: The Power Threat Hypothesis." *Social Forces* 67:605–23.

Bell, Daniel. 1973. *The Coming of Postindustrial Society.* New York: Basic Books.

———. 1976. *The Cultural Contradictions of Capitalism.* New York: Basic Books.

Bennulf, Martin, and Soren Holmberg. 1990. "The Green Breakthrough in Sweden." *Scandinavian Political Studies* 13 (2): 165–84.

Bentler, Peter M. 1990. "Comparative Fit Indices in Structural Models." *Psychological Bulletin* 107:238–46.

Betz, Hans-Georg. 1990. "Value Change in Postmaterialist Politics: The Case of West Germany." *Comparative Political Studies* 23:239–56.

Block, J. 1981. "Some Enduring and Consequential Structures of Personality." In Albert I. Rabin et al. (eds.), *Further Explorations in Personality*, pp. 27–43. New York: Wiley-Interscience.

Böltken, Ferdinand, and Wolfgang Jagodzinski. 1985. "In an Environment of Insecurity: Postmaterialism in the European Community, 1970 to 1980." *Comparative Political Studies* 17:453–84.

Bollen, Kenneth A. 1979. "Political Democracy and the Timing of Development." *American Sociological Review* 44:572–87.

———. 1980. "Issues in the Comparative Measurement of Political Democracy." *American Sociological Review* 45:370–90.

———. 1993. "Liberal Democracy: Validity and Source Biases in Cross-National Measures." *American Journal of Political Science* 37:1207–30.

Bollen, Kenneth A., and Robert Jackman. 1985. "Political Democracy and the Size Distribution of Income." *American Sociological Review* 48:468–79.

Boudon, Raymond. 1973. *Education, Opportunity, and Social Inequality: Changing Prospects in Western Society.* New York: Wiley.

Boynton, Robert, and Gerhard Loewenberg. 1973. "The Development of Public Support for Parliament in Germany." *British Journal of Political Science* 3:169–89.

Brim, Orville G., and Jerome Kagan (eds.). 1980. *Constancy and Change in Human Development.* Cambridge, Mass.: Harvard University Press.

Brunk, Gregory G., Gregory A. Caldeira, and Michael S. Lewis-Beck. 1987. "Capitalism, Socialism and Democracy: An Empirical Inquiry." *European Journal of Political Research* 15:459–70.

Brzezinski, Zbigniew. 1989. *The Grand Failure: The Birth and Death of Communism in the Twentieth Century.* New York: Scribner's.

Bürklin, Wilhelm, Markus Klein, and Achim Russ, 1994. "Dimensionen des Wertewandels: Eine empirische Längsschnittanalyse zur Dimensionalität und der Wandlungsdynamik gesellschaftlicher Wertorientierungen." *Politische Vierteljahresschrift* 35 (4): 579–606.

Burkhart, Ross E., and Michael S. Lewis-Beck. 1994. "Comparative Democracy: The Economic Development Thesis." *American Political Science Review* 88:903–10.

Campbell, Angus, Phillip E. Converse, and Willard Rodgers. 1976. *The Quality of Life.* New York: Russell Sage.

Cardoso, Fernando Henrique, and Enzo Faletto. 1971 (English translation, 1979). *Dependency and Development in Latin America.* Berkeley: University of California Press.

Carkoglu, Ali, and Sean Blinn. 1994. "Issue Dimension Volatility in Election Manifestoes: The Post-Materialist Revolution, Party Competition and Electoral Change in Post-war Democracies." Paper presented at the 1994 annual meeting of the Midwest Political Science Association, Chicago.

Cernea, Michael M. 1993. "Culture and Organization: The Social Sustainability of Induced Development." *Sustainable Development* 1 (2): 18–29.

Chatfield, C. 1989. *The Analysis of Time Series: An Introduction.* London: Chapman and Hall.

Chen, E. Y. K. 1979. *Hyper-growth in Asian Economies.* New York: Holmes and Meier.

Clark, Terry N. 1995. "Who Cares if Social Class Is Dying or Not?" Paper presented at conference on social class at Nuffield College, Oxford, February 1995. Research report no. 353.

Clark, Terry N., Seymour M. Lipset, and Mike Rempel. 1993. "The Declining Political Significance of Social Class." *International Sociology* 8 (3): 293–316.

Clarke, Harold D., and Nitish Dutt. 1991. "Measuring Value Change in Western Industrialized Societies: The Impact of Unemployment." *American Political Science Review* 85:905–20.

Cole, Harold, George Malaith, and Andrew Postlewaite. 1992. "Social Norms, Saving Behavior and Growth." *Journal of Political Economy* 100:1092–1125.

Conradt, David P. 1993. *The German Polity.* 5th ed. New York: Longmans.

Costa, Paul T., Jr., and Robert McCrae. 1980. "Still Stable after All These Years: Personality as a Key to Some Issues in Adulthood and Old Age." In Paul B. Baltes and Orville G. Brim (eds.), *Life-Span Development and Behavior,* vol. 3, pp. 65–102. New York: Academic Press.

Crepaz, Markus. 1990. "The Impact of Party Polarization and Postmaterialism on Voter Turnout—A Comparative Study of 16 Industrial Democracies." *European Journal of Political Research* 18:183–205.

Cusack, Thomas. 1991. "The Changing Contours of Government." Discussion paper, Berlin Science Center.

Dahl, Robert A. 1971. *Polyarchy: Participation and Opposition.* New Haven: Yale University Press.

Dalton, Russell J. 1977. "Was There a Revolution? A Note on Generational versus Life Cycle Explanations of Value Differences." *Comparative Political Studies* 9:459–75.

———. 1991a. "The Dynamics of Party System Change." In Karlheinz Reif and Ronald Inglehart(eds.), *Eurobarometer: The Dynamics of European Public Opinion,* pp. 215–52. New York: St. Martin's.

———. 1991b. "Responsiveness of Parties and Party Systems to the New Politics." In Hans-Dieter Klingemann, Richard Stöss, and Bernhard Wessels (eds.), *Politische Klasse und politische Institutionen,* pp. 145–71. Opladen/Wiesbaden: Westdeutscher Verlag.

———. 1993. *Politics in Germany.* 2d ed. New York: Harper Collins.

Dalton, Russell J., Scott C. Flanagan, and Paul Allen Beck (eds). 1984. *Electoral Change in Advanced Industrial Democracies: Realignment or Dealignment?* Princeton: Princeton University Press.

Davis, James A. 1996. Review essay on Paul R. Abramson and Ronald Inglehart, *Value Change in Global Perspective. Public Opinion Quarterly* 60 (summer): 322–31.

Dawkins, Richard. 1989. *The Selfish Gene.* Revised edition. Oxford: Oxford University Press.

De Graaf, Nan Dirk. 1988. *Postmaterialism and the Stratification Process.* Utrecht: Interdisplinair Sociaal wetenschappelijk Onderzoeksinstitut.

Derrida, Jacques. 1976. *Of Grammatology.* Baltimore: Johns Hopkins University Press.

———. 1979. *Spurs: Nietzsche's Styles.* Chicago: University of Chicago Press.

———. 1981. *Positions.* Chicago: University of Chicago Press.

Deutsch, Karl W. 1964. "Social Mobilization and Political Development." *American Political Science Review* 55:493–514.

Diamond, Jared. 1993. "The Diffusion of Language Groups in Africa." *Discover* 14:53–62.

Diamond, Larry, Juan J. Linz, and Seymour M. Lipset (eds.). 1989. *Democracy in Developing Countries*: vol. 2, *Africa*, vol. 3, *Asia*, vol. 4, *Latin America*. Boulder, Colo.: Lynne Rienner.

Diez Nicolas, Juan. 1994. "Postmaterialismo y desarollo economico en Espana." In Juan Diez-Nicolas and Ronald Inglehart (eds.), *Tendencias Mundiales de Cambio en los Valores Sociales y Politicos: Una Perspectiva Global,* pp. 125–56. Madrid: Fundesco.

Di Palma, Giuseppe. 1990. *To Craft Democracies: An Essay on Democratic Transitions.* Berkeley: University of California Press.

Dollar, David. 1992. "Outward-oriented Developing Economies Really Do Grow More

Rapidly: Evidence from 95 LDCs, 1976–1985." *Economic Development and Cultural Change*. 13 (79): 523–44.

Duch, Raymond M. 1996. Review of Paul R. Abramson and Ronald Inglehart, *Value Change in Global Perspective*. *American Political Science Review* 90:665–67.

Duch, Raymond M., and Michael A. Taylor. 1993. "Postmaterialism and the Economic Condition." *American Journal of Political Science* 37:747–89.

Duncan, Otis Dudley. 1968. "Social Stratification and Mobility: Problems in the Measurement of a Trend." In Eleanor B. Sheldon and Wilbert E. Moore (eds.), *Indicators of Social Change: Concepts and Measurement*, pp. 341–73. New York: Russell Sage.

Duvall, Raymond, Steven Jackson, Bruce M. Russett, Duncan Snidal, and David Sylvan. 1981. "A Formal Model of 'Dependencia Theory:' Structure and Measurement." In Richard L. Merritt and Bruce M. Russett (eds.), *From National Development to Global Community*, pp. 215–61. London: Allen and Unwin.

Easton, David. 1963. *The Political System*. New York: Wiley.

Eckstein, Harry. 1961. *A Theory of Stable Democracy*. Princeton: Princeton University Press.

———. 1988. "A Culturalist Theory of Political Change." *American Political Science Review* 82:789–804.

Elster, Jon. 1982. "Marxism, Functionalism and Game Theory: The Case for Methodological Individualism." *Theory and Society* 11:453–82.

Erikson, Erik H. 1982. *The Life Cycle Completed: A Review*. New York: Norton.

Esman, Milton J., and Norman T. Uphoff. 1984. *Local Organizations: Intermediaries in Rural Development*. Ithaca: Cornell University Press.

Ester, Peter, Loek Halman, and Ruud de Moor. 1993. *The Individualizing Society: Value Change in Europe and North America*. Tilburg: Tilburg University Press.

Fershtman, Chaim, and Yoram Weiss. 1993. "Social Status, Culture and Economic Performance." *Economic Journal* 103:946–59.

Fishbein, Martin, and Icek Ajzen. 1975. *Belief, Attitude, Intention and Behavior*. Reading, Mass.: Addison-Wesley.

Flanagan, Scott. 1982. "Changing Values in Advanced Industrial Societies." *Comparative Political Studies* 14:403–44.

———. 1987. "Changing Values in Advanced Industrial Society Revisited: Towards a Resolution of the Values Debate." *American Political Science Review* 81:1303–19.

Foucault, Michel. 1965 [1961]. *Madness and Civilization*. Translated by Richard Howard. New York: Pantheon.

———. 1972. *The Archaeology of Knowledge*. Translated by A. M. Sheridan Smith. New York: Pantheon.

———. 1977 [1975]. *Discipline and Punish*. Translated by Alan Sheridan. New York: Vintage.

———. 1978. *The History of Sexuality*. Translated by Robert Hurley. New York: Pantheon.

Ganzeboom, Harry B. G., and Henk Flap (eds.). 1989. *New Social Movements and Value Change: Theoretical Developments and Empirical Analyses*. Amsterdam: SISWO.

Gibson, James L., and Raymond M. Duch. 1992. "The Origins of a Democratic Culture in the Soviet Union: The Acquisition of Democratic Values." Paper presented at the 1992 annual meeting of the Midwest Political Science Association, Chicago.

———. 1994. "Postmaterialism and the Emerging Soviet Democracy." *Political Research Quarterly* 47 (1): 5–39.

Glenn, Norval D. 1976. "Cohort Analysis' Futile Quest: Statistical Attempts to Separate Age, Period and Cohort Effects." *American Sociological Review* 41:900–904.

———. 1977. *Cohort Analysis*. Beverly Hills, Calif.: Sage.

———. 1987. "Social Trends in the United States: Evidence from Sample Surveys." *Public Opinion Quarterly* 51:109–26.

Gonick, Lev S., and Robert M. Rosh. 1988. "The Structural Constraints of the World-Economy on National Political Development." *Comparative Political Studies* 21:171–99.

Gouldner, Alvin. 1979. *The Future of the Intellectuals and the Rise of the New Class*. New York: Seabury.

Granato, James, Ronald Inglehart, and David Leblang. 1996a. "The Effect of Cultural Values on Economic Development: Theory, Hypotheses and Some Empirical Tests." *American Journal of Political Science* 40 (3): 607–31.

———. 1996b. "Cultural Values, Stable Democracy and Economic Development: A Reply." *American Journal of Political Science* 40 (3): 680–96.

Granato, James, and Motoshi Suzuki. 1995. "The Use of the Encompassing Principle to Resolve Empirical Controversies in Voting Behavior: An Application to Voter Rationality in Congressional Elections." Typescript.

Greenstein, Fred I. 1969. *Personality and Politics*. Chicago: Markham.

Gubert, Renzo (ed.). 1992. *Persitenze e mutamenti dei Valori degli Italinan nel Contesto Europea*. Trento: Reverdito Edizioni.

Habermas, Jürgen. 1975. *Legitimation Crisis*. Boston: Beacon Press.

———. 1979. Einleitung. In *Stichworte zur "Geistigen Situation der Zeit,"* edited by Jürgen Habermas. Frankfurt: Suhrkamp.

———. 1980. "The Hermeneutic Claim to Universality." In Josef Bleicher (ed.), *Contemporary Hermeneutics*, pp. 114–53. London: Routledge and Kegan Paul.

———. 1984. *The Theory of Communicative Action*. Vol. 1. Boston: Beacon Press.

———. 1987a. *The Philosophical Discourse of Modernity*. Cambridge, Mass.: MIT Press.

———. 1987b. *The Theory of Communicative Action*. Vol. 2. Boston: Beacon Press.

Halman, Loek, Felix Heunk, Rund de Moor, and Harry Zanders. 1987. *Traditie, Secularisatie en Individualisering*. Tilburg: University of Tilburg Press.

Hamilton, David L. 1981. "Stereotyping and Intergroup Behavior: Some Thoughts on the Intergroup Approach." In David L. Hamilton (ed.), *Cognitive Processes in Stereotyping and Intergroup Behavior*, pp. 333–54. Hillsdale, N.J.: Erlbaum.

Harrison, Lawrence E. 1992. *Who Prospers? How Cultural Values Shape Economic and Political Success*. New York: Basic Books.

Heidegger, Martin. 1949. "Über den Humanismus." Frankfurt: Klostermann.

Hein, Simon. 1992. "Trade Strategy and the Dependency Hypothesis: A Comparison of Policy, Foreign Investment and Economic Growth in Latin America and East Asia." *Economic Development and Cultural Change* 13 (79): 495–521.

Hellevik, Ottar. 1993. "Postmaterialism as a Dimension of Cultural Change." *International Journal of Public Opinion Research* 5:211–33.

———. 1994. "Measuring Cultural Orientation: Ranking vs. Rating." *International Journal of Public Opinion Research* 6 (9): 292–95.

Helliwell, John F. 1994. "Empirical Linkages between Democracy and Economic Growth." *British Journal of Political Science* 24:175–98.

Hendry, David, and Jean-François Richard. 1989. "Recent Developments in the Theory of Encompassing." In Bernard Cornet and Henry Tulkens (eds.), *Contributions to Operations Research and Econometrics*, pp. 329–50. Cambridge, Mass.: MIT Press.

Herz. Thomas. 1979. "Der Wandel von Wertvorstellungen in westlichen Industriegesellschaften." *Kölner Zeitschrift für Soziologie und Sozialpsycholoie* 31:282–302.

Hibbs, Douglas A., Douglas Rivers, and Nicholas Vasilatos. 1982. "The Dynamics of Political Support for American Presidents among Occupational and Partisan Groups." *American Journal of Political Science* 26:312–32.

Hirsch, Robert. 1976. *The Social Limits to Growth*. Cambridge, Mass.: Harvard University Press.

Hoffmann-Martinot, Vincent. 1991. "Gruene and Verts: Two Faces of European Ecologism." *West European Politics* 14 (4): 70–95.

Horkheimer, Max, and Theodor W. Adorno. 1972 [1947]. *Dialectic of Enlightenment*. Translated by John Cumming. New York: Seabury.

Hout, Michael, Clem Brooks, and Jeff Manza. 1993. "The Persistence of Classes in Post-Industrial Societies." *International Sociology* 8 (3): 259–77.

Hout, Michael, and Andrew M. Greeley. 1987. "The Center Doesn't Hold: Church Attendance in the United States, 1940–1984." *American Sociology Review* 52 (June): 325–45.

Huber, John. 1989. "Values and Partisanship in Left-Right Orientations: Measuring Ideology." *European Journal of Political Research* 17:599–621.

Huber, John, and Ronald Inglehart. 1995. "Expert Interpretations of Party Space and Party Locations in 42 Societies." *Party Politics* 1 (1): 73–112.

Huntington, Samuel P. 1984. "Will More Countries Become Democratic?" *Political Science Quarterly* 99:193–218.

———. 1991. *The Third Wave: Democratization in the Twentieth Century*. Norman, Okla.: University of Oklahoma Press.

———. 1994. "The Clash of Civilizations?" *Foreign Affairs* 72 (3): 22–49.

Huxley, Aldous L. 1932. *Brave New World*. London.

Hyman, Herbert H. 1972. *Secondary Analysis of Sample Surveys: Principles, Procedures, and Potentialities*. New York: Wiley.

Hyman, Herbert H., and Paul B. Sheatsley. 1954. "'The Authoritarian Personality': A Methodological Critique." In Richard Christie and Marie Jahoda (eds.), *Studies in the Scope and Method of the Authoritarian Personality*, pp. 50–122. Glencoe: Free Press.

Inglehart, Marita R. 1991. *Reactions to Critical Life Events: A Social Psychological Analysis*. New York: Praeger.

Inglehart, Ronald. 1970. "The New Europeans: Inward or Outward Looking?" *International Organization* 24 (1): 129–39.

———. 1971. "The Silent Revolution in Europe." *American Political Science Review* 4:991–1017.

———. 1976. "Changing Values and Attitudes toward Military Service among the American Public." In Nancy Goldman and David Segal (eds.), *The Social Psychology of Military Service*. Beverly Hills: Sage.

———. 1977. *The Silent Revolution: Changing Values and Political Styles*. Princeton: Princeton University Press.

———. 1979. "Value Priorities and Socioeconomic Change." In Samuel Barnes et al. (eds.), *Political Action: Mass Participation in Five Western Democracies*, pp. 305–42. Beverly Hills: Sage.

―――. 1981. "Post-Materialism in an Environment of Insecurity." *American Political Science Review* 75:880–900.

―――. 1985a. "Aggregate Stability and Individual-Level Flux in Mass Belief Systems: The Level of Analysis Paradox." *American Political Science Review* 79:97–116.

―――. 1985b. "New Perspectives on Value Change." *Comparative Political Studies* 17:485–532.

―――. 1988. "The Renaissance of Political Culture." *American Political Science Review* 82 (4): 1203–30.

―――. 1990. *Culture Shift in Advanced Industrial Society*. Princeton: Princeton University Press.

―――. 1994. "Polarized Priorities or Flexible Alternatives? A Comment." *International Journal of Public Opinion Research* 6 (9): 289–92.

―――. 1995. "Public Support for Environmental Protection: The Impact of Objective Problems and Subjective Values in 43 Societies." *PS: Political Science and Politics* (March): 57–71.

Inglehart, Ronald, and Paul Abramson. 1992a. "Generational Replacement and Value Change in Eight West European Societies." *British Journal of Political Science* (April): 183–228.

―――. 1992b. "Value Change in Advanced Industrial Society: Problems in Conceptualization and Measurement." Paper presented at the annual meeting of the Western Political Science Association, San Francisco.

―――. 1993. "Values and Value Change on Five Continents." Paper presented at 1993 annual meeting of the American Political Science Association, Washington, D.C.

―――. 1994. "Economic Security and Value Change." *American Political Science Review* 88:336–54.

Inglehart, Ronald, and Hans-Dieter Klingemann. 1996. "Dimensionen des Wertewandels: Eine Replik." *Politische Vierteljahresschrift* 33 (June): 319–40.

Inglehart, Ronald, Neil Nevitte, and Miguel Basanez. 1996. *The North American Trajectory: Social Institutions and Social Change*. Hawthorne, N.Y: Aldine de Gruyter.

Inglehart, Ronald, and Renata Siemienska. 1988. "Political Values and Dissatisfaction in Poland and the West: A Comparative Analysis." *Government and Opposition* 23 (2): 440–57.

Inkeles, Alex, and Raymond Bauer. 1968. *The Soviet Citizen: Daily Life in a Totalitarian Society*. New York: Atheneum.

Inkeles, Alex, and Larry Diamond. 1980. "Personal Qualities as a Reflection of National Development." In Frank Andrews and Alexander Szalai (eds.), *Comparative Studies in Quality of Life*, pp. 91–109. London: Sage.

Inkeles, Alex, and David Smith. 1974. *Becoming Modern: Individual Change in Six Developing Countries*. Cambridge, Mass.: Harvard University Press.

Jackman, Robert W. 1973. "On the Relationship of Economic Development to Political Performance." *American Journal of Political Science* 36:611–21.

―――. 1987. "The Politics of Economic Growth in Industrial Democracies, 1974–1980." *Journal of Politics* 49:242–56.

Jackman, Robert W., and Ross A. Miller. 1996a. "The Poverty of Political Culture." *American Journal of Political Science* 40 (3): 697–716.

―――. 1996b. "A Renaissance of Political Culture?" *American Journal of Political Science* 40 (3): 632–59.

Jackson, David, and Duane Alwin. 1980. "The Factor Analysis of Ipsative Measures." *Sociological Methods and Research* 9:218–38.

Jackson, James S., and Marita R. Inglehart. 1996. "Reverberation Theory: Stress and Racism in Hierarchically Structured Communities." In S. E. Hobfoll and M. de Vries (eds.), *Stress in Communities: Moving beyond the Individual.* Norwell, Mass.: Kluwer (forthcoming).

Jaeggi, Urs. 1979. "Drinnen und Draussen." In Jürgen Habermas (ed.), *Stichworte zur "Geistigen Situation der Zeit,"* pp. 443–73. Frankfurt: Suhrkamp.

Jennings, M. Kent, and Gregory Markus. 1984. "Partisan Orientations over the Long Haul: Results from the Three-wave Socialization Panel." *American Political Science Review* 78:1000–1018.

Jennings, M. Kent, and Richard G. Niemi. 1981. *Generations and Politics.* Princeton: Princeton University Press.

Kaase, Max, and Kenneth Newton. 1995. *Beliefs in Government.* Oxford: Oxford University Press.

Kesselman, Mark. 1979. Review of Ronald Inglehart, *The Silent Revolution. American Political Science Review* 73:284–86.

Kinder, Donald, and D. Roderick Kiewiet. 1979. "Sociotropic Politics: The American Case." *British Journal of Political Science* 11:129–61.

Kitschelt, Herbert. 1994. *The Transformation of European Social Democracy.* New York: Cambridge University Press.

———. 1995. *The Radical Right in Western Europe: A Comparative Analysis.* Ann Arbor: University of Michigan Press.

Kitschelt, Herbert, and Staf Hellemans. 1990. "The Left-Right Semantics and the New Politics Cleavage." *Comparative Political Studies* 23 (2): 210–38.

Klages, Helmut. 1988. *Wertdynamik: Über die Wandelbarkeit des Selbstverständlichen.* Osnabrück (Texte und Thesen: 212).

———. 1992. "Die gegenwärtige Situation der Wert- und Wertwandelforschung—Probleme und Perspektiven." In Helmut Klages, Hans Jürgen Hippler, and Willi Herbert (eds.), *Werte und Wandel: Ergebnisse und Methoden eniner Forschungstradition,* pp. 5–39. Frankfurt: Campus Verlag.

Klandermans, P. Bert. 1990. "Linking the 'Old' and 'New': Movement Networks in the Netherlands." In Russell J. Dalton and Manfred Kuechler (eds.), *Challenging the Political Order: New Social and Political Movements in Western Democracies.* New York: Oxford University Press.

Klingemann, Hans-Dieter, Richard Hofferbert, and Ian Budge. 1994. *Parties, Policies and Democracy.* Boulder: Westview Press.

Knutsen, Oddbjorn. 1989. "Cleavage Dimensions in Ten West European Countries: A Comparative Empirical Analysis." *Comparative Political Studies* 21 (4): 495–534.

———. 1995. "Party Choice." In Jan W. van Deth and Elinor Scarbrough (eds.), *The Impact of Values,* pp. 461–91. Oxford: Oxford University Press.

Kolb, Eberhard. 1988. *The Weimar Republic.* Trans. P. S. Falla. London: Unwin Hyman.

Kramer, Gerald H. 1971. "Short-Term Fluctuations in U.S. Voting Behavior, 1896–1964." *American Political Science Review* 65:131–43.

Kraus, Stephen J. 1995. "Attitudes and the Prediction of Behavior: A Meta-Analysis of the Empirical Literature." *Personality and Social Psychology Bulletin* 21 (1): 58–75.

Kriesi, Hanspeter. 1989. "New Social Movements and the New Class in the Netherlands." *American Journal of Sociology* 94 (5): 1078–1116.

Kuhn, Thomas. 1962. *The Structure of Scientific Revolutions*. Chicago: University of Chicago Press.

Ladd, Everett C., Jr. 1978. "The New Lines Are Drawn: Class and Ideology in America." *Public Opinion* 1:48–53.

Landell-Mills, Pierre. 1992. "Governance, Cultural Change and Empowerment." *Journal of Modern African Studies* 30 (4): 543–67.

Lane, Robert. 1965. "The Politics of Consensus in an Age of Affluence." *American Political Science Review* 59 (4): 874–95.

LaPiere, R. T. 1934. "Attitudes versus Actions." *Social Forces* 13:230–37.

Leamer, Edward. 1983. "Let's Take the 'Con' out of Econometrics." *American Economic Review* 73:31–43.

Lenski, Gerhard. 1963. *The Religious Factor*. New York: Anchor-Doubleday.

Lerner, Daniel. 1958. *The Passing of Traditional Society: Modernizing the Middle East*. New York: Free Press.

Lesthaeghe, Ron, and Dominique Meekers. 1986. "Value Changes and the Dimensions of Familism in the European Community." *European Journal of Population* 2:225–68.

Levine, Ross, and David Renelt. 1992. "A Sensitivity Analysis of Cross-Country Growth Regressions." *American Economic Review* 82 (4): 942–63.

Levinson, Daniel J., et al. 1979. *The Seasons of a Man's Life*. New York: Knopf.

Lewis-Beck, Michael. 1986. "Comparative Economic Voting: Britain, France, Germany and Italy." *American Journal of Political Science* 30:315–46.

Lijphart, Arend. 1979. "Religious vs. Linguistic vs. Class Voting." *American Political Science Review* 73:4442–58.

———. 1991. "Political Parties." In David Butler (ed.), *Democracy at the Polls*, pp. 214–47. Washington, D.C.: American Enterprise Institute.

Lindblom, Charles. 1977. *Politics and Markets: The World's Political-Economic Systems*. New York: Basic Books.

Lipset, Seymour Martin. 1959. "Social Requisites of Democracy: Economic Development and Political Legitimacy." *American Political Science Review* 53:69–105.

———. 1960. *Political Man*. New York: Doubleday.

———. 1979. "The New Class and the Professoriate." In B. Bruce-Briggs (ed.), *The New Class?* pp. 67–68. New Brunswick: Transaction Books.

———. 1981. *Political Man: The Social Bases of Politics*. Expanded ed. Baltimore: Johns Hopkins University Press.

Lipset, Seymour Martin, Martin Trow, and James S. Coleman. 1956. *Union Democracy*. Glencoe, Ill.: Free Press.

Lucas, Robert. 1988. "On the Mechanics of Economic Development." *Journal of Monetary Economics* 21:3–32.

Lyon, David. 1994. *Postmodernity*. Minneapolis: University of Minnesota Press.

Lyotard, Jean-François. 1984 [1979]. *The Postmodern Condition: A Report on Knowledge*. Translated by Geoff Bennington and Brian Massumi. Minneapolis: University of Minnesota Press.

Manabe, Kazufumi. 1995. "People's Attitudes toward Technology and Environment in China." (In Japanese). *Kwansei Gakuin University Annual Studies* (forthcoming).

Mankiw, Gregory, David Romer, and David Weil. 1992. "A Contribution to the Empirics of Economic Growth." *Quarterly Journal of Economics* 152:407–37.

Markus, Gregory B. 1988. "The Impact of Personal and National Conditions on the Presidential Vote: A Pooled Cross-Sectional Analysis." *American Journal of Political Science* 32:137–54.

Maslow, Abraham K. 1954. *Motivation and Personality*. New York: Harper and Row.

McLanahan, Sara, and Irwin Garfinkel. 1986. *Single Mothers and Their Chidren: A New American Dilemma*. Washington, D.C.: Urban Institute Press.

McLanahan, Sara, and Gary Sandefur. 1994. *Growing up with a Single Parent: What Hurts, What Helps*. Cambridge, Mass.: Harvard University Press.

McClelland, David. 1961. *The Achieving Society*. Princeton: Van Nostrand.

McClelland, David C., et al. 1953. *The Achievement Motive*. New York: Appleton-Century-Crofts.

Meadows, Donella H., Dennis L. Meadows, Jorgen Randers, and William W. Behrens. 1972. *The Limits to Growth*. New York: Universe.

Melich, Anna (ed.). 1991. *Les Valeurs des Suisses*. Berne: Lange.

Michels, Roberto. 1962. *Political Parties: A Sociological Study of the Oligarchical Tendencies of Modern Democracy*. New York: Collier Books.

Milbrath, Lester W., and M. Goel. 1977. *Political Participation*. 2d edition. Chicago: Rand McNally.

Miller, Arthur H. 1974. "Political Issues and Trust in Government: 1964–1970." *American Political Science Review* 68 (3): 951–72.

Minkenberg, Michael. 1990. *Neokonservatismus und Neue Rechte in den USA*. Baden-Baden: Nomos Verlagsgesellschaft.

Mizon, Grayham, and Jean-François Richard. 1986. "The Encompassing Principle and Its Application to Non-nested Hypothesis Tests." *Econometrica* 54:657–78.

Moore, Barrington. 1966. *The Social Origins of Dictatorship and Democracy*. Boston: Beacon Press.

Muller, Edward N. 1988. "Democracy, Economic Development and Income Inequality." *American Sociological Review* 53:50–68.

Muller, Edward N., and Mitchell A. Seligson. 1994. "Civic Culture and Democracy: The Question of Causal Relationships." *American Political Science Review* 88 (3): 635–52.

Müller-Rommel, Ferdinand (ed.). 1990. *New Politics in Western Europe: The Rise and the Success of Green Parties and Alternative Lists*. Boulder: Westview Press.

Nie, Norman, Sidney Verba, and John Petrocik. 1979. *The Changing American Voter*. Cambridge, Mass.: Harvard University Press.

Nieuwbeerta, Paul, and Nan Dirk De Graaf. 1997. "Class Voting and the Influence of Varying Class Structures in 16 Western Countries: 1956–1990." In Geoffrey Evans (ed.), *The End of Class Politics: Class Voting in Comparative Perspective*. Oxford: Oxford University Press (forthcoming).

O'Donnell, Guillermo. 1978. "Reflections on the Pattern of Change in the Bureaucratic Authoritarian State." *Latin American Research Review* 13 (1): 3–38.

O'Donnell, Guillermo, Philippe C. Schmitter, and Laurence Whitehead (eds.). 1986. *Transitions from Authoritarian Rule: Prospects for Democracy*. Baltimore: Johns Hopkins University Press.

Offe, Claus. 1990. "Reflections on the Institutional Self-transformation of Movement Politics: A Tentative Stage Model." In Russell J. Dalton and Manfred Kuechler (eds.), *Challenging the Political Order: New Social and Political Movements in Western Democracies*, pp. 232–50. New York: Oxford University Press.

Olson, Mancur. 1982. *The Rise and Decline of Nations*. New Haven: Yale University Press.

Orizo, Francisco Andres, and Alejandro Sanchez Fernandez. *El Sistema de Valors dels Catalans*. Barcelona: Institut Catala d'Estudis Mediterranis.

Orwell, George. 1949. *1984*. Boston: Harcourt-Brace.

Ostrom, Charles W., Jr. 1990. *Time Series Analysis: Regression Techniques*. 2d edition. Newbury Park, Calif.: Sage.

Powell, G. Bingham. 1982. *Contemporary Democracies: Participation, Stability and Violence*. Cambridge, Mass.: Harvard University Press.

Przeworski, Adam, and Fernando Limongi. 1993. "Political Regimes and Economic Growth." *Journal of Economic Perspectives* 7 (3): 51–69.

Putnam, Robert D., with Robert Leonardi and Rafaella Nanetti. 1993. *Making Democracy Work: Civic Traditions in Modern Italy*. Princeton: Princeton University Press.

Pye, Lucian W. 1990. "Political Science and the Crisis of Authoritarianism." *American Political Science Review* 84 (1): 3–19.

Riffault, Helene (ed.). 1994. *Les Valeurs des Francais*. Paris: Presses Universitaires de France.

Rohrschneider, Robert. 1988. "Citizens' Attitudes toward Environmental Issues: Selfish or Selfless?" *Comparative Political Studies* 21:347–67.

———. 1990. "The Roots of Public Opinion toward New Social Movements: An Empirical Test of Competing Explanations." *American Journal of Political Science* 34 (1): 1–30.

———. 1993. "Environmental Belief Systems in Western Europe: A Hierarchical Model of Constraint." *Comparative Political Studies* 26:3–29.

Rokeach, Milton. 1968. *Beliefs, Attitudes and Values*. San Francisco: Jossey-Bass.

———. 1973. *The Nature of Human Values*. New York: Free Press.

Romer, Paul. 1986. "Increasing Returns and Long-run Growth." *Journal of Political Economy* 94:1002–37.

———. 1990. "Endogenous Technical Change." *Journal of Political Economy* 98:71–102.

Rostow, W. W. 1961. *The Stages of Economic Growth*. Cambridge: Cambridge University Press.

Rotter, Julian B. 1966. "Generalized Expectancies for Internal vs. External Control of Reinforcement." *Psychological Monographs: General and Applied* 80:591–609.

Russett, Bruce, et al. 1964. *World Handbook of Political and Social Indicators*. New Haven: Yale University Press.

Samuelson, Robert J. 1995. *The Good Life and Its Discontents*. New York: Random House.

Scarbrough, Elinor. 1995. "Materialist-Postmaterialist Value Orientations." In Jan W. van Deth and Elinor Scarbrough (eds.), *The Impact of Values*, pp. 123–59. Oxford: Oxford University Press.

Schumacher, E. F. 1973. *Small Is Beautiful: Economics as if People Mattered*. New York: Harper and Row.

Schumpeter, Joseph. 1947. *Capitalism, Socialism and Democracy*. 2d ed. New York: Harper and Brothers.

Shively, W. Phillips. 1991. Feature Review of *Culture Shift in Advanced Industrial Society*. *Journal of Politics* 53:235–38.

Silver, Brian D. 1987. "Political Beliefs of the Soviet Citizen: Sources of Support for Regime Norms." In James R. Millar (ed.), *Politics, Work, and Daily Life in the USSR:*

A Survey of Former Soviet Citizens, pp. 207–35. Cambridge: Cambridge University Press.

Skocpol, Theda. 1982. "Bringing the State Back In." *Items* 36 (1/2): 1–8. Reprinted in Roy Macridis and Bernard Brown (eds.), *Comparative Politics: Notes and Readings* (8th ed., 1996), pp. 57–65. Belmont: Wadsworth.

Sokal, Alan D. 1996. "Transgressing the Boundaries: Toward a Transformative Hermeneutics of Quantam Gravity." *Social Text* 46–47 (summer): 217–52.

Solow, Robert. 1956. "A Contribution to the Theory of Economic Growth." *Quarterly Journal of Economics* 70 (1): 65–94.

Sombart, Werner. 1913. *The Jews and Modern Capitalism*. London: Fisher, Unwin.

Statistiches Bundesamt. 1994. *Datenreport, 1994*. Bonn: Bundeszentrale für politische Bildung.

Swan, Trevor. 1956. "Economic Growth and Capital Accumulation." *Economic Record* 22:334–61.

Szekelyi, Maria, and Robert Tardos. 1993. "Attitudes That Make a Difference: Expectancies and Economic Progress." Discussion papers of the Institute for Research on Poverty, University of Wisconsin.

Tajfel, Henri. 1978. *Differentiation between Social Groups: Studies in the Social Psychology of Intergroup Relations*. London: Academic Press.

Tajfel, Henri, and J. C. Turner. 1979. "An Integrative Theory of Intergroup Conflict." In W. G. Austin and S. Worchel (eds.), *The Social Psychology of Intergroup Relations*, pp. 33–47. Monterey, Calif.: Brooks/Cole.

Tanzi, Vito, and Ludger Schuknecht. 1995 (December). "The Growth of Government and the Reform of the State in Industrial Countries." Washington, D.C.: IMF working paper.

Tawney, Richard Henry. 1955. [1922]. *The Acquisitive Society*. New York: Harcourt, Brace.

———. 1926. *Religion and the Rise of Capitalism: A History*. Gloucester, Mass.: P. Smith.

Taylor, Charles L., and David A. Jodice. 1983. *World Handbook of Political and Social Indicators*. 3d ed. New Haven: Yale University Press.

Teilhard de Chardin, Pierre. 1959. *The Phenomenon of Man*. Translated by Bernard Wall. New York: Harper and Brothers.

Thomassen, Jacques A., and Jan van Deth. 1989. "How New Is Dutch Politics?" *West European Politics* 12:61–78.

Thompson, Michael, Richard Ellis, and Aaron Wildavsky. 1990. *Cultural Theory*. Boulder: Westview Press.

Trump, Thomas M. 1991. "Value Formation and Postmaterialism: Inglehart's Theory of Value Change Reconsidered." *Comparative Political Studies* 24:365–90.

Tufte, Edward R. 1978. *Political Control of the Economy*. Princeton: Princeton University Press.

van Deth, Jan W. 1983a. "The Persistence of Materialist and Post-Materialist Value Orientations." *European Journal of Political Science* 9:407–31.

———. 1983b. "Ranking the Ratings: The Case of Materialist and Postmaterialist Value Orientations." *Political Methodology* 11: 63–79.

———. 1984. *Politieke Waarden*. Amsterdam: CT Press.

———. 1989. "Fighting a Trojan Horse: The Persistence and Change of Political Orientations." In Harry Ganzeboom and Hendrik Flap (eds.), *New Social Movements and Value Change*, pp. 89–112. Amsterdam: SISWO.

Van Deth, Jan W., and Elinor Scarbrough (eds.). 1995. *The Impact of Values*. Oxford: Oxford University Press.

Verba, Sidney, Norman H. Nie, and Jae-On Kim. 1978. *Participation and Political Equality*. Cambridge: Cambridge University Press.

Voye, Liliane, Bernadette Bawin-Legros, Jan Kerkhofs, and Karel Dobbelaere. 1992. *Belges, Hereux et Satisfaits*. Brussels: De Boeck-Wesmael.

Wallerstein, Judith, and Sanrda Blakeslee. 1989. *Second Chances: Men, Women and Children a Decade after Divorce*. New York: Ticknor and Fields.

Watanuki, Joji. 1977. *Politics in Postwar Japanese Society*. Tokyo: Tokyo University Press.

Whitehead, Barbara D. 1993. "Dan Quayle Was Right." *Atlantic Monthly* (April): 47–84.

———. 1946 [1925]. "Politics as a Vocation." In Hans H. Gerth and C. Wright Mills (eds.), *From Max Weber: Essays in Sociology*, pp. 77–128. New York: Oxford University Press.

Weber, Max. 1958 [1904–5]. *The Protestant Ethic and the Spirit of Capitalism*. New York: Scribner's.

Whitehead, Barbara Dafoe. 1993. "Dan Quayle Was Right." *Atlantic Monthly* (April): 47–84.

Wicker, Allan W. 1969. "Attitudes versus Actions: The Relationship of Verbal and Overt Behavioral Responses to Attitudinal Objects." *Journal of Social Issues* 25:41–78.

Wildavsky, Aaron. 1987. "Choosing Preferences by Constructing Institutions: A Cultural Theory of Preference Formation." *American Political Science Review* 81:3–21.

Wiley, Lawrence. 1957. *Village in the Vaucluse*. Cambridge, Mass.: Harvard University Press.

Wilson, Richard W. 1992. *Compliance Ideology: Rethinking Political Culture*. Cambridge: Cambridge University Press.

World Bank. 1993. *World Development Report, 1993*. New York: Oxford University Press.

Zaller, John, and Stanley Feldman. 1992. "A Simple Theory of the Survey Response." *American Journal of Political Science* 36:579–616.

Zulehner, Paul, and Herman Denz. 1993. *Wie Europe lebt und glaubt*. Düsseldorf: Patmos.

INDEX

1981 World Values surveys, 3
1990 World Values surveys, 3

Aberbach, Joel, 238
abortion, 237, 251, 271, 276–78
Abramson, Paul, 34, 47, 112, 124, 137, 140, 141, 242, 273
Achen, Christopher, 194
achievement criteria, 78
achievement motivation, 77, 82, 83, 86, 220–23, 228, 232, 233, 235, 364
achievement motivation and economic growth, 218–24
Adorno, Theodor, 47
advantages, functional, 17
affect balance, 82, 83, 87
affirmative action, 246
Africa, 223, 281
African-Americans, 39, 52
agenda, political, 237
agricultural societies, 17, 30
air pollution, 242
Ajzen, Icek, 51
Albala-Bertrand, Luis, 162
Alford, Robert, 254–56
Alford class voting index, 254–56
Algeria, 208
alienation, 29
Almond, Gabriel, 53, 161, 171, 172
Altemeyer, Bob, 47
Alwin, Duane, 117, 220
analysis, cross-level, 3; functional, 15–18
Andrews, Frank, 61, 64, 178, 209
anti-semitism, 39
Arat, Zehra, 160
Argentina, 199, 201, 278, 284, 299, 317, 322, 336
armed forces, confidence in , 301
ascribed social status, 219
assembly line, 170
Athens, 169
attitudes, impact on behavior, 51–66
Australia, 118–19, 336
authoritarian elites, 175
Authoritarian Personality, 47–48, 116
authoritarian reflex, 38–39
authoritarian regimes, 166–67
authoritarianism, 48
authority, 52–55; deemphasis of, 75–76; norms concerning, 273–75; rational-legal,

73, 75–76, 97, 102; respect for, 39, 43, 44, 83, 274–75, 296, 327; state, 238; traditional, 73, 75, 82, 97
Avogadro, Amedo, 13
Axelrod, Robert, 15, 16

Baker, Kendall, 234
Banfield, Edwin, 172
Barnes, Samuel, 154, 169, 307, 312
Barro, Robert, 229, 230
Barton, Paul, 290
Basanez, Miguel, ix, 94, 345
Baudrillard, Jean, 21
Bean, Clive, 115, 117, 118, 119, 120, 121, 122
Beck, Paul, 242
Beck, Ulrich, 36
Belgium, 140–41, 244
belief system, 37; consequences of, 49; constraint in, 100
Bell, Daniel, 7, 10, 53, 102, 170
Big Bang, 340
big government, 90
birth control, 56, 57, 327
birth rates, 56
Blacks, 39
Blair, Tony, 250
Blakeslee, Sandra, 290
Blinn, Sean, 253
Boeltken, Ferdinand, 131
Bollen, Kenneth, 160, 165
Bonapartism, 55
Bonn, 175
boycott, participation in, 313
Boynton, Robert, 175
Brim, Orville, 34
Brooks, Clem, 255
Brown, Murphy, 290
Brunk, Gregory, 160
Brzezinski, Zbigniew, 162
Budge, Ian, 252
Buerklin, Wilhelm, 113–16, 117, 119, 121
buildings, occupation of, 385
Bulgaria, 165, 178
bureaucracy, 29, 90
bureaucratic authority, rejection of, 78
bureaucratic state, 28, 74
bureaucratization, 8, 73

James Fenimore Cooper

JAMES FENIMORE COOPER was born in Burlington, New Jersey in 1789; his family moved to Cooperstown, New York while he was still an infant. He attended Yale College but was expelled. Sailing before the mast, he saw Europe for the first time on a merchant vessel. In 1808 he became a midshipman in the U. S. Navy. He resigned in 1811 and married. Cooper lived, at various periods, in Westchester and New York City, but spent his later years in Cooperstown. From 1826 to 1833 he traveled extensively in Europe. The Leather-Stocking Tales were published during the period from 1823 to 1841. Arranged according to the chronology of their hero Natty Bumppo, who appears under various sobriquets in all five romances, the sequence is *The Deerslayer* (age 22-24?), *The Last of the Mohicans* (age 35-37?), *The Pathfinder* (age 37-39), *The Pioneers* (age 71-72?), *The Prairie* (age 80-83). With his story *The Pilot* (1823) Cooper set the style for a new genre of sea fiction. A caustic social critic, he wrote *The American Democrat* (1838) as a critique of American civilization at that time. His works have been translated into numerous languages and have been enthusiastically received because of their vigor and robust narration. Never able to ignore a challenge, Cooper spent much of his later life in disputes with and suits against various journals. He died in 1851 at his home in Cooperstown.

A TALE BY

James Fenimore Cooper

THE
DEERSLAYER

or

The First Warpath

Cop. 14

"What terrors round him wait?
Amazement in his van, with Flight combined,
And Sorrow's faded form, and Solitude behind."

With an Afterword by
ALLAN NEVINS

A Signet Ⓢ *Classic*

Published by The New American Library

PREFACE

As has been stated in the preface to the series of the Leather-Stocking Tales, *The Deerslayer* is properly the first in the order of reading, though the last in that of publication. In this book the hero is represented as just arriving at manhood, with the freshness of feeling that belongs to that interesting period of life and with the power to please that properly characterizes youth. As a consequence, he is loved; and, what denotes the real waywardness of humanity more than it corresponds with theories and moral propositions, perhaps, he is loved by one full of art, vanity, and weakness, and loved principally for his sincerity, his modesty, and his unerring truth and probity. The preference he gives to the high qualities named over beauty, delirious passion, and sin, it is hoped, will offer a lesson that can injure none. This portion of the book is intentionally kept down, though it is thought to be sufficiently distinct to convey its moral.

The intention has been to put the sisters in strong contrast: one admirable in person, clever, filled with the pride of beauty, erring, and fallen; the other, barely provided with sufficient capacity to know good from evil, instinct, notwithstanding, with the virtues of woman, reverencing and loving God, and yielding only to the weakness of her sex in admiring personal attractions in one too coarse and unobservant to distinguish or to understand her quiet, gentle feeling in his favor.

As for the scene of this tale, it is intended for, and believed to be, a close description of the Otsego prior to the year 1760, when the first rude settlement was commenced on its banks, at that time only an insignificant clearing near the outlet, with a small hut of squared logs for the temporary dwelling

of the Deputy Superintendent of Indian affairs. The recollections of the writer carry him back distinctly to a time when nine-tenths of the shores of this lake were in the virgin forest, a peculiarity that was owing to the circumstance of the roads running through the first range of valleys removed from the waterside. The woods and the mountains have ever formed a principal source of beauty with this charming sheet of water, enough of the former remaining to this day to relieve the open grounds from monotony and tameness.

In most respects the descriptions of scenery in the tale are reasonably accurate. The rock appointed for the rendezvous between the Deerslayer and his friend the Delaware still remains, bearing the name of the Otsego Rock. The shoal on which Hutter is represented as having built his "castle" is a little misplaced, lying, in fact, nearer to the northern end of the lake, as well as to the eastern shore, than is stated in this book. Such a shoal, however, exists, surrounded on all sides by deep water. In the driest seasons a few rocks are seen above the surface of the lake, and at most periods of the year, rushes mark its locality. In a word, in all but precise position even this feature of the book is accurate. The same is true of the several points introduced, of the bay, of the river, of the mountains, and all the other accessories of the place.

The legend is purely fiction, no authority existing for any of its facts, characters, or other peculiarities beyond that which was thought necessary to secure the semblance of reality. Truth compels us to admit that the book has attracted very little notice and that if its merits are to be computed by its popularity, the care that has been bestowed on this edition might as well be spared. Such, at least, has been its fate in America; whether it has met with better success in any other country we have no means of knowing.

THE
DEERSLAYER

CHAPTER I

ON THE HUMAN imagination events produce the effects of time. Thus, he who has traveled far and seen much is apt to fancy that he has lived long, and the history that most abounds in important incidents soonest assumes the aspect of antiquity. In no other way can we account for the venerable air that is already gathering around American annals. When the mind reverts to the earliest days of colonial history, the period seems remote and obscure, the thousand changes that thicken along the links of recollections throwing back the origin of the nation to a day so distant as seemingly to reach the mists of time; yet, four lives of ordinary duration would suffice to transmit, from mouth to mouth, in the form of tradition, all that civilized man has achieved within the limits of the republic. Although New York alone possesses a population materially exceeding that of either of the four smallest kingdoms of Europe, or materially exceeding that of the entire Swiss Confederation, it is little more than two centuries since the Dutch commenced their settlement, rescuing the region from the savage state. Thus, what seems venerable by an accumulation of changes is reduced to familiarity when we come seriously to consider it solely in connection with time.

This glance into the perspective of the past will prepare the reader to look at the pictures we are about to sketch with less surprise than he might otherwise feel, and a few additional explanations may carry him back in imagination to the precise condition of society that we desire to delineate. It is a matter of history that the settlements on the eastern shore of the Hudson, such as Claverack, Kinderhook, and even Poughkeepsie, were not regarded as safe from Indian incursions a century since; there is still standing on the banks of the same river, within musket shot of the wharves of Albany, a residence of a younger branch * of the Van Rensselaers that has loopholes constructed for defense against the same crafty enemy, although it dates from a period scarcely so distant. Other similar memorials of the infancy of the country are to be found scattered through what is now deemed the very center of American civilization, affording the plainest proofs that all we possess of security from invasion and hostile violence is the growth of but little more than the time that is frequently filled by a single human life.

The incidents of this tale occurred between the years 1740 and 1745, when the settled portions of the colony of New York were confined to the four Atlantic counties, a narrow belt of country on each side of the Hudson, extending from its mouth to the falls near its head, and to a few advanced "neighborhoods" on the Mohawk and the Schoharie. Broad belts of the virgin wilderness not only reached the shores of the first river, but they even crossed it, stretching away into New England, and affording forest covers to the noiseless moccasin of the native warrior as he trod the secret and bloody warpath. A bird's-eye view of the whole region east of the Mississippi must then have offered one vast expanse of woods, relieved by a comparatively narrow fringe of cultivation along the sea, dotted by the glittering surfaces of lakes, and intersected by the waving lines of rivers. In such a vast picture of solemn solitude, the district of country we design to paint sinks into insignificance, though we feel encouraged to proceed by the conviction that, with slight and immaterial

---

* It is no more than justice to say that the Greenbush Van Rensselaers claim to be the oldest branch of that ancient and respectable family.

distinctions, he who succeeds in giving an accurate idea of any portion of this wild region must necessarily convey a tolerably correct notion of the whole.

Whatever may be the changes produced by man, the eternal round of the seasons is unbroken. Summer and winter, seed-time and harvest, return in their stated order with a sublime precision, affording to man one of the noblest of all the occasions he enjoys of proving the high powers of his far-reaching mind, in compassing the laws that control their exact uniformity and in calculating their never-ending revolutions. Centuries of summer suns had warmed the tops of the same noble oaks and pines, sending their heats even to the tenacious roots, when voices were heard calling to each other, in the depths of a forest, of which the leafy surface lay bathed in the brilliant light of a cloudless day in June, while the trunks of the trees rose in gloomy grandeur in the shades beneath. The calls were in different tones, evidently proceeding from two men who had lost their way, and were searching in different directions for their path. At length a shout proclaimed success, and presently a man of gigantic mold broke out of the tangled labyrinth of a small swamp, emerging into an opening that appeared to have been formed partly by the ravages of the wind and partly by those of fire. This little area, which afforded a good view of the sky, although it was pretty well filled with dead trees, lay on the side of one of the high hills, or low mountains, into which nearly the whole surface of the adjacent country was broken.

"Here is room to breathe in!" exclaimed the liberated forester as soon as he found himself under a clear sky, shaking his huge frame like a mastiff that has just escaped from a snowbank. "Hurrah! Deerslayer, here is daylight, at last, and yonder is the lake."

These words were scarcely uttered when the second forester dashed aside the bushes of the swamp and appeared in the area. After making a hurried adjustment of his arms and disordered dress, he joined his companion, who had already begun his dispositions for a halt.

"Do you know this spot?" demanded the one called Deerslayer, "or do you shout at the sight of the sun?"

"Both, lad, both; I know the spot and am not sorry to see so useful a friend as the sun. Now we have got the p'ints of the compass in our minds once more, and 'twill be our own

faults if we let anything turn them topsy-turvy ag'in, as has
just happened. My name is not Hurry Harry if this be not
the very spot where the land hunters camped the last summer
and passed a week. See, yonder are the dead bushes of their
bower, and here is the spring. Much as I like the sun, boy,
I've no occasion for it to tell me it is noon; this stomach of
mine is as good a timepiece as is to be found in the Colony,
and it already p'ints to half-past twelve. So open the wallet
and let us wind up for another six hours' run."

At this suggestion both set themselves about making the
preparations necessary for their usual frugal but hearty meal.
We will profit by this pause in the discourse to give the
reader some idea of the appearance of the men, each of
whom is destined to enact no insignificant part in our legend.
It would not have been easy to find a more noble specimen of
vigorous manhood than was offered in the person of him
who called himself Hurry Harry. His real name was
Henry March; but the frontiersmen having caught the practice of giving sobriquets from the Indians, the appellation of
Hurry was far oftener applied to him than his proper desig-
nation, and not unfrequently he was termed Hurry-scurry, a
nickname he had obtained from a dashing, reckless, offhand
manner and a physical restlessness that kept him so constantly on the move as to cause him to be known along the
whole line of scattered habitations that lay between the
province and the Canadas. The stature of Hurry Harry exceeded six feet four, and being unusually well proportioned,
his strength fully realized the idea created by his gigantic
frame. The face did no discredit to the rest of the man, for it
was both good-humored and handsome. His air was free,
and though his manner necessarily partook of the rudeness
of a border life, the grandeur that pervaded so noble a phy-
sique prevented it from becoming altogether vulgar.

Deerslayer, as Hurry called his companion, was a very different person in appearance as well as in character. In stature,
he stood about six feet in his moccasins, but his frame was
comparatively light and slender, showing muscles, however,
that promised unusual agility, if not unusual strength. His
face would have had little to recommend it except youth,
were it not for an expression that seldom failed to win upon
those who had leisure to examine it and to yield to the
feeling of confidence it created. This expression was simply

that of guileless truth, sustained by an earnestness of purpose and a sincerity of feeling that rendered it remarkable. At times this air of integrity seemed to be so simple as to awaken the suspicion of a want of the usual means to discriminate between artifice and truth, but few came in serious contact with the man without losing this distrust in respect for his opinions and motives.

Both these frontiersmen were still young, Hurry having reached the age of six or eight and twenty, while Deerslayer was several years his junior. Their attire needs no particular description, though it may be well to add that it was composed in no small degree of dressed deerskins, and had the usual signs of belonging to those who pass their time between the skirts of civilized society and the boundless forests. There was, notwithstanding, some attention to smartness and the picturesque in the arrangements of Deerslayer's dress, more particularly in the part connected with his arms and accouterments. His rifle was in perfect condition, the handle of his hunting knife was neatly carved, his powder horn was ornamented with suitable devices lightly cut into the material, and his shot pouch was decorated with wampum. On the other hand, Hurry Harry, either from constitutional recklessness, or from a secret consciousness how little his appearance required artificial aids, wore everything in a careless, slovenly manner, as if he felt a noble scorn for the trifling accessories of dress and ornaments. Perhaps the peculiar effect of his fine form and great stature was increased, rather than lessened, by this unstudied and disdainful air of indifference.

"Come, Deerslayer, fall to and prove that you have a Delaware stomach, as you say you have had a Delaware edication," cried Hurry, setting the example by opening his mouth to receive a slice of cold venison steak that would have made an entire meal for a European peasant: "fall to, lad, and prove your manhood on this poor devil of a doe with your teeth, as you've already done with your rifle."

"Nay, nay, Hurry, there's little manhood in killing a doe, and that too out of season, though there might be some in bringing down a painter or a catamount," returned the other, disposing himself to comply. "The Delawares have given me my name, not so much on account of a bold heart, as on account of a quick eye and an actyve foot. There may not

be any cowardyce in overcoming a deer, but sartain it is there's no great valor."

"The Delawares themselves are no heroes," muttered Hurry through his teeth, the mouth being too full to permit it to be fairly opened, "or they would never have allowed them loping vagabonds, the Mingos, to make them women."

"That matter is not rightly understood—has never been rightly explained," said Deerslayer earnestly, for he was as zealous a friend as his companion was dangerous as an enemy; "the Mengwe fill the woods with their lies and misconstruct words and treaties. I have now lived ten years with the Delawares and know them to be as manful as any other nation, when the proper time to strike comes."

"Harkee, Master Deerslayer, since we are on the subject, we may as well open our minds to each other in a man-to-man way. Answer me one question: you have had so much luck among the game as to have gotten a title, it would seem, but did you ever hit anything human or intelligible? Did you ever pull trigger on an inimy that was capable of pulling one upon you?"

This question produced a singular collision between mortification and correct feeling in the bosom of the youth that was easily to be traced in the workings of his ingenuous countenance. The struggle was short, however, uprightness of heart soon getting the better of false pride and frontier boastfulness.

"To own the truth, I never did," answered Deerslayer, "seeing that a fitting occasion never offered. The Delawares have been peaceable since my sojourn with 'em, and I hold it to be onlawful to take the life of man except in open and generous warfare."

"What! Did you never find a fellow thieving among your traps and skins and do the law on him with your own hands, by way of saving the magistrates trouble, in the settlements, and the rogue himself the cost of the suit?"

"I am no trapper, Hurry," returned the young man proudly. "I live by the rifle, a we'pon at which I will not turn my back on any man of my years atween the Hudson and the St. Lawrence. I never offer a skin that has not a hole in its head besides them which natur' made to see with, or to breathe through."

"Aye, aye, this is all very well, in the animal way, though

it makes but a poor figure alongside of scalps and and-bushes. Shooting an Indian from an and-bush is acting up to his own principles, and now we have what you call a lawful war on our hands, the sooner you wipe that disgrace off your character, the sounder will be your sleep—if it only come from knowing there is one inimy the less prowling in the woods. I shall not frequent your society long, friend Natty, unless you look higher than four-footed beasts to practyse your rifle on."

"Our journey is nearly ended, you say, Master March, and we can part tonight, if you see occasion. I have a fri'nd waiting for me who will think it no disgrace to consort with a fellow creatur' that has never yet slain his kind."

"I wish I knew what has brought that skulking Delaware into this part of the country so early in the season," muttered Hurry to himself in a way to show equally distrust and a recklessness of its betrayal. "Where did you say the young chief was to give you the meeting?"

"At a small, round rock near the foot of the lake, where, they tell me, the tribes are given to resorting to make their treaties and to bury their hatchets. This rock have I often heard the Delawares mention, though lake and rock are equally strangers to me. The country is claimed by both Mingos and Mohicans and is a sort of common territory to fish and hunt through in time of peace, though what it may become in wartime the Lord only knows!"

"Common territory!" exclaimed Hurry, laughing aloud. "I should like to know what Floating Tom Hutter would say to that. He claims the lake as his own property, in vartue of fifteen years' possession, and will not be likely to give it up to either Mingo or Delaware without a battle for it."

"And what will the Colony say to such a quarrel? All this country must have some owner, the gentry pushing their cravings into the wilderness, even where they never dare to ventur', in their own person, to look at the land they own."

"That may do in other quarters of the Colony, Deerslayer, but it will not do here. Not a human being, the Lord excepted, owns a foot of s'ile in this part of the country. Pen was never put to paper, consarning either hill or valley, hereaway, as I've heard old Tom say, time and ag'in, and so he claims the best right to it of any man breathing; and what Tom claims, he'll be very likely to maintain."

"By what I've heard you say, Hurry, this Floating Tom must be an oncommon mortal—neither Mingo, Delaware, nor paleface. His possession, too, has been long, by your tell, and altogether beyond frontier endurance. What's the man's history and natur'?"

"Why, as to old Tom's human natur', it is not much like other men's human natur', but more like a muskrat's human natur', seeing that he takes more to the ways of that animal than to the ways of any other fellow creatur'. Some think he was a free liver on the salt water, in his youth, and a companion of a sartain Kidd, who was hanged for piracy, long afore you and I were born or acquainted, and that he came up into these regions thinking that the king's cruisers could never cross the mountains, and that he might enjoy the plunder peaceably in the woods."

"Then he was wrong, Hurry, very wrong. A man can enjoy plunder *peaceably* nowhere."

"That's much as his turn of mind may happen to be. I've known them that never could enjoy it at all, unless it was in the midst of a jollification, and them ag'in that enjoyed it best in a corner. Some men have no peace if they don't find plunder, and some if they do. Human natur' is crooked in these matters. Old Tom seems to belong to neither set, as he enjoys his—if plunder he has really got—with his darters in a very quiet and comfortable way, and wishes for no more."

"Aye, he has darters, too; I've heard the Delawares, who've hunted thisaway, tell their histories of these young women. Is there no mother, Hurry?"

"There was *once*, as in reason, but she has now been dead and sunk these two good years."

"Anan?" said Deerslayer, looking up at his companion in a little surprise.

"Dead and sunk, I say, and I hope that's good English. The old fellow lowered his wife into the lake, by way of seeing the last of her, as I can testify, being an eyewitness of the ceremony; but whether Tom did it to save digging, which is no easy job among roots, or out of a consait that water washes away sin sooner than 'arth is more than I can say."

"Was the poor woman oncommon wicked, that her husband should take so much pains with her body?"

"Not onreasonable, though she had her faults. I consider

Judith Hutter to have been as graceful and about as likely
to make a good ind as any woman who had lived so long
beyond the sound of church bells; and I conclude old Tom
sunk her as much by way of *saving* pains, as by way of
taking it. There was a little steel in her temper, it's true, and,
as old Hutter is pretty much flint, they struck out sparks once
and a while; but on the whole they might be said to live
amicable like. When they did kindle, the listeners got some
such insights into their past lives as one gets into the darker
parts of the woods when a stray gleam of sunshine finds its
way down to the roots of the trees. But Judith I shall always
esteem, as it's recommend enough to one woman to be the
mother of such a creatur' as her darter, Judith Hutter!"

"Aye, Judith was the name the Delawares mentioned,
though it was pronounced after a fashion of their own. From
their discourse, I do not think the girl would much please my
fancy."

"Thy fancy!" exclaimed March, taking fire equally at the
indifference and at the presumption of his companion. "What
the devil have you to do with a fancy, and that, too, consarning one like Judith? You are but a boy—a sapling that
has scarce got root. Judith has had *men* among her suitors
ever since she was fifteen—which is now near five years—
and will not be apt even to cast a look upon a half-grown
creatur' like you!"

"It is June, and there is not a cloud atween us and the
sun, Hurry, so all this heat is not wanted," answered the
other, altogether undisturbed; "anyone may have a fancy,
and a squirrel has a right to make up his mind touching a
catamount."

"Aye, but it might not be wise, always, to let the catamount know it," growled March. "But you're young and
thoughtless, and I'll overlook your ignorance. Come, Deerslayer," he added, with a good-natured laugh, after pausing a
moment to reflect, "come, Deerslayer, we are sworn fri'nds,
and will not quarrel about a light-minded, jilting jade just
because she happens to be handsome—more especially as
you have never seen her. Judith is only for a man whose
teeth show the full marks, and it's foolish to be afeard of
a boy. What *did* the Delawares say of the hussy?—for an
Indian, after all, has his notions of womankind as well as
a white man."

"They said she was fair to look on and pleasant of speech, but overgiven to admirers and light-minded."

"They are devils incarnate! After all, what schoolmaster is a match for an Indian in looking into natur'? Some people think they are only good on a trail or the warpath, but I say that they are philosophers and understand a man as well as they understand a beaver, and a woman as well as they understand either. Now that's Judith's character to a ribbon! To own the truth to you, Deerslayer, I should have married the gal two years since, if it had not been for two particular things, one of which was this very light-mindedness."

"And what may have been the other?" demanded the hunter, who continued to eat like one that took very little interest in the subject.

"T'other was an insartainty about her having *me*. The hussy is handsome, and she knows it. Boy, not a tree that is growing in these hills is straighter, or waves in the wind with an easier bend, nor did you ever see the doe that bounded with a more nat'ral motion. If that was all, every tongue would sound her praises; but she has such failings that I find it hard to overlook them, and sometimes I swear I'll never visit the lake ag'in."

"Which is the reason that you always come back? Nothing is ever made more sure by swearing about it."

"Ah, Deerslayer, you are a novelty in these partic'lars, keeping as true to edication as if you had never left the settlements. With me the case is different, and I never want to clinch an idee that I do not feel a wish to swear about it. If you know'd all that I know consarning Judith, you'd find a justification for a little cussing. Now, the officers sometimes stray over to the lake from the forts on the Mohawk to fish and hunt, and in then the creatur' seems beside herself! You can see it in the manner in which she wears her finery and the airs she gives herself with the gallants."

"That is unseemly in a poor man's darter," returned Deerslayer gravely. "The officers are all gentry and can only look on such as Judith with evil intentions."

"There's the unsartainty and the damper! I have my misgivings about a particular captain, and Jude has no one to blame but her own folly, if I'm wrong. On the whole, I wish to look upon her as modest and becoming, and yet the clouds that drive among these hills are not more un-

sartain. Not a dozen white men have ever laid eyes upon her since she was a child, and yet her airs, with two or three of these officers, are extinguishers!"

"I would think no more of such a woman but turn my mind altogether to the forest: *that* will not deceive you, being ordered and ruled by a hand that never wavers."

"If you know'd Judith, you would see how much easier it is to say this than it would be to do it. Could I bring my mind to be easy about the officers, I would carry the gal off to the Mohawk by force, make her marry me in spite of her whiffling, and leave old Tom to the care of Hetty, his other child, who, if she be not as handsome or as quick-witted as her sister, is much the most dutiful."

"Is there another bird in the same nest?" asked Deerslayer, raising his eyes with a species of half-awakened curiosity. "The Delawares spoke to me only of one."

"That's nat'ral enough, when Judith Hutter and Hetty Hutter are in question. Hetty is only comely, while her sister, I tell thee, boy, is such another as is not to be found atween this and the sea: Judith is as full of wit and talk and cunning as an old Indian orator, while poor Hetty is at the best but 'compass meant us.'"

"Anan?" inquired again the Deerslayer.

"Why, what the officers call 'compass meant us,' which I understand to signify that she means always to go in the right direction but sometimes doesn't know how. 'Compass' for the p'int, and 'meant us' for the intention. No, poor Hetty is what I call on the varge of ignorance, and sometimes she stumbles on one side of the line and sometimes on t'other."

"Them are beings that the Lord has in his special care," said Deerslayer solemnly, "for he looks carefully to all who fall short of their proper share of reason. The Redskins honor and respect them who are so gifted, knowing that the Evil Spirit delights more to dwell in an artful body than in one that has no cunning to work upon."

"I'll answer for it, then, that he will not remain long with poor Hetty—for the child is just 'compass meant us,' as I have told you. Old Tom has a feeling for the gal, and so has Judith, quick-witted and glorious as she is herself; else would I not answer for her being altogether safe among the sort of men that sometimes meet on the lake shore."

"I thought this water an onknown and little-frequented

sheet," observed the Deerslayer, evidently uneasy at the idea of being too near the world.

"It's all that, lad, the eyes of twenty white men never having been laid on it; still, twenty true-bred frontiersmen— hunters, and trappers, and scouts, and the like—can do a deal of mischief if they try. 'Twould be an awful thing to me, Deerslayer, did I find Judith married after an absence of six months!"

"Have you the gal's faith to incourage you to hope otherwise?"

"Not at all. I know not how it is—I'm good-looking, boy; that much I can see in any spring on which the sun shines— and yet I could never get the hussy to a promise, or even a cordial, willing smile, though she will laugh by the hour. If she *has* dared to marry in my absence, she'll be like to know the pleasures of widowhood afore she is twenty!"

"You would not harm the man she has chosen, Hurry, simply because she found him more to her liking than yourself?"

"Why not? If an inimy crosses my path, will I not beat him out of it! Look at me—am I a man like to let any sneaking, crawling skin trader get the better of me in a matter that touches me as near as the kindness of Judith Hutter? Besides, when we live beyond law, we must be our own judges and executioners. And if a man *should* be found dead in the woods, who is there to say who slew him, even admitting that the Colony took the matter in hand and made a stir about it?"

"If that man should be Judith Hutter's husband, after what has passed, I might tell enough, at least, to put the Colony on the trail."

"You half-grown, venison-hunting bantling! You dare to think of informing against Hurry Harry in so much as a matter touching a mink or a woodchuck!"

"I would dare to speak truth, Hurry, consarning you, or any man that ever lived."

March looked at his companion for a moment in silent amazement; then, seizing him by the throat with both hands, he shook his comparatively slight frame with a violence that menaced the dislocation of some of the bones. Nor was this done jocularly, for anger flashed from the giant's eyes, and there were certain signs that seemed to threaten much more earnestness than the occasion would appear to call for. What-

ever might be the real intention of March, and it is probable there was none settled in his mind, it is certain that he was unusually aroused; most men who found themselves throttled by one of a mold so gigantic, in such a mood, and in a solitude so deep and helpless, would have felt intimidated and tempted to yield even the right. Not so, however, with Deerslayer. His countenance remained unmoved, his hand did not shake, and his answer was given in a voice that did not resort to the artifice of louder tones, even by way of proving its owner's resolution.

"You may shake, Hurry, until you bring down the mountain," he said quietly, "but nothing beside truth will you shake from me. It is probable that Judith Hutter has no husband to slay, and you may never have a chance to waylay one, else would I tell her of your threat in the first conversation I held with the gal."

March released his grip and sat regarding the other in silent astonishment.

"I thought we had been friends," he at length added, "but you've got the last secret of mine that will ever enter your ears."

"I want none, if they are to be like this. I know we live in the woods, Hurry, and are thought to be beyond human laws—and perhaps we are so, in fact, whatever it may be in right—but there is a law, and a lawmaker, that rule across the whole continent. He that flies in the face of either need not call me fri'nd."

"Damme, Deerslayer, if I do not believe you are, at heart, a Moravian, and no fair-minded, plain-dealing hunter, as you've pretended to be!"

"Fair-minded or not, Hurry, you will find me as plain-dealing in deeds as I am in words. But this giving way to sudden anger is foolish and proves how little you have sojourned with the red man. Judith Hutter no doubt is still single, and you spoke but as the tongue ran and not as the heart felt. There's my hand, and we will say and think no more about it."

Hurry seemed more surprised than ever; then he burst forth in a loud, good-natured laugh, which brought tears to his eyes. After this, he accepted the offered hand, and the parties became friends.

" 'Twould have been foolish to quarrel about an idee," March cried as he resumed his meal, "and more like lawyers in the towns than like sensible men in the woods. They tell me, Deerslayer, much ill blood grows out of idees, among the people in the lower counties, and that they sometimes get to extremities upon them."

"That do they—that do they; and about other matters that might better be left to take care of themselves. I have heard the Moravians say that there are lands in which men quarrel even consarning their religion; if they can get their tempers up on such a subject, Hurry, the Lord have marcy on 'em. Howsever, there is no occasion for our following their example, and more especially about a husband that this Judith Hutter may never see, or never wish to see. For my part, I feel more cur'osity about the feeble-witted sister than about your beauty. There's something that comes close to a man's feelin's, when he meets with a fellow creatur' that has all the outward show of an accountable mortal and who fails of being what he seems only through a lack of reason. This is bad enough in a man, but when it comes to a woman, and she a young and maybe a winning creatur', it touches all the pitiful thoughts his natur' has. God knows, Hurry, that such poor things be defenseless enough with all their wits about 'em, but it's a cruel fortun' when that great protector and guide fails 'em."

"Harkee, Deerslayer—you know what the hunters, and trappers, and peltrymen in general be; their best friends will not deny that they are headstrong and given to having their own way, without much bethinking 'em of other people's rights or feelin's—and yet I don't think the man is to be found in all this region who would harm Hetty Hutter if he could; no, not even a redskin."

"Therein, fri'nd Hurry, you do the Delawares, at least, and all their allied tribes, only justice, for a redskin looks upon a being thus struck by God's power as especially under his care. I rejoice to hear what you say, howsever, I rejoice to hear it; but as the sun is beginning to turn toward the a'ternoon's sky, had we not better strike the trail ag'in, and make forward, that we may get an opportunity of seeing these wonderful sisters?"

Harry March giving a cheerful assent, the remnants of the

meal were soon collected; then the travelers shouldered their packs, resumed their arms, and, quitting the little area of light, they again plunged into the deep shadows of the forest.

CHAPTER II

Thou'rt passing from the lake's green side,
And the hunter's hearth away;
For the time of flowers, for the summer's pride,
Daughter! thou canst not stay.

RECORDS OF WOMAN

OUR TWO ADVENTURERS had not far to go. Hurry knew the direction as soon as he had found the open spot and the spring, and he now led on with the confident step of a man assured of his object. The forest was dark, as a matter of course, but it was no longer obstructed by underbrush, and the footing was firm and dry. After proceeding near a mile, March stopped and began to cast about him with an inquiring look, examining the different objects with care and occasionally turning his eyes on the trunks of the fallen trees, with which the ground was well sprinkled, as is usually the case in an American wood, especially in those parts of the country where timber has not yet become valuable.

"*This* must be the place, Deerslayer," March at length observed; "here is a beech by the side of a hemlock, with three pines at hand, and yonder is a white birch with a broken top; yet I see no rock, nor any of the branches bent down, as I told you would be the case."

"Broken branches are onskillful landmarks, as the least exper'enced know that branches don't often break of themselves," returned the other. "They also lead to suspicion and discoveries. The Delawares never trust to broken branches, unless it is in friendly times and on an open trail. As for the beeches and pines and hemlocks, why, they are to be seen on all sides of us, not only by twos and threes, but by forties, and fifties, and hundreds."

24

"Very true, Deerslayer, but you never calculate on position. Here is a beech and a hemlock——"

"Yes, and there is another beech and a hemlock, as loving as two brothers, or, for that matter, more loving than some brothers; and yonder are others, for neither tree is a rarity in these woods. I fear me, Hurry, you are better at trapping beaver and shooting bears than at leading on a blindish sort of a trail. Ha! There's what you wish to find, a'ter all!"

"Now, Deerslayer, this is one of your Delaware pretensions—hang me if I see anything but these trees, which do seem to start up around us in a most onaccountable and perplexing manner."

"Look thisaway, Hurry—here, in a line with the black oak —don't you see the crooked sapling that is hooked up in the branches of the basswood, near it? Now, that sapling was once snow-ridden, and got the bend by its weight, but it never straightened itself, and fastened itself in among the basswood branches in the way you see. The hand of man did that act of kindness for it."

"That hand was mine!" exclaimed Hurry. "I found the slender young thing bent to the airth, like an unfortunate creatur' borne down by misfortune, and stuck it up where you see it. After all, Deerslayer, I must allow, you're getting to have an oncommon good eye for the woods!"

"'Tis improving, Hurry—'tis improving, I will acknowledge; but 'tis still only a child's eye, compared to some I know. There's Tamenund, now, though a man so old that few remember when he was in his prime, Tamenund lets nothing escape his look, which is more like the scent of a hound than the sight of an eye. Then Uncas,* the father of Chingachgook and the lawful chief of the Mohicans, is another that it is almost hopeless to pass unseen. I'm improving, I will allow—I'm improving, but far from being perfect, as yet."

"And who is this Chingachgook of whom you talk so much, Deerslayer?" asked Hurry, as he moved off in the direction of the righted sapling; "a loping redskin, at the best, I make no question."

---

* Lest the similarity of the names should produce confusion, it may be well to say that the Uncas here mentioned is the grandfather of him who plays so conspicuous a part in *The Last of the Mohicans.*

"Not so, Hurry, but the best of loping redskins, as you call 'em. If he had his rights, he would be a great chief; as it is, he is only a brave and just-minded Delaware, respected and even obeyed in some things, 'tis true, but of a fallen race and belonging to a fallen people. Ah, Harry March, 'twould warm the heart within you to sit in their lodges of a winter's night and listen to the traditions of the ancient greatness and power of the Mohicans!"

"Harkee, fri'nd Nathaniel," said Hurry, stopping short to face his companion, in order that his words might carry greater weight with them, "if a man believed all that other people choose to say in their own favor, he might get an oversized opinion of them and an undersized opinion of himself. These redskins are notable boasters, and I set down more than half of their traditions as pure talk."

"There is truth in what you say, Hurry, I'll not deny it, for I've seen it, and believe it. They *do* boast, but then that is a gift from natur', and it's sinful to withstand nat'ral gifts. See, this is the spot you come to find!"

This remark cut short the discourse, and both the men now gave all their attention to the object immediately before them. Deerslayer pointed out to his companion the trunk of a huge linden, or basswood, as it is termed in the language of the country, which had filled its time and fallen by its own weight. This tree, like so many millions of its brethren, lay where it had fallen, and was moldering under the slow but certain influence of the seasons. The decay, however, had attacked its center even while it stood erect in the pride of vegetation, hollowing out its heart, as disease sometimes destroys the vitals of animal life, even while a fair exterior is presented to the observer. As the trunk lay stretched for near a hundred feet along the earth, the quick eye of the hunter detected this peculiarity, and from this and other circumstances he knew it to be the tree of which March was in search.

"Aye, here we have what we want," cried Hurry, looking in at the larger end of the linden. "Everything is as snug as if it had been left in an old woman's cupboard. Come, lend me a hand, Deerslayer, and we'll be afloat in half an hour."

At this call the hunter joined his companion, and the two went to work deliberately and regularly, like men

accustomed to the sort of thing in which they were employed. In the first place, Hurry removed some pieces of bark that lay before the large opening in the tree, which the other declared to be disposed in a way that would have been more likely to attract attention than to conceal the cover, had any straggler passed that way. The two then drew out a bark canoe containing its seats, paddles, and other appliances, even to fishing lines and rods. This vessel was by no means small, but such was its comparative lightness, and so gigantic was the strength of Hurry, that the latter shouldered it with seeming ease, declining all assistance, even in the act of raising it to the awkward position in which he was obliged to hold it.

"Lead ahead, Deerslayer," said March, "and open the bushes; the rest I can do for myself."

The other obeyed, and the men left the spot, Deerslayer clearing the way for his companion, and inclining to the right or to the left as the latter directed. In about ten minutes they both broke suddenly into the brilliant light of the sun on a low, gravelly point that was washed by water on quite half its outline.

An exclamation of surprise broke from the lips of Deerslayer—an exclamation that was low and guardedly made, however, for his habits were much more thoughtful and regulated than those of the reckless Hurry—when, on reaching the margin of the lake, he beheld the view that unexpectedly met his gaze. It was, in truth, sufficiently striking to merit a brief description. On a level with the point lay a broad sheet of water, so placid and limpid that it resembled a bed of the pure mountain atmosphere compressed into a setting of hills and woods. Its length was about three leagues, while its breadth was irregular, expanding to half a league, or even more, opposite to the point, and contracting to less than half that distance more to the southward. Of course, its margin was irregular, being indented by bays and broken by many projecting, low points. At its northern, or nearest end, it was bounded by an isolated mountain, lower land falling off east and west, gracefully relieving the sweep of the outline. Still, the character of the country was mountainous, high hills, or low mountains, rising abruptly from the water on quite nine-tenths of its circuit. The exceptions, indeed, only served

a little to vary the scene, and even beyond the parts of the shore that were comparatively low the background was high, though more distant.

But the most striking peculiarities of this scene were its solemn solitude and sweet repose. On all sides, wherever the eye turned, nothing met it but the mirrorlike surface of the lake, the placid view of heaven, and the dense setting of woods. So rich and fleecy were the outlines of the forest that scarce an opening could be seen, the whole visible earth, from the rounded mountaintop to the water's edge, presenting one unvaried hue of unbroken verdure. As if vegetation were not satisfied with a triumph so complete, the trees over-hung the lake itself, shooting out toward the light; there were miles along its eastern shore where a boat might have pulled beneath the branches of dark, Rembrandt-looking hemlocks, "quivering aspens," and melancholy pines. In a word, the hand of man had never yet defaced or deformed any part of this native scene, which lay bathed in the sun-light, a glorious picture of affluent forest grandeur, softened by the balminess of June and relieved by the beautiful va-riety afforded by the presence of so broad an expanse of water.

"This is grand!—'tis solemn!—'tis an edication of itself, to look upon!" exclaimed Deerslayer, as he stood leaning on his rifle and gazing to the right and left, north and south, above and beneath, in whichever direction his eye could wander. "Not a tree disturbed even by redskin hand, as I can discover, but everything left in the ordering of the Lord, to live and die according to His own designs and laws! Hurry, your Judith ought to be a moral and well-disposed young woman, if she has passed half the time you mention in the center of a spot so favored."

"That's a naked truth, and yet the gal has the vagaries. All her time has not been passed here, howsever, old Tom having the custom, afore I know'd him, of going to spend the winters in the neighborhood of the settlers, or under the guns of the forts. No, no, Jude has caught more than is for her good from the settlers, and especially from the gallantifying officers."

"If she has—if she has, Hurry, this is a school to set her mind right ag'in. But what is this I see off here, abreast of

us, that seems too small for an island and too large for a boat, though it stands in the midst of the water?"

"Why, that is what these gallanting gentry from the forts call Muskrat Castle; old Tom himself will grin at the name, though it bears so hard on his own natur' and character. 'Tis the stationary house, there being two—this, which never moves, and the other, that floats, being sometimes in one part of the lake and sometimes in another. The last goes by the name of the ark, though what may be the meaning of the word is more than I can tell you."

"It must come from the missionaries, Hurry, whom I have heard speak and read of such a thing. They say that the 'arth was once covered with water, and that Noah, with his children, was saved from drowning by building a vessel called an ark, in which he embarked in season. Some of the Delawares believe this tradition, and some deny it, but it behooves you and me, as white men born, to put our faith in its truth. Do you see anything of this ark?"

"'Tis down south, no doubt, or anchored in some of the bays. But the canoe is ready, and fifteen minutes will carry two such paddles as your'n and mine to the castle."

At this suggestion, Deerslayer helped his companion to place the different articles in the canoe, which was already afloat. This was no sooner done than the two frontiersmen embarked and, by a vigorous push, sent the light bark some eight or ten rods from the shore. Hurry now took the seat in the stern, while Deerslayer placed himself forward, and by leisurely but steady strokes of the paddles, the canoe glided across the placid sheet toward the extraordinary-looking structure that the former had styled Muskrat Castle. Several times the men ceased paddling and looked about them at the scene, as new glimpses opened from behind points, enabling them to see further down the lake, or to get broader views of the wooded mountains. The only changes, however, were in the new forms of the hills, the varying curvature of the bays, and the wider reaches of the valley south; the whole earth, apparently, being clothed in a gala dress of leaves.

"This is a sight to warm the heart!" exclaimed Deerslayer, when they had thus stopped for the fourth or fifth time. "The lake seems made to let us get an insight into the noble forests, and land and water alike stand in the beauty of

God's Providence! Do you say, Hurry, that there is no man
who calls himself lawful owner of all these glories?"

"None but the King, lad. He may pretend to some right
of that natur', but he is so far away that his claim will never
trouble old Tom Hutter, who has got possession, and is like
to keep it as long as his life lasts. Tom is no squatter, not
being on land; I call him a floater."

"I invy that man!—I know it's wrong, and I strive ag'in
the feelin', but I invy that man! Don't think, Hurry, that I'm
consarting any plan to put myself in his moccasins, for
such a thought doesn't harbor in my mind, but I can't help a
little invy! 'Tis a nat'ral feelin', and the best of us are but
nat'ral, a'ter all, and give way to such feelin's at times."

"You've only to marry Hetty to inherit half the estate,"
cried Hurry, laughing. "The gal is comely—nay, if it wasn't
for her sister's beauty, she would be even handsome; and
then her wits are so small that you may easily convart her
into one of your own way of thinking in all things. Do *you*
take Hetty off the old fellow's hands, and *I'll* engage he'll give
you an interest in every deer you can knock over within
five miles of his lake."

"Does game abound?" suddenly demanded the other, who
paid but little attention to March's raillery.

"It has the country to itself. Scarce a trigger is pulled on
it; and as for the trappers, this is not a region they greatly
frequent. I ought not to be so much here myself, but Jude
pulls one way while the beaver pulls another. More than a
hundred Spanish dollars has that creatur' cost me the two
last seasons, and yet I could not forego the wish to look upon
her face once more."

"Do the red men often visit this lake, Hurry?" continued
Deerslayer, pursuing his own train of thought.

"Why, they come and go, sometimes in parties and sometimes singly. The country seems to belong to no native tribe
in particular, and so it has fallen into the hands of the
Hutter tribe. The old man tells me that some sharp ones
have been wheedling the Mohawks for an Indian deed, in
order to get a title out of the Colony, but nothing has come
of it, seeing that no one heavy enough for such a trade has
yet meddled with the matter. The hunters have a good life
lease, still, of this wilderness."

"So much the better—so much the better, Hurry. If I was

King of England, the man that felled one of these trees without good occasion for the timber should be banished to a desarted and forlorn region in which no four-footed animal ever trod. Right glad am I that Chingachgook app'inted our meeting on this lake, for hitherto eye of mine never looked on such a glorious spectacle."

"That's because you've kept so much among the Delawares, in whose country there are no lakes. Now, farther north and farther west, these bits of water abound; and you're young and may yet live to see 'em. But though there be other lakes, Deerslayer, there's no other Judith Hutter!"

At this remark his companion smiled, and then he dropped his paddle into the water, as if in consideration of a lover's haste. Both now pulled vigorously until they got within a hundred yards of the "castle," as Hurry familiarly called the house of Hutter, when they again ceased paddling; the admirer of Judith restraining his impatience the more readily, as he perceived that the building was untenanted at the moment. This new pause was to enable Deerslayer to survey the singular edifice, which was of a construction so novel as to merit a particular description.

Muskrat Castle, as the house had been facetiously named by some waggish officer, stood in the open lake at a distance of fully a quarter of a mile from the nearest shore. On every other side the water extended much farther, the precise position being distant about two miles from the northern end of the sheet and near, if not quite, a mile from its eastern shore. As there was not the smallest appearance of any island —the house stood on piles, with the water flowing beneath it —and Deerslayer had already discovered that the lake was of a great depth, he was fain to ask an explanation of this singular circumstance. Hurry solved the difficulty by telling him that on this spot alone a long, narrow shoal, which extended for a few hundred yards in a north and south direction, rose within six or eight feet of the surface of the lake, and that Hutter had driven piles into it and placed his habitation on them for the purpose of security.

"The old fellow was burnt out three times, atween the Indians and the hunters, and in one affray with the redskins he lost his only son, since which time he has taken to the water for safety. No one can attack him here without coming in a boat, and the plunder and scalps would scarce be worth

the trouble of digging out canoes. Then it's by no means
sartain which would whip in such a scrimmage, for old
Tom is well supplied with arms and ammunition, and the
castle, as you may see, is a tight breastwork ag'in light
shot."

Deerslayer had some theoretical knowledge of frontier
warfare, though he had never yet been called on to raise his
hand in anger against a fellow creature. He saw that Hurry
did not overrate the strength of this position from a military
point of view, since it would not be easy to attack it without
exposing the assailants to the fire of the besieged. A good
deal of art had also been manifested in the disposition of the
timber of which the building was constructed, and which
afforded a protection much greater than was usual to the
ordinary log cabins of the frontier. The sides and ends were
composed of the trunks of large pines, cut about nine feet
long and placed upright, instead of being laid horizontally,
as was the practice of the country. These logs were squared
on three sides, and had large tenons on each end. Massive
sills were secured on the heads of the piles, with suitable
grooves dug out of their upper surfaces, which had been
squared for the purpose, and the lower tenons of the upright
pieces were placed in these grooves, giving them a secure
fastening below. Plates had been laid on the upper ends of
the upright logs, and were kept in their places by a similar
contrivance, the several corners of the structure being well
fastened by scarfing and pinning the sills and plates. The
floors were made of smaller logs, similarly squared, and the
roof was composed of light poles, firmly united and well
covered with bark. The effect of this ingenious arrangement
was to give its owner a house that could be approached only
by water, the sides of which were composed of logs closely
wedged together, which were two feet thick in their thinnest
parts, and which could be separated only by a deliberate
and laborious use of human hands, or by the slow operation
of time. The outer surface of the building was rude and
uneven, the logs being of unequal sizes, but the squared
surfaces within gave both the sides and floor as uniform an
appearance as was desired, either for use or show. The
chimney was not the least singular portion of the castle,
as Hurry made his companion observe, while he explained
the process by which it had been made. The material was a

stiff clay, properly worked, which had been put together in a mold of sticks and suffered to harden, a foot or two at a time, commencing at the bottom. When the entire chimney had thus been raised and had been properly bound in with outward props, a brisk fire was kindled, and kept going until it was burned to something like a brick-red. This had not been an easy operation, nor had it succeeded entirely, but by dint of filling the cracks with fresh clay, a safe fireplace and chimney had been obtained in the end. This part of the work stood on the log floor, secured beneath by an extra pile. There were a few other peculiarities about this dwelling, which will better appear in the course of the narrative.

"Old Tom is full of contrivances," added Hurry, "and he set his heart on the success of his chimney, which threatened more than once to give out altogether; but parseverance will even overcome smoke, and now he has a comfortable cabin of it, though it did promise, at one time, to be a chinky sort of a flue to carry flames and fire."

"You seem to know the whole history of the castle, Hurry, chimney and sides," said Deerslayer, smiling. "Is love so overcoming that it causes a man to study the story of his sweetheart's habitation?"

"Partly that, lad, and partly eyesight," returned the good-natured giant, laughing. "There was a large gang of us in at the lake the summer the old fellow built, and we helped him along with the job. I raised no small part of the weight of them uprights with my own shoulders, and the axes flew, I can inform you, Master Natty, while we were bee-ing it among the trees ashore. The old devil is no way stingy about food, and as we had often eat at his hearth, we thought we would just house him comfortably afore we went to Albany with our skins. Yes, many is the meal I've swallowed in Tom Hutter's cabins, and Hetty, though so weak in the way of wits, has a wonderful particular way about a frying pan or a gridiron!"

While the parties were thus discoursing, the canoe had been gradually drawing nearer to the "castle," and was now so close as to require but a single stroke of a paddle to reach the landing. This was at a floored platform in front of the entrance that might have been some twenty feet square.

"Old Tom calls this sort of a wharf his dooryard," observed Hurry, as he fastened the canoe after he and his

companion had left it, "and the gallants from the forts have named it the 'castle court,' though what a 'court' can have to do here is more than I can tell you, seeing that there is no law. 'Tis as I supposed—not a soul within, but the whole family is off on a v'y'ge of discovery!"

While Hurry was bustling about the "dooryard," examining the fishing spears, rods, nets, and other similar appliances of a frontier cabin, Deerslayer, whose manner was altogether more rebuked and quiet, entered the building with a curiosity that was not usually exhibited by one so long trained in Indian habits. The interior of the "castle" was as faultlessly neat as its exterior was novel. The entire space, some twenty feet by forty, was subdivided into several small sleeping rooms, the apartment into which he first entered serving equally for the ordinary uses of its inmates and for a kitchen. The furniture was of the strange mixture that it is not uncommon to find in the remotely situated log tenements of the interior. Most of it was rude and to the last degree rustic, but there was a clock, with a handsome case of dark wood, in a corner, and two or three chairs, with a table and bureau, that had evidently come from some dwelling of more than usual pretension. The clock was industriously ticking, but its leaden-looking hands did no discredit to their dull aspect, for they pointed to the hour of eleven, though the sun plainly showed it was some time past the turn of the day. There was also a dark, massive chest. The kitchen utensils were of the simplest kind and far from numerous, but every article was in its place, and showed the nicest care in its condition.

After Deerslayer had cast a look about him in the outer room, he raised a wooden latch and entered a narrow passage that divided the inner end of the house into two equal parts. Frontier usages being no way scrupulous, and his curiosity being strongly excited, the young man now opened a door, and found himself in a bedroom. A single glance sufficed to show that the apartment belonged to females. The bed was of the feathers of wild geese and filled nearly to overflowing, but it lay in a rude bunk, raised only a foot from the floor. On one side of it were arranged on pegs various dresses of a quality much superior to what one would expect to meet in such a place, with ribbons, and other similar articles to correspond. Pretty shoes, with handsome silver buckles, such

as were then worn by females in easy circumstances, were not wanting, and no less than six fans, of gay colors, were placed half open in a way to catch the eye by their conceits and hues. Even the pillow, on this side of the bed, was covered with finer linen than its companion, and it was ornamented with a small ruffle. A cap, coquettishly decorated with ribbons, hung above it, and a pair of long gloves, such as were rarely used in those days by persons of the laboring classes, were pinned ostentatiously to it, as if with an intention to exhibit them there, if they could not be shown on the owner's arms.

All this Deerslayer saw and noted with a degree of minuteness that would have done credit to the habitual observation of his friends the Delawares. Nor did he fail to perceive the distinction that existed between the appearances on the different sides of the bed, the head of which stood against the wall. On that opposite to the one just described, everything was homely and uninviting, except through its perfect neatness. The few garments that were hanging from the pegs were of the coarsest materials and of the commonest forms, while nothing seemed made for show. Of ribbons there was not one, nor was there either cap or kerchief beyond those which Hutter's daughters might be fairly entitled to wear.

It was now several years since Deerslayer had been in a spot especially devoted to the uses of females of his own color and race. The sight brought back to his mind a rush of childish recollections, and he lingered in the room with a tenderness of feeling to which he had long been a stranger. He bethought him of his mother, whose homely vestments he remembered to have seen hanging on pegs like those which he felt must belong to Hetty Hutter, and he bethought himself of a sister, whose incipient and native taste for finery had exhibited itself somewhat in the manner of that of Judith, though necessarily in a less degree. These little resemblances opened a long hidden vein of sensations, and as he quitted the room, it was with a saddened mien. He looked no further but returned slowly and thoughtfully toward the "dooryard."

"Old Tom has taken to a new calling, and has been trying his hand at the traps," cried Hurry, who had been coolly examining the borderer's implements. "If that is his humor, and you're disposed to remain in these parts, we can make an oncommon comfortable season of it; for, while the old man

and I outknowledge the beaver, you can fish and knock down the deer to keep body and soul together. We always give the poorest hunters half a share, but one as actyve and sartain as yourself might expect a full one."

"Thank'ee, Hurry, thank'ee with all my heart—but I do a little beavering for myself as occasions offer. 'Tis true, the Delawares call me Deerslayer, but it's not so much because I'm pretty fatal with the venison as because that while I kill so many bucks and does, I've never yet taken the life of a fellow creatur'. They say their traditions do not tell of another who had shed so much blood of animals that had not shed the blood of man."

"I hope they don't account you chicken-hearted, lad? A fainthearted man is like a no-tailed beaver."

"I don't believe, Hurry, that they account me as out-of-the-way timorsome, even though they may not account me as out-of-the-way brave. But I'm not quarrelsome, and that goes a great way toward keeping blood off the hands, among the hunters and redskins—and then, Harry March, it keeps blood off the conscience, too."

"Well, for my part I account game, a redskin, and a Frenchman as pretty much the same thing, though I'm as onquarrelsome a man, too, as there is in all the colonies. I despise a quarreler as I do a cur dog, but one has no need to be overscrupulsome when it's the right time to show the flint."

"I look upon him as the most of a man who acts nearest the right, Hurry. But this is a glorious spot, and my eyes never a-weary looking at it!"

" 'Tis your first acquaintance with a lake, and these idees come over us all at such times. Lakes have a general character, as I say, being pretty much water and land and points and bays."

As this definition by no means met the feelings that were uppermost in the mind of the young hunter, he made no immediate answer, but stood gazing at the dark hills and the glassy water in silent enjoyment.

"Have the Governor's or the King's people given this lake a name?" he suddenly asked, as if struck with a new idea. "If they've not begun to blaze their trees, and set up their compasses, and line off their maps, it's likely they've not bethought them to disturb natur' with a name."

"They've not got to that, yet; the last time I went in with skins, one of the King's surveyors was questioning me consarning all the region hereabouts. He had heard that there was a lake in this quarter and had got some general notions about it, such as that there was water and hills, but how much of either he knowed no more than you know of the Mohawk tongue. I didn't open the trap any wider than was necessary, giving him but poor encouragement in the way of farms and clearings. In short, I left on his mind some such opinion of this country as a man gets of a spring of dirty water, with a path to it that is so muddy that one mires afore he sets out. He told me they hadn't got the spot down yet on their maps, though I conclude that is a mistake, for he showed me his parchment, and there is a lake down on it where there is no lake in fact, and which is about fifty miles from the place where it ought to be, if they meant it for this. I don't think my account will encourage him to mark down another, by way of improvement."

Here Hurry laughed heartily, such tricks being particularly grateful to a set of men who dreaded the approaches of civilization as a curtailment of their own lawless empire. The egregious errors that existed in the maps of the day, all of which were made in Europe, was, moreover, a standing topic of ridicule among them; for, if they had not science enough to make any better themselves, they had sufficient local information to detect the gross blunders contained in those that existed. Anyone who will take the trouble to compare these unanswerable evidences of the topographical skill of our fathers a century since with the more accurate sketches of our own time will at once perceive that the men of the woods had a sufficient justification for all their criticism on this branch of the skill of the colonial governments, which did not at all hesitate to place a river or a lake a degree or two out of the way, even though they lay within a day's march of the inhabited parts of the country.

"I'm glad it has no name," resumed Deerslayer, "or, at least, no paleface name, for their christenings always foretell waste and destruction. No doubt, howsever, the redskins have their modes of knowing it, and the hunters and trappers, too; they are likely to call the place by something reasonable and resembling."

"As for the tribes, each has its own tongue and its own

way of calling things, and they treat this part of the world just as they treat all others. Among ourselves we've got to calling the place the 'Glimmerglass,' seeing that its whole basin is so often fringed with pines cast upward from its face, as if it would throw back the hills that hang over it."

"There is an outlet, I know, for all lakes have outlets, and the rock at which I am to meet Chingachgook stands near an outlet. Has *that* no colony name yet?"

"In that particular they've got the advantage of us, having one end, and that the biggest, in their own keeping; they've given it a name which has found its way up to its source, names nat'rally working upstream. No doubt, Deerslayer, you've seen the Susquehanna, down in the Delaware country?"

"That have I, and hunted along its banks a hundred times."

"That and this are the same, in fact, and, I suppose, the same in sound. I am glad they've been compelled to keep the red men's name, for it would be too hard to rob them of both land and name!"

Deerslayer made no answer, but he stood leaning on his rifle, gazing at the view which so much delighted him. The reader is not to suppose, however, that it was the picturesque alone which so strongly attracted his attention. The spot was very lovely, of a truth, and it was then seen in one of its most favorable moments, the surface of the lake being as smooth as glass and as limpid as pure air, throwing back the mountains, clothed in dark pines, along the whole of its eastern boundary, the points thrusting forward their trees even to nearly horizontal lines, while the bays were seen glittering through an occasional arch beneath, left by a vault fretted with branches and leaves. It was the air of deep repose—the solitudes that spoke of scenes and forests untouched by the hands of man—the reign of nature, in a word, that gave so much pure delight to one of his habits and turn of mind. Still, he felt, though it was unconsciously, like a poet also. If he found a pleasure in studying this large and, to him, unusual opening into the mysteries and forms of the woods, as one is gratified in getting broader views of any subject that has long occupied his thoughts, he was not insensible to the innate loveliness of such a landscape either, but felt a portion of that soothing of the spirit which is a common attendant of a scene so thoroughly pervaded by the holy calm of nature.

CHAPTER III

Come, shall we go and kill us venison?
And yet it irks me, the poor dappled fools,—
Being native burghers of this desert city,—
Should, in their own confines, with forked heads
Have their round haunches gored.

SHAKESPEARE

HURRY HARRY THOUGHT more of the beauties of Judith Hutter than of those of the Glimmerglass and its accompanying scenery. As soon as he had taken a sufficiently intimate survey of Floating Tom's implements, therefore, he summoned his companion to the canoe, that they might go down the lake in quest of the family. Previously to embarking, however, Hurry carefully examined the whole of the northern end of the water with an indifferent ship's glass that formed a part of Hutter's effects. In this scrutiny no part of the shore was overlooked; the bays and points, in particular, being subjected to a closer inquiry than the rest of the wooded boundary.

" 'Tis as I thought," said Hurry, laying aside the glass, "the old fellow is drifting about the south end, this fine weather, and has left the castle to defend itself. Well, now we know that he is not up thisaway, 'twill be but a small matter to paddle down and hunt him up in his hiding place."

"Does Master Hutter think it necessary to burrow on this lake?" inquired Deerslayer, as he followed his companion into the canoe. "To my eye it is such a solitude as one might open his whole soul in and fear no one to disarrange his thoughts or his worship."

"You forget your friends, the Mingos, and all the French savages. Is there a spot on 'arth, Deerslayer, to which them disquiet rogues don't go? Where is the lake, or even the deer

lick, that the blackguards don't find out and, having found out, don't sooner or later discolor its water with blood?"

"I hear no good character of them, sartainly, friend Hurry, though I've never been called on, as yet, to meet them, or any other mortal, on the warpath. I dare to say that such a lovely spot as this would not be likely to be overlooked by such plunderers; for though I've not been in the way of quarreling with them tribes myself, the Delawares give me such an account of 'em that I've pretty much set 'em down, in my own mind, as thorough miscreants."

"You may do that with a safe conscience, or, for that matter, any other savage you may happen to meet."

Here Deerslayer protested, and as they went paddling down the lake a hot discussion was maintained concerning the respective merits of the palefaces and the redskins. Hurry had all the prejudices and antipathies of a white hunter, who generally regards the Indian as a sort of natural competitor and, not unfrequently, as a natural enemy. As a matter of course he was loud, clamorous, dogmatic, and not very argumentative. Deerslayer, on the other hand, manifested a very different temper, proving, by the moderation of his language, the fairness of his views, and the simplicity of his distinctions, that he possessed every disposition to hear reason, a strong, innate desire to do justice, and an ingenuousness that was singularly indisposed to have recourse to sophisms to maintain an argument, or to defend a prejudice. Still, he was not altogether free from the influence of the latter feeling. This tyrant of the human mind, which rushes on its prey through a thousand avenues almost as soon as men begin to think and feel, and which seldom relinquishes its iron sway until they cease to do either, had made some impression on even the just propensities of this individual, who probably offered in these particulars a fair specimen of what absence from bad example, the want of temptation to go wrong, and native good feeling can render youth.

"You will allow, Deerslayer, that a Mingo is more than half devil," cried Hurry, following up the discussion with an animation that touched closely on ferocity, "though you want to overpersuade me that the Delaware tribe is pretty much made up of angels. Now, I gainsay that proposal, consarning white men, even. All white men are not fault-

less, and therefore all Indians *can't* be faultless. And so your argument is out at the elbow in the start. But, this is what I call reason. Here's three colors on 'arth—white, black, and red. White is the highest color, and therefore the best man; black comes next, and is put to live in the neighborhood of the white man, as tolerable and fit to be made use of; and red comes last, which shows that those that made 'em never expected an Indian to be accounted as more than half human."

"God made all three alike, Hurry."

"Alike! Do you call a nigger like a white man, or me like an Indian?"

"You go off at half-cock and don't hear me out. God made us all—white, black, and red—and no doubt had his own wise intentions in coloring us differently. Still, he made us, in the main, much the same in feelin's, though I'll not deny that he gave each race its gifts. A white man's gifts are Christianized, while a redskin's are more for the wilderness. Thus, it would be a great offense for a white man to scalp the dead, whereas it's a signal vartue in an Indian. Then ag'in, a white man cannot amboosh women and children in war, while a redskin may. 'Tis *cruel* work, I'll allow, but for them it's *lawful* work, while for *us* it would be grievous work."

"That depends on your inimy. As for scalping, or even skinning a savage, I look upon them pretty much the same as cutting off the ears of wolves for the bounty, or stripping a bear of its hide. And then you're out significantly, as to taking the poll of a redskin in hand, seeing that the very Colony has offered a bounty for the job, all the same as it pays for wolves' ears and crows' heads."

"Aye, and a bad business it is, Hurry. Even the Indians themselves cry shame on it, seeing it's ag'in a white man's gifts. I do not pretend that all that white men do is properly Christianized and according to the lights given them, for then they would be what they *ought* to be—which we know they are not; but I will maintain that tradition, and use, and color, and laws make such a difference in races as to amount to gifts. I do not deny that there are tribes among the Indians that are nat'rally pervarse and wicked, as there are nations among the whites. Now, I account the Mingos as belonging to the first and the Frenchers, in the Canadas, to the last. In a state of lawful warfare such as we have

lately got into, it is a duty to keep down all compassionate feelin's, so far as life goes, ag'in either; but when it comes to scalps, it's a very different matter."

"Just hearken to reason, if you please, Deerslayer, and tell me if the Colony can make an onlawful law? Isn't an onlawful law more ag'in natur' than scalpin' a savage? A law can no more be onlawful than truth can be a lie."

"That *sounds* reasonable, but it has a most onreasonable bearing, Hurry. Laws don't all come from the same quarter. God has given us his'n, and some come from the Colony and others come from the King and Parliament. When the Colony's laws, or even the King's laws, run ag'in the laws of God, they get to be onlawful and ought not to be obeyed. I hold to a white man's respecting white laws, so long as they do not cross the track of a law comin' from a higher authority; and for a red man to obey his own redskin usages under the same privilege. But 'tis useless talking, as each man will think for himself and have his say agreeable to his thoughts. Let us keep a good lookout for your friend Floating Tom, lest we pass him, as he lies hidden under this bushy shore."

Deerslayer had not named the borders of the lake amiss. Along their whole length, the smaller trees overhung the water, with their branches often dipping in the transparent element. The banks were steep, even from the narrow strand, and as vegetation invariably struggles toward the light, the effect was precisely that at which the lover of the picturesque would have aimed, had the ordering of this glorious setting of forest been submitted to his control. The points and bays, too, were sufficiently numerous to render the outline broken and diversified. As the canoe kept close along the western side of the lake, with a view, as Hurry had explained to his companion, of reconnoitering for enemies before he trusted himself too openly in sight, the expectations of the two adventurers were kept constantly on the stretch, as neither could foretell what the next turning of a point might reveal. Their progress was swift, the gigantic strength of Hurry enabling him to play with the light bark as if it had been a feather, while the skill of his companion almost equalized their usefulness, notwithstanding the disparity in natural means.

Each time the canoe passed a point, Hurry turned a look behind him, expecting to see the "ark" anchored, or beached

in the bay. He was fated to be disappointed, however; they had got within a mile of the southern end of the lake, or a distance of quite two leagues from the "castle," which was now hidden from view by half a dozen intervening projections of the land, when he suddenly ceased paddling, as if uncertain in what direction next to steer.

"It is possible that the old chap has dropped into the river," said Hurry, after looking carefully along the whole of the eastern shore, which was about a mile distant and open to his scrutiny for more than half its length; "for he has taken to trapping considerable, of late, and barring flood wood, he might drop down it a mile or so, though he would have a most scratching time in getting back again!"

"Where is this outlet?" asked Deerslayer; "I see no opening in the banks or the trees that looks as if it would let a river like the Susquehanna run through it."

"Aye, Deerslayer, rivers are like human mortals, having small beginnings and ending with broad shoulders and wide mouths. You don't see the outlet because it passes atween high, steep banks, and the pines, and hemlocks, and basswoods hang over it as a roof hangs over a house. If old Tom is not in the 'Rat's Cove,' he must have burrowed in the river; we'll look for him first in the cove, and then we'll cross to the outlet."

As they proceeded, Hurry explained that there was a shallow bay formed by a long, low point that had got the name of the "Rat's Cove," from the circumstance of its being a favorite haunt of the muskrat, and which offered so complete a cover for the "ark" that its owner was fond of lying in it whenever he found it convenient.

"As a man never knows who may be his visitors in this part of the country," continued Hurry, "it's a great advantage to get a good look at 'em before they come too near. Now it's war, such caution is more than commonly useful, since a Canada man or a Mingo might get into his hut afore he invited 'em. But Hutter is a first-rate look-outer and can pretty much scent danger, as a hound scents the deer."

"I should think the castle so open that it would be sartain to draw inimies, if any happened to find the lake; a thing onlikely enough, I will allow, as it's off the trail of the forts and settlements."

"Why, Deerslayer, I've got to believe that a man meets

with inimies easier than he meets with fri'nds. It's skearful to think for how many causes one gets to be your inimy and for how few your fri'nd. Some take up the hatchet because you don't think just as they think; other some because you run ahead of 'em in the same idees; I once know'd a vaga-bond that quarreled with a fri'nd because he didn't think him handsome. Now, you're no monument in the way of beauty yourself, Deerslayer, and yet you wouldn't be so on-reasonable as to become my inimy for just saying so."

"I'm as the Lord made me, and I wish to be accounted no better, nor any worse. Good looks I may not have—that is to say, to a degree that the light-minded and vain crave—but I hope I'm not altogether without some ricommend in the way of good conduct. There's few nobler looking men to be seen than yourself, Hurry, and I know that I am not to expect any to turn their eyes on me when such a one as you can be gazed on; but I do not know that a hunter is less expart with the rifle, or less to be relied on for food, because he doesn't wish to stop at every shining spring he may meet to study his own countenance in the water."

Here Hurry burst into a fit of loud laughter, for while he was too reckless to care much about his own manifest phys-ical superiority, he was well aware of it, and like most men who derive an advantage from the accidents of birth or nature, he was apt to think complacently on the subject, whenever it happened to cross his mind.

"No, no, Deerslayer, you're no beauty, as you will own yourself, if you'll look over the side of the canoe," he cried. "Jude will say *that* to your face, if you start her, for a parter tongue isn't to be found in any gal's head, in or out of the settlements, if you provoke her to use it. My advice to you is never to aggravate Judith, though you may tell any-thing to Hetty, and she'll take it as meek as a lamb. No, Jude will be just as like as not to tell you her opinion con-sarning your looks."

"And if she does, Hurry, she will tell me no more than you have said already——"

"You're not thick'ning up about a small remark, I hope, Deerslayer, when no harm is meant. You are *not* a beauty, as you must know, and why shouldn't fri'nds tell each other these little trifles? If you *was* handsome, or ever like to be, I'd be one of the first to tell you of it; and that ought to

content you. Now, if Jude was to tell me that I'm as ugly as a sinner, I'd take it as a sort of obligation and try not to believe her."

"It's easy for them that natur' has favored to jest about such matters, Hurry, though it is sometimes hard for others. I'll not deny but I've had my cravings toward good looks— yes, I have—but then I've always been able to get them down by considering how many I've known with fair outsides who have had nothing to boast of inwardly. I'll not deny, Hurry, that I often wish I'd been created more comely to the eye, more like such a one as yourself in them particulars, but then I get the feelin' under by remembering how much better off I am in a great many respects than some fellow mortals. I might have been born lame and onfit even for a squirrel hunt; or blind, which would have made me a burden on myself as well as on my fri'nds; or without hearing, which would have totally onqualified me for ever campaigning or scouting, which I look forward to as part of a man's duty in troublesome times. Yes, yes, it's not pleasant, I will allow, to see them that's more comely, and more sought a'ter, and honored than yourself, but it may all be borne, if a man looks the evil in the face, and don't mistake his gifts and his obligations."

Hurry, in the main, was a goodhearted as well as good-natured fellow, and the self-abasement of his companion completely got the better of the passing feeling of personal vanity. He regretted the allusion he had made to the other's appearance and endeavored to express as much, though it was done in the uncouth manner that belonged to the habits and opinions of the frontier.

"I meant no harm, Deerslayer," he answered, in a depre-cating manner, "and hope you'll forget what I've said. If you're not downright handsome, you've a sartain look that says, plainer than any words, that all's right within. Then you set no valie by looks, and will the sooner forgive any little slight to your appearance. I will not say that Jude will greatly admire you, for that might raise hopes that would only breed disapp'intment; but there's Hetty, now, would be just as likely to find satisfaction in looking at *you* as in looking at any other man. Then you're altogether too grave and considerate like to care much about Judith, for though the gal *is* oncommon, she is so general in her admiration

that a man need not be exalted because she happens to smile. I sometimes think the hussy loves herself better than she does anything else breathin'!"

"If she did, Hurry, she'd do no more, I'm afeard, than most queens on their thrones and ladies in the towns," answered Deerslayer, smiling and turning back toward his companion with every trace of feeling banished from his honest-looking and frank countenance. "I never yet know'd even a Delaware of whom you might not say that much. But here is the end of the long p'int you mentioned, and the 'Rat's Cove' can't be far off."

This point, instead of thrusting itself forward like all the others, ran in a line with the main shore of the lake, which here swept within it, in a deep and retired bay, circling around south again, at the distance of a quarter of a mile, and crossed the valley, forming the southern termination of the water. In this bay Hurry felt almost certain of finding the ark, since, anchored behind the trees that covered the narrow strip of the point, it might have lain concealed from prying eyes an entire summer. So complete, indeed, was the cover in this spot that a boat hauled close to the beach, within the point and near the bottom of the bay, could by possibility be seen from only one direction, and that was from a densely wooded shore within the sweep of the water, where strangers would be little apt to go.

"We shall soon see the ark," said Hurry, as the canoe glided around the extremity of the point, where the water was so deep as actually to appear black. "He loves to burrow up among the rushes, and we shall be in his nest in five minutes, although the old fellow may be off among the traps himself."

March proved a false prophet. The canoe completely doubled the point, so as to enable the two travelers to command a view of the whole cove or bay, for it was more properly the last, and no object, but those that nature had placed there became visible. The placid water swept around in a graceful curve, the rushes bent gently toward its surface, and the trees overhung it as usual, but all lay in the soothing and sublime solitude of a wilderness. The scene was such as a poet or an artist would have delighted in, but it had no charm for Hurry Harry, who was burning with impatience to get a sight of his light-minded beauty.

The motion of the canoe had been attended with little or no noise, the frontiersmen habitually getting accustomed to caution in most of their movements, and it now lay on the glassy water appearing to float in air, partaking of the breathing stillness that seemed to pervade the entire scene. At this instant a dry stick was heard cracking on the narrow strip of land that concealed the bay from the open lake. Both the adventurers started, and each extended a hand toward his rifle, the weapon never being out of reach of the arm.

" 'Twas too heavy for any light creatur'," whispered Hurry, "and it sounded like the tread of a man!"

"Not so—not so," returned Deerslayer; " 'twas, as you say, too heavy for one, but it was too light for the other. Put your paddle in the water and send the canoe in to that log; I'll land and cut off the creatur's retreat up the p'int be it a Mingo, or be it only a muskrat."

As Hurry complied, Deerslayer was soon on the shore, advancing into the thicket with a moccasined foot and a caution that prevented the least noise. In a minute he was in the center of the narrow strip of land and moving slowly down toward its end, the bushes rendering extreme watchfulness necessary. Just as he reached the center of the thicket, the dried twigs cracked again, and the noise was repeated at short intervals, as if some creature having life walked slowly toward the point. Hurry heard these sounds also, and pushing the canoe off into the bay, he seized his rifle to watch the result. A breathless minute succeeded, after which a noble buck walked out of the thicket, proceeded with a stately step to the sandy extremity of the point, and began to slake his thirst from the water of the lake. Hurry hesitated an instant; then, raising his rifle hastily to his shoulder, he took sight and fired. The effect of this sudden interruption of the solemn stillness of such a scene was not its least striking peculiarity. The report of the weapon had the usual sharp, short sound of the rifle, but when a few moments of silence had succeeded the sudden crack, during which the noise was floating in air across the water, it reached the rocks of the opposite mountain, where the vibrations accumulated, and were rolled from cavity to cavity for miles along the hills, seeming to awaken the sleeping thunders of the woods. The buck merely shook his head at the report of the rifle and the whistling of the bullet, for never before had he come in contact with man, but

the echoes of the hills awakened his distrust, and, leaping forward, with his four legs drawn under his body, he fell at once into deep water and began to swim toward the foot of the lake. Hurry shouted and dashed forward in chase, and for one or two minutes the water foamed around the pursuer and the pursued. The former was dashing past the point, when Deerslayer appeared on the sand and signed to him to return.

" 'Twas inconsiderate to pull a trigger afore we had reconn'itered the shore and made sartain that no inimies harbored near it," said the latter, as his companion slowly and reluctantly complied. "This much I have l'arned from the Delawares, in the way of schooling and traditions, even though I've never yet been on a warpath. And moreover, venison can hardly be called in season now, and we do not want for food. They call me Deerslayer, I'll own; and perhaps I desarve the name, in the way of understanding the creatur's habits, as well as for sartainty in the aim; but they can't accuse me of killing an animal when there is no occasion for the meat or the skin. I may be a slayer, it's true, but I'm no slaughterer."

" 'Twas an awful mistake to miss that buck!" exclaimed Hurry, doffing his cap and running his fingers through his handsome but matted curls, as if he would loosen his tangled ideas by the process. "I've not done so onhandy a thing since I was fifteen."

"Never lament it; the creatur's death could have done neither of us any good and might have done us harm. Them echoes are more awful in my ears than your mistake, Hurry, for they sound like the voice of natur' calling out ag'in a wasteful and onthinking action."

"You'll hear plenty of such calls, if you tarry long in this quarter of the world, lad," returned the other, laughing. "The echoes repeat pretty much all that is said or done on the Glimmerglass in this calm, summer weather. If a paddle falls, you hear of it sometimes ag'in and ag'in, as if the hills were mocking your clumsiness, and a laugh or a whistle comes out of them pines, when they're in the humor to speak, in a way to make you believe they can r'ally convarse."

"So much the more reason for being prudent and silent. I do not think the inimy can have found their way into these hills yet, for I don't know what they are to gain by it; but all

the Delawares tell me that as courage is a warrior's first vartue, so is prudence his second. One such call, from the mountains, is enough to let a whole tribe into the secret of our arrival."

"If it does no other good, it will warn old Tom to put the pot over and let him know visitors are at hand. Come, lad, get into the canoe, and we will hunt the ark up while there is yet day."

Deerslayer complied, and the canoe left the spot. Its head was turned diagonally across the lake, pointing toward the southeastern curvature of the sheet. In that direction, the distance to the shore, or to the termination of the lake, on the course the two were now steering, was not quite a mile, and their progress being always swift, it was fast lessening, under the skillful but easy sweeps of the paddles. When about halfway across, a slight noise drew the eyes of the men toward the nearest land, and they saw that the buck was just emerging from the lake and wading toward the beach. In a minute the noble animal shook the water from his flanks, gazed upward at the covering of trees, and, bounding against the bank, plunged into the forest.

"That creatur' goes off with gratitude in his heart," said Deerslayer, "for natur' tells him he has escaped a great danger. You ought to have some of the same feelin's, Hurry, to think your eye wasn't truer—that your hand was onsteady—when no good could come of a shot that was intended onmeaningly, rather than in reason."

"I deny the eye and the hand," cried March, with some heat. "You've got a little character, down among the Delawares, there, for quickness and sartainty at a deer, but I should like to see you behind one of them pines and a full-painted Mingo behind another, each with a cocked rifle and a-striving for the chance! Them's the situations, Nathaniel, to try the sight and the hand, for they begin with trying the narves. I never look upon killing a creatur' as an explite, but killing a savage is. The time will come to try your hand, now we've got to blows ag'in, and we shall soon know what a ven'son reputation can do in the field. I deny that either hand or eye was onsteady; it was all a miscalculation of the buck, which stood still when he ought to have kept in motion, and so I shot ahead of him."

"Have it your own way, Hurry; all I contend for is that

it's lucky. I daresay I shall not pull upon a human mortal as steadily or with as light a heart as I pull upon a deer."

"Who's talking of mortals, or of human beings at all, Deerslayer? I put the matter to you on the supposition of an Injin. I daresay any man would have his feelin's when it got to be life or death ag'in another human mortal, but there would be no such scruples in regard to an Injin—nothing but the chance of his hitting you, or the chance of your hitting him."

"I look upon the red men to be quite as human as we are ourselves, Hurry. They have their gifts and their religion, it's true, but that makes no difference in the end, when each will be judged according to his deeds and not according to his skin."

"That's downright missionary, and will find little favor up in this part of the country, where the Moravians don't congregate. Now, skin makes the man. This is reason—else how are people to judge of each other? The skin is put on, over all, in order that when a creatur', or a mortal, is fairly seen, you may know at once what to make of him. You know a bear from a hog, by his skin, and a gray squirrel from a black."

"True, Hurry," said the other, looking back and smiling. "Nevertheless, they are both squirrels."

"Who denies it? But you'll not say that a red man and a white man are both Injins?"

"No, but I *do* say they are both men. Men of different races and colors, and having different gifts and traditions, but, in the main, with the same natur'. Both have souls, and both will be held accountable for their deeds in this life."

Hurry was one of those theorists who believed in the inferiority of all the human race who were not white. His notions on the subject were not very clear, nor were his definitions at all well settled, but his opinions were nonetheless dogmatic or fierce. His conscience accused him of sundry lawless acts against the Indians, and he had found it an exceedingly easy mode of quieting it, by putting the whole family of red men, incontinently, without the category of human rights. Nothing angered him sooner than to deny his proposition—more especially if the denial were accompanied by a show of plausible argument—and he did not listen to his compan-

ion's remarks with much composure of either manner or feeling.

"You're a boy, Deerslayer, misled and misconsaited by Delaware arts and missionary ignorance," he exclaimed, with his usual indifference to the forms of speech, when excited. "*You* may account yourself as a redskin's brother, but *I* hold 'em all to be animals, with nothing human about 'em but cunning. *That* they have, I'll allow, but so has a fox, or even a bear. I'm older than you, and have lived longer in the woods —or, for that matter, have lived always there, and am not to be told what an Injin is or what he is not. If you wish to be considered a savage, you've only to say so, and I'll name you as such to Judith and the old man, and then we'll see how you'll like your welcome."

Here Hurry's imagination did his temper some service, since, by conjuring up the reception his semiaquatic acquaintance would be likely to bestow on one thus introduced, he burst into a hearty fit of laughter. Deerslayer too well knew the uselessness of attempting to convince such a being of anything against his prejudices, to feel a desire to undertake the task, and he was not sorry that the approach of the canoe to the southeastern curve of the lake gave a new direction to his ideas. They were now, indeed, quite near the place that March had pointed out for the position of the outlet, and both began to look for it with a curiosity that was increased by the expectation of finding the ark.

It may strike the reader as a little singular that the place where a stream of any size passed through banks that had an elevation of some twenty feet should be a matter of doubt with men who could not now have been more than two hundred yards distant from the precise spot. It will be recollected, however, that the trees and bushes here as elsewhere fairly overhung the water, making such a fringe to the lake as to conceal any little variations from its general outline.

"I've not been down at this end of the lake these two summers," said Hurry, standing up in the canoe, the better to look about him. "Aye, there's the rock, showing its chin above the water, and I know that the river begins in its neighborhood."

The men now plied the paddles again, and they were presently within a few yards of the rock, floating toward it,

though their efforts were suspended. This rock was not large, being merely some five or six feet high, only half of which elevation rose above the lake. The incessant washing of the water for centuries had so rounded its summit that it resembled a large beehive in shape, its form being more than usually regular and even. Hurry remarked, as they floated slowly past, that this rock was well known to all the Indians in that part of the country and that they were in the practice of using it as a mark to designate the place of meeting, when separated by their hunts and marches.

"And here is the river, Deerslayer," he continued, "though so shut in by trees and bushes as to look more like an and-bush than the outlet of such a sheet as the Glimmerglass."

Hurry had not badly described the place, which did truly seem to be a stream lying in ambush. The high banks might have been a hundred feet asunder, but on the western side a small bit of low land extended so far forward as to diminish the breadth of the stream to half that width. As the bushes hung in the water beneath, and pines that had the stature of church steeples rose in tall columns above, all inclining toward the light until their branches intermingled, the eye, at a little distance, could not easily detect any opening in the shore, to mark the egress of the water. In the forest above, no traces of this outlet were to be seen from the lake, the whole presenting the same connected and seemingly interminable carpet of leaves. As the canoe slowly advanced, sucked in by the current, it entered beneath an arch of trees, through which the light from the heavens struggled by casual openings, faintly relieving the gloom beneath.

"This is a nat'ral and-bush," half-whispered Hurry, as if he felt that the place was devoted to secrecy and watchfulness. "Depend on it, old Tom has burrowed with the ark somewhere in this quarter. We will drop down with the current a short distance and ferret him out."

"This seems no place for a vessel of any size," returned the other. "It appears to me that we shall have hardly room enough for the canoe."

Hurry laughed at the suggestion, and, as it soon appeared, with reason, for the fringe of bushes immediately on the shore of the lake was no sooner passed than the adventurers found themselves in a narrow stream of a sufficient depth of limpid water, with a strong current, and a canopy of leaves,

upheld by arches composed of the limbs of hoary trees. Bushes lined the shores, as usual, but they left sufficient space between them to admit the passage of anything that did not exceed twenty feet in width and to allow of a perspective ahead of eight or ten times that distance.

Neither of our two adventurers used his paddle, except to keep the light bark in the center of the current, but both watched each turning of the stream, of which there were two or three within the first hundred yards, with jealous vigilance. Turn after turn, however, was passed, and the canoe had dropped down with the current some little distance, when Hurry caught a bush and arrested its movement so suddenly and silently as to denote some unusual motive for the act. Deerslayer laid his hand on the stock of his rifle, as soon as he noted this proceeding; but it was quite as much with a hunter's habit as from any feeling of alarm.

"There the old fellow is!" whispered Hurry, pointing with a finger and laughing heartily, though he carefully avoided making a noise; "ratting it away, just as I supposed; up to his knees in the mud and water, looking to the traps and the bait. But for the life of me I can see nothing of the ark, though I'll bet every skin I take this season Jude isn't trusting her pretty little feet in the neighborhood of that black mud. The gal's more likely to be braiding her hair by the side of some spring, where she can see her own good looks and collect scornful feelings ag'in us men."

"You overjudge young women—yes, you do, Hurry—who as often bethink them of their failings as they do of their perfections. I dare to say, this Judith, now, is no such admirer of herself and no such scorner of our sex, as you seem to think, and that she is quite as likely to be sarving her father in the house, wherever that may be, as he is to be sarving her among the traps."

"It's a pleasure to hear truth from a man's tongue, if it be only once in a girl's life," cried a pleasant, rich, and yet soft female voice, so near the canoe as to make both the listeners start. "As for you, Master Hurry, fair words are so apt to choke you that I no longer expect to hear them from your mouth, the last you uttered sticking in your throat and coming near to death. But I'm glad to see you keep better society than formerly and that they who know how to

esteem and treat women are not ashamed to journey in your company."

As this was said, a singularly handsome and youthful female face was thrust through an opening in the leaves, within reach of Deerslayer's paddle. Its owner smiled graciously on the young man; the frown that she cast on Hurry, though simulated and pettish, had the effect to render her beauty more striking by exhibiting the play of an expressive but capricious countenance—one that seemed to change from the soft to the severe, the mirthful to the reproving, with facility and indifference.

A second look explained the nature of the surprise. Unwittingly, the men had dropped alongside of the ark, which had been purposely concealed in bushes cut and arranged for the purpose, and Judith Hutter had merely pushed aside the leaves that lay before a window in order to show her face and speak to them.

CHAPTER IV

> *And that timid fawn starts not with fear,*
> *When I steal to her secret bower;*
> *And that young May violet to me is dear,*
> *And I visit the silent streamlet near,*
> *To look on the lovely flower.*

BRYANT

THE ARK, as the floating habitation of the Hutters was generally called, was a very simple contrivance. A large flat, or scow, composed the buoyant part of the vessel; in its center, occupying the whole of its breadth, and about two-thirds of its length, stood a low fabric, resembling the castle in construction, though made of materials so light as barely to be bulletproof. As the sides of the scow were a little higher than usual, and the interior of the cabin had no more elevation than was necessary for comfort, this unusual addition had neither a very clumsy nor a very obtrusive appearance. It was, in short, little more than a modern canal boat, though more rudely constructed, of greater breadth than common, and bearing about it the signs of the wilderness in its bark-covered posts and roof. The scow, however, had been put together with some skill, being comparatively light, for its strength, and sufficiently manageable. The cabin was divided into two apartments, one of which served for a parlor and the sleeping room of the father, and the other was appropriated to the uses of the daughter. A very simple arrangement sufficed for the kitchen, which was in one end of the scow and removed from the cabin, standing in the open air—the ark being altogether a summer habitation.

The "and-bush," as Hurry in his ignorance of English termed it, is quite as easily explained. In many parts of the lake and river, where the banks were steep and high, the

smaller trees and larger bushes, as has been already mentioned, fairly overhung the stream, their branches not unfrequently dipping into the water. In some instances they grew out in nearly horizontal lines for thirty or forty feet. The water being uniformly deepest near the shores, where the banks were highest and the nearest to a perpendicular, Hutter had found no difficulty in letting the ark drop under one of these covers, where it had been anchored with a view to conceal its position—security requiring some such precautions, in his view of the case. Once beneath the trees and bushes, a few stones fastened to the ends of the branches had caused them to bend sufficiently to dip into the river, and a few severed bushes, properly disposed, did the rest. The reader has seen that this cover was so complete as to deceive two men accustomed to the woods, and who were actually in search of those it concealed; a circumstance that will be easily understood by those who are familiar with the matted and wild luxuriance of a virgin American forest, more especially in a rich soil.

The discovery of the ark produced very different effects on our two adventurers. As soon as the canoe could be got around to the proper opening, Hurry leaped on board, and in a minute was closely engaged in a gay, and a sort of recriminating discourse with Judith, apparently forgetful of the existence of all the rest of the world. Not so with Deerslayer. He entered the ark with a slow, cautious step, examining every arrangement of the cover with curious and scrutinizing eyes. It is true, he cast one admiring glance at Judith, which was extorted by her brilliant and singular beauty, but even this could detain him but a single instant from the indulgence of his interest in Hutter's contrivances. Step by step did he look into the construction of the singular abode, investigate its fastenings and strength, ascertain its means of defense, and make every inquiry that would be likely to occur to one whose thoughts dwelt principally on such expedients. Nor was the cover neglected. Of this he examined the whole minutely, his commendation escaping him more than once in audible comments. Frontier usages admitting of this familiarity, he passed through the rooms, as he had previously done at the castle, and, opening a door, issued into the end of the scow opposite to that where he had left Hurry and Judith. Here he found the other sister, employed on some

coarse needlework, seated beneath the leafy canopy of the cover.

As Deerslayer's examination was by this time ended, he dropped the butt of his rifle, and leaning on the barrel with both hands, he turned toward the girl with an interest the singular beauty of her sister had not awakened. He had gathered from Hurry's remarks that Hetty was considered to have less intellect than ordinarily falls to the share of human beings, and his education among Indians had taught him to treat those who were thus afflicted by Providence with more than common tenderness. Nor was there anything in Hetty Hutter's appearance, as so often happens, to weaken the interest her situation excited. An idiot she could not properly be termed, her mind being just enough enfeebled to lose most of those traits that are connected with the more artful qualities and to retain its ingenuousness and love of truth. It had often been remarked of this girl, by the few who had seen her and who possessed sufficient knowledge to discriminate, that her perception of the right seemed almost intuitive, while her aversion to the wrong formed so distinctive a feature of her mind as to surround her with an atmosphere of pure morality; peculiarities that are not unfrequent with persons who are termed feeble-minded; as if God had forbidden the evil spirits to invade a precinct so defenseless, with the benign purpose of extending a direct protection to those who had been left without the usual aids of humanity. Her person, too, was agreeable, having a strong resemblance to that of her sister, of which it was a subdued and humble copy. If it had none of the brilliancy of Judith's, the calm, quiet, almost holy expression of her meek countenance seldom failed to win on the observer; and few noted it long that did not begin to feel a deep and lasting interest in the girl. She had no color, in common, nor was her simple mind apt to present images that caused her cheek to brighten; though she retained a modesty so innate that it almost raised her to the unsuspecting purity of a being superior to human infirmities. Guileless, innocent, and without distrust, equally by nature and from her mode of life, Providence had nevertheless shielded her from harm by a halo of moral light, as it is said "to temper the wind to the shorn lamb."

"You are Hetty Hutter," said Deerslayer, in the way one puts a question unconsciously to himself, assuming a kind-

ness of tone and manner that were singularly adapted to win the confidence of her he addressed. "Hurry Harry has told me of you, and I know you must be the child."

"Yes, I'm Hetty Hutter," returned the girl, in a low, sweet voice, which nature, aided by some education, had preserved from vulgarity of tone and utterance. "I'm Hetty; Judith Hutter's sister, and Thomas Hutter's youngest daughter."

"I know your history, then, for Hurry Harry talks considerable, and he is free of speech, when he can find other people's consarns to dwell on. You pass most of your life on the lake, Hetty."

"Certainly. Mother is dead; father is gone a-trapping, and Judith and I stay at home. What's *your* name?"

"That's a question more easily asked than it is answered, young woman, seeing that I'm so young and yet have borne more names than some of the greatest chiefs in all America."

"But you've *got* a name—you don't throw away one name before you come honestly by another?"

"I hope not, gal—I hope not. My names have come nat'rally and I suppose the one I bear now will be of no great lasting, since the Delawares seldom settle on a man's ra'al title until such time as he has an opportunity of showing his true natur', in the council or on the warpath—which has never behappened me, seeing, firstly, because I'm not born a redskin, and have no right to sit in *their* councilings, and am much too humble to be called on for opinions from the great of my own color; and, secondly, because this is the first war that has befallen in my time, and no inimy has yet inroaded far enough into the Colony to be reached by an arm even longer than mine."

"Tell me your names," added Hetty, looking up at him artlessly, "and maybe I'll tell you your character."

"There is some truth in that, I'll not deny, though it often fails. Men are deceived in other men's characters, and frequently give 'em names they by no means desarve. You can see the truth of this in the Mingo names, which, in their own tongue, signify the same things as the Delaware names —at least, so they tell me, for I know little of that tribe, unless it be by report—and no one can say they are as honest or as upright a nation. I put no great dependence, therefore, on names."

"Tell me *all* your names," repeated the girl earnestly, for

her mind was too simple to separate things from professions, and she *did* attach importance to a name; "I want to know what to think of you."

"Well, sartain; I've no objection, and you shall hear them all. In the first place, then, I'm Christian, and white-born, like yourself, and my parents had a name that came down from father to son, as is a part of their gifts. My father was called Bumppo; I was named after him, of course, the given name being Nathaniel, or Natty, as most people saw fit to tarm it."

"Yes, yes—Natty—and Hetty—" interrupted the girl quickly, and looking up from her work again, with a smile; "you are Natty, and I'm Hetty—though you are Bumppo, and I'm Hutter. Bumppo isn't as pretty as Hutter, is it?"

"Why, that's as people fancy. Bumppo has no lofty sound, I admit, and yet men have bumped through the world with it. I did not go by this name, howsever, very long, for the Delawares soon found out, or thought they found out, that I was not given to lying, and they called me, firstly, Straighttongue."

"That's a *good* name," interrupted Hetty earnestly and in a positive manner; "don't tell me there's no virtue in names!"

"I do not say *that,* for perhaps I desarved to be so called, lies being no favorites with me, as they are with some. After a while they found out that I was quick of foot, and then they called me the 'Pigeon,' which, you know, has a swift wing and flies in a direct line."

"*That* was a *pretty* name!" exclaimed Hetty; "pigeons are pretty birds!"

"Most things that God has created are pretty, in their way, my good gal, though they get to be deformed by mankind, so as to change their natur's, as well as their appearance. From carrying messages, and striking blind trails, I got, at last, to following the hunters, when it was thought I was quicker and surer at finding the game than most lads, and then they called me the 'Lap-ear,' as, they said, I partook of the sagacity of a hound."

"That's not so pretty," answered Hetty; "I hope you didn't keep *that* name long."

"Not after I was rich enough to buy a rifle," returned the other, betraying a little pride through his usually quiet and subdued manner; "*then* it was seen I could keep a wigwam in ven'son; in time, I got the name of 'Deerslayer,' which is

that I now bear; homely as some will think it, who set more valie on the scalp of a fellow mortal than on the horns of a buck."

"Well, Deerslayer, I'm not one of them," answered Hetty simply. "Judith likes soldiers, and flary coats, and fine feathers, but they're all naught to me. *She* says the officers are great, and gay, and of soft speech, but they make me shudder, for their business is to kill their fellow creatures. I like your calling better, and your last name is a very good one—better than Natty Bumppo."

"This is nat'ral, in one of your turn of mind, Hetty, and much as I should have expected. They tell me your sister is handsome—oncommon, for a mortal—and beauty is apt to seek admiration."

"Did you never see Judith?" demanded the girl, with quick earnestness; "if you never have, go at once and look at her. Even Hurry Harry isn't more pleasant to look at, though *she* is a woman, and *he* is a man."

Deerslayer regarded the girl for a moment with concern. Her pale face had flushed a little, and her eye, usually so mild and serene, brightened as she spoke, in the way to betray the inward impulses.

"Aye, Hurry Harry," he muttered to himself, as he walked through the cabin toward the other end of the boat. "This comes of good looks, if a light tongue has had no consarn in it. It's easy to see which way that poor creatur's feelin's are leanin', whatever may be the case with your Jude's."

But an interruption was put to the gallantry of Hurry, the coquetry of his mistress, the thoughts of Deerslayer, and the gentle feelings of Hetty by the sudden appearance of the canoe of the ark's owner, in the narrow opening among the bushes that served as a sort of moat to his position. It would seem that Hutter, or Floating Tom, as he was familiarly called by all the hunters who knew his habits, recognized the canoe of Hurry, for he expressed no surprise at finding him in the scow. On the contrary, his reception was such as to denote not only gratification but a pleasure, mingled with a little disappointment at his not having made his appearance some days sooner.

"I looked for you last week," he said, in a half-grumbling, half-welcoming manner, "and was disappointed uncommon-

ly that you didn't arrive. There came a runner through to warn all the trappers and hunters that the Colony and the Canadas were again in trouble; I felt lonesome, up in these mountains, with three scalps to see to and only one pair of hands to protect them."

"That's reasonable," returned March, "and 'twas feeling like a parent. No doubt, if I had two such darters as Judith and Hetty, my exper'ence would tell the same story, though, in gin'ral, I am just as well satisfied with having the nearest neighbor fifty miles off as when he is within call."

"Notwithstanding, you didn't choose to come into the wilderness alone, now you knew that the Canada savages are likely to be stirring," returned Hutter, giving a sort of distrustful and, at the same time, inquiring glance at Deerslayer.

"Why should I? They say a bad companion on a journey helps to shorten the path, and this young man I account to be a reasonably good one. This is Deerslayer, old Tom, a noted hunter among the Delawares, and Christian-born, and Christian edicated, too, like you and me. The lad is not parfect, perhaps, but there's worse men in the country that he came from, and it's likely he'll find some that's no better, in this part of the world. Should we have occasion to defend our traps, and the territory, he'll be useful in feeding us all, for he's a reg'lar dealer in ven'son."

"Young man, you are welcome," growled Tom, thrusting a hard, bony hand toward the youth as a pledge of his sincerity. "In such times a whiteface is a friend's, and I count on you as a support. Children sometimes make a stout heart feeble, and these two daughters of mine give me more concern than all my traps, and skins, and rights in the country."

"That's nat'ral!" cried Hurry. "Yes, Deerslayer, you and I don't know it yet by experience, but on the whole I consider that as nat'ral. If we *had* darters, it's more than probable we should have some such feelin's, and I honor the man that owns 'em. As for Judith, old man, I enlist at once as her soldier, and here is Deerslayer to help you to take care of Hetty."

"Many thanks to you, Master March," returned the beauty, in a full, rich voice and with an accuracy of intonation and utterance that she shared in common with her sister, and

which showed that she had been better taught than her father's life and appearance would give reason to expect; "many thanks to you; but Judith Hutter has the spirit and the experience that will make her depend more on herself than on good-looking rovers like you. Should there be need to face the savages, do you land with my father, instead of burrowing in the huts, under the show of defending us females, and——"

"Girl—girl," interrupted the father, "quiet that glib tongue of thine and hear the truth. There are savages on the lake shore already, and no man can say how near to us they may be at this very moment, or when we may hear more from them!"

"If this be true, Master Hutter," said Hurry, whose change of countenance denoted how serious he deemed the information, though it did not denote any unmanly alarm, "if this be true, your ark is in a most misfortunate position, for, though the cover did deceive Deerslayer and myself, it would hardly be overlooked by a full-blooded Injin who was out seriously in s'arch of scalps!"

"I think as you do, Hurry, and wish with all my heart we lay anywhere else, at this moment, than in this narrow, crooked stream, which has many advantages to hide in but which is almost fatal to them that are discovered. The savages are near us, moreover, and the difficulty is to get out of the river without being shot down like deer standing at a lick!"

"Are you sartain, Master Hutter, that the redskins you dread are ra'al Canadas?" asked Deerslayer, in a modest but earnest manner. "Have you seen any, and can you describe their paint?"

"I have fallen in with the signs of their being in the neighborhood, but have seen none of 'em. I was downstream a mile or so, looking to my traps, when I struck a fresh trail, crossing the corner of a swamp and moving northward. The man had not passed an hour, and I know'd it for an Indian footstep by the size of the foot and the intoe even before I found a worn moccasin, which its owner had dropped as useless. For that matter, I found the spot where he halted to make a new one, which was only a few yards from the place where he had dropped the old one."

"That doesn't look much like a redskin on the warpath!"

returned the other, shaking his head. "An exper'enced warrior, at least, would have burned, or buried, or sunk in the river such signs of his passage; and your trail is, quite likely, a peaceable trail. But the moccasin may greatly relieve my mind, if you bethought you of bringing it off. I've come here to meet a young chief myself, and his course would be much in the direction you've mentioned. The trail may have been his'n."

"Hurry Harry, you're well acquainted with this young man, I hope, who has meetings with savages in a part of the country where he has never been before?" demanded Hutter, in a tone and in a manner that sufficiently indicated the motive of the question—these rude beings seldom hesitated, on the score of delicacy, to betray their feelings. "Treachery is an Indian virtue, and the whites that live much in their tribes soon catch their ways and practices."

"True—true as the Gospel, old Tom, but not personable to Deerslayer, who's a young man of truth, if he has no other ricommend. I'll answer for his *honesty*, whatever I may do for his valor in battle."

"I should like to know his errand in this strange quarter of the country."

"That is soon told, Master Hutter," said the young man, with the composure of one who kept a clean conscience. "I think, moreover, you've a *right* to ask it. The father of two such darters, who occupies a lake after your fashion, has just the same right to inquire into a stranger's business in his neighborhood as the Colony would have to demand the reason why the Frenchers put more rijiments than common along the lines. No, no, I'll not deny your right to know why a stranger comes into your habitation or country in times as serious as these."

"If such is your way of thinking, friend, let me hear your story without more words."

" 'Tis soon told, as I said afore, and shall be honestly told. I'm a young man, and, as yet, have never been on a warpath, but no sooner did the news come among the Delawares that wampum and a hatchet were about to be sent into the tribe than they wished me to go out among the people of my own color and get the exact state of things for 'em. This I did, and after delivering my talk to the chiefs, on my return, I met an officer of the Crown on the Schoharie, who

had moneys to send to some of the friendly tribes that live further west. This was thought a good occasion for Chingachgook, a young chief who has never struck a foe, and myself to go on our first warpath in company, and an app'intment was made for us, by an old Delaware, to meet at the rock near the foot of this lake. I'll not deny that Chingachgook has *another* object in view, but it has no consarn with any here and is his secret, and not mine; therefore I'll say no more about it."

" 'Tis something about a young woman," interrupted Judith hastily, then laughing at her own impetuosity and even having the grace to color a little at the manner in which she had betrayed her readiness to impute such a motive. "If 'tis neither war nor a hunt, it must be love."

"Aye, it comes easy for the young and handsome, who hear so much of them feelin's, to suppose that they lie at the bottom of most proceedin's; but on that head I say nothin'. Chingachgook is to meet me at the rock an hour afore sunset tomorrow evening, after which we shall go our way together, molesting none but the King's inimies, who are lawfully our own. Knowing Hurry of old, who once trapped in our hunting grounds, and falling in with him on the Schoharie, just as he was on the p'int of starting for his summer ha'nts, we agreed to journey in company, not so much from fear of the Mingos as from good fellowship and, as he says, to shorten a long road."

"And you think the trail I saw may have been that of your friend, ahead of his time?" said Hutter.

"That's my idee—which may be wrong, but which may be right. If I saw the moccasin, however, I could tell in a minute whether it is made in the Delaware fashion or not."

"Here it is, then," said the quick-witted Judith, who had already gone to the canoe in quest of it. "Tell us what it says: friend or enemy. You look honest, and *I* believe all you say, whatever father may think."

"That's the way with you, Jude, forever finding out friends where I distrust foes," grumbled Tom. "But, speak out, young man, and tell us what you think of the moccasin."

"That's not Delaware-made," returned Deerslayer, examining the worn and rejected covering for the foot with a cautious eye. "I'm too young on a warpath to be positive, but I

should say that moccasin has a northern look and comes from beyond the great lakes."

"If such is the case, we ought not to lie here a minute longer than is necessary," said Hutter, glancing through the leaves of his cover as if he already distrusted the presence of an enemy on the opposite shore of the narrow and sinuous stream. "It wants but an hour or so of night, and to move in the dark will be impossible, without making a noise that would betray us. Did you hear the echo of a piece in the mountains half an hour since?"

"Yes, old man, and heard the piece itself," answered Hurry, who now felt the indiscretion of which he had been guilty, "for the last was fired from my own shoulder."

"I feared it came from the French Indians; still, it may put them on the lookout and be a means of discovering us. You did wrong to fire, in wartime, unless there was good occasion."

"So I begin to think myself, Uncle Tom, and yet, if a man can't trust himself to let off his rifle in a wilderness that is a thousand miles square lest some inimy should hear it, where's the use in carrying one?"

Hutter now held a long consultation with his two guests, in which the parties came to a true understanding of their situation. He explained the difficulty that would exist in attempting to get the ark out of so swift and narrow a stream in the dark without making a noise that could not fail to attract Indian ears. Any strollers in their vicinity would keep near the river or the lake, but the former had swampy shores in many places and was both so crooked and so fringed with bushes that it was quite possible to move by daylight without incurring much danger of being seen. More was to be apprehended, perhaps, from the ear than from the eye, especially as long as they were in the short, straitened, and canopied reaches of the stream.

"I never drop down into this cover, which is handy to my traps and safer than the lake from curious eyes, without providing the means of getting out ag'in," continued this singular being, "and that is easier done by a pull than a push. My anchor is now lying above the suction, in the open lake, and here is a line, you see, to haul us up to it. Without some such help, a single pair of hands would make heavy work in forcing a scow like this upstream. I have a

sort of a crab, too, that lightens the pull on occasion. Jude can use the oar astern, as well as myself, and, when we fear no enemy, to get out of the river gives us but little trouble."

"What should we gain, Master Hutter, by changing the position?" asked Deerslayer, with a good deal of earnestness. "This is a safe cover, and a stout defense might be made from the inside of this cabin. I've never fou't, unless in the way of tradition, but, it seems to me we might beat off twenty Mingos with palisades like them afore us."

"Aye, aye, you've never fought except in traditions—that's plain enough, young man! Did you ever see as broad a sheet of water as this above us before you came in upon it with Hurry?"

"I can't say that I ever did," Deerslayer answered modestly. "Youth is the time to l'arn, and I'm far from wishing to raise my voice in counsel afore it is justified by exper'ence."

"Well, then, I'll teach you the disadvantage of fighting in this position, and the advantage of taking to the open lake. Here, you may see, the savages will know where to aim every shot, and it would be too much to hope that *some* would not find their way through the crevices of the logs. Now, on the other hand, *we* should have nothing but a forest to aim at. Then we are not safe from fire, here, the bark of this roof being little better than so much kindling wood. The castle, too, might be entered and ransacked, in my absence, and all my possessions overrun and destroyed. Once in the lake, we can be attacked only in boats, or on rafts—shall have a fair chance with the enemy—and can protect the castle with the ark. Do you understand this reasoning, youngster?"

"It sounds well—yes, it has a rational sound, and I'll not gainsay it."

"Well, old Tom," cried Hurry, "if we are to move, the sooner we make a beginning, the sooner we shall know whether we are to have our scalps for nightcaps, or not."

As this proposition was self-evident, no one denied its justice. The three men, after a short preliminary explanation, now set about their preparations to move the ark in earnest. The slight fastenings were quickly loosened, and, by hauling on the line, the heavy craft slowly emerged from the cover. It was no sooner free from the encumbrance of the branches than it swung into the stream, sheering quite close to the western shore, by the force of the current. Not a soul on

board heard the rustling of the branches as the cabin came against the bushes and trees of the western bank without a feeling of uneasiness, for no one knew at what moment, or in what place, a secret and murderous enemy might unmask himself. Perhaps the gloomy light that still struggled through the impending canopy of leaves, or found its way through the narrow, ribbonlike opening which seemed to mark, in the air above, the course of the river that flowed beneath, aided in augmenting the appearance of the danger; for it was little more than sufficient to render objects visible without giving up all their outlines at a glance. Although the sun had not absolutely set, it had withdrawn its direct rays from the valley, and the hues of evening were beginning to gather around objects that stood uncovered, rendering those within the shadows of the woods still more somber and gloomy.

No interruption followed the movement, however, and, as the men continued to haul on the line, the ark passed steadily ahead, the great breadth of the scow preventing its sinking into the water and offering much resistance to the progress of the swift element beneath its bottom. Hutter, too, had adopted a precaution, suggested by experience, which might have done credit to a seaman, and which completely prevented any of the annoyances and obstacles which otherwise would have attended the short turns of the river. As the ark descended, heavy stones, attached to the line, were dropped in the center of the stream, forming local anchors, each of which was kept from dragging by the assistance of those above it, until the uppermost of all was reached, which got its "backing" from the anchor, or grapnel, that lay well out in the lake. In consequence of this expedient, the ark floated clear of the encumbrances of the shore, against which it would otherwise have been unavoidably hauled at every turn, producing embarrassments that Hutter, singlehanded, would have found it very difficult to overcome.

Favored by this foresight, and stimulated by the apprehension of discovery, Floating Tom and his two athletic companions hauled the ark ahead with quite as much rapidity as comported with the strength of the line. At every turn in the stream, a stone was raised from the bottom, when the direction of the scow changed to one that pointed toward the stone that lay above. In this manner with the channel buoyed out for him, as a sailor might term it, did Hutter

move forward, occasionally urging his friends, in a low and guarded voice, to increase their exertions, and then, as occasions offered, warning them against efforts that might, at particular moments, endanger all by too much zeal. In spite of their long familiarity with the woods, the gloomy character of the shaded river added to the uneasiness that each felt, and when the ark reached the first bend in the Susquehanna, and the eye caught a glimpse of the broader expanse of the lake, all felt a relief that perhaps none would have been willing to confess. Here the last stone was raised from the bottom and the line led directly toward the grapnel, which, as Hutter had explained, was dropped above the suction of the current.

"Thank God!" ejaculated Hurry, "*there* is daylight, and we shall soon have a chance of *seeing* our inimies, if we are to *feel* 'em."

"That is more than you or any man can say," growled Hutter. "There is no spot so likely to harbor a party as the shore around the outlet, and the moment we clear these trees and get into open water will be the most trying time, since it will leave the enemy a cover while it puts us out of one. Judith, girl—do you and Hetty leave the oar to take care of itself and go within the cabin; be mindful not to show your faces at a window, for they who will look at them won't stop to praise their beauty. And now, Hurry, we'll step into this outer room ourselves and haul through the door, where we shall all be safe, from a surprise at least. Friend Deerslayer, as the current is lighter and the line has all the strain on it that is prudent, do you keep moving from window to window, taking care not to let your head be seen, if you set any value on life. No one knows when or where we shall hear from our neighbors."

Deerslayer complied, with a sensation that had nothing in common with fear but which had all the interest of a perfectly novel and a most exciting situation. For the first time in his life he was in the vicinity of enemies, or had good reason to think so—and that, too, under all the thrilling circumstances of Indian surprises and Indian artifices. As he took his stand at a window, the ark was just passing through the narrowest part of the stream, a point where the water first entered what was properly termed the river, and where the trees fairly interlocked overhead, causing the current to

rush into an arch of verdure—a feature as appropriate and peculiar to the country, perhaps, as that of Switzerland, where the rivers come rushing literally from chambers of ice.

The ark was in the act of passing the last curve of this leafy entrance as Deerslayer, having examined all that could be seen of the eastern bank of the river, crossed the room to look from the opposite window at the western. His arrival at this aperture was most opportune, for he had no sooner placed his eye at a crack than a sight met his gaze that might well have alarmed a sentinel so young and inexperienced. A sapling overhung the water in nearly half a circle, having first grown toward the light and then pressed down into this form by the weight of the snows—a circumstance of common occurrence in the American woods. On this no less than six Indians had already appeared, others standing ready to follow them, as they left room; each evidently bent on running out on the trunk and dropping on the roof of the ark as it passed beneath. This would have been an exploit of no great difficulty, the inclination of the tree admitting of an easy passage, the adjoining branches offering ample support for the hands, and the fall being too trifling to be apprehended. When Deerslayer first saw this party, it was just unmasking itself by ascending the part of the tree nearest to the earth, or that which was much the most difficult to overcome; and his knowledge of Indian habits told him at once that they were all in their war paint and belonged to a hostile tribe.

"Pull, Hurry," he cried. "Pull for your life, and as you love Judith Hutter! Pull, man, pull!"

This call was made to one that the young man knew had the strength of a giant. It was so earnest and solemn that both Hutter and March felt it was not idly given, and they applied all their force to the line simultaneously and at a most critical moment. The scow redoubled its motion and seemed to glide from under the tree as if conscious of the danger that was impending overhead. Perceiving that they were discovered, the Indians uttered the fearful war whoop and, running forward on the tree, leaped desperately toward their fancied prize. There were six on the tree, and each made the effort. All but their leader fell into the river more or less distant from the ark, as they came, sooner or later,

to the leaping place. The chief, who had taken the dangerous post in advance, having an earlier opportunity than the others, struck the scow just within the stern. The fall proving so much greater than he had anticipated, he was slightly stunned, and for a moment he remained half bent and unconscious of his situation. At this instant Judith rushed from the cabin, her beauty heightened by the excitement that produced the bold act, which flushed her cheek to crimson; throwing all her strength into the effort, she pushed the intruder over the edge of the scow, headlong into the river. This decided feat was no sooner accomplished than the woman resumed her sway; Judith looked over the stern to ascertain what had become of the man, and the expression of her eyes softened to concern; next, her cheek crimsoned between shame and surprise at her own temerity; and then she laughed in her own merry and sweet manner. All this occupied less than a minute, when the arm of Deerslayer was thrown around her waist and she was dragged swiftly within the protection of the cabin. This retreat was not effected too soon. Scarcely were the two in safety when the forest was filled with yells, and bullets began to patter against the logs.

The ark being in swift motion all this while, it was beyond the danger of pursuit by the time these little events had occurred; the savages, as soon as the first burst of their anger had subsided, ceased firing, with the consciousness that they were expending their ammunition in vain. When the scow came up over her grapnel, Hutter tripped the latter in a way not to impede the motion; being now beyond the influence of the current, the vessel continued to drift ahead until fairly in the open lake, though still near enough to the land to render exposure to a rifle bullet dangerous. Hutter and March got out two small sweeps, and, covered by the cabin, they soon urged the ark far enough from the shore to leave no inducement to their enemies to make any further attempt to injure them.

CHAPTER V

Why, let the stricken deer go weep,
The hart ungalled play,
For some must watch, while some must sleep,
Thus runs the world away.

SHAKESPEARE

ANOTHER CONSULTATION TOOK place in the forward part of the scow, at which both Judith and Hetty were present. As no danger could now approach unseen, immediate uneasiness had given place to the concern which attended the conviction that enemies were in considerable force on the shores of the lake, and that they might be sure no practicable means of accomplishing their own destruction would be neglected. As a matter of course, Hutter felt these truths the deepest, his daughters having a habitual reliance on his resources, and knowing too little to appreciate fully all the risks they ran, while his male companions were at liberty to quit him at any moment they saw fit. His first remark showed that he had an eye to the latter circumstance, and might have betrayed, to a keen observer, the apprehension that was just then uppermost.

"We've a great advantage over the Iroquois, or the enemy, whoever they are, in being afloat," he said. "There's not a canoe on the lake that I don't know where it's hid, and now yours is here, Hurry, there are but three more on the land, and they're so snug in hollow logs that I don't believe the Indians could find them, let them try ever so long."

"There's no telling that—no one can say that," put in Deerslayer. "A hound is not more sartain on the scent than a redskin when he expects to get anything by it. Let this party see scalps afore 'em, or plunder, or honor, accordin' to their

71

idees of what honor is, and 'twill be a tight log that hides a canoe from their eyes."

"You're right, Deerslayer," cried Harry March; "you're downright Gospel in this matter, and I rej'ice that my bunch of bark is safe enough here, within reach of my arm. I calcilate they'll be at all the rest of the canoes afore tomorrow night, if they are in ra'al 'arnest to smoke you out, old Tom, and we may as well overhaul our paddles for a pull."

Hutter made no immediate reply. He looked about him in silence for quite a minute, examining the sky, the lake, and the belt of forest which enclosed it, as it might be hermetically, like one consulting their signs. Nor did he find any alarming symptoms. The boundless woods were sleeping in the deep repose of nature, the heavens were placid, but still luminous with the light of the retreating sun, while the lake looked more lovely and calm than it had before done that day. It was a scene altogether soothing and of a character to lull the passions into a species of holy calm. How far this effect was produced, however, on the party in the ark must appear in the progress of our narrative.

"Judith," called out the father, when he had taken this close but short survey of the omens, "night is at hand; find our friends food; a long march gives a sharp appetite."

"We're not starving, Master Hutter," March observed, "for we filled up just as we reached the lake, and, for one, I prefar the company of Jude even to her supper. This quiet evening is very agreeable to sit by her side."

"Natur' is natur'," objected Hutter, "and must be fed. Judith, see to the meal, and take your sister to help you. I've a little discourse to hold with you, friends," he continued, as soon as his daughters were out of hearing, "and wish the girls away. You see my situation; I should like to hear your opinions concerning what is best to be done. Three times have I been burnt out already, but that was on the shore; I've considered myself as pretty safe ever since I got the castle built, and the ark afloat. My other accidents, however, happened in peaceable times, being nothing more than such flurries as a man must meet with in the woods; but this matter looks serious, and your ideas would greatly relieve my mind."

"It's my notion, old Tom, that you, and your huts, and your traps, and your whole possessions hereaway are in

desperate jippardy," returned the matter-of-fact Hurry, who saw no use in concealment. "Accordin' to my idees of valie, they're altogether not worth half as much today as they was yesterday, nor would I give more for 'em taking the pay in skins."

"Then I've children!" continued the father, making the allusion in a way that it might have puzzled even an indifferent observer to say was intended as a bait, or as an exclamation of paternal concern; "daughters, as you know, Hurry, and good girls, too, I may say, though I *am* their father."

"A man may say anything, Master Hutter, particularly when pressed by time and circumstances. You've darters, as you say, and one of them hasn't her equal on the frontiers for good looks, whatever she may have for good behavior. As for poor Hetty, she's Hetty Hutter, and that's as much as one can say about the poor thing. Give me Jude, if her conduct was only equal to her looks!"

"I see, Harry March, I can only count on you as a fairweather friend, and I suppose that your companion will be of the same way of thinking," returned the other, with a slight show of pride that was not altogether without dignity. "Well, I must depend on Providence, which will not turn a deaf ear, perhaps, to a father's prayers."

"If you've understood Hurry, here, to mean that he intends to desart you," said Deerslayer, with an earnest simplicity that gave double assurance of its truth, "I *think* you do him injustice, as I *know* you do me, in supposing I would follow him was he so ontruehearted as to leave a family of his own color in such a strait as this. I've come on this lake, Master Hutter, to rende'vous a fri'nd, and I only wish he was here himself, as I make no doubt he will be at sunset tomorrow, when you'd have another rifle to aid you—an inexper'enced one, I'll allow, like my own, but one that has proved true so often ag'in the game, big and little, that I'll answer for its sarvice ag'in mortals."

"May I depend on *you* to stand by me and my daughters, then, Deerslayer?" demanded the old man, with a father's anxiety in his countenance.

"That may you, Floating Tom, if that's your name, and as a brother would stand by a sister—a husband his wife—or a suitor his sweetheart. In this strait you may count on me,

through all adversities, and I think Hurry does discredit to his natur' and wishes, if you can't count on him."

"Not he," cried Judith, thrusting her handsome face out of the door; "his nature is hurry, as well as his name, and he'll hurry off as soon as he thinks his fine figure in danger. Neither 'old Tom' nor his 'gals' will depend much on Master March, now they know him, but *you* they will rely on, Deerslayer, for your honest face and honest heart tell us that what you promise you will perform."

This was said as much perhaps in affected scorn for Hurry as in sincerity. Still, it was not said without feeling. The fine face of Judith sufficiently proved the latter circumstance, and if the conscious March fancied that he had never seen in it a stronger display of contempt—a feeling in which the beauty was apt to indulge—than while she was looking at him, it certainly seldom exhibited more of womanly softness and sensibility than when her speaking blue eyes were turned on his traveling companion.

"Leave us, Judith," Hutter ordered sternly, before either of the young men could reply; "leave us, and do not return until you come with the venison and fish. The girl has been spoiled by the flattery of the officers who sometimes find their way up here, Master March, and you'll not think any harm of her silly words."

"You never said truer syllable, old Tom," retorted Hurry, who smarted under Judith's observations. "The devil-tongued youngsters of the garrison have proved her undoing! I scarce know Jude any longer, and shall soon take to admiring her sister, who is getting to be much more to my fancy."

"I'm glad to hear this, Harry, and look upon it as a sign that you're coming to your right senses. Hetty would make a much safer and more rational companion than Jude, and would be much the most likely to listen to your suit, as the officers have, I greatly fear, unsettled her sister's mind."

"No man need a safer wife than Hetty," said Hurry, laughing, "though I'll not answer for her being of the most rational. But no matter; Deerslayer has not misconceived me when he told you I should be found at my post. I'll not quit *you*, Uncle Tom, just now, whatever may be my feelin's and intentions respecting your eldest darter."

Hurry had a respectable reputation for prowess among his associates, and Hutter heard this pledge with a satisfaction

that was not concealed. Even the great personal strength of such an aid became of moment, in moving the ark, as well as in the species of hand-to-hand conflicts, that were not unfrequent in the woods, and no commander who was hardpressed could feel more joy at hearing of the arrival of reinforcements than the borderer experienced at being told this important auxiliary was not about to quit him. A minute before, Hutter would have been well content to compromise his danger by entering into a compact to act only on the defensive, but no sooner did he feel some security on this point than the restlessness of man induced him to think of the means of carrying the war into the enemy's country.

"High prices are offered for scalps on both sides," he observed, with a grim smile, as if he felt the force of the inducement at the very time he wished to affect a superiority to earning money by means that the ordinary feelings of those who aspire to be civilized men repudiated, even while they were adopted. "It isn't right, perhaps, to take gold for human blood, and yet, when mankind is busy in killing one another, there can be no great harm in adding a little bit of skin to the plunder. What's your sentiments, Hurry, touching these p'ints?"

"That you've made a vast mistake, old man, in calling savage blood, human blood, at all. I think no more of a redskin's scalp than I do of a pair of wolf's ears, and would just as lief finger money for the one as for the other. With *white* people 'tis different, for they've a nat'ral avarsion to being scalped, whereas your Indian shaves his head in readiness for the knife and leaves a lock of hair by way of braggadocio that one can lay hold of in the bargain."

"That's manly, however, and I felt from the first that we had only to get you on our side, to have you heart and hand," returned Tom, losing all his reserve as he gained a renewed confidence in the disposition of his companion. "Something more may turn up from this inroad of the redskins than they bargained for. Deerslayer, I conclude you're of Hurry's way of thinking and look upon money 'arned in this way as being as likely to pass as money 'arned in trapping or hunting."

"I've no such feelin', nor any wish to harbor it, not I," returned the other. "My gifts are not scalpers' gifts, but such as belong to my religion and color. I'll stand by you, old

man, in the ark or in the castle, the canoe or the woods, but I'll not unhumanize my natur' by falling into ways that God intended for another race. If you and Hurry have got any thoughts that lean toward the Colony's gold, go by yourselves in s'arch of it and leave the females to my care. Much as I must differ from you both on all gifts that do not properly belong to a white man, we shall agree that it is the duty of the strong to take care of the weak, especially when the last belong to them that natur' intended man to protect and console by his gentleness and strength."

"Hurry Harry, that is a lesson you might learn and practice on to some advantage," said the sweet but spirited voice of Judith from the cabin, a proof that she had overheard all that had hitherto been said.

"No more of this, Jude," called out the father angrily. "Move further off; we are about to talk of matters unfit for a woman to listen to."

Hutter did not take any steps, however, to ascertain whether he was obeyed or not, but, dropping his voice a little, he pursued the discourse.

"The young man is right, Hurry," he said, "and we can leave the children in his care. Now, my idea is just this— and I think you'll agree that it is rational and correct. There's a large party of these savages on the shore, and though I didn't tell it before the girls, for they're womanish and apt to be troublesome when anything like real work is to be done, there's women among 'em. This I know from moccasin prints, and 'tis likely they are hunters, after all, who have been out so long that they know nothing of the war, or of the bounties."

"In which case, old Tom, why was their first salute an attempt to cut all our throats?"

"We don't know that their design was so bloody. It's natural and easy for an Indian to fall into ambushes and surprises; and no doubt they wished to get on board the ark first and to make their conditions afterward. That a disapp'inted savage should fire at us is in rule, and I think nothing of that. Besides, how often have they burned me out and robbed my traps—aye, and pulled trigger on me in the most peaceful times?"

"The blackguards will do such things, I must allow, and we pay 'em off pretty much in their own c'ine. Women

would not be on the warpath, sartainly, and so far there's reason in your idee."

"Nor would a hunter be in his war paint," returned Deerslayer. "I saw the Mingos and *know* that they are out on the trail of mortal men, not for beaver or deer."

"There you have it ag'in, old fellow," said Hurry. "In the way of an eye, now, I'd as soon trust this young man as trust the oldest settler in the Colony; if he says paint, why paint it was."

"Then a hunting party and a war party have met, for women must have been with 'em. It's only a few days since the runner went through with the tidings of the troubles, and it may be that warriors have come out to call in their women and children and to get an early blow."

"That would stand the courts, and is just the truth," cried Hurry. "You've got it now, old Tom, and I should like to hear what you mean to make out of it."

"The bounty," returned the other, looking up at his attentive companion in a cool, sullen manner, in which, however, heartless cupidity and indifference to the means were far more conspicuous than any feelings of animosity or revenge. "If there's women, there's children; and big and little have scalps; the Colony pays for all alike."

"More shame to it that it should do so," interrupted Deerslayer; "more shame to it that it don't understand its gifts and pay greater attention to the will of God."

"Hearken to reason, lad, and don't cry out afore you understand a case," returned the unmoved Hurry. "The savages scalp your fri'nds, the Delawares, or Mohicans, whichever they may be, among the rest; and why shouldn't we scalp? I will own it would be ag'in right for you and me, now, to go into the settlements and bring out scalps, but it's a very different matter as concerns Indians. A man shouldn't take scalps if he isn't ready to be scalped himself on fitting occasions. One good turn desarves another all the world over. That's reason, and I believe it to be good religion."

"Aye, Master Hurry," again interrupted the rich voice of Judith, "is it religion to say that one *bad* turn deserves another?"

"I'll never reason ag'in you, Judy, for you beat me with beauty, if you can't with sense. Here's the Canadas paying their Injins for scalps, and why not we pay——"

"*Our* Indians!" exclaimed the girl, laughing with a sort of melancholy merriment. "Father, Father! Think no more of this, and listen to the advice of Deerslayer, who *has* a conscience—which is more than I can say or think of Harry March."

Hutter now rose, and, entering the cabin, he compelled his daughters to go into the adjoining room, when he secured both the doors and returned. Then he and Hurry pursued the subject, but as the purport of all that was material in this discourse will appear in the narrative, it need not be related here in detail. The reader, however, can have no difficulty in comprehending the morality that presided over their conference. It was, in truth, that which, in some form or other, rules most of the acts of men, and in which the controlling principle is that one wrong will justify another. Their enemies paid for scalps, and this was sufficient to justify the Colony for retaliating. It is true, the French used the same argument, a circumstance, as Hurry took occasion to observe in answer to one of Deerslayer's objections, that proved its truth, as mortal enemies would not be likely to have recourse to the same reason unless it were a good one. But neither Hutter nor Hurry was a man likely to stick at trifles in matters connected with the right of the aborigines, since it is one of the consequences of aggression that it hardens the conscience, as the only means of quieting it. In the most peaceable state of the country, a species of warfare was carried on between the Indians, especially those of the Canadas and men of their caste, and the moment an actual and recognized warfare existed, it was regarded as the means of lawfully revenging a thousand wrongs, real and imaginary. Then, again, there was some truth and a good deal of expediency in the principle of retaliation, of which they both availed themselves in particular to answer the objections of their juster-minded and more scrupulous companion.

"You must fight a man with his own we'pons, Deerslayer," cried Hurry, in his uncouth dialect and in his dogmatic manner of disposing of all moral propositions. "If he's f'erce, you must be f'ercer; if he's stout of heart, you must be stouter. This is the way to get the better of Christian or savage: by keeping up to this trail you'll get soonest to the ind of your journey."

"That's not Moravian doctrine, which teaches that all are to be judged according to their talents or l'arning: the Injin like an Injin, and the white man like a white man. Some of their teachers say that if you're struck on the cheek, it's a duty to turn the other side of the face and take another blow, instead of seeking revenge, whereby I understand——"

"That's enough!" shouted Hurry. "That's all I want to prove a man's doctrine! How long would it take to kick a man through the Colony—in at one ind, and out at the other—on that principle?"

"Don't mistake me, March," returned the young hunter, with dignity. "I don't understand by this any more than that it's *best* to do this, if *possible*. Revenge is an Injin gift, and forgiveness a white man's. That's all. Overlook all you *can* is what's meant, and not *revenge* all you can. As for kicking, Master Hurry," and Deerslayer's sunburned cheek flushed as he continued, "into the Colony, or out of the Colony, that's neither here nor there, seeing no one proposes it, and no one would be likely to put up with it. What I wish to say is that a redskin's scalping don't justify a paleface's scalping."

"Do as you're done by, Deerslayer; that's ever the Christian parson's doctrine."

"No, Hurry, I've asked the Moravians consarning that, and it's altogether different. 'Do as you *would* be done by,' they tell me, is the *true* saying, while men practyse the *false*. They think all the Colonies wrong that offer bounties for scalps, and believe no blessing will follow the measures. Above all things, they forbid revenge."

"*That* for your Moravians!" cried March, snapping his fingers; "they're the next thing to Quakers. If you'd believe all they tell you, not even a 'rat would be skinned, out of marcy. Who ever heard of marcy on a muskrat!"

The disdainful manner of Hurry prevented a reply, and he and the old man resumed the discussion of their plans in a more quiet and confidential manner. This confidence lasted until Judith appeared, bearing the simple but savory supper. March observed, with a little surprise, that she placed the choicest bits before Deerslayer and that in the little nameless attentions it was in her power to bestow she quite obviously manifested a desire to let it be seen that she deemed him the honored guest. Accustomed, however, to the wayward-

ness and coquetry of the beauty, this discovery gave him
little concern, and he ate with an appetite that was in no
degree disturbed by any moral causes. The easily digested
food of the forests offering the fewest possible obstacles to
the gratification of this great animal indulgence, Deerslayer,
notwithstanding the hearty meal both had taken in the
woods, was in no manner behind his companion in doing justice to the viands.

An hour later the scene had greatly changed. The lake
was still placid and glassy, but the gloom of the hour had succeeded to the soft twilight of a summer evening, and all
within the dark setting of the woods lay in the quiet repose
of night. The forests gave up no song, or cry, or even murmur, but looked down from the hills on the lovely basin they
encircled, in solemn stillness; the only sound that was
audible was the regular dip of the sweeps, at which Hurry
and Deerslayer lazily pushed, impelling the ark toward the
castle. Hutter had withdrawn to the stern of the scow, in
order to steer, but, finding that the young men kept even
strokes and held the desired course by their own skill, he
permitted the oar to drag in the water, took a seat on the
end of the vessel, and lighted his pipe. He had not been thus
placed many minutes ere Hetty came stealthily out of the
cabin or house, as they usually termed that part of the
ark, and placed herself at his feet, on a little bench that she
brought with her. As this movement was by no means unusual in his feeble-minded child, the old man paid no other
attention to it than to lay his hand kindly on her head, in an
affectionate and approving manner, an act of grace that the
girl received in meek silence.

After a pause of several minutes, Hetty began to sing. Her
voice was low and tremulous, but it was earnest and solemn.
The words and the time were of the simplest form, the first
being a hymn that she had been taught by her mother, and
the last one of those natural melodies that find favor with all
classes, in every age, coming from and being addressed to
the feelings. Hutter never listened to this simple strain without finding his heart and manner softened—facts that his
daughter well knew, and by which she had often profited,
through the sort of holy instinct that enlightens the weak of
mind, more especially in their aims toward good.

Hetty's low, sweet tones had not been raised many mo-

ments when the dip of the oars ceased, and the holy strain arose singly on the breathing silence of the wilderness. As if she gathered courage with the theme, her powers appeared to increase as she proceeded, and though nothing vulgar or noisy mingled in her melody, its strength and melancholy tenderness grew on the ear until the air was filled with this simple homage of a soul that seemed almost spotless. That the men forward were not indifferent to this touching interruption was proved by their inaction; nor did their oars again dip until the last of the sweet sounds had actually died among the remarkable shores, which, at that witching hour, would waft even the lowest modulations of the human voice more than a mile. Hutter was much affected, for rude as he was by early habits, and even ruthless as he had got to be by long exposure to the practices of the wilderness, his nature was of that fearful mixture of good and evil that so generally enters into the moral composition of man.

"You are sad tonight, child," said the father, whose manner and language usually assumed some of the gentleness and elevation of the civilized life he had led in youth when he thus communed with this particular child. "We have just escaped from enemies, and ought rather to rejoice."

"You can never do it, Father!" said Hetty, in a low remonstrating manner, taking his hard, knotty hand into both her own. "You have talked long with Harry March, but neither of you have the heart to do it!"

"This is going beyond your means, foolish child; you must have been naughty enough to have listened, or you could know nothing of our talk."

"Why should you and Hurry kill people—especially women and children?"

"Peace, girl, peace. We are at war and must do to our enemies as our enemies would do to us."

"That's not it, Father! I heard Deerslayer say how it was. You must do to your enemies as you *wish* your enemies would do to you. No man wishes his enemies to kill him."

"We kill our enemies in war, girl, lest they should kill us. One side or the other must begin, and them that begin first are most apt to get the victory. You know nothing about these things, poor Hetty, and had best say nothing."

"*Judith* says it is wrong, Father, and Judith has sense, though I have none."

"Jude understands better than to talk to me of these matters, for she has sense, as you say, and knows I'll not bear it. Which would you prefer, Hetty, to have your own scalp taken and sold to the French, or that we should kill our enemies and keep them from harming us?"

"That's not it, Father! Don't kill them, nor let them kill us. Sell your skins, and get more, if you can, but don't sell human blood."

"Come, come, child, let us talk of matters you understand. Are you glad to see our old friend March back again? You like Hurry and must know that one day he may be your brother—if not something nearer."

"That can't be, Father," returned the girl, after a considerable pause. "Hurry has had one father and one mother, and people never have two."

"So much for your weak mind, Hetty. When Jude marries, her husband's father will be her father, and her husband's sister, her sister. If she should marry Hurry, then he will be your brother."

"Judith will never have Hurry," returned the girl mildly but positively; "Judith don't like Hurry."

"That's more than you can know, Hetty. Harry March is the handsomest, and the strongest, and the boldest young man that ever visits the lake, and, as Jude is the greatest beauty, I don't see why they shouldn't come together. He has as much as promised that he will enter into this job with me, on condition that I'll consent."

Hetty began to move her body back and forth and otherwise to express mental agitation, but she made no answer for more than a minute. Her father, accustomed to her manner and suspecting no immediate cause of concern, continued to smoke with the apparent phlegm which would seem to belong to that particular species of enjoyment.

"Hurry *is* handsome, Father," said Hetty, with a simple emphasis, that she might have hesitated about using had her mind been more alive to the inference of others.

"I told you so, child," muttered old Hutter, without removing the pipe from between his teeth. "He's the likeliest youth in these parts; and Jude is the likeliest young woman I've met with since her poor mother was in her best days."

"Is it wicked to be ugly, Father?"

"One might be guilty of worse things—but you're by no means ugly, though not so comely as Jude."

"Is Judith any happier for being so handsome?"

"She may be, child, and she may not be. But talk of other matters, now, for you hardly understand these, poor Hetty. How do you like our new acquaintance, Deerslayer!"

"He isn't handsome, Father. Hurry is far handsomer than Deerslayer."

"That's true, but they say he is a noted hunter! His fame had reached me before I ever saw him, and I did hope he would prove to be as stout a warrior as he is dexterous with the deer. All men are not alike, howsever, child, and it takes time, as I know by experience, to give a man a true wilderness heart."

"Have I got a wilderness heart, Father—and Hurry, is *his* heart true wilderness?"

"You sometimes ask queer questions, Hetty! Your heart is good, child, and fitter for the settlements than for the woods; while your reason is fitter for the woods than for the settlements."

"Why has Judith more reason than I, Father?"

"Heaven help thee, child—this is more than I can answer. God gives sense, and appearance, and all these things, and He grants them as he seeth fit. Dost thou wish for more sense?"

"Not I. The little I have troubles me, for when I think the hardest, then I feel the unhappiest. I don't believe thinking is good for me, though I do wish I was as handsome as Judith!"

"Why so, poor child? Thy sister's beauty may cause her trouble, as it caused her mother before her. It's no advantage, Hetty, to be so marked for anything as to become an object of envy, or to be sought after more than others."

"Mother was good, if she *was* handsome," returned the girl, the tears starting to her eyes, as usually happened when she adverted to her deceased parent.

Old Hutter, if not equally affected, was moody and silent at this allusion to his wife. He continued smoking, without appearing disposed to make any answer, until his simple-minded daughter repeated her remark, in a way to show that she felt uneasiness lest he might be inclined to deny her assertion. Then he knocked the ashes out of his pipe, and,

laying his hand in a sort of rough kindness on the girl's head, he made a reply.

"Thy mother was too good for this world," he said, "though others might not think so. Her good looks did not befriend her, and you have no occasion to mourn that you are not as much like her as your sister. Think less of beauty, child, and more of your duty, and you'll be as happy on this lake as you could be in the King's palace."

"I know it, Father, but Hurry says beauty is everything in a young woman."

Hutter made an ejaculation expressive of dissatisfaction and went forward, passing through the house, in order to do so. Hetty's simple betrayal of her weakness in behalf of March gave him uneasiness on a subject concerning which he had never felt before, and he determined to come to an explanation at once with his visitor; for directness of speech and decision in conduct were two of the best qualities of this rude being, in whom the seeds of a better education seemed to be constantly struggling upward, to be choked by the fruits of a life in which his hard struggles for subsistence and security had steeled his feelings and indurated his nature. When he reached the forward end of the scow, he manifested an intention to relieve Deerslayer at the oar, directing the latter to take his own place aft. By these changes, the old man and Hurry were again left alone, while the young hunter was transferred to the other end of the ark.

Hetty had disappeared when Deerslayer reached his new post, and for some little time he directed the course of the slow-moving craft by himself. It was not long, however, before Judith came out of the cabin, as if disposed to do the honors of the place to a stranger engaged in the service of her family. The starlight was sufficient to permit objects to be plainly distinguished when near at hand, and the bright eyes of the girl had an expression of kindness in them, when they met those of the youth, that the latter was easily enabled to discover. Her rich hair shaded her spirited and yet soft countenance, even at that hour rendering it the more beautiful—as the rose is loveliest when reposing amid the shadows and contrasts of its native foliage. Little ceremony is used in the intercourse of the woods, and Judith had acquired a readiness of address by the admiration that she so generally excited which, if it did not amount to forward-

ness, certainly in no degree lent to her charms the aid of that retiring modesty on which poets love to dwell.

"I thought I should have killed myself with laughing, Deerslayer," the beauty abruptly but coquettishly commenced, "when I saw that Indian dive into the river! He was a good-looking savage, too"—the girl always dwelt on personal beauty as a sort of merit—"and yet one couldn't stop to consider whether his paint would stand water!"

"And I thought they would have killed you with their we'pons, Judith," returned Deerslayer. "It was an awful risk for a female to run in the face of a dozen Mingos!"

"Did *that* make *you* come out of the cabin, in spite of their rifles, too?" asked the girl, with more real interest than she would have cared to betray, though with an indifference of manner that was the result of a good deal of practice united to native readiness.

"Men ar'n't apt to see females in danger and not come to their assistance. Even a Mingo knows that."

This sentiment was uttered with as much simplicity of manner as of feeling, and Judith rewarded it with a smile so sweet that even Deerslayer, who had imbibed a prejudice against the girl in consequence of Hurry's suspicions of her levity, felt its charm, notwithstanding half its winning influence was lost in the feeble light. It at once created a sort of confidence between them, and the discourse was continued on the part of the hunter without the lively consciousness of the character of this coquette of the wilderness with which it had certainly commenced.

"You are a man of deeds and not of words, I see plainly, Deerslayer," continued the beauty, taking her seat near the spot where the other stood, "and I foresee we shall be very good friends. Hurry Harry has, a tongue, and, giant as he is, he talks more than he performs."

"March is your fri'nd, Judith, and fri'nds should be tender of each other, when apart."

"We all know what Hurry's friendship comes to! Let him have his own way in everything and he's the best fellow in the Colony, but 'head him off,' as you say of the deer, and he is master of everything near him but himself. Hurry is no favorite of mine, Deerslayer, and I daresay, if the truth was known, and his conversation about me repeated, it would be found that he thinks no better of me than I own I do of him."

The latter part of this speech was not uttered without uneasiness. Had the girl's companion been more sophisticated, he might have observed the averted face, the manner in which the pretty little foot was agitated, and other signs that, for some unexplained reason, the opinions of March were not quite as much matter of indifference to her as she thought fit to pretend. Whether this was no more than the ordinary working of female vanity, feeling keenly even when it affected not to feel at all, or whether it proceeded from that deeply seated consciousness of right and wrong which God himself has implanted in our breasts that we may know good from evil, will be made more apparent to the reader as we proceed in the tale. Deerslayer felt embarrassed. He well remembered the cruel imputations left by March's distrust, and while he did not wish to injure his associate's suit by exciting resentment against him, his tongue was one that literally knew no guile. To answer without saying more or less than he wished was consequently a delicate duty.

"March has his say of all things in natur', whether of fri'nd or foe," slowly and cautiously rejoined the hunter. "He's one of them that speak as they feel while the tongue's a-going, and that's sometimes different from what they'd speak if they took time to consider. Give me a Delaware, Judith, for one that reflects and ruminates on his idees! Inmity has made 'em thoughtful, and a loose tongue is no riccomend at their council fires."

"I daresay March's tongue goes free enough when it gets on the subject of Judith Hutter and her sister," said the girl, rousing herself as if in careless disdain. "Young women's good names are a pleasant matter of discourse with some that wouldn't dare to be so open-mouthed if there was a brother in the way. Master March may find it pleasant to traduce us, but sooner or later he'll repent!"

"Nay, Judith, this is taking the matter up too much in 'arnest. Hurry has never whispered a syllable ag'in the good name of Hetty, to begin with——"

"I see how it is—I see how it is," impetuously interrupted Judith. "*I* am the one he sees fit to scorch with his withering tongue!—Hetty, indeed!—Poor Hetty!" she continued, her voice sinking into low husky tones that seemed nearly to stifle her in the utterance. "*She* is beyond and above his slanderous malice! Poor Hetty! If God has created her feeble-

minded, the weakness lies altogether on the side of errors of which she seems to know nothing. The earth never held a purer being than Hetty Hutter, Deerslayer."

"I can believe it—yes, I can believe *that*, Judith, and I hope 'arnestly that the same can be said of her handsome sister."

There was a soothing sincerity in the voice of Deerslayer which touched the girl's feelings; nor did the allusion to her beauty lessen the effect with one who knew only too well the power of her personal charms. Nevertheless, the still, small voice of conscience was not hushed, and it prompted the answer which she made after giving herself time to reflect.

"I daresay Hurry had some of his vile hints about the people of the garrisons," she added. "He knows they are gentlemen and can never forgive anyone for being what he feels he can never become himself."

"Not in the sense of a King's officer, Judith, sartainly, for March has no turn thataway, but in the sense of reality, why may not a beaver hunter be as respectable as a governor? Since you speak of it yourself, I'll not deny that he *did* complain of one as humble as you being as much in the company of scarlet coats and silken sashes. But 'twas jealousy that brought it out of him, and I do think that he mourned over his own thoughts as a mother would have mourned over her child."

Perhaps Deerslayer was not aware of the full meaning that his earnest language conveyed. It is certain that he did not see the color that crimsoned the whole of Judith's fine face, nor detect the uncontrollable distress that immediately after changed its hue to a deadly paleness. A minute or two elapsed in profound stillness, the splash of the water seeming to occupy all the avenues of sound, and then Judith arose and grasped the hand of the hunter, almost convulsively, with one of her own.

"Deerslayer," she said hurriedly, "I'm glad the ice is broken between us. They say that sudden friendships lead to long enmities, but I do not believe it will turn out so with us. I know not how it is—but you are the first man I ever met who did not seem to wish to flatter—to wish my ruin—to be an enemy in disguise—never mind; say nothing to Hurry, and another time we'll talk together again."

As the girl released her grasp, she vanished in the house,

leaving the astonished young man standing at the steering oar, as motionless as one of the pines on the hills. So abstracted, indeed, had his thoughts become that he was hailed by Hutter to keep the scow's head in the right direction before he remembered his actual situation.

CHAPTER VI

So spake the apostate Angel, though in pain,
Vaunting aloud, but racked with deep despair!

MILTON

SHORTLY AFTER THE disappearance of Judith, a light southerly air arose, and Hutter set a large square sail, which had
once been the flying topsail of an Albany sloop, but which,
having become threadbare in catching the breezes of Tappan,
had been condemned and sold. He had a light tough spar of
tamarack that he could raise on occasion, and with a little
contrivance his duck was spread to the wind in a sufficiently
professional manner. The effect on the ark was such as to supersede the necessity of rowing, and in about two hours the
castle was seen, in the darkness, rising out of the water, at the
distance of a hundred yards. The sail was then lowered,
and by slow degrees the scow drifted up to the building, and
was secured.

No one had visited the house since Hurry and his companion left it. The place was found in the quiet of midnight, a
sort of type of the solitude of a wilderness. As an enemy
was known to be near, Hutter directed his daughters to abstain from the use of lights, luxuries in which they seldom
indulged during the warm months, lest they might prove
beacons to direct their foes where they might be found.

"In open daylight I shouldn't fear a host of savages behind these stout logs, and they without any cover to skulk
into," added Hutter, when he had explained to his guests the
reasons why he forbade the use of lights; "for I've three or
four trusty weapons always loaded, and Killdeer, in particular, is a piece that never misses. But it's a different thing at
night. A canoe might get upon us unseen in the dark, and the

savages have so many cunning ways of attacking that I look
upon it as bad enough to deal with 'em under a bright sun. I
built this dwelling in order to have 'em at arm's length, in
case we should ever get to blows again. Some people think
it's too open and exposed, but I'm for anchoring out here,
clear of underbrush and thickets, as the surest means of
making a safe berth."

"You was once a sailor, they tell me, old Tom?" said
Hurry, in his abrupt manner, struck by one or two expressions that the other had just used, "and some people believe
you could give us strange accounts of inimies and ship-
wrecks, if you'd a mind to come out with all you know?"

"There are people in this world, Hurry," returned the
other evasively, "who live on other men's thoughts, and some
such often find their way into the woods. What I've been,
or what I've seen in youth, is of less matter now than what
the savages are. It's of more account to find out what will
happen in the next twenty-four hours than to talk over
what happened twenty-four years since."

"That's judgment, Deerslayer; yes, that's sound judgment.
Here's Judith and Hetty to take care of, to say nothing of our
own topknots; for my part, I can sleep as well in the dark
as I could under a noonday sun. To me it's no great matter
whether there is light or not to see to shut my eyes by."

As Deerslayer seldom thought it necessary to answer his
companion's peculiar vein of humor, and Hutter was evidently indisposed to dwell longer on the subject, its discussion ceased with this remark. The latter had something more
on his mind, however, than recollections. His daughters had
no sooner left them, with an expressed intention of going to
bed, than he invited his two companions to follow him
again into the scow. Here the old man opened his project,
keeping back the portion that he had reserved for execution
by Hurry and himself.

"The great object for people posted like ourselves is to
command the water," he commenced. "So long as there is no
other craft on the lake, a bark canoe is as good as a man-
of-war, since the castle will not be easily taken by swimming.
Now, there are but five canoes remaining in these parts, two
of which are mine, and one is Hurry's. These three we have
with us here; one being fastened in the canoe-dock beneath
the house, and the other two being alongside the scow. The

other canoes are housed on the shore, in hollow logs, and the savages, who are such venomous enemies, will leave no likely place unexamined in the morning, if they're serious in s'arch of bounties——"

"Now, friend Hutter," interrupted Hurry, "the Indian don't live that can find a canoe that is suitably wintered. I've done something at this business before now, and Deerslayer here knows that I am one that can hide a craft in such a way that I can't find it myself."

"Very true, Hurry," put in the person to whom the appeal had been made, "but you overlook the sarcumstance that if you couldn't see the trail of the man who did the job, I could. I'm of Master Hutter's mind, that it's far wiser to mistrust a savage's ingenuity than to build any great expectations on his want of eyesight. If these two canoes can be got off to the castle, therefore, the sooner it's done the better."

"Will you be of the party that's to do it?" demanded Hutter, in a way to show that the proposal both surprised and pleased him.

"Sartain. I'm ready to enlist in any enterprise that's not ag'in a white man's lawful gifts. Natur' orders us to defend our lives, and the lives of others, too, when there's occasion and opportunity. I'll follow you, Floating Tom, into the Mingo camp on such an a'r'nd, and will strive to do my duty, should we come to blows; though, never having been tried in battle, I don't like to promise more than I may be able to perform. We all know our wishes, but none know their might till put to the proof."

"That's modest and suitable, lad," exclaimed Hurry. "You've never yet heard the crack of an angry rifle; and let me tell you, 'tis as different from the persuasion of one of your venison speeches as the laugh of Judith Hutter, in her best humor, is from the scolding of a Dutch housekeeper on the Mohawk. I don't expect you'll prove much of a warrior, Deerslayer, though your equal with the bucks and the does don't exist in all these parts. As for the ra'al sarvice, however, you'll turn out rather rearward, according to my consait."

"We'll see, Hurry, we'll see," returned the other meekly, so far as human eye could discover not at all disturbed by these expressed doubts concerning his conduct on a point

on which men are sensitive, precisely in the degree that they feel the consciousness of demerit. "Having never been tried, I'll wait to know before I form any opinion myself, then there'll be sartainty instead of bragging. I've heard of them that was valiant afore the fight who did little in it, and of them that waited to know their own tempers, and found that they weren't as bad as some expected, when put to the proof."

"At any rate, we know you can use a paddle, young man," said Hutter, "and that's all we shall ask of you tonight. Let us waste no more time, but get into the canoe and *do* in place of talking."

As Hutter led the way in the execution of his project, the boat was soon ready, with Hurry and Deerslayer at the paddles. Before the old man embarked himself, however, he held a conference of several minutes with Judith, entering the house for that purpose; then, returning, he took his place in the canoe, which left the side of the ark at the next instant.

Had there been a temple reared to God in that solitary wilderness, its clock would have told the hour of midnight as the party set forth on their expedition. The darkness had increased, though the night was still clear, and the light of the stars sufficed for all the purposes of the adventurers. Hutter alone knew the places where the canoes were hid, and he directed the course, while his two athletic companions raised and dipped their paddles with proper caution, lest the sound should be carried to the ears of their enemies across that sheet of placid water, in the stillness of deep night. But the bark was too light to require any extraordinary efforts, and skill supplying the place of strength, in about half an hour they were approaching the shore at a point near a league from the castle.

"Lay on your paddles, men," said Hutter, in a low voice, "and let us look about us for a moment. We must now be all eyes and ears, for these vermin have noses like bloodhounds."

The shores of the lake were examined closely, in order to discover any glimmering of light that might have been left in a camp; the men strained their eyes, in the obscurity, to see if some thread of smoke was not still stealing along the mountainside as it arose from the dying embers of a fire. Nothing unusual could be traced, and as the position was at some distance from the outlet, or the spot where the

avages had been met, it was thought safe to land. The paddles were plied again, and the bows of the canoe ground pon the gravelly beach with a gentle motion and a sound arely audible. Hutter and Hurry immediately landed, the ormer carrying his own and his friend's rifle, leaving Deerlayer in charge of the canoe. The hollow log lay a little distance up the side of the mountain, and the old man led the vay toward it, using so much caution as to stop at every hird or fourth step to listen if any tread betrayed the presence of a foe. The same deathlike stillness, however, reigned n the midnight scene, and the desired place was reached vithout an occurrence to induce alarm.

"This is it," whispered Hutter, laying a foot on the trunk f a fallen linden. "Hand me the paddles first, and draw the oat out with care, for the wretches may have left it for a ait, after all."

"Keep my rifle handy, butt toward me, old fellow," answered March. "If they attack me loaded, I shall want to unoad the piece at 'em, at least. And feel if the pan is full."

"All's right," muttered the other. "Move slow when you et your load, and let me lead the way."

The canoe was drawn out of the log with the utmost care, aised by Hurry to his shoulder, and the two began to return o the shore, moving but a step at a time, lest they should umble down the steep declivity. The distance was not great, ut the descent was extremely difficult; toward the end of heir little journey, Deerslayer was obliged to land and meet hem, in order to aid in lifting the canoe through the bushes. Vith his assistance the task was successfully accomplished, nd the light craft soon floated by the side of the other canoe. This was no sooner done than all three turned anxiously toward the forest and the mountain, expecting an enemy to reak out of the one, or to come rushing down the other. Still he silence was unbroken, and they all embarked with the aution that had been used in coming ashore.

Hutter now steered broad off toward the center of the lake. Iaving got a sufficient distance from the shore, he cast his rize loose, knowing that it would drift slowly up the lake before the light, southerly air and intending to find it on his eturn. Thus relieved of his tow, the old man held his way lown the lake, steering toward the very point where Hurry ad made his fruitless attempt on the life of the deer. As

the distance from this point to the outlet was less than
mile, it was like entering an enemy's country, and redouble
caution became necessary. They reached the extremity of th
point, however, and landed in safety on the little gravell
beach already mentioned. Unlike the last place at whicl
they had gone ashore, here was no acclivity to ascend, th
mountains looming up in the darkness quite a quarter of
mile further west, leaving a margin of level ground betweer
them and the strand. The point itself, though long and cov
ered with tall trees, was nearly flat and, for some distance
only a few yards in width. Hutter and Hurry landed, as be
fore, leaving their companion in charge of the boat.

In this instance, the dead tree that contained the canoe o
which they had come in quest lay about halfway betweer
the extremity of the narrow slip of land and the place where
it joined the main shore; knowing that there was water so
near him on his left, the old man led the way along the
eastern side of the belt with some confidence, walking bold
ly, though still with caution. He had landed at the poin
expressly to get a glimpse into the bay, to make certain tha
the coast was clear; otherwise, he would have come ashore
directly abreast of the hollow tree. There was no difficulty i
finding the latter, from which the canoe was drawn as be
fore, and, instead of carrying it down to the place where
Deerslayer lay, it was launched at the nearest favorable
spot. As soon as it was in the water, Hurry entered it and
paddled round to the point, whither Hutter also proceeded
following the beach. As the three men had now in their pos
session all the boats on the lake, their confidence was greatly
increased, and there was no longer the same feverish de
sire to quit the shore, or the same necessity for extreme cau
tion. Their position on the extremity of the long, narrow bit
of land added to the feeling of security, as it permitted an
enemy to approach in only one direction, that in their front
and under circumstances that would render discovery, with
their habitual vigilance, almost certain. The three now landed
together and stood grouped in consultation on the gravelly
point.

"We've fairly tree'd the scamps," said Hurry, chuckling
at their success; "if they wish to visit the castle, let 'em wade
or swim! Old Tom, that idee of your'n, in burrowing out in
the lake, was high proof and carries a fine bead. There be

nen who would think the land safer than the water, but after
ill, reason shows it isn't, the beaver, and rats, and other
,'arned creatur's taking to the last when hard-pressed. I call
our position now entrenched, and set the Canadas at defiance."

"Let us paddle along this south shore," said Hutter, "and
see if there's no sign of an encampment—but first, let me
have a better look into the bay, for no one has been far
enough around the inner shore of the point to make sure of
that quarter yet."

As Hutter ceased speaking, all three moved in the direction he had named. Scarce had they fairly opened the bottom
of the bay when a general start proved that their eyes had
lighted on a common object at the same instant. It was no
more than a dying brand, giving out its flickering and failing
light, but at that hour, and in that place, it was at once as
conspicuous as "a good deed in a naughty world." There was
not a shadow of a doubt that this fire had been kindled at an
encampment of the Indians. The situation, sheltered from
observation on all sides but one, and even on that except for
a very short distance, proved that more care had been taken
to conceal the spot than would be used for ordinary purposes,
and Hutter, who knew that a spring was near at hand, as well
as one of the best fishing stations on the lake, immediately
inferred that this encampment contained the women and
children of the party.

"That's not a warrior's encampment," he growled to
Hurry; "and there's bounty enough sleeping around that fire
to make a heavy division of head-money. Send the lad to the
canoes, for there'll come no good of him in such an onset,
and let us take the matter in hand at once, like men."

"There's judgment in your notion, old Tom, and I like
it to the backbone. Deerslayer, do you get into the canoe, lad,
and paddle off into the lake with the spare one, and set it
adrift, as we did with the other; after which you can float
along shore, as near as you can get to the head of the bay,
keeping outside the point, howsever, and outside the rushes,
too. You can hear us when we want you; and if there's any
delay, I'll call like a loon—yes, that'll do it—the call of a
loon shall be the signal. If you hear rifles, and feel like sojer-
ing, why, you may close in and see if you can make the same
hand with the savages that you do with the deer."

"If my wishes could be followed, this matter would not be undertaken, Hurry——"

"Quite true—nobody denies it, boy; but your wishes *can't* be followed; that inds the matter. So just canoe yourself off into the middle of the lake, and by the time you get back there'll be movements in that camp!"

The young man set about complying with great reluctance and a heavy heart. He knew the prejudices of the frontiersmen too well, however, to attempt a remonstrance. The latter, indeed, under the circumstances might prove dangerous, as it would certainly prove useless. He paddled the canoe, therefore, silently, and with the former caution, to a spot near the center of the placid sheet of water, and set the boat just recovered adrift, to float toward the castle before the light, southerly air. This expedient had been adopted, in both cases, under the certainty that the drift could not carry the light barks more than a league or two before the return of light, when they might easily be overtaken. In order to prevent any wandering savage from using them, by swimming off and getting possession, a possible but scarcely a probable event, all the paddles were retained.

No sooner had he set the recovered canoe adrift than Deerslayer turned the bows of his own toward the point on the shore that had been indicated by Hurry. So light was the movement of the little craft, and so steady the sweep of its master's arm, that ten minutes had not elapsed ere it was again approaching the land, having, in that brief time, passed over fully half a mile of distance. As soon as Deerslayer's eye caught a glimpse of the rushes, of which there were many growing in the water a hundred feet from the shore, he arrested the motion of the canoe and anchored his boat by holding fast to the delicate but tenacious stem of one of the drooping plants. Here he remained, awaiting with an intensity of suspense that can be easily imagined the result of the hazardous enterprise.

It would be difficult to convey to the minds of those who have never witnessed it the sublimity that characterizes the silence of a solitude as deep as that which now reigned over the Glimmerglass. In the present instance, this sublimity was increased by the gloom of night, which threw its shadowy and fantastic forms around the lake, the forest, and the hills. It is not easy, indeed, to conceive of any place more

favorable to heighten these natural impressions than that Deerslayer now occupied. The size of the lake brought all within the reach of human senses, while it displayed so much of the imposing scene at a single view, giving up, as it might be, at a glance, a sufficiency to produce the deepest impressions. As has been said, this was the first lake Deerslayer had ever seen. Hitherto, his experience had been limited to the courses of rivers and smaller streams, and never before had he seen so much of that wilderness which he so well loved spread before his gaze. Accustomed to the forest, however, his mind was capable of portraying all its hidden mysteries, as he looked upon its leafy surface. This was also the first time he had been on a trail where human lives depended on the issue. His ears had often drunk in the traditions of frontier warfare, but he had never yet been confronted with an enemy.

The reader will readily understand, therefore, how intense must have been the expectation of the young man as he sat in his solitary canoe, endeavoring to catch the smallest sound that might denote the course of things on shore. His training had been perfect, so far as theory could go, and his self-possession, notwithstanding the high excitement that was the fruit of novelty, would have done credit to a veteran. The visible evidences of the existence of the camp, or of the fire, could not be detected from the spot where the canoe lay, and he was compelled to depend on the sense of hearing alone. He did not feel impatient, for the lessons he had heard taught him the virtue of patience and, most of all, inculcated the necessity of wariness in conducting any covert assault on the Indians. Once he thought he heard the cracking of a dried twig, but expectation was so intense it might mislead him. In this manner minute after minute passed, until the whole time since he left his companions was extended to quite an hour. Deerslayer knew not whether to rejoice in, or to mourn over, this cautious delay, for if it augured security to his associates, it foretold destruction to the feeble and innocent.

It might have been an hour and a half after his companions and he had parted when Deerslayer was aroused by a sound that filled him equally with concern and surprise. The quavering call of a loon arose from the opposite side of the lake, evidently at no great distance from its outlet. There was

no mistaking the note of this bird, which is so familiar to all who know the sounds of the American lakes. Shrill, tremulous, loud, and sufficiently prolonged, it seems the very cry of warning. It is often raised, also, at night—an exception to the habits of most of the other feathered inmates of the wilderness—a circumstance which had induced Hurry to select it as his own signal. There had been sufficient time, certainly, for the two adventurers to make their way by land from the point where they had been left to that whence the call had come, but it was not probable that they would adopt such a course. Had the camp been deserted they would have summoned Deerslayer to the shore, and, did it prove to be peopled, there could be no sufficient motive for circling it, in order to re-embark at so great a distance. Should he obey the signal and be drawn away from the landing, the lives of those who depended on him might be the forfeit—and should he neglect the call, on the supposition that it had been really made, the consequences might be equally disastrous, though from a different cause. In this indecision he waited, trusting that the call, whether feigned or natural, would be speedily renewed. Nor was he mistaken. A very few minutes elapsed before the same shrill warning cry was repeated, and from the same part of the lake. This time, being on the alert, his senses were not deceived. Although he had often heard admirable imitations of this bird, and was no mean adept himself in raising its notes, he felt satisfied that Hurry, to whose efforts in that way he had attended, could never so completely and closely follow nature. He determined, therefore, to disregard that cry and to wait for one less perfect and nearer at hand.

Deerslayer had hardly come to this determination when the profound stillness of night and solitude was broken by a cry so startling as to drive all recollection of the more melancholy call of the loon from the listener's mind. It was a shriek of agony that came either from one of the female sex, or from a boy so young as not yet to have attained a manly voice. This appeal could not be mistaken. Heart-rending terror—if not writhing agony—was in the sounds, and the anguish that had awakened them was as sudden as it was fearful. The young man released his hold of the rush and dashed his paddle into the water; to do, he knew not what—to steer, he knew not whither. A very few moments,

however, removed his indecision. The breaking of branches, the cracking of dried sticks, and the fall of feet were distinctly audible; the sounds appeared to approach the water, though in a direction that led diagonally toward the shore, and a little farther north than the spot that Deerslayer had been ordered to keep near. Following this clue, the young man urged the canoe ahead, paying but little attention to the manner in which he might betray its presence. He had reached a part of the shore where its immediate bank was tolerably high and quite steep. Men were evidently threshing through the bushes and trees on the summit of this bank, following the line of the shore, as if those who fled sought a favorable place for descending. Just at this instant five or six rifles flashed, and the opposite hills gave back, as usual, the sharp reports in prolonged rolling echoes. One or two shrieks, like those which escape the bravest when suddenly overcome by unexpected anguish and alarm, followed, and then the threshing among the bushes was renewed, in a way to show that man was grappling with man.

"Slippery devil!" shouted Hurry with the fury of disappointment—"his skin's greased! I shan't grapple! Take *that* for your cunning!"

The words were followed by the fall of some heavy object among the smaller trees that fringed the bank, appearing to Deerslayer as if his gigantic associate had hurled an enemy from him in this unceremonious manner. Again the flight and pursuit were renewed, and then the young man saw a human form break down the hill and rush several yards into the water. At this critical moment the canoe was just near enough to the spot to allow this movement, which was accompanied by no little noise, to be seen; and feeling that there he must take in his companion, if anywhere, Deerslayer urged the canoe forward to the rescue. His paddle had not been raised twice when the voice of Hurry was heard filling the air with imprecations, and he rolled on the narrow beach literally loaded down with enemies. While prostrate, and almost smothered with his foes, the athletic frontiersman gave his loon call in a manner that would have excited laughter under circumstances less terrific. The figure in the water seemed suddenly to repent his own flight and rushed to the shore to aid his companion, but was met

and immediately overpowered by half a dozen fresh pursuers, who just then came leaping down the bank.

"Let up, you painted riptyles—let up!" cried Hurry, too hard-pressed to be particular about the terms he used. "Isn't it enough that I am withed like a saw log that ye must choke, too!"

This speech satisfied Deerslayer that his friends were prisoners and that to land would be to share their fate. He was already within a hundred feet of the shore when a few timely strokes of the paddle not only arrested his advance but forced him off to six or eight times that distance from his enemies. Luckily for him, all of the Indians had dropped their rifles in the pursuit, or this retreat might not have been effected with impunity, though no one had noted the canoe in the first confusion of the melee.

"Keep off the land, lad," called out Hutter. "The girls depend only on you, now: you will want all your caution to escape these savages. Keep off, and God prosper you, as you aid my children!"

There was little sympathy in general between Hutter and the young man, but the bodily and mental anguish with which this appeal was made served at the moment to conceal from the latter the former's faults. He saw only the father in his sufferings, and he resolved at once to give a pledge of fidelity to his interests and to be faithful to his word.

"Put your heart at ease, Master Hutter," he called out; "the gals shall be looked to, as well as the castle. The inimy has got the shore, 'tis no use to deny, but he hasn't got the water. Providence has the charge of all, and no one can say what will come of it, but, if good will can sarve you and your'n, depend on that much. My exper'ence is small, but my will is good."

"Aye—aye, Deerslayer," returned Hurry, in his stentorian voice, which was losing some of its heartiness, notwithstanding. "Aye, aye, Deerslayer, you *mean* well enough, but what can you *do*? You're no great matter in the best of times, and such a person is not likely to turn out a miracle in the worst. If there's one savage on this lake shore there's forty, and that's an army you ar'n't the man to overcome. The best way, in my judgment, will be to make a straight course to the castle; get the gals into the canoe, with a few eatables; then strike off for the corner of the lake where we came

in and take the best trail for the Mohawk. These devils won't know where to look for you for some hours, and if they did and went off hot in the pursuit, they must turn either the foot or the head of the lake to get at you. That's my judgment in the matter, and if old Tom here wishes to make his last will and testament in a manner favorable to his darters, he'll say the same."

" 'Twill never do, young man," rejoined Hutter. "The enemy has scouts out at this moment, looking for canoes, and you'll be seen and taken. Trust to the castle, and above all things, keep clear of the land. Hold out a week, and parties from the garrisons will drive the savages off."

" 'Twon't be four-and-twenty hours, old fellow, afore these foxes will be rafting off to storm your castle," interrupted Hurry, with more of the heat of argument than might be expected from a man who was bound and a captive and above whom nothing could be called free but his opinions and his tongue. "Your advice has a stout sound, but it will have a fatal tarmination. If you or I was in the house, we might hold out a few days, but remember that this lad has never seen an inimy afore tonight, and is what you yourself called settlement-conscienced; though, for my part, I think the consciences in the settlements pretty much the same as they are out here in the woods. These savages are making signs, Deerslayer, for me to encourage you to come ashore with the canoe, but that I'll never do, as it's ag'in reason and natur'. As for old Tom and myself, whether they'll scalp us tonight, keep us for the torture by fire, or carry us to Canada is more than anyone knows but the devil that advises them how to act. I've such a big and bushy head that it's quite likely they'll indivor to get two scalps off it, for the bounty is a tempting thing, or old Tom and I wouldn't be in this scrape. Aye—there they go with their signs ag'in, but if I advise you to land, may they eat me as well as roast me. No, no, Deerslayer—do you keep off where you are, and after daylight, on no account come within two hundred yards——"

This injunction of Hurry's was stopped by a hand being rudely slapped against his mouth, the certain sign that someone in the party sufficiently understood English to have at length detected the drift of his discourse. Immediately after, the whole group entered the forest, Hutter and Hurry

apparently making no resistance to the movement. Just as the sounds of the cracking bushes were ceasing, however, the voice of the father was again heard.

"As you're true to my children, God prosper you, young man!" were the words that reached Deerslayer's ears; after which he found himself left to follow the dictates of his own discretion.

Several minutes elapsed, in deathlike stillness, when the party on the shore had disappeared in the woods. Owing to the distance—rather more than two hundred yards—and the obscurity, Deerslayer had been able barely to distinguish the group and to see it retiring, but even this dim connection with human forms gave an animation to the scene that was strongly in contrast to the absolute solitude that remained. Although the young man leaned forward to listen, holding his breath and condensing every faculty in the single sense of hearing, not another sound reached his ears to denote the vicinity of human beings. It seemed as if a silence that had never been broken reigned on the spot again; for an instant, even that piercing shriek which had so lately broken the stillness of the forest, or the execrations of March, would have been a relief to the feeling of desertion to which it gave rise.

This paralysis of mind and body, however, could not last long in one constituted mentally and physically like Deerslayer. Dropping his paddle into the water, he turned the head of the canoe and proceeded slowly, as one walks who thinks intently, toward the center of the lake. When he believed himself to have reached a point in a line with that where he had set the last canoe adrift, he changed his direction northward, keeping the light air as nearly on his back as possible. After paddling a quarter of a mile in this direction, a dark object became visible on the lake, a little to the right; and turning on one side for the purpose, he had soon secured his lost prize to his own boat. Deerslayer now examined the heavens, the course of the air, and the position of the two canoes. Finding nothing in either to induce a change of plan, he lay down and prepared to catch a few hours' sleep, that the morrow might find him equal to its exigencies.

Although the hardy and the tired sleep profoundly, even in scenes of danger, it was some time before Deerslayer lost his recollection. His mind dwelt on what had passed, and his

half-conscious faculties kept figuring the events of the night, in a sort of waking dream. Suddenly he was up and alert, for he fancied he heard the preconcerted signal of Hurry summoning him to the shore. But all was still as the grave again. The canoes were slowly drifting northward, the thoughtful stars were glimmering in their mild glory over his head, and the forest-bound sheet of water lay embedded between its mountains, as calm and melancholy as if never troubled by the winds, or brightened by a noonday sun. Once more the loon raised his tremulous cry, near the foot of the lake, and the mystery of the alarm was explained. Deerslayer adjusted his hard pillow, stretched his form in the bottom of the canoe, and slept.

CHAPTER VII

> *Clear, placid Leman! Thy contrasted lake*
> *With the wild world I dwelt in, is a thing*
> *Which warns me, with its stillness, to forsake*
> *Earth's troubled waters for a purer spring.*
> *This quiet sail is as a noiseless wing*
> *To waft me from distraction: once I loved*
> *Torn ocean's roar, but thy soft murmuring*
> *Sounds sweet as if a sister's voice reproved,*
> *That I with stern delights should e'er have been so moved.*

BYRON

DAY HAD FAIRLY dawned before the young man whom we have left in the situation described in the last chapter again opened his eyes. This was no sooner done than he started up and looked about him with the eagerness of one who suddenly felt the importance of accurately ascertaining his precise position. His rest had been deep and undisturbed, and when he awoke, it was with a clearness of intellect and a readiness of resources that were much needed at that particular moment. The sun had not risen, it is true, but the vault of heaven was rich with the winning softness that "brings and shuts the day," while the whole air was filled with the carols of birds, the hymns of the feathered tribe. These sounds first told Deerslayer the risks he ran. The air, for wind it could scarce be called, was still light, it is true, but it had increased a little in the course of the night, and as the canoes were mere feathers on the water, they had drifted twice the expected distance and, what was still more dangerous, had approached so near the base of the mountain that here rose precipitously from the eastern shore, as to render the carols of the birds plainly audible. This was not the worst. The third canoe had taken the same direction, and was slowly drifting toward a point where it must in-

evitably touch, unless turned aside by a shift of wind, or human hands. In other respects, nothing presented itself to attract attention, or to awaken alarm. The castle stood on its shoal, nearly abreast of the canoes, for the drift had amounted to miles in the course of the night, and the ark lay fastened to its piles, as both had been left so many hours before.

As a matter of course, Deerslayer's attention was first given to the canoe ahead. It was already quite near the point, and a very few strokes of the paddle sufficed to tell him that it must touch before he could possibly overtake it. Just at this moment, too, the wind inopportunely freshened, rendering the drift of the light craft much more rapid and certain. Feeling the impossibility of preventing a contact with the land, the young man wisely determined not to heat himself with unnecessary exertions; first looking to the priming of his piece, he proceeded slowly and warily toward the point, taking care to make a little circuit, that he might be exposed on only one side, as he approached.

The canoe adrift, being directed by no such intelligence, pursued its proper way and grounded on a small sunken rock at the distance of three or four yards from the shore. Just at that moment, Deerslayer had got abreast of the point, and turned the bows of his own boat to the land, first casting loose his tow, that his movements might be unencumbered. The canoe hung an instant on the rock; then it rose a hairsbreadth on an almost imperceptible swell of the water, swung around, floated clear, and reached the strand. All this the young man noted, but it neither quickened his pulses nor hastened his hand. If anyone had been lying in wait for the arrival of the waif, he must be seen, and the utmost caution in approaching the shore became indispensable; if no one was in ambush, hurry was unnecessary. The point being nearly diagonally opposite to the Indian encampment, he hoped the last, though the former was not only possible, but probable, for the savages were prompt in adopting all the expedients of their particular modes of warfare, and quite likely had many scouts searching the shores for craft to carry them off to the castle. As a glance at the lake from any height or projection would expose the smallest object on its surface, there was little hope that either of the canoes could pass unseen, and Indian

sagacity needed no instruction to tell which way a boat or a log would drift, when the direction of the wind was known. As Deerslayer drew nearer and nearer to the land, the stroke of his paddle grew slower, his eye became more watchful, and his ears and nostrils almost dilated with the effort to detect any lurking danger. 'Twas a trying moment for a novice, nor was there the encouragement which even the timid sometimes feel, when conscious of being observed and commended. He was entirely alone, thrown on his own resources, and was cheered by no friendly eye, emboldened by no encouraging voice. Notwithstanding all these circumstances, the most experienced veteran in forest warfare could not have behaved better. Equally free from recklessness and hesitation, his advance was marked by a sort of philosophical prudence that appeared to render him superior to all motives but those which were best calculated to effect his purpose. Such was the commencement of a career in forest exploits that afterward rendered this man, in his way, and under the limits of his habits and opportunities, as renowned as many a hero whose name has adorned the pages of works more celebrated than legends simple as ours can ever become.

When about a hundred yards from the shore, Deerslayer rose in the canoe, gave three or four vigorous strokes with the paddle, sufficient of themselves to impel the bark to land, and then quickly laying aside the instrument of labor, he seized that of war. He was in the very act of raising the rifle when a sharp report was followed by the buzz of a bullet that passed so near his body as to cause him involuntarily to start. The next instant Deerslayer staggered and fell his whole length in the bottom of the canoe. A yell—it came from a single voice—followed, and an Indian leaped from the bushes upon the open area of the point, bounding toward the canoe. This was the moment the young man desired. He rose on the instant and leveled his own rifle at his uncovered foe, but his finger hesitated about pulling the trigger on one whom he held at such a disadvantage. This little delay, probably, saved the life of the Indian, who bounded back into the cover as swiftly as he had broken out of it. In the meantime Deerslayer had been swiftly approaching the land, and his own canoe reached the point just as his enemy disappeared. As its movements had not

been directed, it touched the shore a few yards from the other boat; and though the rifle of his foe had to be loaded, there was not time to secure his prize, and to carry it beyond danger, before he would be exposed to another shot. Under the circumstances, therefore, he did not pause an instant, but dashed into the woods and sought a cover.

On the immediate point there was a small open area, partly in native grass and partly beach, but a dense fringe of bushes lined its upper side. This narrow belt of dwarf vegetation passed, one issued immediately into the high and gloomy vaults of the forest. The land was tolerably level for a few hundred feet, and then it rose precipitously in a mountainside. The trees were tall, large, and so free from underbrush that they resembled vast columns, irregularly scattered, upholding a dome of leaves. Although they stood tolerably close together, for their ages and size, the eye could penetrate to considerable distances, and bodies of men, even, might have engaged beneath their cover with concert and intelligence.

Deerslayer knew that his adversary must be employed in reloading, unless he had fled. The former proved to be the case, for the young man had no sooner placed himself behind a tree than he caught a glimpse of the arm of the Indian, his body being concealed by an oak, in the very act of forcing the leathered bullet home. Nothing would have been easier than to spring forward and decide the affair by a close assault on his unprepared foe, but every feeling of Deerslayer revolted at such a step, although his own life had just been attempted from a cover. He was yet unpracticed in the ruthless expedients of savage warfare, of which he knew nothing except by tradition and theory, and it struck him as an unfair advantage to assail an unarmed foe. His color had heightened, his eye frowned, his lips were compressed, and all his energies were collected and ready; but instead of advancing to fire, he dropped his rifle to the usual position of a sportsman in readiness to catch his aim and muttered to himself, unconscious that he was speaking—

"No, no—that may be redskin warfare, but it's not a Christian's gift. Let the miscreant charge, and then we'll take it out like men, for the canoe he *must* not and *shall* not

have. No, no, let him have time to load, and God will take care of the right!"

All this time the Indian had been so intent on his own movements that he was even ignorant that his enemy was in the wood. His only apprehension was that the canoe would be recovered and carried away before he might be in readiness to prevent it. He had sought the cover from habit, but was within a few feet of the fringe of bushes, and could be at the margin of the forest in readiness to fire in a moment. The distance between him and his enemy was about fifty yards, and the trees were so arranged by nature that the line of sight was not interrupted, except by the particular trees behind which each party stood.

His rifle was no sooner loaded than the savage glanced around him and advanced incautiously as regarded the real, but stealthily as respected the fancied position of his enemy, until he was fairly exposed. Then Deerslayer stepped from behind his own cover and hailed him.

"Thisaway, redskin; thisaway if you're looking for me," he called out. "I'm young in war but not so young as to stand on an open beach to be shot down like an owl by daylight. It rests on yourself whether it's peace or war atween us, for my gifts are white gifts, and I'm not one of them that thinks it valiant to slay human mortals, singly, in the woods."

The savage was a good deal startled by this sudden discovery of the danger he ran. He had a little knowledge of English, however, and caught the drift of the other's meaning. He was also too well schooled to betray alarm, but, dropping the butt of his rifle to the earth with an air of confidence, he made a gesture of lofty courtesy. All this was done with the ease and self-possession of one accustomed to consider no man his superior. In the midst of this consummate acting, however, the volcano that raged within caused his eyes to glare and his nostrils to dilate, like those of some wild beast that is suddenly prevented from taking the fatal leap.

"Two canoe," he said, in the deep, guttural tones of his race, holding up the number of fingers he mentioned, by way of preventing mistakes; "one for you—one for me."

"No, no, Mingo, that will never do. You own neither; and neither shall you have, as long as I can prevent it. I know it's

war atween your people and mine, but that's no reason why human mortals should slay each other, like savage creatur's that meet in the woods; go your way, then, and leave me to go mine. The world is large enough for us both, and when we meet fairly in battle, why, the Lord will order the fate of each of us."

"Good!" exclaimed the Indian. "My brother missionary—great talk; all about Manitou."

"Not so—not so, warrior. I'm not good enough for the Moravians and am too good for most of the other vagabonds that preach about in the woods. No, no, I'm only a hunter, as yet, though afore the peace is made, 'tis like enough there'll be occasion to strike a blow at some of your people. Still, I wish it to be done in fair fight and not in a quarrel about the ownership of a miserable canoe."

"Good! My brother very young—but he very wise. Little warrior—great talker. Chief, sometimes, in council."

"I don't know this, nor do I say it, Injin," returned Deerslayer, coloring a little at the ill-concealed sarcasm of the other's manner. "I look forward to a life in the woods, and I only hope it may be a peaceable one. All young men must go on the warpath, when there's occasion, but war isn't needfully massacre. I've seen enough of the last, this very night, to know that Providence frowns on it; I now invite you to go your own way, while I go mine, and hope that we may part fri'nds."

"Good! My brother has two scalp—gray hair under t'other. Old wisdom—young tongue."

Here the savage advanced with confidence, his hand extended, his face smiling, and his whole bearing denoting amity and respect. Deerslayer met his offered friendship in a proper spirit, and they shook hands cordially, each endeavoring to assure the other of his sincerity and desire to be at peace.

"All have his own," said the Indian: "my canoe, mine; your canoe, your'n. Go look: if your'n, you keep; if mine, I keep."

"That's just, redskin, though you must be wrong in thinking the canoe your property. However, seein' is believin', and we'll go down to the shore, where you may look with your own eyes, for it's likely you'll object to trustin' altogether to mine."

The Indian uttered his favorite exclamation of "good!" and then they walked, side by side, toward the shore. There was no apparent distrust in the manner of either, the Indian moving in advance, as if he wished to show his companion that he did not fear turning his back to him. As they reached the open ground, the former pointed toward Deerslayer's boat, and said emphatically—

"No mine—paleface canoe. *This* red man's. No want other man's canoe—want his own."

"You're wrong, redskin, you're altogether wrong. This canoe was left in old Hutter's keeping, and is his'n according to all law, red or white, till its owner comes to claim it. Here's the seats and the stitching of the bark to speak for themselves. No man ever know'd an Injin to turn off such work."

"Good! My brother little ole—big wisdom. Injin no make him. White man's work."

"I'm glad you think so, for holding out to the contrary might have made ill blood atween us, everyone having a right to take possession of his own. I'll just shove the canoe out of reach of dispute at once, as the quickest way of settling difficulties."

While Deerslayer was speaking, he put a foot against the end of the light boat, and giving a vigorous shove, he sent it out into the lake a hundred feet or more, where, taking the true current, it would necessarily float past the point, and be in no further danger of coming ashore. The savage started at this ready and decided expedient, and his companion saw that he cast a hurried and fierce glance at his own canoe, or that which contained the paddles. The change of manner, however, was but momentary, and then the Iroquois resumed his air of friendliness, and a smile of satisfaction.

"Good!" he repeated, with stronger emphasis than ever. "Young head, old mind. Know how to settle quarrel. Farewell, brother. He go to house in water—muskrat house—Injin go to camp; tell chiefs no find canoe."

Deerslayer was not sorry to hear this proposal, for he felt anxious to join the females, and he took the offered hand of the Indian very willingly. The parting words were friendly, and while the red man walked calmly toward the wood, with the rifle in the hollow of his arm, without

once looking back in uneasiness or distrust, the white man moved toward the remaining canoe, carrying his piece in the same pacific manner, it is true, but keeping his eyes fastened on the movements of the other. This distrust, however, seemed to be altogether uncalled for, and, as if ashamed to have entertained it, the young man averted his look and stepped carelessly up to his boat. Here he began to push the canoe from the shore and to make his other preparations for departing. He might have been thus employed a minute when, happening to turn his face toward the land, his quick and certain eye told him at a glance the imminent jeopardy in which his life was placed. The black, ferocious eyes of the savage were glancing on him like those of the crouching tiger through a small opening in the bushes, and the muzzle of his rifle seemed already to be opening in a line with his own body.

Then, indeed, the long practice of Deerslayer as a hunter did him good service. Accustomed to fire with the deer on the bound, and often when the precise position of the animal's body had in a manner to be guessed at, he used the same expedients here. To cock and poise his rifle were the acts of a single moment and a single motion; then, aiming almost without sighting, he fired into the bushes where he knew a body ought to be in order to sustain the appalling countenance which alone was visible. There was not time to raise the piece any higher, or to take a more deliberate aim. So rapid were his movements that both parties discharged their pieces at the same instant, the concussions mingling in one report. The mountains, indeed, gave back but a single echo. Deerslayer dropped his piece and stood, with head erect, steady as one of the pines in the calm of a June morning, watching the result; while the savage gave the yell that has become historical for its appalling influence, leaped through the bushes, and came bounding across the open ground, flourishing a tomahawk. Still Deerslayer moved not, but stood with his unloaded rifle fallen against his shoulders, while, with a hunter's habits, his hands were mechanically feeling for the powder horn and charger. When about forty feet from his enemy, the savage hurled his keen weapon, but it was with an eye so vacant and a hand so unsteady and feeble that the young man caught it by the

handle as it was flying past him. At that instant the Indian staggered and fell his whole length on the ground.

"I know'd it—I know'd it!" exclaimed Deerslayer, who was already preparing to force a fresh bullet into his rifle; "I know'd it must come to this as soon as I had got the range from the creatur's eyes. A man sights suddenly and fires quick when his own life's in danger; yes, I know'd it would come to this. I was about the hundredth part of a second too quick for him, or it might have been bad for me! The riptyle's bullet has just grazed my side—but, say what you will for or ag'in 'em, a redskin is by no means as sartain with powder and ball as a white man. Their gifts don't seem to lie thataway. Even Chingachgook, great as he is in other matters, isn't downright deadly with the rifle."

By this time the piece was reloaded, and Deerslayer, after tossing the tomahawk into the canoe, advanced to his victim and stood over him, leaning on his rifle, in melancholy attention. It was the first instance in which he had seen a man fall in battle—it was the first fellow creature against whom he had ever seriously raised his own hand. The sensations were novel, and regret, with the freshness of our better feelings, mingled with his triumph. The Indian was not dead, though shot directly through the body. He lay on his back, motionless, but his eyes, now full of consciousness, watched each action of his victor—as the fallen bird regards the fowler—jealous of every movement. The man probably expected the fatal blow which was to precede the loss of his scalp, or perhaps he anticipated that this latter act of cruelty would precede his death. Deerslayer read his thoughts, and he found a melancholy satisfaction in relieving the apprehensions of the helpless savage.

"No, no, redskin," he said, "you've nothing more to fear from me. I am of a Christian stock, and scalping is not of my gifts. I'll just make sartain of your rifle and then come back and do you what sarvice I can. Though here I can't stay much longer, as the crack of three rifles will be apt to bring some of your devils down upon me."

The close of this was said in a sort of a soliloquy, as the young man went in quest of the fallen rifle. The piece was found where its owner had dropped it and was immediately put into the canoe. Laying his own rifle at its side, Deerslayer then returned and stood over the Indian again.

"All inmity atween you and me's at an ind, redskin," he said, "and you may set your heart at rest on the score of the scalp, or any further injury. My gifts are white, as I've told you, and I hope my conduct will be white also!"

Could looks have conveyed all they meant, it is probable Deerslayer's innocent vanity on the subject of color would have been rebuked a little, but he comprehended the gratitude that was expressed in the eyes of the dying savage, without in the least detecting the bitter sarcasm that struggled with the better feeling.

"Water!" ejaculated the thirsty and unfortunate creature, "give poor Injin water."

"Aye, water you shall have, if you drink the lake dry. I'll just carry you down to it, that you may take your fill. This is the way, they tell me, with all wounded people—water is their greatest comfort and delight."

So saying, Deerslayer raised the Indian in his arms and carried him to the lake. Here he first helped him to take an attitude in which he could appease his burning thirst, after which he seated himself on a stone, and took the head of his wounded adversary in his own lap, and endeavored to soothe his anguish in the best manner he could.

"It would be sinful in me to tell you your time hadn't come, warrior," he commenced, "and therefore I'll not say it. You've passed the middle age already, and considerin' the sort of lives ye lead, your days have been pretty well filled. The principal thing now is to look forward to what comes next. Neither redskin nor paleface, on the whole, calculates much on sleepin' forever, but both expect to live in another world. Each has his gifts, and will be judged by 'em, and I suppose you've thought these matters over enough not to stand in need of sarmons when the trial comes. You'll find your happy hunting grounds, if you've been a just Injin; if an onjust, you'll meet your desarts in another way. I've my own idees about these things, but you're too old and exper'enced to need any explanations from one as young as I."

"Good!" ejaculated the Indian, whose voice retained its depth even as life ebbed away; "young head—ole wisdom!"

"It's sometimes a consolation, when the ind comes, to know that them we've harmed, or *tried* to harm, forgive us.

I suppose natur' seeks this relief by way of getting a pardon on 'arth, as we never can know whether He pardons, who is all in all, till judgment itself comes. It's soothing to know that *any* pardon at such times, and that, I conclude, is the secret. Now, as for myself, I overlook altogether your designs ag'in my life; first, because no harm came of 'em; next, because it's your gifts, and natur', and trainin', and I ought not to have trusted you at all; and, finally and chiefly, because I can bear no ill will to a dying man, whether heathen or Christian. So put your heart at ease, so far as I'm consarned; you know best what other matters ought to trouble you, or what ought to give you satisfaction in so trying a moment."

It is probable that the Indian had some of the fearful glimpses of the unknown state of being which God in mercy seems at times to afford to all the human race, but they were necessarily in conformity with his habits and prejudices. Like most of his people, and like too many of our own, he thought more of dying in a way to gain applause among those he left than to secure a better state of existence hereafter. While Deerslayer was speaking, his mind was a little bewildered, though he felt that the intention was good, and when he had done, a regret passed over his spirit that none of his own tribe were present to witness his stoicism, under extreme bodily suffering, and the firmness with which he met his end. With the high innate courtesy that so often distingushes the Indian warrior before he becomes corrupted by too much intercourse with the worst class of the white men, he endeavored to express his thankfulness for the other's good intentions and to let him understand that they were appreciated.

"Good!" he repeated, for this was an English word much used by the savages—"good—young head; young *heart,* too. *Old* heart tough; no shed tear. Hear Indian when he die, and no want to lie—what he call him?"

"Deerslayer is the name I bear now, though the Delawares have said that when I get back from this warpath, I shall have a more manly title, provided I can 'arn one."

"That good name for boy—poor name for warrior. He get better quick. No fear *there*"—the savage had strength sufficient, under the strong excitement he felt, to raise a hand and tap the young man on his breast—"eye sartain—

finger lightning—aim, death—great warrior soon. No Deerslayer—Hawkeye—Hawkeye—Hawkeye. Shake hand."

Deerslayer—or Hawkeye, as the youth was then first
named, for in afteryears he bore the appellation throughout
all that region—Deerslayer took the hand of the savage,
whose last breath was drawn in that attitude, gazing in admiration at the countenance of a stranger, who had shown
so much readiness, skill, and firmness in a scene that was
equally trying and novel. When the reader remembers it is
the highest gratification an Indian can receive to see his
enemy betray weakness, he will be better able to appreciate
the conduct which had extorted so great a concession at such
a moment.

"His spirit has fled!" said Deerslayer, in a suppressed,
melancholy voice. "Ah's me! Well, to this we must all
come sooner or later, and he is happiest, let his skin be of
what color it may, who is best fitted to meet it. Here lies
the body of no doubt a brave warrior, and the soul is already flying toward its heaven or hell, whether that be a
happy hunting ground, a place scant of game; regions of
glory, according to Moravian doctrine, or flames of fire!
So it happens, too, as regards other matters! Here have old
Hutter and Hurry Harry got themselves into difficulty, if
they hav'n't got themselves into torment and death, and
all for a bounty that luck offers to me in what many would
think a lawful and suitable manner. But not a farthing of
such money shall cross my hand. White I was born, and
white will I die, clinging to color to the last, even though
the King's Majesty, his governors, and all his councils, both
at home and in the colonies, forget from what they come,
and where they hope to go, and all for a little advantage in
warfare. No, no—warrior, hand of mine shall never molest your scalp, and so your soul may rest in peace on the
p'int of making a decent appearance, when the body comes
to join it, in your own land of spirits."

Deerslayer arose as soon as he had spoken. Then he
placed the body of the dead man in a sitting posture, with
its back against the little rock, taking the necessary care to
prevent it from falling or in any way settling into an attitude that might be thought unseemly by the sensitive,
though wild notions of a savage. When this duty was performed, the young man stood gazing at the grim countenance

of his fallen foe, in a sort of melancholy abstraction. As was his practice, however, a habit gained by living so much alone in the forest, he then began again to give utterance to his thoughts and feelings aloud.

"I didn't wish your life, redskin," he said, "but you left me no choice atween killing or being killed. Each party acted according to his gifts, I suppose, and blame can light on neither. You were treacherous, according to your natur' in war, and I was a little oversightful, as I'm apt to be in trusting others. Well, this is my first battle with a human mortal, though it's not likely to be the last. I have fou't most of the creatur's of the forest, such as bears, wolves, painters and catamounts, but this is the beginning with the redskins. If I was Injin born, now, I might tell of this, or carry in the scalp, and boast of the expl'ite afore the whole tribe; or, if my inimy had only been even a bear, 'twould have been nat-'ral and proper to let everybody know what had happened; but I don't well see how I'm to let even Chingachgook into this secret, so long as it can be done only by boasting with a white tongue. And why should I wish to boast of it a'ter all? It's slaying a human, although he was a savage; and how do I know that he was a just Injin, and that he has not been taken away suddenly to anything but happy hunting grounds. When it's onsartain whether good or evil has been done, the wisest way is not to be boastful—still, I *should* like Chingachgook to know that I haven't discredited the Delawares or my training!"

Part of this was uttered aloud, while part was merely muttered between the speaker's teeth; his more confident opinions enjoying the first advantage, while his doubts were expressed in the latter mode. Soliloquy and reflection received a startling interruption, however, by the sudden appearance of a second Indian on the lake shore, a few hundred yards from the point. This man, evidently another scout, who had probably been drawn to the place by the reports of the rifles, broke out of the forest with so little caution that Deerslayer caught a view of his person before he was himself discovered. When the latter event did occur, as was the case a moment later, the savage gave a loud yell, which was answered by a dozen voices from different parts of the mountainside. There was no longer any time for delay; in another

minute the boat was quitting the shore under long and steady sweeps of the paddle.

As soon as Deerslayer believed himself to be at a safe distance, he ceased his efforts, permitting the little bark to drift, while he leisurely took a survey of the state of things. The canoe first sent adrift was floating before the air, quite a quarter of a mile above him, and a little nearer to the shore than he wished, now that he knew more of the savages were so near at hand. The canoe shoved from the point was within a few yards of him, he having directed his own course toward it on quitting the land. The dead Indian lay in grim quiet where he had left him, the warrior who had shown himself from the forest had already vanished, and the woods themselves were as silent and seemingly deserted as the day they came fresh from the hands of their great Creator. This profound stillness, however, lasted but a moment. When time had been given to the scouts of the enemy to reconnoiter, they burst out of the thicket upon the naked point, filling the air with yells of fury at discovering the death of their companion. These cries were immediately succeeded by shouts of delight when they reached the body and clustered eagerly around it. Deerslayer was a sufficient adept in the usages of the natives to understand the reason of the change. The yell was the customary lamentation at the loss of a warrior, the shout a sign of rejoicing that the conqueror had not been able to secure the scalp, the trophy without which a victory is never considered complete. The distance at which the canoes lay probably prevented any attempts to injure the conqueror, the American Indian, like the panther of his own woods, seldom making any effort against his foe unless tolerably certain it is under circumstances that may be expected to prove effective.

As the young man had no longer any motive to remain near the point, he prepared to collect his canoes, in order to tow them off to the castle. That nearest was soon in tow, and he proceeded in quest of the other, which was all this time floating up the lake. The eye of Deerslayer was no sooner fastened on this last boat than it struck him that it was nearer to the shore than it would have been had it merely followed the course of the gentle current of air. He began to suspect the influence of some unseen current in the water, and he quickened his exertions in order to regain possession

of it before it could drift in to a dangerous proximity to the woods. On getting nearer, he thought that the canoe had a perceptible motion through the water, and, as it lay broadside to the air, that this motion was taking it toward the land. A few vigorous strokes of the paddle carried him still nearer, when the mystery was explained. Something was evidently in motion on the offside of the canoe, or that which was furthest from himself, and closer scrutiny showed that it was a naked human arm. An Indian was lying in the bottom of the canoe and was propelling it slowly but certainly to the shore, using his hand as a paddle. Deerslayer understood the whole artifice at a glance. A savage had swum off to the boat while he was occupied with his enemy on the point, got possession, and was using these means to urge it to the shore.

Satisfied that the man in the canoe could have no arms, Deerslayer did not hesitate to dash close alongside of the retiring boat, without deeming it necessary to raise his own rifle. As soon as the wash of the water, which he made in approaching, became audible to the prostrate savage, the latter sprang to his feet, and uttered an exclamation that proved how completely he was taken by surprise.

"If you've enj'yed yourself enough in that canoe, redskin," Deerslayer coolly observed, stopping his own career in sufficient time to prevent an absolute collision between the two boats—"if you've enj'yed yourself enough in that canoe, you'll do a prudent act by taking to the lake ag'in. I'm reasonable in these matters, and don't crave your blood, though there's them about that would look upon you more as a due bill for the bounty than a human mortal. Take to the lake this minute, afore we get to hot words."

The savage was one of those who did not understand a word of English, and he was indebted to the gestures of Deerslayer and to the expression of an eye that did not often deceive for an imperfect comprehension of his meaning. Perhaps, too, the sight of the rifle that lay so near the hand of the white man quickened his decision. At all events, he crouched like a tiger about to take his leap, uttered a yell, and the next instant his naked body disappeared in the water. When he rose to take breath, it was at the distance of several yards from the canoe, and the hasty glance he threw behind him denoted how much he feared the arrival of a

fatal messenger from the rifle of his foe. But the young man made no indication of any hostile intention. Deliberately securing the canoe to the others, he began to paddle from the shore; by the time the Indian reached the land, and had shaken himself, like a spaniel on quitting the water, his dreaded enemy was already beyond rifle shot, on his way to the castle. As was so much his practice, Deerslayer did not fail to soliloquize on what had just occurred, while steadily pursuing his course toward the point of destination.

"Well, well"—he commenced—" 'twould have been wrong to kill a human mortal without an object. Scalps are of no account with me, and life is sweet and ought not to be taken marcilessly by them that have white gifts. The savage was a Mingo, it's true, and I make no doubt he is, and will be as long as he lives, a ra'al riptyle and vagabond, but that's no reason I should forget my gifts and color. No, no—let him go; if ever we meet ag'in, rifle in hand, why then 'twill be seen which has the stoutest heart and the quickest eye. Hawkeye! That's not a bad name for a warrior, sounding much more manful and valiant than Deerslayer! 'Twouldn't be a bad title to begin with, and it has been fairly 'arned. If 'twas Chingachgook, now, he might go home and boast of his deeds, and the chiefs would name him Hawkeye in a minute; but it don't become white blood to brag, and 'tisn't easy to see how the matter can be known unless I do. Well, well— everything is in the hands of Providence; this affair as well as another; I'll trust to that for getting my desarts in all things."

Having thus betrayed what might be termed his weak spot, the young man continued to paddle in silence, making his way diligently, and as fast as his tows would allow him, toward the castle. By this time the sun had not only risen, but it had appeared over the eastern mountains, and was shedding a flood of glorious light on this as yet unchristened sheet of water. The whole scene was radiant with beauty, and no one unaccustomed to the ordinary history of the woods would fancy it had so lately witnessed incidents so ruthless and barbarous. As he approached the building of old Hutter, Deerslayer thought, or rather *felt,* that its appearance was in singular harmony with all the rest of the scene. Although nothing had been consulted but strength and security, the rude, massive logs, covered with their rough bark, the pro-

jecting roof, and the form would contribute to render the building picturesque in almost any situation, while its actual position added novelty and piquancy to its other points of interest.

When Deerslayer drew nearer to the castle, however, objects of interest presented themselves that at once eclipsed any beauties that might have distinguished the scenery of the lake, and the site of the singular edifice. Judith and Hetty stood on the platform before the door, Hurry's dooryard, awaiting his approach with manifest anxiety, the former from time to time taking a survey of his person and of the canoes through the old ship's spyglass that has been already mentioned. Never probably did this girl seem more brilliantly beautiful than at that moment, the flush of anxiety and alarm increasing her color to its richest tints, while the softness of her eyes, of charm that even poor Hetty shared with her, was deepened by intense concern. Such, at least, without pausing or pretending to analyze motives, or to draw any other very nice distinctions between cause and effect, were the opinions of the young man, as his canoes reached the side of the ark, where he carefully fastened all three before he put his foot on the platform.

CHAPTER VIII

> *His words are bonds, his oaths are oracles;*
> *His love sincere, his thoughts immaculate;*
> *His tears pure messengers sent from his heart;*
> *His heart as far from fraud as heaven from earth.*
>
> SHAKESPEARE

NEITHER OF THE girls spoke as Deerslayer stood before them alone, his countenance betraying all the apprehension he felt on account of the two absent members of their party.

"Father!" Judith at length exclaimed, succeeding in uttering the word as it might be by a desperate effort.

"He's met with misfortune, and there's no use in concealing it," answered Deerslayer, in his direct and simple-minded manner. "He and Hurry are in Mingo hands, and Heaven only knows what's to be the tarmination. I've got the canoes safe, and that's a consolation, since the vagabonds will have to swim for it, or raft off, to come near this place. At sunset we'll be reinforced by Chingachgook, if I can manage to get him into a canoe; then, I think, we two can answer for the ark and the castle, till some of the officers in the garrisons hear of this warpath, which sooner or later must be the case, when we may look for succor from that quarter, if from no other."

"The officers!" exclaimed Judith impatiently, her color deepening and her eye expressing a lively but passing emotion. "Who thinks or speaks of the heartless gallants now? We are sufficient of ourselves to defend the castle—but what of my father and of poor Hurry Harry?"

" 'Tis natural you should feel this consarn for your own parent, Judith, and I suppose it's equally so that you should feel it for Hurry Harry, too."

Deerslayer then commenced a succinct but clear narrative

of all that occurred during the night, in no manner concealing what had befallen his two companions, or his own opinion of what might prove to be the consequences. The girls
listened with profound attention, but neither betrayed that
feminine apprehension and concern which would have followed such a communication when made to those who
were less accustomed to the hazards and accidents of a
frontier life. To the surprise of Deerslayer, Judith seemed the
most distressed, Hetty listening eagerly but appearing to
brood over the facts in melancholy silence, rather than betraying any outward signs of feeling. The former's agitation, the young man did not fail to attribute to the interest
she felt in Hurry, quite as much as to her filial love, while
Hetty's apparent indifference was ascribed to that mental
darkness which, in a measure, obscured her intellect and
which possibly prevented her from foreseeing all the consequences. Little was said, however, by either, Judith and her
sister busying themselves in making the preparations for the
morning meal, as they who habitually attend to such matters toil on mechanically even in the midst of suffering and
sorrow. The plain but nutritious breakfast was taken by all
three in somber silence. The girls ate little, but Deerslayer
gave proof of possessing one material requisite of a good
soldier, that of preserving his appetite in the midst of the
most alarming and embarrassing circumstances. The meal was
nearly ended before a syllable was uttered; then, however,
Judith spoke in the convulsive and hurried manner in which
feeling breaks through restraint, after the latter has become
more painful than even the betrayal of emotion.

"Father would have relished this fish!" she exclaimed. "He
says the salmon of the lakes is almost as good as the salmon of the sea."

"Your father has been acquainted with the sea, they tell
me, Judith," returned the young man, who could not forbear throwing a glance of inquiry at the girl; in common with
all who knew Hutter, he had some curiosity on the subject of
his early history. "Hurry Harry tells me he was once a sailor."

Judith first looked perplexed; then, influenced by feelings
that were novel to her in more ways than one, she became
suddenly communicative, and seemingly much interested in
the discourse.

"If Hurry knows anything of Father's history, I would he

had told it to me!" she cried. "Sometimes I think, too, he was once a sailor, and then again I think he was not. If that chest were open, or if it could speak, it might let us into his whole history. But its fastenings are too strong to be broken like packthread."

Deerslayer turned to the chest in question and, for the first time, examined it closely. Although discolored, and bearing proofs of having received much ill treatment, he saw that it was of materials and workmanship altogether superior to anything of the same sort he had ever before beheld. The wood was dark, rich, and had once been highly polished, though the treatment it had received left little gloss on its surface, and various scratches and indentations proved the rough collisions that it had encountered with substances still harder than itself. The corners were firmly bound with steel, elaborately and richly wrought, while the locks, of which it had no less than three, and the hinges were of a fashion and workmanship that would have attracted attention even in a warehouse of curious furniture. This chest was quite large; when Deerslayer arose and endeavored to raise an end by its massive handle, he found that the weight fully corresponded with the external appearance.

"Did you never see that chest opened, Judith?" the young man demanded with frontier freedom, for delicacy on such subjects was little felt among the people on the verge of civilization in that age, even if it be today.

"Never. Father has never opened it in my presence, if he ever opens it at all. No one here has ever seen its lid raised, unless it be Father; nor do I even know that he has ever seen it."

"Now, you're wrong, Judith," Hetty quietly answered. "Father *has* raised the lid, and *I've* seen him do it."

A feeling of manliness kept the mouth of Deerslayer shut, for while he would not have hesitated about going far beyond what would be thought the bounds of propriety in questioning the elder sister, he had just scruples about taking what might be thought an advantage of the feeble intellect of the younger. Judith, being under no such restraint, however, turned quickly to the last speaker, and continued the discourse.

"When and where did you ever see that chest opened, Hetty?"

"Here, and again and again. Father often opens it when *you* are away, though he don't in the least mind my being by and seeing all he does as well as hearing all he says."

"And what is it that he does, and what does he say?"

"That I cannot tell *you*, Judith," returned the other in a low but resolute voice. "*Father's* secrets are not *my* secrets."

"Secrets! This is stranger still, Deerslayer, that Father should tell them to Hetty and not tell them to me!"

"There's good reason for that, Judith, though you're not to know it. Father's not here to answer for himself, and I'll say no more about it."

Judith and Deerslayer looked surprised, and for a minute the first seemed pained. But suddenly recollecting herself, she turned away from her sister, as if in pity for her weakness, and addressed the young man.

"You've told but half your story," she said, "breaking off at the place where you went to sleep in the canoe—or rather where you rose to listen to the cry of the loon. We heard the call of the loons, too, and thought their cries might bring a storm, though we are little used to tempests on this lake at this season of the year."

"The winds blow and the tempests howl as God pleases, sometimes at one season and sometimes at another," answered Deerslayer; "and the loons speak accordin' to their natur'. Better would it be if men were as honest and frank. After I rose to listen to the birds, finding it could not be Hurry's signal, I lay down and slept. When the day dawned, I was up and stirring as usual, and then I went in chase of the two canoes, lest the Mingos should lay hands on 'em."

"You have not told us all, Deerslayer," said Judith earnestly. "We heard rifles under the eastern mountain; the echoes were full and long, and came so soon after the reports that the pieces must have been fired on or quite near to the shore. Our ears are used to these signs and are not to be deceived."

"They've done their duty, gal, this time; yes, they've done their duty. Rifles have been sighted this morning, aye, and triggers pulled, too, though not as often as they might have been. One warrior has gone to his happy hunting grounds, and that's the whole of it. A man of white blood and white gifts is not to be expected to boast of his expl'ites and to flourish scalps."

Judith listened almost breathlessly, and when Deerslayer,

in his quiet, modest manner, seemed disposed to quit the subject, she rose and, crossing the room, took a seat by his side. The manner of the girl had nothing forward about it, though it betrayed the quick instinct of a female's affection and the sympathizing kindness of a woman's heart. She even took the hard hand of the hunter and pressed it in both her own, unconsciously to herself, perhaps, while she looked earnestly and even reproachfully into his sunburned face.

"You have been fighting the savages, Deerslayer, singly and by yourself!" she said. "In your wish to take care of us —of Hetty—of me, perhaps, you've fought the enemy bravely, with no eye to encourage your deeds, or to witness your fall, had it pleased Providence to suffer so great a calamity!"

"I've fou't, Judith; yes, I *have* fou't the inimy, and that, too, for the first time in my life. These things must be, and they bring with 'em a mixed feelin' of sorrow and triumph. Human natur' is a fightin' natur', I suppose, as all nations kill in battle, and we must be true to our rights and gifts. What has yet been done is no great matter, but should Chingachgook come to the rock this evening, as is agreed atween us, and I get him off it onbeknown to the savages, or, if known to them, ag'in their wishes and designs, then may we all look to something like warfare afore the Mingos shall get possession of either the castle, or the ark, or yourselves."

"Who is this Chingachgook? From what place does he come, and *why* does he come *here?*"

"The questions are nat'ral and right, I suppose, though the youth has a great name already in his own part of the country. Chingachgook is a Mohican by blood, consorting with the Delawares by usage, as is the case with most of his tribe, which has long been broken up by the increase of our color. He is of the family of the great chiefs, Uncas, his father, having been the considerablest warrior and counselor of his people. Even old Tamenund honors Chingachgook, though he is thought to be yet too young to lead in war; and then the nation is so disparsed and diminished that chieftainship among 'em has got to be little more than a name. Well, this war having commenced in 'arnest, the Delaware and I rendezvous'd an app'intment, to meet this evening at sunset on the rendezvous rock at the foot of this very lake, intending to come out on our first hostile expedition ag'in the Mingos. *Why* we come exactly thisaway is our own secret, but thoughtful

young men on a warpath, as you may suppose, do nothing without a calculation and a design."

"A Delaware can have no unfriendly intentions toward us," said Judith, after a moment's hesitation, "and we know you to be friendly."

"Treachery is the last crime I hope to be accused of," returned Deerslayer, hurt at the gleam of distrust that had shot through Judith's mind; "and least of all, treachery to my own color."

"No one suspects *you*, Deerslayer," the girl impetuously cried. "No—no—your honest countenance would be a sufficient surety for the truth of a thousand hearts! If all men had as honest tongues, and no more promised what they did not mean to perform, there would be less wrong done in the world, and fine feathers and scarlet cloaks would not be thought excuses for baseness and deception."

The girl spoke with strong, nay, even with convulsed feeling, and her fine eyes, usually so soft and alluring, flashed fire as she concluded. Deerslayer could not but observe this extraordinary emotion, but with the tact of a courtier, he avoided not only any allusion to the circumstance but succeeded in concealing the effect of his discovery on himself. Judith gradually grew calm again, and as she was obviously anxious to appear to advantage in the eyes of the young man, she was soon able to renew the conversation as composedly as if nothing had occurred to disturb her.

"I have no right to look into your secrets, or the secrets of your friend, Deerslayer," she continued, "and am ready to take all you say on trust. If we can really get another male ally to join us at this trying moment, it will aid us much; I am not without hope that when the savages find we are able to keep the lake, they will offer to give up their prisoners in exchange for skins, or at least for the keg of powder that we have in the house."

The young man had the words "scalps," and "bounty," on his lips, but a reluctance to alarm the feelings of the daughters prevented him from making the allusion he had intended to the probable fate of their father. Still, so little was he practiced in the arts of deception that his expressive countenance was, of itself, understood by the quick-witted Judith, whose intelligence had been sharpened by the risks and habits of her life.

"I understand what you mean," she continued hurriedly, "and what you would say, but for the fear of hurting me —*us*, I mean, for Hetty loves her father quite as well as I do. But this is not as we think of Indians. They never scalp an unhurt prisoner, but would rather take him away alive, unless, indeed, the fierce wish for torturing should get the mastery of them. I fear nothing for my father's scalp and little for his life. Could they steal on us in the night, we should all probably suffer in this way, but men taken in open strife are seldom injured—not, at least, until the time of torture comes."

"That's tradition, I'll allow, and it's accordin' to practice —but, Judith, do you know the 'ar'nd on which your father and Hutter went ag'in the savages?"

"I do, and a cruel errand it was! But what will you have? Men will be men, and some even that flaunt in their gold and silver, and carry the King's commission in their pockets, are not guiltless of equal cruelty." Judith's eye again flashed, but by a desperate struggle she resumed her composure. "I get warm when I think of all the wrong that men do," she added, affecting to smile, an effort in which she only succeeded indifferently well. "All this is silly. What is done is done, and it cannot be mended by complaints. But the Indians think so little of the shedding of blood, and value men so much for the boldness of their undertakings, that, did they know the business on which their prisoners came, they would be more likely to honor than to injure them for it."

"For a time, Judith; yes, I allow *that*, for a time. But, when that feelin' dies away, then will come the love of revenge. We must indivor, Chingachgook and I, we must indivor to see what we can do to get Hurry and your father free, for the Mingos will no doubt hover about this lake some days in order to make the most of their success."

"You think this Delaware can be depended on, Deerslayer?" demanded the girl thoughtfully.

"As much as I can myself. You say you do not suspect *me*, Judith?"

"*You!*" taking his hand again and pressing it between her own with a warmth that might have awakened the vanity of one less simple-minded and more disposed to dwell on his own good qualities, "I would as soon suspect a brother! I have

known you but a day, Deerslayer, but it has awakened the confidence of a year. Your name, however, is not unknown to me, for the gallants of the garrisons frequently speak of the lessons you have given them in hunting, and all proclaim your honesty."

"Do they ever talk of the shooting, gal?" inquired the other eagerly, after, however, laughing in a silent but heartfelt manner. "Do they ever talk of the shooting? I want to hear nothing about my own, for if that isn't sartified to by this time, in all these parts, there's little use in being skillful and sure; but what do the officers say of their own—yes, what do they say of their own? Arms, as they call it, is their trade, and yet there's some among 'em that know very little how to use 'em!"

"Such I hope will not be the case with your friend Chingachgook, as you call him—what is the English of his Indian name?"

"Big Sarpent—so called for his wisdom and cunning. Uncas is his ra'al name—all his family being called Uncas, until they get a title that has been 'arned by deeds."

"If he has all this wisdom, we may expect a useful friend in him, unless his own business in this part of the country should prevent him from serving us."

"I see no great harm in telling you his ar'n'd, a'ter all, and, as you may find means to help us, I will let you and Hetty into the whole matter, trusting that you'll keep the secret as if it was your own. You must know that Chingachgook is a comely Injin, and is much look'd upon and admired by the young women of his tribe, both on account of his family and on account of himself. Now there is a chief that has a daughter called Wah-ta!-Wah, which is intarpreted into Hist-oh!-Hist in the English tongue, the rarest gal among the Delawares and the one most sought a'ter and craved for a wife by all the young warriors of the nation. Well Chingachgook, among others, took a fancy to Wah-ta!-Wah, and Wah-ta!-Wah took a fancy to him." Here Deerslayer paused an instant, for as he got thus far in his tale, Hetty Hutter arose, approached, and stood attentive at his knee, as a child draws near to listen to the legends of its mother. "Yes, he fancied *her,* and she fancied *him,*" resumed Deerslayer, casting a friendly and approving glance at the innocent and interested girl; "and when that is the case, and

all the elders are agreed, it does not often happen that the young couple keep apart. Chingachgook couldn't well carry off such a prize without making inimies among them that wanted her as much as he did himself. A sartain Briarthorn, as we call him in English, or Yocommon, as he is tarmed in Injin, took it most to heart, and we mistrust him of having a hand in all that followed. Wah-ta!-Wah went with her father and mother two moons ago to fish for salmon on the western streams, where it is agreed by all in these parts that fish most abounds, and while thus empl'y'd the gal vanished. For several weeks we could get no tidings of her, but here, ten days since, a runner that came through the Delaware country brought us a message by which we l'arn that Wah-ta!-Wah was stolen from her people—we think, but do not know it, by Briarthorn's sarcumventions—and that she was now with the inimy, who had adopted her, and wanted her to marry a young Mingo. The message said that the party intended to hunt and forage through this region for a month or two afore it went back into the Canadas, and that if we could contrive to get on a scent in this quarter, something might turn up that would lead to our getting the maiden off."

"And how does that concern *you*, Deerslayer?" demanded Judith a little anxiously.

"It consarns me as all things that touches a fri'nd consarns a fri'nd. I'm here as Chingachgook's aid and helper, and if we can get the young maiden he likes back ag'in, it will give me almost as much pleasure as if I had got back my own sweetheart."

"And where, then, is *your* sweetheart, Deerslayer?"

"She's in the forest, Judith—hanging from the boughs of the trees, in a soft rain—in the dew on the open grass —the clouds that float about in the blue heavens—the birds that sing in the woods—the sweet springs where I slake my thirst—and in all the other glorious gifts that come from God's Providence!"

"You mean that, as yet you've never loved one of my sex, but love best your haunts and your own manner of life."

"That's it—that's just it. I am white—have a white heart, and can't, in reason, love a redskinned maiden, who must have a redskin heart and feelin's. No, no, I'm sound enough in them partic'lars and hope to remain so, at least till this

war is over. I find my time too much taken up with Chingachgook's affair to wish to have one of my own on my hands afore that is settled."

"The girl that finally wins you, Deerslayer, will at least win an *honest* heart—one without treachery or guile—and that will be a victory that most of her sex ought to envy."

As Judith uttered this, her beautiful face had a resentful frown on it, while a bitter smile lingered around a mouth that no derangement of the muscles could render anything but handsome. Her companion observed the change, and though little skilled in the workings of the female heart, he had sufficient native delicacy to understand that it might be well to drop the subject.

As the hour when Chingachgook was expected still remained distant, Deerslayer had time enough to examine into the state of the defenses and to make such additional arrangements as were in his power, and which the exigency of the moment seemed to require. The experience and foresight of Hutter had left little to be done in these particulars; still, several precautions suggested themselves to the young man, who may be said to have studied the art of frontier warfare through the traditions and legends of the people among whom he had so long lived. The distance between the castle and the nearest point on the shore prevented any apprehension on the subject of rifle bullets thrown from the land. The house was within musket shot, in one sense, it was true, but aim was entirely out of the question, and even Judith professed a perfect disregard of any danger from that source. So long, then, as the party remained in possession of the fortress, they were safe, unless their assailants could find the means to come off and carry it by fire or storm, or by some of the devices of Indian cunning and Indian treachery. Against the first source of danger Hutter had made ample provision, and the building itself, the bark roof excepted, was not very combustible. The floor was scuttled in several places, and buckets provided with ropes were in daily use, in readiness for any such emergency. One of the girls could easily extinguish any fire that might be lighted, provided it had not time to make much headway. Judith, who appeared to understand all her father's schemes of defense, and who had the spirit to take no unimportant share in the execution of them, explained

all these details to the young man, who was thus saved much time and labor in making his investigations.

Little was to be apprehended during the day. In possession of the canoes and of the ark, no other vessel was to be found on the lake. Nevertheless, Deerslayer well knew that a raft was soon made, and as dead trees were to be found in abundance near the water, did the savages seriously contemplate the risks of an assault, it would not be a very difficult matter to find the necessary means. The celebrated American ax, a tool that is quite unrivaled in its way, was then not very extensively known and the savages were far from expert in the use of its hatchetlike substitute; still, they had sufficient practice in crossing streams by this mode to render it certain they would construct a raft, should they deem it expedient to expose themselves to the risks of an assault. The death of their warrior might prove a sufficient incentive, or it might act as a caution, but Deerslayer thought it more than possible that the succeeding night would bring matters to a crisis, and in this precise way. This impression caused him to wish ardently for the presence and succor of his Mohican friend and to look forward to the approach of sunset with an increasing anxiety.

As the day advanced, the party in the castle matured their plans and made their preparations. Judith was active, and seemed to find a pleasure in consulting and advising with her new acquaintance, whose indifference to danger, manly devotion to herself and sister, guilelessness of manner, and truth of feeling had won rapidly on both her imagination and her affections. Although the hours appeared long in some respects to Deerslayer, Judith did not find them so, and when the sun began to descend toward the pine-clad summits of the western hills, she felt and expressed her surprise that the day should so soon be drawing to a close. On the other hand, Hetty was moody and silent. She was never loquacious, or if she occasionally became communicative, it was under the influence of some temporary excitement that served to arouse her unsophisticated mind; but for hours at a time, in the course of this all-important day, she seemed to have absolutely lost the use of her tongue. Nor did apprehension on account of her father materially affect the manner of either sister. Neither appeared seriously to dread any evil greater than captivity, and once or twice, when Hetty

did speak, she intimated the expectation that Hutter would find the means to liberate himself. Although Judith was less sanguine on this head, she too betrayed the hope that propositions for a ransom would come, when the Indians discovered that the castle set their expedients and artifices at defiance. Deerslayer, however, treated these passing suggestions as the ill-digested fancies of girls, making his own arrangements as steadily and brooding over the future as seriously as if they had never fallen from their lips.

At length the hour arrived when it became necessary to proceed to the place of rendezvous appointed with the Mohican, or Delaware, as Chingachgook was more commonly called. As the plan had been matured by Deerslayer, and fully communicated to his companions, all three set about its execution in concert and intelligently. Hetty passed into the ark, and, fastening two of the canoes together, she entered one and paddled up to a sort of gateway in the palisades that surrounded the building, through which she carried both, securing them beneath the house by chains that were fastened within the building. These palisades were trunks of trees driven firmly into the mud and served the double purpose of a small enclosure that was intended to be used in this very manner, and to keep any enemy that might approach in boats at arm's-length. Canoes thus *docked* were, in a measure, hid from sight, and as the gate was properly barred and fastened, it would not be an easy task to remove them, even in the event of their being seen. Previously, however, to closing the gate, Judith also entered within the enclosure with the third canoe, leaving Deerslayer busy in securing the door and windows inside the building, over her head. As everything was massive and strong, and small saplings were used as bars, it would have been the work of an hour or two to break into the building, when Deerslayer had ended his task, even allowing the assailants the use of any tools but the ax, and to be unresisted. This attention to security arose from Hutter's having been robbed once or twice by the lawless whites of the frontiers, during some of his many absences from home.

As soon as all was fast in the inside of the dwelling, Deerslayer appeared at a trap, from which he descended into the canoe of Judith. When this was done, he fastened the door with a massive staple and stout padlock. Hetty was then re-

ceived in the canoe, which was shoved outside of the palisades. The next precaution was to fasten the gate, and the keys were carried into the ark. The three were now fastened out of the dwelling, which could only be entered by violence, or by following the course taken by the young man in quitting it.

The glass had been brought outside as a preliminary step, and Deerslayer next took a careful survey of the entire shore of the lake, as far as his own position would allow. Not a living thing was visible, a few birds excepted, and even the last fluttered about in the shades of the trees, as if unwilling to encounter the heat of a sultry afternoon. All the nearest points, in particular, were subjected to severe scrutiny, in order to make certain that no raft was in preparation; the result everywhere gave the same picture of calm solitude. A few words will explain the greatest embarrassment belonging to the situation of our party. Exposed themselves to the observation of any watchful eyes, the movements of their enemies were concealed by the drapery of a dense forest. While the imagination would be very apt to people the latter with more warriors than it really contained, their own weakness must be too apparent to all who might chance to cast a glance in their direction.

"Nothing is stirring, howsever," exclaimed Deerslayer, as he finally lowered the glass, and prepared to enter the ark: "If the vagabonds do harbor mischief in their minds, they are too cunning to let it be seen; it's true, a raft may be in preparation in the woods, but it has not yet been brought down to the lake. They can't guess that we are about to quit the castle, and, if they did, they've no means of knowing where we intend to go."

"This is so true, Deerslayer," returned Judith, "that now all is ready, we may proceed at once, boldly and without the fear of being followed—else we shall be behind our time."

"No—no—the matter needs management—for, though the savages are in the dark as to Chingachgook and the rock, they've eyes and legs, and will see in what direction we steer, and will be sartain to follow us. I shall strive to baffle 'em, howsever, by heading the scow in all manner of ways, first in one quarter and then in another, until they get to be a-leg-weary and tired of tramping a'ter us."

So far as it was in his power, Deerslayer was as good as

his word. In less than five minutes after this speech was made, the whole party was in the ark and in motion. There was a gentle breeze from the north, and boldly hoisting the sail, the young man laid the head of the unwieldy craft in such a direction, as, after making a liberal but necessary allowance for leeway, would have brought it ashore a couple of miles down the lake, and on its eastern side. The sailing of the ark was never very swift, though, floating as it did on the surface, it was not difficult to get it in motion, or to urge it along over the water at the rate of some three or four miles in the hour. The distance between the castle and the rock was a little more than two leagues. Knowing the punctuality of an Indian, Deerslayer had made his calculations closely and had given himself a little more time than was necessary to reach the place of rendezvous, with a view to delay or to press his arrival, as might prove most expedient. When he hoisted the sail, the sun lay above the western hills at an elevation that promised rather more than two hours of day, and a few minutes satisfied him that the progress of the scow was such as to equal his expectations.

It was a glorious June afternoon, and never did that solitary sheet of water seem less like an arena of strife and bloodshed. The light air scarce descended as low as the bed of the lake, hovering over it, as if unwilling to disturb its deep tranquillity, or to ruffle its mirrorlike surface. Even the forests appeared to be slumbering in the sun, and a few piles of fleecy clouds had lain for hours along the northern horizon like fixtures in the atmosphere, placed there purely to embellish the scene. A few aquatic fowls occasionally skimmed along the water, and a single raven was visible, sailing high above the trees and keeping a watchful eye on the forest beneath him, in order to detect anything having life that the mysterious woods might offer as prey.

The reader will probably have observed that, amidst the frankness and abruptness of manner which marked the frontier habits of Judith, her language was superior to that used by her male companions, her own father included. This difference extended as well to pronunciation as to the choice of words and phrases. Perhaps nothing so soon betrays the education and association as the modes of speech, and few accomplishments so much aid the charm of female beauty as a graceful and even utterance, while nothing so soon produces

the disenchantment that necessarily follows a discrepancy between appearance and manner as a mean intonation of voice, or a vulgar use of words. Judith and her sister were marked exceptions to all the girls of their class along that whole frontier, the officers of the nearest garrison having often flattered the former with the belief that few ladies of the towns acquitted themselves better than herself in this important particular. This was far from being literally true, but it was sufficiently near the fact to give birth to the compliment. The girls were indebted to their mother for this proficiency, having acquired from her, in childhood, an advantage that no subsequent study or labor can give without a drawback, if neglected beyond the earlier periods of life. Who that mother was, or rather had been, no one but Hutter knew. She had now been dead two summers, and as was stated by Hurry, she had been buried in the lake, whether in indulgence of a prejudice, or from a reluctance to take the trouble to dig her grave, had frequently been a matter of discussion between the rude beings of that region. Judith had never visited the spot, but Hetty was present at the interment, and she often paddled a canoe, about sunset, or by the light of the moon, to the place, and gazed down into the limpid water in the hope of being able to catch a glimpse of a form that she had so tenderly loved from infancy to the sad hour of their parting.

"Must we reach the rock exactly at the moment the sun sets?" Judith demanded of the young man, as they stood near each other, Deerslayer holding the steering oar, and she working with a needle at some ornament of dress that much exceeded her station in life and was altogether a novelty in the woods. "Will a few minutes, sooner or later, alter the matter? It will be very hazardous to remain long as near the shore as that rock!"

"That's it, Judith, that's the very difficulty! The rock's within p'int blank for a shotgun, and 'twill never do to hover about it too close and too long. When you have to deal with an Injin, you must calculate and manage, for a red natur' dearly likes sarcumvention. Now you see, Judith, that I do not steer toward the rock at all, but here to the eastward of it, whereby the savages will be tramping off in that direction, and get their legs a-wearied, and all for no advantage."

"You think, then, they see us and watch our movements, Deerslayer? I was in hopes they might have fallen back into the woods and left us to ourselves for a few hours."

"That's altogether a woman's consait. There's no letup in an Injin's watchfulness when he's on a warpath, and eyes are on us at this minute, though the lake presarves us. We must draw near the rock on a calculation and indivor to get the miscreants on a false scent. The Mingos have good noses, they tell me, but a white man's reason ought always to equalize their instinct."

Judith now entered into a desultory discourse with Deerslayer, in which the girl betrayed her growing interest in the young man, an interest that his simplicity of mind and her decision of character, sustained as it was by the consciousness awakened by the consideration her personal charms so universally produced, rendered her less anxious to conceal than might otherwise have been the case. She was scarcely forward in her manner, though there was sometimes a freedom in her glances that it required all the aid of her exceeding beauty to prevent from awakening suspicions unfavorable to her discretion, if not to her morals. With Deerslayer, however, these glances were rendered less obnoxious to so unpleasant a construction, for she seldom looked at him without discovering much of the sincerity and nature that accompany the purest emotions of woman. It was a little remarkable that, as his captivity lengthened, neither of the girls manifested any great concern for her father; but, as has been said already, their habits gave them confidence, and they looked forward to his liberation by means of a ransom, with a confidence that might in a great degree account for their apparent indifference. Once before, Hutter had been in the hands of the Iroquois, and a few skins had readily effected his release. This event, however, unknown to the sisters, had occurred in a time of peace between England and France, and when the savages were restrained, instead of being encouraged to commit their excesses, by the policy of the different colonial governments.

While Judith was loquacious and caressing in her manner, Hetty remained thoughtful and silent. Once, indeed, she drew near to Deerslayer and questioned him a little closely as to his intentions, as well as concerning the mode of effecting his purpose; but her wish to converse went no further.

As soon as her simple queries were answered—and answered they all were in the fullest and kindest manner—she withdrew to her seat and continued to work on a coarse garment that she was making for her father, sometimes humming a low melancholy air and frequently sighing.

In this manner the time passed away, and when the sun was beginning to glow behind the fringe of pines that bounded the western hill, or about twenty minutes before it actually set, the ark was nearly as low as the point where Hutter and Hurry had been made prisoners. By sheering first to one side of the lake, and then to the other, Deerslayer managed to create an uncertainty as to his object; doubtless, the savages, who were unquestionably watching his movements, were led to believe that his aim was to communicate with them, at or near this spot, and would hasten in that direction, in order to be in readiness to profit by circumstances. This artifice was well managed, since the sweep of the bay, the curvature of the lake, and the low marshy land that intervened would probably allow the ark to reach the rock before its pursuers, if really collected near the point, could have time to make the circuit that would be required to get there by land. With a view to aid this deception, Deerslayer stood as near the western shore as was at all prudent; then, causing Judith and Hetty to enter the house, or cabin, and crouching himself so as to conceal his person by the frame of the scow, he suddenly threw the head of the latter round and began to make the best of his way toward the outlet. Favored by an increase in the wind, the progress of the ark was such as to promise the complete success of this plan, though the crablike movement of the craft compelled the helmsman to keep its head looking in a direction very different from that in which it was actually moving.

CHAPTER IX

Yet art thou prodigal of smiles—
Smiles sweeter than thy frowns are stern:
Earth sends from all her thousand isles,
A shout at thy return.
The glory that comes down from thee
Bathes, in deep joy, the land and sea.

THE SKIES

IT MAY ASSIST the reader in understanding the events we are
about to record if he has a rapidly sketched picture of the
scene, placed before his eyes at a single view. It will be remembered that the lake was an irregularly shaped basin, of
an outline that, in the main, was oval, but with bays and
points to relieve its formality and ornament its shores.
The surface of this beautiful sheet of water was now glittering like a gem, in the last rays of the evening sun, and the
setting of the whole—hills clothed in the richest forest verdure—was lighted up with a sort of radiant smile that is
best described in the beautiful lines we have placed at the
head of this chapter. As the banks, with few exceptions, rose
abruptly from the water, even where the mountain did not
immediately bound the view, there was a nearly unbroken
fringe of leaves overhanging the placid lake—the trees starting out of the acclivities, inclining to the light, until in many
instances they extended their long limbs and straight trunks
some forty or fifty feet beyond the line of the perpendicular.
In these cases we allude only to the giants of the forest—
pines of a hundred or a hundred and fifty feet in height—for
of the smaller growth, very many inclined so far as to steep
their lower branches in the water.

In the position in which the ark had now got, the castle
was concealed from view by the projection of a point, as

indeed was the northern extremity of the lake itself. A respectable mountain, forest-clad and rounded like all the rest, limited the view in that direction, stretching immediately across the whole of the fair scene, with the exception of a deep bay that passed its western end, lengthening the basin for more than a mile. The manner in which the water flowed out of the lake, beneath the leafy arches of the trees that lined the sides of the stream, has already been mentioned, and it has also been said that the rock, which was a favorite place of rendezvous throughout all that region, and where Deerslayer now expected to meet his friend, stood near this outlet, at no great distance from the shore. It was a large, isolated stone that rested on the bottom of the lake, apparently left there when the waters tore away the earth from around it in forcing for themselves a passage down the river, and which had obtained its shape from the action of the elements during the slow progress of centuries. The height of this rock could scarcely equal six feet, and, as has been said, its shape was not unlike that which is usually given to beehives or to a haycock. The latter, indeed, gives the best idea not only of its form but of its dimensions. It stood, and still stands, for we are writing of real scenes, within fifty feet of the bank and in water that was only two feet in depth, though there were seasons in which its rounded apex, if such a term can properly be used, was covered by the lake. Many of the trees stretched so far forward as almost to blend the rock with the shore, when seen from a little distance; one tall pine in particular overhung it in a way to form a noble and appropriate canopy to a seat that had held many a forest chieftain during the long succession of unknown ages in which America and all it contained existed apart in mysterious solitude, a world by itself, equally without a familiar history and without an origin that the annals of man can reach.

When distant some two or three hundred feet from the shore, Deerslayer took in his sail, and he dropped his grapnel as soon as he found the ark had drifted in a line that was directly to windward of the rock. The motion of the scow was then checked, when it was brought head to wind by the action of the breeze. As soon as this was done, Deerslayer "paid out line" and suffered the vessel to "set down" upon the rock as fast as the light air would force it to lee-

ward. Floating entirely on the surface, this was soon effected, and the young man checked the drift when he was told that the stern of the scow was within fifteen or eighteen feet of the desired spot.

In executing this maneuver, Deerslayer had proceeded promptly, for while he did not in the least doubt that he was both watched and followed by the foe, he believed he had distracted their movements by the apparent uncertainty of his own, and he knew they could have no means of ascertaining that the rock was his aim, unless indeed one of the prisoners had betrayed him, a chance so improbable in itself as to give him no concern. Notwithstanding the celerity and decision of his movements, he did not, however, venture so near the shore without taking due precautions to effect a retreat, in the event of its becoming necessary. He held the line in his hand, and Judith was stationed at a loop on the side of the cabin next to the shore, where she could watch the beach and the rocks and give timely notice of the approach of either friend or foe. Hetty was also placed on watch, but it was to keep the trees overhead in view, lest some enemy might ascend one and, by completely commanding the interior of the scow, render the defenses of the hut or cabin useless.

The sun had disappeared from the lake and valley when Deerslayer checked the ark in the manner mentioned. Still it wanted a few minutes to the true sunset, and he knew Indian punctuality too well to anticipate any unmanly haste in his friend. The great question was whether, surrounded by enemies as he was known to be, he had escaped their toils. The occurrences of the last twenty-four hours must be a secret to him, and, like himself, Chingachgook was yet young on a warpath. It was true, he came prepared to encounter the party that withheld his promised bride, but he had no means of ascertaining the extent of the danger he ran, or the precise positions occupied by either friends or foes. In a word, the trained sagacity and untiring caution of an Indian were all he had to rely on, amid the critical risks he unavoidably ran.

"Is the rock empty, Judith?" inquired Deerslayer, as soon as he had checked the drift of the ark, deeming it imprudent to venture unnecessarily near the shore. "Is anything to be seen of the Delaware chief?"

"Nothing, Deerslayer. Neither rock, shore, tree, nor lake seems to have ever held a human form."

"Keep close, Judith—keep close, Hetty—a rifle has a prying eye, a nimble foot, and a desperate fatal tongue. Keep close then, but keep up actyve looks, and be on the alart. 'Twould grieve me to the heart did any harm befall either of you."

"And *you*, Deerslayer!" exclaimed Judith, turning her handsome face from the loop to bestow a gracious and grateful look on the young man; "do *you* 'keep close,' and have a proper care that the savages do not catch a glimpse of you! A bullet might be as fatal to *you* as to one of us, and the blow that you felt would be felt by all."

"No fear of me, Judith—no fear of me, my good gal. Do not look thisaway, although you look so pleasant and comely, but keep your eyes on the rock, and the shore, and the——"

Deerslayer was interrupted by a slight exclamation from the girl, who, in obedience to his hurried gestures as much as in obedience to his words, had immediately bent her looks again in the opposite direction.

"What is't? What is't, Judith?" he hastily demanded. "Is anything to be seen?"

"There is a man on the rock! An Indian warrior in his paint, and armed!"

"Where does he wear his hawk's feather?" eagerly added Deerslayer, relaxing his hold of the line in readiness to drift nearer to the place of rendezvous. "Is it fast to the warlock, or does he carry it above the left ear?"

" 'Tis as you say, above the left ear; he smiles, too, and mutters the word 'Mohican.' "

"God be praised, 'tis the Sarpent at last!" exclaimed the young man, suffering the line to slip through his hands until hearing a light bound in the other end of the craft, he instantly checked the rope and began to haul it in again, under the assurance that his object was effected.

At that moment the door of the cabin was opened hastily, and a warrior, darting through the little room, stood at Deerslayer's side, simply uttering the exclamation "Hugh!" At the next instant Judith and Hetty shrieked, and the air was filled with the yell of twenty savages, who came leaping through

the branches down the bank, some actually falling headlong
into the water in their haste.

"Pull, Deerslayer," cried Judith, hastily barring the door,
in order to prevent an inroad by the passage through which
the Delaware had just entered. "Pull for life and death—the
lake is full of savages wading after us!"

The young man—for Chingachgook immediately came to
his friend's assistance—needed no second bidding, but they
applied themselves to their task in a way that showed how
urgent they deemed the occasion. The great difficulty was in
suddenly overcoming the *vis inertiæ* of so large a mass, for
once in motion, it was easy to cause the scow to skim the
water with all the necessary speed.

"Pull, Deerslayer, for Heaven's sake!" cried Judith again
at the loop. "These wretches rush into the water like hounds
following their prey! Ah!—the scow moves! And now the
water deepens to the armpits of the foremost; still they rush
forward, and will seize the ark!"

A slight scream, and then a joyous laugh followed from
the girl, the first produced by a desperate effort of their pursuers, and the last by its failure; the scow, which had now
got fairly in motion, gliding ahead into deep water with a
velocity that set the designs of their enemies at naught. As
the two men were prevented by the position of the cabin from
seeing what passed astern, they were compelled to inquire of
the girls into the state of the chase.

"What now, Judith? What next? Do the Mingos still follow, or are we quit of 'em for the present?" demanded Deerslayer when he felt the rope yielding, as if the scow was
going fast ahead, and heard the scream and the laugh of
the girl almost in the same breath.

"They have vanished! One, the last, is just burying himself in the bushes of the bank—there, he has disappeared in
the shadows of the trees! You have got your friend, and we
are all safe!"

The two men now made another great effort, pulled the ark
up swiftly to the grapnel, tripped it, and when the scow had
shot some distance and lost its way, they let the anchor drop
again; then, for the first time since their meeting, they ceased
their efforts. As the floating house now lay several hundred
feet from the shore, and offered a complete protection against

bullets, there was no longer any danger, or any motive for immediate exertion.

The manner in which the two friends now recognized each other was highly characteristic. Chingachgook, a noble, tall, handsome, and athletic young Indian warrior, first examined his rifle with care, opening the pan to make sure the priming was not wet; assured of this important fact, he next cast furtive but observant glances around him at the strange habitation and at the two girls; still he spoke not, and most of all did he avoid the betrayal of a womanish curiosity by asking questions.

"Judith and Hetty," said Deerslayer, with an untaught, natural courtesy, "this is the Mohican chief of whom you've heard me speak; Chingachgook, as he is called, which signifies the Big Sarpent; so named for his wisdom, and prudence, and cunning; my 'arliest and latest friend. I know'd it must be he by the hawk's feather over the left ear, most other warriors wearing 'em on the warlock."

As Deerslayer ceased speaking, he laughed heartily, excited more perhaps by the delight of having got his friend safe at his side under circumstances so trying than by any conceit that happened to cross his fancy, and exhibiting this outbreaking of feeling in a manner that was a little remarkable, since his merriment was not accompanied by any noise. Although Chingachgook both understood and spoke English, he was unwilling to communicate his thoughts in it, like most Indians, and when he had met Judith's cordial shake of the hand and Hetty's milder salute in the courteous manner that became a chief, he turned away, apparently to await the moment when it might suit his friend to enter into an explanation of his future intentions and to give a narrative of what had passed since their separation. The other understood his meaning and discovered his own mode of reasoning in the matter by addressing the girls.

"This wind will soon die away altogether, now the sun is down," he said, "and there is no need of rowing ag'in it. In half an hour or so it will either be a flat calm or the air will come off from the south shore, when we will begin our journey back ag'in to the castle; in the meanwhile, the Delaware and I will talk over matters and get correct ideas of each other's notions consarning the course we ought to take."

No one opposed this proposition, and the girls with-

drew into the cabin to prepare the evening meal, while the two young men took their seats on the head of the scow and began to converse. The dialogue was in the language of the Delawares. As that dialect, however, is but little understood, even by the learned, we shall, not only on this but on all subsequent occasions, render such parts as it may be necessary to give closely into liberal English, preserving, as far as possible, the idioms and peculiarities of the respective speakers, by way of presenting the pictures in the most graphic forms to the minds of the readers.

It is unnecessary to enter into the details first related by Deerslayer, who gave a brief narrative of the facts that are already familiar to those who have read our pages. In relating these events, however, it may be well to say that the speaker touched only on the outlines, more particularly abstaining from saying anything about his encounter with, and victory over, the Iroquois, as well as to his own exertions in behalf of the deserted young women. When Deerslayer ended, the Delaware took up the narrative in turn, speaking sententiously and with great dignity. His account was both clear and short, nor was it embellished by any incidents that did not directly concern the history of his departure from the villages of his people and his arrival in the valley of the Susquehanna. On reaching the latter, which was at a point only half a mile south of the outlet, he had soon struck a trail, which gave him notice of the probable vicinity of enemies. Being prepared for such an occurrence, the object of the expedition calling him directly into the neighborhood of the party of Iroquois that was known to be out, he considered the discovery as fortunate, rather than the reverse, and took the usual precautions to turn it to account. First following the river to its source, and ascertaining the position of the rock, he met another trail, and had actually been hovering for hours on the flanks of his enemies, watching equally for an opportunity to meet his mistress and to take a scalp —and it may be questioned which he most ardently desired. He kept near the lake, and occasionally he ventured to some spot where he could get a view of what was passing on its surface. The ark had been seen and watched from the moment it hove in sight, though the young chief was necessarily ignorant that it was to be the instrument of effecting the desired junction with his friend. The uncertainty of its

movements, and the fact that it was unquestionably managed by white men, led him to conjecture the truth, however, and he held himself in readiness to get on board whenever a suitable occasion might offer. As the sun drew near the horizon, he repaired to the rock, where, on emerging from the forest, he was gratified in finding the ark lying apparently in readiness to receive him. The manner of his appearance, and of his entrance into the craft, is known.

Although Chingachgook had been closely watching his enemies for hours, their sudden and close pursuit, as he reached the scow, was as much a matter of surprise to himself as it had been to his friend. He could only account for it by the fact of their being more numerous than he had at first supposed, and by their having out parties, of the existence of which he was ignorant. Their regular and permanent encampment, if the word permanent can be applied to the residence of a party that intended to remain out, in all probability, but a few weeks, was not far from the spot where Hutter and Hurry had fallen into their hands, and, as a matter of course, near a spring.

"Well, Sarpent," asked Deerslayer, when the other had ended his brief but spirited narrative, speaking always in the Delaware tongue, which, for the reader's convenience only, we render into the peculiar vernacular of the speaker.

"Well, Sarpent, as you've been scouting around these Mingos, have you anything to tell us of their captyves; the father of these young women and another, who, I somewhat conclude, is the lovyer of one of 'em."

"Chingachgook has seen them. An old man and a young warrior—the falling hemlock and the tall pine."

"You're not so much out, Delaware; you're not so much out. Old Hutter is decaying, of a sartainty, though many solid blocks might be hewn out of his trunk yet; as for Hurry Harry, so far as height and strength and comeliness go, he may be called the pride of the human forest. Were the men bound, or in any manner suffering torture? I ask on account of the young women, who, I dare to say, would be glad to know."

"It is not so, Deerslayer. The Mingos are too many to cage their game. Some watch, some sleep, some scout, some hunt. The palefaces are treated like brothers today; tomorrow they will lose their scalps."

"Yes, that's red natur', and must be submitted to! Judith and Hetty, here's comforting tidings for you, the Delaware telling me that neither your father nor Hurry Harry is in suffering; but, bating the loss of liberty, as well off as we are ourselves. Of course they are kept in the camp; otherwise they do much as they please."

"I rejoice to hear this, Deerslayer," returned Judith, "and now we are joined by your friend, I make no manner of question that we shall find an opportunity to ransom the prisoners. If there are any women in the camp, I have articles of dress that will catch their eyes; and should the worst come to the worst, we can open the good chest, which, I think, will be found to hold things that may tempt the chiefs."

"Judith," said the young man, looking up at her with a smile and an expression of earnest curiosity that, in spite of the growing obscurity, did not escape the watchful looks of the girl, "can you find it in your heart to part with your own finery to release prisoners, even though one be your own father, and the other is your sworn suitor and lovyer?"

The flush on the face of the girl arose in part from resentment, but more perhaps from a gentler and novel feeling that, with the capricious waywardness of taste, had been rapidly rendering her more sensitive to the good opinion of the youth who questioned her than to that of any other person. Suppressing the angry sensation with instinctive quickness, she answered with a readiness and truth that caused her sister to draw near to listen, though the obtuse intellect of the latter was far from comprehending the workings of a heart as treacherous, as uncertain, and as impetuous in its feelings as that of the spoiled and flattered beauty.

"Deerslayer," answered Judith, after a moment's pause, "I shall be honest with *you*. I confess that the time *has* been when what you call finery was to me the dearest thing on earth, but I begin to feel differently. Though Hurry Harry is naught to me, nor ever can be, I would give all I own to set him free. If I would do this for blustering, bullying, talking Hurry, who has nothing but good looks to recommend him, you may judge what I would do for my own father."

"This sounds well and is according to woman's gifts. Ah's me! The same feelin's is to be found among the young women of the Delawares. I've known 'em, often and often, sacrifice

their vanity to their hearts. 'Tis as it should be—'tis as it should be, I suppose, in both colors. Woman was created for the feelin's, and is pretty much ruled by feelin'!"

"Would the savages let Father go, if Judith and I gave them all our best things?" demanded Hetty, in her innocent, mild manner.

"Their women might interfere, good Hetty; yes, their women might interfere with such an ind in view. But, tell me, Sarpent, how is it as to squaws among the knaves; have they many of their own women in the camp?"

The Delaware heard and understood all that passed, though with Indian gravity and finesse he had sat, with averted face, seemingly inattentive to a discourse in which he had no direct concern. Thus appealed to, however, he answered his friend in his ordinary sententious manner.

"Six," he said, holding up all the fingers of one hand, and the thumb of the other, "besides *this*." The last number denoted his betrothed, whom, with the poetry and truth of nature, he described by laying his hand on his own heart.

"Did you see her, Chief—did you get a glimpse of her pleasant countenance, or come close enough to her ear to sing in it the song she loves to hear?"

"No, Deerslayer—the trees were too many, and leaves covered their boughs like clouds hiding the heavens in a storm. But," and the young warrior turned his dark face toward his friend, with a smile on it that illuminated its fierce-looking paint and naturally stern lineaments with a bright gleam of human feeling; "Chingachgook heard the laugh of Wah-ta! Wah; he knew it from the laugh of the women of the Iroquois. It sounded in his ears like the chirp of the wren."

"Aye, trust a lovyer's ear for that, and a Delaware's ear for all sounds that are ever heard in the woods. I know not why it is so, Judith, but when young men—and I dares to say it may be all the same with young women, too—but when they get to have kind feelin's toward each other, it's wonderful how pleasant they laugh, or the speech becomes to the other person. I've seen grim warriors listening to the chattering and the laughing of young gals as if it was church music such as is heard in the old Dutch church that stands in the great street of Albany, where I've been more than once, with peltry and game."

"And *you*, Deerslayer," said Judith quickly and with more sensibility than marked her usually light and thoughtless manner; "have *you* never felt how pleasant it is to listen to the laugh of the girl you love?"

"Lord bless you, gal!—why I've never lived enough among my own color to drop into them sort of feelin's—no, never! I dares to say they are nat'ral and right, but to me there's no music so sweet as the sighing of the wind in the treetops and the rippling of a stream from a full, sparkling nat*yve* fountain of pure fresh water; unless, indeed," he continued, dropping his head for an instant in a thoughtful manner, "it be the open mouth of a sartain hound when I'm on the track of a fat buck. As for unsartain dogs I care little for their cries, seein' they are as likely to speak when the deer is not in sight as when it is."

Judith walked slowly and pensively away, nor was there any of her ordinary calculating coquetry in the light, tremulous sigh that, unconsciously to herself, arose to her lips. On the other hand, Hetty listened with guileless attention, though it struck her simple mind as singular that the young man should prefer the melody of the woods to the songs of girls, or even to the laugh of innocence and joy. Accustomed, however, to defer in most things to her sister, she soon followed Judith into the cabin, where she took a seat and remained pondering intensely over some occurrence, or resolution, or opinion, which was a secret to all but herself. Left alone, Deerslayer and his friend resumed their discourse.

"Has the young paleface hunter been long on this lake?" demanded the Delaware, after courteously waiting for the other to speak first.

"Only since yesterday noon, Sarpent, though that has been long enough to see and do much."

The gaze that the Indian fastened on his companion was so keen that it seemed to mock the gathering darkness of the night. As the other furtively returned his look, he saw the two black eyes glistening on him, like the balls of the panther, or those of the penned wolf. He understood the meaning of this glowing gaze and answered evasively, as he fancied would best become the modesty of a white man's gifts.

"'Tis as you suspect, Sarpent; yes, 'tis somewhat thata-

way. I *have* fell in with the inimy, and I suppose it may be said I've fou't them, too."

An exclamation of delight and exultation escaped the Indian; then, laying his hand eagerly on the arm of his friend, he asked if there were any scalps taken.

"That I *will* maintain, in the face of all the Delaware tribe, old Tamenund, and your father, the great Uncas, as well as the rest, is ag'in white gifts! *My* scalp is on my head, as you can see, Sarpent, and that was the only scalp that was in danger, when one side was altogether Christian and white."

"Did no warrior fall? Deerslayer did not get his name by being slow of sight, or clumsy with the rifle!"

"In that particular, Chief, you're nearer reason and therefore nearer being right. I may say one Mingo fell."

"A chief!" demanded the other, with startling vehemence.

"Nay, that's more than I know or can say. He was artful, and treacherous, and stouthearted, and may well have gained popularity enough with his people to be named to that rank. The man fou't well, though his eye wasn't quick enough for one who had had his schooling in your company, Delaware."

"My brother and friend struck the body?"

"That was uncalled for, seeing that the Mingo died in my arms. The truth may as well be said at once; he fou't like a man of red gifts, and I fou't like a man with gifts of my own color. God gave me the victory; I couldn't fly in the face of His Providence by forgetting my birth and natur'. White he made me, and white I shall live and die."

"Good! Deerslayer is a paleface and has paleface hands. A Delaware will look for the scalp, and hang it on a pole, and sing a song in his honor, when we go back to our people. The honor belongs to the tribe; it must not be lost."

"This is easy talking, but 'twill not be as easy doing. The Mingo's body is in the hands of his fri'nds and no doubt is hid in some hole, where Delaware cunning will never be able to get at the scalp."

The young man then gave his friend a succinct but clear account of the event of the morning, concealing nothing of any moment and yet touching on everything modestly and with a careful attention to avoid the Indian habit of boasting. Chingachgook again expressed his satisfaction at the honor won by his friend, and then both arose, the hour having ar-

rived when it became prudent to move the ark further from
the land.

It was now quite dark, the heavens having become clouded,
and the stars hid. The north wind had ceased, as was usual,
with the setting of the sun, and a light air arose from the
south. This change favoring the design of Deerslayer, he
lifted his grapnel, and the scow immediately and quite perceptibly began to drift more into the lake. The sail was set,
when the motion of the craft increased to a rate not much
less than two miles in the hour. As this superseded the necessity of rowing—an occupation that an Indian would not be
likely to desire—Deerslayer, Chingachgook, and Judith
seated themselves in the stern of the scow, where the first
governed its movements by holding the oar. Here they dis-
coursed on their future movements and on the means that
ought to be used in order to effect the liberation of their
friends.

In this dialogue Judith held a material part, the Delaware
readily understanding all she said, while his own replies and
remarks, both of which were few and pithy, were occasionally rendered into English by his friend. Judith rose
greatly in the estimation of her companions in the half hour
that followed. Prompt of resolution and firm of purpose, her
suggestions and expedients partook of her spirit and sagacity,
both of which were of a character to find favor with men of
the frontier. The events that had occurred since their meeting, as well as her isolated and dependent situation, induced
the girl to feel toward Deerslayer like the friend of a year instead of an acquaintance of a day, and so completely had
she been won by his guileless truth of character and of
feeling—pure novelties in our sex, as respected her own experience—that his peculiarities excited her curiosity and created a confidence that had never been awakened by any
other man. Hitherto she had been compelled to stand on the
defensive in her intercourse with men—with what success was
best known to herself—but here had she been suddenly
thrown into the society and under the protection of a youth
who evidently as little contemplated evil toward herself as if
he had been her brother. The freshness of his integrity, the
poetry and truth of his feelings, and even the quaintness of
his forms of speech all had their influence and aided in
awakening an interest that she found as pure as it was sud-

den and deep. Hurry's fine face and manly form had never compensated for his boisterous and vulgar turn, and her intercourse with the officers had prepared her to make comparisons under which even his great natural advantages suffered. But this very intercourse with the officers who occasionally came upon the lake to fish and hunt had an effect in producing her present sentiments toward the young stranger. With them, while her vanity had been gratified and her self-love strongly awakened, she had many causes deeply to regret the acquaintance—if not to mourn over it in secret sorrow—for it was impossible for one of her quick intellect not to perceive how hollow was the association between superior and inferior, and that she was regarded as the plaything of an idle hour rather than as an equal and a friend by even the best intentioned and least designing of her scarlet-clad admirers. Deerslayer, on the other hand, had a window in his breast through which the light of his honesty was ever shining, and even his indifference to charms that so rarely failed to produce a sensation piqued the pride of the girl and gave him an interest that another, seemingly more favored by nature, might have failed to excite.

In this manner half an hour passed, during which time the ark had been slowly stealing over the water, the darkness thickening around it, though it was easy to see that the gloom of the forest at the southern end of the lake was getting to be distant, while the mountains that lined the sides of the beautiful basin were overshadowing it, nearly from side to side. There was, indeed, a narrow stripe of water in the center of the lake where the dim light that was still shed from the heavens fell upon its surface in a line extending north and south; along this faint tract—a sort of inverted Milky Way, in which the obscurity was not quite as dense as in other places—the scow held her course, he who steered well knowing that it led in the direction he wished to go. The reader is not to suppose, however, that any difficulty could exist as to the course. This would have been determined by that of the air had it not been possible to distinguish the mountains, as well as by the dim opening to the south, which marked the position of the valley in that quarter, above the plain of tall trees, by a sort of lessened obscurity; the difference between the darkness of the forest and that of the night as seen only in the air. The peculiarities at length caught the attention of

Judith and the Deerslayer, and the conversation ceased, to allow each to gaze at the solemn stillness and deep repose of nature.

" 'Tis a gloomy night," observed the girl, after a pause of several minutes. "I hope we may be able to find the castle."

"Little fear of our missing *that,* if we keep this path in the middle of the lake," returned the young man. "Natur' has made us a road here, and dim as it is, there'll be little difficulty in following it."

"Do you hear nothing, Deerslayer? It seemed as if the water was stirring quite near us!"

"Sartainly something *did* move the water, oncommon like; it must have been a fish. Them creatur's prey upon each other like men and animals on the land; one has leaped into the air and fallen back hard into his own element. 'Tis of little use, Judith, for any to strive to get out of their elements, since it's natur' to stay in 'em, and natur' will have its way. Ha! *That* sounds like a paddle, used with more than common caution!"

At this moment the Delaware bent forward and pointed significantly into the boundary of gloom, as if some object had suddenly caught his eye. Both Deerslayer and Judith followed the direction of his gesture, and each got a view of a canoe at the same instant. The glimpse of this startling neighbor was dim, and to eyes less practiced it might have been uncertain, though to those in the ark the object was evidently a canoe with a single individual in it, the latter standing erect and paddling. How many lay concealed in its bottom, of course, could not be known. Flight, by means of oars, from a bark canoe impelled by vigorous and skillful hands was utterly impracticable, and each of the men seized his rifle in expectation of a conflict.

"I can easily bring down the paddler," whispered Deerslayer, "but we'll first hail him and ask his ar'nd." Then raising his voice, he continued in a solemn manner, "Hold! If you come nearer, I must fire, though contrary to my wishes, and then sartain death will follow. Stop paddling, and answer!"

"Fire, and slay a poor, defenseless girl," returned a soft, tremulous female voice, "and God will never forgive you! Go your way, Deerslayer, and let me go mine."

"Hetty!" exclaimed the young man and Judith in a breath,

and the former sprang instantly to the spot where he had left the canoe they had been towing. It was gone, and he understood the whole affair. As for the fugitive, frightened at the menace, she ceased paddling and remained dimly visible, resembling a spectral outline of a human form, standing on the water. At the next moment the sail was lowered to prevent the ark from passing the spot where the canoe lay. This last expedient, however, was not taken in time, for the momentum of so heavy a craft and the impulsion of the air soon set her by, bringing Hetty directly to windward, though still visible, as the change in the positions of the two boats now placed her in that species of Milky Way which has been mentioned.

"What can this mean, Judith?" demanded Deerslayer. "Why has your sister taken the canoe and left us?"

"You know she is feeble-minded, poor girl! And she has her own ideas of what ought to be done. She loves her father more than most children love their parents—and then——"

"Then, what, gal? This is a trying moment, one in which truth must be spoken."

Judith felt a generous and womanly regret at betraying her sister, and she hesitated ere she spoke again. But once more urged by Deerslayer, and conscious herself of all the risks the whole party was running by the indiscretion of Hetty, she could refrain no longer.

"Then, I fear, poor, weak-minded Hetty has not been altogether able to see the vanity, and madness, and folly that lie hid behind the handsome face and fine form of Hurry Harry. She talks of him in her sleep and sometimes betrays the inclination in her waking moments."

"You think, Judith, that your sister is now bent on some mad scheme to serve her father and Hurry, which will, in all likelihood, give them riptyles, the Mingos, the mastership of a canoe?"

"Such, I fear, will turn out to be the fact, Deerslayer. Poor Hetty has hardly sufficient cunning to outwit a savage."

All this while the canoe, with the form of Hetty erect in one end of it, was dimly perceptible, though the greater drift of the ark rendered it at each instant less and less distinct. It was evident no time was to be lost, lest it should altogether disappear. The rifles were now laid aside as useless,

the two men seizing the oars and sweeping the head of the scow around in the direction of the canoe. Judith, accustomed to the office, flew to the other end of the ark and placed herself at what might be called the helm. Hetty took the alarm at these preparations, which could not be made without noise, and started off like a bird that had been suddenly put up by the approach of unexpected danger.

As Deerslayer and his companion rowed with the energy of those who felt the necessity of straining every nerve, and Hetty's strength was impaired by a nervous desire to escape, the chase would have quickly terminated in the capture of the fugitive had not the girl made several short and unlooked-for deviations in her course. These turnings gave her time, and they had also the effect of gradually bringing both canoe and ark within the deeper gloom cast by the shadows from the hills. They also gradually increased the distance between the fugitive and her pursuers, until Judith called out to her companions to cease rowing, for she had completely lost sight of the canoe.

When this mortifying announcement was made, Hetty was actually so near as to understand every syllable her sister uttered; though the latter had used the precaution of speaking as low as circumstances would allow her to do and make herself heard. Hetty stopped paddling at the same moment and waited the result with an impatience that was breathless, equally from her late exertions and her desire to land. A dead silence immediately fell on the lake, during which the three in the ark were using their senses differently in order to detect the position of the canoe. Judith leaned forward to listen, in the hope of catching some sound that might betray the direction in which her sister was stealing away, while her two companions brought their eyes as near as possible to a level with the water, in order to detect any object that might be floating on its surface. All was vain, however, for neither sound nor sight rewarded their efforts. All this time, Hetty, who had not the cunning to sink into the canoe, stood erect, a finger pressed on her lips, gazing in the direction in which the voices had been heard, resembling a statue of profound and timid attention. Her ingenuity had barely sufficed to enable her to seize the canoe and to quit the ark in the noiseless manner related; and then it appeared to be momentarily exhausted. Even the doublings of the canoe had

been as much the consequence of an uncertain hand and of nervous agitation as of any craftiness or calculation.

The pause continued several minutes, during which Deerslayer and the Delaware conferred together in the language of the latter. Then the oars dipped again, and the ark moved away, rowing with as little noise as possible. It steered westward, a little southerly, or in the direction of the encampment of the enemy. Having reached a point at no great distance from the shore, and where the obscurity was intense, on account of the proximity of the land, it lay there near an hour, in waiting for the expected approach of Hetty, who, it was thought, would make the best of her way to that spot as soon as she believed herself relieved from the danger of pursuit. No success rewarded this little blockade, however, neither appearance nor sound denoting the passage of the canoe. Disappointed at this failure, and conscious of the importance of getting possession of the fortress before it could be seized by the enemy, Deerslayer now took his way toward the castle with the apprehension that all his foresight in securing the canoes would be defeated by this ungarded and alarming movement on the part of the feeble-minded Hetty.

CHAPTER X

——But who in this wild wood
May credit give to either eye or ear?
From rocky precipice or hollow cave,
'Midst the confused sound of rustling leaves,
And crackling boughs, and cries of nightly birds,
Returning seeming answer.

JOANNA BAILLIE

FEAR, AS MUCH as calculation, had induced Hetty to cease paddling when she found that her pursuers did not know in which direction to proceed. She remained stationary until the ark had pulled in near the encampment—as has been related in the preceding chapter—when she resumed the paddle and, with cautious strokes, made the best of her way toward the western shore. In order to avoid her pursuers, however, who, she rightly suspected, would soon be rowing along that shore themselves, the head of the canoe was pointed so far north as to bring her to land on a point that thrust itself into the lake, at the distance of near a league from the outlet. Nor was this altogether the result of a desire to escape; feeble-minded as she was, Hetty Hutter had a good deal of that instinctive caution which so often keeps those whom God has thus visited from harm. She was perfectly aware of the importance of keeping the canoes from falling into the hands of the Iroquois, and long familiarity with the lake had suggested one of the simplest expedients by which this great object could be rendered compatible with her own purpose.

The point in question was the first projection that offered on that side of the lake where a canoe, if set adrift with a southerly air, would float clear of the land, and where it would be no great violation of probabilities to suppose it

might even hit the castle, the latter lying above it almost in a direct line with the wind. Such then was Hetty's intention, and she landed on the extremity of the gravelly point, beneath an overhanging oak, with the express intention of shoving the canoe off from the shore, in order that it might drift up toward her father's insulated abode. She knew, too, from the logs that occasionally floated about the lake that, did it miss the castle and its appendages, the wind would be likely to change before the canoe could reach the northern extremity of the lake, and that Deerslayer might have an opportunity of regaining it in the morning, when no doubt he would be earnestly sweeping the surface of the water and the whole of its wooded shores with the glass. In all this, too, Hetty was less governed by any chain of reasoning than by her habits, the latter often supplying the defects of mind in human beings, as they perform the same office for animals of the inferior classes.

The girl was quite an hour finding her way to the point, the distance and the obscurity equally detaining her, but she was no sooner on the gravelly beach than she prepared to set the canoe adrift, in the manner mentioned. While in the act of pushing it from her, she heard low voices that seemed to come from among the trees behind her. Startled at this unexpected danger, Hetty was on the point of springing into the canoe again, in order to seek safety in flight, when she thought she recognized the tones of Judith's melodious voice. Bending forward so as to catch the sounds more directly— they evidently came from the water—she then understood that the ark was approaching from the south, so close in with the western shore as necessarily to cause it to pass the point within twenty yards of the spot where she stood. Here, then, was all she could desire: the canoe was shoved off into the lake, leaving its late occupant alone on the narrow strand.

When this act of self-devotion was performed, Hetty did not retire. The foliage of the overhanging trees and bushes would have almost concealed her person, had there been light, but in that obscurity it was utterly impossible to discover any object thus shaded at the distance of a few feet. Flight, too was perfectly easy, as twenty steps would effectually bury her in the forest. She remained, therefore, watching with intense anxiety the result of her expedient, intending to call the attention of the others to the canoe with her

voice, should they appear to pass without observing it. The ark approached under its sail again, Deerslayer standing in its bow, with Judith near him, and the Delaware at the helm. It would seem that, in the bay below, it had got too close to the shore in the lingering hope of intercepting Hetty, for as it came nearer, the latter distinctly heard the directions that the young man forward gave to his companion, in order to clear the point.

"Lay her head more off the shore, Delaware," said Deerslayer for the third time, speaking in English, that his fair companion might understand his words; "lay her head well offshore. We have got embayed here and needs keep the mast clear of the trees. Judith, there's a canoe!"

The last words were uttered with great earnestness, and Deerslayer's hand was on his rifle ere they were fairly out of his mouth. But the truth flashed on the mind of the quick-witted girl, and she instantly told her companion that the boat *must* be that in which her sister had fled.

"Keep the scow straight, Delaware; steer as straight as your bullet flies when sent ag'in a buck; there—I have it."

The canoe was seized and immediately secured again to the side of the ark. At the next moment the sail was lowered, and the motion of the ark arrested by means of the oars.

"Hetty!" called out Judith, concern, even affection, betraying itself in her tones. "Are you within hearing, sister— for God's sake answer, and let me hear the sound of your voice again! Hetty! Dear Hetty!"

"I'm here, Judith—here on the shore, where it will be useless to follow me, as I will hide in the woods."

"Oh, Hetty, what is't you do! Remember, 'tis drawing near midnight, and the woods are filled with savages and wild beasts!"

"Neither will harm a poor half-witted girl, Judith. God is as much with me here as he would be in the ark, or in the hut. I am going to help my father and poor Hurry Harry, who will be tortured and slain unless someone cares for them."

"We all care for them and intend tomorrow to send them a flag of truce to buy their ransom. Come back then, sister; trust to us, who have better heads than you and who will do all we can for Father."

"I know your head is better than mine, Judith, for mine is

very weak, to be sure, but I must go to Father and poor Hurry. Do you and Deerslayer keep the castle, sister; leave me in the hands of God."

"God is with us all, Hetty—in the castle, or on the shore —Father as well as ourselves; it is sinful not to trust to His goodness. You can do nothing in the dark, will lose your way in the forest and perish for want of food."

"God will not let that happen to a poor child that goes to serve her father, sister. I must try and find the savages."

"Come back for this night only; in the morning we will put you ashore and leave you to do as you may think right."

"You *say* so, Judith, and you *think* so, but you would not. Your heart would soften, and you'd see tomahawks and scalping knives in the air. Besides, I've got a thing to tell the Indian chief that will answer all our wishes, and I'm afraid I may forget it if I don't tell it to him at once. You'll see that he will let Father go as soon as he hears it!"

"Poor Hetty! What can *you* say to a ferocious savage that will be likely to change his bloody purpose!"

"That which will frighten him and make him let Father go," returned the simple-minded girl positively. "You'll see, sister; you'll see how soon it will bring him to, like a gentle child!"

"Will you tell *me*, Hetty, what you intend to say?" asked Deerslayer. "I know the savages well and can form some idee how far fair words will be likely, or not, to work on their bloody natur's. If it's not suited to the gifts of a redskin, 'twill be of no use, for reason goes by gifts, as well as conduct."

"Well, then," answered Hetty, dropping her voice to a low, confidential tone; for the stillness of the night and the nearness of the ark permitted her to do this and still to be heard. "Well, then, Deerslayer, as you seem a good and honest young man, I will tell *you*. I mean not to say a word to any of the savages until I get face to face with their head chief, let them plague me with as many questions as they please; no—I'll answer none of them, unless it be to tell them to lead me to their wisest man. Then, Deerslayer, I'll tell him that God will not forgive murder and thefts, and that if Father and Hurry did go after the scalps of the Iroquois, he must return good for evil, for so the Bible commands, else he will go into everlasting punishment. When he hears this and feels it to be true, as feel it he must, how

long will it be before he sends Father and Hurry and me to the shore opposite the castle, telling us all three to go our way in peace?"

The last question was put in a triumphant manner, and then the simple-minded girl laughed at the impression she never doubted that her project had made on her auditors. Deerslayer was dumfounded at this proof of guileless feebleness of mind, but Judith had suddenly bethought her of a means of counteracting this wild project, by acting on the very feelings that had given it birth. Without adverting to the closing question, or the laugh, therefore, she hurriedly called to her sister by name, as one suddenly impressed with the importance of what she had to say. But no answer was given to the call.

By the snapping of twigs, and the rustling of leaves, Hetty had evidently quitted the shore, and was already burying herself in the forest. To follow would have been bootless, since the darkness, as well as the dense cover that the woods everywhere afforded, would have rendered her capture next to impossible, there was also the never-ceasing danger of falling into the hands of their enemies. After a short and melancholy discussion, therefore, the sail was again set, and the ark pursued its course toward its habitual moorings, Deerslayer silently felicitating himself on the recovery of the canoe and brooding over his plans for the morrow. The wind rose as the party quitted the point, and in less than an hour they reached the castle. Here all was found as it had been left, and the reverse of the ceremonies had to be taken in entering the building that had been used on quitting it. Judith occupied a solitary bed that night, bedewing the pillow with her tears as she thought of the innocent and hitherto neglected creature who had been her companion from childhood; bitter regrets came over her mind from more causes than one, as the weary hours passed away, making it nearly morning before she lost her recollection in sleep. Deerslayer and the Delaware took their rest in the ark, where we shall leave them enjoying the deep sleep of the honest, the healthful, and fearless, to return to the girl we have last seen in the midst of the forest.

When Hetty left the shore, she took her way unhesitatingly into the woods with a nervous apprehension of being followed. Luckily, this course was the best she could have

hit on to effect her own purpose, since it was the only one that led her from the point. The night was so intensely dark, beneath the branches of the trees, that her progress was very slow, and the direction she went altogether a matter of chance, after the first few yards. The formation of the ground, however, did not permit her to deviate far from the line in which she desired to proceed. On one hand, it was soon bounded by the acclivity of the hill, while the lake on the other served as a guide. For two hours did this singlehearted and simple-minded girl toil through the mazes of the forest, sometimes finding herself on the brow of the bank that bounded the water, and at others struggling up an ascent that warned her to go no further in that direction, since it necessarily ran at right angles to the course on which she wished to proceed. Her feet often slid from beneath her, and she got many falls, though none to do her injury; but by the end of the period mentioned, she had become so weary as to want strength to go any further. Rest was indispensable, and she set about preparing a bed with the readiness and coolness of one to whom the wilderness presented no unnecessary terrors. She knew that wild beasts roamed through all the adjacent forest, but animals that preyed on the human species were rare, and of dangerous serpents there were literally none. These facts had been taught her by her father, and whatever her feeble mind received at all, it received so confidingly as to leave her no uneasiness from any doubts or skepticism. To her the sublimity of the solitude in which she was placed was soothing rather than appalling, and she gathered a bed of leaves with as much indifference to the circumstances that would have driven the thoughts of sleep entirely from the minds of most of her sex as if she had been preparing her place of nightly rest beneath the paternal roof.

As soon as Hetty had collected a sufficient number of the dried leaves to protect her person from the damps of the ground, she kneeled beside the humble pile, clasped her raised hands in an attitude of deep devotion, and in a soft, low, but audible voice repeated the Lord's Prayer. This was followed by those simple and devout verses, so familiar to children, in which she recommended her soul to God, should it be called away to another state of existence ere the return of morning. This duty done, she lay down and disposed herself to sleep. The attire of the girl, though suited to the

season, was sufficiently warm for all ordinary purposes, but the forest is ever cool, and the nights of that elevated region of country have always a freshness about them that renders clothing more necessary than is commonly the case in the summers of a low latitude. This had been foreseen by Hetty, who had brought with her a coarse, heavy mantle, which, when laid over her body, answered all the useful purposes of a blanket. Thus protected, she dropped asleep in a few minutes, as tranquilly as if watched over by the guardian care of that mother who had so recently been taken from her forever—affording, in this particular, a most striking contrast between her own humble couch and the sleepless pillow of her sister.

Hour passed after hour in a tranquillity as undisturbed and a rest as sweet as if angels expressly commissioned for that object watched around the bed of Hetty Hutter. Not once did her soft eyes open, until the gray of the dawn came struggling through the tops of the trees, falling on their lids and, united to the freshness of a summer's morning, giving the usual summons to awake. Ordinarily, Hetty was up ere the rays of the sun tipped the summits of the mountains, but on this occasion her fatigue had been so great and her rest was so profound that the customary warnings failed of their effect. The girl murmured in her sleep, threw an arm forward, smiled as gently as an infant in its cradle, but still slumbered. In making this unconscious gesture, her hand fell on some object that was warm, and, in the half-unconscious state in which she lay, she connected the circumstance with her habits. At the next moment, a rude attack was made on her side, as if a rooting animal were thrusting its snout beneath with a desire to force her position; then, uttering the name of "Judith," she awoke. As the startled girl arose to a sitting attitude, she perceived that some dark object sprang from her, scattering the leaves and snapping the fallen twigs in its haste. Opening her eyes and recovering from the first confusion and astonishment of her situation, Hetty perceived a cub of the common American brown bear balancing itself on its hinder legs and still looking toward her, as if doubtful whether it would be safe to trust itself near her person again. The first impulse of Hetty, who had been mistress of several of these cubs, was to run and seize the little creature as a prize, but a loud growl warned

her of the danger of such a procedure. Recoiling a few steps, the girl looked hurriedly around and perceived the dam watching her movements, with fiery eyes, at no great distance. A hollow tree that had once been the home of bees having recently fallen, the mother, with two more cubs, was feasting on the dainty food that this accident had placed within her reach, while the first kept a jealous eye on the situation of its truant and reckless young.

It would exceed all the means of human knowledge to pretend to analyze the influences that govern the acts of the lower animals. On this occasion, the dam, though proverbially fierce when its young is thought to be in danger, manifested no intention to attack the girl. It quitted the honey and advanced to a place within twenty feet of her, where it raised itself on its hinder legs and balanced its body in a sort of angry, growling discontent, but approached no nearer. Happily, Hetty did not fly. On the contrary, though not without terror, she knelt with her face toward the animal and, with clasped hands and uplifted eyes, repeated the prayer of the previous night. This act of devotion was not the result of alarm; it was a duty she never neglected to perform ere she slept, and when the return of consciousness awoke her to the business of the day. As the girl arose from her knees, the bear dropped on her feet again and, collecting its cubs around her, permitted them to draw their natural sustenance. Hetty was delighted with this proof of tenderness in an animal that has but a very indifferent reputation for the gentler feelings, and as a cub would quit its mother to frisk and leap about in wantonness, she felt a strong desire again to catch it up in her arms and play with it. But admonished by the growl, she had self-command sufficient not to put this dangerous project in execution; and recollecting her errand among the hills, she tore herself away from the group and proceeded on her course, along the margin of the lake, of which she now caught glimpses again through the trees. To her surprise, though not to her alarm, the family of bears arose and followed her steps, keeping a short distance behind her, apparently watching every movement, as if they had a near interest in all she did.

In this manner, escorted by the dam and cubs, the girl proceeded nearly a mile, thrice the distance she had been able to achieve in the darkness during the same period of time.

She then reached a brook that had dug a channel for itself into the earth, and went brawling into the lake, between steep and high banks covered with trees. Here Hetty performed her ablutions; then, drinking of the pure mountain water, she went her way, refreshed and lighter of heart, still attended by her singular companions. Her course now lay along a broad and nearly level terrace, which stretched from the top of the bank that bounded the water to a low acclivity that rose to a second and irregular platform above. This was at a part of the valley where the mountains ran obliquely, forming the commencement of a plain that spread between the hills, southward of the sheet of water. Hetty knew by this circumstance that she was getting near to the encampment, and had she not, the bears would have given her warning of the vicinity of human beings. Snuffing the air, the dam refused to follow any further, though the girl looked back and invited her to come by childish signs and even by direct appeals made in her own sweet voice. It was while making her way slowly through some bushes in this manner, with averted face and eyes riveted on the immovable animals, that the girl suddenly found her steps arrested by a human hand that was laid lightly on her shoulder.

"Where go?" said a soft female voice, speaking hurriedly and in concern. "Indian—red man—savage—wicked warrior —thataway."

This unexpected salutation alarmed the girl no more than the presence of the fierce inhabitants of the woods. It took her a little by surprise, it is true, but she was in a measure prepared for some such meeting, and the creature who stopped her was as little likely to excite terror as any who ever appeared in the guise of an Indian. It was a girl not much older than herself, whose smile was sunny as Judith's in her brightest moments, whose voice was melody itself, and whose accents and manner had all the rebuked gentleness that characterizes the sex among a people who habitually treat their women as the attendants and servitors of the warriors. Beauty among the women of the aboriginal Americans, before they have become exposed to the hardships of wives and mothers, is by no means uncommon. In this particular the original owners of the country were not unlike their more civilized successors, *nature* appearing to have bestowed that delicacy of mien and outline that forms so

great a charm in the youthful female, but of which they are so early deprived—and that, too, as much by the habits of domestic life as from any other cause.

The girl who had so suddenly arrested the steps of Hetty, was dressed in a calico mantle that effectually protected all the upper part of her person, while a short petticoat of blue cloth edged with gold lace, which fell no lower than her knees, leggings of the same, and moccasins of deerskin completed her attire. Her hair fell in long, dark braids down her shoulders and back, and was parted above a low, smooth forehead in a way to soften the expression of eyes that were full of archness and natural feeling. Her face was oval, with delicate features; the teeth were even and white; while the mouth expressed a melancholy tenderness, as if it wore that peculiar meaning in intuitive perception of the fate of a being who was doomed from birth to endure a woman's sufferings, relieved by a woman's affections. Her voice, as has been already intimated, was soft as the sighing of the night air, a characteristic of the females of her race, but which was so conspicuous in herself as to have procured for her the name of Wah-ta!-Wah, which, rendered into English, means Hist-oh!-Hist.

In a word, this was the betrothed of Chingachgook, who, having succeeded in lulling their suspicions, was permitted to wander around the encampment of her captors. This indulgence was in accordance with the general policy of the red man, who well knew, moreover, that her trail could have been followed in the event of flight. It will also be remembered that the Iroquois, or Hurons, as it would be better to call them, were entirely ignorant of the proximity of her lover; a fact, indeed, that she did not know herself.

It is not easy to say which manifested the most self-possession at this unexpected meeting, the paleface or the red girl. But though a little surprised, Wah-ta!-Wah was the most willing to speak and far the readier in foreseeing consequences as well as in devising means to avert them. Her father, during her childhood, had been much employed as a warrior by the authorities of the colony; dwelling for several years near the forts, she had caught a knowledge of the English tongue, which she spoke in the usual abbreviated manner of an Indian, but fluently and without any of the ordinary reluctance of her people.

"Where go?" repeated Wah-ta!-Wah, returning the smile of Hetty, in her own gentle, winning manner. "*Wicked* warrior thataway—*good* warrior far off."

"What's your name?" asked Hetty, with the simplicity of a child.

"Wah-ta!-Wah, I no Mingo—good Delaware—Yengeese * friend. Mingo cruel, and love scalp for blood—Delaware love him for honor. Come here, where no eyes."

Wah-ta!-Wah now led her companion toward the lake, descending the bank so as to place its overhanging trees and bushes between them and any probable observers; nor did she stop until they were both seated, side by side, on a fallen log, one end of which actually lay buried in the water.

"*Why* you come for?" the young Indian eagerly inquired. "*Where* you come from?"

Hetty told her tale in her own simple and truth-loving manner. She explained the situation of her father and stated her desire to serve him and, if possible, to procure his release.

"Why your father come to Mingo camp in night?" asked the Indian girl, with a directness which, if not borrowed from the other, partook largely of its sincerity. "He know it wartime, and he no boy—he no want beard—no want to be told Iroquois carry tomahawk, and knife, and rifle. Why he come nighttime, seize *me* by hair, and try to scalp Delaware girl?"

"You!" said Hetty, almost sickening with horror; "did he seize *you*—did he try to scalp *you?*"

"Why no? Delaware scalp sell for much as Mingo scalp. Governor no tell difference. Wicked t'ing for paleface to scalp. No his gifts, as good Deerslayer alway tell me."

---

* It is singular there should be any question concerning the origin of the well-known sobriquet of "Yankees." Nearly all the old writers who speak of the Indians first known to the colonists make them pronounce the word "English" as "Yengeese." Even at this day, it is a provincialism of New England to say "*E*nglish" instead of "*In*glish," and there is a close conformity of sound between "*E*nglish" and "Yengeese," more especially if the latter word, as was probably the case, be pronounced short. The transition from "Yengeese," thus pronounced, to "Yankees" is quite easy. If the former is pronounced "Yangis," it is almost identical with "Yankees," and Indian words have seldom been spelt as they are pronounced. Thus the scene of this tale is spelled "Ot*s*ego" and is properly pronounced "Ot*s*ago." The liquids of the Indians would easily convert "En" into "Yen."

"And do *you* know the Deerslayer?" said Hetty, coloring with delight and surprise, forgetting her regrets at the moment in the influence of this new feeling. "I know him, too. He is now in the ark, with Judith and a Delaware who is called the Big Serpent. A bold and handsome warrior is this Serpent, too!"

In spite of the rich, deep color that nature had bestowed on the Indian beauty, the telltale blood deepened on her cheeks, until the blush gave new animation and intelligence to her jet-black eyes. Raising a finger in an attitude of warning, she dropped her voice, already so soft and sweet, nearly to a whisper as she continued the discourse.

"Chingachgook!" returned the Delaware girl, sighing out the harsh name in sounds so softly guttural as to cause it to reach the ear in melody. "His father, Uncas—great chief of the Mahicanni—next to old Tamenund! More as warrior, not so much gray hair, and less at council fire. *You* know Serpent?"

"He joined us last evening and was in the ark with me for two or three hours before I left it. I'm afraid, Hist"—Hetty could not pronounce the Indian name of her new friend, but having heard Deerslayer give her this familiar appellation, she used it without any of the ceremony of civilized life—"I'm afraid he has come after scalps as well as my poor father and Hurry Harry!"

"Why he shouldn't, ha? Chingachgook red warrior, very red—scalp make his honor—be sure he take him."

"Then," said Hetty earnestly, "he will be as wicked as any other. God will not pardon in a red man what he will not pardon in a white man."

"No true," returned the Delaware girl, with a warmth that nearly amounted to passion; "no true, I tell you! The Manitou smile and please when he see young warrior come back from the warpath with two, ten, hundred scalp on a pole! Chingachgook father take scalp, grandfather take scalp —all old chief take scalp, and Chingachgook take as many scalp as he can carry himself!"

"Then, Hist, his sleep of nights must be terrible to think of! No one can be cruel and hope to be forgiven."

"No cruel—plenty forgiven," returned Wah-ta!-Wah, stamping her little foot on the stony strand and shaking her head in a way to show how completely feminine feeling, in

one of its aspects, had got the better of feminine feeling in another. "I tell you, Serpent brave; he go home this time with four, yes, *two* scalp."

"And is that his errand here? Did he really come all this distance, across mountains and valleys, rivers and lakes, to torment his fellow creatures and do so wicked a thing?"

This question at once appeased the growing ire of the half-offended Indian beauty. It completely got the better of the prejudices of education and turned all her thoughts to a gentler and more feminine channel. At first, she looked around her suspiciously, as if distrusting eavesdroppers; then she gazed wistfully into the face of her attentive companion; after which this exhibition of girlish coquetry and womanly feeling terminated by her covering her face with both her hands and laughing in a strain that might well be termed the melody of the woods. Dread of discovery, however, soon put a stop to this naïve exhibition of feeling, and removing her hands, this creature of impulses gazed again wistfully into the face of her companion, as if inquiring how far she might trust a stranger with her secret. Although Hetty had no claim to her sister's extraordinary beauty, many thought her countenance the more winning of the two. It expressed all the undisguised sincerity of her character, and it was totally free from any of the unpleasant physical accompaniments that so frequently attend mental imbecility. It is true that one accustomed to closer observation than common might have detected the proofs of her feebleness of intellect in the language of her sometimes vacant eyes, but they were signs that attracted sympathy by their total want of guile, rather than by any other feeling. The effect on Hist, to use the English and more familiar translation of the name, was favorable, and yielding to an impulse of tenderness, she threw her arms around Hetty and embraced her with an outpouring emotion so natural that it was only equaled by its warmth.

"*You* good," whispered the young Indian; "you good, I know. It's so long since Wah-ta!-Wah have a friend—a sister—anybody to speak her heart to! You Hist friend; don't I say trut'!"

"I never had a friend," answered Hetty, returning the warm embrace with unfeigned earnestness; "I've a sister, but no friend. Judith loves me, and I love Judith, but that's

natural and as we are taught in the Bible; but I *should* like to have a *friend!* I'll be your friend, with all my heart, for I like your voice, and your smile, and your way of thinking in everything except about the scalps———"

"No t'ink more of him—no say more of scalp," interrupted Hist soothingly. "You paleface, I redskin; we bring up different fashion. Deerslayer and Chingachgook great friend, and no the same color; Hist and—what your name, pretty paleface?"

"I am called Hetty, though when they spell the name in the Bible, they always spell it Esther."

"What that make?—no good, no harm. No need to spell name at all. Moravian try to make Wah-ta!-Wah spell, but no won't let him. No good for Delaware girl to know too much —know more than warrior sometime; that great shame. My name Wah-ta!-Wah—that say Hist in your tongue. You call him, Hist—I call him, Hetty."

These preliminaries settled to their mutual satisfaction, the two girls began to discourse of their several hopes and projects. Hetty made her new friend more fully acquainted with her intentions in behalf of her father; and, to one in the least addicted to prying into the affairs of others, Hist would have betrayed her own feelings and expectations in connection with the young warrior of her own tribe. Enough was revealed on both sides, however, to let each party get a tolerable insight into the views of the other, though enough still remained in mental reservation to give rise to the following questions and answers, with which the interview in effect closed. As the quickest-witted, Hist was the first with her interrogatories. Folding an arm about the waist of Hetty, she bent her head so as to look up playfully into the face of the other; and, laughing, as if her meaning were to be extracted from her looks, she spoke more plainly.

"Hetty got broder as well as fader?" she said. "Why no talk of broder as well as fader?"

"I have no brother, Hist. I had one once, they say, but he is dead many a year and lies buried in the lake, by the side of Mother."

"No got broder—got a young warrior; love him almost as much as fader, eh? Very handsome and brave-looking; fit to be chief if he *good* as he *seem* to be."

"It's wicked to love any man as well as I love my father,

and so I strive not to do it, Hist," returned the conscientious Hetty, who knew not how to conceal an emotion by an approach to an untruth as venial as an evasion, though powerfully tempted by female shame to err; "though I sometimes think that wickedness will get the better of me, if Hurry comes so often to the lake. I *must* tell you the truth, dear Hist, because you ask me, but I should fall down and die in the woods if he knew it!"

"Why he no ask you himself? Brave-looking—why not bold-speaking? Young warrior ought to ask young girl; no make young girl speak first. Mingo girls too shame for *that*."

This was said indignantly and with the generous warmth a young female of spirit would be apt to feel at what she deemed an invasion of her sex's most valued privilege. It had little influence on the simple-minded, but also just-minded Hetty, who, though inherently feminine in all her impulses, was much more alive to the workings of her own heart than to any of the usages with which convention has protected the sensitiveness of her sex.

"Ask me *what?*" the startled girl demanded, with a suddenness that proved how completely her fears had been aroused. "Ask me if I like him as well as I do my own father? Oh, I hope he will never put such a question to *me*, for I should have to answer, and that would *kill* me!"

"No—no—no kill, *quite* almost," returned the other, laughing in spite of herself. "Make blush come—make shame come, too—but he no stay great while; then feel happier than ever. Young warrior must tell young girl he want to make wife, else never can live in his wigwam."

"Hurry don't want to marry me—nobody will ever want to marry me, Hist."

"How you can know? P'r'aps everybody want to marry you, and by-and-by tongue say what heart feel. Why nobody want to marry you?"

"I am not full-witted, they say. Father often tells me this; and so does Judith sometimes, when she is vexed; but I shouldn't so much mind them as I did Mother. *She* said so *once*, and then she cried as if her heart would break; and so I *know* I'm not full-witted."

Hist gazed at the gentle, simple girl for quite a minute without speaking; then the truth appeared to flash all at once on the mind of the young Indian maid. Pity, reverence, and

tenderness seemed struggling together in her breast; then, rising suddenly, she indicated a wish to her companion that she would accompany her to the camp, which was situated at no great distance. This unexpected change, from the precaution that Hist had previously manifested a desire to use in order to prevent being seen, to an open exposure of the person of her friend, arose from the perfect conviction that no Indian would harm a being whom the Great Spirit had disarmed by depriving it of its strongest defense, reason. In this respect, nearly all unsophisticated nations resemble each other, appearing to offer spontaneously, by a feeling creditable to human nature, that protection by their own forbearance which has been withheld by the inscrutable wisdom of Providence. Wah-ta!-Wah, indeed, knew that in many tribes the mentally imbecile and the mad were held in a species of religious reverence, receiving from the untutored inhabitants of the forest respect and honors, instead of the contumely and neglect that it is their fortune to meet with among the more pretending and sophisticated.

Hetty accompanied her new friend without apprehension or reluctance. It was her wish to reach the camp, and sustained by her motives, she felt no more concern for the consequences than did her companion herself, now the latter was apprised of the character of the protection that the paleface maiden carried with her. Still, as they proceeded slowly along a shore that was tangled with overhanging bushes, Hetty continued the discourse, assuming the office of interrogating, which the other had instantly dropped as soon as she ascertained the character of the mind to which her questions had been addressed.

"But *you* are not half-witted," said Hetty, "and there's no reason why the Serpent should not marry *you*."

"Hist prisoner, and Mingo got big ear. No speak of Chingachgook when they by. Promise Hist that, good Hetty."

"I know—I know," returned Hetty, half-whispering in her eagerness to let the other see she understood the necessity of caution. "I know—Deerslayer and the Serpent mean to get you away from the Iroquois, and you wish me not to tell the secret."

"How you know?" said Hist hastily, vexed at the moment that the other was not even more feeble-minded than was actually the case. "How you know? Better not talk of any

but fader and Hurry; Mingo understand *dat;* he no understand *t'udder.* Promise you no talk about what you no understand."

"But I *do* understand this, Hist, and so I *must* talk about it. Deerslayer as good as told Father all about it in my presence, and as nobody told me not to listen, I overheard it all, as I did Hurry's and Father's discourse about the scalps."

"Very bad for paleface to talk about scalps, and very bad for young woman to hear! Now you love Hist, I know, Hetty, and so, among Injins, when love hardest never talk most."

"That's not the way among white people, who talk most about them they love best. I suppose it's because I'm only half-witted that I don't see the reason why it should be so different among red people."

"That what Deerslayer call gift. One gift to talk, t'udder gift to hold tongue. Hold-tongue your gift, among Mingos. If Sarpent want to see Hist, so Hetty want to see Hurry. Good girl never tell secret of friend."

Hetty understood this appeal, and she promised the Delaware girl not to make any allusion to the presence of Chingachgook, or to the motive of his visit to the lake.

"Maybe he get off Hurry and fader as well as Hist, if let him have his way," whispered Wah-ta!-Wah to her companion in a confiding, flattering way, just as they got near enough to the encampment to hear the voices of several of their own sex, who were apparently occupied in the usual toils of women of their class. "T'ink of dat, Hetty, and put two, twenty finger on mouth. No get friends free without Sarpent do it."

A better expedient could not have been adopted to secure the silence and discretion of Hetty than that which was now presented to her mind. As the liberation of her father and the young frontiersman was the great object of her adventure, she felt the connection between it and the services of the Delaware, and with an innocent laugh, she nodded her head and, in the same suppressed manner, promised a due attention to the wishes of her friend. Thus assured, Hist tarried no longer but immediately and openly led the way into the encampment of her captors.

> *The great King of kings*
> *Hath in the table of his law commanded,*
> *That thou shalt do no murder.*
> *Take heed; for he holds vengeance in his hand,*
> *To hurl upon their heads that break his law.*
>
> SHAKESPEARE

THAT THE PARTY to which Hist compulsorily belonged was not one that was regularly on the warpath was evident by the presence of females. It was a small fragment of a tribe that had been hunting and fishing within the English limits, where it was found by the commencement of hostilities, and, after passing the winter and spring by living on what was strictly the property of its enemies, it chose to strike a hostile blow before it finally retired. There was also deep Indian sagacity in the maneuver which had led them so far into the territory of their foes. When the runner arrived who announced the breaking out of hostilities between the English and French—a struggle that was certain to carry with it all the tribes that dwelt within the influence of the respective belligerents—this particular party of the Iroquois were posted on the shores of the Oneida, a lake that lies some fifty miles nearer to their own frontier than that which is the scene of our tale. To have fled in a direct line for the Canadas would have exposed them to the dangers of a direct pursuit, and the chiefs had determined to adopt the expedient of penetrating deeper into a region that had now become dangerous, in the hope of being able to retire in the rear of their pursuers, instead of having them on their trail. The presence of the women had induced the attempt of this ruse, the strength of these feebler members of the party being unequal to the effort of escaping from the pursuit of warriors. When the

reader remembers the vast extent of the American wilderness at that early day, he will perceive that it was possible for even a tribe to remain months undiscovered in particular portions of it; nor was the danger of encountering a foe, the usual precautions being observed, as great in the woods as it is on the high seas in a time of active warfare.

The encampment being temporary, it offered to the eye no more than the rude protection of a bivouac, relieved in some slight degree by the ingenious expedients which suggested themselves to the readiness of those who passed their lives amid similar scenes. One fire that had been kindled against the roots of a living oak sufficed for the whole party, the weather being too mild to require it for any purpose but cooking. Scattered around this center of attraction were some fifteen or twenty low huts—perhaps kennels would be a better word—into which their different owners crept at night, and which were also intended to meet the exigencies of a storm. These little huts were made of the branches of trees put together with some ingenuity, and they were uniformly topped with bark that had been stripped from fallen trees, of which every virgin forest possesses hundreds in all stages of decay. Of furniture, they had next to none. Cooking utensils of the simplest sort were lying near the fire; a few articles of clothing were to be seen in or around the huts; rifles, horns, and pouches leaned against the trees, or were suspended from the lower branches; and the carcasses of two or three deer were stretched to view on the same natural shambles.

As the encampment was in the midst of a dense wood, the eye could not take in its *tout ensemble* at a glance, but hut after hut started out of the gloomy picture as one gazed about him in quest of objects. There was no center, unless the fire might be so considered—no open area where the possessors of this rude village might congregate—but all was dark, covert, and cunning, like its owners. A few children strayed from hut to hut, giving the spot a little the air of domestic life, and the suppressed laugh and low voices of the women occasionally broke in upon the deep stillness of the somber forest. As for the men, they either ate, slept, or examined their arms. They conversed but little, and then usually apart, or in groups withdrawn from the females; whilst an air of untiring, innate watchfulness and apprehen-

sion of danger seemed to be blended even with their slumbers.

As the two girls came near the encampment, Hetty uttered a slight exclamation on catching a view of the person of her father. He was seated on the ground with his back to a tree, and Hurry stood near him, indolently whittling a twig. Apparently, they were as much at liberty as any others in or about the camp, and one unaccustomed to Indian usages would have mistaken them for visitors, instead of supposing them to be captives. Wah-ta!-Wah led her new friend quite near them and then modestly withdrew, that her own presence might be no restraint on her feelings. But Hetty was not sufficiently familiar with caresses or outward demonstrations of fondness to indulge in any outbreaking of feeling. She merely approached and stood at her father's side without speaking, resembling a silent statue of filial affection. The old man expressed neither alarm nor surprise at her sudden appearance. In these particulars he had caught the stoicism of the Indians, well knowing that there was no more certain mode of securing their respect than by imitating their self-command. Nor did the savages themselves betray the least sign of surprise at this sudden appearance of a stranger among them. In a word, this arrival produced much less visible sensation, though occurring under circumstances so peculiar, than would be seen in a village of higher pretensions to civilization, did an ordinary traveler drive up to the door of its principal inn. Still a few warriors collected, and it was evident, by the manner in which they glanced at Hetty as they conversed together, that she was the subject of their discourse, and probable that the reasons of her unlooked-for appearance were matters of discussion. This phlegm of manner is characteristic of the North American Indian—some say of his white successor also—but in this case, much should be attributed to the peculiar situation in which the party was placed. The force in the ark, the presence of Chingachgook excepted, was well known; no tribe or body of troops was believed to be near; and vigilant eyes were posted around the entire lake, watching, day and night, the slightest movement of those whom it would not be exaggerated now to term the besieged.

Hutter was inwardly much moved by the conduct of Hetty, though he affected so much indifference of manner. He

recollected her gentle appeal to him before he left the ark, and misfortune rendered that of weight which might have been forgotten amid the triumph of success. Then he knew the simple, singlehearted fidelity of his child and understood why she had come and the total disregard of self that reigned in all her acts.

"This is not well, Hetty," he said, deprecating the consequences to the girl herself more than any other evil. "These are fierce Iroquois and are as little apt to forget an injury as a favor."

"Tell me, Father," returned the girl, looking furtively about her, as if fearful of being overheard, "did God let you do the cruel errand on which you came? I want much to know this, that I may speak to the Indians plainly if he did not."

"You should not have come hither, Hetty; these brutes will not understand your nature or your intentions!"

"How was it, Father? Neither you nor Hurry seems to have anything that looks like scalps."

"If that will set your mind at peace, child, I can answer you no. I had caught the young creatur' who came here with you, but her screeches soon brought down upon me a troop of the wildcats that was too much for any single Christian to withstand. If that will do you any good, we are as innocent of having taken a scalp this time as I make no doubt we shall also be innocent of receiving the bounty."

"Thank you for that, Father! Now I can speak boldly to the Iroquois, and with an easy conscience. I hope Hurry, too, has not been able to harm any of the Indians?"

"Why, as to that matter, Hetty," returned the individual in question, "you've put it pretty much in the natyve character of the religious truth. Hurry has not been *able,* and that is the long and short of it. I've seen many squalls, old fellow, both on land and on the water, but never did I feel one as lively and as snappish as that which come down upon us night afore last, in the shape of an Indian hurrah-boys! Why, Hetty, you're no great matter at a reason or an idee that lies a little deeper than common, but you're human and have some human notions—now I'll just ask you to look at these circumstances. Here was old Tom, your father, and myself bent on a legal operation, as is to be seen in the words of the law and the proclamation, thinking no harm, when we were

set upon by critturs that were more like a pack of hungry wolves than mortal savages even, and there they had us tethered like two sheep in less time than it has taken me to tell you the story."

"You are free, now, Hurry," returned Hetty, glancing timidly at the fine, unfettered limbs of the young giant. "You have no cords or withes to pain your arms or legs now."

"Not I, Hetty. Natur' is natur', and freedom is natur', too. My limbs have a free look, but that's pretty much the amount of it, sin' I can't use them in the way I should like. Even these trees have eyes—aye, and tongues, too, for, was the old man here or I to start one single rod beyond our jail limits, sarvice would be put on the bail afore we could 'gird up our loins' for a race; and like as not four or five rifle bullets would be traveling after us, carrying so many invitations to curb our impatience. There isn't a jail in the Colony as tight as this we are now in, for I've tried the vartue of two or three on 'em, and I know the mater'als they are made of, as well as the men that made 'em, takin' down being the next step in schoolin' to puttin' up in all such fabrications."

Lest the reader should get an exaggerated opinion of Hurry's demerits from this boastful and indiscreet revelation, it may be well to say that his offenses were confined to assaults and batteries, for several of which he had been imprisoned, when, as he has just said, he often escaped by demonstrating the flimsiness of the constructions in which he was confined by opening for himself doors in spots where the architects had neglected to place them. But Hetty had no knowledge of jails and little of the nature of crime beyond what her unadulterated and almost instinctive perceptions of right and wrong taught her, and this sally of the rude being who had spoken was lost upon her. She understood his general meaning, however, and answered in reference to that alone.

"It's so best, Hurry," she said. "It is best Father and you should be quiet and peaceable till I have spoken to the Iroquois, when all will be well and happy. I don't wish either of you to follow, but leave me to myself. As soon as all is settled and you are at liberty to go back to the castle, I will come and let you know it."

Hetty spoke with so much simple earnestness, seemed so

confident of success, and wore so high an air of moral feeling and truth that both the listeners felt more disposed to attach an importance to her mediation than might otherwise have happened. When she manifested an intention to quit them, therefore, they offered no obstacle, though they saw she was about to join the group of chiefs who were consulting apart, seemingly on the manner and motive of her own sudden appearance.

When Hist—for so we love best to call her—quitted her companion, she strayed near one or two of the elder warriors who had shown her most kindness in her captivity—the principal man of whom had even offered to adopt her as his child, if she would consent to become a Huron. In taking this direction the shrewd girl did so to invite inquiry. She was too well trained in the habits of her people to obtrude the opinions of one of her sex and years on men and warriors, but nature had furnished a tact and ingenuity that enabled her to attract the attention she desired without wounding the pride of those whom it was her duty to defer to and respect. Even her affected indifference stimulated curiosity, and Hetty had hardly reached the side of her father before the Delaware girl was brought within the circle of the warriors by a secret but significant gesture. Here she was questioned as to the presence of her companion and the motives that had brought her to the camp. This was all that Hist desired. She explained the manner in which she had detected the weakness of Hetty's reason, rather exaggerating than lessening the deficiency in her intellect, and then she related, in general terms, the object of the girl in venturing among her enemies. The effect was all that the speaker expected, her account investing the person and character of their visitor with a sacredness and respect that she well knew would prove her protection. As soon as her own purpose was attained, Hist withdrew to a distance, where, with female consideration and a sisterly tenderness, she set about the preparation of a meal to be offered to her new friend as soon as the latter might be at liberty to partake of it. While thus occupied, however, the ready girl in no degree relaxed in her watchfulness, noting every change of countenance among the chiefs, every movement of Hetty, and the smaller occurrences that could be likely to affect her own interests or that of her new friend.

As Hetty approached the chiefs, they opened their little

circle with an ease and deference of manner that would have done credit to men of more courtly origin. A fallen tree lay near, and the oldest of the warriors made a quiet sign for the girl to be seated on it, taking his place at her side with the gentleness of a father. The others arranged themselves around the two with grave dignity, and then the girl, who had sufficient observation to perceive that such a course was expected of her, began to reveal the object of her visit. The moment she opened her mouth to speak, however, the old chief gave a gentle sign for her to forbear, said a few words to one of his juniors, and then waited in silent patience until the latter had summoned Hist to the party. This interruption proceeded from the chief's having discovered that there existed a necessity for an interpreter, few of the Hurons present understanding the English language, and they but imperfectly.

Wah-ta!-Wah was not sorry to be called upon to be present at the interview, and least of all in the character in which she was now wanted. She was aware of the hazards she ran in attempting to deceive one or two of the party; but was nonetheless resolved to use every means that offered and to practice every artifice that an Indian education could supply to conceal the facts of the vicinity of her betrothed and of the errand on which he had come. One unpracticed in the expedients and opinions of savage life would not have suspected the readiness of invention, the wariness of action, the high resolution, the noble impulses, the deep self-devotion, and the feminine disregard of self, where the affections were concerned, that lay concealed beneath the demure looks, the mild eyes, and the sunny smiles of this young Indian beauty. As she approached them, the grim old warriors regarded her with pleasure, for they had a secret pride in the hope of engrafting so rare a scion on the stock of their own nation, adoption being as regularly practiced and as distinctly recognized among the tribes of America as it ever had been among those nations that submit to the sway of the civil law.

As soon as Hist was seated by the side of Hetty, the old chief desired her to ask "the fair young paleface" what had brought her among the Iroquois, and what they could do to serve her.

"Tell them, Hist, who I am—Thomas Hutter's youngest

daughter; Thomas Hutter, the oldest of their two prisoners; he who owns the castle and the ark, and who has the best right to be thought the owner of these hills and that lake, since he has dwelt so long, and trapped so long, and fished so long among them. They'll know whom you mean by Thomas Hutter, if you tell them *that*. And then tell them that I've come here to convince them they ought not to harm Father and Hurry, but let them go in peace, and to treat them as brothers, rather than as enemies. Now tell them all this plainly, Hist, and fear nothing for yourself or me; God will protect us."

Wah-ta!-Wah did as the other desired; taking care to render the words of her friend as literally as possible into the Iroquois tongue, a language she used with a readiness almost equal to that with which she spoke her own. The chiefs heard this opening explanation with grave decorum, the two who had a little knowledge of English intimating their satisfaction with the interpreter by furtive but significant glances of the eyes.

"And, now, Hist," continued Hetty, as soon as it was intimated to her that she might proceed, "I wish you to tell these red men, word for word, what I am about to say. Tell them first, that Father and Hurry came here with an intention to take as many scalps as they could; for the wicked governor and the province have offered money for scalps—whether of warriors or women, men, or children—and the love of gold was too strong for their hearts to withstand it. Tell them this, dear Hist, just as you have heard it from me, word for word."

Wah-ta!-Wah hesitated about rendering this speech as literally as had been desired, but detecting the intelligence of those who understood English, and apprehending even a greater knowledge than they actually possessed, she found herself compelled to comply. Contrary to what a civilized man would have expected, the admission of the motives and of the errands of their prisoners produced no visible effect on either the countenances or the feelings of the listeners. They probably considered the act meritorious, and that which neither of them would have hesitated to perform in his own person, he would not be apt to censure in another.

"And now, Hist," resumed Hetty, as soon as she perceived

that her first speeches were understood by the chiefs, "you can tell them more. They know that Father and Hurry did not succeed, and therefore they can bear them no grudge for any harm that has been done. If they had slain their children and wives, it would not alter the matter, and I'm not certain that what I am about to tell them would not have more weight had there been mischief done. But ask them first, Hist, if they know there is a God who reigns over the whole earth and is ruler and chief of all who live, let them be red or white, or what color they may?"

Wah-ta!-Wah looked a little surprised at this question, for the idea of the Great Spirit is seldom long absent from the mind of an Indian girl. She put the question as literally as possible, however, and received a grave answer in the affirmative.

"This is right," continued Hetty, "and my duty will now be light. This Great Spirit, as you call our God, has caused a book to be written, which we call a Bible, and in this book have been set down all His commandments, and His holy will and pleasure, and the rules by which all men are to live, and directions how to govern the thoughts even, and the wishes, and the will. Here, this is one of these holy books, and you must tell the chiefs what I am about to read to them from its sacred pages."

As Hetty concluded, she reverently unrolled a small English Bible from its envelope of coarse calico, treating the volume with the sort of external respect that a Romanist would be apt to show to a religious relic. As she slowly proceeded in her task, the grim warriors watched each movement with riveted eyes, and when they saw the little volume appear, a slight expression of surprise escaped one or two of them. But Hetty held it out toward them in triumph, as if she expected the sight would produce a visible miracle; then, without betraying either surprise or mortification at the stoicism of the Indian, she turned eagerly to her new friend in order to renew the discourse.

"This is the sacred volume, Hist," she said, "and these words, and lines, and verses, and chapters all came from God."

"Why Great Spirit no send book to Injin, too?" demanded Hist, with the directness of a mind that was totally unsophisticated.

"Why?" answered Hetty, a little bewildered by a question so unexpected. "Why?—Ah! You know the Indians don't know how to read."

If Hist was not satisfied with this explanation, she did not deem the point of sufficient importance to be pressed. Simply bending her body in gentle admission of the truth of what she heard, she sat patiently awaiting the further arguments of the paleface enthusiast.

"You can tell these chiefs that throughout this book men are ordered to forgive their enemies, to treat them as they would brethren, and never to injure their fellow creatures, more especially on account of revenge, or any evil passion. Do you think you can tell them this so that they will understand it, Hist?"

"Tell him well enough, but he no very easy to understand."

Hist then conveyed the ideas of Hetty in the best manner she could to the attentive Indians, who heard her words with some such surprise as an American of our own times would be apt to betray at a suggestion that the great modern, but vacillating ruler of things human, public opinion, might be wrong. One or two of their number, however, having met with missionaries, said a few words in explanation, and then the group gave all its attention to the communications that were to follow. Before Hetty resumed, she inquired earnestly of Hist if the chiefs had understood her, and receiving an evasive answer, was fain to be satisfied.

"I will now read to the warriors some of the verses that it is good for them to know," continued the girl, whose manner grew more solemn and earnest as she proceeded; "and they will remember that they are the words of the Great Spirit. First, then, ye are commanded to '*Love thy neighbor as thyself.*' Tell them *that,* dear Hist."

"Neighbor for Injin no mean paleface," answered the Delaware girl, with more decision than she had hitherto thought it necessary to use. "Neighbor mean Iroquois for Iroquois, Mohican for Mohican, paleface for paleface. No need tell chief anything else."

"You forget, Hist, these are the words of the Great Spirit, and the chiefs must obey them as well as others. Here is another commandment: '*Whosoever shall smite thee on the right cheek, turn to him the other also.*'"

"What that mean?" demanded Hist, with the quickness of lightning.

Hetty explained that it was an order not to resent injuries, but rather to submit to receive fresh wrongs from the offender.

"And hear this too, Hist," she added: "*'Love your enemies, bless them that curse you, do good to them that hate you, and pray for them which despitefully use you and persecute you.'*"

By this time Hetty had become excited; her eye gleamed with the earnestness of her feelings, her cheeks flushed, and her voice, usually so low and modulated, became stronger and more impressive. With the Bible she had been early made familiar by her mother, and she now turned from passage to passage with surprising rapidity, taking care to cull such verses as taught the sublime lessons of Christian charity and Christian forgiveness. To translate half of what she said, in her pious earnestness, Wah-ta!-Wah would have found impracticable had she made the effort, but wonder held her tongue-tied equally with the chiefs, and the young, simple-minded enthusiast had fairly become exhausted with her own efforts before the other opened her mouth again to utter a syllable. Then, indeed, the Delaware girl gave a brief translation of the substance of what had been both read and said, confining herself to one or two of the more striking of the verses, those that had struck her own imagination as the most paradoxical, and which certainly would have been the most applicable to the case, could the uninstructed minds of the listeners embrace the great moral truths they conveyed.

It will be scarcely necessary to tell the reader the effect that such novel duties would be likely to produce among a group of Indian warriors, with whom it was a species of religious principle never to forget a benefit or to forgive an injury. Fortunately, the previous explanations of Hist had prepared the minds of the Hurons for something extravagant, and most of that which to them seemed inconsistent and paradoxical was accounted for by the fact that the speaker possessed a mind that was constituted differently from those of most of the human race. Still, there were one or two old men who had heard similar doctrines from the missionaries,

and they felt a desire to occupy an idle moment by pursuing a subject that they found so curious.

"This is the Good Book of the palefaces," observed one of these chiefs, taking the volume from the unresisting hand of Hetty, who gazed anxiously at his face while he turned the leaves, as if she expected to witness some visible results from the circumstance. "This is the law by which my white brethren profess to live?"

Hist, to whom this question was addressed, if it might be considered as addressed to anyone in particular, answered simply in the affirmative, adding that both the French of the Canadas and the Yengeese of the British provinces equally admitted its authority and affected to revere its principles.

"Tell my young sister," said the Huron, looking directly at Hist, "that I will open my mouth and say a few words."

"The Iroquois chief go to speak—my paleface friend listen," said Hist.

"I rejoice to hear it!" exclaimed Hetty. "God has touched his heart, and he will now let Father and Hurry go!"

"This is the paleface law," resumed the chief. "It tells him to do good to them that hurt him; when his brother asks him for his rifle, to give him the powder horn, too. Such is the paleface law?"

"Not so—not so," answered Hetty earnestly, when these words had been interpreted. "There is not a word about rifles in the whole book, and powder and bullets give offense to the Great Spirit."

"Why, then, does the paleface use them? If he is ordered to *give* double to him that asks only for one thing, why does he *take* double from the poor Indians, who ask for *no* thing? He comes from beyond the rising sun, with his book in his hand, and he teaches the red man to read it; but why does he forget himself all it says? When the Indian gives, he is never satisfied, and now he offers gold for the scalps of our women and children, though he calls us beasts if we take the scalp of a warrior killed in open war. My name is Rivenoak."

When Hetty had got this formidable question fairly presented to her mind in the translation, and Hist did her duty with more than usual readiness on this occasion, it scarcely need be said that she was sorely perplexed. Abler heads than that of this poor girl have frequently been puzzled by ques-

tions of a similar drift, and it is not surprising that, with all her own earnestness and sincerity, she did not know what answer to make.

"What shall I tell them, Hist?" she asked imploringly. "I *know* that all I have read from the book is true, and yet it wouldn't seem so, would it, by the conduct of those to whom the book was given?"

"Give 'em paleface reason," returned Hist ironically; "that always good for one side; though be bad for t'other."

"No, no, Hist, there can't be two sides to truth—and yet it does seem strange! I'm certain I have read the verses right, and no one would be so wicked as to print the word of God wrong. *That* can never be, Hist."

"Well, to poor Injin girl it seem everything *can* be to palefaces," returned the other coolly. "One time 'ey say white, and one time 'ey say black. Why, *never can be?*"

Hetty was more and more embarrassed until, overcome with the apprehension that she had failed in her object and that the lives of her father and Hurry would be the forfeit of some blunder of her own, she burst into tears. From that moment the manner of Hist lost all its irony and cool indifference, and she became the fond, caressing friend again. Throwing her arms around the afflicted girl, she attempted to soothe her sorrows by the scarcely ever failing remedy of female sympathy.

"Stop cry—no cry," she said, wiping the tears from the face of Hetty, as she would have performed the same office for a child, and stopping to press her, occasionally, to her own warm bosom with the affection of a sister; "why you so trouble? You no make he book, if he be wrong; and you no make he paleface, if he be wicked. There wicked red man and wicked white man—no color all good—no color all wicked. Chiefs know *that* well enough."

Hetty soon recovered from this sudden burst of grief, and then her mind reverted to the purpose of her visit, with its singlehearted earnestness. Perceiving that the grim-looking chiefs were still standing around her in grave attention, she hoped that another effort to convince them of the right might be successful.

"Listen, Hist," she said, struggling to suppress her sobs and to speak distinctly; "tell the chiefs that it matters not what the wicked do—right is right—the words of the Great

Spirit are the words of the Great Spirit—and no one can go
harmless for doing an evil act because another has done it
before him! *'Render good for evil,'* says this book, and that
is the law for the red man as well as for the white man."

"Never hear such law among Delaware, or among Iroquois," answered Hist soothingly. "No good to tell chiefs any
such law as *dat*. Tell 'em somet'ing they believe."

Hist was about to proceed, notwithstanding, when a tap
on the shoulder, from the finger of the oldest chief, caused
her to look up. She then perceived that one of the warriors
had left the group, and was already returning to it with
Hutter and Hurry. Understanding that the two last were
to become parties in the inquiry, she became mute, with the
unhesitating obedience of an Indian woman. In a few sec-
onds the prisoners stood face to face with the principal
men of the captors.

"Daughter," said the senior chief to the young Delaware,
"ask this graybeard why he came into our camp?"

The question was put by Hist, in her own imperfect English, but in a way that was easy to be understood. Hutter was too stern and obdurate, by nature, to shrink from the
consequences of any of his acts, and he was also too familiar
with the opinions of the savages not to understand that nothing was to be gained by equivocation, or an unmanly dread
of their anger. Without hesitating, therefore, he avowed
the purpose with which he had landed, merely justifying it
by the fact that the government of the province had bid
high for scalps. This frank avowal was received by the Iroquois with evident satisfaction, not so much, however, on account of the advantage it gave them in a moral point of view,
as by proving that they had captured a man worthy of occupying their thoughts and of becoming a subject of their
revenge. Hurry, when interrogated, confessed the truth,
though he would have been more disposed to concealment
than his sterner companion, did the circumstances very well
admit of its adoption. But he had tact enough to discover
that equivocation would be useless at that moment, and he
made a merit of necessity by imitating a frankness, which,
in the case of Hutter, was the offspring of habits of indifference, acting on a disposition that was always ruthless
and reckless of personal consequences.

As soon as the chiefs had received the answers to their

questions, they walked away in silence, like men who deemed the matter disposed of, all Hetty's dogmas being thrown away on beings trained in violence from infancy to manhood. Hetty and Hist were now left alone with Hutter and Hurry, no visible restraint being placed on the movements of either, though all four, in fact, were vigilantly and unceasingly watched. As respects the men, care was had to prevent them from getting possession of any of the rifles that lay scattered about, their own included—and there all open manifestations of watchfulness ceased. But they, who were so experienced in Indian practices, knew too well how great was the distance between appearances and reality to become the dupes of this seeming carelessness. Although both thought incessantly on the means of escape, and this without concert, each was aware of the uselessness of attempting any project of the sort that was not deeply laid and promptly executed. They had been long enough in the encampment, and were sufficiently observant to have ascertained that Hist, also, was a sort of captive; presuming on the circumstance, Hutter spoke in her presence more openly than he might otherwise have thought it prudent to do, inducing Hurry to be equally unguarded by his example.

"I'll not blame you, Hetty, for coming on this errand, which was well meant, if not very wisely planned," commenced the father, seating himself by the side of his daughter and taking her hand, a sign of affection that this rude being was accustomed to manifest to this particular child; "but preaching and the Bible are not the means to turn an Indian from his ways. Has Deerslayer sent any message, or has he any scheme by which he thinks to get us free?"

"Aye, that's the substance of it!" put in Hurry. "If you can help us, gal, to half a mile of freedom, or even a good start of a short quarter, I'll answer for the rest. Perhaps the old man may want a little more, but for one of my height and years *that* will meet all objections."

Hetty looked distressed, turning her eyes from one to the other, but she had no answer to give to the question of the reckless Hurry.

"Father," she said, "neither Deerslayer nor Judith knew of my coming until I had left the ark. They are afraid the Iroquois will make a raft and try to get off to the hut, and

think more of defending *that* than of coming to aid you."

"No—no—no," said Hist hurriedly, though in a low voice, and with her face bent toward the earth, in order to conceal from those whom she knew to be watching them the fact of her speaking at all. "No, no no, Deerslayer different man. He no t'ink of defending 'self, with friend in danger. Help one another, and all get to hut."

"This sounds well, old Tom," said Hurry, winking and laughing, though he too used the precaution to speak low. "Give me a ready-witted squaw for a fri'nd, and though I'll not downright defy an Iroquois, I think I would defy the devil."

"No talk loud," said Hist. "Some Iroquois got Yengeese tongue, and all got Yengeese ear."

"Have we a friend in you, young woman?" inquired Hutter, with an increasing interest in the conference. "If so, you may calculate on a solid reward; and nothing will be easier than to send you to your own tribe, if we can once fairly get you off with us to the castle. Give us the ark and the canoes, and we can command the lake, in spite of all the savages in the Canadas. Nothing but artillery could drive us out of the castle, if we can get back to it."

"S'pose 'ey come ashore to take scalp?" retorted Hist, with cool irony, at which the girl appeared to be more expert than is common for her sex.

"Aye, aye—that was a mistake; but there is little use in lamentations, and less still, young woman, in flings."

"Father," said Hetty, "Judith thinks of breaking open the big chest, in hopes of finding something in *that* which may buy your freedom of the savages."

A dark look came over Hutter at the announcement of this fact, and he muttered his dissatisfaction in a way to render it intelligible enough.

"What for no break open chest?" put in Hist. "Life sweeter than old chest—scalp sweeter than old chest. If no tell darter to break him open, Wah-ta!-wah no help him to run away."

"Ye know not what ye ask—ye are but silly girls, and the wisest way for ye both is to speak of what ye understand and to speak of nothing else. I little like this cold neglect of the savages, Hurry; it's a proof that they think of something serious, and if we are to do anything, we must

do it soon. Can we count on this young woman, think you?"

"Listen," said Hist quickly, and with an earnestness that proved how much her feelings were concerned; "Wah-ta!-wah no Iroquois—all over Delaware—got Delaware heart—Delaware feeling. She prisoner, too. One prisoner help t'udder prisoner. No good to talk more, now. Darter stay with fader—Wah-ta!-wah come and see friend—all look right—*then* tell what he do."

This was said in a low voice, but distinctly, and in a manner to make an impression. As soon as it was uttered, the girl arose and left the group, walking composedly toward the hut she occupied, as if she had no further interest in what might pass between the palefaces.

CHAPTER XII

She speaks much of her father; says she hears
There's tricks i' the world; and hems, and beats her heart;
Spurns enviously at straws: speaks things in doubt,
That carry but half sense; her speech is nothing,
Yet the unsuspected use of it doth move
The hearers to collection;——

SHAKESPEARE

WE LEFT THE occupants of the castle and the ark buried in sleep. Once or twice, in the course of the night, it is true, Deerslayer or the Delaware arose and looked out upon the tranquil lake, when, finding all safe, each returned to his pallet and slept like a man who was not easily deprived of his natural rest. At the first signs of the dawn, the former arose, however, and made his personal arrangements for the day, though his companion, whose nights had not been tranquil or without disturbance of late, continued on his blanket until the sun had fairly risen. Judith, too, was later than common that morning, for the earlier hours of the night had brought her little of either refreshment or sleep. But ere the sun had shown himself over the eastern hills, these too were up and afoot; even the tardy, in that region, seldom remained on their pallets after the appearance of the great luminary.

Chingachgook was in the act of arranging his forest toilet, when Deerslayer entered the cabin of the ark and threw him a few coarse, but light summer vestments that belonged to Hutter.

"Judith hath given me them for your use, Chief," said the latter, as he cast the jacket and trousers at the feet of the Indian; "for it's ag'in all prudence and caution to be seen in your war dress and paint. Wash off all them fiery

streaks from your cheeks, put on these garments, and here is a hat, such as it is, that will give you an awful on-civilized sort of civilization, as the missionaries call it. Remember that Hist is at hand, and what we do for the maiden must be done while we are doing for others. I know it's ag'in your gifts and your natur' to wear clothes, unless they are cut and carried in a red man's fashion, but make a virtue of necessity and put these on at once, even if they do rise a little in your throat."

Chingachgook, or the Serpent, eyed the vestments with strong disgust, but he saw the usefulness of the disguise, if not its absolute necessity. Should the Iroquois discover a red man in or about the castle, it might, indeed, place them more on their guard and give their suspicions a direction toward their female captive. Anything was better than a failure, as it regarded his betrothed, and after turning the different garments around and around, examining them with a species of grave irony, affecting to draw them on in a way that defeated itself, and otherwise manifesting the reluctance of a young savage to confine his limbs in the usual appliances of civilized life, the chief submitted to the directions of his companion and finally stood forth, so far as the eye could detect, a red man in color alone. Little was to be apprehended from this last peculiarity, however, the distance from the shore and the want of glasses preventing any very close scrutiny, and Deerslayer himself, though of a brighter and fresher tint, had a countenance that was burned by the sun to a hue scarcely less red than that of his Mohican companion. The awkwardness of the Delaware in his new attire caused his friend to smile more than once that day, but he carefully abstained from the use of any of those jokes which would have been bandied among white men on such an occasion; the habits of a chief, the dignity of a warrior on his first path, and the gravity of the circumstances in which they were placed united to render so much levity out of season.

The meeting at the morning meal of the three islanders, if we may use the term, was silent, grave, and thoughtful. Judith showed by her looks that she had passed an unquiet night, while the two men had the future before them, with its unseen and unknown events. A few words of courtesy passed between Deerslayer and the girl in the course of the breakfast, but no allusion was made to their situation. At

length, Judith, whose heart was full and whose novel feelings disposed her to entertain sentiments more gentle and tender than common, introduced the subject, and this in a way to show how much of her thoughts it had occupied in the course of the last sleepless night.

"It would be dreadful, Deerslayer," the girl abruptly exclaimed, "should anything serious befall my father and Hetty! We cannot remain quietly here and leave them in the hands of the Iroquois, without bethinking us of some means of serving them."

"I'm ready, Judith, to sarve them and all others who are in trouble, could the way to do it be pointed out. It's no trifling matter to fall into redskin hands, when men set out on an a'r'nd like that which took Hutter and Hurry ashore—that I know as well as another—and I wouldn't wish my worst inimy in such a strait, much less them with whom I've journeyed, and eat, and slept. Have you any scheme that you would like to have the Sarpent and me indivor to carry out?"

"I know of no other means to release the prisoners than by bribing the Iroquois. They are not proof against presents, and we might offer enough, perhaps, to make them think it better to carry away what to them will be rich gifts than to carry away poor prisoners—if, indeed, they should carry them away at all!"

"This is well enough, Judith; yes, it's well enough, if the inimy is to be bought, and we can find articles to make the purchase with. Your father has a convenient lodge, and it is most cunningly placed, though it doesn't seem overstocked with riches that will be likely to buy his ransom. There's the piece he calls Killdeer might count for something, and I understand there's a keg of powder about, which might be a makeweight, sartain; and yet two able-bodied men are not to be bought off for a trifle—besides——"

"Besides what?" demanded Judith impatiently, observing that the other hesitated to proceed, probably from a reluctance to distress her.

"Why, Judith, the Frenchers offer bounties as well as our own side; and the price of two scalps would purchase a keg of powder and a rifle; though I'll not say one of the latter altogether as good as Killdeer there, which your father va'nts as oncommon and onequaled, like. But fair powder, and a

pretty sartain rifle; then the red men are not the expartest in firearms and don't always know the difference atwixt that which is ra'al and that which is seeming."

"This is horrible!" muttered the girl, struck by the homely manner in which her companion was accustomed to state his facts. "But you overlook my own clothes, Deerslayer; they, I think, might go far with the women of the Iroquois."

"No doubt they would; no doubt they would, Judith," returned the other, looking at her keenly, as if he would ascertain whether she were really capable of making such a sacrifice. "But are you sartain, gal, you could find it in your heart to part with your own finery for such a purpose? Many is the man who has thought he was valiant till danger stared him in the face; I've known them too that consaited they were kind and ready to give away all they had to the poor, when they've been listening to other people's hardheartedness, but whose fists have clenched as tight as the riven hickory, when it came to downright offerings of their own. Besides, Judith, you're handsome—oncommon in that way, one might observe and do no harm to the truth—and they that have beauty like to have that which will adorn it. Are you sartain you could find it in your heart to part with your own finery?"

The soothing allusion to the personal charms of the girl was well-timed to counteract the effect produced by the distrust that the young man expressed of Judith's devotion to her filial duties. Had another said as much as Deerslayer, the compliment would most probably have been overlooked in the indignation awakened by the doubts, but even the unpolished sincerity that so often made this simple-minded hunter bare his thoughts had a charm for the girl; and, while she colored, and for an instant her eyes flashed fire, she could not find it in her heart to be really angry with one whose very soul seemed truth and manly kindness. Look her reproaches she did; but conquering the desire to retort, she succeeded in answering in a mild and friendly manner.

"You must keep all your favorable opinions for the Delaware girls, Deerslayer, if you seriously think thus of those of your own color," she said, affecting to laugh. "But, *try* me; if you find that I regret either ribbon or feather, silk or muslin, then may you think what you please of my heart and say what you think."

"That's justice! The rarest thing to find on 'arth is a truly just man. So says Tamenund, the wisest prophet of the Delawares, and so all must think that have occasion to see, and talk, and act among mankind. I love a just man, Sarpent; his eyes are never covered with darkness toward his inimies, while they are all sunshine and brightness toward his fri'nds. He uses the reason that God has given him, and he uses it with a feelin' of his being ordered to look at, and to consider things as they *are*, and not as he *wants* them to be. It's easy enough to find men who *call* themselves just, but it's wonderfully oncommon to find them that are the very thing, in fact. How often have I seen Indians, gal, who believed they were lookin' into a matter agreeable to the will of the Great Spirit when, in truth, they were only striving to act up to their own will and pleasure, and this, half of the time, with a temptation to go wrong that could no more be seen by themselves than the stream that runs in the next valley can be seen by us through yonder mountain; though any looker-on might have discovered it as plainly as we can discover the parch that are swimming around this hut."

"Very true, Deerslayer," rejoined Judith, losing every trace of displeasure in a bright smile; "very true; and I hope to see you act on this love of justice in all matters in which I am concerned. Above all, I hope you will judge for yourself and not believe every evil story that a prating idler like Hurry Harry may have to tell that goes to touch the good name of any young woman who may not happen to have the same opinions of his face and person that the blustering gallant has of himself."

"Hurry Harry's idees do not pass for gospel with me, Judith, but even worse than he may have eyes and ears," returned the other gravely.

"Enough of this!" exclaimed Judith, with flashing eye and a flush that mounted to her temples, "and more of my father and his ransom. 'Tis as you say, Deerslayer; the Indians will not be likely to give up their prisoners without a heavier bribe than my clothes can offer, and Father's rifle and powder. There is the chest."

"Aye, there is the chist, as you say, Judith; and when the question gets to be between a secret and a scalp, I should think most men would prefar keeping the last. Did your fa-

ther ever give you any downright command consarning that chist?"

"Never. He has always appeared to think its locks, and its steel bands, and its strength its best protection."

" 'Tis a rare chist, and altogether of curious build," returned Deerslayer, rising and approaching the thing in question, on which he seated himself, with a view to examine it with greater ease. "Chingachgook, this is no wood that comes of any forest that you or I have ever trailed through! 'Tisn't the black walnut, and yet it's quite as comely, if not more so, did the smoke and the treatment give it fair play."

The Delaware drew near, felt of the wood, examined its grain, endeavored to indent the surface with a nail, and passed his hand curiously over the steel bands, the heavy padlocks, and the other novel peculiarities of the massive box.

"No—nothing like this grows in these regions," resumed Deerslayer. "I've seen all the oaks, both the maples, the elms, the basswood, all the walnuts, the butternuts, and every tree that has a substance and color, wrought into some form or other, but never have I before seen such a wood as this! Judith, the chist itself would buy your father's freedom; or Iroquois cur'osity isn't as strong as redskin cur'osity, in general, especially in the matter of woods."

"The purchase might be cheaper made, perhaps, Deerslayer. The chest is full, and it would be better to part with half than to part with the whole. Besides, Father—I know not why —but Father values that chest highly."

"He would seem to prize what it holds more than the chist itself, judging by the manner in which he treats the outside and secures the inside. Here are three locks, Judith; is there no key?"

"I've never seen one, and yet key there must be, since Hetty told us *she* had often seen the chest opened."

"Keys no more lie in the air, or float on the water, than humans, gal; if there is a key, there must be a place in which it is kept."

"That is true, and it might not be difficult to find it, did we dare to search!"

"This is for you, Judith, it is altogether for you. The chist is your'n, or your father's, and Hutter is your father, not mine. Cur'osity is a woman's, not a man's failing, and

there you have got all the reasons before you. If the chist has articles for ransom, it seems to me they would be wisely used in redeeming their owner's life, or even in saving his scalp, but that is a matter for your judgment, and not for ourn. When the lawful owner of a trap, or a buck, or a canoe, isn't present, his next of kin becomes his ripresenta-tyve, by all the laws of the woods. We therefore leave you to say whether the chist shall or shall not be opened."

"I hope you do not believe I can hesitate when my father's life's in danger, Deerslayer!"

"Why, it's pretty much putting a scolding ag'in tears and mourning. It's not onreasonable to foretell that old Tom may find fault with what you've done when he sees himself once more in his hut here, but there's nothing unusual in men's falling out with what has been done for their own good; I dare to say that even the moon would seem a different thing from what it now does, could we look at it from the other side."

"Deerslayer, if we can find the key, I will authorize you to open the chest and to take such things from it as you may think will buy Father's ransom."

"First find the key, gal; we'll talk of the rest a'terward. Sarpent, you've eyes like a fly and a judgment that's seldom out; can you help us in calculating where Floating Tom would be apt to keep the key of a chist that he holds to be as private as this?"

The Delaware had taken no part in the discourse until he was thus directly appealed to, when he quitted the chest, which had continued to attract his attention, and cast about him for the place in which a key would be likely to be concealed under such circumstances. As Judith and Deerslayer were not idle the while, the whole three were soon engaged in an anxious and spirited search. As it was certain that the desired key was not to be found in any of the common drawers or closets, of which there were several in the building, none looked there, but all turned their inquiries to those places that struck them as ingenious hiding places, more likely to be used for such a purpose. In this manner the outer room was thoroughly but fruitlessly examined; then they entered the sleeping apartment of Hutter. This part of the rude building was better furnished than the rest of the structure, containing several articles that had been especially

devoted to the service of the deceased wife of its owner, but as Judith had all the rest of the keys, it was soon rummaged, without bringing to light the particular key desired.

They now entered the bedroom of the daughters. Chingachgook was immediately struck with the contrast between the articles, and the arrangement of that side of the room that might be called Judith's, and that which more properly belonged to Hetty. A slight exclamation escaped him, and pointing in each direction, he alluded to the fact in a low voice, speaking to his friend in the Delaware tongue.

"As you think, Sarpent," answered Deerslayer, whose remarks we always translate into English, preserving as much as possible of the peculiar phraseology and manner of the man. " 'Tis just so, as anyone may see, and 'tis all founded in natur'. One sister loves finery, some say, overmuch, while t'other is as meek and lowly as God ever created goodness and truth. Yet, after all, I daresay that Judith has her vartues and Hetty has her failin's."

"And the 'Feeble-mind' has seen the chest opened?" inquired Chingachgook, with curiosity in his glance.

"Sartain; that much I've heard from her own lips; for that matter, so have you. It seems her father doesn't misgive *her* discretion, though he does that of his eldest darter."

"Then the key is hid only from the Wild Rose?" for so Chingachgook had begun gallantly to term Judith, in his private discourse with his friend.

"That's it! That's just it! One he trusts, and the other he doesn't. There's red and white in that, Sarpent, all tribes and nations agreeing in trusting some and refusing to trust other some. It depends on character and judgment."

"Where could a key be put, so little likely to be found by the Wild Rose, as among coarse clothes?"

Deerslayer started, and turning to his friend with admiration expressed in every lineament of his face, he fairly laughed, in his silent but hearty manner, at the ingenuity and readiness of the conjecture.

"Your name's well bestowed, Sarpent—yes, 'tis well bestowed! Sure enough, where would a lover of finery be so little likely to s'arch as among garments as coarse and unseemly as these of poor Hetty? I dares to say Judith's delicate fingers haven't touched a bit of cloth as rough and oncomely as that petticoat, now, since she first made acquaintance

with the officers! Yet, who knows? The key may be as likely to be on the same peg as in any other place. Take down the garment, Delaware, and let us see if you are ra'ally a prophet."

Chingachgook did as desired, but no key was found. A coarse pocket, apparently empty, hung on the adjoining peg, and this was next examined. By this time the attention of Judith was called in that direction, and she spoke hurriedly, like one who wished to save unnecessary trouble.

"These are only the clothes of poor Hetty, dear simple girl!" she said. "Nothing we seek would be likely to be there."

The words were hardly out of the handsome mouth of the speaker when Chingachgook drew the desired key from the pocket. Judith was too quick of apprehension not to understand the reason a hiding place so simple and exposed had been used. The blood rushed to her face—as much with resentment, perhaps, as with shame—and she bit her lip, though she continued silent. Deerslayer and his friend now discovered the delicacy of men of native refinement, neither smiling, or even by a glance betraying how completely he understood the motives and ingenuity of this clever artifice. The former, who had taken the key from the Indian, led the way into the adjoining room and, applying it to a lock, ascertained that the right instrument had actually been found. There were three padlocks, each of which, however, was easily opened by this single key. Deerslayer removed them all, loosened the hasps, raised the lid a little to make certain it was loose, and then he drew back from the chest several feet, signing to his friend to follow.

"This is a family chist, Judith," he said, "and 'tis like to hold family secrets. The Sarpent and I will go into the ark, and look to the canoes, and paddles, and oars, while you can examine it by yourself and find out whether anything that will be a makeweight in a ransom is or is not among the articles. When you've got through, give us a call, and we'll all sit in council together, touching the valie of the articles."

"Stop, Deerslayer," exclaimed the girl, as he was about to withdraw; "not a single thing will I touch—I will not even raise the lid—unless you are present. Father and Hetty have seen fit to keep the inside of this chest a secret from me, and I am much too proud to pry into their hidden treasures,

unless it were for their own good. But on no account will I open the chest alone. Stay with me, then; I want witnesses of what I do."

"I rather think, Sarpent, that the gal is right! Confidence and reliance beget security, but suspicion is like to make us all wary. Judith has a right to ask us to be present, and should the chist hold any of Master Hutter's secrets, they will fall into the keeping of two as close-mouthed young men as are to be found. We *will* stay with you, Judith—but first let us take a look at the lake and the shore, for this chist will not be emptied in a minute."

The two men now went out on the platform, and Deerslayer swept the shore with the glass, while the Indian gravely turned his eye on the water and the woods in quest of any sign that might betray the machinations of their enemies. Nothing was visible, and assured of their temporary security, the three collected around the chest again with the avowed object of opening it.

Judith had held this chest, and its unknown contents, in a species of reverence as long as she could remember. Neither her father nor her mother ever mentioned it in her presence, and there appeared to be a silent convention that in naming the different objects that occasionally stood near it, or even lay on its lid, care should be had to avoid any allusion to the chest itself. Habit rendered this so easy and so much a matter of course that it was only quite recently the girl had begun even to muse on the singularity of the circumstance. But there had never been sufficient intimacy between Hutter and his eldest daughter to invite confidence. At times, he was kind, but in general, with her more especially, he was stern and morose. Least of all had his authority been exercised in a way to embolden his child to venture on the liberty she was about to take without many misgivings of the consequences, although the liberty proceeded from a desire to serve himself. Then Judith was not altogether free from a little superstition on the subject of this chest, which had stood a sort of tabooed relic before her eyes from childhood to the present hour. Nevertheless, the time had come when it would seem that this mystery was to be explained, and that under circumstances, too, which left her very little choice in the matter.

Finding that both her companions were watching her

movements in grave silence, Judith placed a hand on the lid and endeavored to raise it. Her strength, however, was insufficient, and it appeared to the girl, who was fully aware that all the fastenings were removed, that she was resisted in an unhallowed attempt by some supernatural power.

"I cannot raise the lid, Deerslayer," she said; "had we not better give up the attempt and find some other means of releasing the prisoners?"

"Not so, Judith; not so, gal. No means are as sartain and easy as a good bribe," answered the other. "As for the lid, 'tis held by nothing but its own weight, which is prodigious for so small a piece of wood, loaded with iron as it is."

As Deerslayer spoke, he applied his own strength to the effort and succeeded in raising the lid against the timbers of the house, where he took care to secure it by a sufficient prop. Judith fairly trembled as she cast her first glance at the interior, and she felt a temporary relief in discovering that a piece of canvas that was carefully tucked in around the edges effectually concealed all beneath it. The chest was apparently well stored, however, the canvas lying within an inch of the lid.

"Here's a full cargo," said Deerslayer, eyeing the arrangement, "and we had needs go to work leisurely and at our ease. Sarpent, bring some stools, while I spread this blanket on the floor, and then we'll begin work orderly and in comfort."

The Delaware complied; Deerslayer civilly placed a stool for Judith, took one himself, and commenced the removal of the canvas covering. This was done deliberately and in as cautious a manner as if it were believed that fabrics of a delicate construction lay hidden beneath. When the canvas was removed, the first articles that came in view were some of the habiliments of the male sex. These were of fine materials, and according to the fashions of the age, were gay in colors and rich in ornaments. One coat, in particular, was of scarlet, and had buttonholes worked in gold thread. Still it was not military but was part of the attire of a civilian of condition at a period when social rank was rigidly respected in dress. Chingachgook could not refrain from an exclamation of pleasure, as soon as Deerslayer opened this coat and held it up to view; notwithstanding all his trained self-command, the splendor of the vestment was too much for the philosophy of an Indian. Deerslayer turned quickly,

and he regarded his friend with a momentary displeasure, as this burst of weakness escaped him; then he soliloquized, as was his practice whenever any strong feeling suddenly got the ascendancy.

" 'Tis his gift! Yes, 'tis the gift of a redskin to love finery, and he is not to be blamed. This is an extr'ornary garment, too, and extr'ornary things get up extr'ornary feelin's. I think this will do, Judith, for the Indian heart is hardly to be found in all America that can withstand colors like these and glitter like that. If this coat was ever made for your father, you've come honestly by the taste for finery, you have."

"That coat was never made for Father," answered the girl quickly. "It is much too long, while Father is short and square."

"Cloth was plenty, if it was, and glitter cheap," answered Deerslayer, with his silent, joyous laugh. "Sarpent, this garment was made for a man of your size, and I should like to see it on your shoulders."

Chingachgook, nothing loath, submitted to the trial, throwing aside the coarse and threadbare jacket of Hutter to deck his person in a coat that was originally intended for a gentleman. The transformation was ludicrous, but as men are seldom struck with incongruities in their own appearance any more than in their own conduct, the Delaware studied this change in a common glass, by which Hutter was in the habit of shaving, with grave interest. At that moment he thought of Hist, and we owe it to truth to say, though it may militate a little against the stern character of a warrior to own it, that he wished he could be seen by her in his present improved aspect.

"Off with it, Sarpent—off with it," resumed the inflexible Deerslayer. "Such garments as little become you as they would become me. Your gifts are for paint, and hawk's feathers, and blankets, and wampum; and mine are for doublets of skins, tough leggings, and sarviceable moccasins. I say moccasins, Judith, for though white, living as I do in the woods, it's necessary to take to some of the practyces of the woods, for comfort's sake and cheapness."

"I see no reason, Deerslayer, why one man may not wear a scarlet coat as well as another," returned the girl. "I wish I could see *you* in this handsome garment."

"See me in a coat fit for a lord! Well, Judith, if you wait till that day, you'll wait until you see me beyond reason and memory. No—no—gal, my gifts are my gifts, and I'll live and die in 'em, though I never bring down another deer or spear another salmon. What have I done that you should wish to see *me* in such a flaunting coat, Judith?"

"Because I think, Deerslayer, that the false-tongued and falsehearted young gallants of the garrison ought not alone to appear in fine feathers, but that truth and honesty have *their* claims to be honored and exalted."

"And what exaltification—" the reader will have remarked that Deerslayer had not very critically studied his dictionary —"would it be to me, Judith, to be bedizened and bescarleted like a Mingo chief that has just got his presents up from Quebec? No—no—I'm well as I am, and if not, I can be no better. Lay the coat down on the blanket, Sarpent, and let us look further into the chist."

The tempting garment, one surely that was never intended for Hutter, was laid aside, and the examination proceeded. The male attire, all of which corresponded with the coat in quality, was soon exhausted, and then succeeded female. A beautiful dress of brocade, a little the worse from negligent treatment, followed, and this time open exclamations of delight escaped the lips of Judith. Much as the girl had been addicted to dress, and favorable as had been her opportunities of seeing some little pretension in that way among the wives of the different commandants and other ladies of the forts, never before had she beheld a tissue or tints to equal those that were now so unexpectedly placed before her eyes. Her rapture was almost childish; nor would she allow the inquiry to proceed until she had attired her person in a robe so unsuited to her habits and her abode. With this end, she withdrew into her own room, where, with hands practiced in such offices, she soon got rid of her own neat gown of linen and stood forth in the gay tints of the brocade. The dress happened to fit the fine, full person of Judith, and certainly it had never adorned a being better qualified by natural gifts to do credit to its really rich hues and fine texture. When she returned, both Deerslayer and Chingachgook, who had passed the brief time of her absence in taking a second look at the male garments, arose in surprise, each permitting exclamations of wonder and pleasure

to escape him in a way so unequivocal as to add new luster to the eyes of Judith, by flushing her cheeks with a glow of triumph. Affecting, however, not to notice the impression she had made, the girl seated herself with the stateliness of a queen, desiring that the chest might be looked into further.

"I don't know a better way to treat with the Mingos, gal," cried Deerslayer, "than to send you ashore as you be, and to tell 'em that a queen has arrived among 'em! They'll give up old Hutter, and Hurry, and Hetty, too, at such a spectacle!"

"I thought your tongue too honest to flatter, Deerslayer," returned the girl, gratified at this admiration more than she would have cared to own. "One of the chief reasons of my respect for you was your love for truth."

"And 'tis truth, solemn truth, Judith, and nothing else. Never did eyes of mine gaze on as glorious a lookin' creatur' as you be yourself at this very moment! I've seen beauties in my time, too, both white and red, and them that was renowned and talked of, far and near, but never have I beheld one that could hold any comparison with what you are at this blessed instant, Judith. Never."

The glance of delight which the girl bestowed on the frank-speaking hunter in no degree lessened the effect of her charms, and as the humid eyes blended with it a look of sensibility, perhaps Judith never appeared more truly lovely than at what the young man had called that "blessed instant." He shook his head, held it suspended a moment over the open chest like one in doubt, and then proceeded with the examination.

Several of the minor articles of female dress came next, all of a quality to correspond with the gown. These were laid at Judith's feet, in silence, as if she had a natural claim to their possession. One or two, such as gloves and lace, the girl caught up and appended to her already rich attire in affected playfulness, but with the real design of decorating her person as far as circumstances would allow. When these two remarkable suits, male and female they might be termed, were removed, another canvas covering separated the remainder of the articles from the part of the chest which they had occupied. As soon as Deerslayer perceived this arrangement, he paused, doubtful of the propriety of proceeding any further.

"Every man has his secrets, I suppose," he said, "and all men have a right to their enj'yment. We've got low enough in this chist, in my judgment, to answer our wants, and it seems to me we should do well by going no further and by letting Master Hutter have to himself and his own feelin's all that's beneath this cover."

"Do you mean, Deerslayer, to offer these clothes to the Iroquois as ransom?" demanded Judith quickly.

"Sartain. What are we prying into another man's chist for, but to sarve its owner in the best way we can? This coat, alone, would be very apt to gain over the head chief of the riptyles, and if his wife or darter should happen to be out with him, that there gownd would soften the heart of any woman that is to be found atween Albany and Montreal. I do not see that we want a larger stock in trade than them two articles."

"To you it may seem so, Deerslayer," returned the disappointed girl, "but of what use could a dress like this be to any Indian woman? She could not wear it among the branches of the trees; the dirt and smoke of the wigwam would soon soil it; and how would a pair of red arms appear thrust through these short, laced sleeves!"

"All very true, gal, and you might go on and say it is altogether out of time, and place, and season in this region at all. What is it to us how the finery is treated, so long as it answers our wishes? I do not see that your father can make any use of such clothes, and it's lucky he has things that are of no valie to himself that will bear a high price with others. We can make no better trade for him than to offer these duds for his liberty. We'll throw in the light frivol'ties and get Hurry off in the bargain!"

"Then you think, Deerslayer, that Thomas Hutter has no one in his family—no child—no daughter—to whom this dress may be thought becoming, and whom you could wish to see in it once and a while, even though it should be at long intervals, and only in playfulness?"

"I understand you, Judith—yes, I now understand your meaning, and I think I can say, your wishes. That you are as glorious in that dress as the sun when it rises or sets in a soft October day, I'm ready to allow; and that you greatly become it is a good deal more sartain than that it becomes you. There's gifts in clothes as well as in other things. Now

I do not think that a warrior on his first path ought to lay on the same awful paints as a chief that has had this vartue tried, and knows from exper'ence he will not disgrace his pretensions. So it is with all of us, red or white. You are Thomas Hutter's darter, and that gownd was made for the child of some governor, or a lady of high station, and it was intended to be worn among fine furniture and in rich company. In my eyes, Judith, a modest maiden never looks more becoming than when becomingly clad, and nothing is suitable that is out of character. Besides, gal, if ther's a creatur' in the colony that can afford to do without finery and to trust to her own good looks and sweet countenance, it's yourself."

"I'll take off the rubbish this instant, Deerslayer," cried the girl, springing up to leave the room, "and never do I wish to see it on any human being again."

"So it is with 'em all, Sarpent," said the other, turning to his friend and laughing, as soon as the beauty had disappeared. "They like finery, but they like their natyve charms most of all. I'm glad the gal has consented to lay aside her furbelows, howsever, for it's ag'in reason for one of her class to wear 'em; and then she *is* handsome enough, as I call it, to go alone. Hist would show oncommon likely, too, in such a gownd, Delaware!"

"Wah-ta!-Wah is a redskin girl, Deerslayer," returned the Indian. "Like the young of the pigeon, she is to be known by her own feathers. I should pass by without knowing her, were she dressed in such a skin. It's wisest always to be so clad that our friends need not ask us for our names. The 'Wild Rose' is very pleasant, but she is no sweeter for so many colors."

"That's it! That's natur', and the true foundation for love and protection. When a man stops to pick a wild strawberry, he does not expect to find a melon, and when he wishes to gather a melon, he's disapp'inted if it proves to be a squash—though squashes *be* often brighter to the eye than melons. That's it, and it means, stick to your gifts and your gifts will stick to you."

The two men had now a little discussion together, touching the propriety of penetrating any further into the chest of Hutter, when Judith reappeared, divested of her robes, and in her own simple linen frock again.

"Thank you, Judith," said Deerslayer, taking her kindly

by the hand, "for I know it went a little ag'in the nat'ral cravings of woman to lay aside so much finery as it might be in a lump. But you're more pleasing to the eye as you stand, you be, than if you had a crown on your head and jewels dangling from your hair. The question now is whether to lift this covering, to see what will be ra'ally the best bargain we can make for Master Hutter, for we must do as we think *he* would be willing to do, did he stand here in our places."

Judith looked very happy. Accustomed as she was to adulation, the humble homage of Deerslayer had given her more true satisfaction than she had ever yet received from the tongue of man. It was not the terms in which this admiration had been expressed, for *they* were simple enough, that produced so strong an impression; nor yet their novelty, or their warmth of manner, nor any of those peculiarities that usually give value to praise; but it was the unflinching truth of the speaker that carried his words so directly to the heart of the listener. This is one of the great advantages of plain dealing and frankness. The habitual and wily flatterer may succeed until his practices recoil on himself and, like other sweets, his aliment cloys by its excess; but he who deals honestly, though he often necessarily offend, possesses a power of praising that no quality but sincerity can bestow, since his words go directly to the heart, finding their support in the understanding. Thus it was with Deerslayer and Judith; so soon and so deeply did this simple hunter impress those who knew him with a conviction of his unbending honesty, that all he uttered in commendation was as certain to please, as all he uttered in the way of rebuke was as certain to rankle and excite enmity where his character had not awakened a respect and affection that in another sense rendered it painful. In afterlife, when the career of this untutored being brought him in contact with officers of rank and others entrusted with the care of the interests of the state, this same influence was exerted on a wider field; even generals listening to his commendations with a glow of pleasure that it was not always in the power of their official superiors to awaken. Perhaps Judith was the first individual of his own color who fairly submitted to this natural consequence of truth and fair-dealing, on the part of Deerslayer. She had actually pined for his praise, and she had now received it;

and that in the form which was most agreeable to her weaknesses and habits of thought. The result will appear in the course of the narrative.

"If we knew all that chest holds, Deerslayer," returned the girl, when she had a little recovered from the immediate effect produced by his commendations of her personal appearance, "we could better determine on the course we ought to take."

"That's not onreasonable, gal, though it's more a paleface than a redskin gift, to be prying into other people's secrets."

"Curiosity is natural, and it is expected that all human beings should have human failings. Whenever I've been at the garrisons, I've found that most in and about them had a longing to learn their neighbor's secrets."

"Yes, and sometimes to fancy them, when they couldn't find 'em out! That's the difference atween an Indian gentleman and a white gentleman. The Sarpent, here, would turn his head aside, if he found himself onknowingly lookin' into another chief's wigwam; whereas, in the settlements, while all pretend to be great people, most prove they've got betters, by the manner in which they talk of their consarns. I'll be bound, Judith, you wouldn't get the Sarpent, there, to confess there was another in the tribe so much greater than himself, as to become the subject of his ideas, and to empl'y his tongue in conversations about his movements, and ways, and food, and all the other little matters that occupy a man when he's not empl'y'd in his greater duties. He who does this is but little better than a blackguard in the grain, and them that encourages him is pretty much of the same kidney, let them wear coats as fine as they may, or of what dye they please."

"But this is not another man's wigwam; it belongs to my father. These are his things, and they are wanted in his service."

"That's true, gal, that's true, and it carries weight with it. Well, when all is before us, we may, indeed, best judge which to offer for the ransom and which to withhold."

Judith was not altogether as disinterested in her feelings as she affected to be. She remembered that the curiosity of Hetty had been indulged in connection with this chest, while her own had been disregarded, and she was not sorry to possess an opportunity of being placed on a level with her

less gifted sister in this one particular. It appearing to be admitted all around that the inquiry into the contents of the chest ought to be renewed, Deerslayer proceeded to remove the second covering of canvas.

The articles that lay uppermost, when the curtain was again raised on the secrets of the chest, were a pair of pistols, curiously inlaid with silver. Their value would have been considerable in one of the towns, though as weapons, in the woods, they were a species of arms seldom employed; never, indeed, unless it might be by some officer from Europe, who visited the colonies, as many were then wont to do, so much impressed with the superiority of the usages of London as to fancy they were not to be laid aside on the frontiers of America. What occurred on the discovery of these weapons will appear in the succeeding chapter.

CHAPTER XIII

> *An oaken, broken, elbow chair;*
> *A candle-cup without an ear;*
> *A battered, shattered, ash bedstead;*
> *A box of deal without a lid;*
> *A pair of tongs, but out of joint;*
> *A back-sword poker, without point:*
> *A dish which might good meat afford once;*
> *An Ovid, and an old Concordance.*
>
> DEAN SWIFT'S *Inventory*

No SOONER DID Deerslayer raise the pistols than he turned to the Delaware and held them up for his admiration.

"Child gun," said the Serpent, smiling, while he handled one of the instruments as if it had been a toy.

"Not it, Sarpent; not it. 'Tis made for a man, and would satisfy a giant if rightly used. But stop; white men are remarkable for their carelessness in putting away firearms in chists and corners. Let me look if care has been given to these."

As Deerslayer spoke, he took the weapon from the hand of his friend and opened the pan. The last was filled with priming, caked like a bit of cinder, by time, moisture, and compression. An application of the ramrod showed that both the pistols were charged, although Judith could testify that they had probably lain for years in the chest. It is not easy to portray the surprise of the Indian at this discovery, for he was in the practice of renewing his priming daily and of looking to the contents of his piece at other short intervals.

"This is white neglect," said Deerslayer, shaking his head, "and scarce a season goes by that someone in the settlements doesn't suffer from it. It's extr'ornary too, Judith—yes, it's downright extr'ornary—that the owner shall fire his piece at a deer, or some other game, or perhaps at an inimy, and

twice out of three times he'll miss, but let him catch an accident with one of these forgotten charges, and he makes it sartain death to a child, or a brother, or a fri'nd! Well, we shall do a good turn to the owner if we fire these pistols for him; and as they're novelties to you and me, Sarpent, we'll try our hands at a mark. Freshen that priming, and I'll do the same with this, and then we'll see who is the best man with a pistol; as for the rifle, that's long been settled atween us."

Deerslayer laughed heartily at his own conceit, and in a minute or two they were both standing on the platform, selecting some object in the ark for their target. Judith was led by curiosity to their side.

"Stand back, gal, stand a little back; these we'pons have been long loaded," said Deerslayer, "and some accident may happen in the discharge."

"Then *you* shall not fire them! Give them both to the Delaware—or it would be better to unload them without firing."

"That's ag'in usage—and some people say ag'in manhood, though I hold to no such silly doctrine. We must fire 'em, Judith; yes, we must fire 'em; though I foresee that neither will have any great reason to boast of his skill."

Judith, in the main, was a girl of great personal spirit, and her habits prevented her from feeling any of the terror that is apt to come over her sex at the report of firearms. She had discharged many a rifle and had even been known to kill a deer, under circumstances that were favorable to the effort. She submitted, therefore, falling a little back by the side of Deerslayer, giving the Indian the front of the platform to himself. Chingachgook raised the weapon several times, endeavored to steady it by using both hands, changed his attitude from one that was awkward to another still more so, and finally drew the trigger with a sort of desperate indifference, without having, in reality, secured any aim at all. The consequence was that, instead of hitting the knot which had been selected for the mark, he missed the ark altogether, the bullet skipping along the water like a stone that was thrown by hand.

"Well done, Sarpent—well done," cried Deerslayer, laughing with his noiseless glee. "You've hit the lake, and that's an expl'ite, for some men! I know'd it, and as much as

said it, here, to Judith, for your short we'pons don't belong to redskin gifts. You've hit the lake, and that's better than only hitting the air! Now, stand back, and let us see what white gifts can do with a white we'pon. A pistol isn't a trifle, but color is color."

The aim of Deerslayer was both quick and steady, and the report followed almost as soon as the weapon rose. Still the pistol hung fire, as it is termed, and fragments of it flew in a dozen directions, some falling on the roof of the castle, others in the ark, and one in the water. Judith screamed, and when the two men turned anxiously toward the girl, she was as pale as death, trembling in every limb.

"She's wounded—yes, the poor gal's wounded, Sarpent, though one couldn't foresee it, standing where she did. We'll lead her into a seat, and we must do the best for her that our knowledge and skill can afford."

Judith allowed herself to be supported to a seat, swallowed a mouthful of the water that the Delaware offered to her in a gourd, and, after a violent fit of trembling that seemed ready to shake her fine frame to dissolution, she burst into tears.

"The pain must be borne, poor Judith—yes, it must be borne," said Deerslayer soothingly; "though I am far from wishing you not to weep, for weeping often lightens galish feelin's. Where can she be hurt, Sarpent? I see no signs of blood, nor any rent of skin or garments."

"I am uninjured, Deerslayer," stammered the girl through her tears. "It's fright—nothing more, I do assure you; and, God be praised, no one, I find, has been harmed by the accident."

"This is extr'ornary!" exclaimed the unsuspecting and simple-minded hunter. "I thought, Judith, you'd been above settlement weaknesses, and that you was a gal not to be frightened by the sound of a bursting we'pon. No—I didn't think you so skeary! *Hetty* might well have been startled, but you've too much judgment and reason to be frightened when the danger's all over. They're pleasant to the eye, Chief, and changeful, but very unsartain in their feelin's!"

Shame kept Judith silent. There had been no acting in her agitation, but all had fairly proceeded from sudden and uncontrollable alarm—an alarm that she found almost as inexplicable to herself as it proved to be to her companions.

Wiping away the traces of tears, however, she smiled again, and was soon able to join in the laugh at her own folly.

"And you, Deerslayer," she at length succeeded in saying, "are you, indeed, altogether unhurt? It seems almost miraculous that a pistol should have burst in your hand, and you escape without the loss of a limb, if not of life!"

"Such wonders ar'n't oncommon, at all, among wornout arms. The first rifle they gave me played the same trick, and yet I lived through it, though not as onharmless as I've got out of this affair. Thomas Hutter is master of one pistol less than he was this morning, but as it happened in trying to sarve him, there's no ground of complaint. Now, draw near and let us look further into the inside of the chist."

Judith, by this time, had so far got the better of her agitation as to resume her seat, and the examination went on. The next article that offered was enveloped in cloth, and, on opening it, it proved to be one of the mathematical instruments that were then in use among seamen, possessing the usual ornaments and fastenings in brass. Deerslayer and Chingachgook expressed their admiration and surprise at the appearance of the unknown instrument, which was bright and glittering, having apparently been well cared for.

"This goes beyond the surveyors, Judith," Deerslayer exclaimed, after turning the instrument several times in his hands. "I've seen all their tools often—and wicked and heartless enough are they, for they never come into the forest but to lead the way to waste and destruction—but none of them have as designing a look as this! I fear me, after all, that Thomas Hutter has journeyed into the wilderness with no fair intentions toward its happiness. Did you ever see any of the cravings of a surveyor about your father, gal?"

"He is no surveyor, Deerslayer, nor does he know the use of that instrument, though he seems to own it. Do you suppose that Thomas Hutter ever wore that coat? It is as much too large for him as this instrument is beyond his learning."

"That's it—that must be it, Sarpent; the old fellow, by some onknown means, has fallen heir to another man's goods! They say he has been a mariner, and no doubt this chist and all it holds—Ha! What have we here? This far outdoes the brass and black wood of the tool!"

Deerslayer had opened a small bag from which he was

taking, one by one, the pieces of a set of chessmen. They were of ivory, much larger than common, and exquisitely wrought. Each piece represented the character or thing after which it is named; the knights being mounted; the castles stood on elephants; and even the pawns possessed the heads and busts of men. The set was not complete, and a few fractures betrayed bad usage, but all that was left had been carefully put away and preserved. Even Judith expressed wonder as these novel objects were placed before her eyes, and Chingachgook fairly forgot his Indian dignity in admiration and delight. The latter took up each piece and examined it with never-tiring satisfaction, pointing out to the girl the more ingenious and striking portions of the workmanship. But the elephants gave him the greatest pleasure. The "hughs" that he uttered as he passed his fingers over their trunks and ears and tails were very distinct; nor did he fail to note the pawns, which were armed as archers. This exhibition lasted several minutes, during which time Judith and the Indian had all the rapture to themselves. Deerslayer sat silent, thoughtful, and even gloomy, though his eyes followed each movement of the two principal actors, noting every new peculiarity about the pieces as they were held up to view. Not an exclamation of pleasure nor a word of condemnation passed his lips. At length his companions observed his silence, and then, for the first time since the chessmen had been discovered, did he speak.

"Judith," he asked earnestly, but with a concern that amounted almost to tenderness of manner, "did your parents ever talk to you of religion?"

The girl colored, and the flashes of crimson that passed over her beautiful countenance were like the wayward tints of a Neapolitan sky in November. Deerslayer had given her so strong a taste for truth, however, that she did not waver in her answer, replying simply and with sincerity:

"My *mother* did, often," she said; "my father *never*. I thought it made my mother sorrowful to speak of our prayers and duties, but my father has never opened his mouth on such matters before or since her death."

"That I can believe—that I can believe. He has no God—no such God as it becomes a man of white skin to worship, or even a redskin. Them things are idols!"

Judith started, and for a moment she seemed seriously hurt. Then she reflected, and in the end she laughed.

"And you think, Deerslayer, that these ivory toys are my father's gods? I have heard of idols, and know what they are."

"Them are idols!" repeated the other positively. "Why should your father keep 'em if he doesn't worship 'em?"

"Would he keep his gods in a bag and locked up in a chest? No, no, Deerslayer, my poor father carries his god with him wherever he goes, and that is in his own cravings. These things may really be idols—I think they are, myself, from what I have heard and read of idolatry—but they have come from some distant country, like all the other articles, and have fallen into Thomas Hutter's hands when he was a sailor."

"I'm glad of it—I am downright glad to hear it, Judith, for I do not think I could have mustered the resolution to strive to help a white idolator out of his difficulties! The old man is of my color and nation, and I wish to sarve him, but as one who denied all his gifts in the way of religion, it would have come hard to do so. That animal seems to give you great satisfaction, Sarpent, thought it's an idolatrous head, at the best."

"It is an elephant," interrupted Judith. "I've often seen pictures of such animals at the garrisons, and mother had a book in which there was a printed account of the creature. Father burned that, with all the other books, for he said mother loved reading too well. This was not long before mother died, and I've sometimes thought that the loss hastened her end."

This was said equally without levity and without any deep feeling. It was said without levity, for Judith was saddened by her recollections, and yet she had been too much accustomed to live for self and for the indulgence of her own vanities to feel her mother's wrongs very heavily. It required extraordinary circumstances to awaken a proper sense of her situation and to stimulate the better feelings of this beautiful but misguided girl, and these circumstances had not yet occurred in her brief existence.

"Elephant, or no elephant, 'tis an idol," returned the hunter, "and not fit to remain in Christian keeping."

"Good for Iroquois!" said Chingachgook, parting with one

of the castles with reluctance as his friend took it from him to replace it in the bag. "Elephon buy whole tribe—buy Delaware, almost!"

"Aye, that it would, as anyone who comprehends redskin natur' must know," answered Deerslayer; "but the man that passes false money, Sarpent, is as bad as he who makes it. Did you ever know a just Injin that wouldn't scorn to sell a coonskin for the true marten, or to pass off a mink for a beaver. I know that a few of these idols, perhaps *one* of them elephants, would go far toward buying Thomas Hutter's liberty, but it goes ag'in conscience to pass such counterfeit money. Perhaps no Injin tribe, hereaway, is downright idolaters, but there's some that come so near it that white gifts ought to be particular about encouraging them in their mistake."

"If idolatry is a *gift*, Deerslayer, and *gifts* are what you seem to think them, idolatry in such people can hardly be a sin," said Judith, with more smartness than discrimination.

"God grants no such gifts to any of his creatur's, Judith," returned the hunter seriously. "*He* must be adored, under some name or other, and not creatur's of brass or ivory. It matters not whether the Father of all is called God or Manitou, Deity or Great Spirit, he is nonetheless our common Maker and Master; nor does it count for much whether the souls of the just go to Paradise or happy hunting grounds, since He may send each his own way, as suits His own pleasure and wisdom; but it curdles my blood when I find human mortals so bound up in darkness and consait as to fashion the 'arth, or wood, or bones—things made by their own hands—into motionless, senseless effigies, and then fall down before them and worship 'em as a Deity!"

"After all, Deerslayer, these pieces of ivory may not be idols at all. I remember, now, to have seen one of the officers at the garrison with a set of fox and geese made in some such a design as these; and here is something hard, wrapped in cloth, that may belong to your idols."

Deerslayer took the bundle the girl gave him, and unrolling it, he found the board within. Like the pieces, it was large, rich, and inlaid with ebony and ivory. Putting the whole in conjunction, the hunter, though not without many misgivings, slowly came over to Judith's opinion, and finally admitted that the fancied idols must be merely the curi-

ously carved men of some unknown game. Judith had the
tact to use her victory with great moderation, nor did she
once, even in the most indirect manner, allude to the ludicrous mistake of her companion.

This discovery of the uses of the extraordinary-looking little images settled the affair of the proposed ransom. It was
agreed generally—and all understood the weaknesses and
tastes of Indians—that nothing could be more likely to tempt
the cupidity of the Iroquois than the elephants, in particular. Luckily, the whole of the castles were among the pieces,
and these four tower-bearing animals it was finally determined should be the ransom offered. The remainder of the
men, and, indeed, all the rest of the articles in the chest, were
to be kept out of view and to be resorted to only as a last
appeal. As soon as these preliminaries were settled, everything but those intended for the bribe was carefully replaced in the chest, and all the covers were "tucked in" as
they had been found; it was quite possible, could Hutter
have been put in possession of the castle again, that he
might have passed the remainder of his days in it, without
even suspecting the invasion that had been made on the pri-
vacy of the chest. The rent pistol would have been the most
likely to reveal the secret, but this was placed by the side
of its fellow, and all were pressed down as before—some
half a dozen packages in the bottom of the chest not having
been opened at all. When this was done, the lid was lowered,
the padlocks replaced, and the key turned. The latter was
then replaced in the pocket from which it had been taken.

More than an hour was consumed in settling the course
proper to be pursued and in returning everything to its place.
The pauses to converse were frequent, and Judith, who experienced a lively pleasure in the open, undisguised admiration with which Deerslayer's honest eye gazed at her handsome face, found the means to prolong the interview with a
dexterity that seems to be innate in female coquetry. Deerslayer, indeed, appeared to be the first who was conscious of
the time that had been thus wasted, and to call the attention of his companions to the necessity of doing something
toward putting the plan of ransoming into execution. Chingachgook had remained in Hutter's bedroom, where the elephants were laid, to feast his eyes with the images of animals
so wonderful and so novel. Perhaps an instinct told him that

his presence would not be as acceptable to his companions as this holding himself aloof, for Judith had not much reserve in the manifestations of her preferences, and the Delaware had not got so far as one betrothed without acquiring some knowledge of the symptoms of the master passion.

"Well, Judith," said Deerslayer, rising, after the interview had lasted much longer than even he himself suspected, " 'tis pleasant convarsing with you and settling all these matters, but duty calls us another way. All this time, Hurry and your father, not to say Hetty——"

The word was cut short in the speaker's mouth, for, at that critical moment, a light step was heard on the platform or courtyard, a human figure darkened the doorway, and the person last mentioned stood before him. The low exclamation that escaped Deerslayer and the slight scream of Judith were hardly uttered when an Indian youth, between the ages of fifteen and seventeen, stood beside her. These two entrances had been made with moccasined feet and consequently almost without noise, but unexpected and stealthy as they were, they had not the effect to disturb Deerslayer's self-possession. His first measure was to speak rapidly in Delaware to his friend, cautioning him to keep out of sight, while he stood on his guard; the second was to step to the door to ascertain the extent of the danger. No one else, however, had come, and a simple contrivance, in the shape of a raft, that lay floating at the side of the ark at once explained the means that had been used in bringing Hetty off. Two dead, dry, and consequently buoyant logs of pine were bound together with pins and withes, and a little platform of riven chestnut had been rudely placed on their surfaces. Here Hetty had been seated on a billet of wood, while the young Iroquois had rowed the primitive and slow-moving, but perfectly safe craft from the shore. As soon as Deerslayer had taken a close survey of this raft, and satisfied himself nothing else was near, he shook his head, and muttered in his soliloquizing way——

"This comes of prying into another man's chist! Had we been watchful and keen-eyed, such a surprise could never have happened; and getting this much from a boy teaches us what we may expect when the old warriors set themselves fairly about their sarcumventions. It opens the way, hows-

ever, to a treaty for the ransom, and I will hear what Hetty
has to say."

Judith, as soon as her surprise and alarm had a little
abated, discovered a proper share of affectionate joy at the
return of her sister. She folded her to her bosom and kissed
her, as had been her wont in the days of their childhood and
innocence. Hetty herself was less affected, for to her there
was no surprise, and her nerves were sustained by the purity
and holiness of her purpose. At her sister's request she took
a seat and entered into an account of her adventures since
they had parted. Her tale commenced just as Deerslayer returned, and he also became an attentive listener, while the
young Iroquois stood near the door, seemingly as indifferent
to what was passing as one of its posts.

The narrative of the girl was sufficiently clear until she
reached the time where we left her in the camp, after the
interview with the chiefs and at the moment when Hist
quitted her in the abrupt manner already stated. The sequel
of the story may be told in her own language.

"When I read the texts to the chiefs, Judith, you could not
have seen that they made any changes on their minds," she
said, "but if seed is planted, it *will* grow. God planted the
seeds of all the trees——"

"Aye, that did he—that did he," muttered Deerslayer;
"and a goodly harvest has followed."

"God planted the seeds of all the trees," continued Hetty,
after a moment's pause, "and you see to what a height and
shade they have grown! So it is with the Bible. You may
read a verse this year, and forget it, and it will come back
to you a year hence, when you least expect to remember it."

"And did you find anything of this among the savages,
poor Hetty?"

"Yes, Judith, and sooner and more fully than I had even
hoped. I did not stay long with Father and Hurry, but went
to get my breakfast with Hist. As soon as we had done, the
chiefs came to us, and *then* we found the fruits of the seed
that had been planted. They said what I had read from the
good book was right—it *must* be right—it sounded *right*, like
a sweet bird singing in their ears, and they told me to come
back and say as much to the great warrior who had slain
one of their braves; to tell it to you and to say how happy
they should be to come to church here, in the castle, or to

come out in the sun and hear me read more of the sacred volume; to tell you that they wish you would lend them some canoes, that they can bring Father and Hurry and their women to the castle, that we might all sit on the platform there and listen to the singing of the paleface Manitou —there, Judith, did you ever know of anything that so plainly shows the power of the Bible as *that?*"

"If it were true, 'twould be a miracle, indeed, Hetty. But all this is no more than Indian cunning and Indian treachery, striving to get the better of us by management, when they find it is not to be done by force."

"Do you doubt the Bible, sister, that you judge the savages so harshly?"

"I do not doubt the Bible, poor Hetty, but I much doubt an Indian and an Iroquois. What do you say to this visit, Deerslayer?"

"First let me talk a little with Hetty," returned the party appealed to. "Was this raft made a'ter you had got your breakfast, gal, and did you walk from the camp to the shore opposite to us, here?"

"Oh, no, Deerslayer. The raft was ready made, and in the water—could that have been by a miracle, Judith?"

"Yes—yes—an Indian miracle," rejoined the hunter. "They're expart enough in them sort of miracles. And you found the raft ready made to your hands, and in the water, and in waiting like for its cargo?"

"It was all as you say. The raft was near the camp, and the Indians put me on it, and had ropes of bark, and they dragged me to the place opposite to the castle, and then they told that young man to row me off, here."

"And the woods are full of the vagabonds, waiting to know what is to be the upshot of the miracle. We comprehend this affair, now, Judith—but I'll first get rid of this young Canadian bloodsucker, and then we'll settle our own course. Do you and Hetty leave us together, first bringing me the elephants, which the Sarpent is admiring; for 'twill never do to let this loping deer be alone a minute, or he'll borrow a canoe without asking."

Judith did as desired, first bringing the pieces and retiring with her sister into their own room. Deerslayer had acquired some knowledge of most of the Indian dialects of that region, and he knew enough of the Iroquois to hold a dialogue in

the language. Beckoning to the lad, therefore, he caused him
to take a seat on the chest, when he placed two of the castles
suddenly before him. Up to that moment, this youthful savage had not expressed a single intelligible emotion or fancy.
There were many things in and about the place that were
novelties to him, but he had maintained his self-command
with philosophical composure. It is true, Deerslayer had detected his dark eye scanning the defenses and the arms, but
the scrutiny had been made with such an air of innocence, in
such a gaping, indolent, boyish manner, that no one but a
man who had himself been taught in a similar school would
have even suspected his object. The instant, however, the
eyes of the savage fell upon the wrought ivory and the
images of the wonderful, unknown beasts, surprise and admiration got the mastery of him. The manner in which the
natives of the South Sea Islands first beheld the toys of
civilized life has been often described, but the reader is not
to confound it with the manner of an American Indian under
similar circumstances. In this particular case, the young
Iroquois, or Huron, permitted an exclamation of rapture to
escape him, and then he checked himself, like one who had
been guilty of an indecorum. After this, his eyes ceased to
wander but became riveted on the elephants, one of which,
after a short hesitation, he even presumed to handle. Deerslayer did not interrupt him for quite ten minutes, knowing
that the lad was taking such note of the curiosities as would
enable him to give the most minute and accurate description
of their appearance to his seniors on his return. When he
thought sufficient time had been allowed to produce the desired effect, the hunter laid a finger on the naked knee of the
youth and drew his attention to himself.

"Listen," he said, "I want to talk with my young friend
from the Canadas. Let him forget that wonder for a minute."

"Where t'other pale brother?" demanded the boy, looking
up and letting the idea that had been most prominent in his
mind, previously to the introduction of the chessmen, escape
him involuntarily.

"He sleeps—or if he isn't fairly asleep, he is in the room
where the men do sleep," returned Deerslayer. "How did
my young friend know there was another?"

"See him from the shore. Iroquois have got long eyes—see
beyond the clouds—see the bottom of the great spring!"

"Well, the Iroquois are welcome. Two palefaces are prisoners in the camp of your fathers, boy."

The lad nodded, treating the circumstance with great apparent indifference, though a moment after he laughed, as if exulting in the superior address of his own tribe.

"Can you tell me, boy, what your chiefs intend to do with these captyves; or haven't they yet made up their minds?"

The lad looked a moment at the hunter with a little surprise; then he coolly put the end of his forefinger on his own head, just above the left ear, and passed it around his crown, with an accuracy and readiness that showed how well he had been drilled in the peculiar art of his race.

"When?" demanded Deerslayer, whose gorge rose at this cool demonstration of indifference to human life. "And why not take them to your wigwams?"

"Road too long and full of palefaces. Wigwam full, and scalps sell high. Small scalp, much gold."

"Well, that explains it—yes, that does explain it. There's no need of being any plainer. Now, you know, lad, that the oldest of your prisoners is the father of these two young women; the other is the suitor of one of them. The gals nat'rally wish to save the scalps of such fri'nds, and they will give them two ivory creatur's as ransom; one for each scalp. Go back and tell this to your chiefs, and bring me the answer before the sun sets."

The boy entered zealously into this project, and with a sincerity that left no doubt of his executing his commission with intelligence and promptitude. For a moment he forgot his love of honor and all his clannish hostility to the British and their Indians, in his wish to have such a treasure in his tribe, and Deerslayer was satisfied with the impression he had made. It is true, the lad proposed to carry one of the elephants with him, as a specimen of the other, but to this his brother negotiator was too sagacious to consent, well knowing that it might never reach its destination if confided to such hands. This little difficulty was soon arranged, and the boy prepared to depart. As he stood on the platform, ready to step aboard the raft, he hesitated and turned short with a proposal to borrow a canoe, as the means most likely to shorten the negotiation. Deerslayer quietly refused the request, and, after lingering a little longer, the boy rowed slowly away from the castle, taking the direction of a thicket

on the shore that lay less than half a mile distant. Deer-slayer seated himself on a stool and watched the progress of the ambassador, sometimes closely scanning the whole line of shore, as far as eye could reach; then, placing an elbow on a knee, he remained a long time with his chin resting on the hand.

During the interview between Deerslayer and the lad, a different scene took place in the adjoining room. Hetty had inquired for the Delaware, and being told why and where he remained concealed, she joined him. The reception which Chingachgook gave his visitor was respectful and gentle. He understood her character, and no doubt his disposition to be kind to such a being was increased by the hope of learning some tidings of his betrothed. As soon as the girl entered, she took a seat and invited the Indian to place himself near her; then she continued silent, as if she thought it decorous for him to question her, before she consented to speak on the subject she had on her mind. But, as Chingachgook did not understand this feeling, he remained respectfully atten-tive to anything she might be pleased to tell him.

"You are Chingachgook—the Great Serpent of the Dela-wares, arn't you?" the girl at length commenced, in her own simple way, losing her self-command in the desire to proceed, but anxious first to make sure of the individual.

"Chingachgook," returned the Delaware with grave dig-nity. "That say Great Sarpent in Deerslayer tongue."

"Well, that is my tongue. Deerslayer, and Father, and Judith, and I, and poor Hurry Harry—do you know Henry March, Great Serpent? I know you don't, however, or *he* would have spoken of *you*, too."

"Did any tongue name Chingachgook, Drooping Lily?"—for so the chief had named poor Hetty. "Was his name sung by a little bird among the Iroquois?"

Hetty did not answer at first, but with that indescribable feeling that awakens sympathy and intelligence among the youthful and unpracticed of her sex, she hung her head, and the blood suffused her cheek ere she found her tongue. It would have exceeded her stock of intelligence to explain this embarrassment, but though poor Hetty could not reason on every emergency, she could always feel. The color slowly receded from her cheek, and the girl looked up archly at the

Indian, smiling with the innocence of a child, mingled with the interest of a woman.

"My sister, the Drooping Lily, hear such bird!" Chingachgook added, and this with a gentleness of tone and manner that would have astonished those who sometimes heard the discordant cries that often came from the same throat—these transitions from the harsh and guttural to the soft and melodious not being infrequent in ordinary Indian dialogues. "My sister's ears were open—has she lost her tongue?"

"You *are* Chingachgook—you *must* be, for there is no other red man here—and she thought Chingachgook would come."

"Chin-gach-gook," pronouncing the name slowly and dwelling on each syllable; "Great Sarpent, Yengeese tongue."

"Chin-gach-gook," repeated Hetty, in the same deliberate manner. "Yes, so Hist called it, and you *must* be the chief."

"Wah-ta!-Wah," added the Delaware.

"Wah-ta!-Wah, or Hist-oh!-Hist. I think Hist prettier than Wah, and so I call her Hist."

"Wah very sweet in Delaware ears!"

"You make it sound differently from me. But never mind; I *did* hear the bird you speak of sing, Great Serpent."

"Will my sister say words of song? What she sing most—how she look—often she laugh?"

"She sang Chin-gach-gook oftener than anything else, and she laughed heartily when I told how the Iroquois waded into the water after us and couldn't catch us. I hope these logs haven't ears, Serpent!"

"No fear logs; fear sister next room. No fear Iroquois; Deerslayer stuff his eyes and ears with strange beast."

"I understand you, Serpent, and I understand Hist. Sometimes I think I'm not half as feeble-minded as they say I am. Now, do you look up at the roof and I'll tell you all. But you frighten me, you look so eager when I speak of Hist."

The Indian controlled his looks and affected to comply with the simple request of the girl.

"Hist told me to say, in a very low voice, that you mustn't trust the Iroquois in anything. They are more artful than any Indians she knows. Then she says that there is a large bright star that comes over the hill about an hour after dark—Hist had pointed out the planet Jupiter, without knowing it—and just as that star comes in sight, she will be on the point

where I landed last night, and that you must come for her, in a canoe."

"Good—Chingachgook understand well enough, now, but he understand better if my sister sing to him ag'in."

Hetty repeated her words, more fully explaining what star was meant and mentioning the part of the point where he was to venture ashore. She now proceeded in her own unsophisticated way to relate her intercourse with the Indian maid and to repeat several of her expressions and opinions that gave great delight to the heart of her betrothed. She particularly renewed her injunctions to be on their guard against treachery, a warning that was scarcely needed, however, as addressed to men as wary as those to whom it was sent. She also explained, with sufficient clearness—for on all such subjects the mind of the girl seldom failed her—the present state of the enemy and the movements they had made since morning. Hist had been on the raft with her until it quitted the shore, and was now somewhere in the woods, opposite to the castle, and did not intend to return to the camp until night approached, when she hoped to be able to slip away from her companions, as they followed the shore on their way home, and conceal herself on the point. No one appeared to suspect the presence of Chingachgook, though it was necessarily known that an Indian had entered the ark the previous night, and it was suspected that he had since appeared in and about the castle in the dress of a paleface. Still some little doubt existed on the latter point, for, as this was the season when white men might be expected to arrive, there was some fear that the garrison of the castle was increasing by these ordinary means. All this had Hist communicated to Hetty while the Indians were dragging them along shore; the distance, which exceeded six miles, affording abundance of time.

"Hist don't know, herself, whether they suspect her or not, or whether they suspect *you,* but she hopes neither is the case. And now, Serpent, since I have told you so much from your betrothed," continued Hetty, unconsciously taking one of the Indian's hands and playing with the fingers, as a child is often seen to play with those of a parent, "you must let me tell you something from myself. When you marry Hist, you must be kind to her, and smile on her, as you do now

on me, and not look cross, as some of the chiefs do at their squaws. Will you promise this?"

"Always good to Wah—too tender to twist hard, else she break."

"Yes, and smile, too; you don't know how much a girl craves smiles from them she loves. Father scarce smiled on me once while I was with him—and, Hurry—yes—Hurry talked loud, and laughed, but I don't think *he* smiled once either. You know the difference between a smile and a laugh?"

"Laugh, best. Hear Wah laugh, think bird sing?"

"I know that; her laugh *is* pleasant, but *you* must smile. And then, Serpent, you mustn't make her carry burdens and hoe corn, as so many Indians do, but treat her more as the palefaces treat their wives."

"Wah-ta!-Wah no paleface—got red skin, red heart, red feelin's. All red; no paleface. *Must* carry papoose."

"Every woman is willing to carry her child," said Hetty, smiling, "and there is no harm in *that*. But you must love Hist, and be gentle, and good to her, for she is gentle and good herself."

Chingachgook gravely bowed, and then he seemed to think this part of the subject might be dismissed. Before there was time for Hetty to resume her communications, the voice of Deerslayer was heard calling on his friend, in the outer room. At this summons the Serpent arose to obey, and Hetty joined her sister.

CHAPTER XIV

"A stranger animal," cries one,
"Sure never lived beneath the sun;
A lizard's body, lean and long,
A fish's head, a serpent's tongue,
Its foot, with triple claw disjoined;
And what a length of tail behind!"

MERRICK

THE FIRST ACT of the Delaware on rejoining his friend was to proceed gravely to disencumber himself of his civilized attire and to stand forth an Indian warrior again. The protest of Deerslayer was met by his communicating the fact that the presence of an Indian in the hut was known to the Iroquois, and that his maintaining the disguise would be more likely to direct suspicions to his real object than if he came out openly as a member of a hostile tribe. When the latter understood the truth, and was told that he had been deceived in supposing the chief had succeeded in entering the ark undiscovered, he cheerfully consented to the change, since further attempt at concealment was useless. A gentler feeling than the one avowed, however, lay at the bottom of the Indian's desire to appear as a son of the forest. He had been told that Hist was on the opposite shore, and nature so far triumphed over all distinctions of habit, and tribes, and people as to reduce this young savage warrior to the level of a feeling which would have been found in the most refined inhabitant of a town, under similar circumstances. There was a mild satisfaction in believing that she he loved could see him, and as he walked out on the platform in his scanty native attire, an Apollo of the wilderness, a hundred of the tender fancies that fleet through lovers' brains beset his imagination and softened his heart.

226

All this was lost on Deerslayer, who was no great adept in the mysteries of Cupid, but whose mind was far more occupied with the concerns that forced themselves on his attention than with any of the truant fancies of love. He soon recalled his companion, therefore, to a sense of their actual condition by summoning him to a sort of council of war, in which they were to settle their future course. In the dialogue that followed, the parties mutually made each other acquainted with what had passed in their several interviews. Chingachgook was told the history of the treaty about the ransom, and Deerslayer heard the whole of Hetty's communications. The latter listened with generous interest to his friend's hopes and promised cheerfully all the assistance he could lend.

" 'Tis our main ar'n'd, Sarpent, as you know, this battling for the castle and old Hutter's darters coming in as a sort of accident. Yes—yes—I'll be actyve in helping little Hist, who's not only one of the best and handsomest maidens of the tribe, but the *very* best and handsomest. I've always encouraged you, Chief, in that liking; it's proper, too, that a great and ancient race like your'n shouldn't come to an end. If a woman of red skin and red gifts could get to be near enough to me to wish her for a wife, I'd s'arch for just such another, but that can *never* be; no, that can *never* be. I'm glad Hetty has met with Hist, howsever, for though the first is a little short of wit and understanding, the last has enough for both. Yes, Sarpent," laughing heartily, "put 'em together and two smarter gals isn't to be found in all York Colony!"

"I will go to the Iroquois camp," returned the Delaware gravely. "No one knows Chingachgook but Wah, and a treaty for lives and scalps should be made by a chief! Give me the strange beasts, and let me take a canoe."

Deerslayer dropped his head and played with the end of a fish pole in the water, as he sat dangling his legs over the edge of the platform, like a man who was lost in thought by the sudden occurrence of a novel idea. Instead of directly answering the proposal of his friend, he began to soliloquize; a circumstance, however, that in no manner rendered his words more true, as he was remarkable for saying what he thought, whether the remarks were addressed to himself or to anyone else.

"Yes—yes," he said, "this must be what they call love! I've heard say that it sometimes upsets reason altogether, leaving a young man as helpless, as to calculation and caution, as a brute beast. To think that the Sarpent should be so lost to reason, and cunning, and wisdom! We must, sartainly, manage to get Hist off, and have 'em married as soon as we get back to the tribe, or this war will be of no more use to the chief than a hunt a little oncommon and extr'ornary. Yes—yes—he'll never be the man he was till this matter is off his mind and he comes to his senses, like all the rest of mankind. Sarpent, you can't be in airnest, and therefore I shall say but little to your offer. But you're a chief, and will soon be sent out on the warpath at the head of parties, and I'll just ask if you'd think of putting your forces into the inimy's hands afore the battle is fou't?"

"Wah!" ejaculated the Indian.

"Aye—Wah!—I know well enough it's Wah, and altogether Wah! Ra'ally, Sarpent, I'm consarned and mortified about you! I never heard so weak an idea come from a chief, and he, too, one that's already got a name for being wise, young and inexper'enced as he is. Canoe you shan't have, so long as the v'ice of fri'ndship and warning can count for anything."

"My paleface friend is right. A cloud came over the face of Chingachgook, and weakness got into his mind, while his eyes were dim. My brother has a good memory for good deeds and a weak memory for bad. He will forget."

"Yes, that's easy enough. Say no more about it, Chief, but if another of them clouds blow near you, do your endivor to get out of its way. Clouds are bad enough in the weather, but when they come to the reason, it gets to be serious. Now, sit down by me here and let us calculate our movements a little, for we shall soon either have a truce and a peace, or we shall come to an actyve and bloody war. You see the vagabonds can make logs sarve their turn as well as the best raftsmen on the rivers, and it would be no great expl'ite for them to invade us in a body. I've been thinking of the wisdom of putting all old Tom's stores into the ark, of barring and locking up the castle, and of taking to the ark altogether. That is movable, and by keeping the sail up and shifting places, we might worry through a great many

nights without them Canada wolves finding a way into our sheepfold."

Chingachgook listened to this plan with approbation. Did the negotiation fail, there was now little hope that the night would pass without an assault; and the enemy had sagacity enough to understand, that, in carrying the castle, they would probably become masters of all it contained, the offered ransom included, and still retain the advantages they had hitherto gained. Some precaution of the sort appeared to be absolutely necessary, for now the numbers of the Iroquois were known, a night attack could scarcely be successfully met. It would be impossible to prevent the enemy from getting possession of the canoes and the ark, and the latter itself would be a hold in which the assailants would be as effectually protected against bullets as were those in the building. For a few minutes both the men thought of sinking the ark in the shallow water, of bringing the canoes into the house, and of depending altogether on the castle for protection. But reflection satisfied them that, in the end, this expedient would fail. It was so easy to collect logs on the shore and to construct a raft of almost any size that it was certain the Iroquois, now they had turned their attention to such means, would resort to them seriously, so long as there was the certainty of success by perseverance. After deliberating maturely and placing all the considerations fairly before them, the two young beginners in the art of forest warfare settled down into the opinion that the ark offered the only available means of security. This decision was no sooner come to than it was communicated to Judith. The girl had no serious objection to make, and all four set about the measures necessary to carrying the plan into execution.

The reader will readily understand that Floating Tom's worldly goods were of no great amount. A couple of beds, some wearing apparel, the arms and ammunition, a few cooking utensils, and the mysterious but half-examined chest formed the principal items. These were all soon removed, the ark having been hauled on the eastern side of the building, so that the transfer could be made without being seen from the shore. It was thought unnecessary to disturb the heavier and coarser articles of furniture, as they were not required in the ark and were of but little value in themselves. As great caution was necessary in removing the different objects,

most of which were passed out of a window with a view to conceal what was going on, it required two or three hours before all could be effected. By the expiration of that time the raft made its appearance, moving from the shore. Deerslayer immediately had recourse to the glass, by the aid of which he perceived that two warriors were on it, though they appeared to be unarmed. The progress of the raft was slow; a circumstance that formed one of the great advantages that would be possessed by the scow in any future collision between them, the movements of the latter being comparatively swift and light. As there was time to make the dispositions for the reception of the two dangerous visitors, everything was prepared for them long before they had got near enough to be hailed. The Serpent and the girls retired into the building, where the former stood near the door, well provided with rifles, while Judith watched the proceedings without through a loop. As for Deerslayer, he had brought a stool to the edge of the platform, at the point toward which the raft was advancing, and taken his seat, with his rifle leaning carelessly between his legs.

As the raft drew nearer, every means possessed by the party in the castle was resorted to in order to ascertain if their visitors had any firearms. Neither Deerslayer nor Chingachgook could discover any, but Judith, unwilling to trust to simple eyesight, thrust the glass through the loop and directed it toward the hemlock boughs that lay between the two logs of the raft, forming a sort of flooring, as well as a seat for the use of the rowers. When the heavy-moving craft was within fifty feet of him, Deerslayer hailed the Hurons, directing them to cease rowing, it not being his intention to permit them to land. Compliance, of course, was necessary, and the two grim-looking warriors instantly quitted their seats, though the raft continued slowly to approach until it had driven in much nearer to the platform.

"Are ye chiefs?" demanded Deerslayer, with dignity. "Are ye chiefs?—or have the Mingos sent me warriors without names, on such an ar'n'd? If so, the sooner ye go back, the sooner the one will be likely to come that a warrior can talk with."

"Hugh!" exclaimed the elder of the two on the raft, rolling his glowing eyes over the different objects that were visible in and about the castle, with a keenness that showed how

ittle escaped him. "My brother is very proud, but Rivenoak (we use the literal translation of the term, writing as we do n English) is a name to make a Delaware turn pale."

"That's true, or it's a lie, Rivenoak, as it may be, but I am not likely to turn pale, seeing that I was born pale. What's your ar'n'd, and why do you come among light bark canoes on logs that are not even dug out?"

"The Iroquois are not ducks, to walk on water! Let the palefaces give them a canoe, and they'll come in a canoe."

"That's more rational than likely to come to pass. We have out four canoes, and being four persons, that's only one for each of us. We thank you for the offer, howsever, though we ask leave not to accept it. You are welcome, Iroquois, on your logs!"

"Thanks—my young paleface warrior—he has got a name —how do the chiefs call him?"

Deerslayer hesitated a moment, and a gleam of pride and human weakness came over him. He smiled, muttered between his teeth, and then looking up proudly, he said:

"Mingo, like all are young and actyve, I've been known by different names at different times. One of your warriors, whose spirit started for the happy grounds of your people as ately as yesterday morning, thought I desarved to be known by the name of Hawkeye, and this because my sight happened to be quicker than his own, when it got to be life or death atween us."

Chingachgook, who was attentively listening to all that passed, heard and understood this proof of passing weakness in his friend, and on a future occasion he questioned him more closely concerning the transaction on the point where Deerslayer had first taken human life. When he had got the whole truth, he did not fail to communicate it to the tribe, from which time the young hunter was universally known among the Delawares by an appellation so honorably earned. As this, however, was a period posterior to all the incidents of this tale, we shall continue to call the young hunter by the name under which he has been first introduced to the reader. Nor was the Iroquois less struck with the vaunt of the white man. He knew of the death of his comrade and had no difficulty in understanding the allusion, the intercourse between the conqueror and his victim on that occasion having been seen by several savages on the shore of the lake,

who had been stationed at different points just within the margin of the bushes to watch the drifting canoes, and who had not time to reach the scene of action ere the victor had retired. The effect on this rude being of the forest was an exclamation of surprise; then such a smile of courtesy and wave of the hand succeeded as would have done credit to Asiatic diplomacy. The two Iroquois spoke to each other in low terms, and both drew near the end of the raft that was closest to the platform.

"My brother, Hawkeye, has sent a message to the Hurons," resumed Rivenoak, "and it has made their hearts very glad. They hear he has images of beasts with two tails! Will he show them to his friends?"

"Inimies would be truer," returned Deerslayer, "but sound isn't sense and does little harm. Here is one of the images; I toss it to you under faith of treaties. If it's not returned, the rifle will settle the p'int atween us."

The Iroquois seemed to acquiesce in the conditions, and Deerslayer arose and prepared to toss one of the elephants to the raft, both parties using all the precaution that was necessary to prevent its loss. As practice renders men expert in such things, the little piece of ivory was soon successfully transferred from one hand to the other, and then followed another scene on the raft in which astonishment and delight got the mastery of Indian stoicism. These two grim old warriors manifested even more feeling as they examined the curiously wrought chessman than had been betrayed by the boy, for in the case of the latter, recent schooling had interposed its influence, while the men, like all who are sustained by well-established characters, were not ashamed to let some of their emotions be discovered. For a few minutes they apparently lost the consciousness of their situation in the intense scrutiny they bestowed on a material so fine, work so highly wrought, and an animal so extraordinary. The lip of the moose is, perhaps, the nearest approach to the trunk of the elephant that is to be found in the American forest, but this resemblance was far from being sufficiently striking to bring the new creature within the range of their habits and ideas, and the more they studied the image, the greater was their astonishment. Nor did these children of the forest mistake the structure on the back of the elephant for a part of the animal. They were familiar with horses and

oxen, and had seen towers in the Canadas, and found nothing surprising in creatures of burden. Still, by a very natural association, they supposed the carving meant to represent that the animal they saw was of a strength sufficient to carry a fort on its back, a circumstance that in no degree lessened their wonder.

"Has my paleface brother any more such beasts?" at last the senior of the Iroquois asked in a sort of petitioning manner.

"There's more where them came from, Mingo," was the answer; "one is enough, however, to buy off fifty scalps."

"One of my prisoners is a great warrior—tall as a pine—strong as the moose—active as a deer—fierce as the panther. Someday he'll be a great chief and lead the army of King George!"

"Tut—tut—Mingo; Hurry Harry is Hurry Harry, and you'll never make more than a corporal of him, if you do that. He's tall enough, of a sartainty, but that's of no use, as he only hits his head ag'in the branches as he goes through the forest. He's strong, too, but a strong body isn't a strong head, and the king's generals are not chosen for their sinews. He's swift, if you will, but a rifle bullet is swifter. And as for f'erceness, it's no great ricommend to a soldier, they that think they feel the stoutest, often givin' out at the pinch. No—no—you'll never make Hurry's scalp pass for more than a good head of curly hair, and a rattlepate beneath it!"

"My old prisoner very wise—king of the lake—great warrior, wise counselor!"

"Well, there's them that might gainsay all this, too, Mingo. A very wise man wouldn't be apt to be taken in so foolish a manner as befell Master Hutter, and if he gives good counsel, he must have listened to very bad in that affair. There's only one king of this lake, and he's a long way off and isn't likely ever to see it. Floating Tom is some such king of this region, as the wolf that prowls through the woods is king of the forest. A beast with two tails is well worth two such scalps!"

"But my brother has another beast? He will give two," holding up as many fingers, "for old father."

"Floating Tom is no father of mine, but he'll fare none the worse for that. As for giving two beasts for his scalp, and each beast with two tails, it is quite beyond reason. Think

yourself well off, Mingo, if you make a much worse trade."

By this time the self-command of Rivenoak had got the better of his wonder, and he began to fall back on his usual habits of cunning, in order to drive the best bargain he could. It would be useless to relate more than the substance of the desultory dialogue that followed, in which the Indian manifested no little management, in endeavoring to recover the ground lost under the influence of surprise. He even affected to doubt whether any original for the image of the beast existed and asserted that the oldest Indian had never heard a tradition of any such animal. Little did either of them imagine at the time that long ere a century elapsed, the progress of civilization would bring even much more extraordinary and rare animals into that region, as curiosities to be gazed at by the curious, and that the particular beast about which the disputants contended would be seen laving its sides and swimming in the very sheet of water on which they had met.* As is not uncommon on such occasions, one of the parties got a little warm in the course of the discussion, for Deerslayer met all the arguments and prevarications of his subtle opponent with his own cool directness of manner and unmoved love of truth. What an elephant was he knew little better than the savage, but he perfectly understood that the carved pieces of ivory must have some such value in the eyes of an Iroquois as a bag of gold, or a package of beaver skins, would in those of a trader. Under the circumstances, therefore, he felt it to be prudent not to concede too much at first, since there existed a nearly unconquerable obstacle to making the transfers, even after the contracting parties had actually agreed upon the terms. Keeping this difficulty in view, he held the extra chessmen in reserve as a means of smoothing any difficulty in the moment of need.

At length the savage pretended that further negotiation was useless, since he could not be so unjust to his tribe as to part with the honor and emoluments of two excellent, full-grown male scalps for a consideration so trifling as a toy like that he had seen—and he prepared to take his departure. Both parties now felt as men are wont to feel when a bargain

---

*The Otsego is a favorite place for the caravankeepers to let their elephants bathe. The writer has seen two at a time, since the publication of this book, swimming about in company.

that each is anxious to conclude is on the eve of being broken off in consequence of too much pertinacity in the way of management. The effect of the disappointment was very different, however, on the respective individuals. Deerslayer was mortified and filled with regret, for he not only felt for the prisoners, but he also felt deeply for the two girls. The conclusion of the treaty, therefore, left him melancholy and full of regret. With the savage, his defeat produced the desire of revenge. In a moment of excitement, he loudly announced his intention to say no more, and he felt equally enraged with himself and with his cool opponent, that he had permitted a paleface to manifest more indifference and self-command than an Indian chief. When he began to urge his raft away from the platform, his countenance lowered, and his eye glowed even while he affected a smile of amity and a gesture of courtesy, at parting.

It took some little time to overcome the *vis inertiæ* of the logs, and while this was doing by the silent Indian, Rivenoak stalked over the hemlock boughs that lay between the logs, in sullen ferocity, eyeing keenly the while the hut, the platform, and the person of his late disputant. Once he spoke in low, quick terms to his companion, and he stirred the boughs with his feet, like an animal that is restive. At that moment the watchfulness of Deerslayer had a little abated, for he sat musing on the means of renewing the negotiation without giving too much advantage to the other side. It was, perhaps, fortunate for him that the keen and bright eyes of Judith were as vigilant as ever. At the instant when the young man was least on his guard, and his enemy was the most on the alert, she called out in a warning voice to the former, most opportunely giving the alarm.

"Be on your guard, Deerslayer," the girl cried. "I see rifles, with the glass, beneath the hemlock brush, and the Iroquois is loosening them with his feet!"

It would seem that the enemy had carried their artifices so far as to employ an agent who understood English. The previous dialogue had taken place in his own language, but it was evident, by the sudden manner in which his feet ceased their treacherous occupation, and in which the countenance of Rivenoak changed from sullen ferocity to a smile of courtesy, that the call of the girl was understood. Signing to his companion to cease his efforts to set the logs

in motion, he advanced to the end of the raft which was nearest to the platform and spoke.

"Why should Rivenoak and his brother leave any cloud between them?" he said. "They are both wise, both brave, and both generous; they ought to part friends. One beast shall be the price of one prisoner."

"And, Mingo," answered the other, delighted to renew the negotiation on almost any terms and determined to clench the bargain if possible by a little extra liberality, "you'll see that a paleface knows how to pay a full price, when he trades with an open heart and an open hand. Keep the beast that you had forgotten to give back to me, as you was about to start, and which I forgot to ask for, on account of consarn at parting in anger. Show it to your chiefs. When you bring us our fri'nds two more shall be added to it—and"—hesitating a moment in distrust of the expediency of so great a concession, then deciding in its favor—"and, if we see them afore the sun sets, we may find a fourth to make up an even number."

This settled the matter. Every gleam of discontent vanished from the dark countenance of the Iroquois, and he smiled as graciously, if not as sweetly, as Judith Hutter herself. The piece already in his possession was again examined, and an ejaculation of pleasure showed how much he was pleased with this unexpected termination of the affair. In point of fact, both he and Deerslayer had momentarily forgotten what had become of the subject of their discussion, in the warmth of their feelings, but such had not been the case with Rivenoak's companion. This man retained the piece, and had fully made up his mind, were it claimed under such circumstances as to render its return necessary, to drop it in the lake, trusting to his being able to find it again at some future day. This desperate expedient, however, was no longer necessary, and after repeating the terms of agreement and professing to understand them, the two Indians finally took their departure, moving slowly toward the shore.

"Can any faith be put in such wretches?" asked Judith, when she and Hetty had come out on the platform, and were standing at the side of Deerslayer, watching the dull movement of the logs. "Will they not rather keep the toy they have and send us off some bloody proofs of their getting

the better of us in cunning, by way of boasting? I've heard of acts as bad as this."

"No doubt, Judith; no manner of doubt, if it wasn't for Indian natur'. But I'm no judge of a redskin if that two-tailed beast doesn't set the whole tribe in some such stir as a stick raises in a beehive! Now, there's the Sarpent, a man with narves like flint and no more cur'osity in everyday consarns than is befitting prudence. Why, he was so overcome with the sight of the creatur', carved as it is in bone, that I felt ashamed for him! That's just their gifts, however, and one can't well quarrel with a man for his gifts, when they are lawful. Chingachgook will soon get over his weakness, and remember that he's a chief, and that he comes of a great stock, and has a renowned name to support and uphold; but, as for yonder scamps, there'll be no peace among 'em, until they think they've got possession of everything of the natur' of that bit of carved bone that's to be found among Thomas Hutter's stores!"

"They only know of the elephants and can have no hopes about the other things."

"That's true, Judith; still, covetousness is a craving feelin'. They'll say, if the palefaces have these curious beasts with two tails, who knows but they've got some with three, or, for that matter, with four! That's what the schoolmasters call nat'ral arithmetic, and 'twill be sartain to beset the feelin's of savages. They'll never be easy till the truth is known."

"Do you think, Deerslayer," inquired Hetty, in her simple and innocent manner, "that the Iroquois won't let Father and Hurry go? I read to them several of the very best verses in the whole Bible, and you see what they have done already."

The hunter, as he always did, listened kindly and even affectionately to Hetty's remarks; then he mused a moment in silence. There was something like a flush on his cheek as he answered, after quite a minute had passed.

"I don't know whether a white man ought to be ashamed or not to own he can't read, but such is my case, Judith. You are skillful, I find, in all such matters, while I have only studied the hand of God, as it is seen in the hills and the valleys, the mountaintops, the streams, the forest, and the springs. Much l'arning may be got in this way, as well as out of books, and yet I sometimes think it is a white man's

gift to read! When I hear from the mouths of the Moravians the words of which Hetty speaks, they raise a longing in my mind, and I think I *will* know how to read 'em myself; but the game in summer, and the traditions, and lessons in war, and other matters have always kept me behindhand."

"Shall I teach you, Deerslayer?" asked Hetty earnestly. "I'm weak-minded, they say, but I can read as well as Judith. It might save your life, to know how to read the Bible to the savages, and it will certainly save your soul, for Mother told me *that* again and again!"

"Thankee, Hetty—yes, thankee, with all my heart. There are like to be too stirring times for much idleness; but, after it's peace, and I come to see you ag'in on this lake, then I'll give myself up to it, as if 'twas pleasure and profit in a single business. Perhaps I ought to be ashamed, Judith, that 'tis so, but truth is truth. As for these Iroquois, 'tisn't very likely they'll forget a beast with two tails on account of a varse or two from the Bible. I rather expect they'll give up the prisoners and trust to some sarcumvention or other to get 'em back ag'in, with us and all in the castle, and the ark in the bargain. Howsever, we must humor the vagabonds first, to get your father and Hurry out of their hands, and next, to keep the peace atween us, until such time as the Sarpent there can make out to get off his betrothed wife. If there's any sudden outbreakin' of anger and ferocity, the Indians will send off all their women and children to the camp at once, whereas, by keeping 'em calm and trustful, we may manage to meet Hist at the spot she has mentioned. Rather than have the bargain fall through now, I'd throw in half a dozen of them effigy bow-and-arrow men, such as we've in plenty in the chist."

Judith cheerfully assented, for she would have resigned even the flowered brocade, rather than not redeem her father and please Deerslayer.

The prospects of success were now so encouraging as to raise the spirits of all in the castle, though a due watchfulness on the movements of the enemy was maintained. Hour passed after hour, notwithstanding, and the sun had once more begun to fall toward the summits of the western hills, and yet no signs were seen of the return of the raft. By dint of sweeping the shore with the glass, Deerslayer at length discovered a place in the dense and dark woods where, he

entertained no doubt, the Iroquois were assembled in considerable numbers. It was near the thicket whence the raft had issued, and a little rill that trickled into the lake announced the vicinity of a spring. Here, then, the savages were probably holding their consultation, and the decision was to be made that went to settle the question of life or death for the prisoners. There was one ground for hope in spite of the delay, however, that Deerslayer did not fail to place before his anxious companions. It was far more probable that the Indians had left their prisoners in the camp than that they had encumbered themselves by causing them to follow through the woods a party that was out on a merely temporary excursion. If such was the fact, it required considerable time to send a messenger the necessary distance and to bring the two white men to the spot where they were to embark. Encouraged by these reflections, a new stock of patience was gathered, and the declension of the sun was viewed with less alarm.

The result justified Deerslayer's conjecture. Not long before the sun had finally disappeared, the two logs were seen coming out of the thicket again; as it drew near, Judith announced that her father and Hurry, both of them pinioned, lay on the bushes in the center. As before, the Indians were rowing. The latter seemed to be conscious that the lateness of the hour demanded unusual exertions, and contrary to the habits of their people, who are ever averse to toil, they labored hard at the rude substitutes for oars. In consequence of this diligence the raft occupied its old station in about half the time that had been taken in the previous visits.

Even after the conditions were so well understood, and matters had proceeded so far, the actual transfer of the prisoners was not a duty to be executed without difficulty. The Iroquois were compelled to place great reliance on the good faith of their foes, though it was reluctantly given, and was yielded to necessity rather than to confidence. As soon as Hutter and Hurry should be released the party in the castle numbered two to one, as opposed to those on the raft, and escape by flight was out of the question, as the former had three bark canoes, to say nothing of the defenses of the house and the ark. All this was understood by both parties, and it is probable the arrangement never could have been

completed had not the honest countenance and manner of Deerslayer wrought their usual effect on Rivenoak.

"My brother knows I put faith in *him*," said the latter as he advanced with Hutter, whose legs had been released to enable the old man to ascend to the platform. "One scalp —one more beast."

"Stop, Mingo," interrupted the hunter, "keep your prisoner a moment. I have to go and seek the means of payment."

This excuse, however, though true in part, was principally a fetch. Deerslayer left the platform, and entering the house, he directed Judith to collect all the arms and to conceal them in her own room. He then spoke earnestly to the Delaware, who stood on guard as before near the entrance of the building, put the three remaining castles in his pocket, and returned.

"You are welcome back to your old abode, Master Hutter," said Deerslayer, as he helped the other up on the platform, slyly passing into the hand of Rivenoak at the same time another of the castles. "You'll find your darters right glad to see you, and here's Hetty come herself to say as much in her own behalf."

Here the hunter stopped speaking and broke out into a hearty fit of his silent and peculiar laughter. Hurry's legs were just released, and he had been placed on his feet. So tightly had the ligatures been drawn that the use of his limbs was not immediately recovered, and the young giant presented, in good sooth, a very helpless and a somewhat ludicrous picture. It was this unusual spectacle, particularly the bewildered countenance, that excited the merriment of Deerslayer.

"You look like a girdled pine in a clearin', Hurry Harry, that is rocking in a gale," said Deerslayer, checking his unseasonable mirth more from delicacy to the others than from any respect to the liberated captive. "I'm glad, however, to see that you haven't had your hair dressed by any of the Iroquois barbers in your late visit to their camp."

"Harkee, Deerslayer," returned the other a little fiercely; "it will be prudent for you to deal less in mirth and more in friendship on this occasion. Act like a Christian, for once, and not like a laughing gal in a country school when the master's back is turned, and just tell me whether there's any feet or not at the end of these legs of mine. I think I can see

them, but as for feelin', they might as well be down on the banks of the Mohawk as where they seem to be."

"You've come off whole, Hurry, and that's not a little," answered the other, secretly passing to the Indian the remainder of the stipulated ransom and making an earnest sign, at the same moment, for him to commence his retreat. "You've come off whole, feet and all, and are only a little numb from a tight fit of the withes. Natur' 'll soon set the blood in motion, and then you may begin to dance, to celebrate what I call a most wonderful and onexpected deliverance from a den of wolves."

Deerslayer released the arms of his friends, as each landed, and the two were now stamping and limping about on the platform, growling and uttering denunciations as they endeavored to help the returning circulation. They had been tethered too long, however, to regain the use of their limbs in a moment; and the Indians being quite as diligent on their return as on their advance, the raft was fully a hundred yards from the castle when Hurry, turning accidentally in that direction, discovered how fast it was getting beyond the reach of his vengeance. By this time he could move with tolerable facility, though still numb and awkward. Without considering his own situation, however, he seized the rifle that leaned against the shoulder of Deerslayer and attempted to cock and present it. The young hunter was too quick for him. Seizing the piece he wrenched it from the hands of the giant; not, however, until it had gone off in the struggle, when pointed directly upward. It is probable that Deerslayer could have prevailed in such a contest, on account of the condition of Hurry's limbs, but the instant the gun went off, the latter yielded and stumped toward the house, raising his legs at each step quite a foot from the ground, from an uncertainty of the actual position of his feet. But he had been anticipated by Judith. The whole stock of Hutter's arms, which had been left in the building as a resource in the event of a sudden outbreaking of hostilities, had been removed, and was already secreted, agreeably to Deerslayer's directions. In consequence of this precaution, no means offered by which March could put his designs in execution.

Disappointed in his vengeance, Hurry seated himself, and like Hutter, for half an hour he was too much occupied in endeavoring to restore the circulation and in regaining the

use of his limbs to indulge in any other reflections. By the end of this time the raft had disappeared, and night was beginning to throw her shadows once more over the whole sylvan scene. Before darkness had completely set in, and while the girls were preparing the evening meal, Deerslayer related to Hutter an outline of the events that had taken place and gave him a history of the means he had adopted for the security of his children and property.

Chapter XV

As long as Edwarde rules thys lande,
Ne quiet you wylle know;
Your sonnes and husbandes shall be slayne,
And brookes with bloode shall flowe.

You leave youre goode and lawfulle kynge,
Whenne ynne adversitye;
Like me, untoe the true cause stycke,
And for the true cause dye.

CHATTERTON

THE CALM OF evening was again in singular contrast, while its gathering gloom was in as singular unison with the passions of men. The sun was set, and the rays of the retiring luminary ceased to gild the edges of the few clouds that had sufficient openings to admit the passage of its fading light. The canopy overhead was heavy and dense, promising another night of darkness, but the surface of the lake was scarcely disturbed by a ripple. There was a little air, though it scarce deserved to be termed wind. Still, being damp and heavy, it had a certain force. The party in the castle were as gloomy and silent as the scene. The two ransomed prisoners felt humbled and dishonored, but their humility partook of the rancor of revenge. They were far more disposed to remember the indignity with which they had been treated during the last few hours of their captivity than to feel grateful for the previous indulgence. Then that keen-sighted monitor conscience, by reminding them of the retributive justice of all they had endured, goaded them rather to turn the tables on their enemies than to accuse themselves. As for the others, they were thoughtful equally from regret and joy. Deerslayer and Judith felt most of the former sensation, though from very different causes, while Hetty for the mo-

ment was perfectly happy. The Delaware had also lively pictures of felicity in the prospect of so soon regaining his betrothed. Under such circumstances, and in this mood, all were taking the evening meal.

"Old Tom!" cried Hurry, bursting into a fit of boisterous laughter, "you looked amazin'ly like a tethered bear as you was stretched on them hemlock boughs, and I only wonder you didn't growl more. Well, it's over, and syth's and lamentations won't mend the matter! There's the blackguard Rivenoak, he that brought us off, has an oncommon scalp, and I'd give as much for it myself as the Colony. Yes, I feel as rich as the governor in these matters now, and will lay down with them doubloon for doubloon. Judith, darling, did you mourn for me much when I was in the hands of the Philipsteins?"

The last were a family of German descent on the Mohawk to whom Hurry had a great antipathy and whom he had confounded with the enemies of Judea.

"Our tears have raised the lake, Harry March, as you might have seen by the shore!" returned Judith, with a feigned levity that she was far from feeling. "That Hetty and I should have grieved for Father was to be expected, but we fairly rained tears for you."

"We *were* sorry for poor Hurry, as well as for Father, Judith!" put in her innocent and unconscious sister.

"True, girl, true, but we feel sorrow for everybody that's in trouble, you know," returned the other in a quick, admonitory manner and a low tone. "Nevertheless, we are glad to see you, Master March, and out of the hands of the Philipsteins, too."

"Yes, they're a bad set, and so is the other brood of 'em, down on the river. It's a wonderment to me how you got us off, Deerslayer; and I forgive you the interference that prevented my doin' justice on that vagabond, for this small sarvice. Let us into the secret, that we may do you the same good turn, at need. Was it by lying, or by coaxing?"

"By neither, Hurry, but by buying. We paid a ransom for you both, and that, too, at a price so high you had well be on your guard ag'in another captyvement, lest our stock of goods shouldn't hold out."

"A ransom! Old Tom has paid the fiddler, then, for nothing of mine would have bought off the hair, much less the skin. I didn't think men as keen set as them vagabonds

would let a fellow up so easy, when they had him fairly at a close hug and floored. But money is money, and somehow it's unnat'ral hard to withstand. Injin, or white man, 'tis pretty much the same. It must be owned, Judith, there's a considerable of human natur' in mankind ginirally, arter all!"

Hutter now rose, and signing to Deerslayer, he led him to an inner room, where, in answer to his questions, he first learned the price that had been paid for his release. The old man expressed neither resentment nor surprise at the inroad that had been made on his chest, though he did manifest some curiosity to know how far the investigation of its contents had been carried. He also inquired where the key had been found. The habitual frankness of Deerslayer prevented any prevarication, and the conference soon terminated by the return of the two to the outer room, or that which served for the double purpose of parlor and kitchen.

"I wonder if it's peace or war between us and the savages!" exclaimed Hurry, just as Deerslayer, who had paused for a single instant, listened attentively, and was passing through the outer door without stopping. "This givin' up captives has a friendly look, and when men have traded together, on a fair and honorable footing, they ought to part fri'nds, for that occasion, at least. Come back, Deerslayer, and let us have your judgment, for I'm beginnin' to think more of you, since your late behavior, than I used to do."

"There's an answer to your question, Hurry, since you're in such haste to come ag'in to blows."

As Deerslayer spoke, he threw on the table, on which the other was reclining with one elbow, a sort of miniature fagot, composed of a dozen sticks bound tightly together with a deerskin thong. March seized it eagerly, and holding it close to a blazing knot of pine that lay on the hearth, and which gave out all the light there was in the room, ascertained that the ends of the several sticks had been dipped in blood.

"If this isn't plain English," said the reckless frontiersman, "it's plain Injin! Here's what they call a dicliration of war, down at York, Judith. How did you come by this defiance, Deerslayer?"

"Fairly enough. It lay, not a minut' since, in what you call Floatin' Tom's dooryard."

"How came it there? It never fell from the clouds, Judith,

as little toads sometimes do, and then it don't rain. You must prove where it come from, Deerslayer, or we shall suspect some design to skear them that would have lost their wits long ago, if fear could drive 'em away."

Deerslayer had approached a window, and cast a glance out of it on the dark aspect of the lake. As if satisfied with what he beheld, he drew near Hurry and took the bundle of sticks into his own hand, examining it attentively.

"Yes, this is an Indian declaration of war, sure enough," he said, "and it's a proof how little you're suited to be on the path it has traveled, Harry March, that it has got here, and you never the wiser as to the means. The savages may have left the scalp on your head, but they must have taken off the *ears;* else you'd have heard the stirring of the water made by the lad as he come off ag'in, on his two logs. His ar'n'd was to throw these sticks at our door, as much as to say, we've struck the warpost since the trade, and the next thing will be to strike *you.*"

"The prowling wolves! But hand me that rifle, Judith, and I'll send an answer back to the vagabonds through their messenger."

"Not while I stand by, Master March," coolly put in Deerslayer, motioning for the other to forbear. "Faith is faith, whether given to a redskin or to a Christian. The lad lighted a knot and came off fairly, under its blaze, to give us this warning, and no man here should harm him while empl'yed on such an ar'n'd. There's no use in words, for the boy is too cunning to leave the knot burning, now his business is done, and the night is already too dark for a rifle to have any sartainty."

"That may be true enough, as to a gun, but there's virtue still in a canoe," answered Hurry, passing toward the door with enormous strides, carrying a rifle in his hands. "The being doesn't live that shall stop me from following and bringing back that riptyle's scalp. The more on 'em that you crush in the egg, the fewer there'll be to dart at you in the woods!"

Judith trembled like the aspen, she scarce knew why herself, though there was the prospect of a scene of violence; for, if Hurry was fierce and overbearing in the consciousness of his vast strength, Deerslayer had about him the calm determination that promises greater perseverance, and a reso-

lution more likely to effect its object. It was the stern, resolute eye of the latter, rather than the noisy vehemence of the first, that excited her apprehensions. Hurry soon reached the spot where the canoe was fastened, but not before Deerslayer had spoken in a quick, earnest voice to the Serpent, in Delaware. The latter had been the first, in truth, to hear the sounds of the oars, and he had gone upon the platform in jealous watchfulness. The light satisfied him that a message was coming, and when the boy cast his bundle of sticks at his feet, it neither moved his anger nor induced surprise. He merely stood at watch, rifle in hand, to make certain that no treachery lay behind the defiance. As Deerslayer now called to him, he stepped into the canoe and, quick as thought, removed the paddles. Hurry was furious when he found that he was deprived of the means of proceeding. He first approached the Indian with loud menaces, and even Deerslayer stood aghast at the probable consequences. March shook his sledge-hammer fists and flourished his arms, as he drew near the Indian, and all expected he would attempt to fell the Delaware to the earth; one of them, at least, was well aware that such an experiment would be followed by immediate bloodshed. But even Hurry was awed by the stern composure of the chief, and he, too, knew that such a man was not to be outraged with impunity; he therefore turned to vent his rage on Deerslayer, where he foresaw no consequences so terrible. What might have been the result of this second demonstration, if completed, is unknown, since it was never made.

"Hurry," said a gentle, soothing voice at his elbow, "it's wicked to be so angry, and God will not overlook it. The Iroquois treated you well, and they didn't take *your* scalp, though you and Father wanted to take *theirs*."

The influence of mildness on passion is well known. Hetty, too, had earned a sort of consideration that had never before been enjoyed by her, through the self-devotion and decision of her recent conduct. Perhaps her established mental imbecility, by removing all distrust of a wish to control, aided her influence. Let the cause be as questionable as it might, the effect was sufficiently certain. Instead of throttling his old fellow traveler, Hurry turned to the girl and poured out a portion of his discontent, if none of his anger, in her attentive ears.

" 'Tis too bad, Hetty!" he exclaimed; "as bad as a county jail, or a lack of beaver, to get a creatur' into your very trap and then to see it get off. As much as six first-quality skins in valie has paddled off on them clumsy logs, when twenty strokes of a well-turned paddle would overtake 'em. I say in valie, for as to the boy in the way of natur', he is only a boy and is worth neither more nor less than one. Deerslayer, you've been ontrue to your fri'nds in letting such a chance slip through my fingers as well as your own."

The answer was given quietly, but with a voice as steady as a fearless nature and the consciousness of rectitude could make it. "I should have been ontrue to the right, had I done otherwise," returned the Deerslayer steadily; "and neither you nor any other man has authority to demand that much of me. The lad came on a lawful business, and the meanest redskin that roams the woods would be ashamed of not respecting his ar'n'd. But he's now far beyond your reach, Master March, and there's little use in talking, like a couple of women, of what can no longer be helped."

So saying, Deerslayer turned away, like one resolved to waste no more words on the subject, while Hutter pulled Harry by the sleeve and led him into the ark. There they sat long in private conference. In the meantime, the Indian and his friend had their secret consultation, for though it wanted some three or four hours to the rising of the star, the former could not abstain from canvassing his scheme and from opening his heart to the other. Judith, too, yielded to her softer feelings and listened to the whole of Hetty's artless narrative of what occurred after she had landed. The woods had few terrors for either of these girls, educated as they had been, and accustomed as they were to look out daily at their rich expanse, or to wander beneath their dark shades, but the elder sister felt that she would have hesitated about thus venturing alone into an Iroquois camp. Concerning Hist, Hetty was not very communicative. She spoke of her kindness and gentleness and of the meeting in the forest, but the secret of Chingachgook was guarded with a shrewdness and fidelity that many a sharper-witted girl might have failed to display.

At length the several conferences were broken up by the reappearance of Hutter on the platform. Here he assembled the whole party and communicated as much of his intentions

as he deemed expedient. Of the arrangement made by Deer-slayer, to abandon the castle during the night and to take refuge in the ark, he entirely approved. It struck him, as it had the others, as the only effectual means of escaping destruction. Now that the savages had turned their attention to the construction of rafts, no doubt could exist of their at least making an attempt to carry the building, and the message of the bloody sticks sufficiently showed their confidence in their own success. In short, the old man viewed the night as critical, and he called on all to get ready as soon as possible, in order to abandon the dwelling, temporarily at least, if not forever.

These communications made, everything proceeded promptly and with intelligence: the castle was secured in the manner already described, the canoes were withdrawn from the dock and fastened to the ark by the side of the other; the few necessaries that had been left in the house were transferred to the cabin, the fire was extinguished, and all embarked.

The vicinity of the hills, with their drapery of pines, had the effect to render nights that were obscure darker than common on the lake. As usual, however, a belt of comparative light was stretched through the center of the sheet, while it was within the shadows of the mountains that the gloom rested most heavily on the water. The island or castle stood in this belt of comparative light, but still the night was so dark as to cover the departure of the ark. At the distance of an observer on the shore, her movements could not be seen at all, more particularly as a background of dark hillside filled up the perspective of every view that was taken diagonally or directly across the water. The prevalent wind on the lakes of that region is west, but owing to the avenues formed by the mountains, it is frequently impossible to tell the true direction of the currents, as they often vary within short distances and brief differences of time. This is truer in light, fluctuating puffs of air than in steady breezes, though the squalls of even the latter are familiarly known to be uncertain and baffling in all mountainous regions and narrow waters. On the present occasion, Hutter himself (as he shoved the ark from her berth at the side of the platform) was at a loss to pronounce which way the wind blew. In common, this

difficulty was solved by the clouds, which, floating high
above the hilltops, as a matter of course obeyed the currents, but now the whole vault of heaven seemed a mass
of gloomy wall. Not an opening of any sort was visible,
and Chingachgook was already trembling lest the nonappearance of the star might prevent his betrothed from being
punctual to her appointment. Under these circumstances, Hutter hoisted his sail, seemingly with the sole intention of
getting away from the castle, as it might be dangerous to
remain much longer in its vicinity. The air soon filled the
cloth, and when the scow was got under command, and the
sail was properly trimmed, it was found that the direction
was southerly, inclining toward the eastern shore. No better
course offering for the purposes of the party, the singular
craft was suffered to skim the surface of the water in this
direction for more than an hour, when a change in the
currents of the air drove them over toward the camp.

Deerslayer watched all the movements of Hutter and Harry
with jealous attention. At first he did not know whether to
ascribe the course they held to accident or to design, but
he now began to suspect the latter. Familiar as Hutter was
with the lake, it was easy to deceive one who had little
practice on the water, and let his intentions be what they
might, it was evident, ere two hours had elapsed, that the
ark had got over sufficient space to be within a hundred
rods of the shore, directly abreast of the known position
of the camp. For a considerable time previously to reaching this point, Hurry, who had some knowledge of the
Algonquin language, had been in close conference with the
Indian, and the result was now announced by the latter
to Deerslayer, who had been a cold, not to say distrusted
looker-on of all that passed.

"My old father and my young brother, the Big Pine"—
for so the Delaware had named March—"want to see Huron
scalps at their belts," said Chingachgook to his friend. "There
is room for some on the girdle of the Serpent, and his
people will look for them when he goes back to his village.
Their eyes must not be left long in a fog, but they must
see what they look for. I know that my brother has a white
hand; he will not strike even the dead. He will wait for us;
when we come back, he will not hide his face from shame

for his friend. The great Serpent of the Mohicans must be worthy to go on the warpath with Hawkeye."

"Aye, aye, Sarpent, I see how it is; that name's to stick, and in time, I shall get to be known by it instead of Deerslayer; well, if such honors will come, the humblest of us all must be willing to abide by 'em. As for your looking for scalps, it belongs to your gifts, and I see no harm in it. Be marciful, Sarpent, howsever; be marciful, I beseech of you. It surely can do no harm to a redskin's honor to show a little marcy. As for the old man, the father of two young women, who might ripen better feelin's in his heart, and Harry March here, who, pine as he is, might better bear the fruit of a more Christianized tree—as for *them* two, I leave them in the hands of the white man's God. Wasn't it for the bloody sticks, no man should go ag'in the Mingos this night, seein' that it would dishonor our faith and characters, but them that crave blood can't complain if blood is shed at their call. Still, Sarpent, you can be *marciful.* Don't begin your career with the wails of women and the cries of children. Bear yourself so that Hist will smile, not weep, when she meets you. Go, then, and the Manitou presarve you!"

"My brother will stay here with the scow. Wah will soon be standing on the shore waiting, and Chingachgook must hasten."

The Indian then joined his two co-adventurers, and first lowering the sail, they all three entered a canoe and left the side of the ark. Neither Hutter nor March spoke to Deerslayer concerning their object, or the probable length of their absence. All this had been confided to the Indian, who had acquitted himself of the trust with characteristic brevity. As soon as the canoe was out of sight, and that occurred ere the paddles had given a dozen strokes, Deerslayer made the best dispositions he could to keep the ark as nearly stationary as possible; then he sat down in the end of the scow, to chew the cud of his own bitter reflections. It was not long, however, before he was joined by Judith, who sought every occasion to be near him, managing her attack on his affections with the address that was suggested by native coquetry, aided by no little practice, but which received much of its most dangerous power from the touch of feeling that threw around her manner, voice, accents,

thoughts, and acts, the indescribable witchery of natural tenderness. Leaving the young hunter exposed to these dangerous assailants, it has become our more immediate business to follow the party in the canoe to the shore.

The controlling influence that led Hutter and Hurry to repeat their experiment against the camp was precisely that which had induced the first attempt, a little heightened, perhaps, by the desire of revenge. But neither of these two rude beings, so ruthless in all things that touched the rights and interests of the red man, though possessing veins of human feeling on other matters, was much actuated by any other desire than a heartless longing for profit. Hurry had felt angered at his sufferings when first liberated, it is true, but that emotion soon disappeared in the habitual love of gold, which he sought with the reckless avidity of a needy spendthrift, rather than with the ceaseless longings of a miser. In short, the motive that urged them both so soon to go against the Hurons was a habitual contempt of their enemy, acting on the unceasing cupidity of prodigality. The additional chances of success, however, had their place in the formation of the second enterprise. It was known that a large portion of the warriors—perhaps all—were encamped for the night abreast of the castle, and it was hoped that the scalps of helpless victims would be the consequence. To confess the truth, Hutter in particular—he who had just left two daughters behind him—expected to find few besides women and children in the camp. This fact had been but slightly alluded to in his communications with Hurry, and with Chingachgook it had been kept entirely out of view. If the Indian thought of it at all, it was known only to himself.

Hutter steered the canoe; Hurry had manfully taken his post in the bows; Chingachgook stood in the center. We say stood, for all three were so skilled in the management of that species of frail bark as to be able to keep erect positions in the midst of the darkness. The approach to the shore was made with great caution, and the landing effected in safety. The three now prepared their arms and began their tigerlike approach upon the camp. The Indian was on the lead, his two companions treading in his footsteps, with a stealthy cautiousness of manner that rendered their progress almost literally noiseless. Occasionally a dried

twig snapped under the heavy weight of the gigantic Hurry, or the blundering clumsiness of the old man, but had the Indian walked on air, his step could not have seemed lighter. The great object was first to discover the position of the fire, which was known to be the center of the whole encampment. At length the keen eye of Chingachgook caught a glimpse of this important guide. It was glimmering at a distance among the trunks of trees. There was no blaze, but merely a single smoldering brand, as suited the hour, the savages usually retiring and rising with the revolutions of the sun.

As soon as a view was obtained of this beacon, the progress of the adventurers became swifter and more certain. In a few minutes they got to the edge of the circle of little huts. Here they stopped to survey their ground and to concert their movements. The darkness was so deep as to render it difficult to distinguish anything but the glowing brand, the trunks of the nearest trees, and the endless canopy of leaves that veiled the clouded heaven. It was ascertained, however, that a hut was quite near, and Chingachgook attempted to reconnoiter its interior. The manner in which the Indian approached the place that was supposed to contain enemies resembled the wily advances of the cat on the bird. As he drew near, he stooped to his hands and knees, for the entrance was so low as to require this attitude even as a convenience. Before trusting his head inside, however, he listened long to catch the breathing of sleepers. No sound was audible, and this human Serpent thrust his head in at the door, or opening, as another serpent would have peered in on the nest. Nothing rewarded the hazardous experiment, for after feeling cautiously with a hand, the place was found to be empty.

The Delaware proceeded in the same guarded manner to one or two more of the huts, finding all in the same situation. He then returned to his companions and informed them that the Hurons had deserted their camp. A little further inquiry corroborated this fact, and it only remained to return to the canoe. The different manner in which the adventurers bore the disappointment is worthy of a passing remark. The chief, who had landed solely with the hope of acquiring renown, stood stationary, leaning against a tree, waiting the pleasure of his companions. He was mor-

tified, and a little surprised, it is true, but he bore all with dignity, falling back for support on the sweeter expectations that still lay in reserve for that evening. It was true, he could not now hope to meet his mistress with the proofs of his daring and skill on his person, but he might still hope to meet her, and the warrior who was zealous in the search might always hope to be honored. On the other hand, Hutter and Hurry, who had been chiefly instigated by the basest of all human motives, the thirst of gain, could scarce control their feelings. They went prowling among the huts, as if they expected to find some forgotten child or careless sleeper; and again and again did they vent their spite on the insensible huts, several of which were actually torn to pieces and scattered about the place. Nay, they even quarreled with each other, and fierce reproaches passed between them. It is possible some serious consequences might have occurred had not the Delaware interfered to remind them of the danger of being so unguarded and of the necessity of returning to the ark. This checked the dispute, and in a few minutes they were paddling sullenly back to the spot where they hoped to find that vessel.

It has been said that Judith took her place at the side of Deerslayer soon after the adventurers departed. For a short time the girl was silent, and the hunter was ignorant which of the sisters had approached him, but he soon recognized the rich, full-spirited voice of the elder, as her feelings escaped in words.

"This is a terrible life for women, Deerslayer!" she exclaimed. "Would to Heaven I could see an end of it!"

"The life is well enough, Judith," was the answer, "being pretty much as it is used or abused. What would you wish to see in its place?"

"I should be a thousand times happier to live nearer to civilized beings—where there are farms and churches, and houses built as it might be by Christian hands, and where my sleep at night would be sweet and tranquil! A dwelling near one of the forts would be far better than this dreary place where we live!"

"Nay, Judith, I can't agree too lightly in the truth of all this. If forts are good to keep off inimies, they sometimes hold inimies of their own. I don't think 'twould be for your good, or the good of Hetty, to live near one, and if

I *must* say what I think, I'm afeard you are a little too near as it is." Deerslayer went on in his own steady, earnest manner, for the darkness concealed the tints that colored the cheeks of the girl almost to the brightness of crimson, while her own great efforts suppressed the sounds of the breathing that nearly choked her. "As for farms, they have their uses, and there's them that like to pass their lives on 'em; but what comfort can a man look for in a clearin' that he can't find in double quantities in the forest? If air, and room, and light are a little craved, the windrows and the streams will furnish 'em, or here are the lakes for such as have bigger longings in that way; but where are you to find your shades, and laughing springs, and leaping brooks, and vinerable trees a thousand years old in a clearin'? You don't find *them*, but you find their disabled trunks, marking the 'arth like headstones in a graveyard. It seems to me that the people who live in such places must be always thinkin' of their own inds and of univarsal decay—and that, too, not of the decay that is brought about by time and natur', but the decay that follows waste and violence. Then, as to churches, they are good, I suppose, else wouldn't good men uphold 'em. But they are not altogether necessary. They call 'em the temples of the Lord, but, Judith, the whole 'arth is a temple of the Lord to such as have the right mind. Neither forts nor churches make people happier of themselves. Moreover, all is contradiction in the settlements, while all is concord in the woods. Forts and churches almost always go together, and yet they're downright contradictions, churches being for peace and forts for war. No, no—give me the strong places of the wilderness, which is the trees, and the churches, too, which are arbors raised by the hand of natur'."

"Woman is not made for scenes like these, Deerslayer; scenes of which we shall have no end as long as this war lasts."

"If you mean women of white color, I rather think you're not far from the truth, gal; but as for the females of the red men, such visitations are quite in character. Nothing would make Hist, now, the bargained wife of yonder Delaware, happier than to know that he is at this moment prowling around his nat'ral inimies, striving after a scalp."

"Surely, surely, Deerslayer, she cannot be a woman and

not feel concern when she thinks the man she loves is in danger!"

"She doesn't think of the danger, Judith, but of the honor; and when the heart is desperately set on such feelin's, why, there is little room to crowd in fear. Hist is a kind, gentle, laughing, pleasant creatur', but she loves honor as well as any Delaware gal I ever know'd. She's to meet the Sarpent an hour hence, on the p'int where Hetty landed, and no doubt she has her anxiety about it, like any other woman; but she'd be all the happier did she know that her lover was at this moment waylaying a Mingo for his scalp."

"If you really believe this, Deerslayer, no wonder you lay so much stress on gifts. Certain am I that no white girl could feel anything but misery while she believed her betrothed in danger of his life! Nor do I suppose even you, unmoved and calm as you ever seem to be, could be at peace if you believed *your* Hist in danger."

"That's a different matter—'tis altogether a different matter, Judith. Woman is too weak and gentle to be intended to run such risks, and man *must* feel for her. Yes, I rather think that's as much red natur' as it's white. But I have no Hist, nor am I like to have, for I hold it wrong to mix colors anyway except in friendship and sarvices."

"In that you are and feel as a white man should! As for Hurry Harry, I do think it would be all the same to him whether his wife were a squaw or a governor's daughter, provided she was a little comely and could help to keep his craving stomach full."

"You do March injustice, Judith; yes, you do. The poor fellow dotes on *you,* and when a man has ra'ally set his heart on such a creatur', it isn't a Mingo, or even a Delaware gal, that'll be likely to unsettle his mind. You may laugh at such men as Hurry and I, for we're rough and unteached in the way of books and other knowledge, but we've our good p'ints as well as our bad ones. An honest heart is not to be despised, gal, even though it be not varsed in all the niceties that please a female fancy."

"*You*, Deerslayer! And *do* you—*can* you, for an instant, suppose I place *you* by the side of Harry March? No, no. I am not so far gone in dullness as that. No one—man or woman—could think of naming your honest heart, manly nature, and simple truth with the boisterous selfishness,

greedy avarice, and overbearing ferocity of Henry March. The very best that can be said of him is to be found in his name of Hurry-scurry, which, if it means no great harm, means no great good. Even my father, following his feelings with the other, as he is doing at this moment, well knows the difference between you. This I *know*, for he has said as much to me in plain language."

Judith was a girl of quick sensibilities and of impetuous feelings, and being under few of the restraints that curtail the manifestations of maiden emotions among those who are educated in the habits of civilized life, she sometimes betrayed the latter with a freedom that was so purely natural as to place it as far above the wiles of coquetry as it was superior to its heartlessness. She had now even taken one of the hard hands of the hunter and pressed it between both her own with a warmth and earnestness that proved how sincere was her language. It was perhaps fortunate that she was checked by the very excess of her feelings, since the same power might have urged her on to avow *all* that her father had said—the old man not having been satisfied with making a comparison favorable to Deerslayer, as between the hunter and Hurry, but having actually, in his blunt, rough way, briefly advised his daughter to cast off the latter entirely and to think of the former as a husband. Judith would not willingly have said this to any other man, but there was so much confidence awakened by the guileless simplicity of Deerslayer that one of her nature found it a constant temptation to overstep the bounds of habit. She went no further, however, immediately relinquishing the hand and falling back on a reserve that was more suited to her sex and, indeed, to her natural modesty.

"Thankee, Judith, thankee with all my heart," returned the hunter, whose humility prevented him from placing any flattering interpretation on either the conduct or the language of the girl. "Thankee as much as if it was all true. Harry's sightly—yes, he's as sightly as the tallest pine of these mountains, and the Sarpent has named him accordingly; howsever, some fancy good looks, and some fancy good conduct, only. Hurry has one advantage, and it depends on himself whether he'll have t'other or—Heark! That's your father's voice, gal, and he speaks like a man who's riled at something."

"God save us from any more of these horrible scenes!"

exclaimed Judith, bending her face to her knees and endeavoring to exclude the discordant sounds by applying her hands to her ears. "I sometimes wish I had no father!"

This was bitterly said, and the repinings which extorted the words were bitterly felt. It is impossible to say what might next have escaped her had not a gentle, low voice spoken at her elbow.

"Judith, I ought to have read a chapter to Father and Hurry!" said the innocent but terrified speaker, "and *that* would have kept them from going again on such an errand. Do you call to them, Deerslayer, and tell them I want them, and that it will be good for them both if they'll return and hearken to my words."

"Ah's me! Poor Hetty, you little know the cravin's for gold and revenge if you believe they are so easily turned aside from their longin's! But this is an oncommon business in more ways than one, Judith! I hear your father and Hurry growling like bears, and yet no noise comes from the mouth of the young chief. There's an ind of secresy, and yet his whoop, which ought to ring in the mountains, accordin' to rule in such sarcumstances, is silent!"

"Justice may have alighted on him, and his death have saved the lives of the innocent."

"Not it—not it—the Sarpent is not the one to suffer if *that's* to be the law. Sartainly there has been no onset, and 'tis most likely that the camp's deserted and the men are coming back disapp'inted. That accounts for the growls of Hurry and the silence of the Sarpent."

Just at this instant a fall of a paddle was heard in the canoe, for vexation made March reckless. Deerslayer felt convinced that his conjecture was true. The sail being down, the ark had not drifted far, and ere many minutes he heard Chingachgook, in a low, quiet tone, directing Hutter how to steer in order to reach it. In less time than it takes to tell the fact, the canoe touched the scow, and the adventurers entered the latter. Neither Hutter nor Hurry spoke of what had occurred. But the Delaware, in passing his friend, merely uttered the words "fire's out," which, if not literally true, sufficiently explained the truth to his listener.

It was now a question as to the course to be steered. A short, surly conference was held, when Hutter decided that the wisest way would be to keep in motion as the

means most likely to defeat any attempt at a surprise—announcing his own and March's intention to requite themselves for the loss of sleep during their captivity by lying down. As the air still baffled and continued light, it was finally determined to sail before it, let it come in what direction it might, so long as it did not blow the ark upon the strand. This point settled, the released prisoners helped to hoist the sail, and then they threw themselves on two of the pallets, leaving Deerslayer and his friend to look after the movements of the craft. As neither of the latter was disposed to sleep, on account of the appointment with Hist, this arrangement was acceptable to all parties. That Judith and Hetty remained up also in no manner impaired the agreeable features of this change.

For some time the scow rather drifted than sailed along the western shore, following a light, southerly current of the air. The progress was slow—not exceeding a couple of miles in the hour—but the two men perceived that it was not only carrying them toward the point they desired to reach, but at a rate that was quite as fast as the hour yet rendered necessary. But little was said the while even by the girls, and that little had more reference to the rescue of Hist than to any other subject. The Indian was calm to the eye, but as minute after minute passed his feelings became more and more excited, until they reached a state that might have satisfied the demands of even the most exacting mistress. Deerslayer kept the craft as much in the bays as was prudent, for the double purpose of sailing within the shadows of the woods and of detecting any signs of an encampment they might pass on the shore. In this manner they doubled one low point, and were already in the bay that was terminated north by the goal at which they aimed. The latter was still a quarter of a mile distant when Chingachgook came silently to the side of his friend and pointed to a place directly ahead. A small fire was glimmering just within the verge of the bushes that lined the shore on the southern side of the point—leaving no doubt that the Indians had suddenly removed their camp to the very place, or at least the very projection of land, where Hist had given them the rendezvous!

CHAPTER XVI

I hear thee babbling to the vale
Of sunshine and of flowers,
But unto me thou bring'st a tale
Of visionary hours.

WORDSWORTH

THE DISCOVERY MENTIONED at the close of the preceding chapter was of great moment in the eyes of Deerslayer and his friend. In the first place, there was the danger, almost the certainty, that Hutter and Hurry would make a fresh attempt on this camp should they awake and ascertain its position. Then there was the increased risk of landing to bring off Hist; and there were the general uncertainty and additional hazards that must follow from the circumstance that their enemies had begun to change their positions. As the Delaware was aware that the hour was near when he ought to repair to the rendezvous, he no longer thought of trophies torn from his foes; one of the first things arranged between him and his associate was to permit the two others to sleep on, lest they should disturb the execution of their plans by substituting some of their own. The ark moved slowly, and it would have taken fully a quarter of an hour to reach the point, at the rate at which they were going, thus affording time for a little forethought. The Indians, in the wish to conceal their fire from those who were thought to be still in the castle, had placed it so near the southern side of the point as to render it extremely difficult to shut it in by the bushes, though Deerslayer varied the direction of the scow, both to the right and to the left, in the hope of being able to effect that object.

"There's one advantage, Judith, in finding that fire so near the water," he said, while executing these little maneuvers; "it shows the Mingos believe we are in the hut, and our coming on 'em from this quarter will be an onlooked-for event.

260

But 'tis lucky Harry March and your father are asleep, else we should have 'em prowling after scalps ag'in. Ha! There —the bushes are beginning to shut in the fire—and now it can't be seen at all!"

Deerslayer waited a little to make certain that he had at last gained the desired position; then he gave the signal agreed on, and Chingachgook let go the grapnel and lowered the sail.

The situation in which the ark now lay had its advantages and its disadvantages. The fire had been hid by sheering toward the shore, and the latter was nearer perhaps than was desirable. Still, the water was known to be very deep farther off in the lake, and anchoring in deep water, under the circumstances in which the party was placed, was to be avoided, if possible. It was also believed no raft could be within miles; and, though the trees in the darkness appeared almost to overhang the scow, it would not be easy to get off to her without using a boat. The intense darkness that prevailed so close in with the forest, too, served as an effectual screen, and so long as care was had not to make a noise, there was little or no danger of being detected. All these things Deerslayer pointed out to Judith, instructing her as to the course she was to follow in the event of an alarm, for it was thought to the last degree inexpedient to arouse the sleepers, unless it might be in the greatest emergency.

"And now, Judith, as we understand one another, it is time the Sarpent and I had taken to the canoe," the hunter concluded. "The star has not risen yet, it's true, but it soon must, though none of us are likely to be any the wiser for it, tonight, on account of the clouds. Howsever, Hist has a ready mind, and she's one of them that doesn't always need to have a thing afore her to see it. I'll warrant you she'll not be either two minutes or two feet out of the way, unless them jealous vagabonds, the Mingos, have taken the alarm and put her as a stool pigeon to catch us; or have hid her away in order to prepare her mind for a Huron instead of a Mohican husband."

"Deerslayer," interrupted the girl earnestly, "this is a most dangerous service; why do *you* go on it at all?"

"Anan! Why you know, gal, we go to bring off Hist, the Sarpent's betrothed—the maid he means to marry, as soon as we get back to the tribe."

"That is all right for the Indian—but *you* do not mean

to marry Hist—*you* are not betrothed, and why should *two* risk their lives and liberties to do that which one can just as well perform?"

"Ah!—now I understand you, Judith—yes, now I begin to take the idee. You think as Hist is the Sarpent's betrothed, as they call it, and not mine, it's altogether his affair; and as one man can paddle a canoe, he ought to be left to go after his gal alone! But you forget this is our ar'n'd here, on the lake, and it would not tell well to forget an ar'n'd just at the pinch. Then, if love does count for so much with some people, particularly with young women, fri'ndship counts for something, too, with other some. I dares to say the Delaware can paddle a canoe by himself and can bring off Hist by himself, and perhaps he would like that quite as well as to have me with him, but he couldn't sarcumvent sarcumventions, or stir up an ambushment, or fight with the savages, and get his sweetheart at the same time, as well by himself as if he had a fri'nd with him, to depend on, even if that fri'nd is no better than myself. No—no—Judith, you wouldn't desart one that counted on *you*, at such a moment, and you can't in reason expect me to do it."

"I fear—I believe you are right, Deerslayer, yet I wish you were not to go! Promise me one thing, at least, and that is not to trust yourself among the savages, or to do anything more than to save the girl. That will be enough for once, and with that you ought to be satisfied."

"Lord bless you, gal, one would think it was Hetty that's talking, not the quick-witted and wonderful Judith Hutter! But fright makes the wise silly and the strong weak. Yes, I've seen proofs of that time and ag'in! Well, it's kind and softhearted in you, Judith, to feel this consarn for a fellow creatur', and I shall always say that you are kind and of true feelin's, let them that invy your good looks tell as many idle stories of you as they may."

"Deerslayer!" hastily said the girl, interrupting him, though nearly choked by her emotions, "do you believe all you hear about a poor motherless girl? Is the foul tongue of Hurry Harry to blast my life?"

"Not it, Judith—not it. I've told Hurry it wasn't manful to backbite them he couldn't win by fair means, and that even an Indian is always tender, touching a young woman's good name."

"If I had a brother, he wouldn't dare to do it!" exclaimed Judith, her eyes flashing fire. "But finding me without any protector but an old man, whose ears are getting to be as dull as his feelings, he has his way as he pleases."

"Not exactly that, Judith; no, not exactly that, neither! *No* man, brother or stranger, would stand by and see as fair a gal as yourself hunted down without saying a word in her behalf. Hurry's in 'arnest in wanting to make you his wife, and the little he does let out ag'in you comes more from jealousy, like, than from anything else. Smile on him when he awakes, and squeeze his hand only half as hard as you squeezed mine a bit ago, and my life on it, the poor fellow will forget everything but your comeliness. Hot words don't always come from the heart, but oftener from the stomach than anywhere else. Try him, Judith, when he wakes, and see the vartue of a smile."

Deerslayer laughed, in his own manner, as he concluded, and then he intimated to the patient-looking, but really impatient Chingachgook his readiness to proceed. As the young man entered the canoe, the girl stood immovable as stone, lost in the musings that the language and manner of the other were likely to produce. The simplicity of the hunter had completely put her at fault, for in her narrow sphere Judith was an expert manager of the other sex, though in the present instance she was far more actuated by impulses, in all she had said and done, than by calculation. We shall not deny that some of Judith's reflections were bitter, though the sequel of the tale must be referred to, in order to explain how merited, or how keen were her sufferings.

Chingachgook and his paleface friend set forth on their hazardous and delicate enterprise with a coolness and method that would have done credit to men who were on their twentieth instead of being on their first warpath. As suited his relation to the pretty fugitive in whose service they were engaged, the Indian took his place in the head of the canoe, while Deerslayer guided its movements in the stern. By this arrangement, the former would be the first to land and, of course, the first to meet his mistress. The latter had taken his post without comment, but in secret influenced by the reflection that one who had so much at stake as the Indian might not possibly guide the canoe with the same steadiness and intelligence as another who had more com-

mand of his feelings. From the instant they left the side of the ark, the movements of the two adventurers were like the maneuvers of highly drilled soldiers who for the first time were called on to meet the enemy in the field. As yet, Chingachgook had never fired a shot in anger, and the debut of his companion in warfare is known to the reader. It is true, the Indian had been hanging about his enemy's camp for a few hours, on his first arrival, and he had even once entered it, as related in the last chapter, but no consequences had followed either experiment. Now, it was certain that an important result was to be effected, or a mortifying failure was to ensue. The rescue, or the continued captivity of Hist, depended on the enterprise. In a word, it was virtually the maiden expedition of these two ambitious young forest soldiers, and while one of them set forth, impelled by sentiments that usually carry men so far, both had all their feelings of pride and manhood enlisted in their success.

Instead of steering in a direct line to the point, then distant from the ark less than a quarter of a mile, Deerslayer laid the head of his canoe diagonally toward the center of the lake, with a view to obtain a position from which he might approach the shore, having his enemies in his front only. The spot where Hetty had landed and where Hist had promised to meet them, moreover, was on the upper side of the projection rather than on the lower, and to reach it would have required the adventurers to double nearly the whole point, close in with the shore, had not this preliminary step been taken. So well was the necessity for this measure understood that Chingachgook quietly paddled on, although it was adopted without consulting him and apparently was taking him in a direction nearly opposite to that one might think he most wished to go. A few minutes sufficed, however, to carry the canoe the necessary distance when both the young men ceased paddling, as it were by instinctive consent, and the boat became stationary.

The darkness increased rather than diminished, but it was still possible, from the place where the adventurers lay, to distinguish the outlines of the mountains. In vain did the Delaware turn his head eastward to catch a glimpse of the promised star, for notwithstanding that the clouds broke a little near the horizon in that quarter of the heavens, the curtain continued so far drawn as effectually to conceal all

behind it. In front, as was known by the formation of land above and behind it, lay the point, at a distance of about a thousand feet. No signs of the castle could be seen, nor could any movement in that quarter of the lake reach the ear. The latter circumstance might have been equally owing to the distance, which was several miles, or to the fact that nothing was in motion. As for the ark, though scarcely further from the canoe than the point, it lay so completely buried in the shadows of the shore that it would not have been visible even had there been many degrees more of light than actually existed.

The adventurers now held a conference in low voices, consulting together as to the probable time. Deerslayer thought it wanted yet some minutes to the rising of the star, while the impatience of the chief caused him to fancy the night further advanced and to believe that his betrothed was already waiting his appearance on the shore. As might have been expected, the opinion of the latter prevailed, and his friend disposed himself to steer for the place of rendezvous. The utmost skill and precaution now became necessary in the management of the canoe. The paddles were lifted and returned to the water in a noiseless manner, and when within a hundred yards of the beach, Chingachgook took in his altogether, laying his hand on his rifle in its stead. As they got still more within the belt of darkness that girded the woods, it was seen that they were steering too far north, and the course was altered accordingly. The canoe now seemed to move by instinct, so cautious and deliberate were all its motions. Still it continued to advance, until its bows grated on the gravel of the beach, at the precise spot where Hetty had landed, and whence her voice had issued, the previous night, as the ark was passing. There was, as usual, a narrow strand, but bushes fringed the woods and, in most places, overhung the water.

Chingachgook stepped upon the beach and cautiously examined it, for some distance, on each side of the canoe. In order to do this, he was often obliged to wade to his knees in the lake. No Hist rewarded his search. When he returned, he found his friend also on the shore. They next conferred in whispers, the Indian apprehending that they must have mistaken the place of rendezvous. Deerslayer thought it was probable they had mistaken the hour. While he was yet

speaking, he grasped the arm of the Delaware, caused him to turn his head in the direction of the lake, and pointed toward the summits of the eastern mountains. The clouds had broken a little, apparently behind rather than above the hills, and the selected star was glittering among the branches of a pine. This was every way a flattering omen, and the young men leaned on their rifles, listening intently for the sound of approaching footsteps. Voices they often heard, and mingled with them were the suppressed cries of children and the low but sweet laugh of Indian women. As the native Americans are habitually cautious and seldom break out in loud conversation, the adventurers knew by these facts that they must be very near the encampment. It was easy to perceive that there was a fire within the woods by the manner in which some of the upper branches of the trees were illuminated, but it was not possible, where they stood, to ascertain exactly how near it was to themselves. Once or twice it seemed as if stragglers from around the fire were approaching the place of rendezvous, but these sounds were either altogether illusion, or those who had drawn near returned again without coming to the shore. A quarter of an hour was passed in this state of intense expectation and anxiety, when Deerslayer proposed that they should circle the point in the canoe and, by getting a position close in where the camp could be seen, reconnoiter the Indians and thus enable themselves to form some plausible conjectures for the nonappearance of Hist. The Delaware, however, resolutely refused to quit the spot, plausibly enough offering as a reason the disappointment of the girl, should she arrive in his absence. Deerslayer felt for his friend's concern and offered to make the circuit of the point by himself, leaving the latter concealed in the bushes to await the occurrence of any fortunate event that might favor his views. With this understanding, then, the parties separated.

As soon as Deerslayer was at his post again, in the stern of the canoe, he left the shore with the same precautions and in the same noiseless manner as he had approached it. On this occasion he did not go far from the land, the bushes affording a sufficient cover, by keeping as close in as possible. Indeed, it would not have been easy to devise any means more favorable to reconnoitering around an Indian camp than those afforded by the actual state of things.

The formation of the point permitted the place to be circled on three of its sides, and the progress of the boat was so noiseless as to remove any apprehensions from an alarm through sound. The most practiced and guarded foot might stir a bunch of leaves or snap a dried stick in the dark, but a bark canoe could be made to float over the surface of smooth water almost with the instinctive readiness, and certainly with the noiseless movements, of an aquatic bird.

Deerslayer had got nearly in a line between the camp and the ark before he caught a glimpse of the fire. This came upon him suddenly and a little unexpectedly, at first causing an alarm, lest he had incautiously ventured within the circle of light it cast. But, perceiving at a second glance that he was certainly safe from detection so long as the Indians kept near the center of the illumination, he brought the canoe to a state of rest, in the most favorable position he could find, and commenced his observations.

We have written much, but in vain, concerning this extraordinary being, if the reader requires now to be told that, untutored as he was in the learning of the world, and simple as he ever showed himself to be in all matters touching the subtleties of conventional taste, he was a man of strong, native, poetical feeling. He loved the woods for their freshness, their sublime solitudes, their vastness, and the impress that they everywhere bore of the divine hand of their Creator. He rarely moved through them without pausing to dwell on some peculiar beauty that gave him pleasure, though seldom attempting to investigate the causes, and never did a day pass without his communing in spirit, and this, too, without the aid of forms or language, with the infinite source of all he saw, felt, and beheld. Thus constituted in a moral sense, and of a steadiness that no danger could appall or any crisis disturb, it is not surprising that the hunter felt a pleasure at looking on the scene he now beheld that momentarily caused him to forget the object of his visit. This will more fully appear when we describe it.

The canoe lay in front of a natural vista, not only through the bushes that lined the shore but of the trees also, that afforded a clear view of the camp. It was by means of this same opening that the light had been first seen from the ark. In consequence of their recent change of ground, the Indians had not yet retired to their huts, but had been de-

layed by their preparations, which included lodging as well as food. A large fire had been made, as much to answer the purpose of torches as for the use of their simple cookery, and at this precise moment it was blazing high and bright, having recently received a large supply of dried brush. The effect was to illuminate the arches of the forest and to render the whole area occupied by the camp as light as if hundreds of tapers were burning. Most of the toil had ceased, and even the hungriest child had satisfied its appetite. In a word, the time was that moment of relaxation and general indolence which is apt to succeed a hearty meal, and when the labors of the day have ended. The hunters and the fishermen had been equally successful, and food, that one great requisite of savage life, being abundant, every other care appeared to have subsided in the sense of enjoyment dependent on this all-important fact.

Deerslayer saw at a glance that many of the warriors were absent. His acquaintance, Rivenoak, however, was present, being seated in the foreground of a picture that Salvator Rosa would have delighted to draw, his swarthy features illuminated as much by pleasure as by the torchlike flame, while he showed another of the tribe one of the elephants that had caused so much sensation among his people. A boy was looking over his shoulder in dull curiosity, completing the group. More in the background, eight or ten warriors lay half recumbent on the ground, or sat with their backs inclining against trees, so many types of indolent repose. Their arms were near them, sometimes leaning against the same trees as themselves, or were lying across their bodies, in careless preparation. But the group that most attracted the attention of Deerslayer was that composed of the women and children. All the females appeared to be collected together, and almost as a matter of course, their young were near them. The former laughed and chatted in their rebuked and quiet manner, though one who knew the habits of the people might have detected that everything was not going on in its usual train. Most of the young women seemed to be lighthearted enough, but one old hag was seated apart, with a watchful, soured aspect, which the hunter at once knew betokened that some duty of an unpleasant character had been assigned her by the chiefs. What that duty was he had no means of knowing, but he felt satisfied it must

be in some measure connected with her own sex, the aged among the women generally being chosen for such offices and no other.

As a matter of course, Deerslayer looked eagerly and anxiously for the form of Hist. She was nowhere visible, though the light penetrated to considerable distances in all directions around the fire. Once or twice he started, as he thought he recognized her laugh, but his ears were deceived by the soft melody that is so common to the Indian female voice. At length the old woman spoke loud and angrily, and then he caught a glimpse of one or two dark figures, in the background of trees, which turned, as if obedient to the rebuke, and walked more within the circle of the light. A young warrior's form first came fairly into view, then followed two youthful females, one of whom proved to be the Delaware girl. Deerslayer now comprehended it all. Hist was watched, possibly by her young companion, certainly by the old woman. The youth was probably some suitor of either her or her companion, but even his discretion was distrusted under the influence of his admiration. The known vicinity of those who might be supposed to be her friends, and the arrival of a strange red man on the lake, had induced more than the usual care, and the girl had not been able to slip away from those who watched her, in order to keep her appointment. Deerslayer traced her uneasiness by her attempting, once or twice, to look up through the branches of the trees, as if endeavoring to get glimpses of the star she had herself named as the sign for meeting. All was vain, however, and after strolling about the camp a little longer, in affected indifference, the two girls quitted their male escort and took seats among their own sex. As soon as this was done, the old sentinel changed her place to one more agreeable to herself, a certain proof that she had hitherto been exclusively on watch.

Deerslayer now felt greatly at a loss how to proceed. He well knew that Chingachgook could never be persuaded to return to the ark without making some desperate effort for the recovery of his mistress, and his own generous feelings well disposed him to aid in such an undertaking. He thought he saw the signs of an intention among the females to retire for the night; and should he remain, and the fire continue to give out its light, he might discover the particular hut, or

arbor, under which Hist reposed, a circumstance that would
be of infinite use in their future proceedings. Should he remain, however, much longer where he was, there was
great danger that the impatience of his friend would drive
him into some act of imprudence. At each instant, indeed,
he expected to see the swarthy form of the Delaware appearing in the background, like the tiger prowling around the
fold. Taking all things into consideration, therefore, he came
to the conclusion it would be better to rejoin his friend and
endeavor to temper his impetuosity by some of his own coolness and discretion. It required but a minute or two to put
this plan in execution, the canoe returning to the strand
some ten or fifteen minutes after it had left it.

Contrary to his expectations, perhaps, Deerslayer found
the Indian at his post, from which he had not stirred, fearful
that his betrothed might arrive during his absence. A conference followed, in which Chingachgook was made acquainted with the state of things in the camp. When Hist
named the point as the place of meeting, it was with the expectation of making her escape from the old position and
of repairing to a spot that she expected to find without any
occupants, but the sudden change of localities had discon-
certed all her plans. A much greater degree of vigilance
than had been previously required was now necessary, and
the circumstance that an aged woman was on watch also
denoted some special grounds of alarm. All these considerations, and many more that will readily suggest themselves to
the reader, were briefly discussed before the young men
came to any decision. The occasion, however, being one that
required acts instead of words, the course to be pursued was
soon chosen.

Disposing of the canoe in such a manner that Hist must
see it, should she come to the place of meeting previously to
their return, the young men looked to their arms and prepared
to enter the wood. The whole projection into the lake contained about two acres of land, and the part that formed
the point, and on which the camp was placed, did not com-
pose a surface of more than half that size. It was principally
covered with oaks, which, as is usual in the American forests,
grew to a great height without throwing out a branch and
then arched in a dense and rich foliage. Beneath, except the
fringe of thick bushes along the shore, there was very little

underbrush, though, in consequence of their shape, the trees were closer together than is common in regions where the ax has been freely used, resembling tall, straight, rustic columns, upholding the usual canopy of leaves. The surface of the land was tolerably even, but it had a small rise near its center, which divided it into a northern and southern half. On the latter the Hurons had built their fire, profiting by the formation to conceal it from their enemies, who, it will be remembered, were supposed to be in the castle, which bore northerly. A brook also came brawling down the sides of the adjacent hills and found its way into the lake on the southern side of the point. It had cut for itself a deep passage through some of the higher portions of the ground, and, in later days, when the spot has become subjected to the uses of civilization, by its windings and shaded banks, it has become no mean accessory in contributing to the beauty of the place. This brook lay west of the encampment, and its waters found their way into the great reservoir of that region on the same side, quite near to the spot chosen for the fire. All these peculiarities, so far as circumstances allowed, had been noted by Deerslayer and explained to his friend.

The reader will understand that the little rise in the ground that lay behind the Indian encampment greatly favored the secret advance of the two adventurers. It prevented the light of the fire diffusing itself on the ground directly in the rear, although the land fell away toward the water, so as to leave what might be termed the left, or eastern flank of the position unprotected by this covering. We have said "unprotected," though that is not properly the word, since the knoll behind the huts and the fire offered a cover for those who were now stealthily approaching, rather than any protection to the Indians. Deerslayer did not break through the fringe of bushes immediately abreast of the canoe, which might have brought him too suddenly within the influence of the light, since the hillock did not extend to the water, but he followed the beach northerly until he had got nearly on the opposite side of the tongue of land, which brought him under the shelter of the low acclivity and, consequently, more in shadow.

As soon as the friends emerged from the bushes, they stopped to reconnoiter. The fire was still blazing behind the little ridge, casting its light upward into the tops of the trees,

producing an effect that was more pleasing than advanta-
geous. Still, the glare had its uses, for while the background
was in obscurity, the foreground was in strong light, exposing the savages and concealing their foes. Profiting by
the latter circumstance, the young men advanced cautiously
toward the ridge, Deerslayer in front, for he insisted on this
arrangement, lest the Delaware should be led by his feelings
into some indiscretion. It required but a moment to reach
the foot of the little ascent, and then commenced the most
critical part of the enterprise. Moving with exceeding caution, and trailing his rifle, both to keep its barrel out of view
and in readiness for service, the hunter put foot before foot,
until he had got sufficiently high to overlook the summit, his
own head being alone brought into the light. Chingachgook
was at his side, and both paused to take another close
examination of the camp. In order, however, to protect themselves against any straggler in the rear, they placed their
bodies against the trunk of an oak, standing on the side next
the fire.

The view that Deerslayer now obtained of the camp was
exactly the reverse of that he had perceived from the water.
The dim figures which he had formerly discovered must have
been on the summit of the ridge, a few feet in advance of
the spot where he was now posted. The fire was still blazing
brightly, and around it were seated on logs thirteen warriors,
which accounted for all whom he had seen from the canoe.
They were conversing with much earnestness among themselves, the image of the elephant passing from hand to hand.
The first burst of savage wonder had abated, and the question now under discussion was the probable existence, the history and habits of so extraordinary an animal. We have not
leisure to record the opinions of these rude men on a subject
so consonant to their lives and experience, but little is haz-
arded in saying that they were quite as plausible, and far
more ingenious, than half the conjectures that precede the
demonstrations of science. However much they may have
been at fault as to their conclusions and inferences, it is certain that they discussed the questions with a zealous and
most undivided attention. For the time being, all else was
forgotten, and our adventurers could not have approached
at a more fortunate instant.

The females were collected near each other, much as

Deerslayer had last seen them, nearly in a line between the place where he now stood and the fire. The distance from the oak against which the young men leaned and the warriors was about thirty yards; the women may have been half that number of yards nigher. The latter, indeed, were so near as to make the utmost circumspection as to motion and noise indispensable. Although they conversed in their low, soft voices, it was possible, in the profound stillness of the woods, even to catch passages of the discourse, and the lighthearted laugh that escaped the girls might occasionally have reached the canoe. Deerslayer felt the tremor that passed through the frame of his friend when the latter first caught the sweet sounds that issued from the plump, pretty lips of Hist. He even laid a hand on the shoulder of the Indian, as a sort of admonition to command himself. As the conversation grew more earnest, each leaned forward to listen.

"The Hurons have more curious beasts than that," said one of the girls contemptuously, for, like the men, they conversed of the elephant and his qualities. "The Delawares will think this creature wonderful, but tomorrow no Huron tongue will talk of it. Our young men will find him if the animal dares to come near our wigwams!"

This was in fact addressed to Wah-ta!-Wah, though she who spoke uttered her words with an assumed diffidence and humility that prevented her looking at the other.

"The Delawares are so far from letting such creatures come into their country," returned Hist, "that no one has even seen their images there! Their young men would frighten away the *images* as well as the *beasts*."

"The Delaware young men!—the nation is women—even the deer walk when they hear their hunters coming! Who has ever heard the name of a young Delaware warrior?"

This was said in good humor and with a laugh, but it was also said bitingly. That Hist so felt it was apparent by the spirit betrayed in her answer.

"Who has ever heard the name of a young Delaware!" she repeated earnestly. "Tamenund, himself, though now as old as the pines on the hill, or as the eagles in the air, was once young; his name was heard from the great salt lake to the sweet waters of the west. What is the family of Uncas? Where is another as great, though the palefaces have plowed

up its graves and trodden on its bones? Do the eagles fly as high, is the deer as swift, or the panther as brave? Is there no young warrior of that race? Let the Huron maidens open their eyes wider, and they may see one called Chingachgook, who is as stately as a young ash and as tough as the hickory."

As the girl used her figurative language and told her companions to "open their eyes and they would see" the Delaware, Deerslayer thrust his fingers into the sides of his friend and indulged in a fit of his hearty, benevolent laughter. The other smiled, but the language of the speaker was too flattering and the tones of her voice too sweet for him to be led away by any accidental coincidence, however ludicrous. The speech of Hist produced a retort, and the dispute, though conducted in good humor and without any of the coarse violence of tone and gesture that often impairs the charms of the sex in what is called civilized life, grew warm and slightly clamorous. In the midst of this scene the Delaware caused his friend to stoop so as completely to conceal himself, and then he made a noise so closely resembling the little chirrup of the smallest species of the American squirrel that Deerslayer himself, though he had heard the imitation a hundred times, actually thought it came from one of the little animals skipping about over his head. The sound is so familiar in the woods that none of the Hurons paid it the least attention. Hist, however, instantly ceased talking and sat motionless. Still, she had sufficient self-command to abstain from turning her head. She had heard the signal by which her lover so often called her from the wigwam to the stolen interview, and it came over her senses and her heart, as the serenade affects the maiden in the land of song.

From that moment Chingachgook felt certain that his presence was known. This was effecting much, and he could now hope for a bolder line of conduct on the part of his mistress than she might dare to adopt under an uncertainty of his situation. It left no doubt of her endeavoring to aid him in his effort to release her. Deerslayer arose as soon as the signal was given, and though he had never held that sweet communion which is known only to lovers, he was not slow to detect the great change that had come over the manner of the girl. She still affected to dispute, though it was no longer with spirit and ingenuity, but what she said was uttered more as a lure to draw her antagonists on to an easy

conquest than with any hopes of succeeding herself. Once or twice, it is true, her native readiness suggested a retort or an argument that raised a laugh and gave her a momentary advantage, but these little sallies, the offspring of mother wit, served the better to conceal her real feelings and to give to the triumph of the other party a more natural air than it might have possessed without them. At length the disputants became wearied, and they rose in a body as if about to separate. It was now that Hist, for the first time, ventured to turn her face in the direction whence the signal had come. In doing this, her movements were natural but guarded, and she stretched her arm and yawned, as if overcome with a desire to sleep. The chirrup was again heard, and the girl felt satisfied as to the position of her lover, though the strong light in which she herself was placed, and the comparative darkness in which the adventurers stood, prevented her from seeing their heads, the only portions of their forms that appeared above the ridge at all. The tree against which they were posted had a dark shadow cast upon it by the intervention of an enormous pine that grew between it and the fire, a circumstance which alone would have rendered objects within its cloud invisible at any distance. This Deerslayer well knew, and it was one of the reasons why he had selected this particular tree.

The moment was near when it became necessary for Hist to act. She was to sleep in a small hut, or bower, that had been built near the spot where she stood, and her companion was the aged hag already mentioned. Once within the hut, with this sleepless old woman stretched across the entrance, as was her nightly practice, the hope of escape was nearly destroyed—and she might, at any moment, be summoned to her bed. Luckily, at this instant, one of the warriors called to the old woman by name and bade her bring him water to drink. There was a delicious spring on the northern side of the point; the hag took a gourd from a branch and, summoning Hist to her side, moved toward the summit of the ridge, intending to descend and cross the point to the natural fountain. All this was seen and understood by the adventurers, and they fell back into the obscurity, concealing their persons by trees, until the two females had passed them. In walking, Hist was held tightly by the hand. As she moved by the tree that hid Chingachgook and his friend, the former

felt for his tomahawk, with the intention to bury it in the brain of the woman. But the other saw the hazard of such a measure, since a single scream might bring all the warriors upon them, and he was averse to the act on considerations of humanity. His hand, therefore, prevented the blow. Still, as the two moved past, the chirrup was repeated, and the Huron woman stopped and faced the tree whence the sounds seemed to proceed, standing, at the moment, within six feet of her enemies. She expressed her surprise that a squirrel should be in motion at so late an hour and said it boded evil. Hist answered that she had heard the same squirrel three times within the last twenty minutes, and that she supposed it was waiting to obtain some of the crumbs left from the late supper. This explanation appeared satisfactory, and they moved toward the spring, the men following stealthily and closely. The gourd was filled, and the old woman was hurrying back, her hand still grasping the wrist of the girl, when she was suddenly seized so violently by the throat as to cause her to release her captive and to prevent her making any sound other than a sort of gurgling, suffocating noise. The Serpent passed his arm around the waist of his mistress and dashed through the bushes with her, on the north side of the point. Here he immediately turned along the beach and ran toward the canoe. A more direct course could have been taken, but it might have led to a discovery of the place of embarking.

Deerslayer kept playing on the throat of the old woman, like the keys of an organ, occasionally allowing her to breathe, and then compressing his fingers again nearly to strangling. The brief intervals for breath, however, were well improved, and the hag succeeded in letting out a screech or two that served to alarm the camp. The tramp of the warriors as they sprang from the fire was plainly audible, and at the next moment three or four of them appeared on the top of the ridge, drawn against the background of light, resembling the dim shadows of the phantasmagoria. It was now quite time for the hunter to retreat. Tripping up the heels of his captive, and giving her throat a parting squeeze, quite as much in resentment at her indomitable efforts to sound the alarm as from any policy, he left her on her back and moved toward the bushes, his rifle at a poise, and his head over his shoulders, like a lion at bay.

CHAPTER XVII

> *There, ye wise saints, behold your light, your star,*
> *Ye would be dupes and victims, and ye are,*
> *Is it enough? or, must I, while a thrill*
> *Lives in your sapient bosoms, cheat you still?*
>
> MOORE

THE FIRE, THE CANOE, and the spring near which Deerslayer commenced his retreat would have stood in the angles of a triangle of tolerably equal sides. The distance from the fire to the boat was a little less than the distance from the fire to the spring, while the distance from the spring to the boat was about equal to that between the two points first named. This, however, was in straight lines—a means of escape to which the fugitives could not resort. They were obliged to have recourse to a detour in order to get the cover of the bushes, and to follow the curvature of the beach. Under these disadvantages, then, the hunter commenced his retreat—disadvantages that he felt to be so much the greater from his knowledge of the habits of all Indians, who rarely fail in cases of sudden alarm, more especially when in the midst of cover, immediately to throw out flankers with a view to meet their foes at all points and, if possible, to turn their rear. That some such course was now adopted, he believed from the tramp of feet, which not only came up the ascent, as related, but were also heard, under the faint impulse, diverging not only toward the hill in the rear, but toward the extremity of the point, in a direction opposite to that he was about to take himself. Promptitude consequently became a matter of the last importance, as the parties might meet on the strand before the fugitive could reach the canoe.

Notwithstanding the pressing nature of the emergency, Deerslayer hesitated a single instant ere he plunged into the

bushes that lined the shore. His feelings had been awakened by the whole scene, and a sternness of purpose had come over him to which he was ordinarily a stranger. Four dark figures loomed on the ridge, drawn against the brightness of the fire, and an enemy might have been sacrificed at a glance. The Indians had paused to gaze into the gloom in search of the screeching hag, and with many a man less given to reflection than the hunter, the death of one of them would have been certain. Luckily, he was more prudent. Although the rifle dropped a little toward the foremost of his pursuers, he did not aim or fire, but disappeared in the cover. To gain the beach, and to follow it around to the place where Chingachgook was already in the canoe with Hist, anxiously waiting his appearance, occupied but a moment. Laying his rifle in the bottom of the canoe, Deerslayer stooped to give the latter a vigorous shove from the shore, when a powerful Indian leaped through the bushes, alighting like a panther on his back. Everything was now suspended by a hair, a false step ruining all. With a generosity that would have rendered a Roman illustrious throughout all time—but which, in the career of one so simple and humble, would have been forever lost to the world, but for this unpretending legend—Deerslayer threw all his force into a desperate effort, shoved the canoe off with a power that sent it a hundred feet from the shore as it might be in an instant, and fell forward into the lake himself, face downward, his assailant necessarily following him.

Although the water was deep within a few yards of the beach, it was not more than breast high as close in as the spot where the two combatants fell. Still, this was quite sufficient to destroy one who had sunk under the great disadvantages in which Deerslayer was placed. His hands were free, however, and the savage was compelled to relinquish his hug to keep his own face above the surface. For half a minute there was a desperate struggle, like the floundering of an alligator that has just seized some powerful prey, and then both stood erect, grasping each other's arms, in order to prevent the use of the deadly knife in the darkness. What might have been the issue of this severe personal struggle cannot be known, for half a dozen savages came leaping into the water to the aid of their friend, and Deerslayer

yielded himself a prisoner with a dignity that was as remarkable as his self-devotion.

To quit the lake and lead their new captive to the fire occupied the Indians but another minute. So much engaged were they all with the struggle and its consequences that the canoe was unseen, though it still lay so near the shore as to render every syllable that was uttered perfectly intelligible to the Delaware and his betrothed; the whole party left the spot, some continuing the pursuit after Hist, along the beach, though most proceeded to the light. Here Deerslayer's antagonist so far recovered his breath and his recollection, for he had been throttled nearly to strangulation, as to relate the manner in which the girl had got off. It was now too late to assail the other fugitives, for no sooner was his friend led into the bushes than the Delaware placed his paddle into the water, and the light canoe glided noiselessly away, holding its course toward the center of the lake, until safe from shot, after which it sought the ark.

When Deerslayer reached the fire, he found himself surrounded by no less than eight grim savages, among whom was his old acquaintance Rivenoak. As soon as the latter caught a glimpse of the captive's countenance, he spoke apart to his companions, and a low but general exclamation of pleasure and surprise escaped them. They knew that the conqueror of their late friend, he who had fallen on the opposite side of the lake, was in their hands, and subject to their mercy or vengeance. There was no little admiration mingled in the ferocious looks that were thrown on the prisoner, an admiration that was as much excited by his present composure as by his past deeds. This scene may be said to have been the commencement of the great and terrible reputation that Deerslayer, or Hawkeye, as he was afterward called, enjoyed among all the tribes of New York and Canada; a reputation that was certainly more limited in its territorial and numerical extent than those which are possessed in civilized life, but which was compensated for what it wanted in these particulars, perhaps, by its greater justice and the total absence of mystification and management.

The arms of Deerslayer were not pinioned, and he was left the free use of his hands, his knife having been first removed. The only precaution that was taken to secure his person was untiring watchfulness, and a strong rope of bark

that passed from ankle to ankle, not so much to prevent his walking as to place an obstacle in the way of his attempting to escape by any sudden leap. Even this extra provision against flight was not made until the captive had been brought to the light and his character ascertained. It was, in fact, a compliment to his prowess, and he felt proud of the distinction. That he might be bound when the warriors slept he thought probable, but to be bound in the moment of capture showed that he was already, and thus early, attaining a name. While the young Indians were fastening the rope, he wondered if Chingachgook would have been treated in the same manner, had he too fallen into the hands of the enemy. Nor did the reputation of the young paleface rest altogether on his success in the previous combat, or in his discriminating and cool manner of managing the late negotiation, for it had received a great accession by the occurrences of the night. Ignorant of the movements of the ark, and of the accident that had brought their fire into view, the Iroquois attributed the discovery of their new camp to the vigilance of so shrewd a foe. The manner in which he ventured upon the point, the abstraction or escape of Hist, and most of all the self-devotion of the prisoner, united to the readiness with which he had sent the canoe adrift, were so many important links in the chain of facts on which his growing fame was founded. Many of these circumstances had been seen, some had been explained, and all were understood.

While this admiration and these honors were so unreservedly bestowed on Deerslayer, he did not escape some of the penalties of his situation. He was permitted to seat himself on the end of a log, near the fire, in order to dry his clothes, his late adversary standing opposite, now holding articles of his own scanty vestments to the heat, and now feeling his throat, on which the marks of his enemy's fingers were still quite visible. The rest of the warriors consulted together, near at hand, all those who had been out having returned to report that no signs of any other prowlers near the camp were to be found. In this state of things, the old woman, whose name was Shebear, in plain English, approached Deerslayer with her fists clenched and her eyes flashing fire. Hitherto she had been occupied with screaming, an employment at which she had played her part with no small degree of success, but having succeeded in effectually

alarming all within reach of a pair of lungs that had been strengthened by long practice, she next turned her attention to the injuries her own person had sustained in the struggle. These were in no manner material, though they were of a nature to arouse all the fury of a woman who had long ceased to attract by means of the gentler qualities, and who was much disposed to revenge the hardships she had so long endured as the neglected wife and mother of savages on all who came within her power. If Deerslayer had not permanently injured her, he had temporarily caused her to suffer, and she was not a person to overlook a wrong of this nature on account of its motive.

"Skunk of the palefaces," commenced this exasperated and semipoetic fury, shaking her fist under the nose of the impassable hunter, "you are not even a woman. Your friends, the Delawares, are only women, and you are their sheep. Your own people will not own you, and no tribe of red *men* would have you in their wigwams; you skulk among petticoated warriors. *You* slay our brave friend who has left us?—no—his great soul scorned to fight you and left his body rather than have the shame of slaying *you!* But the blood that you spilled when the spirit was not looking on has not sunk into the ground. It must be buried in your groans—what music do I hear? Those are not the wailings of a red man!—no red warrior groans so much like a hog. They come from a paleface throat—a Yengeese bosom—and sound as pleasant as girls singing. Dog—skunk—woodchuck —mink—hedgehog—pig—toad—spider—Yengee—"

Here the old woman, having expended her breath and exhausted her epithets, was fain to pause a moment, though both her fists were shaken in the prisoner's face and the whole of her wrinkled countenance was filled with fierce resentment. Deerslayer looked upon these impotent attempts to arouse him as indifferently as a gentleman in our own state of society regards the vituperative terms of a blackguard: the one party feeling that the tongue of an old woman could never injure a warrior, and the other knowing that mendacity and vulgarity can only permanently affect those who resort to their use; but he was spared any further attack at present by the interposition of Rivenoak, who shoved aside the hag, bidding her quit the spot, and prepared to take his seat at the side of his prisoner. The old woman

withdrew, but the hunter well understood that he was to be the subject of all her means of annoyance, if not of positive injury, so long as he remained in the power of his enemies, for nothing rankles so deeply as the consciousness that an attempt to irritate has been met by contempt, a feeling that is usually the most passive of any that is harbored in the human breast. Rivenoak quietly took the seat we have mentioned, and, after a short pause, he commenced a dialogue, which we translate, as usual, for the benefit of those readers who have not studied the North American languages.

"My paleface friend is very welcome," said the Indian, with a familiar nod and a smile so covert it required all Deerslayer's vigilance to detect, and not a little of his philosophy to detect unmoved; "he is welcome. The Hurons keep a hot fire to dry the white man's clothes."

"I thank you, Huron, or Mingo, as I most like to call you," returned the other; "I thank you for the welcome, and I thank you for the fire. Each is good in its way, and the last is very good, when one has been in a spring as cold as the Glimmerglass. Even Huron warmth may be pleasant, at such a time, to a man with a Delaware heart."

"The paleface—but my brother has a name? So great a warrior would not have lived without a name?"

"Mingo," said the hunter, a little of the weakness of human nature exhibiting itself in the glance of his eye and the color on his cheek, "Mingo, *your* brave called me Hawkeye, I suppose on account of a quick and sartain aim, when he was lying with his head in my lap, afore his spirit started for the happy hunting grounds."

" 'Tis a good name! The hawk is sure of his blow. Hawkeye is not a woman; why does he live with the Delawares?"

"I understand you, Mingo, but we look on all that as a sarcumvention of some of your subtle devils, and deny the charge. Providence placed me among the Delawares young; and, 'bating what Christian usages demand of my color and gifts, I hope to live and die in their tribe. Still, I do not mean to throw away altogether my natyve rights, and shall strive to do a paleface's duty in redskin society."

"Good; a Huron is a redskin, as well as a Delaware. Hawkeye is more of a Huron than of a woman."

"I suppose you know, Mingo, your own meaning; if you don't, I make no question, 'tis well known to Satan. But if

you wish to get anything out of me, speak plainer, for bargains cannot be made blindfolded or tongue-tied."

"Good; Hawkeye has not a forked tongue, and he likes to say what he thinks. He is an acquaintance of the Muskrat"—this was a name by which all the Indians designated Hutter—"and he has lived in his wigwam; but he is not a friend. He wants no scalps, like a miserable Indian, but fights like a stouthearted paleface. The Muskrat is neither white nor red; neither a beast nor a fish. He is a water snake; sometimes in the spring and sometimes on the land. He looks for scalps like an outcast. Hawkeye can go back and tell him how he has outwitted the Hurons, how he has escaped, and when his eyes are in a fog, when he can't see as far as from his cabin to the woods, then Hawkeye can open the door for the Hurons. And how will the plunder be divided? Why, Hawkeye will carry away the most, and the Hurons will take what he may choose to leave behind him. The scalps can go to Canada, for a paleface has no satisfaction in *them*."

"Well, well, Rivenoak—for so I hear 'em tarm you—this is plain English enough, though spoken in Iroquois. I understand all you mean, now, and must say it outdevils even Mingo deviltry! No doubt, 'twould be easy enough to go back and tell the Muskrat that I had got away from you, and gain some credit, too, by the expl'ite."

"Good; that is what I want the paleface to do."

"Yes—yes—that's plain enough. I know what you want me to do, without more words. When inside the house, and eating the Muskrat's bread, and laughing and talking with his pretty darters, I might put his eyes into so thick a fog that he couldn't even see the door, much less the land."

"Good! Hawkeye should have been born a Huron! His blood is not more than half white!"

"There you're out, Huron; yes, there you're as much out as if you mistook a wolf for a catamount. I'm white in blood, heart, natur', and gifts, though a little redskin in feelin's and habits. But when old Hutter's eyes are well befogged, and his pretty darters, perhaps, in a deep sleep, and Hurry Harry, the Great Pine, as you Indians tarm him, is dreaming of anything but mischief, and all suppose Hawkeye is acting as a faithful sentinel, all I have to do is to set a torch somewhere in sight for a signal, open the door, and let in the Hurons to knock 'em all on the head."

"Surely my brother is mistaken; he *cannot* be white! He is worthy to be a great chief among the Hurons!"

"That is true enough, I dares to say, if he could do all this. Now, hearkee, Huron, and for once hear a few honest words from the mouth of a plain man. I am a Christian born, and them that come of such a stock and that listen to the words that were spoken to their fathers, and will be spoken to their children, until 'arth and all it holds perishes, can never lend themselves to such wickedness. Sarcumventions in war may be, and *are*, lawful, but sarcumventions, and deceit, and treachery among fri'nds are fit only for the paleface devils. I know that there are white men enough to give you this wrong idea of our natur', but such are ontrue to their blood and gifts, and ought to be, if they are not, outcasts and vagabonds. No upright paleface could do what you wish, and to be as plain with you as I wish to be, in my judgment no upright Delaware either; with a Mingo it may be different."

The Huron listened to his rebuke with obvious disgust; but he had his ends in view, and was too wily to lose all chance of effecting them by a precipitate avowal of resentment. Affecting to smile, he seemed to listen eagerly, and he then pondered on what he had heard.

"Does Hawkeye love the Muskrat?" he abruptly demanded; "or does he love his daughters?"

"Neither, Mingo. Old Tom is not a man to gain my love; as for the darters, they are comely enough to gain the liking of any young man; but there's reason ag'in any very great love for either. Hetty is a good soul, but natur' has laid a heavy hand on her mind, poor thing!"

"And the Wild Rose!" exclaimed the Huron—for the fame of Judith's beauty had spread among those who could travel the wilderness as well as the highway, by means of old eagles' nests, rocks, and riven trees, known to them by report and tradition, as well as among the white borderers—"Is she not sweet enough to be put in the bosom of my brother?"

Deerslayer had far too much of the innate gentleman to insinuate aught against the fair fame of one who, by nature and position, was so helpless; and as he did not choose to utter an untruth, he preferred being silent. The Huron mistook the motive and supposed that disappointed affection lay at the bottom of his reserve. Still bent on cor-

upting or bribing his captive in order to obtain possession of the treasures with which his imagination filled the castle, he persevered in his attack.

"Hawkeye is talking with a friend," he continued. "He knows that Rivenoak is a man of his word, for they have traded together, and trade opens the soul. My friend has come here on account of a little string, held by a girl, that can pull the whole body of the stoutest warrior?"

"You are nearer the truth now, Huron, than you've been afore, since we began to talk. This is true. But one end of that string was not fast to my heart, nor did the Wild Rose hold the other."

"This is wonderful! Does my brother love in his head and not in his heart? And can the Feeble Mind pull so hard against so stout a warrior?"

"There it is ag'in; sometimes right and sometimes wrong! The string you mean is fast to the heart of a great Delaware —one of the Mohican stock in fact, living among the Delawares since the dispersion of his own people, and of the family of Uncas—Chingachgook by name, or Great Sarpent. He has come here, led by the string, and I've followed, or rather come afore, for I got here first pulled by nothing stronger than fri'ndship, which is strong enough for such as are not niggardly of their feelin's and are willing to live a little for their fellow creatur's, as well as for themselves."

"But a string has two ends—one is fast to the mind of a Mohican, and the other——?"

"Why, the other was here close to the fire, half an hour since. Wah-ta!-Wah held it in her hand, if she didn't hold it to her heart."

"I understand what you mean, my brother," returned the Indian gravely, for the first time catching a direct clue to the adventures of the evening. "The Great Serpent being strongest, pulled the hardest, and Hist was forced to leave us."

"I don't think there was much pulling about it," answered the other, laughing, always in his silent manner, with as much heartiness as if he were not a captive and in danger of torture or death. "I don't think there was much pulling about it; no, I don't. Lord help you, Huron, he likes the gal, and the gal likes him, and it surpassed Huron sarcumven-

tions to keep two young people apart, when there was so strong a feelin' to bring 'em together."

"And Hawkeye and Chingachgook came into our camp on this errand only?"

"That's a question that'll answer itself, Mingo! Yes, if a question could talk, it would answer itself to your perfect satisfaction. For what else should we come? And yet, it isn't exactly so, neither, for we didn't come into your camp at all, but only as far as that pine, there, that you see on the other side of the ridge, where we stood watching your movements and conduct as long as we liked. When we were ready, the Sarpent gave his signal, and then all went just as it should, down to the moment when yonder vagabond leaped upon my back. Sartain; we came for that, and for no other purpose, and we got what we came for; there's no use in pretending otherwise. Hist is off with a man who's the next thing to her husband, and come what will to me, *that's* one good thing determined."

"What sign or signal told the young maiden that her lover was nigh?" asked the old Huron, with more curiosity than it was usual for him to betray.

Deerslayer laughed again and seemed to enjoy the success of the exploit with as much glee as if he had not been its victim.

"Your squirrels are great gadabouts, Mingo!" he cried, still laughing; "yes, they're sartainly great gadabouts! When other folks' squirrels are at home and asleep, yourn keep in motion among the trees and chirrup and sing in a way that even a Delaware gal can understand their music! Well, there's four-legged squirrels, and there's two-legged squirrels, and give me the last when there's a good tight string atween two hearts. If one brings 'em together, t'other tells when to pull hardest."

The Huron looked vexed, though he succeeded in suppressing any violent exhibition of resentment. He soon quitted his prisoner and, joining the rest of his warriors, communicated the substance of what he had learned. As in his own case admiration was mingled with anger at the boldness and success of their enemies. Three or four of them ascended the little acclivity and gazed at the tree where it was understood the adventurers had posted themselves, and one even descended and examined for footprints around its

roots, in order to make sure that the statement was true. The result confirmed the story of the captive, and they all returned to the fire with increased wonder and respect. The messenger, who had arrived with some communication from the party above while the two adventurers were watching the camp, was now dispatched with some answer, and doubtless bore with him the intelligence of all that had happened.

Down to this moment, the young Indian who had been seen walking in company with Hist and another female had made no advances to any communication with Deerslayer. He had held himself aloof from his friends even, passing near the bevy of younger women who were clustering together, apart as usual, and conversed in low tones on the subject of the escape of their late companion. Perhaps it would be true to say that these last were pleased as well as vexed at what had just occurred. Their female sympathies were with the lovers, while their pride was bound up in the success of their own tribe. It is possible, too, that the superior personal advantages of Hist rendered her dangerous to some of the younger part of the group, and they were not sorry to find she was no longer in the way of their own ascendency. On the whole, however, the better feeling was most prevalent, for neither the wild condition in which they lived, the clannish prejudices of tribes, nor their hard fortunes as Indian women could entirely conquer the inextinguishable leaning of their sex to the affections. One of the girls even laughed at the disconsolate look of the swain who might fancy himself deserted, a circumstance that seemed suddenly to arouse his energies and induced him to move toward the log on which the prisoner was still seated, drying his clothes.

"This is Catamount!" said the Indian, striking his hand boastfully on his naked breast as he uttered the words, in a manner to show how much weight he expected them to carry.

"This is Hawkeye," quietly returned Deerslayer, adopting the name by which he knew he would be known in future among all the tribes of the Iroquois. "My sight is keen: is my brother's leap long?"

"From here to the Delaware villages. Hawkeye has stolen my wife: he must bring her back, or his scalp will hang on a pole and dry in my wigwam."

"Hawkeye has stolen nothing, Huron. He doesn't come of a thieving breed, nor has he thieving gifts. Your wife, as

you call Wah-ta!-Wah, will never be the wife of any redskin of the Canadas; her mind is in the cabin of a Delaware, and her body has gone to find it. The catamount is actyve, I know, but its legs can't keep pace with a woman's wishes."

"The Serpent of the Delawares is a dog; he is a poor bull-pout that keeps in the water; he is afraid to stand on the hard earth like a brave Indian!"

"Well, well, Huron, that's pretty impudent, considering it's not an hour since the Sarpent stood within a hundred feet of you, and would have tried the toughness of your skin with a rifle bullet, when I pointed you out to him, hadn't I laid the weight of a little judgment on his hand. You may take in timersome gals in the settlements with your cata-mount whine, but the ears of a man can tell truth from on-truth."

"Hist laughs at him! She sees he is lame, and a poor hunter, and he has never been on a warpath. She will take a man for a husband, not a fool."

"How do you know that, Catamount? How do you know that?" returned Deerslayer, laughing. "She has gone into the lake, you see, and maybe she prefers a trout to a mongrel cat. As for warpaths, neither the Sarpent nor I have much exper'ence, we are ready to own, but if you don't call this one, you must tarm it what the gals in the settlements tarm it, the high road to matrimony. Take my advice, Catamount, and s'arch for a wife among the Huron women; you'll never get one with a willing mind from among the Delawares."

Catamount's hand felt for his tomahawk, and when the fingers reached the handle, they worked convulsively, as if their owner hesitated between policy and resentment. At this critical moment Rivenoak approached and, by a gesture of authority, induced the young man to retire, assuming his former position himself on the log, at the side of Deerslayer. Here he continued silent for a little time, maintaining the grave reserve of an Indian chief.

"Hawkeye is right," the Iroquois at length began; "his sight is so strong that he can see truth in a dark night, and our eyes have been blinded. He is an owl, darkness hiding nothing from him. He ought not to strike his friends. He is right."

"I'm glad you think so, Mingo," returned the other, "for a traitor, in my judgment, is worse than a coward. I care

as little for the Muskrat as one paleface ought to care for
another, but I care too much for him to ambush him in the
way you wished. In short, according to my ideas, any
sarcumvention, except open-war sarcumventions, are ag'in
both law and what we whites call 'gospel,' too."

"My paleface brother is right; he is no Indian to forget
his Manitou and his color. The Hurons know that they have
a great warrior for their prisoner, and they will treat him as
one. If he is to be tortured, his torments shall be such as no
common man can bear; if he is to be treated as a friend, it
will be the friendship of chiefs."

As the Huron uttered this extraordinary assurance of consideration, his eye furtively glanced at the countenance of
his listener, in order to discover how he stood the compliment; though his gravity and apparent sincerity would have
prevented any man but one practiced in artifices from detecting his motives. Deerslayer belonged to the class of the
unsuspicious, and acquainted with the Indian notions of what
constituted respect, in matters connected with the treatment
of captives, he felt his blood chill at the announcement, even
while he maintained an aspect so steeled that his quick-
sighted enemy could discover in it no signs of weakness.

"God has put me in your hands, Huron," the captive at
length answered, "and I suppose you will act your will on
me. I shall not boast of what I can do, under torment, for
I've never been tried, and no man can say till he has been,
but I'll do my endivors not to disgrace the people among
whom I got my training. Howsever, I wish you now to bear
witness that I'm altogether of white blood, and, in a nat'ral
way, of white gifts, too, so, should I be overcome and forget
myself, I hope you'll lay the fault where it properly belongs,
and in no manner put it on the Delawares, or their allies
and friends the Mohicans. We're all created with more or
less weakness, and I'm afeard it's a paleface's to give in under
great bodily torment, when a redskin will sing his songs and
boast of his deeds in the very teeth of his foes!"

"We shall see. Hawkeye has a good countenance, and he
is tough—but why should he be tormented when the Hurons
love him? He is not born their enemy, and the death of one
warrior will not cast a cloud between them forever."

"So much the better, Huron, so much the better. Still I
don't wish to owe anything to a mistake about each other's

meaning. It is so much the better that you bear no malice
for the loss of a warrior who fell in war, and yet it is ontrue
that there is no inmity—lawful inmity I mean, atween us.
So far as I have redskin feelin's at all, I've Delaware feelin's,
and I leave you to judge for yourself how far they are likely
to be fri'ndly to the Mingos—"

Deerslayer ceased, for a sort of specter stood before him
that put a stop to his words, and, indeed, caused him for a
moment to doubt the fidelity of his boasted vision. Hetty
Hutter was standing at the side of the fire, as quietly as if
she belonged to the tribe.

As the hunter and the Indian sat watching the emotions
that were betrayed in each other's countenance, the girl had
approached unnoticed, doubtless ascending from the beach
on the southern side of the point, or that next to the spot
where the ark had anchored, and had advanced to the fire
with the fearlessness that belonged to her simplicity, and
which was certainly justified by the treatment formerly received from the Indians. As soon as Rivenoak perceived
the girl she was recognized, and calling to two or three of
the younger warriors, the chief sent them out to reconnoiter,
lest her appearance should be the forerunner of another attack. He then motioned to Hetty to draw near.

"I hope your visit is a sign that the Sarpent and Hist are
in safety, Hetty," said Deerslayer, as soon as the girl had
complied with the Huron's request. "I don't think you'd come
ashore ag'in on the ar'n'd that brought you here afore."

"Judith told me to come this time, Deerslayer," Hetty replied. "She paddled me ashore herself, in a canoe, as soon
as the Serpent had shown her Hist and told his story. How
handsome Hist is tonight, Deerslayer, and how much happier
she looks than when she was with the Hurons!"

"That's natur', gal; yes, that may be set down as human
natur'. She's with her betrothed and no longer fears a Mingo
husband. In my judgment, Judith herself would lose most of
her beauty if she thought she was to bestow it all on a Mingo!
Content is a great fortifier of good looks; and I'll warrant
you, Hist is contented enough, now she is out of the hands
of these miscreants and with her chosen warrior! Did you
say that your sister told you to come ashore—why should
Judith do that?"

"She bid me come to see you and to try and persuade the

savages to take more elephants to let you off; but I've brought the Bible with me—*that* will do more than all the elephants in Father's chest!"

"And your father, good little Hetty—and Hurry; did they know of your ar'n'd?"

"Nothing. Both are asleep, and Judith and the Serpent thought it best they should not be woke, lest they might want to come again after scalps, when Hist had told them how few warriors and how many women and children there were in the camp. Judith would give me no peace till I had come ashore to see what had happened to *you*."

"Well, that's remarkable as consarns Judith! Why should she feel so much unsartainty about me? Ah, I see how it is now; yes, I see into the whole matter now. You must understand, Hetty, that your sister is oneasy lest Harry March should wake and come blundering here into the hands of the inimy ag'in, under some idee that, being a traveling comrade, he ought to help me in this matter! Hurry is a blunderer, I will allow, but I don't think he'd risk as much for my sake as he would for his own."

"Judith don't care for Hurry, though Hurry cares for her," replied Hetty innocently but quite positively.

"I've heard you say as much as that afore; yes, I've heard that from you afore, gal; and yet it isn't true. One don't live in a tribe not to see something of the way in which liking works in a woman's heart. Though no way given to marrying myself, I've been a looker-on among the Delawares, and this is a matter in which paleface and redskin gifts are all as one the same. When the feelin' begins, the young woman is thoughtful and has no eyes or ears onless for the warrior that has taken her fancy; then follows melancholy and sighing and such sort of actions; after which, especially if matters don't come to plain discourse, she often flies around to backbiting and fault-finding, blaming the youth for the very things she likes best in him. Some young creatur's are forward in this way of showing their love, and I'm of opinion Judith is one of 'em. Now, I've heard her as much as deny that Hurry was good-looking, and the young woman who could do *that* must be far gone indeed."

"The young woman who liked Hurry would own that he is handsome. *I* think Hurry *very* handsome, Deerslayer, and I'm sure everybody must think so that has eyes. Judith don't

like Harry March, and that's the reason she finds fault with him."

"Well—well—my good little Hetty, have it your own way, if we should talk from now till winter, each would think as at present, so there's no use in words. I must believe that Judith is much wrapped up in Hurry and that, sooner or later, she'll have him; and this, too, all the more from the manner in which she abuses him; and I dare to say, you think just the contrary. But mind what I now tell you, gal, and pretend not to know it," continued this being, who was so obtuse on a point on which men are usually quick enough to make discoveries, and so acute in matters that would baffle the observation of much the greater portion of mankind; "I see how it is with them vagabonds. Rivenoak has left us, you see, and is talking yonder with his young men; and though too far to be *heard*, I can *see* what he is telling them. Their orders is to watch your movements, and to find where the canoe is to meet you, to take you back to the ark, and then to seize all and what they can. I'm sorry Judith sent you, for I suppose she wants you to go back ag'in."

"All that's settled, Deerslayer," returned the girl in a low, confidential, and meaning manner; "you may trust me to outwit the best Indian of them all. I know I am feeble-minded, but I've got *some* sense, and you'll see how I'll use it in getting back, when my errand is done!"

"Ah's me! Poor girl; I'm afeard all that's easier said than done. They're a venomous set of riptyles, and their p'ison's none the milder for the loss of Hist. Well, I'm glad the Sarpent was the one to get off with the gal, for now ther'll be two happy, at least; whereas, had *he* fallen into the hands of the Mingos, there'd be two miserable and another far from feelin' as a man likes to feel."

"Now you put me in mind of a part of my errand that I had almost forgotten, Deerslayer. Judith told me to ask you what you thought the Hurons would do with you if you couldn't be bought off, and what *she* had best do to serve you. Yes, this was the most important part of the errand—what she had best do in order to serve you."

"That's as *you* think, Hetty, but it's no matter. Young women are apt to lay most stress on what most touches their feelin's; but no matter; have it your own way, so you be but careful not to let the vagabonds get the mastery of a

canoe. When you get back to the ark, tell 'em to keep close and to keep moving too, most especially at night. Many hours can't go by without the troops on the river hearing of this party, and then your fri'nds may look for relief. 'Tis but a day's march from the nearest garrison, and true soldiers will never lie idle with the foe in their neighborhood. This is my advice, and you may say to your father and Hurry that scalp-hunting will be a poor business now, as the Mingos are up and awake, and nothing can save 'em 'till the troops come, except keeping a good belt of water atween 'em and the savages."

"What shall I tell Judith about you, Deerslayer? I know she will send me back again, if I don't bring her the truth about *you*."

"Then tell her the *truth*. I see no reason Judith Hutter shouldn't hear the *truth* about me as well as a *lie*. I'm a captyve in Indian hands, and Providence only knows what will come of it! Hark'ee, Hetty"—dropping his voice and speaking still more confidentially—"you *are* a little weak-minded, it must be allowed, but you know something of Injins. Here I am in their hands, after having slain one of their stoutest warriors, and they've been endivoring to work upon me, through fear of consequences, to betray your father and all in the ark. I understand the blackguards as well as if they told it all out plainly with their tongues. They hold up avarice afore me on one side, and fear on t'other, and think honesty will give way atween 'em both. But let your father and Hurry know 'tis all useless; as for the Sarpent, *he* knows it already."

"But what shall I tell *Judith*? She will certainly send me back if I don't satisfy her mind."

"Well, tell Judith the same. No doubt the savages will try the torments to make me give in and to revenge the loss of their warrior, but I must hold out ag'in nat'ral weakness in the best manner I can. You may tell Judith to feel no consarn on my account—it will come hard, I know, seeing that a white man's gifts don't run to boasting and singing under torment, for he generally feels smallest when he suffers most—but you may tell her not to have any consarn. I think I shall make out to stand it; and she may rely on this, let me give in as much as I may, and prove completely that I am white, by wailings, and howlings, and even

tears, yet I'll never fall so far as to betray my fri'nds. When it gets to burning holes in the flesh with heated ramrods, and to hacking the body, and tearing the hair out by the roots, natur' may get the upper hand, so far as groans and complaints are consarned, but there the triumph of the vagabonds will ind; nothing short of God's abandoning him to the devils can make an honest man ontrue to his color and duty."

Hetty listened with great attention, and her mild but speaking countenance manifested a strong sympathy in the anticipated agony of the supposititious sufferer. At first she seemed at a loss how to act; then, taking a hand of Deerslayer's, she affectionately recommended to him to borrow her Bible and to read it while the savages were inflicting their torments. When the other honestly admitted that it exceeded his power to read, she even volunteered to remain with him and to perform this holy office in person. The offer was gently declined, and Rivenoak being about to join them, Deerslayer requested the girl to leave him, first enjoining her again to tell those in the ark to have full confidence in his fidelity. Hetty now walked away and approached the group of females with as much confidence and self-possession as if she were a native of the tribe. On the other hand, the Huron resumed his seat by the side of his prisoner, the one continuing to ask questions with all the wily ingenuity of a practical Indian counselor, the other baffling him by the very means that are known to be the most efficacious in defeating the finesse of the more pretending diplomacy of civilization, or by confining his answers to the truth, and the truth only.

CHAPTER XVIII

Thus died she; never more on her
Shall sorrow light, or shame. She was not made
Through years or moons the inner weight to bear,
Which colder hearts endure till they are laid
By age in earth; her days and pleasures were
Brief but delightful—such as had not stayed
Long with her destiny; but she sleeps well
By the sea-shore whereon she loved to dwell.

BYRON

THE YOUNG MEN who had been sent out to reconnoiter, on the sudden appearance of Hetty, soon returned to report their want of success in making any discovery. One of them had even been along the beach as far as the spot opposite to the ark, but the darkness completely concealed that vessel from his notice. Others had examined in different directions, and everywhere the stillness of night was added to the silence and solitude of the woods. It was consequently believed that the girl had come alone, as on her former visit, and on some similar errand. The Iroquois were ignorant that the ark had left the castle, and there were movements projected, if not in the course of actual execution by this time, which also greatly added to the sense of security. A watch was set, therefore, and all but the sentinels disposed themselves to sleep.

Sufficient care was had to the safekeeping of the captive without inflicting on him any unnecessary suffering; as for Hetty, she was permitted to find a place among the Indian girls in the best manner she could. She did not find the friendly offices of Hist, though her character not only bestowed impunity from pain and captivity, but procured for her a consideration and an attention that placed her, on the score of comfort, quite on a level with the wild but gentle beings around her. She was supplied with a skin, and made

her own bed on a pile of boughs a little apart from the huts. Here she was soon in a profound sleep, like all around her.

There were now thirteen men in the party, and three kept watch at a time. One remained in shadow, not far from the fire, however. His duty was to guard the captive, to take care that the fire neither blazed up so as to illuminate the spot, nor yet became wholly extinguished, and to keep an eye generally on the state of the camp. Another passed from one beach to the other, crossing the base of the point, while the third kept moving slowly around the strand on its outer extremity, to prevent a repetition of the surprise that had already taken place that night. This arrangement was far from being usual among savages, who ordinarily rely more on the secrecy of their movements than on vigilance of this nature, but it had been called for by the peculiarity of the circumstances in which the Hurons were now placed. Their position was known to their foes, and it could not easily be changed at an hour which demanded rest. Perhaps, too, they placed most of their confidence on the knowledge of what they believed to be passing higher up the lake, and which, it was thought, would fully occupy the whole of the palefaces, who were at liberty, with their solitary Indian ally. It was also probable Rivenoak was aware that, in holding his captive, he had in his own hands the most dangerous of all his enemies.

The precision with which those accustomed to watchfulness, or lives of disturbed rest, sleep is not the least of the phenomena of our mysterious being. The head is no sooner on the pillow than consciousness is lost; and yet, at a necessary hour the mind appears to arouse the body as promptly as if it had stood sentinel over it the while. There can be no doubt that they who are thus roused awake by the influence of thought over matter, though the mode in which this influence is exercised must remain hidden from our curiosity until it shall be explained, should that hour ever arrive, by the entire enlightenment of the soul on the subject of all human mysteries. Thus it was with Hetty Hutter. Feeble as the immaterial portion of her existence was thought to be, it was sufficiently active to cause her to open her eyes at midnight. At that hour she awoke, and leaving her bed of skin and boughs, she walked innocently and openly to the embers of the fire, stirring the latter, as the coolness of the night and

the woods, in connection with an exceedingly unsophisticated bed, had a little chilled her. As the flame shot up, it lighted the swarthy countenance of the Huron on watch, whose dark eyes glistened under its light, like the balls of the panther that is pursued to his den with burning brands. But Hetty felt no fear, and she approached the spot where the Indian stood. Her movements were so natural and so perfectly devoid of any of the stealthiness of cunning or deception that he imagined she had merely arisen on account of the coolness of the night, a common occurrence in a bivouac, and the one of all others, perhaps, the least likely to excite suspicion. Hetty spoke to him, but he understood no English. She then gazed near a minute at the sleeping captive and moved slowly away in a sad and melancholy manner.

The girl took no pains to conceal her movements. Any ingenious expedient of this nature quite likely exceeded her powers; still, her step was habitually light and scarcely audible. As she took the direction of the extremity of the point, or the place where she had landed in the first adventure, and where Hist had embarked, the sentinel saw her light form gradually disappear in the gloom without uneasiness or changing his own position. He knew that others were on the lookout, and he did not believe that one who had twice come into the camp voluntarily, and had already left it openly, would take refuge in flight. In short, the conduct of the girl excited no more attention than that on any person of feeble intellect would excite in civilized society, while her person met with more consideration and respect.

Hetty certainly had no very distinct notions of the localities, but she found her way to the beach, which she reached on the same side of the point as that on which the camp had been made. By following the margin of the water, taking a northern direction, she soon encountered the Indian who paced the strand as sentinel. This was a young warrior, and when he heard her light tread coming along the gravel, he approached swiftly, though with anything but menace in his manner. The darkness was so intense that it was not easy to discover forms, within the shadows of the woods, at the distance of twenty feet, and quite impossible to distinguish persons until near enough to touch them. The young Huron manifested disappointment when he found whom he had met,

for, truth to say, he was expecting his favorite, who had promised to relieve the *ennui* of a midnight watch with her presence. This man was also ignorant of English, but he was at no loss to understand why the girl should be up at that hour. Such things were usual in an Indian village and camp, where sleep is as irregular as the meals. Then poor Hetty's known imbecility, as in most things connected with the savages, stood her friend on this occasion. Vexed at his disappointment, and impatient of the presence of one he thought an intruder, the young warrior signed for the girl to move forward, holding the direction of the beach. Hetty complied, but as she walked away, she spoke aloud in English, in her usual soft tones, which the stillness of the night made audible at some little distance.

"If you took me for a Huron girl, warrior," she said, "I don't wonder you are so little pleased. I am Hetty Hutter, Thomas Hutter's daughter, and have never met any man at night, for Mother always said it was wrong, and modest young women should never do it; modest young women of the palefaces, I mean; for customs are different in different parts of the world, I know. No, no, I'm Hetty Hutter, and wouldn't meet even Hurry Harry, though he should fall down on his knees and ask me! Mother said it was wrong."

By the time Hetty had said this, she reached the place where the canoes had come ashore, and owing to the curvature of the land and the bushes, would have been completely hid from the sight of the sentinel, had it been broad day. But another footstep caught the lover's ear, and he was already nearly beyond the sound of the girl's silvery voice. Still Hetty, bent only on her own thoughts and purposes, continued to speak, though the gentleness of her tones prevented the sounds from penetrating far into the woods. On the water they were more widely diffused.

"Here I am, Judith," she added, "and there is no one near me. The Huron on watch has gone to meet his sweetheart, who is an Indian girl, you know, and never had a Christian mother to tell her how wrong it is to meet a man at night—"

Hetty's voice was hushed by a "hist!" that came from the water, and then she caught a dim view of the canoe, which approached noiselessly and soon grated on the shingle with its bow. The moment the weight of Hetty was felt in the

light craft, the canoe withdrew, stern foremost, as if possessed of life and volition, until it was a hundred yards from the shore. Then it turned, and making a wide sweep, as much to prolong the passage as to get beyond the sound of voices, it held its way toward the ark. For several minutes nothing was uttered; but, believing herself to be in a favorable position to confer with her sister, Judith, who alone sat in the stern, managing the canoe with a skill little short of that of a man, began a discourse which she had been burning to commence ever since they quitted the point.

"Here we are safe, Hetty," she said, "and may talk without the fear of being overheard. You must speak low, however, for sounds are heard far on the water in a still night. I was so close to the point, some of the time while you were on it, that I have heard the voices of the warriors, and I heard your shoes on the gravel of the beach even before you spoke."

"I don't believe, Judith, the Hurons know I have left them."

"Quite likely they do not, for a lover makes a poor sentry, unless it be to watch for his sweetheart! But tell me, Hetty, did you see and speak with Deerslayer?"

"Oh, yes—there he was seated near the fire, with his legs tied, though they left his arms free to move them as he pleased."

"Well, what did he tell you, child? Speak quick; I am dying to know what message he sent me."

"What did he tell me? Why, what do you think, Judith; he told me that he couldn't read! Only think of that! A white man, and not know how to read his Bible, even! He never could have had a mother, sister!"

"Never mind *that,* Hetty. All men can't read; though Mother knew so much, and taught us so much, Father knows very little about books, and he can barely read the Bible, you know."

"Oh! I never thought fathers *could* read much, but *mothers* ought all to read, else how can they teach their children? Depend on it, Judith, Deerslayer could never have had a mother, else he would know how to read."

"Did you tell him *I* sent you ashore, Hetty, and how much concern I feel for his misfortune?" asked the other impatiently.

"I believe I did, Judith, but you know I am feeble-minded,

and I may have forgotten. I *did* tell him you brought me ashore. And he told me a great deal that I was to say to you, which I remember well, for it made my blood run cold to hear him. He told me to say that his friends—I suppose you are one of them, sister—?"

"How can you torment me thus, Hetty! Certainly, I am one of the truest friends he has on earth."

"Torment you! Yes, now I remember all about it. I am glad you used that word, Judith, for it brings it all back to my mind. Well, he said he might be *tormented* by the savages, but he would try to bear it as becomes a Christian white man, and that no one need be afeard—why does Deerslayer call it afeard, when Mother has always taught us to say afraid?"

"Never mind, dear Hetty, never mind *that* now," cried the other, almost gasping for breath. "Did Deerslayer really tell you that he thought the savages would put him to the torture? Recollect well now, Hetty, for this is a most awful and serious thing."

"Yes, he did; and I remember it by your speaking about my tormenting you. Oh! I felt very sorry for him, and Deerslayer took all so quietly and without noise! Deerslayer is not as handsome as Hurry Harry, Judith, but he is more quiet."

"He's worth a million Hurrys! Yes, he's worth all the young men who ever came upon the lake put together," said Judith, with an energy and positiveness that caused her sister to wonder. "He is *true*. There is no lie about Deerslayer. *You*, Hetty, may not know what a merit it is in a man to have truth, but when you get—no—I hope you will never know it. Why should one like you be ever made to learn the hard lesson to distrust and hate!"

Judith bowed her face, dark as it was, and unseen as she must have been by any eye but that of Omniscience, between her hands and groaned. This sudden paroxysm of feeling, however, lasted but for a moment, and she continued more calmly, still speaking frankly to her sister, whose intelligence and whose discretion in anything that related to herself she did not in the least distrust. Her voice, however, was low and husky, instead of having its former clearness and animation.

"It is a hard thing to fear truth, Hetty," she said, "and yet do I more dread Deerslayer's truth than any enemy! One cannot tamper with such truth—so much honesty—such

obstinate uprightness! But we are not altogether unequal, sister—Deerslayer and I? He is not altogether my superior?"

It was not usual for Judith so far to demean herself as to appeal to Hetty's judgment. Nor did she often address her by the title of sister, a distinction that is commonly given by the junior to the senior, even where there is perfect equality in all other respects. As trifling departures from habitual deportment oftener strike the imagination than more important changes, Hetty perceived the circumstances and wondered at them in her own simple way.

Her ambition was a little quickened, and the answer was as much out of the usual course of things as the question, the poor girl attempting to refine beyond her strength.

"Superior, Judith!" she repeated with pride. "In what *can* Deerslayer be *your* superior? Are you not Mother's child— and does he know how to read—and wasn't Mother before any woman in all this part of the world? I should think, so far from supposing himself *your* superior, he would hardly believe himself *mine*. You are handsome, and he is ugly——"

"No, not ugly, Hetty," interrupted Judith. "Only plain. But his honest face has a look in it that is far better than beauty. In my eyes Deerslayer is handsomer than Hurry Harry."

"Judith Hutter, you frighten me! Hurry is the handsomest mortal in the world—even handsomer than you are yourself, because a man's good looks, you know, are always better than a woman's good looks."

This little innocent touch of natural taste did not please the elder sister at the moment, and she did not scruple to betray it.

"Hetty, you now speak foolishly, and had better say no more on this subject," she answered. "Hurry is not the handsomest mortal in the world, by many; and there are officers in the garrisons"—Judith stammered at the words —"there are officers in the garrisons near us far comelier than he. But, why do you think me the equal of Deerslayer —speak of *that*, for I do not like to hear you show so much admiration of a man like Hurry Harry, who has neither feelings, manners, nor conscience. *You* are too good for *him*, and he ought to be told it at once."

"*I!* Judith, how you forget! Why *I* am not beautiful and am feeble-minded."

"You are *good*, Hetty, and that is more than can be said of Henry March. He may have a *face*, and a *body*, but he has no *heart*. But enough of this, for the present. Tell me what raises me to an equality with Deerslayer."

"To think of you asking me this, Judith! He can't read, and you can. He don't know how to talk, but speaks worse than Hurry even—for, sister, Hurry doesn't always pronounce his words right! Did you ever notice *that?*"

"Certainly, he is as coarse in speech as in everything else. But I fear you flatter me, Hetty, when you think I can be justly called the equal of a man like Deerslayer. It is true, I have been better taught; in one sense am more comely; and perhaps might look higher; but then his truth—his truth—makes a fearful difference between us! Well, I will talk no more of this, and we will bethink us of the means of getting him out of the hands of the Hurons. We have Father's chest in the ark, Hetty, and might try the temptation of more elephants, though I fear such baubles will not buy the liberty of a man like Deerslayer. I am afraid Father and Hurry will not be as willing to ransom Deerslayer as Deerslayer was to ransom them!"

"Why not, Judith? Hurry and Deerslayer are friends, and friends should always help one another."

"Alas, poor Hetty, you little know mankind! Seeming friends are often more to be dreaded than open enemies, particularly by females. But you'll have to land in the morning and try again what can be done for Deerslayer. Tortured he *shall* not be, while Judith Hutter lives and can find means to prevent it."

The conversation now grew desultory, and was drawn out, until the elder sister had extracted from the younger every fact that the feeble faculties of the latter permitted her to retain and to communicate. When Judith was satisfied—though she could never be said to be satisfied, whose feelings seemed to be so interwoven with all that related to the subject as to have excited a nearly inappeasable curiosity —but when Judith could think of no more questions to ask, without resorting to repetition, the canoe was paddled toward the scow. The intense darkness of the night and the deep shadows which the hills and forest cast upon the water rendered it difficult to find the vessel, anchored, as it had been, as close to the shore as a regard to safety rendered

prudent. Judith was expert in the management of a bark canoe, the lightness of which demanded skill rather than strength, and she forced her own little vessel swiftly over the water the moment she had ended her conference with Hetty and had come to the determination to return. Still no ark was seen. Several times the sisters fancied they saw it, looming up in the obscurity, like a low black rock, but on each occasion it was found to be either an optical illusion, or some swell of the foliage on the shore. After a search that lasted half an hour, the girls were forced to the unwelcome conviction that the ark had departed.

Most young women would have felt the awkwardness of their situation, in a physical sense, under the circumstances in which the sisters were left, more than any apprehensions of a different nature. Not so with Judith, however, and even Hetty felt more concern about the motives that might have influenced her father and Hurry than any fears for her own safety.

"It cannot be, Hetty," said Judith, when a thorough search had satisfied them both that no ark was to be found, "it cannot be that the Indians have rafted, or swum off, and surprised our friends as they slept?"

"I don't believe that Hist and Chingachgook would sleep until they had told each other all they had to say after so long a separation—do you, sister?"

"Perhaps not, child. There was much to keep them awake, but one Indian may have been surprised even when not asleep, especially as his thoughts may have been on other things. Still, we should have heard a noise, for in a night like this an oath of Hurry Harry's would have echoed in the eastern hills like a clap of thunder."

"Hurry *is* sinful and thoughtless about his words, Judith," Hetty meekly and sorrowfully answered.

"No—no; 'tis impossible the ark could be taken and I not hear the noise. It is not an hour since I left it, and the whole time I have been attentive to the smallest sound. And yet it is not easy to believe a father would willingly abandon his children!"

"Perhaps Father has thought us in our cabin asleep, Judith, and has moved away to go home. You know we often move the ark in the night."

"This is true, Hetty, and it must be as you suppose. There

is a little more southern air than there was, and they have gone up the lake—"

Judith stopped, for as the last word was on her tongue, the scene was suddenly lighted, though only for a single instant, by a flash. The crack of a rifle succeeded, and then followed the roll of the echo along the eastern mountains. Almost at the same moment a piercing female cry arose in the air in a prolonged shriek. The awful stillness that succeeded was, if possible, more appalling than the fierce and sudden interruption of the deep silence of midnight. Resolute as she was both by nature and habit, Judith scarce breathed, while poor Hetty hid her face and trembled.

"That was a woman's cry, Hetty," said the former solemnly, "and it was a cry of anguish! If the ark has moved from this spot, it can only have gone north with this air, and the gun and shriek came from the point. Can anything have befallen Hist?"

"Let us go and see, Judith; she may want our assistance —for, besides herself, there are none but men in the ark."

It was not a moment for hesitation, and ere Judith had ceased speaking her paddle was in the water. The distance to the point in a direct line was not great, and the impulses under which the girls worked were too exciting to allow them to waste the precious moments in useless precautions. They paddled incautiously for them, but the same excitement kept others from noting their movements. Presently a glare of light caught the eye of Judith through an opening in the bushes, and steering by it she so directed the canoe as to keep it visible, while she got as near the land as was either prudent or necessary.

The scene that was now presented to the observation of the girls was within the woods, on the side of the declivity so often mentioned and in plain view from the boat. Here all in the camp were collected, some six or eight carrying torches of fat-pine, which cast a strong but funereal light on all beneath the arches of the forest. With her back supported against a tree, and sustained on one side by the young sentinel whose remissness had suffered Hetty to escape, sat the female whose expected visit had produced his delinquency. By the glare of the torch that was held near her face, it was evident that she was in the agonies of death, while the blood that trickled from her bared bosom

betrayed the nature of the injury she had received. The pungent, peculiar smell of gunpowder, too, was still quite perceptible in the heavy, damp night air. There could be no question that she had been shot. Judith understood it all at a glance. The streak of light had appeared on the water a short distance from the point, and either the rifle had been discharged from a canoe hovering near the land, or it had been fired from the ark in passing. An incautious exclamation or laugh may have produced the assault, for it was barely possible that the aim had been assisted by any other agent than sound. As to the effect, that was soon still more apparent, the head of the victim dropping and the body sinking in death. Then all the torches but one were extinguished—a measure of prudence—and the melancholy train that bore the body to the camp was just to be distinguished by the glimmering light that remained.

Judith sighed heavily and shuddered as her paddle again dipped and the canoe moved cautiously around the point. A sight had afflicted her senses, and now haunted her imagination, that was still harder to be borne than even the untimely fate and passing agony of the deceased girl. She had seen, under the strong glare of all the torches, the erect form of Deerslayer, standing, with commiseration and, as she thought, with shame depicted on his countenance, near the dying female. He betrayed neither fear nor backwardness, *himself*, but it was apparent by the glances cast at him by the warriors that fierce passions were struggling in *their* bosoms. All this seemed to be unheeded by the captive, but it remained impressed on the memory of Judith throughout the night.

No canoe was met hovering near the point. A stillness and darkness, as complete as if the silence of the forest had never been disturbed, or the sun had never shone on that retired region, now reigned on the point, and on the gloomy water, the slumbering woods, and even the murky sky. No more could be done, therefore, than to seek a place of safety, and this was only to be found in the center of the lake. Paddling, in silence, to that spot, the canoe was suffered to drift northerly, while the girls sought such repose as their situation and feelings would permit.

CHAPTER XIX

> *Stand to your arms, and guard the door—all's lost*
> *Unless that fearful bell be silenced soon.*
> *The officer hath missed his path, or purpose,*
> *Or met some unforeseen and hideous obstacle.*
> *Anselmo, with thy company proceed*
> *Straight to the tower; the rest remain with me.*

> MARINO FALIERO

THE CONJECTURE OF Judith Hutter concerning the manne
in which the Indian girl had met her death was accurat
in the main. After sleeping several hours, her father an
March awoke. This occurred a few minutes after she ha
left the ark to go in quest of her sister, and when of cours
Chingachgook and his betrothed were on board. From th
Delaware the old man learned the position of the camp
and the recent events, as well as the absence of his daugh
ters. The latter gave him no concern, for he relied greatl
on the sagacity of the eldest and the known impunity wit
which the younger passed among the savages. Long familiar
ity with danger, too, had blunted his sensibilities. Nor di
he seem much to regret the captivity of Deerslayer, fo
while he knew how material his aid might be in a de
fense, the difference in their views on the morality of th
woods had not left much sympathy between them. He woul
have rejoiced to know the position of the camp before i
had been alarmed by the escape of Hist, but it would b
too hazardous now to venture to land; and he reluctantl
relinquished for the night the ruthless designs that captivit
and revenge had excited him to entertain. In this moo
Hutter took a seat in the head of the scow, where he wa
quickly joined by Hurry, leaving the Serpent and Hist i
quiet possession of the other extremity of the vessel.

"Deerslayer has shown himself a boy in going among the savages at this hour and letting himself fall into their hands like a deer that tumbles into a pit," growled the old man, perceiving as usual the mote in his neighbor's eyes while he overlooked the beam in his own. "If he is left to pay for his stupidity with his own flesh, he can blame no one but himself."

"That's the way of the world, Old Tom," returned Hurry. "Every man must meet his own debts and answer for his own sins. I'm amazed, however, that a lad as skillful and watchful as Deerslayer should have been caught in such a trap! Didn't he know any better than to go prowling about a Huron camp, at midnight, with no place to retreat to but a lake? Or did he think himself a buck that, by taking to the water, could throw off the scent and swim himself out of difficulty? I had a better opinion of the boy's judgment, I'll own; but we must overlook a little ignorance in a raw hand. I say, Master Hutter, do you happen to know what has become of the gals? I see no signs of Judith or Hetty, though I've been through the ark and looked into all its living creatur's."

Hutter briefly explained the manner in which his daughters had taken to the canoe, as it had been related by the Delaware, as well as the return of Judith after landing her sister and her second departure.

"This comes of a smooth tongue, Floating Tom," exclaimed Hurry, grating his teeth in pure resentment—"this comes of a smooth tongue, and a silly gal's inclinations—and you had best look into the matter! You and I were both prisoners"—Hurry could recall that circumstance *now* —"you and I were both prisoners, and yet Judith never stirred an inch to do us any service! She is bewitched with this lank-looking Deerslayer, and he, and she, and you, and all of us had best look to it. I am not a man to put up with such a wrong quietly, and do say, all the parties had best look to it! Let's up kedge, old fellow, and move nearer to this point, and see how matters are getting on."

Hutter had no objections to this movement, and the ark was got under way in the usual manner, care being taken to make no noise. The wind was passing northward, and the sail soon swept the scow so far up the lake as to render the dark outlines of the trees that clothed the point dimly

visible. Floating Tom steered, and he sailed along as near
the land as the depth of the water and the overhanging
branches would allow. It was impossible to distinguish anything that stood within the shadows of the shore, but the
forms of the sail and of the hut were discerned by the
young sentinel on the beach, who has already been mentioned. In the moment of sudden surprise, a deep Indian
exclamation escaped him. In that spirit of recklessness and
ferocity that formed the essence of Hurry's character, this
man dropped his rifle and fired. The ball was sped by accident, or by that overruling Providence which decides the
fates of all, and the girl fell. Then followed the scene with
the torches, which has just been described.

At the precise moment when Hurry committed this act
of unthinking cruelty, the canoe of Judith was within a
hundred feet of the spot from which the ark had so lately
moved. Her own course has been described, and it has now
become our office to follow that of her father and his companions. The shriek announced the effects of the random
shot of March, and it also proclaimed that the victim was a
woman. Hurry himself was startled at these unlooked-for
consequences, and for a moment he was sorely disturbed
by conflicting sensations. At first he laughed, in reckless
and rude-minded exultation, and then conscience, that moni-
ter planted in our breasts by God and which receives its
more general growth from the training bestowed in the
tillage of childhood, shot a pang to his heart. For a minute
the mind of this creature, equally of civilization and bar-
barism, was a sort of chaos as to feeling, not knowing what
to think of its own act; then the obstinacy and pride of
one of his habits interposed to assert their usual ascendency.
He struck the butt of his rifle on the bottom of the scow
with a species of defiance and began to whistle a low air
with an affectation of indifference. All this time the ark was
in motion, and it was already opening the bay above the
point, and was consequently quitting the land.

Hurry's companions did not view his conduct with the
same indulgence as that with which he appeared disposed
to regard it himself. Hutter growled out his dissatisfaction,
for the act led to no advantage, while it threatened to
render the warfare more vindictive than ever, and none censure motiveless departures from the right more severely than

the mercenary and unprincipled. Still, he commanded himself, the captivity of Deerslayer rendering the arm of the offender of double consequence to him at that moment. Chingachgook arose, and for a single instant the ancient animosity of tribes was forgotten in a feeling of color, but he recollected himself in season to prevent any of the fierce consequences that for a passing moment he certainly meditated. Not so with Hist. Rushing through the hut, or cabin, the girl stood at the side of Hurry, almost as soon as his rifle touched the bottom of the scow, and with a fearlessness that did credit to her heart, she poured out her reproaches with the generous warmth of a woman.

"What for you shoot?" she said. "What Huron gal do dat you kill her? What you t'ink Manitou *say?* What you t'ink Manitou *feel?* What Iroquois *do?* No get honor—no get camp—no get prisoner—no get battle—no get scalp—no get not'ing at all. Blood come after blood! How you feel your wife killed? Who pity you when tear come for moder or sister? You big as great pine—Huron gal little slender birch—why you fall on her and crush her? You t'ink Huron forget it? No, redskin never forget. Never forget friend; never forget enemy. Red man Manitou in *dat.* Why you so wicked, great paleface?"

Hurry had never been so daunted as by this close and warm attack of the Indian girl. It is true that she had a powerful ally in his conscience, and while she spoke earnestly, it was in tones so feminine as to deprive him of any pretext for unmanly anger. The softness of her voice added to the weight of her remonstrance by lending to the latter an air of purity and truth. Like most vulgar-minded men, he had only regarded the Indians through the medium of their coarser and fiercer characteristics. It had never struck him that the affections are human; that even high principles —modified by habits and prejudices, but not the less elevated within their circle—can exist in the savage state; and that the warrior who is most ruthless in the field can submit to the softest and gentlest influences in the moments of domestic quiet. In a word, it was the habit of his mind to regard all Indians as being only a slight degree removed from the wild beasts that roamed the woods, and to feel disposed to treat them accordingly, whenever interest or caprice supplied a motive or an impulse. Still, though daunted

by these reproaches, the handsome barbarian could hardly be said to be penitent. He was too much rebuked by conscience to suffer an outbreak of temper to escape him, and perhaps he felt that he had already committed an act that might justly bring his manhood in question. Instead of resenting, or answering the simple but natural appeal of Hist, he walked away like one who disdained entering into a controversy with a woman.

In the meanwhile the ark swept onward, and by the time the scene with the torches was enacting beneath the trees, it had reached the open lake; Floating Tom causing it to sheer further from the land with a sort of instinctive dread of retaliation. An hour now passed in gloomy silence, no one appearing disposed to break it. Hist had retired to her pallet, and Chingachgook lay sleeping in the forward part of the scow. Hutter and Hurry alone remained awake, the former at the steering oar, while the latter brooded over his own conduct with the stubbornness of one little given to a confession of his errors and the secret goadings of the worm that never dies. This was at the moment when Judith and Hetty reached the center of the lake, and had lain down to endeavor to sleep in their drifting canoe.

The night was calm, though so much obscured by clouds. The season was not one of storms, and those which did occur in the month of June on that embedded water, though frequently violent, were always of short continuance. Nevertheless, there was the usual current of heavy, damp night air, which, passing over the summits of the trees, scarcely appeared to descend so low as the surface of the glassy lake, but kept moving a short distance above it, saturated with the humidity that constantly arose from the woods and apparently never proceeding far in any one direction. The currents were influenced by the formation of the hills, as a matter of course—a circumstance that rendered even fresh breezes baffling, and which reduced the feebler efforts of the night air to a sort of capricious and fickle sighings of the woods. Several times the head of the ark pointed east, and once it was actually turned toward the south again, but on the whole, it worked its way north, Hutter making always a fair wind, if wind it could be called, his principal motive appearing to be a wish to keep in motion, in order to defeat any treacherous design of his enemies. He now

felt some little concern about his daughters, and perhaps as much about the canoe, but on the whole, this uncertainty did not much disturb him, as he had the reliance already mentioned on the intelligence of Judith.

It was the season of the shortest nights, and it was not long before the deep obscurity which precedes the day began to yield to the returning light. If any earthly scene could be presented to the senses of man that might soothe his passions and temper his ferocity, it was that which grew upon the eyes of Hutter and Hurry as the hours advanced, changing night to morning. There were the usual soft tints of the sky in which neither the gloom of darkness nor the brilliancy of the sun prevails, and under which objects appear more unearthly and, we might add, holy than at any other portion of the twenty-four hours. The beautiful and soothing calm of eventide has been extolled by a thousand poets, and yet it does not bring with it the far-reaching and sublime thoughts of the half hour that precedes the rising of a summer's sun. In the one case the panorama is gradually hid from the sight, while in the other its objects start out from the unfolding picture, first dim and misty, then marked in in solemn background; next seen in the witchery of an *increasing,* a thing as different as possible from the *decreasing* twilight, and finally mellow, distinct, and luminous as the rays of the great center of light diffuse themselves in the atmosphere. The hymns of birds, too, have no novel counterpart in the retreat to the roost, or the flight to the nest, and these invariably accompany the advent of the day, until the appearance of the sun itself

Bathes in deep joy, the land and sea.

All this, however, Hutter and Hurry witnessed without experiencing any of that calm delight which the spectacle is wont to bring when the thoughts are just and the aspirations pure. They not only witnessed it, but they witnessed it under circumstances that had a tendency to increase its power and to heighten its charms. Only one solitary object became visible, in the returning light, that had received its form or uses from human taste or human desires, which as often deform as beautify a landscape. This was the castle, all the rest being native and fresh from the

hand of God. That singular residence, too, was in keeping
with the natural objects of the view, starting out from the
gloom—quaint, picturesque, and ornamental. Nevertheless,
the whole was lost on the observers, who knew no feeling
of poetry, had lost their sense of natural devotion in lives
of obdurate and narrow selfishness, and had little other
sympathy with nature than that which originated with her
lowest wants.

As soon as the light was sufficiently strong to allow of a
distinct view of the lake, and more particularly of its shores,
Hutter turned the head of the ark directly toward the castle,
with the avowed intention of taking possession for the day at
least, as the place most favorable for meeting his daughters
and for carrying on his operations against the Indians. By
this time, Chingachgook was up, and Hist was heard stirring
among the furniture of the kitchen. The place for which they
steered was distant only a mile, and the air was sufficiently
favorable to permit it to be neared by means of the sail. At
this moment, too, to render the appearances generally auspi-
cious, the canoe of Judith was seen floating northward in the
broadest part of the lake, having actually passed the scow
in the darkness, in obedience to no other power than that of
the elements. Hutter got his glass and took a long and anxious
survey to ascertain if his daughters were in the light craft
or not, and a slight exclamation like that of joy escaped him
as he caught a glimpse of what he rightly conceived to be a
part of Judith's dress above the top of the canoe. At the next
instant, the girl arose, and was seen gazing about her, like
one assuring herself of her situation. A minute later, Hetty
was seen on her knees, in the other end of the canoe, repeating the prayers that had been taught her in childhood
by a misguided but repentant mother. As Hutter laid down
the glass, still drawn to its focus, the Serpent raised it to
his eye and turned it toward the canoe. It was the first time
he had ever used such an instrument, and Hist understood
by his "hugh!" the expression of his face, and his entire
mien that something wonderful had excited his admiration.
It is well known that the American Indians, more particularly
those of superior character and stations, singularly maintain
their self-possession and stoicism in the midst of the flood
of marvels that present themselves in their occasional visits
to the abodes of civilization; Chingachgook had imbibed

enough of this impassibility to suppress any very undignified manifestation of surprise. With Hist, however, no such law was binding, and when her lover managed to bring the glass in a line with a canoe, and her eye was applied to the smaller end, the girl started back in alarm; then she clapped her hands with delight, and a laugh, the usual attendant of untutored admiration, followed. A few minutes sufficed to enable this quick-witted girl to manage the instrument for herself, and she directed it at every prominent object that struck her fancy. Finding a rest in one of the windows, she and the Delaware first surveyed the lake, then the shores, the hills, and finally the castle attracted their attention. After a long, steady gaze at the latter, Hist took away her eye and spoke to her lover in a low, earnest manner. Chingachgook immediately placed his eye to the glass, and his look even exceeded that of his betrothed, in length and intensity. Again they spoke together confidentially, appearing to compare opinions, after which the glass was laid aside, and the young warrior quitted the cabin to join Hutter and Hurry.

The ark was slowly but steadily advancing, and the castle was materially within half a mile, when Chingachgook joined the two white men in the stern of the scow. His manner was calm, but it was evident to the others, who were familiar with the habits of the Indians, that he had something to communicate. Hurry was generally prompt to speak, and according to custom, he took the lead on this occasion.

"Out with it, redskin," he cried, in his usual rough manner. "Have you discovered a chipmunk in a tree, or is there a salmon trout swimming under the bottom of the scow? You find what a paleface can do in the way of eyes, now, Sarpent, and mustn't wonder that they can see the land of the Indians from afar off."

"No good to go to castle," put in Chingachgook with emphasis, the moment the other gave him an opportunity of speaking. "Huron there."

"The Devil he is! If this should turn out to be true, Floating Tom, a pretty trap were we about to pull down on our heads! Huron there!—well, this may be so, but no signs can I see of anything near or about the old hut but logs, water, and bark—'bating two or three windows and one door."

Hutter called for the glass and took a careful survey of the spot before he ventured an opinion at all; then he somewhat

cavalierly expressed his dissent from that given by the Indian.

"You've got this glass wrong end foremost, Delaware," continued Hurry; "neither the old man nor I can see any trail in the lake."

"No trail—water make no trail," said Hist eagerly. "Stop boat—no go too near—Huron there!"

"Aye, that's it! Stick to the same tale and more people will believe you. I hope, Sarpent, you and your gal will agree in telling the same story arter marriage as well as you do now. Huron there!—whereabouts is he to be seen—in the padlock, or the chains, or the logs? There isn't a jail in the Colony that has a more lock-up look about it than old Tom's *chiente;* and I know something about jails from exper'ence."

"No see moccasin," said Hist impatiently, "why no *look*—and see him."

"Give me the glass, Harry," interrupted Hutter, "and lower the sail. It is seldom that an Indian woman meddles, and when she does, there is generally a cause for it. There *is,* truly, a moccasin floating against one of the piles, and it may or may not be a sign that the castle hasn't escaped visitors in our absence. Moccasins are no rarities, however, for I wear 'em myself, and Deerslayer wears 'em, and you wear 'em, March; and for that matter, so does Hetty, quite as often as she wears shoes; though I never yet saw Judith trust her pretty foot in a moccasin."

Hurry had lowered the sail, and by this time the ark was within two hundred yards of the castle, setting in nearer and nearer each moment, but at a rate too slow to excite any uneasiness. Each now took the glass in turn, and the castle and everything near it was subjected to a scrutiny still more rigid than ever. There the moccasin lay, beyond a question, floating so lightly and preserving its form so well that it was scarcely wet. It had caught by a piece of the rough bark of one of the piles on the exterior of the water palisade that formed the dock already mentioned, which circumstance alone prevented it from drifting away before the air. There were many modes, however, of accounting for the presence of the moccasin without supposing it to have been dropped by an enemy. It might have fallen from the platform even while Hutter was in possession of the place and drifted to the spot where it was now seen, remaining unnoticed until detected by

the acute vision of Hist. It might have drifted from a distance
up or down the lake, and accidentally become attached to the
pile or palisade. It might have been thrown from a window
and alighted in that particular place; or it might certainly
have fallen from a scout or an assailant during the past
night, who was obliged to abandon it to the lake in the deep
obscurity which then prevailed.

All these conjectures passed from Hutter to Hurry, the
former appearing disposed to regard the omen as a little
sinister, while the latter treated it with his usual reckless
disdain. As for the Indian, he was of opinion that the moccasin should be viewed as one would regard a trail in the
woods which might or might not equally prove to be threatening. Hist, however, had something available to propose.
She declared her readiness to take a canoe, proceed to the
palisade, and bring away the moccasin, when its ornaments
would show whether it came from the Canadas or not. Both
the white men were disposed to accept this offer, but the
Delaware interfered to prevent the risk. If such a service
was to be undertaken, it best became a warrior to expose
himself in its execution, and he gave his refusal to let his
betrothed proceed much in the quiet but brief manner in
which an Indian husband issues his commands.

"Well, then, Delaware, go yourself if you're so tender of
your squaw," put in the unceremonious Hurry. "That moccasin must be had, or Floating Tom will keep off here at
arm's length till the hearth cools in his cabin. It's but a little
deerskin arter all, and cut thisaway or thataway, it's not a
skearcrow to frighten true hunters from their game. What
say you, Sarpent, shall you or I canoe it?"

"Let red man go. Better eyes than paleface—know Huron
trick better, too."

"That I'll gainsay, to the hour of my death! A white man's
eyes, and a white man's nose, and for that matter his sight
and ears, are all better than an Injin's, when fairly tried.
Time and ag'in have I put that to the proof, and what is
proved is sartain. Still I suppose the poorest vagabond going,
whether Delaware or Huron, can find his way to yonder
hut and back ag'in; and so, Sarpent, use your paddle and welcome."

Chingachgook was already in the canoe, and he dipped the
implement the other named into the water just as Hurry's

limber tongue ceased. Wah-ta!-Wah saw the departure of her
warrior on this occasion with the submissive silence of an
Indian girl, but with most of the misgivings and apprehensions
of her sex. Throughout the whole of the past night, and
down to the moment when they used the glass together in
the hut, Chingachgook had manifested as much manly tenderness toward his betrothed as one of the most refined
sentiments could have shown under similar circumstances,
but now every sign of weakness was lost in an appearance
of stern resolution. Although Hist timidly endeavored to
catch his eye as the canoe left the side of the ark, the pride
of a warrior would not permit him to meet her fond and
anxious looks. The canoe departed, and not a wandering
glance rewarded her solicitude.

Nor were the Delaware's care and gravity misplaced, under
the impressions with which he proceeded on this enterprise.
If the enemy had really gained possession of the building, he
was obliged to put himself under the very muzzles of their
rifles, as it were, and this too without the protection of any
of that cover which forms so essential an ally in Indian warfare. It is scarcely possible to conceive of a service more
dangerous, and had the Serpent been fortified by the experience of ten more years—or had his friend, the Deerslayer, been present—it would never have been attempted,
the advantages in no degree compensating for the risk. But
the pride of an Indian chief was acted on by the rivalry of
color, and it is not unlikely that the presence of the very
creature from whom his ideas of manhood prevented his
receiving a single glance, overflowing as he was with the love
she so well merited, had no small influence on his determination.

Chingachgook paddled steadily toward the palisades, keeping his eye on the different loops of the building. Each instant he expected to see the muzzle of a rifle protruded, or
to hear its sharp crack, but he succeeded in reaching the
piles in safety. Here he was, in a measure, protected, having
the heads of the palisades between him and the hut; the
chances of any attempt on his life, while thus covered, were
greatly diminished. The canoe had reached the piles with its
head inclining northward, at a short distance from the moccasin. Instead of turning to pick up the latter, the Delaware
slowly made the circuit of the whole building, deliberately

examining every object that should betray the presence of enemies, or the commission of violence. Not a single sign could be discovered, however, to confirm the suspicions that had been awakened. The stillness of desertion pervaded the building; not a fastening was displaced; not a window had been broken. The door looked as secure as at the hour when it was closed by Hutter, and even the gate of the dock had all the customary fastenings. In short, the most wary and jealous eye could detect no other evidence of the visit of enemies than that which was connected with the appearance of the floating moccasin.

The Delaware was now greatly at a loss how to proceed. At one moment, as he came round in front of the castle, he was on the point of stepping up on the platform, and of applying his eye to one of the loops, with a view of taking a direct personal inspection of the state of things within; but he hesitated. Though of little experience in such matters, himself, he had heard so much of Indian artifices through traditions, had listened with such breathless interest to the narration of the escapes of the elder warriors, and, in short, was so well schooled in the theory of his calling, that it was almost as impossible for him to make any gross blunder on such an occasion, as it was for a well-grounded scholar, who had commenced correctly, to fail in solving his problem in mathematics. Relinquishing the momentary intention to land, the chief slowly pursued his course round the palisades. As he approached the moccasin—having now nearly completed the circuit of the building—he threw the ominous article into the canoe, by a dexterous and almost imperceptible movement of his paddle. He was now ready to depart; but retreat was even more dangerous than the approach, as the eye could no longer be riveted on the loops. If there was really anyone in the castle, the motive of the Delaware in reconnoitering must be understood; and it was the wisest way, however perilous it might be, to retire with an air of confidence, as if all distrust were terminated by the examination. Such, accordingly, was the course adopted by the Indian, who paddled deliberately away, taking the direction of the ark, suffering no nervous impulse to quicken the motions of his arms, or to induce him to turn even a furtive glance behind him.

No tender wife, reared in the refinements of the highest

civilization, ever met a husband on his return from the field, with more of sensibility in her countenance than Hist discovered as she saw the Great Serpent of the Delawares step, unharmed, into the ark. Still, she repressed her emotions, though the joy that sparkled in her dark eyes, and the smile that lighted her pretty mouth spoke a language that her betrothed could understand.

"Well, Sarpent," cried Hurry, always the first to speak, "what news from the muskrats? Did they show their teeth, as you surrounded their dwelling?"

"I no like him," sententiously returned the Delaware. "Too still. So still, can see silence!"

"That's downright Injin—as if anything could make less noise than nothing! If you've no better reason than this to give, Old Tom had better hoist his sail and go and get his breakfast under his own roof. What has become of the moccasin?"

"Here," returned Chingachgook, holding up his prize for the general inspection.

The moccasin was examined, and Hist confidently pronounced it to be Huron, by the manner in which the porcupine's quills were arranged on its front. Hutter, and the Delaware, too, were decidedly of the same opinion. Admitting all this, however, it did not necessarily follow that its owners were in the castle. The moccasin might have drifted from a distance, or it might have fallen from the foot of some scout who had quitted the place when his errand was accomplished. In short, it explained nothing, while it awakened so much distrust.

Under the circumstances, Hutter and Hurry were not men to be long deterred from proceeding by proofs as slight as that of the moccasin. They hoisted the sail again, and the ark was soon in motion, heading toward the castle. The wind, or air, continued light, and the movement was sufficiently slow to allow of a deliberate survey of the building as the scow approached.

The same deathlike silence reigned, and it was difficult to fancy that anything possessing animal life could be in or around the place. Unlike the Serpent, whose imagination had acted through his traditions until he was ready to perceive an artificial in a natural stillness, the others saw nothing to apprehend in a tranquillity that, in truth, merely denoted

the repose of inanimate objects. The accessories of the scene, too, were soothing and calm, rather than exciting. The day had not yet advanced so far as to bring the sun above the horizon, but the heavens, the atmosphere, and the woods and lake were all seen under that softened light which immediately precedes his appearance and which, perhaps, is the most witching period of the four-and-twenty hours. It is the moment when everything is distinct, even the atmosphere seeming to possess a liquid lucidity, the hues appearing gray and softened, with the outlines of objects diffused, and the perspective just as moral truths that are presented in their simplicity without the meretricious aids of ornament or glitter. In a word, it is the moment when the senses seem to recover their powers in the simplest and most accurate forms, like the mind emerging from the obscurity of doubts into the tranquillity and peace of demonstration. Most of the influence that such a scene is apt to produce on those who are properly constituted in a moral sense was lost on Hutter and Hurry, but both the Delawares, though too much accustomed to witness the loveliness of morningtide to stop to analyze their feelings, were equally sensible of the beauties of the hour, though it was probably in a way unknown to themselves. It disposed the young warrior to peace, and never had he felt less longings for the glory of the combat than when he joined Hist in the cabin the instant the scow rubbed against the side of the platform. From the indulgence of such gentle emotions, however, he was aroused by a rude summons from Hurry, who called on him to come forth and help to take in the sail and to secure the ark.

Chingachgook obeyed, and by the time he had reached the head of the scow, Hurry was on the platform, stamping his feet, like one glad to touch what, by comparison, might be called terra firma, and proclaiming his indifference to the whole Huron tribe in his customary noisy, dogmatical manner. Hutter had hauled a canoe up to the head of the scow, and was already about to undo the fastenings of the gate, in order to enter within the dock. March had no other motive in landing than a senseless bravado, and having shaken the door in a manner to put its solidity to the proof, he joined Hutter in the canoe and began to aid him in opening the gate. The reader will remember that this mode of entrance was rendered necessary by the manner in which the

owner of this singular residence habitually secured it whenever it was left empty; more particularly at moments when
danger was apprehended. Hutter had placed a line in the
Delaware's hand, on entering the canoe, intimating that the
other was to fasten the ark to the platform and to lower
the sail. Instead of following these directions, however, Chingachgook left the sail standing, and throwing the bight of
the rope over the head of a pile, he permitted the ark to drift
around until it lay against the defenses in a position where
it could be entered only by means of a boat, or by passing
along the summits of the palisades—the latter being an exploit that required some command of the feet, and which
was not to be attempted in the face of a resolute enemy.

In consequence of this change in the position of the scow,
which was effected before Hutter had succeeded in opening
the gate of his dock, the ark and the castle lay, as sailors
would express it, yardarm and yardarm, kept asunder some
ten or twelve feet by means of the piles. As the scow pressed
close against the latter, their tops formed a species of breastwork that rose to the height of a man's head, covering in a
certain degree the parts of the scow that were not protected
by the cabin. The Delaware surveyed this arrangement with
great satisfaction, and as the canoe of Hutter passed through
the gate into the dock, he thought that he might defend his
position against any garrison in the castle for a sufficient
time, could he but have had the helping arm of his friend
Deerslayer. As it was, he felt comparatively secure and no
longer suffered the keen apprehensions he had lately experienced in behalf of Hist.

A single shove sent the canoe from the gate to the trap beneath the castle. Here Hutter found all fast, neither padlock, nor chain, nor bar having been molested. The key was
produced, the locks removed, the chain loosened, and the
trap pushed upward. Hurry now thrust his head in at the
opening; the arms followed, and the colossal legs rose without any apparent effort. At the next instant, his heavy foot
was heard stamping in the passage above—that which separated the chambers of the father and daughters, and into
which the trap opened. He then gave a shout of triumph.

"Come on, old Tom," the reckless woodsman called out
from within the building. "Here's your tenement, safe and
sound; aye, and as empty as a nut that has passed half an

hour in the paws of a squirrel! The Delaware brags of being able to *see* silence; let him come here, and he may *feel* it in the bargain."

"Any silence where you are, Hurry Harry," returned Hutter, thrusting his head in at the hole as he uttered the last word, which instantly caused his voice to sound smothered to those without—"any silence where you are ought to be both seen and felt, for it's unlike any other silence."

"Come, come—old fellow; hoist yourself up, and we'll open doors and windows and let in the fresh air to brighten up matters. Few words, in troublesome times, make men the best fri'nds. Your darter Judith is what I call a misbehaving young woman, and the hold of the whole family on me is so much weakened by her late conduct that it wouldn't take a speech as long as the ten commandments to send me off to the river, leaving you and your traps, your ark and your children, your manservants and your maidservants, your oxen and your asses, to fight this battle with the Iroquois by yourselves. Open that window, Floating Tom, and I'll blunder through and do the same job to the front door."

A moment of silence succeeded, and a noise like that produced by the fall of a heavy body followed. A deep execration from Hurry succeeded, and then the whole interior of the building seemed alive. The noises that now so suddenly —and, we may add, so unexpectedly, even to the Delaware —broke the stillness within could not be mistaken. They resembled those that would be produced by a struggle between tigers in a cage. Once or twice the Indian yell was given, but it seemed smothered, and as if it proceeded from exhausted or compressed throats, and in a single instance, a deep and another shockingly revolting execration came from the throat of Hurry. It appeared as if bodies were constantly thrown upon the floor with violence, as often rising to renew the struggle. Chingachgook felt greatly at a loss what to do. He had all the arms in the ark, Hutter and Hurry having proceeded without their rifles, but there was no means of using them, or of passing them to the hands of their owners. The combatants were literally caged, rendering it almost as impossible, under the circumstances, to get out as to get into the building. Then there was Hist to embarrass his movements and to cripple his efforts. With a view to relieve himself from this disadvantage, he told the girl to take the re-

maining canoe and to join Hutter's daughters, who were incautiously but deliberately approaching, in order to save herself and to warn the others of their danger. But the girl positively and firmly refused to comply. At that moment, no human power, short of an exercise of superior physical force, could have induced her to quit the ark. The exigency of the moment did not admit of delay, and the Delaware, seeing no possibility of serving his friends, cut the line and, by a strong shove, forced the scow some twenty feet clear of the piles. Here he took the sweeps and succeeded in getting a short distance to windward, if any direction could be thus termed in so light an air, but neither the time nor his skill at the oars allowed the distance to be great. When he ceased rowing, the ark might have been a hundred yards from the platform, and half that distance to the southward of it, the sail being lowered. Judith and Hetty had now discovered that something was wrong, and were stationary a thousand feet further north.

All this while the furious struggle continued within the house. In scenes like these, events thicken in less time than they can be related. From the moment when the first fall was heard within the building to that when the Delaware ceased his awkward attempts to row, it might have been three or four minutes, but it had evidently served to weaken the combatants. The oaths and execrations of Hurry were no longer heard, and even the struggles had lost some of their force and fury; nevertheless, they still continued with unabated perseverance. At this instant the door flew open and the fight was transferred to the platform, the light, and the open air.

A Huron had undone the fastenings of the door, and three or four of his tribe rushed after him upon the narrow space, as if glad to escape from some terrible scene within. The body of another followed, pitched headlong through the door with terrific violence. Then March appeared, raging like a lion at bay, and for an instant freed from his numerous enemies. Hutter was already a captive and bound. There was now a pause in the struggle which resembled a lull in a tempest. The necessity of breathing was common to all, and the combatants stood watching each other, like mastiffs that have been driven from their holds and are waiting for a favorable opportunity of renewing them. We shall profit by this pause

to relate the manner in which the Indians had obtained possession of the castle; and this the more willingly because it may be necessary to explain to the reader why a conflict which had been so close and fierce should have also been so comparatively bloodless.

Rivenoak and his companion, particularly the latter, who had appeared to be a subordinate and occupied solely with his raft, had made the closest observations in their visits to the castle; even the boy had brought away minute and valuable information. By these means the Hurons obtained a general idea of the manner in which the place was constructed and secured, as well as of details that enabled them to act intelligently in the dark. Notwithstanding the care that Hutter had taken to drop the ark on the east side of the building, when he was in the act of transferring the furniture from the former to the latter, he had been watched in a way to render the precaution useless. Scouts were on the lookout on the eastern as well as on the western shore of the lake, and the whole proceeding had been noted. As soon as it was dark, rafts like that already described approached from both shores to reconnoiter, and the ark had passed within fifty feet of one of them without its being discovered, the men it held lying at their length on the logs, so as to blend themselves and their slow-moving machine with the water. When these two sets of adventurers drew near the castle, they encountered each other, and after communicating their respective observations, they unhesitatingly approached the building. As had been expected, it was found empty. The rafts were immediately sent for a reinforcement to the shore, and two of the savages remained to profit by their situation. These men succeeded in getting on the roof and, by removing some of the bark, in entering what might be termed the garret. Here they were found by their companions. Hatchets now opened a hole through the square logs of the upper floor, through which no less than eight of the most athletic of the Indians dropped into the room beneath. Here they were left, well supplied with arms and provisions, either to stand a siege, or to make a sortie, as the case might require. The night was passed in sleep, as is usual with Indians in a state of inactivity. The returning day brought them a view of the approach of the ark, through the loops, the only manner in which light and air were now

admitted, the windows being closed most effectually with plank, rudely fashioned to fit. As soon as it was ascertained that the two white men were about to enter by the trap, the chief, who directed the proceedings of the Hurons, took his measures accordingly. He removed all the arms from his own people, even to the knives, in distrust of savage ferocity, when awakened by personal injuries, and he hid them where they could not be found without a search. Ropes of bark were then prepared, and taking their stations in the three different rooms, they all waited for the signal to fall upon their intended captives. As soon as the party had entered the building, men without replaced the bark of the roof, removed every sign of their visit with care, and then departed for the shore. It was one of these who had dropped his moccasin, which he had not been able to find again, in the dark. Had the death of the girl been known, it is probable nothing could have saved the lives of Hurry and Hutter, but that event occurred after the ambush was laid, and at a distance of several miles from the encampment near the castle. Such were the means that had been employed to produce the state of things we shall continue to describe.

CHAPTER XX

> *Now all is done that man can do,*
> *And all is done in vain!*
> *My love! my native land, adieu,*
> *For I must cross the main;*
>   *My dear,*
> *For I must cross the main.*
>
> SCOTTISH BALLAD

IN THE LAST chapter we left the combatants breathing in their narrow lists. Accustomed to the rude sports of wrestling and jumping then so common in America, more especially on the frontiers, Hurry possessed an advantage, in addition to his prodigious strength, that had rendered the struggle less unequal than it might otherwise appear to be. This alone had enabled him to hold out so long against so many enemies, for the Indian is by no means remarkable for his skill or force in athletic exercises. As yet, no one had been seriously hurt, though several of the savages had received severe falls; and he, in particular, who had been thrown bodily upon the platform, might be said to be temporarily *hors de combat*. Some of the rest were limping, and March himself had not entirely escaped from bruises, though want of breath was the principal loss that both sides wished to repair.

Under circumstances like those in which the parties were placed, a truce, let it come from what cause it might, could not well be of long continuance. The arena was too confined, and the distrust of treachery too great, to admit of this. Contrary to what might be expected in his situation, Hurry was the first to recommence hostilities. Whether this proceeded from policy or an idea that he might gain some advantage by making a sudden and unexpected assault, or was

the fruit of irritation and his undying hatred of an Indian, it is impossible to say. His onset was furious, however, and at first it carried all before it. He seized the nearest Huron by the waist, raised him entirely from the platform, and hurled him into the water as if he had been a child. In half a minute, two more were at his side, one of whom received a grave injury by falling on the friend who had just preceded him. But four enemies remained, and in a hand-to-hand conflict, in which no arms were used but those which nature had furnished, Hurry believed himself fully able to cope with that number of redskins.

"Hurrah, Old Tom!" he shouted; "the rascals are taking to the lake, and I'll soon have 'em all swimming!" As these words were uttered, a violent kick in the face sent back the injured Indian, who had caught at the edge of the platform and was endeavoring to raise himself to its level, helplessly and hopelessly into the water. When the affray was over, his dark body was seen, through the limpid element of the Glimmerglass, lying, with outstretched arms, extended on the bottom of the shoal on which the castle stood, clinging to the sands and weeds as if life were to be retained by this frenzied grasp of death. A blow sent into the pit of another's stomach doubled him up like a worm that had been trodden on; but two able-bodied foes remained to be dealt with. One of these, however, was not only the largest and strongest of the Hurons, but he was also the most experienced of the warriors present, and that one whose sinews were the best strung in fights and by marches on the warpath. This man fully appreciated the gigantic strength of his opponent, and had carefully husbanded his own. He was also equipped in the best manner for such a conflict, standing in nothing but his breechcloth, the model of a naked and beautiful statue of agility and strength. To grasp him required additional dexterity and unusual force. Still, Hurry did not hesitate; but the kick that had actually destroyed one fellow creature was no sooner given than he closed in with this formidable antagonist, endeavoring to force him into the water also. The struggle that succeeded was truly frightful. So fierce did it immediately become, and so quick and changeful were the evolutions of the athletes, that the remaining savage had no chance for interfering, had he possessed the desire; but wonder and apprehension held him

spellbound. He was an inexperienced youth, and his blood curdled as he witnessed the fell strife of human passions, exhibited, too, in an unaccustomed form.

Hurry first attempted to throw his antagonist. With this view he seized him by the throat and an arm and tripped with the quickness and force of an American borderer. The effect was frustrated by the agile movements of the Huron, who had clothes to grasp by and whose feet avoided the attempt with a nimbleness equal to that with which it was made. Then followed a sort of melee, if such a term can be applied to a struggle between two in which no efforts were distinctly visible, the limbs and bodies of the combatants assuming so many attitudes and contortions as to defeat observation. This confused but fierce rally lasted less than a minute, however, when Hurry, furious at having his strength baffled by the agility and nakedness of his foe, made a desperate effort, which sent the Huron from him, hurling his body violently against the logs of the hut. The concussion was so great as momentarily to confuse the latter's faculties. The pain, too, extorted a deep groan—an unusual concession to agony to escape a red man in the heat of battle. Still, he rushed forward again to meet his enemy, conscious that his safety rested on his resolution. Hurry now seized the other by the waist, raised him bodily from the platform, and fell with his own great weight on the form beneath. This additional shock so far stunned the sufferer that his gigantic white opponent now had him completely at his mercy. Passing his hands round the throat of his victim, he compressed them with the strength of a vice, fairly doubling the head of the Huron over the edge of the platform, until the chin was uppermost, with the infernal strength he expended. An instant sufficed to show the consequences. The eyes of the sufferer seemed to start forward, his tongue protruded, and his nostrils dilated nearly to splitting. At this instant a rope of bark, having an eye, was passed dexterously within the two arms of Hurry; the end threaded the eye, forming a noose, and his elbows were drawn together behind his back with a power that all his gigantic strength could not resist. Reluctantly, even under such circumstances, did the exasperated borderer see his hands drawn from their deadly grasp, for all the evil passions were then in the ascendant. Almost at the same instant, a similar fastening

secured his ankles, and his body was rolled to the center of the platform as helplessly, and as cavalierly, as if it were a log of wood. His rescued antagonist, however, did not rise, for while he began again to breathe, his head still hung helplessly over the edge of the logs, and it was thought at first that his neck was dislocated. He recovered gradually only, and it was hours before he could walk. Some fancied that neither his body nor his mind ever totally recovered from this near approach to death.

Hurry owed his defeat and capture to the intensity with which he had concentrated all his powers on his fallen foe. While thus occupied, the two Indians he had hurled into the water mounted to the heads of the piles along which they passed and joined their companion on the platform. The latter had so far rallied his faculties as to have got the ropes, which were in readiness for use as the others appeared, and they were applied in the manner related, as Hurry lay pressing his enemy down with his whole weight, intent only on the horrible office of strangling him. Thus were the tables turned in a single moment; he who had been so near achieving a victory that would have been renowned for ages, by means of tradition, throughout all that region, lying helpless, bound, and a captive. So fearful had been the efforts of the paleface, and so prodigious the strength he exhibited, that even as he lay, tethered like a sheep before them, they regarded him with respect, and not without dread. The helpless body of their stoutest warrior was still stretched on the platform; and, as they cast their eyes toward the lake in quest of the comrade that had been hurled into it so unceremoniously, and of whom they had lost sight in the confusion of the fray, they perceived his lifeless form clinging to the grass on the bottom, as already described. These several circumstances contributed to render the victory of the Hurons almost as astounding to themselves as a defeat.

Chingachgook and his betrothed witnessed the whole of this struggle from the ark. When the three Hurons were about to pass the cords around the arms of the prostrate Hurry, the Delaware sought his rifle, but before he could use it, the white man was bound, and the mischief was done. He might still bring down an enemy, but to obtain the scalp was impossible; and the young chief, who would so freely risk his own life to obtain such a trophy, hesitated about

taking that of a foe without such an object in view. A glance at Hist and the recollection of what might follow checked any transient wish for revenge. The reader has been told that Chingachgook could scarcely be said to know how to manage the oars of the ark at all, however expert he might be in the use of the paddle. Perhaps there is no manual labor at which men are so bungling and awkward as in their first attempts to pull an oar, even the experienced mariner, or boatman, breaking down in his efforts to figure with the celebrated rullock of the gondolier. In short, it is temporarily an impracticable thing for a beginner to succeed with a single oar, but in this case it was necessary to handle two at the same time, and those of great size. Sweeps, or large oars, however, are sooner rendered of use by the raw hand than lighter implements, and this was the reason that the Delaware had succeeded in moving the ark as well as he did in a first trial. That trial, notwithstanding, sufficed to produce distrust, and he was fully aware of the critical situation in which Hist and himself were now placed, should the Hurons take to the canoe that was still lying beneath the trap, and come against them. At one moment he thought of putting Hist into the canoe in his own possession and of taking to the eastern mountain, in the hope of reaching the Delaware villages by direct flight. But many considerations suggested themselves to put a stop to this indiscreet step. It was almost certain that scouts watched the lake on both sides, and no canoe could possibly approach the shore without being seen from the hills. Then a trail could not be concealed from Indian eyes, and the strength of Hist was unequal to a flight sufficiently sustained to outstrip the pursuit of trained warriors. This was a part of America in which the Indians did not know the use of horses, and everything would depend on the physical energies of the fugitives. Last, but far from being least, were the thoughts connected with the situation of Deerslayer, a friend who was not to be deserted in his extremity.

Hist, in some particulars, reasoned and even felt differently, though she arrived at the same conclusions. Her own danger disturbed her less than her concern for the two sisters, in whose behalf her womanly sympathies were now strongly enlisted. The canoe of the girls, by the time the struggle on the platform had ceased, was within three hun-

dred yards of the castle, and here Judith ceased paddling, the evidences of strife first becoming apparent to the eyes. She and Hetty were standing erect, anxiously endeavoring to ascertain what had occurred, but unable to satisfy their doubts, from the circumstance that the building, in a great measure, concealed the scene of action.

The parties in the ark and in the canoe were indebted to the ferocity of Hurry's attack for their momentary security. In any ordinary case, the girls would have been immediately captured; a measure easy of execution now that the savages had a canoe, were it not for the rude check the audacity of the Hurons had received in the recent struggle. It required some little time to recover from the effects of this violent scene, and this so much the more because the principal man of the party, in the way of personal prowess at least, had been so great a sufferer. Still, it was of the last importance that Judith and her sister should seek immediate refuge in the ark, where the defenses offered a temporary shelter at least; and the first step was to devise the means of inducing them to do so. Hist showed herself in the stern of the scow and made many gestures and signs, in vain, in order to induce the girls to make a circuit to avoid the castle and to approach the ark from the eastward. But these signs were distrusted or misunderstood. It is probable Judith was not yet sufficiently aware of the real state of things to put full confidence in either party. Instead of doing as desired, she rather kept more aloof, paddling slowly back to the north, or into the broadest part of the lake, where she could command the widest view and had the fairest field for flight before her. At this instant the sun appeared above the pines of the eastern range of mountains, and a light southerly breeze arose, as was usual enough at that season and hour.

Chingachgook lost no time in hoisting the sail. Whatever might be in reserve for him, there could be no question that it was every way desirable to get the ark at such a distance from the castle as to reduce his enemies to the necessity of approaching the former in the canoe, which the chances of war had so inopportunely, for his wishes and security, thrown into their hands. The appearance of the opening duck seemed first to arouse the Hurons from their apathy, and by the time the head of the scow had fallen off before the wind,

which it did unfortunately in the wrong direction, bringing it within a few yards of the platform, Hist found it necessary to warn her lover of the importance of covering his person against the rifles of his foes. This was a danger to be avoided under all circumstances, and so much the more because the Delaware found that Hist would not take to the cover herself, so long as he remained exposed. Accordingly Chingachgook abandoned the scow to its own movements, forced Hist into the cabin, the doors of which he immediately secured, and then he looked about him for the rifles.

The situation of the parties was now so singular as to merit a particular description. The ark was within sixty yards of the castle, a little to the southward, or to windward of it, with its sail full, and the steering oar abandoned. The latter, fortunately, was loose, so that it produced no great influence on the crablike movements of the unwieldy craft. The sail being set, as sailors term it, flying, or having no braces, the air forced the yard forward, though both sheets were fast. The effect was threefold on a boat with a bottom that was perfectly flat and that drew merely some three or four inches of water. It pressed the head slowly around to leeward, it forced the whole fabric bodily in the same direction at the same time, and the water that unavoidably gathered under the lee also gave the scow a forward movement. All these changes were exceedingly slow, however, for the wind was not only light, but it was baffling as usual, and twice or thrice the sail shook. Once it was absolutely taken aback.

Had there been any keel to the ark, it would inevitably have run foul of the platform, bows on, when it is probable nothing could have prevented the Hurons from carrying it, more particularly as the sail would have enabled them to approach under cover. As it was, the scow wore slowly round, barely clearing that part of the building. The piles projecting several feet, *they* were not cleared, but the head of the slow-moving craft caught between two of them by one of its square corners, and hung. At this moment the Delaware was vigilantly watching through a loop for an opportunity to fire, while the Hurons kept within the building, similarly occupied. The exhausted warrior reclined against the hut, there having been no time to remove him, and Hurry lay, almost as helpless as a log, tethered like a sheep on its way to

the slaughter, near the middle of the platform. Chingachgook could have slain the first at any moment, but his scalp would have been safe, and the young chief disdained to strike a blow that could lead to neither honor nor advantage.

"Run out one of the poles, Sarpent, if Sarpent you be," said Hurry, amid the groans that the tightness of the ligatures was beginning to extort from him. "Run out one of the poles, and shove the head of the scow off, and you'll drift clear of us—and, when you've done that good turn for *your-self,* just finish this gagging blackguard for *me.*"

The appeal of Hurry, however, had no other effect than to draw the attention of Hist to his situation. This quick-witted creature comprehended it at a glance. His ankles were bound with several turns of stout bark rope, and his arms above the elbows were similarly secured behind his back, barely leaving him a little play of the hands and wrists. Putting her mouth near a loop, she said in a low but distinct voice:

"Why you don't roll here, and fall in scow? Chingachgook shoot Huron if he chase!"

"By the Lord, gal, that's a judgmatical thought, and it shall be tried, if the starn of your scow will come a little nearer. Put a bed at the bottom for me to fall on."

This was said at a happy moment, for, tired of waiting, all the Indians made a rapid discharge of their rifles, almost simultaneously, injuring no one, though several bullets passed through the loops. Hist had heard part of Hurry's words, but most of what he said was lost in the sharp reports of the firearms. She undid the bar of the door that led to the stern of the scow, but did not dare to expose her person. All this time the head of the ark hung, but by a gradually decreasing hold, as the other end swung slowly round, nearer and nearer to the platform. Hurry, who now lay with his face toward the ark, occasionally writhing and turning over like one in pain, evolutions he had performed ever since he was secured, watched every change, and at last he saw that the whole vessel was free, and was beginning to grate slowly along the sides of the piles. The attempt was desperate, but it seemed the only chance for escaping torture and death, and it suited the reckless daring of the man's character. Waiting to the last moment, in order that the stern of the scow might fairly rub against the platform, he began to writhe again, as if in intolerable suffering, execrating all Indians in general,

and the Hurons in particular, and then he suddenly and rapidly rolled over and over, taking the direction of the stern of the scow. Unfortunately, Hurry's shoulders required more space to revolve in than his feet, and by the time he reached the edge of the platform, his direction had so far changed as to carry him clear of the ark altogether; and the rapidity of his revolutions, and the emergency, admitting of no delay, he fell into the water. At this instant, Chingachgook, by an understanding with his betrothed, drew the fire of the Hurons again, not a man of whom saw the manner in which one whom they knew to be effectually tethered had disappeared. But Hist's feelings were strongly interested in the success of so bold a scheme, and she watched the movements of Hurry as the cat watches the mouse. The moment he was in motion she foresaw the consequences, and this the more readily as the scow was now beginning to move with some steadiness, and she bethought her of the means of saving him. With a sort of instinctive readiness, she opened the door at the very moment the rifles were ringing in her ears; protected by the intervening cabin, she stepped into the stern of the scow in time to witness the fall of Hurry into the lake. Her foot was unconsciously placed on the end of one of the sheets of the sail, which was fastened aft, and catching up all the spare rope with the awkwardness but also with the generous resolution of a woman, she threw it in the direction of the helpless Hurry. The line fell on the head and body of the sinking man, and he not only succeeded in grasping separate parts of it with his hands, but he actually got a portion of it between his teeth. Hurry was an expert swimmer, and tethered as he was, he resorted to the very expedient that philosophy and reflection would have suggested. He had fallen on his back, and instead of floundering and drowning himself by desperate efforts to walk on the water, he permitted his body to sink as low as possible, and was already submerged, with the exception of his face, when the line reached him. In this situation he might possibly have remained until rescued by the Hurons, using his hands as fishes use their fins, had he received no other succor; but the movement of the ark soon tightened the rope, and of course he was dragged gently ahead, holding even pace with the scow. The motion aided in keeping his face above the surface of the water, and it would have been possible for one ac-

customed to endurance to have been towed a mile in this singular but simple manner.

It has been said that the Hurons did not observe the sudden disappearance of Hurry. In his present situation he was not only hid from view by the platform, but as the ark drew slowly ahead, impelled by a sail that was now filled, he received the same friendly service from the piles. The Hurons, indeed, were too intent on endeavoring to slay their Delaware foe by sending a bullet through some one of the loops or crevices of the cabin to bethink them at all of one whom they fancied so thoroughly tied. Their great concern was the manner in which the ark rubbed past the piles, although its motion was lessened at least one half by the friction, and they passed into the northern end of the castle, in order to catch opportunities of firing through the loops of that part of the building. Chingachgook was similarly occupied, and remained as ignorant as his enemies of the situation of Hurry. As the ark grated along, the rifles sent their little clouds of smoke from one cover to the other, but the eyes and movements of the opposing parties were too quick to permit any injury to be done. At length one side had the mortification, and the other the pleasure, of seeing the scow swing clear of the piles altogether, when it immediately moved away, with a materially accelerated motion, toward the north.

Chingachgook now first learned from Hist the critical condition of Hurry. To have exposed either of their persons in the stern of the scow would have been certain death, but, fortunately, the sheet to which the man clung led forward to the foot of the sail. The Delaware found means to unloosen it from the cleat aft, and Hist, who was already forward for that purpose, immediately began to pull upon the line. At this moment Hurry was towing fifty or sixty feet astern, with nothing but his face above water. As he was dragged out clear of the castle and the piles, he was first perceived by the Hurons, who raised a hideous yell and commenced a fire on what may very well be termed the "floating mass." It was at the same instant, that Hist began to pull upon the line forward—a circumstance that probably saved Hurry's life, aided by his own self-possession and border readiness. The first bullet struck the water directly on the spot where the broad chest of the young giant was visible

through the pure element, and might have pierced his heart had the angle at which it was fired been less acute. Instead of penetrating the lake, however, it glanced from its smooth surface, rose, and actually buried itself in the logs of the cabin, near the spot at which Chingachgook had shown himself the minute before, while clearing the line from the cleat. A second, and a third, and a fourth bullet followed, all meeting with the same resistance from the surface of the water, though Hurry sensibly felt the violence of the blows they struck upon the lake so immediately above and so near his breast. Discovering their mistake, the Hurons now changed their plan and aimed at the uncovered face, but by this time Hist was pulling on the line, the target advanced, and the deadly missiles still fell upon the water. In another moment the body was dragged past the end of the scow and became concealed. As for the Delaware and Hist, they worked perfectly covered by the cabin, and in less time than it requires to tell it they had hauled the huge frame of Hurry to the place they occupied. Chingachgook stood in readiness with his keen knife, and bending over the side of the scow, he soon severed the bark that bound the limbs of the borderer. To raise him high enough to reach the edge of the boat and to aid him in entering were less easy tasks, as Hurry's arms were still nearly useless, but both were done in time, when the liberated man staggered forward and fell, exhausted and helpless, into the bottom of the scow. Here we shall leave him to recover his strength and the due circulation of his blood, while we proceed with the narrative of events that crowd upon us too fast to admit of any postponement.

The moment the Hurons lost sight of the body of Hurry, they gave a common yell of disappointment, and three of the most active of their number ran to the trap and entered the canoe. It required some little delay, however, to embark with their weapons, to find the paddles, and, if we may use a phrase so purely technical, "to get out of dock." By this time Hurry was in the scow, and the Delaware had his rifles again in readiness. As the ark necessarily sailed before the wind, it had got by this time quite two hundred yards from the castle, and was sliding away each instant, further and further, though with a motion so easy as scarcely to stir the water. The canoe of the girls was quite a quarter of a mile distant from the ark, obviously keeping aloof, in ignorance

of what had occurred and in apprehension of the consequences of venturing too near. They had taken the direction of the eastern shore, endeavoring at the same time to get to windward of the ark and, in a manner, between the two parties, as if distrusting which was to be considered a friend and which an enemy. The girls, from long habit, used the paddles with great dexterity; Judith, in particular, had often sportively gained races in trials of speed with the youths that occasionally visited the lake.

When the three Hurons emerged from behind the palisades and found themselves on the open lake, and under the necessity of advancing unprotected on the ark, if they persevered in the original design, their ardor sensibly cooled. In a bark canoe, they were totally without cover, and Indian discretion was entirely opposed to such a sacrifice of life as would most probably follow any attempt to assault an enemy entrenched as effectually as the Delaware. Instead of following the ark, therefore, these three warriors inclined toward the eastern shore, keeping at a safe distance from the rifles of Chingachgook. But this maneuver rendered the position of the girls exceedingly critical. It threatened to place them, if not between two fires, at least between two dangers, or what they conceived to be dangers; instead of permitting the Hurons to enclose her in what she fancied a sort of net, Judith immediately commenced her retreat in a southern direction, at no very great distance from the shore. She did not dare to land; if such an expedient were to be resorted to at all, she could only venture on it in the last extremity. At first the Indians paid little or no attention to the other canoe, for, fully apprised of its contents, they deemed its capture of comparatively little moment, while the ark, with its imaginary treasures, the persons of the Delaware and of Hurry, and its means of movement on a large scale, was before them. But this ark had its dangers as well as its temptations, and after wasting nearly an hour in vacillating evolutions, always at a safe distance from the rifle, the Hurons seemed suddenly to take their resolution and began to display it by giving eager chase to the girls.

When this last design was adopted, the circumstances of all parties, as connected with their relative positions, were materially changed. The ark had sailed and drifted quite half a mile, and was nearly that distance due north of the

castle. As soon as the Delaware perceived that the girls avoided him, unable to manage his unwieldy craft, and knowing that flight from a bark canoe, in the event of pursuit, would be a useless expedient if attempted, he had lowered his sail, in the hope it might induce the sisters to change their plan and to seek refuge in the scow. This demonstration produced no other effect than to keep the ark nearer to the scene of action and to enable those in her to become witnesses of the chase. The canoe of Judith was about a quarter of a mile south of that of the Hurons, a little nearer to the east shore, and about the same distance to the southward of the castle as it was from the hostile canoe, a circumstance which necessarily put the last nearly abreast of Hutter's fortress. With the several parties thus situated, the chase commenced.

At the moment when the Hurons so suddenly changed their mode of attack, their canoe was not in the best possible racing trim. There were but two paddles, and the third man was so much extra and useless cargo. Then the difference in weight between the sisters and the other two men, more especially in vessels so extremely light, almost neutralized any difference that might proceed from the greater strength of the Hurons and rendered the trial of speed far from being as unequal as it might seem. Judith did not commence her exertions until the near approach of the other canoe rendered the object of the movement certain, and then she excited Hetty to aid her with her utmost skill and strength.

"Why should we run, Judith?" asked the simple-minded girl; "the Hurons have never harmed *me*, nor do I think they ever will."

"That may be true as to you, Hetty, but it will prove very different with me. Kneel down and say your prayer, and rise and do your utmost to help escape. Think of me, dear girl, too, as you pray."

Judith gave these directions from a mixed feeling; first, because she knew that her sister ever sought the support of her Great Ally, in trouble; and next, because a sensation of feebleness and dependence suddenly came over her own proud spirit in that moment of apparent desertion and trial. The prayer was quickly said, however, and the canoe was soon in rapid motion. Still, neither party resorted to their greatest exertions from the outset, both knowing that the

chase was likely to be arduous and long. Like two vessels of war that are preparing for an encounter, they seemed desirous of first ascertaining their respective rates of speed, in order that they might know how to graduate their exertions, previous to the great effort. A few minutes sufficed to show the Hurons that the girls were expert and that it would require all their skill and energies to overtake them.

Judith had inclined toward the eastern shore at the commencement of the chase with a vague determination of landing and flying to the woods as a last resort, but as she approached the land, the certainty that scouts must be watching her movements made her reluctance to adopt such an expedient unconquerable. Then she was still fresh, and had sanguine hopes of being able to tire out her pursuers. With such feelings, she gave a sweep with her paddle, and sheered off from the fringe of dark hemlocks, beneath the shades of which she was so near entering, and held her way again, more toward the center of the lake. This seemed the instant favorable for the Hurons to make their push, as it gave them the entire breadth of the sheet to do it in; and this, too, in the widest part, as soon as they had got between the fugitives and the land. The canoes now flew, Judith making up for what she wanted in strength by her great dexterity and self-command. For half a mile the Indians gained no material advantage, but the continuance of so great exertions for so many minutes sensibly affected all concerned. Here the Indians resorted to an expedient that enabled them to give one of their party time to breathe, by shifting their paddles from hand to hand, and this, too, without sensibly relaxing their efforts. Judith occasionally looked behind her, and she saw this expedient practiced. It caused her immediately to distrust the result, since her powers of endurance were not likely to hold out against those of men who had the means of relieving each other; still she persevered, allowing no very visible consequences immediately to follow the change.

As yet, the Indians had not been able to get nearer to the girls than two hundred yards, though they were what seamen would term "in their wake," or in a direct line behind them, passing over the same track of water. This made the pursuit what is technically called a "stern chase," which is proverbially a "long chase," the meaning of which is that in consequence of the relative positions of the parties, no

change becomes apparent except that which is a direct gain in the nearest possible approach. "Long" as this species of chase is admitted to be, however, Judith was enabled to perceive that the Hurons were sensibly drawing nearer and nearer, before she had gained the center of the lake. She was not a girl to despair, but there was an instant when she thought of yielding, with the wish of being carried to the camp where she knew the Deerslayer to be a captive; but the considerations connected with the means she hoped to be able to employ in order to procure his release immediately interposed, in order to stimulate her to renewed exertions. Had there been anyone there to note the progress of the two canoes, he would have seen that of Judith flying swiftly away from its pursuers, as the girl gave it freshly impelled speed, while her mind was thus dwelling on her own ardent and generous schemes. So material, indeed, was the difference in the rate of going between the two canoes for the next five minutes that the Hurons began to be convinced all their powers must be exerted, or they would suffer the disgrace of being baffled by women. Making a furious effort, under the mortification of such a conviction, one of the stronger of their party broke his paddle at the very moment when he had taken it from the hand of a comrade to relieve him. This at once decided the matter, a canoe containing three men, and having but one paddle, being utterly unable to overtake fugitives like the daughters of Thomas Hutter.

"There, Judith!" exclaimed Hetty, who saw the accident —"I hope, now, you will own that praying is useful! The Hurons have broke a paddle, and they never *can* overtake us."

"I never denied it, poor Hetty, and sometimes wish, in bitterness of spirit, that I had prayed more myself, and thought less of my beauty. As you say, we are now safe, and need only go a little south, and take breath."

This was done, the enemy giving up the pursuit as suddenly as a ship that has lost an important spar, the instant the accident occurred. Instead of following Judith's canoe, which was now lightly skimming over the water toward the south, the Hurons turned their bows toward the castle, where they soon arrived and landed. The girls, fearful that some spare paddles might be found in or about the buildings, continued on; nor did they stop until so distant from their enemies as to give them every chance of escape, should the chase be

renewed. It would seem that the savages meditated no such design, but at the end of an hour their canoe, filled with men, was seen quitting the castle and steering toward the shore. The girls were without food, and they now drew nearer to the buildings and the ark, having finally made up their minds, from its maneuvers, that the latter contained friends.

Notwithstanding the seeming desertion of the castle, Judith approached it with extreme caution. The ark was now quite a mile to the northward, but sweeping up toward the buildings; this, too, with a regularity of motion that satisfied Judith a white man was at the oars. When within a hundred yards of the building, the girls began to encircle it, in order to make sure that it was empty. No canoe was nigh, and this emboldened them to draw nearer and nearer, until they had gone around the piles and reached the platform.

"Do you go into the house, Hetty," said Judith, "and see that the savages are gone. They will not harm you; and if any of them are still here, you can give me the alarm. I do not think they will fire on a poor defenseless girl, and I at least may escape, until I shall be ready to go among them of my own accord."

Hetty did as desired—Judith retiring a few yards from the platform the instant her sister landed, in readiness for flight. But the last was unnecessary, not a minute elapsing before Hetty returned to communicate that all was safe.

"I've been in all the rooms, Judith," said the latter earnestly, "and they are empty, except Father's; he is in his own chamber, sleeping, though not as quietly as we could wish."

"Has anything happened to Father?" demanded Judith, as her foot touched the platform, speaking quick, for her nerves were in a state to be easily alarmed.

Hetty seemed concerned, and she looked furtively about her, as if unwilling anyone but a child should hear what she had to communicate, and even that *she* should learn it abruptly.

"You know how it is with Father sometimes, Judith," she said. "When overtaken with liquor, he doesn't always know what he says or does—and he seems to be overtaken with liquor now."

"That is strange! Would the savages have drunk with him

and then leave him behind? But 'tis a grievous sight to a child, Hetty, to witness such a failing in a parent, and we will not go near him till he wakes."

A groan from the inner room, however, changed this resolution, and the girls ventured near a parent, whom it was no unusual thing for them to find in a condition that lowers a man to the level of brutes. He was seated, reclining in a corner of a narrow room, with his shoulders supported by the angle, and his head fallen heavily on his chest. Judith moved forward, with a sudden impulse, and removed a canvas cap that was forced so low on his head as to conceal his face and, indeed, all but his shoulders. The instant this obstacle was taken away, the quivering and raw flesh, the bared veins and muscles, and all the other disgusting signs of mortality as they are revealed by tearing away the skin, showed he had been scalped, though still living.

CHAPTER XXI

> *Lightly they'll talk of the spirit that's gone,*
> *And o'er his cold ashes upbraid him;*
> *But nothing he'll reck, if they'll let him sleep on,*
> *In the grave where a Briton has laid him.*

DISPUTED

THE READER MUST imagine the horror that daughters would experience at unexpectedly beholding the shocking spectacle that was placed before the eyes of Judith and Esther, as related in the close of the last chapter. We shall pass over the first emotions, the first acts of filial piety, and proceed with the narrative by imagining rather than relating most of the revolting features of the scene. The mutilated and ragged head was bound up, the unseemly blood was wiped from the face of the sufferer, the other appliances required by appearances and care were resorted to, and there was time to inquire into the more serious circumstances of the case. The facts were never known until years later, in all their details, simple as they were; but they may as well be related here, as it can be done in a few words. In the struggle with the Hurons, Hutter had been stabbed by the knife of the old warrior who had used the discretion to remove the arms of everyone but himself. Being hard pushed by his sturdy foe, his knife settled the matter. This occurred just as the door was opened and Hurry burst out upon the platform, as has been previously related. This was the secret of neither party's having appeared in the subsequent struggle, Hutter having been literally disabled, and his conqueror being ashamed to be seen with the traces of blood about him, after having used so many injunctions to convince his young warriors of the necessity of taking their prisoners alive. When the three Hurons returned from the chase, and it was determined

to abandon the castle and join the party on the land, Hutter was simply scalped, to secure the usual trophy, and was left to die by inches, as has been done in a thousand similar instances by the ruthless warriors of this part of the American continent. Had the injury of Hutter been confined to his head, he might have recovered, however; it was the blow of the knife that proved mortal.

There are moments of vivid consciousness, when the stern justice of God stands forth in colors so prominent as to defy any attempts to veil them from the sight, however unpleasant they may appear, or however anxious we may be to avoid recognizing it. Such was now the fact with Judith and Hetty, who both perceived the decrees of a retributive Providence, in the manner of their father's suffering, as a punishment for his own recent attempts on the Iroquois. This was seen and felt by Judith with the keenness of perception and sensibility that were suited to her character, while the impression made on the simpler mind of her sister was perhaps less lively, though it might well have proved more lasting.

"Oh, Judith!" exclaimed the weak-minded girl as soon as their first care had been bestowed on the sufferer. "Father went for scalps himself, and now where is his own? The Bible might have foretold this dreadful punishment!"

"Hush—Hetty—hush, poor sister—he opens his eyes; he may hear and understand you. 'Tis as you say and think, but 'tis too dreadful to speak of!"

"Water—" ejaculated Hutter, as it might be by a desperate effort that rendered his voice frightfully deep and strong for one as near death as he evidently was. "Water—foolish girls—will you let me die of thirst?"

Water was brought and administered to the sufferer—the first he had tasted in hours of physical anguish. It had the double effect of clearing his throat and of momentarily reviving his sinking system. His eyes opened with that anxious, distended gaze which is apt to accompany the passage of a soul surprised by death, and he seemed disposed to speak.

"Father—" said Judith, inexpressibly pained by his deplorable situation, and this so much the more from her ignorance of what remedies ought to be applied. "Father, can we do anything for you? Can Hetty and I relieve your pain?"

"Father!" slowly repeated the old man. "No, Judith—no, Hetty—I'm no father. *She* was your mother, but I'm no father. Look in the chest—'tis all there—give me more water."

The girls complied, and Judith, whose early recollections extended further back than her sister's, and who on every account had more distinct impressions of the past, felt an uncontrollable impulse of joy as she heard these words. There had never been much sympathy between her reputed father and herself, and suspicions of this very truth had often glanced across her mind, in consequence of dialogues she had overheard between Hutter and her mother. It might be going too far to say she had never loved him, but it is not so to add that she rejoiced it was no longer a duty. With Hetty the feeling was different. Incapable of making all the distinctions of her sister, her very nature was full of affection, and she *had* loved her reputed parent, though far less tenderly than the real parent, and it grieved her now to hear him declare he was not naturally entitled to that love. She felt a double grief, as if his death and his words together were twice depriving her of parents. Yielding to her feelings, the poor girl went aside and wept.

The very opposite emotions of the two girls kept both silent for a long time. Judith gave water to the sufferer frequently, but she forbore to urge him with questions, in some measure out of consideration for his condition but; if truth must be said, quite as much lest something he should add in the way of explanation might disturb her pleasing belief that she was not Thomas Hutter's child. At length Hetty dried her tears and came and seated herself on a stool by the side of the dying man, who had been placed at his length on the floor, with his head supported by some worn vestments that had been left in the house.

"Father," she said—"you let me *call* you Father, though you say you are not one—Father, shall I read the Bible to you? Mother always said the Bible was good for people in trouble. She was often in trouble herself, and then she made me read the Bible to her—for Judith wasn't as fond of the Bible as I am—and it always did her good. Many is the time I've known Mother begin to listen with the tears streaming from her eyes and end with smiles and gladness. Oh, Father, you don't know how much good the Bible can do, for you've never tried it; now, I'll read a chapter, and

it will soften your heart, as it softened the hearts of the Hurons."

While poor Hetty had so much reverence for, and faith in, the virtue of the Bible, her intellect was too shallow to enable her fully to appreciate its beauties, or to fathom its profound and sometimes mysterious wisdom. That instinctive sense of right, which appeared to shield her from the commission of wrong and even cast a mantle of moral loveliness and truth around her character, could not penetrate abstrusities, or trace the nice affinities between cause and effect, beyond their more obvious and indisputable connection, though she seldom failed to see the latter and to defer to all their just consequences. In a word, she was one of those who feel and act correctly, without being able to give a logical reason for it, even admitting revelation as her authority. Her selections from the Bible, therefore, were commonly distinguished by the simplicity of her own mind and were oftener marked for containing images of known and palpable things than for any of the higher cast of moral truths with which the pages of that wonderful book abound—wonderful and unequaled, even without referring to its divine origin, as a work replete with the profoundest philosophy, expressed in the noblest language. Her mother, with a connection that will probably strike the reader, had been fond of the book of Job, and Hetty had, in a great measure, learned to read by the frequent lessons she had received from the different chapters of this venerable and sublime poem—now believed to be the oldest book in the world. On this occasion the poor girl was submissive to her training, and she turned to that well-known part of the sacred volume with the readiness with which the practiced counsel would cite his authorities from the stores of legal wisdom. In selecting the particular chapter, she was influenced by the caption, and she chose that which stands in our English version as, *"Job excuseth his desire of death."* This she read steadily, from beginning to end, in a sweet, low, and plaintive voice, hoping devoutly that the allegorical and abstruse sentences might convey to the heart of the sufferer the consolation he needed. It is another peculiarity of the comprehensive wisdom of the Bible that scarce a chapter, unless it be strictly narrative, can be turned to that does not contain some searching truth that is applicable to

the condition of every human heart, as well as to the temporal state of its owner, either through the workings of that heart or even in a still more direct form. In this instance, the very opening sentence—*"Is there not an appointed time to man on earth?"*—was startling, and as Hetty proceeded, Hutter applied, or fancied he could apply, many aphorisms and figures to his own worldly and mental condition. As life is ebbing fast, the mind clings eagerly to hope, when it is not absolutely crushed by despair. The solemn words, *"I have sinned; what shall I do unto thee, O thou preserver of men? Why hast thou set me as a mark against thee, so that I am a burden to myself?"* struck Hutter more perceptibly than the others; and, though too obscure for one of his blunted feelings and obtuse mind either to feel or to comprehend in their fullest extent, they had a directness of application to his own state that caused him to wince under them.

"Don't you feel better now, Father?" asked Hetty, closing the volume. "Mother was always better when she had read the Bible."

"Water," returned Hutter, "give me water, Judith. I wonder if my tongue will always be so hot! Hetty, isn't there something in the Bible about cooling the tongue of a man who was burning in hellfire?"

Judith turned away, shocked, but Hetty eagerly sought the passage, which she read aloud to the conscience-stricken victim of his own avaricious longings.

"That's it, poor Hetty; yes, that's it. My tongue wants cooling, *now; what will it be hereafter?"*

This appeal silenced even the confiding Hetty, for she had no answer ready for a confession so fraught with despair. Water, so long as it could relieve the sufferer, it was in the power of the sisters to give, and, from time to time it was offered to the lips of the sufferer, as he asked for it. Even Judith prayed. As for Hetty, as soon as she found that her efforts to make her father listen to her texts were no longer rewarded with success, she knelt at his side and devoutly repeated the words which the Saviour has left behind him as a model for human petitions. This she continued to do, at intervals, as long as it seemed to her that the act could benefit the dying man. Hutter, however, lingered longer than the girls had believed possible when they first found him.

At times he spoke intelligibly, though his lips oftener moved in utterance of sounds that carried no distinct impressions to the mind. Judith listened intently, and she heard the words "husband," "death," "pirate," "law," "scalps," and several others of a similar import, though there was no sentence to tell the precise connection in which they were used. Still they were sufficiently expressive to be understood by one whose ears had not escaped all the rumors that had been circulated to her reputed father's discredit, and whose comprehension was as quick as her faculties were attentive.

During the whole of the painful hour that succeeded, neither of the sisters bethought her sufficiently of the Hurons to dread their return. It seemed as if their desolation and grief placed them above the danger of such an interruption; when the sound of oars was at length heard, even Judith, who alone had any reason to apprehend the enemy, did not start but at once understood that the ark was near. She went upon the platform fearlessly, for should it turn out that Hurry was not there, and that the Hurons were masters of the scow also, escape was impossible. Then she had the sort of confidence that is inspired by extreme misery. But there was no cause for any new alarm—Chingachgook, Hist, and Hurry all standing in the open part of the scow, cautiously examining the building to make certain of the absence of the enemy. They, too, had seen the departure of the Hurons, as well as the approach of the canoe of the girls to the castle, and presuming on the latter fact, March had swept the scow up to the platform. A word sufficed to explain that there was nothing to be apprehended, and the ark was soon moored in her old berth.

Judith said not a word concerning the condition of her father, but Hurry knew her too well not to understand that something was more than usually wrong. He led the way, though with less of his confident, bold manner than usual, into the house, and penetrating to the inner room, found Hutter lying on his back, with Hetty sitting at his side, fanning him with pious care. The events of the morning had sensibly changed the manner of Hurry. Notwithstanding his skill as a swimmer and the readiness with which he had adopted the only expedient that could possibly save him, the helplessness of being in the water, bound hand and foot, had produced some such an effect on him as the near

approach of punishment is known to produce on most criminals, leaving a vivid impression of the horrors of death upon his mind, and this, too, in connection with a picture of bodily helplessness, the daring of this man being far more the offspring of vast physical powers than of the energy of the will, or even of natural spirit. Such heroes invariably lose a large portion of their courage with the failure of their strength, and though Hurry was now unfettered and as vigorous as ever, events were too recent to permit the recollection of his late deplorable condition to be at all weakened. Had he lived a century, the occurrences of the few momentous minutes during which he was in the lake would have produced a chastening effect on his character, if not always on his manner.

Hurry was not only shocked when he found his late associate in this desperate situation, but he was greatly surprised. During the struggle in the building, he had been far too much occupied himself to learn what had befallen his comrade, and as no deadly weapon had been used in his particular case, but every effort had been made to capture him without injury, he naturally believed that Hutter had been overcome, while he owed his own escape to his great bodily strength and to a fortunate concurrence of extraordinary circumstances. Death, in the silence and solemnity of a chamber, was a novelty to him. Though accustomed to scenes of violence, he had been unused to sit by the bedside and watch the slow beating of the pulse as it gradually grew weaker and weaker. Notwithstanding the change in his feelings, the manners of a life could not be altogether cast aside in a moment, and the unexpected scene extorted a characteristic speech from the borderer.

"How now, old Tom," he said, "have the vagabonds got you at an advantage, where you're not only down, but are likely to be kept down! I thought you a captyve, it's true, but never supposed you so hard run as this!"

Hutter opened his glassy eyes and stared wildly at the speaker. A flood of confused recollections rushed on his wavering mind at the sight of his late comrade. It was evident that he struggled with his own images and knew not the real from the unreal.

"Who are you?" he asked in a husky whisper, his failing strength refusing to aid him in a louder effort of his voice.

'Who are you? You look like the mate of the *Snow*—he was a giant, too, and near overcoming us."

"I'm your mate, Floating Tom, and your comrade, but have nothing to do with any snow. It's summer now, and Harry March always quits the hills as soon after the frosts set in as is convenient."

"I know you—Hurry-scurry—I'll sell you a scalp! A sound one, and of a full-grown man—what'll you give?"

"Poor Tom! That scalp business hasn't turned out at all profitable, and I've pretty much concluded to give it up and to follow a less bloody calling."

"Have you got any scalp? Mine's gone—how does it feel to have a scalp? I know how it feels to lose one—fire and flames about the brain—and a wrenching at the heart—no, no—kill *first*, Hurry, and scalp *afterward*."

"What does the old fellow mean, Judith? He talks like one that is getting tired of the business as well as myself. Why have you bound up his head? Or have the savages tomahawked him about the brains?"

"They have done that for *him* which you and he, Harry March, would have so gladly done for *them*. His skin and hair have been torn from his head to gain money from the Governor of Canada, as you would have torn theirs from the heads of the Hurons to gain money from the Governor of York."

Judith spoke with a strong effort to appear composed, but it was neither in her nature, nor in the feeling of the moment, to speak altogether without bitterness. The strength of her emphasis, indeed, as well as her manner, caused Hetty to look up reproachfully.

"These are high words to come from Thomas Hutter's darter, as Thomas Hutter lies dying before her eyes," retorted Hurry.

"God be praised for that! Whatever reproach it may bring on my poor mother, I am *not* Thomas Hutter's daughter."

"Not Thomas Hutter's darter! Don't disown the old fellow in his last moments, Judith, for *that's* a sin the Lord will never overlook. If you're not Thomas Hutter's darter, whose darter be you?"

This question rebuked the rebellious spirit of Judith, for in getting rid of a parent whom she felt it was a relief to find she might own she had never loved, she overlooked

the important circumstance that no substitute was ready to supply his place.

"I cannot tell you, Harry, who my father was," she answered more mildly. "I hope he was an honest man, at least."

"Which is more than you think was the case with old Hutter? Well, Judith, I'll not deny that hard stories were in circulation consarning Floating Tom, but who is there that doesn't get a scratch when an inimy holds the rake? There's them that say hard things of *me,* and even *you,* beauty as you be, don't always escape."

This was said with a view to set up a species of community of character between the parties, and, as the politicians are wont to express it, with ulterior intentions. What might have been the consequences with one of Judith's known spirit, as well as her assured antipathy to the speaker, it is not easy to say, for just then Hutter gave unequivocal signs that his last moment was nigh. Judith and Hetty had stood by the dying bed of their mother, and neither needed a monitor to warn them of the crisis, and every sign of resentment vanished from the face of the first. Hutter opened his eyes and even tried to feel about him with his hands, a sign that sight was failing. A minute later his breathing grew ghastly; a pause totally without respiration followed; and then succeeded the last, long-drawn sigh, on which the spirit is supposed to quit the body. This sudden termination of the life of one who had hitherto filled so important a place in the narrow scene on which he had been an actor put an end to all discussion.

The day passed by without further interruption, the Hurons, though possessed of a canoe, appearing so far satisfied with their success as to have relinquished all immediate designs on the castle. It would not have been a safe undertaking, indeed, to approach it under the rifles of those it was now known to contain, and it is probable that the truce was more owing to this circumstance than to any other. In the meanwhile, the preparations were made for the interment of Hutter. To bury him on the land was impracticable, and it was Hetty's wish that his body should lie by the side of that of her mother, in the lake. She had it in her power to quote one of his speeches, in which he himself had called the lake the "family burying ground," and luckily this was done without the knowledge of her

sister, who would have opposed the plan, had she known it, with unconquerable disgust. But Judith had not meddled with the arrangement, and every necessary disposition was made without her privity or advice.

The hour chosen for the rude ceremony was just as the sun was setting, and a moment and a scene more suited to paying the last office to one of calm and pure spirit could not have been chosen. There are a mystery and a solemn dignity in death that dispose the living to regard the remains of even a malefactor with a certain degree of reverence. All worldly distinctions have ceased; it is thought that the veil has been removed and that the character and destiny of the departed are now as much beyond human opinions as they are beyond human ken. In nothing is death more truly a leveler than in this, since, while it may be impossible absolutely to confound the great with the low, the worthy with the unworthy, the mind feels it to be arrogance to assume a right to judge of those who are believed to be standing at the judgment seat of God. When Judith was told that all was ready, she went upon the platform, passive to the request of her sister, and then she first took heed of the arrangement. The body was in the scow, enveloped in a sheet, and quite a hundredweight of stones, which had been taken from the fireplace, were enclosed with it in order that it might sink. No other preparation seemed to be thought necessary, though Hetty carried her Bible beneath her arm.

When all were on board the ark, this singular habitation of the man whose body it now bore to its final abode was set in motion. Hurry was at the oars. In his powerful hands, indeed, they seemed little more than a pair of sculls which were wielded without effort, and as he was expert in their use, the Delaware remained a passive spectator of the proceedings. The progress of the ark had something of the stately solemnity of a funeral procession, the dip of the oars being measured and the movement slow and steady. The wash of the water, as the blades rose and fell, kept time with the efforts of Hurry, and might have been likened to the measured tread of mourners. Then the tranquil scene was in beautiful accordance with a rite that ever associates with itself the idea of God. At that instant the lake had not even a single ripple on its glassy surface, and the broad

panorama of woods seemed to look down on the holy tranquillity of the hour and ceremony in melancholy stillness. Judith was affected to tears, and even Hurry, though he hardly knew why, was troubled. Hetty preserved the outward signs of tranquillity, but her inward grief greatly surpassed that of her sister, since her affectionate heart loved more from habit and long association than from the usual connections of sentiment and taste. She was sustained by religious hope, however, which in her simple mind usually occupied the space that worldly feelings filled in that of Judith, and she was not without an expectation of witnessing some open manifestation of divine power on an occasion so solemn. Still, she was neither mystical nor exaggerated, her mental imbecility denying both. Nevertheless, her thoughts had generally so much of the purity of a better world about them that it was easy for her to forget earth altogether and to think only of heaven. Hist was serious, attentive, and interested, for she had often seen the interments of the palefaces, though never one that promised to be as peculiar as this, while the Delaware, though grave and also observant in his demeanor, was stoical and calm.

Hetty acted as pilot, directing Hurry how to proceed to find that spot in the lake which she was in the habit of terming "mother's grave." The reader will remember that the castle stood near the southern extremity of a shoal that extended near half a mile northerly, and it was at the furthest end of this shallow water that Floating Tom had seen fit to deposit the remains of his wife and child. His own were now in the course of being placed at their side. Hetty had marks on the land by which she usually found the spot, although the position of the buildings, the general direction of the shoal, and the beautiful transparency of the water all aided her, the latter even allowing the bottom to be seen. By these means the girl was enabled to note their progress, and at the proper time she approached March, whispering—

"Now, Hurry, you can stop rowing. We have passed the stone on the bottom, and mother's grave is near."

March ceased his efforts, immediately dropping the kedge, and taking the warp in his hand in order to check the scow. The ark turned slowly around under this restraint, and when it was quite stationary, Hetty was seen at its

tern, pointing into the water, the tears streaming from her yes in ungovernable natural feeling. Judith had been present t the interment of her mother, but she had never visited he spot since. This neglect proceeded from no indifference o the memory of the deceased—for she had loved her *mother*, and bitterly had she found occasion to mourn her oss—but she was averse to the contemplation of death, and there had been passages in her own life since the day of that interment which increased this feeling and rendered her, if possible, still more reluctant to approach the spot that contained the remains of one whose severe lessons of female morality and propriety had been deepened and rendered doubly impressive by remorse for her own failings. With Hetty, the case had been very different. To her simple and innocent mind, the remembrance of her mother brought no other feeling than one of gentle sorrow, a grief that is so often termed luxurious, even, because it associates with itself the images of excellence and the purity of a better state of existence. For an entire summer she had been in the habit of repairing to the place after nightfall, and carefully anchoring her canoe so as not to disturb the body, she would sit and hold fancied conversations with the deceased, sing sweet hymns to the evening air, and repeat the orisons that the being who now slumbered below had taught her in infancy. Hetty had passed her happiest hours in this indirect communion with the spirit of her mother, the wildness of Indian traditions and Indian opinions unconsciously to herself mingling with the Christian lore received in childhood. Once she had even been so far influenced by the former as to have bethought her of performing some of those physical rites at her mother's grave, which the red men are known to observe, but the passing feeling had been obscured by the steady, though mild light of Christianity, which never ceased to burn in her gentle bosom. Now her emotions were merely the natural outpourings of a daughter that wept for a mother whose love was indelibly impressed on the heart, and whose lessons had been too earnestly taught to be easily forgotten by one who had so little temptation to err.

There was no other priest than nature at that wild and singular funeral rite. March cast his eyes below, and through the transparent medium of the clear water, which was al-

most as pure as air, he saw what Hetty was accustomed to call "mother's grave." It was a low, straggling mound of earth, fashioned by no spade, out of a corner of which gleamed a bit of the white cloth that formed the shroud of the dead. The body had been lowered to the bottom and Hutter brought earth from the shore and let it fall upon it until all was concealed. In this state the place had remained until the movement of the waters revealed the solitary sign of the uses of the spot that has just been mentioned.

Even the most rude and brawling are chastened by the ceremonies of a funeral. March felt no desire to indulge his voice in any of its coarse outbreakings, and was disposed to complete the office he had undertaken in decent sobriety. Perhaps he reflected on the retribution that had alighted on his late comrade, and bethought him of the frightful jeopardy in which his own life had so lately been placed. He signified to Judith that all was ready, received her directions to proceed, and, with no other assistant than his own vast strength, raised the body and bore it to the end of the scow. Two parts of a rope were passed beneath the legs and shoulders, as they are placed beneath coffins and then the corpse was slowly lowered beneath the surface of the lake.

"Not *there*—Harry March—no, not *there*," said Judith shuddering involuntarily. "Do not lower it quite so near the spot where mother lies!"

"Why not, Judith?" asked Hetty earnestly. "They lived together in life, and should lie together in death."

"No—no—Harry March, further off—further off. Poor Hetty, you know not what you say. Leave me to order this."

"I know I am weak-minded, Judith, and that you are clever—but surely a husband should be placed near a wife. Mother always said that this was the way they bury in Christian churchyards."

This little controversy was conducted earnestly but in smothered voices, as if the speakers feared that the dead might overhear them. Judith could not contend with her sister at such a moment, but a significant gesture from her induced March to lower the body at a little distance from that of his wife; then he withdrew the cords, and the act was performed.

"There's an end of Floating Tom!" exclaimed Hurry, bending over the scow and gazing through the water at the body. "He was a brave companion on a scout and a notable hand with traps. Don't weep, Judith—don't be overcome, Hetty, for the righteousest of us all must die, and when the time comes, lamentations and tears can't bring the dead to life. Your father will be a loss to you, no doubt—most fathers are a loss, especially to onmarried darters—but there's a way to cure that evil, and you're both too young and handsome to live long without finding it out. When it's agreeable to hear what an honest and onpretending man has to say, Judith, I should like to talk a little with you, apart."

Judith had scarce attended to this rude attempt of Hurry's at consolation, although she necessarily understood its general drift and had a tolerably accurate notion of its manner. She was weeping at the recollection of her mother's early tenderness, and painful images of long-forgotten lessons and neglected precepts were crowding her mind. The words of Hurry, however, recalled her to the present time, and abrupt and unseasonable as was their import, they did not produce those signs of distaste that one might have expected, from the girl's character. On the contrary, she appeared to be struck with some sudden idea, gazed intently for a moment at the young man, dried her eyes, and led the way to the other end of the scow, signifying her wish for him to follow. Here she took a seat and motioned for March to place himself at her side. The decision and earnestness with which all this was done a little intimidated her companion, and Judith found it necessary to open the subject herself.

"You wish to speak to me of marriage, Harry March," she said, "and I have come here, over the grave of my parents, as it might be—no, no—over the grave of my poor, dear, dear mother to hear what you have to say."

"This is oncommon, and you have a skearful way with you this evening, Judith," answered Hurry, more disturbed than he would have cared to own; "but truth is truth, and it shall come out, let what will follow. You well know, gal, that I've long thought you the comeliest young woman my eyes ever beheld, and that I've made no secret of that fact, either

here on the lake, out among the hunters and trappers, or in the settlements."

"Yes—yes, I've heard this before, and I suppose it to be true," answered Judith, with a sort of feverish impatience.

"When a young man holds such language of any particular young woman, it's reasonable to calculate he sets store by her."

"True—true, Hurry—all this you've told me again and again."

"Well, if it's agreeable, I should think a woman couldn't hear it too often. They all tell me this is the way with your sex—that nothing pleases them more than to repeat, over and over, for the hundredth time, how much you like 'em, unless it be to talk to 'em of their good looks!"

"No doubt—we like both, on most occasions: but this is an uncommon moment, Hurry, and vain words should not be too freely used. I would rather hear you speak plainly."

"You shall have your own way, Judith, and I some suspect you always will. I've often told you that I not only like you better than any other young women going—or for that matter, better than *all* the young women going—but you must have observed, Judith, that I've never asked you, in up-and-down tarms, to marry me."

"I have observed both," returned the girl, a smile struggling about her beautiful mouth in spite of the singular and engrossing intentness which caused her cheeks to flush and lighted her eyes with a brilliancy that was almost dazzling. "I have observed both and have thought the last remarkable for a man of Harry March's decision and fearlessness."

"There's been a reason, gal, and it's one that troubles me even now—nay, don't flush up so, and look fierylike, for there are thoughts which will stick long in any man's mind, as there be words that will stick in his throat—but then, ag'in, there's feelin's that will get the better of 'em all, and to these feelin's I find I must submit. You've no longer a father, or a mother, Judith, and it's morally impossible that you and Hetty could live here alone, allowing it was peace and the Iroquois was quiet; but as matters stand, not only would you starve, but you'd both be prisoners, or scalped, afore a week was out. It's time to think of a change and a husband, and if you'll accept of me, all that's past shall be forgotten, and there's an end on't."

Judith had difficulty in repressing her impatience until his rude declaration and offer were made, which she evidently wished to hear and which she now listened to with a willingness that might well have excited hope. She hardly allowed the young man to conclude, so eager was she to bring him to the point and so ready to answer.

"There, Hurry, that's enough," she said, raising a hand, as if to stop him. "I understand you as well as if you were to talk a month. You prefer me to other girls, and you wish me to become your wife."

"You put it in better words than I can do, Judith, and I wish you to fancy them said, just as you most like to hear 'em."

"They're plain enough, Hurry, and 'tis fitting they should be so. This is no place to trifle or deceive in. Now listen to my answer, which shall be, in every tittle, as sincere as your offer. There is a reason, March, why I should never——"

"I suppose I understand you, Judith, but if I'm willing to overlook that reason, it's no one's consarn but mine. Now don't brighten up like the sky at sundown, for no offense is meant, and none should be taken."

"I do not brighten up, and will *not* take offense," said Judith, struggling to repress her indignation in a way she had never found it necessary to exert before. "There is a reason why I should not, *cannot,* ever be your wife, Hurry, that you seem to overlook, and which it is my duty now to tell you, as plainly as you have asked me to consent to become so. I do not, and I am certain that I never shall, love you well enough to marry you. No man can wish for a wife who does not prefer him to all other men, and when I tell you this frankly, I suppose you yourself will thank me for my sincerity."

"Oh, Judith, them flaunting, gay, scarlet-coated officers of the garrisons have done all this mischief!"

"Hush, March, do not calumniate a daughter over her mother's grave. Do not, when I only wish to treat you fairly, give me reason to call for evil on your head, in bitterness of heart! Do not forget that I am a woman, and that you are a man, and that I have neither father nor brother to revenge your words."

"Well, there is something in the last, and I'll say no more. Take time, Judith, and think better on this."

"I want no time; my mind has long been made up, and I have only waited for you to speak plainly, to answer plainly.

We now understand each other, and there is no use in saying any more."

The impetuous earnestness of the girl awed the young man for never before had he seen her so serious and determined In most of their previous interviews she had met his advances with evasion or sarcasm, but these Hurry had mistaken for female coquetry and had supposed might easily be converted into consent. The struggle had been with himself about offering; he had never seriously believed it possible that Judith would refuse to become the wife of the handsomest man on all that frontier. Now that the refusal came and that in terms so decided as to put all caviling out of the question, if not absolutely dumfounded, he was so much mortified and surprised as to feel no wish to attempt to change her resolution.

"The Glimmerglass has now no great call for me," he exclaimed after a minute's silence. "Old Tom is gone; the Hurons are as plenty on shore as pigeons in the woods, and altogether it is getting to be an onsuitable place."

"Then leave it. You see it surrounded by dangers, and there is no reason why you should risk your life for others Nor do I know that you can be of any service to us. Go tonight; we'll never accuse you of having done anything forgetful or unmanly."

"If I do go, 'twill be with a heavy heart on your account Judith; I would rather take you with me."

"That is not to be spoken of any longer, March; but I will land you in one of the canoes as soon as it is dark, and you can strike a trail for the nearest garrison. When you reach the fort, if you send a party—"

Judith smothered the words, for she felt that it was humiliating to be thus exposing herself to the comments and reflections of one who was not disposed to view her conduct in connection with all in these garrisons with an eye of favor. Hurry, however, caught the idea, and without perverting it, as the girl dreaded, he answered to the purpose.

"I understand *what* you would say, and *why* you don't say it," he replied. "If I get safe to the fort, a party shall start on the trail of these vagabonds, and I'll come with it myself, for I should like to see you and Hetty in a place of safety before we part forever."

"Ah, Harry March, had you always spoken thus, felt

thus, my feelings toward you might have been different!"

"Is it too late now, Judith? I'm rough and a woodsman, but we all change under different treatment from what we have been used to."

"It *is* too late, March. I can never feel toward you, or any other man but *one*, as you would wish to have me. There, I've said enough, surely, and you will question me no further. As soon as it is dark, I or the Delaware will put you on the shore; you will make the best of your way to the Mohawk and the nearest garrison and send all you can to our assistance. And, Hurry, we are now friends, and I may trust you, may I not?"

"Sartain, Judith, though our fri'ndship would have been all the warmer could you look upon me as I look upon you."

Judith hesitated, and some powerful emotion was struggling within her. Then, as if determined to look down all weaknesses and accomplish her purposes at every hazard, she spoke more plainly.

"You will find a captain of the name of Warley at the nearest post," she said, pale as death and even trembling as she spoke; "I think it likely he will wish to head the party; I would greatly prefer it should be another. If Captain Warley *can* be kept back, 'twould make me very happy."

"That's easier said than done, Judith, for those officers do pretty much as they please. The major will order, and captains, and lieutenants, and ensigns must obey. I know the officer you mean; a red-faced, gay, oh!-be-joyful sort of a gentleman, who swallows Madeira enough to drown the Mohawk, and yet a pleasant talker. All the gals in the valley admire him, and they say he admires all the gals. I don't wonder he is your dislike, Judith, for he's a very gin'ral lover, if he isn't a gin'ral officer."

Judith did not answer, though her frame shook, and her color changed from pale to crimson and from crimson back again to the hue of death.

"Alas, my poor mother!" she ejaculated mentally, instead of uttering it aloud. "We are over thy grave, but little dost thou know how much thy lessons have been forgotten; thy care neglected; thy love defeated."

As this goading of the worm that never dies was felt, she arose and signified to Hurry that she had no more to communicate.

Chapter XXII

> ―――That point
> In misery, which makes the oppressed man
> Regardless of his own life, makes him too
> Lord of the oppressor's――――
>
> COLERIDGE

ALL THIS TIME Hetty had remained seated in the head of the scow, looking sorrowfully into the water which held the body of her mother as well as that of the man whom she had been taught to consider her father. Hist stood near her in gentle quiet, but had no consolation to offer in words. The habits of her people taught her reserve in this respect, and the habits of her sex induced her to wait patiently for a moment when she might manifest some soothing sympathy by means of acts, rather than of speech. Chingachgook held himself a little aloof, in grave reserve, looking like a warrior but feeling like a man.

Judith joined her sister with an air of dignity and solemnity it was not her practice to show, and though the gleamings of anguish were still visible on her beautiful face, when she spoke, it was firmly and without tremor. At that instant Hist and the Delaware withdrew, moving toward Hurry, in the other end of the boat.

"Sister," said Judith kindly, "I have much to say to you. We will get into this canoe, and paddle off to a distance from the ark—the secrets of two orphans ought not to be heard by every ear."

"Certainly, Judith, by the ears of their parents. Let Hurry lift the grapnel, and move away with the ark, and leave us here, near the graves of Father and Mother, to say what we may have to say."

"Father!" repeated Judith slowly, the blood for the first

360

time since her parting with March, mounting to her cheeks; "He was no father of ours, Hetty! *That* we had from his own mouth, and in his dying moments."

"Are you glad, Judith, to find you had no father? He took care of us, and fed us, and clothed us, and loved us; a father could have done no more. I don't understand why he wasn't a father."

"Never mind, dear child, but let us do as you have said. It may be well to remain here and let the ark move a little away. Do you prepare the canoe, and I will tell Hurry and the Indians our wishes."

This was soon and simply done, the ark moving with measured strokes of the sweeps a hundred yards from the spot, leaving the girls floating seemingly in air, above the place of the dead, so buoyant was the light vessel that held them, and so limpid the element by which it was sustained.

"The death of Thomas Hutter," Judith commenced after a short pause had prepared her sister to receive her communications, "has altered all our prospects, Hetty. If he was *not* our father, we are *sisters* and must feel alike and live together."

"How do I know, Judith, that you wouldn't be as glad to find I am not your sister as you are in finding that Thomas Hutter, as you call him, was not your father? I am only half-witted, and few people like to have half-witted relations; and then I'm not handsome—at least, not as handsome as you—and you may wish a handsomer sister."

"No, no, Hetty. *You* and you only are my sister—my heart, and my love for you, tell me that—and Mother was my mother—of that, too, am I glad and proud, for she was a mother to be proud of—but Father was not father!"

"Hush, Judith! His spirit may be near; it would grieve it to hear his children talking so, and that, too, over his very grave. Children should never grieve parents, Mother often told me, and especially when they are dead!"

"Poor Hetty! They are happily removed beyond all cares on our accounts. Nothing that *I* can do or say will cause Mother any sorrow *now*—there is some consolation in that, at least!—and nothing *you* can say or do will make her smile, as she used to smile on your good conduct when living."

"You don't know that, Judith. Spirits can see, and Mother may see as well as any spirit. She always told us that God

saw all we did and that we should do nothing to offend *him*, and now *she* has left us, I strive to do nothing that can displease *her*. Think how her spirit would mourn and feel sorrow, Judith, did it see either of us doing what is not right; and spirits *may* see, after all, especially the spirits of parents that feel anxious about their children."

"Hetty, Hetty—you know not what you say!" murmured Judith, almost livid with emotion. "The dead *cannot* see and know nothing of what passes here! But we will not talk of this any longer. The bodies of Mother and Thomas Hutter lie together in the lake, and we will hope that the spirits of both are with God. That we, the children of one of them, remain on earth is certain; it is now proper to know what we are to do in future."

"If we are not Thomas Hutter's children, Judith, no one will dispute our right to his property. We have the castle, and the ark, and the canoes, and the woods, and the lakes, the same as when he was living, and what can prevent us from staying here and passing our lives just as we ever have done?"

"No, no—poor sister. This can no longer be. Two girls would not be safe here, even should these Hurons fail in getting us into their power. Even Father had as much as he could sometimes do to keep peace upon the lake, and we should fail altogether. We must quit this spot, Hetty, and remove into the settlements."

"I am sorry you think so, Judith," returned Hetty, dropping her head on her bosom and looking thoughtfully down at the spot where the funeral pile of her mother could just be seen. "I am *very* sorry to hear it. I would rather stay here where, if I wasn't born, I've passed my life. I don't like the settlements—they are full of wickedness and heartburnings, while God dwells unoffended in these hills! I love the trees, and the mountains, and the lake, and the springs—all that His bounty has given us—and it would grieve me sorely, Judith, to be forced to quit them. You are handsome and not at all half-witted, and one day you will marry, and then you will have a husband, and I a brother, to take care of us, if women can't really take care of themselves in such a place as this."

"Ah! If this *could* be so, Hetty, then, indeed, I could *now* be a thousand times happier in these woods than in the settlements! *Once* I did not feel thus, but *now* I do. Yet where

is the man to turn this beautiful place into such a Garden of Eden for us?"

"Harry March loves you, sister," returned poor Hetty, unconsciously picking the bark off the canoe as she spoke. "He would be glad to be your husband, I'm sure, and a stouter and a braver youth is not to be met with the whole country around."

"Harry March and I understand each other, and no more need be said about *him*. There is one—but no matter. It is all in the hands of Providence, and we must shortly come to some conclusion about our future manner of living. Remain here—that is, remain here alone, we cannot—and perhaps no occasion will ever offer for remaining in the manner you think of. It is time, too, Hetty, we should learn all we can concerning our relations and family. It is not probable we are altogether without relations, and they may be glad to see us. The old chest is now our property, and we have a right to look into it and learn all we can by what it holds. Mother was so very different from Thomas Hutter that, now I know we are not his children, I burn with a desire to know whose children we can be. There are papers in that chest, I am certain, and those papers may tell us all about our parents and natural friends."

"Well, Judith, you know best, for you are cleverer than common, Mother always said, and I am only half-witted. Now Father and Mother are dead, I don't much care for any relations but you, and don't think I could love them I never saw as well as I ought. If you don't like to marry Hurry, I don't see who you can choose for a husband, and then I fear we shall have to quit the lake after all."

"What do you think of Deerslayer, Hetty?" asked Judith, bending forward like her unsophisticated sister and endeavoring to conceal her embarrassment in a similar manner. "Would he not make a brother-in-law to your liking?"

"Deerslayer!" repeated the other, looking up in unfeigned surprise. "Why, Judith, Deerslayer isn't in the least comely, and is altogether unfit for one like you!"

"He is not ill-looking, Hetty, and beauty in a man is not of much matter."

"Do you think so, Judith? I know that beauty is of no great matter, in man or woman, in the eyes of God; Mother has often told me so, when she thought I might have been

sorry I was not as handsome as you—though she needn't have been uneasy on that account, for I never coveted anything that is yours, sister; but tell me so she did; still, beauty is very pleasant to the eye, in both. I think, if I were a man, I should pine more for good looks than I do as a girl. A handsome man is a more pleasing sight than a handsome woman."

"Poor child! You scarce know what you say or what you mean! Beauty in our sex is something, but in man it passes for little. To be sure, a man ought to be tall, but others are tall as well as Hurry; and active—I think I know those that are more active; and strong—well, he hasn't all the strength in the world; and brave—I am certain I can name a youth who is braver."

"This is strange, Judith. I didn't think the earth held a handsomer, or a stronger, or a more active, or a braver man than Hurry Harry. I am sure *I* never met his equal in either of these things."

"Well, well, Hetty—say no more of this. I dislike to hear *you* talking in this manner. 'Tis not suitable to your innocence, and truth, and warmhearted sincerity. Let Harry March go. He quits us tonight, and no regret of mine will follow him, unless it be that he has stayed so long and to so little purpose."

"Ah, Judith, that is what I've long feared, and I did *so* hope he might be my brother-in-law!"

"Never mind it now; let us talk of our poor mother and of Thomas Hutter."

"Speak kindly, then, sister, for you can't be quite certain that spirits don't both hear and see. If Father wasn't father, he was good to us and gave us food and shelter. We can't put any stones over their graves here in the water to tell people all this, and so we ought to say it it with our tongues."

"They will care little for that, girl. 'Tis a great consolation to know, Hetty, that if Mother ever did commit any heavy fault when young, she lived sincerely to repent of it; no doubt her sins were forgiven her."

" 'Tisn't right, Judith, for children to talk of their parents' sins. We had better talk of our own."

"Talk of your sins, Hetty! If there ever was a creature on earth without sin, it is you! I wish I could say or think the same of myself; but we shall see. No one knows what changes

affection for a good husband can make in a woman's heart. I don't think, child, I have even now the same love for finery I once had."

"It would be a pity, Judith, if you did think of clothes over your parents' graves! We will never quit this spot, if you say so, and will let Hurry go where he pleases."

"I am willing enough to consent to the last, but cannot answer for the first, Hetty. We must live, in future, as becomes respectable young women, and cannot remain here to be the talk and jest of all the rude and foul-tongued trappers and hunters that may come upon the lake. Let Hurry go by himself, and then I'll find the means to see Deerslayer, when the future shall be soon settled. Come, girl, the sun has set and the ark is drifting away from us; let us paddle up to the scow and consult with our friends. This night I shall look into the chest, and tomorrow shall determine what we are to do. As for the Hurons, now we can use our stores without fear of Thomas Hutter, they will be easily bought off. Let me get Deerslayer once out of their hands, and a single hour shall bring things to an understanding."

Judith spoke with decision, and she spoke with authority, a habit she had long practiced toward her feeble-minded sister. But while thus accustomed to have her way by the aid of manner and a readier command of words, Hetty occasionally checked her impetuous feelings and hasty acts by the aid of those simple moral truths that were so deeply engrafted in all her own thoughts and feelings, shining through both with a mild and beautiful luster that threw a sort of holy halo around so much of what she both said and did. On the present occasion, this healthful ascendency of the girl of weak intellect over her of a capacity that, in other situations, might have become brilliant and admired, was exhibited in the usual simple and earnest manner.

"You forget, Judith, what has brought us here," she said reproachfully. "This is Mother's grave, and we have just laid the body of Father by her side. We have done wrong to talk so much of ourselves at such a spot, and ought now to pray God to forgive us and ask *Him* to teach us where we are to go and what we are to do."

Judith involuntarily laid aside her paddle, while Hetty dropped on her knees and was soon lost in her devout but simple petitions. Her sister did not pray. This she had long

ceased to do directly, though anguish of spirit frequently
wrung from her mental and hasty appeals to the great source
of benevolence for support, if not for a change of spirit. Still,
she never beheld Hetty on her knees that a feeling of tender
recollection, as well as of profound regret at the deadness of
her own heart, did not come over her. Thus had she herself
done in childhood and even down to the hour of her ill-
fated visits to the garrisons; and she would willingly have
given worlds, at such moments, to be able to exchange her
present sensations for that confiding faith, those pure aspirations, and the gentle hope that shone through every lineament and movement of her otherwise less-favored sister. All
she could do, however, was to drop her head to her bosom
and assume in her attitude some of that devotion in which
her stubborn spirit refused to unite.

When Hetty rose from her knees, her countenance had a
glow and serenity that rendered a face that was always agreeable positively handsome. Her mind was at peace, and her
conscience acquitted her of a neglect of duty.

"Now you may go, if you want to, Judith," she said. "God
has been kind to me and lifted a burden off my heart. Mother
had many such burdens, she used to tell me, and she always
took them off in this way. 'Tis the only way, sister, such
things can be done. You may raise a stone, or a log, with
your hands, but the heart *must* be lightened by prayer. I
don't think you pray as often as you used to do when younger, Judith!"

"Never mind—never mind, child," answered the other
huskily; " 'tis no matter, now. Mother is gone, and Thomas
Hutter is gone, and the time has come when we must think
and act for ourselves."

As the canoe moved slowly away from the place under the
gentle impulsion of the elder sister's paddle, the younger sat
musing, as was her wont whenever her mind was perplexed
by any idea more abstract and difficult of comprehension
than common.

"I don't know what you mean by future, Judith," she at
length suddenly observed. "Mother used to call heaven the
future, but you seem to think it means next week, or tomorrow!"

"It means both, dear sister—everything that is yet to come,
whether in this world or another. It is a solemn word, Hetty,

and most so, I fear, to them that think the least about it. Mother's future is eternity; ours may yet mean what will happen while we live in this world—is not that a canoe just passing behind the castle? Here, more in the direction of the point, I mean; it is hid, now; but certainly I saw a canoe stealing behind the logs."

"I've seen it some time," Hetty quietly answered, for the Indians had few terrors for her, "but I did not think it right to talk about such things over Mother's grave. The canoe came from the camp, Judith, and was paddled by a single man; he seemed to be Deerslayer, and no Iroquois."

"Deerslayer!" returned the other, with much of her native impetuosity. "That can't be! Deerslayer is a prisoner, and I have been thinking of the means of setting him free. Why did you fancy it Deerslayer, child?"

"You can look for yourself, sister; there comes the canoe in sight again, on this side of the hut."

Sure enough, the light boat had passed the building, and was now steadily advancing toward the ark, the persons on board of which were already collecting in the head of the scow to receive their visitor. A single glance sufficed to assure Judith that her sister was right and that Deerslayer was alone in the canoe. His approach was so calm and leisurely, however, as to fill her with wonder, since a man who had effected his escape from enemies, by either artifice or violence, would not be apt to move with the steadiness and deliberation with which his paddle swept the water. By this time the day was fairly departing, and objects were already seen dimly under the shores. In the broad lake, however, the light still lingered, and around the immediate scene of the present incidents, which was less shaded than most of the sheet, being in its broadest part, it cast a glare that bore some faint resemblance to the warm tints of an Italian or Grecian sunset. The logs of the hut and ark had a sort of purple hue, blended with the growing obscurity, and the bark of the hunter's boat was losing its distinctness, in colors richer but more mellowed than those it showed under a bright sun. As the two canoes approached each other—for Judith and her sister had plied their paddles so as to intercept the unexpected visitor ere he reached the ark—even Deerslayer's sunburned countenance wore a brighter aspect than common, under the pleasing tints that seemed to dance in the

atmosphere. Judith fancied that delight at meeting her had some share in this unusual and agreeable expression. She was not aware that her own beauty appeared to more advantage than common from the same natural cause, nor did she understand what it would have given her so much pleasure to know, that the young man actually thought her, as she drew near, the loveliest creature of her sex, his eyes had ever dwelt on.

"Welcome—welcome, Deerslayer!" exclaimed the girl as the canoes floated at each other's sides. "We have had a melancholy—a frightful day—but your return is, at least, one misfortune the less. Have the Hurons become more humane and let you go, or have you escaped from the wretches by your own courage and skill?"

"Neither, Judith—neither one nor t'other. The Mingos are Mingos still, and will live and die Mingos; it is not likely their natur's will ever undergo much improvement. Well, they've *their* gifts, and we've our'n, Judith, and it doesn't much become either to speak ill of what the Lord has created, though if the truth must be said, I find it a sore trial to think kindly or to talk kindly of them vagabonds. As for outwitting them, that might have been done, and it *was* done, too, atween the Sarpent, yonder, and me, when we were on the trail of Hist"—here the hunter stopped to laugh in his own silent fashion—"but it's no easy matter to sarcumvent the sarcumvented. Even the fa'ans get to know the tricks of the hunters afore a single season is over, and an Indian whose eyes have once been opened by a sarcumvention never shuts them ag'in in precisely the same spot. I've known whites to do that, but never a redskin. What they l'arn comes by practice, and not by books, and of all schoolmasters, exper'ence gives lessons that are the longest remembered."

"All this is true, Deerslayer; but if you have not escaped from the savages, how came you here?"

"That's a nat'ral question, and charmingly put. You *are* wonderful handsome this evening, Judith, or Wild Rose, as the Sarpent calls you, and I may as well say it, since I honestly think it. You may well call them Mingos savages, too, for savage enough do they feel, and savage enough will they act, if you once give them an opportunity. They feel their loss here, in the late scrimmage, to their hearts' cores,

nd are ready to revenge it on any creatur' of English blood
hat may fall in their way. Nor, for that matter, do I much
hink they would stand at taking their satisfaction out of a
Dutchman."

"They have killed Father; that ought to satisfy their
wicked cravings for blood," observed Hetty reproachfully.

"I know it, gal—I know the whole story—partly from
what I've seen from the shore, since they brought me up
from the point, and partly from their threats ag'in myself,
and their other discourse. Well, life is unsartain at the best,
and we all depend on the breath of our nostrils for it from
day to day. If you've lost a staunch fri'nd, as I make no
doubt you have, Providence will raise up new ones in his
stead, and since our acquaintance has begun in this oncommon manner, I shall take it as a hint that it will be a
part of my duty in futur', should the occasion offer, to see
you don't suffer for want of food in the wigwam. I can't
bring the dead to life, but as to feeding the living, there's
few on all this frontier can outdo me, though I say it in the
way of pity and consolation like, and in no particular in
the way of boasting!"

"We understand you, Deerslayer," returned Judith hastily,
"and take all that falls from your lips as it is meant, in kindness and friendship. Would to heaven all men had tongues
as true and hearts as honest!"

"In that respect men *do* differ, of a sartainty, Judith. I've
known them that wasn't to be trusted any further than you
can see them, and others ag'in whose messages, sent with a
small piece of wampum, perhaps, might just as much be
depended on as if the whole business was finished afore your
face. Yes, Judith, you never said truer words than when you
said some men might be depended on and some others
might not."

"You are an unaccountable being, Deerslayer," returned
the girl, not a little puzzled by the childish simplicity of
character that the hunter so often betrayed—a simplicity so
striking that it frequently appeared to place him nearly on
a level with the fatuity of poor Hetty, though always relieved by the beautiful moral truth that shone through all
that this unfortunate girl both said and did. "You are a most
unaccountable man, and I often do not know how to under-

stand you. But never mind, just now; you have forgotten to tell us by what means you are here."

"I!—oh! That's not very onaccountable, if I am myself, Judith. I'm out on furlough."

"Furlough! That word has a meaning among the soldiers that I understand; I cannot tell what it signifies when used by a prisoner."

"It means just the same. You're right enough; the soldiers do use it, and just in the same way as I use it. A furlough is when a man has leave to quit a camp, or a garrison, for a sartain specified time, at the end of which he is to come back and shoulder his musket, or submit to his torments, just as he may happen to be a soldier or a captyve. Being the last, I must take the chances of a prisoner."

"Have the Hurons suffered you to quit them in this manner, without watch or guard?"

"Sartain—I couldn't have come in any other manner, unless, indeed, it had been by a bold rising, or a sarcumvention."

"What pledge have they that you will ever return?"

"My word," answered the hunter simply. "Yes, I own I gave 'em *that*, and big fools would they have been to let me come without it! Why, in that case, I shouldn't have been obliged to go back and ondergo any deviltries their fury may invent, but might have shouldered my rifle, and made the best of my way to the Delaware villages. But, Lord, Judith, they know'd this, just as well as you and I do, and would no more let me come away without a promise to go back than they would let the wolves dig up the bones of their fathers!"

"Is it possible you mean to do this act of extraordinary self-destruction and recklessness?"

"Anan!"

"I ask if it can be possible that you expect to be able to put yourself again in the power of such ruthless enemies by keeping your word?"

Deerslayer looked at his fair questioner for a moment with stern displeasure. Then the expression of his honest and guileless face suddenly changed, lighting as by a quick illumination of thought, after which he laughed in his ordinary manner.

"I didn't understand you, at first, Judith; no, I didn't. You believe that Chingachgook and Hurry Harry won't

suffer it, but you don't know mankind thoroughly yet, I see. The Delaware would be the last man on 'arth to offer any objections to what he knows is a duty; as for March, he doesn't care enough about any creatur' but himself to spend many words on such a subject. If he did, 'twould make no great difference, howsever; but not he—for he thinks more of his gains than of even his own word. As for my promises, or your'n, Judith, or anybody else's, they give him no consarn. Don't be under any oneasiness, therefore, gal; I shall be allowed to go back according to the furlough; and if difficulties was made, I've not been brought up, and edicated, as one may say, in the woods, without knowing how to look 'em down."

Judith made no answer for some little time. All her feelings as a woman—and as a woman who, for the first time in her life, was beginning to submit to that sentiment which has so much influence on the happiness or misery of her sex—revolted at the cruel fate that she fancied Deerslayer was drawing down upon himself, while the sense of right, which God has implanted in every human breast, told her to admire an integrity as indomitable and unpretending as that which the other so unconsciously displayed. Argument, she felt, would be useless, nor was she, at that moment, disposed to lessen the dignity and high principle that were so striking in the intentions of the hunter by any attempt to turn him from his purpose. That something might yet occur to supersede the necessity for this self-immolation she tried to hope, and then she proceeded to ascertain the facts in order that her own conduct might be regulated by her knowledge of circumstances.

"When is your furlough out, Deerslayer?" she asked, after both canoes were heading toward the ark and moving, with scarcely a perceptible effort of the paddles, through the water.

"Tomorrow noon; not a minute afore; and you may depend on it, Judith, I shan't quit what I call Christian company to go and give myself up to them vagabonds an instant sooner than is downright necessary. They begin to fear a visit from the garrisons, and wouldn't lengthen the time a moment; and it's pretty well understood atween us that, should I fail in my ar'n'd, the torments are to take place

when the sun begins to fall, that they may strike upon their home trail as soon as it is dark."

This was said solemnly, as if the thought of what was believed to be in reserve duly weighed on the prisoner's mind, and yet so simply and without a parade of suffering as rather to repel than to invite any open manifestations of sympathy.

"Are they bent on revenging their losses?" Judith asked faintly, her own high spirit yielding to the influence of the other's quiet but dignified integrity of purpose.

"Downright, if I can judge of Indian inclinations by the symptoms. They think, howsever, I don't suspect their designs, I do believe; but one that has lived so long among men of redskin gifts is no more likely to be misled in Injin feelin's than a true hunter is like to lose his trail, or a staunch hound his scent. My own judgment is greatly ag'in my own escape, for I see the women are a good deal enraged on behalf of Hist, though I say it, perhaps, that shouldn't say it—seein' that I had a considerable hand myself in getting the gal off. Then there was a cruel murder in their camp last night, and that shot might just as well have been fired into my breast. Howsever, come what will, the Sarpent and his wife will be safe, and that is some happiness, in any case."

"Oh, Deerslayer, they will think better of this, since they have given you until tomorrow noon to make up your mind!"

"I judge not, Judith; yes, I judge not. An Injin is an Injin, gal, and it's pretty much hopeless to think of swarving him when he's got the scent and follows it with his nose in the air. The Delawares, now, are a half-christianized tribe —not that I think such sort of Christians much better than your whole-blooded disbelievers—but, nevertheless, what good half-christianizing can do to a man some among 'em have got, and yet revenge clings to their hearts like the wild creepers here to the tree! Then I slew one of the best and boldest of their warriors, they say, and it *is* too much to expect that they should captivate the man who did this deed in the very same scouting on which it was performed, and they take no account of the matter. Had a month or so gone by, their feelin's would have been softened down, and we might have met in a more friendly way; but it is as it is. Judith, this is talking of nothing but myself and my own

consarns, when you have had trouble enough, and may want to consult a fri'nd a little about your own matters. Is the old man laid in the water, where I should think his body would like to rest?"

"It is, Deerslayer," answered Judith almost inaudibly. "That duty has just been performed. You are right in thinking that I wish to consult a friend, and that friend is yourself. Hurry Harry is about to leave us; when he is gone, and we have got a little over the feelings of this solemn office, I hope you will give me an hour alone. Hetty and I are at a loss what to do."

"That's quite natural, coming as things have, suddenly and fearfully. But here's the ark, and we'll say more of this when there is a better opportunity."

CHAPTER XXIII

The winde is great upon the highest hilles;
The quiet life is in the dale below;
Who tread on ice shall slide against their willes;
They want not cares, that curious arts should know;
Who lives at ease and can content him so,
Is perfect wise, and sets us all to schoole:
Who hates this lore may well be called a foole.

CHURCHYARD

THE MEETING BETWEEN Deerslayer and his friends in the ark was grave and anxious. The two Indians, in particular, read in his manner that he was not a successful fugitive, and a few sententious words sufficed to let them comprehend the nature of what their friend had termed his "furlough." Chingachgook immediately became thoughtful, while Hist, as usual, had no better mode of expressing her sympathy than by those little attentions which mark the affectionate manner of woman.

In a few minutes, however, something like a general plan for the proceedings of the night was adopted, and to the eye of an uninstructed observer, things would be thought to move in their ordinary train. It was now getting to be dark, and it was decided to sweep the ark up to the castle and secure it in its ordinary berth. This decision was come to in some measure on account of the fact that all the canoes were again in the possession of their proper owners, but principally from the security that was created by the representations of Deerslayer. He had examined the state of things among the Hurons, and felt satisfied that they meditated no further hostilities during the night, the loss they had met having indisposed them to further exertions for the moment. Then, he had a proposition to make—the object of

his visit—and if this were accepted, the war would at once terminate between the parties, and it was improbable that the Hurons would anticipate the failure of a project on which their chiefs had apparently set their hearts by having recourse to violence previously to the return of their messenger.

As soon as the ark was properly secured, the different members of the party occupied themselves in their several peculiar manners, haste in council or in decision no more characterizing the proceedings of the border whites than it did those of their red neighbors. The women busied themselves in preparations for the evening meal, sad and silent, but ever attentive to the first wants of nature.

Hurry set about repairing his moccasins by the light of a blazing knot; Chingachgook seated himself in gloomy thought; while Deerslayer proceeded, in a manner equally free from affectation and concern, to examine "Killdeer," the rifle of Hutter that has been already mentioned, and which subsequently became so celebrated in the hands of the individual who was now making a survey of its merits. The piece was a little longer than usual, and had evidently been turned out from the workshop of some manufacturer of a superior order. It had a few silver ornaments, though on the whole it would have been deemed a plain piece by most frontiersmen; its great merit consisting in the accuracy of its bore, the perfection of the details, and the excellence of the metal. Again and again did the hunter apply the breech to his shoulder and glance his eye along the sights, and as often did he poise his body and raise the weapon slowly, as if about to catch an aim at a deer, in order to try the weight and to ascertain its fitness for quick and accurate firing. All this was done by the aid of Hurry's torch, simply, but with an earnestness and abstraction that would have been found touching by any spectator who happened to know the real situation of the man.

" 'Tis a glorious we'pon, Hurry!" Deerslayer at length exclaimed, "and it may be thought a pity that it has fallen into the hands of women. The hunters have told me of its expl'ites, and by all I have heard I should set it down as sartain death in exper'enced hands. Hearken to the tick of this lock—a wolf trap hasn't a livelier spring; pan and cock speak together, like two singing masters undertaking a psalm

in meetin'. I never *did* see so true a bore, Hurry, that's sartain."

"Aye, Old Tom used to give the piece a character, though he wasn't the man to particularize the ra'al natur' of any sort of firearms in practice," returned March, passing the deer's thongs through the moccasin with the coolness of a cobbler. "He was no marksman, that we must all allow, but he had his good p'ints as well as his bad ones. I have had hopes that Judith might consait the idee of giving Killdeer to me."

"There's no saying what young women may do, that's a truth, Hurry, and I suppose you're as likely to own the rifle as another. Still, when things are so very near perfection, it's a pity not to reach it entirely."

"What do you mean by that? Would not that piece look as well on my shoulder as on any man's?"

"As for looks, I say nothing. You are both good-looking and might make what is called a good-looking couple. But the true p'int is as to conduct. More deer would fall in one day, by that piece, in some men's hands than would fall in a week in your'n, Hurry! I've seen you try; you remember the buck, t'other day?"

"That buck was out of season, and who wishes to kill venison out of season? I was merely trying to frighten the creatur', and I think you will own that he was pretty well skeared, at any rate."

"Well, well, have it as you say. But this is a lordly piece, and would make a steady hand and quick eye the King of the Woods."

"Then keep it, Deerslayer, and become King of the Woods," said Judith earnestly, who had heard the conversation, and whose eye was never long averted from the honest countenance of the hunter. "It can never be in better hands than it is at this moment; there I hope it will remain these fifty years."

"Judith, you can't be in 'arnest!" exclaimed Deerslayer, taken so much by surprise as to betray more emotion than it was usual for him to manifest on ordinary occasions. "Such a gift would be fit for a ra'al king to make—yes, and for a ra'al king to receive."

"I never was more in earnest in my life, Deerslayer, and I am as much in earnest in the wish as in the gift."

"Well, gal, well, we'll find time to talk of this ag'in. You mustn't be downhearted, Hurry, for Judith is a sprightly young woman, and she has a quick reason; she knows that the credit of her father's rifle is safer in my hands than it can possibly be in your'n, and therefore you mustn't be downhearted. In other matters, more to your liking, too, you'll find she'll give you the preference."

Hurry growled out his dissatisfaction, but he was too intent on quitting the lake and in making his preparations to waste his breath on a subject of this nature. Shortly after, the supper was ready; it was eaten in silence, as is so much the habit of those who consider the table as merely a place of animal refreshment. On this occasion, however, sadness and thought contributed their share to the general desire not to converse, for Deerslayer was so far an exception to the usages of men of his cast as not only to wish to hold discourse on such occasions, but as often to create a similar desire in his companions.

The meal ended, and the humble preparations removed, the whole party assembled on the platform to hear the expected intelligence from Deerslayer on the subject of his visit. It had been evident he was in no haste to make his communications, but the feelings of Judith would no longer admit of delay. Stools were brought from the ark and the hut, and the whole six placed themselves in a circle, near the door, watching each other's countenances as best they could by the scanty means that were furnished by a lovely, starlit night. Along the shore, beneath the mountains, lay the usual body of gloom, but in the broad lake no shadow was cast, and a thousand mimic stars were dancing in the limpid element that was just stirred enough by the evening air to set them all in motion.

"Now, Deerslayer," commenced Judith, whose impatience resisted further restraint; "tell us all the Hurons have to say, and the reason why they have sent you on parole, to make us some offer."

"Furlough, Judith; furlough is the word; and it carries the same meaning with a captyve at large as it does with a soldier who has leave to quit his colors. In both cases the word is passed to come back—and now I remember to have heard that's the ra'al signification, 'furlough' meaning a 'word' passed for the doing of anything, or the like. Parole,

I rather think, is Dutch and has something to do with the tattoos of the garrisons. But this makes no great difference, since the vartue of a pledge lies in the idee, not in the word. Well, then, if the message must be given, it must, and perhaps there is no use in putting it off. Hurry will soon be wanting to set out on his journey to the river, and the stars rise and set just as if they cared for neither Injin nor message. Ah's me! 'Tisn't a pleasant, and I know it's a useless ar'n'd, but it must be told."

"Hearkee, Deerslayer," put in Hurry a little authoritatively; "you're a sensible man in a hunt, and as good a fellow on a march as a sixty-miler-a-day could wish to meet with, but you're oncommon slow about messages, especially them that you think won't be likely to be well received. When a thing is to be told, why, tell it, and don't hang back like a Yankee lawyer pretending he can't understand a Dutchman's English, just to get a double fee out of him."

"I understand you, Hurry, and well are you named to-night, seeing you've no time to lose. But let us come at once to the p'int, seeing that's the object of this council— for council it may be called, though women have seats among us. The simple fact is this. When the party came back from the castle, the Mingos held a council, and bitter thoughts were uppermost, as was plainly to be seen by their gloomy faces. No one likes to be beaten, a redskin as little as a paleface. Well, when they had smoked upon it, and made their speeches, and their council fire had burnt low, the matter came out. It seems the elders among 'em consaited I was a man to be trusted on a furlough. They're wonderful obsarvant, them Mingos; *that* their worst inimies must allow; but they consaited I was such a man; and it isn't often," added the hunter, with a pleasing consciousness that his previous life justified this implicit reliance on his good faith, "it isn't often they consait anything so good of a paleface; but so they did with me, and therefore they didn't hesitate to speak their minds, which is just this: You see the state of things. The lake and all on it, they fancy, lie at their marcy. Thomas Hutter is deceased, and as for Hurry, they've got the idee he has been near enough to death today not to wish to take another look at him this summer. Therefore, they account all your forces as reduced to Chingachgook and the two young women, and while they know the Dela-

ware to be of a high race, and a born warrior, they know he's now on his first warpath. As for the gals, of course they set them down much as they do women in gin'ral."

"You mean that they despise us!" interrupted Judith, with eyes that flashed so brightly as to be observed by all present.

"That will be seen in the ind. They hold that all on the lake lies at their marcy, and therefore they send by me this belt of wampum"—showing the article in question to the Delaware, as he spoke—"with these words: Tell the Sarpent, they say, that he has done well for a beginner; he may now strike across the mountains for his own villages, and no one shall look for his trail. If he has found a scalp, let him take it with him; the Huron braves have hearts and can feel for a young warrior who doesn't wish to go home empty-handed. If he is nimble, he is welcome to lead out a party in pursuit. Hist, howsever, must go back to the Hurons; when she left them in the night, she carried away, by mistake, that which doesn't belong to her."

"That *can't* be true!" said Hetty earnestly. "Hist is no such girl—but one that gives everybody his due—"

How much more she would have said in remonstrance cannot be known, inasmuch as Hist, partly laughing and partly hiding her face in shame, put her own hand across the speaker's mouth in a way to check the words.

"You don't understand Mingo messages, poor Hetty," resumed Deerslayer, "which seldom mean what lies exactly uppermost. Hist has brought away with her the inclinations of a young Huron, and they want her back again, that the poor young man may find them where he last saw them! The Sarpent, they say, is too promising a young warrior not to find as many wives as he wants, but this one he cannot have. That's their meaning, and nothing else, as I understand it."

"They are very obliging and thoughtful in supposing a young woman can forget all her own inclinations in order to let this unhappy youth find his!" said Judith ironically, though her manner became more bitter as she proceeded. "I suppose a woman is a woman, let her color be white or red, and your chiefs know little of a woman's heart, Deerslayer, if they think it can ever forgive when wronged, or ever forget when it fairly loves."

"I suppose that's pretty much the truth with some women,

Judith, though I've known them that could do both. The
next message is to you. They say the Muskrat, as they call
your father, has dove to the bottom of the lake; that he will
never come up again; and that his young will soon be in want
of wigwams, if not of food. The Huron huts, they think,
are better than the huts of York; they wish you to come
and try them. Your color is white, they own, but they think
young women who've lived so long in the woods would lose
their way in the clearin's. A great warrior among them has
lately lost his wife, and he would be glad to put the Wild
Rose on her bench at his fireside. As for the Feeble-mind, she
will always be honored and taken care of by red warriors.
Your father's goods, they think, ought to go to enrich the
tribe, but your own property, which is to include everything
of a female natur', will go, like that of all wives, into the
wigwam of the husband. Moreover, they've lost a young
maiden by violence lately, and 'twill take two palefaces to
fill her seat."

"And do *you* bring such a message to *me?*" exclaimed
Judith, though the tone in which the words were uttered
had more in it of sorrow than of anger. "Am I a girl to
be an Indian's slave?"

"If you wish my honest thoughts on this p'int, Judith,
I shall answer that I don't think you'll willingly ever become any man's slave, redskin or white. You're not to think
hard, howsever, of my bringing the message, as near as I
could, in the very words in which it was given to me. Them
was the conditions on which I got my furlough, and a
bargain is a bargain, though it is made with a vagabond.
I've told you what *they've* said, but I've not yet told you
what I think you ought, one and all, to answer."

"Aye, let's hear that, Deerslayer," put in Hurry. "My
cur'osity is up on that consideration, and I should like
right well to hear your idees of the reasonableness of the
reply. For my part, though, my own mind is pretty much
settled on the p'int of my own answer, which shall be
made known as soon as necessary."

"And so is mine, Hurry, on all the different heads, and
on no one is it more sartainly settled than on your'n. If
I was you, I should say—'Deerslayer, tell them scamps they
don't know Harry March! He is human, and having a white
skin he has also a white natur', which natur' won't let him

desart females of his own race and gifts in their greatest need. So set me down as one that will refuse to come into your treaty, though you should smoke a hogshead of tobacco over it."

March was a little embarrassed at this rebuke, which was uttered with sufficient warmth of manner and with a point that left no doubt of the meaning. Had Judith encouraged him, he would not have hesitated about remaining to defend her and her sister, but under the circumstances a feeling of resentment rather urged him to abandon them. At all events, there was not a sufficiency of chivalry in Hurry Harry to induce him to hazard the safety of his own person, unless he could see a direct connection between the probable consequences and his own interests. It is no wonder, therefore, that his answer partook equally of his intention and of the reliance he so boastingly placed on his gigantic strength, which, if it did not always make him courageous, usually made him impudent as respects those with whom he conversed.

"Fair words make long friendships, Master Deerslayer," he said a little menacingly. "You're but a stripling, and you know by exper'ence what you are in the hands of a man. As you're not me, but only a go-between sent by the savages to us Christians, you may tell your empl'yers that they do know Harry March, which is a proof of their sense as well as his. He's human enough to follow human natur', and that tells him to see the folly of one man's fighting a whole tribe. If females desart him, they must expect to be desarted by him, whether they're of his own gifts or another man's gifts. Should Judith see fit to change her mind, she's welcome to my company to the river, and Hetty with her; but shouldn't she come to this conclusion, I start as soon as I think the enemy's scouts are beginning to nestle themselves in among the brush and leaves for the night."

"Judith will not change her mind, and she does not ask your company, Master March," returned the girl, with spirit.

"That p'int's settled, then," resumed Deerslayer, unmoved by the other's warmth. "Hurry Harry must act for himself and do that which will be most likely to suit his own fancy. The course he means to take will give him an easy race, if it don't give him an easy conscience. Next comes the question with Hist—what say you, gal?—will you desart

your duty, too, and go back to the Mingos and take a Huron husband; and all, not for the love of the man you're to marry, but for the love of your own scalp?"

"Why you talk so to Hist?" demanded the girl, half offended. "You t'ink a redskin girl made like captain's lady, to laugh and joke with any officer that come?"

"What I think, Hist, is neither here nor there, in this matter. I must carry back your answer, and in order to do so, it is necessary that you should send it. A faithful messenger gives his ar'n'd, word for word."

Hist no longer hesitated to speak her mind fully. In the excitement she rose from her bench, and naturally recurring to that language in which she expressed herself the most readily, she delivered her thoughts and intentions beautifully and with dignity in the tongue of her own people.

"Tell the Hurons, Deerslayer," she said, "that they are as ignorant as moles; they don't know the wolf from the dog. Among my people, the rose dies on the stem where it budded; the tears of the child fall on the graves of its parents; the corn grows where the seed has been planted. The Delaware girls are not messengers, to be sent like belts of wampum from tribe to tribe. They are honeysuckles that are sweetest in their own woods; their own young men carry them away in their bosoms because they are fragrant; they are sweetest when plucked from their native stems. Even the robin and the marten come back, year after year, to their old nests; shall a woman be less truehearted than a bird? Set the pine in the clay, and it will turn yellow; the willow will not flourish on the hill; the tamarack is healthiest in the swamp; the tribes of the sea love best to hear the winds that blow over the salt water. As for a Huron youth, what is he to a maiden of the Lenni Lenape? He may be fleet, but her eyes do not follow him in the race; they look back toward the lodges of the Delawares. He may sing a sweet song for the girls of Canada, but there is no music for Wah but in the tongue she has listened to from childhood. Were the Huron born of the people that once roamed the shores of the salt lake, it would be in vain, unless he were of the family of Uncas. The young pine will rise to be as high as any of its fathers. Wah-ta!-Wah has but one heart, and it can love but one husband."

Deerslayer listened to this characteristic message, which

was given with an earnestness suited to the feelings from which it sprang, with undisguised delight, meeting the ardent eloquence of the girl, as she concluded, with one of his own heartfelt, silent, and peculiar fits of laughter.

"That's worth all the wampum in the woods!" he exclaimed. "You don't understand it, I suppose, Judith; but if you'll look into your feelin's, and fancy that an inimy had sent to tell you to give up the man of your ch'ice, and to take up with another that wasn't the man of your ch'ice, you'll get the substance of it, I'll warrant! Give me a woman for ra'al eloquence, if they'll only make up their minds to speak what they *feel*. By speakin', I don't mean chatterin', howsever; for most of them will do *that* by the hour; but comin' out with their honest, deepest feelin's, in proper words. And now, Judith, having got the answer of a redskin girl, it is fit I should get that of a paleface, if, indeed, a countenance that is as blooming as your'n can in any wise so be tarmed. You are well named the Wild Rose, and so far as color goes, Hetty ought to be called the Honeysuckle."

"Did this language come from one of the garrison gallants, I should deride it, Deerslayer; but coming from *you*, I know it can be depended on," returned Judith, deeply gratified by his unmeditated and characteristic compliments. "It is too soon, however, to ask my answer; the Great Serpent has not yet spoken."

"The Sarpent? Lord; I could carry back his speech without hearing a word of it! I didn't think of putting the question to him at all, I will allow; though 'twould be hardly right either, seeing that truth is truth, and I'm bound to tell these Mingos the fact, and nothing else. So, Chingachgook, let us hear *your* mind on this matter—are you inclined to strike across the hills toward your village, to give up Hist to a Huron, and to tell the chiefs at home, that if they're actyve and successful they may possibly get *on* the end of the Iroquois trail some two or three days a'ter the inimy has got *off* of it?"

Like his betrothed, the young chief arose, that his answer might be given with due distinctness and dignity. Hist had spoken with her hands crossed upon her bosom, as if to suppress the emotions within; but the warrior stretched an

arm before him, with a calm energy that aided in giving emphasis to his expressions.

"Wampum should be sent for wampum," he said, "a message must be answered by a message. Hear what the Great Serpent of the Delawares has to say to the pretended wolves from the great lakes, that are howling through our woods. They are no wolves; they are dogs that have come to get their tails and ears cropped by the hands of the Delawares. They are good at stealing young women: bad at keeping them. Chingachgook takes his own where he finds it; he asks leave of no cur from the Canadas. If he has a tender feeling in his heart, it is no business of the Hurons. He tells it to her who most likes to know it; he will not bellow it in the forest for the ears of those that only understand yells of terror. What passes in his lodge is not for the chiefs of his own people to know; still less for Mingo rogues—"

"Call 'em vagabonds, Sarpent," interrupted Deerslayer, unable to restrain his delight—"yes, just call 'em up-and-down vagabonds, which is a word easily intarpreted, and the most hateful to all their ears, it's so true. Never fear me; I'll give 'em your message, syllable for syllable, sneer for sneer, idee for idee, scorn for scorn—and they desarve no better at your hands. Only call 'em vagabonds, once or twice, and that will set the sap mounting in 'em, from their lowest roots to the uppermost branches."

"Still less for Mingo vagabonds!" resumed Chingachgook, quite willingly complying with his friend's request. "Tell the Huron dogs to howl louder, if they wish a Delaware to find them in the woods, where they burrow like foxes, instead of hunting like warriors. When they had a Delaware maiden in their camp, there was a reason for hunting them up; now they will be forgotten, unless they make a noise. Chingachgook don't like the trouble of going to his villages for more warriors; he can strike their runaway trail; unless they hide it under ground, he will follow it to Canada, alone. He will keep Wah-ta!-Wah with him to cook his game; they two will be Delawares enough to scare all the Hurons back to their own country."

"That's a grand dispatch, as the officers call them things!" cried Deerslayer; " 'twill set all the Huron blood in motion; most particularly that part where he tells 'em Hist, too,

will keep on their heels till they're fairly driven out of the country. Ah's me! Big words arn't always big deeds, notwithstanding. The Lord send that we be able to be only one half as good as we promise to be. And now, Judith, it's your turn to speak, for them miscreants will expect an answer from each person, poor Hetty, perhaps, excepted."

"And why not Hetty, Deerslayer? She often speaks to the purpose; the Indians may respect her words, for they feel for people in her condition."

"That is true, Judith, and quick-thoughted in you. The redskins *do* respect misfortunes of all kinds, and Hetty's in particular. So, Hetty, if you have anything to say, I'll carry it to the Hurons as faithfully as if it was spoken by a schoolmaster or a missionary."

The girl hesitated a moment, and then she answered in her own gentle, soft tones, as earnestly as any who had preceded her.

"The Hurons can't understand the difference between white people and themselves," she said, "or they wouldn't ask Judith and me to go and live in their villages. God has given one country to the red men, and another to us. He meant us to live apart. Then Mother always said that we should never dwell with any but Christians, if possible, and *that* is a reason why we can't go. This lake is ours, and we won't leave it. Father's and Mother's graves are in it, and even the worst Indians love to stay near the graves of their fathers. I will come and see them again, if they wish me to to, and read more out of the Bible to them, but I can't quit Father's and Mother's graves."

"That will do—that will do, Hetty, just as well as if you sent them a message twice as long," interrupted the hunter. "I'll tell 'em all you've said and all you mean, and I'll answer for it, that they'll be easily satisfied. Now, Judith, your turn comes next, and then this part of my ar'n'd will be tarminated for the night."

Judith manifested a reluctance to give her reply that had awakened a little curiosity in the messenger. Judging from her known spirit, he had never supposed the girl would be less true to her feelings and principles than Hist or Hetty, and yet there was a visible wavering of purpose that rendered him slightly uneasy. Even now, when directly required to speak, she seemed to hesitate; nor did she open her lips until

the profound silence told her how anxiously her words were expected. Then, indeed, she spoke, but it was doubtingly and with reluctance.

"Tell me, first—tell *us*, first, Deerslayer," she commenced, repeating the words merely to change the emphasis. "What effect will our answers have on *your* fate? If you are to be the sacrifice of our spirit, it would have been better had we all been more wary as to the language we use. What, then, are likely to be the consequences to yourself?"

"Lord, Judith, you might as well ask me which way the wind will blow next week, or what will be the age of the next deer that will be shot! I can only say that their faces look a little dark upon me, but it doesn't thunder every time a black cloud rises, nor does every puff of wind blow up rain. That's a question, therefore, much more easily put than answered."

"So is this message of the Iroquois to me," answered Judith, rising, as if she had determined on her own course for the present. "My answer shall be given, Deerslayer, after you and I have talked together alone, when the others have laid themselves down for the night."

There was a decision in the manner of the girl that disposed Deerslayer to comply, and this he did the more readily as the delay could produce no material consequences, one way or the other. The meeting now broke up, Hurry announcing his resolution to leave them speedily. During the hour that was suffered to intervene, in order that the darkness might deepen before the frontiersman took his departure, the different individuals occupied themselves in their customary modes, the hunter, in particular, passing most of the time in making further inquiries into the perfection of the rifle already mentioned.

The hour of nine soon arrived, however, and then it had been determined that Hurry should commence his journey. Instead of making his adieus frankly and in a generous spirit, the little he thought it necessary to say was uttered sullenly and in coldness. Resentment at what he considered Judith's obstinacy was blended with mortification at the career he had run since reaching the lake; as is usual with the vulgar and narrow-minded, he was more disposed to reproach others with his failures than to censure himself. Judith gave him her hand, but it was quite as much in glad-

ness as with regret, while the two Delawares were not sorry to find he was leaving them. Of the whole party, Hetty alone betrayed any real feeling. Bashfulness and the timidity of her sex and character kept even her aloof, so that Hurry entered the canoe, where Deerslayer was already waiting for him, before she ventured near enough to be observed. Then, indeed, the girl came into the ark and approached its end just as the little bark was turning from it, with a movement so light and steady as to be almost imperceptible. An impulse of feeling now overcame her timidity, and Hetty spoke.

"Goodbye, Hurry"—she called out in her sweet voice— "goodbye, dear Hurry. Take care of yourself in the woods, and don't stop once till you reach the garrison. The leaves on the trees are scarcely plentier than the Hurons around the lake, and they'd not treat a strong man like you as kindly as they treat me."

The ascendency which March had obtained over this feeble-minded but right-thinking and right-feeling girl arose from a law of nature. Her senses had been captivated by his personal advantages, and her moral communications with him had never been sufficiently intimate to counteract an effect that must have been otherwise lessened, even with one whose mind was as obtuse as her own. Hetty's instinct of right, if such a term can be applied to one who seemed taught by some kind spirit how to steer her course with unerring accuracy between good and evil, would have revolted at Hurry's character on a thousand points, had there been opportunities to enlighten her; but while he conversed and trifled with her sister, at a distance from herself, his perfection of form and feature had been left to produce their influence on her simple imagination and naturally tender feelings without suffering by the alloy of his opinions and coarseness. It is true, she found him rough and rude, but her father was that, and most of the other men she had seen, and that which she believed to belong to all of the sex struck her less unfavorably in Hurry's character than it might otherwise have done. Still, it was not absolutely love that Hetty felt for Hurry, nor do we wish so to portray it, but merely that awakening sensibility and admiration, which, under more propitious circumstances, and always supposing no untoward revelations of character on the part of the young man had supervened to prevent it, might soon have

ripened into that engrossing feeling. She felt for him an incipient tenderness, but scarcely any passion. Perhaps the
nearest approach to the latter that Hetty had manifested
was to be seen in the sensitiveness which had caused her to
detect March's predilection for her sister, for among Judith's
many admirers, this was the only instance in which the dull
mind of the girl had been quickened into an observation of
the circumstance.

Hurry received so little sympathy at his departure that
the gentle tones of Hetty, as she thus called after him,
sounded soothingly. He checked the canoe and, with one
sweep of his powerful arm, brought it back to the side of
the ark. This was more than Hetty, whose courage had risen
with the departure of her hero, expected, and she now shrank
timidly back at his unexpected return.

"You're a good gal, Hetty, and I can't quit you without
shaking hands," said March kindly. "Judith, a'ter all, isn't
worth as much as you, though she may be a trifle better
looking. As to wits, if honesty and fair dealing with a young
man is a sign of sense in a young woman, you're worth a
dozen Judiths—aye, and for that matter, most young women
of my acquaintance."

"Don't say anything against Judith, Harry," returned
Hetty imploringly. "Father's gone, and Mother's gone, and
nobody's left but Judith and me, and it isn't right for sisters
to speak evil, or to hear evil, of each other. Father's in the
lake, and so is Mother, and we should all fear God, for
we don't know when we may be in the lake, too."

"That sounds reasonable, child, as does most you say.
Well, if we ever meet again, Hetty, you'd find a fri'nd in
me, let your sister do what she may. I was no great fri'nd of
your mother, I'll allow, for we didn't think alike on most
p'ints; but then your father, Old Tom, and I fitted each other
as remarkably as a buckskin garment will fit any reasonable-
built man. I've always been unanimous of opinion that old
Floating Tom Hutter, at the bottom, was a good fellow, and
will maintain that ag'in all inimies for his sake, as well as
for your'n."

"Goodbye, Hurry," said Hetty, who now wanted to hasten
the young man off as ardently as she had wished to keep him
only the moment before, though she could give no clearer
account of the latter than of the former feeling; "goodbye,

Hurry; take care of yourself in the woods; don't halt till you reach the garrison. I'll read a chapter in the Bible for you, before I go to bed, and think of you in my prayers."

This was touching a point on which March had no sympathies, and without more words he shook the girl cordially by the hand and re-entered the canoe. In another minute the two adventurers were a hundred feet from the ark, and half a dozen had not elapsed before they were completely lost to view. Hetty sighed deeply and rejoined her sister and Hist.

For some time Deerslayer and his companion paddled ahead in silence. It had been determined to land Hurry at the precise point where he is represented, in the commencement of our tale, as having embarked, not only as a place little likely to be watched by the Hurons, but because he was sufficiently familiar with the signs of the woods at that spot to thread his way through them in the dark. Thither, then, the light craft proceeded, being urged as diligently and as swiftly as two vigorous and skillful canoemen could force their little vessel through, or rather *over*, the water. Less than a quarter of an hour sufficed for the object, and at the end of that time, being within the shadows of the shore and quite near the point they sought, each ceased his efforts in order to make their parting communications out of earshot of any straggler who might happen to be in the neighborhood.

"You will do well to persuade the officers at the garrison to lead out a party ag'in these vagabonds as soon as you get in, Hurry," Deerslayer commenced; "and you'll do better if you volunteer to guide it up yourself. You know the paths, and the shape of the lake, and the natur' of the land, and can do it better than a common, gin'ralizing scout. Strike at the Huron camp first and follow the signs that will then show themselves. A few looks at the hut and the ark will satisfy you as to the state of the Delaware and the women; at any rate, there'll be a fine opportunity to fall on the Mingo trail and to make a mark on the memories of the blackguards that they'll be apt to carry with 'em a long time. It won't be likely to make much difference with me, since *that* matter will be determined afore tomorrow's sun has set, but it may make a great change in Judith and Hetty's hopes and prospects!"

"And as for yourself, Nathaniel," Hurry inquired with more interest than he was accustomed to betray in the welfare of others—"and as for yourself, what do you think is likely to turn up?"

"The Lord, in his wisdom, only can tell, Henry March! The clouds look black and threatening, and I keep my mind in a state to meet the worst. Vengeful feelin's are uppermost in the hearts of the Mingos, and any little disapp'intment about the plunder, or the prisoners, or Hist may make the torments sartain. The Lord, in his wisdom, can only detarmine my fate, or you'rn!"

"This is a black business and ought to be put a stop to in some way or other," answered Hurry, confounding the distinctions between right and wrong, as is usual with selfish and vulgar men. "I heartily wish old Hutter and I had scalped every creatur' in their camp the night we first landed with that capital object! Had you not held back, Deerslayer, it might have been done; then you wouldn't have found yourself, at the last moment, in the desperate condition you mention."

" 'Twould have been better had you said you wished you had never attempted to do what it little becomes any white man's gifts to undertake, in which case, not only might we have kept from coming to blows, but Thomas Hutter would now have been living, and the hearts of the savages would be less given to vengeance. The death of that young woman, too, was oncalled for, Henry March, and leaves a heavy load on our names, if not on our consciences!"

This was so apparent, and it seemed so obvious to Hurry himself, at the moment, that he dashed his paddle into the water and began to urge the canoe toward the shore, as if bent only on running away from his own lively remorse. His companion humored this feverish desire for change, and in a minute or two the bows of the boat grated lightly on the shingle of the beach. To land, shoulder his pack and rifle, and to get ready for his march occupied Hurry but an instant, and with a growling adieu he had already commenced his march, when a sudden twinge of feeling brought him to a dead stop and, immediately after, to the other's side.

"You cannot mean to give yourself up ag'in to them murdering savages, Deerslayer!" he said, quite as much in

angry remonstrance as with generous feeling. " 'Twould be the act of a madman or a fool!"

"There's them that thinks it madness to keep their words, and there's them that don't, Hurry Harry. You may be one of the first, but I'm one of the last. No redskin breathing shall have it in his power to say that a Mingo minds his word more than a man of white blood and white gifts in anything that consarns me. I'm out on a furlough, and if I've strength and reason, I'll go in on a furlough afore noon tomorrow!"

"What's an Injin, or a word passed, or a furlough taken from creatur's like them that have neither souls nor names?"

"If they've got neither souls nor names, you and I have both, Harry March, and one is accountable for the other. This furlough is not, as you seem to think, a matter altogether atween me and the Mingos, seeing it is a solemn bargain made atween me and God. He who thinks that he can say what he pleases in his distress, and that 'twill all pass for nothing because 'tis uttered in the forest and into red men's ears, knows little of his situation, and hopes, and wants. The words are said to the ears of the Almighty. The air is His breath, and the light of the sun is little more than a glance of His eye. Farewell, Harry; we may not meet ag'in, but I would wish you never to treat a furlough, or any other solemn thing that your Christian God has been called on to witness, as a duty so light that it may be forgotten according to the wants of the body, or even according to the cravings of the spirit."

March was now glad again to escape. It was quite impossible that he could enter into the sentiments that ennobled his companion, and he broke away from both with an impatience that caused him secretly to curse the folly that could induce a man to rush, as it were, on his own destruction. Deerslayer, on the contrary, manifested no such excitement. Sustained by his principles, inflexible in the purpose of acting up to them, and superior to any unmanly apprehension, he regarded all before him as a matter of course and no more thought of making any unworthy attempt to avoid it than a Moslem thinks of counteracting the decrees of Providence. He stood calmly on the shore, listening to the reckless tread with which Hurry betrayed his progress through the bushes, shook his head in dissatisfaction at the want of caution, and then stepped quietly into his canoe. Before he

dropped the paddle again into the water, the young man gazed about him at the scene presented by the starlit night. This was the spot where he had first laid his eyes on the beautiful sheet of water on which he floated. If it was then glorious in the bright light of summer's noontide, it was now sad and melancholy under the shadows of night. The mountains rose around it, like black barriers to exclude the outer world, and the gleams of pale light that rested on the broader parts of the basin were no bad symbols of the faintness of the hopes that were so dimly visible in his own future. Sighing heavily, he pushed the canoe from the land and took his way back, with steady diligence, toward the ark and the castle.

CHAPTER XXIV

> *Thy secret pleasures turned to open shame;*
> *Thy private feasting to a public fast;*
> *Thy smoothing titles to a ragged name;*
> *Thy sugared tongue to bitter wormwood taste;*
> *Thy violent vanities can never last.*
>
> RAPE OF LUCRECE

JUDITH WAS ON the platform, awaiting the return of Deerslayer with stifled impatience, when the latter reached the hut. Hist and Hetty were both in a deep sleep on the bed usually occupied by the two daughters of the house, and the Delaware was stretched on the floor of the adjoining room, his rifle at his side, and a blanket over him, already dreaming of the events of the last few days. There was a lamp burning in the ark, for the family was accustomed to indulge in this luxury on extraordinary occasions, and possessed the means, the vessel being of a form and material to render it probable it had once been an occupant of the chest.

As soon as the girl got a glimpse of the canoe, she ceased her hurried walk up and down the platform and stood ready to receive the young man whose return she had now been anxiously expecting for some time. She helped him to fasten the canoe and, by aiding in the other little similar employments, manifested her desire to reach a moment of liberty as soon as possible. When this was done, in answer to an inquiry of his, she informed him of the manner in which their companions had disposed of themselves. He listened attentively, for the manner of the girl was so earnest and impressive as to apprise him that she had something on her mind of more than common concern.

"And now, Deerslayer," Judith continued, "you see I have lighted the lamp and put it in the cabin of the ark. That

393

is never done with us, unless on great occasions, and I consider this night as the most important of my life. Will you follow me and see what I have to show you—hear what I have to say?"

The hunter was a little surprised, but making no objections, both were soon in the scow, in the room that contained the light. Here two stools were placed at the side of the chest, with the lamp on another, and a table nearby to receive the different articles as they might be brought to view. This arrangement had its rise in the feverish impatience of the girl, which could brook no delay that it was in her power to obviate. Even all the padlocks were removed, and it only remained to raise the heavy lid and to expose the treasures of this long-secreted hoard.

"I see, in part, what all this means," observed Deerslayer; "yes, I see through it, in part. But why is not Hetty present? Now Thomas Hutter is gone, she is one of the owners of these cur'osities, and ought to see them opened and handled."

"Hetty sleeps," answered Judith hastily. "Happily for her, fine clothes and riches have no charms. Besides, she has this night given her share of all that the chest may hold to me, that I may do with it as I please."

"Is poor Hetty composs enough for that, Judith?" demanded the just-minded young man. "It's a good rule, and a righteous one, never to take when those that give don't know the valie of their gifts, and such as God has visited heavily in their wits ought to be dealt with as carefully as children that haven't yet come to their understandings."

Judith was hurt at this rebuke, coming from the person it did, but she would have felt it far more keenly, had not her conscience fully acquitted her of any unjust intentions toward her feeble-minded but confiding sister. It was not a moment, however, to betray any of her usual mountings of the spirit, and she smothered the passing sensation in the desire to come to the great object she had in view.

"Hetty will not be wronged," she mildly answered; "she even knows not only what I am about to do, Deerslayer, but *why* I do it. So take your seat, raise the lid of the chest, and this time we will go to the bottom. I shall be disappointed if something is not found to tell us more of the history of Thomas Hutter and my mother."

"Why Thomas Hutter, Judith, and not your father? The

dead ought to meet with as much reverence as the living!"

"I have long suspected that Thomas Hutter was not *my* father, though I did think he might have been Hetty's, but now we know he was the father of neither. He acknowledged that much in his dying moments. I am old enough to remember better things than we have seen on this lake, though they are so faintly impressed on my memory that the earlier part of my life seems like a dream."

"Dreams are but miserable guides when one has to determine about realities, Judith," returned the other admonishingly. "Fancy nothing and hope nothing on their account; though I've known chiefs that thought 'em useful."

"I expect nothing for the future from them, my good friend, but cannot help remembering what has been. This is idle, however, when half an hour of examination may tell us all, or even more than I want to know."

Deerslayer, who comprehended the girl's impatience, now took his seat and proceeded once more to bring to light the different articles that the chest contained. As a matter of course, all that had been previously examined were found where they had been last deposited, and they excited much less interest or comment than when formerly exposed to view. Even Judith laid aside the rich brocade with an air of indifference, for she had a far higher aim before her than the indulgence of vanity and was impatient to come at the still hidden, or rather unknown, treasures.

"All these we have seen before," she said, "and will not stop to open. The bundle under your hand, Deerslayer, is a fresh one; that we will look into. God send it may contain something to tell poor Hetty and myself who we really are."

"Aye, if some bundles could speak, they might tell wonderful secrets," returned the young man, deliberately undoing the folds of another piece of coarse canvas in order to come at the contents of the roll that lay on his knees; "though this doesn't seem to be one of that family, seeing 'tis neither more nor less than a sort of flag—though of what nation, it passes my l'arnin' to say."

"That flag must have some meaning to it," Judith hurriedly interposed. "Open it wider, Deerslayer, that we may see the colors."

"Well, I pity the ensign that has to shoulder this cloth and to parade it about in the field. Why 'tis large enough,

Judith, to make a dozen of them colors the King's officers set so much store by. These can be no ensign's colors, but a gin'ral's!"

"A ship might carry it, Deerslayer, and ships I know do use such things. Have you never heard any fearful stories about Thomas Hutter's having once been concerned with the people they call buccaneers?"

"Buck-and-near! Not I—not I—I never heard him mentioned as good at a buck, far off or nearby. Hurry Harry did tell me something about its being supposed that he had formerly, in some way or other, dealings with sartain sea-robbers; but, Lord, Judith, it can't surely give you any satisfaction to make out that ag'in your mother's own husband, though he isn't your father?"

"Anything will give me satisfaction that tells me who I am and helps to explain the dreams of childhood. My mother's husband! Yes, he must have been that, though why a woman like *her* should have chosen a man like *him* is more than mortal reason can explain. You never saw Mother, Deerslayer, and can't feel the vast, vast difference there was between them!"

"Such things *do* happen, howsever—yes, they *do* happen—though why Providence lets them come to pass is more than I understand. I've knew the f'ercest warriors with the gentlest wives of any in the tribe, and awful scolds fall to the lot of Injins fit to be missionaries."

"That was not it, Deerslayer, that was not it. Oh! If it should prove that—no; I cannot wish she should not have been his wife at all. *That* no daughter can wish for her own mother! Go on, now, and let us see what the square-looking bundle holds."

Deerslayer complied, and he found that it contained a small trunk of pretty workmanship, but fastened. The next point was to find a key, but search proving ineffectual, it was determined to force the lock. This Deerslayer soon effected by the aid of an iron instrument, and it was found that the interior was nearly filled with papers. Many were letters; some fragments of manuscripts, memorandums, accounts, and other similar documents. The hawk does not pounce upon the chicken with a more sudden swoop than Judith sprang forward to seize this mine of hitherto concealed knowledge. Her education, as the reader will have perceived,

was far superior to her situation in life, and her eye glanced over page after page of the letters with a readiness that her schooling supplied and with an avidity that found its origin in her feelings. At first, it was evident that the girl was gratified, and, we may add, with reason; for the letters, written by females, in innocence and affection, were of a character to cause her to feel proud of those with whom she had every reason to think she was closely connected by the ties of blood. It does not come within the scope of our plan to give more of these epistles, however, than a general idea of their contents, and this will best be done by describing the effect they produced on the manner, appearance, and feeling of her who was so eagerly perusing them.

It has been said already that Judith was much gratified with the letters that first met her eye. They contained the correspondence of an affectionate and intelligent mother to an absent daughter, with such allusions to the answers as served, in a great measure, to fill up the vacuum left by the replies. They were not without admonitions and warnings, however, and Judith felt the blood mounting to her temples, and a cold shudder succeeding, as she read one in which the propriety of the daughter's indulging in as much intimacy, as had evidently been described in one of the daughter's own letters, with an officer "who came from Europe, and who could hardly be supposed to wish to form an honorable connection in America," was rather coldly commented on by the mother. What rendered it singular was the fact that the signatures had been carefully cut from every one of these letters, and wherever a name occurred in the body of the epistles, it had been erased with so much diligence as to render it impossible to read it. They had all been enclosed in envelopes, according to the fashion of the age, and not an address either was to be found. Still, the letters themselves had been religiously preserved, and Judith thought she could discover traces of tears remaining on several. She now remembered to have seen the little trunk in her mother's keeping, previously to her death, and she supposed it had first been deposited in the chest, along with the other forgotten, or concealed objects, when the letters could no longer contribute to that parent's grief or happiness.

Next came another bundle, and these were filled with the protestations of love, written with passion certainly, but also

with that deceit which men so often think it justifiable to use to the other sex. Judith had shed tears abundantly over the first packet, but now she felt a sentiment of indignation and pride better sustaining her. Her hand shook, however, and cold shivers again passed through her frame as she discovered a few points of strong resemblance between these letters and some it had been her own fate to receive. Once, indeed, she laid the packet down, bowed her head to her knees, and seemed nearly convulsed. All this time Deerslayer sat, a silent but attentive observer of everything that passed. As Judith read a letter, she put it into his hands to hold, until she could peruse the next; but this seemed in no degree to enlighten her companion, as he was totally unable to read. Nevertheless, he was not entirely at fault in discovering the passions that were contending in the bosom of the fair creature by his side, and as occasional sentences escaped her in murmurs, he was nearer the truth, in his divinations or conjectures, than the girl would have been pleased at discovering.

Judith had commenced with the earliest letters, luckily for a ready comprehension of the tale they told, for they were carefully arranged in chronological order, and to anyone who would take the trouble to peruse them, they would have revealed a sad history of gratified passion, coldness, and, finally, of aversion. As she obtained the clue to their import, her impatience could not admit of delay, and she soon got to glancing her eyes over a page, by way of coming at the truth in the briefest manner possible. By adopting this expedient, one to which all who are eager to arrive at results without encumbering themselves with details are so apt to resort, Judith made a rapid progress in this melancholy revelation of her mother's failings and punishment. She saw that the period of her own birth was distinctly referred to, and even learned that the homely name she bore was given her by the father of whose person she retained so faint an impression as to resemble a dream. This name was not obliterated from the text of the letters, but stood as if nothing was to be gained by erasing it. Hetty's birth was mentioned once, and in that instance the name was the mother's; but ere this period was reached came the signs of coldness, shadowing forth the desertion that was so soon to follow. It was in this stage of the correspondence that her mother had

recourse to the plan of copying her own epistles. They were but few, but were eloquent with the feelings of blighted affection and contrition. Judith sobbed over them until again and again she felt compelled to lay them aside from sheer physical inability to see, her eyes being literally obscured with tears. Still she returned to the task with increasing interest, and finally succeeded in reaching the end of the latest communication that had probably ever passed between her parents.

All this occupied fully an hour, for near a hundred letters were glanced at, and some twenty had been closely read. The truth now shone clear upon the acute mind of Judith, so far as her own birth and that of Hetty were concerned. She sickened at the conviction, and for the moment, the rest of the world seemed to be cut off from her, and she had now additional reasons for wishing to pass the remainder of her life on the lake, where she had already seen so many bright and so many sorrowing days.

There yet remained more letters to examine. Judith found these were a correspondence between her mother and Thomas Hovey. The originals of both parties were carefully arranged, letter and answer, side by side, and they told the early history of the connection between the ill-assorted pair far more plainly than Judith wished to learn it. Her mother made the advances toward a marriage, to the surprise, not to say horror, of her daughter, and she actually found a relief when she discovered traces of what struck her as insanity, or a morbid disposition, bordering on that dire calamity, in the earlier letters of that ill-fated woman. The answers of Hovey were coarse and illiterate, though they manifested a sufficient desire to obtain the hand of a woman of singular personal attractions, and whose great error he was willing to overlook for the advantage of possessing one every way so much his superior, and who, it also appeared, was not altogether destitute of money. The remainder of this part of the correspondence was brief, and it was soon confined to a few communications on business, in which the miserable wife hastened the absent husband in his prepara-tions to abandon a world which there was a sufficient reason to think was as dangerous to one of the parties as it was disagreeable to the other. But a single expression had es-caped her mother, by which Judith could get a clue to the

motives that had induced her to marry Hovey, or Hutter; and this she found was that feeling of resentment which so often tempts the injured to inflict wrongs on themselves, by way of heaping coals on the heads of those through whom they have suffered. Judith had enough of the spirit of that mother to comprehend this sentiment, and for a moment did she see the exceeding folly which permitted such revengeful feelings to get the ascendency.

There what may be called the historical part of the papers ceased. Among the loose fragments, however, was an old newspaper that contained a proclamation offering a reward for the apprehension of certain freebooters by name, among which was that of Thomas Hovey. The attention of the girl was drawn to the proclamation, and to this particular name, by the circumstance that black lines had been drawn under both in ink. Nothing else was found among the papers that could lead to a discovery of either the name or the place of residence of the wife of Hutter. All the dates, signatures, and addresses had been cut from the letters, and wherever a word occurred in the body of the communications that might furnish a clue, it was scrupulously erased. Thus Judith found all her hopes of ascertaining who her parents were defeated, and she was obliged to fall back on her own resources and habits for everything connected with the future. Her recollection of her mother's manners, conversation, and sufferings filled up many a gap in the historical facts she had now discovered, and the truth in its outlines stood sufficiently distinct before her to take away all desire, indeed, to possess any more details. Throwing herself back in her seat, she simply desired her companion to finish the examination of the other articles in the chest, as it might yet contain something of importance.

"I'll do it, Judith; I'll do it," returned the patient Deerslayer; "but if there's many more letters to read, we shall see the sun ag'in afore you've got through with the reading of them! Two good hours have you been looking at them bits of papers!"

"They tell me of my parents, Deerslayer, and have settled my plans for life. A girl may be excused who reads about her *own* father and mother, and that too for the first time in her life! I am sorry to have kept you waiting."

"Never mind me, gal; never mind me. It matters little

whether I sleep or watch; but though you be pleasant to look at, and are so handsome, Judith, it is not altogether agreeable to sit so long to behold you shedding tears. I know that tears don't kill, and that some people are better for shedding a few now and then—especially women—but I'd rather see you smile any time, Judith, than see you weep."

This gallant speech was rewarded with a sweet, though a melancholy smile, and then the girl again desired her companion to finish the examination of the chest. The search necessarily continued some time, during which Judith collected her thoughts and regained her composure. She took no part in the search, leaving everything to the young man, looking listlessly herself, at the different articles that came uppermost. Nothing further of much interest or value, however, was found. A sword or two, such as were then worn by gentlemen, some buckles of silver, or so richly plated as to appear silver, and a few handsome articles of female dress composed the principal discoveries. It struck both Judith and the Deerslayer, notwithstanding, that some of these things might be made useful in effecting a negotiation with the Iroquois, though the latter saw a difficulty in the way that was not so apparent to the former. The conversation was first renewed in connection with this point.

"And now, Deerslayer," said Judith, "we may talk of yourself and of the means of getting you out of the hands of the Hurons. Any part, or all of what you have seen in the chest, will be cheerfully given by me and Hetty to set you at liberty."

"Well, that's ginerous,—yes, 'tis downright freehearted, and freehanded and ginerous. This is the way with women; when they take up a fri'ndship, they do nothing by halves, but are as willing to part with their property as if it had no valie in their eyes. Howsever, while I thank you both, just as much as if the bargain was made and Rivenoak or any of the other vagabonds was here to accept and close the treaty, there's two principal reasons why it can never come to pass, which may be as well told at once, in order no onlikely expectations may be raised in you, or any onjustifiable hopes in me."

"What reason *can* there be, if Hetty and I are willing to part with the trifles for your sake, and the savages are willing to receive them?"

"That's it, Judith—you've got the ideas, but they're a little out of their places, as if a hound should take the back'ard instead of the leading scent. That the Mingos will be willing to receive them things, or any more like 'em you may have to offer, is probable enough, but whether they'll pay valie for 'em is quite another matter. Ask yourself, Judith, if anyone should send you a message to say that, for such or such a price, you and Hetty might have that chist and all it holds, whether you'd think it worth your while to waste many words on the bargain?"

"But this chest and all it holds are already ours; there is no reason why we should purchase what is already our own."

"Just so the Mingos calculate! They say the chist is theirs already; or as good as theirs, and they'll not thank anybody for the key."

"I understand you, Deerslayer; surely we are yet in possession of the lake, and we can keep possession of it until Hurry sends troops to drive off the enemy. This we may certainly do, provided you will stay with us, instead of going back and giving yourself up a prisoner again, as you now seem determined on."

"That Hurry Harry should talk in this way is natr'al and according to the gifts of the man. He knows no better, and therefore he is little likely to feel or to act any better; but, Judith, I put it to your heart and conscience—would you, *could* you think of me as favorably as I hope and believe you now do, was I to forget my furlough and not go back to the camp?"

"To think *more* favorably of you than I now do, Deerslayer, would not be easy; but I might continue to think *as* favorably—at least it seems so—I hope I could; for a world wouldn't tempt me to let you do anything that might change my real opinion of you."

"Then don't try to entice me to overlook my furlough, gal! A furlough is a sacred thing among warriors and men that carry their lives in their hands, as we of the forests do, and what a grievous disapp'intment would it be to old Tamenund, and to Uncas, the father of the Sarpent, and to my other fri'nds in the tribe, if I was so to disgrace myself on my very first warpath! This you will parceive, moreover, Judith, is without laying any stress on nat'ral gifts and a white man's

duties, to say nothing of conscience. The last is king with me, and I try never to dispute his orders."

"I believe you are right, Deerslayer," returned the girl, after a little reflection and in a saddened voice; "a man like *you* ought not to act as the selfish and dishonest would be apt to act; *you* must indeed go back. We will talk no more of this, then; should I persuade you to anything for which you would be sorry hereafter, my own regret would not be less than yours. You shall not have it to say, Judith—I scarce know by what name to call myself now!"

"And why not?—why not, gal? Children take the names of their parents nat'rally and by a sort of gift, like; and why shouldn't you and Hetty do as others have done afore ye? Hutter was the old man's name, and Hutter should be the name of his darters—at least until you are given away in lawful and holy wedlock."

"I am Judith, and Judith only," returned the girl positively, "until the law gives me a right to another name. Never will I use that of Thomas Hutter again; nor, with my consent, shall Hetty! Hutter was not his own name, I find, but had he a thousand rights to it, it would give none to me. *He* was not my father, thank heaven, though I may have no reason to be proud of him that *was!*"

"This is strange," said Deerslayer, looking steadily at the excited girl, anxious to know more but unwilling to inquire into matters that did not properly concern him; "yes, this is very strange and oncommon! Thomas Hutter wasn't Thomas Hutter, and his darters weren't his darters! Who, then, could Thomas Hutter be, and who are his darters?"

"Did you never hear anything whispered against the former life of this person, Deerslayer?" demanded Judith. "Passing, as I did, for his child, such reports reached even me."

"I'll not deny it, Judith; no, I'll not deny it. Sartain things have been said, as I've told you, but I'm not very credible as to reports. Young as I am, I've lived long enough to l'arn there's two sorts of characters in the world—them that is 'arned by deeds, and them that is 'arned by tongues—and so I prefer to see and judge for myself, instead of letting every jaw that chooses to wag become my judge. Hurry Harry spoke pretty plainly of the whole family, as we journeyed thisaway; and he did hint something consarning Thomas Hutter's having been a free liver on the water, in his younger

days. By free liver, I mean that he made free to live on other men's goods."

"He told you he was a pirate—there is no need of mincing matters between friends. Read that, Deerslayer, and you will see that he told you no more than the truth. This Thomas Hovey was the Thomas Hutter you knew, as is seen by these letters."

As Judith spoke, with a flushed cheek and eyes dazzling with the brilliancy of excitement, she held the newspaper toward her companion, pointing to the proclamation of a Colonial governor, already mentioned.

"Bless you, Judith!" answered the other, laughing; "you might as well ask me to print that—or for that matter to write it. My edication has been altogether in the woods; the only book I read, or care about reading, is the one which God has opened afore all his creatur's in the noble forests, broad lakes, rolling rivers, blue skies, and the winds, and tempests, and sunshine, and other glorious marvels of the land! This book I can read, and I find it full of wisdom and knowledge."

"I crave your pardon, Deerslayer," said Judith earnestly, more abashed than was her wont, in finding that she had inadvertently made an appeal that might wound her companion's pride. "I had forgotten your manner of life, and least of all did I wish to hurt your feelings."

"Hurt my feelin's!—why should it hurt my feelin's to ask me to read when I can't read? I'm a hunter—and, I may now begin to say, a warrior—and no missionary, and therefore books and papers are of no account with such as I. No, no, Judith"—and here the young man laughed cordially—"not even for wads, seeing that your true deerkiller always uses the hide of a fa'an, if he's got one, or some other bit of leather suitably prepared. There's some that *do* say all that stands in print is true, in which case I'll own an unl'arned man must be somewhat of a loser; nevertheless, it can't be truer than that which God has printed with His own hand, in the sky, and the woods, and the rivers, and the springs."

"Well, then, Hutter, or Hovey, was a pirate, and being no father of mine, I cannot wish to call him one. His name shall no longer be my name."

"If you dislike the name of that man, there's the name

of your mother, Judith. Her name may sarve you just as good a turn."

"I do not know it. I've looked through those papers, Deerslayer, in the hope of finding some hint by which I might discover who my mother was, but there is no more trace of the past in that respect than the bird leaves in the air."

"That's both oncommon and onreasonable. Parents are bound to give their offspring a name, even though they give 'em nothing else. Now, I come of a humble stock, though we have white gifts and a white natur', but we are not so poorly off as to have no name. Bumppo we are called, and I've heard it said," a touch of human vanity glowing on his cheek, "that the time has been when the Bumppos had more standing and note among mankind than they have just now."

"They never deserved them more, Deerslayer, and the name is a good one; either Hetty or myself would a thousand times rather be called Hetty Bumppo or Judith Bumppo than to be called Hetty or Judith Hutter."

"That's a moral impossible," returned the hunter good-humoredly, "unless one of you should so far demean herself as to marry me."

Judith could not refrain from smiling when she found how simply and naturally the conversation had come around to the very point at which she had aimed to bring it. Although far from unfeminine or forward either in her feelings or her habits, the girl was goaded by a sense of wrongs not altogether merited, incited by the helplessness of a future that seemed to contain no resting place, and still more influenced by feelings that were as novel to her as they proved to be active and engrossing. The opening was too good, therefore, to be neglected, though she came to the subject with much of the indirectness and, perhaps, justifiable address of a woman.

"I do not think Hetty will ever marry, Deerslayer," she said, "if your name is to be borne by either of us, it must be borne by me."

"There's been handsome women, too, they tell me, among the Bumppos, Judith, afore now, and should you take up with the name, oncommon as you be, in this particular, them that knows the family won't be altogether surprised."

"This is not talking as becomes either of us, Deerslayer, for whatever is said on such a subject beyween man and

woman should be said seriously and in sincerity of heart. Forgetting the shame that ought to keep girls silent until spoken to, in most cases, I will deal with you as frankly as I know one of your generous nature will most like to be dealt by. Can you—do you think, Deerslayer, that you could be happy with such a wife as a woman like myself would make?"

"A woman like you, Judith! But where's the sense in trifling about such a thing? A woman like you, that is handsome enough to be a captain's lady, and fine enough, and, so far as I know, edication enough, would be little apt to think of becoming my wife. I suppose young gals that feel themselves to be smart and know themselves to be handsome find a sartain satisfaction in passing their jokes ag'in them that's neither, like a poor Delaware hunter."

This was said good-naturedly, but not without a betrayal of feeling which showed that something like mortified sensibility was blended with the reply. Nothing could have occurred more likely to awaken all Judith's generous regrets, or to aid her in her purpose, by adding the stimulant of a disinterested desire to atone to her other impulses, and clothing all under a guise so winning and natural as greatly to lessen the unpleasant feature of a forwardness unbecoming the sex.

"You do me injustice if you suppose I have any such thought or wish," she answered earnestly. "Never was I more serious in my life, or more willing to abide by any agreement that we may make tonight. I have had many suitors, Deerslayer—nay, scarce an unmarried trapper or hunter has been in at the lake these four years who has not offered to take me away with him, and I fear some that were married, too——"

"Aye, I'll warrant that!" interrupted the other. "I'll warrant all that! Take 'em as a body, Judith, 'arth don't hold a set of men more given to theirselves, and less given to God and the law."

"Not one of them would I—could I listen to; happily for myself, perhaps, has it been that such was the case. There have been well-looking youths among them, too, as you may have seen in your acquaintance, Henry March."

"Yes, Harry is sightly to the eye, though, to my idees, less so to the judgment. I thought at first you meant to have

him, Judith, I did, but afore he went, it was easy enough to verify that the same lodge wouldn't be big enough for you both."

"You have done me justice in that at least, Deerslayer. Hurry is a man I could never marry, though he were ten times more comely to the eye and a hundred times more stout of heart than he really is."

"Why not, Judith—why not? I own I'm cur'ous to know why a youth like Hurry shouldn't find favor with a maiden like you."

"Then you shall know, Deerslayer," returned the girl, gladly availing herself of the opportunity of extolling the qualities which had so strongly interested her in her listener —hoping by these means covertly to approach the subject nearest her heart. "In the first place, looks in a man are of no importance with a woman, provided he is manly, and not disfigured or deformed."

"There I can't altogether agree with you," returned the other thoughtfully, for he had a very humble opinion of his own personal appearance. "I have noticed that the comeliest warriors commonly get the best-looking maidens of the tribe for wives; the Sarpent, yonder, who is sometimes wonderful in his paint, is a gin'ral favorite with all the Delaware young women, though he takes to Hist himself as if she was the only beauty on 'arth."

"It may be so with Indians, but it is different with white girls. So long as a young man has a straight and manly frame that promises to make him able to protect a woman and to keep want from the door, it is all they ask of the figure. Giants like Hurry may do for grenadiers, but are of little account as lovers. Then as to the face, an honest look, one that answers for the heart within, is of more value than any shape, or color, or eyes, or teeth, or trifles like them. The last may do for girls, but who thinks of them at all in a hunter, or a warrior, or a husband! If there are women so silly, Judith's not among them."

"Well, this is wonderful! I always thought that handsome liked handsome, as riches love riches!"

"It may be so with you men, Deerslayer, but it is not always so with us women. We like stouthearted men, but we wish to see them modest, sure on a hunt or the warpath, ready to die for the right and unwilling to yield to the

wrong. Above all, we wish for honesty—tongues that are not used to say what the mind does not mean, and hearts that feel a little for others as well as for themselves. A true-hearted girl could die for such a husband, while the boaster and the double-tongued suitor gets to be as hateful to the sight as he is to the mind."

Judith spoke bitterly and with her usual force, but her listener was too much struck with the novelty of the sensations he experienced to advert to her manner. There was something so soothing to the humility of a man of his temperament to hear qualities that he could not but know he possessed himself thus highly extolled by the loveliest female he had ever beheld that, for the moment, his faculties seemed suspended in a natural and excusable pride. Then it was that the idea of the possibility of such a creature as Judith becoming his companion for life first crossed his mind. The image was so pleasant and so novel that he continued completely absorbed by it for more than a minute, totally regardless of the beautiful reality that was seated before him, watching the expression of his upright and truth-telling countenance with a keenness that gave her a very fair, if not an absolutely accurate clue to his thoughts. Never before had so pleasing a vision floated before the mind's eye of the young hunter, but accustomed most to practical things and little addicted to submitting to the power of his imagination, even while possessed of so much true poetical feeling in connection with natural objects in particular, he soon recovered his reason and smiled at his own weakness, as the fancied picture faded from his mental sight and left him the simple, untaught, but highly moral being he was, seated in the ark of Thomas Hutter, at midnight, with the lovely countenance of its late owner's reputed daughter beaming on him with anxious scrutiny by the light of the solitary lamp.

"You're wonderful handsome, and enticing, and pleasing to look on, Judith!" he exclaimed, in his simplicity, as fact resumed its ascendency over fancy. "Wonderful! I don't remember ever to have seen so beautiful a gal, even among the Delawares, and I'm not astonished that Hurry Harry went away soured as well as disapp'inted!"

"Would you have had me, Deerslayer, become the wife of such a man as Henry March?"

"There's that which is in his favor, and there's that which is ag'in him. To my taste, Hurry wouldn't make the best of husbands, but I fear that the tastes of most young women hereaway wouldn't be so hard upon him."

"No—no—Judith without a name would never consent to be called Judith March! Anything would be better than *that!*"

"Judith Bumppo wouldn't sound as well, gal, and there's many names that would fall short of March in pleasing the ear."

"Ah, Deerslayer, the pleasantness of the sound in such cases does not come through the ear, but through the heart. Everything is agreeable when the heart is satisfied. Were Natty Bumppo Henry March, and Henry March Natty Bumppo, I might think the name of March better than it is: or were he you, I should fancy the name of Bumppo horrible!"

"That's just it—yes, that's the reason of the matter. Now, I'm nat'rally avarse to sarpents, and I hate even the word—which, the missionaries tell me, comes from human natur' on account of a sartain sarpent at the creation of the 'arth that outwitted the first woman—yet ever since Chingachgook has 'arned the title he bears, why the sound is as pleasant to my ears as the whistle of the whippoorwill of a calm evening—it is. The feelin's make all the difference in the world, Judith, in the natur' of sounds; aye, even in that of looks, too."

"This is so true, Deerslayer, that I am surprised you should think it remarkable that a girl, who may have some comeliness herself, should not think it necessary that her husband should have the same advantage, or what you fancy an advantage. To me, looks in a man are nothing, provided his countenance be as honest as his heart."

"Yes, honesty is a great advantage, in the long run, and they that are the most apt to forget it, in the beginning, are the most apt to l'arn it in the ind. Nevertheless, there's more, Judith, that look to present profit than to the benefit that is to come after a time. One they think a sartainty, and the other an onsartainty. I'm glad, howsever, that *you* look at the thing in its true light and not in the way in which so many is apt to deceive themselves."

"I do thus look at it, Deerslayer," returned the girl with emphasis, still shrinking with a woman's sensitiveness from

a direct offer of her hand, "and can say, from the bottom of my heart, that I would rather trust my happiness to a man whose truth and feelings may be depended on than to a false-tongued and falsehearted wretch that had chests of gold and houses and lands—yes, though he were even seated on a throne!"

"These are brave words, Judith; they're downright brave words; but do you think that the feelin's would keep 'em company, did the ch'ice actually lie afore you? If a gay gallant in a scarlet coat stood on one side, with his head smelling like a deer's foot, his face smooth and blooming as your own, his hands as white and soft as if God hadn't bestowed 'em that man might live by the sweat of his brow, and his step as lofty as dancing teachers and a light heart could make it—and on the other side stood one that has passed his days in the open air till his forehead is as red as his cheek, had cut his way through swamps and bushes till his hand was as rugged as the oaks he slept under, had trodden on the scent of game till his step was as stealthy as the catamount's, and had no other pleasant odor about him than such as natur' gives in the free air and the forest—now, if both these men stood here as suitors for your feelin's, which do you think would win your favor?"

Judith's fine face flushed, for the picture that her companion had so simply drawn of a gay officer of the garrisons had once been particularly grateful to her imagination, though experience and disappointment had not only chilled all her affections, but given them a backward current, and the passing image had a momentary influence on her feelings; but the mounting color was succeeded by a paleness so deadly as to make her appear ghastly.

"As God is my judge," the girl solemnly answered, "did both these men stand before me, as I may say one of them does, my choice, if I know my own heart, would be the latter. I have no wish for a husband who is any way better than myself."

"This is pleasant to listen to and might lead a young man, in time, to forget his own onworthiness, Judith! Howsever, you hardly think all that you say. A man like me is too rude and ignorant for one that has had such a mother to teach her; vanity is nat'ral, I do believe, but vanity like that would surpass reason!"

"Then you do not know of what a woman's heart is capable! Rude *you* are not, Deerslayer! Nor can one be called ignorant that has studied what is before his eyes as closely as you have done. When the affections are concerned, all things appear in their pleasantest colors, and trifles are overlooked, or are forgotten. When the heart feels a sunshine, nothing is gloomy—even dull-looking objects seeming gay and bright—and so it would be between you and the woman who should love you, even though your wife might happen in some matters to possess what the world calls the advantage over you."

"Judith, you come of people altogether above mine in the world, and onequal matches, like onequal fri'ndships, can't often tarminate kindly. I speak of this matter altogether as a fanciful thing, since it's not very likely that *you*, at least, would be able to treat it as a matter that can ever come to pass."

Judith fastened her deep blue eyes on the open, frank countenance of her companion, as if she would read his soul. Nothing there betrayed any covert meaning, and she was obliged to admit to herself that he regarded the conversation as argumentative, rather than positive, and that he was still without any active suspicion that her feelings were seriously involved in the issue. At first she felt offended; then she saw the injustice of making the self-abasement and modesty of the hunter a charge against him; this novel difficulty gave a piquancy to the state of affairs that rather increased her interest in the young man. At that critical instant, a change of plan flashed on her mind, and with a readiness of invention that is peculiar to the quick-witted and ingenious, she adopted a scheme by which she hoped effectually to bind him to her person. This scheme partook equally of her fertility of invention and of the decision and boldness of her character. That the conversation might not terminate too abruptly, however, or any suspicion of her design exist, she answered the last remark of Deerslayer as earnestly and as truly as if her original intention remained unaltered.

"I, certainly, have no reason to boast of parentage, after what I have seen this night," said the girl, in a saddened voice. "I had a mother, it is true, but of her name, even, I am ignorant; as for my father, it is better perhaps that I

should never know who he was, lest I speak too bitterly of
him!"

"Judith," said Deerslayer, taking her hand kindly and with
a manly sincerity that went directly to the girl's heart, " 'tis
better to say no more tonight. Sleep on what you've seen and
felt; in the morning, things that now look gloomy may look
more cheerful. Above all, never do anything in bitterness,
or because you feel as if you'd like to take revenge on yourself for other people's backslidings. All that has been said
or done atween us this night is your secret, and shall never
be talked of by me, even with the Sarpent; and you may
be sartain if he can't get it out of me, no man can. If your
parents have been faulty, let the darter be less so; remember that you're young, and the youthful may always hope
for better times; that you're more quick-witted than usual,
and such gin'rally get the better of difficulties; and that as for
beauty, you're oncommon; this is an advantage with all. It
is time to get a little rest, for tomorrow is like to prove a
trying day to some of us."

Deerslayer arose as he spoke, and Judith had no choice
but to comply. The chest was closed and secured, and they
parted in silence, she to take her place by the side of Hist
and Hetty, and he to seek a blanket on the floor of the cabin
he was in. It was not five minutes ere the young man was in a
deep sleep, but the girl continued awake for a long time.
She scarce knew whether to lament or to rejoice at having
failed in making herself understood. On the one hand, were
her womanly sensibilities spared; on the other, was the disappointment of defeated, or at least of delayed expectations,
and the uncertainty of a future that looked so dark. Then
came the new resolution and the bold project for the morrow; and when drowsiness finally shut her eyes, they closed
on a scene of success and happiness that was pictured by
the fancy, under the influence of a sanguine temperament
and a happy invention.

CHAPTER XXV

But, mother, now a shade has past
Athwart my brightest visions here,
A cloud of darkest gloom has wrapt
The remnant of my brief career!
No song, no echo can I win;
The sparkling fount has dried within.

MARGARET DAVIDSON

HIST AND HETTY arose with the return of light, leaving Judith still buried in sleep. It took but a minute for the first to complete her toilet. Her long, coal-black hair was soon adjusted in a simple knot, the calico dress belted tight to her slender waist, and her little feet concealed in their gaudily-ornamented moccasins. When attired, she left her companion employed in household affairs and went herself on the platform, to breathe the pure air of the morning. Here she found Chingachgook studying the shores of the lake, the mountains, and the heavens with the sagacity of a man of the woods and the gravity of an Indian.

The meeting between the two lovers was simple but affectionate. The chief showed a manly kindness, equally removed from boyish weakness and haste, while the girl betrayed in her smile and half-averted looks the bashful tenderness of her sex. Neither spoke, unless it were with the eyes, though each understood the other as fully as if a vocabulary of words and protestations had been poured out. Hist seldom appeared to more advantage than at that moment, for just from her rest and ablutions, there was a freshness about her youthful form and face that the toils of the wood do not always permit to be exhibited by even the juvenile and pretty. Then Judith had not only imparted some of her own skill in the toilet during their short inter-

course, but she had actually bestowed a few well-selected ornaments from her own stores that contributed not a little to set off the natural graces of the Indian maid. All this the lover saw and felt, and for a moment his countenance was illuminated with a look of pleasure; but it soon grew grave again and became saddened and anxious. The stools used the previous night were still standing on the platform; placing two against the walls of the hut, he seated himself on one, making a gesture to his companion to take the other. This done, he continued thoughtful and silent for quite a minute, maintaining the reflecting dignity of one born to take his seat at the council fire, while Hist was furtively watching the expression of his face, patient and submissive, as became a woman of her people. Then the young warrior stretched his arm before him, as if to point out the glories of the scene at that witching hour when the whole panorama, as usual, was adorned by the mellow distinctness of early morning, sweeping with his hand slowly over lake, hills, and heavens. The girl followed the movement with pleased wonder, smiling as each new beauty met her gaze.

"Hugh!" exclaimed the chief, in admiration of a scene so unusual even to him, for this was the first lake he had ever beheld. "This is the country of the Manitou! It is too good for Mingos, Hist, but the curs of that tribe are howling in packs through the woods. They think that the Delawares are asleep, over the mountains."

"All but one of them is, Chingachgook. There is one here, and he is of the blood of Uncas!"

"What is one warrior against a tribe? The path to our villages is very long and crooked, and we shall travel it under a cloudy sky. I am afraid, too, Honeysuckle of the Hills, that we shall travel it alone!"

Hist understood the allusion, and it made her sad—though it sounded sweet to her ears to be compared, by the warrior she so loved, to the most fragrant and the pleasantest of all the wildflowers of her native woods. Still, she continued silent, as became her when the allusion was to a grave interest that men could best control, though it exceeded the power of education to conceal the smile that gratified feeling brought to her pretty mouth.

"When the sun is thus," continued the Delaware, pointing

to the zenith by simply casting upward a hand and finger by a play of the wrist, "the great hunter of our tribe will go back to the Hurons to be treated like a bear that they roast and skin, even on full stomachs."

"The Great Spirit may soften their hearts and not suffer them to be so bloody-minded. I have lived among the Hurons, and know them. They have hearts, and will not forget their own children, should they fall into the hands of the Delawares."

"A wolf is forever howling; a hog will always eat. They have lost warriors; even their women will call out for vengeance. The paleface has the eyes of an eagle and can see into a Mingo's heart; he looks for no mercy. There is a cloud over his spirit, though it is not before his face."

A long, thoughtful pause succeeded, during which Hist stealthily took the hand of the chief, as if seeking his support, though she scarce ventured to raise her eyes to a countenance that was now literally becoming terrible, under the conflicting passions and stern resolution that were struggling in the breast of its owner.

"What will the son of Uncas do?" the girl at length timidly asked. "He is a chief, and is already celebrated in council, though so young; what does his heart tell him is wisest? Does the head, too, speak the same words as the heart?"

"What does Wah-ta!-Wah say, at a moment when my dearest friend is in danger. The smallest birds sing the sweetest; it is always pleasant to hearken to their songs. I wish I could hear the Wren of the Woods in my difficulty; its note would reach deeper than the ear."

Again Hist experienced the profound gratification that the language of praise can always awaken when uttered by those we love. The "Honeysuckle of the Hills" was a term often applied to the girl by the young men of the Delawares, though it never sounded so sweet in her ears as from the lips of Chingachgook; but the latter alone had ever styled her the Wren of the Woods. With him, however, it had got to be a familiar phrase, and it was past expression pleasant to the listener, since it conveyed to her mind the idea that her advice and sentiments were as acceptable to her future husband as the tones of her voice and modes of conveying them were agreeable, uniting the two things most

prized by an Indian girl, as coming from her betrothed, admiration for a valued physical advantage, with respect for
her opinion. She pressed the hand she held between both her
own, and answered:

"Wah-ta!-Wah says that neither she nor the Great Serpent could ever laugh again, or ever sleep without dreaming
of the Hurons, should the Deerslayer die under a Mingo
tomahawk, and they do nothing to save him. She would
rather go back and start on her long path alone than let such
a dark cloud pass before her happiness."

"Good! The husband and the wife will have but one heart;
they will see with the same eyes and feel with the same
feelings."

What further was said need not be related here. That the
conversation was of Deerslayer and his hopes has been seen
already, but the decision that was come to will better appear in the course of the narrative. The youthful pair were
yet conversing when the sun appeared above the tops of the
pines, and the light of a brilliant American day streamed
down into the valley, bathing "in deep joy" the lake, the
forests, and the mountainsides. Just at this instant Deerslayer came out of the cabin of the ark and stepped upon the
platform. His first look was at the cloudless heavens; then
his rapid glance took in the entire panorama of land and
water, when he had leisure for a friendly nod at his friends
and a cheerful smile for Hist.

"Well," he said, in his usual composed manner and pleasant voice, "he that sees the sun set in the west and wakes
arly enough in the morning will be sartain to find him
coming back ag'in in the east, like a buck that is hunted
around his ha'nts. I daresay, now, Hist, you've beheld this
time and ag'in, and yet it never entered into your galish mind
to ask the reason?"

Both Chingachgook and his betrothed looked up at the
luminary with an air that betokened sudden wonder, and
then they gazed at each other, as if to seek the solution
of the difficulty. Familiarity deadens the sensibilities, even
as connected with the gravest natural phenomena, and never
before had these simple beings thought of inquiring into a
movement that was of daily occurrence, however puzzling
it might appear on investigation. When the subject was thus
suddenly started, it struck both alike and at the same in-

stant, with some such force as any new and brilliant proposition in the natural sciences would strike the scholar. Chingachgook alone saw fit to answer.

"The palefaces know everything," he said; "can they tell us why the sun hides his face, when he goes back, at night?"

"Aye, that is downright redskin l'arnin'," returned the other, laughing, though he was not altogether insensible to the pleasure of proving the superiority of his race by solving the difficulty, which he set about doing, in his own peculiar manner. "Hark'ee, Sarpent," he continued more gravely, though too simply for affectation; "this is easierly explained than an Indian brain may fancy. The sun, while he seems to keep traveling in the heavens, never budges, but it is the 'arth that turns round; and anyone can understand, if he is placed on the side of a mill wheel, for instance, when it's in motion, that he must sometimes see the heavens, while he is at other times under water. There's no great secret in that, but plain natur', the difficulty being in setting the 'arth in motion."

"How does my brother know that the earth turns round?" demanded the Indian. "Can he see it?"

"Well, that's been a puzzler, I will own, Delaware, for I've often tried, but never could fairly make it out. Sometimes I've consaited that I could, and then ag'in I've been obliged to own it an onpossibility. Howsever, turn it does, as all my people say, and you ought to believe 'em, since they can foretell eclipses and other prodigies that used to fill the tribes with terror, according to your own traditions of such things."

"Good. This is true; no red man will deny it. When a wheel turns, my eyes can see it—they do not see the earth turn."

"Aye, that's what I call sense obstinacy! Seeing is believing, they say, and what they can't see, some men won't in the least give credit to. Nevertheless, Chief, that isn't quite as good reason as it may at first seem. You believe in the Great Spirit, I know, and yet, I conclude, it would puzzle you to show where you see Him!"

"Chingachgook can see Him everywhere—everywhere in good things—the Evil Spirit in bad. Here, in the lake; there, in the forest; yonder, in the clouds; in Hist, in the son of

Uncas, in Tamenund, in Deerslayer. The Evil Spirit is in the Mingos. That I know; I do not see the earth turn round."

"I don't wonder they call you the Sarpent, Delaware; no, I don't! There's always a meaning in your words, and there's often a meaning in your countenance, too! Not withstanding, your answers doesn't quite meet my idee. That God is obsarvable in all nat'ral objects is allowable, but then he is not parceptible in the way I mean. *You* know there is a Great Spirit by his works, and the palefaces know that the 'arth turns round by its works. This is the reason of the matter, though how it is to be explained is more than I can exactly tell you. This I know: all my people consait that fact, and what all the palefaces consait is very likely to be true."

"When the sun is in the top of that pine tomorrow, where will my brother Deerslayer be?"

The hunter started, and he looked intently, though totally without alarm, at his friend. Then he signed for him to follow and led the way into the ark, where he might pursue the subject unheard by those whose feelings he feared might get the mastery over their reason. Here he stopped and pursued the conversation in a more confidential tone.

"'Twas a little onreasonable in you, Sarpent," he said, "to bring up such a subject afore Hist, and when the young woman of my own color might overhear what was said. Yes, 'twas a little more onreasonable than most things that you do. No matter; Hist didn't comprehend, and the other didn't hear. Howsever, the question is easier put than answered. No mortal can say where he will be when the sun rises tomorrow. I will ask you the same question, Sarpent, and should like to hear what answer you can give."

"Chingachgook will be with his friend, Deerslayer; if he be in the land of spirits, the Great Serpent will crawl at his side; if beneath yonder sun, its warmth and light shall fall on both."

"I understand you, Delaware," returned the other, touched with the simple self-devotion of his friend. "Such language is as plain in one tongue as in another; it comes from the heart, and goes to the heart, too. 'Tis well to think so, and it may be well to *say* so, for that matter, but it would not be well to *do* so, Sarpent. You are no longer alone in life, for though you have the lodges to change and other

ceremonies to go through afore Hist becomes your lawful wife, yet are you as good as married in all that bears on the feelin's, and joy, and misery. No, no; Hist must not be desarted because a cloud is passing atween you and me a little onexpectedly and a little darker than we may have looked for."

"Hist is a daughter of the Mohicans: she knows how to obey her husband. Where he goes she will follow. *Both* will be with the Great Hunter of the Delawares when the sun shall be in the pine tomorrow."

"The Lord bless and protect you! Chief, this is downright madness. Can either or both of you alter a Mingo natur'? Will your grand looks, or Hist's tears and beauty, change a wolf into a squirrel, or make a catamount as innocent as a fa'an! No, Sarpent, you will think better of this matter, and leave me in the hands of God. A'ter all, it's by no means sartain that the scamps design the torments, for they may yet be pitiful and bethink them of the wickedness of such a course—though it *is* but a hopeless expectation to look forward to a Mingo's turning aside from evil, and letting marcy get uppermost in his heart. Nevertheless, no one knows to a sartainty what will happen, and young creatur's like Hist ar'n't to be risked on unsartainties. This marrying is altogether a different undertaking from what some young men fancy. Now, if you was single, or as good as single, Delaware, I should expect you to be actyve and stirring about the camp of the vagabonds from sunrise to sunset, sarcumventing and contriving, as restless as a hound off the scent, and doing all manner of things to help me and to distract the inimy; but two are often feebler than one, and we must take things as they are and not as we want 'em to be."

"Listen, Deerslayer," returned the Indian, with an emphasis so decided as to show how much he was in earnest. "If Chingachgook was in the hands of the Hurons, what would my paleface brother do? Sneak off to the Delaware villages and say to the chiefs, and old men, and young warriors—'See; here is Wah-ta!-wah; she is safe, but a little tired; and here is the Son of Uncas, not as tired as the Honeysuckle, being stronger, but just as safe.' Would he do this?"

"Well, that's oncommon ingen'ous; it's cunning enough for

a Mingo himself. The Lord only knows what put it into your head to ask such a question. What would I do? Why, in the first place, Hist wouldn't be likely to be in my company at all, for she would stay as near you as possible, and therefore all that part about *her* couldn't be said without talking nonsense. As for her being tired, that would fall through, too, if she didn't go, and no part of your speech would be likely to come from me: so you see, Sarpent, reason is ag'in you, and you may as well give it up, since to hold out ag'in reason is no way becoming a chief of your character and repitation."

"My brother is not himself; he forgets that he is talking to one who has sat at the council fires of his nation," returned the other kindly. "When men speak, they should say that which does not go in at one side of the head and out at the other. Their words shouldn't be feathers, so light that a wind which does not ruffle the water can blow them away. He has not answered my question; when a chief puts a question, his friend should not talk of other things."

"I understand you, Delaware; I understand well enough what you mean, and truth won't allow me to say otherwise. Still, it's not as easy to answer as you seem to think, for this plain reason. You wish me to say what I would do if I had a betrothed, as you have, here on the lake, and a fri'nd yonder, in the Huron camp, in danger of the torments. That's it, isn't it?"

The Indian bowed his head silently and always with unmoved gravity, though his eye twinkled at the sight of the other's embarrassment.

"Well, I never had a betrothed, never had the kind of feelin's toward any young woman that you have toward Hist, though the Lord knows my feelin's kind enough toward 'em all! Still, my heart, as they call it, in such matters isn't touched, and therefore I can't say what I would do. A fri'nd pulls strong; that I know by exper'ence, Sarpent; but by all that I've seen and heard consarning love, I'm led to think that a betrothed pulls stronger."

"True; but the betrothed of Chingachgook does not pull toward the lodges of the Delawares; she pulls toward the camp of the Hurons."

"She's a noble gal, for all her little feet and hands that an't bigger than a child's, and a voice that's as pleasant as a

mocker's; she's a noble gal, and like the stock of her sires! Well, what is it, Sarpent?—for I conclude she hasn't changed her mind and means to give herself up and turn Huron wife. What is it you want?"

"Wah-ta!-wah will never live in the wigwam of an Iroquois," answered the Delaware drily. "She has little feet, but they can carry her to the villages of her people; she has small hands, too, but her mind is large. My brother will see what we can do when the time shall come, rather than let him die under Mingo torments."

"Attempt nothing heedlessly, Delaware," said the other earnestly. "I suppose you must and will have your way; on the whole, it's right you should, for you'd neither be happy unless something was undertaken. But attempt nothing heedlessly. I didn't expect you'd quit the lake while my matter remained in unsartainty; but remember, Sarpent, that no torments that Mingo ingenuity can invent, no ta'ntings and revilings, no burnings and roastings and nail-tearings, nor any other onhuman contrivance, can so soon break down my spirit as to find that you and Hist have fallen into the power of the inimy in striving to do something for my good."

"The Delawares are prudent. The Deerslayer will not find them running into a strange camp with their eyes shut."

Here the dialogue terminated. Hetty announced that the breakfast was ready, and the whole party were soon seated around the simple board, in the usual primitive manner of borderers. Judith was the last to take her seat, pale, silent, and betraying in her countenance that she had passed a painful if not a sleepless night. At this meal scarce a syllable was exchanged, all the females manifesting want of appetite, though the two men were unchanged in this particular. It was early when the party arose, and there still remained several hours before it would be necessary for the prisoner to leave his friends. The knowledge of this circumstance, and the interest all felt in his welfare, induced the whole to assemble on the platform again, in the desire to be near the expected victim, to listen to his discourse, and, if possible, to show their interest in him by anticipating his wishes. Deerslayer himself, so far as human eyes could penetrate, was wholly unmoved, conversing cheerfully and naturally, though he avoided any direct allusion to the ex-

pected and great event of the day. If any evidence could be discovered of his thoughts reverting to that painful subject at all, it was in the manner in which he spoke of death and the last great change.

"Grieve not, Hetty," he said—for it was while consoling this simple-minded girl for the loss of her parents that he thus betrayed his feelings—"since God has app'inted that all must die. Your parents, or them you fancied your parents, which is the same thing, have gone afore you; this is only in the order of natur', my good gal, for the aged go first and the young follow. But one that had a mother like your'n, Hetty, can be at no loss to hope the best as to how matters will turn out in another world. The Delaware here and Hist believe in happy hunting grounds and have idees befitting their notions and gifts as redskins, but we who are of white blood hold altogether to a different doctrine. Still, I rather conclude our heaven is their land of spirits and that the path which leads to it will be traveled by all colors alike. 'Tis onpossible for the wicked to enter on it, I will allow; but fri'nds can scarce be separated, though they are not of the same race on 'arth. Keep up your spirits, poor Hetty, and look forward to the day when you will meet your mother ag'in, and that without pain or sorrowing."

"I do expect to see Mother," returned the truth-telling and simple girl, "but what will become of Father?"

"That's a nonplusser, Delaware," said the hunter in the Indian dialect; "yes, that is a downright nonplusser! The Muskrat was not a saint on 'arth, and it's fair to guess he'll not be much of one hereafter! Howsever, Hetty"—dropping into the English by an easy transition—"we must all hope for the best. That is wisest, and it is much the easiest to the mind, if one can only do it, I ricommend to you trusting to God and putting down all misgivings and fainthearted feelin's. It's wonderful, Judith, how different people have different notions about the futur', some fancying one change and some fancying another. I've known white teachers that have thought all was spirit hereafter, and them ag'in that believed the body will be transported to another world, much as the redskins themselves imagine, and that we shall walk about in the flesh, and know each other, and talk together, and be fri'nds there as we've been fri'nds here."

"Which of these opinions is most pleasing to *you*, Deer-

slayer?" asked the girl, willing to indulge his melancholy mood, and far from being free from its influence
herself. "Would it be disagreeable to think that you should
meet all who are now on this platform in another world?
Or have you known enough of us here to be glad to see us
no more?"

"The last would make death a bitter portion; yes, it would.
It's eight good years since the Sarpent and I began to hunt
together, and the thought that we were never to meet ag'in
would be a hard thought to me. He looks forward to the
time when he shall chase a sort of spirit deer, in company,
on plains where there's no thorns, or brambles, or marshes,
or other hardships to overcome; whereas, I can't fall into
all these notions, seeing that they appear to be ag'in reason. Spirits can't eat, nor have they any use for clothes, and
deer can only rightfully be chased to be slain, or slain,
unless it be for the venison or the hides. Now I find it hard
to suppose that blessed spirits can be put to chasing game
without an object, tormenting the dumb animals just for the
pleasure and agreeableness of their own amusements. I never
yet pulled a trigger on buck or doe, Judith, unless when
food or clothes was wanting."

"The recollection of which, Deerslayer, must now be a great
consolation to you."

"It is the thought of such things, my fri'nds, that enables a man to keep his furlough. It might be done without
it, I own; for the worst redskins sometimes do their duty
in this matter; but it makes that which might otherwise be
hard, easy, if not altogether to our liking. Nothing truly
makes a bolder heart than a light conscience."

Judith turned paler than ever, but she struggled for self-
command and succeeded in obtaining it. The conflict had
been severe, however, and it left her so little disposed to
speak that Hetty pursued the subject. This was done in the
simple manner natural to the girl.

"It would be cruel to kill the poor deer," she said, "in this
world or any other, when you don't want their venison or
their skins. No good white man and no good red man
would do it. But it's wicked for a Christian to talk about
chasing anything in Heaven. Such things are not done before the face of God, and the missionary that teaches these
doctrines can't be a true missionary. He must be a wolf in

sheep's clothing. I suppose you know what a sheep is, Deerslayer?"

"That I do, gal; and a useful creature it is to such as like cloths better than skins for winter garments. I understand the natur' of sheep, though I've had but little to do with 'em —and the natur' of wolves too, and can take the idee of a wolf in the fleece of a sheep, though I think it would be likely to prove a hot jacket for such a beast in the warm months."

"And sin and hypocrisy are hot jackets, as *they* will find who put them on," returned Hetty positively, "so the wolf would be no worse off than the sinner. Spirits don't hunt, nor trap, nor fish, nor do anything that vain men undertake, since they've none of the longings of this world to feed. Oh, Mother told me all that years ago, and I didn't wish to hear it denied."

"Well, my good Hetty, in that case you'd better not broach your doctrine to Hist when she and you are alone and the young Delaware maiden is inclined to talk religion. It's her fixed idee, I know, that the good warriors do nothing but hunt and fish in the other world, though I don't believe that she fancies any of them are brought down to trapping, which is no empl'yment for a brave. But of hunting and fishing, accordin' to her notion, they've their fill, and that, too, over the most agreeablest hunting grounds and among game that is never out of season, and which is just actyve and instinctyve enough to give a pleasure to death. So I wouldn't ricommend it to you to start Hist on that idee."

"Hist can't be so wicked as to believe any such thing," returned the other earnestly. "No Indian hunts after he is dead."

"No wicked Indian, I grant you; no wicked Indian sartainly. He is obliged to carry the ammunition, and to look on without sharing in the sport, and to cook, and to light the fires, and to do everything that isn't manful. Now mind, I don't tell you these are my idees, but they are Hist's idees, and therefore for the sake of peace, the less you say to her ag'in 'em the better."

"And what are your ideas of the fate of an Indian in the other world?" demanded Judith, who had just found her voice.

"Ah, gal, anything but that! I am too Christianized to

expect anything so fanciful as hunting and fishing after death; nor do I believe there is one Manitou for the redskin and another for a paleface. You find different colors on arth, as anyone may see, but you don't find different natur's. Different gifts, but only one natur'."

"In what is a gift different from a nature? Is not nature itself a gift from God?"

"Sartain; that's quick-thoughted and creditable, Judith, though the main idee is wrong. A natur' is the creatur' itself; its wishes, wants, idees, and feelin's, as all are born in him. This natur' never can be changed in the main, though it may undergo some increase or lessening. Now, gifts come of sarcumstances. Thus, if you put a man in a town, he gets town gifts; in a settlement, settlement gifts; in a forest, gifts of the woods. A soldier has soldierly gifts, and a missionary preaching gifts. All these increase and strengthen until they get to fortify natur', as it might be, and excuse a thousand acts and idees. Still, the creatur' is the same at the bottom, just as a man who is clad in regimentals is the same as the man that is clad in skins. The garments make a change to the eye and some change in the conduct, perhaps, but none in the man. Herein lies the apology for gifts, seein' that you expect different conduct from one in silks and satins from one in homespun, though the Lord, who didn't make the dresses but who made the creatur's themselves, looks only at His own work. This isn't ra'al missionary doctrine, but it's as near it as a man of white color need be. Ah's me! Little did I think to be talking of such matters today, but it's one of our weaknesses never to know what will come to pass. Step into the ark with me, Judith, for a minute. I wish to converse with you."

Judith complied with a willingness she could scarce conceal. Following the hunter into the cabin, she took a seat on a stool, while the young man brought Killdeer, the rifle she had given him, out of a corner, and placed himself on another, with the weapon laid upon his knees. After turning the piece around and around and examining its lock and its breech with a sort of affectionate assiduity, he laid it down and proceeded to the subject which had induced him to desire the interview.

"I understand you, Judith, to say that you gave me this rifle," he said. "I agreed to take it because a young woman

can have no particular use for firearms. The we'pon has a great name, and it desarves it, and ought of right to be carried by some known and sure hand, for the best reputation may be lost by careless and thoughtless handling."

"Can it be in better hands than those in which it is now Deerslayer? Thomas Hutter seldom missed with it: with you it must turn out to be——"

"Sartain death!" interrupted the hunter, laughing. "I once know'd a beaver man that had a piece he called by that very name, but 'twas all boastfulness, for I've seen Delawares that were as true with arrows at a short range. Howsever, I'll not deny my gifts—for *this* is a gift, Judith, and not natur'— but I'll not deny my gifts, and therefore allow that the rifle couldn't well be in better hands than it is at present. But how long will it be likely to remain there? Atween us, the truth may be said, though I shouldn't like to have it known to the Sarpent and Hist; but to *you* the truth may be spoken. since *your* feelin's will not be as likely to be tormented by it as those of them that have known me longer and better. How long am I like to own this rifle or any other? That is a serious question for our thoughts to rest on, and should that happen which is so likely to happen, Killdeer would be without an owner."

Judith listened with apparent composure, though the conflict within came near overpowering her. Appreciating the singular character of her companion, however, she succeeded in appearing calm, though, had not his attention been drawn exclusively to the rifle, a man of his keenness of observation could scarce have failed to detect the agony of mind with which the girl had hearkened to his words. Her great self-command, notwithstanding, enabled her to pursue the subject in a way still to deceive him.

"What would you have me do with the weapon," she asked, "should that which you seem to expect take place?"

"That's just what I wanted to speak to you about, Judith —that's just it. There's Chingachgook, now, though far from being parfect sartainty with a rifle—for few redskins ever get to be *that*—though far from being parfect sartainty, he is respectable and is coming on. Nevertheless, he is my fri'nd, and all the better fri'nd, perhaps, because there never can be any hard feelin's atween us, touchin' our gifts, his'n bein' red and mine bein' altogether white. Now, I should like to

leave Killdeer to the Sarpent, should anything happen to keep me from doing credit and honor to your precious gift, Judith."

"Leave it to whom you please, Deerslayer; the rifle is your own, to do with as you please; Chingachgook shall have it, should you never return to claim it, if that be your wish."

"Has Hetty been consulted in this matter? Property goes from the parent to the children, and not to one child in par-tic'lar."

"If you place your right on that of the law, Deerslayer, I fear none of us can claim to be the owner. Thomas Hutter was no more the father of Esther than he was the father of Judith. Judith and Esther we are, truly, having no other name."

"There may be law in that, but there's no great reason, gal. Accordin' to the custom of families, the goods are your'n, and there's no one here to gainsay it. If Hetty would only say that she is willing, my mind would be quite at ease in the matter. It's true, Judith, that your sister has neither your beauty nor your wit, but we should be the tenderest of the rights and welfare of the most weak-minded."

The girl made no answer, but, placing herself at a window, she summoned her sister to her side. When the question was put to Hetty, her simple-minded and affectionate nature cheerfully assented to the proposal to confer on Deerslayer a full right of ownership to the much-coveted rifle. The latter now seemed perfectly happy, for the time being, at least, and after again examining and re-examining his prize, he ex-pressed a determination to put its merits to a practical test before he left the spot. No boy could have been more eager to exhibit the qualities of his trumpet or his crossbow than this simple forester was to prove those of his rifle. Returning to the platform, he first took the Delaware aside and in-formed him that this celebrated piece was to become his property in the event of anything serious befalling himself.

"This is a new reason why you should be wary, Sarpent, and not run into any oncalculated danger," the hunter added, "for it will be a victory of itself, to a tribe, to own such a piece as this! The Mingos will turn green with envy, and what is more, they will not ventur' heedlessly near a village where it is known to be kept. So look well to it, Delaware, and remember that you've now to watch over a thing that

has all the valie of a creatur', without its failin's. Hist may
be, and should be precious to you, but Killdeer will have
the love and veneration of your whole people."

"One rifle like another, Deerslayer," returned the Indian in
English, the language used by the other, a little hurt at his
friend's lowering his betrothed to the level of a gun. "All
kill; all wood and iron. Wife dear to heart; rifle good to
shoot."

"And what is a man in the woods, without something to
shoot with?—a miserable trapper, or a forlorn broom and
basketmaker, at the best. Such a man may hoe corn and
keep soul and body together, but he can never know
the savory morsels of venison, or tell a bear's ham from a
hog's. Come, my fri'nd, such another occasion may never
offer ag'in, and I feel a strong craving for a trial with this
celebrated piece. You shall bring out your own rifle, and I
will just sight Killdeer in a careless way, in order that we
may know a few of its secret vartues."

As this proposition served to relieve the thoughts of the
whole party, by giving them a new direction, while it was
likely to produce no unpleasant result, everyone was willing
to enter into it, the girls bringing forth the firearms with an
alacrity bordering on cheerfulness. Hutter's armory was well
supplied, possessing several rifles, all of which were habitually kept loaded, in readiness to meet any sudden demand for their use. On the present occasion it only remained
to freshen the primings, and each piece was in a state for
service. This was soon done, as all assisted in it, the females
being as expert in this part of the system of defense as their
male companions.

"Now, Sarpent, we'll begin in an humble way, using old
Tom's commoners first and coming to your we'pon and Killdeer as the winding-up observations," said Deerslayer, delighted to be again, weapon in hand, ready to display his
skill. "Here's birds in abundance, some in, and some over
the lake, and they keep at just a good range, hovering
around the hut. Speak your mind, Delaware, and p'int out
the creatur' you wish to alarm. Here's a diver, nearest in,
off to the eastward, and that's a creatur' that buries itself at
the flash, and will be like enough to try both piece and
powder."

Chingachgook was a man of few words. No sooner was

the bird pointed out to him than he took his aim and fired. The duck dived at the flash, as had been expected, and the bullet skipped harmlessly along the surface of the lake, first striking the water within a few inches of the spot where the bird had so lately swum. Deerslayer laughed cordially and naturally, but at the same time he threw himself into an attitude of preparation and stood keenly, watching the sheet of placid water. Presently a dark spot appeared, and then the duck arose to breathe, and shook its wings. While in this act, a bullet passed directly through its breast, actually turning it over lifeless, on its back. At the next moment Deerslayer stood with the breech of his rifle on the platform, as tranquil as if nothing had happened, though laughing in his own peculiar manner.

"There's no great trial of the pieces in that!" he said, as if anxious to prevent a false impression of his own merit. "No, that proof's neither for nor ag'in the rifles, seeing it was all quickness of hand and eye. I took the bird at a disadvantage, or he might have got under again, afore the bullet reached him. But the Sarpent is too wise to mind such tricks, having long been used to them. Do you remember the time, Chief, when you thought yourself sartain of the wild goose, and I took him out of your very eyes, as it might be, with a little smoke! Howsever such things pass for nothing atween fri'nds, and young folk will have their fun, Judith. Aye, here's just the bird we want, for it's as good for the fire as it is for the aim, and nothing should be lost that can be turned to just account. There, farther north, Delaware."

The latter looked in the required direction, and he soon saw a large black duck, floating in stately repose on the water. At that distant day, when so few men were present to derange the harmony of the wilderness, all the smaller lakes with which the interior of New York so abounds were places of resort for the migratory aquatic birds, and this sheet, like the others, had once been much frequented by all the varieties of the duck, by the goose, the gull, and the loon. On the appearance of Hutter, the spot was comparatively deserted for other sheets, more retired and remote, though some of each species continued to resort thither, as indeed they do to the present hour. At that instant, a hundred birds were visible from the castle, sleeping on the water, or laving their feathers in the limpid element, though no other offered so fa-

vorable a mark as that Deerslayer had just pointed out to his friend. Chingachgook, as usual, speared his words and proceeded to execution. This time his aim was more careful than before, and his success in proportion. The bird had a wing crippled, and fluttered along the water screaming, materially increasing its distance from its enemies.

"That bird must be put out of pain," exclaimed Deerslayer, the moment the animal endeavored to rise on the wing, "and this is the rifle and the eye to do it."

The duck was still floundering along when the fatal bullet overtook it, severing the head from the neck as neatly as if it had been done with an ax. Hist had indulged in a low cry of delight at the success of the young Indian, but now she affected to frown and resent the greater skill of his friend. The chief, on the contrary, uttered the usual exclamation of pleasure, and his smile proved how much he admired and how little he envied.

"Never mind the gal, Sarpent; never mind Hist's feelin's, which will neither choke nor drown, slay nor beautify," said Deerslayer, laughing. " 'Tis nat'ral for women to enter into their husband's victories and defeats, and you are as good as man and wife, so far as prejudice and friendship go. Here is a bird overhead that will put the pieces to the proof; I challenge you to an upward aim, with a flying target. That's a ra'al proof, and one that needs sartain rifles, as well as sartain eyes."

The species of eagle that frequents the water and lives on fish was also present, and one was hovering at a considerable height above the hut, greedily watching for an opportunity to make a swoop, its hungry young elevating their heads from a nest that was in sight in the naked summit of a dead pine. Chingachgook silently turned a new piece against this bird and, after carefully watching his time, fired. A wider circuit than common denoted that the messenger had passed through the air at no great distance from the bird, though it missed its object. Deerslayer, whose aim was not more true than it was quick, fired as soon as it was certain his friend had missed, and the deep swoop that followed left it momentarily doubtful whether the eagle was hit or not. The marksman himself, however, proclaimed his own want of success, calling on his friend to seize another rifle, for he saw signs on the part of the bird of an intention to quit the spot.

"I made him wink, Sarpent; I do think his feathers were ruffled, but no blood has yet been drawn, nor is that old piece fit for so nice and quick a sight. Quick, Delaware, you've now a better rifle; Judith, bring out Killdeer, for this is the occasion to try his merits, if he has 'em!"

A general movement followed, each of the competitors got ready, and the girls stood in eager expectation of the result. The eagle had made a wide circuit after his low swoop, and fanning his way upward, once more hovered nearly over the hut, at a distance even greater than before. Chingachgook gazed at him and then expressed his opinion of the impossibility of striking a bird at that great height, and while he was so nearly perpendicular as to the range. But a low murmur from Hist produced a sudden impulse, and he fired. The result showed how well he had calculated, the eagle not even varying his flight, sailing around and around in his airy circle, and looking down, as if in contempt, at his foes.

"Now, Judith," cried Deerslayer, laughing, with glistening and delighted eyes, "we'll see if Killdeer isn't Killeagle, too! Give me room, Sarpent, and watch the reason of the aim, for by reason anything may be l'arned."

A careful sight followed, and was repeated again and again, the bird continuing to rise higher and higher. Then followed the flash and the report. The swift messenger sped upward, and at the next instant, the bird turned on its side and came swooping down, now struggling with one wing and then with the other, sometimes whirling in a circuit, next fanning desperately as if conscious of its injury, until, having described several complete circles around the spot, it fell heavily into the end of the ark. On examining the body, it was found that the bullet had pierced it about halfway between one of its wings and the breastbone.

CHAPTER XXVI

Upon two stony tables, spread before her,
She leaned her bosom, more than stony hard;
There slept the impartial judge, and strict restorer
Of wrong or right, with pain or with reward;
There hung the score of all our debts, the card
Where good, and bad, and life, and death, were painted,
Was never heart of mortal so untainted,
But when the roll was read, with thousand terrors fainted.

GILES FLETCHER

"WE'VE DONE AN unthoughtful thing, Sarpent—yes, Judith, we've done an unthoughtful thing in taking life with an object no better than vanity!" exclaimed Deerslayer, when the Delaware held up the enormous bird, by its wings, and exhibited the dying eyes riveted on its enemies with the gaze that the helpless ever fasten on their destroyers. " 'Twas more becomin' two boys to gratify their feelin's in this onthoughtful manner than two warriors on a warpath, even though it be their first. Ah's me! Well, as a punishment I'll quit you at once, and when I find myself alone with them bloody-minded Mingos, it's more than like I'll have occasion to remember that life is sweet, even to the beasts of the woods and the fowls of the air. Here, Judith; there's Killdeer; take him back ag'in, and keep him for some hand that's more desarving to own such a piece."

"I know of none as deserving as your own, Deerslayer," answered the girl in haste; "none but yours shall keep the rifle."

"If it depended on skill, you might be right enough, gal, but we should know *when* to use firearms as well as *how* to use 'em. I haven't l'arnt the first duty yet, it seems, so keep the peace till I have. The sight of a dyin' and distressed creatur', even though it be only a bird, brings wholesome

432

thoughts to a man who don't know how soon his own time may come, and who *is* pretty sartain that it will come afore the sun sets; I'd give back all my vain feelin's and rej'icin's in hand and eye if that poor eagle was only on its nest ag'in with its young, praisin' the Lord, for anything that we can know about the matter, for health and strength!"

The listeners were confounded with this proof of sudden repentance in the hunter, and that, too, for an indulgence so very common that men seldom stop to weigh its consequences or the physical suffering it may bring on the unoffending and helpless. The Delaware understood what was said, though he scarce understood the feelings which had prompted the words, and by way of disposing of the difficulty, he drew his keen knife and severed the head of the sufferer from its body.

"What a thing is power!" continued the hunter, "and what a thing it is to have it and not to know how to use it! It's no wonder, Judith, that the great so often fail of their duties, when even the little and the humble find it so hard to do what's right and not to do what's wrong. Then, how one evil act brings others a'ter it! Now, wasn't it for this furlough of mine, which must soon take me back to the Mingos, I'd find this creatur's nest, if I traveled the woods a fortnight—though an eagle's nest is soon found by them that understands the bird's natur'—but I'd travel a fortnight rather than not find it, just to put the young, too, out of their pain."

"I'm glad to hear you say this, Deerslayer," observed Hetty, "and God will be more apt to remember your sorrow for what you've done than the wickedness itself. I thought how wicked it was to kill harmless birds while you were shooting and meant to tell you so, but—I don't know how it happened—I was so curious to see if you *could* hit an eagle at so great a height that I forgot altogether to speak till the mischief was done."

"That's it; that's just it, my good Hetty. We can all see our faults and mistakes when it's too late to help them! Howsever, I'm glad you didn't speak, for I don't think a word or two would have stopped me just at that moment; and so the sin stands in its nakedness, not aggravated by any unheeded calls to forbear. Well, well, bitter thoughts are hard to be borne at all times, but there's times when they're harder than at others."

Little did Deerslayer know, while thus indulging in feelings that were natural to the man and so strictly in accordance with his own unsophisticated and just principles, that, in the course of the inscrutable Providence which so uniformly and yet so mysteriously covers all events with its mantle, the very fault he was disposed so severely to censure, was to be made the means of determining his own earthly fate. The mode and the moment in which he was to feel the influence of this interference it would be premature to relate, but both will appear in the course of the succeeding chapters. As for the young man, he now slowly left the ark, like one sorrowing for his misdeeds, and seated himself in silence on the platform. By this time the sun had ascended to some height, and its appearance, taken in connection with his present feelings, induced him to prepare to depart. The Delaware got the canoe ready for his friend as soon as apprised of his intention, while Hist busied herself in making the few arrangements that were thought necessary to his comfort. All this was done without ostentation but in a way that left Deerslayer fully acquainted with, and equally disposed to appreciate, the motive. When all was ready, both returned to the side of Judith and Hetty—neither of whom had moved from the spot where the young hunter sat.

"The best fri'nds must often part," the last began, when he saw the whole party grouped around him. "Yes, fri'ndship can't alter the ways of Providence, and let our feelin's be as they may, we must part. I've often thought there's moments when our words dwell longer on the mind than common, and when advice is remembered, just because the mouth that gives it isn't likely to give it ag'in. No one knows what will happen in the world, and therefore it may be well, when fri'nds separate under a likelihood that the parting may be long, to say a few words in kindness, as a sort of keepsakes. If all but one will go into the ark, I'll talk to each in turn, and what is more, I'll listen to what you may have to say back ag'in; for it's a poor counselor that won't take as well as give."

As the meaning of the speaker was understood, the two Indians immediately withdrew as desired, leaving the sisters, however, still standing at the young man's side. A look of Deerslayer's induced Judith to explain.

"You can advise Hetty as you land," she said hastily, "I intend that she shall accompany you to the shore."

"Is this wise, Judith? It's true that, under common sarcumstances, a feeble mind is a great protection among redskins, but when their feelin's are up, and they're bent on revenge, it's hard to say what may come to pass. Besides——"

"What were you about to say, Deerslayer?" asked Judith, whose gentleness of voice and manner amounted nearly to tenderness, though she struggled hard to keep her emotions and apprehensions in subjection.

"Why, simply that there are sights and doin's that one even as little gifted with reason and memory as Hetty, here, might better not witness. So, Judith, you would do well to let me land alone and to keep your sister back."

"Never fear for me, Deerslayer," put in Hetty, who comprehended enough of the discourse to know its general drift; "I'm feeble-minded, and that, they say, is an excuse for going anywhere, and what that won't excuse will be overlooked on account of the Bible I always carry. It is wonderful, Judith, how all sorts of men, the trappers as well as the hunters, red men as well as white, Mingos as well as Delawares, do reverence and fear the Bible!"

"I think you have not the least ground to fear any injury, Hetty," answered the sister, "and therefore I shall insist on your going to the Huron camp with our friend. Your being there can do no harm, not even to yourself, and may do great good to Deerslayer."

"This is not a moment, Judith, to dispute, and so have the matter your own way," returned the young man. "Get yourself ready, Hetty, and go into the canoe, for I've a few parting words to say to your sister, which can do you no good."

Judith and her companion continued silent until Hetty had so far complied as to leave them alone, when Deerslayer took up the subject as if it had been interrupted by some ordinary occurrence, and in a very matter-of-fact way.

"Words spoken at parting, and which may be the last we ever hear from a fri'nd, are not soon forgotten," he repeated, "and so, Judith, I intend to speak to you like a brother, seein' I'm not old enough to be your father. In the first place, I wish to caution you ag'in your inimies, of which two may be said to ha'nt your very footsteps and to beset your ways. The

first is oncommon good looks, which is as dangerous a foe to some young women as a whole tribe of Mingos could prove, and which calls for great watchfulness; not to admire and praise, but to distrust and sarcumvent. Yes, good looks may be sarcumvented and fairly outwitted, too. In order to do this, you've only to remember that they melt like the snows, and when once gone, they never come back ag'in. The seasons come and go, Judith; if we have winter, with storms and frosts, and spring, with chills and leafless trees, we have summer, with its sun and glorious skies, and fall, with its fruits and a garment thrown over the forest that no beauty of the town could rummage out of all the shops in America. 'Arth is an eternal round, the goodness of God bringing back the pleasant when we've had enough of the onpleasant. But it's not so with good looks. *They* are lent for a short time in youth, to be used and not abused, and as I never met with a young woman to whom Providence has been as bountiful as it has to you, Judith, in this partic'lar, I warn you, as it might be with my dyin' breath, to beware of the inimy—fri'nd or inimy, as we deal with the gift."

It was so grateful to Judith to hear these unequivocal admissions of her personal charms that much would have been forgiven to the man who made them, let him be who he might. But at that moment, and from a far better feeling, it would not have been easy for Deerslayer seriously to offend her, and she listened with a patience which, had it been foretold only a week earlier, it would have excited her indignation to hear.

"I understand your meaning, Deerslayer," returned the girl, with a meekness and humility that a little surprised her listener, "and hope to be able to profit by it. But you have mentioned only one of the enemies I have to fear; who, or what, is the other?"

"The other is givin' way afore your own good sense and judgment, I find, Judith; yes, he's not as dangerous as I supposed. Howsever, havin' opened the subject, it will be as well to end it honestly. The first inimy you have to be watchful of, as I've already told you, Judith, is oncommon good looks, and the next is an oncommon knowledge of the sarcumstance. If the first is bad, the last doesn't, in any way, mend the matter, so far as safety and peace of mind are consarned."

How much longer the young man would have gone on in his simple and unsuspecting, but well-intentioned manner, it might not be easy to say, had he not been interrupted by his listener's bursting into tears and giving way to an outbreak of feeling which was so much the more violent from the fact that it had been with so much difficulty suppressed. At first her sobs were so violent and uncontrollable that Deerslayer was a little appalled, and he was abundantly repentant from the instant that he discovered how much greater was the effect produced by his words than he had anticipated. Even the austere and exacting are usually appeased by the signs of contrition, but the nature of Deerslayer did not require proofs of intense feeling so strong, in order to bring him down to a level with the regrets felt by the girl herself. He arose as if an adder had stung him, and the accents of the mother that soothes her child were scarcely more gentle and winning than the tones of his voice, as he now expressed his contrition at having gone so far.

"It was well meant, Judith," he said, "but it was not intended to hurt your feelin's so much. I have overdone the advice, I see; yes, I've overdone it, and I crave your pardon for the same. Fri'ndship's an awful thing! Sometimes it chides us for not having done enough, and then ag'in it speaks in strong words for havin' done too much. Howsever, I acknowledge I've overdone the matter, and as I've a ra'al and strong regard for you, I rej'ice to say it, inasmuch as it proves how much better you are than my own vanity and consaits had made you out to be."

Judith now removed her hands from her face, her tears had ceased, and she unveiled a countenance so winning, with the smile which rendered it even radiant, that the young man gazed at her for a moment with speechless delight.

"Say no more, Deerslayer," she hastily interposed; "it pains me to hear you find fault with yourself. I know my own weakness all the better, now I see that you have discovered it; the lesson, bitter as I have found it for a moment, shall not be forgotten. We will not talk any longer of these things, for I do not feel myself brave enough for the undertaking, and I should not like the Delawares, or Hist, or even Hetty to notice my weakness. Farewell, Deerslayer, may God bless and protect you as your honest heart deserves blessing and protection, and as I must think He will."

Judith had so far regained the superiority that properly belonged to her better education, high spirit, and surpassing personal advantages as to preserve the ascendency she had thus accidentally obtained, and effectually prevented any return to the subject that was as singularly interrupted as it had been singularly introduced. The young man permitted her to have everything her own way, and when she pressed his hard hand in both her own, he made no resistance, but submitted to the homage as quietly, and with quite as matter of course a manner, as a sovereign would have received a similar tribute from a subject, or the mistress from her suitor. Feeling had flushed the face and illuminated the whole countenance of the girl, and her beauty was never more resplendent than when she cast a parting glance at the youth. That glance was filled with anxiety, interest, and gentle pity. At the next instant she darted into the hut and was seen no more, though she spoke to Hist from a window to inform her that their friend expected her appearance.

"You know enough of redskin natur', and redskin usages, Wah-ta!-Wah, to see the condition I am in on account of this furlough," commenced the hunter, in Delaware, as soon as the patient and submissive girl of that people had moved quietly to his side; "you will therefore best onderstand how onlikely I am ever to talk with you ag'in. I've but little to say, but that little comes from long livin' among your people and from havin' obsarved and noted their usages. The life of a woman is hard at the best, but I must own, though I'm not opinionated in favor of my own color, that it is harder among the red men than it is among the palefaces. This is a p'int on which Christians may well boast, if boasting can be set down for Christianity in any manner or form, which I rather think it cannot. Howsever, all women have their trials. Red women have their'n in what I should call the nat'ral way, while white women take 'em inoculated like. Bear your burden, Hist, becomingly, and remember, if it be a little toilsome, how much lighter it is than that of most Indian women. I know the Sarpent well—what I call cordially—and he will never be a tyrant to anything he loves, though he will expect to be treated himself like a Mohican chief. There will be cloudy days in your lodge, I suppose, for they happen under all usages and among all people, but by keepin' the windows of the heart open, there will always be

room for the sunshine to enter. You come of a great stock yourself, and so does Chingachgook. It's not very likely that either will ever forget the sarcumstance and do anything to disgrace your forefathers. Nevertheless, likin' is a tender plant and never thrives long when watered with tears. Let the 'arth around your married happiness be moistened by the dews of kindness."

"My pale brother is very wise; Wah will keep in her mind all that his wisdom tells her."

"That's judicious and womanly, Hist. Care in listening and stoutheartedness in holding to good counsel is a wife's great protection. And, now, ask the Sarpent to come and speak with me for a moment, and carry away with you all my best wishes and prayers. I shall think of you, Hist, and of your intended husband, let what may come to pass, and always wish you well, here and hereafter, whether the last is to be according to Indian idees or Christian doctrines."

Hist shed no tear at parting. She was sustained by the high resolution of one who had decided on her course; but her dark eyes were luminous with the feelings that glowed within, and her pretty countenance beamed with an expression of determination that was in marked and singular contrast to its ordinary gentleness. It was but a minute ere the Delaware advanced to the side of his friend with the light, noiseless tread of an Indian.

"Come thisaway, Sarpent, here more out of sight of the women," commenced the Deerslayer, "for I've several things to say that mustn't so much as be suspected, much less overheard. *You* know too well the natur' of furloughs and Mingos to have any doubts or misgivin's consarnin' what is likely to happen when I get back to the camp. On them two p'ints, therefore, a few words will go a great way. In the first place, Chief, I wish to say a little about Hist, and the manner in which you red men treat your wives. I suppose it's accordin' to the gifts of your people that the women should work and the men hunt, but there's such a thing as moderation in all matters. As for huntin', I see no good reason why any limits need be set to *that,* but Hist comes of too good a stock to toil like a common drudge. One of your means and standin' need never want for corn, or potatoes, or anything that the fields yield; therefore, I hope the hoe will never be put into the hands of any wife of your'n.

You know I am not quite a beggar, and all I own, whether in ammunition, skins, arms, or calicoes, I give to Hist, should I not come back to claim them by the end of the season. This will set the maiden up and will buy labor for her for a long time to come. I suppose I needn't tell you to love the young woman, for that you do already, and whomsoever the man ra'ally loves he'll be likely enough to cherish. Nevertheless, it can do no harm to say that kind words never rankle, while bitter words do. I know you're a man, Sarpent, that is less apt to talk in his own lodge than to speak at the council fire, but forgetful moments may overtake us all, and the practyce of kind doin' and kind talkin' is a wonderful advantage in keepin' peace in a cabin, as well as on a hunt."

"My ears are open," returned the Delaware gravely; "the words of my brother have entered so far that they never can fall out again. They are like rings that have no end and cannot drop. Let him speak on; the song of the wren and the voice of a friend never tire."

"I will speak a little longer, Chief, but you will excuse it for the sake of old companionship, should I now talk about myself. If the worst comes to the worst, it's not likely there'll be much left of me but ashes, so a grave would be useless and a sort of vanity. On that score I'm no way partic'lar, though it might be well enough to take a look at the remains of the pile, and should any bones or pieces be found, 'twould be more decent to gather them together and bury them than to let them lie for the wolves to gnaw at and howl over. These matters can make no great difference in the ind, but men of white blood and Christian feelin's have rather a gift for graves."

"It shall be done as my brother says," returned the Indian gravely. "If his mind is full, let him empty it in the bosom of a friend."

"Thank you, Sarpent; my mind's easy enough; yes, it's tolerable easy. Idees will come uppermost that I'm not apt to think about in common, it's true, but by striving ag'in some and lettin' others come out, all will be right in the long run. There's one thing, howsever, Chief, that *does* seem to be *on*reasonable, and ag'in natur', though the missionaries say it's true; and bein' of my religion and color, I feel bound to believe them. They say an Injin may torment and tortur' the body to the heart's content, and scalp, and cut, and tear,

and burn, and consume all his inventions and deviltries, until nothin' is left but ashes, and they shall be scattered to the four winds of heaven, yet, when the trumpet of God shall sound, all will come together ag'in, and the man will stand forth in his flesh the same creatur' as to looks, if not as to feelin's, that he was afore he was harmed!"

"The missionaries are good men; they mean well," returned the Delaware courteously; "they are not great medicines. They think all they say, Deerslayer; that is no reason why warriors and orators should be all ears. When Chingachgook shall see the father of Tamenund standing in his scalp, and paint, and warlock, then will he believe the missionaries."

"Seein' *is* believin', of a sartainty. Ah's me! And some of us may see these things sooner than we thought. I comprehend your meanin' about Tamenund's father, Sarpent, and the idee's a close idee. Tamenund is now an elderly man—say eighty, every day of it—and his father was scalped, and tormented, and burned when the present prophet was a youngster. Yes, if one could see *that* come to pass, there wouldn't be much difficulty in yieldin' faith to all that the missionaries say. Howsever, I'm not ag'in the opinion now, for you must know, Sarpent, that the great principle of Christianity is to believe *without* seeing, and a man should always act up to his religion and principles, let them be what they may."

"That is strange for a wise nation," said the Delaware, with emphasis. "The red man looks hard, that he may *see* and understand."

"Yes, that's plauserble and is agreeable to mortal pride, but it's not as deep as it seems. If we could understand *all* we see, Sarpent, there might be not only sense but safety in refusin' to give faith to any *one* thing that we might find oncomprehensible, but when there's so many things about which it may be said we know nothing at all, why, there's little use and no reason in bein' difficult touchin' anyone in partic'lar. For my part, Delaware, all my thoughts haven't been on the game, when outlyin' in the hunts and scoutin's of our youth. Many's the hour I've passed, pleasantly enough, too, in what is tarmed conterplation by my people. On such occasions the mind is actyve, though the body seems lazy and listless. An open spot on a mountainside, where a wide look can be had at the heavens and the 'arth, is a most judicious

place for a man to get a just idee of the power of the Maritou, and of his own littleness. At such times there isn't any great disposition to find fault with little difficulties in the way of comprehension, as there are so many big ones to hide them. Believin' comes easy enough to me at such times, and if the Lord made man first out of 'arth, as they tell me it is written in the Bible, then turns him into dust at death, I see no great difficulty in the way to bringin' him back in the body, though ashes be the only substance left. These things lie beyond our understandin', though they may and do lie so close to our feelin's. But of all the doctrines, Sarpent, that which disturbs me, and disconsarts my mind the most, is the one which teaches us to think that a pale-face goes to one heaven and a redskin to another; it may separate in death them which lived much together and loved each other well in life!"

"Do the missionaries teach their white brethren to think it is so?" demanded the Indian, with serious earnestness. "The Delawares believe that good men and brave warriors will hunt together in the same pleasant woods, let them belong to whatever tribe they may; that all the unjust Indians, and cowards, will have to sneak in with the dogs and the wolves to get venison for their lodges."

" 'Tis wonderful how many consaits mankind have consarnin' happiness and misery hereafter!" exclaimed the hunter, borne away by the power of his own thoughts. "Some believe in burnin's and flames, and some think punishmen is to eat with the wolves and dogs. Then, ag'in, some fancy heaven to be only the carryin' out of their own 'arthly longin's while others fancy it all gold and shinin' lights! Well, I've an idee of my own, in that matter, which is just this, Sarpent Whenever I've done wrong, I've gin'rally found 'twas owin to some blindness of the mind, which hid the right from view, and when sight has returned, then has come sorrow and repentance. Now, I consait that, after death, when the body is laid aside, or, if used at all, is purified and withou its longin's, the spirit sees all things in their ra'al light and never becomes blind to truth and justice. Such bein' the case all that has been done in life is beheld as plainly as the sur is seen at noon; the good brings joy while the evil brings sorrow. There's nothin' onreasonable in that, but it's agree able to every man's experience."

"I thought the palefaces believed *all* men were wicked; who then could ever find the white man's heaven?"

"That's ingen'ous, but it falls short of the missionary teachin's. You'll be Christianized one day, I make no doubt, and then 'twill all come plain enough. You must know, Sarpent, that there's been a great deed of salvation done that, by God's help, enables all men to find a pardon for their wickedness, and *that* is the essence of the white man's religion. I can't stop to talk this matter over with you any longer, for Hetty's in the canoe, and the furlough takes me away; but the time will come, I hope, when you'll *feel* these things; for, after all, they must be *felt* rather than reasoned about. Ah's me! Well, Delaware, there's my hand; you know it's that of a fri'nd, and will shake it as such, though it never has done you one half the good its owner wishes it had."

The Indian took the offered hand and returned its pressure warmly. Then falling back on his acquired stoicism of manner, which so many mistake for constitutional indifference, he drew up in reserve and prepared to part from his friend with dignity. Deerslayer, however, was more natural; nor would he have at all cared about giving way to his feelings, had not the recent conduct and language of Judith give him some secret, though ill-defined apprehensions of a scene. He was too humble to imagine the truth concerning the actual feelings of that beautiful girl, while he was too observant not to have noted the struggle she had maintained with herself, and which had so often led her to the very verge of discovery. That something extraordinary was concealed in her breast he thought obvious enough, and through a sentiment of manly delicacy that would have done credit to the highest human refinement, he shrank from any exposure of her secret that might subsequently cause regret to the girl herself. He therefore determined to depart now, and that without any further manifestations of feeling either from himself or from others.

"God bless you, Sarpent—God bless you!" cried the hunter as the canoe left the side of the platform. "Your Manitou and my God only know when and where we shall meet ag'in; I shall count it a great blessing, and a full reward for any little good I may have done on 'arth, if we shall be permitted to know each other and to consort together here-

after as we have so long done in these pleasant woods afore us!"

Chingachgook waved his hand. Drawing the light blanket he wore over his head, as a Roman would conceal his grief in his robes, he slowly withdrew into the ark, in order to indulge his sorrow and his musings alone. Deerslayer did not speak again until the canoe was halfway to the shore. Then he suddenly ceased paddling at an interruption that came from the mild, musical voice of Hetty.

"Why do *you* go back to the Hurons, Deerslayer?" demanded the girl. "They say *I* am feeble-minded, and such they never harm; but you have as much sense as Hurry Harry; and more too, Judith thinks, though I don't see how that can well be."

"Ah, Hetty, afore we land I must convarse a little with you, child; and that, too, on matters touching your own welfare, principally. Stop paddling—or, rather, that the Mingos needn't think we are plotting and contriving, and so treat us accordingly, just dip your paddle lightly, and give the canoe a little motion and no more. That's just the idee and the movement; I see you're ready enough at an appearance, and might be made useful at a sarcumvention, if it was lawful now to use one—that's just the idee and the movement! Ah's me! Desait and a false tongue are evil things and altogether onbecoming our color, Hetty, but it *is* a pleasure and a satisfaction to outdo the contrivances of a redskin in the strife of lawful warfare. My path has been short, and is like soon to have an end, but I can see that the wanderings of a warrior arn't altogether among brambles and difficulties. There's a bright side to a warpath, as well as to most other things, if we'll only have the wisdom to see it and the ginerosity to own it."

"And why should your warpath, as you call it, come so near to an end, Deerslayer?"

"Because, my good girl, my furlough comes so near to an end. They're likely to have pretty much the same tarmination as regards time—one following on the heels of the other as a matter of course."

"I don't understand your meaning, Deerslayer," returned the girl, looking a little bewildered. "Mother always said people ought to speak more plainly to me than to most other persons because I'm feeble-minded. Those that are feeble-

minded don't understand as easily as those that have sense."

"Well then, Hetty, the simple truth is this. You know that I'm now a captyve to the Hurons, and captyves can't do, in all things, as they please——"

"But how can you be a captive," eagerly interrupted the girl, "when you are out here on the lake, in Father's bark canoe, and the Indians are in the woods, with no canoe at all? *That* can't be true, Deerslayer!"

"I wish with all my heart and soul, Hetty, that you was right and that I was wrong, instead of your bein' all wrong and my bein' only too near the truth. Free as I seem to your eyes, gal, I'm bound hand and foot, in ra'ality."

"Well, it *is* a great misfortune not to have sense! Now, I can't see, or understand, that you are a captive, or bound in any manner. If you are bound, with what are your hands and feet fastened?"

"With a furlough, gal; that's a thong that binds tighter than any chain. One *may* be broken, but the other can't. Ropes and chains allow of knives, and desait, and contrivances, but a furlough can be neither cut, slipped, nor sarcumvented."

"What sort of a thing is a furlough, then, if it be stronger than hemp or iron? I never saw a furlough."

"I hope you may never feel one, gal; the tie is altogether in the feelin's in these matters, and therefore is to be felt and not seen. You can understand what it is to give a promise, I dare to say, good little Hetty?"

"Certainly. A promise is to say you will do a thing, and that binds you to be as good as your word. Mother always kept her promises to me, and then she said it would be wicked if I didn't keep my promises to her and to everybody else."

"You have had a good mother in some matters, child, whatever she may have been in other some. That is a promise, and as you say, it must be kept. Now, I fell into the hands of the Mingos last night, and they let me come off to see my fri'nds and send messages in to my own color, if any such feel consarn on my account, on condition that I shall be back when the sun is up today, and take whatever their revenge and hatred can contrive, in the way of torments, in satisfaction for the life of a warrior that fell by my rifle, as well as for that of the young woman shot by Hurry, and

other disapp'intments met with on and about this lake. What is called a promise atween a mother and darter, or even atween strangers, in the settlements is called a furlough, when given by one soldier to another on a warpath. And now I suppose you understand my situation, Hetty?"

The girl made no answer for some time, but she ceased paddling altogether, as if the novel idea distracted her mind too much to admit of other employment. Then she resumed the dialogue earnestly and with solicitude.

"Do you think the Hurons will have the heart to do what you say, Deerslayer?" she asked. "I have found them kind and harmless."

"That's true enough as consarns one like you, Hetty, but it's a very different affair when it comes to an open inimy, and he too the owner of a pretty sartain rifle. I don't say that they bear me special malice on account of any expl'its already performed, for that would be bragging, as it might be, on the varge of the grave, but it's no vanity to believe that they know one of their bravest and cunnin'est chiefs fell by my hands. Such bein' the case, the tribe would reproach them if they failed to send the spirit of a paleface to keep the company of the spirit of their red brother—always supposin' that he can catch it. I look for no marcy, Hetty, at their hands, and my principal sorrow is that such a calamity should befall me on my first warpath: that it would come sooner or later, every soldier counts on and expects."

"The Hurons shall *not* harm you, Deerslayer," cried the girl, much excited. " 'Tis wicked as well as cruel; I have the Bible here to tell them so. Do you think I would stand by and see you tormented?"

"I hope not, my good Hetty, I hope not; and, therefore, when the moment comes, I expect you will move off and not be a witness of what you can't help, while it would grieve you. But I haven't stopped the paddles to talk of my own afflictions and difficulties, but to speak a little plainly to you, gal, consarnin' your own matters."

"What can you have to say to me, Deerslayer! Since Mother died, few talk to me of such things."

"So much the worse, poor gal; yes, 'tis so much the worse, for one of your state of mind needs frequent talking to in order to escape the snares and desaits of this wicked world.

You haven't forgotten Hurry Harry, gal, so soon, I calculate?"

"I!—I forget Henry March!" exclaimed Hetty, starting. "Why should I forget him, Deerslayer, when he is our friend, and only left us last night? Then, the large bright star that Mother loved so much to gaze at was just over the top of yonder tall pine on the mountain as Hurry got into the canoe, and when you landed him on the point near the east bay, it wasn't more than the length of Judith's handsomest ribbon above it."

"And how can you know how long I was gone, or how far I went to land Hurry, seein' you were not with us, and the distance was so great, to say nothing of the night?"

"Oh! I knew when it was well enough," returned Hetty positively. "There's more ways than one for counting time and distance. When the mind is engaged, it is better than any clock. Mine is feeble, I know, but it goes true enough in all that touches poor Hurry Harry. Judith will never marry March, Deerslayer."

"That's the p'int, Hetty; that's the very p'int I want to come to. I suppose you know that it's nat'ral for young people to have kind feelin's for one another, more especially when one happens to be a youth and t'other a maiden. Now one of your years and mind, gal, that has neither father nor mother, and who lives in a wilderness frequented by hunters and trappers, needs to be on her guard against evils she little dreams of."

"What harm can it be to think well of a fellow creature?" returned Hetty simply, though the conscious blood was stealing to her cheeks in spite of a spirit so pure that it scarce knew why it prompted the blush. "The Bible tells us to love them who despitefully use us, and why shouldn't we like them that do not?"

"Ah! Hetty, the love of the missionaries isn't the sort of likin' I mean. Answer me one thing, child: do you believe yourself to have mind enough to become a wife and a mother?"

"That's not a proper question to ask a young woman, Deerslayer, and I'll not answer it," returned the girl, in a reproving manner—much as a parent rebukes a child for an act of indiscretion. "If you have anything to say about Hurry, I'll hear *that*—but you must not speak evil of him; he is absent, and 'tis unkind to talk evil of the absent."

"Your mother has given you so many good lessons, Hetty, that my fears for you are not as great as they were. Nevertheless, a young woman without parents, in your state of mind, and who is not without beauty, must always be in danger in such a lawless region as this. I would say nothin' amiss of Hurry, who, in the main, is not a bad man for one of his callin', but you ought to know one thing, which it may not be altogether pleasant to tell you but which must be said. March has a desperate likin' for your sister Judith."

"Well, what of that? Everybody admires Judith, she's so handsome, and Hurry has told me again and again how much he wishes to marry her. But that will never come to pass, for Judith don't like Hurry. She likes another and talks about him in her sleep, though you need not ask me who he is, for all the gold in King George's crown, and all the jewels, too, wouldn't tempt me to tell you his name. If sisters can't keep each other's secrets, who can?"

"Sartainly; I do not wish you to tell me, Hetty, nor would it be any advantage to a dyin' man to know. What the tongue says when the mind's asleep, neither head nor heart is answerable for."

"I wish I knew why Judith talks so much in her sleep about officers, and honest hearts, and false tongues, but I suppose she don't like to tell me, as I'm feeble-minded. Isn't it odd, Deerslayer, that Judith don't like Hurry—he, who is the bravest-looking youth that ever comes upon the lake and is as handsome as she is herself. Father always said they would be the comeliest couple in the country, though Mother didn't fancy March any more than Judith. There's no telling what will happen, they say, until things actually come to pass."

"Ah's me! Well, poor Hetty, 'tis of no great use to talk to them that can't understand you, and so I'll say no more about what I did wish to speak of, though it lay heavy on my mind. Put the paddle in motion ag'in, gal, and we'll push for the shore, for the sun is nearly up and my furlough is almost out."

The canoe now glided ahead, holding its way toward the point where Deerslayer well knew that his enemies expected him, and where he now began to be afraid he might not arrive in season to redeem his plighted faith. Hetty, perceiving his impatience, without very clearly comprehending

its cause, however, seconded his efforts in a way that soon rendered their timely return no longer a matter of doubt. Then, and then only, did the young man suffer his exertions to flag, and Hetty began again to prattle in her simple, confiding manner, though nothing further was uttered that it may be thought necessary to relate.

CHAPTER XXVII

Thou hast been busy, Death, this day, and yet
But half thy work is done! The gates of hell
Are thronged, yet twice ten thousand spirits more,
Who, from their warm and healthful tenements,
Fear no divorce, must, ere the sun go down,
Enter the world of woe!——

SOUTHEY

ONE EXPERIENCED IN the signs of the heavens would have seen that the sun wanted but two or three minutes of the zenith when Deerslayer landed on the point where the Hurons were now encamped, nearly abreast of the castle. This spot was similar to the one already described, with the exception that the surface of the land was less broken and less crowded with trees. Owing to these two circumstances, it was all the better suited to the purpose for which it had been selected, the space beneath the branches bearing some resemblance to a densely wooded lawn. Favored by its position and its spring, it had been much resorted to by savages and hunters, and the natural grasses had succeeded their fires, leaving an appearance of sward in places, a very unusual accompaniment of the virgin forest. Nor was the margin of water fringed with bushes, as on so much of its shore, but the eye penetrated the woods immediately on reaching the strand, commanding nearly the whole area of the projection.

If it was a point of honor with the Indian warrior to redeem his word, when pledged to return and meet his death at a given hour, so was it a point of characteristic pride to show no womanish impatience, but to reappear as nearly as possible at the appointed moment. It was well not to exceed the grace accorded by the generosity of the enemy, but it was better to meet it to a minute. Something of this dramatic

ffect mingles with most of the graver usages of the American
borigines, and, no doubt, like the prevalence of a similar
eeling among people more sophisticated and refined, may be
eferred to a principle of nature. We all love the wonderful,
nd when it comes attended by chivalrous self-devotion and
a rigid regard to honor, it presents itself to our admiration
n a shape doubly attractive. As respects Deerslayer, though
e took a pride in showing his white blood by often deviat-
ng from the usages of the red men, he frequently dropped
nto their customs, and oftener into their feelings, uncon-
ciously to himself, in consequence of having no other arbi-
ers to appeal to than their judgments and tastes. On the
resent occasion, he would have abstained from betraying a
everish haste by a too speedy return, since it would have
ontained a tacit admission that the time asked for was more
han had been wanted; but, on the other hand, had the
dea occurred to him, he would have quickened his move-
ents a little, in order to avoid the dramatic appearance of
eturning at the precise instant set as the utmost limit of his
bsence. Still, accident had interfered to defeat the last in-
ention, for when the young man put his foot on the point
nd advanced with a steady tread toward the group of chiefs
hat was seated in grave array on a fallen tree, the oldest of
heir number cast his eye upward at an opening in the trees
nd pointed out to his companions the startling fact that the
un was just entering a space that was known to mark the
enith. A common but low exclamation of surprise and ad-
niration escaped every mouth, and the grim warriors looked
t each other, some with envy and disappointment, some
vith astonishment, at the precise accuracy of their victim, and
thers with a more generous and liberal feeling. The Amer-
can Indian always deemed his moral victories the noblest,
rizing the groans and yielding of his victim under torture
nore than the trophy of his scalp—and the trophy itself
nore than his life. To slay, and not to bring off the proof
f victory, indeed, was scarcely deemed honorable, even
hese rude and fierce tenants of the forest, like their more
urtured brethren of the court and the camp, having set up
or themselves imaginary and arbitrary points of honor, to
upplant the conclusions of the right and the decisions of
eason.

The Hurons had been divided in their opinions concerning

the probability of their captive's return. Most among them
indeed, had not expected it possible for a paleface to com
back voluntarily and meet the known penalties of an India
torture, but a few of the seniors expected better things from
one who had already shown himself so singularly cool
brave, and upright. The party had come to its decision, how
ever, less in the expectation of finding the pledge redeeme
than in the hope of disgracing the Delawares by casting int
their teeth the delinquency of one bred in their village
They would have greatly preferred that Chingachgook shoul
be their prisoner and prove the traitor, but the paleface scio
of the hated stock was no bad substitute for their purpose:
failing in their designs against the ancient stem. With a view
to render the triumph as signal as possible, in the event o
the hour's passing without the reappearance of the hunte
all the warriors and scouts of the party had been called in
and the whole band, men, women, and children, was now
assembled at this single point to be a witness of the expecte
scene. As the castle was in plain view, and by no mean
distant, it was easily watched by daylight, and it being
thought that its inmates were now limited to Hurry, the
Delaware, and the two girls, no apprehensions were felt o
their being able to escape unseen. A large raft, having a
breastwork of logs, had been prepared, and was in actua
readiness to be used against either ark or castle, as occasion
might require, so soon as the fate of Deerslayer was deter
mined, the seniors of the party having come to the opinion
that it was getting to be hazardous to delay their departure
for Canada beyond the coming night. In short, the band
waited merely to dispose of this single affair, ere it brough
matters to a crisis and prepared to commence its retrea
toward the distant waters of Ontario.

It was an imposing scene, into which Deerslayer now
found himself advancing. All the older warriors were seated
on the trunk of the fallen tree, waiting his approach with
grave decorum. On the right stood the young men, armed
while the left was occupied by the women and children. In
the center was an open space of considerable extent, always
canopied by leaves, but from which the underbrush, dead
wood, and other obstacles had been carefully removed. The
more open area had probably been much used by former
parties, for this was the place where the appearance of a

ward was the most decided. The arches of the woods, even
at high noon, cast their somber shadows on the spot, which
the brilliant rays of the sun that struggled through the leaves
contributed to mellow and, if such an expression can be used,
to illuminate. It was probably from a similar scene that the
mind of man first got its idea of the effects of Gothic tracery
and churchly hues; this temple of nature producing some
such effect, so far as light and shadows were concerned, as
the well-known offspring of human invention.

As was not unusual among the tribes and wandering bands
of the aborigines, two chiefs shared in nearly equal degrees
the principal and primitive authority that was wielded over
these children of the forest. There were several who might
claim the distinction of being chief men, but the two in question were so much superior to all the rest in influence that,
when they agreed, no one disputed their mandates, and when
they were divided, the band hesitated, like men who had
lost their governing principle of action. It was also in conformity with practice—perhaps we might add, in conformity
with nature, that one of the chiefs was indebted to his mind
for his influence, whereas the other owed his distinction altogether to qualities that were physical. One was a senior, well
known for eloquence in debate, wisdom in council, and prudence in measures, while his great competitor, if not his
rival, was a brave, distinguished in war, notorious for ferocity, and remarkable, in the way of intellect, for nothing but
the cunning and expedients of the warpath. The first was
Rivenoak, who has already been introduced to the reader,
while the last was called le Panthère, in the language of
the Canadas, or the Panther, to resort to the vernacular of
the English colonies. The appellation of the fighting chief
was supposed to indicate the qualities of the warrior, agreeably to a practice of the red man's nomenclature: ferocity,
cunning, and treachery being, perhaps, the distinctive features of his character. The title had been received from the
French, and was prized so much the more from that circumstance, the Indian submitting profoundly to the greater intelligence of his paleface allies, in most things of this nature.
How well the sobriquet was merited will be seen in the
sequel.

Rivenoak and the Panther sat side by side, awaiting the
approach of their prisoner, as Deerslayer put his moccasined

foot on the strand; nor did either move or utter a syllable until the young man had advanced into the center of the area, and proclaimed his presence with his voice. This was done firmly, though in the simple manner that marked the character of the individual.

"Here I am, Mingos," he said, in the dialect of the Delawares, a language that most present understood; "here I am, and there is the sun. One is not more true to the laws of natur' than the other has proved true to his word. I am your prisoner; do with me what you please. My business with man and 'arth is settled; nothing remains now but to meet the white man's God, accordin' to a white man's duties and gifts."

A murmur of approbation escaped even the women at this address, and for an instant there was a strong and pretty general desire to adopt into the tribe one who owned so brave a spirit. Still there were dissenters from this wish, among the principal of whom might be classed the Panther, and his sister, le Sumac, so called from the number of her children, who was the widow of le Loup Cervier, now known to have fallen by the hand of the captive. Native ferocity held one in subjection, while the corroding passion of revenge prevented the other from admitting any gentler feeling at the moment. Not so with Rivenoak. This chief arose stretched his arm before him in a gesture of courtesy, and paid his compliments with an ease and dignity that a prince might have envied. As, in that band, his wisdom and eloquence were confessedly without rivals, he knew that on himself would properly fall the duty of first replying to the speech of the paleface.

"Paleface, you are honest," said the Huron orator. "My people are happy in having captured a man and not a skulking fox. We now know you; we shall treat you like a brave. If you have slain one of our warriors and helped to kill others, you have a life of your own ready to give away in return. Some of my young men thought that the blood of a paleface was too thin, that it would refuse to run under the Huron knife. You will show them it is not so; your heart is stout as well as your body. It is a pleasure to make such a prisoner; should my warriors say that the death of le Loup Cervier ought not to be forgotten, that he cannot travel toward the land of spirits alone, and that his enemy must

be sent to overtake him, they will remember that he fell by the hand of a brave, and send you after him with such signs of our friendship as shall not make him ashamed to keep your company. I have spoken; you know what I have said."

"True enough, Mingo, all true as the gospel," returned the simple-minded hunter; "you *have* spoken, and I *do* know not only what you have *said*, but, what is still more important, what you *mean*. I dare to say your warrior, the Lynx, was a stouthearted brave, and worthy of your fri'ndship and respect, but I do not feel unworthy to keep his company, without any passport from your hands. Nevertheless, here I am, ready to receive judgment from your council, if, indeed, the matter was not determined among you afore I got back."

"My old men would not sit in council over a paleface until they saw him among them," answered Rivenoak, looking around him a little ironically; "they said it would be like sitting in council over the winds; they go where they will and come back as they see fit, and not otherwise. There was one voice that spoke in your favor, Deerslayer, but it was alone, like the song of the wren whose mate has been struck by the hawk."

"I thank that voice whosoever it may have been, Mingo, and will say it was as true a voice, as the rest were lying voices. A furlough is as binding on a paleface, if he be honest, as it is on a redskin; and was it not so, I would never bring disgrace on the Delawares, among whom I may be said to have received my edication. But words are useless and lead to braggin' feelin's; here I am; act your will on me."

Rivenoak made a sign of acquiescence, and then a short conference was privately held among the chiefs. As soon as the latter ended, three or four young men fell back from among the armed group and disappeared. Then it was signified to the prisoner that he was at liberty to go at large on the point until a council was held concerning his fate. There was more of seeming than of real confidence, however, in this apparent liberality, inasmuch as the young men mentioned already formed a line of sentinels across the breadth of the point, inland, and escape from any other part was out of the question. Even the canoe was removed beyond this line of sentinels, to a spot where it was considered safe

from any sudden attempt. These precautions did not proceed from a failure of confidence, but from the circumstance that the prisoner had now complied with all the required conditions of his parole, and it would have been considered a commendable and honorable exploit to escape from his foes. So nice, indeed, were the distinctions drawn by the savages, in cases of this nature, that they often gave their victims a chance to evade the torture, deeming it as creditable to the captors to overtake, or to outwit a fugitive, when his exertions were supposed to be quickened by the extreme jeopardy of his situation, as it was for him to get clear from so much extraordinary vigilance.

Nor was Deerslayer unconscious or forgetful of his rights and of his opportunities. Could he now have seen any probable opening for an escape, the attempt would not have been delayed a minute. But the case seemed desperate. He was aware of the line of sentinels, and felt the difficulty of breaking through it unharmed. The lake offered no advantages, as the canoe would have given his foes the greatest facilities for overtaking him; else would he have found it no difficult task to swim as far as the castle. As he walked about the point, he even examined the spot to ascertain if it offered no place of concealment, but its openness, its size, and the hundred watchful glances that were turned toward him, even while those who made them affected not to see him, prevented any such expedient from succeeding. The dread and disgrace of failure had no influence on Deerslayer, who deemed it ever a point of honor to reason and feel like a white man, rather than as an Indian, and who felt it a sort of duty to do all he could that did not involve a dereliction from principle in order to save his life. Still he hesitated about making the effort, for he also felt that he ought to see the chance of success before he committed himself.

In the meantime the business of the camp appeared to proceed in its regular train. The chiefs consulted apart, admitting no one but the Sumac to their councils; for she, the widow of the fallen warrior, had an exclusive right to be heard on such an occasion. The young men strolled about in indolent listlessness, awaiting the result with Indian impatience, while the females prepared the feast that was to celebrate the termination of the affair, whether it proved fortunate or otherwise for our hero. No one betrayed feeling,

and an indifferent observer, beyond the extreme watchfulness of the sentinels, would have detected no extraordinary movement or sensation to denote the real state of things. Two or three old women put their heads together, and it appeared unfavorably to the prospect of Deerslayer, by their scowling looks and angry gestures, but a group of Indian girls were evidently animated by a different impulse, as was apparent by stolen glances that expressed pity and regret. In this condition of the camp an hour soon glided away.

Suspense is, perhaps, the feeling, of all others that is most difficult to be supported. When Deerslayer landed, he fully expected in the course of a few minutes to undergo the tortures of an Indian revenge, and he was prepared to meet his fate manfully, but the delay proved far more trying than the nearer approach of suffering, and the intended victim began seriously to meditate some desperate effort at escape, as it might be from sheer anxiety to terminate the scene, when he was suddenly summoned to appear, once more, in front of his judges, who had already arranged the band in its former order in readiness to receive him.

"Killer of the Deer," commenced Rivenoak, as soon as his captive stood before him, "my aged men have listened to wise words; they are ready to speak. You are a man whose fathers came from beyond the rising sun; we are children of the setting sun; we turn our faces toward the Great Sweet Lakes when we look toward our villages. It may be a wise country and full of riches toward the morning, but it is very pleasant toward the evening. We love most to look in that direction. When we gaze at the east we feel afraid, canoe after canoe bringing more and more of your people in the track of the sun, as if their land was so full as to run over. The red men are few already; they have need of help. One of our best lodges has lately been emptied by the death of its master; it will be a long time before his son can grow big enough to sit in his place. There is his widow! She will want venison to feed her and her children, for her sons are yet like the young of the robin before they quit the nest. By your hand has this great calamity befallen her. She has two duties; one to le Loup Cervier, and one to his children. Scalp for scalp, life for life, blood for blood, is one law; to feed her young another. We know you, Killer of the Deer. You are honest; when you say a thing, it is so. You have

but one tongue, and that is not forked like a snake's. Your head is never hid in the grass; all can see it. What you say, that will you do. You are just. When you have done wrong, it is your wish to do right again as soon as you can. Here is the Sumac; she is alone in her wigwam, with children crying around her for food—yonder is a rifle; it is loaded and ready to be fired. Take the gun; go forth and shoot a deer; bring the venison and lay it before the widow of le Loup Cervier; feed her children; call yourself her husband. After which, your heart will no longer be Delaware but Huron; le Sumac's ears will not hear the cries of her children; my people will count the proper number of warriors.

"I feared this, Rivenoak," answered Deerslayer, when the other had ceased speaking; "yes, I did dread that it would come to this. Howsever, the truth is soon told, and that will put an end to all expectations on this head. Mingo, I'm white, and Christian-born; 'twould ill become me to take a wife, under redskin forms, from among heathen. That which I wouldn't do in peaceable times and under a bright sun, still less would I do behind clouds, in order to save my life. I may never marry; most likely Providence, in putting me up here in the woods, has intended I should live single, without a lodge of my own: but should such a thing come to pass, none but a woman of my own color and gifts shall darken the door of my wigwam. As for feeding the young of your dead warrior, I would do that cheerfully, could it be done without discredit, but it cannot, seeing that I can never live in a Huron village. Your own young men must find the Sumac in venison, and the next time she marries, let her take a husband whose legs are not long enough to overrun territory that don't belong to him. We fou't a fair battle, and he fell; in this there is nothin' but what a brave expects, and should be ready to meet. As for getting a Mingo heart, as well might you expect to see gray hairs on a boy, or the blackberry growing on the pine. No, no, Huron; my gifts are white, so far as wives are consarned; it is Delaware in all things touchin' Injins."

These words were scarcely out of the mouth of Deerslayer before a common murmur betrayed the dissatisfaction with which they had been heard. The aged women, in particular, were loud in their expressions of disgust, and the gentle Sumac herself, a woman quite old enough to be our

hero's mother, was not the least pacific in her denunciations. But all the other manifestations of disappointment and discontent were thrown into the background by the fierce resentment of the Panther. This grim chief had thought it a degradation to permit his sister to become the wife of a paleface of the Yengeese at all, and had only given a reluctant consent to the arrangement—one by no means unusual among the Indians, however—at the earnest solicitations of the bereaved widow; and it goaded him to the quick to find his condescension slighted, the honor he had with so much regret been persuaded to accord condemned. The animal from which he got his name does not glare on his intended prey with more frightful ferocity than his eyes gleamed on the captive, nor was his arm backward in seconding the fierce resentment that almost consumed his breast.

"Dog of the palefaces!" he exclaimed in Iroquois, "go yell among the curs of your own evil hunting grounds!"

The denunciation was accompanied by an appropriate action. Even while speaking his arm was lifted and the tomahawk hurled. Luckily the loud tones of the speaker had drawn the eye of Deerslayer toward him, else would that moment have probably closed his career. So great was the dexterity with which this dangerous weapon was thrown, and so deadly the intent, that it would have riven the skull of the prisoner, had he not stretched forth an arm and caught the handle in one of its turns with a readiness quite as remarkable as the skill with which the missile had been hurled. The projectile force was so great, notwithstanding, that when Deerslayer's arm was arrested, his hand was raised above and behind his own head, and in the very attitude necessary to return the attack. It is not certain whether the circumstance of finding himself unexpectedly in this menacing posture and armed, tempted the young man to retaliate, or whether sudden resentment overcame his forbearance and prudence. His eye kindled, however, and a small red spot appeared on each cheek, while he cast all his energy into the effort of his arm and threw back the weapon at his assailant. The unexpectedness of this blow contributed to its success, the Panther neither raising an arm nor bending his head to avoid it. The keen little ax struck the victim in a perpendicular line with the nose, directly between the eyes, literally braining him on the spot. Sallying forward, as the serpent

darts at its enemy even while receiving its own death wound, this man of powerful frame fell his length into the open area formed by the circle, quivering in death. A common rush to his relief left the captive for a single instant quite without the crowd, and willing to make one desperate effort for life, he bounded off with the activity of a deer. There was but a breathless instant, then the whole band, old and young, women and children, abandoning the lifeless body of the Panther where it lay, raised the yell of alarm and followed in pursuit.

Sudden as had been the event which induced Deerslayer to make this desperate trial of speed, his mind was not wholly unprepared for the fearful emergency. In the course of the past hour, he had pondered well on the chances of such an experiment and had shrewdly calculated all the details of success and failure. At the first leap, therefore, his body was completely under the direction of an intelligence that turned all its efforts to the best account and prevented everything like hesitation or indecision at the important instant of the start. To this alone was he indebted for the first great advantage, that of getting through the line of sentinels unharmed. The manner in which this was done, though sufficiently simple, merits a description.

Although the shores of the point were not fringed with bushes, as was the case with most of the others on the lake, it was owing altogether to the circumstance that the spot had been so much used by hunters and fishermen. This fringe commenced on what might be termed the mainland, and was as dense as usual, extending in long lines both north and south. In the latter direction, then, Deerslayer held his way, and as the sentinels were a little without the commencement of this thicket before the alarm was clearly communicated to them, the fugitive had gained its cover. To run among the bushes, however, was out of the question, and Deerslayer held his way for some forty or fifty yards in the water, which was barely knee deep, offering as great an obstacle to the speed of his pursuers as it did to his own. As soon as a favorable spot presented, he darted through the line of bushes and issued into the open woods.

Several rifles were discharged at Deerslayer while in the water, and more followed as he came out into the comparative exposure of the clear forest. But the direction of his

line of flight, which partially crossed that of the fire, the haste with which the weapons had been aimed, and the general confusion that prevailed in the camp prevented any harm from being done. Bullets whistled past him, and many cut twigs from the branches at his side, but not one touched even his dress. The delay caused by these fruitless attempts was of great service to the fugitive, who had gained more than a hundred yards on even the leading men of the Hurons, ere something like concert and order had entered into the chase. To think of following with rifle in hand was out of the question, and after emptying their pieces in vague hopes of wounding their captive, the best runners of the Indians threw them aside, calling out to the women and boys to recover and load them again, as soon as possible.

Deerslayer knew too well the desperate nature of the struggle in which he was engaged to lose one of the precious moments. He also knew that his only hope was to run in a straight line, for as soon as he began to turn, or double, the greater number of his pursuers would put escape out of the question. He held his way, therefore, in a diagonal direction up the acclivity, which was neither very high nor very steep, in this part of the mountain, but which was sufficiently toilsome for one contending for life to render it painfully oppressive. There, however, he slackened his speed to recover breath, proceeding even at a quick walk, or a slow trot, along the more difficult parts of the way. The Hurons were whooping and leaping behind him; but this he disregarded, well knowing they must overcome the difficulties he had surmounted, ere they could reach the elevation to which he had attained. The summit of the first hill was now quite near him, and he saw, by the formation of the land, that a deep glen intervened before the base of a second hill could be reached. Walking deliberately to the summit, he glanced eagerly about him in every direction in quest of a cover. None offered in the ground, but a fallen tree lay near him, and desperate circumstances required desperate remedies. This tree lay in a line parallel to the glen, at the brow of the hill; to leap on it, and then to force his person as close as possible under its lower side, took but a moment. Previously to disappearing from his pursuers, however, Deerslayer stood on the height and gave a cry of triumph, as if exulting at the

sight of the descent that lay before him. In the next instant he was stretched beneath the tree.

No sooner was this expedient adopted than the young man ascertained how desperate had been his own efforts by the violence of the pulsations in his frame. He could hear his heart beat, and his breathing was like the action of a bellows in quick motion. Breath was gained, however, and the heart soon ceased to throb as if about to break through its confinement. The footsteps of those who toiled up the opposite side of the acclivity were now audible, and presently voices and treads announced the arrival of the pursuers. The foremost shouted as they reached the height; then, fearful that their enemy would escape under favor of the descent, each leaped upon the fallen tree and plunged into the ravine, trusting to get a sight of the pursued, ere he reached the bottom. In this manner, Huron followed Huron, until Natty began to hope the whole had passed. Others succeeded, however, until quite forty had leaped over the tree; and then he counted them, as the surest mode of ascertaining how many could be behind. Presently all were in the bottom of the glen, quite a hundred feet below him, and some had even ascended part of the opposite hill, when it became evident an inquiry was making as to the direction he had taken. This was the critical moment, and one of nerves less steady, or of a training that had been neglected, would have seized it to rise and fly. Not so with Deerslayer. He still lay quiet, watching with jealous vigilance every movement below and fast regaining his breath.

The Hurons now resembled a pack of hounds at fault. Little was said, but each man ran about examining the dead leaves, as the hound hunts for the lost scent. The great number of moccasins that had passed made the examination difficult, though the intoe of an Indian was easily to be distinguished from the freer and wider step of a white man. Believing that no more pursuers remained behind, and hoping to steal away unseen, Deerslayer suddenly threw himself over the tree and fell on the upper side. This achievement appeared to be effected successfully, and hope beat high in the bosom of the fugitive. Rising to his hands and feet after a moment lost in listening to the sounds in the glen, in order to ascertain if he had been seen, the young man next scrambled to the top of the hill, a distance of only ten yards, in

the expectation of getting its brow between him and his pursuers, and himself so far under cover. Even this was effected, and he rose to his feet, walking swiftly but steadily along the summit in a direction opposite to that in which he had first fled. The nature of the calls in the glen, however, soon made him uneasy, and he sprang upon the summit, again, in order to reconnoiter. No sooner did he reach the height than he was seen, and the chase renewed. As it was better footing on the level ground, Deerslayer now avoided the side hill, holding his flight along the ridge, while the Hurons, judging from the general formation of the land, saw that the ridge would soon melt into the hollow, and kept to the latter, as the easiest mode of heading the fugitive. A few, at the same time, turned south, with a view to prevent his escaping in that direction, while some crossed his trail toward the water, in order to prevent his retreat by the lake, running southerly.

The situation of Deerslayer was now more critical than it ever had been. He was virtually surrounded on three sides, having the lake on the fourth. But he had pondered well on all the chances and took his measures with coolness, even while at the top of his speed. As is generally the case with the vigorous bordermen, he could outrun any single Indian among his pursuers, who were principally formidable to him on account of their numbers and the advantages they possessed in position, and he would not have hesitated to break off in a straight line at any spot, could he have got the whole band again fairly behind him. But no such chance did, or indeed could now offer, and when he found that he was descending toward the glen, by the melting away of the ridge, he turned short, at right angles to his previous course, and went down the declivity with tremendous velocity, holding his way toward the shore. Some of his pursuers came panting up the hill, in direct chase, while most still kept on, in the ravine, intending to head him at its termination.

Deerslayer had now a different, though a desperate project in view. Abandoning all thoughts of escape by the woods, he made the best of his way toward the canoe. He knew where it lay: could it be reached, he had only to run the gauntlet of a few rifles, and success would be certain. None of the warriors had kept their weapons, which would have retarded their speed, and the risk would come either from the uncer-

tain hands of the women, or from those of some well-grown boy—though most of the latter were already out in hot pursuit. Everything seemed propitious to the execution of this plan, and the course being a continued descent, the young man went over the ground at a rate that promised a speedy termination to his toil.

As Deerslayer approached the point, several women and children were passed, but though the former endeavored to cast dried branches between his legs, the terror inspired by his bold retaliation on the redoubted Panther was so great that none dared come near enough seriously to molest him. He went by all triumphantly and reached the fringe of bushes. Plunging through these, our hero found himself once more in the lake and within fifty feet of the canoe. Here he ceased to run, for he well understood that his breath was now all-important to him. He even stooped, as he advanced, and cooled his parched mouth by scooping up water in his hand to drink. Still the moments pressed, and he soon stood at the side of the canoe. The first glance told him that the paddles had been removed! This was a sore disappointment after all his efforts, and for a single moment he thought of turning and of facing his foes by walking with dignity into the center of the camp again. But an infernal yell, such as the American savage alone can raise, proclaimed the quick approach of the nearest of his pursuers, and the instinct of life triumphed. Preparing himself duly, and giving a right direction to its bows, he ran off into the water bearing the canoe before him, threw all his strength and skill into a last effort, and cast himself forward so as to fall into the bottom of the light craft, without materially impeding its way. Here he remained on his back, both to regain his breath and to cover his person from the deadly rifle. The lightness, which was such an advantage in paddling the canoe, now operated unfavorably. The material was so like a feather that the boat had no momentum; else would the impulse in that smooth and placid sheet have impelled it to a distance from the shore that would have rendered paddling with the hands safe. Could such a point once be reached, Deerslayer thought he might get far enough out to attract the attention of Chingachgook and Judith, who would not fail to come to his relief with other canoes, a circumstance that promised everything. As the young man lay in the bottom of the canoe,

he watched its movements by studying the tops of the trees on the mountainside, and judged of his distance by the time and the motion. Voices on the shore were now numerous, and he heard something said about manning the raft, which fortunately for the fugitive lay at a considerable distance on the other side of the point.

Perhaps the situation of Deerslayer had not been more critical that day than it was at this moment. It certainly had not been one half as tantalizing. He lay perfectly quiet for two or three minutes, trusting to the single sense of hearing, confident that the noise in the lake would reach his ears, did anyone venture to approach by swimming. Once or twice he fancied that the element was stirred by the cautious movement of an arm, and then he perceived it was the wash of the water on the pebbles of the strand; for, in mimicry of the ocean, it is seldom that those little lakes are so totally tranquil as not to possess a slight heaving and setting on their shores. Suddenly all the voices ceased, and a deathlike stillness pervaded the spot, a quietness as profound as if all lay in the repose of inanimate life. By this time the canoe had drifted so far as to render nothing visible to Deerslayer, as he lay on his back, except the blue void of space, and a few of those brighter rays that proceed from the effulgence of the sun, marking his proximity. It was not possible to endure this uncertainty long. The young man well knew that the profound stillness foreboded evil, the savages never being so silent as when about to strike a blow, resembling the stealthy foot of the panther ere he takes his leap. He took out a knife, and was about to cut a hole through the bark in order to get a view of the shore, when he paused from a dread of being seen in the operation, which would direct the enemy where to aim their bullets. At this instant a rifle *was* fired, and the ball pierced both sides of the canoe, within eighteen inches of the spot where his head lay. This was close work, but our hero had too lately gone through that which was closer to be appalled. He lay still half a minute longer, and then he saw the summit of an oak coming slowly within his narrow horizon.

Unable to account for this change, Deerslayer could restrain his impatience no longer. Hitching his body along with the utmost caution, he got his eye at the bullethole, and fortunately commanded a very tolerable view of the point.

The canoe, by one of those imperceptible impulses that so
often decide the fate of men as well as the course of things,
had inclined southerly, and was slowly drifting down the
lake. It was lucky that Deerslayer had given it a shove
sufficiently vigorous to send it past the end of the point ere
it took this inclination, or it must have gone ashore again.
As it was, it drifted so near it as to bring the tops of two
or three trees within the range of the young man's view,
as has been mentioned, and, indeed, to come in quite as
close proximity with the extremity of the point as was at
all safe. The distance could not much have exceeded a hundred feet, though fortunately a light current of air from the
southwest began to set it slowly offshore.

Deerslayer now felt the urgent necessity of resorting to
some expedient to get further from his foes and, if possible, to apprise his friends of his situation. The distance
rendered the last difficult, while the proximity to the point
rendered the first indispensable. As was usual in such craft, a
large, round, smooth stone was in each end of the canoe
for the double purpose of seats and ballast; one of these was
within reach of his feet. The stone he contrived to get so far
between his legs as to reach it with his hands, and then he
managed to roll it to the side of its fellow in the bows, where
the two served to keep the trim of the light boat, while he
worked his own body as far aft as possible. Before quitting
the shore, and as soon as he perceived that the paddles were
gone, Deerslayer had thrown a bit of dead branch into the
canoe, and this was within reach of his arm. Removing the
cap he wore, he put it on the end of this stick, and just let
it appear over the edge of the canoe, as far as possible from
his own person. This ruse was scarcely adopted before the
young man had a proof how much he had underrated the
intelligence of his enemies. In contempt of an artifice so
shallow and commonplace, a bullet was fired directly through
another part of the canoe, which actually raised his skin. He
dropped the cap, and instantly raised it immediately over his
head, as a safeguard. It would seem that this second artifice
was unseen, or what was more probable, the Hurons, feeling
certain of recovering their captive, wished to take him alive.
Deerslayer lay passive a few minutes longer, his eye at
the bullethole, however, and much did he rejoice at seeing
that he was drifting gradually further and further from the

hore. When he looked upward, the treetops had disappeared, but he soon found that the canoe was slowly turning, so as to prevent his getting a view of anything at his peephole but of the two extremities of the lake. He now bethought him of the stick, which was crooked, and offered some facilities for rowing, without the necessity of rising. The experiment succeeded, on trial, better even than he had hoped, though his great embarrassment was to keep the canoe straight. That his present maneuver was seen soon became apparent by the clamor on the shore, and a bullet entering the stern of the canoe, traversed its length, whistling between the arms of our hero, and passed out at the head. This satisfied the fugitive that he was getting away with tolerable speed and induced him to increase his efforts. He was making a stronger push than common when another messenger from the point broke the stick outboard and at once deprived him of his oar. As the sound of voices seemed to grow more and more distant, however, Deerslayer determined to leave all to the drift, until he believed himself beyond the reach of bullets. This was nervous work, but it was the wisest of all the expedients that offered; and the young man was encouraged to persevere in it by the circumstance that he felt his face fanned by the air, a proof that there was a little more wind.

Chapter XXVIII

Nor widows' tears, nor tender orphans' cries
Can stop th' invaders' force;
Nor swelling seas, nor threatening skies,
Prevent the pirate's course:
Their lives to selfish ends decreed,
Through blood and rapine they proceed,
No anxious thoughts of ill-repute,
Suspend the impetuous and unjust pursuit;
But power and wealth obtained, guilty and great,
Their fellow-creatures' fears they raise, or urge their hate.

CONGREVE

BY THIS TIME Deerslayer had been twenty minutes in the canoe, and he began to grow a little impatient for some signs of relief from his friends. The position of the boat still prevented his seeing in any direction, unless it were up or down the lake; and, though he knew that his line of sight must pass within a hundred yards of the castle, it, in fact, passed that distance to the westward of the buildings. The profound stillness troubled him also, for he knew not whether to ascribe it to the increasing space between him and the Indians, or to some new artifice. At length, wearied with fruitless watchfulness, the young man turned himself on his back, closed his eyes, and awaited the result in determined acquiescence. If the savages could so completely control their thirst for revenge, he was resolved to be as calm as themselves and to trust his fate to the interposition of the currents and air.

Some additional ten minutes may have passed in this quiescent manner, on both sides, when Deerslayer thought he heard a slight noise, like a low rubbing against the bottom of his canoe. He opened his eyes of course, in expectation of seeing the face or arm of an Indian rising from the water, and found that a canopy of leaves was impending directly

over his head. Starting to his feet, the first object that met his eye was Rivenoak, who had so far aided the slow progress of the boat as to draw it on the point, the grating on the strand being the sound that had first given our hero the alarm. The change in the drift of the canoe had been altogether owing to the baffling nature of the light currents of air, aided by some eddies in the water.

"Come," said the Huron, with a quiet gesture of authority to order his prisoner to land; "my young friend has sailed about till he is tired; he will forget how to run again, unless he uses his legs."

"You've the best of it, Huron," returned Deerslayer, stepping steadily from the canoe and passively following his leader to the open area of the point; "Providence has helped you in an onexpected manner. I'm your prisoner ag'in, and I hope you'll allow that I'm as good at breaking jail as I am at keeping furloughs."

"My young friend is a moose!" exclaimed the Huron. "His legs are very long; they have given my young men trouble. But he is not a fish; he cannot find his way in the lake. We did not shoot him; fish are taken in nets, and not killed by bullets. When he turns moose again, he will be treated like a moose."

"Aye, have your talk, Rivenoak; make the most of your advantage. 'Tis your right, I suppose, and I know it is your gift. On that p'int there'll be no words atween us, for all men must and ought to follow their gifts. Howsever, when your women begin to ta'nt and abuse me, as I suppose will soon happen, let 'em remember that if a paleface struggles for life so long as it's lawful and manful, he knows how to loosen his hold on it decently, when he feels that the time has come. I'm your captyve; work your will on me."

"My brother has had a long run on the hills and a pleasant sail on the water," returned Rivenoak more mildly, smiling, at the same time, in a way that his listener knew denoted pacific intentions. "He has seen the woods; he has seen the water; which does he like best? Perhaps he has seen enough to change his mind and make him hear reason."

"Speak out, Huron. Something is in your thoughts, and the sooner it is said, the sooner you'll get my answer."

"That is straight! There is no turning in the talk of my paleface friend, though he is a fox in running. I will speak

to him; his ears are now open wider than before, and his eyes are not shut. The Sumac is poorer than ever. Once she had a brother and a husband. She had children, too. The time came, and the husband started for the happy hunting grounds without saying farewell; he left her alone with his children. This he could not help, or he would not have done it; le Loup Cervier was a good husband. It was pleasant to see the venison, and wild ducks, and geese, and bear's meat that hung in his lodge in winter. It is now gone; it will not keep in warm weather. Who shall bring it back again? Some thought the brother would not forget his sister, and that, next winter, he would see that the lodge should not be empty. We thought this; but the Panther yelled and followed the husband on the path of death. They are now trying which shall first reach the happy hunting grounds. Some think the Lynx can run fastest, and some think the Panther can jump the furthest. The Sumac thinks both will travel so fast and so far that neither will ever come back. Who shall feed her and her young? The man who told her husband and her brother to quit her lodge, that there might be room for him to come into it. He is a great hunter, and we know that the woman will never want."

"Aye, Huron, this is soon settled, accordin' to your notions, but it goes sorely ag'in the grain of a white man's feelin's. I've heard of men's saving their lives thisaway, and I've know'd them that would prefer death to such a sort of captivity. For my part, I do not seek my end, nor do I seek matrimony."

"The paleface will think of this while my people get ready for the council. He will be told what will happen. Let him remember how hard it is to lose a husband and a brother. Go: when we want him, the name of Deerslayer will be called."

This conversation had been held with no one near but the speakers. Of all the band that had so lately thronged the place, Rivenoak alone was visible. The rest seemed to have totally abandoned the spot. Even the furniture, clothes, arms, and other property of the camp had entirely disappeared, and the place bore no other proofs of the crowd that had so lately occupied it than the traces of their fires and resting places and the trodden earth that still showed the marks of their feet. So sudden and unexpected a change caused

Deerslayer a good deal of surprise and some uneasiness, for he had never known it to occur, in the course of his experience among the Delawares. He suspected, however, and rightly, that a change of encampment was intended, and that the mystery of the movement was resorted to in order to work on his apprehensions.

Rivenoak walked up the vista of trees, as soon as he ceased speaking, leaving Deerslayer by himself. The chief disappeared behind the covers of the forest, and one unpracticed in such scenes might have believed the prisoner left to the dictates of his own judgment. But the young man, while he felt a little amazement at the dramatic aspect of things, knew his enemies too well to fancy himself at liberty, or a free agent. Still, he was ignorant how far the Hurons meant to carry their artifices, and he determined to bring the question as soon as practicable to the proof. Affecting an indifference he was far from feeling, he strolled about the area, gradually getting nearer and nearer to the spot where he had landed, when he suddenly quickened his pace, though carefully avoiding all appearance of flight, and, pushing aside the bushes, he stepped upon the beach. The canoe was gone, nor could he see any traces of it after walking to the northern and southern verges of the point and examining the shores in both directions. It was evidently removed beyond his reach and knowledge, and under circumstances to show that such had been the intention of the savages.

Deerslayer now better understood his actual situation. He was a prisoner on the narrow tongue of land, vigilantly watched beyond a question, and with no other means of escape than that of swimming. He again thought of this last expedient, but the certainty that the canoe would be sent in chase, and the desperate nature of the chances of success, deterred him from the undertaking. While on the strand, he came to a spot where the bushes had been cut and thrown into a small pile. Removing a few of the upper branches, he found beneath them the dead body of the Panther. He knew that it was kept until the savages might find a place to inter it, when it would be beyond the reach of the scalping knife. He gazed wistfully toward the castle, but there all seemed to be silent and desolate, and a feeling of

loneliness and desertion came over him to increase the gloom of the moment.

"God's will be done!" murmured the young man, as he walked sorrowfully away from the beach, entering again beneath the arches of the wood; "God's will be done, on 'arth as it is in heaven! I did hope that my days would not be numbered so soon! But it matters little, a'ter all. A few more winters, and a few more summers, and 'twould have been over, accordin' to natur'. Ah's me! The young and actyve seldom think death possible, till he grins in their faces and tells 'em the hour is come!"

While this soliloquy was being pronounced, the hunter advanced into the area, where, to his surprise, he saw Hetty alone, evidently awaiting his return. The girl carried the Bible under her arm, and her face, over which a shadow of gentle melancholy was usually thrown, now seemed sad and downcast. Moving nearer, Deerslayer spoke.

"Poor Hetty," he said; "times have been so troublesome of late that I'd altogether forgotten you; we meet, as it might be, to mourn over what is to happen. I wonder what has become of Chingachgook and Wah?"

"Why did you kill the Huron, Deerslayer?" returned the girl reproachfully. "Don't you know your commandments, which say, 'Thou shalt not kill!' They tell me you have now slain the woman's husband and brother."

"It's true, my good Hetty, 'tis gospel truth, and I'll not deny what has come to pass. But, you must remember, gal, that many things are lawful in war which would be onlawful in peace. The husband was shot in open fight— or open so far as I was consarned, while he had a better cover than common—and the brother brought his end on himself by casting his tomahawk at an unarmed prisoner. Did you witness that deed, gal?"

"I saw it and was sorry it happened, Deerslayer, for I hoped you wouldn't have returned blow for blow, but good for evil."

"Ah, Hetty, that may do among the missionaries, but 'twould make an onsartain life in the woods. The Panther craved my blood, and he was foolish enough to throw arms into my hands at the very moment he was striving a'ter it. 'Twould have been ag'in natur' not to raise a hand in such a trial, and 'twould have done discredit to my training and

gifts. No, no; I'm as willing to give every man his own as another, and so I hope you'll testify to them that will be likely to question you as to what you've seen this day."

"Deerslayer, do you mean to marry Sumac, now she has neither husband nor brother to feed her?"

"Are such your ideas of matrimony, Hetty? Ought the young to wive with the old—the paleface with the redskin—the Christian with the heathen? It's ag'in reason and natur', and so you'll see, if you think of it a moment."

"I've always heard Mother say," returned Hetty, averting her face, more from a feminine instinct than from any consciousness of wrong, "that people should never marry until they loved each other better than brothers and sisters—and I suppose that is what you mean. Sumac *is* old and you *are* young."

"Aye, and she's red and I'm white. Besides, Hetty, suppose you was a wife, now, having married some young man of your own years, and state, and color—Hurry Harry, for instance"—Deerslayer selected this example simply from the circumstance that he was the only young man known to both—"and that he had fallen on a warpath, would you wish to take to your bosom for a husband the man that slew him?"

"Oh! no, no, no," returned the girl, shuddering. "*That* would be wicked as well as heartless! No Christian girl could or would do that. I never shall be the wife of Hurry, I know, but were he my husband, no man should ever be it again after his death."

"I thought it would get to this, Hetty, when you come to understand sarcumstances. 'Tis a moral impossibility that I should ever marry Sumac, and though Injin weddin's have no priests and not much religion, a white man who knows his gifts and duties can't profit by that and so make his escape at the fitting time. I do think death would be more nat'ral like, and welcome, than wedlock with this woman."

"Don't say it too loud," interrupted Hetty impatiently. "I suppose she will not like to hear it. I'm sure Hurry would rather marry even me than suffer torments, though I *am* feeble-minded, and I am sure it would kill me to think he'd prefer death to being my husband."

"Aye, gal; you an't Sumac, but a comely young Christian

with a good heart, pleasant smile, and kind eye. Hurry might be proud to get you, and that, too, not in misery and sorrow, but in his best and happiest days. Howsever, take my advice and never talk to Hurry about these things; he's only a borderer, at the best."

"I wouldn't tell him for the world!" exclaimed the girl, looking about her like one affrighted and blushing she knew not why. "Mother always said young women shouldn't be forward and speak their minds before they're asked; oh, I never forget what mother told me. 'Tis a pity Hurry is so handsome, Deerslayer; I do think fewer girls would like him then, and he would sooner know his own mind."

"Poor gal, poor gal, it's plain enough how it is; but the Lord will bear in mind one of your simple heart and kind feelin's! We'll talk no more of these things; if you had reason, you'd be sorrowful at having let others so much into your secret. Tell me, Hetty, what has become of all the Hurons, and why they let you roam about the p'int, as if you, too, was a prisoner?"

"I'm no prisoner, Deerslayer, but a free girl, and go when and where I please. Nobody dare hurt *me*! If they did, God would be angry—as I can show them in the Bible. No—no—Hetty Hutter is not afraid; *she's* in good hands. The Hurons are up yonder in the woods and keep a good watch on us both, I'll answer for it, since all the women and children are on the lookout. Some are burying the body of the poor girl who was shot, so that the enemy and the wild beasts can't find it. I told 'em that Father and Mother lay in the lake, but I wouldn't let them know in what part of it, for Judith and I don't want any of their heathenish company in our burying ground."

"Ah's me! Well, it *is* an awful dispatch to be standing here, alive and angry, and with the feelin's up and furious, one hour, and then to be carried away at the next and put out of sight of mankind in a hole in the 'arth. No one knows what will happen to him on a warpath, that's sartain."

Here the stirring of leaves and the cracking of dried twigs interrupted the discourse and apprised Deerslayer of the approach of his enemies. The Hurons closed around the spot that had been prepared for the coming scene, and in the center of which the intended victim now stood, in a circle —the armed men being so distributed among the feebler

members of the band that there was no safe opening through which the prisoner could break. But the latter no longer contemplated flight, the recent trial having satisfied him of his inability to escape when pursued so closely by numbers. On the contrary, all his energies were aroused in order to meet his expected fate with a calmness that should do credit to his color and his manhood, one equally removed from recreant alarm and savage boasting.

When Rivenoak reappeared in the circle, he occupied his old place at the head of the area. Several of the elder warriors stood near him, but now that the brother of Sumac had fallen, there was no longer any recognized chief present whose influence and authority offered a dangerous rivalry to his own. Nevertheless, it is well known that little which could be called monarchical or despotic entered into the politics of the North American tribes, although the first colonists, bringing with them to this hemisphere the notions and opinions of their own countries, often dignified the chief men of those primitive nations with the titles of kings and princes. Hereditary influence did certainly exist, but there is much reason to believe it existed rather as a consequence of hereditary merit and acquired qualifications than as a birthright. Rivenoak, however, had not even this claim —having risen to consideration purely by the force of talents, sagacity, and, as Bacon expresses it in relation to all distinguished statesmen, "by a union of great and mean qualities," a truth of which the career of the profound Englishman himself furnishes so apt an illustration.

Next to arms, eloquence offers the great avenue to popular favor, whether it be in civilized or savage life, and Rivenoak had succeeded, as so many have succeeded before him, quite as much by rendering fallacies acceptable to his listeners as by any profound or learned expositions of truth, or the accuracy of his logic. Nevertheless, he had influence, and was far from being altogether without just claims to its possession. Like most men who reason more than they feel, the Huron was not addicted to the indulgence of the mere ferocious passions of his people: he had been commonly found on the side of mercy in all the scenes of vindictive torture and revenge that had occurred in his tribe since his own attainment to power. On the present occasion, he was reluctant to proceed to extremities, although the provocation

was so great; still, it exceeded his ingenuity to see how that alternative could well be avoided. Sumac resented her rejection more than she did the deaths of her husband and brother, and there was little probability that the woman would pardon a man who had so unequivocally preferred death to her embraces. Without her forgiveness, there was scarce a hope that the tribe could be induced to overlook its loss, and even to Rivenoak himself, much as he was disposed to pardon, the fate of our hero now appeared to be almost hopelessly sealed.

When the whole band was arrayed around the captive, a grave silence, so much the more threatening from its profound quiet, pervaded the place. Deerslayer perceived that the women and boys had been preparing splinters of the fat pine roots, which he well knew were to be stuck into his flesh and set in flames, while two or three of the young men held the thongs of bark with which he was to be bound. The smoke of a distant fire announced that the burning brands were in preparation, and several of the elder warriors passed their fingers over the edges of their tomahawks, as if to prove their keenness and temper. Even the knives seemed loosened in their sheaths, impatient for the bloody and merciless work to begin.

"Killer of the Deer," recommenced Rivenoak, certainly without any signs of sympathy or pity in his manner, though with calmness and dignity; "Killer of the Deer, it is time that my people knew their minds. The sun is no longer over our heads; tired of waiting on the Hurons, he has begun to fall near the pines on this side of the valley. He is traveling fast toward the country of our French fathers; it is to warn his children that their lodges are empty, and that they ought to be at home. The roaming wolf has his den, and he goes to it when he wishes to see his young. The Iroquois are not poorer than the wolves. They have villages, and wigwams, and fields of corn; the good spirits will be tired of watching them alone. My people must go back and see to their own business. There will be joy in the lodges when they hear our whoop from the forest! It will be a sorrowful whoop; when it is understood, grief will come after it. There will be one scalp whoop, but there will be only one. We have the fur of the Muskrat; his body is among the fishes. Deerslayer must say whether another

scalp shall be on our pole. Two lodges are empty; a scalp, living or dead, is wanted at each door."

"Then take 'em dead, Huron," firmly, but altogether without dramatic boasting, returned the captive. "My hour is come, I do suppose; and what must be, must. If you are bent on the tortur', I'll do my indivors to bear up ag'in it, though no man can say how far his natur' will stand pain, until he's been tried."

"The paleface cur begins to put his tail between his legs!" cried a young and garrulous savage, who bore the appropriate title of the Corbeau Rouge; a sobriquet he had gained from the French, by his facility in making unseasonable noises, and an undue tendency to hear his own voice; "he is no warrior; he has killed the Loup Cervier when looking behind him not to see the flash of his own rifle. He grunts like a hog, already; when the Huron women begin to torment him, he will cry like the young of the catamount. He is a Delaware woman, dressed in the skin of a Yengeese!"

"Have your say, young man; have your say," returned Deerslayer, unmoved; "you know no better, and I can overlook it. Talking may aggravate women, but can hardly make knives sharper, fire hotter, or rifles more sartain."

Rivenoak now interfered, reproving the Red Crow for his premature interference and then directing the proper persons to bind the captive. This expedient was adopted, not from any apprehensions that he would escape, or from any necessity that was yet apparent, of his being unable to endure the torture with his limbs free, but from an ingenious design of making him feel his helplessness and of gradually sapping his resolution, by undermining it, as it might be, little by little. Deerslayer offered no resistance. He submitted his arms and legs, freely if not cheerfully, to the ligaments of bark, which were bound around them, by order of the chief, in a way to produce as little pain as possible. These directions were secret, and given in a hope that the captive would finally save himself from any serious bodily suffering, by consenting to take the Sumac for a wife. As soon as the body of Deerslayer was withed in bark sufficiently to create a lively sense of helplessness, he was literally carried to a young tree, and bound against it, in a way that effectually prevented him from moving, as well as from fall-

ing. The hands were laid flat against the legs, and thongs
were passed over all, in a way nearly to incorporate the
prisoner with the tree. His cap was then removed, and he
was left half-standing, half-sustained by his bonds, to face
the coming scene in the best manner he could.

Previously to proceeding to anything like extremities, it
was the wish of Rivenoak to put his captive's resolution to
the proof, by renewing the attempt at a compromise. This
could be effected only in one manner, the acquiescence of
the Sumac being indispensably necessary to a compromise of
her right to be revenged. With this view, then, the woman
was next desired to advance, and to look to her own interest; no agent being considered as efficient as the principal
herself in this negotiation. The Indian females, when girls,
are usually mild and submissive, with musical tones, pleasant voices, and merry laughs; but toil and suffering generally deprive them of most of these advantages by the
time they have reached an age which the Sumac had long
before passed. To render their voices harsh, it would seem
to require active, malignant passions, though when excited
their screams can rise to a sufficiently conspicuous degree of
discordancy to assert their claim to possess this distinctive
peculiarity of the sex. The Sumac was not altogether without
feminine attraction, however, and had so recently been
deemed handsome in her tribe, as not to have yet learned
the full influence that time and exposure produce on man
as well as on woman. By an arrangement of Rivenoak's
some of the women around her had been employing the time
in endeavoring to persuade the bereaved widow that there
was still a hope Deerslayer might be prevailed on to enter
her wigwam, in preference to entering the world of spirits,
and this, too, with a success that previous symptoms
scarcely justified. All this was the result of a resolution on
the part of the chief to leave no proper means unemployed,
in order to get the greatest hunter that was then thought to
exist in all that region, transferred to his own nation, as
well as a husband for a woman who he felt would be likely
to be troublesome, were any of her claims to the attention
and care of the tribe overlooked.

In conformity with this scheme the Sumac had been secretly advised to advance into the circle, and to make her
appeal to the prisoner's sense of justice before the band had

recourse to the last experiment. The woman, nothing loath, consented; for there was some such attraction, in becoming the wife of a noted hunter, among the females of the tribes, as is experienced by the sex in more refined life when they bestow their hands on the affluent. As the duties of a mother were thought to be paramount to all other considerations, the widow felt none of that embarrassment in preferring her claims, to which even a female fortune hunter among ourselves might be liable. When she stood forth before the whole party, therefore, the children that she led by the hand fully justified all she did.

"You see me before you, cruel paleface," the woman commenced; "your spirit must tell you my errand. I have found you; I cannot find le Loup Cervier, nor the Panther; I have looked for them in the lake, in the woods, in the clouds. I cannot say where they have gone."

"No man knows, good Sumac, no man knows," interposed the captive. "When the spirit leaves the body it passes into a world beyond our knowledge, and the wisest way for them that are left behind is to hope for the best. No doubt both your warriors have gone to the happy hunting grounds, and at the proper time you will see 'em ag'in in their improved state. The wife and sister of braves must have looked forward to some such tarmination of their 'arthly careers."

"Cruel paleface, what had my warriors done that you should slay them? They were the best hunters and the boldest young men of their tribe; the Great Spirit intended that they should live until they withered like the branches of the hemlock, and fell of their own weight."

"Nay, nay, good Sumac," interrupted the Deerslayer, whose love of truth was too indomitable to listen to such hyperbole with patience, even though it came from the torn breast of a widow—"Nay, nay, good Sumac, this is a little outdoing redskin privileges. Young man was neither, any more than you can be called a young woman; and as to the Great Spirit's intending that they should fall otherwise than they did, that's a grievous mistake, inasmuch as what the Great Spirit intends is sartain to come to pass. Then, ag'in, it's plain enough neither of your fri'nds did me any harm: I raised my hand ag'in 'em on account of what they were *striving* to do, rather than what they did. This is nat'ral law, 'to do, lest you should be done by.'"

"It is so. Sumac has but one tongue; she can tell but one story. The paleface struck the Hurons, lest the Hurons should strike him. The Hurons are a just nation; they will forget it. The chiefs will shut their eyes, and pretend not to have seen it. The young men will believe the Panther and the Lynx have gone to far-off hunts; and the Sumac will take her children by the hand, and go into the lodge of the paleface, and say, 'See; these are *your* children—they are also mine; feed us, and we will live with you.'"

"The tarms are onadmissible, woman; and, though I feel for your losses, which must be hard to bear, the tarms cannot be accepted. As to givin' you ven'son, in case we lived near enough together, that would be no great expl'ite, but as for becomin' your husband, and the father of your children, to be honest with you, I feel no callin' thataway."

"Look at this boy, cruel paleface; he has no father to teach him to kill the deer, or to take scalps. See this girl; what young man will come to look for a wife in a lodge that has no head? There are more among my people in the Canadas, and the Killer of Deer will find as many mouths to feed as his heart can wish for."

"I tell you, woman," exclaimed Deerslayer, whose imagination was far from seconding the appeal of the widow, and who began to grow restive under the vivid pictures she was drawing, "all this is nothing to me. People and kindred must take care of their own fatherless, leaving them that have no children to their own loneliness. As for me, I have no offspring, and I want no wife. Now, go away, Sumac; leave me in the hands of your chiefs; for my color, and gifts, and natur' itself cry out ag'in the idee of taking you for a wife."

It is unnecessary to expatiate on the effect of this downright refusal of the woman's proposals. If there was anything like tenderness in her bosom—and no woman was, probably, ever entirely without that feminine quality—it all disappeared at this plain announcement. Fury, rage, mortified pride, and a volcano of wrath, burst out at one explosion, converting her into a sort of maniac, as it might be at the touch of a magician's wand. Without deigning a reply in words, she made the arches of the forest ring with screams, and then flew forward at her victim, seizing him by the hair, which she appeared resolute to draw out by the roots.

was some time before her grasp could be loosened. For-
nately for the prisoner, her rage was blind, since his total
elplessness left him entirely at her mercy; had it been bet-
r directed, it might have proved fatal before any relief
ould have been offered. As it was, she did succeed in
renching out two or three handfuls of hair, before the
oung men could tear her away from her victim.

The insult that had been offered to the Sumac was deemed
n insult to the whole tribe; not so much, however, on
ccount of any respect that was felt for the woman, as
n account of the honor of the Huron nation. Sumac, her-
elf, was generally considered to be as acid as the berry
rom which she derived her name; and now that her great
upporters, her husband and brother, were both gone, few
ared about concealing their aversion. Nevertheless, it had
ecome a point of honor to punish the paleface who dis-
ained a Huron woman, and more particularly, one who
oolly preferred death to relieving the tribe from the sup-
ort of a widow and her children. The young men showed
n impatience to begin to torture, that Rivenoak under-
tood; and as his elder associates manifested no disposition
o permit any longer delay, he was compelled to give the
ignal for the infernal work to proceed.

CHAPTER XXIX

The ugly bear now minded not the stake,
Nor how the cruel mastiffs do him tear;
The stag lay still, unroused from the brake,
The foamy boar feared not the hunter's spear;
All thing was still in desert, bush, and briar.

EARL OF DORSET

IT WAS ONE of the common expedients of the savages, on such occasions, to put the nerves of their victims to the severest proofs. On the other hand, it was a matter of Indian pride to betray no yielding to terror or pain, but for the prisoner to provoke his enemies to such acts of violence as would soonest produce death. Many a warrior had been known to bring his own sufferings to a more speedy termination by taunting reproaches and reviling language, when he found that his physical system was giving way under the agony of sufferings produced by a hellish ingenuity that might well eclipse all that has been said of the infernal devices of religious persecution. This happy expedient of taking refuge from the ferocity of his foes in their passions was denied Deerslayer, however, by his peculiar notions of the duty of a white man, and he had stoutly made up his mind to endure everything, in preference to disgracing his color.

No sooner did the young men understand that they were at liberty to commence than some of the boldest and most forward among them sprang into the arena, tomahawk in hand. Here they prepared to throw that dangerous weapon, the object being to strike the tree as near as possible to the victim's head without absolutely hitting him. This was so hazardous an experiment that none but those who were

nown to be exceedingly expert with the weapon were allowed
o enter the lists at all, lest an early death interfere with
he expected entertainment. In the truest hands, it was seldom
hat the captive escaped injury in these trials, and it often
iappened that death followed, even when the blow was not
oremeditated. In the particular case of our hero, Rivenoak and
he older warriors were apprehensive that the example of the
Panther's fate might prove a motive with some fiery spirit,
suddenly to sacrifice his conqueror, when the temptation of
effecting it in precisely the same manner, and possibly with
he identical weapon with which the warrior had fallen,
offered. This circumstance, of itself, rendered the or-
deal of the tomahawk doubly critical for the Deerslayer.

It would seem, however, that all who now entered what
we shall call the lists were more disposed to exhibit their
own dexterity than to resent the deaths of their comrades.
Each prepared himself for the trial with the feelings of
rivalry rather than with the desire for vengeance, and for
he first few minutes the prisoner had little more connection with the result than grew out of the interest that necessarily attached itself to a living target. The young men
were eager, instead of being fierce, and Rivenoak thought
he still saw signs of being able to save the life of the captive,
when the vanity of the young men had been gratified, always
admitting that it was not sacrificed to the delicate experi-
ments that were about to be made.

The first youth who presented himself for the trial was
called the Raven, having as yet had no opportunity of obtaining a more warlike sobriquet. He was remarkable for high
pretension rather than for skill or exploits, and those who
knew his character thought the captive in imminent danger
when he took his stand, and poised the tomahawk. Nevertheless, the young man was good-natured, and no thought was
uppermost in his mind other than the desire to make a better
cast than any of his fellows. Deerslayer got an inkling of this
warrior's want of reputation by the injunctions that he had
received from the seniors, who, indeed, would have objected
to his appearing in the arena at all, but for an influence derived from his father, an aged warrior of great merit, who
was then in the lodges of the tribe. Still, our hero maintained
an appearance of self-possession. He had made up his mind
that his hour was come, and it would have been a mercy,

instead of a calamity, to fall by the unsteadiness of the first
hand that was raised against him. After a suitable number
of flourishes and gesticulations that promised much more
than he could perform, the Raven let the tomahawk quit
his hand. The weapon whirled through the air with the usual
evolutions, cut a chip from the sapling to which the prisoner
was bound, within a few inches of his cheek, and stuck
in a large oak that grew several yards behind him. This was
decidedly a bad effort, and a common sneer proclaimed as
much, to the great mortification of the young man. On the
other hand, there was a general but suppressed murmur of
admiration at the steadiness with which the captive stood the
trial. The head was the only part he could move, and this
had been purposely left free, that the tormentors might have
the amusement, and the tormented endure the shame, of
dodging and otherwise attempting to avoid the blows. Deerslayer disappointed these hopes by a command of nerve that
rendered his whole body as immovable as the tree to which
he was bound. Nor did he even adopt the natural and
usual expedient of shutting his eyes: the firmest and oldest
warrior of the red men never having more disdainfully
denied himself this advantage under similar circumstances.

The Raven had no sooner made his unsuccessful and puerile
effort than he was succeeded by le Daim-Mose, or the
Moose, a middle-aged warrior who was particularly skillful
in the use of the tomahawk, and from whose attempt the
spectators confidently looked for gratification. This man had
none of the good nature of the Raven, but he would gladly
have sacrificed the captive to his hatred of the palefaces
generally, were it not for the greater interest he felt in his
own success as one particularly skillful in the use of the
weapon. He took his stand quietly but with an air of confidence, poised his little ax but a single instant, advanced a
foot with a quick motion, and threw. Deerslayer saw the keen
instrument whirling toward him and believed all was over,
still he was not touched. The tomahawk had actually bound
the head of the captive to the tree by carrying before it some
of his hair, having buried itself deep beneath the soft bark.
A general yell expressed the delight of the spectators, and the
Moose felt his heart soften a little toward the prisoner
whose steadiness of nerve alone enabled him to give this
evidence of his consummate skill.

Le Daim-Mose was succeeded by the Bounding Boy, or
le Garçon qui Bondi, who came leaping into the circle
like a hound or a goat at play. This was one of those elastic
youths whose muscles seemed always in motion, and who
either affected, or who from habit was actually unable to
move in any other manner, than by showing the antics just
mentioned. Nevertheless, he was both brave and skillful,
and had gained the respect of his people by deeds in war as
well as success in the hunts. A far nobler name would long
since have fallen to his share, had not a Frenchman of
rank inadvertently given him this sobriquet, which he religiously preserved as coming from his great father, who
lived beyond the wide salt lake. The Bounding Boy skipped
about in front of the captive, menacing him with his tomahawk, now on one side and now on another, and then again
in front, in the vain hope of being able to extort some sign
of fear by this parade of danger. At length Deerslayer's
patience became exhausted by all this mummery, and he
spoke for the first time since the trial had actually commenced.

"Throw away, Huron!" he cried, "or your tomahawk will
forget its ar'n'd. Why do you keep loping about like a fa'an
that's showing its dam how well it can skip, when you're a
warrior grown, yourself, and a warrior grown defies you and
all your silly antics? Throw, or the Huron gals will laugh
in your face."

Although not intended to produce such an effect, the last
words aroused the "Bounding" warrior to fury. The same
nervous excitability which rendered him so active in his
person made it difficult to repress his feelings, and the
words were scarcely past the lips of the speaker than the
tomahawk left the hand of the Indian. It was cast without
good will, and with a fierce determination to slay. Had the
intention been less deadly, the danger might have been
greater. The aim was uncertain, and the weapon glanced near
the cheek of the captive, slightly cutting the shoulder in its
evolutions. This was the first instance in which any other
object than that of terrifying the prisoner and of displaying
skill had been manifested, and the Bounding Boy was immediately led from the arena and was warmly rebuked for
his intemperate haste, which had come so near defeating all
the hopes of the band.

To this irritable person succeeded several other young warriors, who not only hurled the tomahawk but who cast the knife, a far more dangerous experiment, with reckless indifference; yet they always manifested a skill that prevented any injury to the captive. Several times Deerslayer was grazed, but in no instance did he receive what might be termed a wound. The unflinching firmness with which he faced his assailants, more especially in the sort of rally with which this trial terminated, excited a profound respect in the spectators, and when the chiefs announced that the prisoner had well withstood the trials of the knife and the tomahawk, there was not a single individual in the band who really felt any hostility toward him, with the exception of Sumac and the Bounding Boy. These two discontented spirits got together, it is true, feeding each other's ire, but, as yet, their malignant feelings were confined very much to themselves, though there existed the danger that the others, ere long, could not fail to be excited by their own efforts into that demoniacal state which usually accompanied all similar scenes among the red men.

Rivenoak now told his people that the paleface had proved himself to be a man. He might live with the Delawares, but he had not been made woman with that tribe. He wished to know whether it was the desire of the Hurons to proceed any further. Even the gentlest of the females, however, had received too much satisfaction in the late trials to forgo their expectations of a gratifying exhibition, and there was but one voice in the request to proceed. The politic chief, who had some such desire to receive so celebrated a hunter into his tribe as a European minister has to devise a new and available means of taxation, sought every plausible means of arresting the trial in season, for he well knew, if permitted to go far enough to arouse the more ferocious passions of the tormentors, it would be as easy to dam the waters of the great lakes of his own region as to attempt to arrest them in their bloody career. He therefore called four or five of the best marksmen to him and bid them put the captive to the proof of the rifle, while at the same time he cautioned them touching the necessity of their maintaining their own credit, by the closest attention to the manner of exhibiting their skill.

When Deerslayer saw the chosen warriors step into the

circle, with their arms prepared for service, he felt some such relief as the miserable sufferer who has long endured the agonies of disease feels at the certain approach of death. Any trifling variance in the aim of this formidable weapon would prove fatal, since, the head being the target, or rather the point it was desired to graze without injury, an inch or two of difference in the line of projection must at once determine the question of life or death.

In the torture by the rifle there was none of the latitude permitted that appeared in the case of even Gesler's apple, a hairsbreadth being, in fact, the utmost limits that an expert marksman would allow himself on an occasion like this. Victims were frequently shot through the head by too eager or unskillful hands, and it often occurred that, exasperated by the fortitude and taunts of the prisoner, death was dealt intentionally in a moment of ungovernable irritation. All this Deerslayer well knew, for it was in relating the traditions of such scenes, as well as of the battles and victories of their people, that the old men beguiled the long winter evenings in their cabins. He now fully expected the end of his career and experienced a sort of melancholy pleasure in the idea that he was to fall by a weapon as much beloved as the rifle. A slight interruption, however, took place before the business was allowed to proceed.

Hetty Hutter witnessed all that passed, and the scene at first had pressed upon her feeble mind in a way to paralyze it entirely, but by this time she had rallied, and was growing indignant at the unmerited suffering the Indians were inflicting on her friend. Though timid and shy as the young of the deer on so many occasions, this right-feeling girl was always intrepid in the cause of humanity, the lessons of her mother, and the impulses of her own heart—perhaps we might say the promptings of that unseen and pure spirit that seemed ever to watch over and direct her actions—uniting to keep down the apprehensions of woman and to impel her to be bold and resolute. She now appeared in the circle, gentle, feminine, even bashful in mien, as usual, but earnest in her words and countenance, speaking like one who knew herself to be sustained by the high authority of God.

"Why do you torment Deerslayer, red men?" she asked. "What has he done that you trifle with his life? Who has given you the right to be his judges? Suppose one of your

knives or tomahawks had hit him; what Indian among you all could cure the wound you would make? Besides, in harming Deerslayer, you injure your own friend; when Father and Hurry Harry came after your scalps, he refused to be of the party and stayed in the canoe by himself. You are tormenting your friend, in tormenting this young man!"

The Hurons listened with grave attention, and one among them who understood English translated what had been said into their native tongue. As soon as Rivenoak was made acquainted with the purport of her address, he answered it in his own dialect, the interpreter conveying it to the girl in English.

"My daughter is very welcome to speak," said the stern old orator, using gentle intonations and smiling as kindly as if addressing a child. "The Hurons are glad to hear her voice; they listen to what she says. The Great Spirit often speaks to men with such tongues. This time her eyes have not been open wide enough to see all that has happened. Deerslayer did not come for our scalps, that is true; why did he not come? Here they are, on our heads; the warlocks are ready to be taken hold of; a bold enemy ought to stretch out his hand to seize them. The Iroquois are too great a nation to punish men that take scalps. What they do themselves, they like to see others do. Let my daughter look around her and count my warriors. Had I as many hands as four warriors, their fingers would be fewer than my people, when they came into your hunting grounds. Now a whole hand is missing. Where are the fingers? Two have been cut off by this paleface; my Hurons wish to see if he did this by means of a stout heart or by treachery, like a skulking fox, or like a leaping panther."

"You know yourself, Huron, how one of them fell. I saw it, and you all saw it, too. 'Twas too bloody to look at; but it was not Deerslayer's fault. Your warrior sought his life, and he defended himself. I don't know whether the good book says that it was right, but all men will do that. Come, if you want to know which of you can shoot best, give Deerslayer a rifle, and then you will find how much more expert he is than any of your warriors; yes, than *all* of them together!"

Could one have looked upon such a scene with indifference, he would have been amused at the gravity with which

the savages listened to the translation of this unusual request. No taunt, no smile mingled with their surprise, for Hetty had a character and a manner too saintly to subject her infirmity to the mockings of the rude and ferocious. On the contrary, she was answered with respectful attention.

"My daughter does not always talk like a chief at a council fire," returned Rivenoak, "or she would not have said this. Two of my warriors have fallen by the blows of our prisoner; their grave is too small to hold a third. The Hurons do not like to crowd their dead. If there is another spirit about to set out for the far-off world, it must not be the spirit of a Huron; it must be the spirit of a paleface. Go, daughter, and sit by Sumac, who is in grief; let the Huron warriors show how well they can shoot; let the paleface show how little he cares for their bullets."

Hetty's mind was unequal to a sustained discussion, and accustomed to defer to the directions of her seniors, she did as told, seating herself passively on a log by the side of the Sumac and averting her face from the painful scene that was occurring within the circle.

The warriors, as soon as this interruption had ceased, resumed their places and again prepared to exhibit their skill, as there was a double object in view, that of putting the constancy of the captive to the proof and that of showing how steady were the hands of the marksmen under circumstances of excitement. The distance was small and, in one sense, safe. But in diminishing the distance taken by the tormentors, the trial to the nerves of the captive was essentially increased. The face of Deerslayer, indeed, was just removed sufficiently from the ends of the guns to escape the effects of the flash, and his steady eye was enabled to look directly into their muzzles, as it might be, in anticipation of the fatal messenger that was to issue from each. The cunning Hurons well knew this fact, and scarce one leveled his piece without first causing it to point as near as possible at the forehead of the prisoner, in the hope that his fortitude would fail him and that the band would enjoy the triumph of seeing a victim quail under their ingenious cruelty. Nevertheless, each of the competitors was still careful not to injure, the disgrace of striking prematurely being second only to that of failing altogether in attaining the object. Shot after shot was made, all the bullets coming in close prox-

imity to the Deerslayer's head without touching it. Still, no one could detect even the twitching of a muscle on the part of the captive, or the slightest winking of an eye. This indomitable resolution, which so much exceeded everything of its kind that any present had before witnessed, might be referred to three distinct causes. The first was resignation to his fate, blended with natural steadiness of deportment, for our hero had calmly made up his mind that he must die, and preferred this mode to any other; the second was his great familiarity with this particular weapon, which deprived it of all the terror that is usually connected with the mere form of the danger; and the third was this familiarity carried out in practice, to a degree so nice as to enable the intended victim to tell, within an inch, the precise spot where each bullet must strike, for he calculated its range by looking in at the bore of the piece. So exact was Deerslayer's estimation of the line of fire that his pride of feeling finally got the better of his resignation, and when five or six had discharged their bullets into the tree, he could not refrain from expressing his contempt at their want of hand and eye.

"You may call this shooting, Mingos," he exclaimed, "but we've squaws among the Delawares, and I have known Dutch gals on the Mohawk, that could outdo your greatest indivors. Ondo these arms of mine, put a rifle into my hands, and I'll pin the thinnest warlock in your party to any tree you can show me, and this at a hundred yards: aye, or at two hundred, if the object can be seen, nineteen shots in twenty: or for that matter, twenty in twenty, if the piece is creditable and trusty!"

A low menacing murmur followed this cool taunt, the ire of the warriors kindled at listening to such a reproach from one who so far disdained their efforts as to refuse even to wink, when a rifle was discharged as near his face as could be done without burning it. Rivenoak perceived that the moment was critical, and still retaining his hope of adopting so noted a hunter into his tribe, the politic old chief interposed in time, probably, to prevent an immediate resort to that portion of the torture which must necessarily have produced death, through extreme bodily suffering, if in no other manner. Moving into the center of the irritated group, he addressed them with his usual wily logic and plausible man-

ner, at once suppressing the fierce movement that had commenced.

"I see how it is," he said. "We have been like the palefaces when they fasten their doors at night, out of fear of the red man. They use so many bars that the fire comes and burns them before they can get out. We have bound the Deerslayer too tight; the thongs keep his limbs from shaking and his eyes from shutting. Loosen him; let us see what his own body is really made of."

It is often the case, when we are thwarted in a cherished scheme, that any expedient, however unlikely to succeed, is gladly resorted to, in preference to a total abandonment of the project. So it was with the Hurons. The proposal of the chief found instant favor, and several hands were immediately at work cutting and tearing the ropes of bark from the body of our hero. In half a minute Deerslayer stood as free from bonds as when, an hour before, he had commenced his flight on the side of the mountain. Some little time was necessary that he should recover the use of his limbs, the circulation of the blood having been checked by the tightness of the ligatures, and this was accorded to him by the politic Rivenoak, under the pretense that his body would be more likely to submit to apprehension if its true tone were restored, though really with a view to give time to the fierce passions which had been awakened in the bosoms of his young men to subside. This ruse succeeded, and Deerslayer, by rubbing his limbs, stamping his feet, and moving about, soon regained the circulation, recovering all his physical powers as effectually as if nothing had occurred to disturb them.

It is seldom men think of death in the pride of their health and strength. So it was with Deerslayer. Having been helplessly bound, and, as he had every reason to suppose, so lately on the very verge of the other world, to find himself so unexpectedly liberated, in possession of his strength, and with a full command of limb, acted on him like a sudden restoration to life, reanimating hopes that he had once absolutely abandoned. From that instant all his plans changed. In this he simply obeyed a law of nature, for while we have wished to represent our hero as being resigned to his fate, it has been far from our intention to represent him as anxious to die. From the instant that his buoyancy of feeling revived,

his thoughts were keenly bent on the various projects that presented themselves as modes of evading the designs of his enemies, and he again became the quick-witted, ingenious, and determined woodsman, alive to all his own powers and resources. The change was so great that his mind resumed its elasticity, and, no longer thinking of submission, it dwelt only on the devices of the sort of warfare in which he was engaged.

As soon as Deerslayer was released, the band divided itself in a circle around him, in order to hedge him in, and the desire to break down his spirit grew in them, precisely as they saw proofs of the difficulty there would be in subduing it. The honor of the band was now involved in the issue, and even the sex lost all its sympathy with suffering, in the desire to save the reputation of the tribe. The voices of the girls, soft and melodious as nature had made them, were heard mingling with the menaces of the men, and the wrongs of Sumac suddenly assumed the character of injuries inflicted on every Huron female. Yielding to this rising tumult, the men drew back a little, signifying to the females that they left the captive for a time in their hands, it being a common practice, on such occasions, for the women to endeavor to throw the victim into a rage by their taunts and revilings, and then to turn him suddenly over to the men in a state of mind that was little favorable to resisting the agony of bodily suffering. Nor was this party without the proper instruments for effecting such a purpose. Sumac had a notoriety as a scold, and one or two crones, like the She Bear, had come out with the party, most probably as the conservators of its decency and moral discipline, such things occurring in savage as well as civilized life. It is unnecessary to repeat all that ferocity and ignorance could invent for such a purpose, the only difference between this outbreaking of feminine anger and a similar scene among ourselves consisting in the figures of speech and the epithets; the Huron women called their prisoner by the names of the lower and least respected animals that were known to themselves.

But Deerslayer's mind was too much occupied to permit him to be disturbed by the abuse of excited hags, and their rage necessarily increasing with his indifference, as his indifference increased with their rage, the furies soon rendered themselves impotent by their own excesses. Perceiving that

the attempt was a complete failure, the warriors interfered to put a stop to this scene, and this so much the more, because preparations were now seriously making for the commencement of the real tortures, or that which would put the fortitude of the sufferer to the test of severe bodily pain. A sudden and unlooked-for announcement that proceeded from one of the lookouts, a boy ten or twelve years old, however, put a momentary check to the whole proceedings. As this interruption has a close connection with the dénouement of our story, it shall be given in a separate chapter.

But Deerslayer's mind was too much occupied to permit him to be disturbed by the abuse of excited bags, and their rage necessarily increasing with his indifference, as his indifference increased with their rage, the furies soon rendered themselves impotent by their own excesses. Perceiving that

CHAPTER XXX

So deem'st thou—so each mortal deems
Of that which is from that which seems;
*   But other harvest here*
Than that which peasant's scythe demands,
Was gathered in by sterner hands,
*   With bayonet, blade, and spear.*

SCOTT

IT EXCEEDED DEERSLAYER'S power to ascertain what had produced the sudden pause in the movements of his enemies, until the fact was revealed in the due course of events. He perceived that much agitation prevailed among the women in particular, while the warriors rested on their arms in a sort of dignified expectation. It was plain no alarm was excited, though it was not equally apparent that a friendly occurrence produced the delay. Rivenoak was evidently apprised of all, and by a gesture of his arm he appeared to direct the circle to remain unbroken, and for each person to await the issue in the situation he or she then occupied. It required but a minute or two to bring an explanation of this singular and mysterious pause, which was soon terminated by the appearance of Judith on the exterior of the line of bodies, and her ready admission within its circle.

If Deerslayer was startled by this unexpected arrival, well knowing that the quick-witted girl could claim none of that exemption from the penalties of captivity that was so cheerfully accorded to her feeble-minded sister, he was equally astonished at the guise in which she came. All her ordinary forest attire, neat and becoming as this usually was, had been laid aside for the brocade that has been already mentioned, and which had once before wrought so great and magical an effect in her appearance. Nor was this all. Accus-

tomed to see the ladies of the garrison in the formal gala attire of the day, and familiar with the more critical niceties of these matters, the girl had managed to complete her dress in a way to leave nothing strikingly defective in its details, or even to betray an incongruity that would have been detected by one practiced in the mysteries of the toilet. Head, feet, arms, hands, bust, and drapery were all in harmony, as female attire was then deemed attractive and harmonious, and the end she aimed at, that of imposing on the uninstructed senses of the savages by causing them to believe their guest was a woman of rank and importance, might well have succeeded with those whose habits had taught them to discriminate between persons. Judith, in addition to her rare native beauty, had a singular grace of person, and her mother had imparted enough of her own deportment to prevent any striking or offensive vulgarity of manner, so that, sooth to say, the gorgeous dress might have been worse bestowed in nearly every particular. Had it been displayed in a capital, a thousand might have worn it before one could have been found to do more credit to its gay colors, glossy satins, and rich laces than the beautiful creature whose person it now aided to adorn.

The effect of such an apparition had not been miscalculated. The instant Judith found herself within the circle, she was, in a degree, compensated for the fearful personal risk she ran by the unequivocal sensation of surprise and admiration produced by her appearance. The grim old warriors uttered their favorite exclamation, "Hugh!" The younger men were still more sensibly overcome, and even the women were not backward in letting open manifestations of pleasure escape them. It was seldom that these untutored children of the forest had ever seen any white female above the commonest sort, and as to dress, never before had so much splendor shone before their eyes. The gayest uniforms of both French and English seemed dull compared with the luster of the brocade, and while the rare personal beauty of the wearer added to the effect produced by its hues, the attire did not fail to adorn that beauty in a way which surpassed even the hopes of its wearer. Deerslayer himself was astounded, and this quite as much by the brilliant picture the girl presented as at the indifference to consequences with which she had braved the danger of the step she had taken. Under such

circumstances, all waited for the visitor to explain her object, which to most of the spectators seemed as inexplicable as her appearance.

"Which of these warriors is the principal chief?" demanded Judith of Deerslayer, as soon as she found it was expected that she should open the communication; "my errand is too important to be delivered to any of inferior rank. First explain to the Hurons what I say; then give an answer to the question I have put."

Deerslayer quietly complied, his auditors greedily listening to the interpretation of the first words that fell from so extraordinary a vision. The demand seemed perfectly in character for one who had every appearance of an exalted rank herself. Rivenoak gave an appropriate reply by presenting himself before his fair visitor in a way to leave no doubt that he was entitled to all the consideration he claimed.

"I can believe this, Huron," resumed Judith, enacting her assumed part with a steadiness and dignity that did credit to her powers of imitation, for she strove to impart to her manner the condescending courtesy she had once observed in the wife of a general officer, at a similar though a more amicable scene. "I can believe you to be the principal person of this party; I see in your countenance the marks of thought and reflection. To you, then, I must make my communication."

"Let the Flower of the Woods speak," returned the old chief courteously, as soon as her address had been translated so that all might understand it. "If her words are as pleasant as her looks, they will never quit my ears; I shall hear them long after the winter in Canada has killed the flowers and frozen all the speeches of summer."

This admiration was grateful to one constituted like Judith, and contributed to aid her self-possession quite as much as it fed her vanity. Smiling involuntarily, or in spite of her wish to seem reserved, she proceeded in her plot.

"Now, Huron," she continued, "listen to my words. Your eyes tell you that I am no common woman. I will not say I am queen of this country; *she* is afar off, in a distant land; but under our gracious monarchs there are many degrees of rank; one of these I fill. What that rank is precisely it is unnecessary for me to say, since you would not understand it. For that information you must trust your eyes. You *see*

what I am; you must *feel* that in listening to my words, you listen to one who can be your friend or your enemy, as you treat her."

This was well uttered, with a due attention to manner and a steadiness of tone that was really surprising, considering all the circumstances of the case. It was well, though simply rendered into the Indian dialect, too, and it was received with a respect and gravity that augured favorably for the girl's success. But Indian thought is not easily traced to its sources. Judith waited with anxiety to hear the answer, filled with hope even while she doubted. Rivenoak was a ready speaker, and he answered as promptly as comported with the notions of Indian decorum, that peculiar people seeming to think a short delay respectful, inasmuch as it manifests that the words already heard have been duly weighed.

"My daughter is handsomer than the wild roses of Ontario; her voice is pleasant to the ear as the song of the wren," answered the cautious and wily chief, who of all the band stood alone in not being fully imposed on by the magnificent and unusual appearance of Judith, but who distrusted even while he wondered. "The hummingbird is not much larger than the bee, yet its feathers are as gay as the tail of the peacock. The Great Spirit sometimes puts very bright clothes on very little animals. Still, He covers the moose with coarse hair. These things are beyond the understanding of poor Indians, who can only comprehend what they see and hear. No doubt my daughter has a very large wigwam somewhere about the lake that the Hurons have not found on account of their ignorance?"

"I have told you, Chief, that it would be useless to state my rank and residence, inasmuch as you would not comprehend them. You must trust to your eyes for this knowledge; what red man is there that cannot see? This blanket that I wear is not the blanket of a common squaw; these ornaments are such as the wives and daughters of chiefs only appear in. Now listen and hear why I have come alone among your people, and hearken to the errand that has brought me here. The Yengeese have young men as well as the Hurons—and plenty of them, too—this you well know."

"The Yengeese are as plenty as the leaves on the trees! This every Huron knows and feels."

"I understand you, Chief. Had I brought a party with me, it might have caused trouble. My young men and your young men would have looked angrily at each other, especially had my young men seen that paleface bound for the tortures. He is a great hunter and is much loved by all the garrisons, far and near. There would have been blows about him, and the trail of the Iroquois back to the Canadas would have been marked with blood."

"There is so much blood on it now," returned the chief, gloomily, "that it blinds our eyes. My young men see that it is all Huron."

"No doubt; and more Huron blood would be spilled, had I come surrounded with palefaces. I have heard of Rivenoak and have thought it would be better to send him back in peace to his village, that he might leave his women and children behind him; if he then wished to come for our scalps, we would meet him. He loves animals made of ivory and little rifles. See; I have brought some with me to show him. I am his friend. When he has packed up these things among his goods, he will start for his village before any of my young men can overtake him, and then he will show his people in Canada what riches they can come to seek, now that our great fathers across the salt lake have sent each other the war hatchet. I will lead back with me this great hunter, of whom I have need to keep my house in venison."

Judith, who was sufficiently familiar with Indian phraseology, endeavored to express her ideas in the sententious manner common to those people, and she succeeded even beyond her own expectations. Deerslayer did her full justice in the translation, and this so much the more readily since the girl carefully abstained from uttering any direct untruth, a homage she paid to the young man's known aversion to falsehood, which he deemed a meanness altogether unworthy of a white man's gifts. The offering of the two remaining elephants and of the pistols already mentioned, one of which was all the worse for the recent accident, produced a lively sensation among the Hurons generally, though Rivenoak received it coldly, notwithstanding the delight with which he had first discovered the probable existence of a creature with two tails. In a word, this cool and sagacious savage was not

so easily imposed on as his followers, and with a sentiment of honor that half the civilized world would have deemed supererogatory, he declined the acceptance of a bribe that he felt no disposition to earn by a compliance with the donor's wishes.

"Let my daughter keep her two-tailed hog, to eat when venison is scarce," he dryly answered; "and the little gun, which has two muzzles. The Hurons will kill deer when they are hungry, and they have long rifles to fight with. This hunter cannot quit my young men now; they wish to know if he is as stouthearted as he boasts himself to be."

"That I deny, Huron," interrupted Deerslayer, with warmth; "yes, that I downright deny as ag'in truth and reason. No man has heard me *boast*, and no man shall, though ye flay me alive, and then roast the quivering flesh, with your own infarnal devices and cruelties! I may be humble, and misfortunate, and your prisoner, but I'm no boaster, by my very gifts."

"My young paleface *boasts* he is *no* boaster," returned the crafty chief; "he *must* be right. I hear a strange bird singing. It has very rich feathers. No Huron ever before saw such feathers. They will be ashamed to go back to their village and tell their people that they let their prisoner go on account of the song of this strange bird, and not be able to give the *name* of the bird. They do not know how to say whether it is a wren or a catbird. This would be a great disgrace; my young men would not be allowed to travel in the woods without taking their mothers with them to tell them the names of the birds."

"You can ask my name of your prisoner," returned the girl. "It is Judith; and there is a great deal of the history of Judith in the palefaces' best book, the Bible. If I am a bird of fine feathers, I have also my name."

"No," answered the wily Huron, betraying the artifice he had so long practiced by speaking in English, with tolerable accuracy; "I not ask prisoner. He tired; he want rest. I ask my daughter with feeble mind. She speak truth. Come here, daughter; you answer. *Your* name, Hetty?"

"Yes, that's what they call me," returned the girl; "though t's written Esther, in the Bible."

"He write *him* in Bible, too? All write in Bible. No matter —what *her* name?"

"That's Judith, and it's so written in the Bible, though father sometimes called her Jude. That's my sister Judith, Thomas Hutter's daughter—Thomas Hutter, whom you called the Muskrat; though he was *no* muskrat, but a man, like yourselves—he lived in a house on the water, and that was enough for *you*."

A smile of triumph gleamed on the hard, wrinkled countenance of the chief when he found how completely his appeal to the truth-loving Hetty had succeeded. As for Judith herself, the moment her sister was questioned, she saw that all was lost, for no sign or even entreaty could have induced the right-feeling girl to utter a falsehood. To attempt to impose a daughter of the Muskrat on the savages as a princess or a great lady she knew would be idle, and she saw her bold and ingenious expedient for liberating the captive fail, through one of the simplest and most natural causes that could be imagined. She turned her eye on Deerslayer, therefore, as if imploring him to interfere, to save them both.

"It will not do, Judith," said the young man, in answer to this appeal, which he understood, though he saw its uselessness; "it will not do. 'Twas a bold idea, and fit for a general's lady; but yonder Mingo"—Rivenoak had withdrawn to a little distance, and was out of earshot—"but yonder Mingo is an oncommon man, and not to be deceived by any unnat'ral sarcumventions. Things must come afore him in their right order to draw a cloud afore *his* eyes! 'Twas too much to attempt making him fancy that a queen or a great lady lived in these mountains, and no doubt he thinks the fine clothes you wear are some of the plunder of your own father—or, at least, of him who once passed for your father—as quite likely it was, if all they say is true."

"At all events, Deerslayer, my presence here will save you for a time. They will hardly attempt torturing you before my face!"

"Why not, Judith? Do you think they will treat a woman of the palefaces more tenderly than they treat their own? It's true that your sex will most likely save you from the torments, but it will not save your liberty, and may not save your scalp. I wish you hadn't come, my good Judith; it can do no good to me, while it may do great harm to yourself."

"I can share your fate," the girl answered, with generous

enthusiasm. "They shall not injure you while I stand by, if in my power to prevent it—besides——"

"Besides what, Judith? What means have you to stop Injin cruelties, or to avart Injin deviltries?"

"None, perhaps, Deerslayer," answered the girl, with firmness, "but I can suffer with my friends—die with them if necessary."

"Ah, Judith—suffer you may, but die you will not until the Lord's time shall come. It's little likely that one of your sex and beauty will meet with a harder fate than to become the wife of a chief, if indeed your white inclinations can stoop to match with an Injin. 'Twould have been better had you stayed in the ark or the castle; but what has been done is done. You was about to say something when you stopped at 'besides'?"

"It might not be safe to mention it here, Deerslayer," the girl hurriedly answered, moving past him carelessly, that she might speak in a low tone; "half an hour is all in all to us. None of your friends are idle."

The hunter replied merely by a grateful look. Then he turned toward his enemies, as if ready again to face the torments. A short consultation had passed among the elders of the band, and by this time they also were prepared with their decision. The merciful purpose of Rivenoak had been much weakened by the artifice of Judith, which, failing of its real object, was likely to produce results the very opposite of those she had anticipated. This was natural, the feeling being aided by the resentment of an Indian, who found how near he had been to becoming the dupe of an inexperienced girl. By this time Judith's real character was fully understood— the widespread reputation of her beauty contributed to the exposure. As for the unusual attire, it was confounded with the profound mystery of the animals with two tails and, for the moment, lost its influence.

When Rivenoak, therefore, faced the captive again, it was with an altered countenance. He had abandoned the wish of saving him, and was no longer disposed to retard the more serious part of the torture. This change of sentiment was, in effect, communicated to the young men, who were already eagerly engaged in making their preparations for the contemplated scene. Fragments of dried wood were rapidly collected near the sapling, the splinters which it was intended to thrust

into the flesh of the victim, previous to lighting, were all collected, and the thongs were already produced that were again to bind him to the tree. All this was done in profound silence, Judith watching every movement with breathless expectation, while Deerslayer himself stood seemingly as unmoved as one of the pines of the hills. When the warriors advanced to bind him, however, the young man glanced at Judith, as if to inquire whether resistance or submission were most advisable. By a significant gesture she counseled the last, and in a minute he was once more fastened to the tree, a helpless object of any insult or wrong that might be offered. So eagerly did everyone now act that nothing was said. The fire was immediately lighted in the pile, and the end of all was anxiously expected.

It was not the intention of the Hurons absolutely to destroy the life of their victim by means of fire. They designed merely to put his physical fortitude to the severest proofs it could endure, short of that extremity. In the end, they fully intended to carry his scalp with them into their village, but it was their wish first to break down his resolution and to reduce him to the level of a complaining sufferer. With this view, the pile of brush and branches had been placed at a proper distance, or one at which it was thought the heat would soon become intolerable, though it might not be immediately dangerous. As often happened, however, on these occasions, this distance had been miscalculated, and the flames began to wave their forked tongues in a proximity to the face of the victim that would have proved fatal in another instant, had not Hetty rushed through the crowd, armed with a stick, and scattered the blazing pile in a dozen directions. More than one hand was raised to strike the presumptuous intruder to the earth, but the chiefs prevented the blows by reminding their irritated followers of the state of her mind. Hetty, herself, was insensible to the risk she ran; as soon as she had performed this bold act, she stood looking about her in frowning resentment, as if to rebuke the crowd of attentive savages for their cruelty.

"God bless you, dearest sister, for that brave and ready act," murmured Judith, herself unnerved so much as to be incapable of exertion. "Heaven itself has sent you on its holy errand."

" 'Twas well meant, Judith," rejoined the victim; " 'twas

excellently meant, and 'twas timely, though it may prove on-timely in the ind! What is to come to pass must come to pass soon, or 'twill quickly be too late. Had I drawn in one mouthful of that flame in breathing, the power of man couldn't save my life, and you see that this time they've so bound my forehead as not to leave my head the smallest chance. 'Twas well meant, but it might have been more marci-ful to let the flames act their part."

"Cruel, heartless Hurons!" exclaimed the still indignant Hetty. "Would you burn a man and a Christian as you would burn a log of wood! Do you never read your Bibles? Or do you think God will forget such things?"

A gesture from Rivenoak caused the scattered brands to be collected; fresh wood was brought, even the women and chil-dren busying themselves eagerly in the gathering of dried sticks. The flame was just kindling a second time when an *Indian* female pushed through the circle, advanced to the heap, and with her foot dashed aside the lighted twigs in time to prevent the conflagration. A yell followed this second dis-appointment, but when the offender turned toward the circle and presented the countenance of Hist, it was succeeded by a common exclamation of pleasure and surprise. For a min-ute, all thought of pursuing the business in hand was forgot-ten, and young and old crowded around the girl, in haste to demand an explanation of her sudden and unlooked-for re-turn. It was at this critical instant that Hist spoke to Judith in a low voice, placed some small object, unseen, in her hand, and then turned to meet the salutations of the Huron girls, with whom she was personally a great favorite. Judith re-covered her self-possession and acted promptly. The small, keen-edged knife that Hist had given to the other was passed by the latter into the hands of Hetty, as the safest and least-suspected medium of transferring it to Deerslayer. But the feeble intellect of the last defeated the well-grounded hopes of all three. Instead of first cutting loose the hands of the vic-tim and then concealing the knife in his clothes, in readiness for action at the most available instant, she went to work her-self, with earnestness and simplicity, to cut the thongs that bound his head, that he might not again be in danger of in-haling flames. Of course this deliberate procedure was seen, and the hands of Hetty were arrested ere she had more than liberated the upper portion of the captive's body, not in-

cluding his arms, below the elbows. This discovery at once
pointed distrust toward Hist, and to Judith's surprise, when
questioned on the subject, that spirited girl was not disposed
to deny her agency in what had passed.

"Why should I not help the Deerslayer?" the girl demanded, in the tones of a firm-minded woman. "He is the
brother of a Delaware chief; my heart is all Delaware. Come
forth, miserable Briarthorn, and wash the Iroquois paint
from your face; stand before the Hurons, the crow that you
are; you would eat the carrion of your own dead rather than
starve. Put him face to face with Deerslayer, chiefs and
warriors; I will show you how great a knave you have been
keeping in your tribe."

This bold language, uttered in their own dialect and with a
manner full of confidence, produced a deep sensation among
the Hurons. Treachery is always liable to distrust, and though
the recreant Briarthorn had endeavored to serve the enemy
well, his exertions and assiduities had gained for him little
more than toleration. His wish to obtain Hist for a wife had
first induced him to betray her and his own people, but serious rivals to his first project had risen up among his new
friends, weakening still more their sympathies with treason.
In a word, Briarthorn had been barely permitted to remain in
the Huron encampment, where he was as closely and as jeal-
ously watched as Hist herself, seldom appearing before the
chiefs and sedulously keeping out of view of Deerslayer, who
until this moment was ignorant even of his presence. Thus
summoned, however, it was impossible to remain in the background. "Wash the Iroquois paint from his face," he did not,
for when he stood in the center of the circle, he was so disguised in these new colors that at first the hunter did not
recognize him. He assumed an air of defiance, notwithstanding, and haughtily demanded what any could say against
"Briarthorn."

"Ask yourself that," continued Hist, with spirit, though her
manner grew less concentrated, and there was a slight air of
abstraction that became observable to Deerslayer and Judith, if to no others. "Ask that of your own heart, sneaking
woodchuck of the Delawares; come not here with the face
of an innocent man. Go look in the spring; see the colors of
your enemies on your lying skin; and then come back and
boast how you ran from your tribe and took the blanket of

the French for your covering. Paint yourself as bright as the hummingbird, you will still be black as the crow."

Hist had been so uniformly gentle while living with the Hurons that they now listened to her language with surprise. As for the delinquent, his blood boiled in his veins, and it was well for the pretty speaker that it was not in his power to execute the revenge he burned to inflict on her, in spite of his pretended love.

"Who wishes Briarthorn?" he sternly asked. "If this pale-face is tired of life: if afraid of Indian torments, speak, Rivenoak; I will send him after the warriors we have lost."

"No, Chief, no, Rivenoak," eagerly interrupted Hist. "The Deerslayer fears nothing; least of all a crow! Unbind him— cut his withes—place him face to face with this cawing bird; then let us see which is tired of life."

Hist made a forward movement, as if to take a knife from a young man and perform the office she had mentioned in person, but an aged warrior interposed at a sign from Rivenoak. This chief watched all the girl did with distrust, for, even while speaking in her most boastful language and in the steadiest manner, there was an air of uncertainty and expectation about her that could not escape so close an observer. She acted well, but two or three of the old men were equally satisfied that it was merely acting. Her proposal to release Deerslayer, therefore, was rejected, and the disappointed Hist found herself driven back from the sapling at the very moment she fancied herself about to be successful. At the same time the circle, which had got to be crowded and confused, was enlarged and brought once more into order. Rivenoak now announced the intention of the old men again to proceed, the delay having been continued long enough, and leading to no result.

"Stop, Huron; stay, Chiefs!" exclaimed Judith, scarce knowing what she said, or why she interposed, unless to obtain time; "for God's sake, a single minute longer——"

The words were cut short by another and a still more extraordinary interruption. A young Indian came bounding through the Huron ranks, leaping into the very center of the circle, in a way to denote the utmost confidence, or a temerity bordering on foolhardiness. Five or six sentinels were still watching the lake at different and distant points, and it was the first impression of Rivenoak that one of these

had come in with tidings of import. Still, the movements of
the stranger were so rapid, and his war dress, which scarcely
left him more drapery than an antique statue, had so little
distinguishing about it that at the first moment it was impossible to ascertain whether he were friend or foe. Three leaps
carried this warrior to the side of Deerslayer, whose withes
were cut in the twinkling of an eye, with a quickness and precision that left the prisoner perfect master of his limbs. Not
till this was effected did the stranger bestow a glance on any
other object; then he turned and showed the astonished
Hurons the noble brow, fine person, and eagle eye of a young
warrior in the paint and panoply of a Delaware. He held a
rifle in each hand, the butts of both resting on the earth,
while from one dangled its proper pouch and horn. This
was Killdeer, which, even as he looked boldly and in
defiance on the crowd around him, he suffered to fall back
into the hands of its proper owner. The presence of two
armed men, though it was in their midst, startled the Hurons.
Their rifles were scattered about against the different trees,
and their only weapons were their knives and tomahawks.
Still, they had too much self-possession to betray fear. It
was little likely that so small a force would assail so strong
a band, and each man expected some extraordinary proposition to succeed so decisive a step. The stranger did not seem
disposed to disappoint them; he prepared to speak.

"Hurons," he said, "this earth is very big. The great lakes
are big, too; there is room beyond them for the Iroquois;
there is room for the Delawares on this side. I am
Chingachgook, the son of Uncas; the kinsman of Tamenund.
This is my betrothed; that paleface is my friend. My heart
was heavy when I missed him; I followed him to your camp
to see that no harm happened to him. All the Delaware girls
are waiting for Wah; they wonder that she stays away so
long. Come, let us say farewell, and go on our path."

"Hurons, this is your mortal enemy, the Great Serpent of
them you hate!" cried Briarthorn. "If he escape, blood will
be in your moccasin prints from this spot to the Canadas. *I*
am *all* Huron."

As the last words were uttered, the traitor cast his knife
at the naked breast of the Delaware. A quick movement of
the arm on the part of Hist, who stood near, turned aside
the blow, the dangerous weapon burying its point in a pine.

At the next instant, a similar weapon glanced from the hand of the Serpent, and quivered in the recreant's heart. A minute had scarcely elapsed from the moment in which Chingachgook bounded into the circle and that in which Briarthorn fell, like a log, dead in his tracks. The rapidity of events prevented the Hurons from acting, but this catastrophe permitted no further delay. A common exclamation followed, and the whole party was in motion. At this instant, a sound unusual to the woods was heard, and every Huron, male and female, paused to listen, with ears erect and faces filled with expectation. The sound was regular and heavy, as if the earth were struck with beetles. Objects became visible among the trees of the background, and a body of troops was seen advancing with measured tread. They came upon the charge, the scarlet of the king's livery shining among the bright green foliage of the forest.

The scene that followed is not easily described. It was one in which wild confusion, despair, and frenzied efforts were so blended as to destroy the unity and distinctness of the action. A general yell burst from the enclosed Hurons; it was succeeded by the hearty cheers of England. Still, not a musket or rifle was fired, though that steady, measured tramp continued, and the bayonet was seen gleaming in advance of a line that counted nearly sixty men. The Hurons were taken at a fearful disadvantage. On three sides was the water, while their formidable and trained foes cut them off from flight on the fourth. Each warrior rushed for his arms, and then all on the point, man, woman, and child, eagerly sought the covers. In this scene of confusion and dismay, however, nothing could surpass the discretion and coolness of Deerslayer. His first care was to place Judith and Hist behind trees; he looked for Hetty, but she had been hurried away in the crowd of Huron women. This effected, he threw himself on a flank of the retiring Hurons, who were inclining off toward the southern margin of the point, in the hope of escaping through the water. Deerslayer watched his opportunity, and finding two of his recent tormentors in a range, his rifle first broke the silence of the terrific scene. The bullet brought down both at one discharge. This drew a general fire from the Hurons, and the rifle and war cry of the Serpent were heard in the clamor. Still the trained men returned no answering volley, the whoop and piece of Hurry

alone being heard on their side, if we except the short, prompt word of authority and that heavy, measured, and menacing tread. Presently, however, the shrieks, groans, and denunciations that usually accompany the use of the bayonet followed. That terrible and deadly weapon was glutted in vengeance. The scene that succeeded was one of those, of which so many have occurred in our own times, in which neither age nor sex forms an exemption to the lot of a savage warfare.

Chapter XXXI

The flower that smiles to-day
    To-morrow dies;
All that we wish to stay,
    Tempts and then flies:
What is this world's delight?—
Lightning that mocks the night,
Brief even as bright.

Shelley

THE PICTURE NEXT presented by the point of land that the unfortunate Hurons had selected for their last place of encampment need scarcely be laid before the eyes of the reader. Happily for the more tender-minded and the more timid, the trunks of the trees, the leaves, and the smoke had concealed much of that which passed, and night shortly after drew its veil over the lake and the whole of that seemingly interminable wilderness, which may be said to have then stretched, with far and immaterial interruptions, from the banks of the Hudson to the shores of the Pacific Ocean. Our business carries us into the following day, when light returned upon the earth, as sunny and as smiling as if nothing extraordinary had occurred.

When the sun rose on the following morning, every sign of hostility and alarm had vanished from the basin of the Glimmerglass. The frightful event of the preceding evening had left no impression on the placid sheet, and the untiring hours pursued their course in the placid order prescribed by the powerful hand that set them in motion. The birds were again skimming the water, or were seen poised on the wing high above the tops of the tallest pines of the mountains, ready to make their swoops in obedience to the irresistible laws of their nature. In a word, nothing was changed but

the air of movement and life that prevailed in and around the castle. Here, indeed, was an alteration that must have struck the least observant eye. A sentinel, who wore the light infantry uniform of a royal regiment, paced the platform with measured tread, and some twenty men of the same corps lounged about the place, or were seated in the ark. Their arms were stacked under the eye of their comrade on post. Two officers stood examining the shore with the ship's glass so often mentioned. Their looks were directed to that fatal point, where scarlet coats were still to be seen gliding among the trees, and where the magnifying power of the instrument also showed spades at work and the sad duty of interment going on. Several of the common men bore proofs on their persons that their enemies had not been overcome entirely without resistance, and the youngest of the two officers on the platform, wore an arm in a sling. His companion, who commanded the party, had been more fortunate. He it was that used the glass in making the reconnaissances in which the two were engaged.

A sergeant approached to make a report. He addressed the senior of these officers as Captain Warley, while the other was alluded to as Mr. ——, which was equivalent to Ensign —— Thornton. The former, it will at once be seen, was the officer who had been named with so much feeling in the parting dialogue between Judith and Hurry. He was, in truth, the very individual with whom the scandal of the garrisons had most freely connected the name of this beautiful but indiscreet girl. He was a hard-featured, red-faced man of about five-and-thirty, but of a military carriage and with an air of fashion that might easily impose on the imagination of one as ignorant of the world as Judith.

"Craig is covering us with benedictions," observed this person to his young ensign, with an air of indifference, as he shut the glass and handed it to his servant; "to say the truth, not without reason; it is certainly more agreeable to be here in attendance on Miss Judith Hutter than to be burying Indians on a point of the lake, however romantic the position or brilliant the victory. By the way, Wright, is Davis still living?"

"He died about ten minutes since, your Honor," returned the sergeant to whom this question was addressed. "I knew how it would be as soon as I found the bullet had touched

the stomach. I never knew a man who could hold out long, if he had a hole in his stomach."

"No; it is rather inconvenient for carrying away anything very nourishing," observed Warley, gaping. "This being up two nights *de suite*, Arthur, plays the devil with a man's faculties! I'm as stupid as one of those Dutch parsons on the Mohawk—I hope your arm is not painful, my dear boy?"

"It draws a few grimaces from me, sir, as I suppose you see," answered the youth, laughing at the very moment his countenance was a little awry with pain. "But it may be borne. I suppose Graham can spare a few minutes, soon, to look at my hurt."

"She is a lovely creature, this Judith Hutter, after all, Thornton, and it shall not be my fault, if she is not seen and admired in the parks!" resumed Warley, who thought little of his companion's wound. "Your arm, eh! Quite true. Go into the ark, Sergeant, and tell Dr. Graham I desire he would look at Mr. Thornton's injury as soon as he has done with the poor fellow with the broken leg. A lovely creature! And she looked like a queen in that brocade dress in which we met her. I find all changed here; father and mother both gone, the sister dying, if not dead, and none of the family left but the beauty! This has been a lucky expedition all around, and promises to terminate better than Indian skirmishes in general."

"Am I to suppose, sir, that you are about to desert your colors in the great corps of bachelors and close the campaign with matrimony?"

"I, Tom Warley, turn Benedict! Faith, my dear boy, you little know the corps you speak of, if you fancy any such thing. I do suppose there *are* women in the colonies that a captain of light infantry need not disdain, but they are not to be found up here on a mountain lake, or even down on the Dutch river where we are posted. It is true my uncle, the general, once did me the favor to choose a wife for me, in Yorkshire, but she had no beauty—and I would not marry a princess unless she were handsome."

"If handsome, you would marry a beggar?"

"Aye, these are the notions of an ensign! Love in a cottage—doors—and windows—the old story, for the hundredth time. The twenty——th don't *marry*. We are not a marrying corps, my dear boy. There's the colonel, old Sir Edwin ——,

now; though a full general, he has never thought of a wife; and when a man gets as high as a lieutenant general without matrimony, he is pretty safe. Then the lieutenant colonel is *confirmed,* as I tell my cousin, the bishop. The major is a widower, having tried matrimony for twelve months in his youth, and we look upon him now as one of our most certain men. Out of ten captains, but one is in the dilemma, and he, poor devil, is always kept at regimental headquarters, as a sort of *memento mori* to the young men as they join. As for the subalterns, not one has ever yet had the audacity to speak of introducing a wife into the regiment. But your arm is troublesome, and we'll go ourselves and see what has become of Graham."

The surgeon who had accompanied the party was employed very differently from what the captain supposed. When the assault was over, and the dead and wounded were collected, poor Hetty had been found among the latter. A rifle bullet had passed through her body, inflicting an injury that was known at a glance to be mortal. How this wound was received no one knew; it was probably one of those casualties that ever accompany scenes like that related in the previous chapter. The Sumac, all the elderly women, and some of the Huron girls had fallen by the bayonet, either in the confusion of the melee, or from the difficulty of distinguishing the sexes where the dress was so simple. Much the greater portion of the warriors suffered on the spot. A few had escaped, however, and two or three had been taken unharmed. As for the wounded, the bayonet saved the surgeon much trouble. Rivenoak had escaped with life and limb, but was injured and a prisoner. As Captain Warley and his ensign went into the ark, they passed him, seated in dignified silence, in one end of the scow, his head and leg bound, but betraying no visible signs of despondency or despair. That he mourned the loss of his tribe is certain; still, he did it in a manner that best became a warrior and a chief.

The two soldiers found their surgeon in the principal room of the ark. He was just quitting the pallet of Hetty with an expression of sorrowful regret on his hard, pock-marked, Scottish features that it was not usual to see there. All his assiduity had been useless, and he was compelled reluctantly to abandon the expectation of seeing the girl sur-

vive many hours. Dr. Graham was accustomed to deathbed scenes, and ordinarily they produced but little impression on him. In all that relates to religion, his was one of those minds which, in consequence of reasoning much on material things, logically and consecutively, and overlooking the total want of premises which such a theory must ever possess, through its want of a primary agent, had become skeptical; leaving a vague opinion concerning the origin of things, that with high pretensions to philosophy, failed in the first of all philosophical principles, a cause. To him religious dependence appeared a weakness, but when he found one gentle and young like Hetty, with a mind beneath the level of her race, sustained at such a moment by these pious sentiments, and that, too, in a way that many a sturdy warrior and reputed hero might have looked upon with envy, he found himself affected by the sight to a degree that he would have been ashamed to confess. Edinburgh and Aberdeen, then as now, supplied no small portion of the medical men of the British service, and Dr. Graham, as indeed his name and countenance equally indicated, was by birth a North Briton.

"Here is an extraordinary exhibition for a forest, and one but half gifted with reason," he observed, with a decided Scotch accent, as Warley and the ensign entered; "I just hope, gentlemen, that when we three shall be called on to quit the twenty——th, we may be found as resigned to go on the half pay of another existence as this poor demented chiel!"

"Is there no hope that she can survive the hurt?" demanded Warley, turning his eyes toward the pallid Judith, on whose cheeks, however, two large spots of red had settled as soon as he came into the cabin.

"No more than there is for Chairlie Stuart. Approach and judge for yourselves, gentlemen; ye'll see faith exemplified in an exceeding and wonderful manner. There is a sort of *arbitrium* between life and death in actual conflict in the poor girl's mind that renders her an interesting study to a philosopher. Mr. Thornton, I'm at your service now; we can just look at the arm in the next room, while we speculate as much as we please on the operations and sinuosities of the human mind."

The surgeon and ensign retired, and Warley had an opportunity of looking about him more at leisure and with a better

understanding of the nature and feelings of the group collected in the cabin. Poor Hetty had been placed on her own simple bed, and was reclining in a half-seated attitude, with the approaches of death on her countenance, though they were singularly dimmed by the luster of an expression in which all the intelligence of her entire being appeared to be concentrated. Judith and Hist were near her, the former seated in deep grief, the latter standing in readiness to offer any of the gentle attentions of feminine care. Deerslayer stood at the end of the pallet, leaning on Killdeer, unharmed in person; all the fine, martial ardor that had so lately glowed in his countenance having given place to the usual look of honesty and benevolence, qualities of which the expression was now softened by manly regret and pity. The Serpent was in the background of the picture, erect and motionless as a statue, but so observant that not a look of the eye escaped his own keen glance. Hurry completed the group, being seated on a stool near the door, like one who felt himself out of place in such a scene, but who was ashamed to quit it unbidden.

"Who is that in scarlet?" asked Hetty, as soon as the captain's uniform caught her eye. "Tell me, Judith, is it the friend of Hurry?"

" 'Tis the officer who commands the troops that have rescued us all from the hands of the Hurons," was the low answer of the sister.

"Am I rescued, too? I thought they said I was shot, and about to die. Mother is dead, and so is Father; but you are living, Judith, and so is Hurry. I was afraid Hurry would be killed, when I heard him shouting among the soldiers."

"Never mind—never mind, dear Hetty," interrupted Judith, sensitively alive to the preservation of her sister's secret, more, perhaps, at such a moment than at any other. "Hurry is well, and Deerslayer is well, and the Delaware is well, too."

"How came they to shoot a poor girl like me and let so many men go unharmed? I didn't know that the Hurons were so wicked, Judith!"

" 'Twas an accident, poor Hetty; a sad accident it has been! No one would willingly have injured *you*."

"I'm glad of that—I thought it strange: I am feeble-minded, and the red men have never harmed me before. I

should be sorry to think that they had changed their minds. I am glad, too, Judith, that they haven't hurt Hurry. Deerslayer, I don't think God will suffer anyone to harm. It was very fortunate the soldiers came as they did though, for fire *will* burn!"

"It was, indeed, fortunate, my sister; God's holy name be forever blessed for the mercy."

"I daresay, Judith, you know some of the officers; you used to know so many."

Judith made no reply; she hid her face in her hands and groaned. Hetty gazed at her in wonder, but naturally supposing her own situation was the cause of this grief, she kindly offered to console her sister.

"Don't mind me, dear Judith," said the affectionate and pure-hearted creature. "I don't suffer, if I do die; why, Father and Mother are both dead, and what happens to *them* may well happen to *me*. You know I am of less account than any of the family; therefore, few will think of me after I'm in the lake."

"No, no, no—poor, dear, dear Hetty!" exclaimed Judith in an uncontrollable burst of sorrow. "I, at least, will ever think of you, and gladly—oh, how gladly—would I exchange places with you, to be the pure, excellent, sinless creature you are!"

Until now, Captain Warley had stood leaning against the door of the cabin; when this outbreak of feeling, and perchance of penitence, escaped the beautiful girl, he walked slowly and thoughtfully away, even passing the ensign, then suffering under the surgeon's care, without noticing him.

"I have got my Bible here, Judith!" returned her sister in a voice of triumph. "It's true, I can't read any longer; there's something the matter with my eyes—*you* look dim and distant—and so does Hurry, now I look at him; well, I never could have believed that Henry March would have so dull a look. What can be the reason, Judith, that I see so badly today? I, who Mother always said had the best eyes in the whole family. Yes, that was it; my mind was feeble—what people call half-witted—but my eyes were *so* good."

Again Judith groaned; this time no feeling of self, no retrospect of the past, caused the pain. It was the pure, heartfelt sorrow of sisterly love, heightened by a sense of the meek humility and perfect truth of the being before her.

At that moment, she would gladly have given up her own
life to save that of Hetty. As the last, however, was beyond
the reach of human power, she felt there was nothing left
her but sorrow. At this moment Warley returned to the cabin,
drawn by a secret impulse he could not withstand, though he
felt, just then, as if he would gladly abandon the American
continent forever, were it practicable. Instead of pausing at
the door, he now advanced so near the pallet of the sufferer
as to come more plainly within her gaze. Hetty could still
distinguish large objects, and her look soon fastened on him.

"Are you the officer that came with Hurry?" she asked.
"If you are, we ought all to thank you, for though I am
hurt, the rest have saved their lives. Did Harry March tell
you where to find us and how much need there was for your
services?"

"The news of the party reached us by means of a friendly
runner," returned the captain, glad to relieve his feelings by
this appearance of a friendly communication, "and I was
immediately sent out to cut it off. It was fortunate, certainly,
that we met Hurry Harry, as you call him, for he acted as a
guide, and it was not less fortunate that we heard a firing,
which I now understand was merely a shooting at the mark,
for it not only quickened our march but called us to the right
side of the lake. The Delaware saw us on the shore, with
the glass, it would seem, and he and Hist, as I find his squaw
is named, did us excellent service. It was, really, altogether a
fortunate concurrence of circumstances, Judith."

"Talk not to me of anything fortunate, sir," returned the
girl huskily, again concealing her face. "To me the world is
full of misery. I wish never to hear of marks, or rifles, or
soldiers, or *men* again."

"Do you know my sister?" asked Hetty, ere the rebuked
soldier had time to rally for an answer. "How came you to
know that her name is Judith? You are right, for that *is* her
name; and I am Hetty; Thomas Hutter's daughters."

"For Heaven's sake, dearest sister; for *my* sake, beloved
Hetty," interposed Judith imploringly, "say no more of
this."

Hetty looked surprised, but accustomed to comply, she
ceased her awkward and painful interrogatories of Warley,
bending her eyes toward the Bible, which she still held between her hands, as one would cling to a casket of precious

stones in a shipwreck or a conflagration. Her mind now reverted to the future, losing sight, in a great measure, of the scenes of the past.

"We shall not long be parted, Judith," she said; "when *you* die, you must be brought and buried in the lake, by the side of Mother, too."

"Would to God, Hetty, that I lay there at this moment!"

"No, that cannot be, Judith; people must die before they have any right to be buried. 'Twould be wicked to bury you, or for you to bury yourself while living. Once I thought of burying myself; God kept me from that sin."

"You! You, Hetty Hutter, think of such an act?" exclaimed Judith, looking up in uncontrollable surprise, for she well knew nothing passed the lips of her conscientious sister that was not religiously true.

"Yes, I did, Judith, but God has forgotten—no, he *forgets* nothing—but he has *forgiven* it," returned the dying girl, with the subdued manner of a repentant child. " 'Twas after Mother's death; I felt I had lost the best friend I had on earth, if not the *only* friend. 'Tis true, you and Father were kind to me, Judith, but I was so feeble-minded I knew I should only give you trouble; and then you were so often ashamed of such a sister and daughter; and 'tis hard to live in a world where all look upon you as below them. I thought then if I could bury myself by the side of Mother, I should be happier in the lake than in the hut."

"Forgive me—pardon me, dearest Hetty; on my bended knees, I beg you to pardon me, sweet sister, if any word or act of mine drove you to so maddening and cruel a thought."

"Get up, Judith; kneel to God—don't kneel to me. Just so I felt when mother was dying. I remembered everything I had said and done to vex her, and could have kissed her feet for forgiveness. I think it must be so with all dying people, though now I think of it, I don't remember to have had such feelings on account of Father."

Judith arose, hid her face in her apron, and wept. A long pause—one of more than two hours—succeeded, during which Warley entered and left the cabin several times, apparently uneasy when absent and yet unable to remain. He issued various orders, which his men proceeded to execute, and there was an air of movement in the party, more especially as Mr. Craig, the lieutenant, had got through the un-

pleasant duty of burying the dead and had sent for instructions from the shore, desiring to know what he was to do
with his detachment. During this interval, Hetty slept a little, and Deerslayer and Chingachgook left the ark to confer
together. But at the end of the time mentioned, the surgeon
passed upon the platform, and with a degree of feeling his
comrades had never before observed in one of his habits, he
announced that the patient was rapidly drawing near her
end. On receiving this intelligence, the group collected again,
curiosity to witness such a death—or a better feeling—
drawing to the spot men who had so lately been actors in a
scene seemingly of so much greater interest and moment.
By this time Judith had got to be inactive, through grief,
and Hist alone was performing the little offices of feminine
attention that are so appropriate to the sickbed. Hetty herself had undergone no other apparent change than the general failing that indicated the near approach of dissolution.
All that she possessed of mind was as clear as ever, and in
some respects, her intellect was perhaps more than usually
active.

"Don't grieve for me so much, Judith," said the gentle
sufferer, after a pause in her remarks; "I shall soon see
Mother; I think I see her *now;* her face is just as sweet and
smiling as it used to be! Perhaps when I'm dead, God will
give me all my mind, and I shall become a more fitting companion for Mother than I ever was before."

"You will be an angel in heaven, Hetty," sobbed the sister;
"no spirit there will be more worthy of its holy residence!"

"I don't understand it quite; still, I know it must be all
true; I've read it in the Bible. How dark it's becoming! Can
it be night so soon? I can hardly see you at all; where is
Hist?"

"I here, poor girl; why you no see me?"

"I do see you, but I couldn't tell whether 'twas you or
Judith. I believe I shan't see you much longer, Hist."

"Sorry for that, poor Hetty. Never mind; paleface got a
heaven for girl as well as for warrior."

"Where's the Serpent? Let me speak to him; give me his
hand; so; I feel it. Delaware, you will love and cherish this
young Indian woman; I know how fond she is of *you,* and
you must be fond of *her.* Don't treat her as some of your

people treat their wives; be a real husband to her. Now bring Deerslayer near me; give me *his* hand."

This request was complied with, and the hunter stood by the side of the pallet, submitting to the wishes of the girl with the docility of a child.

"I feel, Deerslayer," she resumed, "though I couldn't tell why—but I feel that you and I are not going to part forever. 'Tis a strange feeling! I never had it before; I wonder what it comes from!"

" 'Tis God encouraging you in extremity, Hetty; as such, it ought to be harbored and respected. Yes, we *shall* meet ag'in, though it may be a long time first, and in a far distant land."

"Do you mean to be buried in the lake, too? If so, that may account for the feeling."

" 'Tis little likely, gal, 'tis little likely; but there's a region for Christian souls where there's no lakes nor woods, they say, though why there should be none of the *last* is more than I can account for, seeing that pleasantness and peace is the object in view. My grave will be found in the forest, most likely, but I hope my spirit will not be far from your'n."

"So it must be, then. I am too weak-minded to understand these things, but I *feel* that you and I will meet again. Sister, where are you? I can't see now anything but darkness. It must be night, surely!"

"Oh, Hetty, I am here at your side; these are my arms that are around you," sobbed Judith. "Speak, dearest; is there anything you wish to say, or have done, in this awful moment!"

By this time Hetty's sight had entirely failed her. Nevertheless, death approached with less than usual of its horrors, as if in tenderness to one of her half-endowed faculties. She was pale as a corpse, but her breathing was easy and unbroken, while her voice, though lowered almost to a whisper, remained clear and distinct. When her sister put this question, however, a blush diffused itself over the features of the dying girl, so faint, however, as to be nearly imperceptible, resembling that hue of the rose which is thought to portray the tint of modesty, rather than the dye of the flower in its richer bloom. No one but Judith detected this expression of feeling, one of the gentle expressions of womanly sensibility,

even in death. On her, however, it was not lost, nor did she conceal from herself the cause.

"Hurry is here, dearest Hetty," whispered the sister, with her face so near the sufferer as to keep the words from other ears. "Shall I tell him to come and receive your good wishes?"

A gentle pressure of the hand answered in the affirmative, and then Hurry was brought to the side of the pallet. It is probable that this handsome but rude woodsman had never before found himself so awkwardly placed, though the inclination which Hetty felt for him (a sort of secret yielding to the instincts of nature, rather than any unbecoming impulse of an ill-regulated imagination) was too pure and unobtrusive to have created the slightest suspicion of the circumstance in his mind. He allowed Judith to put his hard, colossal hand between those of Hetty, and stood waiting the result in awkward silence.

"This is Hurry, dearest," whispered Judith, bending over her sister, ashamed to utter the words so as to be audible to herself; "speak to him and let him go."

"What shall I say, Judith?"

"Nay, whatever your own pure spirit teaches, my love. Trust to that, and you need fear nothing."

"Goodbye, Hurry," murmured the girl, with a gentle pressure of his hand. "I wish you would try and be more like Deerslayer."

These words were uttered with difficulty; a faint flush succeeded them for a single instant, then the hand was relinquished, and Hetty turned her face aside as if done with the world. The mysterious feeling that bound her to the young man, a sentiment so gentle as to be almost imperceptible to herself, and which could never have existed at all had her reason possessed more command over her senses, was forever lost in thoughts of a more elevated, though scarcely of a purer character.

"Of what are you thinking, my sweet sister?" whispered Judith; "tell me, that I may aid you at this moment."

"Mother—I see Mother, now, and bright beings around her in the lake. Why isn't Father there? It's odd that I can see Mother when I can't see *you!* Farewell, Judith."

The last words were uttered after a pause, and her sister had hung over her some time in anxious watchfulness before she perceived that the gentle spirit had departed. Thus died

Hetty Hutter, one of those mysterious links between the material and immaterial world, which, while they appear to be deprived of so much that is esteemed and necessary for this state of being, drawn so near to, and offer so beautiful an illustration of, the truth, purity, and simplicity of another.

CHAPTER XXXII

A baron's chylde to be begylde! it were a cursed dede:
To be felawe with an outlawe! Almighty God forbede!
Yea, better were, the poor squyère, alone to forest yede,
Than ye sholde say, another day, that by my cursed dede
Ye were betrayed: wherefore, good mayde, the best rede that I can
Is, that I to the grene wode go, alone, a banyshed man.

NOTBROWNE MAYDE

THE DAY THAT followed proved to be melancholy, though one of much activity. The soldiers, who had so lately been employed in interring their victims, were now called on to bury their own dead. The scene of the morning had left a saddened feeling on all the gentlemen of the party, and the rest felt the influence of a similar sensation, in a variety of ways and from many causes. Hour dragged on after hour until evening arrived, and then came the last melancholy offices in honor of poor Hetty Hutter. Her body was laid in the lake by the side of that of the mother she had so loved and reverenced; the surgeon, though actually an unbeliever, so far complied with the received decencies of life as to read the funeral service over her grave, as he had previously done over those of the other *Christian* slain. It mattered not; that all-seeing eye which reads the heart could not fail to discriminate between the living and the dead, and the gentle soul of the unfortunate girl was already far removed beyond the errors or deceptions of any human ritual. These simple rites, however, were not wholly wanting in suitable accompaniments. The tears of Judith and Hist were shed freely, and Deerslayer gazed upon the limpid water that now flowed over one whose spirit was even purer than its own mountain springs with glistening eyes. Even the Delaware turned aside to conceal his weakness, while the

common men gazed on the ceremony with wondering eyes and chastened feelings.

The business of the day closed with this pious office. By order of the commanding officer, all retired early to rest, for it was intended to begin the march homeward with the return of light. One party, indeed, bearing the wounded, the prisoners, and the trophies, had left the castle in the middle of the day under the guidance of Hurry, intending to reach the fort by shorter marches. It had been landed on the point so often mentioned, or that described in our opening pages, and when the sun set, was already encamped on the brow of the long, broken, and ridgy hills that fell away toward the valley of the Mohawk. The departure of this detachment had greatly simplified the duty of the succeeding day, disencumbering its march of its baggage and wounded and otherwise leaving him who had issued the order greater liberty of action.

Judith held no communication with any but Hist, after the death of her sister, until she retired for the night. Her sorrow had been respected, and both the females had been left with the body, unintruded on to the last moment. The rattling of the drum broke the silence of that tranquil water, and the echoes of the tattoo were heard among the mountains so soon after the ceremony was over as to preclude the danger of interruption. That star which had been the guide of Hist rose on a scene as silent as if the quiet of nature had never yet been disturbed by the labors or passions of man. One solitary sentinel, with his relief, paced the platform throughout the night; and morning was ushered in, as usual, by the martial beat of the reveille.

Military precision succeeded to the desultory proceedings of bordermen, and when a hasty and frugal breakfast was taken, the party began its movement toward the shore with a regularity and order that prevented noise or confusion. Of all the officers, Warley alone remained. Craig headed the detachment in advance, Thornton was with the wounded, and Graham accompanied his patients, as a matter of course. Even the chest of Hutter with all the more valuable of his effects, was borne away, leaving nothing behind that was worth the labor of a removal. Judith was not sorry to see that the captain respected her feelings and that he occupied himself entirely with the duty of his command, leav-

ing her to her own discretion and feelings. It was understood by all that the place was to be totally abandoned, but beyond this, no explanations were asked or given.

The soldiers embarked in the ark, with the captain at their head. He had inquired of Judith in what way she chose to proceed, and understanding her wish to remain with Hist to the last moment, he neither molested her with requests nor offended her with advice. There was but one safe and familiar trail to the Mohawk, and on that, at the proper hour, he doubted not that they should meet in amity, if not in renewed intercourse.

When all were on board, the sweeps were manned, and the ark moved in its sluggish manner toward the distant point. Deerslayer and Chingachgook now lifted two of the canoes from the water and placed them in the castle. The windows and door were then barred, and the house was left, by means of the trap, in the manner already described. On quitting the palisades, Hist was seen in the remaining canoe, where the Delaware immediately joined her, and paddled away, leaving Judith standing alone on the platform. Owing to this prompt proceeding Deerslayer found himself alone with the beautiful and still weeping mourner. Too simple to suspect anything, the young man swept the light boat around and received its mistress in it, when he followed the course already taken by his friend.

The direction to the point led diagonally past, and at no great distance from, the graves of the dead. As the canoe glided by, Judith, for the first time that morning, spoke to her companion. She said but little, merely uttering a simple request to stop for a minute or two, ere she left the place.

"I may never see this spot again, Deerslayer," she said, "and it contains the bodies of my mother and sister! Is it not possible, think you, that the innocence of one of these beings may answer in the eyes of God for the salvation of both?"

"I don't understand it so, Judith, though I'm no missionary and am but poorly taught. Each spirit answers for its own backslidings, though a hearty repentance will satisfy God's laws."

"Then *must* my poor, poor mother, be in heaven!—bitterly —bitterly—has she repented of her sins. Surely her sufferings

in this life ought to count as something against her sufferings in the next!"

"All this goes beyond me, Judith. I strive to do right, here, as the surest means of keeping all right, hereafter. Hetty was oncommon, as all that know'd her must allow, and her soul was as fit to consort with angels the hour it left its body as that of any saint in the Bible!"

"I do believe you only do her justice! Alas! Alas! That there should be so great differences between those who were nursed at the same breast, slept in the same bed, and dwelt under the same roof! But, no matter—move the canoe a little further east, Deerslayer—the sun so dazzles my eyes that I cannot see the graves. This is Hetty's, on the right of Mother's?"

"Sartain—you asked that of us; and all are glad to do as you wish, Judith, when you do that which is right."

The girl gazed at him near a minute in silent attention; then she turned her eyes backward, at the castle.

"This lake will soon be entirely deserted," she said, "and this, too, at a moment when it will be a more secure dwelling place than ever. What has so lately happened will prevent the Iroquois from venturing again to visit it for a long time to come."

"That it will! Yes, that may be set down as settled. I do not mean to pass thisaway ag'in so long as the war lasts, for to my mind, no Huron moccasin will leave its print on the leaves of this forest until their traditions have forgotten to tell their young men of their disgrace and rout."

"And do you so delight in violence and bloodshed? I had thought better of you, Deerslayer—believed you one who could find his happiness in a quiet domestic home, with an attached and loving wife ready to study your wishes, and healthy and dutiful children anxious to follow in your footsteps and to become as honest and just as yourself."

"Lord, Judith, what a tongue you're mistress of! Speech and looks go hand in hand, like, and what one can't do, the other is pretty sartain to perform! Such a gal, in a month, might spoil the stoutest warrior in the Colony."

"And am I then so mistaken? Do you really love war, Deerslayer, better than the hearth and the affections?"

"I understand your meaning, gal; yes, I do understand what you mean, I believe, though I don't think you alto-

gether understand *me*. Warrior I may now call myself, I suppose, for I've both fou't and conquered, which is sufficient for the name; neither will I deny that I've feelin's for the callin', which is both manful and honorable, when carried on accordin' to nat'ral gifts—but I've no relish for blood. Youth is youth, howsever, and a Mingo is a Mingo. If the young men of this region stood by and suffered the vagabonds to overrun the land, why, we might as well all turn Frenchers at once and give up country and kin. I'm no fire-eater, Judith, or one that likes fightin' for fightin's sake, but I can see no great difference atween *givin' up territory afore a war, out of a dread of war, and givin' it up a'ter a war because we can't help it—onless it be that the last is the most manful and honorable.*"

"No woman would ever wish to see her husband or brother stand by and submit to insult and wrong, Deerslayer, however she might mourn the necessity of his running into the dangers of battle. But you've done enough already in clearing this region of the Hurons, since to you is principally owing the credit of our late victory. Now, listen to me patiently, and answer me with that native honesty which it is as pleasant to regard in one of your sex as it is unusual to meet with."

Judith paused, for now that she was on the very point of explaining herself, native modesty asserted its power, notwithstanding the encouragement and confidence she derived from the great simplicity of her companion's character. Her cheeks, which had so lately been pale, flushed, and her eyes lighted with some of their former brilliancy. Feeling gave expression to her countenance and softness to her voice, rendering her who was always beautiful trebly seductive and winning.

"Deerslayer," she said after a considerable pause, "this is not a moment for affectation, deception, or a want of frankness of any sort. Here, over my mother's grave, and over the grave of truth-loving, truth-telling Hetty, everything like unfair dealing seems to be out of place. I will therefore speak to you without any reserve and without any dread of being misunderstood. You are not an acquaintance of a week, but it appears to me as if I had known you for years. So much, and so much that is important, has taken place within that short time that the sorrows, and dan-

gers, and escapes of a whole life have been crowded into a few days; they who have suffered and acted together in such scenes ought not to feel like strangers. I know that what I am about to say might be misunderstood by most men, but I hope for a generous construction of my course from you. We are not here dwelling among the arts and deceptions of the settlements, but young people who have no occasion to deceive each other, in any manner or form. I hope I make myself understood?"

"Sartain, Judith; few converse better than yourself, and none more agreeable, like. Your words are as pleasant as your looks."

"It is the manner in which you have so often praised those looks that gives me courage to proceed. Still, Deerslayer, it is not easy for one of my sex and years to forget all her lessons of infancy, all her habits, and her natural diffidence, and say openly what her heart feels!"

"Why not, Judith? Why shouldn't women as well as men deal fairly and honestly by their fellow creatur's? I see no reason why you should not speak as plainly as myself, when there is anything ra'ally important to be said."

This indomitable diffidence, which still prevented the young man from suspecting the truth, would have completely discouraged the girl had not her whole soul, as well as her whole heart, been set upon making a desperate effort to rescue herself from a future that she dreaded with a horror as vivid as the distinctness with which she fancied she foresaw it. This motive, however, raised her above all common considerations, and she persevered even to her own surprise, if not to her great confusion.

"I will—I *must* deal as plainly with you as I would with poor, dear Hetty, were that sweet child living!" she continued, turning pale, instead of blushing, the high resolution by which she was prompted reversing the effect that such a procedure would ordinarily produce on one of her sex; "yes, I will smother all other feelings in the one that is now uppermost! You love the woods and the life that we pass here, in the wilderness, away from the dwellings and towns of the whites."

"As I loved my parents, Judith, when they was living! This very spot would be all creation to me, could this war be fairly over once, and the settlers kept at a distance."

"Why quit it, then? It has no owner—at least none
who can claim a better right than mine, and *that* I freely
give to you. Were it a kingdom, Deerslayer, I think I should
delight to say the same. Let us then return to it, after we
have seen the priest at the fort, and never quit it again, until
God calls us away to that world where we shall find the
spirits of my poor mother and sister."

A long, thoughtful pause succeeded, Judith having covered her face with both her hands after forcing herself to
utter so plain a proposal, and Deerslayer musing equally in
sorrow and surprise on the meaning of the language he had
just heard. At length the hunter broke the silence, speaking in
a tone that was softened to gentleness by his desire not to
offend.

"You haven't thought well of this, Judith," he said; "no,
your feelin's are awakened by all that has lately happened,
and believin' yourself to be without kindred in the world,
you are in too great haste to find some to fill the places of
them that's lost."

"Were I living in a crowd of friends, Deerslayer, I should
still think as I now think, say as I now say," returned Judith,
speaking with her hands still shading her lovely face.

"Thank you, gal—thank you, from the bottom of my heart.
Howsever, I am not one to take advantage of a weak moment, when you're forgetful of your own great advantages,
and fancy 'arth and all it holds is in this little canoe. No—
no—Judith, 'twould be onginerous in me; what you've offered can never come to pass!"

"It all may be, and that without leaving cause of repentance to any," answered Judith, with an impetuosity of
feeling and manner that at once unveiled her eyes. "We
can cause the soldiers to leave our goods on the road till
we return, when they can easily be brought back to the
house; the lake will be no more visited by the enemy, this
war at least; all your skins may be readily sold at the garrison; there *you* can buy the few necessaries we shall want,
for I wish never to see the spot again; and Deerslayer,"
added the girl, smiling with a sweetness and nature that
the young man found it hard to resist, "as a proof how
wholly I am and wish to be yours—how completely I desire to be nothing but your wife—the very first fire that we
kindle after our return shall be lighted with the brocade

dress and fed by every article I have that you may think unfit for the woman you wish to live with!"

"Ah's me! You're a winning and a lovely creatur', Judith; yes, you *are* all that, and no one can deny it and speak truth. These pictur's are pleasant to the thoughts, but they mightn't prove so happy as you now think 'em. Forget it all, therefore, and let us paddle after the Sarpent and Hist, as if nothing had been said on the subject."

Judith was deeply mortified, and what is more, she was profoundly grieved. Still, there was a steadiness and quiet in the manner of Deerslayer, that completely smothered her hopes, and told her that for once, her exceeding beauty had failed to excite the admiration and homage it was wont to receive. Women are said seldom to forgive those who slight their advances, but this high-spirited and impetuous girl entertained no shadow of resentment, then or ever, against the fair-dealing and ingenuous hunter. At the moment, the prevailing feeling was the wish to be certain that there was no misunderstanding. After another painful pause, therefore, she brought the matter to an issue by a question too direct to admit of equivocation.

"God forbid that we lay up regrets in afterlife through any want of sincerity now," she said. "I hope we understand each other at least. You will not accept me for a wife, Deerslayer?"

" 'Tis better for both that I shouldn't take advantage of your own forgetfulness, Judith. We can never marry."

"You do not love me—cannot find it in your heart, perhaps, to esteem me, Deerslayer!"

"Everything in the way of fri'ndship, Judith—everything, even to sarvices and life itself. Yes, I'd risk as much for you, at this moment, as I would risk in behalf of Hist, and that is sayin' as much as I can say of any darter of woman. I do not think I feel toward either—mind I say *either*, Judith—as if I wished to quit Father and Mother—if Father and Mother was livin'; which, however, neither is—but if both was livin', I do not feel toward any woman as if I wish'd to quit 'em in order to cleave unto *her*."

"This is enough!" answered Judith in a rebuked and smothered voice; "I understand all that you mean. Marry you cannot, without loving, and that love you do not feel for me. Make no answer if I am right, for I shall under-

stand your silence. *That* will be painful enough of itself."

Deerslayer obeyed her, and he made no reply. For more than a minute the girl riveted her bright eyes on him as if to read his soul, while he sat playing with the water, like a corrected schoolboy. Then Judith herself dropped the end of her paddle and urged the canoe away from the spot with a movement as reluctant as the feelings which controlled it. Deerslayer quietly aided the effort, however, and they were soon on the trackless line taken by the Delaware.

In their way to the point, not another syllable was exchanged between Deerslayer and his fair companion. As Judith sat in the bow of the canoe, her back was turned toward him, else it is probable the expression of her countenance might have induced him to venture some soothing terms of friendship and regard. Contrary to what would have been expected, resentment was still absent, though the color frequently changed from the deep flush of mortification to the paleness of disappointment. Sorrow, deep, heartfelt sorrow, however, was the predominant emotion, and this was betrayed in a manner not to be mistaken.

As neither labored hard at the paddle, the ark had already arrived, and the soldiers had disembarked before the canoe of the two loiterers reached the point. Chingachgook had preceded it, and was already some distance in the wood, at a spot where the two trails, that to the garrison and that to the villages of the Delawares, separated. The soldiers, too, had taken up their line of march, first setting the ark adrift again, with a reckless disregard of its fate. All this Judith saw, but she heeded it not. The Glimmerglass had no longer any charms for her, and when she put her foot on the strand, she immediately proceeded on the trail of the soldiers without casting a single glance behind her. Even Hist was passed unnoticed, that modest young creature shrinking from the averted face of Judith, as if guilty herself of some wrongdoing.

"Wait you here, Sarpent," said Deerslayer as he followed in the footsteps of the dejected beauty, while passing his friend. "I will just see Judith among her party and come and j'ine you."

A hundred yards had hid the couple from those in front, as well as those in the rear, when Judith turned and spoke.

"This will do, Deerslayer," she said sadly. "I understand

your kindness, but shall not need it. In a few minutes I shall reach the soldiers. As you cannot go with me on the journey of life, I do not wish you to go further on this. But stop; before we part, I would ask you a single question. And I require of you as you fear God and reverence the truth not to deceive me in your answer. I know you do not love another, and I can see but one reason why you cannot, *will* not love me. Tell me, then, Deerslayer"—the girl paused, the words she was about to utter seeming to choke her; then, rallying all her resolution, with a face that flushed and paled at every breath she drew, she continued—"tell me, then, Deerslayer, if anything light of me that Henry March has said may not have influenced your feelings?"

Truth was the Deerslayer's polar star. He ever kept it in view, and it was nearly impossible for him to avoid uttering it, even when prudence demanded silence. Judith read his answer in his countenance, and with a heart nearly broken by the consciousness of undeserving, she signed to him an adieu and buried herself in the woods. For some time Deerslayer was irresolute as to his course, but in the end he retraced his steps and joined the Delaware. That night the three "camped" on the headwaters of their own river, and the succeeding evening they entered the village of the tribe, Chingachgook and his betrothed in triumph, their companion honored and admired but in a sorrow that it required months of activity to remove.

The war that then had its rise was stirring and bloody. The Delaware chief rose among his people until his name was never mentioned without eulogiums, while another Uncas, the last of his race, was added to the long line of warriors who bore that distinguished appellation. As for the Deerslayer, under the sobriquet of Hawkeye, he made his fame spread far and near, until the crack of his rifle became as terrible to the ears of the Mingos as the thunders of the Manitou. His services were soon required by the officers of the crown, and he especially attached himself in the field to one in particular, with whose afterlife he had a close and important connection.

Fifteen years had passed away, ere it was in the power of the Deerslayer to revisit the Glimmerglass. A peace had intervened, and it was on the eve of another, and still more important war, when he and his constant friend, Chingachgook,

were hastening to the forts to join their allies. A stripling accompanied them, for Hist already slumbered beneath the pines of the Delawares, and the three survivors had now become inseparable. They reached the lake just as the sun was setting. Here all was unchanged; the river still rushed through its bower of trees; the little rock was wasting away by the slow action of the waves in the course of centuries; the mountains stood in their native dress, dark, rich, and mysterious; while the sheet glistened in its solitude, a beautiful gem of the forest.

The following morning the youth discovered one of the canoes drifted on the shore in a state of decay. A little labor put it in a state for service, and they all embarked with a desire to examine the place. All the points were passed, and Chingachgook pointed out to his son the spot where the Hurons had first encamped and the point whence he had succeeded in stealing his bride. Here they even landed, but all traces of the former visit had disappeared. Next they proceeded to the scene of the battle, and there they found a few of the signs that linger around such localities. Wild beasts had disinterred many of the bodies, and human bones were bleaching in the rains of summer. Uncas regarded all with reverence and pity, though traditions were already rousing his young mind to the ambition and sternness of a warrior.

From the point, the canoe took its way toward the shoal, where the remains of the castle were still visible, a picturesque ruin. The storms of winter had long since unroofed the house, and decay had eaten into the logs. All the fastenings were untouched, but the seasons rioted in the place, as if in mockery at the attempt to exclude them. The palisades were rotting, as were the piles, and it was evident that a few more recurrences of winter, a few more gales and tempests, would sweep all into the lake and blot the building from the face of that magnificent solitude. The graves could not be found. Either the elements had obliterated their traces, or time had caused those who looked for them to forget their position.

The ark was discovered stranded on the eastern shore, where it had long before been driven, with the prevalent northwest winds. It lay on the sandy extremity of a long, low point that is situated about two miles from the outlet,

and which is itself fast disappearing before the action of the elements. The scow was filled with water, the cabin unroofed, and the logs were decaying. Some of its coarser furniture still remained, and the heart of Deerslayer beat quick as he found a ribbon of Judith's fluttering from a log. It recalled all her beauty and, we may add, all her failings. Although the girl had never touched his heart, the Hawkeye, for so we ought now to call him, still retained a kind and sincere interest in her welfare. He tore away the ribbon and knotted it to the stock of Killdeer, which had been the gift of the girl herself.

A few miles farther up the lake another of the canoes was discovered, and on the point where the party finally landed were found those which had been left there upon the shore. That in which the present navigation was made, and the one discovered on the eastern shore, had dropped through the decayed floor of the castle, drifted past the falling palisades, and had been thrown as waifs upon the beach.

From all these signs, it was probable the lake had not been visited since the occurrence of the final scene of our tale. Accident or tradition had rendered it again a spot sacred to nature, the frequent wars and the feeble population of the colonies still confining the settlements within narrow boundaries. Chingachgook and his friend left the spot with melancholy feelings. It had been the region of their first warpath, and it carried back the minds of both to scenes of tenderness as well as to hours of triumph. They held their way toward the Mohawk in silence, however, to rush into new adventures as stirring and as remarkable as those which had attended their opening career on this lovely lake. At a later day they returned to the place, where the Indian found a grave.

Time and circumstances have drawn an impenetrable mystery around all else connected with the Hutters. They lived, erred, died, and are forgotten. None connected had felt sufficient interest in the disgraced and disgracing to withdraw the veil, and a century is about to erase even the recollection of their names. The history of crime is ever revolting, and it is fortunate that few love to dwell on its incidents. The sins of the family have long since been arraigned at the judgment seat of God, or are registered for the terrible settlement of the last great day.

The same fate attended Judith. When Hawkeye reached the garrison on the Mohawk, he inquired anxiously after that lovely but misguided creature. None knew her—even her person was no longer remembered. Other officers had again and again succeeded the Warleys and Craigs and Grahams, though an old sergeant of the garrison, who had lately come from England, was enabled to tell our hero that Sir Robert Warley lived on his paternal estates and that there was a lady of rare beauty in the lodge who had great influence over him, though she did not bear his name. Whether this was Judith, relapsed into her early failing, or some other victim of the soldier's, Hawkeye never knew, nor would it be pleasant or profitable to inquire. We live in a world of transgressions and selfishness, and no pictures that represent us otherwise can be true, though, happily for human nature, gleamings of that pure spirit in whose likeness man has been fashioned are to be seen, relieving its deformities and mitigating if not excusing its crimes.

AFTERWORD

Every eminent novelist has the power of varying his themes and of producing masterworks in a variety of moods. James Fenimore Cooper is no exception. Critics sometimes speak carelessly of his famous quintet of Leatherstocking Tales as if each book were part of a unitary whole. The fact is that although the five novels are bound together by the personality of Leatherstocking (alias Deerslayer, Hawkeye, and Natty Bumppo), and although in four of the five the conflict of red man with white furnishes most of the action, the books differ widely in scene, spirit, and incident.

The Deerslayer is as much the most romantic of Cooper's narratives of the American frontier as *Rob Roy* is the most romantic of Walter Scott's tales of the Scottish border; in Leatherstocking, Chingachgook, the former pirate Tom Hutter, the Indian Rivenoak, and the spirited Judith Hutter, Cooper offers a group of characters as memorable as the captivating girl Di Vernon, the dashing outlaw Rob Roy, and the delightfully canny Baillie Nicol Jarvie in Scott's immortal work. Both books are linked with history: *The Deerslayer* with events in the province of New York 1740-1745, *Rob Roy* more directly with the Jacobite insurrection of 1715 and the ensuing repressions. In both we have sharp contrasts between human groups; Cooper painted the warfare of savages and settlers, Scott the collisions of Highlanders and Lowlanders. In both, nature plays a central role, and Cooper did nearly as well by Lake Otsego and its wild surroundings as Scott did by Loch Lomond and the craggy Highlands.

It is easy to understand why *The Deerslayer* was Cooper's own favorite among the Leatherstocking Tales. It is distinguished not only by its romantic (at times melodramatic) quality and its range of character studies, but by other merits: its success in catching the freshness of youth in Leatherstocking and Chingachgook, here shown at the beginning of their careers; the quaint passages of philosophic musing that Cooper puts into Leatherstocking's mouth; the vivid painting

of scenes on and about the lake where he had spent so much
of his boyhood; and the masterly handling of suspense, so
that interest never flags. The book is not so poetic as *The
Prairie,* which deals with Leatherstocking's old age; it offers
no such realistic study of life and manners in a frontier setting,
as does *The Pioneers;* it is less closely woven into the texture
of colonial history than *The Last of the Mohicans;* but it
enacts the most rapid drama of all Cooper's tales.

Unquestionably Cooper was still near the height of his
powers when he published *The Deerslayer.* As early as 1821,
when he wrote *The Spy,* the first American novel with qualities of real greatness, he had proved his ability to create a
striking character and to tell a stirring story. In the next half
dozen years he had executed his best work in *The Pilot*—the
first true sea novel ever written—*The Pioneers, The Last of
the Mohicans,* and *The Prairie.* Then, his first three Leatherstocking books done, he turned to other themes than the
forest, the Indian, and the ambush. He went abroad; he
became interested in social controversy; he involved himself
in suits over lands and libels; he even made foolish forays into
satire. His best work in this period lay in such naval stories as
The Two Admirals. Then with renewed inspiration he unexpectedly brought out *The Pathfinder* and *The Deerslayer*
in 1840-41.

It was remarkable that after so long an interval Cooper
should return with unabated gusto to the fortunes of Leatherstocking and Chingachgook. In so doing he proved that the
true home of his romantic instincts was not the ocean and
not such semihistorical episodes as those of *Mercedes of
Castile,* but the forest. It is a little hard for readers of *The
Deerslayer* to follow such critics as Carl Van Doren when
they speak of the woods as a romantic sanctuary, a temple
breathing holy calm, and a teacher of peace, virtue, and
order. In these pages the wilderness seems to me full of
treachery, peril, and battle. Its recesses attract outlaws like
Tom Hutter and brute adventurers like the scalp-hunter
Hurry Harry; its thickets afford lurking places for vindictive,
bloody-minded savages. But Cooper loved the beauty and
sublimity of the scenes he describes in his opening paragraphs,
when a bird's-eye view of the whole region east of the Mississippi presented one vast expanse of greenery, dotted in its
"solemn solitude" by glittering lakes and intersected by

wandering river lines. He puts his feeling into a speech that Leatherstocking directs at Judith Hutter.

> As for farms, they have their uses, and there's them that like to pass their lives on 'em; but what comfort can a man look for in a clearin' that he can't find in double quantities in the forest? If air, and room, and light are a little craved, the windrows and the streams will furnish 'em, or here are the lakes for such as have bigger longings in that way; but where are you to find your shades, and laughing springs, and leaping brooks, and vinerable trees, a thousand years old, in a clearin'? Then as to churches, they are good, I suppose . . . but Judith, the whole arth is a temple of the Lord to such as have the right mind.

It was remarkable also that Cooper, in the enterprise of recreating Leatherstocking in youth after already having depicted him in prime manhood and in old age, should succeed so well in harmonizing the early and the later appearances of his hero. At practically every point the young man is consistent with the central figure of the later tales; as consistent, at least, as any man of twenty-three can be with himself at forty and at seventy. We see here the same true-minded, open-hearted, generous personage that we meet later—a good deal more naïve and more candidly talkative, as he ought to be. Though this prologue to the other four books has a freshness and liveliness all its own, it blends harmoniously with them. The youthful Leatherstocking who so hotly denounces the red followers of Rivenoak ("a venomous set of riptyles") for their cunning ferocity is the same man who in *The Last of the Mohicans* fiercely denounces Montcalm for permitting the massacre of helpless British prisoners at Fort William Henry.

At the same time Cooper here enlarges our conception of Leatherstocking. The young man is fresh from the influence of the Moravian missionaries; they have confirmed his natural piety, humanity, and sense of justice; and in his lament over the first foe he has had to kill we feel a genuine grief. It is a true idealist who utters a sad soliloquy as he straightens the limbs of the Indian who had attempted to put a bullet in his back.

"I didn't wish your life, redskin," he said, "but you left me no choice between killing or being killed. Each party acted

according to his gifts, I suppose, and blame can light on neither. You were treacherous, according to your natur' in war, and I was a little oversightful, as I'm apt to be in trusting others. Well, this is my first battle with a human mortal . . . . I have fou't most of the creatur's of the forest, such as bears, wolves, painters, and catamounts, but this is the beginning with the redskins . . . . And why should I wish to boast of it a'ter all? It's slaying a human, although he was a savage; and how do I know that he was a just Injin, and that he has not been taken away suddenly to anything but happy hunting grounds?"

An equal impression of idealism and moral depth springs from Leatherstocking's short disquisitions on a future life, in which he devoutly believes; on the relativity of ethics—"A white man's gifts are Christianized, while a redskin's are more for the wilderness"; and on the superiority of God's law to that of King and Parliament: whenever they come into conflict, then man-made laws "get to be onlawful, and ought not to be obeyed." Leatherstocking has worked out his own philosophy, too, on the relations of man and woman, as he shows in his heart-to-heart talk with Judith when he rejects her virtual proposal of marriage; they are unsuited to each other, he declares, and that ends the matter. He is a little in love with Wah-ta!-Wah, the lovely girl pledged to Chingachgook, but he puts all thought of her aside in justice to his friend and to his ideas of racial purity.

One pre-eminent merit of *The Deerslayer* lies in the originality and skill of Cooper's plot. It is essentially simple, never confusing the reader, but it suffices to furnish a tightly woven narrative full of variety, color, and unexpected turns. Never do we meet a violation of probability like several that mar *The Last of the Mohicans*. It is true that Mark Twain carped at one initial scene in *The Deerslayer*, the escape of Hutter's ark from the Indian-beset tributary of Lake Otsego in which it had been moored. But Clemens forgot that Cooper described the stream as one with a swift current, and the Indians had but an uncertain means of dropping aboard. Taken in all its major parts, the story claims our faith.

And what a story it is! Certainly Cooper had one of his best inspirations when he invented in Hutter a refugee from law and order, a miscreant with a terrible past to conceal, who has immured himself and his two motherless daughters in a castle built on a shoal in the deep waters of Lake Otsego, with

an attendant ark to communicate at need with the almost trackless shores. It was a logical second step to bring Leatherstocking upon the scene just as hostile Indians, the Mingoes, made an encampment upon the lake's shore. And it was a triumph of romantic imagination to make the purpose of Leatherstocking's visit a rendezvous with Chingachgook, a Delaware chieftain and his closest friend, who was in hot pursuit of the Mingoes who had kidnapped his sweetheart.

The plot provides a well-varied conflict of whites and Indians in a natural setting of exceptional picturesqueness. It provides also, in its dramatis personae, a wealth of contrasts. They include the contrast between Hutter's beautiful and strong-minded but reputedly wanton daughter, Judith, and her pure but half-witted sister, Hetty; the contrast between the Christian rectitude and pacifism of Leatherstocking and the pagan ruthlessness of Hurry, anxious only to take Mingo scalps while keeping his own; the contrast between the two Indians who throw their strong energies into the action—Chingachgook, fearless, determined, and sleeplessly alert, but reluctant to kill, and Rivenoak, an embodiment of Indian fiendishness at its worst. In the background we dimly discern two still larger contrasts: that between the untouched wilderness and the onset of civilization represented by settlers, hunters, and a garrison of troops, and the contrast between British and French civilizations as the rival powers struggle for mastery of the continent.

In no other book does Cooper so dexterously maintain suspense as in *The Deerslayer*, nor is all the suspense warlike. Interest is never keener than when Judith, Leatherstocking, and Chingachgook open Thomas Hutter's mysterious chest and find not only his treasures but further proofs of his former life on the far side of the law. The two love stories, Judith's ill-omened attachment for Leatherstocking and Chingachgook's ultimately successful passion for Wah-ta!-Wah, add a somewhat tame suspense of a special sort; love was never Cooper's forte. But the final events carry interest to a breathless point. Our only regret is that it should be broken, and the tale ended, by a rather disappointing *deus ex machina*, the arrival of a powerful body of redcoats just as knives have been sharpened and wood lighted for the final phase of Leatherstocking's torture.

The Deerslayer throws special light on two charges often brought against Cooper's handling of his materials and does

much to strengthen his position against them. Both require notice, but both may be summarily dismissed.

One charge is that Cooper's presentation of the Indians and Indian life is at once superficial and excessively favorable, that he popularized that romantic view of the noble red man violently denounced by Theodore Roosevelt in *The Winning of the West*. The fact is that Cooper never pretended to give a realistic, and still less a scientific, depiction of the aborigines. He knew that some of them *were* men of noble character—as noble as Massasoit or Logan or Chief Joseph; he knew that others, and especially those corrupted or embittered by white men, had the devilish traits depicted in some of the Mingoes. Cooper had never lived with the Indians, nor studied the lore accumulated by men who knew them well, nor explored the rudiments of the science of ethnology. As a writer of romance, he naturally made his good Indians all too good and his bad Indians all too bad. His real weakness was that he rendered them figures of melodrama, not of the real world. He never even studied the subject historically, so that he gives a highly distorted view of the respective roles played by the Algonquin (Delaware) and the Iroquois (Mingo) tribes in our colonial history.

His view was that which he put into the words of Wah-ta!-Wah: "Mingo is cruel and loves scalp for blood—Delaware love him for honor." On the side he presents the honest, chivalrous, humane Chingachgook and Uncas, and on the other Satanic types whose sadistic cruelties freeze the blood. Their clash sometimes give birth to melodrama that almost equals the wild stories by Charles Brockden Brown, and surpasses the extravagance of Richard Montgomery Bird's *Nick o' the Woods*—to cite only our early novels.

The Indian has been so generally maligned that Cooper performed a real service in his presentation of Chingachgook and Uncas, who had their counterparts in many tribes. He must also be credited with a just appreciation of two great Indian superiorities, to which he was the first widely-read author to do justice. He comprehended the remarkable gift of eloquence possessed by some red leaders, and in *The Deerslayer* and several other novels he gives us memorable examples. He understood also that while the Indian was inferior to the white frontiersman in markmanship and in the use of most of the white man's other tools, he was far superior in

woodcraft. He could read the clouds, he could spell the meaning of a bent twig, he could understand the nature of wild bird and beast, with a precision impossible to any civilized rival.

The other charge most frequently brought against Cooper, that he was unable to depict a true woman and gave his readers colorless, namby-pamby heroines instead of the resourceful, intrepid women and daughters of our real frontier, gains credence from his weaker novels. It is forcefully refuted by *The Deerslayer*, however, and a single reading of that book throws it out of court. Cooper's gentlefolk were likely to be insipid. Judith Hutter, however, no more belonged to the gentlefolk than Leatherstocking himself, and in every critical situation she shows force of character and decision. She is mistress of the castle and the ark; she hesitates not a second when an Indian raider has to be pushed off the boat to drown; she loses neither nerve nor hope when pursued across Lake Otsego by another canoe sped by lusty savages. We may well believe that the hints of loose conduct given currency by Hurry were slanders born of his chagrin when she refuses him. Her protection of her weak-minded sister, her influence over her father, her true womanliness in her conversations with Leatherstocking—all these instances and more do her credit. She has her faults, but lack of strength, enterprise, and vigor were not among them.

But even Judith is surpassed, in courage, steadfastness, and above all in energy of speech, by the true heroine of the novel, Wah-ta!-Wah, or Hist. The two most impassioned pieces of eloquence in the volume are Hist's excoriation of Hurry Harry for his needless slaying of a Huron girl and her spirited repudiation of any idea that she might leave her own people for a union with a Mingo brave. Of this latter speech Leatherstocking justly observed: "That's worth all the wampum in the woods."

It is a rich, an intensely exciting, and, despite its patches of theatricality, an elevating romance that Cooper has given us in *The Deerslayer;* the story of an America now so far lost in time and change that it is hard to believe it ever existed. But it did exist, and some memory of it, in our all too artificial day, ought to be cherished by the nation.

Allan Nevins

The Huntington Library

SELECTED BIBLIOGRAPHY

Other Works by James Fenimore Cooper

The Spy, 1821   Novel
The Pioneers, 1823   Novel
The Pilot, 1824   Novel
The Last of the Mohicans, 1826   Novel (Signet Classic 148)
The Prairie, 1827   Novel
The Red Rover, 1827   Novel
Notions of the Americans, 1828   Social Criticism
The Bravo, 1831   Novel
The Monikins, 1835   Satire
Sketches of Switzerland, Parts I and II, 1836   Travel
Gleanings in Europe (England, France, Italy), 1837-38
  Travel
The American Democrat, 1838   Social Criticism
Homeward Bound, 1838   Novel
Home as Found, 1838   Novel
The History of the Navy of the United States of America,
  1839
The Pathfinder, 1840   Novel (Signet CP88)
The Wing-and-Wing, 1842   Novel
Wyandotte, 1843   Novel
Afloat and Ashore, 1844   Novel
Satanstoe, 1845   Novel
The Chainbearer, 1845,   Novel
The Redskins, 1846   Novel
The Crater, 1847   Novel
The Oak Openings, 1848   Novel
The Sea Lions, 1849   Novel
The Ways of the Hour, 1850   Novel

Selected Biography and Criticism

Beard, James Franklin (ed.). *The Letters and Journals of James Fenimore Cooper*. 2 vols. Cambridge, Mass.: Harvard University Press; London: Oxford University Press, 1960.

Boynton, Henry W. *James Fenimore Cooper*. New York and London: D. Appleton-Century Co., 1931.

Cooper, James Fenimore (grandson of the novelist) (ed.). *Correspondence of James Fenimore Cooper*. New Haven, Conn.: Yale University Press, 1922.

Cunningham, Mary E. (ed.). *James Fenimore Cooper: A Reappraisal*. Cooperstown, N. Y.: New York State Historical Association, 1954.

Dondore, Dorothy Anne. *The Prairie and the Making of Middle America: Four Centuries of Description*. Cedar Rapids, Iowa: The Torch Press, 1926.

Grossman, James. *James Fenimore Cooper*. New York: William Sloane Associates, Inc.; London: Methuen & Co., Ltd., 1949.

Hazard, Lucy Lockwood. *The Frontier in American Literature*. New York: Thomas Y. Crowell Co., 1927; New York: Barnes & Noble, Inc., 1941.

Leisy, Ernest E. *The American Historical Novel*. Norman, Okla.: University of Oklahoma Press, 1950.

Lounsbury, Thomas R. *James Fenimore Cooper* (American Men of Letters Series). Boston: Houghton Mifflin & Co., 1882.

Outland, Ethel R. *The Effingham Libels on Cooper*. Madison, Wisc.: University of Wisconsin Press, 1929.

Parrington, Vernon L. *Main Currents in American Thought*. 3 vols. New York: Harcourt, Brace & Co., 1927.

Ross, John F. *The Social Criticism of Fenimore Cooper*. Berkeley, Calif.: University of California Press, 1933.

Rourke, Constance. *American Humor*. New York: Harcourt, Brace & Co., 1931.

Spiller, Robert E., and others. *Literary History of the United States*. 3 vols. New York and London: The Macmillan Company, 1948.

————, *Fenimore Cooper: Critic of His Time*. New York: Minton, Balch & Co.; London: G. P. Putnam's Sons, 1931.

Van Doren, Carl. *The American Novel*. New York: The Macmillan Company, 1921.

Waples, Dorothy. *The Whig Myth of James Fenimore Cooper*. New Haven: Yale University Press; London: Oxford University Press, 1938.

Winters, Yvor. *Maule's Curse: Seven Studies in the History of American Obscurantism*. New York: New Directions, 1938.

A NOTE ON THE TEXT

The text of this edition is based on the W. A. Townsend and Company edition published in 1859 and reprinted by the Riverside Press in their collected edition of Cooper's works in 1872. The spelling and punctuation have been brought into conformity with modern American usage.

About the Author

Ronald Inglehart is Professor of Political Science and Program Director at the Institute for Social Research at the University of Michigan. Among his books are *The Silent Revolution: Changing Values and Political Styles among Western Publics* and *Culture Shift in Advanced Industrial Society,* both published by Princeton University Press.